HISTORIC
CITIES
OF THE
AMERICAS

HISTORIC CITIES OF THE AMERICAS

An Illustrated Encyclopedia

Volume 1: The Caribbean, Mexico, and Central America

David F. Marley

A B C • C L I O

Santa Barbara, California • Denver, Colorado • Oxford, England

Library of Congress Cataloging-in-Publication Data

Marley, David.
    Historic cities of the Americas : an illustrated encyclopedia / David F. Marley
        p. cm.
    Includes bibliographical references and index.
    ISBN 1-57607-027-1 (hardback : alk. paper)   ISBN 1-57607-574-5 (e-book)
1. Cities and towns—America—History—Encyclopedias. 2. City and town life—America—
History—Encyclopedias. 3. Urbanization—America—History—Encyclopedias. I. Title.
    HT121.M37 2005
    307.76'097—dc22

                                                            2005019012

07 06 05   10 9 8 7 6 5 4 3 2 1

This book is also available on the World Wide Web as an e-book. Visit http://
www.abc-clio.com for details.
ABC-CLIO, Inc.
130 Cremona Drive, P.O. Box 1911
Santa Barbara, California 93116–1911

This book is printed on acid-free paper.
Manufactured in the United States of America

To my mother, Lilly May Marley (née Rolston),
who created loving homes in:

Angola, Indiana
Sudbury, Ontario
Rosario, Honduras
El Dorado, Salvador
Camborne, England
Caquipec, Guatemala
Stamford, Connecticut
Mexico City, Mexico
and Windsor, Ontario

Contents

Preface and Acknowledgments, xix

HISTORIC CITIES OF THE AMERICAS
An Illustrated Encyclopedia

Volume 1: The Caribbean, Mexico, and Central America

Volume 2: North America and South America

Contents

Preface and Acknowledgments

God made the country, and man made the town.
—William Cowper (1731–1800)

The aim of this work is to provide a reference tool detailing seminal events in the evolution of some of the most famous cities in the New World. Often, historical overviews offer a cursory account of early development, compressed into a few pages preceding a more fulsome description of modern urban growth. *Historic Cities of the Americas* seeks to upend and compensate this trend of uneven scope by instead furnishing more expansive paragraphs upon each phase of a metropolis' historical progression, enhanced with antique maps and photographs.

Common themes naturally abound among many of these urban compilations, especially when considered along regional lines. The indigenous peoples who inhabited the Americas prior to the arrival of the first Europeans usually observed a seminomadic lifestyle, either shifting their settlements frequently with the change of each season or every few years as local resources became depleted. Some exceptions occurred in fertile, well-watered, agricultural pockets with tolerable year-round climates, such as at **Mexico City** or **Oaxaca**, and to a lesser extent at the coastal outlet of **Campeche**. Yet the first European explorers were nonetheless to only rarely encounter any significant urban concentration. While sailing back across the Atlantic aboard the *Niña* after his initial contact, Christopher Columbus prepared a report on 15 February 1493, which read in part:

> When I reached Cuba, I followed its north coast westwards, and found it so extensive that I thought this must be the mainland, the province of Cathay. Since there were no towns or villages on the coast, but only small groups of houses whose inhabitants fled as soon as we approached, I continued on my course, thinking that I should undoubtedly come to some great towns or cities.

He was disappointed, and even the small toehold that he had ensconced in the peaceful Arawak village near modern **Cap-Haïtien** after the wreck of his flagship *Santa María* was to be completely eradicated by the time he returned with a group of colonists.

The Spaniards therefore created their own distinct trio of Antillean cities at **Santo Domingo**, **San Juan de Puerto Rico**, and **Santiago de Cuba** over the next couple of decades as they gradually subdued and occupied the hapless archipelago. But it was the discovery of vast Indian nations on the American mainland that truly spawned the birth and far-reaching influence of major metropolises within the Spanish empire, starting with Hernán Cortés's creation of the nonexistent **Veracruz**—a legal stratagem designed to win himself freedom from the authority of the governor of Cuba.

Yet Cortés's subsequent subjugation of the lands and peoples of Mexico and Central America was nonetheless to be characterized by a single-minded focus upon city building, for as the historian Charles Gibson has noted: "Spaniards were city-minded people; municipalities were sometimes created as the first political act of *conquistadores,* the assumption being that colonial life could not begin until formalized through municipal authority." Consequently, in addition to taking over such densely populated concentrations as Mexico City and Oaxaca, **Panama** and **Guatemala** also came to be delegated as subcapitals for the viceroyalty, while even wholly new Spanish-style cities were to be created upon empty lands at **Puebla** and **Guadalajara**. Mineral strikes at the remote mining camps of **Guanajuato** and **Zacatecas** eventually became solidified as cities, despite their inhospitable environs, while **Monterrey** struggled to survive for more than two centuries before burgeoning. The rise in value and volume of plate-fleet traffic also coalesced significant numbers of inhabitants at such torrid, yet strategically vital seaports as **Havana**, **Acapulco**, and **Portobelo**.

This migration of permanent Spanish residents over to the American mainland also left behind a void in the Antilles, which came to be filled during the seventeenth century by interlopers from rival West European nations. A private British company established **Bridgetown** on Barbados, while a Dutch venture erected **Willemstad** on Curaçao; these advance bases in turn facilitated the proliferation of Crown outposts ever deeper into the West Indies, such as at **Fort-de-France**, **Kingston**, **Nassau**, **Port-au-Prince**, and **Port of Spain**. Profits from the sugar trade eventually allowed the latter to attain considerable influence and importance during the eighteenth century before fading into abeyance once Spanish-American independence was achieved and the global economy diversified. A century of turmoil, poverty, or neglect would hamper the development of virtually every city in this book until modernization was at last reached.

The author would like to acknowledge the kind assistance

received from Dr. Basil Kingstone, head of the French Department, and Dr. Ronald Welch of the Geography Department of the University of Windsor, Ontario, Canada; Dr. William O. Autry of Goshen College, Indiana; the entire staff of the Archivo General de la Nación in Mexico City; Dr. Pedro González García, director of the Archive of Indies in Seville; Dr. José Ignacio González Aller, director of the Museo Naval in Madrid; Ms. Joan Dalton, Mr. Robert Elliott, Ms. Lou Ann Greenham, Ms. Karen Needham, Ms. Mita Sen-Roy, Ms. Maureen Souchuk, Mr. Graham Staffen, and Mr. Donald Tupling of the Leddy Library of the University of Windsor.

—David F. Marley
Windsor, Ontario
March 2005

CARIBBEAN

All these islands are so utterly at Your Highnesses' command, that it only remains to . . .
make them work, sow seed and do whatever else is necessary, and build a town . . .

—from Christopher Columbus's initial report,
written while returning to Spain (February 1493)

Bahamas

Nassau

Once a neglected backwater of the British empire, yet today a glittering international resort.

Background (600–1646)

Almost 2,000 years ago, Arawak-speaking tribes were driven out of what is now Venezuela by more aggressive Carib rivals pushing northwest out of the Amazons. They created a seaborne wave of refugees that gradually spread up through the Antilles, in turn supplanting its even more primitive *Ciboney* (literally, "People of the Rock") or *Guanajatabey* ("Cave Dwellers") before eventually coalescing into a distinct new island culture that has been labeled Taino by modern archaeologists. A branch of these Arawak-speaking Tainos reached the Bahamas around 600 C.E., establishing themselves in modest numbers throughout its south-central portions, while adopting the local name *Lucayos*, or Small-Island People. They subsisted mainly by fishing and the cultivation of manioc.

Despite being the first inhabitants to greet Christopher Columbus when he made his transatlantic landfall at San Salvador Island on 12 October 1492, the Lucayans were subsequently ignored as the Spaniards probed southeastward and instead subjugated a much larger and wealthier Taino island that they christened Hispaniola or Santo Domingo (modern Haiti and the Dominican Republic). European-bred epidemics nonetheless decimated the Lucayans, along with most other Caribbean nations, after which the new regional overlords began carrying off survivors to serve as slaves in their Dominican gold mines—a policy sanctioned by the Spanish Crown as of May 1509, which effectively finished depopulating the Lucayan archipelago within the next three years. When the explorer Juan Ponce de León passed through in quest of the legendary Fountain of Youth in 1513, he encountered only a single elderly woman still living in the Lucayas. (The name "Bahamas" is apparently a latter-day corruption of the Spanish nautical term *Baja mar,* or Shallow Sea, as the shoal waters around the islands became labeled on pilots' charts.)

Aerial view of Nassau harbor, ca. 1926, looking east toward Montagu Bay in the distance. At left lies Hog—modern Paradise—Island, while the city itself sits on New Providence Island to the right. (Moseley, *The Bahamas Handbook*)

The archipelago was to remain largely depopulated until 1565, when a band of interlopers from western France attempted to secure a tiny foothold on Abaco—which they dubbed Lucayoneque—as a compliment to a colony already being developed across the Strait of Florida near modern-day Jacksonville by Jean Ribault and René Goulaine de Laudonnière. Yet the outpost on Florida was soon eradicated by a Spanish counterexpedition; a French relief vessel that reached Abaco shortly thereafter found no trace of its settlers.

Private colonization efforts nonetheless persisted throughout the Antilles and North America during the early seventeenth century, the English Crown even granting Sir Robert Heath title in October 1629 to all unclaimed lands south of Virginia—including the Bahamas—although he then proved unable to act upon that license. A second French attempt was also authorized four years later, when King Louis XIII's chief minister, Cardinal Armand-Jean du Plessis de Richelieu, ceded four strategically placed islands (known at the time as Abaco, Inaugua, Mariguana, and Gilatur) to Guillaume de Caen, adding the right to bear the honorific title of Baron des Bahames; however, nothing came of this grant either, mostly because the Huguenot (Protestant) de Caen was ordered to set-

tle only Catholic Frenchmen into his new colony, hampering its implementation.

Eventually, two vessels sent by Gov. William Sayle of the private English settlement on Bermuda reconnoitered the Bahamas in 1644, after which he successfully petitioned his shareholders in London to establish a separate colony of Calvinist zealots in this archipelago. Armed with a permit "for the Plantation of the Islands of Eleutheria (the Greek word for 'Freedom,' soon bastardized into Eleuthera), formerly called Buhama in America," Sayle appeared off Segatoo Island in the spring of 1648 with seventy settlers aboard his 50-ton *William,* and a 6-ton shallop. This initial establishment endured considerable hardship, starting when the flagship was wrecked crossing the reefs near Governor's Bay, which compelled Sayle to sail with eight men aboard his shallop to obtain help from Virginia. In 1649 his fledgling colony was further joined by sixty more Puritans and republicans expelled from Bermuda, while a desperately needed shipload of provisions donated by Puritan sympathizers in Boston was received in March 1650, prompting Sayle to send back 10 tons of *braziletto* wood in gratitude. (When sold at public auction, the resultant £124 provided a substantial portion of Harvard College's endowment.)

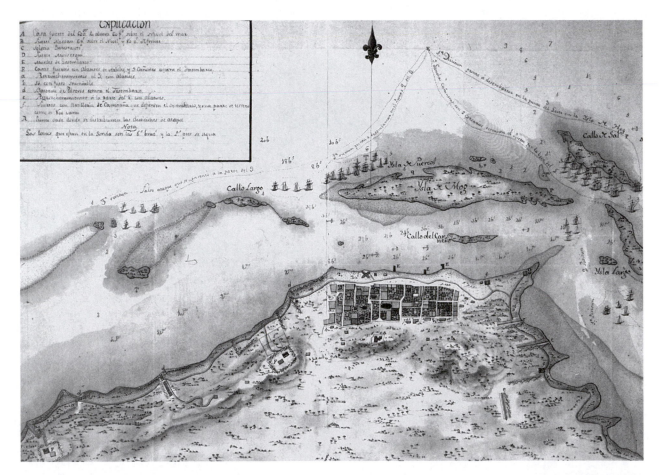

Map of New Providence Island and its immediate approaches, as surveyed during the Spanish occupation of 1782–1783. (Archive of Indies, Seville)

Gradually, these few dozen Bahamian pioneers began scratching out a living and even expanded onto adjoining islands, a smaller one due west of Eleuthera being occupied about 1666; until then it had been unofficially called Sayle's Island because the governor had allegedly twice ridden out storms in a sheltered harbor on its northeastern shore. Yet upon becoming inhabited it was renamed New Providence, in memory of another earlier Calvinist colony on Providencia, or Santa Catalina Island, 150 miles east of Nicaragua's Mosquito Coast, which had been extirpated by a Spanish expedition a quarter century earlier.

Early Struggles as "Charles Town" (1666–1694)

Despite measuring only 58 square miles, and being rather flat and covered with brushwood and lagoons, this newly inhabited island was surrounded by crystalline waters and enjoyed one of the most delightful climates in the archipelago—being neither too rainy, as occurred farther to its northwest, nor too hot and arid, as to its southeast. Its anchorage also proved to be exceptionally good, approachable via the deep-water passages dubbed "Tongue of the Ocean" or Providence Channel, and protected from southeasterly gales and hurricanes by an 80-foot ridge rising just 400 yards south of its beach; the harbor also offered respite from sea currents because of a 5-mile-long offshore cay (which was to be christened Hog Island by Gov. Nicholas Trott in the mid-1690s, apparently in memory of his family estate and birthplace of Hog Bay, Bermuda). Although vessels of more than 500 tons could not easily traverse its 14-foot-deep, reef-lined bar, the inner roads stretched 3.5 miles long by 1/3 of a mile wide, with high and low tides ranging from 18 to 24 feet in depth.

Soon a ramshackle collection of huts built from the nearby palmetto copses began sprawling just inside the bar, each plot surrounded by its own colorful garden or orchard, the whole untidy agglomeration being named Charles Town in honor of the recently restored Stuart monarch Charles II in England. By early 1670 it was estimated that half of the 1,000 English residents of the Bahamas were eking out a hardscrabble existence on New Providence Island, when they were unexpectedly reinforced by survivors from Capt. John Russell's *Port Royal*, wrecked on Abaco Island while conveying a large party of settlers and supplies to the Carolinas. This unforeseen landing inspired Russell's London-based backers—six high-born friends of the king known collectively as the Lords Proprietors of Carolina—to rewrite the Bahamian company charter that same November, displacing its original Puritan shareholders in favor of themselves.

Residents of the islands nonetheless retained much of their autonomy, a primitive log stockade being completed at Charles Town by 1672; the community also became unofficially recognized as the archipelago's capital despite conflicting claims from Harbour and Exuma islands. Nothing more was done to encourage the development of the Bahamian chain, though, and its settlers languished rather forlornly over the next few years, supplementing their meager fishing and agricultural activities by scavenging for wrecks or ambergris and trading with any vessel that chanced to call.

This eagerness to please casual visitors meant that West Indian privateers soon found Charles Town a most obliging bolt-hole in which to dispose of their booty, although such illicit proclivities also attracted unwanted attention. In March 1683, for example, the French *flibustier* Bréhal—seconded by the English mercenaries John Markham of New York, Thomas Paine, Conway Wooley, plus the Dutch-born Jan Corneliszoon (also of New York)—sailed from New Providence Island to raid Spanish Saint Augustine. In retaliation, the Cuban corsair captain Juan de Larco made a stealthy descent with 200 men aboard a pair of vessels on 19 January 1684 ("Old Style," or "O.S."; according to our "New Style" or modern Gregorian calendar, it would have been 29 January). Having seized a woodcutting sloop off Andros, de Larco compelled its master to pilot them through the less frequented eastern approach, so that his 150 raiders disgorged suddenly at daybreak within a half mile of Charles Town itself, while his corsair ships bore down upon the six vessels anchored in its harbor.

Charles Town's population consisted of approximately 400 men capable of bearing arms—although scarcely half actually possessed any guns—plus perhaps 200 women, a like number of children, and 200 slaves. Taken utterly by surprise, they were incapable of mounting an effective defense. Former governor Robert Clarke was wounded and captured as he attempted to mount a feeble countercharge, while his recently arrived successor, Robert Lilburne, fled from his bedroom in the Wheel of Fortune Inn into the jungle, along with most other residents. The 10-gun New England frigate *Good Intent* of Capt. William Warren and another anchored vessel managed to escape across the bar, leaving the Spaniards to pillage the remaining four and quickly ransack the town, loading their plunder aboard their largest prize before torching the rest and sailing away that same evening. De Larco thereupon hastened across to northern Eleuthera and visited a like treatment upon its English settlement, before returning to Charles Town on 15 November 1684 (O.S.) to torch its buildings and carry off numerous residents to Havana.

Frightened by this devastating sweep, a couple of hundred survivors sought refuge on Jamaica, while another fifty from northern Eleuthera were temporarily resettled at Casco in Maine. The Bahamas subsequently remained devoid of any recognizable English presence until December 1686, when a small contingent from Jamaica under the preacher Thomas Bridges reoccupied New Providence Island, and more colonists gradually joined them. The archipelago revived fully after the New England salvor William Phips raised an immense fortune in bullion from the nearby Ambrosian Bank (modern Silver Bank, north of the Dominican Republic) in the spring of 1687

Major Hurricanes in the Bahamas, 1780–1919

4–6 October 1780	25–27 August 1856
3–5 October 1796	10–12 November 1857
5–6 September 1801	16–19 October 1858
7–9 September 1804	13–15 August 1861
23–24 July 1813	27–28 August 1862
22–24 August 1813	23–25 October 1865
20–22 August 1821	1 October 1866
1–2 September 1821	11 October 1870
13–14 August 1830	20 October 1870
14–15 August 1835	26 August 1871
2–3 August 1837	6 October 1873
5–8 September 1838	8 September 1883
2–4 August 1842	3 September 1888
5–6 October 1844	11 August 1899
10–11 October 1846	11 October 1903
22–23 August 1848	13 September 1908
18–20 August 1853	8 September 1919

from the Spanish vice flagship *Nuestra Señora de la Pura y Limpia Concepción,* which had sunk in 1641. The resultant treasure-hunting fever made the Bahamas an attractive prospect once more. Phips's patron—Christopher Monk, 2nd Duke of Albemarle—even attempted to take over the archipelago's lease from his fellow proprietors back in London, although he was balked by the new king, James II, who preferred having the islands transformed into a Crown colony.

This latter notion was postponed when that English monarch was driven from the throne in November 1688 and succeeded by the Protestant Queen Mary and her Dutch consort William, Prince of Orange-Nassau, after which an overseas war erupted, with England, Holland, and Spain being ranged against France. New Providence Island was consequently left largely to its own devises once again, profiting as a lawless privateer base during the ensuing hostilities (known to history as King William's War, the War of the League of Augsburg, the War of the Grand Alliance, or the Nine Years' War). Its remote locale, coupled with its insignificance and absentee rulers, meant that the ruffianly Col. Cadwallader Jones could even act as self-proclaimed "governor" from 1690 to 1693, refusing to acknowledge the authority of William and Mary.

Creation of "Nassau" (1695–1717)

Eventually, though, Jones was succeeded in August 1694 by the more loyal and ambitious Nicholas Trott. Allegiance to the Crown was restored, so that the island capital could begin to undergo a modest reformation by commencing construction of a 28-gun wooden fort, as well as implementing a rational street plan. The town was officially renamed Nassau the next year, in honor of the Queen's foreign-born consort. By the time that Trott's term ended in November 1696, Nassau boasted 160 houses, being assigned a vice admiralty court as of February 1697, complete with judge, registrar, and marshal appointed from London, who arrived that same July.

The court was needed because of continuing venality in island administration, Trott having lost his post for receiving the notorious pirate Henry Every, a renegade who had mutinied and carried off an English salvage ship from La Coruña, Spain. Every thereupon launched a year-and-a-half rampage through the Far East, during which time he robbed the Mogul trader *Ganj-i-Sawai* of £200,000 off Bombay. Hoping to escape back into civilian life, Every and his 200 cutthroats dropped anchor in late April 1696 at Royal Island off Eleuthera, sending a boat with four spokesmen the 50 miles into Nassau allegedly to offer Trott a £1,000 bribe to permit their stolen flagship *Fancy* into port and its crew to disperse. Upon acceptance, Every sailed into Nassau harbor masquerading as "Henry Bridgeman" and *Fancy* as an "interloper," or unlicensed slaver from the Guinea Coast, with an unregistered cargo of ivory and slaves. He and Trott then struck a deal for disposal of the ship. Every gave *Fancy* over to the governor's care, after which it was stripped of everything of value—including its 46 guns, 100 barrels of powder, many small arms, 50 tons of ivory, sails, blocks, etc.—and allowed to drift ashore two days later, being pounded to pieces by the surf. With this telltale piece of evidence destroyed, Every and his men disappeared from the Bahamas aboard passing ships.

Imposing honest administration upon this unruly, unfrequented colony proved so difficult that Nassau's new governor, Nicholas Webb, even quit office for Newcastle in Delaware in 1699, his chosen successor—the mulatto privateer Read Elding—being arrested in October 1701 by another disreputable figure, Elias Haskett; Elding was quickly released by a band of his supporters, who in turn deposed and banished Haskett. Such tumultuous, ineffectual leadership was to cost Nassau dearly when another round of hostilities erupted back in Europe in May 1702: Queen Anne's War or the War of the Spanish Succession, with England and Holland arrayed against France and Spain. Officials at Saint-Domingue (Haiti) and Santiago de Cuba, who viewed New Providence Island as a mutual menace, raised a joint expedition of French *boucaniers* and 150 Spanish soldiers aboard two frigates commanded by Claude Le Chesnaye and Blas Moreno Mondragón, materializing off Nassau in October 1703. More than a hundred startled residents were killed in this opening onslaught, while another eighty to a hundred—including Acting Gov. Ellis Lightwood—were carried away as captives two weeks later, along with thirteen prizes and twenty-two cannons, while the town's half-rotted palmetto-and-lime fortification was thrown down.

When the new governor-designate, Edward Birch, landed at Nassau early in 1704, he became so distraught at beholding its ruined state—survivors not having even a "shift to cover their nakedness," according to his report—that he did not bother unfurling his company-issued commission before taking ship back to England a few months later. Another enemy raid in 1706 left only twenty-seven families still cringing inside makeshift huts on New Providence Island, and no more than 400 to 500 English residents scattered throughout the entire archipelago. These survivors suffered considerable distress from more descents during the remainder of this conflict, while their scant overseas trade dried up and no new governors or assistance came out from England.

The cessation of hostilities in 1713 brought little relief, as hundreds of West Indian privateers—suddenly bereft of legitimate employment—drifted into the sparsely populated Bahamas to continue preying upon nearby shipping lanes, selling their booty to accomplices ashore. Rogue captains such as Benjamin Hornigold, "Calico Jack" Rackham, and Edward Teach (alias "Blackbeard") were so powerful that when Nassau's vice admiralty judge, Thomas Walker, brought Hornigold's lieutenant Daniel Stilwell to trial for robbing a Spanish vessel in 1715, an enraged Hornigold crossed over from Eleuthera and released the prisoner and his men from jail, threatening to burn Walker's house about his ears. The judge fled in August 1716, after more pirates had entered the port and brazenly emplaced their guns within Fort Nassau's crudely reconstructed embrasures, menacing the harbor and town.

International grievances against this burgeoning "pirate republic" at last goaded the British government into reviving its former plan of bringing the Bahamas directly under Crown rule.

Crown Capital (1718–1775)

Woodes Rogers, a battle-scarred privateer who had circumnavigated the globe and captured a Manila galleon—as well as incidentally rescuing the marooned Scottish master Alexander Selkirk from the Juan Fernández Islands, thereby furnishing the inspiration for Daniel Defoe's *Robinson Crusoe*—was selected to effect this difficult transition. He sailed from England with 250 new colonists aboard the 460-ton former Indiaman *Delicia*, backed by the frigates HMSS *Milford* and *Rose*, plus the naval sloops *Buck* and *Shark*. News of his appointment had preceded him, along with a promised amnesty for pirates, so that the more recalcitrant spirits such as Blackbeard had already forsaken the Bahamas for easier hunting grounds.

Still, when Rogers's expedition arrived outside Nassau's bar on the afternoon of 26 July 1718 (O.S.), Charles Vane's pirate flagship remained defiantly at anchor, so that the governor-designate sent *Rose* and *Shark* to take soundings after nightfall. Vane responded by loosing a recently captured French prize against them in flames, before getting under way next dawn for Abaco. With this lone threat removed, Rogers came ashore by midmorning, being greeted by an honor guard of 300 boozy buccaneers under Hornigold and other captains, who swore fealty to the Crown. Rogers promptly assumed office and began civic improvements to Nassau, such as repairing its shoddily rebuilt fortress, erecting a new barracks and eastern battery, granting 120-square-foot plots in town to each new settler family—plus 25 acres outside for gardens—as well as many other needed public works.

However, progress was soon suspended by the eruption of the War of the Quadruple Alliance in December 1718, with England, Holland, France, and Austria being ranged against Spain. Although heavily outnumbered elsewhere, the Spaniards in Cuba were able to mount a strong expedition against Nassau, the privateer captains Francisco Cornejo and José Cordero appearing outside the harbor on 24 February 1720 (O.S.) with 1,200 to 1,300 men crammed aboard three frigates, plus nine sloops and brigantines. Reluctant to steer directly across its bar because of the intimidating presence inside of *Delicia* and the 24-gun frigate HMS *Flamborough*, these raiders instead circled east before disembarking three contingents under captains Fernando Castro, Francisco de León, and Julián Barroso, who inflicted considerable damage among outlying properties before finally being expelled a few weeks later by the 500 militiamen that Rogers had gathered at Nassau. Yet the Spanish continued to roam unchecked throughout the islands, making off with at least a hundred

View southeastward across the old town's central core, ca. 1926, with Christ Church visible at left, at the corner of King and George streets—a building entirely reconstructed as of 1837–1840 and elevated into a cathedral upon the consecration of Nassau's first bishop in 1861. Photo taken from atop the New Colonial Hotel, where Fort Nassau's barracks had once stood. (Moseley, *The Bahamas Handbook*)

slaves and much booty, before peace was restored in March 1721.

Rogers became so ill and indebted that he returned to London that same year and did not resume office until eight years later; George Phenney took his place, and under Phenney's administration the Bahamas began to enjoy some of the benefits of Britain's rise as a global power: local shipbuilding increased, for example, while the first small commercial plantations were also created. The population of New Providence Island grew from 427 whites and 233 blacks in February 1722 to 633 whites and 409 blacks by October 1731, while its first formal church—a prefabricated wooden structure imported from England—was erected southeast of Fort Nassau. Upon Rogers's return, a representative legislature had also been convened for the first time on 29 September 1729 (O.S.), and some other minor progress was achieved; however, his death from yellow fever in 1732 retarded development.

Rogers's successor, Richard Fitzwilliam, did not arrive until two years later, and he proved to be haughty and unpopular. Resentment against his rule climaxed on the evening of 15 March 1736 (O.S.), when forty ill-used soldiers mutinied at Fort Nassau, firing upon Fitzwilliam when he attempted to intervene from his residence at Government House, a quarter mile away. These rebels then freed a jailed French pilot, nailed up the fort's seaward guns, and boarded a large sloop to escape for Havana. Unskilled sailors, they were overtaken at daybreak next day by a pursuing sloop and brought back into Nassau, where a dozen were hanged and the remainder flogged and transported.

Ironically, it was to be the outbreak of yet another conflict in 1739—the War of Jenkins's Ear against Spain—that helped Nassau blossom into a bustling town of more than 2,000 people spread among 400 homes, because of the large numbers of prizes brought in by privateers. Over the nine years of this struggle, 117 enemy vessels were condemned at its vice admiralty court, worth £750,000; many other lesser seizures were also made. As a result of this economic upsurge, Nassau's fortifications multiplied as well, 17-gun Fort Montagu—named after the Duke of Montagu and intended to guard the harbor's eastern entrance—being commenced as of June 1741. The fort was completed the next year, under the direction of the newly appointed "Chief Engineer to fortify the Bahama Islands," Peter Henry Bruce. An 8-gun battery was also installed at the eastern end of town, while old Fort Nassau's artillery was augmented to fifty-four cannon and twenty-six mortars; also, its structure was almost entirely rebuilt with the addition of a

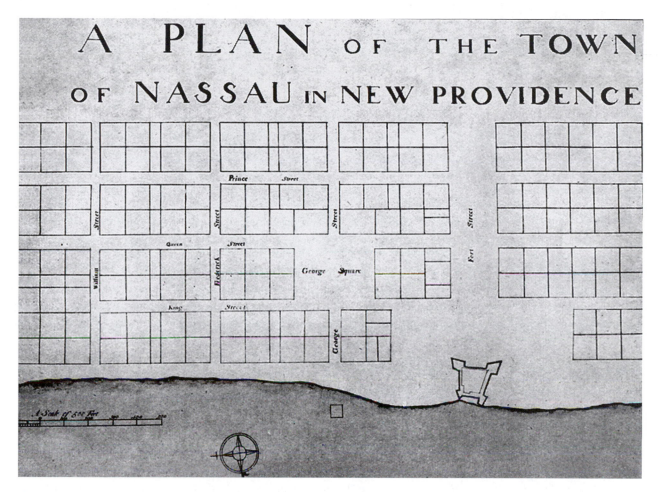

The growing town's grid pattern, ca. 1739, showing how streets were to radiate out from Fort Nassau; north is toward bottom. (Moseley, *The Bahamas Handbook*)

600-man barracks, bombproof magazine, pair of wells, and so forth. Civic improvements were also made: Christ Church was rebuilt in stone; a public or "free" school with a salaried master was established; roads were cleared; and many thatched dwellings were replaced by buildings of plank and shingle.

By the time these hostilities ceased in 1748, Gov. John Tinker could report that New Providence Island had "increased most surprisingly in strength and wealth, and the town of Nassau grown populous." Although the privateering boom was thus abruptly curtailed, seaborne commerce raiding resumed on an even grander scale with the outbreak of the Seven Years' War in 1756. Peace again brought about a severe depression after 1763, the Bahamian treasury becoming bankrupt and its law courts forced to close; yet, according to a census taken in 1773, New Providence Island's population now stood at 1,024 whites and 1,800 "reputed blacks." That same year, its long-suffering garrison—their numbers reduced to a peacetime low of only 23 disgruntled soldiers—was reinforced by a company of regular troops, while 500 local slaves were also conscripted to toil away at its fortifications.

American and Spanish Invasions (1776–1783)
Despite such work, the city was easily carried when the Thirteen American Colonies revolted against Britain three years later. The fledgling U.S. Navy mounted its first ever overseas strike when Commo. Esekial Hopkins appeared outside Hog Island from Delaware on 3 March 1776—a Sunday morning—with his 24-gun flagship *Alfred* under Capt. John Paul Jones and 20-gun frigate *Columbus;* 14-gun brigs *Andrew Doria* and *Cabot;* 12-gun sloop *Providence;* 10-gun sloop *Hornet;* 8-gun schooner *Wasp;* plus two Bahamian sloops captured off Abaco Island. Notwithstanding ample warnings received of a possible raid, Gov. Montfort Browne was taken completely aback when this sighting was reported to him, clad in his nightshirt at the door of Government House. Shaken, he ordered warning guns fired from Fort Nassau to assemble New Providence's militia, which discharges deterred the

Americans from "standing straight in," or sailing directly into port (although two guns actually tumbled from their decrepit mountings, and few volunteers mustered).

Hopkins instead opted to circle through the Narrows into Montagu Bay, 3 miles from Nassau, where he disembarked 200 marines and 50 sailors under Capt. Samuel Nicholas in Fox Hill Creek, a mile east of Fort Montagu. The British governor attempted to counter by hastening two detachments overland, one to confront the invaders, the other to strengthen Fort Montagu; both, however, melted ignominiously back into their homes, and the U.S. forces entered Nassau unopposed next morning to receive Browne's surrender. Hopkins's squadron thereupon anchored in the harbor and spent the next fortnight stripping the defenses of more than a hundred cannons, plus a considerable amount of war materiel, before finally departing homeward with the governor and a dozen other prominent officials as prisoners.

Deprived of its heavy ordnance, Nassau remained vulnerable to enemy penetrations for the next few years. An American privateer cut out some prizes from its harbor later in 1776, threatening to rake the town, and two years afterward, Lieut. Rathbun of the sloop USS *Providence* also stole into port and occupied Fort Nassau in an attempt to lure HMS *Gayton* under its guns, being frustrated when some loyal subjects signaled that vessel not to cross its bar. Although initially sympathetic toward the Thirteen Colonies, Bahamian sentiment turned against the United States after that country became allied with the islanders' traditional foes of France and Spain in August 1778 and June 1779, respectively. Nassau's naval strength gradually recuperated with the appointment of John Maxwell as governor in 1780, reflected in an increase in privateering captures.

Two years later the Bahamian capital faced an even sterner test when a Hispano-U.S. expedition of fifty-nine vessels escorted by the 40-gun frigate *South Carolina* under Commo. Alexander Gillon materialized from Cuba on the evening of 5 May 1782, bearing a 1,800-man army under Lt. Gen. Juan Manuel de Caxigal, governor of Havana. A surrender demand was sent ashore next afternoon, which Maxwell accepted by 7 May, whereby the Spaniards acquired Nassau plus seventy-seven anchored vessels without suffering a single casualty. Gillon set sail for Philadelphia on 14 May, while Caxigal departed a few days later, leaving behind a 300-man occupying force under Capt. Antonio Claraco y Sanz, plus seven small men-of-war crewed by 150 sailors under Capt. Raymundo Andrés.

New Providence Island remained under Spanish control for the next eleven months, until a dispatch-sloop arrived from Cuba on 10 April 1783 with news that peace preliminaries had been signed back in Europe—one clause directing that the Bahamas be restored to British control in exchange for Florida. However, before any such transfer could be formalized, the twenty-five-year-old Loyalist militia colonel Andrew Deveaux, Jr.—exiled from Beaufort, South Carolina, because of the American patriots' triumph— approached New Providence Island on 13 April with a small flotilla of volunteers and Bahamian out-islanders, intent on recapturing Nassau. Its Spanish garrison initially mistook these vessels for smugglers and so were astonished to see a heavily armed landing party storm ashore next dawn, overrunning Fort Montagu and three guard boats. Claraco retreated inside Fort Nassau and requested a truce, which Deveaux rescinded next day. The Spaniards thereupon scuttled their remaining warships on 16 April and huddled miserably within the stronghold, until finally agreeing to be repatriated to Cuba two days later.

Loyalist Sanctuary (1784–1815)

Deveaux's well-publicized victory attracted many other displaced American Loyalists over the next several years, during which 100,000 quit the United States rather than remain under republican rule. Of these, 1,600 whites and 5,700 free blacks or slaves resettled in the Bahamas, receiving land plus other incentives, thereby trebling the colony's population and quadrupling the number of inhabited islands to a dozen. Although a majority of these migrants settled on out-islands, many took up residence in Nassau, injecting much-needed enhancements into the sleepy port town, whose streets had not yet even been paved. John Wells, for example, a printer and bookseller driven out of Charleston, South Carolina, in August 1784, founded Nassau's first newspaper—the weekly *Bahama Gazette*—while John Russell (formerly of St. John's, East Florida) erected a thriving shipyard on Hog Island. Generally speaking, these transplanted merchants and planters brought more professional business practices to the Bahamas, so that its economy no longer depended exclusively upon the boom-and-bust cycles of privateering and salvage.

However, the clearance of thousands of acres on New Providence and other islands for the installation of commercial plantations also extinguished many previous liberties, blacks in particular finding their former easygoing lifestyle restricted by harsh new slave laws as well as odious racial constraints. The census of 1788 recorded 131 "old white" households and 1,024 "old slaves" still living on New Providence Island, compared with 165 "new white" households and 1,264 "new slaves." Exports of cash crops such as cotton had already risen twelvefold from fifteen years previously, while the volume of Nassau's seaborne traffic—including slavers—rose as well. The city's road system was overhauled to service its growing number of warehouses—stout stone structures with tiny windows below and airy, wooden living quarters above—so that Nassau began assuming its present contours, spreading into a grid pattern a mile long and quarter mile deep along the waterfront. Its old

Bourse had been replaced as of 1787 by an open-air, colonnaded, commercial mart called Vendue House, while a public market was inaugurated two years later. Schools, shops, taverns, and even a lending library had been created, while well-to-do homes now began dotting the upper slopes of the ridge south of town.

The French Revolution of 1789 touched off a major slave insurrection in northern Saint-Domingue (Haiti) two years later, plus a gradual descent into global conflict by January 1793 that engendered sufficient concern throughout the Antilles that ten companies of the 47th (Lancashire) Infantry Regiment were sent to Nassau as early as 1790. Gov. John Murray—Earl of Dunmore and Viscount Fincastle, as well as the last royal governor of Virginia—had moreover decided that old Fort Nassau should be replaced by an entirely new, moated citadel west of the expanded town, being named Fort Charlotte in honor of George III's queen when it was completed in 1794. An additional stronghold called Fort Fincastle was erected atop the highest point above town—Bennet's or Society Hill—as well as a 4-gun battery dubbed Fort Murray on Hog Island. There were also lesser redoubts at Potter's Cay between Nassau and Hog Island, Clifton Point at the westernmost extremity of New Providence Island, and Winton at its eastern end. Thanks to such efforts, the capital was spared any threats during the ensuing two decades of warfare, although constant fears of a slave revolt gripped many planters, and a yellow fever epidemic claimed hundreds of lives in 1796.

Nassau once again thrived in its traditional role of privateer base, more than 500 vessels worth millions of pounds being condemned at its vice admiralty court during the years 1803 to 1815 alone—more than half intercepted during the War of 1812 against the United States. The town came to reflect this bonanza, an elegant, octagonal, two-story jail having been completed in 1799 (it is said to have been modeled after the Old Powder Magazine at Williamsburg, Virginia, and since 1879 has housed Nassau's Public Library and Museum). In addition, the new St. Matthew's Anglican Church was consecrated in July 1802; a beautiful new complex of government offices was built of coral limestone along Bay Street between 1803 and 1805, allegedly based upon the design of Governor Tryon's famed winged palace at New Bern, North Carolina; an imposing new Government House was erected between 1803 and 1806; and a public hospital was created in 1809.

Many private mansions were also built, of flat stonework and plastered in pastel shades of pink, blue, green, or yellow

Nassau and Hog Island, as seen from atop Fort Charlotte early in 1860; colored lithograph based upon an original drawing by Lieutenant A. Samson of the 1st West Indian Regiment. (Day & Son, London)

Overgrown ruins of Fort Charlotte, ca. 1913. (Lloyd, *Twentieth Century Impressions of the West Indies*)

with distinctive coigns picked out in white, plus expensive glass windowpanes, while even lesser dwellings had now become solid structures combining wood and stone, with cedar-shingle roofs. By 1807 the population of New Providence Island stood at 1,720 whites, 1,035 free mulattos and blacks, and 3,280 slaves. The cornerstone for a circular, 70-foot limestone lighthouse was also laid at the western tip of Hog Island on 2 October 1816, its octagonal lantern imported from England going into operation eleven months later.

Stagnation (1816–1897)

As at the conclusion of previous conflicts, though, the end of the Napoleonic and American wars brought about economic depression, from which the Bahamas could not so easily rebound, because its cotton exports had also been crippled by general exhaustion of thin topsoils; also, its medium and small tenant farms could not hope to compete against the huge commercial plantations feeding international markets from elsewhere in the world. By 1826 the total population of the Bahamian archipelago stood at a mere 16,413 people.

During this decline, Nassau's municipal limits were expanded to incorporate former black shantytowns such as Delancey Town (named after Stephen de Lancey, an American Loyalist who had served as lieutenant-colonel of the 1st Battalion of the New Jersey Volunteers), Bain's Town, and Grant's Town—the latter so named because it was taken over in 1829,

during the administration of Gov. Sir Lewis Grant. Parliament's abolition of slavery throughout the British West Indies in 1834 effectively ended the last vestiges of the Bahamian plantation-based economy, estate owners being compensated for their emancipated slaves, while the latter resettled onto small plots. Although the archipelago's population expanded from 21,794 residents in 1838 to 26,491 by 1845, the vast majority still languished in considerable poverty. Exports of sponges, pineapples, and other tropical fruits provided minor profits during the mid-1840s, but not enough for Nassau to regain its former luster.

A disastrous tornado struck the city on 30 March 1850, followed by a cholera epidemic in 1851–1852. Concerned by this seemingly hopeless slide in their fortunes, local officials—having noted how their city's natural beauty was attractive to yachtsmen from wintry North America—decided to encourage such visits by requesting that international steamship companies establish regular routes between Nassau and the North American market. They even offered the Cunard Line a "bounty" or subsidy of £3,000 per annum as of early 1859 to operate a monthly mail service between the island capital and New York City, while simultaneously committing £25,000 to the construction of a grand new hotel (the Royal Victoria) that would overlook the harbor.

Before any such measures could take effect, though, port activities were unexpectedly revived by the outbreak of the

The rakish Confederate blockade-runner *Advance* lying empty off Nassau, 1863. (Confederate Navy Archives)

U.S. Civil War two years later, as more than 400 Confederate blockade-runners subsequently called at this neutral anchorage during the four years of that conflict. Many of Nassau's largest buildings were rebuilt or replaced during this boom period—such as new warehouses, coaling bunkers, private mansions, a prison, and a public cemetery. But the inevitable recession set in again once the war concluded in the spring of 1865, followed by a devastating hurricane that struck the city on 1 October 1866, with 60-foot waves surging over Hog Island into the anchorage to wreak extensive damage.

Writing ten years after the Civil War's conclusion, a Nassauvian noted: "Since the termination of the war, all is dullness and depression," so that the Bank of the Bahamas (established in 1836) went bankrupt by 1885. Gov. Sir Ambrose Shea attempted to reverse the depression by encouraging commercial extraction of sisal hemp from agave cactus plants during the late 1880s, yet his scheme failed. Hoping to improve business contacts abroad, the local legislature had even passed an act in 1873 "for establishing telegraphic communication between the Bahama Islands and parts beyond the limits of the government"; however, it was not until eighteen years later that

a £30,000 loan was raised, so that a cable could be laid between Nassau and Jupiter, Florida, and operations initiated by February 1892.

A professional police force had also been created at Nassau that previous year of 1891, constables being recruited at Barbados and other Caribbean islands to replace the peacekeeping duties of the troops of the 1st West India Regiment, who were repatriated to Jamaica. When Florida's citrus groves were decimated by the Great Freeze of 1894–1895, Bahamian authorities hoped to entice some U.S. growers over to their own frost-free islands, yet that notion soon faded as well.

Evolution as Tourist Destination (1898–Present)

Finally, the government committed itself to fomenting tourism as a prime Nassauvian industry when it passed a "Hotel and Steam Service Act" in 1898, granting subsidies for winter passenger service with Miami as well as the operation of two hotels: the old Royal Victoria and a new one to be called the Colonial. Both were taken over by the Florida East Coast Hotel Company. The breathtaking beauty and wondrous climate of New Providence's beaches lent themselves to sea bathing, sports, dining, music, and other amusements for vacationers. As ancillary steps, the first telephones appeared at Nassau in 1907; electric lighting arrived two years later, plus a wireless telegraph station by 1913. Nevertheless, the island populace dwindled from 13,554 people in 1911 to only 12,975 a decade later, mostly because of emigration by impoverished black residents who did not benefit directly from the tourist influx and preferred venturing abroad to seek better economic opportunities. Many sought work on Florida's railway construction projects or digging the Panama Canal.

This trend was reversed when the legislature sought to expand Nassau's tourist appeal by catering to a broader market in the United States, therefore committing funds to improving the city infrastructure, which in turn spawned a work boom. Dredging operations to deepen Nassau's roadstead commenced in 1922 and were completed six years later, when the 13,000-ton New York passenger liner *Munargo* berthed directly at Prince George Wharf, rather than anchoring offshore as had been the previous practice. But such enhancements also created considerable upheaval, attracting so many migrants from even poorer Caribbean nations that social and racial tensions increased and some anti-immigrant legislation was enacted. The global Great Depression, which started with the New York stock market crash of October 1929,

brought an abrupt halt to all middle-class tourism from the United States, as only extremely wealthy Americans such as Andrew Mellon, J. P. Morgan, Howard Hughes, Fred Fisher, Vincent Astor, and the like could still winter at Nassau aboard their luxury yachts.

By 1931, the number of New Providence Island's inhabitants had rebounded to 19,765, yet the economy remained hamstrung, being further slowed by the outbreak of World War II in September 1939. When the Duke of Windsor—formerly England's King Edward VIII, who had abdicated his throne three years previously for the sake of "the woman I love," U.S. divorcee Wallis Warfield-Simpson—was appointed governor of the Bahamas in July 1940 because of political embarrassments in London over his pro-German proclivities, he encountered such widespread poverty that make-work projects were arranged to help ease local unemployment. A month later, London also authorized Washington to establish bases on British possessions throughout the Western Hemisphere, one such air base being installed on Grand Exuma Island. Early in March 1942, a few sinkings were made by Axis submarines in Bahamian waters, further deepening the islands' isolation.

Eventually the war ended and tourism revived, greatly abetted by the advent of modern commercial air travel, so that Nassau's population quickly surged from 29,391 people in

Street scene in Nassau, ca. 1914. (Lloyd, *Twentieth Century Impressions of the West Indies*)

A Nassauvian police sergeant, ca. 1926. (Moseley, *The Bahamas Handbook*)

1943 to 46,920 by 1957. Two years later the pace of development quickened even further when the wealthy, young U.S. entrepreneur Huntington Hartford II—grandson of the founder of the Great Atlantic and Pacific Tea Company, or A & P, at that time the fifth-largest corporation in the United States—purchased most of Hog Island for $9.5 million with the intent of converting it into a luxury resort. He spent another $10 million on hotels and beautification projects, officially changing its name to Paradise Island in May 1962, while trying to secure a casino license. Foiled in that latter effort, Hartford sold majority shares in January 1966 to the U.S. developers James M. Crosby and I. G. Davis, Jr., who eventually obtained the requisite gambling license and furthermore completed a 1,500-foot-long, 70-foot-high bridge from Nassau out to Paradise Island by March 1967, which facilitated access to the thousands of new hotel rooms being made available.

There were now approximately 85,000 residents on New Providence Island, representing 80 percent of the total Bahamian populace, plus more than a million passengers streaming through Nassau's International Airport every year. In 1973 the Bahamas gained full independence from Britain, and its new government continued to develop the tourist industry, whose proceeds flowed mostly into the rapidly modernizing capital. According to the census undertaken in 1990, the city of Nassau had a population of 172,196 inhabitants—not including its suburbs, which had become very extensive.

For further reading on the history of Nassau or the Bahamas, please consult the Select Bibliography at the end of this volume.

Barbados

Bridgetown

Originally a strategically placed naval base during the Age of Sail because of its commanding position to windward of the Lesser Antilles.

Background (380–1627)

Archaeologists believe that this small, low-lying, coral island was originally populated around 380 C.E. by aboriginal groups, which have been dubbed "Saladoid-Barrancoids" after the location of digs that first revealed their existence. These peoples later migrated northward from what is today Venezuela, only to in turn be supplanted some two centuries later by another Venezuelan tribe of the Ignerian cultural group called Arawaks, who retained possession of the island until ca. 1200, when they too were displaced by yet a third wave of more aggressive tribesmen: the Caribs. Like all their predecessors, this latter group also settled down to a subsistence existence based upon fishing and the cultivation of root crops, their numbers on the island eventually peaking at perhaps 10,000 inhabitants.

When Christopher Columbus and other Spanish explorers entered the Caribbean during the late 1490s, they chose to establish their headquarters on Hispaniola (modern-day Haiti and the Dominican Republic), largely ignoring this easternmost island, except for chance visits or slaving raids over the ensuing decades. Barbados was given the Spanish nickname *Isla de los Barbados* (Island of the Bearded Ones), apparently because of its "bearded" fig trees. The slaving raids, coupled with devastating epidemics unwittingly unleashed throughout the archipelago by the Europeans' arrival, soon drove the Caribs to recongregate farther south. Thus, when the Portuguese seaman Pedro da Campos called at Barbados in 1536, he found it deserted and left behind "hogs to breed there for future wanderers."

Because of its low silhouette—only 166–167 square miles of land mass plus the encircling reefs, some of which extend more than 2.5 miles out to sea—the Spaniards never considered Barbados suitable for colonization, especially after the vastly richer Aztec and Incan empires of the American mainland were conquered during the 1520s and 1530s. Sailors from other West European nations therefore found this island still empty when they began penetrating into the West Indies during the latter half of the sixteenth century and so started using it as a stopover to refresh their provisions before venturing deeper into the Caribbean, recognizing it as a safe haven for sailing ships to make an initial landfall after traversing the Atlantic.

During the early decades of the seventeenth century, private companies furthermore began forming in England, Holland, and France to secure footholds in the Americas and develop these as commercial outposts, so that it was not long before Barbados became occupied. The English captain Simon Gordon—a subordinate of Thomas Warner, who had been driven out of Guyana and become one of the cofounders of St. Kitts—claimed to have landed on this easternmost island as early as 1620. Three Dutch West India Company ships under Pieter Schouten also visited Barbados in mid-March 1624, during his reconnaissance of the Caribbean, and a Dutch war fleet under Adm. Piet Heyn refreshed there as well in July 1626.

Yet it was to be the English who actually secured the island, their efforts having been initiated a few years previously when King James I granted title to "Barbadoes" (as it was to be commonly spelled throughout this early era) to one of his favorites, the Duke of Marlborough. That nobleman in turn delegated the practical details of colonization to a protégé, Sir William Courteen, who sent Capt. John Powell out on a scouting mission with the ship *Olive Blossom* early in 1625. When Powell reported back favorably, the vessel *William and John* was equipped to carry out the first eighty colonists under Powell's younger brother Henry, who sighted the island on 17 February 1627 ("Old Style," or "O.S."; 27 February according to our "New Style" Gregorian calendar) and disembarked to commence clearing the densely forested land for cultivation with the aid of ten black slaves captured en route. A small community called "Jamestown" (modern Holetown) was soon created, with William Dean acting as its private governor.

Foundation and Early Development (1628–1651)

However, this initial settlement did not become the island's capital because the death of King James two years previously had prompted his successor, Charles I, to grant another title to one of his own favorites: the heavily indebted James Hay, Earl of Carlisle and Viscount Doncaster. He in turn ceded 10,000 acres of Barbados to a London merchant syndicate headed by Sir Marmaduke Rawdon, in exchange for the discharge of his debts. A second group of sixty-four colonists consequently arrived at the island on 5 July 1628 (O.S.) under Charles Wolverstone and ensconced themselves on its southwestern shores, claiming 100-acre properties on the relatively low-lying flatlands radiating out from a sweeping, unenclosed harbor that they christened "Carlisle Bay" in honor of their patron.

Although most of this second party dispersed inland to commence clearing properties and erecting crude wattle shelters, an unplanned settlement also sprang up around their coastal "Careenage," or landing beach, which commanded a narrow and shallow roadstead. This harbor was actually an arm of the sea, protected from currents and storms by its low headland and dotted with numerous inlets suitable for unloading or servicing ships. High tides moreover flowed as far up the "Indian River" (modern Constitution River) as the future Harmony Hall, permitting sloops to travel up to a mile incountry to deliver or receive heavy cargoes. Because of these natural advantages a town rapidly evolved along this shoreline with the official name of Doncaster, yet much more commonly known as the "Bridge Town" or "Indian Bridgetown" because of the remnants of an ancient span found across this waterway's narrowest portion. A wooden bridge was promptly built to replace it and a street plan laid out—reputedly by Capt. John Swan, one of Wolverstone's subordinates, for whom Swan Street was named.

By the time a Dutch fleet under Adm. Adriaen Janszoon Pater visited in November 1629, there were 1,600 to 1,800 English residents on the island, although divided into two bickering factions; Carlisle and Courteen were also locked in bitter litigation back in London, and both fledgling groups endured so much neglect during this early era that it was later remembered as the "Starving Time." Eventually, though, Carlisle's suit prevailed, after which the island economy improved and thousands more migrants began arriving from England. They were attracted by Barbados's fertile terrain and wondrous climate, its tropical warmth being offset by cool Atlantic trade winds, even during the dry season of December through May. Bridgetown flourished accordingly, and English-style cottages made of sawn timber with thatched gables began to multiply, while English and Dutch vessels called regularly in Carlisle Bay to "lighter," or ferry cargoes to and from shore were aided through the 4- to 9-foot shallows of the Careenage by local boatmen. A council and assembly were constituted by 1639, confirming the town's status as island capital.

The outbreak of the English Civil War three years later between Charles and Parliament further benefited Barbados, as that bitter contest encouraged even more families from both sides to seek to escape into a neutral setting. (It was alleged that Barbadian impartiality was such that if anyone on the

View southwestward across Bridgetown's Careenage, showing oceangoing steamships anchored out in the deeper waters of Carlisle Bay, ca. 1918; photo taken from the Clock Tower atop the House of Assembly. (Henry Walter Parkinson)

island uttered the names of either contending faction—"Cavalier" or "Roundhead"—they had to buy all who heard a meal of young pig and turkey.) By 1643 the island's population had skyrocketed to approximately 37,000 whites and 6,000 blacks, roughly 11,200 of the former being small-time freeholders scattered throughout the interior of the island, each employing two or three indentured servants or slaves to produce modest yields of indigo, cotton, or tobacco on their plots, which they then exported through Bridgetown.

Compared with other West Indian colonies, Barbados was so stable and populous that its energetic private governor, Francis, Lord Willoughby of Parham, was even able to raise 300 men at Bridgetown to be dispatched late in 1650 under Anthony Rowse to secure Surinam as a Barbadian subcolony. The governor could also order the erection of a stronghold on Little Island so as to cover the Carlisle Bay anchorage, which when completed, six years later, became known as Fort Willoughby.

Parliamentary Rule (1652–1659)

Yet events in England were to intrude upon the island's neutrality once the defeated Charles had been executed in January 1649 and the triumphant Oliver Cromwell had formed a new "Commonwealth" government, which set about procuring the allegiance of all overseas British colonies. As a result, a seven-ship parliamentary squadron under Commo. Sir George Ayscue arrived off Barbados on the evening of 15 October 1651 (O.S.), dividing to penetrate Carlisle and Austin's bays simultaneously the next morning. Capt. Richard Pack, Ayscue's second in command, surprised fourteen Dutch traders in the former anchorage by sending aboard men to subdue and overtake the crews, sailing out twelve of these ships despite counterfire from its shore batteries, while Ayscue was shelled passing Needham's Point to rejoin him.

Hoping to subdue the island without bloodshed, Ayscue sent an officer inshore next day, calling for Barbados's submission "for the use of the Parliament of England." Willoughby, who had arrived from his plantation 12 miles outside Bridgetown and assembled a force of 400 riders and 6,000 militiamen, replied that he knew "no supreme authority over Englishmen" but the exiled King Charles II. Ayscue thereupon instituted a blockade, intercepting all merchantmen arriving at Bridgetown—mostly Dutch vessels. This unwittingly contributed to a downturn in diplomatic relations between London and The Hague and hastened the eruption of the First Anglo-Dutch War the next year.

The Barbadian stalemate ensued until news arrived from England on 8 November 1651 (O.S.) of Cromwell's victory over the last Royalist army at Worcester; buoyed by these tidings, Ayscue sent 200 seamen on a nocturnal raid two weeks later that destroyed the 4-gun Holetown battery and came away with thirty prisoners. Island morale was further sapped when the parliamentary warships *John* and *Guinea* arrived early in

December with thirteen more vessels, bound to subdue Virginia. Ayscue employed 550 men early on the morning of 7 December to attack the small fort at Speight's Bay (pronounced "Spike's" Bay, also known as Little Bristol; modern Speightstown). Although its defenders had been forewarned and totaled three cavalry troops and 1,200 infantrymen, they nonetheless broke in the darkness, leaving behind four cannon and eighty prisoners. Ayscue ordered the latter released, to spread sedition among Willoughby's ranks.

The Virginia squadron departed by 14 December 1651 (O.S.), after which Ayscue began a secret correspondence with Col. Sir Thomas Modyford, whose militia regiment was stationed near his plantation on Austin's Bay. Despite his being a Royalist, Modyford believed that the impasse was ruining the island economy, so he agreed to turn his 800 men inland, allowing Ayscue's troops to come ashore on 3 January 1652 (O.S.). The 2,000 parliamentary infantrymen and 100 cavalrymen were contained by 2,000 foot and 400 riders a quarter mile distant under Willoughby. Yet a week of steady rain averted any immediate clash, after which the monarchists asked for terms. These proved generous, no punishments being imposed, while the Barbadians would be allowed to retain their local council and general assembly, with limited powers of taxation.

The articles of capitulation were therefore signed at the Mermaid Inn near Austin's Bay on 11 January 1652 (O.S.), all strongholds being surrendered the next day. Ayscue installed his aide, Daniel Searle, as island governor on 17 January and sailed away by mid-March. This surrender document became known as the Charter of Barbados, as it enumerated the colonists' rights in place of the Earl of Carlisle's original private patent, which had been abrogated by the Commonwealth's abolition of the monarchy.

However, Bridgetown's trade still continued to languish as the First Anglo-Dutch War erupted back in Europe in May 1652, hampering transatlantic traffic for the next two years. At the cessation of hostilities, the town consisted of 300 to 400 wooden structures housing perhaps 2,000 residents, mostly employed among its warehouses or inns. In an effort to speed its commercial revival, Searle instituted some modest municipal reforms: first, by having the legislature pass an act in 1654 to provide unimpeded access to all wharves or landing spots, followed by another two years later "for the making good and clearing ye streets and lands in and about ye Indian Bridge Towne"; a third act in April 1657 defined land plots more clearly, as well as creating a public market.

However, the port was to benefit most notably from a boom in the island's sugarcane industry as Dutch refugees arrived from Brazil with specialized knowledge about tropical cultivation as well as the erection of wind-powered mills for refining harvests. Bridgetown soon began profiting from lucrative exports, plus the importation of African field hands. Unfortunately, society was to be irrevocably transformed by this eco-

Bridgetown as seen from offshore, ca. 1905. (Keane, *Central and South America*)

nomic makeover, as sugar crops required much vaster estates, as well as major capital investments in expensive milling machinery and slaves. Many small landholders—already discouraged by their recent setbacks—consequently began quitting Barbados, 3,500 volunteering to emigrate to the recently conquered Jamaica or to North America. This trend accelerated over the next couple of decades, as small-scale farmers could not compete with the increasingly rich sugar operators and so became displaced by ever-larger plantations.

Therefore, although the volume and value of Bridgetown's traffic soared, the island changed from a diverse community into a single-crop economy. On 9 February 1659 (O.S.), the capital also suffered its first major conflagration, with more than 200 dwellings and warehouses being reduced to ashes and its bridge severely damaged. Hoping to prevent future outbreaks, a statute was enacted in April 1660 prohibiting thatched roofs on houses and encouraging the use of shingles, as well as directing every householder whose premises contained a courtyard to sink a well; but with land tenure now so uncertain, many impoverished residents simply rebuilt with whatever materials were at hand.

Royal Restoration and Dutch Bombardment (1660–1667)

After Cromwell's death in England, his Commonwealth collapsed and Charles II was peacefully installed on the English throne in the spring of 1660, and Thomas Modyford was appointed as Barbados's first royal governor by late June. A private claim was also filed on behalf of Carlisle's heirs to resurrect his original patent over the island, yet that title was eventually ceded to the Crown in exchange for a 4.5 percent duty on all export produce, which was to be paid to the heirs. The island capital's name was officially changed from Doncaster to St. Michael's, its parish name, although "Bridgetown" still continued to prevail. In December 1660 it was furthermore reported that Willoughby was to be restored to his old position of governor-general of the English Antilles, so that Modyford resigned (although he remained as speaker of the Barbadian General Assembly until he too was knighted and promoted to the governorship of Jamaica three years later).

Despite a steady drain of island residents, Bridgetown revived under Willoughby's vigorous leadership, so much so that by June 1664 he was able to send 1,500 men aboard five ships—in addition to 600 Caribs in seventeen canoes—to expel a small French garrison from Saint Lucia. Relations with The Netherlands then took another downturn, both nations mobilizing their navies and clashing in West Africa and North America. On the morning of 19 April 1665 (O.S.), intent on inaugurating hostilities with a surprise attack, Dutch admiral Michiel Adriaenszoon de Ruyter suddenly materialized off Barbados. His five warships and seven frigates stood directly into Carlisle Bay next morning, surprising twenty-nine merchantmen and a single man-of-war about to weigh. Ignoring the fire from shore batteries and anchored vessels, de Ruyter

Panoramic view of Bridgetown, as engraved in 1695 by Jan Kip, based upon an original drawing by Samuel Copen. (Library of Congress)

moved to within point-blank range and crashed out heavy volleys over the next several hours, destroying much of the convoy. However, he could not dent Bridgetown's defenses, while his 68-gun flagship *Spiegel* and other warships sustained considerable damage. The Dutch therefore withdrew to the neutral French island of Martinique to effect repairs.

Notwithstanding the shock of this attack, Barbados recovered and fared rather well during the initial phases of this, the Second Anglo-Dutch War, by quickly overrunning the nearby islands of Sint Eustatius, Sabá, and Tobago. In January 1666, though, France joined The Netherlands, and three months afterward the English residents on St. Kitts were overwhelmed by their French neighbors. Learning of this defeat, Willoughby commandeered a merchant convoy in mid-July that was about to depart Bridgetown, using it to load a relief force of more than 1,000 men aboard nineteen vessels. But while steering northwestward to gather further strength from Nevis, Montserrat, and Antigua, his fleet was swallowed wholesale by a hurricane. Deprived of fighting men by this calamitous loss, Bridgetown waited anxiously until a fleet could be hastened out from England under Rear Adm. Sir John Harman in the spring of 1667. Shortly thereafter, a new governor-general—William Willoughby, younger brother of the deceased Francis—arrived with 800 soldiers plus abundant supplies of artillery, powder, and shot for the city batteries, so that it survived the remaining few months of this conflict undisturbed.

Sugar Capital and Naval Base (1668–1765)
Barbados's wealth had now multiplied fortyfold since 1640, while its slave population had risen to 30,000 by 1668, although the number of white residents had almost fallen to half—20,000—through emigration. The percentage of landowners contracted even more precipitously, to a mere 2,639 by 1679—of whom 120 were wealthy estate owners, controlling virtually all the arable land. As a result, the sugar trade now dominated Bridgetown's economy, its port servicing a steady stream of inbound slavers and outbound merchant convoys. For the remainder of the seventeenth century, the

volume of island exports exceeded that of any other British Caribbean territory and would prove "more valuable than the total from North America."

Increasingly crowded, the town suffered another fire that broke out on the evening of Saturday, 18 April 1668 (O.S.), in a garret on premises belonging to the merchants John Bushel and Francis Bond. Flames quickly spread to the adjacent public magazine, whose 170 barrels of gunpowder detonated, raining fiery destruction throughout most other neighborhoods. More than 800 of Bridgetown's 1,000 structures and its bridge were destroyed, so that the legislature—obliged to convene in some of the surviving taverns, the Roebuck proving a particular favorite—ordered that reconstruction be carried out in noncombustible stone wherever possible. The old wooden stockade called James Fort was to be resurrected by 1670 as a 20-gun stone fortress.

Lamentably, though, another conflagration erupted around 8:00 P.M. on 24 January 1673 (O.S.) in "New England Row"—modern Broad Street—claiming forty more houses plus a substantial proportion of the town's food supplies. The restored bridge also suffered some damage, as well as from a hurricane in 1675, while the magazine was not entirely rebuilt until eight years afterward, by the local contractor Simon Cooper. He was also hired by the assembly to erect a second 20-foot-wide span across the town's waterway, which when completed in November 1681 became known as the "East Bridge" (later replaced by Victoria Bridge, eventually renamed the Charles Duncan O'Neal Bridge). The older Indian span henceforth became known as the "West Bridge" until washed away by heavy flooding in January 1700.

Bridgetown's importance as a naval base was also underscored during the late seventeenth and early eighteenth centuries, as its position 100 miles east of the Windward Islands ensured that advance warning of any hostile developments in Europe reached Barbados first, giving it a tactical advantage over its neighbors. The prevailing flow of winds and sea currents from east to west furthermore facilitated descents by Barbadian sailing ships against all other Antillean targets, while hampering any counterattacks in the opposite direction. Lastly, Carlisle Bay provided Royal Navy warships with a deep, semi-sheltered anchorage in which to ride out storms, plus accessible copses from which to draw hardwood timbers such as cedar and mahogany for repairs.

(Even rum could be made available to crews. Prior to having been deployed in the West Indies, English warships had traditionally carried cider, beer, and brandy for their men's consumption while operating in home waters, but these first two spirits decayed in the warm tropics; local sugar-derived stimulants had therefore been sporadically substituted. The policy of purchasing Barbadian rum was apparently made official after Adm. Sir John Narborough—the commissioner of the navy responsible for the Victualling Department in London—visited Bridgetown in November 1687 aboard his 48-gun HMS *Foresight* and bought "600 odd gallons of rum to be served to our ship's company in lieu of brandy," thus recommending this practice throughout the service.)

During King William's War, or the War of the League of Augsburg, from 1689 to 1697, Bridgetown served as a staging point for major strikes against St. Kitts, Guadeloupe, Martinique, and in relief of Cartagena, without being directly threatened in turn. Once peace was restored the port resumed its sugar and slaving trade until visited by a large fleet under Vice Adm. John Benbow in November 1701. His presence caused Paris to counter that next January with thirty-eight French warships dispatched to reinforce Martinique under Vice Adm. François-Louis Rousselet, Comte de Château-Renault. As relations worsened in Europe the French admiral was instructed to launch a preemptive attack against Bridgetown, but he felt such an enterprise beyond his fleet's capabilities—having only 2,200 troops, a third of the estimated English numbers on Barbados. He consequently opted to support France's Spanish allies by sailing to Havana and escorting the Mexican plate-fleet across the Atlantic.

When Queen Anne's War, or the War of the Spanish Succession, finally erupted in the summer of 1702, the Barbadian capital again proved to be a valuable regional stronghold. Commo. Hovenden Walker arrived in January 1703 with 4,000 soldiers, who after losing a quarter of their number to death, desertion, or illness, unsuccessfully assailed Guadeloupe six weeks later; yet despite that failure Bridgetown remained safe throughout the ensuing ten years of hostilities, nor was its trade crippled. According to a census undertaken two years after peace was restored in 1713, the island's population consisted of 16,888 white residents—of whom 4,097 lived in Bridgetown or its immediate environs, called St. Michael's Parish, while slave numbers had swollen to approximately 40,000.

The port grew in prosperity over the next few decades as island commerce continued to escalate, notwithstanding the six-month blockade imposed as of October 1720 by the pirate Bartholomew Roberts. Barbados's neat, cultivated appearance

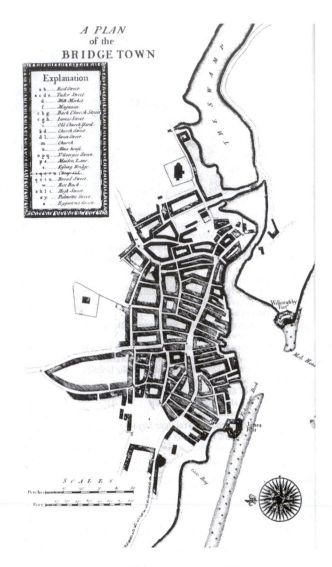

Bridgetown, ca. 1717–1721, as surveyed by William Mayo; north is toward lower left, while the entrance is guarded by Forts James and Willoughby. (Barbados Museum)

and old-fashioned customs had long ago earned it the nickname of "Little England," while its society was headed by estate holders who were actually present as resident managers, rather than absentee owners as in other Caribbean colonies. Bridgetown therefore began to benefit from innovations such as the causeway erected to replace its Old Indian Bridge, ca. 1721 (but which unwittingly blocked off the flow into the Careenage, slowly silting up its channel). A new town hall was also completed by 1730 to accommodate the legislature, law courts, and jail—prisoners having previously escaped from the more rudimentary confinement in James Fort—and a printing press was imported that same year by David Harry of Philadelphia. He used it to publish a two-page weekly called the *Barbados Gazette,* edited as of 1731 by Samuel Keimer, a former associate of Benjamin Franklin.

Bridgetown maintained strong ties with North America throughout the colonial era, regularly exporting sugar, rum, and molasses to Philadelphia and the Chesapeake Bay in exchange for foodstuffs, building materials, and livestock. Social interaction had also begun very early on. Henry Winthrop, second son of John Winthrop, governor of the Massachusetts Bay Company, had been a member of Barbados's first party of settlers in 1627, while many other New England families had relatives on the island. Barbadian émigrés had moreover resettled all along the Atlantic seaboard, while members of the island elite sent their children north for schooling. Conversely, winter-weary North Americans visited Barbados for its sunny and healthful clime, such as a nineteen-year-old George Washington, who in 1751 accompanied his older half brother Lawrence—terminally ill with tuberculosis—or the painter William Johnston, who moved to the island in 1760 to live out his remaining years.

Sugar cultivation was stimulated throughout the West Indies by Parliament's passage of the Molasses Act in 1733, as well as by the Sugar Act six years later, both measures having been engineered by monopolistic interests in London. The resultant upsurge in trade indirectly benefited Bridgetown: a school called Codrington College was opened by 1742 from a

"George Washington House" in Bridgetown, as it appeared ca. 1940. (Library of Congress)

bequest left forty years prior by Sir Christopher Codrington. Naval facilities were also upgraded after relations between England and France began to deteriorate again in December 1743, Commo. Charles Knowles arriving as station commander and rebuilding its defenses in anticipation of an outbreak, with the assistance of Gov. Sir Thomas Robinson and military engineer John Trail.

Hostilities erupted the next spring, being remembered as King George's War, or the War of the Austrian Succession. Commo. Fitzroy Henry Lee arrived as new station commander in May 1745, being succeeded that same September by Vice Adm. Isaac Townsend—who, despite bringing a considerable fleet into Carlisle Bay, could not persuade regional governors to unite for an offensive against French Saint Lucia. Barbados had become equally reluctant to aid its British West Indian neighbors, Bridgetown's shippers complaining about the inconvenience of sharing convoys with other Leeward Islanders, retarding their own consignments to North America or London. Such self-interest was further exacerbated by the fact that Barbados's agricultural system had by now become so highly developed that the island no longer had to import many African slaves, its population of field hands having become largely self-sustaining.

Once peace returned in 1748, a pair of misfortunes befell the town. First, a new stone span was completed to replace its old wooden bridge in April 1751, only to promptly collapse; then, on Sunday, 8 February 1756, a fire broke out among some cotton bales in Joseph Blackman's storehouse on Canary Street (so named because as early as the seventeenth century, its establishments had specialized in wines imported from the Canary Islands; later it was renamed St. George Street in honor of the February 1861 visit by Prince Alfred, Duke of Edinburgh, aboard HMS *St. George*). This blaze moved swiftly westward and engulfed James Fort, before veering north toward Cheapside, then eastward so as to consume virtually everything along the south side of Broad Street. By the time the flames finally abated next dawn, some 160 houses had been reduced to cinders.

War against France resumed in May 1756, Bridgetown being once more pressed into service as a naval base and staging area, despite another accidental fire sparked by someone frying fish at 2:00 A.M. on Saturday, 25 February 1758; this fire destroyed ninety dwellings on Roebuck Street. A fleet of sixty troop transports stood into Carlisle Bay on 3 January 1759 with more than 3,700 soldiers under Maj.-Gen. Peregrine Thomas Hopson, departing a fortnight later to overrun Guadeloupe and Marie-Galante. Rear Adm. George Brydges Rodney brought another, even larger formation into Carlisle Bay in November–December 1761, conveying 13,000 troops under Maj. Gen. Robert Monckton, who sailed on 5 January 1762 to subdue Martinique. A third enormous fleet under Vice Adm. Sir George Pocock and Lt. Gen. George Keppel, Earl of Albemarle, paused briefly at Bridgetown in late April 1762, before proceeding deep into the Caribbean to conquer Havana.

Codrington College, as it appeared, ca. 1907, framed by some magnificent "cabbage" palms. (Aspinall, *Pocket Guide to the West Indies*)

Bridgetown profited from victualling and repairing these massive fleets, as well as from intercepted prizes brought in for adjudication by privateers.

Setbacks and Resurgence (1766–1815)

A brief economic slowdown occurred once peace was restored in 1763, followed by a calamitous conflagration that started after a clerk employed by William Chate on High Street fell asleep with a candle burning at 11:30 P.M. on 13 May 1766. Fanned by a strong northeasterly breeze, its flames swept so frighteningly through the town that a few houses were even intentionally blown up, in a desperate bid to stem their advance. By the time this blaze had burned itself out the next morning, more than 26 acres of Bridgetown lay in smoldering ruins: from High Street in the east to the Old Churchyard (St. Mary's) in the west, and from Swan Street in the north as far down as the waterfront, some 1,140 buildings were destroyed—including 418 private dwellings and all public offices. Property losses were estimated at the then enormous sum of £500,000.

Survivors crowded into the few unaffected areas east of High Street so that reconstruction might commence, but that sector too went up in flames from another accidental fire, ignited on the evening of 27 December 1766 in Paul Bedford's

store on Lees Alley (modern Ricketts Street). Damage from this second conflagration was assessed at an additional £100,000, the widespread devastation prompting the Barbadian legislature to pass an act the following year that explicitly revised future building features: for example, certain narrow alleys were to be closed off and some streets widened, altering the town's layout; all structures were to be reerected of stone or brick rather than wood, "with roofs of copper, slate, tile, sawed stone, or block tin, and no other materials"; and so forth. Gradually the port struggled back to life, its recuperation being further assisted by a large-scale project in December 1772 to provide uniform access to all its wharves and to dredge its sea channel.

When Edward Hay arrived the next year to assume office as governor, he found a total of 18,532 white inhabitants on the island, 534 free mulattos or blacks, and 68,908 slaves. The outbreak of the American Revolutionary War in 1775 contributed to a difficult period for Bridgetown: most of its trade with North America was abruptly curtailed; drought simultaneously reduced agricultural productivity on the island; and another devastating fire swept through the capital in 1776—the only improvement being that during the subsequent reconstruction of Bridgetown, its East Bridge was replaced by a new 40-foot-wide span. Barbados's economic plight nonetheless became so critical that only the timely arrival of relief convoys from London early in 1778 prevented a famine.

The region also became the focus of some noteworthy naval actions. The 64-gun HMS *Yarmouth* of Capt. Nicholas Vincent chased a U.S. squadron off the island on 7 March 1778, during which pursuit the 32-gun frigate USS *Randolph* of Capt. Nicholas Biddle exploded and went down with almost all its 315 hands. That same August, France allied itself with the Thirteen Colonies, and Barbadians became further worried as Martinique immediately launched an offensive that captured Dominica. Reinforcements were consequently rushed out from London, which Rear Adm. Sir Samuel Barrington used to mass a counterexpedition in Carlisle Bay, setting sail on 11 December with 4,000 soldiers under Maj.-Gen. Sir William Meadows to invade Saint Lucia. However, a powerful French fleet under Vice Adm. Charles-Henri, Comte d'Estaing, remained poised at Martinique throughout this campaign, so that Bridgetown lived in continuous fear of invasion, while its trade declined from ballooning insurance premiums on all commercial consignments.

Another memorable incident occurred in January 1779, when the American privateer *Cumberland* of Capt. John Manley was captured off Barbados's eastern coast, its 117 men being interned in Bridgetown's jail—from which the American officers escaped on the night of 23 February by climbing down a rope ladder and disappearing among the anchored vessels. More ominously, the British fleet blockading Martinique under Vice Adm. John "Foul Weather Jack" Byron withdrew that same June to cover the departure of merchant convoys from the Leeward Islands, allowing D'Estaing to sortie with twenty-five ships-of-the-line and a host of auxiliaries to threaten Barbados. Fortunately, contrary winds diverted the French against Grenada, before this enemy fleet could be overtaken and mauled on 6 July by Byron's twenty-one ships-of-the-line, after which both formations quit the West Indies altogether, leaving Bridgetown in a state of unease.

Spain also declared war against Great Britain, in June 1779, and invasion fears revived until Gen. John Vaughan arrived to bolster the Barbadian garrison in February 1780—a reinforcement that proved timely, as Vice Adm. Luc-Urbain du Bouexic, Comte de Guichen, quit Martinique on 13 April with a large fleet and 3,000 troops under the governor-general of the French West Indies, Claude-François-Amour, Marquis de Bouillé du Chariol, who attempted yet another thrust, but was repelled three days later opposite Dominica by Rodney's fleet. Some anxiety recurred at Bridgetown when a huge Spanish fleet under Adm. José Solano y Bote joined de Guichen at Martinique in early June, but that combined host steered west toward Saint-Domingue (Haiti) and Cuba.

Despite being spared any direct assault, Barbados was struck by a hurricane on the evening of 10 October 1780, and its capital was reduced to a sodden mass of rubble over the next forty-eight hours, only 30 of its 1,200 structures emerg-

ing unscathed. Even Government House—believed to be storm-proof because of its circular design, barricaded windows, plus 3-foot-thick walls—had its roof, doors, and shutters torn off within the first twelve hours, compelling Gov. James Cunningham and his family to flee from its flooded cellar into the lee of a stone battery. The naval hospital at Temple Yard was also heavily damaged when a loose ship drove into it, twenty-three seamen becoming entombed amid its ruins. Plantations suffered wholesale destruction as well, and a total of 4,326 deaths were recorded on the island. (After the storm, 800 Spanish prisoners labored tirelessly under Capt. Pedro Santiago of the Aragón Regiment to help alleviate the distress of the frightened survivors, moving Cunningham to write to London that they "conducted themselves more like friends than enemies; I therefore mean to show them every indulgence in my power.")

As the battered town began to rebuild for the second time in fourteen years, hostilities broadened further as Britain declared war against The Netherlands on 20 December 1780, so that Rodney and Vaughan next January occupied the Dutch Antillean outposts of Sint Eustatius, Sint Maarten, Saba, Essequibo, Demerara, and Berbice. The French responded after a strong fleet arrived at Martinique in April 1781 under Adm. François-Joseph-Paul, Comte de Grasse Tilly, who detached a squadron next month to overwhelm Tobago, despite two counterexpeditions mounted from Barbados by Rodney. Even after de Grasse departed for Chesapeake Bay to help Gen. George Washington defeat the besieged British army at Yorktown, Governor-General de Bouillé was able to lead a small fleet from Martinique that same November to wrench Sint Eustatius, Sint Maarten, and Saba back from the English.

Bridgetown's plight continued when de Grasse's fleet returned from Virginia to spearhead another thrust that captured St. Kitts in January 1782, Rear Adm. Samuel Hood's British fleet vainly trying to reply by transporting reinforcements across from Barbados and Antigua. Yet Demerara and Essequibo were recaptured as well, plus the English island of Montserrat by late February. The Barbadian capital, still undergoing extensive reconstruction, feared that it too would suffer an invasion until Rodney finally returned with his fleet and defeated de Grasse in a huge battle near The Saintes on 12 April, ending such menaces for the remaining year of the conflict.

Still, the island's commerce had been ground to a halt, and by the time hostilities ceased in the spring of 1783, its population had been reduced to 16,157 whites, roughly 800 free mulattos or blacks, and 62,258 slaves. Bridgetown was able to recuperate from its material damages, the temporary downturn in its naval and privateering revenues, as well as its lost North American trade, thanks to a fortunate spike in global sugar prices. That increase became even more pronounced after production on Saint-Domingue collapsed altogether in 1791, the result of disruptions occasioned by the French Revolution. The

Barbadian port boomed as the radical Directorate in Paris executed Louis XVI on 21 January 1793, then followed that act with a declaration of war against England and Spain. The port's trade stood in little danger, as the French navy had already been decimated by republican purges; furthermore, renewed service as a naval base helped it to thrive once more.

A small squadron under Vice Adm. Sir John Laforey set sail in mid-April 1793 to seize French Tobago; another departed Bridgetown later that same month under Rear Adm. Alan Gardner to make an unsuccessful bid with a contingent of French monarchists to wrest Martinique from republican control. A much larger expedition then reached Carlisle Bay from England in late January 1794 under Vice Adm. Sir John Jervis (later the Earl of St. Vincent) and Lt. Gen. Sir Charles Grey who proceeded to overrun Martinique and several other islands, after which fighting shifted away from Barbados for more than a year. Unfortunately, though, Bridgetown suffered one of its worst floods on 8 November 1795, when after almost forty-eight hours of unrelenting rain, the gully that carried waters from the central island parishes into Constitution River ran higher than had ever previously been known, meeting with the spring tide to inundate the town to a depth of 5 feet in several areas, as well as washing away both bridges. The Barbadian capital was saved from utter destruction only when its river overflowed just above the urban area, cascading through Nelson Street toward the open sea.

As the sodden capital struggled to recover, another expedition under Rear Adm. Sir Hugh Cloberry Christian and Lt. Gen. Sir Ralph Abercromby reached Carlisle Bay on 21 April 1796, scooping up enemy islands so effectively that invasion fears at Barbados ceased for the remainder of this contest. Not even Spain's declaration of war against England in October 1796 could disturb Bridgetown's commerce; its convoys still departed on a regular basis, while its prize court benefited from an upsurge in adjudications of privateer prizes. American warships and merchantmen also began calling in large numbers once again, as the United States had been drawn into a quasi war against France, deploying a squadron in December 1798 to escort shipping in and out of the Antilles.

Britain and France agreed to a truce in the autumn of 1801, signing a treaty by March 1802; however, fighting flared anew only fourteen months later, so that Commo. Samuel Hood (a cousin of Admiral Hood) and Lt. Gen. William Grinfield entered Carlisle Bay on 17 June 1803 with yet another expedition to capture Saint Lucia and Tobago. A second British thrust that same September secured Demerara, Essequibo, and Berbice, while a third campaign out of Barbados saw 2,000 troops under Maj. Gen. Sir Charles Green overwhelm Surinam by April 1804.

A brief invasion fear gripped Bridgetown in February 1805, when Rear Adm. Edouard-Thomas de Burgues, Comte de Missiessy, reached Martinique with eleven warships and 3,300 men. This arrival inspired French West Indian forces to raid numerous nearby British islands, until Rear Adm. Sir Alexander Forrester Inglis Cochrane reached Carlisle Bay on 3 April with his own squadron, having pursued Missiessy across the Atlantic. The latter promptly withdrew, but an enormous Franco-Spanish battle fleet then gained Martinique on 14 May under Vice Adm. Pierre-Charles-Silvestre de Villeneuve, his intent apparently being to conquer the British West Indies.

Bridgetown fell into a panic because of this formidable threat, little realizing that Villeneuve's true objective was to lure Royal Navy fleets across the ocean in his wake, then race back to Europe to cover Napoleon's projected invasion of England. Barbadians did not feel safe until Vice Adm. Horatio, Viscount Nelson, reached Carlisle Bay on 4 June 1805 with his own battle fleet. He quickly incorporated two local ships-of-the-line and 2,000 militiamen into his force, then steered southwest toward Trinidad in quest of his enemy. Learning that the combined Franco-Spanish fleet had headed north from Martinique, the British admiral subsequently reversed course, disembarked his Barbadian contingent, then refreshed supplies at Antigua before sailing out into the Atlantic in Villeneuve's pursuit, eventually defeating him at the Battle of Trafalgar. Bridgetown regained some equanimity and reacted calmly when another Royal Navy squadron under Vice Adm. Sir John Thomas Duckworth entered Carlisle Bay on 12 January 1806, having chased a small French force under Vice Adm. Corentin de Leissègues across the Atlantic, annihilating this prey a few weeks later off Santo Domingo.

In other noteworthy incidents, the South American revolutionary Francisco de Miranda also used Barbados as a staging area for his unsuccessful bid to foment a revolt in Venezuela in August 1806; Cochrane and Gen. Henry Bowyer organized an expedition to sail from Bridgetown against the Danish West Indies in December 1807, after learning that war had been declared against that nation back in Europe. Then a much larger formation transported an army from Carlisle Bay under Lt. Gen. George Beckwith to conquer Martinique in February 1809, as well as the Saintes, Guadeloupe, Saint Martin, and Sint Eustatius.

Thanks to the Royal Navy's dominance everywhere on the high seas, Bridgetown spent the last few years of the Napoleonic conflict undisturbed by foreign threats. A great deal of naval and military construction had also been undertaken in town, such as the completion of a new naval hospital at Cheapside in 1805, plus a grand new cruciform marketplace in November 1810. Sugar convoys still departed regularly, although prices on international markets had begun falling worrisomely because of increased competition from other sources. An alliance had also been forged with Spain in 1808, diverting many commercial shippers to the much larger South American markets; a further setback occurred when the War of 1812 broke out, once again costing Bridgetown its U.S. trade.

Nevertheless, the Barbadian capital emerged noticeably enhanced from these two decades of struggle, featuring many fine Georgian mansions adorned with attractive verandas and terraces. However, the Crown's wartime expenditures were abruptly curtailed once Napoleon was defeated in Europe in the spring of 1814. Many British garrisons were withdrawn so that France's rival West Indian colonies could be restored upon the ascension of Louis XVIII to the throne in Paris. The American war also concluded early in 1815, and Bridgetown's wartime boom ended, as the Royal Navy presence in the Antilles was drastically scaled back, and no more privateering ventures were authorized.

Stagnation (1816–1860)

A census taken in 1816 recorded nearly 20,000 inhabitants living in Bridgetown and its adjoining St. Michael's Parish, of whom 5,038 were classified as whites, 1,933 as free mulattoes or blacks, and the remainder as slaves, out of a total Barbadian population of 16,020 whites, 3,007 free mulattoes or blacks, and approximately 77,000 slaves. However, the island economy did not bounce back to its previous levels of peacetime prosperity, inasmuch as the overseas price of sugar continued to sag, and local plantations could no longer compete with the much larger operations on the American or African mainlands. Transatlantic shipping patterns had moreover changed, and Bridgetown's once strategically placed seaport now found itself awkwardly situated to attract new clients. Little other industry existed to lure additional business, so that an economic malaise set in.

The capital's worries deepened when several thousand slave laborers, their expectations of freedom having been raised through false rumors, revolted in St. Philip Parish on the evening of 14 April 1816. This insurrection quickly spread into three adjoining parishes, before militiamen and British troops could suppress it, two days later. Some 400 individuals were slain or executed during this outburst, mostly blacks, while another 130 were exiled to Honduras. A hurricane then swept through Bridgetown on 21 October 1817, followed by a major flood on 14 October 1819; lastly, a fire erupted at the Bullhead Alley residence of a baker named Watts around 1:00 P.M. on Sunday, 10 June 1821. It consumed a large number of buildings, while many others had to be pulled down to prevent the flames from spreading.

Three years later, some good fortune at last smiled upon the island capital when a new diocese was created, and St. Michael's Parish Church was elevated to the status of a cathedral with the consecration of Dr. William Hart Coleridge as the first Anglican bishop for Barbados and the Leeward Islands in 1825. A second church—St. Mary's—was also created that same year, and this enhanced prestige inspired a few leading citizens to propose incorporating Bridgetown as a city. A committee was appointed as of 3 December 1825 to prepare a petition requesting such a royal charter from London. Unfortunately, another conflagration erupted in January 1826 at the residence of a Bridgetown coach painter named McCarra,

who as a sergeant-major in a militia artillery company, had brought home a cartridge box after a parade that subsequently exploded. Fanned by a strong easterly wind, this blaze swept through the neighborhood, destroying 166 homes before burning itself out. In the aftermath to this calamity, Bridgetown's shaken citizenry passed a resolution on 15 February 1826 declaring that it was "inexpedient to incorporate the Town of St. Michael."

Another massive hurricane struck on the evening of 10 August 1831, and Barbadian society was further convulsed when free blacks and "people of colour" were granted full rights and suffrage on instructions from London in 1832; the old plantation system finally ended with the full emancipation of all remaining slaves six years later. However, the implementation of this policy simply freed thousands of retainers into a depressed island economy, without any skills or means of support. Many soon found themselves mired in abject poverty, eking out a meager subsistence as seasonal laborers or tenant farmers. Their plight was further aggravated when the sugar industry collapsed altogether after Britain started to equalize importation duties in 1845, replacing its old monopoly network with a "free trade" series of reforms throughout the empire that benefited many, yet lowered still further the exports from such forlorn outposts as Bridgetown.

With impoverished squatters now pressing in upon its outskirts, the Barbadian capital endured yet more catastrophes. On the night of 3–4 February 1846, another fire broke out and spread from 20 Swan Street, despite the fact that 32 houses were either torn down or blown up in a desperate bid to check its advance. Ten acres of the lower town were consumed by dawn, comprising 180 dwellings, and that area—known for a time thereafter as the Burnt District—was purchased the next year by the Crown in vain hopes of redeveloping it, although no financing could be raised. The poor Greenfields district was also consumed by a fire on 17 February 1853, losing 97 tenements; a person died of cholera on Fairchild Street on 14 May 1854, proving to be the first victim of an epidemic that claimed more than 18,000 lives throughout the island before abating that September. Another calamitous blaze erupted in the Palmetto Street lumberyard of John and George Alleyne on the night of 14 February 1860, destroying Bridgetown as far south as its upper wharf before crossing the Careenage and razing both sides of Bay Street right up to Shurland's Alley.

Tentative Modernization (1861–1945)

Once again, the government purchased the devastated sector—known as the New Burnt District—and cleared it so as to expand the public buildings, as well as enlarging and improving the area around Trafalgar Square. And in order to provide some recourse against future outbreaks of fire, the recently created Waterworks Company also began laying pipes throughout town that same December, its first tap being

View of the Swing Bridge and reconstructed public buildings, ca. 1880. The massive new Clock Tower atop the entrance to the East Wing of Barbados's House of Assembly started to sink and crack shortly after this photo was taken, having to be dismantled in 1884 so as to be reerected atop the West Wing two years later. (W. G. Cooper)

opened on Nelson's Statue, a spigot protruding from the base of the statue and emptying into a public fountain, by 29 March 1861. This service was extended shortly thereafter into private homes, and by October 1861 there were 490 hydrants and 105 standpipes scattered throughout Bridgetown, greatly enhancing firefighting capabilities.

These constituted the first significant urban improvements made in several decades. They were followed by a few others, such as an iron "swing bridge" imported from London in 1865—although its two segments did not meet perfectly when assembled, so that one side had to be replaced by an immovable concrete substitute, delaying the inaugural until 18 April 1872. The span, moreover, was damaged by a hurricane in 1898 and renamed the Chamberlain Swing Bridge upon being reopened in December 1900, in appreciation of the assistance voted to the island by the government of British prime minister Joseph Chamberlain. Gas lighting was inaugurated on the

evening of 14 January 1876, while construction of a private railroad line toward Speightstown began in June 1877. Its Bridgetown-to-Carrington portion was completed by October 1881, and its full 24-mile extension as far as Belleplaine in St. Andrew Parish was finished by March 1883, one month after the capital's first telephones had been installed by the Tropical American Telephone Company.

Yet the attempt to save administrative costs by merging Barbados and the British Leeward Islands into a union with the Windward Islands met with violent local opposition, culminating in the so-called Confederation Riots of 1876. The price of sugar plunged again on the London markets eight years later, creating another serious economic downturn for the impoverished island. Nevertheless, Bridgetown's first horse-drawn "trams," or streetcars, were introduced that following year, running to Hastings Rocks and Fontabelle; a major new private dry dock was completed on the waterfront

Throng of laborers along Bridgetown's waterfront, waiting to sail to participate in the Panama Canal project, ca. 1907. (Henry Walter Parkinson)

by 1893. Still, the vast majority of Barbadians remained mired in poverty, while a tiny white elite proved unable to create any viable new industries. (According to a census taken in 1891, 122,717 of the 182,867 residents on Barbados were classified as black.) The island was then hard hit by a massive hurricane in 1898, whose devastation was so extensive that considerable financial assistance was required from the British government. During this reconstruction phase, Bridgetown's old wooden East or Victoria Bridge was replaced by an iron span, completed in 1901–1902.

Bridgetown's economy nonetheless remained prostrate, for in addition to its depleted commercial traffic, the port's role as a strategic naval base had long since withered away—the advent of steam warships having rendered its leeward position irrelevant except as a coaling station. What's more, the Royal Navy had introduced a "blue water" strategy by the end of the nineteenth century whereby powerful fleets operated directly out of Britain rather than overseas bases. Barbados's prospects

thus remained so grim that tens of thousands of islanders emigrated to seek employment abroad when the Panama Canal project began in 1904; almost a quarter of the total population departed over the next few years.

Some modest steps toward modernization nonetheless continued: Bridgetown's first buses appeared and made daily runs toward Speightstown by 1907, while electric power was introduced as of June 1911. Another large fire had erupted, around noon of 20 July 1910 in the cooperage of Musson, Son, and Company, doing great damage to the poor district called Golden Square and lower Bay Street before finally being quenched. World War I created a brief commercial upsurge, yet the port's economy stalled again at its conclusion, then was further exacerbated by the global effects of the Great Depression of October 1929. Bridgetown's streetcar company had already gone out of business by July 1925, and its railway service to Belleplaine did the same a dozen years afterward. Such unremitting poverty led to disturbances in July 1937.

Modern Era (1946–Present)

World War II had little direct effect upon Bridgetown, most Allied operations for the Eastern Caribbean being headquartered at Trinidad, which had long since outstripped Barbados in size, wealth, and importance. Nevertheless, the profusion of large-scale U.S. construction and logistical projects throughout the theater helped galvanize many islanders, who once this conflict ceased sought to alleviate their plight by charting a more independent course for their nation. A conference of West Indian labor leaders therefore met on Barbados in September 1945 to devise a common strategy, resulting in the formation of the Caribbean Labor Congress, from which organization would emerge numerous future leaders such as Grantley Adams of Barbados, Albert Gomes of Trinidad, Norman Manley of Jamaica, and Vere Bird of Antigua.

London was willing to oblige the islander movement, hoping to divest itself of disparate and unproductive colonial holdovers by reorganizing them into a semiautonomous federation that could then be welcomed into the Commonwealth. Washington also favored West Indian independence, so as to eliminate the last vestiges of European influence in the Americas and expand U.S. commercial interests. Barbados simultaneously began to share in a burgeoning tourism boom throughout the region, especially after work started on deepening Bridgetown's harbor to receive cruise ships as of 1955. (That project was temporarily delayed when Hurricane Janet roared through on 22 September of that same year.) The city began sprawling as a result, spreading northwestward and southeastward into an elliptical-shaped metropolitan area along the coastline, because growth inland was checked by a steep coral terrace a couple of miles away, beyond which lay fertile agricultural fields.

Aspirations for a West Indian Federation were dashed when this measure was voted down in Jamaica and Trinidad in September 1961 and January 1962, respectively, ending the experiment. Each island thereupon went its separate way, Barbados achieving full sovereignty and independence from Britain by 30 November 1966. Four years later, its government announced a plan to reverse Bridgetown's traditional dominance by decentralizing many government and commercial functions, redistributing them to other points. Still, Greater Bridgetown's inhabitants numbered close to 100,000 people—46 percent of the total island populace—according to the census taken in 1980–1981, although only 7,466 actually resided within the old city limits. And even at such a recent date, a majority of its dwellings still consisted of wooden structures, usually raised upon loose rock pile foundations to reduce the destructive effects of termites or other vermin; many also used pit latrines, not being connected to the sewers.

For further reading materials on the history of Bridgetown and Barbados, please consult the Select Bibliography at the end of this volume.

Cuba

Havana

A capital set beside one of the finest natural harbors in the world and which achieved its earliest fame as a plate-fleet base.

Discovery (1508–1518)

The first European to sight this vast bottleneck harbor and its dramatic stone headland was Capt. Sebastián de Ocampo, a veteran of Christopher Columbus's initial Caribbean penetrations, who in 1508 was ordered by Gov. Nicolás de Ovando of Santo Domingo to determine whether various Cuban sightings in fact represented one continuous island. De Ocampo set sail with two caravels and began reconnoitering its northern coastline, working westward until he arrived outside this particular bay, which he entered via its 300-yard-wide and almost mile-long channel, to refresh his provisions and effect repairs.

The passage opened up into a placid inner anchorage measuring 2.5 miles in length and width, whose shorelines abounded with cedar, mahogany, oak, ebony, teak, pines, and tar, essential elements for fixing and caulking hulls. Freshwater was accessible from several discharging streams, as well as fruits and food from its fertile, dark-red clay soil, so that de Ocampo named this well-favored sanctuary Puerto de Carenas, or Careening Port, upon his chart, before proceeding westward with his reconnaissance. Within a few more months, he was able to circle round and confirm for Governor de Ovando that Cuba did actually consist of a single island.

Three years later, 330 Spanish conquistadors and a host of native auxiliaries left Santo Domingo under Deputy Gov. Diego Velázquez de Cuéllar to subjugate eastern Cuba, in the process creating a succession of coastal towns over the next few years. Sometime in 1514 the sixth such municipality was established by Velázquez's subordinate Pánfilo de Narváez. It was at Gato Lagoon inside the mouth of the Onicaxinal or Hondo River, near Batabanó on the island's southern coast—a swampy place christened San Cristóbal de la Habana, or Saint Christopher of the Havana, the latter possibly being a corruption of Habaguanex, the name of the regional Taino overlord. (Columbus had also recorded *Avan* as a Cuban provincial name during his initial contact; in the future, the town's name would be spelled as "Habana" or "Havana," the version La Habana eventually coming to predominate among Spaniards, while "Havana" was adopted by the English.) As Saint Christopher's feast day fell on 25 July in the Church calendar, this formal act of possession may possibly have been celebrated on 25 July 1514, although no confirmation has ever been discovered.

The tiny outpost failed to prosper, as most Spaniards remained clustered farther east around the original island capital of Santiago de Cuba, near the source of supplies and reinforcements flowing across from Santo Domingo. Cuba also proved to be a disappointment for the conquistadors, having little mineral wealth, while its primitive Taino inhabitants were unaccustomed to regimented labor, and so sickened and perished in large numbers as slaves. Rumors soon circulated of an immensely rich empire farther west—the Aztecs of Mexico—which Governor Velázquez confirmed by sending a scouting expedition around northern Cuba in 1517. An army was therefore mustered at Santiago de Cuba under one of the governor's protégés, Hernán Cortés, to conquer a foothold.

But this subordinate gathered so many eager adherents that Velázquez began to suspect him of intending to seize this opulent prize for himself, so he tried to replace Cortés. The latter thereupon weighed anchor without permission on 18 November 1518, coasting along southern Cuba to gain more recruits from isolated outposts such as Havana, before striking out toward Cozumel on 18 February 1519 to initiate his epic two-year subjugation of the Aztec empire. Numerous vessels followed in his wake, and a new route to Europe was also pioneered when Cortés—desirous of sending Alonso Hernández

View northeastward across Havana's entrance channel, ca. 1913. At left lies the open sea, with El Morro Castle sitting atop its rocky headland and the ancient La Punta Fortress in center-foreground. The long shape of San Carlos Castle looms above the city atop La Cabaña Heights at center-right, while the inner bay lies out of camera range at right. (Lloyd, *Twentieth Century Impressions of Cuba*)

Portocarreo and Francisco de Montejo as emissaries to Emperor Charles I in Spain, with missives and chests of Mexican treasure justifying his defection—ordered them to sail directly into the Atlantic without touching at either Santiago or Santo Domingo, which were controlled by his jealous rivals.

The pilot, Antón de Alaminos, consequently steered across the Gulf of Mexico to northern Cuba, refreshing provisions from 23 to 26 August 1519 at Mariel—where Montejo owned an estate—before standing out into the open ocean via the "Bahama Channel" (modern Straits of Florida). A new navigational pattern had unwittingly been created, whereby ships sailing westward from the Antilles toward Mexico would follow Cortés's route along southern Cuba, then return eastward out of the Gulf to emerge on Cuba's northwestern shoreline, where a city would soon spring up.

Foundation and Early Evolution (1519–1560)

A few settlers had already traversed the island from their neglected San Cristóbal de la Habana outpost to erect shacks at an inlet 3 miles west of de Ocampo's Puerto de Carenas and dam up its river (called Casiguagas by local inhabitants, but which the Spaniards renamed de los Almendares, or "of the Almond Trees"). This tiny seaside enclave later became known as Chorrera—today lying within modern Havana's Puentes Grandes sector—although its transplanted residents referred to their new settlement as San Cristóbal de la Habana, apparently to indicate that it fell within their original town charter.

Shortly thereafter, they shifted their community into Puerto de Carenas itself, this third—and final—foundation of San Cristóbal de la Habana allegedly being consecrated by a religious service and *cabildo*, or council, meeting at the foot of a giant *ceiba*, or silk-cottonwood, tree, where the modern Templete stands. These ceremonies are believed to have occurred on 16 November 1519 (traditionally observed as the city's foundation date), and it is recorded that a few Spaniards were residing on the low and fertile shoreline inside the bay when Juan Ponce de León arrived in June 1521, mortally wounded from his attempt to find the Fountain of Youth in Florida.

However, Havana was not to flourish until a decade later, when increasing numbers of shipmasters realized that it offered an ideal stopover before striking out into the North Atlantic. The prevailing winds traversed its narrow channel perpendicularly, thus facilitating entry and egress by sailing ships; wood, water, and food such as fish, turtles, fruit, corn, coconuts, and potatoes were readily available, along with campsites at which to rest weary crews; its climate was temperate and healthful by Caribbean standards, its heat and humidity being moderated by breezes and proximity to the cool North American continental mass. Rainfall was spread out from May through December, and the Gulf Stream—the world's strongest ocean current, flowing past at speeds up to

6 miles an hour—helped propel emerging vessels toward the Straits of Florida.

Soon, so much traffic was calling that governors started regular visits from their nominal island capital of Santiago, located 500 miles away. Foreign interest was also sparked, the first enemy descent occurring when a French corsair vessel materialized outside Havana's entrance on 15 March 1537, having ventured into the Antilles as part of a recurrent Franco-Spanish dynastic struggle in Europe known as the Hapsburg-Valois Wars. Gov. Gonzalo de Guzmán commandeered three of five anchored merchantmen—the 200-ton *Trinidad,* the *Santa Catalina,* and the *San Miguel*—to sortie under Lt. Juan Velázquez. He overtook this intruder off Mariel three days later, only to blunder aground and be boarded, so that the Frenchmen returned into Havana's harbor to extort ransom from its hapless villagers.

Alarmed by the ease of this penetration, de Guzmán requested artillery from Spain to fortify the entrance. Yet before any could arrive, another French corsair robbed and torched the town's few wooden structures in May 1538. When word of this second depredation reached Santiago, the new governor, Hernando de Soto—a veteran of Francisco Pizarro's conquest of Peru, who had arrived on 7 June—dispatched his military engineer Mateo Aceituno with 100 men to throw up a 6-gun battery and cover the narrowest stretch of Havana's channel. De Soto's main fleet then followed in September–October, wintering for six months, before the governor set sail on his ill-fated attempt to conquer Florida.

Much construction was initiated during his brief tenure so that Havana's original 6-gun battery could become transformed into a 12-gun fort called Castillo de la Fuerza by 1540. Crown officials felt sufficiently secure to order Mexico's bullion safeguarded inside the fort by October 1541, until a battle squadron could be sent from Spain (relations with France having once again deteriorated). When hostilities flared openly next spring, the king dispatched even more armaments to bolster Havana's defenses, which helped repel an attack on 31 October 1543 by a homeward-bound French privateering squadron that disgorged more than 200 men a mile and a half away at San Lázaro Inlet. These rovers advanced confidently across open country, only to be surprised by the heavy counterfire from La Fuerza fortress, leaving behind 20 dead in their flight.

Next year, Havana's strategic importance was underscored when the Crown announced that all sailings out of Seville would be coalesced into two annual convoys with naval escorts, a wartime decree that laid the framework for the plate-fleet system. Because of its position at the confluence of the best homeward-bound sea-lanes, Havana was designated as a rendezvous for all such formations, significantly boosting the town's infrastructure: yards and copper foundries, for example, were installed for the first time. A small French raider men-

Painting of Havana's inner harbor in 1889, by the visiting Mexican landscape artist José María Velasco. (Private Collection, Mexico City)

aced its approaches in January 1546, then another in March 1553, but the defenses were now sufficiently imposing to deter such minor threats. The *Real Audiencia,* or Royal Tribunal, at Santo Domingo even authorized Cuban governors to forsake their official seat of residence at Santiago for extended periods to supervise port operations; Dr. Gonzalo Pérez de Angulo duly took up semipermanent residence at Havana as of July 1553.

But unfortunately, no convoys appeared the next year, and residents were alarmed to spot two sails at dawn on 10 July 1555. These ships disgorged several score of armed men at San Lázaro Inlet under the notorious Huguenot (French Protestant) corsair Jacques de Sores. Advancing swiftly, the raiders attacked La Fuerza citadel from its unguarded rear, burning the wooden door and compelling its two dozen defenders under the alcaide, Juan de Lobera, to surrender by dawn of 12 July. The Huguenots then brought their four vessels "in to careen" (or into the harbor to be safely beached and tilted up on dry land to repair their hulls), while demanding a ransom of 30,000 pesos, cassava bread, and meat in order to spare Havana's buildings—plus 500 pesos for each Spanish captive and another 100 for every slave. Having escaped inland, Pérez de Angulo launched an unsuccessful counterattack at dawn of 18 July with 35 Spanish, 220 black, and 80 Indian volunteers, during which the startled corsairs slaughtered all 30 Spanish prisoners, except Lobera. Angered by this assault, de Sores subsequently retaliated by leveling the town, hanging numerous slaves by their heels around Havana's outskirts and torching farms as far as 5 miles inland, before retiring back out to sea on 5 August with the citadel's twelve cannon.

Shorn of their defenses, Havana's survivors were powerless to prevent a trio of French ships from re-entering on 4 October 1555, disembarking fifty men who encamped amid the ruins. They were then followed by another dozen enemy craft over the next several days, foraging deep inland for booty—principally hides from abandoned cattle ranches—before departing three weeks later.

Havana did not begin to recuperate until peace with France was restored in February 1556. The plate-fleet of Adm. Alvaro Sánchez de Aviles arrived from Cartagena, Colombia, on 1 June to throw up some extemporized defenses, manning them with 100 sailors. Their presence provided the few score residents sufficient reassurance to start tentative reconstruction efforts of their own, a more permanent resurrection occurring after the 120-ton hired vessel *Espíritu Santo* of Capt. Diego Hernández appeared from Spain late in 1558 with a party of engineers under Bartolomé Sánchez. Sánchez set about rebuilding La Fuerza citadel as of 1 December with plans drawn up by Ochoa de Luyando. Civilian numbers rebounded to perhaps 100 families over the next few years, as fears of another invasion gradually subsided.

Emergence as Plate-Fleet Terminal (1561–1620)

The Crown reconfirmed Havana's status in the plate-fleet circuit by a royal decree issued on 16 July 1561 that codified transatlantic sailing patterns. Galleons had also begun to increase in size thanks to innovations in naval architecture inspired by Adm. Alvaro de Bazán, eliminating smaller West Indian harbors such as Santo Domingo or San Juan de Puerto Rico from consideration as ports of call. Furthermore, the volume of specie flowing out of Mexico soared dramatically, due to a new amalgamation treatment for silver ores called the *patio* process, which added so significantly to monetary volumes that more resources had to be committed for Havana's preservation.

As a result, a royal engineer named Francisco de Calona arrived in June 1562, having been hired to replace the irascible and unpopular Sánchez and to reinvigorate work on La Fuerza citadel. The next year, de Calona was also ordered by Gov. Diego de Mazariegos to replace the two-man lookout shack atop El Morro headland with a 40-foot whitewashed stone tower to serve as an observation platform and beacon for approaching galleons (its construction being financed through a new harbor tax).

The Crown also reacted vigorously when several hundred Huguenot settlers established a colony in the summer of 1564 near modern Jacksonville, overlooking the Straits of Florida. It was deemed such a threat to homeward-bound silver convoys that a counterexpedition hastened out from Spain in Sep-

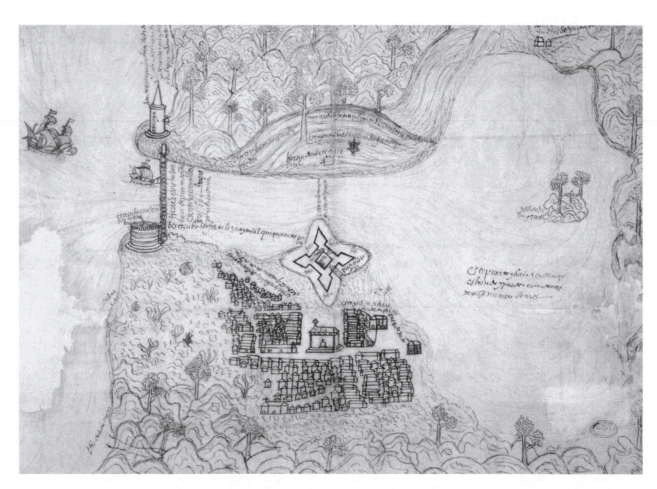

Crude pen-and-ink drawing of Havana, ca. 1584–1586; north is toward upper left. The Real Fuerza citadel at center has been accurately rendered, although the log boom across the harbor entrance had not yet been installed, nor had the round La Punta fortress been constructed. (Archive of Indies, Seville)

tember 1565 under Adm. Pedro Menéndez de Aviles, who not only annihilated this intruder compound, but also reinforced Havana's still incomplete La Fuerza stronghold with 200 troops under Capt. Baltasar de Barreda. Adm. Francisco García Osorio de Sandoval was moreover installed as Cuba's new governor, to counter several more French thrusts over the next few years.

Apparently now safe from foreign depredations, and with subsidies from the Mexican exchequer and an increasingly lucrative stream of plate-fleet arrivals, the town experienced such a boom that modern scholars have described Havana as "the fastest growing urban center in the Americas from 1570 to 1620." Seville's Guild of Masters and Pilots was already referring to Havana as the "key" to the Straits of Florida, an expression that became expanded into the residents' boast that their port was the *Llave del Nuevo Mundo,* or Key to the New World. A full-blown community began to emerge, the San Juan de Dios Convent, for example, being commenced as of 1570. Three years later—amid a smallpox epidemic engendered by the deposit of some sick slaves—the Hospital Real de San Felipe y Santiago was completed (later becoming known as the Caridad, or charity hospital), and the original *Iglesia Parroquial,* or parish church, was entirely rebuilt in bricks and mortar by June 1574.

Because anchored fleets depleted the freshwater supply from Jagüey at the foot of La Cabaña heights, in addition to the few wells within the town itself—necessitating the precarious ferrying of this commodity from La Chorrera by boat—a 3-mile-long aqueduct dubbed the *Zanja Real,* or Royal Ditch, was started under de Calona's supervision in May 1575, diverting water through a *husillo* (siphon). (This project was delayed less than a year later by problems in surmounting Aróstegui Hill and other natural barriers, as well as from widespread damage wrought by a hurricane that swept across the island on 14 August 1576.) The king's engineer was moreover charged with the erection of a *real aduana,* or royal customs-house, on Havana's waterfront in 1576. He completed the reconstruction of the city's citadel by April 1577, producing a new stone fortress with four equal bastions dubbed the *Real Fuerza,* or Royal Stronghold, to distinguish it from the previous *Fuerza Vieja,* or Old Stronghold. A second story with living quarters was also commenced in 1578, to convert the edifice into the Cuban governor's official residence at Havana.

By the last two decades of the sixteenth century, its harbor had become the lynchpin for all plate-fleets departing Spanish America. Convoys from Veracruz and Cartagena, as well as smaller detachments from Honduras and other lesser Caribbean ports, would rendezvous in Havana's ample anchorage by midsummer to weather the West Indian hurricane season of late summer or early autumn; if danger threatened, they might winter and resume their voyage the next spring. Merchants and aristocrats traveling as passengers paid handsomely for amenities during their layovers, while ranchers sold

salted meat and bacon to crews and exported hides. Agricultural production on the plain west of town increased as a result, farmers tapping water from the expanding Zanja Real project to irrigate their fields and power the mills that ground corn and wheat (although still in such modest quantities that supplementary foodstuffs would have to be imported from Mexico for decades to come).

Shipwrights also found steady employment, even laying down their own vessels (such as the royal frigates constructed for Menéndez de Aviles in 1573–1575, which included a prototype 600-ton galleass called the *San Cristóbal*). Incessant demand for skilled labor furthermore meant that Havana became a considerable slave entrepot, with entrepreneurs making purchases as investments and renting out their extra retainers as seasonal contract workers until they could be sold at a profit.

In the spring of 1585, Gov. Gabriel de Luján and alcaide Diego Hernández de Quiñones received warnings from Spain that Sir Francis Drake was about to lead a large privateering sweep through the Antilles. Five frigates were immediately delegated to patrol the Dry Tortuga Keys off Florida, while munitions were hastened out from Cadiz to replenish Havana's magazines; also, the plate-fleet of Adm. Juan de Guzmán was instructed not to put to sea, but rather to winter over at Veracruz. Drake eventually materialized off Havana on 26 May 1586, but his crews, weakened by disease, did not attempt disembarkation. Governor de Luján shadowed the movements of this enemy formation with 1,000 men ashore, until the raiders

Modern watercolor by Guillermo G. de Aledo of a sixteenth-century Spanish galleon being wrecked on a Florida reef; salvage vessels and divers were routinely dispatched from Havana to retrieve cargoes from such lost vessels. (Museo Naval, Madrid)

disappeared northeastward on 29 May. Sea traffic had nonetheless been sufficiently dislocated that famine briefly threatened Havana, before ten barks arrived from Mexico in November 1587 with provisions and 200 reinforcements.

Hostilities erupted openly with the defeat of the Invincible Armada in the English Channel the next summer, so that when the new Cuban governor, Juan de Texeda, arrived from Spain in mid-1589, he was accompanied by the Italian-born military engineer Batista Antonelli, who on 27 June commenced the foundations for a pair of strongholds to cover both sides of Havana's entrance: a huge castle atop the northwestern tip of El Morro headland, which was to be called *Tres Reyes,* or the Three Wise Men, plus the smaller, round, moated redoubt of *San Salvador,* or Holy Savior, on the *Punta,* or Point of lowland opposite. (Both official names failed to take hold, however; the forts became better known as El Morro and La Punta.) De Texeda had also brought out materials for launching six 80-ton royal frigates, while Havana's municipal council simultaneously purchased a private lot next to the *aduana,* or customs house, from Juan Bautista de Rojas, to begin erecting Crown offices and a jail.

The resultant construction boom, as well as expenditures by thousands of plate-fleet passengers and seamen repeatedly idled in port because of English rovers, helped Havana profit throughout the ensuing decade and a half of the Elizabethan war, so that its population swelled to approximately 3,000 residents. Four of the six royal frigates were commissioned by February 1591, escorting a portion of that year's bullion consignment across to Spain, while several large merchantmen were also launched. Adm. Diego de Ribera furthermore sortied from Havana that same May with eleven vessels and 2,000 men—a fraction of his anchored fleet—to patrol the Cuban coastline against a purported concentration of English privateers.

Water from the Zanja Real project finally reached the town center in 1592, discharging into Plaza de la Ciénega (modern Cathedral Square, at a spot still called Callejón del Chorro, or Stream Alley). Although erratic and unhygienic, this flow helped ease townspeople's needs, and it provided some modest municipal revenue: a tax assessed for vessels to refill their casks. King Phillip II granted Havana the title of city via a royal writ issued on 20 December 1592, accompanied by a crest adorned with a golden key and three silver forts upon a blue background—emblematic of its role as "Key to the New World," guarded by El Morro, La Punta, and Real Fuerza.

Three years later, a planter named Vicente Santa María erected the first sugar mill within its district and commenced small-scale exports of that lucrative product. Havana's first theatrical production was also celebrated beside the Real Fuerza in 1598, honoring Gov. Juan Maldonado's saint day; a foundry was furthermore installed next year. Although the city remained unthreatened by enemy invasion, Gov. Pedro de Valdés nonetheless ordered Cristóbal de Roda—Antonelli's nephew and successor as military engineer—to draw up an ambitious plan for erecting stone ramparts around the city in 1603, a plan shelved because of its high cost.

By the time a peace treaty was concluded with England in August 1604, Havana had become a somewhat crowded port city, its main square lined with a few mansions featuring high ceilings, inner courtyards, and whitewashed exteriors in pastel hues to help deflect the sun's heat. Finely carved balconies, shutters, doors, and banisters were added from local hardwoods such as red cedar, while wealthy citizens had their own private wells or rooftop cisterns to catch rain; poorer residents supplemented the rather haphazard flow in the public fountains by buying freshwater from street vendors. Stout warehouses were clustered along Havana's shoreline, and a visitor observed a few years later that ships, "of no matter what size, are practically moored to the houses."

Downpours such as the storm that struck on 1 September 1605 transformed the narrow and unpaved streets into unhealthful quagmires. Yellow fever—a virus carried by the *Aedes aegypti (stegomya)* mosquito, which flourishes in warm climes and breeds in stagnant water containers with solid sides and flat bottoms, such as cisterns or wooden ship casks—proved especially endemic, being frequently renewed by infusions of nonimmunized blood when plate-fleets arrived at Havana. Other contagious diseases, such as smallpox and typhus, added to the city's woes, producing a much higher death rate than in the Cuban hinterland.

Another royal decree on 8 October 1607 elevated Havana to the status of island capital, Santiago being reduced to administering only the eastern third of Cuba, while governors were henceforth to be addressed as *Capitán-General.* Naval construction at the Havana yards was also resumed by another royal order issued on 21 December of that same year. Adm. Juan Enríquez de Borja came out from Spain in September 1608 to assume command over five newly launched 650-ton galleons that formed the core of a new *Armada de Barlovento,* or Windward Fleet, in the Caribbean. An Augustinian convent was furthermore completed at Havana that same year, while exports diversified through the production of small amounts of tobacco and cacao on surrounding farms. The private contractor Capt. Alonso de Herrera had completed three more galleons for the Crown by 1619, the total population for the city and its district being estimated the following year by Bishop Alonso Enríquez de Armendáriz as 7,000 Spanish congregants and 460 black slaves.

Dutch Blockades (1621–1648)

A stern test was to be endured after the United Provinces of The Netherlands declared war against Spain on 1 April 1621, and the Westindische Compagnie (West Indian Company) sent a trio of warships under Pieter Schouten to reconnoiter the Caribbean three years later. One vessel became separated from his main body, then chanced upon the annual Honduran detachment rounding the western tip of Cuba in

"Disinfection Service" vehicle in the streets of Havana, ca. 1913; more than four decades previously, mosquitoes had been identified as the source of yellow-fever epidemics by the Cuban researcher Dr. Carlos J. Finlay. (Lloyd, *Twentieth Century Impressions of Cuba*)

July 1624, capturing the vice flagship *San Juan Bautista* of Capt. Francisco Hernández y Moreno. When sailed to The Netherlands, the wealth derived from that single prize tempted other Dutch commanders to waylay traffic heading into Havana.

Consequently, Adm. Boudewijn Hendricksz materialized offshore with twenty-three vessels on 19 June 1626, having timed his cruise through the West Indies to arrive by midsummer, when the silver convoys traditionally moved toward the Cuban capital. Its defenders were spared any immediate action, as Hendricksz died unexpectedly on 2 July, and his successor, Adriaen Claeszoon, could not maintain the blockading fleet intact; yet shortly after this enemy departed and the Mexican treasure convoy entered, a second Dutch formation took up station off the Dry Tortuga Bank under Piet Heyn. Heyn's fourteen ships proved no match for the thirteen powerful galleons of the Tierra Firme convoy of Adm. Tomás de Larraspuru, which streamed past them into Havana, yet such threats would nonetheless intensify.

Lookouts were redoubled, and the *sargento mayor* (military commander), Diego Vázquez de Hinestrosa, prepared three coast guard vessels with 150 men to sally from Havana in aid of distressed galleons. Adm. Hendrick Jacobszoon Lucifer's

three Zeeland vessels surprised another Honduran convoy opposite Cojímar on 8 July 1627, taking its vice flagship, although the flagship managed to stagger safely into Havana four days later. Vázquez de Hinestrosa hurried out to sea with his new flotilla and spent the next month escorting vessels into port, but Lucifer's prize again netted such a profit back in The Netherlands—1.2 million guilders—that the Dutch planned an even more ambitious strike for next summer.

A dozen ships under Pieter Adriaanszoon Ita appeared off the Dry Tortugas, sighted another pair of Honduran galleons opposite Mariel on 1 August 1628, and chased them toward the Cuban capital. The galleons' commander, Alvaro de la Cerda—forewarned of this enemy presence—had reinforced his crews with 100 musketeers before departing. The Spaniards put up a stout fight, but were finally forced aground less than 3 miles west of La Punta fortress. Vázquez de Hinestrosa sallied to their rescue but was driven back as well; the Honduran vice flagship thereupon erupted in flames, while the flagship was towed off into the Straits of Florida by the triumphant Ita.

This dramatic encounter convinced Capt. Gen. Lorenzo de Cabrera y Corvera that the Dutch blockade had concluded for that summer, so he wrote the plate-fleet commander at Veracruz to set sail—little realizing that a second, more powerful

Dutch fleet had stealthily followed the first across the Caribbean and now lay off the Dry Tortugas under Heyn. Heyn's thirty-one ships closed upon Havana on 22 August 1628, intercepting the belated warnings that Cabrera attempted to send across the Gulf. The Mexican convoy therefore blundered into Heyn's fleet on 8 September, most lesser vessels being snapped up before the treasure galleons—flagship *Santa Ana María* of Adm. Juan de Benavides y Bazán, vice flagship *Santa Gertrudis* of Capt. Baltasar de Amezquita, plus *San Juan Bautista* and *Nuestra Señora de la Antigua*—were chased into Matanzas Bay by evening, where all four ran aground. More than 300 Spaniards perished and another 600 were wounded while desperately trying to ferry their bullion ashore, as Dutch ships fired upon their boats in the moonlight. The next morning the stranded galleons were boarded and a year's Mexican silver production—valued at 11.5 million guilders—was seized. Spain was plunged into financial crisis by this loss.

Havana's authorities strengthened their harbor defenses after this spectacular coup, fearful that their city would also come under attack. Efforts included the erection of a bell tower atop the Real Fuerza Palace to give warning of any stealthy approach via the entrance channel. A bronze figure was cast a few years later by the local artificer Gerónimo Martín Pinzón to crown this tower as a weather vane, bearing the emblem of the Knights of Calatrava—of which order the new captain general, Juan Bitrián de Viamonte, was a member. (This statue became known as the Giraldilla, the diminutive form of Giralda, and the nickname already borne by the tower of Seville's cathedral.)

Although the Cuban capital was not assaulted, it was still menaced by blockaders: Adm. Adriaen Janszoon Pater and Vice Adm. Jan Janszoon van Hoorn hovered offshore with twenty-six ships from June to September 1629, obliging all plate-fleets to cancel their sailings, despite Madrid's urgent need for bullion. Ita then combined with Commos. Dierick Ruyters and Jan Gijsbertszoon Booneter to mount another watch outside Havana in late August 1630, compelling that year's Tierra Firme convoy commander—Admiral de Larraspuru—to the risky expedient of steering directly from Cartagena out of the Caribbean via the Windward and Caicos passages, a gamble that succeeded when he reached Spain with 7 million pesos in silver. Although Booneter reappeared off Cuba with a squadron in April–May 1631, and Adm. Maarten Thijssen did the same in August 1632 with twenty-two ships, the Dutch eventually became discouraged.

Their interest revived after the one-legged privateer Cornelis Corneliszoon Jol—famed among the Dutch as Houtebeen (Peg-Leg) and among Spaniards as *Pie de Palo*—trailed the Tierra Firme convoy of Vice Adm. Francisco de Mexía across from Cartagena in August 1637, his small Dutch vessels powerless to snap up any prizes because of the intimidating escort provided by Adm. Carlos de Ibarra's battle fleet. Jol waited outside Havana for a second opportunity: four Spanish warships

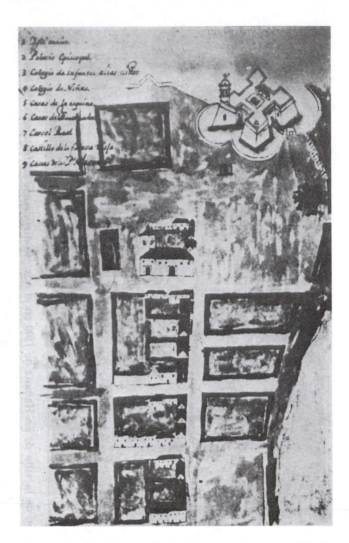

The city core in 1691; note the Real Fuerza Palace crowned by its Giraldilla weather vane at upper left, while the Iglesia Parroquial or "Parish Church" appears at center. (Biblioteca Nacional José Martí, Havana)

and sixteen merchantmen that emerged on 6 September. But after falling in behind them, the Dutch privateers saw another thirty-three Spanish vessels exiting and, fearful of becoming trapped between the two formations, sheered off with only a tiny prize.

Nonetheless, Jol returned to Holland and persuaded the West India Company to finance another major expedition, with which he rematerialized off the Dry Tortugas by late July 1638. To mask his true strength, Jol divided his twenty-eight ships into four equal squadrons, thereby deceiving Capt.-Gen. Francisco Riaño y Gamboa into believing that repeated Cuban sightings of seven Dutch vessels represented but a single small squadron, rather than segments of a much larger fleet. As a result, Riaño wrote reassurances to the distant plate-fleet commanders, so that the Tierra Firme convoy of Admiral de Ibarra (now ennobled as Vizconde de Centenera) reached Cabañas by the afternoon of 30 August, expecting to encounter only a small Dutch blockading squadron—but instead sighting eighteen enemy sail. Surprised, the seven Spanish galleons and seven merchantmen fended off Dutch attacks for four days, until de Ibarra reversed course for Veracruz (a decision for which he was subsequently awarded the additional title of Marqués de Taracena). Jol waited vainly for his vanished prey until 17 September before his fleet disbanded.

He returned with another thirty-six sail in early September 1640, sending a single vessel to look into Havana before settling down to another blockade. But the new captain-general, Alvaro de Luna Sarmiento, had already written to warn treasure fleet commanders of Jol's presence, so that the Dutch remained idly off the coast until the afternoon of 11 September, when they were hit by a four-day storm out of the north-northwest. Four blockading ships were wrecked between the capital and Mariel, and another three were driven deep into the Old Bahama Channel. Havana's garrison commander, Lucas Carvajal, salvaged numerous guns and equipment from the wrecks, as well as capturing 261 survivors (another 100 Dutchmen having drowned). After attempting to ransom his men, Jol departed on 28 September.

Havana was not threatened again for the remaining eight years of this conflict, although concerns over a potential disembarkation at Chorrera—which would sever the city's main water supply—prompted Captain-General de Luna to order a small fort erected at that inlet; it was named Santa Dorotea de Luna in his honor upon being completed in May 1646. Another redoubt was finished at Cojímar around that same time, while a tower was added at Bacuranao four years later and El Morro Castle's drawbridges and cellars were fully installed. Still, when the port was menaced by a lone buccaneer ship in late August 1648, Capt. Gen. Diego de Villalba y Toledo could only press two private galleons into service, which ran aground and were wrecked upon exiting.

Hapsburg Decay (1649–1700)

Peace with The Netherlands was restored by January 1648, but Spain emerged as a ruined power, fighting on feebly against France while hampered by a revolt in Catalonia, hostility from neighboring Portugal, and the collapse of its imperial economy. For the Cuban capital, the Crown's bankruptcy signified a drastic curtailment in plate-fleet traffic, as well as the elimination of naval contracts at its city yards. To make matters worse, an epidemic struck Havana in the spring of 1649—allegedly brought in by a ship from Cartagena—claiming one-third of its unhappy populace. A huge British expedition also captured Jamaica half a dozen years later, allowing Vice Adm. William Goodson to hover threateningly off the Cuban capital in the summer of 1656.

With their maritime business blighted and animal husbandry crippled because of the depleted demand to feed crews, many *habaneros* turned to other agricultural pursuits, so that small sugar and tobacco farms multiplied throughout its district. Among the few large-scale projects undertaken by the Crown was the erection of new municipal offices, a jail, and a slaughterhouse in 1668, plus the commencement of a 3-mile circuit of stone walls in January 1671 to enclose the capital within a 350-acre compound—a vast endeavor justified by the growing boldness of West Indian buccaneers, who had recently sacked Portobelo, Maracaibo, and other fortified Spanish-American coastal towns. The royal engineer Juan de Ciscara (alternate spelling: Siscara) consequently arrived from Santiago de Cuba to supervise these labors, initiating the construction of ramparts 5 feet thick by almost 40 feet high. (Because of fitful royal finances and recurrent labor shortages, the entire perimeter was not completed until sixty-nine years later.)

The city experienced modest growth during this lean interlude, reflected by the erection of Santo Angel Custodio Church on Angel Hill in 1679; San Lázaro Hospital for lepers, which opened in July 1681; Santa Teresa Monastery, founded in 1687; Santa Catalina Monastery, completed two years afterward; as well as the San Felipe Neri Convent, founded in 1693. However, it was not until the deformed and invalid Hapsburg monarch Charles II died in Spain on 30 November 1700 and was succeeded by the sixteen-year-old French Bourbon prince Philip of Anjou that the Spanish empire's decline finally began to be reversed.

Bourbon Revival (1701–1761)

Fearful that a union between Spain and France would concentrate too much power, other European nations contested this succession, so that Vice Adm. John Benbow prowled into the Caribbean with ten Royal Navy warships late in 1701. Believing that this deployment portended a preemptive strike against a Spanish plate-fleet, Paris and Madrid sent out a huge French counterexpedition in January 1702 under Vice Adm. François-Louis Rousselet, Comte de Château-Renault, who entered Havana on 9 April. Leaving his main body at anchor, Château-Renault proceeded to Veracruz with a squadron to escort the bullion convoy of Adm. Luis Manuel de Velasco; during his absence, the French commander's fleet suffered hundreds of losses resulting from disease, death, and desertion. Château-Renault rejoined on 7 July and set sail two weeks later from Havana with his fleet and twenty-seven Spanish merchantmen, only to be captured at Vigo Bay, Spain, by an Anglo-Dutch fleet under Adm. Sir George Rooke. This interception sparked the War of the Spanish Succession, or Queen Anne's War.

In addition to its traditional role as a plate-fleet haven, the Cuban capital was to become transformed into a regional naval base during the ensuing hostilities: four vessels, for example, were dispatched by Capt.-Gen. Pedro Nicolás Benítez de Lugo with more than 200 troops in December 1702, to help lift the Anglo-American investiture of St. Augustine (Florida); a passing British battle-fleet under Vice Adm. John Graydon peered

Workers rolling cigars in a tobacco factory, ca. 1913; the man at center was a lector, hired to entertain them by reading newspaper excerpts aloud. (Lloyd, *Twentieth Century Impressions of Cuba*)

into Havana on 20 July 1703; a small French expedition under Pierre Le Moyne d'Iberville entered in the summer of 1706, suffering heavy losses to disease, before d'Iberville succumbed on 8 July and six vessels sortied under his subordinate Capt. Jacques Lefebvre to ferry 200 Cuban troops and two field-pieces to help invade South Carolina; the 44-gun *Thétis* of Jean-François de Choiseul, Comte de Beaupré and the governor of Saint-Domingue (Haiti), was battered into submission 3 miles outside Havana on the night of 5–6 May 1711 by the block-aders HMSS *Windsor* of Capt. George Paddon and *Weymouth* of Richard Lestock.

The Cuban capital was assigned an even more significant naval role once that conflict ceased in 1713, as the reform-minded colonial and marine minister at Madrid, Bernardo Tinajero de la Escalera, concerned by the vulnerability of Spain's yards to enemy attack—as well as by their lack of tall trees after years of overexploitation—proposed that ten ships-of-the-line and two smaller vessels be privately contracted at Havana. Such work would not only prove less costly to the Crown because of Cuba's lower pay scales, but the resultant ves-sels would also be of stouter manufacture, thanks to the durable tropical hardwoods available around the bay.

This project could not be immediately implemented because of the government's pallid financial condition, as well as unrest on farms outside Havana, where—after four and a half months of discontent against an unpopular new royal monopoly on tobacco—*vegueros* (tobacco workers) blocked roads leading into the capital on 24 August 1717. The city gar-rison refused to support Capt.-Gen. Vicente Raja, who was compelled to flee to Spain and leave the government in the hands of a deputy. Matters worsened after Madrid was drawn into war next year against the Quadruple Alliance of England, France, Holland, and Austria, resulting in more alarms for the Cuban capital. Some 100 privateersmen from Francisco and José Cornejo's anchored vessels even mutinied in Havana's bay on 11 September 1720, landing at Luyanó Beach to march toward Jesús del Monte Convent demanding their unpaid wages. The new captain-general, Gregorio Guazo Calderón, surrounded that sanctuary with two companies of troops and compelled the rebels to retreat, hanging their ringleaders three days later.

Peace with the Quadruple Alliance was restored by spring of 1721, yet Havana was damaged by a hurricane and earth-quake the next year, and then another tobacco rebellion occurred in 1723. Guazo sent two companies of mounted infantry on that occasion to disperse the 500 armed protesters marching against the capital, killing one and hanging eight others at dawn of 21 February 1723. Sufficient calm was restored for the Belgian-born Charles Havré to import the city's first printing press that same year, although true stability was not achieved until Adm. Antonio Gaztañeta y de Iturribálzaga arrived from Spain with 2,000 troops in August 1726; Havana's Royal Tobacco Factory was inaugurated the next year.

War with England briefly threatened in April 1727, Adm. Francis Hosier appearing outside the Cuban capital with his battle fleet, before that dispute was resolved. The city populace was counted at 21,310 residents by 1728, and its ancient San Jerónimo College was elevated to the status of a university on 5 January of that same year, in accordance with the papal brief *Aeternal Sapiental,* issued six years previously. Maritime traffic rebounded and tobacco farming increased throughout the hinterland, as farms expanded farther west into the Nueva Filipina district (soon to be renamed Pinar del Río).

But Havana was to enjoy its most steady economic growth thanks to an upsurge in naval construction, five ships-of-the-line having already been launched, while the 70-gun *Conquistador* was completed in 1729; the 64-gun *Gallo Indiano* and *Nuestra Señora del Carmen* (alias *Andalucía*) the next year; the 66-gun *San Cristóbal* or *Constante* in 1731; and the 70-gun *San José* (alias *Africa*) the ensuing year—despite a hurricane that had struck in 1730, destroying the San Francisco de Paula Hospital and numerous other city structures. Output would have been even greater had not the private yards been so rudimentary: hulls were still being laid down on a flat expanse of wasteland southwest of the city, and launchings were so clumsy that crowds gathered to be entertained for days on end by the spectacle of oxen and boats straining away, trying to pull a finished hull into the water.

Consequently, the Crown decided to professionalize Havana's industry by sending out trained specialists such as the master shipwright Juan de Acosta and naval commissioner Lorenzo de Montalvo, who—with support from Capt.-Gen. Juan Francisco de Güemes y Horcasitas and station commander Adm. Rodrigo de Torres y Morales—replaced the

Havana and its district in May 1733; north is toward bottom left. (Archive of Indies, Seville)

untidy sprawl of private shops as of 1735 with a single *astillero real* (royal shipyard) called La Tenaza, including new stocks and slipways to facilitate assembly and launchings. Private contractors continued to be employed within this complex, but under supervision from royal officials. Material acquisitions were also rationalized, heavy mahogany and cedar for hulls being drawn from Havana's immediate environs, while lighter pine for masts was imported from other Cuban ports or Pensacola; costs were reduced by using a couple of hundred slaves on the most labor-intensive tasks. Ironwork and canvas was imported from Spain, while newly commissioned warships sailed unarmed across the Atlantic to receive their ordinance at Cadiz, rather than deplete meager Cuban inventories.

The arsenal soon became the largest employer and consumer of goods on the island, furthermore attracting attention when the War of Jenkins's Ear, or King George's War, threatened to erupt back in Europe. Commo. Charles Brown's Jamaican squadron materialized off the Cuban capital in September 1739, HMS *Shoreham* of Capt. Edward Boscawen pressing into its approaches to destroy two sloops and capture a third, while landing a party at nearby Puerto María to burn a mass of lumber on 26 September. Capt.-Gen. de Güemes y Horca-

sitas retaliated by confiscating all English trade goods in Havana on 2 October, then repelled more disembarkations at Bacuranao, Jaruco, and Bahía Honda before London finally declared war against Spain on 30 October.

Havana once again helped relieve the beleaguered St. Augustine by dispatching expeditions in the summers of 1740 and 1742, as well as serving as a base for blockade-runners. Adm. de Torres slipped out late in October 1744 with four ships-of-the-line and a frigate, speeding 8 million pesos in Mexican bullion across to Spain, saving its government from bankruptcy. Although sporadically threatened, the Cuban capital's batteries discouraged any direct enemy assault, its greatest losses occurring when a storm swept over the island on 30 June 1741 and a bolt of lightning struck the 70-gun flagship *San Ignacio* or *Invencible* at San Francisco Dock; the superstructure caught fire, spreading to the magazine and sparking such a violent explosion that stone ramparts were shorn off, buildings throughout the city were peppered with flying debris, and nine other moored warships suffered extensive damage—although only 16 people were actually killed and 21 injured.

Havana otherwise prospered throughout this decadelong

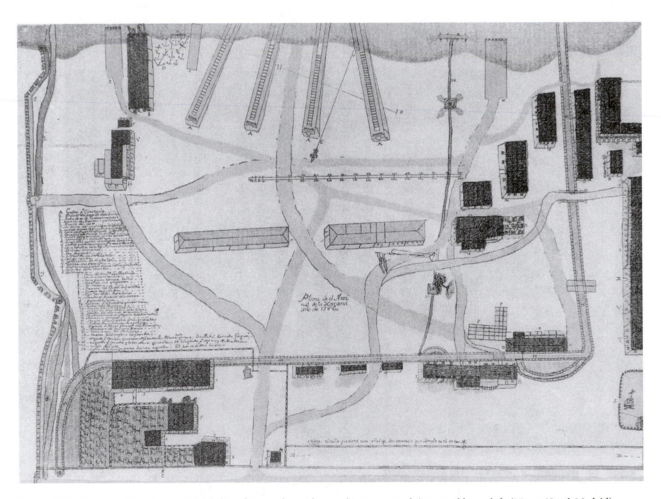

Pen-and-ink drawing with watercolor highlights of Havana's naval arsenal in 1788; north is toward lower left. (Museo Naval, Madrid)

conflict, thanks to regular silver subsidies from Mexico, which financed the launchings of fourteen large ships-of-the-line from its yard (compared with only a single one in all of Spain). But as fighting wound down in the autumn of 1748, the flow of Mexican treasure became menaced when Adm. Charles Knowles's Jamaican squadron took up station off Florida's Tortuga Bank, hoping to intercept one last Veracruz convoy before peace was concluded. The new naval commander at Havana—Vice Adm. Andrés Reggio Branciforte Saladino y Colonna, Knight Grand Cross of the Order of San Genaro—put to sea on 2 October, his undermanned crews supplemented by a regiment of troops and several hundred conscripts aboard.

After a tentative sweep, Reggio returned four days later to await his enemy a dozen miles off Havana. A mass of ships came up over the western horizon out of the Gulf on 11 October 1748, proving to be a Jamaican convoy bound for England, which the Spaniards chased, little realizing that Knowles was beating upwind that same night from the Tortuga Bank.

The two formations sighted each other east of Havana on 12 October 1748, the English overtaking the Spaniards by 2:00 P.M. and capturing *Conquistador* before fighting ceased around midnight. *Africa* had drifted helplessly into the night, while the five other Spanish warships limped back into the Cuban capital with more than 150 dead and a like number wounded. Next morning the victors reassembled outside, Knowles leading part of his squadron eastward on 14 October to locate the dis-

masted *Africa* the next afternoon in a small, unguarded bay 25 miles away. When its crew perceived the English entered, they cut their flagship's cables and set it ablaze, to drift ashore and blow up an hour later. Knowles reunited with his formation off Havana, but a sloop arrived on 16 October with news that a treaty had been signed in Europe; he therefore deposited his prisoners ashore and made off toward Jamaica with his lone prize.

Although two more ships-of-the-line were launched at the city yards in 1749, plus three more in 1750, the Crown contract with the private Havana Company was allowed to lapse so that production might be temporarily shifted back to Spain, where a new generation of royal warships was being designed by shipwrights hired out of Britain. The economy of the Cuban capital was kept vibrant by minor launchings and a revival of seaborne trade, thanks to a significant upsurge in its sugar production. Still, the city's population nonetheless remained virtually static at 22,828 residents according to a census taken in 1755, with another 5,153 people scattered throughout its immediate jurisdiction.

More specialists came out from Spain toward the end of the 1750s to resume large-scale naval production, including the Irish-born Matthew and Ignatius Mullen (a father-and-son team known to the Spaniards as *Mateo* and *Ignacio Mullan*). The *astillero real* was further improved by the addition of a water-powered sawmill to cut lumber, so that two 64-gun

Spanish Squadron under Vice Adm. Andrés Reggio Branciforte Saladino y Colonna, Havana, 1748

Ship	Guns	Men	Commander
San Francisco de Asis (flag; alias *Africa*)	74	710	Juan Antonio de la Colina
San José (vice-flag; alias *Invencible*)	74	700	Rear Adm. Benito Antonio de Spínola or Espínola
Jesús, María y José (alias *Conquistador*)	64	610	Tomás de San Justo
Santa Teresa de Jesús (alias *Dragón*)	64	610	Manuel de Paz
Nuestra Señora del Rosario (alias *Nueva España*)	64	610	Fernando Varela
Real Familia	64	610	Marcos Forestal
Galga (privateer frigate)	36	300	Pedro de Garaycoechea

British Squadron under Command of Admiral Charles Knowles, Havana, 1748

Ship	Guns	Tons	Men	Commander
Cornwal (flag)	80	1,350	600	Taylor
Tilbury	58	1,124	400	Charles Powlett
Strafford	60	1,067	400	David Brodie
Warwick	60	951	400	Thomas Innes
Canterbury	58	1,117	400	Clarke
Lennox	56	1,096	400	Charles Holmes
Oxford	50	767	300	Edmund Toll

Modern depiction of the 80-gun Spanish ship-of-the-line *San Alejandro,* better known as the *Fénix* or *Phoenix,* one of several score warships built at Havana. Launched in 1749 and captured by the British thirty-one years later, *Fénix's* wooden hull proved so durable that she was not broken up until 1836. (Museo Naval, Madrid)

ships-of-the-line were launched in 1759, plus another pair two years later. Sugar plantations had meanwhile mushroomed so notably around the city that yard managers now found themselves competing with estate-owners for wood: the boiling of syrup from cane-stalks consuming 15 million cubic feet annually by 1760—the same amount required to build a dozen ships-of-the-line. Royal decrees had therefore been issued as early as 1749 to help conserve vital cedar copses.

In Europe, Madrid secretly aligned itself with Paris in the summer of 1761, intending to join the ongoing French and Indian War against Britain the next spring. Troops and warships were sent out to bolster Havana's defenses against that anticipated rupture, the city garrison augmenting to 300 regular cavalrymen, 3,500 infantry, and 70 gunners, plus another 1,000 marines and 4,000 sailors aboard ten ships-of-the-line. The British cabinet, however, unexpectedly learned of this secret alliance and declared war against Spain on 24 December 1761, dispatching a huge offensive a few months later to surprise the Cuban capital.

English Occupation (1762–1763)

El Morro's lookouts spotted a huge mass of shipping 20 miles east of Havana on the morning of 6 June 1762, but Capt.-Gen. Juan de Prado dismissed it as merely a Jamaican merchant-convoy bound toward England. However, the British formation—42 warships manned by 14,000 seamen under Vice Adm. Sir George Pocock, plus another 3,000 sailors working

160 hired transports conveying a 12,500-man invasion army under Lt.-Gen. George Keppel, Earl of Albemarle—continued to close, until the capital's garrison belatedly scrambled to arms. The English fleet meanwhile divided, one column seeking a suitable spot east of the city to disembark Albemarle's army, while Pocock pressed westward with his heavy warships in a feint.

A sudden storm delayed the English landing, but de Prado deployed his best soldiers—grenadiers and pickets of the Aragón, España, and Havana regiments, plus 200 marines—to counter Pocock's false westward thrust, thus allowing Albemarle to come ashore uncontested the next morning at Bacuranao and Cojímar, striking southward with his army to occupy Guanabacoa by noon of 8 June 1762. The captain-general reconcentrated his forces around the capital, now rapidly emptying as thousands of civilians fled, only to see Albemarle reverse his advance next morning, returning to establish a seaside beachhead at Miraguanes Point. This digression allowed Capt. Luis Vicente de Velasco time to bolster El Morro Castle with the 400 sailors of his warship *Reina,* augmenting its strength to more than 1,000 men, while three block-ships were also scuttled in the channel to impede penetration.

Pocock's detachment secured the 6-gun fortress at La Chorrera, while Albemarle's main army scaled La Cabaña Heights above the city by 1:00 A.M. of 11 June 1762, pressing on toward El Morro at the tip of the headland. This castle proved to be a formidable obstacle, though, its southeastern face protected by a trench 100 feet wide and 60 feet deep—invisible from out at sea and thus unknown to the British—while its escarpment was solid rock, making it impossible to dig siege-trenches. Albemarle's drive stalled, sappers and sailors dragging artillery through torrential downpours up to these heights over the next ten days, while Cuban guerrillas menaced the invaders' encampments, and disease appeared. The first British mortars did not open fire against El Morro until 22 June, and despite suffering steady losses, the defenders were reinforced by boat-parties stealing out of Havana every night.

Pocock detached a squadron to capture Mariel, west of the capital, and de Prado staged an unsuccessful counterattack against Albemarle's siege-works at dawn of 29 June 1762. HMSS *Dragon, Cambridge, Marlborough,* and *Stirling Castle* sailed in to engage El Morro at point-blank range on 1 July but withdrew badly battered. With more than 3,500 men now sick, Albemarle commandeered cotton-bales from a passing Jamaican convoy and used these to extemporize fascines atop the stark promontory, thereby allowing his engineers to drive to the very edge of El Morro's moat by 20 July, from where sappers darted across to begin mining its northeastern bastion. Some 1,500 Cuban militiamen slipped out of Havana before sunrise on 22 July, again to assault the English encampments.

On 28 July 1762, several thousand reinforcements from New York and New England began materializing, so reinvigorating to the British besiegers that they blew El Morro's northeastern

Havana's cathedral during the British occupation, August–September, 1762; oil painting by Dominique Serres the Elder. (National Maritime Museum, Greenwich, England)

bastion at 1:00 P.M. of 30 July, overwhelming its 800 remaining defenders, who had retired into their subterranean quarters to eat. De Velasco fell mortally wounded along with 342 others, while 326 were captured and 37 others wounded. Albemarle redeployed his batteries so that artillery fire now rained down into the hapless city from both La Cabaña and El Morro, while 2,000 New Englanders advanced overland from San Lázaro in a pincer movement to occupy Jesús del Monte, tightening the besiegers' stranglehold.

The English called upon de Prado to capitulate on 10 August 1762 and were rebuffed. Albemarle thereupon ordered his guns to resume pounding Havana the next day, panicking La Punta's garrison into abandoning their exposed position. The captain general therefore requested terms that same afternoon, which were finalized by 13 August, so that 936 Spanish regulars marched out of the ruined city the next day, along with a large naval contingent, leaving behind 2,000 sick or injured comrades. Approximately 3,800 Spaniards had perished during this siege, while the British reported 2,764 casualties of their own resulting from death, wounds, desertion, or capture, with many hundreds of others remaining ill.

As de Prado's authority had encompassed not only the city, but also the entire western half of Cuba—from Sagua to Cape San Antonio—redcoats were sent to occupy a few other towns, convincing Havana's refugees to begin filtering back into their devastated capital. The British occupiers proved benign, Albemarle even hosting balls to introduce his young subalterns among society. The captive city revived remarkably, and while its fate was being negotiated back in Europe, scores of British merchantmen entered to sell or acquire goods. During the eleven months that Havana remained in English hands, its economy boomed thanks to an influx of inexpensive imports—including roughly 10,000 slaves—as well as notable exports of sugar.

Colonial Heyday (1763–1795)

The Cuban capital was restored to Spain in exchange for Florida, so that Ambrosio Funes de Villalpando, Conde de Ricla, arrived as new captain general on 6 July 1763. Battle damage was repaired, and Havana continued to prosper under his tenure. He had been accompanied by the Belgian-born engineer Agustín Crame (originally Cramer) and

Silvestre Abarca, who together supervised a costly series of defense projects. El Morro, La Punta, Real Fuerza, La Chorrera, San Lázaro, Cojímar, and the city ramparts were all to be strengthened, while three new strongholds were to be created: a huge fort atop the strategic La Cabaña Heights, commenced in November 1763 and named Castillo San Carlos, or San Carlos Castle, in honor of King Charles III; Atarés Castle atop Soto Hill, protecting the landward approaches to the naval arsenal inside the bay; and Príncipe Castle atop Aróstegui Hill to the west, commenced in 1774 and completed twenty years later (and eventually converted into a penitentiary). At least 4,000 hired *jornaleros* (day laborers) toiled upon El Morro and La Punta over the next three years.

Shipbuilding also resumed on a grand scale, a naval treasury being established to provide Crown financing (rather than rely upon private investors as before), while a naval intendancy was also founded in December 1763 to coordinate all production matters under the veteran Montalvo. The three sunken block-ships were raised while the gutted *astillero real* was being rebuilt, a graving facility and iron forge being added after the removal of the old Royal Tobacco Warehouse. The 98-gun warships *San Carlos* and *San Fernando* were consequently launched by 1765, a 64-gun ship next year, the 98-gun *San Luís* in 1767, plus a pair of 74-gun ships the following year.

The city weathered a hurricane on 15 October 1768—remembered as the *tormenta de Santa Teresa,* or "Saint Theresa's storm," having struck on that particular church feast day—that collapsed a portion of the ramparts and ninety-six houses, inflicting 159 casualties. Still, the economy thrived thanks to the fortification projects, increased sugar exports, and resurrected shipyard (which employed about 600 permanent workers and several hundred day laborers). Havana launched the Royal Spanish Navy's most substantial vessels, including the 130-gun *Santísima Trinidad*—completed in March 1769—which remained the world's largest warship until its loss at the Battle of Trafalgar thirty-six years later. The Cuban *astillero* soon grew so big that its cordage and rope warehouses were shifted across Havana's harbor, while the powder magazine was removed to its far end for safety.

Crown engineers had also strictly enforced the ban against civilian structures outside Havana's walls, clearing a 3/4-mile expanse west of the city that was renamed the Campo Marte (that is, Parade Ground, later Parque de Colón or Columbus's Park, and then Plaza de la Fraternidad or Fraternity Square). Capt.-Gen. Felipe de Fondesviela, Marqués de la Torre, then beautified this clearance by installing a tree-lined promenade called the *Prado* from the refurbished ramparts out to the harbor mouth in 1772, plus another called *Alameda de Paula* along the inner harbor. A street-paving system was also tested the next year, using wooden blocks cut from trees so hard as to be nicknamed *quiebra-hachas* (ax-breakers), but which unfortunately proved to be treacherously slippery when wet.

The Prado or "Paseo de Martí," ca. 1925; note the harbor entrance and El Morro lighthouse visible at its far end, plus the fine edifices built of white coral limestone. (Carpenter, *Lands of the Caribbean*)

The transfer of Havana's Parish Church into San Felipe Neri, then into the former Jesuit Church (originally built 1656–1724), proved more successful, as the old sanctuary on the eastern side of the Plaza de Armas (Main Square) was demolished in 1773 to make way for a magnificent new Palacio de los Capitanes-Generales (Captains-General Palace), completed in December 1791. It was remodeled in 1835 and 1851, eventually becoming the Ayuntamiento (Municipal Building). The Royal Tobacco Factory was expanded as well, military hospitals and barracks were added, private mansions multiplied, and the old Casa de Comedias Theater was replaced by a grand new Coliseo in Paula Square in 1775. So much construction was done that the supervisor of fortification projects complained to the Marqués de la Torre in March 1777 of difficulties securing day laborers.

Property grew scarce and the city became crowded as poor rural migrants were attracted, as well as an influx of slaves and Spanish immigrants from overseas, virtually doubling the population to 40,737 inhabitants by 1778, with another 9,457 people scattered throughout its suburbs (out of a total of 175,000 on the entire island). Trade was spurred by the monarchy's easing of old mercantilist restrictions, so that by the time Spain joined the Thirteen American Colonies in their war against Britain in June 1779, Havana could confidently dispatch contingents in support of Bernardo de Gálvez's capture of Mobile (Alabama) early in 1780. Adm. José Solano y Bote also reached Havana from Spain that same August with a dozen ships-of-the-line, plus sixty transports bearing 10,000 troops under Lt.-Gen. Victorio de Navía Osorio, who so strained accommodations that *barracones* (large barracks) had to be extemporized along the Prado. De Gálvez departed on 16 October with 3,800 men aboard fourteen warships and fifty transports to attack British Pensacola but was driven back by a storm; a second successful crossing with a smaller force in late February 1781 was followed that same April by an expedition under Solano and French Commo. François Aymar, Baron de Monteil, who assisted de Gálvez in subduing Pensacola.

The Cuban capital benefited significantly from assembling such offensives, one final force of 2,000 soldiers sortieing in April 1782 aboard sixty vessels—including the 40-gun U.S. frigate *South Carolina* of Commo. Alexander Gillon—to capture Nassau in the Bahamas. Extensive contacts with American merchants helped offset Havana's difficulty in securing provisions, especially flour, from its traditional Mexican sources throughout this conflict. The city also profited as shipyard expenditures peaked at 10.6 million pesos in 1783, many vessels being repaired or refitted in addition to the new launchings. Work continued even after peace was restored, four new 112-gun ships-of-the-line, three 98-gunners, plus a dozen other warships being laid down as of 1786.

Public lighting was introduced that same year, while overseas trade boomed. The number of merchantmen circulating between the Cuban capital and Cadiz quadrupled during 1787–1789. A splendid new Casa Real de Correos (Royal Post Office) was completed by the military engineer Antonio Fernández de Trevejos y Zaldívar, overlooking Havana's main square; its main church was also elevated to a cathedral when the city's first bishop was consecrated in November 1789. The first daily newspaper—the *Papel Periódico de La Habana*—appeared on Sunday, 24 October 1790.

Cuba's economy was further stimulated by the collapse of French sugar production on Saint-Domingue (Haiti) next year, because of the emergence of a radical new government in Paris that dislocated transatlantic sales and stirred slave unrest. Prices skyrocketed so steeply on European markets that Cuban plantation-owners expanded operations to take advantage of this windfall, abetted by official efforts to streamline exports out of Havana. The importation of African slaves also soared, new arrivals being housed in the disused wartime *barracones* along the Prado, while the capital's suburban populace more than quadrupled during this growth spurt.

Havana endured another great storm on 21–22 June 1792, but damages were promptly replaced thanks to its commercial success. Not even a declaration of war against Spain by the new Republic of France in January 1793 could dampen the capital's prospects: a local chapter of the Real Sociedad Económica de Amigos del País—that is, the Royal Economic Society of Friends of the Nation—was formed that same month, dedicated to advancements such as the acquisition four years later of the first steam engine from England, installed at the Seybabo Mill to facilitate sugarcane processing. Business leaders were also granted the right by the Crown to form their own Consulado (merchant guild) in 1794, the year in which Havana's first public library also opened.

But when the 74-gun *Asia* was launched in 1795, it proved to be the last major warship built at city yards, because Madrid submitted to advancing French republican armies in August of that same year, ceding Santo Domingo as a token of submission. The loss of that sister colony was underscored when Commo. Gabriel de Aristizábal docked his 74-gun warship *San Lorenzo* at Havana's Caballería Wharf on 15 January 1796, having brought Columbus's remains from the Santo Domingo Cathedral for reinterment in the Cuban capital. (However, a second lead-lined box of bones was discovered under the Dominican cathedral's floor in 1877, inscribed with the words "First Admiral"; most modern scholars believe that this latter box—auctioned at London in September 1973—most probably contained Columbus's remains, while de Aristizábal had mistakenly removed those of his son and successor. The disputed bones were removed from Havana's cathedral when the Spaniards withdrew from Cuba in 1898.)

Blockade and Transition (1796–1822)

Madrid realigned itself with the French Directorate in August 1796, then joined the ongoing hostilities against England as of 6 October, forcing Havana into change. Royal Navy squadrons quickly imposed a blockade, so that sugar exports and slave imports sagged. Local officials struggled to find commercial outlets, neutral U.S. vessels providing one alternative, although they could not fully compensate for lost peacetime volumes, nor guarantee delivery. On 16 November 1798, the 74-gun English blockader HMS *Carnatic* intercepted the warship USS *Baltimore* of Cmdr. Isaac Phillips, impressing fifty-five seamen. Although all but five were restored shortly thereafter, the incident led to strong protests from President John Quincy Adams. Another foreigner who braved the British blockade of Havana was the German naturalist Alexander, Baron von Humboldt, who arrived in mid-December 1800 at the beginning of his celebrated Spanish-American tour.

In addition to diminished trade, Havana's yards were also idled by the utter collapse of Crown finances, a predicament that was not alleviated even after peace with England was restored in March 1802, as fighting flared anew only twenty months later, the port again being blockaded. One of the few municipal enhancements enacted during that difficult interlude came when Bishop José Díaz de Espada y Fernández de Landa created the city's first cemetery in February 1806, so that bodies no longer had to be buried in churches, from where many diseases emanated.

The French emperor Napoleon I sent an army into Spain in the summer of 1808 to depose Ferdinand VII in favor of his brother Joseph Bonaparte, a crude usurpation of power rejected by Cuba and virtually every other New World colony. Support was instead thrown behind an interim junta established at Aranjuez to uphold the captive monarch's cause, uniting with Great Britain against their mutual foe; yet although the Royal Navy blockade was lifted as a result of this realignment, and Havana's trade resurged with English assistance, Crown subsidies from Mexico were nonetheless curtailed after an independence movement also gripped that nation as of September 1810.

No such insurrectionist manifestations occurred in the Cuban capital, because of its prosperity and sizable garrison, supplemented by eighteen companies of loyal "Ferdinand VII" Militia Volunteers raised by its veteran captain-general, Salvador del Muro y Salazar, Marqués de Someruelos (who would remain in office continuously from May 1799 until 1812). There were 42,805 inhabitants within the city walls according to the census of 1810, plus another 53,278 scattered throughout its municipality. A hurricane that struck on 24–28 October of that same year sank seventy anchored vessels and washed away numerous shoreside avenues, while leaving streets inundated for a fortnight thereafter.

A public marketplace was inaugurated just outside the capital in July 1817 (later becoming known as Plaza del Vapor, or Steamer Square), while free trade was permitted aboard foreign vessels as of the following January, and the San Alejandro Academy of Fine Arts opened under the artistic direction of the French-born painter Jean-Baptiste Vermay—recommended to Bishop de Espada by the great master Francisco de Goya y Lucientes. The foreign-built *Neptune,* the first steamship ever seen in Cuban waters, entered the harbor on 20 February 1819 to initiate regular traffic between Havana and Matanzas.

When Spanish regiments destined for service against the Latin American insurgency mutinied near Seville on 9 March 1820 and compelled Ferdinand VII to restore the liberal constitution of 1812, Capt.-Gen. Juan Manuel de Cajigal grudgingly did the same at Havana on 16 April; yet conservatives soon drove the liberals from power in Spain, and the royalist cause faded on the American mainland. The Cuban capital's role in the old imperial administration was irretrievably altered by the emergence of hostile new republics on the mainland, which not only severed Havana's traditional subsidies and maritime traffic, but also eliminated all need for future naval production. Repression was furthermore tightly imposed locally after Francisco Dionisio Vives arrived to assume office as captain-general in 1823, being determined to prevent any insurgent sentiment taking root in Cuba.

Late Spanish Era (1823–1897)

Havana was now reduced to complete dependency upon its sugar and tobacco exports, the combined population of the city and its district standing at 109,228 by 1826—little changed from the previous sixteen years. Madrid sought to reverse its Continental losses by assembling an expedition of fifteen ships at Havana that set sail on 7 July 1829 to reconquer Mexico with 3,500 troops under Brig. Isidro Barradas. But hopes of support from monarchist sympathizers in that country proved illusory, the small force being quickly surrounded and defeated in the state of Veracruz.

A few desultory efforts were subsequently made to improve the Cuban capital's infrastructure, its first railway track being laid down as of 1832—in sections by competing British and U.S. interests—eventually extending 45 miles from its harborfront to sugar refineries in the Güines Valley. This project was interrupted when a cholera epidemic struck the city's San Lázaro suburb on 25 February 1833, claiming at least 7,830 lives by the end of April (including those of the painter Vermay and his wife).

Havana's Parque Central or "Central Park" at the end of the Upper Prado, ca. 1913. (Lloyd, *Twentieth Century Impressions of Cuba*)

Havana was to be lifted out of its postepidemic depression by the energetic new Capt.-Gen. Miguel Tacón y Rosique, who arrived in March 1834 and immediately reinvigorated life through a series of municipal improvements: new avenues, sewers, and public markets were built; streets were cleaned and illuminated; houses were enumerated; the new Fernando VII Aqueduct reached the urban core by 1835, relegating the old Zanja Real to mere use for farm irrigation and mill-power; forces of *serenos* (night-watchmen) and firefighters were created; a new prison was erected at the far end of the Prado; work commenced on a splendid new private theater in 1836 (named the Gran Teatro Tacón upon its completion the following year); and the first 30-mile stretch of railway as far as Bejucal went into service by November 1837. Although Tacón was in office scarcely four years, his reforms marked a significant watershed in Havana's modernization and beautification, the capital becoming not only more orderly, but also cleaner, thus reducing contagious disease. Although only 48,860 people still lived inside its old ramparts by 1841, another 135,648 now occupied the sprawl of suburbs outside.

A few more improvements were made over the ensuing decade, such as Capt.-Gen. Jerónimo Valdés's secularization in August 1842 of the old Dominican-run San Jerónimo University, which became reconstituted as the Real y Literaria Universidad de La Habana; in addition, the beacon atop El Morro Castle was replaced with a modern 100-foot light-tower in July 1845 by his successor, Capt.-Gen. Leopoldo O'Donnell y Jores. A hurricane swept over the capital on 10–11 October 1846, leveling the Coliseo Theater and numerous other structures, after which the population went into reversal—from a high of 218,836 residents to 214,449 by 1851, 210,063 five years later, and 205,676 by 1861. An Academia de Ciencias (Academy of Sciences) was established at the capital in 1860, emphasizing the study of medicine, pharmacy, and natural history in order to bolster Cuba's sugar industry.

Because of its proximity to the United States, Havana benefited by serving as a neutral haven for Confederate smugglers and Federal blockaders during the U.S. Civil War. Early during that struggle, Capt. Charles Wilkes of the screw-sloop USS *San Jacinto* (an Antarctic explorer resentful of the lackluster patrol duty assigned him) schemed with Consul-General Robert Wilson Shufeldt to intercept the British mail packet *Trent* as it exited the Cuban capital for London, removing the rebel diplomatic passengers James M. Mason and John Slidell on 8 November 1861. This detainment sparked a serious international confrontation, Britain reinforcing its North American fleets and garrisons while threatening to deny Union states essential war materials such as saltpeter, until President Abraham Lincoln informed London that Wilkes had acted without authorization and the two delegates were freed.

Havana also briefly served as a naval base when Madrid joined London and Paris in a military intervention against Mexico to collect on defaulted foreign debts. Adm. Joaquín

The Academy of Sciences building in Havana, ca. 1913. (Lloyd, *Twentieth Century Impressions of Cuba*)

Gutiérrez de Rubalcava assembled thirteen warships, five hired merchantmen, and five horse transports at the Cuban capital, before setting sail with 5,800 soldiers under Gen. Manuel Gasset y Mercader on 29 November 1861 to seize Veracruz. A second contingent of 2,000 troops under Gen. Juan Prim y Prats followed on 3 January 1862, accompanied by a British squadron under Commo. Hugh Dunlop, plus a French warship and three frigates under Adm. Jean-Pierre Edmond Jurien de la Gravière. Spain and Britain soon withdrew from the enterprise, leaving the French to occupy Mexico alone.

Thanks to these revivals in Havana's traffic, an accidental conflagration that consumed ten wooden docks and warehouses in its Regla wharf district in July 1863 was promptly redressed by city authorities, sufficient funds being available to also commence work the next month on tearing down the old, thick ramparts to make way for urban expansion. The Confederate surrender in the spring of 1865 conversely caused a severe economic downturn, many *habaneros* finding their economic plight compounded by burdensome Spanish taxes in addition to the often corrupt and harsh government by royal administrators. Wishing to gain a voice in island policy, equality with peninsular Spaniards in appointments and privileges, and a gradual abolition of slavery, Cuban and Puerto Rican reformers attended a board of inquiry in Madrid the next year to air their grievances, only to be disappointed when it collapsed in 1867, sparking calls for outright independence.

Activity at the Caballería Wharves, ca. 1913. (Lloyd, *Twentieth Century Impressions of Cuba*)

One such Cuban separatist—the wealthy planter Carlos Manuel de Céspedes—raised a revolt in the eastern La Demajagua District as of 10 October 1868 that was to smolder throughout the countryside over the following decade. Havana remained cowed by its Spanish garrison, the few proindependence outbursts—such as a crowd inside the Villanueva Theater cheering for "Céspedes and a free Cuba" on the evening of 21–22 January 1869—being put down through brutal purges. Hundreds of the capital's most liberal exponents, including a youthful José Martí, were summarily detained, executed, or exiled.

The ragtag rural rebels finally accepted the Convention of Zanjón in February 1878, seemingly winning all their demands—amnesty, abolition of slavery, colonial autonomy—although Madrid was to honor those terms only selectively. The capital's population slowly rebounded from 199,349 people in 1881 to 200,134 five years later, and 211,795 by 1891; electric lighting was moreover introduced during 1889–1890. Yet notwithstanding an upsurge in the number of inhabitants to 230,707 by 1896, many still yearned for freedom and tacitly supported another rural rebellion, which exploded east of Cuba and spread westward, despite the tens of thousands of troops dispatched to the island by Madrid.

American Occupations (1898–1909)

Amid such tensions, a riot erupted in Havana when uniformed Spanish officers ransacked proindependence Cuban newspapers on 12 January 1898, prompting the U.S. consul-general to request assistance from Washington. Three days later, a cordon of Spanish troops was deployed to defend the U.S. consulate from pro-Spanish zealots; then the 6,700-ton battleship USS *Maine* of Capt. Charles D. Sigsbee entered on 25 January to protect U.S. interests. However, it suddenly exploded at anchor at 9:40 P.M. on 15 February, claiming the lives of 266 of its 354 crew members. A naval court of inquiry was appointed five days later by President William McKinley to travel to the Cuban capital and investigate, reporting back to Congress by 28 March. Although unable to determine the exact cause of the detonation, its members concluded that it had most likely originated outside rather than inside the ship, suggesting a Spanish mine.

Resolutions threatening war against Spain and recognizing Cuban independence were consequently introduced into Congress on 29 March 1898, and despite Madrid's willingness to accede to virtually every U.S. demand, hostilities commenced as of 21 April. Next day, the 1,400-ton gunboat *Nashville* captured the Spanish steamer *Buenaventura* as it approached

Havana out of the Gulf of Mexico and imposed a blockade. The twelve-year-old, 1,130-ton Spanish cruiser *Conde de Venadito* sortied with the equally ancient 570-ton torpedo gunboat *Nueva España* on 14 May to engage the 1,000-ton gunboats *Vicksburg* and *Annapolis* east of the port—soon supported by the auxiliaries *Mayflower, Wasp, Tecumseh,* and *Osceola*—which drove the Spaniards back under the protection of Santa Clara Battery by nightfall. Another action occurred at midnight of 4–5 July, when the armed yacht *Hawk* intercepted the 4,380-ton mail steamer *Alfonso XIII* 7 miles outside Havana, chasing it aground near Mariel by 1:30 A.M.

Other Spanish forces were routed elsewhere, so that a truce was concluded by 12 August 1898, whereby Madrid agreed to relinquish Cuba by 10 December—although "to the United States in trust for its inhabitants," rather than directly to the rebels themselves. Havana and its district changed hands when Gen. John R. Brooke assumed office as military governor on 1 January 1899, focusing his initial efforts on restoring essential services for its unhappy citizenry. Some municipal and fiscal activities were revived by the end of that same year, when Brooke was succeeded by the youthful medical brigadier Leonard E. Wood (a former Rough Rider and friend of Theodore Roosevelt, who had enjoyed great success as military governor of Santiago and Oriente Province).

Wood continued civic improvements through such measures as the University of Havana's transfer from its old colonial grounds of San Jerónimo to a modern campus on Aróstegui Hill, as well as upgrading public health, postal, and telegraphic services. Trade resurged, and the population swelled from 238,278 inhabitants in 1898 to 257,172 by 1901, despite a yellow-fever outbreak—which was contained when Dr. Walter Reed confirmed the Cuban physician Carlos J. Finlay's earlier research that identified mosquitoes as carriers, so that sanitary officer Maj. William C. Gorgas could adopt effective countermeasures. Wood had also overseen the convention that reorganized Cuba's government along U.S. lines in November 1900, as well as the election of Tomás Estrada Palma—a conservative who had resided in the United States for almost two decades—as president on 31 December 1901.

Notwithstanding the undoubted improvements made to their municipal infrastructure, most *habaneros* were relieved to see U.S. forces withdraw after Estrada Palma's inauguration on 20 May 1902, although a strong U.S. influence nonetheless remained, inasmuch as corporations had purchased sizable sugar properties throughout Cuba's interior. Farmers displaced by large-scale mechanization and modernization projects migrated into the capital, swelling its population to 294,671 people by 1906, and despite an apparently vibrant economy, so much poverty persisted that popular opinion turned against Estrada Palma. When he stood for reelection, blatant fraud secured victory over his Liberal opponents, prompting a walkout by Faustino "Pino" Guerra and other opposition legislators.

A guerrilla revolt therefore exploded in the countryside on 16 August 1906, and some factions called for another U.S. intervention. President Theodore Roosevelt, however, was reluctant to oblige for both domestic and international considerations. Eventually, though, an armored train was ambushed west of the capital on 8 September, compelling Roosevelt to send the cruiser USS *Denver* of Cmdr. John Colwell into Havana's harbor four days later to "protect American interests." But Colwell and Cmdr. William F. Fullam of the USS *Marietta*, dispatched into Cienfuegos, were eager to show what naval strength might accomplish, and so interpreted their orders very broadly.

After an interview with Estrada Palma on 13 September 1906, Colwell brought 130 armed sailors and a fieldpiece ashore at Havana, only to be angrily recalled by Roosevelt the next day. Secretary of State William Howard Taft then arrived from Florida aboard the cruiser USS *Des Moines* in hopes of brokering a resolution, but Estrada Palma's cabinet resigned on the evening of 28 September rather than agree to hold new elections. Washington therefore reluctantly sent more than 2,000 marines ashore the next day from the battleship USS *Louisiana* and other vessels, while a 6,000-man U.S. occupation army followed on 6 October under Brig. Frederick Funston. Charles E. Magoon—former governor of the Panama Canal Zone—was appointed Cuba's provisional captain-general a week later.

Havana remained peacefully under U.S. rule for the next

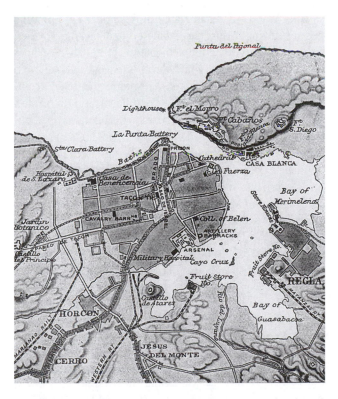

Map of the city and its environs, ca. 1905. (Keane, *Central and South America*)

U.S. naval squadron at anchor within Havana's harbor on 22 September 1906, immediately prior to being ordered to dislodge the Cuban government. (U.S. Naval Historical Center, Washington, D.C.)

two years, its economy reviving despite a hurricane that wreaked great damage on 17 October 1906 plus a wave of strikes and financial panic the following year, when laborers demanded to be paid in U.S. currency. To alleviate the chronic seasonal unemployment every May through December after the sugar and tobacco crops had been harvested, Magoon instituted a vigorous series of highway projects, harbor dredging, civic construction, and so forth. Havana's waterfront was enhanced by clearing the clutter of piers from the Punta as far as the south end of Almeda de Paula, thereby facilitating cargo handling. Electric streetcar service was also extended into the suburbs; telephone services were augmented; water lines were added as far as Marianao, Camp Columbia, and Guanabacoa; sewers were dug; and streets were paved.

When the Liberal former general José Miguel Gómez was elected Cuba's president on 28 January 1909, a second U.S. withdrawal began with Camp Columbia outside Havana evacuated that same April. (The next year, the *Maine*'s remains were raised, then towed out to sea two years later to be committed to the deep.)

Modern Growth (1910–Present)
The capital, whose economy remained quite robust and whose population was measured at 334,454 inhabitants in 1911, now began to sprawl southwestward and into the foothills, engulfing such satellite communities as Venado, Jesús del Monte, and Luyana, while even towns across the bay such as Marianao and Guanabacoa became virtual suburbs. Wider streets were also cut through the old colonial core and along city shorelines to reduce traffic congestion.

Another crisis arose when Conservative president Mario García Menocal sought reelection in November 1916, despite having pledged not to do so, then proclaimed himself the victor in defiance of a seeming win by his Liberal opponent. The Cuban Supreme Court ruled against García Menocal in January 1917, calling for new elections in Oriente and Santa Clara provinces, but the president did not respond; a coup therefore erupted at dawn of 11 February, when a few soldiers unsuccessfully mutinied at Camp Columbia.

However, other uprisings claimed the garrisons of Santiago, Camagüey, and Guantánamo, while former president Gómez raised a revolt in Santa Clara Province and Pino Guerra, and Baldomero Acosta (a former major league baseball player for the Washington Senators) took to the field in western Cuba. U.S. gunboats once more disembarked blue-jackets to protect U.S. interests, but Washington—on the brink of joining World War I against Germany—branded the revolt a "lawless and unconstitutional" distraction, and so moved to end it. Marine companies were landed, freeing García Menocal's forces to push across the island from Havana to defeat Gómez by 7 March 1917. The so-called Sugar Revolt concluded eleven days later, when the triumphant García Menocal—at Washington's insistence—promulgated a general amnesty for all rebels.

Once World War I had ended in November 1918, Havana began receiving an upsurge of tourists out of the United States, cruise ship visits being supplemented as of 1920 by seaplanes of Aeromarine Airways, which flew passengers and mail from the Florida Keys. Six years later, in response to European competition, the U.S. Congress authorized Pan American Airlines to initiate regular flights into the Cuban capital, whose populace had now mushroomed from 360,517 inhabitants in 1919 to 432,353 by 1925, despite a financial crisis precipitated by a dramatic drop in the price of sugar. Less than two months after being sworn into office as president on 20 May 1925, Gen. Gerardo Machado y Morales and his minister of public works, Dr. Carlos Miguel de Céspedes, inaugurated an ambitious construction scheme for the entire island, which included plans for a regulated expansion of Havana, erection of monumental structures, and upgrading of its outdated aqueduct system.

The Malecón (Sea-Wall) promenade leading out to the rich western suburbs was beautified with numerous new parks and edifices, while narrow streets in the old colonial core were made one-way so as to improve motor vehicle flow; a broad new avenue was cleared, running directly up to the presidential palace and named Avenida de las Misiones because it was to be lined by foreign missions. In 1928, the Ministry of Public Works also purchased the historic and beautiful Convent of Santa Clara—built in 1644—to convert it into their

Mounted traffic policemen, ca. 1913; note the Prussian-style helmets and mustaches, universally popular prior to World War I. (Lloyd, *Twentieth Century Impressions of Cuba*)

headquarters, while the grandiose Palacio del Congreso (Congressional Palace) was completed in Central Park and the university was enhanced.

Unfortunately, this ambitious program was abruptly curtailed by the Great Depression after the New York stock market crash of October 1929, which caused the price of Cuban sugar and tobacco to plummet on international markets, as well as to dry up tourism. Poor rural migrants continued to press into Havana, though, its population swelling to 542,522 people by 1931, at a time when unemployment levels were peaking at 50 percent and municipal resources were nonexistent; the first vast slums consequently appeared, and poverty became deep-seated. Public transportation, education, police enforcement, and medical care could not keep pace, so that widespread disillusionment led to strikes and riots in which at least 1,000 people died and 300 residences were ransacked, bringing about Machado's downfall by 13 August 1933.

Several months of intermittent strife ensued, until Col. Carlos Mendieta was recognized as interim president, with José Barnet winning election in December 1935, although real power gravitated to the army's chief-of-staff, Gen. Fulgencio

Batista. Some stability and prosperity were restored to Havana as the 1930s drew to a close, although tensions were brewing in distant Europe. (In a poignant byplay, the passenger liner *St. Louis* arrived at Havana in the summer of 1939 with 930 Jewish refugees, seeking asylum from Nazi persecution; they were denied entry and returned to Europe upon the eve of World War II.)

Batista won the presidency outright on 10 October 1940, then joined the United States against the Axis powers of Germany, Italy, and Japan after the Pearl Harbor attack of 7 December 1941. Cuba saw little direct military participation, except for a few early incidents such as the sinking of two American merchantmen and the damaging of another pair 12 miles off its northern coast by the German *U-126* of Lt. Ernst Bauer on 11–13 March 1942. The submarine menace soon faded, though, and Havana profited by serving as a transshipment point for the war effort, its population reaching 659,883 inhabitants by 1943 (out of 4,778,583 on the island). Next year, Batista went abroad after the election of his Liberal opponent Ramón Grau San Martín, who tried to erase many corrupt practices and democratize Cuba's government.

Leftist tendencies became even more pronounced after Grau was succeeded in 1948 by his secretary of the interior, Carlos Prío Socarras. A Conservative reaction then coalesced around Batista, who reassumed power through a bloodless military coup on 10 March 1952, suspending Cuba's constitution and disbanding congress until elections could be held two years later—which the unscrupulous dictator won, uncontested. Resistance percolated on all sides, Havana—a teeming metropolis of 785,455 residents by January 1953, with thousands more people living in adjoining towns, such as the 226,252 in Marianao—providing especially fertile ground for social unrest and union activism. Its universities had also became hotbeds of agitation, while even Washington viewed Batista with disfavor, not least because of his association with U.S. crime syndicates running Cuba's notoriously libertine casinos and brothels.

Military and police concentrations allowed Batista to repress overt disobedience in the capital, but not in the countryside. As of December 1956, an especially tenacious guerrilla band fought from the remote mountain jungles of the Sierra Maestra of eastern Cuba, led by the former University of Havana law student and agitator Fidel Castro Ruz. Other groups also beset the regime, until finally Washington sus-

pended aid shipments to Batista in March 1958 because of his repeated human rights violations. A general strike that same April failed to dislodge the dictator, but his demoralized army could not halt twin guerrilla offensives out of eastern and western Cuba. When the column of Argentine-born medical doctor Ernesto ("Ché") Güevara de la Cerna captured Santa Clara on 28 December, Batista fled three nights later.

Castro's guerrillas entered Havana in triumph on 8 January 1959, and his revolutionary movement soon revealed radical new plans for its urban development. Almost immediately, expropriations in favor of the emergent socialist state undermined private property ownership, and thousands of upper- and middle-class citizens who resisted were either arrested or driven into exile. After Castro openly embraced communism in mid-1960, diplomatic relations with Washington were severed on 4 January 1961, and Cuba was embargoed by the U.S. government. It subsequently turned to the Soviet Union and its Warsaw Pact satellites in Eastern Europe for material and ideological support.

Castro clamped totalitarian controls over every aspect of national life, and among many other social innovations set about deliberately decentralizing many functions previously performed in Havana. His goal was to lessen the capital's finan-

"Physical culture" class at a girls' school, ca. 1913. (Lloyd, *Twentieth Century Impressions of Cuba*)

cial and administrative predominance, as well as to reverse migration waves into its metropolis—whose populace had grown from 1,362,000 inhabitants in 1958 to 1,755,000 by September 1970, representing more than 21 percent of Cuba's total population. Such drastic changes proved both good and bad, the city's worst slums disappearing and conditions improving for many thousands of poorer residents, who gained access to utilitarian housing, education, and medical facilities. Uncontrolled sprawl also ceased, unlike in many other contemporary Caribbean or Latin American nations, but Havana also stagnated as all private initiative was stifled. Its colonial sectors decayed, while vast new housing projects erected to its east soon revealed many inadequacies that could not be rectified in such a tightly controlled society.

A small but steady stream of *habaneros* chose perilous methods of escape across the Straits of Florida into the United States, highlighted by the five-month "Mariel Boat-Lift," which started when emigration restrictions were temporarily lifted as of 21 April 1980, allowing 120,000 people to depart through that small fishing town. The capital's colonial core—commonly known as *La Vieja Habana* (Old Havana)—was declared a World Heritage Site by the United Nations Educational, Scientific, and Cultural Organization (UNESCO) in Paris on 14 December 1982, and five years later the Cuban government unveiled a plan to renovate many of its most historic structures, as well as improve general housing conditions to preserve it as a viable residential community. By 1993, Havana's total population was estimated at 2,176,000 inhabitants.

For further reading materials on the history of Havana or Cuba, please consult the Select Bibliography at the end of this volume; additional sources on Caribbean urban history can be found under "Regional Studies and Journals," as well as under "General Works on Latin America."

Santiago

Original island capital, located deep within a great natural harbor along Cuba's southeastern coast.

Foundation and Early Heyday (1515–1526)

After Christopher Columbus's initial exploratory probe through the Caribbean in late 1492, he returned the next year to establish an outpost on Hispaniola—modern Haiti and the Dominican Republic—expecting to transform it into an advance base for tapping into the rich trade of Japan or China. But his belief in having contacted Asia proved illusory, so that his disgruntled Spanish followers soon turned instead to subjugating and exploiting the primitive inhabitants of the Antillean archipelago.

Having crushed all resistance on Hispaniola, Deputy Gov. Diego Velázquez de Cuéllar decided in November 1511 to pursue the beaten Arawak chieftain Hatuey across to Cuba, disembarking 330 conquistadors and some native auxiliaries from four ships at a place dubbed Puerto de Palmas (Port of Palms), near modern Guantánamo Bay. Shortly thereafter, another contingent followed under Velázquez's subordinate Pánfilo de Narváez, who routed and burned Hatuey at the stake, so that Velázquez could found the first Spanish settlement on Cuba by early 1512: Nuestra Señora de la Asunción de Baracoa (Our Lady of the Assumption at Baracoa).

From this northeastern outpost, detachments pushed through the 5,500-foot central mountain ranges, eventually emerging onto the rugged southern shoreline and discovering a magnificent landlocked bay, 6 miles long by 3 miles wide. Its barren, encircling hills protected this vast anchorage from storms, while a long and sinuous access-channel—with rocky escarpments only 200 yards wide at their narrowest point—promised excellent defense against enemy raiders. Given the Catholic kings' expressed desire for a permanent port on Cuba's southeastern coast, Velázquez decided to shift his capital from Baracoa to this new locale in late July or early August 1515, naming his new settlement Santiago de Cuba (Saint James of Cuba).

Town plots were duly distributed among his subordinates, clustered around a limestone hill, plus outlying estates and vassal serfs, after which an *alcalde mayor* (municipal magistrate) and a *cabildo* (town council) were elected. Shacks were soon being erected upon individual plots, plus a communal log fort, warehouse, church, and smelter to treat the small pockets of gold that dotted streams throughout the mountainous interior. Ships began calling at the port bringing more volunteers, who pressed deeper into Cuba until the entire island was subdued. Santiago prospered by serving as the springboard and shipyard for these ventures, so that a few sturdy stone and wooden dwellings came to be added. Its hot and hilly environs also proved to be a good breeding ground for horses, cattle, sheep, and pigs, as well as being suitable for planting small amounts of sugar and tobacco.

There were perhaps 2,000 Spaniards living in and around Santiago Bay by February 1517, when Velázquez dispatched Francisco Hernández de Córdoba round Cuba's northern coast to investigate rumors of a rich empire farther west: the Aztecs of Mexico. Hernández de Córdoba limped home two months later with enough finely wrought gold to confirm this new land's wealth and sophistication, so that a second probe was dispatched under the governor's nephew, Juan de Grijalva. A third member of Velázquez's entourage—Santiago's thirty-four-year-old alcalde Hernán Cortés, owner of Cuvanacan estate on the Duabán River—was directed to raise a larger expedition to secure a foothold in the newfound territory until the governor could follow with a full-blown conquistador army.

Cortés had Santiago's town crier announce his departure, and within two weeks he had gathered more than 300 volunteers aboard seven vessels. Suspecting that the charismatic alcalde harbored his own secret designs upon the opulent prize of Mexico, Velázquez tried to supersede Cortés, only to see him

Panoramic view northward from Santiago's sea-entrance, ca. 1913; the city proper lies just out of sight at far right, 6 miles inland from the Caribbean. (Lloyd, *Twentieth Century Impressions of Cuba*)

abruptly weigh anchor on 18 November 1518 and sail slowly along southern Cuba, gathering more recruits and defying Velázquez's recalls. After assembling 580 men, sixteen horses, plus several hundred Cuban porters and black slaves, the renegade finally steered his eleven vessels toward Cozumel in mid-February 1519 to initiate his epic two-year conquest of the Aztec empire. Other vessels followed in his wake, while Velázquez angrily confiscated Cortés's Cuban properties in retaliation. But the governor's wrath turned to alarm when he learned that same autumn that the usurper had contrived to send Mexican treasure directly to Spain, seeking the favor of King Charles I. When Velázquez's favorite, Pánfilo de Narváez, returned to Santiago from Spain, the governor consequently instructed him to raise another army to capture and execute Cortés.

De Narváez stripped the Cuban capital's district of most of its remaining able-bodied Spaniards in the process, clearing the bay on 5 March 1520 with 1,400 men crammed aboard eighteen vessels. Santiago had been struck by a smallpox epidemic that previous November, and its population would never recuperate: de Narváez was defeated by Cortés's surprise counterattack against his Mexican base camp on the night of 28–29 May 1520, incorporating the entire Cuban contingent into his command. Cortés moreover subdued all Aztec resistance within a year, so that most remaining island residents began departing to partake in the dazzling wealth of the mainland, along with new migrants arriving from Castille—

who were disenchanted by Santiago's torrid climate, accentuated by the mountains that shut out the easterly trade breezes.

Consequently, when official notification arrived from Spain in 1522 that Santiago had been elevated to the full status of a city—complete with its own coat-of-arms—the news rang hollow, as the once-vibrant community had now become drastically reduced in size and importance. Velázquez died in October 1524, allegedly of a fit of apoplexy, and was buried within the capital's church, leaving his relative Martín de Rojas to assume the mantle of Cuban governor; yet the latter had to devote most of his time and energy to wringing a meager livelihood from his tenantless properties, and the depleted city suffered a final blow when fire raced through it early in 1526, reducing most edifices to ashes.

Abandonment (1526–1607)

Santiago's decline was briefly checked by the first five-year term of de Rojas's successor, Gonzalo de Guzmán—another Velázquez relation, appointed governor by the Crown as of August 1526—under whose leadership the few dozen remaining citizens began to profit modestly from sales of meat and food to ships bound toward Veracruz, as well as from exports of a few hides and sugar. Wheat cultivation was also encouraged by Madrid to help provide sustenance for transient ship crews.

The city, deep within its bay, nonetheless remained a seldom visited stopover: when Cuba's first bishop, Fr. Miguel

Santiago and its anchorage, ca. 1913. (Lloyd, *Twentieth Century Impressions of Cuba*)

Ramírez de Salamanca, arrived at Santiago to take up official residence in 1529, he found the capital reduced to a clutch of dwellings, its few Spanish residents often absent, tending to ranches or small mines scattered throughout the hilly interior and returning into their city homes only upon occasion. The next September some copper deposits were discovered when a bell-maker traveling toward Mexico was taken to a hill named El Cardenillo, west of Santiago, to conduct assays; yet lack of financial resources, technical expertise, or skilled manpower impeded any immediate exploitation, and relations between the municipality's handful of councilors and Governor de Guzmán also remained highly strained.

In an attempt to improve conditions, the Crown granted tax exemptions, as well as providing minor funding to clear roads and import slaves; yet Santiago could not compete with the allure of the bustling new port of Havana, which had sprung up 500 miles farther west to service Spanish galleons homeward bound from Mexico. According to one authority, there were scarcely 300 Spaniards and 500 African slaves left on all of Cuba by 1532, while the island capital was moreover swept by an accidental fire that consumed a third of Santiago's buildings on 4 December 1535.

Inasmuch as Spain was involved in a prolonged dynastic struggle against France back in Europe—known as the Hapsburg-Valois Wars—the hapless city also made an easy target for rovers prowling into the Antilles. A French corsair vessel entered Santiago Bay and carried off some anchored merchantmen on 31 May 1537, while another 80-man interloper pillaged an exiting brigantine on 4 April 1538, then next morning stood into the harbor to engage the anchored caravel *Magdalena* of Diego Pérez and a small 2-gun shore battery. Maritime traffic came to a virtual standstill until Hernando de Soto, a veteran of Francisco Pizarro's conquest of Peru and recently created knight of the Order of Santiago, arrived from Spain as Cuba's new governor on 7 June; however, his 950-man, nine-vessel expedition was actually intended to subjugate Florida, so that after scouring Santiago's district for food and mounts, he merely appointed the city mayor Lic. Bartolomé Ortíz as deputy governor before departing for Havana on 15 September.

The capital's prospects remained so moribund that even the former governor de Rojas abandoned Santiago for Peru in 1543, while a twenty-man French vessel was able to penetrate its bay again on 7 September, looting a merchantman and attempting a disembarkation. Juanes de Avila arrived as new Cuban governor and ordered a modest strengthening of city defenses, holding a muster in February 1544 that revealed that 200 militiamen could be raised from throughout Santiago's district. He also attempted to bolster its local economy by requesting more Crown concessions to encourage development of sugar mills and treatment-plants for copper ores, as the mines located 8 miles northwest of the city at Santiago del Prado (also known as Santiago del Cobre, modern El Cobre) had become expropriated as royal properties.

Yet discouraged estate owners no longer bothered maintaining city homes, and no municipal infrastructure existed. Even the bishop vacated Santiago's see for Spain, while de Avila himself spent most of his term at Havana—despite having married the wealthiest widow at Santiago, Guiomar de Guzmán. Havana's greater traffic volumes also meant that the Crown subsidized construction of that port's defenses, while Santiago was left to the meager protection of its lone waterfront battery. Another small band of French raiders stole into its bay under cover of darkness and seized a caravel at dawn on 17 April 1546, and when Lic. Antonio de Cháves arrived to be sworn into office as new island governor that same 4 June, he too delegated a local deputy before departing for Havana the next year. His successor, Dr. Gonzalo Pérez de Angulo, did the same after his own inaugural in November 1549, and such prolonged absences were sanctioned by the *Real Audiencia* (Royal Tribunal) at Santo Domingo three years later.

On the night of 30 June–1 July 1554, the Huguenot corsairs Jacques de Sores and peg-legged François le Clerc (nicknamed *Jambe de Bois* in French, or *Pie de Palo* in Spanish) led four ships and four smaller consorts into Santiago Bay under cover of darkness, slipping ashore 300 men who occupied the sleeping city at dawn and remained in possession for a month and a half, appropriating much smelted copper from Santiago del Prado, as well as holding the new bishop and a half dozen prominent captives until a ransom of 80,000 pesos could be raised. The interlopers thereupon threw down Santiago's paltry defenses and burned several buildings, sparing the church in exchange for all the silver plate it contained, before retiring on 16 August.

Santiago nearly succumbed altogether as a result of this raid, its leading citizens refusing to rebuild and instead recongregating farther west, hoping to re-establish themselves in the more remote lowlands around Bayamo. When another French squadron entered Santiago Bay and occupied the city ruins for a fortnight in June 1558, they could extort only 400 pesos before exiting. Santiago del Prado was nonetheless reoccupied that same year, its mining operations becoming more professionalized once the German engineer Jan Tetzel was contracted in 1560 to help tap its copper deposits, with fifty slaves furnished by the Crown. Adm. Pedro Menéndez de Aviles furthermore attempted to resurrect Santiago's city garrison by installing fifty soldiers and four artillery pieces seven years later, although the office of deputy governor was nevertheless transferred to Bayamo as of 1568, followed by the bishopric in 1574.

Ironically, the region's residents were now reduced to dealing with foreign smugglers to meet their needs, discreetly bartering hides and produce in quiet inlets in exchange for European manufactures or African slaves; visits by commercial Spanish vessels had become a rarity. Yet despite its diminished importance, Santiago suffered yet another descent in May 1586, when a French corsair—angry because his father had been executed at Bayamo the previous month—led two vessels into its bay to torch the city church, San Francisco Monastery, and the few remaining dwellings, before being driven off by a relief column that Deputy Gov. Hernán Manrique Gómez de Rojas marched across from Bayamo.

The Crown tried to help Santiago reconstitute itself by allotting monies from the Mexican exchequer to rebuild its religious institutions, as well as rescinding duties on its Antillean commerce. Still, no real revival occurred until the latter phases of Spain's conflict against Elizabethan England, when a foundry was installed at Havana to manufacture artillery and metalwork, requiring copper shipments from Santiago del Prado. The city served as a refining center and transshipment point for these cargoes, enjoying such an economic boom that it was accorded the privilege in 1602 of receiving annual visits by a small merchantman detached from the plate-fleets bound toward Mexico, so that its citizenry might supplement their exports with small quantities of ebony and dyewoods.

This sudden upsurge in prosperity again attracted enemy attention, Santiago being surprised in May 1603 by the ship *Elizabeth and Cleeve* of Capt. Christopher Reeve and a smaller pinnace, which stole into the bay to relieve its reconstructed church of assorted booty before departing. But now, with more lucrative trade to protect, residents petitioned the Crown to have fortifications erected, their plea proving to be fortunately timed: once peace with England was declared in August 1604, King Philip III was determined to extirpate all communities along Santo Domingo's northwestern coast and southeastern Cuba that had maintained contacts with foreign smugglers.

Santiago was briefly considered for such extinction, but it was spared, instead receiving a number of families uprooted from Gonaives (Haiti). Its long-diminished status was nevertheless underscored by a royal decree issued on 8 October 1607, recognizing Havana as Cuba's official capital. Santiago was henceforth to become subordinate to it and to govern only the eastern third of the island.

Revival as Provincial Capital (1608–1654)

Capt. Juan de Villaverde Ureta was promoted from Havana's garrison commander to governor of Santiago, arriving by 2 December 1608. However, his term in office would prove difficult, all efforts at improving living conditions—by such projects as diverting water into the city—being hampered by a lack of revenue. The copper mines had been placed under the control of the captains-general at Havana, and demand for ore had plummeted upon the war's cessation. Moreover, Bayamo still exceeded the nominal provincial capital in both size and wealth, while Santiago suffered a further setback when it was swept by fire early in 1613.

Villaverde died that same March, and shortly thereafter eighty soldiers appeared, having been sent from Havana to arrest the bishop for excommunicating Capt.-Gen. Gaspar Ruiz de Pereda over a dispute, as well as to investigate rumors of renewed smuggling and illegal foreign residents. The city's decline became so palpable that the next two governors—Juan García de Navia, who served from 1614 to 1617, and Rodrigo de Velasco, from 1618 to 1623—spent most of their terms at Bayamo. Santiago Bay's proposed fortification had also been deferred, so that when Capt. Alonso de Contreras, knight of the Order of San Juan, visited the harbor with his warship for four days in the spring of 1619, he had to throw up his own small shore battery. The next year, Bishop Alonso Enríquez de Armendáriz estimated that there were 1,500 congregants at Bayamo, yet only 250 at Santiago, plus a like number at its copper mines.

Nevertheless, fortune once more favored the provincial capital, when the Cauto River around Bayamo began silting up during the late 1620s and early 1630s, initiating a gradual economic tilt back toward Santiago. Sugarcane cultivation increased throughout the district, its high profit margin attracting more seaborne traders, while copper mining resurged once Francisco de Salazar inherited the royal contract from his father-in-law in 1639, complete with the services of 269 slaves. Santiago's first permanent stone churches and structures consequently began to emerge, as well as a formal street plan.

But as Spain had become embroiled in hostilities against The Netherlands, the city's resurrection once more made it worthy of enemy attack: On 15 March 1635, the Dutch ships *Otter* of peg-legged Capt. Cornelis Corneliszoon Jol and *Brack* of Capt. Cornelis Janszoon van Uytgeest penetrated Santiago Bay, masquerading as Spanish men-of-war. The unsuspecting

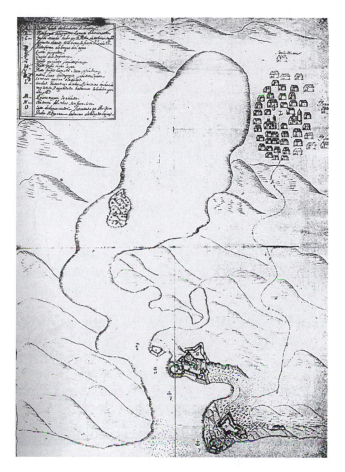

Crude map of Santiago Bay, ca. 1669, showing the new forts erected to guard its harbor entrance, plus the city itself at upper right. (Archive of Indies, Seville)

honor of the governor. It was completed a few years later (although most commonly referred to as the *Morro,* a generic Spanish term for any seaside keep). A garrison of royal troops was also assigned to the city proper.

Devastation and Resurrection (1655–1688)

Santiago received an unexpected boost after a huge English offensive was dispatched into the West Indies by the Lord Protector Oliver Cromwell in the spring of 1655, securing Jamaica as a permanent British base. Approximately two-thirds of its 1,500 displaced Spanish inhabitants and slaves were resettled in Santiago's environs, from where they launched a series of raids over the next several years in hopes of reclaiming their lost island.

As a result, twenty English vessels—including one tiny craft commanded by the twenty-seven-year-old militia captain Henry Morgan—materialized outside Santiago Bay under Commo. Christopher Myngs at daybreak of 18 October 1662, throwing 1,000 heavily armed men ashore 2 miles east of its entrance at Aguadores by nightfall. Advancing through the darkened jungle by torchlight, this column emerged 3 miles southeast of Santiago the next morning, brushing aside 170 Spanish regulars and two fieldpieces assembled at Las Lagunas by Gov. Pedro de Morales, as well as 200 militiamen under Cristóbal Arnaldo de Issasi (a former Jamaican guerrilla leader). The next day, Myngs detached a contingent to occupy the undefended San Pedro de la Roca harbor-castle as well, so that the English flotilla could enter unchallenged. The invaders then spent the next five days pursuing Spanish civilians into the interior, hoping to extort ransoms. But—frustrated in this design—they used 700 barrels of powder from Santiago's magazines to raze all its principal buildings and the harbor-castle, before departing on 25 October with seven prizes.

Once again, frightened citizens hesitated to rebuild their homes, while Santiago's economy was also left crippled because copper production had ceased altogether, the Crown's offer of a generous new lease on the mines in 1663 finding no takers. It was not to be until Pedro de Bayona Villanueva—Santiago's former *sargento mayor* (garrison commander) from 1654 to 1659—arrived from Spain to assume office as governor in June 1664, accompanied by the military engineer Juan de Siscara (alternate spelling: Ciscara) that the city falteringly began its recuperation.

Both officers reported that they found Santiago "as the enemy left it," flattened and defenseless, so that a stone citadel christened Fuerte Real de San Francisco (Royal Fort of Saint Francis) was initiated atop the ruined foundations of the old Franciscan convent at the city's devastated core. It was to provide some measure of security for property owners wanting to resume residence. The San Pedro harbor-castle was also repaired and strengthened by the addition of the Estrella and Santa Catalina batteries at water level, although all these projects proceeded only fitfully because of frequent interruptions

capital did not realize its danger until these interlopers opened fire upon the pilot-boat, killing Capt. Juan de Inza and capturing his crew. Fourteen militiamen rallied to the city battery, allowing Gov. Juan de Amezqueta Quijano to fire back as the rovers searched a half dozen anchored vessels for copper. Most proving to be empty, the Dutch offered to spare them for a price, which the governor refused. As reinforcements continued to stream into Santiago from the surrounding hills, Jol and Van Uytgeest retreated that same evening with one fully laden frigate.

When a similar incursion recurred on 4 August 1636, the authorities requested help from Madrid, and the Crown dispatched the military engineer Juan Bautista Antonelli to inspect Santiago Bay and advise as to construction of its long-postponed defenses. Arriving in June 1638, he examined the shorelines accompanied by its new governor, Pedro de la Roca y Borja, and agreed that the most advantageous site for a redoubt was atop the 200-foot stony headland at the harbor-mouth. Funds were duly allocated from the Mexican exchequer, and work commenced by 1643 on a small citadel named Castillo de la Roca de San Pedro (Castle of San Pedro Rock) in

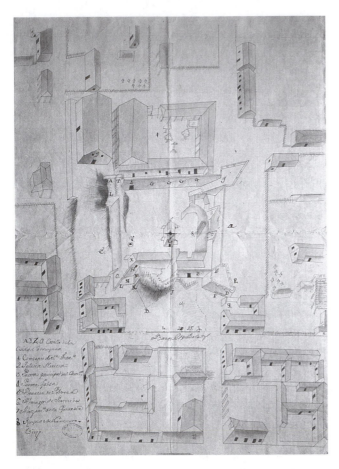

Fort San Francisco as it appeared in 1729, just prior to undergoing repairs ordered by Gov. Pedro Ignacio Jiménez; also note the new Franciscan church adjacent to this stronghold. (Archive of Indies, Seville)

in money shipments from Mexico. Still, the defensive measures were sufficient to deter a small Dutch squadron from braving the entrance on 2 May 1667, as well as a dozen ships and 700 buccaneers under Morgan on 1 March 1668.

Over the next few decades Santiago led an uneasy existence, serving both as an advance base for Spanish attacks against Jamaica and French-held Saint-Domingue (modern Haiti), as well as an entrepot for clandestine deals with foreign traders seeking its meats, hides, tobacco, sugar, and dyewoods. An earthquake rattled the city in 1675, and the French buccaneer Pierre de Frasquenay tried another surprise attack on 9 November 1677, disembarking 400 *flibustiers* at Justicia Inlet to march inland under cover of darkness, guided by a simple-minded Spanish captive named Juan Perdomo—who led the raiders by such a meandering path that one column mistakenly fired upon another in the gloom, killing fourteen of their own men and revealing their presence.

A much heavier earthquake damaged the city's partially reconstructed defenses and buildings on 11 February 1679, tempting the Breton corsair Pierre Bart into making one more

disembarkation at nearby Sabana la Mar, which proved abortive. However, when a buccaneer fleet sacked Veracruz four years later, Santiago's authorities were galvanized—despite feeble municipal revenues—into completing San Francisco citadel and installing fourteen artillery pieces, for fear that their own city might share the same fate. In December 1686, Madrid also dispatched judge Lic. Tomás Pizarro Cortés to conduct an investigation into the region's illegal contacts with foreign traders, temporarily banishing Gov. Gil Correoso Catalán to Baracoa while these inquiries were held. But little was accomplished, as Santiago's residents were now quite dependent upon smuggling to supplement their livelihoods.

Flourishment (1689–1766)

Concern over enemy descents was finally eased during King William's War, or the War of the League of Augsburg, during which Spain was allied with Britain and Holland against France. Santiago remained unthreatened while these hostilities raged between 1689 and 1697, emerging so invigorated that during the next conflict—the War of the Spanish Succession, or Queen Anne's War, from 1702 to 1713—its governor, Juan, Barón de Chávez, was able to raise 150 volunteers and sail in October 1703 with a large number of French *boucaniers* from Saint-Domingue aboard a pair of frigates commanded by Blas Moreno Mondragón and Claude Le Chesnaye, to raze the English settlement of New Providence (Nassau) in the Bahamas. This expedition returned with thirteen prizes, between 80 and 100 captives, plus twenty-two guns used to strengthen the harbor defenses. An elated Crown the next year elevated Santiago to the rank of *Muy Noble y Muy Leal Ciudad,* or Very Noble and Very Loyal City.

Tobacco and sugar exports blossomed modestly over the next few decades, thanks to economic incentives introduced by Spain's new Bourbon monarchy, a prosperity that came to be reflected in the enhanced opulence of Santiago's cathedral, as well as the opening in 1722 of San Basilio el Magno Seminary—the city's first institution of higher learning. By the time that the War of Jenkins's Ear erupted against England late in 1739, the provincial capital had grown sufficiently to be featured in a significant strategic role, for the first time in its history.

Harbor defenses were refurbished on Crown orders, and coastal batteries augmented to more than sixty cannons, measures that proved amply justified when eight warships from Vice Adm. Edward Vernon's Jamaican squadron materialized offshore on 31 July 1741, being the vanguard for forty transports bearing 3,400 redcoats under Brig. Thomas Wentworth, hovering more than 60 miles farther east in hopes of invading the city. Judging Santiago Bay's entrance impervious to bombardment, the British instead disembarked their troops in Guantánamo Bay on the night of 4–5 August. Santiago's governor, Francisco Caxigal de la Vega, meanwhile bolstered his 350-man garrison and 600 urban militiamen with rural contingents and sortied to thwart the invasion host when the British attempted to advance over the difficult intervening terrain. Wentworth's army sickened in its fortified encampment, finally growing so decimated—with 2,260 redcoats fever stricken by 5 December—that the entire expedition reembarked four days later.

Santiago's garrison was further cheered by the arrival in mid-February 1742 of 1,500 reinforcements from Spain—the Portugal Infantry Regiment and Almansa Dragoons under Cols. Francisco Villavicencio and Alonso de Arcos Moreno—then spent the next six years untroubled except for sporadic British blockades, while privateering captures compensated for interrupted commercial traffic. Caxigal de la Vega used artillery from the prizes to arm the batteries at Juragua la Grande and Juragua la Chica, while also erecting new barracks and a slaughterhouse within Santiago.

Late during that conflict, Rear Adm. Charles Knowles sailed from Jamaica with the intent of bursting directly into Santiago Bay with his squadron, but upon rushing its entrance on the morning of 9 April 1748—spearheaded by Capt. Digby Dent's 60-gun HMS *Plymouth*—the English became becalmed. Arcos Moreno, now promoted to brigadier and governor, responded by having a 200-ton ship warped out of the inner bay to support a 10-inch cable stretched between shorelines, so that when a breeze finally did spring up that afternoon, the *Plymouth* sheered off and Knowles led his squadron back toward Jamaica the next day.

Peace found Santiago on a firmer economic footing than ever before, while the restoration of merchant traffic was to usher in a boom in tobacco, timber, and sugar exports. Its urban populace had swelled to 15,471 inhabitants by 1755, and the visitor Nicolás José de Ribera described the city two years

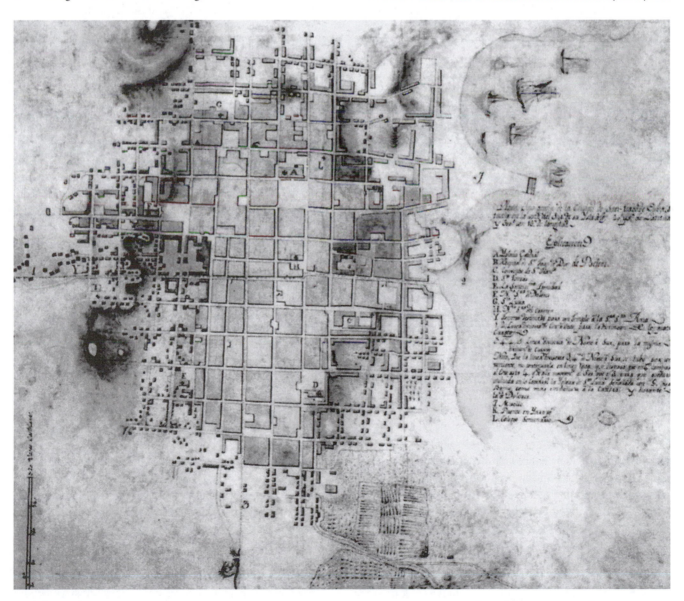

Santiago and its immediate environs in 1751, as surveyed by Baltasar Díaz de Priego; north is toward left. (Archive of Indies, Seville)

afterward as "a large town of very civilized people," enjoying regular maritime contacts with Cartagena, Portobello, and Campeche. When Madrid secretly aligned itself with Paris in 1761, promising to join the ongoing French and Indian War against Britain the next spring, the Spanish Crown took special care to bolster Santiago's defenses against the anticipated rupture: Commo. Juan Benito de Erasún duly entered on 31 January 1762 with his 70-gun flagship *Monarca, Arrogante* of Alexo Gutiérrez de Rubalcava, and *Galicia* of José de Aguirre, as well as the 44-gun frigate *Pallas* of Juan Bautista Rafael de Aramburu and brig *Cazador* of Antonio Contreras.

Monarca struck a rock while working into Santiago Bay, however, taking on several inches of water an hour at anchor; then an enormous British expedition swept down upon Havana, besieging the Cuban capital as of early June 1762. Santiago's governor, Lorenzo de Madariaga, attempted to assist by dispatching three companies of marines and a like number of regular troops under Lt.-Col. Vicente Jústiz to Jagua aboard *Arrogante*, but Havana surrendered before this small relief force could even be marched across the island. On 9 September, five French ships-of-the-line and two frigates under Rear Adm. Charles, Comte de Blénac-Courbon, also reached Santiago from Cap-François (modern Cap-Haïtien) with 600 more Spanish regulars detached from Santo Domingo as reinforcements, but as Havana and the western third of Cuba remained firmly in English hands, nothing more could be effected.

While Havana's fate was being negotiated in Europe over the next ten months, Santiago was not threatened, its citizens even profiting from the scores of British merchantmen prowling offshore, discreetly offering many items—including slaves—at low prices, as well as seeking to purchase local goods. Eventually Havana was restored in exchange for Florida, and after a Spanish captain-general reassumed office in the capital by July 1763, the Crown authorized a vigorous program of military construction as of the next year, expanding and improving Santiago's harbor defenses. The authority of its governors was moreover extended to include Baracoa, Holguín, El Cobre, Bayamo, and many other lesser towns, so as to impose a more complete administrative control over eastern Cuba.

Disaster and Revival (1767–1822)

The city was struck by another massive earthquake on 11 June 1767, leveling virtually every major structure and causing numerous deaths and injuries. Santiago's economy was now sufficiently robust, though, to ensure its full recovery, aided by financial and material backing from the Crown, so that the city's population was measured at 18,374 inhabitants by 1774, and its trade—spurred by a general easing of the old mercantilist restrictions throughout the empire—continued a steady increase. Not even the disruptions caused by Spain's alliance with the Thirteen American Colonies as of June 1779, assisting in their rebellion against Britain, could dampen the

resurgent city's prospects, and its privateer vessels regularly plied the nearby Windward Passage.

Santiago's traditional trade resumed once these hostilities ceased four years later, only the creation of a separate new bishopric at Havana in 1788 detracting somewhat from its prestige by reducing its ancient ecclesiastical authority. The city also failed to benefit significantly from the collapse of sugar production on neighboring Saint-Domingue in 1791, which sparked a vast upsurge elsewhere on Cuba to take advantage of the dramatically enhanced prices overseas. But because of its mountainous terrain, Santiago was ill suited for such large-scale cultivation, the biggest sugar plantation in its district employing fifty slaves at most, while producing only 250 hogsheads of raw sugar a year. The city's populace therefore remained relatively static throughout this boom period, being measured at 20,761 residents in 1792.

However, the quality of urban life had nonetheless improved, Santiago's first press being imported from Spain that same year by the printer Matías Alqueza. This era was also to be remembered as the heyday of its cathedral music-master and presbyter Esteban Salas y Castro Montes de Oca, who left an exceptional body of baroque choral compositions.

Santiago was not initially affected when the Republic of France declared war against Spain in January 1793, although Madrid did eventually succumb to a French invasion and realigned itself with the radical Directorate in Paris three years afterward—a switch that precipitated hostilities against England by October 1796, so that the Royal Navy clamped a blockade upon Cuba. Santiago's authorities therefore had to seek alternative outlets for its tobacco and timber exports (often resorting to neutral U.S. vessels), while also encouraging a resumption of privateering. Peace returned briefly in March 1802, but fighting flared anew only twenty months later back in Europe, so that Cuba once again became blockaded.

More important for the city's development, though, black Haitian rebels defeated the last French army outside Cap-François on 18 November 1803, precipitating a panic-stricken flight by its surviving white residents, who put to sea aboard tiny vessels and steered for Santiago as the nearest haven. It is estimated that over the next few months, 20,000 to 22,000 desperate French refugees (including their family dependents and slaves) reached the city, where many chose to remain, despite their somewhat cool reception because of the strain placed upon all supplies, services, and housing. Being experienced West Indian residents, however, many soon established successful businesses in town, as well as introducing coffee trees—a valuable new cash crop—into the surrounding hills. They also proved valuable privateers, bringing in numerous prizes (including the American brig *Columbia,* captured by Capt. Antoine Bouchet's sloop *Coquette* early in 1804, eliciting heated protests from Gov. William C. Claiborne of Louisiana).

Not surprisingly, such a massive influx transformed and invigorated Santiago. When the next census was taken in July

Santiago's eighteenth-century cathedral and main plaza, ca. 1901. (Library of Congress)

1808, the city population had jumped to 33,881, of whom 7,749 were of French origin (2,642 of the latter being white, the remainder black). The city's first newspaper had also appeared three years before: *El amigo de los cubanos (The Cubans' Friend)*, so called because it was subsidized by the local chapter of the Sociedad Económica de Amigos del País (Economic Society of Friends of the Nation). Some anti-Gallic sentiment resurfaced when Emperor Napoleon I sent an army into Spain in the summer of 1808, deposing King Ferdinand VII in favor of his own brother Joseph Bonaparte; but a pair of French privateers anchored in Santiago Bay were nonetheless allowed to escape upon receipt of this news, and the city otherwise benefited from Spain's return to its British alliance, which resulted in the lifting of the Royal Navy blockade.

The ensuing period of loosened imperial ties also allowed Santiago's authorities to pursue a semiautonomous course, yet without steering toward full independence—such as occurred elsewhere in Spanish America, where mixed-heritage Creoles had long resented the preferments accorded peninsular-born Spaniards and where the introduction of greater self-govern-ment soon escalated into calls for outright liberty. Rebellions erupted in Mexico and numerous other Latin American colonies as of September 1810, but Cuba did not experience any such uprising, instead remaining loyal to Spain throughout the ensuing fifteen-year struggle for freedom.

The worst troubles to affect Santiago started in late May 1816, when it was learned that seven republican privateers—mostly American or British West Indian mercenaries who were already familiar with eastern Cuba, and had taken out South American commissions after being left unemployed by the conclusion of the War of 1812—were prowling off Point Maisí. The city's governor, Brig. Eusebio Escudero, dispatched patrols, and Capt. José Cepeda brought the captive twenty-three-man American schooner *Margariteña* of Isaiah Homer back into Santiago Bay by 3 October. More than a dozen insurgent privateers under an American leader called Thomas Taylor, in command of the 20-gun brig *Patriot* and corvette *Zephyr*, retaliated by blockading the harbor entrance as of 21 February 1817, demanding to exchange some Spanish prisoners for their colleagues. Failing to extort an agreement, however, they

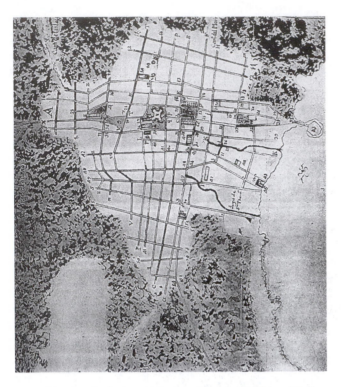

Map of Santiago in 1813; north is toward bottom. (Archive of Indies, Seville)

dispersed by mid-April, and this privateer menace did not finally ease until the British and U.S. navies intervened a few years later to restore order throughout the region.

Late Colonial Era (1823–1897)

The defeat of Spain's last armies on the Latin American mainland produced profound changes for both Santiago and Cuba, which became severed not only from much of their traditional maritime traffic, but also from all royal subsidies. Madrid could not compensate for such monetary losses, so that the island economy was now reduced to merely its sugar, tobacco, and agricultural exports—at a time when prices were spiraling downward on international markets, and the entire Caribbean was becoming mired in a protracted depression.

Although affected by this downturn, Santiago was nonetheless fortunate in that demand for metal overseas—spurred by the emergence of the Industrial Revolution in both Europe and North America—led to a revival of its nearby mining operations. The city governor was even ordered to reincorporate Santiago del Prado in May 1832 as a new town called Nuestra Señora de la Caridad de El Cobre (Our Lady of Charity of El Cobre). Thanks to foreign investment and the application of more modern techniques, this site soon evolved into a significant producer of iron, copper, manganese, and zinc, eventually spawning the establishment of foundries, narrow-gauge railroads, and shipping facilities around Santiago Bay.

Such development was briefly interrupted when the Liberal administration in Madrid ordered elections held throughout Cuba in 1836, which order Capt.-Gen. Miguel Tacón y Rosique refused to obey at Havana, arguing that such a political contest ran counter to the island's "best interests." But Santiago's governor, Gen. Manuel Lorenzo, seemingly secure within his newly prosperous eastern capital, not only disputed this annulment, but also led his own district into a short-lived rebellion by unilaterally electing three deputies to the Cortes (Parliament) in Madrid. However, threatened three months afterward with a military expedition sent from Havana by Tacón, as well as fears of a naval blockade and a possible mutiny among his disillusioned followers, Lorenzo capitulated and sailed for Europe aboard the British frigate HMS *Vestal*. A civil war subsequently engulfed Spain as well, during which Tacón was ordered to expel Santiago's archbishop, an action that contributed to his own recall in 1837.

Santiago resumed its peaceful evolution, based upon a small but burgeoning complex of foundries, soap-works, tan-yards, and tobacco factories that supplemented its traditional exports of coffee, cacao, sugar, rum, and cabinet woods. As a result of such economic growth, the city soon expanded into the encircling hills, despite having to create some tortuous streets in order to master the steep ascents. Most of its dwellings remained single-story structures that suffered another destructive earthquake, in 1852. And because of its remoteness from the central authorities in Havana, the eastern province also played a leading role in the rural unrest that started with the Ten Years War in October 1868, as many Cubans had now come to openly resent self-serving Spanish rule.

Santiago's garrison prevented any outburst within the city itself, but outlying districts were often contested. A diplomatic furor also occurred when the New York–registered *Virginius*—commanded by Joseph Fry and crewed by 52 sailors, chiefly Americans and Englishmen but bearing 103 Cuban insurgents under Gen. Bernabé Varona—was captured off Morant Bay, Jamaica, on 31 October 1873 by the Spanish warship *Tornado*. Carried into Santiago for adjudication, 53 of these captives received a summary trial and were executed on 4–8 November, including Fry and some of his Anglo-American crewmen. Washington lodged a heated protest, and the British frigate HMS *Niobe* of Capt. Lambton Lorraine appeared offshore, threatening to bombard the defenses if any more men were shot. Madrid agreed on 8 December to hand over *Virginius* and its surviving crew members to a U.S. warship eight days later, and although the U.S. attorney general eventually ruled that this vessel was the legal property of Cuban insurgents—hence subject to capture by Spanish forces—Madrid nonetheless paid an indemnity of $80,000 on 27 February 1875 to compensate for the execution of its seamen.

Three years afterward the Cuban insurgency wound down when its exhausted rural rebels were obliged to accept the Con-

View looking down San Basilio Street toward Santiago's anchorage, ca. 1913; note the steep incline. (Lloyd, *Twentieth Century Impressions of Cuba*)

supposedly steering toward Puerto Rico but actually making for Santiago.

Unaware of Cervera's approach, the U.S. auxiliary warships *Saint Louis* and *Wompatuck* stood in close to the entrance of Santiago Bay after nightfall on 16 May 1898, attempting to raise and sever the two underwater telegraphic cables running to Jamaica. The Spanish shore batteries opened fire and a pair of vessels sortied, obliging the U.S. ships to retire, although they resumed their efforts and succeeded in cutting one cable the next morning before vanishing eastward. Cervera's squadron slipped into the harbor undetected at 5:30 A.M. on 19 May, although their arrival provided scant relief to the beleaguered 9,000-man garrison of Gen. Arsenio Linares, whose pay was already ten months in arrears and whose stores were ill prepared to meet the demands of an additional 2,200 seamen. Cervera's warships moreover proved to be a military liability, useless against the encircling Cuban guerrilla bands, while attracting a major U.S. assault.

vention of Zanjón, seemingly achieving all their demands—amnesty, the abolition of slavery, colonial autonomy—although those terms were to be honored only superficially; Madrid soon resumed dictating policies. Unrest therefore built anew, exploding into another eastern rural rebellion when constitutional guarantees were suspended by the captain-general at Havana in late February 1895. This time the insurrection quickly spread westward, despite the tens of thousands of troops that Madrid dispatched to Cuba. Santiago's reinforced garrison soon found itself isolated and the city's economy was crippled, while the harsh counterinsurgency methods applied in the countryside not only steeled rebel resolve, but also further provoked a U.S. intervention.

American Siege and Occupations (1898–1917)

Tensions between Washington and Madrid escalated to the point where war was declared by late April 1898. The U.S. Navy immediately imposed a blockade upon Santiago and all other major ports, while maintaining close watch for a squadron that Rear Adm. Pascual Cervera y Topete was bringing across the Atlantic from the Cape Verde Islands as belated reinforcements. On 14 May these Spanish warships—the 7,000-ton cruisers *Infanta María Teresa, Vizcaya,* and *Almirante Oquendo;* the 6,840-ton *Cristóbal Colón;* and the 380-ton destroyers *Furor* and *Plutón*—were sighted resupplying at Curaçao before disappearing again the next evening,

Rear Adm. Pascual Cervera y Topete, commander of the Spanish squadron trapped inside Santiago Bay, May–July 1898. (Lloyd, *Twentieth Century Impressions of Cuba,* 1913)

On 26 May 1898, Commo. Winfield Scott Schley arrived 20 miles outside the harbor with his battleships *Iowa, Massachusetts,* and *Texas;* the armored cruisers *Brooklyn* and *Marblehead;* the armed auxiliaries *Vixen, Hawk,* and *Eagle;* plus the collier *Merrimac.* After being joined that same evening by the cruiser *Minneapolis,* as well as the armed auxiliaries *Saint Paul* and *Yale,* Schley cruised indecisively offshore for another two days before finally sighting Cervera's men-of-war anchored inside on the morning of 29 May. Two days later, the U.S. squadron exchanged fire with the coastal defenses, after which Rear Adm. William Thomas Sampson arrived on 1 June to assume overall command, and the Spaniards stretched a boom across the entrance to impede a penetration.

Wishing to seal Cervera inside, the U.S. fleet scuttled the *Merrimac* in the channel at 3:30 A.M. on 3 June, although it came to rest a little out of position, so that a narrow passage was still left out to the sea. Sampson's fleet then shelled the defenses on 6 June yet could inflict only minor damage. Sampson realized that it was impossible to force an entry, so U.S. strategists decided to switch tactics by disembarking an army farther east. Sampson's smaller vessels therefore penetrated Guantánamo Bay and contacted the Cuban guerrilla forces of Gen. Calixto García, a marine force securing this potential landing spot by 16 June. Four days later the 17,000-man Fifth Corps of Maj.-Gen. William Rufus Shafter arrived off Santiago from Tampa aboard thirty-two crowded transports, beginning their disembarkation 17 miles farther east at Daiquirí on 17 June, while Sampson's fleet shelled various coastal strongholds as a diversion. The town of Siboney was soon overrun, and Shafter's army linked up with 4,000 Cuban insurgents.

Admiral Sampson expected this force to push due west along the coast and outflank its batteries, so that his fleet might then enter Santiago Bay and annihilate the Spanish squadron, but Shafter opted to push northwestward and assault the city first. His timetable was accelerated when Cuban scouts reported on 28 June 1898 that 8,000 Spanish troops had broken out of a rebel encirclement at Manzanillo and were pressing eastward to reinforce Santiago. The U.S. commander therefore launched a three-pronged attack against Linares's defensive positions at dawn on 1 July, sending secondary units along the coast and up the Siboney Road toward San Juan Hill (actually a low ridge just east of Santiago), while his main thrust—6,200 men of Brig. Henry W. Lawton's 2nd Infantry Division—circled northward and stormed the village of El Caney along the Guantánamo Road.

This crossroads was held by 520 Spaniards barricaded behind trenches and a blockhouse who checked Lawton's attack for the better part of a day, before finally being overwhelmed. In the meantime, thirty-nine-year-old Col. Theodore Roosevelt's 1st Volunteer "Rough Riders" Cavalry Regiment, along with the 1st, 6th, 10th, and 16th Cavalry regiments, plus a battery of Gatling guns, carried San Juan Hill after a bitter struggle. Both sides emerged shaken by their losses, Shafter

having endured 1,100 casualties. The Spaniards—whose losses were even greater—had been driven back into their second line of trenches on the less favorable lower ground just east of Santiago, and a severely wounded Linares had been succeeded by Gen. José Toral. Convinced that the city was doomed, Madrid telegraphed Adm. Cervera on 2 July 1898 with orders to escape with his squadron; he consequently recalled the 1,200 sailors who had been helping man the defenses ashore and removed the entrance mines after nightfall so as to clear a passage out to sea.

His sortie began at 9:30 A.M. on Sunday morning, 3 July 1898, being immediately detected by Schley's vice flagship *Brooklyn,* as well as the battleships *Iowa, Indiana, Oregon,* and *Texas* (Sampson having gone east with *New York* to confer ashore with Shafter, while *Massachusetts* was recoaling at Guantánamo). *Brooklyn, Texas,* and *Iowa* opened fire before Cervera's column had even begun turning westward, striking the Spanish flagships *Infanta María Teresa* and *Oquendo* repeatedly and driving them aground 6 and 8 miles, respectively, from the entrance by 10:00 A.M. *Vizcaya* was set ablaze and ran ashore at Aserraderos an hour and a quarter later, while the destroyers *Furor* and *Plutón* were sunk near Cabrera Point. Only *Colón* (mounting two dummy 10-inch guns) led *Brooklyn* and *Oregon* on a 50-mile run before finally being forced aground that afternoon opposite Turquino Peak. All the Spanish ships were lost and their crews either killed or captured, compared with only a single U.S. seaman dead and another injured.

Shaken by this lopsided slaughter, Santiago's garrison was further demoralized when the Manzanillo relief column slipped into the city from El Cobre that same evening, proving to be a mere 3,500 weary troops under Col. Federico Escario rather than the anticipated 8,000 fresh reinforcements. Shafter thereupon called on Toral to surrender but was rejected, and some 20,000 civilians—about half the city's populace—were allowed to evacuate toward El Caney in anticipation of a direct assault. The elderly cruiser *Reina Mercedes* was scuttled to reblock the harbor entrance at 11:30 P.M. on 4 July 1898, after which Shafter began extending his siege lines, eventually gaining the western shores of the bay and trapping the defenders. From their high ground, the U.S. troops shelled the gutted city until 14 July, when Toral was once again asked to capitulate and—after telegraphing Madrid—agreed to terms. Shafter rode in to raise the Stars and Stripes above the governor's palace by noon of 17 July.

Not only had the city's 12,000-man garrison surrendered but, in addition, so had another 18,000 Spanish troops and militiamen scattered around a half-dozen lesser outposts throughout eastern Cuba. But the Cuban general García was not included in this arrangement, nor were his rebels allowed to enter Santiago for fear of exacting vengeance. The youthful medical brigadier Leonard E. Wood—a Rough Rider and close friend of Roosevelt—was instead installed as military

View across the American-occupied city from its inland heights, ca. 1901. (Library of Congress)

governor on 20 July 1898, over objections from rebel spokesmen that at least the city administration "should be turned over to Cubans." Shafter agreed to share some civic duties, and the rebel general Demetrio Castillo was temporarily installed as mayor, but the U.S. forces remained distrustful of the ragtag and mostly black insurgents, believing that only the former Spanish municipal officials could help implement Santiago's resurrection.

As a result, Castillo was removed a few days later in favor of the former Spanish mayor Leonardo Ros, at which point García's insulted followers retired into the hills around Holguín and Gibara. Notwithstanding this rancorous split, Wood proved to be an able administrator for the half-empty city, whose few thousand surviving residents were still suffering so badly from pestilence and famine that the death toll was exceeding 200 people a day. Water and sanitation systems had been destroyed, and food trade into the produce market was at a standstill; moreover, there remained tensions with country dwellers, some defeated Spaniards treating all Cubans with bitter vindictiveness, while some rural rebels wished to avenge years of repression. No public funds were available, the municipal government and courts were abandoned, and all roads leading inland were dangerous.

Wood began by recruiting citizens to clear Santiago's streets of bodies and debris, thereby checking the spread of disease. He then turned to repairing its docks and bridges, initially paying wages for this work in rations before substituting checks as the economy gradually revived. The city had started to come

back to life by mid-September 1898, so that General García was allowed to make a ceremonial visit on 22 September; still the United States refused to relinquish control, though, and a month later Wood's authority was expanded to encompass all of eastern Cuba. Despite smoldering pockets of resistance inland, he succeeded in pacifying Santiago's immediate hinterland by consulting frequently with local leaders, generously distributing supplies, ending merchant profiteering, encouraging farmers to resume cultivation, and reconstituting some Cuban rebels into a rural police force.

As for Santiago itself, the wealthy rum merchant Emilio Bacardí was appointed mayor in November 1898, while its law courts and municipal taxation system were also restored. A new seawall was erected along its waterfront, the wharf was extended, and the anchorage dredged; the jail, slaughterhouses, markets, and military hospital were all renovated; an ice-plant, an orphanage, and a grammar school for girls were built; limestone highways were laid inland; and plans were drawn up for a new municipal water system. By the time Wood was promoted to major-general and departed in December 1899 to assume office as Cuba's captain-general at Havana, Santiago was well on its way to economic recovery.

Yet despite being grateful for such improvements to their city's infrastructure, most residents of Santiago still yearned for true independence, while its black inhabitants—almost 57 percent of the populace—chafed under the racism too often manifest by many U.S. occupiers. Eventually national elections were held on 31 December 1901, and Tomás Estrada Palma—

The city's famous "Padre Pico" steps, ca. 1913. (Lloyd, *Twentieth Century Impressions of Cuba*)

a conservative who had lived in the United States for roughly twenty years—emerged as Cuba's new president, so that U.S. troops could depart Santiago in May 1902. A strong American commercial influence nonetheless remained, as corporations had made sizable purchases of sugar properties in Oriente Province and began tapping upland forest areas through clear-cutting and burn-offs, their expansion efforts supplemented by the Cuban Railway Company. But much poverty and dissatisfaction also persisted, and Estrada Palma was soon regarded as little more than a U.S. puppet; when his reelection bid in 1905–1906 was marred by fraud, Liberal opponents raised a revolt in August 1906 that caused U.S. investors and some Cuban factions to call for another intervention.

President Theodore Roosevelt eventually felt constrained to act in October 1906, so that Cuba and Santiago remained peacefully under U.S. rule for another two years, during which time a new customshouse and pier were constructed for the city, its water system was repaired and extended, its hospital was modernized, and numerous disputed town lots held by the Church were purchased for the government. According to a census taken in 1907, Santiago's population had stabilized at 45,470 inhabitants, with another 8,144 people scattered throughout its immediate municipality. The Liberal former general José Miguel Gómez was elected president and installed into office at Havana in January 1909, leading to a second U.S. withdrawal.

Santiago resumed its former existence, but a third crisis arose in November 1916, when conservative president Mario García Menocal sought reelection—despite having pledged not to—then proclaimed himself the victor, despite his apparent defeat at the hands of his Liberal opponent. The Cuban Supreme Court ruled against García Menocal and in January 1917 called for new votes in Oriente and Santa Clara provinces, but the president proved slow to comply; a nationwide coup therefore erupted at dawn of 11 February—being suppressed at Havana, although succeeding in winning over Santiago's garrison under Col. Rigoberto Fernández, as well as those at Camagüey and Guantánamo and certain rural areas of Santa Clara and other provinces.

The U.S. gunboat *Petrel* of Cmdr. Dudley Knox consequently arrived outside Santiago Bay from Guantánamo at dawn of 15 February 1917 to once again protect American interests, initially agreeing to prevent any government vessels from entering the harbor, in exchange for a rebel pledge not to block its channel with scuttled ships. However, Washington—teetering on the brink of joining World War I against Germany—had little patience with this distracting revolt in Cuba, branding it "lawless and unconstitutional" four days later. Knox's arrangement with the Santiago rebels was quickly disavowed, and companies of marines were disembarked to protect American-owned sugar plantations in Oriente Province. This display of U.S. disapproval allowed García Menocal to push troops across the island from Havana, so that the rebel authorities in Santiago requested that the cruisers USS *San Francisco* and *Olympia,* plus the gunboat *Machias,* land 500 marines in the city on 8 March to prevent any excesses when the government army of Col. Miguel Varona entered.

This third U.S. occupation of Santiago proved transitory, the marines quickly fanning out to El Cobre and other more threatened spots before this so-called Sugar Revolt was concluded ten days later when the triumphant president—at Washington's insistence—promulgated a general amnesty for all rebels. He nevertheless asked Washington to keep 1,600 marines stationed in Oriente Province as peacekeepers over

the next six years, supposedly to protect the region's new American-owned sugar plantations but actually to help the central government to control this remote and restive province.

Modern Era (1918–Present)

The city doubled in size over the next two decades, despite the economic crises that blighted the Cuban economy during 1920–1921 and after the New York stock market crash of October 1929. Some measure of stability and prosperity eventually returned as the 1930s drew to a close, though, and Gen. Fulgencio Batista assumed office as president in October 1940 and joined the U.S. war effort against Germany, Italy, and Japan after the Pearl Harbor attack of 7 December 1941. Santiago saw little direct military involvement during World War II, yet it profited from increased demands for its metals and produce in North America, despite the inability of ocean-going ships drawing more than 14 feet of water to berth directly at its wharves. Its population also continued to grow during the postwar era, rising from 118,266 people in 1943 (with another 2,300 in its outlying suburbs) to 163,237 a decade later.

Cuba's national politics became increasingly polarized when the Liberal administration of Pres. Ramón Grau San Martín from 1944 to 1948 was followed by the more leftist Pres. Carlos Prío Socarras from 1948 to 1952. He provoked a conservative reaction that soon coalesced around Batista, who seized power again through a bloodless military coup on 10 March 1952, suspended the constitution, and installed a repressive regime. Resistance to this unscrupulous dictator sprang up throughout the countryside, and Santiago—because of its remoteness—was once more to become prominently featured.

At dawn of 26 July 1953, 111 poorly armed followers of the former University of Havana law student and political agitator Fidel Castro Ruz entered the city in a disguised convoy of cars, hoping to surprise the 1,000-man garrison of Col. Alberto del Río Chaviano while they were still recuperating inside Moncada Barracks from the Carnival celebrations of the previous night. However, the assault was defeated after an hour-long firefight during which nineteen troops and three rebels were killed, and the outraged soldiery thereupon hunted down, tortured, and executed approximately eighty rebels and sympathizers over the next several days. Eventually, a delegation of city notables—including Santiago's bishop, university rector, a judge, and the wealthy department store owner Enrique Canto—appealed to Batista to halt the brutal measures. Castro was caught hiding in the woods of Gran Piedad Mountain along with a few other rebels and was tried that same October, being sentenced to fifteen years' incarceration on Isla de Pinos. But a groundswell of public sentiment resulted in his being amnestied by mid-May 1955, at which time he went into exile in Mexico to plot another coup.

Hotel erected in Santiago's main square by the Cuban railway company, as it appeared ca. 1925. (Carpenter, *Lands of the Caribbean*)

Bullet-scarred exterior of the Moncada Barracks after Castro's failed assault, July 1953.

Anti-Batista outbursts and work stoppages nonetheless persisted throughout Cuba, and a rebel group called the 26 of July Movement kept Castro's cause alive in Oriente Province by setting off several bombs in Santiago late in 1955 that injured six people and maintained a climate of fear. The city's national senator Rolando Masferrer had also organized a political countergroup, a private army of urban toughs nicknamed Los Tigres, as part of a broader fascistic movement aimed at supplanting Cuba's feeble democratic institutions with an outright dictatorship. Turmoil heightened when some 300 uniformed rebels under Frank País—wearing the red-and-black armbands of the 26 of July Movement—captured Santiago's police headquarters, customshouse, and other official buildings during a dawn raid on 30 November 1956, only to melt away and repeat this tactic the next day, bringing civic life for the 189,000 inhabitants to a virtual standstill. Two days later it was learned that Castro had returned from exile, disembarking near Belic from the yacht *Granma* with eighty-two followers to march up into the Sierra Maestra range and inaugurate a guerrilla campaign.

Batista responded by airlifting 280 soldiers under Col.

Pedro Barrera into Santiago, and Castro was lucky to survive a chance encounter with a patrol on 5 December 1956 before escaping deep into the highlands with fewer than twenty men. Government control gradually eroded over the next several months as the 26 of July Movement detonated more bombs within the city, while Castro gained adherents in the mountains and launched hit-and-run raids. When the eight-car motorcade of U.S. ambassador Earl Smith visited Santiago's main square on 31 July 1957, he was greeted by a throng of women protestors bearing anti-Batista grievances. Strikes and unrest also gripped many other parts of Cuba, so undermining Batista's regime that large guerrilla bands at last began operating boldly north of the city in early November 1958, cutting off the main highway toward Havana the next month, while precipitating a flood of refugees into Santiago.

The dictator had by now become so discredited that he abruptly resigned and flew into exile from Havana on New Year's Eve 1958, Masferrer being simultaneously warned by telephone so that he too could slip out of Santiago aboard his yacht that same night. Therefore, when Castro advanced upon the city with his guerrillas on 1 January 1959, he was surprised

Milkmen in the streets of Santiago, ca. 1925. (Carpenter, *Lands of the Caribbean*)

that Santiago's garrison and two anchored frigates surrendered without a fight. In a euphoric speech before a huge throng assembled in the main square late that same night, he triumphantly proclaimed that Santiago—the "bulwark of liberty"—would become the new national capital under his regime.

Practical considerations kept him from carrying out this design once he gained Havana a week later, and a chaotic transition then engulfed the battered country as Castro sought to uproot and completely transform its society by imposing Communist doctrines. Washington reacted by embargoing Cuba, while the CIA organized a counterinvasion and—in an attempt to deceive the new Cuban leadership that this landing would occur in Oriente Province—even penetrated Santiago Bay at dawn of 13 March 1961 with a small boat, peppering its refinery with small cannons and machine-gun fire in the hope of sparking an explosion. A pair of B-26 bombers with false markings also struck the city airfield at dawn on 15 April, destroying two parked warplanes. Castro ordered the arrest of many thousands of potential opponents throughout Cuba over the next two days, then defeated the actual disembarkation in the Bahía de Cochinos (Bay of Pigs) west of Cienfuegos.

The confrontational atmosphere gradually subsided, but many thousands of Cubans nonetheless fled as a socialist administration took full control over every aspect of civic life, with support from the Soviet Union and its Warsaw Pact satellites in Eastern Europe. Despite such difficulties, Santiago benefited from Castro's desire to decentralize many functions previously performed in Havana, so as to lessen the capital's traditional predominance over the island; the eastern city's population increased from 259,000 inhabitants in 1967 to an estimated 430,500 by 1993, while its industrial sectors also expanded. Living conditions for its poorest residents improved through access to utilitarian housing, education, and medical facilities. But conversely, all private initiative was discouraged, and Santiago's development stagnated, with the exception of cumbersome state projects.

For further reading on the history of Santiago or Cuba, please consult the
    Select Bibliography at the end of this volume.

Curaçao

Willemstad
Entrepot located less than 60 miles from the South American mainland, which evolved into the capital of the "Five Sisters" of The Netherlands Antilles: Aruba, Bonaire, Saba, Sint Eustatius, and the southern half of Sint Maarten.

Spanish Indifference (1499–1519)
Curaçao was initially sighted by the explorer Alonso de Ojeda in late July or early August 1499, as he probed westward from the Gulf of Paria toward Cape de la Vela. His Florentine-born colleague Amerigo Vespucci also visited the island that same autumn, dubbing it—along with neighboring Aruba and Bonaire—the Islas de los Gigantes (Islands of the Giants), because of some exceptionally tall Caquetí Indians that he chanced to encounter. However, as Curaçao was but a dry, brown, flattish island roughly 40 miles long by 10 miles wide, surrounded by menacing coral reefs, with barren hills rising to 1,200 feet in its northwestern quadrant, it proved to be an untempting prospect for Spanish settlement when compared with other lusher and more accessible West Indian isles.

Even after the Spaniards began expanding out of their original stronghold on Santo Domingo during the early sixteenth century and conquering private fiefdoms throughout the Antillean archipelago, sparsely populated and distant Curaçao held little allure. Its torrid climate was scarcely eased by an average annual rainfall of 20 inches; in addition, streams were few and far between, resulting in a sun-baked landscape so stark and arid that only a few thousand Carib residents could eke out a subsistence existence by harvesting maize and bean crops from its few fertile glens, supplemented by fishing activities. And given that conquistadors preferred exploitable mineral deposits, or arable lands worked by thousands of vassals, Curaçao was ignored over the next couple of decades, except for *indiero,* or slave-catching expeditions—the raid by Capt. Diego de Salazar in 1515 netting 2,000 local inhabitants, who were taken north to toil in the Dominican mines and plantations.

Colonization (1520–1633)
It was not until the reformist royal factor at Santo Domingo, Juan de Ampíes, intervened that Curaçaoans at last became

Aerial view looking eastward across Willemstad, ca. 1910; part of ancient Fort Amsterdam appears in the right foreground, with the Waaigat stretching away in the middle distance. (Foto Fischer Archive, Curaçao)

73

exempt from such predatory treatment, becoming designated *indios guaitiaos* (friendly Indians) who could not legally be enslaved. De Ampíes was furthermore authorized by the Crown in 1520 to repopulate the island grouping still known as Los Gigantes with Christianized Caquetís, so that Gonzalo de Sevilla arrived on Curaçao the next year with a small group of settlers to initiate such a project. But that attempt lasted only a year and a half, as the conquest of the wealthy Aztec empire by Hernán Cortés in the spring of 1521 sparked a massive wave of emigration westward from the Antilles to Mexico. Consequently, Curaçao remained uninhabited until the summer of 1527, when de Ampíes's son disembarked with a second small group of Spanish colonists to found another short-lived settlement: it ended when news arrived of Francisco Pizarro's subjugation of the equally rich Incan empire of Peru, precipitating a second wave of West Indian depopulations.

A permanent Spanish presence was not established on Curaçao until the late 1530s, when de Ampíes's son-in-law Lázaro Bejarano returned with livestock as an additional means of support, his group prospering sufficiently that they were able to erect the island's first whitewashed, stone-and-brick church by 1542. Animal husbandry flourished by allowing livestock to range freely, while residents clustered in ranches scattered along the western or lee shore. A town had also emerged on the southeastern bank of Santa Anna Bay, whose spacious and landlocked inner harbor was acknowledged as the island's biggest and best anchorage. Although plate-fleet traffic from Spain routinely bypassed such a minor colony, small vessels called in Santa Anna Bay as they plied along the Venezuelan coast, pausing to refresh their wood and water as well as barter for meat, hides, and salt.

Foreign interlopers began being clandestinely welcomed as well, stealing into the Spanish West Indies in ever-increasing numbers to trade or mount attacks during times of European conflict. The few Spaniards on Curaçao seemed to have been spared, at least initially, as these rovers realized that visits to the unpatrolled offshore community were mutually beneficial. Records of these early contacts remain sketchy, French corsairs being known to have called at Curaçao in the early 1560s. The English slaver John Hawkins traded with Bejarano himself in May 1565, describing the island as "one great cattle ranch." His compatriot and associate John Lovell also visited, in the spring of 1567, with the young Francis Drake serving aboard; three of Hawkins's ships returned the following year.

Crown authorities in Spain sought to curtail all such illegal contacts, and the countermeasures they imposed elsewhere in the New World eventually soured relations to a point where Curaçao also would be attacked. In 1571 the Huguenot rover Jean Bontemps disembarked seventy men to pillage the island; he was defeated, dying of an arrow wound to his throat when confronted in a teeming rainstorm by a force of local inhabitants led by the Spanish residents Antonio and Gonzalo Bar-

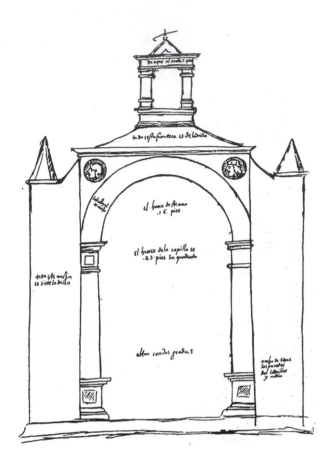

Modern copy of a sketch executed in 1548, depicting the facade of the church erected six years previously on Curaçao by Lázaro Bejarano. (Archive of Indies, Seville)

budo. (Bontemps's head was later sent to Santo Domingo as a ghoulish war trophy.) When the Bristol merchant Andrew Barker attempted to take on water for his barks *Ragged Staff* and *Bear* in September 1576, he suffered fourteen men wounded from ambush. An even worse fate befell another boatload of fourteen Frenchmen in 1584—eleven being slain and one captured by thirty islanders.

Yet despite such isolated clashes, clandestine trade persisted even after full-scale hostilities erupted between Spain and Elizabethan England in 1588, dragging on for fifteen years. And despite being unsupported by the Crown and almost never visited by Spanish ships, the tiny community inside Santa Anna Bay fared rather well during this struggle, their ranches and herds multiplying. By 1620, although the total island populace had grown to only 160 Spanish residents and several hundred native inhabitants, they nevertheless boasted some 10,000 head of cattle, 14,000 sheep, 2,000 goats, as well as 6,000 horses and mules.

The lonely settlement became especially vulnerable once European powers began establishing rival Antillean outposts during the early seventeenth century, particularly after the

United Provinces of The Netherlands declared war against Spain on 1 April 1621. Three years later, the private Westindische Compagnie (West Indian Company, WIC) dispatched a trio of ships under Pieter Schouten to reconnoiter the Caribbean for potential bases, and one such Dutch toehold was installed on the island of Sint Maarten—only to be eradicated by a passing Spanish plate-fleet in the summer of 1633. The WIC directors in Amsterdam responded by outfitting another expedition the next year under Johannes van Walbeeck, with orders to take "possession of the island of Curaçao in order to have a suitable place where one might obtain salt, wood and other matters, and from the same place attack the enemy."

Dutch Conquest (1634–1648)

Guided by Jan Janszoon Otzen, who had been brought to the island as a Spanish captive a few years previously, van Walbeeck's ships *Groot Hoorn, Eenhoorn, Brack, Engel Gabriel,* and two sloops sighted Curaçao and the large cross marking the entrance into Santa Anna Bay on 6 July 1634; however, they were carried farther west by the strong winds and currents, having to circle patiently back, capturing a Spanish bark and being joined by another Dutch ship during this digression as well as a buccaneer vessel under a renegade Cuban mulatto named Diego de los Reyes. The expedition

reappeared off Curaçao by 28 July, its ships filing unopposed through the narrow entrance into the vast inner harbor of Santa Anna Bay (quickly redubbed the Schottegat by these would-be invaders).

The Spanish residents living inside—now reduced to forty men, women, and children under the governorship of Lope López de Morla, plus fewer than 500 Christianized local inhabitants—were startled by the bold entry of this 400-man squadron, of whom 225 were soldiers under Pierre le Grand (a French Huguenot mercenary who had previously served with the Dutch in Brazil). López therefore ordered some fifty Indian archers to man a trench opposite Santa Anna's landing beach, while offering to negotiate. Van Walbeeck instead reconnoitered the inner shoreline, then started disembarking troops from seven boats at dawn of 30 July 1634, while de los Reyes distracted López by parleying from offshore. By the time the Spaniards realized that this was intended as a full-blown invasion, rather than just a pillaging raid, the Dutch were already ashore. The next day López set Santa Anna's few buildings and wood stockpiles ablaze, tainted its wells with offal, and retreated inland with his followers.

Because the lone town had been rendered uninhabitable, the Dutch encamped near some wells on the opposite side of the bay, while detachments tried to run down the elusive residents.

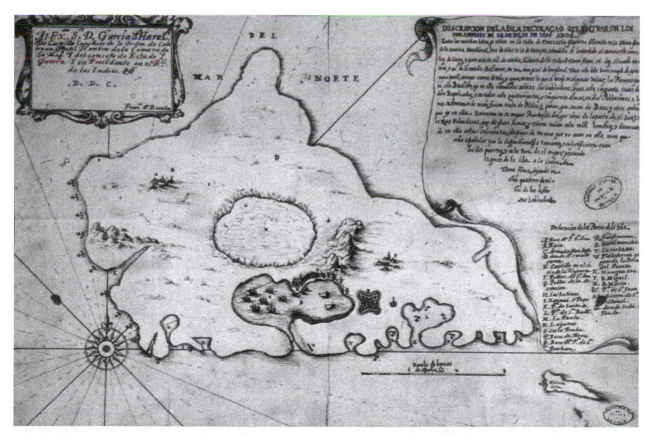

Crude Spanish map of Curaçao in 1634, drawn by Francisco de Ruesta in anticipation of an attempted reconquest of the island from the Dutch; note the prominence accorded both Santa Anna and Santa Barbara bays. (Archive of Indies, Seville)

These pursuit columns suffered a setback when one was attacked at Santa Barbara by native archers in a rainstorm on 5 August 1634, losing twenty-five men because their powder was damp. Yet the Dutch managed to overrun the tiny northern hamlet of Ascensión twelve days later, nailing numerous surrender demands addressed to López upon trees. He finally was cornered in the San Cristóbal Hills (modern St. Christoffelberg) on 21 August and compelled to capitulate. Thirty-two Spaniards and 402 loyal Indians were deported with him to the Venezuelan port of Coro aboard the yachts *Eenhoorn* and *Brack* and a fishing boat. Some seventy-five islanders chose to remain amid the conquerors, while an initial Dutch survey also recorded 750 horses, a few cattle, plus countless goats and sheep that were left upon the island.

Shortly after disembarking, van Walbeeck had begun preparing for an anticipated Spanish counterexpedition by throwing up a battery called the Waterfort to cover Santa Ana Bay's strategic harbor entrance. This decision would effectively shift Curaçao's town from its original, indefensible position on the southeastern shores of the inner bay out to the narrow *Punta,* or "point," that commanded the entry (the Spanish term was soon corrupted into *Punda* by the Dutch). Their initial seaside redoubt consisted of a single, 5-foot-high rampart made of brick and lime—materials brought by the invaders themselves—topped by a double wooden palisade filled with earth and exposed on its landward side.

Six months after the Waterfort's completion, the Dutch initiated construction of a much larger and more permanent fort nearby, using rocks, coral, and clay to create a stronghold that would house the entire Dutch force; a chain was also stretched across the harbor mouth. Soldiers detailed to such labors almost mutinied twice, resentful at having to toil in such unaccustomed heat. A few Dutch privateers had meanwhile appeared, using this new base to strike against Spanish targets, while administrative support of the recently conquered island was officially delegated by other Dutch provinces to the Amsterdam Chamber of the WIC on 20 April 1635.

Madrid's response proved to be much slower and ineffectual than expected, Adm. Lope de Hoces y Córdoba not reaching Cumaná, Venezuela, with three warships until 9 May 1636 after a stopover in Brazil. Sixteen days later he was joined by Commo. Sancho de Urdanivia's four store-ships and four tartans from Spain, so as to mount a joint operation against occupied Curaçao. As their siege-train had been lost when de Urdanivia's fifth store-ship wrecked on Matalino Island, the Spanish commanders instead opted to proceed straight into Cartagena.

The Dutch had by now finished an imposing harbor-castle christened "Fort Amsterdam," with walls 15 feet high and 8 feet thick, its seaward ramparts being built of *ijsse* bricks brought in as ballast by arriving ships. The compound it enclosed was ample enough to accommodate a WIC warehouse, offices, living quarters, a magazine, a church, a well, and everything necessary to withstand a protracted siege, so that Dutch civilians—made uneasy by frequent Spanish threats—tended to cluster near this reassuring bulwark on its seaside promontory rather than clear a new town site deeper inside the Schottegat.

Van Walbeeck was succeeded as island "director," or governor, by Jacob Pieterszoon Tolck, with civil and military authority combined, and a squadron of warships was placed at his disposal to prosecute the war against the Spaniards. Tolck ordered an additional small stronghold—named Fort Tolcksburg upon its completion—erected to protect Santa Barbara Bay farther to the southeast, plus another redoubt just east of Santa Anna Bay to defend Fort Amsterdam's landward flank, and became sufficiently secure to dispatch raids against the nearby Venezuelan and Colombian coasts. His successor, Jan Claeszoon van Campen, continued this aggressive policy by sending four small vessels with 250 to 275 men under Commo. Hendrik Gerristz in October 1641 to raid the Spanish towns inside the Laguna de Maracaibo.

Venezuela's governor, Ruy Fernández de Fuenmayor, retaliated by leading 300 men out of La Guaira a year later to fall upon Bonaire, whose 40-man Dutch detachment set fire to their tiny keep and fled to advise yet another new director at Willemstad: Pieter Stuyvesant (the future governor of New Netherland, or New York). He in turn avenged this counterstroke by sending a pair of Dutch ships to assail Puerto Cabello and Coro in November, where they took 2,500 cattle, sheep, and goats to restock Bonaire. Stuyvesant also welcomed 1,000 English freebooters under Commo. William Jackson, providing them with a pilot for a destructive sweep through the Laguna de Maracaibo.

Yet Stuyvesant's attempt to reconquer the former WIC base of Sint Maarten early in 1644 was repelled, costing him his right leg. And when 450 WIC personnel under David Adam Wiltschut, expelled by the Portuguese from São Luis—the Dutch outpost in the Brazilian region of Maranhão—unexpectedly reached Curaçao that same April, the island was still not capable of accommodating so many additional people, provisions being so scarce that many of these newcomers had to be shipped on to New Netherland in North America (whose administration would subsequently govern Curaçao, when the peg-legged Stuyvesant was appointed joint director).

Still, a small town had begun to take shape in the shadow of Fort Amsterdam, being named *Willemstad,* or William's Town, in honor of the young son of the United Provinces' stadholder, Frederik Hendrik, who later succeeded his father as Willem II. While the island's WIC offices continued to be headquartered within the original compound, private buildings had by now sprung up on the narrow stretch of land just to its north, being limited on the west by Santa Anna Bay, to the north by the Waaigat River, and to the east by a new defensive wall. Streets were laid out along the best lines of fire radiating from the fort, and this ancillary community did not truly

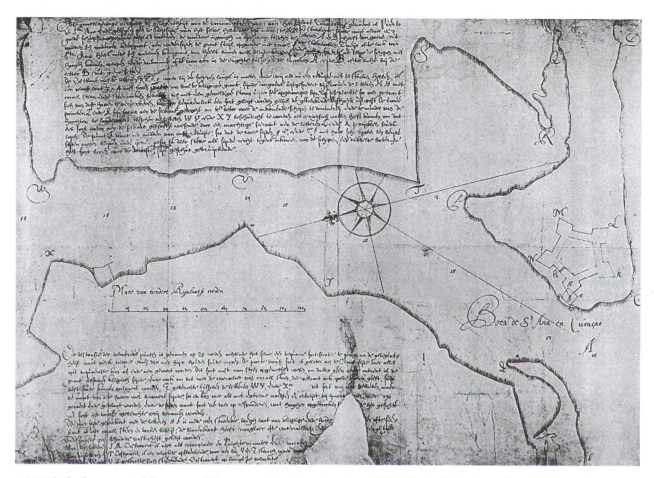

A 1634 draft of a pentagonal fort to guard the entrance into Santa Anna Bay, which is depicted branching off into the Waaigat at top and Schottegat at extreme left; north is toward lower left. After construction started, practical considerations dispensed with Fort Amsterdam's southwestern bastion, its seaward face being left squared off. (Algemeen Rijksarchief, The Hague)

begin to thrive until peace was concluded between The Netherlands and Spain in January 1648, allowing for a greater economic purpose to take hold on the island.

Slaving Station (1649–1713)

Given that Curaçao's harsh landscape was largely unsuitable for planting New World cash crops such as sugar or tobacco—being dismissed by one contemporary Dutch chronicler as that "cursed little barren island"—the WIC directorate instead hoped to transform it into a slave depot, believing that by offering such coveted human merchandise, their factors might also gain access to otherwise closed markets throughout the Caribbean and Spanish America so as to sell additional products. A concerted effort commenced once hostilities wound down, greatly impelled by the fortuitous resettlement on the island of Jewish exiles driven from Portugal's American empire.

The first Sephardic Jews had reached Curaçao from Holland in 1651, under a leader named João de Yllan, but they had failed to prosper. However, a second group arrived from Pernambuco in Brazil three years afterward and founded a successful congregation called Mikvé Israel by 1656. Their synagogue was built on the *Hoop,* or "Hope," Plantation on the northwestern shores of the Schottegat (site of the modern Beth Haim Cemetery), and they were in turn able three years later to bring out twelve more families from Holland—about seventy persons—supposedly to form an agrarian community under a charter granted to Isaac da Costa. Yet, as so many were familiar with Latin customs and the language, they proved infinitely more adept at selling into Venezuela and other Hispanic-American colonies, which were starved of imports because of Madrid's restrictive mercantilist policies.

The bankrupt Spanish Crown's ban on foreign purchases was finally breached in 1662, when *asiento,* or monopoly, rights to furnish slaves to its empire were sold to the Genoese commercial house of Domingo Grillo and Ambrosio Lomelín, who in turn contracted with the Dutch of Curaçao for the acquisition of 24,000 slaves over seven years, to be delivered at diverse ports. Willemstad was consequently to grow into one of the largest slave marts in the Caribbean, exporting

Mikvé Israel Synagogue, completed in 1731–1732, as it appeared ca. 1955; it is the oldest such temple in the Western Hemisphere. (Ozinga, *De monumenten van Curaçao*)

much other merchandise besides, so that its trading houses multiplied. The town soon consisted of twenty-six densely packed blocks of brick or stone dwellings with wooden verandas and shutters, crowded along narrow streets crisscrossing in no discernible pattern. Its finest homes faced the Waterkant, the waterfront (along modern Handelskade), as well as along the Heerenstraat parallel to it, plus the curving Breestraat along Fort Amsterdam's northern face. The ground floors of most edifices were used as warehouses or shops, while the second and third floors were given over to living quarters.

A hospital for the poor had been created as early as 1659, while water had to be ferried into the bustling community from wells around the Schottegat and sold door-to-door. Two nearby pens contained as many as 3,000 slaves at a time, while regional produce was also exported to Holland, especially salt from Bonaire. When New Netherland was lost to the English and became New York City after the Second Anglo-Dutch War of 1665–1667, Willemstad's booming trade meant that it was elevated to the status of capital of The Netherlands Antilles, its previously secondary office of vice director being upgraded to a resident governor, answerable only to the Amsterdam chamber. Because of the many opportunities available for personal gain, this office proved to be a coveted posting, as the gover-

nor and his hand-picked Raad (council) dominated all business and civic affairs.

Willemstad's burgeoning prosperity attracted enemies as well, for although it had not been threatened by British forces during the first two Anglo-Dutch Wars—because of its difficult sea approaches and the reputed impregnability of its harbor-castle, described by Col. Theodore Cary of Jamaica as the "strongest Dutch fort in the Indies"—the French nevertheless decided to test its strength when news of the outbreak of a Franco-Dutch conflict reached the Antilles in the summer of 1672. Jean-Charles de Baas-Castelmore, governor-general for the French West Indies, led a force from the Windward Islands to a rendezvous off Saint Croix, hoping to combine with a contingent from Saint-Domingue (modern Haiti) for a joint descent against Curaçao.

However, de Baas was disappointed when only one Dominican ship arrived, others having been wrecked on Puerto Rico, so that he could materialize off southern Curaçao on 13 March 1673 with but the 70-gun royal flagship *Belliqueux* of Captain Dumé d'Amplimont, the frigates *Sibylle* and *Fée*, plus three transports, disembarking a small army near Santa Barbara Bay the next day. After skirmishing half-heartedly against the defenders of tiny Fort Tolcksburg, the governor-general—discouraged by reports of Acting Gov. Jan

Doncker's strong Dutch concentration at Willemstad, plus numerous ships lying inside the Schottegat—re-embarked his men by 16 March. Doncker, a merchant and council member pressed into office because of the death of Gov. Dirck Otterinck, was rewarded for this successful defense by being confirmed as governor by the Amsterdam chamber, then spent his six-year term completing all defenses and promoting the agricultural development of the island; its populace had suffered considerable want when the flow of Dutch supply ships had been interrupted by these hostilities.

Moreover, the WIC itself had by the end of December 1674 endured so many losses that it had to be dissolved and reconstituted on a smaller scale. Curaçao and its subordinate islands of Aruba and Bonaire were consequently reincorporated under a reduced charter, and Willemstad was declared a free port the next year, in the hope of encouraging sales of slaves and other commodities to neutrals, in spite of the ongoing war with France. A second, even more serious threat loomed during the closing phases of this conflict when the French admiral Jean,

Comte d'Estrées, having already annihilated the Dutch garrison on Tobago, sailed westward against Curaçao with eighteen royal warships and more than a dozen privateer vessels, only to suffer a massive shipwreck while passing the Aves Islands group on the evening of 11 May 1678, losing seven large warships, a half-dozen lesser consorts, 500 men, and his siege-train, so that he limped away toward Haiti.

By the time peace was concluded in August 1678, the global power of The Netherlands had become eclipsed, although Willemstad was able to resume its role as a major slave depot for the West Indies, importing and distributing thousands of African captives every year. However, the transient nature of such traffic did not materially improve Willemstad, the needs of its few permanent citizens being often ignored by officials appointed from Holland who looked to their personal aggrandizement before being rotated out at the end of a brief tenure. For example, the damage inflicted by a 1681 hurricane was only indifferently repaired, so as not to deplete company profits. The island's few fertile pockets and

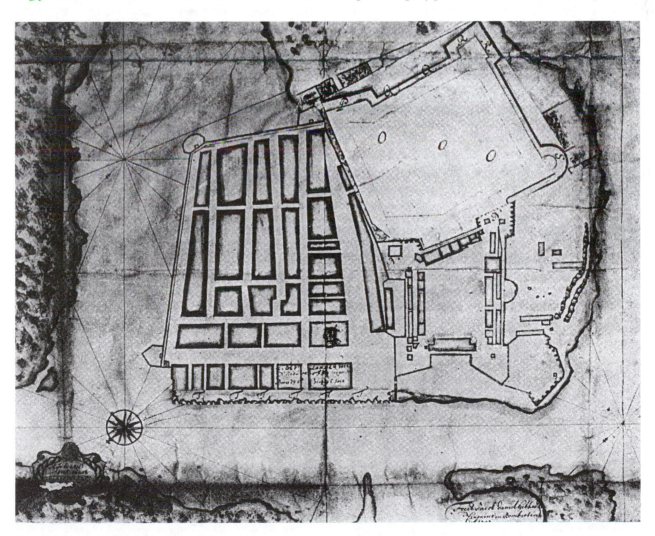

First reliable map of Willemstad and Fort Amsterdam, as surveyed in 1707 by the artillery officer Jacob Daniel Gebhardt; north is toward lower left. (Algemeen Rijksarchief, The Hague)

arid climate did not otherwise allow for the development of alternate sources of income, its being noted in 1683 that while 1,800 slaves were employed in domestic service on Curaçao, only 600 were engaged in agricultural cultivation. And when the Spanish *asiento* was canceled four years afterward, 5,000 slaves were left unsold at Willemstad.

The islanders' narrow economic self-interest became manifest when King William's War, or the War of the League of Augsburg, erupted two years later, with The Netherlands, Britain, and Spain arrayed against France. Curaçao did not support its English allies—or even other Dutch colonies—during the subsequent Antillean campaigns, instead concentrating upon smuggling as many slaves and goods as possible into Spanish America. Such conduct was even sustained when Queen Anne's War, or the War of the Spanish Succession, started in May 1702, for although England and Holland were on this occasion aligned against France and Spain, Curaçao's unique priorities meant that the greatest threat to its trade was posed by English ships intercepting smugglers plying from Willemstad to the Venezuelan and Colombian coastlines. The English Council of Trade and Plantations in London angrily complained that same December that "the Dutch from Curaçao drive a constant trade with the Spaniards, as if there was no war," so that the WIC directorate made a few conciliatory gestures—while secretly instructing Gov. Nicolaas van Beek to recall all his privateering commissions, for fear that too zealous a Dutch blockade of Spanish America might alienate their clientele.

Willemstad had now expanded beyond its original boundaries, a few new homes having been built north of the Waaigat, in a suburb that would soon become known as Scharloo. Villas had also appeared east of the town's old Punda wall and along the Steenenpad (Stone Path), in a section that would be called Pietermaai after sea Capt. Pieter de Mey (or Maai), the first property owner to erect a house there, around 1710. And most particularly, spacious new one-story homes were rising on the previously uninhabited shoreline opposite the town, on the northwestern stretch of Santa Anna Bay, which was still referred to by its original Spanish name of Otrabanda or its Dutch equivalent, Overzijde, meaning the "Other Side." Governor van Beek bolstered Willemstad's defenses by erecting a new wall with two bastions called Forts Oranje and Bloedfort along the northern edge of Punda, as well as by restoring a portion of the town's eastern wall, which had collapsed in 1690 through neglect. He also installed a new iron chain across the harbor mouth. His successor, Jacob Beck, who arrived in 1704, further requested that the WIC station two warships in the port as protection against enemy privateers and finance the erection of a pair of bastions on the Punta Brava side of the entrance to protect the new Otrabanda enclave.

Such measures proved timely because the French launched a West Indian offensive during the closing stages of Queen Anne's War, or the War of the Spanish Succession. A small fleet under Commo. Jacques Cassard—having already ravaged Montserrat, Suriname, Berbice, and Sint Eustatius—paraded past Willemstad on 6 February 1713, looking for a spot to disembark their troops. But Curaçao's luck held: the French flagship *Neptune* struck a reef, taking seventeen siege-pieces and 1,000 mortar shells to the bottom, while another warship was carried too far west by winds and currents. Cassard and the Martinican militia colonel François de Collart were therefore only able to bring a reduced landing force ashore at St. Kruis Bay twelve days later, suffering some fifty casualties—including the French commodore, who was wounded in a foot and had to be superseded by Capt. Anne Henry de Bandeville de Saint Périer of *Téméraire*.

The invaders' strength consisted of 560 soldiers, 320 West Indian buccaneers, and 180 sailors, with which to subdue 800 Dutch troops and militiamen under Gov. Jeremias van Collen. Few of the latter were regulars, though, and they were hampered by shortages of guns and ammunition, so that van Collen merely tried to delay the French advance overland. They nonetheless had outflanked a Dutch company entrenched atop a hill by 22 February 1713, sending it reeling back across Santa Anna Bay into Willemstad, so that Bandeville could occupy Otrabanda and install three small mortars. But the attackers were otherwise powerless to invest in Fort Amsterdam, which was additionally protected by three large Dutch ships anchored in the intervening gap of water. The French therefore threatened to wreak havoc among the island's unguarded farms, so that van Collen accepted Bandeville's terms on 3 March, whereby the invaders evacuated Curaçao without pillaging in exchange for a ransom of 115,000 Spanish pesos. A yellow-fever epidemic then struck the capital that same year.

Trade Entrepot (1714–1791)

Peace was declared shortly thereafter in Europe, The Netherlands emerging with their naval power so diminished that large-scale slaving contracts were henceforth appropriated by British and French rivals. Willemstad's role as a major slave base came to an abrupt end, its compounds containing only eighty-eight African captives by 1720. A protracted drought had also ruined the island's corn harvest, and pirates were snapping up vessels headed for its port. Sorties by island privateers helped ease this latter danger, and Willemstad's merchants soon discovered that there was still abundant demand on the Spanish-American mainland for their contraband goods. Cacao, coffee, hides, indigo, tobacco, and other produce could also be brought back and re-exported profitably to Europe, so that smuggling with Venezuela soon became the port's principal business. This *kleine vaart* (short-range) trade not only allowed the town to survive, but also fueled urban development: proceeds benefited the local citizenry much more directly than working for the distant Amsterdam chamber, which was soon complaining about the expense of maintaining 200 administrators and a like number of soldiers at Willemstad while collecting only a few meager dues on the residents' newfound traffic.

Some 1,200 vessels were shortly calling at the port every year, and its clandestine trade soared with the outbreak of the War of Jenkins's Ear between England and Spain late in 1739, as neutral Dutch vessels could service both belligerents and Spanish-American needs peaked because of the Royal Navy blockade. Proposals to better fortify Willemstad during this struggle were rejected by its citizens, who did not wish to bear any additional expenses or inconvenience and who felt vindicated when their harbor was not threatened. It even served as a sanctuary for the English squadron of Commo. Charles Knowles, which entered in March 1743 to repair and reprovision after being mauled during a failed bombardment of La Guaira.

Merchants and sea captains, suddenly grown rich during this nine-year boom, did commission so many new private mansions—town-houses in the Pietermaai suburb, as well as grand *landhuizen* (country villas) along Curaçao's southern shoreline—that WIC officials complained about the stones being pilfered from their vital fortification projects by contractors. The island's twenty plantations also began to increase in number, while Willemstad's Jewish community in particular flourished because of their long-standing relationship with Latin-American customers. Jewish numbers rose to 1,500 individuals spread among 280 families, representing fully half the total white populace. A new synagogue was established in Otrabanda, leading to disputes with members of the original 1692 temple on Joode Kerckstraat in Punda.

Cessation of hostilities late in 1748 brought on depression and a wave of bankruptcies for Curaçao, plus a frightening slave revolt in June 1750 on the WIC's Hato Plantation on the northern coast—which also served as the summer resort for governors—before being crushed through thirty-four executions. Willemstad's business surged again when the French and Indian War started six years later, the Dutch again profiting from their neutrality. Interceptions at sea, however, required the expense of stationing a squadron in port, under Rear Adm. Joost Sels, as of 1759, while Spanish-America was not blockaded and therefore increased its demands until the very last year of this struggle in 1762. Another downturn subsequently ensued, followed by a still greater boom as of 1775, when Willemstad's trading companies—frequent clients of North American suppliers in the past—began discreetly selling arms to the colonial rebels in their Revolutionary War against British rule.

Willemstad profited handsomely during the first few years of this struggle, being shaken only by the sudden explosion

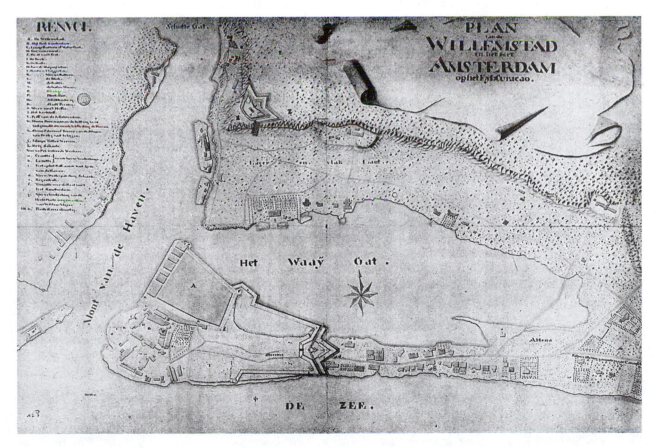

Map of Willemstad and its immediate surroundings, drafted in November 1751 to accompany Lt.-Gen. G. A. van Burmania's proposal for the town's expansion eastward, so as to improve its defensibility; this project was not authorized. (Algemeen Rijksarchief, The Hague)

and death of more than 200 men aboard the anchored Dutch warship *Alphen* on 15 September 1778. However, commerce was severely curtailed when Britain declared war against The Netherlands twenty-seven months afterward and imposed a blockade—although Fort Amsterdam's reputed impregnability spared the town any direct assault when Adm. Sir George Brydges Rodney descended from Barbados with a huge English fleet in February 1781, escorting a troop convoy with 3,000 redcoats under Gen. John Vaughan. The troops overran Sint Eustatius, Sint Maarten, Saba, Essequibo, Demerara, and Berbice, so that Willemstad remained in uneasy isolation for the remaining two years of this conflict, although unexpectedly visited when the French ally Commo. Louis-Antoine, Comte de Bougainville, limped into harbor in mid-April 1782 with his 80-gun flagship *Auguste* and four other warships to effect repairs after being battered by Rodney's fleet during the Battle of the Saintes.

Yet another depression gripped the port once general peace was restored early in 1783; this economic downturn proved so deep that numerous merchants emigrated in search of better prospects, and Willemstad's population declined noticeably. Those citizens who remained behind had by now come to openly resent the WIC's outdated practice of exacting taxes and fees without having contributed significantly to the island's prosperity for several decades. Discontent coalesced into a political faction called the "Patriots"—mostly young or lower-class elements who, inspired by liberal ideals emanating from

Europe, called for change—while conservative "Orangists" defended the status quo. Debate eventually grew so shrill that the states-general dispatched two inspectors, Willem A. J. Grovestins and W. C. Boeij, to report upon conditions throughout the Dutch West Indies.

They reached Willemstad at the end of August 1789 and departed that same December, recording an urban populace of 2,001 Dutch residents, 1,423 Jews, 2,615 free mulattoes, and 5,359 slaves spread among 924 houses in Punda, Pietermaai, Scharloo, and Otrabanda. (A dialect called Papiamento was already developing among the town's lower classes, being a blend of Hispano-Portuguese, African, and Dutch.) The resultant Grovestins-Boeij report also enumerated inherent deficiencies of WIC rule, which the states-general acknowledged by refusing to extend its charter the following year, so that a century and a half of company rule ended when a Committee of Deputies for West Indian Affairs was set up by the Dutch government as of 1791.

British Occupations (1792–1815)

Yet before any significant policy changes could be implemented at Willemstad, The Netherlands were rent by a great sociopolitical upheaval precipitated by the French Revolution of 1789, whose professed ideals of "liberty, equality, and fraternity" found a strong echo not only in the home country, but also among the disgruntled populace of the tiny island outpost. Dissension deepened when it was learned four years

Capt. Charles Brisbane's Royal Navy frigates surprise Willemstad at dawn, 1 January 1807. (Author's collection)

later that the United Provinces had declared war against France, Gov. Johannes de Veer and other senior officials striving to contain pro-French demonstrations on Curaçao until word finally arrived that a revolutionary army had penetrated Holland in mid-January 1795 and the troops were greeted as liberators, while the stadholder, Willem V, Prince of Orange, had fled into exile in England.

Emboldened by this dramatic deposal, the pro-French "Patriot" faction began clashing with Willemstad's Orangist garrison, until both groups were distracted by a slave revolt that same August on the Knip Plantation of western Curaçao. Once it was quelled, the political schism worsened as conflicting orders arrived from overseas: Willem writing to urge support of British efforts against revolutionary France, while the states-general did the opposite, furthermore abolishing the hereditary office of stadholder by proclaiming the Batavian Republic as of August 1796. De Veer consequently resigned and was briefly succeeded by the pro-English acting-governor, Jacob Beaujon, who was so hamstrung by the pro-French Raad that he too made way for militia captain Johann Rudolf Lauffer. Yet despite the latter's revolutionary proclivities and approval for the erection of a new stronghold dubbed Fort Republiek atop Sablica Hill to command the entire length of Santa Anna Bay, Lauffer observed such a strict neutrality as even to deport suspected French agents from Willemstad—believing that Curaçao's economic self-interest would be best served by some measure of independence in the war-torn West Indies.

Therefore, although Willemstad received the 54-gun French frigate *Vengeance* after it was mauled by Capt. Thomas Truxtun's 36-gun U.S. frigate *Constellation* in February 1800, Lauffer refused to admit two Guadeloupan brigs and three schooners that attempted to enter Santa Anna Bay on 23 July—allegedly to reinforce their Dutch allies against an English threat, yet actually to fully impose the Franco-Batavian alliance upon the reluctant islanders. Negotiations with these uninvited visitors dragged on for several weeks, until the French built up their strength to more than 1,200 men aboard thirteen vessels, then moved up the coast on 3 September to seize St. Michiel Bay, disembarking their troops to march overland and occupy Otrabanda four days later, from where they opened fire against Willemstad.

Outnumbered and beleaguered, Lauffer and the Raad contrived to contact the blockading frigate HMS *Nereide* of Capt. Frederick Watkins, preferring to submit to the English allies of the exiled stadholder than to the French. A treaty surrendering control over the colony was consequently signed on 13 September 1800, and the invaders were compelled to lift their siege by dawn of 23 September, leaving behind great destruction. Watkins thereupon ordered the arrest of all French inhabitants on Curaçao, however loyal, and some merchant warehouses were ransacked before Vice Adm. Lord Hugh Seymour could arrive from Jamaica with Royal Navy reinforcements in Octo-

ber. Upon departing six weeks later, the admiral left Lauffer in charge of civilian affairs under a British military governor, which occupation would continue until the Treaty of Amiens was signed a year and a half later, and Batavian officials arrived from Holland on 22 December 1802 aboard the 36-gun frigate *Kenau Hasselaar* to officially restore Dutch rule as of 13 January 1803.

Willemstad had been left on the brink of economic ruin by this protracted ordeal, and its plight worsened after word arrived in June 1803 that hostilities had resumed in Europe, for the British—having familiarized themselves with Fort Amsterdam's weaknesses during their tenure—no longer regarded it as impregnable. A squadron materialized shortly thereafter and disgorged 120 men in Piscadero Bay to overrun Otrabanda, although they could not then subdue Willemstad, so withdrew a few days later. A tight blockade was nonetheless imposed, trade grinding to a standstill while prices soared, with shortages and hunger appearing. Pierre-Jean Changuion arrived as the new Batavian-appointed governor in August 1804, and he fended off another pair of British disembarkations the following spring, so that the islanders' situation seemed to be improving. Yet the French emperor Napoleon I ended the Batavian Republic in November 1806 by crowning his brother Louis Bonaparte as king of Holland, while seven British warships under Sir William Bolton again threatened Curaçao the next month.

After the latter departed over the horizon, Governor Changuion and most Dutch officers confidently dispersed to enjoy the Christmas holidays, unaware that Capt. Charles Brisbane's 38-gun frigate HMS *Arethusa* was rendezvousing off Aruba with the 44-gun *Anson*, 38-gun *Latona*, and the *Fisgard*, intending to burst into Santa Anna Bay by surprise at dawn of New Year's Day. Towing a landing force in boats, these warships stood directly into Willemstad's channel at sunrise of 1 January 1807, catching the sentinels completely by surprise. Ignoring the few desultory rounds fired from the batteries, and the anchored *Kenau Hasselaar* of Captain Evertsz and the 22-gun corvette *Suriname* of Captain van Nes, the English moored opposite their preselected targets and sent a surrender demand ashore. As Changuion was with his family at his Blenheim plantation, no reply could be given. Brisbane therefore ordered his vessels to open fire by 6:15 A.M., silencing all resistance with several point-blank broadsides, so that redcoats could swarm into the town and citadel unopposed. By the time the governor appeared, it only remained to negotiate the final terms for surrendering Fort Republiek. Brisbane's brilliant stroke had won him the island, a knighthood, and the governorship of St. Vincent, at a cost of 3 British killed and 14 wounded, compared with some 200 Dutch casualties.

The occupiers immediately started bolstering the defenses to preclude any possible counterattack (Fort Republiek being renamed "Fort George"), then settled in for a protracted stay. Their second tenure in Willemstad was to have a much more

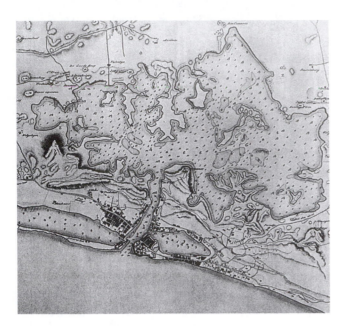

Highly detailed map of the Schottegat, Santa Anna Bay, the Waaigat, and Willemstad, published in Amsterdam in 1836. (University of Leiden Library)

profound and beneficial effect, as commerce resurged with the elimination of the Royal Navy blockades, and Willemstad became accessible to British and international markets as a free port. Changuion had even been asked to stay on as civilian governor, yet he preferred to return to Holland to stand trial for his defeat. The English therefore installed a benign administration under military governor Sir James Cockburn, who treated the populace so well that many merchants who had previously emigrated to other islands in discouragement now returned. Dry-docks also sprang up around Santa Anna Bay to repair the numerous ships sheltering during hurricane seasons, and a few fast schooners were built. The first weekly newspaper, the *Curaçaosche Courant,* even appeared by 1811.

When Napoleon invaded Spain in the summer of 1808 to install his brother Joseph Bonaparte as king, Cockburn sent a trade delegation to Caracas to open relations with the Spaniards, so that Curaçao's traffic into Venezuela might be resumed. This initiative benefited Willemstad so handsomely that its merchants thanked the governor with a written memorandum that same September pledging allegiance to King George and rewarded Cockburn personally with £6,000 "as a trivial indemnity." After Venezuela revolted against Spanish rule two years later, his successor, John Hodgson, struggled to maintain this trade intact by placating both royalist and patriot factions on the South American mainland. He also provided sanctuary at the end of August 1812 to Simón Bolívar and fifty other defeated patriot leaders. Bolívar's famous Cartagena Manifesto allegedly was prepared in his Otrabanda house before he departed that same November to initiate the cam-

paign that would result in the foundation of the Second Venezuelan Republic.

In Europe, meanwhile, Napoleon was beaten in October 1813 at the Battle of Leipzig, allowing the Low Countries to rise against their French overlords and welcome back Prince Willem VI of Orange by that same December. Once the emperor was captured and banished to the Mediterranean isle of Elba in May 1814, London established relations with the new Dutch government that same August, promising to restore its West Indian islands.

News of this prospective transfer did not generate great enthusiasm when it was announced in Willemstad in October 1814, seeming to portend a reimposition of old and unsuccessful practices. Nor was it welcome in Venezuela, whose hard-pressed republican rulers had come to depend upon covert British support through Curaçao. Napoleon's escape from Elba in February 1815 postponed the matter, as Europe was plunged back into crisis until his final defeat at Waterloo and subsequent deportation to the remote South Atlantic island of St. Helena. That same September, the Prince of Orange was formally crowned as Willem I, King of The Netherlands, and an expedition duly cleared to reclaim Curaçao.

Stagnation (1816–1913)

Vice Adm. Albert Kikkert, who had once served as Willemstad's harbor commander and had married into a prominent island family, arrived with 300 soldiers aboard the warship *Prins van Orange* on 27 January 1816, consummating the switch back to Dutch authority by 4 March. He also bore the new title of "governor-general of the Curaçao Islands," being represented on Aruba and Bonaire by subordinate governors, and he reconstituted the Raad at Willemstad by appointing two government employees and four merchants to regulate all civilian matters, such as the tiny police force, schools, street maintenance, markets, ferries, churches, and even the manumission of slaves. A Council of Civil and Criminal Justice was moreover created to sit as a court, while the old island militia was reorganized into an 820-man regiment, spread among five companies segregated by race. Even Fort George was renamed as Fort Nassau.

In economic matters, Kikkert and The Hague were anxious to maintain Curaçao's lucrative trade into Venezuela, as the Caribbean otherwise offered few commercial prospects. The new island government could not even meet its own expenses, and it had inherited heavy debts, representing a drain upon Dutch resources. Because the Venezuelan patriots had been expelled that previous year by a huge royal counterexpedition sent out from Spain under Gen. Pablo Morillo y Morillo, the Curaçaoan administration tried to curry favor with the restored Spanish rulers by extraditing several republicans who had fled to their island. Insurgent privateers under the Curaçao-born Commo. Philippus Ludovicus Brion (in Spanish, Felipe Luis Brion) thereupon retaliated by intercepting a

Spanish ship as it departed Willemstad that same June, after which Brion and Bolívar appeared outside the harbor in an attempt to persuade the Dutch to recognize their cause.

The Hague refused to be swayed, though, so that while shipping between Curaçao and Spanish-controlled ports continued, many craft were intercepted by the insurgents, necessitating the dispatch of naval forces from Holland in 1817. The Spanish monarchist cause then went into decline in Venezuela and was defeated by May 1821, Morillo and more than 2,000 Loyalists fleeing into Willemstad aboard a flotilla of seventy boats escorted by the frigate *Ligera* of Captain Angel Laborde y Navarro and subsequently attempting to blockade Bolívar's republic by issuing privateering commissions to mercenaries. Willemstad's merchants—already disappointed by the loss of their Spanish-controlled trade, lack of good relations with the new patriot regime, and the inroads being made by their British rivals—protested against such a counterproductive policy, even stoning the exiled Morillo's house during a riot.

Dutch authorities therefore decided to recognize the republican government the next year, while the British sent a squadron to sweep the Venezuelan coast of privateers, so that all traffic might proceed safely. Yet the fledgling republic soon proved to be a commercial disappointment, as it disintegrated into such economic and political chaos that the hopes of Willemstad's merchants faded, so that many chose to emigrate. Although regular mail service with Amsterdam was inaugurated in 1825, the focus of attention shifted so completely away from Curaçao's capital that when The Netherlands Antilles were realigned into a single jurisdiction in 1828, the office of governor-general was transferred to Paramaribo in Suriname, which also received a new Hoge Raad (High Council), Willemstad being demoted to a mere vice governorship.

Reinier Frederik van Raders conducted several experiments to develop alternative exports from Curaçao's small farms or salt pans during his tenure from 1836 to 1846, but to little avail. Another administrative overhaul separated the impoverished island from Paramaribo's control in 1845, so that

Willemstad once again became the capital over Aruba and Bonaire. Yet The Hague constantly trimmed subsidies, and Willemstad's dependence upon trade into Venezuela entered an uneasy phase when the former president José Antonio Páez raised a revolt in June 1849 against his successor, José Tadeo Monagas. The latter—believing that this rival movement was headquartered on Curaçao, where Páez had been popular—retaliated by seizing various Dutch merchantmen anchored in Venezuelan ports. This diplomatic confrontation was not resolved until Holland sent a half-dozen warships to blockade La Guaira and Puerto Cabello, which (coupled with separate British threats against Venezuela's proposed moratorium on its foreign debt) obliged Monagas to back down and pay an indemnization.

Full trade access was not restored, though, so that the island went into another depression, its population declining by January 1854 to only 3,400 whites, 8,000 free *hende di coló* (people of color), plus 7,200 slaves. The next year tensions recurred when some Curaçaoan Jewish businessmen were robbed during rioting at Coro, so that Dutch men-of-war again had to sail out of Willemstad to exact compensation. Living conditions in the tiny island capital were moderately improved when its seventeenth-century walls were finally demolished in 1861, allowing the urban area to expand eastward. Slavery was also abolished by the states-general as of 1 July 1863, marking an end to such labor-intensive enterprises as plantations—which had already declined in number from 362 in 1828 to about 100—and the stark *salinjas* (salt pans).

Trade with Venezuela improved after Gen. Juan C. Falcón won its presidency the next year, contracting the commercial house of Abraham J. Jesurun of Willemstad to provide large amounts of arms and other commodities. But the return to power of Monagas led to yet another downturn, persisting even after his death in December 1868. In an ill-judged effort to appease Caracas's repeated complaints about Venezuelan exiles plotting sedition from Willemstad, The Hague ordered its new governor, Abraham M. de Rouville, to expel four prominent

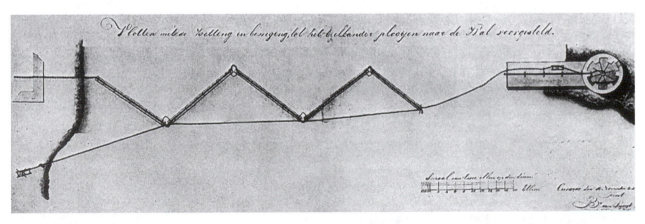

Diagram of the capstan used to extend and retract the boom across the entrance into Santa Anna Bay, November 1835. (Ministerie van Rijksdelen Overzee, The Netherlands)

exiles in January 1870—a decision that backfired when one deportee, Antonio Guzmán Blanco, disembarked in his homeland and rallied so much support that he fought his way into the presidency by that same April, remaining in power over the next eighteen years.

Guzmán Blanco's resentment against his expulsion from Curaçao led to the detention of numerous Dutch vessels, so that The Hague had to send out a man-of-war and even fired Governor de Rouville as a scapegoat. His friend, the popular island attorney general Willem K. C. Sassen (nicknamed Papachi [Daddy] Sassen by islanders), was also dismissed on 24 November 1871, and when a mob of well-wishers congregated before his Otrabanda house that evening, they were dispersed by police fire on orders from Gov. H. François G. Wagner, an incident that resulted in one death and nineteen wounded. Relations with Guzmán Blanco were tentatively patched up in August 1872, so that some coastal traffic could resume. Phosphate was also discovered two years later by the English engineer John Godden on the southern slopes of Tafelberg (Table Mountain) in southeastern Curaçao, spawning a minor ore export boom through Fuik Bay. The island economy otherwise depended upon fishing and very modest quantities of hides, tropical woods (such as the tannin-producing *dividivi* pods), tobacco, cacao, shoes, straw hats woven from palmettos, as well as oranges and orange liqueur shipped to North America and Europe. Only two or three ships arrived at Willemstad annually from The Netherlands, although the

Koninklijke West Indische Maildienst—Royal West Indian Mail Service (KWIM)—finally inaugurated regular steamship service as of 1882.

Guzmán Blanco was eventually deposed in October 1888, so that relations with Venezuela improved over the next six years and trade regained a certain stability. Foreign warships occasionally called at Willemstad, its most unexpected visitors materializing on the morning of 14 May 1898, when the battle-squadron of Rear Adm. Pascual Cervera y Topete appeared from across the Atlantic, steering toward Cuba as reinforcements during the Spanish-American War. Cervera's 7,000-ton flagship *Infanta María Teresa* and cruiser *Vizcaya* entered the harbor to recoal and reprovision, while the cruisers *Almirante Oquendo* and *Cristóbal Colón* and two destroyers hovered anxiously outside. All departed the next evening, pretending to steer north-northeast toward Puerto Rico but actually making for Santiago de Cuba, where they were eventually destroyed. Willemstad was also visited by German and British warships during the Venezuelan debt crisis of 1902–1903.

Refinery Port (1914–1939)

Curaçao began the twentieth century as a half-forgotten colonial outpost steeped in poverty, with meager trade, and its agricultural output so crippled by persistent droughts that hunger was a problem. Its plight began to be ameliorated once regional movement increased when the Panama Canal dig commenced, the coral reefs outside Willemstad blasted and

Imperial German heavy cruiser *Vineta* entering Santa Anna Bay to anchor in the distant Schottegat during a courtesy visit, ca. 1902–1910; note the Emmabrug or Queen Emma pontoon-bridge swung open at left. The Otrabanda suburb forms the backdrop to this photograph, while Willemstad itself lies just out of camera-range at right. (Mariners' Museum, Newport News)

mud banks dredged so that oceangoing ships of up to 35,000 tons might enter and coal from bunkers, newly installed to cater to the future trans-Isthmian traffic.

More important, the Dutch-British "Shell" consortium, along with the General Asphalt Company of the United States, obtained concessions from Caracas to explore for oilfields in the nearby Laguna de Maracaibo in 1913. After confirming the potential wealth of these deposits by drilling the first well the next year, a Shell representative visited Curaçao in hopes of finding a broad yet safe expanse of land upon which to establish a refinery and tank farm. Impressed by the terrain inside the sheltered yet accessible Schottegat anchorage, as well as Curaçao's sociopolitical stability, the company secured permission from local authorities and The Hague to purchase three plantations on the north shore of the Schottegat by 1915 where they started to build a plant. (Because it was situated on a peninsula that had once been an island, the plant became known as the Isla Peninsula Plant; Shell eventually purchased almost all the land around the Schottegat.)

Construction progressed slowly, as World War I had erupted in Europe, and notwithstanding Holland's neutrality, global shortages of industrial materials were experienced. The number of ships visiting Willemstad also plunged, from 1,500 in 1913 to 500 five years later, while two Dutch men-of-war had to be stationed in its harbor as a precaution. Its refinery could not initiate production until 23 May 1918, and then on such a limited basis that only 14,000 tons of petroleum were processed that first year, because two 800-ton tankers were all the transportation available to convey crude oil from the Laguna into Willemstad. The problem was resolved when a separate company, the Curaçaose Scheepvaart Maatschappij—Curaçao Navigation Company (CSM)—began custom-building much larger tankers of sufficiently shallow draft to traverse the Laguna's 13-foot bar.

By 1922 refinement had reached full capacity of more than 200,000 barrels a day, and Willemstad was to be transformed almost beyond recognition by revenues derived from this oil boom. Its infrastructure was modernized and general standards of living raised—albeit at the cost of an unsightly sprawl of industrial plants, a sudden influx of new residents, the loss of genteel colonial-era ways, and a permanent bluish smog. Yet for the first time since the Dutch had resumed control over the island more than a century earlier, Curaçao's budget had a positive balance, requiring no subsidies from The Netherlands, and it was upgraded from the status of a colony to that of a dominion or territory.

However, few benefits initially accrued to the capital's populace, many of whom were poor and black, while Dutch managers or engineers hired for specialty work at the refinery soon made themselves unpopular, being nicknamed *macambas* in the Papiamento dialect because of their condescending attitude toward the local inhabitants, their notably higher pay scale, and a propensity to depart as soon as their contracts expired. Such discriminatory practices fostered resentment, and the first sparks of labor unrest occurred when Willemstad's dockers—angered by a pay cut imposed after the KWIM mail service was absorbed by the Koninklijke Nederlandsche Stoomboot Maatschappij (Royal Netherlandic Steamship Company)—went on strike on 1 April 1922. This strike eventually boiled over into a bloody riot at 10:45 A.M. on 17 July during which the KWIM offices were sacked, four people killed, and nineteen injured before troops and police could restore order.

Despite the strains placed upon Willemstad's social services and housing by such sudden industrialization, the Schottegat refinery and its storage facilities continued to expand in 1927, the total workforce rising to 6,000 employees. A new bunkering port was also added at Caracas Bay, a gasoline port was added at Bullen Bay, and an even larger refinery complex was built in Saint Nicolaas Bay on neighboring Aruba. Curaçao's phosphate mining industry furthermore revived during this decade, coming to employ a couple thousand workers.

The great concentration of foreign laborers around Willemstad spawned occasional incidents, none more dramatic than the one on the evening of Saturday, 8 June 1929, when about forty poorly armed Venezuelans led by Rafael Simón Urbina drove two buses into the Waterfort military camp and killed three Dutch soldiers by surprise, before capturing another thirty. Some 200 more Venezuelans thereupon appeared in cars and emptied the arsenal, while hundreds more closed off the pontoon bridge across Santa Anna Bay and occupied the streets around Fort Amsterdam. At dawn the next day, Urbina compelled Gov. Lenoard Frytier to allow his followers to set sail with thirteen hostages aboard the commandeered steamer *Maracaibo,* disembarking near Coro to use this stolen weaponry in an unsuccessful bid to topple the Venezuelan dictator Juan Vicente Gómez. When the shaken Dutch governor returned into Willemstad with the rescued hostages on the evening of 9 June, he declared a month-long state of martial law in fear of the remaining 2,300 Venezuelan workers on the island; a warship also arrived from Holland shortly thereafter to become permanently stationed against any future coups.

After a sharp economic downturn caused by the New York stock market crash of October 1929, which brought on a worldwide "Great Depression" and reduced demand for gasoline and oil so much as to cause the Schottegat refinery to lay off half its employees, the island economy rebounded during the second half of the 1930s. One symbol of the return to prosperity was the arrival in 1934 of a three-engined Fokker F-18 passenger plane, inaugurating regular air service by the Dutch Koninklijke Luchvaart Maatschappij—Royal Airline Company (KLM). A few hotels also began to appear in Willemstad, while tentative social reforms such as accident and health insurance for workers were passed. Yet another auspicious sign was the resurgence of Curaçao's population, which rose from 55,463 inhabitants in 1935 to 73,943 eight years later, of whom

View northward across Willemstad's rooftops, ca. 1942, showing the oil-tanks and industrial sprawl just beyond Santa Anna Bay within the hazy Schottegat. (Hiss, *Netherlands America*)

roughly half were concentrated around the capital and its immediate environs.

World War II and the Modern Era (1940–Present)

When France and Britain declared war against Germany in September 1939 to deflect Nazi aggression against Poland, a brief "phony war" ensued, in which neither side launched a major offensive; however, that impasse was abruptly ruptured when a German army invaded Holland on 10 May 1940, driving through the neutral nation so as to outflank the French border defenses. Upon receipt of radio reports of this treacherous attack, martial law was proclaimed at Willemstad. Some 300 Germans were interned—although the German consul and several ships had cleared port as early as March—and a few merchantmen were seized after efforts to scuttle several of them by their crews had been frustrated. Because of the great logistical importance attached to Curaçao's refinery complex, British troops of the King's Shropshire Light Infantry furthermore arrived from Jamaica, persuading local authorities to continue resisting Germany by processing oil in alliance with England and the government-in-exile of Queen Wilhelmina.

Willemstad and its refineries were therefore taken over for the Allied cause, production remaining so high that some 10,000 ships entered Santa Anna Bay the next year, 4,000 of them tankers. After the entry of the United States into the conflict following the December 1941 bombing of Pearl Harbor, three A-20A Havoc medium bombers of the U.S. 59th Bomber

Squadron flew in to become stationed as of mid-January 1942 on the island's small grass aerodrome, called Hato Field. U.S. infantry and coastal artillery units arrived as well on 11 February, officially replacing the British contingent as of the next day.

These first U.S. units had not yet fully settled in when the German submarine *U-67* of Lt. Gunther Muller-Stockheim inaugurated a new offensive code-named Operation "Neuland" in West Indian waters by torpedoing three tankers anchored outside Willemstad at 4:35 A.M. on 16 February 1942, although only the 3,100-ton *Rafaela* actually burned and sank, the other two being hit by duds. The shock of this attack and a simultaneous strike against Saint Nicolaas Bay in Aruba nonetheless paralyzed all oil shipments for the next several weeks, as well as halting the importation of foodstuffs and materiel, since civilian merchantmen went on strike until some life-saving methods and defensive measures could be improvised against U-boat attacks.

U.S. Rear Adm. Jesse B. Oldendorf arrived on 1 March 1942 to set about building up regional strength and to protect the flow of oil. In the process, the island's economy was to be greatly stimulated by such massive construction projects as the conversion of Hato Field into an aerodrome with numerous concrete runways and a proliferation of coastal batteries. When ship traffic resumed, a few German commanders tested these defenses. For example, *U-130* of Ernst Kals attempted to shell the camouflaged refinery at Bullen Point on 19 April, only to be chased off by U.S. artillery and planes; on the evening of 18 August, *U-217* of Kurt Reichenburg-Klinke followed the American tanker *Esso Concord* through the outer ring of reefs and fired three torpedoes after it had tied up at the jetty, missing and instead blasting the stone mole; while on the evening of 12 November, *U-163* of Lt. Cmdr. Kurt-Eduard Engelmann torpedoed the 2,000-ton destroyer USS *Erie* as it hovered 4 miles outside Willemstad escorting a large approaching convoy, forcing the blazing American warship to beach just beyond Piscadero Point.

Yet German submarines were soon driven from Caribbean waters and defeated at sea by relentless air patrols, so that Willemstad was not threatened again for the remaining two and a half years of the conflict, permitting its refineries to produce the bulk of high-octane fuels used by Allied forces. Island society was also irrevocably changed during this interlude, partly because of the severed ties with occupied Holland, as well as the palpable influence exerted by the sizable American presence. When The Hague sought to reassert its authority following the liberation of Europe in May 1945, the relationship between home country and overseas colony had changed, demands for autonomy now coming to the fore. Political parties emerged, universal suffrage was introduced, and the former system of Dutch-appointed governors made way as of 1950 to locally elected Regeringsraden (Government Councils) for Suriname and The Netherlands Antilles, headquartered respectively at Paramaribo and Willemstad. These bodies would rule over local matters, supported by Dutch fiscal, diplomatic, and military resources, while furthermore being represented in the states-general at The Hague.

Unfortunately, this political compromise was crippled by a steep decline in Curaçao's oil production, as Venezuela successfully pressured international firms to shift their refinement capacity over to the undeveloped Maracaibo mainland. Consequently, the number of workers employed in the Schottegat complex plunged from 13,000 people in 1952—processing almost 40,000 tons of petroleum daily—to a mere 3,880 by 1968, which enormous loss of income and tax revenues was coincidentally exacerbated by the island's population explosion, the totals rising from 81,300 residents in 1945 to 118,858 ten years later, of whom 49,250 lived in or around Willemstad.

Both Curaçaoan and Dutch officials struggled to offset such mass layoffs by once more declaring the city a free port, as well as by encouraging the development of tourism and banking industries. Yet lush Aruba proved to be a much more attractive destination for cruise ships and international air travelers, while the U.S. Congress passed legislation in 1964 to curtail all offshore investments. Unemployment on the island rose to 20 to 25 percent and popular discontent boiled over, the stores of Willemstad's business district being gutted when 4,000 strikers—incensed at the wage disparities still existing between Royal Shell employees and local subcontractors—ran rampant on 30 May 1969, looting and torching many buildings before being put down by Dutch marines and the police.

Despite considerable financial support from The Hague, Shell finally closed its outdated petroleum installations in 1985. Eight years later the island's population was measured at 160,000, of whom perhaps 75 percent lived in and around Willemstad, although only 2,300 to 2,400 actually within its tiny colonial-era core. Nevertheless, its distinctive architecture and colorful history led the city to become designated as a World Heritage Site by the United Nations Educational, Scientific, and Cultural Organization in 1997, while the wealthy entrepreneur Jacob Gelt Dekker commenced the Kura Hulanda Anthropological Museum in its Otrabanda district the next year as a precursor to several new luxury hotels intended to house tourists drawn by Willemstad's singular past.

For further reading on Willemstad or The Netherlands Antilles, please consult the Select Bibliography at the end of this volume.

Dominican Republic

Santo Domingo

First European-built capital in the New World, which has struggled to survive against successive encroachments.

Initial Establishment (1496–1502)

On his second voyage into the Caribbean, Christopher Columbus returned late in 1493 with 1,500 settlers and installed an outpost the next January called Isabela on the northern coast of what he had dubbed *La Española* (The Spanish Island), erroneously assuming that it would serve as his trading base with nearby Asia. Conditions at this sun-baked and infertile camp proved harsh, though, and as the months passed without either Japan or China being encountered, most of its disillusioned Spanish residents turned against the Columbus brothers and dispersed around the island.

Three summers later, during one of the admiral's periodic absences in Spain, his brother Bartholomew abandoned Isabela and led a group of loyal retainers around to the southern shore to found a new town near some recently discovered mines at the mouth of the Haina River. A settlement called Santo Domingo was duly constituted there on 4 August 1496, its name apparently chosen because that particular date fell on a Sunday—in Spanish, *Domingo*—as well as coinciding with Saint Dominic's Day on the Church calendar—and furthermore honoring Columbus's deceased father, Domenico.

Relocation and Early Evolution (1502–1519)

The initial wooden shantytown was flattened by a hurricane in July 1502, prompting the newly arrived royal governor, Nicolás de Ovando, to order all of Santo Domingo's inhabitants to shift once again, this time 10 miles farther east to the western banks of some coral cliffs rising above a small natural harbor at the Ozama River mouth. New plots were allocated there in a gridiron pattern, a defensive perimeter was commenced, and a hospital called San Nicolás de Bari and other public buildings began to appear, the town soon evolving into the seat of Crown authority for all of the Spanish West Indies; hopes of tapping into Far Eastern trade had by now become supplanted by a desire to subjugate and exploit the American archipelago itself.

In 1503, de Ovando ordered work started by Juan de Rabé on a huge stone tower along Santo Domingo's waterfront, to be called the Torre del Homenaje, which was completed two years later. The city diocese was also recognized by the papal bull *Illius fulciti praesidio* of 1504, construction of a solid new church commencing two years later that would be dedicated to the governor's patronymic, San Nicolás. His successor, Diego Columbus (son and heir to the great admiral), expanded upon this policy of erecting imposing structures so as to exemplify Spanish permanence in the New World by having a splendid new *alcázar* (private palace) built on a low eminence in 1510. It in turn encouraged the creation of other large, stone, private dwellings capable of resisting both the weather and military assaults. The next year, a three-judge *Real Audiencia* (Royal Tribunal) was installed to hear cases from throughout the Caribbean outposts—rather than referring them across the Atlantic to Spain, as had previously been practiced. In that same year of 1511, the city was also elevated into a bishopric,

Panoramic view of Santo Domingo and its Ozama River Bridge, ca. 1922–1924. (Library of Congress)

so that a massive Gothic-style cathedral was commenced as of 1520 and completed twenty years later.

More important, though, Santo Domingo had come to serve as a clearinghouse for most vessels traveling in and out of the Caribbean, as well as a springboard for military expeditions pushing across to the American mainland. Virtually every famous future conquistador—Juan Ponce de León, Vasco Núñez de Balboa, Hernán Cortés, Pedro de Alvarado, and Francisco Pizarro, to name but a few—called at this strategic port city before proceeding on their respective quests, Santo Domingo the only Spanish colony sufficiently developed to furnish provisions, men, ships, and Crown authorization to sustain such enterprises. Its plantations and cattle ranches had rendered the capital agriculturally self-sufficient, while harvests processed in its coastal sugar mills—plus a little gold extracted from inland mines—provided the basis for a modest yet steady transatlantic trade.

Downturn (1520–1585)

Ironically, the immense gains achieved from these mainland campaigns were to detract from Santo Domingo's luster and relegate the city to second-class status within a few decades. When glowing reports began circulating of the fabulous wealth of the Aztec empire in Mexico, the entire Caribbean archipelago was emptied of adventurers in the early 1520s, all hoping to win vast estates and rich mines by partaking in its subjugation. The capital of Santo Domingo was reduced by this exodus to a population of roughly 3,000 people spread among 500 households, until municipal authorities grew so desperate that they banned any further emigration on pain of death. Nevertheless, a second wave of departures occurred when the equally wealthy Incan empire of Peru was encountered during the mid-1530s.

Not that life immediately turned bad for the few hundred householders left behind, as Santo Domingo's elite still enjoyed imported luxuries, splendid homes, and even indulged in artistic pursuits. Gonzalo Fernández de Oviedo, for example, was commissioned in August 1532 to write a general history of the Spanish West Indies, while the wealthy Hernando Gorjón gave an endowment five years later toward the establishment of a university (which was not actually founded until 1551 and remained unrecognized by the Crown until seven years after that date). Yet, within the broad scope of the Spanish-American empire, Santo Domingo had become a backwater, both mainland kingdoms being quickly elevated to independent viceroyalties—Mexico in 1527, Peru by 1540—so as to be administered directly from Spain.

Worse still, Santo Domingo's strategic role in servicing transient ships faded as transatlantic galleons became ever larger and convoys more numerous, so that they could no longer enter its small harbor safely after the 1550s. Instead, they preferred merely to pause in Ocoa Bay to refresh provisions before proceeding toward their mainland destinations

Diagram of an intersection near the city's San Francisco Convent in 1531; the angled street had recently been opened, provoking a complaint by Juan de Mosquera against Alfonso Iñiquez for this infringement upon his property. (Archive of Indies, Seville)

of Veracruz or Nombre de Dios. Only small vessels called, usually to pick up a few thousand hides and small amounts of sugar. City residents suffered a further calamity when a hurricane struck their island on 29 August 1552, sinking or dismasting most of Santo Domingo's vessels and causing extensive damage ashore; a heavy earthquake followed on 20 November 1562, although its worst effects were confined to the central highlands.

Nevertheless, discouraged Dominicans continued to move away steadily and were not replaced by new migrants, so that there were only 300 Spanish households left in the capital by 1568. And as the sixteenth century advanced, it became increasingly difficult for even 200-ton vessels to traverse Santo Domingo's bar, which was silting up; many islanders had therefore turned to bartering with foreign smugglers in remote inlets, especially along its northwestern coast, while the capital stagnated from commercial isolation and royal neglect.

Strategic Outpost (1586–1654)

When frictions between Catholic Spain and Protestant England flared into open warfare in the mid-1580s, Santo Domingo found itself so diminished in strength as to present a tempting target. On the morning of 10 January 1586—according to our "New Style," or modern Gregorian calendar, although New Year's Day by the "Old Style" Julian calendar was still employed in England—Sir Francis Drake materialized offshore with twenty-three vessels bearing 2,300 men. Having intercepted a Spanish bark with a Greek pilot en route, the great rover also knew that the best disembarkation point lay at the Haina River mouth, so that he proceeded there by evening to land 800 troops under the command of Christopher Carleill.

The next day, the English fleet feinted against Santo Domingo from out at sea, so that its defenders scuttled two ships in a vain attempt to block up its entrance. They were consequently utterly taken aback when Carleill's small army approached overland by noon, so abandoned their city—whose defensive circuit was not yet completed, negating any hope of an effective Spanish resistance. The invaders occupied Santo Domingo over the next month, then burned many residences in an effort to extort ransoms from inhabitants who were hiding in the interior. After receiving 25,000 ducats, Drake departed on 11 February 1586 to attack Cartagena.

Although some efforts were made to strengthen the defenses after the English departed, the island was to be repeatedly menaced by blockaders during the remaining eighteen years of the Elizabethan War, while a hurricane inflicted additional damage upon the half-empty capital in 1591, bringing down the Santa Bárbara Church and other edifices. By the beginning of the seventeenth century only 200 households had been reconstituted at Santo Domingo. This number was to be rather unexpectedly augmented, however, after peace was restored in August 1604, as Gov. Antonio Osorio (his title traditionally given as *Presidente de la Audiencia* or "Tribunal President") was ordered by King Philip III to lead a few hundred soldiers to torch the towns along the island's northwestern coast the next summer, forcibly transferring their residents to the southern shoreline so as to come under direct *Audiencia* supervision, because of their inveterate traffic with foreign smugglers.

Santo Domingo's city council had protested against this Draconian measure on 26 August 1604, Mayor Francisco Serrano Pimentel and Secretary Baltasar de Sepúlveda presenting a petition to Osorio arguing that the island would benefit more from increased ship traffic from Spain and the importation of African slaves. Yet their concerns were ignored, and the abrupt influx of refugees added to the capital's woes by straining its limited resources, resulting in serious overcrowding and famine. According to a census taken in October 1606—the year after Osorio's sweep—approximately half of the 5,000 Spaniards on the island were at that time crammed into Santo Domingo and

Hand-tinted engraving of Sir Francis Drake's famous assault against Santo Domingo in January 1586; published two years later in Leyden by Batista Boazio. (British Museum and National Maritime Museum, Greenwich)

its immediate environs, spread among 648 households and twelve sugar mills, ninety-five cattle ranches, and 120 farms (out of a total of roughly 16,000 people on the whole island, of whom 11,000 were slaves). Because of the difficulties that continued to tax the capital's resources, its populace declined again by half over the next twenty years, as many unhappy inhabitants opted to emigrate to start afresh elsewhere.

Worse still, the abandoned properties and livestock left along the island's northwestern coast were taken over by foreign interlopers, facilitating permanent annexation. In November 1630 a small expedition sortied from Santo Domingo to eliminate an English outpost on Tortuga Island. Yet more trespassers kept appearing, so that this operation had to be repeated four years later. Santo Domingo's populace all the while continued to dwindle, its export traffic having long since withered away; only eleven stores were authorized to import merchandise into the city from overseas. Residents had to rely upon local craftsmen for their needs, many of whom were free mulattoes or blacks, while the economy grew ever more dependent upon the annual *situados* (subsidies) sent by the Mexican exchequer, mostly in the form of payrolls for Crown and Church officials, as well as the 300-man garrison and occasional military projects.

Second English Assault and Aftermath (1655–1683)

The impoverished and somnolent island became the target of yet another huge offensive when the so-called Western Design, an expedition organized by England's lord protector, Oliver Cromwell, arrived in the West Indies with the intent of securing a major regional base. At 1:00 P.M. on 23 April 1655, 16 English warships under Adm. William Penn, plus two dozen transports bearing 2,500 soldiers and 5,000 Antillean volunteers under Gen. Robert Venables, materialized offshore, taking the capital's defenders completely by surprise. While Penn bore down upon the city with his men-of-war as a diversion, Vice Adm. William Goodson led the transports westward, seeking a suitable disembarkation point. Because of English fears of shoals, they were landed at Nizao, a distance of 30 miles, which allowed time for the Spaniards—300 regulars and 400 militiamen within the capital, plus 1,300 volunteer horsemen from the surrounding ranches—to recover from their initial shock and brace for an assault under the recently arrived Gov. Bernardino de Meneses Bracamonte Zapata, Conde de Peñalba.

The English troops, unused to campaigning in tropical weather, were not able to forge back through the trackless jungle until 27 April 1655, so sick and enfeebled as to require refreshment from their waiting fleet before resuming their final drive against Santo Domingo's outer defenses on 4 May. The next afternoon they were bloodily checked 2 miles short of the city walls by 250 Spanish musketeers and 300 Dominican lancers gathered around Fort San Gerónimo (alternate

Detailed map signed by Gov. Antonio Osorio in January 1608, depicting some proposed changes and additions to the city's outer defenses; north is toward bottom. (Archive of Indies, Seville)

spelling: Jerónimo), bringing an effective halt to the invasion. As sickness was now rampant within the English ranks, the attackers began re-embarking by 8 May, departing four days later and leaving behind more than 600 graves, 200 prisoners, and two siege-guns.

Santo Domingo had suffered only thirty men killed and a like number wounded, and the governor furthermore completed a fortified gatehouse in its walls to repel any future assaults (remembered as the Puerta del Conde—Count's Gate—later renamed the 27 de Febrero Bastion). Yet although the English had failed to overrun the island, they nevertheless seized nearby Jamaica, and other foreign strongholds subsequently began multiplying throughout the West Indies. Madrid sought to contest such encroachments by using Santo Domingo as an advance military base, but Spanish power was by now too depleted to expel the rival colonies.

The city itself was furthermore subjected to a smallpox epidemic, cacao blight, and hurricane in 1666; another storm two years later; a second epidemic in 1669; a third hurricane in September 1672; plus an earthquake in May 1673 that killed two dozen residents, this toll not any higher because most still spent their days eking out a meager livelihood by tending to their crops in the countryside. The Dominicans were also powerless to prevent small bands of French settlers from claiming the entire northwestern portion of the island, an occupation that was uneasily confirmed when the Treaty of Ratisbonne was signed in Europe in August 1684.

Resurgence (1684–1794)

Ironically, though, this French intrusion upon the island helped revive the Spanish capital, as local beef and produce were profitably smuggled across the border in exchange for currency and imported European goods, while worried ministers in Madrid redoubled subsidies to Santo Domingo's neglected garrison and promoted emigration from the Canary Islands and other Catholic lands in the hope of bolstering the Dominican population. More than 1,600 new settlers arrived on the Spanish half of the island in the seven years after 1684, instilling such confidence that when the War of the League of Augsburg, or King William's War, erupted in Europe four years later and the French thrust across the island to seize the northern Dominican city of Santiago de los Caballeros, a powerful counterexpedition could be organized in the capital.

Gov. Francisco de Segura Sandoval y Castilla rallied 2,600 militiamen, and on 21 December 1690 dispatched them around the eastern tip of the island aboard a half-dozen warships of Spain's *Armada de Barlovento* (Windward Fleet) under Adm. Jacinto Lope Gijón. Meanwhile, the governor led another 700 riders directly overland to recapture Santiago de los Caballeros, then rendezvoused with the first contingent near Manzanillo Bay in January 1691 to annihilate Cap-François (modern Cap-Haïtien). A second such strike was launched when two English warships—the 46-gun HMS *Hampshire* bearing Col. Peter Beckford from Jamaica and the detached frigate HMS *Swan* from Commo. Robert Wilmot's fleet at St. Kitts—arrived separately at Santo Domingo early in 1695 to propose a joint Anglo-Spanish descent against the French half of the island. De Segura's successor as *Audiencia* president, Gov. Gil Correoso Catalán, accepted and received a visit from four warships with Wilmot and his military colleague Col. Luke Lillingston, then agreed to lead 1,500 Dominican troops overland to meet the main English force at Bayahá by 12 May and together wreak havoc among the French settlements.

Not only were Santo Domingo's residents reassured by these successful operations, but in addition, island tensions subsided once peace was restored and Spain's last Hapsburg monarch—the deformed invalid Charles II—died on 30 November 1700, being succeeded by the sixteen-year-old French Bourbon prince Philip of Anjou. The resultant diplomatic realignment caused relations with the Dominicans' Gallic neighbors to stabilize as border disputes became better regulated; the Spaniards even prospered from the sale of cattle and foodstuffs to the rapidly expanding French plantations. By 1718 there were 18,400 residents on the Spanish half of the island, compared with 130,000 French inhabitants—mostly slaves—eight years later.

Despite being outnumbered and overshadowed by their wealthier neighbors during this boom period, Santo Domingo nonetheless flourished, its population rising to an estimated 8,000 people by 1740. The War of Jenkins's Ear, which lasted for the next eight years, caused some economic dislocation, yet much worse was to befall the residents in 1751: their city was battered by heavy hurricanes between 2 and 6 June and 21 and 25 August, as well as by earthquakes that struck on the afternoon of 18 October and the morning of 21 November. Some 180 soldiers furthermore gathered before its cathedral at dawn on 13 July 1757, angry at their twenty-eight months' arrears in pay; sixty surged into the Santa Bárbara Bastion to point its artillery menacingly into the city, and after a tense round of negotiations, Gov. Francisco Rubio y Peñaranda managed to placate the mutineers with a small stipend.

Still, compared with a century earlier, Santo Domingo was able to shrug off such setbacks with relative ease. The city garrison had for some time played a prominent economic, social, and political role, and it was further reinforced from Spain early in 1762 by the Second Battalions of the Granada and Murcia Infantry regiments after Madrid allied itself with Paris in the ongoing French and Indian War against London. Consequently, Commo. Juan Benito de Erasún paused with his squadron to deliver these troops before proceeding to take up station at Santiago de Cuba. Yet these 600 regulars remained at Santo Domingo only briefly, as an enormous British expedition then swept through the West Indies that same summer to invest Havana, so that these reinforcements were instead marched overland to Cap-François to be ferried across to Cuba by a French squadron.

Santo Domingo's exports soared once peace returned, and the island's agricultural productivity rose, abetted by a loosening of trade restrictions and other reforms emanating out of Madrid. Many beautiful masonry homes were consequently erected during this period, and the city expanded, notwithstanding more heavy storms that struck on 27 August 1775 and from 14 to 17 October 1780. Overseas traffic was also dislocated during the American War of Independence, yet the census of 1782–1783 revealed that the urban populace had almost doubled to 14,000 inhabitants, with another 51,000 people distributed around the Spanish half of the island.

Unfortunately, this flowering proved all too brief, as the entire island was about to become engulfed in turmoil as an indirect result of the 1789 Revolution in Paris, which pitted monarchists against republicans on the French half of the island, while more than 500,000 mulattoes and blacks also sought to gain their liberty. At first the neutral Spaniards had surreptitiously encouraged such in fighting, hoping to weaken their traditional rivals, and when the radical revolutionaries in Paris declared war against Spain in January 1793, a column of Dominican troops advanced that same August to help black Haitian rebels secure Cap-François and other northern towns. However, these rebels soon grew so strong that they no longer needed Spanish aid, while Spain was defeated back in Europe by a French invasion, being compelled to sign the Treaty of

Map of the city, published in Madrid by the royal geographer Tomás López in 1785; north is toward left. In his caption at lower right, López acknowledged consulting earlier cartographic works by Thomas Jefferys, Jacques-Nicolas Bellin, and Juan Gros in compiling this print. (Museo Naval, Madrid)

Basle in July 1795—one of whose terms stated that Santo Domingo was to be ceded to France in exchange for an evacuation of the Spanish homeland by the victorious invaders.

French Occupations (1795–1809)

News of this arrangement reached the city on 17 October 1795, with devastating effect. Most residents were appalled at the prospect of passing under French rule, while whites were furthermore apprehensive of the mulatto and black armies now unleashed in neighboring Saint-Domingue. Local despair peaked when the Spanish commodore Gabriel de Aristizábal opened Columbus's tomb in the cathedral on 20 December, removing the famous explorer's remains to be transported to Havana aboard his 74-gun warship *San Lorenzo* for reinterment, rather than leave them behind. (It appears that he failed in his intent, as a second box of bones was discovered in 1877 under the cathedral floor, inscribed with the words "First Admiral." Most scholarly opinion

believes that this latter box—auctioned off in London in September 1973—most likely contained Columbus's actual remains, while de Aristizábal had mistakenly removed those of his son and successor.)

A clause in the Treaty of Basle allowed Dominicans to emigrate to Cuba, so that thousands now availed themselves of that option. But when Madrid also declared war—at France's behest—against Britain in October 1796, this flow of migrants was abruptly cut off by the imposition of a Royal Navy blockade throughout the West Indies. Santo Domingo was left forlorn and isolated, although still nominally in Spanish hands, as its French neighbors were so racked by internal strife as to be unable to implement the occupation of the eastern half of the island.

The capital's unhappiness deepened when a hurricane roared through on 19–20 September 1798. Then, a little more than a year later, the *Audiencia* abandoned the island altogether for the Cuban city of Puerto Príncipe (modern Cam-

Columbus's empty tomb in Santo Domingo Cathedral, as it appeared ca. 1925. (Carpenter, *Lands of the Caribbean*)

agüey), leaving only Gov. Joaquín García Moreno with 650 soldiers as Santo Domingo's last remaining Spanish authorities. Eventually, the black republican Gen. Toussaint-Louverture marched across the island against the half-deserted capital with 10,000 poorly disciplined troops early in 1801, so that García Moreno capitulated Haina on 25 January, followed by the San Gerónimo Citadel and Santo Domingo the next day without bloodshed. Satisfied with his prize, Toussaint-Louverture soon retired westward, leaving behind a small garrison. The Spanish governor sailed away from the city with his soldiers on 22 February.

However, as peace with England was restored later that same year, Napoleon Bonaparte then sent out a huge counter-expedition to reclaim both halves of the island for France. Gen. Charles-Victor-Emmanuel Leclerc duly arrived at Samaná Bay on 29 January 1802 with 20,000 soldiers, and one of his columns advanced directly overland toward Santo Domingo against token black resistance, being greeted almost as liberators by its few remaining Spanish inhabitants when they entered on 25 February. The city's plight scarcely improved,

though, as war with Britain flared anew only fifteen months later—leading to a reimposition of the Royal Navy blockade—while disease so drastically thinned the ranks of recent French arrivals that black resistance became reanimated. The occupiers of the western half of the island were exterminated, and Haiti's full independence was proclaimed by 1 January 1804, after which the new black strongman—Gov.-Gen. Jean-Jacques Dessalines—assumed the title of Emperor Jacques I by October and launched a massive invasion of the eastern half of the island the following February.

Dessalines and his 21,000 Haitian troops reached Santo Domingo's gates by 8 March 1805, besieging its heavily outnumbered French holdouts under Gen. Jean-Louis Ferrand. The garrison was fortuitously spared by a chance sighting on 26 March of a passing French squadron under Rear Adm. Edouard-Thomas de Burgues, Comte de Missiessy, which Jacques feared portended an invasion of Haiti during his absence. (Actually, Missiessy was homeward bound for France, having quit Martinique on 22 March to exit the Caribbean.) The Haitians therefore raised their siege and fell back through the interior, annihilating numerous towns during their retirement.

Ferrand's lonely garrison was heartened early the next year by a visit from eight warships under Vice Adm. Corentin de Leissègues, but a more powerful British pursuit squadron under Vice Adm. Sir John Thomas Duckworth overtook them at anchor on the morning of 6 February 1806. Leissègues ordered his commanders to slip their cables and run westward before the wind, past Point Nizao, in the hope of gaining shelter under the Ocoa Bay batteries; the fleeing men-of-war were overhauled shortly after 10:00 A.M., however, and an hour and a half later Leissègues steered his battered 120-gun flagship *Impérial* in toward the coast, to run aground. The 84-gun *Diomede* soon followed suit, while the 84-gun *Alexandre* as well as the 74-gun *Brave* and *Jupitre* had already surrendered to the British. Duckworth stood away toward Jamaica with his prizes, leaving Santo Domingo disconsolate.

The unity between French garrison troops and Spanish residents against their mutual enemies fractured after Emperor Napoleon I sent an army into Spain in the summer of 1808, deposing Ferdinand VII in favor of his brother Joseph Bonaparte. This crude usurpation of power was rejected by most Latin American vassals, so that on 7 November—after four months' careful planning—rural residents led by the rich *hacendado* (estate-owner) Juan Sánchez Ramírez rose against their former allies. At Sabana de Palo Hincado, a plain about a mile and a half west of the town of Seibo (known to the French as Seybo), some 2,000 Dominican insurgents annihilated 600 of Ferrand's troops, a defeat that drove the governor to suicide.

Sánchez Ramírez thereupon marched upon Santo Domingo itself, arriving outside by 27 November 1808, but a lack of heavy siege artillery prevented his ill-equipped followers from storming the ramparts, held by 1,200 surviving

Engraved map by the military engineer George de Bois St. Lys of the Anglo-Dominican siege of the French garrison holding the city of Santo Domingo, 27 November 1808–7 July 1809; inserted in Gilbert Guillermin's *Précis historique des derniers événemens de la partie de l'est de Saint-Domingue depuis le 10 août 1808, jusqu'a la capitulation de Santo-Domingo.* (Paris, Arthus-Bertrand, 1811)

French defenders under Brigadier J. Barquier. Sánchez Ramírez therefore installed his headquarters at Jainamosa on the eastern banks of the Ozama, and an eight-month encirclement ensued, supported by a Royal Navy blockade out of Jamaica. Finally, British Maj.-Gen. Hugh Lyle Carmichael disembarked 30 miles west of the city at Polingue on 28 June 1809 with four regiments of redcoats and persuaded Sánchez Ramírez (despite having 400 of his best 600 Puerto Rican regulars sick) to advance two days later and seize San Carlos Church on the capital's outskirts to cut off communications between the main garrison and outlying Fort San Gerónimo. The Dominicans also secured a nearby beach, from which to unload materiel from Capt. William Price Cumby's supporting Royal Navy squadron.

The demoralized French defenders had already requested an armistice once and been rebuffed, and they repeated this proposal on 1 July 1809, just as the first British troops arrived overland (having been delayed by torrential downpours). As negotiations progressed, Carmichael maintained pressure on Barquier by installing heavy siege-batteries around the city circuit, then massed his forces for an assault. The capitulation was finalized on 6 July, although the French pointedly surrendered to the British rather than to the Dominican guerrillas. Redcoats moved into Fort San Gerónimo and the battered city the next day, their defenders being subsequently evacuated to Jamaica. But the Dominicans were annoyed to learn that they would

have to pay the English 400,000 pesos in order to recuperate their capital, a sum that was not raised until a month later.

Fleeting Independence (1809–1821)

This hard-fought campaign to expel the French from Santo Domingo became known as the *guerra de la reconquista,* or "war of reconquest," and the city resumed its former role as capital over the eastern half of the island, while reaffirming its loyalty to Spain. Seaborne trade also experienced a modest revival as the Royal Navy blockade was lifted, and British and Antillean ships could now enter port, although the Dominicans' dire poverty limited the volume of such commerce. So many skilled residents had fled abroad that the devastated city even struggled to rebuild its infrastructure, its population being measured at scarcely 8,000 people by 1812—the same number as seventy years previously—with another 54,000 rural inhabitants scattered throughout the interior.

Madrid was unable to dispatch Carlos Urrutia y Matos to assume office as the new governor until May 1813, because in addition to the lengthy struggle to drive the French from Spain, disgruntled Spanish-American Creoles had also launched separatist insurgencies in viceroyalties from Mexico as far south as Buenos Aires, seeking the overthrow of the old imperial system in favor of outright independence. The tiny Dominican elite did not share such sentiments, yet as royalist fortunes waned upon the continent, and Haitian power increased alarmingly on the western half of the island—especially after its bickering mulatto-black factions were reunited in October 1820 under Pres. Jean-Pierre Boyer—a quasi-liberal movement finally emerged on its Spanish half.

Late in 1821 the leader José Núñez de Cáceres proclaimed Santo Domingo's adhesion to the new "Republic of Gran Colombia," created by Simón Bolívar, but the determination of the island elite to perpetuate their privileged status by maintaining intact all colonial-era institutions such as social hierarchy, land titles, and slavery doomed this limited experiment in liberty to failure two months later. (It is remembered as the *Independencia Efímera,* or "Ephemeral Independence".) Haitians in particular resented their neighbors' continuation of slave holding practices and feared that Santo Domingo might eventually become a bridgehead for their own future resubjugation; Boyer therefore called upon Dominican blacks and mulattoes early the next year to assert their complete freedom from Spanish rule, then marched in support upon the capital of Santo Domingo with a large army.

Haitian Occupation (1822–1843)

Boyer and his menacing host arrived at the town of San Carlos just outside the city on 8 February 1822, being received the next morning with Santo Domingo's keys. For the next two decades the eastern half of the island was to remain under Haitian rule, and the city—no longer a capital—languished from neglect. Although its black and mulatto citizens undoubtedly benefited from their emancipation, and some minor trade fitfully continued, the Haitian government had neither the resources nor the inclination to address its numerous municipal deficiencies. Even language differences aggravated its problems, Santo Domingo's university closing down because of a lack of Spanish-speaking teachers and students.

Resentment against Haitian occupation eventually began to coalesce in the countryside, a secret nationalistic society called La Trinitaria being organized in 1838 under the leadership of Juan Pablo Duarte, gradually spreading its influence throughout the subject nation from its northern base of Santiago de los Caballeros. When Boyer was deposed in Port-au-Prince on 13 March 1843, the resultant succession struggle in Haiti gave the Dominicans an opportunity to seize the Puerta del Conde Bastion at Santo Domingo on 27 February 1844 and once more proclaim their independence.

Uneasy Capital of the First Republic (1844–1860)

The new government was promptly beset by a three-pronged Haitian invasion, successfully repelled by a Dominican army under the command of the wealthy rancher Gen. Pedro Santana. Fearful of more attacks, he and a number of likeminded conservatives in the National Junta then proposed that the overmatched new "Dominican Republic" request aid from France in exchange for status as a protectorate—or at least territorial concessions for a coaling station at Samaná Bay, a long-standing French interest. In order to prevent such submission to a foreign power, the more liberal and nationalistic Trinitario faction from the north staged a coup in Santo Domingo on 9 June 1844, deposing the junta leader Tomás de Bobadilla and other leading conservatives. But the liberals' attempt to impose Esteban Roca as commander of the army was rejected by its rank-and-file, so that Santana was reinstated.

He thereupon marched on the capital with 2,000 loyal troops, installing a conservative administration by mid-July 1844, which in turn drew up a constitution that accorded dictatorial powers to Santana through Article 210 (which allowed a president to govern by decree so long as a Haitian threat existed). Envoys were dispatched to France, Britain, Spain, and other nations in the hope of achieving annexation, but without success, as each power checked the designs of the others. Therefore, despite having regained its freedom and standing as a capital, Santo Domingo continued to suffer from uncertainty and neglect, the latter exacerbated by the indifference displayed to its municipal shortcomings by both rural-based conservatives and northern-based liberals. Export traffic in mahogany, meat, and hides remained negligible (and largely controlled by Britain), but at least the republic's 5,200 white inhabitants, 135,000 mulattoes, and 34,000 blacks enjoyed a subsistence existence thanks to their numerous small farms.

Fears of a Haitian reoccupation finally eased two years later, so that Santana completed his term by August 1848 and retired to his El Prado estate. He was succeeded as president by Manuel Jiménez González, who disbanded the army in a cost-cutting move, only to have the aggressive new Haitian ruler Faustin Soulouque invade early the next year with 10,000 troops. The Dominicans' plight deteriorated so rapidly that panic gripped their long-suffering capital, until Santana emerged from retirement and defeated the Haitians at the Battle of Las Carreras on 21 April 1849, driving them back across the border. He then marched back into Santo Domingo for a second time and installed the mulatto landowner Buenaventura Báez as president on 24 September, while he himself retained control over military affairs.

Hostility with Haiti was to persist until 1851, when a truce was finally mediated by Britain, France, and the United States. Santana reassumed the presidency when Báez's term expired in February 1853, then drove him into exile so as not to impede subsequent efforts to incorporate the fledgling republic into the United States. Serious negotiations began when the American envoy William Cazneau reached Santo Domingo aboard the warship USS *Columbia* in July 1854, ostensibly to acknowledge its independence (already recognized by Britain, France, Denmark, and Holland) and negotiate a commercial treaty. Yet after protracted debates in the Dominican congress, annexation was rejected that same December because of doubts raised by the entrenched slavery of the U.S. South. Many black and mulatto Dominicans feared that slavery would be extended into their own country if Santana succeeded in ceding their nation to the United States.

Haiti had likewise been fearful that U.S. annexation might result in a re-establishment of slavery, so that Emperor Faustin invaded the Dominican interior with a 30,000-man Haitian army in November 1855, only to be expelled by January 1856. Santana thereupon redoubled his efforts to transfer the republic to American control, even offering U.S. agents the opportunity of carrying out a naturalization drive such as that introduced by the recently arrived Spanish representative at Santo Domingo, Antonio María Segovia, who had granted citizenship to hundreds of local adherents, but when it had become obvious that Santana could not consummate his plan for U.S. absorption, he resigned in May 1856, making way for a triumphal return by Báez that same October.

Divisions deepened further when tobacco growers and merchants in the north, leery of the reinstated mulatto president's personal designs upon their increasingly lucrative business, revolted and seized Santiago de los Caballeros in July 1857, as well as calling Santana out of retirement. The conservative former president marched upon the capital for a third time and besieged it for little over a year, until Báez surrendered and went into exile once more. But Santana's return to power prompted Haiti to invade yet again in 1859, and despite being checked militarily, the island economy was now so ruined that its conservative president—having despaired of securing Washington's intervention—turned to Spain.

Secret negotiations soon secured Madrid's approval, so that Spanish troops, immigrants, and warships began to marshal in Cuba by the summer of 1860. In order to prepare the Dominicans for such a dramatic change in national status, demonstrations were organized at Santo Domingo as of October, and Santana's final conditions for annexation were quietly accepted the following month: namely, that slavery was not to be reimposed, that the Dominican Republic was to be treated as an equal province, that Dominicans were to be employed in the colonial bureaucracy and militia, and that all Dominican laws enacted since 1844 were to be honored.

Spanish Reoccupation (1861–1865)

These machinations climaxed when Santana proclaimed the Dominican Republic's annexation by Spain on 18 March 1861, and a stream of Spanish warships, troops, bureaucrats, and priests began disembarking at Santo Domingo. At first they were greeted as redeemers by prominent Dominicans longing for a stable economic environment and an end to Haitian invasions; yet the mass of mulatto and black citizenry—never consulted about this abrupt transfer—feared a loss of their meager liberties and livelihoods. Annexation was nonetheless formally approved by the Cortes (Parliament) at Madrid a couple of months afterward, with Santana's appointment as governor, his ennoblement as Marqués de las Carreras and welcomed into the senate, as well as being invested with the orders of Isabel la Católica and Carlos III.

Disillusionment soon set in on both sides, though, the Spaniards being appalled at Santo Domingo's utter destitution and lack of public services—lacking even the most basic of amenities, Santana having openly boasted of delivering a country "without lawyers or newspapers"—so that a vast upgrade would be required, siphoning funds away from Cuban and Puerto Rican projects. The new rulers were also bigoted against its black and mulatto residents, regarding them as illiterate and incompetent, while furthermore alienating rural dwellers through their plan of redistributing land among Spanish immigrants.

For their part, wealthy Dominicans resented the new taxes that were enacted; the discriminatory duties levied against foreign carriers so that Spanish shippers might benefit (but which instead caused island commerce to decline); the arbitrary imposition of unfavorable currency exchange rates; and their exclusion from all influential posts, Santana himself being forced to resign his governorship by January 1862. The heavy-handed efforts of Archbishop Bienvenido Monzón to reimpose strict Catholic observances and persecute Protestant converts also stirred a good deal of ill will, especially among the lower classes, already uneasy because of the racist undercurrent to this new regime.

Rebellions soon erupted in the interior, worsening after the

Spaniards furthermore tried to reintroduce a state-run tobacco monopoly in the north, provoking such widespread resistance that it escalated into the so-called *guerra de restauración* (war of restoration). Santiago de los Caballeros fell to rebel forces by mid-1863, where the Dominicans installed a provisional government, then pressed the Spanish back inside Santo Domingo by the end of that same year. As losses continued to mount—roughly 7,500 invaders eventually succumbing, although only 6 percent because of Dominican military action, the rest from yellow fever—and Washington began exerting heavy pressure on Madrid, the Spaniards finally decided to abandon the island. A bill ordering a troop withdrawal was passed by the Cortes on 1 May 1865, and Santo Domingo was restored to local rule three months afterward.

Political Prize (1865–1915)

Despite regaining its freedom, the capital would continue to experience difficulties, beginning when Pedro Antonio

Fort San Gerónimo, ca. 1925, as seen from offshore. By this date, the original sixteenth-century redoubt had been often modified and converted into a penitentiary. (Carpenter, *Lands of the Caribbean*)

Pimentel, the head of the provisional government at Santiago de los Caballeros, attempted to march triumphantly upon Santo Domingo in August 1865 only to be checked by rival southern forces under José María Cabral. The unity achieved while acting against the Spanish intervention quickly dissolved into two rancorous factions: northern *Azules* (Blues), many of whom were liberal former Santanistas, ranged against the rural and more conservative *Rojos* (Reds) of the ranchlands and woods of the south and west, who generally supported former president Báez.

When Cabral arranged the latter's return to power in February 1866, a series of coups and countercoups ensued, during which the unhappy capital changed hands a half dozen times over the next two years. Matters were further complicated when Frederick Seward, son and assistant to U.S. secretary of state William Seward, visited Santo Domingo along with Adm. David D. Porter during the winter of 1866–1867, in the hope of leasing a coaling station at Samaná Bay from Báez (who proved amenable, although that thirty-year arrangement was eventually voted down by the abolitionist lobby in the U.S. Congress led by Senator Charles Sumner, despite support from the prominent African American leader Frederick Douglass).

After Báez returned to office for a fourth time in January 1868, he resorted to an increasingly authoritarian policy of repression to retain power, and furthermore tried to solve his nation's perennial state of "absolute penury" by reviving the old dream of American annexation. The new U.S. administration of President Ulysses S. Grant displayed a like interest as of 1869, even dispatching a dozen warships to prop up Báez's regime when it was threatened by Haitian-backed rebels, but this assistance was not enough, the Dominican president finally being deposed in 1873.

More chaos ensued, sixteen different administrations assuming power at Santo Domingo between January 1874 and October 1879. Finally, Ulises Heureaux won the presidency and retained it until his assassination in July 1899, at which time the nation plunged back into another six years of anarchy, and its capital was once again contested as a political prize. For example, former president Alexandro Woss y Gil rebelled against the provisional government of Gen. Horacio Vásquez in April 1903, driving him from the city; a second revolt erupted shortly thereafter at Puerto Plata, so that Gen. Carlos Morales advanced across the island and, after a brief siege, compelled Woss to surrender the capital by 24 November.

Washington became concerned because such frequent dislocations also entailed financial losses for foreign nationals, furnishing an excuse for military interventions by Britain, Germany, France, Italy, or Spain. In an effort to limit such encroachments in the New World, the U.S. government pressured the Dominicans in 1905 to allow American personnel to take over customs collection and debt payments, regardless of which faction held temporary sway in the capital. This "Dominican Customs Receivership" was to be controlled by an appointee of the U.S. president, remitting 45 percent of total revenues to the island government while retaining 55 percent to pay off all foreign claimants, so that the United States became the republic's sole creditor.

This drastic measure, coupled with a large bank loan and the election of the popular president Ramón Cáceres in 1906, ushered in an interlude of relative stability and prosperity for Santo Domingo, so that the capital was able to take a few modest steps toward reconstruction and modernization. Unfortunately, Cáceres was assassinated in November 1911, plunging the republic back into political and economic anarchy. Washington attempted to restore order the following year by cutting off customs funds and sending a special commission—backed by 750 marines—to impose a border treaty with Haiti, as well as other reforms upon the squabbling Dominican factions. The United States also forced the resignation of President Eladio Victoria in favor of interim rule by Archbishop Adolfo A. Nouel, yet disorder nonetheless persisted. Nouel's successor— Gen. José Bordas Valdéz—was ousted as well, in August 1914, paving the way for the election of President Juan Isidro Jiménez.

With World War I now raging in Europe, a worried Democratic administration under President Woodrow Wilson became so concerned with preserving the neutrality of the Americas that it forced Jiménez to accept a U.S. director of public works and a financial adviser, who together managed most of the republic's disbursements, rather than permit them to be diverted into the traditional patronage payoffs. Such an overt surrender of economic independence engendered deep-seated Dominican resentment, as well as an anti-Jiménez backlash, but Washington escalated its demands by insisting early in 1915 that the luckless president also disband the army in favor of a U.S.-controlled constabulary. This latest demand led to calls for Jiménez's impeachment and threats of open rebellion at Santo Domingo.

American Occupation (1916–1924)

This crisis climaxed when Jiménez ordered the arrest on 14 April 1916 of several key supporters of his insubordinate war minister, Gen. Desiderio Arias, who promptly mutinied and commandeered the capital's main arsenal at Fort Ozama with 250 troops. A two-week standoff ensued until the rebellious general surrounded the Chamber of Deputies on 1 May, calling for the president's immediate ouster; Jiménez responded by advancing from his country estate with 800 loyal troops and divesting Arias of all authority.

The transport *Prairie* and gunboat *Castine* consequently arrived off the nervous city from U.S.-occupied Haiti on the afternoon of 3 May 1916, offering to disembark their marines in Jiménez's support. The latter demurred, asking only for weaponry. But Washington ignored this request and two mornings later ordered 150 marines under Capt. Frederic ("Dopey") Wise to land and seize Fort San Gerónimo, then march the 2 miles into the capital to defend the U.S. and Haitian legations as well as the Customs Receivership—whose offices were located "in a strategic position on the heights overlooking the city." Unwilling to cooperate with Wise in besieging his mutinous general inside Fort Ozama, Jiménez resigned the presidency on 7 May.

Five days later, the dispatch-vessel *Dolphin* and store-ship *Culgoa* also arrived at Santo Domingo from Port-au-Prince with Rear Adm. William B. Caperton plus two additional marine companies under Maj. Newt H. Hall; a third company appeared the next day from Guantánamo Bay aboard the collier *Hector*. Now with 400 men ashore, the American commander ordered Arias to evacuate his stronghold by Monday, 15 May 1916, when the entire capital was to be occupied. He and his mutineers duly retired northwestward, offering to submit to any president selected by the Chamber of Deputies. American reinforcements continued to arrive, though, and the northern coastal towns of Monte Cristi and Puerto Plata were seized by 1 June, after which Col. Joseph ("Uncle Joe") H. Pendleton pushed into the interior and subdued Arias's last concentration around Santiago by 6 July.

Having thus gained control over the whole republic, the United States imposed strict conditions upon an interim president chosen by its fragmented chamber—the highly regarded medical doctor, lawyer, and university professor Dr. Francisco Henríquez y Carvajal—who subsequently refused to acquiesce

Gen. Desiderio Arias as he appeared, ca. 1920. (Franck, *Roaming through the West Indies*)

to these many demands. Friction also developed between the capital's 21,000 mostly mulatto and black residents and marine patrols, resulting in a serious clash when a contingent sent in November 1916 to arrest Gen. Ramón Batista in the Villa Duarte suburb suffered two dead and several wounded from an ambush, sparking an angry marine reprisal that saw these attackers killed, several houses destroyed, and numerous Dominicans randomly beaten. Consequently, when the legislative session legally expired on 29 November, Washington took the final step of having naval captain Harry S. Knapp proclaim martial law, and the capital's populace grudgingly resigned itself to a lengthy U.S. occupation.

Tensions eased considerably after the United States became distracted by entering World War I in the spring of 1917, and the island economy experienced an upsurge by contributing to the war effort. Once transatlantic hostilities ceased, in November 1918, the U.S. administration furthermore turned to improving public services such as education, health, and sanitation throughout the island. Santo Domingo in particular benefited from numerous work projects, such as the modernization and extension of its primitive road network running inland; the upgrading of its telegraph and telephone communications; the rehabilitation of its harbor, docks, and customshouse; the erection of a new bridge across the Ozama; and the construction or restoration of many municipal edifices. Even a red-light district was allocated in the Barahona-Monte Cristi sector.

Unfortunately, the collapse of commodity prices in New York drove the island economy into depression by late 1920, halting such labors and idling almost 5,000 workers. The U.S. presidential campaign also featured the Dominican occupation as a partisan political issue, so that the new Republican administration of President Warren G. Harding proved unwilling to perpetuate it. After protracted negotiations the U.S. military government handed administrative duties over to a provisional Dominican government in October 1922 in anticipation of a withdrawal. Once the elderly Gen. Horacio Vásquez and Federíco Henríquez y Carvajal were elected president and vice president, respectively, and installed into office by 12 July 1924, the last marine companies departed Santo Domingo on 18 September.

Transformation into "Ciudad Trujillo" (1925–1961)

Although they were relieved to see the U.S. troops depart, city residents had benefited materially from the occupation, and Santo Domingo's infrastructure continued to be improved even after their withdrawal—a long-needed sewer system and aqueduct, for example, finally being completed. The capital's economy was also boosted by the modern new American-built highway leading into the northern farmlands, which so facilitated overland transportation that significant amounts of agricultural produce could be diverted down for export through its port for the first time. Vásquez illegally extended his four-year term in 1928 to partake in this bounty, but his health started to deteriorate shortly thereafter, and the world economy collapsed with the New York stock market crash of October 1929. The resultant Great Depression sparked a rebellion in the north of the Dominican Republic by late February of the next year, and an ill-armed insurgent host under Rafael Estrella Ureña drove upon the capital from Santiago de los Caballeros with surprising ease.

This advance was covertly assisted by the brigadier commanding the 1,300-man National Guard—a ruthlessly ambitious former telegraph operator and sugar plantation guard named Rafael Leónidas Trujillo Molina—who betrayed his president by encouraging and even secretly arming these rebels. Once Vásquez fell, Trujillo cowed Estrella Ureña into running as his vice presidential candidate, while unleashing armed henchmen against all other potential rivals; the ensuing election was marred by coercion and fraud, Trujillo winning the presidency in mid-August 1930 with more votes than there were eligible voters. A massive hurricane then swept over the island that same 3 September, killing 2,000 people and injuring 8,000, while leveling most of Santo Domingo's buildings within the span of a couple of hours, including its lone U.S.-built bridge across the Ozama River. In order to hasten recovery from such widespread devastation, the newly installed president took to ruling by decree, ignoring constitutional niceties and thereby tightening his grip on power.

These emergency powers allowed Trujillo to condemn many old obstructive properties in Santo Domingo, thus improving its street patterns by replacing the ancient colonial layout with a more open design, eventually resulting in a more modern and beautiful capital. A new seaside boulevard, for example, would stretch as far as Fort San Gerónimo, while space was also cleared to permit easier access to the reconstructed Ozama Bridge. But Trujillo's real aim was to bring all economic activity under state control, and he soon dispensed with political parties and unions as well. The Partido Dominicano (Dominican Party), which he founded in August 1931, was the only political entity allowed to exist, being funded by such extortionate methods as automatic 10 percent pay deductions from all government employees. Inspired by the totalitarian models then ruling Italy, Spain, Germany, and Russia, Trujillo clamped a tight dictatorship upon the republic through a system of police surveillance and pervasive socioeconomic control.

The devastated capital slowly began to rebuild, and according to a census taken in May 1935, its population had rebounded to 71,297 inhabitants, with another 22,910 scattered throughout the surrounding district. Some measure of the pervasive fear that this despotic rule now evoked was exemplified the following month, when the sycophantic National Congress proposed that the capital be renamed Ciudad Trujillo (Trujillo City); after a brief show of reluctant refusal from the dictator, a bill was passed on 11 January 1936—while the president was ostensibly on vacation—officially changing its name from Santo Domingo, National District, into Trujillo City, District of Santo Domingo. Of more practical benefit, its harbor was dredged, and a new 2,000-foot breakwater was completed by mid-August 1938, projecting from the Torrecilla headland opposite so as to allow ships of up to 30,000 tons' displacement to berth and process cargoes directly at the city wharves.

Trujillo maintained an assiduously pro-U.S. international policy so as to retain favor in Washington; that stood the Dominican Republic in good stead after the Japanese attacked Pearl Harbor on 7 December 1941. The very next day, Trujillo declared war in support of the United States, and his nation and capital prospered throughout the remainder of these hostilities, thanks to increased demand for island exports. Economic growth and modernization continued even after World War II ended in 1945, as American firms were granted generous concessions to invest on the island, and sugar prices soared.

These gains allowed Trujillo to conduct ever more ambitious public works projects in the city and countryside, most of which—such as increased agricultural productivity, an expanded highway network, better harbors, and so forth—personally benefited the despot, his family, or cronies. Eventually they amassed about 60 percent of the republic's total assets—including its best lands, sugar mills, cement works, airlines, shipping concerns, tobacco fields—and employed a majority of its populace, either directly or indirectly through the government apparatus that they controlled. By the early 1950s, Trujillo was one of the richest men in the world, with a personal fortune estimated at several hundred million dollars—even though his nation had one of the lowest standards of living in the Western Hemisphere.

The capital had expanded beyond its old colonial boundaries during this upsurge, spreading into the low surrounding hills. Migrants from the countryside had swelled its population to 181,553 residents by 1950, a trend that would continue to accelerate. But many of these recent arrivals were crammed into impoverished slums because of such rapid and unplanned growth, as well as the unmoved sociopolitical system. Aware of a changing international climate and the championing of democracy by the United States, Trujillo sought to deflect criticism by not standing for reelection in May 1952, although he retained command over the armed forces and fielded his brother and war minister—Gen. Hector Bienvenido Trujillo Molina—as the sole and uncontested candidate.

Gradually, this oligarchic avarice and brutal repression engendered a domestic opposition from among the capital's emerging middle class, the Catholic Church, and urban laborers, as well as deepening repugnance abroad. When sugar prices plummeted and the Cuban dictator Fulgencio Batista fled to Ciudad Trujillo in January 1959, pressure began to mount for removal of the Dominican regime as well. Washington wished

Aerial view of Ciudad Trujillo in 1946, just as the rebuilt city was initiating its post–World War II boom. (Library of Congress)

to replace an embarrassing political liability with a more democratic government so as to preclude any further socialist revolutions in the Caribbean, while Dominican elements hoped to liberalize their society and gain access to power. Critical comments from the Venezuelan president Rómulo Betancourt goaded Rafael Trujillo into sanctioning an assassination attempt against him on 24 June 1960, which failed and precipitated a retaliatory trade embargo against the Dominican Republic by the Organization of American States (OAS).

In a gesture of appeasement, Hector Trujillo resigned the Dominican presidency on 3 August 1960, being succeeded by his vice president, Joaquín Antonio Balaguer—Rafael Trujillo's former presidential secretary and minion. Unimpressed by this cosmetic change, Washington severed diplomatic relations on 26 August, tightened the embargo, and furnished weapons to the dictator's enemies through covert agents of the Central Intelligence Agency (CIA). On 30 May 1961, Rafael Trujillo was

shot along the highway just west of the capital while en route to his latest mistress; but his assassins failed to announce his death and immediately seize power, allowing his lightly wounded chauffeur time to hitch a ride back into the city with a warning. The dictator's eldest son—Rafael "Ramfis" Trujillo, Jr.—consequently returned from Paris and executed most of the two dozen conspirators.

But pressure against the new dictator nonetheless escalated over the next several months, and street demonstrations in the capital climaxed with serious rioting in late October 1961 that obliged Ramfis's hated uncles Hector and José Arismendi Trujillo to go into exile. They returned a couple of weeks later in a final bid to retain power, but could not avert Ramfis's resignation on 14 November; after emptying the national treasury of tens of millions of dollars, the Trujillos flew to Miami five days later, while a U.S. aircraft carrier task force hovered offshore. Balaguer remained in office as president despite the demonstrations that had also erupted against him as of 21 November, accompanied by widespread looting of Trujillo businesses and mansions. Two days later, the National Congress voted to change the name of the capital back to Santo Domingo.

U.S. Intervention (1962–1966)

In the troubled city, Balaguer shared power with a provisional seven-man Consejo de Estado (Council of State) composed of opposition politicians, businessmen, and clergymen until mid-January 1962, when rioting obliged him to leave the country as well (although with considerable respect, due to his steps toward democratization and relinquishment of the former dictator's properties). Some semblance of normalcy returned to the capital as diplomatic and trade relations were restored abroad, so that peaceful elections could be held that same December, being won in a landslide by Prof. Juan D. Bosch, candidate of the moderate left-of-center Partido Revolucionario Dominicano (Dominican Revolutionary Party), who had spent half his life in exile.

Yet after assuming office in late February 1963, his efforts to liberalize the republic's administration provoked a reaction from more conservative elements such as landowners, businessmen, the Church, and the military. Washington furthermore viewed with suspicion his attempts to secure financial support from European sources, while U.S. investors feared that their properties were about to be expropriated. The ineptness of this new government also bred much economic hardship, so that a general strike occurred on 20 September 1963; five days later, the National Palace was surrounded by mutinous troops and Bosch was deported to Puerto Rico. The National Congress was dissolved as well, and the republic was governed by a "triumvirate" of conservative officeholders until 24 April 1965, when they too were deposed by a bloodless military coup.

However, this second group of plotters was in turn surprised when a group of young army colonels took over this rebellion the next day by rousing thousands of civilian supporters into the streets of Santo Domingo with a call for Bosch's return. Brig. Elías Wessín y Wessín—a member of this second cabal of conspirators and commander of 1,500 troops and thirty tanks at San Isidro Air Base, 20 miles outside the capital—countered by sending four of his P-51 fighters to strafe the presidential palace on the afternoon of 25 April 1965, then the next day attempted to fight his way into the city out of the east with his armored column. But his progress was unexpectedly checked at Duarte Bridge by rebel troops and armed civilians under the skillful leadership of Col. Francisco Caamaño Deñó, who, despite suffering hundreds of casualties and great material damage during fierce exchanges of gunfire, succeeded in repelling Wessín's assault, so that their popular uprising appeared on the verge of success.

At this point, the administration of U.S. president Lyndon Baines Johnson—convinced that the insurrection enjoyed stealthy Communist backing—decided to intervene. The aircraft carrier USS *Boxer* and transports bearing 1,500 marines therefore materialized off the embattled city at dawn on 27 April 1965, protecting the evacuation of about 1,000 American civilians and 1,400 other nationals from Haina the following day. As sputtering combat persisted around the capital, Washington thereupon committed to a full-scale intervention by disembarking 1,700 marines on 30 April and airlifting 2,500 paratroopers into San Isidro Air Base to impose a cease-fire within a 9-square-mile "internationalized zone" that encompassed all foreign legations within the city.

The arrival of more U.S. troops (their numbers eventually swelled to almost 23,000 throughout the island) stifled all overt fighting, but Caamaño Deñó's rebels were nonetheless left in control of the capital, while the east bank of the Ozama River was held by the military junta—now nominally headed by Col. Antonio Imbert Barrera, one of Trujillo's assassins and supposedly a more palatable figurehead than Wessín. A tense standoff ensued, OAS-brokered negotiations being punctuated by occasional exchanges of gunfire, such as the weeklong outburst that erupted after junta planes destroyed the rebel radio station on 13 May 1965, or the bloody outbreak of 15 June, when twenty-one people were slain within the beleaguered city and its customshouse was set ablaze. An agreement was finally hammered out on 31 August, whereby both Caamaño and Wessín went abroad to diplomatic postings, so that this impasse could end and Santo Domingo might begin recuperating from a confrontation that had claimed some 3,000 lives.

U.S. soldiers and a few thousand Latin American troops, known collectively as the Fuerza Interamericana de Pacificación (Inter-American Pacification Force), remained as peacekeepers in the Dominican Republic until June 1966, when Balaguer was elected president, so that the last foreign contingents could withdraw by 27 September.

Modern Era (1967–Present)

World opprobrium against the heavy-handed U.S. intervention prompted Washington to lavish assistance upon this new regime, so as to showcase the benefits of free enterprise. Balaguer also revised the Dominican constitution to permit greater foreign investment and ownership, thereby hoping to win back American investors; sugar prices simultaneously soared on international markets as well, increasing export values. Together, these measures helped to produce an economic spurt and expansion for the capital, exemplified by a great deal of private construction and public works projects, plus the restoration of its old colonial-era core so as to attract tourism.

Such activities contributed to an explosive growth in population, which reached 671,402 inhabitants by 1970, representing 16.7 percent of the republic's total and far outstripping the second-largest city, Santiago de los Caballeros (which had

U.S. troops patrolling the streets of Santo Domingo, May 1965. (U.S. Department of Defense Visual Information Center)

only 150,000). Yet the inherent social inequities meant that the greatest gains were confined to the upper and middle classes, while a majority of urban residents continued to live in slums blighted by high unemployment, infant mortality, illiteracy, and malnutrition rates. Dissent naturally festered in such sectors, countered by police repression. Conditions eased somewhat after the U.S. administration of President Jimmy Carter urged Balaguer to honor the electoral results of May 1978, which produced a victory for the opposition PRD candidate, a wealthy rancher named Antonio Guzmán.

Already sprawling well beyond its original boundaries, Santo Domingo continued its demographic explosion as droves of rural peasants migrated into the capital in search of better prospects. Many erected makeshift huts of wood or tin in the shantytowns that spread ever farther around its outskirts, most such squatter communities lacking the benefits of electricity, running water, or sewers. Their flimsy dwellings suffered extensive damage when Hurricane David swept over the island at the end of August 1979, killing more than 1,000 people and injuring 10,000, so that extensive reconstruction was required. Nevertheless, the total population—for this, the oldest European-built city in the Americas—mushroomed from 1.3 million to 2.135 million inhabitants between 1980 and 1993.

For further reading on the history of Santo Domingo or the Dominican Republic, please consult the Select Bibliography at the end of this volume.

Haiti

Cap-Haïtien

First European settlement in the New World, which became a preeminent French colonial seaport and has borne a half dozen names during its long and turbulent history.

Spanish Foundation (1492–1579)

During Christopher Columbus's initial penetration into the Antilles, he touched at the Bahamas and Cuba before sighting a coastline that so closely resembled Spain that he dubbed it *La Isla Española* or "The Spanish Island" (a term later Anglicized into "Hispaniola"). While anchored off a large bay on the night of 24 December 1492, his flagship *Santa María* accidentally drifted onto a reef and became wrecked, so that the explorer and his crew sought sanctuary ashore the next day at the village of the regional Taino-speaking Arawak chieftain Guacanagarí.

These castaways were generously received, as the natives hoped that the powerful strangers might in turn protect them from the Caribs, a rival seafaring people who had raided for generations. Large canoes therefore helped strip the stranded *Santa María* of everything of value—including its timbers—and lightered these goods into Guacanagarí's village, where they were stored in his main lodge. With only the small caravel *Niña* now left to him (*Pinta* under Martín Alonso Pinzón having become separated a few days previously), Columbus decided to leave some volunteers behind in Guacanagarí's village, while returning to Spain with the remainder of his crew.

The chieftain proved amenable, so that his village core was ceded to the Spaniards, who used *Santa María*'s timbers to commence erecting a fortified enclosure complete with moat, palisade, and most probably a watchtower. Columbus named this outpost Villa y Puerto de Navidad (Town and Port of Christmas; sometimes rendered as Natividad), in honor of the auspicious date on which he and his castaways had been received. Modern archaeologists believe that it most likely lay just southwest of what is today the city of Cap-Haïtien, at a spot

Aerial view of Cap-Haïtien, ca. 1930–1940; note the encroaching hills. (Library of Congress)

107

now known as En Bas-Saline. Even before it was completed, the explorer assigned a thirty-six-man garrison under his subordinates Diego de Arana, Pedro Gutiérrez, and Rodrigo de Escobedo, then departed for Spain on 4 January 1493. Two days later *Niña* overtook *Pinta* east of present-day Monte Cristi, so that both vessels sailed back across the Atlantic together.

When the admiral returned to the West Indies later that same year with five ships and a dozen caravels bearing 1,500 settlers (as well as several score horses and domesticated animals, plus sugar-cane and other seedlings for planting), he paused during his passage along northern Hispaniola to inspect Monte Christi, in the belief that it might prove a better base than the Navidad site, which he deemed incapable of sustaining such a large colony because its terrain was "all swampy and unsuitable for habitation." Columbus's misgivings deepened after the fleet dropped anchor off Navidad a couple of days later, finding its stockade destroyed and garrison vanished, with Guacanagarí and his friendly Taino tribesmen shifted farther up the coast because the enemy chieftains Caonabó and Mayreni had mounted an assault during the explorer's absence.

Shaken by this massacre and now distrustful of the Indians, the Spaniards scouted for a more defensible locale, forsaking Navidad in favor of a site farther east that they named *La Isabela* on 6 January 1494 in honor of the Spanish queen Isabel. From that spot, Columbus continued probing in the erroneous belief that he was near Asia and that Isabela would become his trading base once commercial relations were established with either Japan or China. But as months elapsed with only more primitive islands being encountered, its settlers—many being undesirables banished from Spain—grew disillusioned by the harsh conditions at their sun-baked and infertile camp, and so turned against the Columbus brothers and dispersed around the island. Three summers later, the admiral's brother Bartholomew abandoned Isabela altogether and led a few loyal retainers around to Hispaniola's southern shore to found a permanent new capital called Santo Domingo.

Nicolás de Ovando arrived as Crown-appointed governor for the Spanish West Indies in the summer of 1502 and set about reorganizing its government so as to exploit the Antillean archipelago. In the ensuing rush to register private land claims, a small group of settlers ventured less than a mile inland from Columbus's original seaside stockade of Navidad to found a new town called Puerto Real (Port Royal), one of thirteen such new communities sanctioned by de Ovando in 1503. This particular settlement lay on the periphery of a vast plain (later called the Plaine du Nord—North Plain, in French) that proved ideally suited for breeding cattle and cultivating crops. Produce could then be lightered downriver to the small native village that had once again sprung up near Navidad's ruins, Tainos having resumed their traditional fishing in its sheltered bay to supplement their harvests of manioc and yucca.

This seaside hamlet was known to the Spaniards as El Guarico, and its residents were often conscripted to serve as stevedores whenever ships arrived, off-loading goods and conveying them inland to Puerto Real, as well as bringing back goods for export. Both the native village along the coast and the Spanish town inland remained relatively small, though, their numbers contracting even further after the island experienced a serious depopulation drain on account of the conquest of neighboring Cuba in 1511, which lured away many adventurers. In addition, a smallpox epidemic claimed thousands of Taíno lives seven years later, and the subjugation of the dazzling Mexican and Peruvian empires in the early 1520s and 1530s drew away the bulk of sea traffic and reduced Hispaniola to a half-forgotten backwater.

Unable to attract any replacement settlers or valuable trade, nor compensate for the eradication of its indigenous laborers through purchases of expensive African slaves, Puerto Real failed to develop into anything more than a cluster of roughly sixty stone structures. It was laid out in a grid pattern around a central square dominated by a single church, a few municipal offices, and a large slaughterhouse on the outskirts. El Guarico fared even worse, the deaths of so many of its Taino fishermen and lack of regular Spanish sea traffic causing it to dwindle into a mere clutch of grass shacks.

Its broad natural harbor therefore lay virtually uninhabited when the first foreign raiders began penetrating into the West Indies. France and Spain were locked in a recurrent dynastic struggle back in Europe known as the Hapsburg-Valois Wars, so that French rovers pushed into the Antilles as early as 1537 to seek out targets. But they also found many forlorn Spanish communities eager for clandestine trade, and so returned during intervals of peace to barter European goods and African slaves for New World produce. The northwestern coast of Hispaniola proved a particularly favorite stopover for such smugglers, who could anchor in its many secluded inlets to refresh provisions and receive discreet visits from customers in boats. As early as July 1551, the peninsula east of Puerto Plata was being openly referred to in Spanish correspondence as Cabo Francés (French Cape; modern Cabo Francés Viejo in the Dominican Republic), because of the interlopers so often found brazenly riding at anchor there.

El Guarico, with its undefended anchorage, convenient lookout point atop its nearby headland, and isolated ranching community deeper inland, also became a popular port of call, the Spaniards of Puerto Real selling so many thousand hides and so much meat and tallow to French masters that official island exports sagged appreciably, goading the authorities of Santo Domingo, Seville, and Madrid into a Draconian measure: to curtail such illicit contacts, King Philip II commanded in 1579 that Puerto Real be vacated and its residents dispersed among adjoining jurisdictions. Only four Crown-controlled towns—Puerto Plata, Monte Christi, Bayahá, and La Yaguana (modern Léogâne, Haiti)—were allowed to subsist on this

Map of northwestern Hispaniola drawn by Christopher Columbus in 1493; although sketchy, it accurately depicts the coastal outline and identifies such spots as Tortuga Island, Natividad, and Monte Christi. (Biblioteca del Palacio de Liria de la Casa Ducal de Alba, Madrid)

particular coastline; El Guarico Bay was consequently forsaken by the Spaniards for a second time.

Abandonment (1580–1669)

Although uninhabited, the anchorage nonetheless continued to attract foreign seamen and soon became known as the new Cabo Francés. Regional smuggling increased during the war against Elizabethan England from 1588 to 1603 because of disruptions to Spanish transatlantic traffic occasioned by British privateers. With the cessation of hostilities, Philip III ordered Gov. Antonio Osorio to sweep along Hispaniola's northwestern shore with a few hundred soldiers in the summer of 1605, torching all four towns and compelling their citizens to relocate to the southern coast of the island, so as to come under direct Crown supervision.

This withdrawal merely aggravated the problem, though, as foreign vessels could now anchor anywhere along the northwestern coast with impunity, and their crews could disembark with impunity to tap the abandoned clearances and livestock. A fortified intruder stronghold was eventually established on the offshore Île-à-Tortue, or Tortuga Island, a quarter century later, and a French adventurer named Jérémie Deschamps de Moussac et du Rausset arrived in the spring of 1659 with authorization from both Paris and London to act as its private "governor." He in turn appointed his nephew Frédéric Deschamps de la Place to act as his deputy, then transferred across to Hispaniola's uninhabited western mainland to found new settlements at Petit-Goâve and Léogâne in 1663.

French Crown rule was imposed over this private colony after du Rausset tried to sell it to English interests on Jamaica, being instead imprisoned in the Bastille the next year and persuaded to make over his ownership to the newly created Com-

pagnie des Indes Occidentales (West Indian Company), a firm backed by France's chief royal minister Jean-Baptiste Colbert. Its directors named the Léogâne planter Bertrand d'Ogeron, Sieur de la Bouère, as their new governor; he assumed leadership over approximately 700 to 800 French settlers spread between both the mainland and Tortuga communities by June 1665.

French Refoundation (1670–1710)

This colony flourished during d'Ogeron's eleven-year tenure, many engagés (indentured settlers) migrating out from Europe, so that more mainland tracts could be cleared and occupied. One such significant gain occurred in 1670, when twelve colonists led by the former flibustier Pierre le Long departed Tortuga—then in the grips of a violent protest against the restrictive trade policies of the Compagnie—to re-establish a fishing and agricultural settlement at the old El Guarico site, which they christened Cap-François (being the accepted seventeenth-century spelling for "French Cape"; the name later evolved into Cap-Français).

Over the next couple of decades, this small beachfront community profited as a transshipment point as its settlers pushed into and began developing the vast and fertile North Plain. Tortuga lay virtually abandoned by 1685, as most of the 4,500 French colonists and their 3,500 slaves had now recongregated into three mainland enclaves, each with its own agricultural zone: Léogâne/Petit-Goâve, Cap-François, and Port-de-Paix. Growth was so promising that the first royal army and naval companies were assigned to Saint-Domingue three years later. But when Louis XIV became embroiled in hostilities against Spain, Britain, and other members of the League of Augsburg in April 1689 (a conflict known to English America as King

William's War), the few hundred residents of Cap-François found themselves in an exposed frontline position and endured two devastating attacks.

The first occurred after the island's governor, Pierre-Paul Tarin de Cussy, led a cross-border incursion into Spanish territory in the summer of 1690, burning the town of Santiago de los Caballeros. The Spaniards retaliated by rallying 2,600 militiamen at their capital of Santo Domingo, then sailing around the eastern tip of the island that same December aboard a half-dozen warships under Adm. Jacinto Lope Gijón; another 700 Spanish cavalrymen advanced overland under Gov. Francisco de Segura Sandoval y Castilla to resecure Santiago de los Caballeros. The two contingents then rendezvoused near Manzanillo Bay on 14 January 1691 to press westward against Cap-François.

When news of this invasion reached de Cussy, he offered battle at Savane de la Limonade (Lemonade Plain), 7 miles southeast of Cap-François, without awaiting reinforcements from the other French settlements, despite being outnumbered by 3,000 men to his 1,000. Underestimating the Spaniards' resolve, the defenders relied upon their superior musketry, only to be crushed in an hour-and-a-half clash on the morning of 21 January 1691 when the attackers suddenly sprang 300 hidden lancers from the tall grass as the French companies were reloading, producing a close-quarters melee in which de Cussy and more than 400 of his followers were slain, compared with only 47 Spanish dead and 130 wounded. The Spaniards then rampaged unchecked through Cap-François and its district the next day, burning everything of value, before making off with 130 slaves and two prize ships. When the royal naval officer Jean-Baptiste Ducasse came ashore two weeks later, he found de Cussy's corpse and hundreds others still rotting upon the battlefield, most survivors having fled Cap-François.

After reporting to Paris, Ducasse returned to Port-de-Paix in August 1691 with two warships and a corvette, anchoring until he received confirmation from the king on 1 October to act as Saint-Domingue's new French governor. He then concentrated island militia into Cap-François, sufficiently restoring its citizenry's morale to reassume occupancy by February 1692 and start rebuilding a few edifices. However, a second invasion occurred when an English expedition under Commo. Robert Wilmot and Col. Luke Lillingston combined with another large Spanish force out of Santo Domingo to pierce the border again on 24 May 1695. This time, Cap-François's 300 defenders under the *flibustier* chieftain Laurens de Graaf merely moved aside, allowing their partially reconstructed town to be razed five days later by landing parties from four enemy warships, after which the allied army forged westward and massacred Port-de-Paix's garrison on 15 July before dissolving their association.

As a result of these twin disasters, Léogâne—being more distant and thus less vulnerable to attack—was confirmed as de facto French capital three years later, when a *subdelegation*

(subsidiary bureau) of the West Indian *Intendance* (the Crown office charged with civilian administration) was transferred across from Martinique. Saint-Domingue's northern establishments were nevertheless reoccupied because of their great economic potential, Cap-François being resurrected and its residents bolstered by a visit early in March 1697 by the fleet of Adm. Bernard-Jean-Louis de Saint-Jean, Baron de Pointis, whose fourteen ships and 4,000 men had come out from France to mount the last offensive of the war against Cartagena (Colombia). Greater relief was provided when the Treaty of Rijswyck was signed in September of that same year, acknowledging French sovereignty over the western third of the island, thus diminishing the threat of future Spanish incursions.

Tobacco farms multiplied in the interior and Cap-François's trade resurged once peace was restored, its small urban core beginning to radiate out from its original wharf (where D'Estaing's Fountain would later be erected), a growth that was channeled into a grid pattern by royal surveyors. Although no longer enjoying the status of island capital, Cap-François nonetheless had a distinct geographic advantage over Léogâne, as it lay so far to windward as to receive the first visits by any arriving merchantmen, so that it quickly outstripped its rival in economic development. Cap-François's Hôpital de la Charité (Charity Hospital, operated by the Order of Saint Jean-de-Dieu, better known as the Brothers of Charity) opened as early as 1698, and not even a slave revolt two years later and an earthquake in 1701 could check the town's evolution; it was judged sufficiently prosperous to be granted its own *Conseil Supérieur* (high court) that same year and became legally reconstituted into a city in 1711.

Colonial Splendor (1711–1791)

Cap-François suffered another earthquake in 1713, but it emerged from this event and the War of the Spanish Succession otherwise unscathed. The following year the island's prestige was enhanced when Saint-Domingue was granted its own independent office of Governor-General for the French Leeward Islands, ending its subordination to the governor-generals of the Windward Islands at Martinique. A resident intendant was also added in 1719, both officials being headquartered at Petit-Goâve, while the third-ranking *Ordonnateur* (naval commissioner) came to be installed at Cap-François because of its superior transoceanic contacts. Life in the northern port city blossomed so significantly that a printer from Dijon named Joseph Payet was licensed to establish a press by 1724 (soon suspended for publishing pornographic materials). The municipality continued to expand despite occasional setbacks, such as the severe drought of 1726, floods in 1732, and another earthquake two years later.

An accidental fire on the night of 20–21 September 1734 had a much more profound impact, however, as half of the wooden structures of Cap-François were consumed, leading

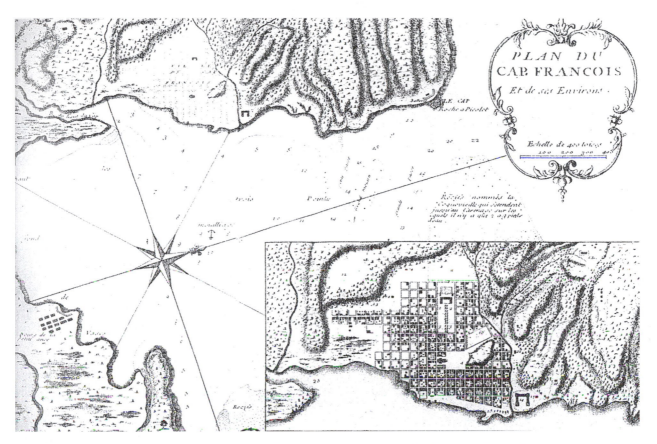

Map of the harbor of Cap-François as engraved by d'Anville, plus an insert showing its urban layout, ca. 1728. Half this city's structures, which were mostly built of wood, were to burn to the ground six years afterward. (Charlevoix, *Histoire de l'Isle Espagnole ou S. Domingue*)

municipal authorities to decree that all future edifices be made of stone. The city's appearance altered dramatically as a result, especially as these sturdy new structures were soon being whitewashed to deflect the sun's heat. A water conduit was also completed the next year to help fight fires and to meet other civic needs, the flow being brought down from the northern foothills and discharged into a 20-foot stone fountain at the center of the reconstructed Place d'Armes (the Main Square; it was lined by elms and boasted a painted fence, turnstiles, and gravel walkways). A few other urban amenities were implemented, and the resurrected city even began achieving a certain fame abroad, while referred to throughout the island simply as "Le Cap." Its citizens successfully weathered another drought in 1743, a pair of earthquakes on 18 and 21 November 1751, plus more droughts in 1754 and 1757.

When the French and Indian War erupted against England, the port's newfound prominence caused it to be blockaded by Royal Navy squadrons operating in the Caribbean. On 21 October 1757, Commo. Guy-François de Coëtnempren, Comte de Kersaint, sortied with his 70-gun flagship *Intrépide* and the *Sceptre,* the 64-gun *Opiniâtre,* the 50-gun *Greenwich,* the 44-gun *Outarde,* as well as the 32-gun frigates *Sauvage* and *Licorne* to chase away a trio of British warships, so that a large

merchant convoy might emerge and sail for France. Despite their inferior numbers, the 60-gun English men-of-war *Augusta* of Commo. Arthur Forrest, *Dreadnought* of Capt. Maurice Suckling, and *Edinburgh* of Capt. William Langdon put up a stout fight before retiring two and a half hours later, so that the wounded Kersaint could bring out his charges.

Concerned about possibly being targeted for a British invasion, the authorities erected huge *casernes* (barracks) in the foothills west of Cap-Français on property recently expropriated from the Jesuits and that eventually evolved into a vast compound capable of housing 1,300 troops, as well as offices for every senior Crown official on the island. But although Martinique was beset by a British expedition in 1759 and completely overrun three years later, Saint-Domingue was spared any enemy landings; its worst losses occurred when another departing convoy was decimated by a trio of Royal Navy blockaders in October 1760. During the closing phase of the war, Rear Adm. Charles, Comte de Blénac Courbon, arrived on 17 March 1762 with his 80-gun flagship *Duc de Bourgogne;* the 74-gun *Hector, Diadème,* and *Défenseur;* the 64-gun *Protée, Dragon,* and *Brillant;* the 32-gun frigates *Diligente* and *Zéphyre;* and the 26-gun frigates *Opale* and *Calypse. Dragon* struck a reef while entering the Cap-Français anchorage and went down with 50 hands, but the vessels otherwise safely disgorged 3,000 troops of the Juercy, Foix, and Boulognois regiments as reinforcements. De Blénac then departed on 7 September, ferrying 600 Spanish troops across to Santiago de Cuba, before rendezvousing with a homeward-bound French convoy out of the Bight of Léogâne.

Hostilities ceased shortly thereafter and—given France's loss of India, Canada, and Louisiana by the terms of the peace treaty—Saint-Domingue now remained as the Crown's principal overseas colony; it therefore received exceptional stimulus over the next few decades. This dramatic escalation in the island's fortunes came to be reflected at Cap-Français, its largest city: for example, the printer Antoine Marie of Nantes reestablished a press late in 1763 and issued the port's first weekly newspaper—the *Affiches Américaines* ("American Bulletins")—by that following February. A private theater called the Comédie du Cap, which had operated in Rue Vaudreuil since 1740, also was transformed into a public institution as of 1764, while a magnificent new 1,500-seat theater was completed within the next two years in the very heart of the city at Place de Montarcher; it proved so popular that its company of twelve male and eight female actors staged or hosted some 2,000 operatic, musical, or theatrical performances every year.

The island economy was furthermore bolstered when 100,000 coffee trees were imported in 1765 to be planted on inland slopes, representing a wholesale commitment by the Crown to this valuable new cash crop. The colony's old small and medium-size farms were soon supplanted by huge new plantations designed to harvest sugar, indigo, cotton, and coffee in commercial quantities, and to achieve such an escalation, tens of thousands of slaves were imported from Africa.

The scope of overseas trade also broadened two years later when foreign imports were allowed for the first time through Cape Saint Nicholas Mole, while virtually every major port in France was allowed to trade directly with Saint-Domingue as of 1771, vastly augmenting the flow of goods through Cap-Français.

A heavy earthquake rattled the city on 3 June 1770, leveling many structures—including its cathedral, which was replaced the following year by a solid, two-story edifice made of Nantes stone; it cost 1.8 million colonial livres and was specially designed to resist such phenomena. Cap-Français was also infected with smallpox when a slave ship sank in its roadstead in 1772, the survivors swimming ashore to start an epidemic that claimed 1,200 lives. The city nonetheless rebounded, its population of 6,353 inhabitants in 1771 tripling within the next seventeen years. Its first paved streets date from 1776, as well as its first house numbers and street signs, while a grand new Vauxhall tea-house opened in the Carénage neighborhood to its north, where fashionable balls and other mass entertainments could be held.

Maritime traffic multiplied so rapidly that a hundred ships might be found at anchor at any given time, red flags marking the harbor entrance and a pilot-boat greeting arrivals, as well as escorting masters before the Crown authorities. Cargoes were disgorged into twenty-seven private warehouses lining the harbor front's Quai Saint-Louis, while naval dockyards had also been erected along the Quai d'Argout and at the northern Carénage; there furthermore existed several other wharves, a lighthouse, and numerous artillery batteries.

The city played a significant strategic role when France allied itself with the Thirteen American Colonies in August

Panoramic view of Cap-Français, looking southeastward across the city from "behind the prison" on its northern fringe; etching engraved by Nicolas Ponce from an original drawing by Ferdinand de la Brunière and included in Médéric-Louis-Élie Moreau de Saint-Méry's *Recueil de vues des lieux principaux de la colonie françoise de Saint-Domingue,* published in Paris in 1791. (National Maritime Museum, Greenwich)

1778, aiding their struggle to win freedom from England. Island officials were transferred across from Port-au-Prince into Cap-Français for the duration of those hostilities, helping it serve as a major base for French battle fleets operating in the West Indies. Vice Adm. Charles-Henri, Comte d'Estaing, arrived with a large convoy on 31 July 1779, pausing sixteen days before continuing north to reinforce the American rebels; his subordinate, Commo. Toussaint Guillaume Picquet de la Motte (better known as the Comte de Lamotte Picquet), returned the next spring with four warships, chasing away Commo. Sir William Cornwallis's trio of British blockaders; Vice Adm. Luc Urbain du Bouexic, Comte de Guichen, visited and left behind ten warships under Commo. François Aymar, Baron de Monteil, when he departed to escort a Spanish convoy on 16 August 1780; and Adm. François-Joseph Paul, Comte de Grasse Tilly, arrived with a 200-ship convoy on 8 July 1781 and remained less than a month before departing with 3,200 troops and a small siege train to reinforce the Franco-American armies in North America.

During Grasse Tilly's visit, the 74-gun *Intrépide* caught fire and exploded, killing or injuring forty-two crewmen and damaging Cap-Français's wharves; water conduits were consequently extended down to a new seaside D'Estaing Fountain that same year to provide ready access for firefighting purposes as well as to enable boat crews to resupply more easily, without having to manhandle heavy casks through the city streets. As many as 600 ships could be found at anchor during this conflict, while the Hôpital de la Charité was also expanded enormously, its wards being augmented to tend to 1,000 patients. Eventually, though, the main French battle fleet in the West Indies was defeated by Adm. Sir George Rodney at the Battle of the Saintes on 12 April 1782, its survivors limping into Cap-Français thirteen days later to regroup under the wounded Commo. Louis-Philippe de Rigaud, Marquis de Vaudreuil, before departing on 4 July to escort a Spanish contingent as far as Havana and then steer north up the Atlantic seaboard.

Once peace was restored in March 1783, Cap-Français experienced yet another economic upsurge when it was sanctioned to receive foreign merchantmen as of August 1784, while its importation of African slaves mushroomed so appreciably that by the end of that same decade there were approximately 560,000 inhabitants crowded onto the island, nearly 90 percent of whom were blacks toiling among 7,800 plantations, compared to only 32,000 whites, plus 28,000 mulatto or black freemen (called *affranchis,* or "enfranchised"). Crown officials had once more resumed their peacetime offices at Port-au-Prince, and all island courts were merged into a single *Conseil Supérieur* (high court) at the capital in 1787; yet when a census was taken two years later, Cap-Français still remained the largest, busiest, and wealthiest city on Saint-Domingue, its population standing at 18,850 residents—double the number for Port-au-Prince. A Société Royale des Sciences et des Arts (Royal Society of Sciences and Arts) was also formed in the northern port city in 1789, and a contemporary observer noted: "Le Cap sets the tone; it is the Paris of our island."

Saint-Domingue was now recognized as the richest commercial colony in the world, exporting roughly half the sugar and coffee consumed in Europe while netting more profits than all of Spanish America combined. It was estimated that one person in eight in France derived a living from this island traffic, the bulk of which—approximately 1,200 annual vessels—put into Cap-Français. As a result, the city was at the peak of its colonial splendor, consisting of fifty-six streets crisscrossed in a grid pattern and encompassing 260 blocks that contained nearly 1,400 houses (only 150 of which were made of wood). Some 300 edifices stood two stories high, and there were a few of triple stories; fashionable white neighborhoods clustered around its main square, with luxury boutiques lining the Rue du Gouvernement (Government Street). Water was distributed through nine fountains dotted around the city, conveyed via aqueducts or underground pipes imported from France.

Free blacks lived in the more crowded southwestern quadrant, known as Petite-Guinée (Little Guinea); on market Sundays, as many as 15,000 slaves congregated there to buy and sell produce in its Place de Clugny, where public executions were also held. The cemetery and abattoir were also located on the south side, the latter being an open-air shed measuring 150 by 30 feet in which on average twenty-two cattle, ten sheep, twenty-five goats, and thirty pigs were killed daily. *La fossette* (the dump) furthermore lay along the city's southern fringe, although some refuse and sewage were discharged into a ravine near the prison to its north, to be carried out to sea upon the tide.

Devastation (1791–1803)

The revolutionary changes unleashed when a mob stormed the Bastille in Paris on 14 July 1789 eventually dissolved this island society, in the process inflicting great suffering upon Cap-Français. Initially, wealthy white *grand blancs* tried to uphold the traditional regime that ensured their privileged status, while bourgeois *petit blancs* and Creole *affranchis* embraced certain egalitarian ideals in the hope of personal advancement, while ignoring the plight of almost a half-million slaves scattered throughout the island. Conflicting decrees emanated from the chaotic Estates-General assembly in Paris; then a slave insurrection erupted in the Limbé district outside Cap-Français at dawn on 23 August 1791, prompting the newly installed governor-general, Philibert François Rouxel de Blanchelande, to recall all whites and loyal blacks into the city, which was menaced by 15,000 rebels under their leader "Zamba" Boukman Dutty on 30–31 August.

Too ill-armed to brave its defenses, though, the rebels instead razed 50 miles of surrounding countryside, destroying 200 sugar and 1,200 coffee plantations by mid-September

Panoramic view of Cap-Français's harbor, as seen from the road leading toward Petite-Anse; Ponce etching from an original de la Brunière drawing, for inclusion in Moreau de Saint-Méry's *Recueil de vues,* published in Paris in 1791. (National Maritime Museum, Greenwich)

1791. "From Le Cap," it has been written, "the whole horizon was a wall of fire." Other uprisings ensued around the island, and trade came to a virtual standstill, which the increasingly radical administration in Paris could not alleviate. Cap-Français was assaulted on 22–23 January 1792 by a black rebel army under Georges Biassou, who wished to secure ammunition and supplies. Some semblance of central authority was restored when the twenty-eight-year-old Jacobin commissioner Léger-Félicité Sonthonax arrived from France that same September with 6,000 troops. But although he was welcomed by mulattoes—who had been granted special status by the new government—he made no concessions to either rebellious blacks or disgruntled whites, who were suspected of harboring royalist sympathies. The black insurrection outside Cap-Français therefore persisted, while transatlantic commerce worsened after the Directorate in Paris executed Louis XVI on 21 January 1793 and declared war against England and Spain.

Sonthonax and his fellow commissioner Étienne Polvérel sailed against Port-au-Prince early in April 1793 to put down an anti-Republican mutiny, then hastened back into Cap-Français two months later to suppress a similar conspiracy and to confront a cross-border invasion launched by Gov. Joaquín García Moreno of Santo Domingo in support of the local black rebel leaders Biassou and Jean-François "Papillon" Petecou. Some 1,000 anti-Republican political prisoners being held aboard ships out in Cap-Français's harbor suddenly rose against their captors on 20 June, streaming ashore with 2,000 sailors to seize the city arsenal, compelling Sonthonax and Polvérel to flee the next day. Cap-Français was plunged into anarchy as prisons were thrown open and thousands of slaves

joined in an orgy of destruction. Desperate to regain control, Sonthonax and Polvérel promised freedom and citizenship to any slave willing to fight for the Republican cause, so that a 3,000-man contingent under the maroon leader Pierrot—part of the Hispano-black army encamped in the hills—fought its way into the burning city by 22 June.

Yet when the commissioners returned five days later, black troops were disillusioned to learn that this Republican offer had extended only to combatants, not their families or loved ones; leaders such as Biassou therefore refused to be swayed and instead occupied the charred ruins of Cap-Français along with their Spanish allies in August 1793, pacifying the rebellious North Plain by year's end. A former slave coachman born as François Dominique Toussaint—but now serving as "Brigadier" Toussaint-Louverture—withdrew his 4,000 black soldiers from the Spanish alliance, and a month and a half after a British expedition had seized Port-au-Prince in May 1794, he restored Cap-Français and its district to the French Republican general Étienne Laveaux in exchange for a pledge of total abolition of slavery.

However, although nominally under French control once again, as well as being elevated to de facto island capital and beset by little active campaigning, Cap-Français nonetheless remained isolated by the British naval blockade; also, most of its skilled residents had either perished or fled, and inland plantations could not resume production. The city garrison furthermore fell out among themselves, a mulatto faction arresting Laveaux on 20 March 1796, feeling that he had become too closely aligned with black interests. Toussaint-Louverture marched from Gonaïves at the head of his 10,000-man army to free the French general two days later, being rewarded on

1 April by appointment as "deputy governor" over the Republican-controlled areas of Saint-Domingue. Sonthonax returned from France that same May, only to be deported from Cap-Français in August 1797 by Toussaint-Louverture, who ruled the hapless city alone until a new commissioner—Gen. Thomas Hédouville—arrived on 29 March 1798.

Concerned by Toussaint-Louverture's increasingly entrenched power and rapprochement with the English (who agreed to withdraw from Port-au-Prince shortly thereafter), Hédouville attempted to undermine the black chieftain by favoring his mulatto rivals; however, when the French general went so far as to order the arrest of Toussaint-Louverture's adopted nephew Moïse that same summer, the deputy-governor's brutal subordinate Jean-Jacques Dessalines—nicknamed the "Tiger"—was sent marching against Cap-Français, where a mob drove the commissioner from the island by 22 October 1798. Toussaint-Louverture's independent bent became even more pronounced during France's so-called "Quasi-War" against the United States, as U.S. commerce raiders were welcomed at his northern port city, while French privateers were discouraged.

Late in October 1801, the chieftain suppressed a rebellion by disgruntled black laborers on the North Plain, executing scores of ringleaders (including Moïse). Shortly thereafter, Britain and France agreed to a cessation of hostilities back in Europe, which allowed Paris to move toward reasserting full control over Saint-Domingue. The youthful Gen. Charles Victor Emmanuel Leclerc consequently reached Samaná Bay on 29 January 1802 with a 20,000-man expedition (as well as his wife, Pauline, Napoleon Bonaparte's youngest sister), and four days later materialized before Cap-Français, threatening to storm ashore on 3 February with 5,000 troops. Col. Henry Christophe, commander of its black garrison, requested forty-eight hours to consult with Toussaint-Louverture, which was refused; he therefore put the unhappy city to the torch on 7 February and retired into the interior. Such defiance proved short-lived, though, as French units pressed ashore all around the island, stamping out southern resistance within a week, while most northern leaders requested amnesties by late April or early May.

Leclerc established his headquarters at Cap-Français, although his wife opted to move into a palace just outside of Port-au-Prince with their three-year-old son after yellow fever broke out in the north. Black discontent was reanimated after reports began circulating in late July 1802 that Paris had restored slavery on Guadeloupe, reopened the transatlantic slave trade, and denied persons of color the title of "citizen." The French occupying force on Saint-Domingue, which had dwindled by more than a third because of disease, tried to stifle all aspirations at liberty through gruesome massacres, as well as by treacherously deporting Toussaint-Louverture to France (where he died of pneumonia in the Alpine fortress of Joux). Rebellions nonetheless flared anew, rendering the island unsafe, while yellow fever decimated the French ranks. Leclerc himself succumbed at Cap-Français on the night of 2 November, being succeeded as governor-general by Gen. Donatien Marie Joseph de Vimeur, Vicomte de Rochambeau.

Vainly hoping to hold on in the south, Rochambeau traveled to Port-au-Prince in March 1803, but his campaign was interrupted two months later by news that England had resumed hostilities against France, so that the governor-general—accompanied by many frightened French refugees—returned into Cap-Français by June to confront yet another Royal Navy blockade. The city soon became beleaguered by black land forces as well, desperation driving the 74-gun warships *Duquesne* and *Duguay-Trouin,* as well as the frigate *Guerrière,* to slip out of harbor on the squally Sunday evening of 24 July in a bid to elude Capt. John Loring's British squadron. Colonial rule finally ended when Rochambeau's surviving troops were decisively beaten by black contingents at Vertières outside Cap-Français on 18 November, prompting the French general to surrender to the British blockaders and the city's last white residents to exit in precipitous flight.

Early Independent Era (1804–1810)

Through sheer weight of numbers, the black northern faction had emerged triumphant on the island; their leader, Dessalines, proposed depriving Port-au-Prince of its status as capital, in favor of a grand new city to be constructed in the Artibonite district and named after himself. A new nation was also proclaimed as of 1 January 1804, called Haiti—one of two ancient names that Taino-speaking Arawak natives had used for their realm, signifying "Mountainous Land" (the other term being *Quisqueya,* or "Mother of the Earth"). In order to crush all dissent, the black general thereupon led his army on a pitiless march throughout the fledgling country, massacring surviving whites, plus mulattoes or blacks of suspect loyalty.

This campaign of terror concluded with Dessalines returning into Cap-Français—now renamed *Cap-Haïtien*—and anointing himself Emperor Jacques I on 8 October 1804, while issuing a series of decrees intended to organize his administration. Notwithstanding the port's lost trade, decimated populace, ruined infrastructure, overgrown roads, abandoned plantations, and dispersed former slaves, Dessalines had promised Leclerc that it would be revived, and even incorporated the phrase *Je renais de mes cendres* ("I am reborn from my ashes") into his coat-of-arms. Reconstruction of the shattered city therefore commenced, as well as a colossal project to create a nearby stronghold in case of another sudden invasion. For the latter task, the emperor commissioned the French architect La Ferrière to design a formidable redoubt deep within the jungle, 15 miles south of Cap-Haïtien, atop a 2,600-foot limestone ridge called Mount Bonnêt-à-l'Évêque; from its eminence, lookouts could see for 30 miles on a clear day, as far as Monte Christi.

However, none of these works could be completed before the megalomaniacal emperor was assassinated outside Port-au-Prince at dawn on 17 October 1806, and the young nation was torn apart after mulatto delegates produced a constitution two months later, proffering its presidency—with severely limited powers—to Gen. Henry Christophe, successor in command of the black armies of the north. Rather than accept office under such restrictions, he launched an offensive into the south with 10,000 men, aiming to win full control over the government, but was repelled from the capital by its mulatto leader, Anne-Alexandre Sabès Pétion.

Christophe therefore returned to Cap-Haïtien in January 1807, where a council composed of seven of his generals and two civilians granted him full executive, legislative, administrative, and military powers as president of a new "Republic of the North." Pétion was elected president of a new "Republic of the South" on 9 March, and the country became formally divided, Cap-Haïtien serving as northern capital. Christophe hoped that by transforming his territory into a prosperous state, he might win over the southerners; but when Pétion was re-elected on 9 March 1811, the northern strongman decided on sterner measures.

"Cap-Henry" Interlude (1811–1820)

Two and a half weeks later, Christophe declared himself "King Henry I" and promulgated a new constitution on 4 April 1811

that transformed his northern republic into a hereditary monarchy, complete with an aristocracy composed of four princes, eight dukes, twenty-two counts, thirty-seven barons, and fourteen knights. Amid the many effusions offered up by his leery subjects to mark this occasion, Cap-Haïtien became renamed *Cap-Henry*, the "Royal and Military Orders of Saint-Henry" were created, coins were struck bearing the monarch's likeness, and the strict new "Code Henry" was instituted as of 24 February 1812, controlling virtually every aspect of daily life.

Economic revival being of paramount importance to the black king, work was made compulsory, idleness being punished by his dreaded personal guards, the Dahomeys. In addition to becoming conscripted to resurrect agricultural plantations, thousands of former slaves were also delegated to build nine royal palaces—the ornate Sans-Souci proving to be the king's favorite, erected 10 miles south of Cap-Henry at Milot—and to complete the extremely difficult La Ferrière fortification project initiated by Dessalines. This remarkable citadel was finished by 1817, reputedly at a cost of 20,000 lives. Its 10-foot-thick walls, bristling with 275 cannon, overlooked a 200-foot precipice and boasted numerous internal features that would allow 1,500 troops to withstand a three-year siege.

The northern kingdom's economy had furthermore improved so notably under Henry's despotic rule that 150 foreign merchant vessels called at Cap-Henry that same year. Yet

Aerial view of the overgrown ruins of La Ferrière Citadel, as they appeared, ca. 1940. (Frederic Lewis, *Lands and Peoples*)

The remnants of Sans-Souci Palace outside Cap-Haïten, ca. 1925. (Niles, *Black Haiti*)

despite these and many other accomplishments—such as rebuilding Cap-Henry's hospital and barracks and the repaving of its streets—the monarch naturally became increasingly hated. On 15 August 1820, while attending Assumption Day Mass in the small church at La Limonade, he collapsed from a massive stroke. While vainly attempting to recuperate from paralysis in Sans-Souci Palace, his enemies began defecting to the party of Jean-Pierre Boyer, newly elected president of the Republic of the South. Advised to abdicate in favor of Crown Prince Victor, Henry refused; but eventually he sent his queen, Marie-Louise, plus the princesses Améthyste and Athénaïse, aboard a British warship commanded by Admiral Sir Home Popham before committing suicide by firing a golden bullet through his heart on 8 October. The next day, rioters killed Prince Victor and began tearing away all vestiges of Henry's despotic rule, while his capital resumed its former name of Cap-Haïtien.

Declining Fortunes (1821–1887)
Upon visiting the northern port city shortly thereafter, Boyer was acclaimed president of a reunited Haiti, then early in

1822 called upon the neighboring Dominicans to proclaim their independence from Spain as well, marching into Santo Domingo at the head of a large army by 9 February to bring the entire island under his rule. The quarter century of Boyer's reign helped cement Port-au-Prince's status as Haiti's capital, although Cap-Haïtien clung to some pretensions of power, despite the Caribbean archipelago's general descent into poverty and backwardness.

A heavy earthquake caused extensive damage to the city's ancient stone buildings on 7 May 1842; the next January, though, Boyer was driven into exile, and the accumulated resentment felt by poor black peasants against the callousness of mulatto rule afforded Cap-Haïtien a brief return to prominence: when the mulatto president Charles "Rivière" Hérard, Sr., was driven from office by a popular insurrection and the Spanish part of the island seceded from Haitian domination in February 1844, the octogenarian Philippe Guerrier—formerly Duc de l'Avancé in Henry's black northern monarchy—was acclaimed as a compromise president, although he died shortly thereafter. Louis Pierrault—another older, illiterate, black northern general—succeeded to office on 16 April 1845, and so disliked and distrusted the mulatto elite at Port-au-Prince that he rode back to Cap-Haïtien a month later, ordering that Haiti's national government be transferred there as of 1 November. But before any such move could be implemented, Pierrault was deposed by a mutiny, and Port-au-Prince was grudgingly restored to its status of capital in March 1846.

Haiti's economic malaise improved modestly after Fabre-Nicolas Geffard, Duc de Tabara and chief-of-staff for the Emperor Faustin Soulouque, deposed that self-proclaimed despot in January 1859 and inaugurated a relatively enlightened administration. Even relations with the Holy See were patched up by March 1860, permitting the Bishop of Lervia to visit Cap-Haïtien and establish a suffragan see a year and a half later. Because of its proximity to the United States, the impoverished city also benefited by serving as a neutral port-of-call during the American Civil War, receiving both Confederate blockade-runners and Federal navy ships. Yet Geffard's regime was powerless to alleviate the commercial slump that ensued once the war concluded, and so he was driven from office by mid-March 1867.

Cap-Haïtien enjoyed another brief resurgence when discontent among rural black peasants swept the army of northern strongman Gen. Sylvain Salnave into Port-au-Prince, to be acclaimed "Protector of the Republic" by a frenzied mob on 3 May 1867. The mulatto-dominated Constituent Assembly invested him with provisional powers three days later, then began deliberating his permanent installation; tired of waiting, Salnave sent his troops on 14 June to frighten the legislators into confirming him for a four-year term. When a motion was subsequently introduced on 11 October to inquire into his detention of Gen. Léon Montas at Cap-Haïtien, a throng burst into the legislature three days later and chased out the delegates.

Although Salnave could crush political opposition in the national capital, he fared less well against a northeastern rebellion that erupted when his enemies raised a force of *caco* guerrillas (originally a Spanish nickname for renegade slaves) and struck from the dense border jungles outside Cap-Haïtien. Despite personally assuming command over counterinsurgency operations, Salnave failed to stamp out the revolt, eventually becoming besieged within Port-au-Prince. His isolated garrisons fell one by one, Gonaïves capitulating by the end of August 1869, followed by Port-de-Paix on 24 October, Jacmel on 4 November, and Cap-Haïtien on 14 November, leading to his fall from power a month later.

A brief interlude of peace ensued under the mulatto presidents Nissage Saget and Michel Domingue, the latter launching a nationwide modernization program under his ambitious vice president and nephew, Septimus "Vava" Rameau. Msgr. Constant-Mathurin Hillion, who was invested as Cap-Haïtien's first Catholic bishop on 24 May 1874, supplemented Rameau's governmental efforts by initiating the reconstruction of the port city's ruined French colonial church to serve as his cathedral, as well as by erecting a presbytery and a pair of schools. Unfortunately, though, fiscal problems soon crippled the national program, after which a smallpox epidemic reached Cap-Haïtien aboard a boat from Monte Christi in August 1881, claiming thousands of victims over the next six months.

Opposition Springboard (1888–1914)

Cap-Haïtien unwittingly entered a new phase of national prominence when its garrison under Gen. Séïde Thélémaque rose on 5 August 1888 in support of a broad revolt spearheaded by the black former president Boisrond Canal, marching uncontested into Port-au-Prince eighteen days later—only to be scattered and Thélémaque killed by a surprise counterattack by the capital's garrison under Gen. Anselme Prophète on the night of 28–29 September. Feeling once more betrayed and resentful against the decades of secondary status under mulatto politicians, Cap-Haïtien formally seceded from the government, proclaiming its own separate République Septentrionale (Northern Republic) on 7 October, to be defended by a newly raised army under Gen. Louis Mondestin Florvil Hyppolite.

Eight days later, the National Assembly in Port-au-Prince elected Sen. François-Denis Légitime as southern "chief of state," civil war erupting when General Prophète penetrated into the north with his army on 9 December 1888. His campaign soon bogged down, though, and Hyppolite was eventually able to counterattack into the south by early August 1889, driving his opponents into exile and claiming the presidency of a reunited Haiti. Cap-Haïtien benefited from this victory by the black northern faction, as well as from the rise of coffee prices on international markets, which helped to buoy its exports and secure foreign loans.

Ironically, though, Port-au-Prince profited even more and its populace doubled in size under the direction of such able northern administrators as Etienne Mathon—who was appointed as the capital's mayor —and who proved more comfortable than southern officials in dealing with foreign contractors, having ample experience because of Cap-Haïtien's frequent seaborne contacts. In contrast, the northern city's growth was constrained by its surrounding hills and dispersed hinterland farms, while Port-au-Prince soon expanded beyond its old boundaries and vastly outstripped its rival in population and economic activity.

Hyppolite died of natural causes in March 1896, and malfeasance then paralyzed the government. Another succession struggle in 1902 saw Cap-Haïtien's elderly garrison commander, Nord Alexis, opposed by Anténor Firmin for the district seat in the National Legislature. Firmin was forced to flee to Gonaïves aboard the dispatch vessel *Crête-à-Pierrot* after his house was ransacked by a mob; then—after gathering adherents and attempting to march back against Le Cap—he was defeated by Alexis, who led his 7,000-man army directly into Port-au-Prince by 14 December 1902 to claim the presidency. Financial woes ended his regime six years later, and another *caco* insurrection in the northeast was spearheaded in February 1911 by Jean-Jacques Dessalines Michel Cincinnatus Leconte, who marched into the capital by 6 August. Yet another northern *caco* uprising drove the rich Port-au-Prince lawyer Michel Oreste from office at the end of January 1914, Gen. Charles Oreste Zamor entering the capital with his army on the evening of 7 February to be acclaimed president the next day. He too resigned, on 28 October, making way for the elderly *caco* leader Davilmar Théodore's victorious army eleven days later.

Concerned by this unstable cycle of regime changes—at a time when World War I had just exploded in Europe—U.S. Secretary of State William Jennings Bryan dispatched the gunboat *Machias* into Port-au-Prince on 17 December 1914 to seize Haiti's gold reserves and convey them to New York for safekeeping. This act so weakened Théodore's prestige that Gen. Vibrun Guillaume Sam mounted yet another revolt at Cap-Haïtien on 15 January 1915, being joined a few days later by 1,000 *caco* guerrillas under "General" Metellus. U.S. Rear Adm. William Caperton visited this northern port city eight days later, but merely to shadow Sam's progression southward "to prevent excesses." Théodore fled Port-au-Prince by 22 February, allowing Sam to enter uncontested and be acclaimed Haiti's new ruler three days later.

A rival leader, Dr. Rosalvo Bobo, thereupon launched still another revolt in the north that same May 1915, his revolutionaries laying such close siege to Cap-Haïtien that the French cruiser *Descartes* disembarked a landing party to prevent any massacre of its foreign residents. The cruiser USS *Washington* and armed yacht *Eagle* also dropped anchor in its harbor by 1 July to protect American interests.

U.S. Occupation (1915–1934)

Sam was suddenly killed amid a bloody insurrection in the capital on 27 July 1915, which decided Washington to intervene directly. Hundreds of marines were disembarked at Port-au-Prince, and *Eagle* and the gunboat *Nashville* ended Cap-Haïtien's siege in early August by inviting the rebel leader Bobo aboard the U.S. transport *Jason* to be conveyed into the capital. Expecting to arrive as president, Bobo was instead defeated by the U.S.-backed candidate Philippe Sudre Dartiguenave in a hastily arranged election on 12 August, so that he departed into exile while Dartiguenave became Haiti's puppet figurehead.

Four days later a sizable marine garrison was landed at Cap-Haïtien, and U.S. officials assumed permanent administrative duties over the city's 25,000 residents. A ragtag army of *caco* rebels nonetheless continued to resist in the surrounding mountains, so that Col. Eli Cole initiated an antiguerrilla sweep by pushing 4 miles inland from Cap-Haïtien with 130 marines on 27 September 1915, fighting his way into Haut-du-Cap. The next day, Quartier-Morin, 5 miles farther east along the coast, was also occupied; then the senior marine commandant for all of Haiti—Col. Littleton W. T. "Tony" Waller—sailed east from Cap-Haïtien with another marine company

aboard *Nashville* on 4 October, disembarking to seize Fort Liberté and the border town of Ouanaminthe.

A protracted jungle campaign simmered over the next four years, until the former *caco* Jean-Baptiste Conzé was bribed to lead a small party of marines into the principal rebel encampment of Charlemagne Masséna Péralte near Grande Rivière on the night of 30–31 October 1919, shooting that charismatic leader. After Péralte's chief lieutenant, Benoît Brataville, was also surprised and killed by a marine patrol near Las Cahobas on 18 May 1920, local resistance effectively ended. Most residents of Cap-Haïtien had long since resigned themselves to the U.S. occupation, their opposition instead coalescing peacefully around patriot philosophers such as the Reverend Descartes Albert, who founded the Ligue du Bien Public (League for the Public Good) to record complaints against U.S. abuses.

Municipal services had been upgraded by the American occupiers, and agricultural exports increased during this interlude of imposed stability. Urban expansion was hampered by a swamp south of the city, as well as the precipitous hills to its north and west. The only material damages sustained occurred when a heavy hurricane swept through Cap-Haïtien in 1928. Residents were nonetheless relieved when the newly elected

Modern street scene in Cap-Haitien; note the narrow, eighteenth-century grid pattern. (Franz-Marc Frei/Corbis)

U.S. president Franklin D. Roosevelt, during a state visit to meet with Haitian president Sténio Vincent, announced at a banquet in the city's Union Club on 5 July 1934 that the marines would be withdrawn the following month, so that nineteen years of occupation ended when the 2nd Marine Regiment was recalled on 15 August and full autonomy was restored to the island.

Modern Era (1935–Present)

The city emerged from this ordeal more healthful and prosperous, yet economically dependent upon exports of produce to the United States and France—the latter declining notably because of naval dangers occasioned during World War II (1939–1945). Soaring coffee prices on foreign exchanges produced a postwar revival and favorable balance of trade, yet Cap-Haïtien found itself reduced to a secondary role in Haitian politics. According to the census of August 1950, its populace stood at a mere 24,229 residents—less than one-fifth the capital's numbers—with another 510,000 people scattered throughout its heavily rural *département* (although many country dwellers had apparently been missed by the enumerators). Its street pattern remained largely unchanged from colonial days, many buildings still facing each other at 20- to 30-foot distances, not including their overhanging bal-

conies. Most edifices were still built of masonry, although many wooden-frame constructions had also begun to spring up, the vast majority of residents being crowded into communal quarters with little access to running water or sewers.

Cap-Haïtien lagged even further behind during the subsequent population explosion and mass migrations from depressed rural areas into urban concentrations, for although the number of its inhabitants almost doubled to 45,688 people by 1971, the capital's total now approached half a million. Cap-Haïtien's harbor, despite docks upgraded to receive ships drawing as much as 24 feet of water, handled only about one-ninth of the island's trade. Local exports consisted chiefly of bananas, pineapples, sugarcane, coffee, cacao, and sisal (rope fiber). Some light industrial development occurred within the city limits; a stock-feeding station was erected on its boundaries, and a modest tourist trade developed—drawn by such nearby historic monuments as Sans-Souci Palace, La Citadelle Laferrière, and the nearly ruined palace briefly occupied by Napoleon's sister Pauline.

Cap-Haïtien's population was measured at 75,519 inhabitants by 1986, and in a throwback to its old role of alternative capital, it was used eight years later to receive President Jean-Bertrand Aristide, who visited Cap-Haïtien on 30 September

Marines of the 2nd LAR Battalion guarding the parade route of President Jean-Bertrand Aristide during his visit to Cap-Haïtien prior to being restored into office, 30 September 1994. Note the concrete edifices. (U.S. Department of Defense Visual Information Center)

Marines lining the route of Pres. Aristide during his brief visit to Cap-Haïtien, 30 September 1994. (U.S. Department of Defense Visual Information Center)

1994, prior to being restored into office. Also, its former police chief Guy Philippe orchestrated a coup attempt on 17 December 2001 when he sent two dozen gunmen in a failed assault against the Presidential Palace at Port-au-Prince.

For further reading materials on the history of Cap-Haïtien or Haiti, please consult the Select Bibliography at the end of this volume; additional sources on Caribbean urban history can be found under "Regional Studies and Journals," as well as under "General Works on the French in the Americas."

Port-au-Prince

City that, notwithstanding its belated foundation and violent history, has emerged as this republic's dominant metropolis.

Antecedents (1502–1748)

On his second penetration into the Antilles, Christopher Columbus arrived in late 1493 with 1,500 Spanish settlers to establish an outpost on the northwestern coast of this island, assuming that it would serve as his trading base with Asia, which he erroneously believed to lie nearby. However, after it had become evident that the Far East was not close by, the outpost's residents—disillusioned by their miserable living conditions—dispersed to carve out individual coastal holdings during the early 1500s.

One such group resettled west of Lake Xaragua (modern Etang Saumâtre) and founded a short-lived hamlet called Santa María de la Vera Paz (Saint Mary of the True Peace); a few years later, a new village dubbed Santa María del Puerto (Saint Mary of the Port) was also erected on the headland of La Yaguana—a Spanish rendering of its original Arawak name—which managed to eke out a humble existence based upon animal husbandry and agriculture, despite being torched by French rovers in 1543.

Almost half a century later, during Spain's war against Elizabethan England, La Yaguana was surprised two hours before sunrise on 27 May 1592 by a 110-man boat party from Christopher Newport's flagship *Golden Dragon* and three other privateer vessels, who torched its 150 buildings before sailing away. A still more drastic event was to occur once peace was restored in 1603, as King Philip III—vexed by the coastal residents' pernicious trade with foreign smugglers—ordered Santo Domingo's governor, Antonio Osorio, to sweep along Hispaniola's northern and western shorelines with a few hundred soldiers in the summer of 1605, torching every town and compelling all inhabitants to relocate to the southern coast, under direct Crown supervision.

Ironically, this Draconian measure only encouraged more foreign incursions, as the abandoned properties and livestock tempted seaborne interlopers into permanent occupation. Starting from a fortified offshore stronghold on Tortuga Island, a detachment of *boucaniers* (buccaneers—that is, cattle-hunters who cured their meat in *boucans,* or "smoke-houses") transferred ashore at Trou-Bordet around 1650, erecting a hilltop strong-house dubbed l'Hôpital (The Hospital) on the southern side of Cul-de-Sac Bay (near modern Turgeau Heights). Nine years later, an officer named Jérémie Deschamps de Moussac et du Rausset arrived at Tortuga Island with authorization from both Paris and London to act as its private "governor," and soon afterward founded yet another new mainland settlement—Petit-Goâve—to take advantage of its broad and fertile surrounding plains.

By 1663 a second hamlet, dubbed Léogâne (the French rendering of La Yaguana), had also been established nearby, by another thirty migrants; then, in June 1665, one of Léogâne's estate-holders—Bertrand d'Ogeron, Sieur de la Bouère, a retired marine regiment captain and shareholder in an earlier colonizing company—was appointed governor over the entire French half of the island by the newly created Compagnie des Indes Occidentales (Company of the West Indies) in Paris, which was backed by the chief royal minister Jean-Baptiste

Panoramic view of Port-au-Prince's waterfront, ca. 1890. (Jacques Taupiac, Album)

Colbert. Despite considerable resentment on Tortuga against this corporation's trade monopoly, its *boucaniers* even mutinying against d'Ogeron in the spring of 1670, his eleven-year tenure nonetheless proved remarkably successful; the colony flourished as numerous *engagés* (indentured laborers) were brought out from France to clear and work Saint-Domingue's mainland. By the time d'Ogeron resumed his private life at Léogâne in 1674, the total French population had multiplied from 700 or 800 residents to roughly 5,000.

Although Cap-François (modern Cap-Haïtien) soon emerged as the busiest and largest town, Léogâne and Petit-Goâve shared the title of administrative capital because they were farther removed from seaborne raiders and better sheltered from hurricanes behind the island's central mountain range. Léogâne's inhabitants had initially been concentrated at a spot called l'Ester (The Inlet), with a few others living some miles away at Petite-Rivière (Little River); both communities—plus a few lesser ones scattered in between—composed the "parish of Léogâne" and were ministered to by the Dominican Order.

However, their geographic dispersal meant that they could never be coalesced into a defensible whole, so that Petit-Goâve was fortified to act as a single stronghold during times of war—most especially after the harrowing Anglo-Spanish descent against the island's northern coastline in the spring of 1695. Still, Petit-Goâve did not prove entirely satisfactory as a capital, as it was too far west from the rich farmlands on Cul-de-Sac Plain for easy overland access, while furthermore blighted by an insalubrious reputation.

In 1714, Saint-Domingue was granted its own independent office of Governor-General for the French Leeward Islands, thus ending its previous subordination to the governor-generals of the French Windward Islands at Martinique, while the role of its intendant (a Crown official charged with civil administration) was also separated from that of Martinique five years later. Such developments required an expanded Crown presence on Saint-Domingue, which could not be installed within the limited confines of either Léogâne or Petit-Goâve, so that the notion of creating an entirely new capital was raised as early as 1723: specifically, an anchorage east of Léogâne known as the Port-du-Prince (Port of the *Prince*) was suggested, its name—soon transposed into Port-au-Prince—recalling an incident from the recent war with Britain in which the 30-gun royal transport *Prince de Frise* of Lieutenant de Saint-André had sought sanctuary from English pursuers in 1706 by anchoring and erecting batteries on its small offshore isles.

Nevertheless, it would not be until Charles Brunier, Marquis de Larnage, arrived as governor-general in November 1737 that such a project was actively implemented. Concerned by escalating Anglo-Spanish frictions in the New World, which threatened to plunge the entire Caribbean into a general conflict and compromise French commercial interests, Larnage inspected the Port-au-Prince shoreline with his military engineer de La Lance and—impressed by its healthful surroundings, defensible terrain, and proximity to the large plantations of Cul-de-Sac Plain—proposed constructing a city centered around the abandoned buccaneer stronghold of l'Hôpital atop Fortin Hill (modern Bel-Air). Before work could be authorized from Paris, however, the War of Jenkins's Ear erupted between Britain and Spain in the autumn of 1739, and a year later the

View westward across the Bord-de-Mer or "Seashore" waterfront district, ca. 1890. (Jacques Taupiac, *Album*)

French Crown dispatched a huge fleet into the Antilles to attack English outposts in support of their Spanish cousins—albeit without any formal declaration of war against London.

This expedition's vanguard reached Port-Saint-Louis (modern Les Cayes in southwestern Haiti) on 7 November 1740 under Vice Adm. Antoine François de Pardaillan de Gondrin, Marquis d'Antin, who proposed a joint operation with regional Spanish forces. However, disease quickly decimated d'Antin's crews, so that by the time his last squadron joined on 8 January 1741, his strength was considerably depleted. Saint-Domingue was then alarmed to learn ten days later that a British counterexpedition of two dozen warships under Rear Adm. Sir Chaloner Ogle and 100 transports bearing 8,000 redcoats under Brig. Thomas Wentworth was straggling past Cape Tiburón to reinforce Jamaica. Its Royal Navy escorts even exchanged shots with four French men-of-war hastening to rejoin d'Antin at Port-Saint-Louis after visiting Petit-Goâve, so that—disheartened by the arrival of this enormous British reinforcement and his own fleet's debilitation—the French admiral decided to quit the Antilles without attempting any hostilities, sailing for France on 7 February while leaving seven ships-of-the-line behind at Petit-Goâve under Commo. Jacques, Comte de Roquefeuil.

Although no fighting had yet erupted, an outbreak still seemed imminent, so that Larnage continued to fortify Saint-Domingue's ports—and amid these labors, he laid the groundwork for Port-au-Prince's foundation by ordering his military engineer Meynier and private contractor Pierre Morel to erect a 14-gun battery on l'Islet, a cay a half-mile off that bay's uninhabited shoreline, by early 1742. Additional batteries were then installed near Sarthe on the plain, at l'Habitation Ferron near Martissant (later becoming the Hôtel Beau-Rivage), and at l'Habitation Piémont—dubbed Fort Bagatelle—which together encircled the future city-site below l'Hôpital. Larnage even instructed Morel to commence work on a stone aqueduct to bring water from the Charbonnière River, and he issued decrees to the inhabitants of the nearby villages of Cul-de-Sac and Trou-Bourdet on 6 February 1743 and 3 June 1743, respectively, to begin selling their properties in anticipation of moving into a new island capital. An ordinance was even passed that same 29 October affixing the limits for Port-au-Prince's parish, effectively signaling the city's creation.

Yet although town plots were delineated by the surveyor du Coudreau, no civilian transfer could take place, as the Crown was distracted when hostilities against England actually commenced on 17 March 1744, so that this civilian project fell into abeyance. Larnage ordered another 6-gun emplacement called the Batterie des Trois-Joseph (Battery of the Three Josephs) erected atop Fortin Hill, before succumbing to gangrene and gout at Petit-Goâve's main citadel of Fort-Royal on 19 November 1746. The war with Britain then dragged on for another two years, so that it was not until late 1748 that Hubert de Brienne, Comte de Conflans, could reach Saint-Domingue as the island's new governor-general.

Foundation and Early Evolution (1749–1789)

The notion of erecting a new island capital was regalvanized when the Grande-Rivière River overflowed its banks on 3 June 1749, inundating the town of Cul-de-Sac; for rather than rebuild upon its sodden ground, the inhabitants petitioned de Conflans to implement his predecessor's design. Ten days later a new set of ordinances was issued; the surveyor Duport visited the site to make a few changes in its original delineation, then he supervised the actual distribution of land grants as residents began the six-month process of transferring their households. Merchants were assigned shoreline properties so as to have ready access to the wharves, while blacks were settled inland. Most structures were initially made of wood brought from Gonâve Island or the Barradères by ship, plus whatever stone could be garnered from Fortin Hill.

A royal order signed by Louis XV on 26 November 1749 confirmed Port-au-Prince as the new island capital, after which de Conflans and the intendant Simon-Pierre Maillart purchased an adjacent estate called l'Habitation Bretton des Chapelles and its 237 slaves on 20 April 1750, on which the military engineer de Verville was directed to install Crown offices, barracks for six marine companies, and a round powder magazine (which, for safety's sake, was to be erected just beyond the city limits). Setbacks occurred when a hurricane roared through on 6 July 1751, followed by another that same 20 September, as well as a series of strong tremors starting on 18 October and climaxing with a major quake at 8:00 A.M. on 21 November; the latter, although it claimed no lives, leveled three-quarters of the 100 painstakingly erected structures and damaged the rest.

Reconstruction began shortly thereafter under a vigorous new intendant, Laporte de Lalanne, so that the Crown courts could be transferred from Léogâne and reconstituted as the Conseil Súperior de Port-au-Prince by July 1752, along with the Amirauté (Admiralty) tribunal. Labors were further spurred by another downturn in Anglo-French relations during the mid-1750s, prompting the Crown to authorize increased expenditures on fortifications and resulting in the strengthening of both l'Islet and Trois-Joseph Batteries (dubbed Fort-l'Islet and Fort Saint-Joseph, respectively), as well as the creation of the 15-gun Fort Sainte-Claire to cover the city's waterfront. This latter defense was named after the wife of the new governor-general, Joseph Hyacinthe Rigaud, Marquis de Vaudreuil.

War against Britain erupted in May 1756, and although French commerce suffered significantly over the ensuing seven years, the fledgling capital's geographic position deep inside the Bight of Léogâne spared it any direct assault. Street-paving

The crowded Mouillage or "Anchorage" before Port-au-Prince in the eighteenth century, looking eastward toward Cul-de-Sac Plain and the distant highlands in the center of the island. (Bibliothèque Nationale, Paris)

ordinances were passed in November 1757, notwithstanding that ongoing conflict, while shade trees were planted to beautify Port-au-Prince's emergent boulevards; numerous other public works were also undertaken. Private construction efforts kept pace, so that by 1761 there were 392 dwellings within the city limits, plus dozens more under construction—including several splendid, two-storied town houses with broad verandas commissioned by wealthy plantation owners, atop the panoramic folds of Fortin Hill—while the first theater and newspaper made their appearance. By the time hostilities ceased in February 1763, the capital boasted some 680 dwellings.

The loss of India, Canada, and Louisiana in the subsequent peace negotiations meant that Saint-Domingue became France's principal overseas colony, and so received exceptional stimulus—including the importation of 100,000 coffee trees two years later, which would generate a valuable new cash export. Port-au-Prince benefited as a result, despite the epidemic late in 1765 that claimed 207 residents' lives, plus 447 of its soldiers and sailors. But the earthquake that struck at 7:15 P.M. on 3 June 1770 destroyed almost every building, burying some 200 people amid the rubble and spawning another epidemic. Bereft of water because of its shattered aqueduct,

most city inhabitants shifted temporarily into the countryside while reconstruction was undertaken. Municipal authorities, moreover—having noted how collapsing stone edifices had claimed many lives—decreed on 8 August that all future dwellings should be rebuilt of wood—albeit upon stone foundations, so as to minimize future calamities.

About one-quarter of the lost buildings had been replaced by the end of 1770, and a new aqueduct was completed three years afterward. The city gradually revived, its dwellings numbering 787 by 1775 and its public theater reopening by January 1778 with a performance of Favart's comic opera *Les Trois Sultanes.* Port-au-Prince was emptied of Crown officials and garrison troops when France allied itself with the Thirteen American Colonies against Britain in August 1778, more strategically placed Cap-Français serving as de facto capital for the duration of the conflict. And although Port-au-Prince was unscathed by any fighting, a fire remembered as *l'incendie de la Saint-Pierre* (the Saint Peter's Day Fire) broke out along its waterfront on the night of 29–30 June 1784, reducing eighty-three buildings to ashes.

They were soon rebuilt, however, as Saint-Domingue experienced a great postwar economic upsurge—being licensed to receive foreign merchantmen for the first time, as well as to

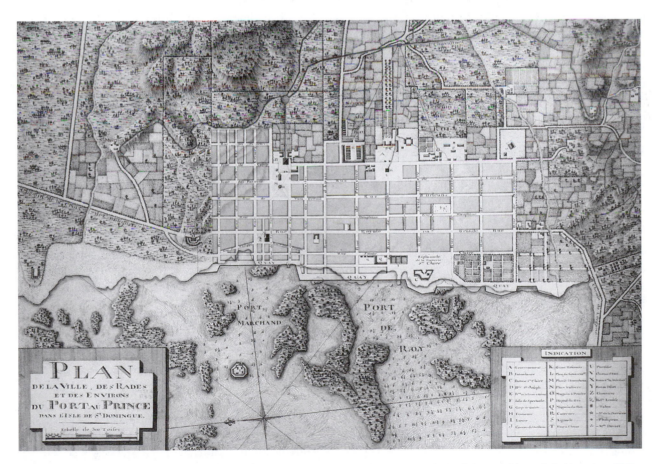

Map of Port-au-Prince, ca. 1785, attributed to the French military engineer George Bois St. Lys; north is toward lower left. (American Philosophical Society, Philadelphia)

import record numbers of African slaves, greatly incrementing the island's agricultural output. Numerous urban improvements were introduced, especially during the administration of the vigorous intendant François de Barbé, Marquis de Marbois. A hurricane that struck on 16 August 1788 damaged or flattened a tenth of Port-au-Prince's edifices, yet these material losses were promptly replaced. Next year, its population was estimated at 1,800 whites, 400 *affranchis* (enfranchised) free mulattoes or blacks, 4,000 slaves, and 1,000 troops spread among 895 dwellings—as well as an average of 2,200 sailors on leave at any given time from the ships anchored in the *port marchand* (merchant port) at the north end of its harbor or the warships in the fortified *port du Roi* (king's port) to its south.

Revolutionary Turmoil (1790–1794)

Saint-Domingue was now the richest colony in the world, a leader in both coffee and sugar exports and a lynchpin for France's economy. Port-au-Prince—although still only half the size of its sister city of Cap-Français—was at the peak of its colonial splendor when news was received in mid-September 1789 of the storming of the Bastille in Paris, undermining the authority of the newly appointed governor-general, Louis Ambroise Thomassin, Comte de Peynier, as the chaotic "democracy" of the Estates-General was unleashed. Emboldened by this overseas upheaval, the capital's white citizenry proclaimed their own Comité de l'Ouest (Committee of the West) to represent their interests before the revolutionary assemblage, yet the latter—inspired by high-minded ideals regarding the "Rights of Man," as well as personal appearances by the mulatto coffee merchant Jacques Vincent Ogé and his colleague Julien Raymond—instead extended universal suffrage to Saint-Domingue's *affranchis* as of 8 March 1790.

The white-dominated Committee of the West refused to implement such a socially unsettling decree, so countered by sporting *pompons rouges* (red pompons) in their hats, rather than the red, white, and blue cockades worn by their more radical compatriots in Paris. A conservative countercoup thereupon erupted at Port-au-Prince, when the aristocratic Col. Thomas Antoine de Mauduit, Chevalier du Plessis, issued pompons in the traditional white color of the Bourbon kings to his 110th Colonial Regiment, then disbanded the Comité de l'Ouest on the night of 29–30 July 1790. City defenses were also manned against any possible assault, yet despite this apparent collapse of local revolutionary resolve—plus the crushing of a northern insurrection of black slaves that same October, led by Ogé and Jean-Baptiste Chavannes—monarchist sentiment on the island remained very thin, while France itself continued to descend into full-blown republicanism.

This schism was to be driven home when the ships-of-the-line *Borée* and *Fougueux*, frigates *Uranie* and *Prudente,* plus the transport *Nantais* appeared off Port-au-Prince on 3 March 1791, bearing almost 2,000 highly politicized soldiers of the 9th Normandie and 48th D'Artois Infantry regiments. Contacted by local delegations of white antimonarchists, they streamed ashore belligerently that same night, being greeted as saviors by a "revolutionary" mob, while Loyalists fled and Mauduit was seized. The next afternoon the colonel was hacked to pieces, and the city was gripped by even more excesses over the next few days, climaxing when 2,000 men dislodged the frightened troops of the 110th Regiment from their fortified barracks on 2 May.

Yet revolutionary euphoria was dampened when another decree dated 15 May 1791 was received from the Assembly in Paris, extending full citizenship to free-born mulattoes or blacks. Once more unwilling to implement such a liberal policy, the remaining whites were alarmed when embittered *affranchis* began withdrawing from the capital after the Bastille Day celebrations that 14 July, to initiate a revolt one week later among La Coupe Hills to its southeast. Black slaves proved even more resentful of white racialism, a massive uprising exploding on Saint-Domingue's north-central plain on 22 August, during which Cap-Français became besieged. Fearful of enduring a similar black uprising on Cul-de-Sac Plain, its plantation owners came to terms with the mulatto rebels among La Coupe Hills by 7 September, in exchange for armed support against any possible insurrection.

Urban whites isolated within Port-au-Prince, their recently arrived revolutionary "saviors" now decimated by disease, had little choice but to concur and struck a like deal on 24 October 1791, uneasily admitting 1,500 mulatto troops under Anne-Alexandre Sabès Pétion who marched in through Saint-Joseph Gate. Racial animosity soon surfaced, though, a minor confrontation between a black drummer and a revolutionary gunner touching off a full-scale assault against Pétion's garrison within L'Intendance on 21 November, driving it into the countryside by nightfall with scores of lives lost on both sides. Sparks from artillery salvos caused a general conflagration remembered as *l'incendie de la Sainte-Cécile* (being Saint Cecilia's Day on the Church calendar) which consumed about half of Port-au-Prince's 1,000 buildings by dawn—including its Comédie Theater and Robert Hospital, although the worst damage was suffered among the commercial and Bel-Air districts. This inferno was accompanied by dreadful scenes of carnage directed against mulattoes and blacks, plus indiscriminate looting.

Angered by this white "Jacobin racism," as one historian has labeled it, the mulatto troops regrouped at Croix des Bouquets and imposed a loose siege upon the capital, as well as severing its Turgeau and Martissans aqueducts. A stalemate ensued despite a sally on 22 March 1792 by 1,000 white troops in two columns, who overran Croix des Bouquets and La Charbonnière, only to be driven back eight days later by black reinforcements from Cul-de-Sac Plain. The siege was then pressed home more tightly, until the former governor-general, Philibert François de Rouxel de Blanchelande, materialized offshore in

Admiral de Grimoüard quelling a revolutionary outburst aboard his flagship *Borée* at anchor in Port-au-Prince harbor, 11 December 1791. (*L'Amiral de Grimoüard au Port-au-Prince*)

late June with several warships, bearing orders from the National Assembly in Paris to arrest Port-au-Prince's disobedient leadership. Acting in concert with the mulatto besiegers, Blanchelande arranged a peaceful capitulation of the city, coming ashore to greet 1,000 mulatto troops as they marched in through the Saint-Joseph and Léogâne gates on 5 July 1792.

Port-au-Prince revived briefly, some rubble being cleared away and replaced by a few new stone buildings, while merchantmen under American, British, and Dutch flags called to trade. The island's stability seemed assured when the Jacobin commissioners Léger-Félicité Sonthonax and Étienne Polvérel disembarked with 6,000 fresh soldiers at Cap-Français on 19 September 1792 to begin reforming the colonial administration; yet rural blacks in Cul-de-Sac Plain—disappointed at perceiving no freedom from their enslavement—revolted again in late January 1793, after which overseas news arrived that the captive Louis XVI had been executed, France had been proclaimed a republic, and war had been declared against England and Spain.

Port-au-Prince's merchant traffic abruptly ceased, and the new local white leader—Auguste, formerly Marquis de Borel—aligned himself with rural black rebels to expel the

mulatto garrison from the city. The Jacobin commissioners retaliated from Cap-Français by dispatching a half-dozen warships, which appeared offshore on 4 April 1793 to support a siege by 2,000 mostly mulatto troops. Now boasting 3,000 defenders—of whom a majority were black—Borel was able to reject surrender demands from Sonthonax and Polvérel, so that they sailed against its defenses at dawn of 12 April and unleashed a seven-hour bombardment that killed thirty-three people (including a dozen women and children) and caused the merchant guild to bribe Borel into absconding to Jamaica, thereby allowing the besiegers to enter the next evening and the commissioners to disembark by the morning of 14 April.

Port-au-Prince was thereupon purged of its most intractable white elements, almost 1,000 individuals being detained or deported over the next few weeks on a variety of charges, while many others simply fled. Mulattoes received municipal and military appointments, while the city regiment was reconstituted as of 19 April 1793 into a 2,000-man *légion de l'égalité* (equality legion), adopting the name Légion de l'Ouest (Legion of the West). Yet blacks continued to be excluded from advancement, contributing to republican setbacks elsewhere on the island. In a desperate bid to gain their

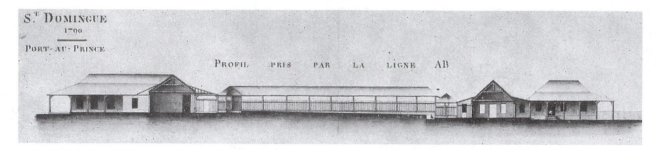

Cutaway view of L'Intendance by the military engineer Lieutenant-Colonel Frémond de La Merveillère, 1790. (Archives Nationales, Paris)

support, Sonthonax proclaimed the abolition of slavery throughout northern Saint-Domingue on 29 August, extended into Port-au-Prince's jurisdiction by 21 September, although many local mulattoes and whites still resisted such change.

In a demonstration of its loyalty, Port-au-Prince was renamed Port-Républicain on 23 September 1793, but a foreign complication was added when a British expedition under Commo. John Ford and Lt. Col. John Whitelocke appeared from Jamaica and occupied the ports of Jérémie and Cap-du-Môle, being greeted as redeemers by their white and mulatto residents. In order to maximize their appeal, this small English force furthermore announced that it was acting "in name of the French Crown" rather than as enemies of revolutionary France, and the 32-gun frigate HMS *Penelope* of Capt. Bartholomew Samuel Rowley even materialized off Port-au-Prince on 2 January 1794, hoping to arrange that city's capitulation as well.

Although Sonthonax rebuffed this overture, his republican administration was sore beset: on 4 February 1794, the National Convention in Paris abolished slavery throughout France's overseas colonies, sparking a violent reaction from Montbrun and his mulatto garrison within Port-au-Prince, who—feeling that their hard-won status was being capriciously sacrificed to assuage black rebels—killed or captured the depleted remnants of the 48th D'Artois Regiment on the night of 16–17 March, as well as temporarily detaining Sonthonax. Many white noncombatants were also slaughtered, while several hundred local black rebels under leaders such as Alaou and Hyacinthe were assassinated over the next few days.

British Occupation (1794–1798)
Bolstered by three fresh regiments, the English moved to take advantage of this republican setback, Commo. Ford appearing off Port-au-Prince's harbor on 30 May 1794 with his 64-gun flagship *Europa,* plus three other ships-of-the-line and a half-dozen lesser warships, escorting twelve transports bearing 1,465 redcoats. These troops were to assault the capital in concert with two approaching land columns raised by exiled French monarchists, 1,000 troops marching from Léogâne under the Baron de Montalembert plus another 1,200 from

l'Arcahaie under the former planter Hanus de Jumécourt and his black adjutant, Jean-Baptiste Lapointe.

The defenders could count upon only 1,200 mulatto troops, 400 of whom were detached by Montbrun the next day to prevent an immediate British disembarkation north of the city—two frigates and some transports having anchored menacingly at Fossé Cove—while he personally reinforced Fort Bizoton on the southern perimeter and assigned Pétion to hold Fort-l'Islet within the bay. Sonthonax meanwhile clandestinely summoned Montbrun's bitter rival Martial Besse from Jacmel to assume the post of second in command, complicating matters. On 1 June 1794, the 64-gun Royal Navy warships *Belliqueux* and *Sceptre,* plus the frigate *Penelope,* forged into Port-Sallé Bay and pounded Fort Bizoton for four hours, while 300 redcoats disembarked and linked up with 500 monarchist militiamen under Montalembert. A heavy downpour curtailed fighting at 6:00 P.M., but the British clambered through a breach and carried Fort Bizoton at bayonet point.

Thrice wounded, Montbrun retreated into Port-au-Prince with a few survivors, being succeeded the next day by Besse. The Légion de l'Ouest balked at obeying his orders, though, and with the English and monarchists massing to press home their attack, it was decided to abandon the capital. A stream of refugees emerged from the landward gates around noon, composed mostly of 2,000 mulatto noncombatants fleeing toward Nérette and Jacmel. On 3 June 1794, the 32-gun frigates *Hermione* and *Iphigenia* bore down upon Pointe-à-Fortin (modern Pointe-de-la-Saline) and bombarded Fort Touron, whose garrison scarcely resisted. Port-au-Prince's last defenders now being on the verge of open flight, its remaining white residents congregated inside Fort Saint-Joseph on its northern fringe, or aboard some of the twenty-two merchantmen anchored in its harbor, to avoid the anticipated orgy of looting or house-to-house fighting. Entreaties were sent out to the besiegers, and outlying fortifications were surrendered by nightfall.

On the morning of 4 June 1794, the British disembarked along the city waterfront while monarchist columns pressed through the Léogâne and Saint-Joseph gates, exacting vengeance until the English imposed order. Although having

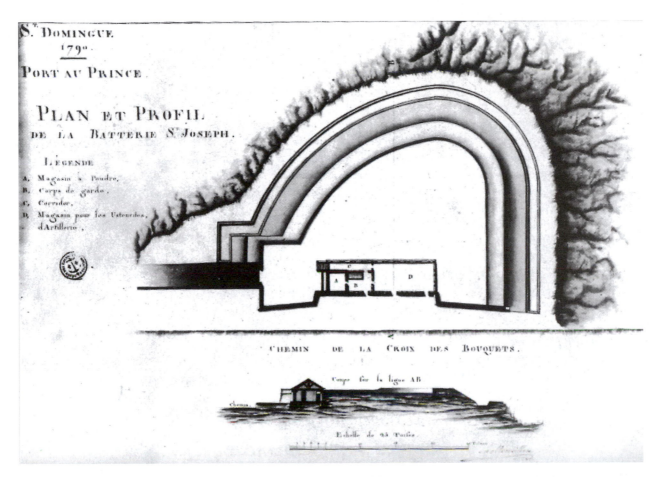

Diagram and cutaway view by Frémond de La Merveillère of Fort Saint-Joseph on the city's northern boundary, 1790; north is toward right. (Archives Nationales, Paris)

ostensibly seized the capital to restore French royal authority—even renaming it Port-au-Prince—the city's administration was actually exercised by British military officers. Yet despite their most conciliatory efforts, their occupation was doomed to failure because poor whites, mulattoes, and blacks could not abide any return to prerevolutionary practices in which they had enjoyed no role beyond servitude. The English were also too few in number to subdue the hostile hinterland, especially after being reduced by tropical diseases. (Within two months, 40 officers and almost 600 redcoats had perished, and of the 828 still alive by the end of 1794, most lay in hospital.)

A ring of redoubts was therefore commenced in the hills around Port-au-Prince, while some mulatto and black auxiliary units were raised—although their loyalty to the English and French crowns remained highly suspect, and they were unable to contain the countermovement that developed inland. Léogâne was reconquered by André Rigaud, who allied himself with Louis-Jacques Bauvais to besiege Fort Bizoton by March 1795; two months' investiture failed to dislodge its British garrison, though, so that the siege was lifted, although the black guerrillas who dominated Cul-de-Sac Plain and the

heights east of the capital subsequently pressed in as close as La Charbonnière and l'Hôpital to interrupt the city's vital water supply, before the English were reinforced and sallied from Port-au-Prince to chase them away.

Heartened by this success, 2,000 redcoats and 1,200 monarchists emerged from the capital to assail Léogâne on 20 March 1796 aboard transports escorted by the 74-gun HMSS *Leviathan* and *Swiftsure,* the 64-gun *Africa,* the 32-gun frigates *Ceres* and *Iphigenia,* plus numerous lesser warships. Mulatto units holding that town under Pétion resisted stoutly, compelling the attackers to retire the following morning; yet Port-au-Prince's plight was nonetheless alleviated by these twin thrusts, so that some monarchist planters even began reclaiming estates on Cul-de-Sac Plain. This resumption of cultivation in turn attracted merchantmen into port, creating such a boom in the sale of agricultural implements and other goods during the latter half of 1796 that London sent out John Graves Simcoe (recent founder of York in Upper Canada; *see* "Toronto" entry under the "Canada" country heading in Volume Two) to determine whether the conquered portions of Saint-Domingue might be permanently annexed by Britain.

It was finally decided that this would prove too expensive, both in human and financial terms, so that English interest waned. The black northern warlord Toussaint-Louverture had also begun to emerge as the most powerful commander on the island, being appointed "general-in-chief" by the French commissioner Sonthonax on 1 May 1797. Determined to expel all foreign intruders from the south, Toussaint-Louverture launched an invasion, helping a 2,000-man mulatto army under Pétion eradicate the 300 isolated black monarchist militiamen defending Fort de La Coupe by mid-February 1798. All British outposts were consequently withdrawn inside the capital, and a month later Brig. Thomas Maitland reached Port-au-Prince to arrange for its evacuation. He requested terms from Toussaint-Louverture on 23 April, and the last redcoats and monarchists rowed out to a waiting convoy on 8 May—setting sail the next day as the 1st and 8th Demi-Brigades marched into the capital under Col. Christophe Morney to reclaim it under its old name of Port-Républicain.

Black and French Invasions (1798–1803)

Southern mulattoes nonetheless resented the intervention of northern black forces, especially as Morney ordered Pétion to withdraw his Légion de l'Ouest from the recaptured capital to Léogâne, so that Toussaint-Louverture might make a triumphal entry on 14 May 1798 and install his own garrison. The power of his northern armies made the warlord dangerous to oppose, however, and he even flouted the authority of the newly arrived republican commissioner, Gen. Thomas Hédouville.

When the commissioner was driven from Cap-Français on 22 October 1798, he spitefully appointed the mulatto leader Rigaud as "general-in-chief of the South," thus rendering him nominally independent from Toussaint-Louverture. Rigaud subsequently began challenging the warlord's military appointments at Léogâne and Jacmel in mid-February 1799, prompting Toussaint-Louverture to deliver a menacing speech to a mulatto assembly in Port-Républicain's cathedral on 21 February before traveling northward to prepare for war against the southerners. Rigaud rebelled openly by 15 June, but Port-Républicain remained firmly in the grip of its black garrison, while Toussaint-Louverture and his subordinates Henry Christophe and Jean-Jacques Dessalines conducted a genocidal campaign throughout the south, so bitter that it was dubbed the "War of the Knives." Mulatto strongholds at Jacmel and Les Cayes eventually fell by August 1800, Rigaud fleeing into exile in France. The victorious Toussaint-Louverture was accorded a hero's welcome while passing through Port-Républicain the next month, although many of its mulatto citizenry were subsequently executed by Dessalines on suspicion of disloyalty.

Still, the city had not been directly assaulted, and it was able to conduct considerable trade aboard neutral American vessels until late in 1801, when France signed a peace treaty with Great Britain. This truce allowed First Consul Napoleon Bonaparte,

eager to reverse Toussaint-Louverture's independent tendencies, to send out a massive expedition to reclaim the entire island. Gen. Charles Victor Emmanuel Leclerc materialized at Samaná Bay on 29 January 1802, and a detachment of 3,000 soldiers anchored off Lamentin in Port-Républicain's harbor by the afternoon of 3 February. The city's surprised black garrison commander, Brig. Louis Daure Lamartinière, prepared to resist with his 2,400 troops yet found that not all were loyal, plus there was scant support among the roughly 20,000 inhabitants. Denied permission to come ashore, the French nevertheless disembarked at dawn on 5 February and advanced rapidly upon the capital. They brushed aside feeble resistance to enter by that same evening, finding that Lamartinière's black northern soldiers had butchered white and mulatto residents alike and set numerous fires before retreating.

As the island's new governor-general, Leclerc visited Port-Républicain in March 1802, yet chose to establish his headquarters at Cap-Français in early April; however, his wife Pauline (Napoleon's youngest sister) opted to move back to Port-Républicain a couple of weeks later, occupying a suburban palace with their three-year-old son because yellow fever had broken out in the north. Cowed by the overwhelming display of French might, black leaders such as Christophe, Toussaint-Louverture, and Dessalines surrendered soon after. But the will to resist was reanimated later that same summer by reports that Paris had restored slavery on Guadeloupe, reopened the transatlantic slave trade, and denied persons of color the title of "citizen." Leclerc's European troops were moreover suffering heavily from disease, and the contagion spread into Port-Républicain. The governor-general himself died at Cap-Français on 2 November, being succeeded by the governor of Port-Républicain, Gen. Donatien Marie Joseph de Vimeur, Vicomte de Rochambeau.

Terrified by their shrinking numbers, the French resorted to cruel punishments to repress the restive black populace, yet rural revolts quickly multiplied throughout the north, moving into the south by early January 1803. Determined to contain this spreading insurgency, Rochambeau returned from Cap-Français into Port-Républicain on 20 March 1803, but his design of conducting numerous executions within the city, then leading a campaign of terror through Cul-de-Sac Plain, was interrupted by news that England had renewed its hostilities against France as of May, necessitating his return into Cap-Français the next month to confront the threat of yet another Royal Navy blockade.

His departure from Port-Républicain was accompanied by many southern refugees, and within a month black guerrillas swept across Cul-de-Sac Plain and overran the city's Croix des Bouquets outpost, while an army of 5,000 mulatto and black rebels under Pierre Cangé advanced out of the southwest to invest Fort Bizoton. Famine now gripped the beleaguered city, while many of its 1,400 mulatto and black militia defenders deserted. By 22 September 1803, Port-Républicain was com-

Market scene at Port-au-Prince, ca. 1905. (Keane, *Central and South America*)

pletely encircled by 15,000 insurgents under Dessalines, who installed his headquarters atop Turgeau Heights. Two days later a battery erected by Pétion on Phelippeau Hill near l'Hôpital opened fire, dueling with the city batteries until Fort Bizoton had to be evacuated on 2 October and the authorities requested terms. Desperate in defeat, French citizens sailed perilously out of harbor aboard a flotilla of small boats six days later, while victorious rebel armies marched into the gutted city.

Capital of the "Republic of the South" (1804–1821)

Although the city now regained its former name of Port-au-Prince and its native son Pétion was appointed as governor, political power was held by the black northern faction, which deprived the recaptured city of its status as capital in favor of L'Habitation Marchand-Laville in the Artibonite district. There, Dessalines intended to erect a grand new city named after himself. Rochambeau and the last French troops were defeated outside Cap-Français by 18 November 1803, allowing the triumphant black general to proclaim a new nation as of 1 January 1804: Haiti (one of two ancient names that Taino natives had used for the island, signifying "Mountainous Land," the other term being *Quisqueya* or "Mother of the Earth").

In a bid to discourage any future reconquest by France, Dessalines led his army on a pitiless march throughout the country, massacring all surviving whites and people of suspect loyalties. Port-au-Prince was purged on 16–25 March 1804, despite discreet efforts by Pétion and other mulattoes to spare the innocent. This campaign of terror concluded with Dessalines anointing himself Emperor Jacques I at Cap-Haïtien on 8 October, then issuing a series of decrees to organize his fledgling nation—one of which declared that Port-au-Prince was to be shifted several miles inland to L'Habitation Dérance, amid La Selle Hills in the Trou-Coucou district, so as to be safer from foreign influences or invasions. Practical considerations impeded implementation of this decree until the megalomaniac's rule ended with his assassination at dawn on 17 October 1806 while riding across Larnage Bridge into the outskirts of Port-au-Prince (remembered ever after as the Pont-Rouge—Red Bridge).

The ensuing succession struggle split the young nation asunder, mulatto delegates manipulating a constitutional conference at Port-au-Prince to produce a democratic constitution on 27 December 1806, whose presidency—with severely limited powers—was offered to Christophe, commander of the black armies of the north. Rather than accept office under such strictures, the latter launched a 10,000-man offensive into the south, aiming to wrest full control over the government. Pétion countersallied from Port-au-Prince at the head of 3,000 men, hoping to surprise Christophe at Sibert on 1 January 1807, only to be defeated; Port-au-Prince therefore had to mount a desperate resistance under the guerrilla chieftain Yayou, until Pétion could return and repel Christophe's major assault on 8 January. The northerners thereupon withdrew, sowing a path of destruction across Cul-de-Sac Plain, to acclaim Christophe as president of the "Republic of the North" at Cap-Haïtien, while Pétion was proclaimed "President of the Republic of the South" on 9 March.

Anticipating further hostilities, Port-au-Prince's defenses were strengthened and its garrison augmented to 8,000 men; yet when no invasion ensued, other enhancements were implemented, such as the construction of a 400-bed military hospital and medical school in 1808. Christophe, meanwhile, hoped that by transforming his northern territory into a prosperous state, he might win over reluctant southerners; yet when Pétion was re-elected by his southern legislature on 9 March 1811, the northern strongman decided on more direct action. Two and a half weeks afterward, he declared himself "King Henry I," then next year launched another invasion of the south with 15,000 troops. Jean-Pierre Boyer led a counter-column out of Port-au-Prince in March 1812 to attempt to stem this onslaught, being defeated at Santo and driven back into the capital. Henry's army arrived and deployed for a protracted siege, its batteries opening fire by 6 April; still, more than two months of pounding failed to reduce the defenses, so that the northern king ordered a retirement by 14 June.

Port-au-Prince was repaired and enjoyed an interlude of modest prosperity, although smitten by a hurricane in October 1816 and the chance detonation of its Bel-Air powder magazine on 10 June 1817. Pétion died of natural causes on 29 March 1818, being succeeded by the election of Boyer by the Senate the following day. The southern capital was then ravaged by an accidental fire that started at noon on 15 August 1820, claiming almost 300 wooden buildings—coincidentally, King Henry collapsed that same day from a stroke while attending church outside Cap-Henry, being left paralyzed. His adherents began cautiously defecting to Boyer, so that after the stricken monarch finally committed suicide on 8 October, rioters killed his heir-apparent and tore away all vestiges of his despotic rule, so that the two halves of Haiti could be reunited. Early in 1822, Boyer furthermore called upon the neighboring Dominicans to proclaim their independence from Spain and marched into Santo Domingo with a large army on 9 February to bring the entire island under single rule.

Island Capital (1822–1843)

The quarter century of Boyer's reign would help Port-au-Prince to begin to recuperate from its many hardships, despite a conflagration that burned more than 200 of its buildings on 16 December 1822. Two years later, several hundred black migrants arrived from the United States, settling along an extension of Rohan Street that was redubbed Rue Américaine (American Street), while the total urban popula-

tion began edging up toward 25,000. In July 1825 a French fleet arrived bearing official recognition of Haiti's independence, although this acknowledgement unfortunately saddled the impoverished young nation with heavy indemnization payments.

The stone arsenal just southwest of Port-au-Prince exploded on the morning of 2 February 1827, claiming more than thirty lives; the city's shabby and insalubrious condition led Boyer in September 1831 to renew the notion of creating a whole new capital some 6 miles inland at La Coupe-Charbonnière, to be named Ville-Pétion (gradually devolving into Pétionville) in honor of his precursor. Lack of funds, though, rendered that project largely stillborn, only 2 government edifices ever being completed plus a few private homes of influential politicians. Losses occasioned by the fire that broke out in Port-au-Prince on the afternoon of 8 July 1832, leveling 16 entire blocks and more than 300 dwellings in its southern sector, added to the government's insolvency, so that the capital was to remain at its original site.

The city suffered some minor damage from an earthquake that rattled Haiti on 7 May 1842, then much worse damage when another major fire broke out at 3:00 P.M. on 9 January 1843 in the Daumesnil Pharmacy on the Grand' Rue; the flames, fanned by a west wind, consumed a dozen blocks by nightfall, including more than 300 residences, 50 stores, and 5 pharmacies. Less than three weeks after this tragedy, an insurrection also erupted at Les Cayes, quickly gaining momentum in the countryside until Boyer went aboard the English corvette *Scylla* with his family on the evening of 13 March to sail away into exile on Jamaica.

Political Prize (1843–1888)

Despite such an ignominious end, Boyer's reign had nonetheless cemented Port-au-Prince's status as the Haitian capital, which would withstand the sociopolitical disintegration that was about to ensue. Its citizenry anxiously greeted the insurgent army of the mulatto leader Charles "Rivière" Hérard, Sr., which entered shortly thereafter and peacefully reimposed the name of "Port-Républicain," in honor of an apparent restoration of democratic rule. Yet Hérard would prove unable to govern, the Spanish half of the island seceding by February 1844, while discontented black Haitian peasants also revolted against the ascendancy of yet another mulatto president.

Hoping to avert an assault against the capital, its municipal authorities consequently availed themselves of Hérard's absence at his Arcahaie base camp to acclaim the octogenarian Philippe Guerrier—formerly the "Duc de l'Avancé" in Henry's black northern monarchy—as the new national president, leaving Hérard no choice but to board the British corvette *Spartan* on 2 June 1844 and follow Boyer into exile. Guerrier retired to his private home at Saint-Marc and died on 15 April 1845, being succeeded the next day by another older, illiterate black northern general: Louis Pierrault. At his inaugural the capital reclaimed its former name of Port-au-Prince but was then surprised when Pierrault—who openly disliked and distrusted Port-au-Princians—rode away to Cap-Haïtien one month later, ordering that the Haitian government be transferred there as of 1 November. Port-au-Prince received a further setback when a fire erupted around its Saint-Joseph Gate on the night of 10–11 November, claiming many buildings despite prompt assistance from the crews of two visiting French warships.

Insulted by Pierrault's departure, Port-au-Prince embraced the subsequent mutiny spearheaded at Saint-Marc by Gen. Jean-Baptiste Riché and was rewarded by being restored as Haitian capital when he was installed as president on 24 March 1846. Eleven months later, he too succumbed to disease and was succeeded by the commander of his guard, Faustin Soulouque. Annoyed by the constant manipulations engineered by mulatto politicians, this illiterate black general unleashed a brutal onslaught against them on Sunday afternoon, 16 April 1848, massacring scores of Port-au-Prince's leading citizens over the next three days, while hundreds more were driven into foreign consulates or aboard neutral vessels.

His power now unchallenged, Soulouque tried reducing the neighboring Dominicans by military means, and despite meeting with utter failure during his attempt at reconquest, he was acclaimed Emperor Faustin I by August 1849. Two and a half years of costly preparations for his investiture thereupon ensued, including the purchase of a custom-made golden crown and regalia from the Parisian jeweler Rouvenat, plus the erection of a huge wooden temple draped with linen southeast of the capital's Fort Riché. Finally, his imperial guard were issued splendid new uniforms on Sunday, 4 April 1852, and two weeks of ceremonies climaxed with Soulouque's coronation.

Notwithstanding this extravagance, Port-au-Prince remained blighted by poverty and squalor throughout his reign, losing 100 buildings to another fire that started in the Myrthil Bruno Pharmacy on 12 June 1857. Eventually wearying of Faustin's megalomania, the populace at Gonaïves revolted on 22 December 1858, led by Fabre Nicolas Geffard, Duc de Tabara and chief of staff of the imperial guard. His insurgents marched triumphantly into the capital on 15 January 1859, while the emperor and his family fled into the French consulate, then afterward sailed to Jamaica aboard the British frigate HMS *Melbourne*. Geffard was elected president by the Senate five days later and promised to uphold republican forms of government.

His administration began promisingly enough, with some simple yet long overdue improvements along the capital's waterfront—street repairs, digging of drains, the erection of a long wooden jetty and customs shed—that were intended to benefit commercial traffic, which had grown appreciably

Soulouque's coronation as Emperor Faustin I, April 1852. *(Album imperial d'Haiti)*

over the past decade. Port-au-Prince now had a population of approximately 29,000 residents, who were pleased to see the Rue du Port (Port Street) paved over with stones (thus becoming known as Rue Pavée—Paved Street); old, open-air colonial aqueducts were also replaced with iron pipes; and two dozen petroleum lamps were installed along Quai and Arsenal streets by October of that same year. In 1861, Mark Bird—the American pastor of the Wesleyan mission—imported a gas lighting system from the United States, and a telegraph system was tested by the government in 1862. Of more practical benefit, the first coastal steamboats began carrying passengers from Fort-L'Islet in June 1863; municipal garbage pickup was instituted as of October 1864; Port-au-Prince's first public park—Place Geffard, formerly Place Pétion—was inaugurated on the 30th of that same month; while horse-drawn coaches began providing public transport as far as Bizoton and Pétionville. Theaters, hotels, and schools all multiplied throughout this prosperous period as well.

Regrettably, another major conflagration erupted, in the Théâtre National on Bonne-Foi Street, at 7:00 P.M. on 28 February 1865, destroying almost 400 buildings, many in Port-au-Prince's vital business district. Another even more terrible fire started around 8:00 A.M. on 19 March 1866 in a wholesale store owned by John Hepburn, a U.S. black who had immigrated to Haiti thirty-one years previously. This latter blaze—remembered as *l'incendie Hepburn* (the Hepburn Fire)—swept through the capital's central core, entirely consuming fifteen blocks and damaging another thirteen. Among the 1,500 buildings lost were the Senate, Ministry of the Interior, Trea-

sury, Post Office, Fort Per, and part of the National Print Office. An additional tragedy ensued when the city arsenal suddenly detonated at 4:00 A.M. on 12 September 1866.

Geffard's regime was powerless to alleviate the people's misery, and they consequently turned against the president. On the night of 22–23 January 1867, his favorite guard unit—the Tirailleurs-Carabiniers (Carbine-Riflemen)—peppered the Presidential Palace with rounds; although driven back into Fort Lamarre and crushed the next dawn by a loyal battalion under Col. Tibérius Zamor, this elite unit's mutiny nonetheless signaled Geffard's unpopularity. Another more serious revolt broke out shortly thereafter at Saint-Marc, obliging the president and his family to slip aboard the French warship *Destin* on the night of 12–13 March and sail away into Jamaican exile, while angry mobs ransacked their homes.

The leaders of this Saint-Marc uprising—Nissage Saget and Victorin Chevallier—entered the capital shortly thereafter and established an interim government; however, popular support swung behind the northern strongman Gen. Sylvain Salnave, who ten days after his army marched in from Cap-Haïtien was acclaimed "Protector of the Republic" by a frenzied black mob on 3 May 1867. The mulatto-dominated Constituent Assembly invested him with provisional powers three days later, then began deliberating his permanent election; tired of waiting, though, Salnave sent his troops on 14 June to frighten the legislators into confirming him for a four-year term. When a motion was subsequently introduced on 11 October to inquire into the detention of Gen. Léon Montas at Cap-Haïtien—on Salnave's orders—a throng burst into the

Fort Lamarre—at right—as it appeared while undergoing repairs, ca. 1890. (*Histoire du gouvernement du Général Légitime*)

legislature three days later and chased out its delegates, gutting the building.

Yet although Salnave could easily suppress opposition in the capital, he could not do so in the remote northeastern jungles, where his enemies launched a struggle with *caco* guerrillas (originally a Spanish nickname for renegade slaves). Despite personally assuming command in the field, the president failed to defeat this insurrection, which emboldened others. As a result, Saget rose in revolt in the central Artibonite district in April 1868, while a band of young mulattoes even stormed the Port-au-Prince prison to free its political detainees. This latter coup was put down by the city garrison, and Salnave disembarked two days later to personally punish this bold affront to his authority by allowing black mobs to ransack mulatto-owned stores throughout Port-au-Prince.

Rural rebellions nonetheless continued to sprout, and John Lynch's *cacos* pressed in on Drouillard, north of the unhappy capital, by May 1868, while Pétion Faubert occupied Pétionville to its east and General Normil controlled Carrefour to its south. Salnave prepared to withstand a siege, abetted by Port-au-Prince's black populace. Early in June, Lynch overran Fort Gommier atop Bel-Air Hill, only to be ejected by a counterattack, but Faubert took up an entrenched position 3 miles east at Saint-Amand on Gros-Morne Hill, prompting Salnave to torch more than a half-mile of shanties outside the capital's ramparts, so as to clear a field of fire between Pont Rouge and the Saint-Joseph Gate. A stalemate thereupon ensued, broken

a month later when Salnave called upon black rural peasants to threaten the besiegers' rear, Normil being obliged to retire westward to Petit-Goâve so that presidential forces could reclaim the hills around La Charbonnière. Faubert and Lynch lifted their siege as well by 1 September, withdrawing toward Saint-Marc.

Although spared the horrors of a direct assault, the city nevertheless remained in great distress under the increasingly desperate and distrustful Salnave. His garrison at Gonaïves capitulated by the end of August 1869, followed by Port-de-Paix on 24 October, Jacmel on 4 November, and Cap-Haïtien by 14 November. Rebel forces, now with British and French backing, closed in upon the capital once more, where Salnave braced to make a last stand. On the night of 17–18 December, two rebel vessels glided into Port-au-Prince's harbor and boarded the recently purchased warship *Terreur*, while 1,000 troops were disgorged to fight their way into the city. Its surprised 3,000-man garrison was furthermore struck by twin land assaults at dawn, while hysterical civilians tried to escape southward. Fort Eveillard's powder magazine exploded, leveling much of Bel-Air, before this rebel onslaught could be checked at nightfall. However, the rebel warships began shelling the Presidential Palace at dawn of Sunday, 19 December (their aim directed by a gunner loaned from a British warship), until Salnave fled toward Pétionville with a few loyal adherents.

Behind him, powder magazines within the Presidential Palace and Fort Lerebours detonated, sparking a massive

Column of *caco* cavalrymen moving along Port-au-Prince's "John Brown" Avenue, early during the twentieth century. (Collection Edmond Mangonès)

conflagration that reduced hundreds of the capital's emptied structures to ashes. The victorious rebels exacted harsh vengeance upon black residents as well, executing hundreds over the next several months for their complicity in Salnave's reign of terror. The fugitive president was caught attempting to escape into the Dominican Republic and was brought back to face a summary trial on 15 January 1870, being convicted of "murder and arson" and paraded through the city's most ravaged sectors before being tied to a blood-red post within the Presidential Palace's ruins and garroted. Passions eventually subsided, Saget being elected president by the National Assembly on 19 March 1870, so that reconstruction could gradually get under way.

A curious after-note occurred on 11 June 1872, when a German warship visited Port-au-Prince to demand $15,000 in compensation from the Haitian government for losses suffered by two of their nationals during the recent civil war; a pair of Haitian steamers were seized by German marines that same evening to exert greater pressure until payment was made. More serious were three fires that erupted on 27 April and 3–4 June 1873, as well as 11–12 April 1874, the first consuming four city blocks and leaving 150 families homeless; the second claimed about thirty buildings in a single block; while the third once more gutted the city's commercial district, although effectively contained by the newly created *pompiers de Saint-Martial* (Saint-Martial firemen).

Saget had already appointed his elderly colleague Gen. Michel Domingue as commander in chief of the Haitian Army and retired to Saint-Marc, paving the way for Domingue to be elected president as of 11 June 1874. Much of his administration's innovations would be driven by his ambitious vice president and nephew, Septimus "Vava" Rameau, who promised a nationwide modernization program and created the Banque Nationale d'Haïti (National Bank of Haiti) that same October to help finance such labors. (Unfortunately, the American firm of H. Lazare failed to provide the requisite funds, so that this institution's impact was severely limited and disillusionment soon set in.) Private enterprise introduced some improvements as well, such as the first Haitian railroad, laid in 1874 to bring lumber from Cul-de-Sac Plain.

However, much of the capital's Saint-Joseph sector was leveled by a conflagration on the night of 11–12 February 1875, after which criticism of Domingue and Rameau redoubled. The regime consequently ordered the arrest on 1 May of its three leading opponents—Gen. Broussais Brice, Pierre Momplaisir-Pierre, and Boisrond Canal—plus the banishment of another forty individuals. Dissension nonetheless grew, finally bursting forth on 7 March 1876 when Gen. Louis Tanis revolted with the Jacmel garrison. Support for the government quickly evaporated, so that Rameau went to the closed National Bank in Port-au-Prince on Easter Saturday afternoon, 15 April, to carry its silver deposits away to Les Cayes. Detected by a crowd, he was

Pierre Momplaisir-Pierre, Boisrond Canal, and Gen. Broussais Brice, Sr. (Victor Meignan, *Aux Antilles,* 1882)

chased into the Presidential Palace, from where he and Domingue and their families attempted to reach the sanctuary of the French legation. The vice president was shot dead in the street, and Domingue was wounded by a bayonet thrust, although he managed to gain the anchored French warship *Sané* to sail away into exile at Saint Thomas. Mobs meanwhile looted the bank, customs warehouses, and mansions of known associates of the deposed leader.

Canal was subsequently elected president, yet the capital continued to languish because of the government's insolvency. One of its few innovations was the inauguration of the first horse-drawn streetcar service in mid-January 1878, tracks being laid and operated by a private New York firm. But while President Canal was on an inspection tour of southern Haiti, Tanis launched another rebellion on 14 March in support of the National Party's leader, Gen. Louis Etienne Félicité Lysius Salomon, Jr.—former Duc de Saint-Louis du Sud and finance minister under Emperor Faustin—who had recently returned to Port-au-Prince after twenty years' exile in Europe. Troops loyal to Canal resisted from Fort Eveillard under Gen. Jean Chrysostome François, his artillery opening fire upon Tanis's headquarters in Fort National, while terrified civilians fled from out of this cross fire. Three days of exchanges concluded when the mutineers escaped upon news of the president's imminent return into the capital.

Little more than a year later, though, Canal fell out with his own Liberal Party rival, Boyer Bazelais. After a legislative dispute on 30 June 1879, General François took a police detachment to arrest Bazelais at his home on Rue Pavée, only to be greeted by gunfire. A tense, three-day standoff ensued, full-pitch fighting resuming on the afternoon of 4 July that caused numerous buildings to go up in flames and a disguised Bazelais to seek sanctuary in the Spanish consulate. However, outraged Liberals rallied at Gonaïves to drive out Canal, who—now without party backing—appointed the National Party general Richelieu Duperval on 17 July to maintain order in the capital before sailing away to Saint Thomas.

Generals Joseph Lamoth and Hériston Hérissé temporarily assumed power at Port-au-Prince, denying the capital to the Liberals until the sixty-six-year-old National Party leader Salomon disembarked in early October 1879 to a tumultuous reception, being elected president by the National Assembly on the 23rd of that same month. Although he was to spend much of his term at his beautiful country Villa "Solitude" in the nearby Turgeau foothills, Salomon nonetheless succeeded in reforming the army and city police (whose numbers rose from 180 to 250 officers, for an urban population now approaching 40,000 people), as well as by re-establishing the National Bank in September 1880, thanks to a large loan from a Parisian credit company.

Tragically, a smallpox epidemic struck the capital in October 1881, claiming more than 4,000 victims within the next four months; then the Liberal exile Bazelais disembarked at Miragoâne on 27 March 1883, raising a revolt in southern Haiti. Six months of guerrilla strikes around Jacmel and Jérémie increased tension within Port-au-Prince, until a group of zealous young mulatto Liberals attempted a coup on the morning of 22 September, killing a pair of senior officers before being put down. This incident provoked panic throughout the tense city, and soldiers opened fire indiscriminately against mulattoes while black mobs ransacked businesses. Fires—some deliberately set—took hold, and a fifth of the capital was consumed during the ensuing two nights of looting, until order could finally be restored by summary executions carried out by Gen. Boisrond Canal, Jr.

The Liberal threat to smoldering Port-au-Prince eased when it was learned that Bazelais had died of dysentery on the campaign trail, so that some rebuilding could commence. In order to reduce the crowded clusters of wooden structures that fed such conflagrations, the city's boundaries were expanded for the first time, two new *quartiers* (wards) being incorporated and christened Salomon and Derrière l'Exposition—this latter name because it extended southward from behind the National Exposition grounds. Mercifully, the capital enjoyed a few years of peace, and some modest improvements could be made, thanks to a rise in coffee prices on international exchanges. In October 1885, for example, the first of more than 100 naphtha streetlights were installed, while a new produce market dubbed the *marché Saint-Louis* or *Wharf-Zherbes*—this latter a garbling of the term Wharf-des-Herbes—was inaugurated the following year west of Fort Per, along the waterfront between Bonne-Foi and Miracles streets. An iron lighthouse was also completed offshore on l'Islet by May 1888.

When the elderly president Salomon was rumored to be contemplating treatment abroad for his rheumatism, a coup attempt occurred in the capital on 24 May 1888, hoping to depose him in favor of the National Party senators François Denis Légitime and François Manigat; it failed, though, and the latter were obliged to flee. A suspicious fire then broke out during a session of the Chamber of Deputies on 4 July, destroying that building along with the nearby Ministry of the Interior, National Print Office, civil courts, as well as numerous schools and other structures. (Fearful of becoming compromised by battling what seemed to be a politically motivated and retaliatory blaze, most Port-au-Princians refused to muster, so that seamen from the French warship *Bison* and passenger liner *Ville de Nazaire* had to contain the flames.) Arson also broke out three days later at the house of Minister of Justice Arteaud—a close personal friend and ally of Légitime—consuming more than 100 edifices before burning itself out.

Finally, word arrived that the Cap-Haïtien garrison of Gen. Séïde Thélémaque had risen in favor of former president Canal on 5 August 1888, prompting several contingents in Port-au-Prince to do the same five days later, so that Salomon departed into exile aboard the British warship *Canada*. Légitime returned from Jamaica on 15 August, disembarking

Panoramic view looking westward across Port-au-Prince; note the horse-drawn tram heading down "Miracles" Street toward the waterfront, an American-owned service that ceased operations as of April 1888. (Paul Déléage, *Haïti en 1886*)

from the ship *Alvo* to a delirious welcome at Port-au-Prince. But General Thélémaque also marched into the capital eight days later with 8,000 to 9,000 northern troops, encamping to await the outcome of the legislative elections of 30 September.

Tensions escalated between the northern militiamen and the city garrison under Gen. Anselme Prophète, erupting into heavy machine gun fire on the night of 28–29 September 1888, during which Thélémaque was killed and his army scattered. Feeling once more betrayed by mulatto politicians in the capital, Cap-Haïtien seceded on 7 October, proclaiming its own République Septentrionale (Northern Republic), backed by an army under Gen. Louis Mondestin Florvil Hyppolite. Eight days later, the National Assembly in Port-au-Prince countered by electing Légitime as "Chief of State," and civil war erupted openly when General Prophète penetrated into the northern district of Artibonite on 9 December with his army.

Tentative Modernization (1889–1914)
Prophète's campaign soon slowed, and Hyppolite's army counterattacked into Cul-de-Sac Plain by early August 1889. Dreading a vengeful northern penetration into the capital, many Port-au-Princians fled, compelling Légitime to depart into exile again on 22 August aboard the French warship *Kerguelen*. The next day, Hyppolite's victorious army entered the half-empty city, and once he was acclaimed president at Gonaïves on 9 October 1889, his iron-fisted rule actually improved urban life by imposing order and stability. High coffee prices on international markets also buoyed Haiti's economy, helping to secure large loans to finance a series of public projects, while northern administrators—such as Port-au-Prince's newly appointed mayor, Etienne Mathon—proved more comfortable dealing with foreign contractors, having experience because of Cap-Haïtien's more accessible geographic position.

The capital's first modern government offices emerged as a result, with metal frames imported from the famous Eiffel factory in Paris. Telegraph services were also inaugurated; muddy streets were paved over with gravel (a few concrete sidewalks being poured along main thoroughfares); wooden bridges were replaced by brick spans; an iron-wrought city slaughterhouse and market were erected; petroleum street lamps were introduced; proper docks were created at the Bizoton Navy Yard; a hydroelectric generator was installed in the National Palace; shade trees were planted; new railroad tracks were laid; the city water system was overhauled; and even telephone service was attempted. Thanks to this outburst of activity, the population of Port-au-Prince and its immediate environs surged to perhaps 70,000 residents, including many foreigners, spread among 6,000 buildings and 2,000 shacks.

Yet notwithstanding such progress, the hot-tempered

Panoramic view looking toward Panthéon Square from atop the Saint-Martial Observatory, ca. 1891. (Gentil Tippenhauer, *Die Insel*)

general—his northern Creole nickname of *Mabial* implying wrathfulness—reacted brutally when he was interrupted at Mass by an attempt to release political detainees from Port-au-Prince's prison on 28 May 1891. Galloping through the streets on his horse, he ordered his garrison to carry out scores of summary executions over the next three days, precipitating a flight of prominent refugees that was not reversed until a general amnesty was promulgated on 12 December. The city also suffered considerable damage when a fire started on the afternoon of 30 November 1894 in the home of Mrs. Méline Augustin (nicknamed *Ti Méline*—Little Méline) that destroyed much of the Bel-Air district and was remembered as *l'incendie Ti Méline* (Little Méline's Fire).

Still, political power passed rather peacefully when Hyppolite died suddenly of natural causes on 24 March 1896, although malfeasance and maladministration subsequently slowed the pace of the capital's modernization and Haiti's foreign debt spiraled out of control. As a harbinger of future difficulties, the German warships *Stein* and *Charlotte* appeared off Port-au-Prince on 6 December 1897 to intimidate President Tirésias Augustin Simon Sam into rescinding a fine levied against a Haitian-born German national, Emil Lüders; a severe fire also broke out on the night of 28–29 December, causing considerable damage to the city's Saint-Joseph Parish. When Sam's term finally expired in May 1902, he was chased aboard the liner *Olinde Rodrigues* by a Port-au-Princian mob.

The ensuing succession struggle ended when the elderly garrison commander for Cap-Haïtien, Nord Alexis, led his 7,000-man army into Port-au-Prince on 14 December 1902 to lay claim to the presidency four days later. Economic woes continued to hamper his administration, although a few improvements were made in the capital by Mayor Sténio Vincent—such as the creation of new water reservoirs, the introduction of limited electric lighting, and the laying of new railroad lines. However, a bad fire occurred on 20–21 July 1906, then another even worse conflagration on 5 July 1908, claiming 1,200 structures in the capital's central core while leaving 12,000 of its 80,000 residents destitute and homeless.

François Antoine Simon mounted a revolt at Les Cayes that drove Alexis aboard the French cruiser *Duguay-Trouin* by 2 December 1908, his luggage being pillaged by an angry throng of Port-au-Princians as he departed. Simon entered the next day with his troops and was elected president by the National Assembly on 17 December. With the nation bankrupt, he too sought foreign loans to implement his ambitious economic plans—most particularly the development of bananas as an export crop—so that the National Bank of Haiti was reorganized and underwritten with funds from French, German, and American institutions. One of the side benefits of Simon's efforts was the installation of electric lighting throughout the capital, as well as the construction of a wharf out to L'Islet Island to better receive oceangoing ships; yet popular discontent led

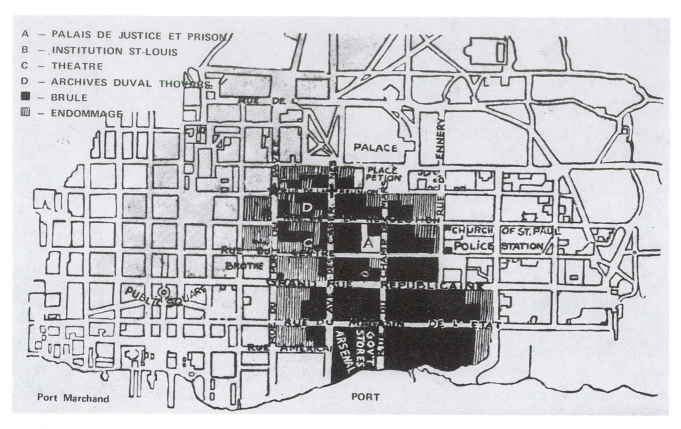

Map of the city areas either destroyed or damaged—in shades of black or gray, respectively—by the fire of 5 July 1908; north is toward left. (Roger Gaillard)

to another *caco* insurrection in northeastern Haiti by February 1911, spearheaded by Jean-Jacques Dessalines Michel Cincinnatus Leconte. A rebel army under Gen. Stivern Péralte reached Pétionville by 1 August, compelling Simon and his family to flee through a hostile crowd to Port-au-Prince's waterfront the next day and sail away into exile.

Leconte marched into the capital on 6 August 1911 and eight days later was confirmed as president by the National Assembly. Although uneasy under its new ruler, Port-au-Prince continued to enjoy some modest signs of progress, despite a general economic slowdown. Leconte was suddenly killed on 8 August 1912, when the powder magazine beside the National Palace accidentally exploded, leveling this building and others nearby. His successor, Tancrède Auguste, did not rule long, expiring of natural causes on 2 May 1913 and being succeeded by the rich Port-au-Princian lawyer and senator Michel Oreste. Lacking any military support, this civilian was powerless to confront yet another *caco* uprising in northeastern Haiti early the following year, so resigned by 27 January 1914 to go into exile aboard the German cruiser *Vineta*. German, U.S., and French marines disembarked to protect their nationals' interests in the lawless capital until Gen. Charles Oreste Zamor

could march in with his army on the evening of 7 February, being acclaimed president the next day.

But Haiti's decline gathered still further speed, Zamor resigning by 28 October 1914 amid the usual scenes of pillage. Eleven days later, the elderly *caco* leader Davilmar Théodore marched into the capital with his army and secured the presidency, but the economy had by that stage utterly collapsed. U.S. secretary of state William Jennings Bryan—concerned by such regional instability when World War I had just exploded in Europe—dispatched the gunboat *Machias* into Port-au-Prince on 17 December, landing fifty marines to seize the half-million dollars in gold reserves from Haiti's National Bank and carry them to the National City Bank in New York City for safekeeping.

This humiliating step signaled Théodore's doom, as Gen. Vibrun Guillaume Sam revolted at Cap-Haïtien on 15 January 1915, being joined a few days later by 1,000 *caco* guerrillas under "General" Metellus. U.S. Rear Adm. William Caperton reached this northern port on 23 January to shadow Sam's army in its progression toward the capital "to prevent excesses." With his treasury gone and supporters fallen away, Théodore quit Port-au-Prince aboard a Dutch liner by noon of 22 February, Sam entering uncontested and being acclaimed Haiti's new ruler three days later.

U.S. Occupation (1915–1934)

Sam's seizure of power was unexpectedly challenged when the former police chief, Charles de Delva, escaped from his asylum inside the Portuguese embassy at dawn of 27 July 1915 and torched the Presidential Palace with thirty-six armed followers. Wounded in a leg, Sam in turn sought sanctuary within the French embassy, while his own police chief, Charles Oscar Étienne, massacred 200 political detainees and fled into the Dominican embassy. An enraged mob dragged the latter back out into the street and hacked him to pieces, Sam sharing the same fate next morning—a savage outburst that goaded the U.S. government into intervening directly in Haitian affairs.

At 11:40 A.M. on 28 July 1915, the cruiser USS *Washington* reappeared off riot-torn Port-au-Prince and that same evening set 170 marines and 170 sailors ashore at Bizoton Navy Yard under marine captain George van Orden, who marched the 2 miles eastward into the capital and restored some semblance of order, at a cost of two Haitians dead and ten wounded. The next evening, this landing force was augmented by the arrival of the troop transport *Jason*, bearing another marine company from Guantánamo Bay. A feeble Haitian counterattack struck the detachment holding Fort Lerebours just south of Port-au-Prince at 8:00 P.M. on 29 July, being repelled with six attackers dead and two wounded; two U.S. sailors died, one being William Gompers, nephew of the famous labor leader Samuel Gompers.

The battleship *Connecticut* of Capt. E. H. Durell arrived from Philadelphia with five companies of the 2nd Marine Regiment under Col. Eli Cole on 4 August 1915 to secure Port-au-Prince fully and disband all factions. Soon afterward *Jason* entered with yet another northern revolutionary leader—Dr. Rosalvo Bobo—who expected to be acclaimed as president; however, he was then defeated by the U.S.-backed candidate Philippe Sudre Dartiguenave in a hastily arranged election on 12 August, which maneuver added to Haitian resentment against this U.S. intervention. Outright opposition was stifled, however, by the appearance on 13 August of the armored cruiser *Tennessee* with an additional 850 men and thirty-five machine guns of the 1st Marine Regiment under Col. Littleton W. T. Waller. Three days later, the United States assumed permanent administrative duties at Cap-Haïtien and all other ports, effectively bringing Haiti under U.S. domination; only a ragtag army of *caco* rebels retired into the mountainous interior to wage a feeble guerrilla struggle.

Port-au-Prince remained under U.S. martial rule for the next few years, its tranquillity being briefly shattered when the rebel Antoine Pierre Paul attempted to overthrow Dartiguenave by firing into the Presidential Palace at dawn on 5 January 1916; however, this coup was repressed by a swift marine

The American-installed president, Philippe Sudre Dartiguenave, as he appeared, ca. 1920. (Franck, *Roaming Through the West Indies*)

response, five rebels being killed and many others arrested. The capital's residents, like most other Haitians, then resigned themselves to American occupation, expecting it to last for the duration of World War I. When that global conflict ceased in November 1918, unrest quickly developed inland, as Haitian factions began jockeying for power in anticipation of a U.S. withdrawal. Yet such guerrilla activity—especially in the northeastern jungles bordering the Dominican Republic, led by the escaped former general Charlemagne Masséna Péralte—instead caused Washington to rescind its evacuation plans, out of fear that the nation would slide back into anarchy.

Sweeps by heavily reinforced marine units against Charlemagne's elusive *cacos* during the summer of 1919 were punctuated by a dawn assault by 300 guerrillas against the northern gates of Port-au-Prince itself on 6 October, although the

A Haitian gendarme or "policeman" under the American regime, ca. 1920; eight years later, this force was melded with the army to produce the Garde d'Haïti or "Haitian Guard." (Franck, *Roaming Through the West Indies*)

forewarned defenders easily halted this attack with machine gun fire, killing thirty *cacos*. A turncoat was then bribed to lead a marine hunting party into Charlemagne's remote jungle camp on the night of 30–31 October, slaying that charismatic leader. In one last gesture of defiance, his subordinate Benoît Brataville attempted another assault against the capital before sunrise on 15 January 1920, but more than 100 of these 300 attackers were killed.

Washington's policy had hardened into a long-term commitment to improving Haitian material conditions before withdrawing, so as to leave behind a "stable democracy." On 15 May 1922, Dartiguenave was peacefully succeeded as president by Louis Borno, and an agreement was signed whereby his

government was to receive loans from the United States in exchange for allowing American civilian administrators to manage their application. The capital benefited from such imposed assistance, Washington wishing to transform it into a showpiece. Its first public telephones were installed as early as June 1922, while the Bellevue Reservoir was expanded the following year; water distribution gradually spread throughout the city by the laying of steel pipes. A new power plant was installed near the ruins of Fort Sainte-Claire by September 1923, replacing the decrepit unit that had supplied the city's 380 electric streetlights from Bizoton; a decree was furthermore passed on 26 August 1924 expanding the capital's boundaries, so that Port-au-Prince—whose population had increased from an estimated 77,000 people in 1918 to 91,250 by 1928—almost doubled in size as well, annexing some outlying suburbs.

Main avenues around the Bord-de-Mer (Waterfront) section were paved over with thick concrete to permit heavy vehicular traffic, while narrower neighborhood streets were asphalted, both measures facilitating the appearance of the city's first private buses and taxis. In all, some thirty-three miles of urban paving were completed during the 1920s, not counting newly opened streets nor a highway running to Pétionville (which had become transformed into a resort). Lighthouses and harbor buoys were modernized as well, their old oil and kerosene lamps being replaced by more powerful designs.

Many new public buildings were erected: a Palais des Finances (Finance Ministry); a Hôtel de Ville (City Hall, designed by the Haitian architect Georges Baussan and civic engineer Pierre Nazon); an Ecole Centrale d'Agriculture (Central Agricultural School) at Damien; a Quartier Générale de la Gendarmerie (General Police Headquarters); a Bureau des Télégraphes et Téléphones (Office of Telegraphs and Telephones); an Ecole de Médecine (Medical School); a Bureau administratif de la Douane (Customs and Excise Office); a Palais de Justice (Hall of Justice); the Magasins généraux de l'Etat (Bonded Government Warehouses); and a Bureau du Port (Port Office). All were completed between 1924 and 1929, before the Great Depression in the United States brought an abrupt halt to such projects.

As the city's lowest-lying neighborhoods had chronically suffered severe inundations during the rainy seasons, 15 miles of reinforced-concrete drains were laid in 1926 to divert flash-flood waters from the Babiole and Desprez ravines into the Bois-de-Chênes lowlands. Even Port-au-Prince's first radio station began transmitting on 22 October of that same year, while city parks were beautified and the remains of the dead leaders Pétion and Dessalines were solemnly exhumed and reinterred in a mausoleum. A broad new concrete wharf was completed by 1929, while air passenger service from Bowen Field was inaugurated as of September of the same year (the inaugural flight being attended by Col. Charles Lindbergh and

Rue du Quai or "Wharf Street" lined with peaceful protestors awaiting the arrival of the Forbes Commission on 28 February 1930; note its recently poured concrete paving. (Collection Edmond Mangonès)

his wife; Pan American Airways' tiny Fokker–7s were soon replaced in their regular runs to Florida and Puerto Rico by Sikorsky 543 "flying boats," and still later by forty-four-seat "American Clippers").

But despite such welcome improvements to the infrastructure, Haitians remained unhappy with this foreign presence, especially as such efforts were repeatedly marred by racist attitudes among some Americans. The curt announcement by President George Freeman of the Ecole Centrale d'Agriculture that student grants would be reduced sparked a protest on 31 October 1929 that deepened when Perkins Johnson, director of Port-au-Prince's customshouse, struck an employee on 2 December, provoking a temporary walkout by most government employees. Consequently, Marine Col. R. M. Cutts proclaimed martial law one week later, resulting in a tragic confrontation at Croix-Marchaterre near Les Cayes in January 1930, when rural peasants—launching their own independent protest against recently imposed alcohol and tobacco taxes—were fired upon by a jittery marine contingent, suffering more than twenty dead and fifty wounded.

President Herbert Hoover dispatched a commission from Washington to investigate matters under Cameron Forbes, former governor-general of the Philippines, whose five members all spoke French and reached Port-au-Prince aboard the cruiser USS *Rochester* on the afternoon of 28 February 1930. After listening to numerous complaints, they defused the crisis by proposing that the Haitian Assembly elect an interim president to replace Borno—seventy-year-old Eugène Roy

being chosen on 21 April—while furthermore recommending that the office of marine "high commissioner" be abolished and Haiti gradually restored to local rule. The capital experienced a rash of arson fires during this tense period until Roy could actually assume office, the villas of both the senior marine colonel and lieutenant-colonel being burned, along with the Parisiana Theater—where the Assembly had conducted its vote. Yet on the appointed day, Borno quit the Presidential Palace to a chorus of jeers, and eight days later he flew out of Chancerelles Airfield with his son Henri aboard a Pan American Airways flight, bound for exile in France.

Legislative elections—the first in more than thirty years—were held on 14 October 1930, and the Assembly convened in the capital by 17 November to select a new president from among their number. Sténio Vincent, the fifty-six-year-old former mayor of Port-au-Prince, emerged victorious the next day and began pressuring Washington to end its occupation, seconded by diplomatic complaints from Latin American governments. Franklin D. Roosevelt finally acceded, as part of his "Good Neighbor" policy toward the Western Hemisphere. In May 1934, a U.S. fleet composed of the aircraft carrier *Saratoga* and twenty-eight other vessels under Rear Adm. John Hallegan paid a five-day courtesy call at Port-au-Prince, after which Roosevelt announced—during a meeting with the Haitian president at Cap-Haïtien on 5 July—that the marines would be withdrawn the following month. Military authority was transferred to the Garde d'Haïti (Haitian Guard) during a ceremony held at the capital's Champ-de-Mar parade grounds on

The wooden Parisiana Theater being consumed by a fire set by an arsonist on the morning of 30 April 1930. (Collection Edmond Mangonès)

1 August, and two weeks later the last U.S. servicemen departed.

Modern Growth (1935–Present)

Although few enhancements were to be added to Port-au-Prince over the next decade and a half, residents were nonetheless relieved to regain their national autonomy. The Haitian economy remained dependent upon agricultural exports to the United States and France, the latter declining notably because of interruptions occasioned by naval dangers during the World War II years of 1939 to 1945. Soaring coffee prices on foreign exchanges produced a postwar revival and favorable balance of trade by 1949, when Port-au-Prince celebrated the bicentenary of its foundation by hosting an international exposition. Its importance as the political capital persisted with such incidents as the bloodless deposal of President Dumarsais Estimé by Col. Paul E. Magloire in May 1950. That same year, a census revealed its population to have reached 134,117 inhabitants.

Like other Caribbean and Latin American cities, Port-au-Prince subsequently began to experience a remarkable expansion, as increased birthrates plus the introduction of some limited mechanization—reducing the demand for field hands—produced mass migrations from depressed rural areas into the capital, almost quadrupling its urban populace

to 494,000 by 1971. Such a huge influx of new residents would have strained the resources of any municipal government, much less the cash-starved administration vainly striving to control such explosive growth. Because of the city's warm climate, even crude huts sufficed to provide squatters with some shelter, so that slums soon mushroomed southwest of Port-au-Prince, as well as in its light-industrial sector to the north. Wealthier citizens escaped into new developments to the southeast, nearer Turgeau, while commercial and governmental offices came to predominate within the old city core.

This unbridled demographic growth continued to accelerate after President François "Papa Doc" Duvalier died in office on 21 April 1971, being succeeded as president-for-life by his nineteen-year-old son Jean-Claude "Baby Doc" Duvalier. Within the next five years, the capital's population attained 638,800 inhabitants, the vast majority mired in abject poverty, without running water, electricity, or other amenities. Public transportation remained woefully inadequate for such a sprawl of people, being supplemented by *tap-taps*—extemporized private vehicles made out of brightly painted wooden bodies attached atop old automobile frames. Undeterred, new migrants continued to pour into the metropolitan area, few tall buildings being erected because of a lack of capitalization and modern construction experience, so that the city instead continued to spread out into its surrounding

U.S. Marines trooping aboard the transport *Argonne* to withdraw from Haiti, 15 August 1934. (Collection Georges Corvington)

foothills, engulfing nearby towns. By the mid-1980s, even such formerly remote places as Carrefour, Bizoton, and Pétionville had become virtual suburbs, interconnected by crowded highways.

After several months of disgruntled street disturbances and mounting international pressure, "Baby Doc" Duvalier fled Port-au-Prince on the night of 7 February 1986, flying into exile in France with his wife and twenty relations aboard a U.S. Air Force transport. He was temporarily replaced by a five-man junta commanded by his army chief-of-staff, Lt. Gen. Henri Namphy, who also overthrew civilian president Leslie Manigat when the latter attempted to dismiss him from his post on 19 June 1988. Three months later Namphy was himself deposed in turn by Brig. Prosper Avril, and municipal services continued to suffer. By 1990 there were an estimated 690,000 residents crammed within the old boundaries of Port-au-Prince, and well over a million people if its entire metropolitan area were included.

Four years later yet another dramatic political confrontation gripped the capital, when after three years of unavailing diplomatic efforts to restore the democratically elected Jean-Bertrand Aristide as president—including the imposition of a naval blockade, plus freezing of Haitian assets in the United States—U.S. president William J. Clinton authorized a full-scale military intervention dubbed Operation "Uphold Democracy." A fleet of twenty-three warships set sail on 22 Septem-

ber 1994, while the next day a trio of emissaries (former U.S. president Jimmy Carter; former chief of the Joint Chiefs of Staff, Gen. Colin Powell; plus Senator San Nunn of Georgia, chairman of the Armed Services Committee) flew into Port-au-Prince to offer inducements to Lt.-Gen. Raoul Cédras, his second-in-command Brig. Philippe Biamby, and Police Chief Lt.-Col. Joseph-Michel François to go into exile.

The U.S. task force under Adm. Paul D. Miller appeared off the coast by 26 September 1994, consisting of the nuclear aircraft carriers *America* and *Eisenhower*, bearing more than 100 helicopters and 4,000 troops between them; the helicopter carrier *Wasp*, conveying an additional 2,000 marines; the amphibious assault vessels *Nashville* and *Mount Whitney;* the guided missile destroyer *Comte de Grasse;* the guided missile frigates *Aubrey Fitch*, *Oliver Hazard Perry*, and *Clifton Sprague;* plus fourteen other transports and support vessels. These quickly threw 19,000 men ashore, encountering no opposition from Haiti's 7,000-man army, which was ordered not to resist because of Cédras's last-minute acceptance of Washington's terms. After a three-week occupation during which U.S. peacekeeping forces and other United Nations troops fully secured the island, Aristide returned to Port-au-Prince on 15 October, while Cédras flew off into exile in Panama.

For further reading on the history of Port-au-Prince or Haiti, please consult the Select Bibliography at the end of this volume.

Jamaica

Kingston

Seaside capital that has been relocated twice before finally evolving into its modern configuration.

First European Contacts (1494–1523)

Christopher Columbus, having ventured west-southwestward from his initial Spanish settlement on Haiti in hopes of finding the ephemeral Asian mainland, sighted the northern coast of Jamaica on 5 May 1494, deeming it to be the most beautiful island he had yet encountered in the Antilles. After refitting his trio of ships in an inlet, then coasting westward as far as Montego Bay, the explorer nine days later proceeded toward Cuba. He returned three months afterward to circle slowly around Jamaica's southern shoreline, visiting with the chieftain at Bahía de la Vaca (Cow Bay, modern Portland Bay), before gliding past what would later become Kingston and Point Morant, then departing again on 19 August.

Despite recognizing Jamaica as fertile and densely populated, the Spaniards were disappointed by the island's lack of material wealth and therefore showed little inclination to occupy it. Only a few transient ships called, Rodrigo de Bastidas and Juan de la Cosa pausing briefly in 1501 to repair damage that their vessels had suffered from teredo worms during their reconnaissance of the South American mainland, while Columbus himself was marooned on Jamaica's north coast in late June 1503, waiting more than a year to be rescued from Santo Domingo.

Spanish colonization efforts were eventually spurred when the Crown designated Jamaica as an advance base for resupplying Diego de Nicuesa's and Alonso de Ojeda's expeditions of 1509, which were intended to settle Panama and Colombia, respectively. Feeling that the grant of the island for such use infringed upon Columbus's prior claim, his son and heir, Diego Columbus, consequently dispatched sixty men from Santo Domingo under a retainer named Juan de Esquivel to reaffirm his title over Jamaica. King Fernando II subsequently reversed himself and recognized Columbus's act of possession in a letter dated 28 February 1510; a town called Sevilla la Nueva (The New Seville)—de Esquivel a native of the Andalusian port—had been founded on the site of Christopher Columbus's early north-shore encampment, near modern Saint Ann's Bay.

A blockhouse and stockade were duly erected from felled trees, after which its settlers gradually fanned out from this coastal foothold to carve out inland farms, clashing with the local inhabitants. But as Jamaica possessed no deposits of precious metals and soon became depopulated as islanders fled disease or enslavement, the Spaniards also began quitting the island in disappointment, lured away by more promising prospects such as Diego Velázquez's campaign to conquer Cuba during the winter of 1511–1512. The Crown therefore attempted to bolster Jamaica's colonization efforts by appointing Francisco de Garay as the island's new governor late in 1514, and he arrived to assume office as of 15 May 1515. The island's name was also officially changed, to Santiago de Jamaica (Saint James of Jamaica), its original Arawak name having apparently signified "Isle of Springs." De Esquivel's original stockade at Sevilla la Nueva soon included a church and

Panoramic view northeastward across Kingston's waterfront, ca. 1914, looking toward the distant Blue Mountains. (Lloyd, *Twentieth Century Impressions of the West Indies*)

View southwestward across Kingston's anchorage, toward Palisadoes Spit and some British cruisers lying at anchor, 1913. (Lloyd, *Twentieth Century Impressions of the West Indies*)

several scores of shacks with thatched roofs, while its maritime traffic serviced new settlements springing up along the coast; Spanish settlers had moreover introduced domesticated animals, such as cattle, horses, pigs, and sheep, which began to multiply.

But the discovery of the immensely wealthy Mexican empire in 1519 effectively drained the island again, many residents being tempted to emigrate in quest of such dazzling riches—even Governor de Garay himself, who upon learning of the Aztecs' existence, had dispatched four vessels to reconnoiter the Gulf of Mexico in the hope of at least claiming its northern province of Pánuco. When Hernán Cortés, already engaged in subduing the Mexican overlords, absorbed this rival expedition into his ranks, de Garay vainly outfitted two more such contingents, before finally quitting Jamaica on 23 June 1523 at the head of 144 horsemen, 300 archers, 200 harquebusiers, and 200 swordsmen crammed aboard eleven vessels, determined to seize a Mexican toehold by dint of arms. He failed and died in absentia three years later, leaving Jamaica forlorn over the loss of its governor and so many able-bodied men, its remaining residents being unable to attract replacements because of the rush of adventurers directly to Mexico.

Emergence of Santiago de la Vega (1523–1589)

During the very last year of Governor de Garay's tenure, some Jamaican settlers had shifted around to the island's southern shore to occupy a fertile expanse that they recognized was sheltered from the prevailing northeasterly winds and hurricanes of the West Indies by a protective crescent of hills rising to some 2,000 feet. The rich fields of this plain also sloped gently upward from a fine natural harbor that was called Caguaya by its indigenous fishermen and whose 10 square miles of deepwater anchorage were additionally guarded from sea currents and storms by a 2-mile spit of land serving as a breakwater.

These Spaniards therefore disembarked in 1523 to push in from this coastal outlet, clearing farmlands to its west as well as creating a cluster of homes some 6 to 7 miles from the sea. Harvests could be ferried back down the Cobre (Copper) River for export aboard the small ships that called in what would later become known as Hunt's Bay. An overland trail was also cut, so that this inland town of Santiago de la Vega (Saint James of the Plain) evolved over the next few years into the most populous Spanish concentration on the island, displacing Seville la Nueva as its capital by 1534.

The King's House at Spanish Town, Jamaica's former capital of Santiago de la Vega, ca. 1914. (Lloyd, *Twentieth Century Impressions of the West Indies*)

Yet despite the benign climate and ideal conditions for cultivation, settlers found this southern port even farther removed from the main Caribbean sea routes, which now flowed past the island's northern face, running directly from Puerto Rico and Santo Domingo toward Cuba and Mexico. There was also another new equally inaccessible route farther east, which had been opened into Panama after the conquest of the spectacularly wealthy Incan empire of Peru by Francisco Pizarro in the early 1530s.

As a result, Caguaya was usually to receive only a single 120-ton ship from the far side of the Atlantic every year, plus a few dozen tiny West Indian traders. In 1546, Columbus's descendant and nominal island owner—the Duque de Veragua, a permanent resident of Spain—attempted to repopulate his family's neglected Jamaican outpost by sending out Capt. Cristóbal de Peña with a small group of additional settlers; yet such modest reinforcement could scarcely compensate for the colony's lack of appeal, when compared with the silver-rich destinations of Veracruz or Panama. Ironically, Caguaya was to become even more ignored as Spanish transatlantic traffic swelled in volume and ever-larger galleons were introduced during the latter half of the sixteenth century; masters of such large vessels grew even more reluctant to be diverted to Jamaica and brave its reef-lined approaches merely for the sake of its modest agricultural produce.

As a result, Santiago de la Vega's inhabitants—like many other bypassed Spanish communities in the New World—resorted to clandestine contacts with foreign smugglers to meet their needs. A couple of skirmishes were recorded in the summer of 1556, when local authorities attempted to crack down on Jamaica's illegal traffic by arresting a few Frenchmen who had come to trade. Still, officially sanctioned visits by vessels detached from the plate-fleets became increasingly sporadic: a 120-ton ship called in 1557, a 220-ton merchantman in 1560, a trio of 120-ton vessels in 1563, a single 120-tonner in 1565, another pair five years later, a single ship in 1571, then not another until 1580, plus one more in 1582.

By November 1582, Santiago de la Vega's abbot, Francisco Márquez de Villalobos, reported to his superiors in Spain that the town's population consisted of only 100 inhabitants and that their economy was so moribund because of a lack of seaborne contacts that they concentrated mostly on ensuring their basic subsistence. When a French slaver chanced to maroon 150 Africans on the island six years later, they were eagerly redistributed among the few Spanish landowners, who were otherwise bereft of laborers.

First English Descents (1590–1603)

The weakness of this struggling community invited attack by even the smallest privateering expedition after hostilities erupted against Elizabethan England in 1588. One of the first West Indian actions of that conflict occurred when a Spanish convoy out of Santo Domingo, escorted by Capt. Vicente González's galleon, was chased into Caguaya Bay on 13 July 1590 by the 160-ton *Little John* of Christopher Newport and 35-ton pinnace *John Evangelist* of William Lane, which were part of a larger English flotilla under Capt. Abraham Cocke prowling off Haiti's southwestern Cape Tiburón. Two of these Spanish merchantmen ran aground while trying to gain the harbor and were refloated by the pursuing rovers, although the remaining six or seven huddled under the safety of its few harbor guns until Newport and Lane withdrew the following morning.

Jamaica was also victimized by a trio of privateering vessels under Capt. James Langton in mid-February 1594 that intercepted two Spanish barks offshore and combined their cargoes aboard a single one, before dispatching that prize toward England. Capts. Amyas Preston and George Somers paused off the Jamaican coast as well with their three sickly vessels on 12 July the next summer, remaining four days before continuing for the Caymans.

However, the most serious assault occurred when seven vessels under Sir Anthony Sherley reconnoitered as far west as Point Negril on 1 February 1597, before boldly anchoring in Caguaya Bay three days later to set 230 armed men ashore who marched inland to overrun Santiago de la Vega. Its townspeople considered resisting, but upon perceiving the invaders' firepower they instead abandoned their dwellings and melted into the jungle hills. The English occupied Santiago for forty days, stripping its 100 or so primitive structures of valuables, before threatening to put all to the torch unless a ransom of beef and cassava was paid. The Spaniards deemed their thatched wooden edifices unworthy of such meager ransom, yet eventually they gave something so that the English might depart.

Disturbed by the ease of this capture, Crown officials in Madrid sent out some artillery pieces, 400 cannonballs, 150 harquebuses, and 50 muskets in August 1597 to bolster Jamaica's defenses. The island's governor, Fernando Melgarejo de Córdoba, also briefly entertained the notion of fortifying Santiago de la Vega itself, before discarding such a possibility as beyond the means of its tiny, impoverished community; a census taken that same September revealed only 730 inhabitants on the entire island. Instead, the ordnance received from Spain was to be used to create four new batteries at various beaches around its seaport of Caguaya Bay, furthermore bolstered by the digging of numerous seaside gun trenches.

These new harbor defenses did not deter a joint Anglo-French disembarkation on 24 January 1603, when eight vessels under the veteran captains Michael Geare and Christopher Newport paused to set a force ashore; yet Melgarejo was at least able to await these raiders at another new emplacement less than a mile outside Santiago, opening fire with its single artillery-piece and stampeding a cattle herd through the surprised privateer vanguard, compelling them to retire. A lesser descent in May of that same year by the London ship *Elizabeth and Cleeve* of Capt. Christopher Reeve and a small pinnace was also repelled.

Spanish Imperial Backwater (1604–1655)

Once this naval war with England ceased in August 1604, Jamaica experienced a modest rebound, a census taken in July 1611 indicating that the island's total population had grown to 523 Spanish residents with 173 children, 558 black slaves and 107 of their offspring, 75 transients, plus 74 Christianized Indians. Approximately 500 of these individuals resided at Santiago de la Vega, serviced by its modest church, in addition to monasteries established by the orders of Nuestra Señora de Belén and San Jerónimo. Yet the inhabitants' isolation remained largely unchanged, as overseas contacts continued to languish because of a lack of Spanish commercial traffic—a deficiency that would only worsen as the home country's power steadily eroded during the seventeenth century.

Into this vacuum moved foreign seamen, who soon began establishing rival Antillean outposts to windward of the lonely Spanish colony. On 28 March 1643—Palm Saturday—a sloop hurried into Caguaya from Coro, Venezuela, with an urgent warning that Jamaica was about to be attacked by an English expedition under Commo. William Jackson, who had already rampaged through the Laguna de Maracaibo in retaliation for Spain's eradication of England's Providence Island settlement a few years before. Jackson's eleven vessels appeared on 3 April, Easter Friday, disembarking 500 men who brushed aside the feeble Spanish resistance and penetrated inland to occupy Santiago de la Vega for more than a month, eventually sparing its humble dwellings for a ransom of 7,000 pesos, 200 head of cattle, plus some cassava.

Frightened citizens requested weaponry once again from Spain, but the bankrupt Crown could do little more than authorize their absentee overlord, the Duque de Veragua, to send out a private consignment of arms. No such shipment ever arrived, however, and Jamaica's inhabitants were then further decimated by a smallpox epidemic in 1650 that claimed the lives of approximately 50 Spaniards and 100 slaves. The next year, survivors complained that they only had five small and ancient artillery-pieces and 300 ill-assorted firearms with which to defend the 1,500 men, women, children, and slaves left on the island; they therefore begged that funds be provided from the Royal Exchequer to erect a small fortress at Cayo Carena (Careening Key) at the westernmost tip of Caguaya's land-spit—only to learn that Spain's financial destitution precluded even such modest assistance.

English Conquest (1655)

Jamaica's fate was abruptly altered when two turtle hunters spotted a huge fleet rounding Point Morant on 9 May 1655 and hastened to warn Gov. Juan Ramírez de Arellano at Santiago de la Vega. (This event actually occurred on 19 May according to our modern Gregorian calendar, yet it was 9 May by the "Old Style" Julian calendar still employed by the English.) The islanders were caught completely off guard by this unannounced English aggression. At dawn the next day, the invaders hove to outside Caguaya Bay, Adm. William Penn transferring from his 60-gun flagship *Swiftsure* aboard the lighter 12-gun galley *Martin* to lead a flotilla of lesser craft inside by 10:00 A.M. Despite grounding a few times amid the shallows, as well as a brief exchange of shots with the battery covering the inner anchorage—soon to be renamed "Passage Fort," which was abandoned by its handful of inexperienced Spanish defenders under Francisco de Proenza, a local *hacendado* (estate owner)—Penn disembarked a contingent unopposed at Esquivel. The next day, he advanced to occupy Santiago de la Vega, obliging the defeated Ramírez to request a parley.

The British land commander, Gen. Robert Venables, despite being sick, came ashore on 15 May 1655 to announce that the entire island was to be permanently annexed by Britain and that its Spanish inhabitants had a fortnight to depart. Ramírez reluctantly signed this capitulation two days later and set sail shortly thereafter, although not all Spaniards recognized the surrender. More defiant spirits rallied at the inland town of Guatibacoa to ally themselves with the *cimarrones* (renegade black slaves) of the mountainous interior and wage a guerrilla campaign.

The English meanwhile deposited several thousand soldiers who secured Caguaya Bay and Santiago de la Vega, which they dubbed "Cagway" and "Spanish Town," respectively; however, as they were already suffering from tropical diseases contracted during an earlier unsuccessful assault against Santo Domingo, plus a scarcity of provisions, these occupiers soon began succumbing by the hundreds. Within a year, the first 7,000 English arrivals would be reduced to 2,500, and because of this fearsome outbreak, Penn hastily left for England on 25 June with twenty warships, leaving a mere dozen behind under Vice Adm. William Goodson as a permanent squadron.

Creation of Port Royal (1655–1691)

Given their precarious hold upon the island, with Spanish and black guerrillas roaming the foothills just beyond their coastal camps, the dwindling number of healthy Englishmen decided to commence work a couple of weeks later on a 20-gun, rectangular sea-castle at the western tip of Caguaya's land-spit, so as at least to secure their sea communications. By quarrying limestone out of the Port Henderson Hills on the mainland opposite, they were able to construct a stout new stronghold that was christened Fort Cromwell in October 1655.

Compared with this strategic necessity, the defense of a couple of hundred adobe-brick, thatched-roof dwellings at Santiago de la Vega was of secondary importance—although they too were encircled by a wooden palisade that same November, while the old Spanish battery on the western side of Hunt's Bay was transformed into Passage Fort. Yet most construction efforts remained concentrated at Cagway Point, whose stone citadel was deemed sufficiently complete by January 1656 to receive a regiment withdrawn from Spanish Town, notwithstanding the fact that the troops had to bivouac amid the spit's low scrubland dunes in 100 tents. Still, this site was deemed healthier than the capital because of its cool sea breezes and sandy subsoil, which precluded the formation of stagnant puddles. A round stone tower was also commenced inside Fort Cromwell's circuit by March 1656, and as fears of a Spanish reconquest gradually receded, thousands of settlers began arriving from the Leeward Islands to replace the sickly soldiery, fanning out to cultivate the surrounding Liguanea Plain.

As this new phase of the island's development occurred, extemporized huts and shacks gave way to more permanent structures, most now clustered around Cagway's anchorage rather than the original Spanish capital of Santiago de la Vega. This geographical shift gained further impetus after the Commonwealth commissioner William Brayne noted in July 1657 that there was "the fair beginning of a town upon the point of this harbor," where he intended "all our storehouses and trade shall be, which will soon make it a flourishing place."

Consequently, a new governor's residence and large state storehouse were erected on Cagway Point rather than inland at Santiago, while private plots were surveyed in 60-foot lengths by Nicholas Keene to face Cagway's inner harbor. An oak-planked temple called Christchurch was commenced in early January 1658, and a smithy's forge the next month. By August there were at least three rows of houses occupying the point, and as an added precaution against surprise attack, Maj. Richard Stevens erected a line of *pallisadoes* (palisades) across the spit's eastern end, radiating from a stout gatehouse. An oak-planked courthouse was also erected for the emergent town, and Fort Cromwell increased its ordnance to seventy-five guns.

By the middle of 1659 private land was becoming scarce on Cagway Point, despite the disadvantage of having to ferry drinking water and fresh food out from the mainland in canoes. The last serious Spanish attempt to reconquer the island had already been defeated on the northern coast, after which the guerrilla leader Cristóbal Arnaldo de Issasi had quit his Blue Mountain hideout in discouragement. By the summer of 1660 plantations were blossoming across Liguanea Plain,

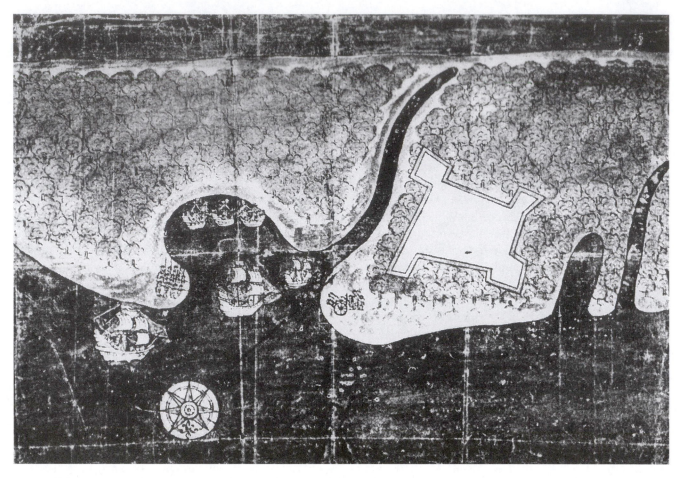

Crude Spanish map of the new English fortress being installed at Port Royal, ca. 1655–1660; note that its contours have been fairly well rendered, although the harbor shorelines are greatly distorted. (Archive of Indies, Seville)

trade with England and New England was growing apace, and Cagway Point boasted roughly 200 houses—many built of brick—plus a permanent population of 600 to 700 people, not including its garrison nor hundreds of transient seafarers.

In August 1660, reports from London indicated that the Commonwealth had collapsed and that Charles II had been restored to the throne, so that Fort Cromwell was renamed "Fort Charles" and Cagway became "Port Royal." Jamaica's first royal governor—Thomas, 7th Baron Windsor of Stanwell—did not actually arrive to assume office until August 1662, being well received, as he had brought out the Cromwellian army's back pay, discharging more than 1,000 surviving soldiers with full wages and a gratuity. This official furthermore convened a legislative assembly at the old capital of Spanish Town, as well as establishing a vice admiralty court so that local cases would not have to be adjudicated across the Atlantic. But his most welcome innovation was the issuance of privateering commissions against the regional Spaniards, despite the nominal peace existing with that nation back in Europe.

Aggrieved by the continuous threat of counterinvasion and other hostile acts by their Spanish-American neighbors, some 1,300 men—many of them discharged soldiers, including a twenty-seven-year-old militia captain named Henry Morgan—eagerly volunteered in September 1662 for a raid against Santiago de Cuba, led by Jamaica's naval commander-in-chief, Commo. Christopher Myngs. The easy success of this venture encouraged the island council to authorize another such assault on 12 December of that same year against Campeche, which also triumphed. Port Royal was consequently to flourish as a major privateering base over the ensuing decade, Morgan emerging as "admiral" of a host of freebooters drawn from throughout the West Indies, leading them on large-scale descents against Portobelo in 1668, Maracaibo the next year, and Panama in 1671.

The Jamaican port witnessed a commensurate rise in peaceful traffic as well, with more than 200 merchantmen calling at its anchorage between January 1668 and January 1670, while Port Royal's permanent populace grew to "714 free men, 529 free women, 426 free children, and 312 slaves" by 1673—

that is, 1,981 inhabitants spread among roughly 800 dwellings. Seven years later, the town's population had continued to rise so impressively that it was estimated at almost 3,000 people: "a little over 2,000 whites and about 850 blacks."

Nevertheless, smaller Spanish Town still remained the island's legal capital, and the plantation owners who had come to dominate Jamaican affairs deplored the excesses committed by the Port Royal privateers, whose bellicosity threatened the peaceful expansion of sugar, cacao, and tobacco exports. Thanks to the disproportionate political power wielded by this elite—only large landowners were permitted to sit as representatives in the assembly or on the council—they were able to vote to curtail buccaneer raids during the early 1670s, while simultaneously encouraging the importation of African slaves so as to clear and operate ever larger estates around the island. Such policies not only altered Jamaica's demographics—its white populace declining from roughly 12,000 people in 1680 to 7,000 by 1700, while its slave population rose from 15,000 to 40,000 during that same period—but furthermore diminished Port Royal's importance, as new outlets were created to export island produce.

To add to its woes, Port Royal was buffeted by a pair of hurricanes in 1683–1684, producing extensive flooding and erosion. Still, it remained Jamaica's largest and busiest town, as well as the region's principal naval base, its defenses having been augmented by the erection of Forts James, Carlisle, and Rupert, as well as a 16-gun battery known as Morgan's Line.

Earthquake and Transferal to Kingston (1692–1722)

Because of its difficult approaches and numerous batteries, Port Royal had never been threatened during the frequent outbursts of seventeenth-century warfare. Yet at 11:40 A.M. on Wednesday, 7 June 1692, an earthquake struck with such ferocity that much of the northern section of the town slid into the harbor, at least two rows of its buildings and some 2,000 of its 6,500 inhabitants being swallowed in 30 to 40 feet of water. Another 2,000 people succumbed as a result of the tidal wave that followed almost immediately thereafter, swamping many of the remaining dwellings and even bursting open the graveyard, adding to the subsequent spread of disease. Such a dramatic catastrophe was widely interpreted abroad as divine punishment, Port Royal's lurid past as a buccaneer roost leading some moralists to label it "the wickedest place on earth"—although it had not been previously known as exceptionally licentious when compared with other seaports of that age.

Nevertheless, many frightened survivors temporarily shifted to "the Rock" (modern Rockfort) at the eastern extreme of the bay in the aftermath of this calamity, while council members examined several sites along the inner shoreline for a new urban locale, rejecting Delacree Pen where the ferry connecting Port Royal to Liguanea Plain had traditionally deposited its passengers as too marshy and unhealthful. A hog crawl farther east was therefore selected and purchased for £2,000 from its absentee proprietor, Col. William Beeston, after which a gridiron-pattern of blocks measuring a half-mile wide by three-quarters of a mile deep was laid out by John Goffe, and 809 lots were assigned for distribution.

Within six weeks of Port Royal's devastation, the name of this new settlement appeared in council minutes as "Kingston"; yet despite a decree directing that all surviving property holders were to erect a house "worth £50" within three years of receiving their new allotment, little construction actually commenced; most Port Royal residents were at first inclined to rebuild on their original land-spit. A further complication arose when Beeston arrived early in 1693, armed with a knighthood and title as the island's new lieutenant-governor, and immediately contested the council's unilateral purchase of his hog crawl, so that it reverted to his ownership. He thereupon began privately selling lots at £5 apiece, while at the same time using his official position to constitute Kingston into a parish—a church soon was begun on the southeast corner of King Street and the new settlement's "Parade," or main square—as well as ordering the island secretary, receiver-general, and naval agent to transfer their operations ashore from Port Royal, so that merchants and others must also transpose their businesses.

Beeston's blatant profit mongering naturally retarded Kingston's development, as did the fact that Jamaica remained distracted by ongoing hostilities against France known as King William's War. The destruction of all harbor defenses except for Fort Charles and part of Morgan's Line by the earthquake and tidal wave soon tempted the French of Saint-Domingue (Haiti) to mount an invasion attempt under their governor, Jean-Baptiste Ducasse, who materialized off Jamaica's eastern tip on the morning of 17 June 1694 with twenty-two vessels bearing more than 3,100 men. The bulk of this fleet anchored in Cow Bay, 15 miles east of the devastated Port Royal, hoping that they had taken the defenders by surprise; yet upon realizing that the English had been forewarned and were prepared to resist, Ducasse contented himself with plundering isolated coastal communities as far west as Carlisle Bay, before departing in late July.

Once hostilities ceased, more than three years later, Port Royal resumed its former role of port of entry, while Kingston burgeoned as a civilian community, achieving a population of approximately 5,000 by 1700. Merchants had soon recognized that their warehouses were safer upon the mainland, their homes less crowded, and overland access to their inland markets less impeded. Port Royal had the further misfortune to be leveled yet again, this time by an accidental blaze that consumed virtually every building in January 1703. Thirteen days after that conflagration, the island council tried once more to orchestrate a complete shift across to the mainland by passing the so-called Kingston Act, which prohibited the resettling of Port Royal and remitted house taxes in Kingston for seven

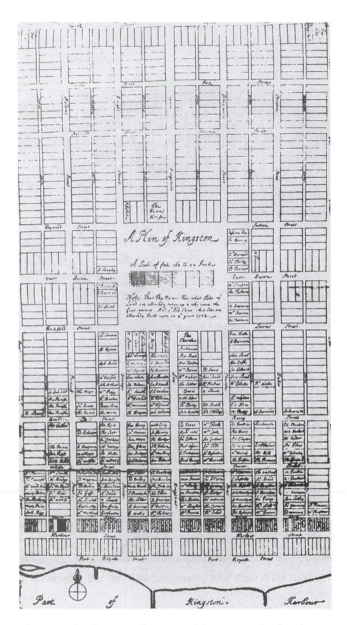

Plan drawn by Christian Lilly in 1702 of the new mainland settlement of Kingston; note the town's long narrow shape, as well as the cluster of early properties south of its main square or Parade, so as to be nearest the three "finger" wharves along its waterfront. (Institute of Jamaica)

base remained intact, with its dockyard, hospital, repair shops, and so forth still ensconced at Port Royal. The exposed establishments on the spit again suffered considerable damage from a hurricane on 28 August 1712, plus another even more violent storm exactly ten years later that flattened half of Port Royal and killed about 400 residents. Henceforth, Kingston was to become the island's dominant town—although without a commensurate political or judicial power, which was still retained at tiny Spanish Town—while naval administration was concentrated at Port Royal.

Colonial Preeminence (1723–1815)

The growth of the West Indian sugar industry was stimulated by Parliament's passage of the Molasses Act in 1733, as well as the Sugar Act six years later, both measures having been engineered by monopoly interests in London. The resultant upsurge in trade volumes solidified Kingston's primacy on the island, as it was to import vast numbers of slaves and British manufactures destined for inland plantations, as well as export bountiful harvests and serve as Jamaica's financial center. The 86,500 resident slaves in 1734 quadrupled in number over the next six decades, while annual sugar exports rose from 33,000 hogsheads in 1739 to almost 100,000 a year during that same interval.

Waterfront properties consequently came into great demand, so that Kingston expanded eastward between its shoreline and Windward Road (any growth westward being precluded by the encroaching mangroves of Delacree Pen and Greenwich Farm). Many new structures were also added, such as the Sephardic synagogue erected at the corner of Princess Street and Water Lane in 1750. Harbor defenses were augmented as well, especially after the eruption of the War of Jenkins's Ear or King George's War late in 1739; a 12-gun battery nicknamed the Twelve Apostles was completed the following year atop a small promontory to cover the channel running past the Port Henderson Hills (this new passage having been opened up by the 1692 earthquake). A lengthier project was initiated as well, on a formidable new defense to sweep the narrows leading into the inner harbor from Mosquito Point, becoming named Fort Augusta in honor of England's Queen; it was completed despite a hurricane that struck the port in 1744 and an accidental explosion within its compound five years afterward.

By 1755, Kingston encompassed more than 1,400 urban lots covering 340 acres, its population having roughly doubled in size to almost 10,000 inhabitants. Fine two-storied Georgian town houses made of stone and brick and featuring columned verandas, high-pitched shingle roofs, and shuttered windows lined East Queen Street, East Street, and Hanover Street, while its merchants had become so wealthy and influential as to outmaneuver the island's planter-legislators at Spanish Town and transfer the title of capital to Kingston—a short-lived victory, though, as the seat of government was restored to Spanish

years. Yet the original offshore site still offered the better anchorage, as well as being regarded as a more healthful and more defensible locale, so that the merchants succeeded in getting the plantation owners' Kingston Act disallowed through lengthy legal arguments and appeals to London.

Port Royal consequently remained the focus of maritime activity, although Kingston was by now so clearly in the ascendancy that the offshore town began serving as a mere transshipment point for mainland businesses, its commercial importance being gradually siphoned off. Only the Royal Navy

Town by 1758 at the instigation of the king-in-council. (The planter-legislators subsequently set about systematically depriving Kingston of public offices over the next few decades, so that its administration might never grow too independent again. Officials such as the receiver-general, the island secretary, and the comptroller consequently had to continue conducting business out of their private homes, inconveniently scattered throughout the town.)

Kingston served as an important naval and privateering base when Britain declared war against France in May 1756, profiting so significantly from the sale of provisions to arriving English fleets and London-bound convoys (plus the disposal of hundreds of prizes) that the restoration of peace early in 1763 caused a temporary economic downturn. Fort Augusta's magazine was furthermore struck by lighting, exploding with such violence that 300 garrison troops were killed, while a heavy earthquake also rumbled through the harbor in September 1771, damaging many buildings. Still, Kingston recuperated swiftly, a survey the following year registering 1,665 houses within the town—four times as many as at Spanish Town.

The American War of Independence, which broke out in 1775, proved somewhat more difficult, for the severance of trade with the Thirteen Colonies hurt Jamaica's economy. The island itself was furthermore threatened when France joined these hostilities as an American ally in 1778, provoking a brief invasion scare at Kingston. Worse still was the alarm of early 1782, when a huge French fleet under Adm. François-Joseph Paul, Comte de Grasse Tilly—fresh from his victory at Chesapeake Bay—reached Martinique to overwhelm the British West Indian islands of St. Kitts and Montserrat. So great was de Grasse's menace that the Jamaican governor, Archibald Campbell, was warned that it was "certain that your island will be attacked at latest in April," and panic gripped Kingston. Forces were placed upon full alert, and a feverish round of defensive measures were undertaken, including the dismantling of the town's lone foundry, "lest it should prove serviceable to the enemy." However, de Grasse was intercepted and defeated at the Battle of the Saintes on 12 April by Adms. George Rodney and Samuel Hood, whose fleets entered Kingston triumphantly, to the immense relief of its inhabitants.

The town endured another postwar depression once peace

"A Draught of the Harbours of Port Royal and Kingston," ca. 1756, by Richard Jones. (Brown, *The Civil History of Jamaica*)

was concluded in January 1783, and it also successfully weathered a hurricane that struck four years later. In 1788, Kingston's population was measured at a robust 26,478—some 9 percent of the island's total inhabitants—and of whom 6,539 were classified as white, 3,280 as "free colored," and 16,659 as black slaves. Kingston was to enjoy its greatest colonial splendor after the emergence of a radical new government in Paris caused sugar production on neighboring Saint-Domingue (Haiti) to collapse by 1791; the ruin of that rival supplier created such a shortfall upon international markets as to dramatically inflate prices. When the new French Republic furthermore declared war against Britain and most other major European monarchies in January 1793, Kingston resumed its role as a major Caribbean naval base, while the Royal Navy's supremacy at sea ensured the safety of its own traffic.

Kingston also welcomed many French West Indian refugees, both white and black, who settled around its periphery and came to monopolize its market gardening. Notwithstanding the obvious distractions created by the war, some minor attempts were made to ameliorate municipal life as well, such as draining the swamps on Kingston's western fringe. The introduction of so-called Bourbon cane into Jamaican fields in 1800 augmented yields so much that sugar output achieved a record of 150,000 hogsheads five years later. By 1802, Kingston was granted the privilege of its own mayor and corporation, while its population was estimated at more than 30,000 by 1807, spread among some 3,000 permanent dwellings plus hundreds of shacks. Given the increasingly crowded conditions along its waterfront, as well as profits accrued from a dozen boom years of war, wealthy citizens began moving out of the urban core into grand new mansions north of the Parade, or into the foothills to enjoy "a more pure and salubrious air."

However, London's abolition of the African slave trade in 1808 closed Kingston's *vendues* (marts) along Harbour and Barry streets, while a new alliance with Spain simultaneously opened up the vast Spanish-American market to British vessels, so that the city was increasingly obliged to rely upon its "free port" status to lure ships into harbor. More than 400 vessels of foreign registry visited Kingston during 1813, helping prop up an otherwise declining economy; it also received a significant contribution from the 10,000 blacks who gathered for market every Sunday—traditionally, the slaves' day of rest.

Stagnation (1816–1906)

A number of buildings burned accidentally at Port Royal in 1815, yet it was to be the restoration of peace in Europe that same year that ironically precipitated Kingston's steepest decline. Upon Napoleon's surrender, Royal Navy expenditures were abruptly curtailed at all overseas bases, while the volume of Jamaica's lone major export—sugar—had been steadily falling since 1805 and would be hard pressed thereafter to compete internationally once full world trade resumed. The

independence of most South and Central American nations from restrictive Spanish rule in the early 1820s furthermore lured many English and foreign shippers into bypassing Kingston altogether, as they could now gain direct commercial access to the vast, untapped American mainland.

Naturally, Kingston was to remain the largest and most prosperous city in the British West Indies, boasting a total parish population of approximately 35,000 by 1828; yet its seaborne traffic was considerably diminished in value, crippling any hopes of significant revival or future development. Little industry existed on Jamaica beyond some tanning, lime quarrying, cabinetmaking, a pair of small foundries, and a pottery. Because of the city's dimmed prospects, the number of Kingstonians would fail to increase for the first time during the decade of the 1830s, despite some otherwise positive social changes enacted by London. For example, free blacks, "people of colour," and Jews were all granted full rights and suffrage as of 1832, while the process of emancipating Jamaica's last remaining slaves began two years afterward and concluded by 1838. Many of the latter, though, chose to "burrow into the interior" once they became free, clearing tiny properties in the mountains to eke out a subsistence existence as peasants, rather than remain upon the coast.

Kingston suffered a devastating fire in 1843, and the island's sugar industry utterly collapsed two years later, after Britain started to equalize importation duties with the aim of inaugurating an era of free imperial trade. Shorn of its last economic prop, Jamaica's overseas trade was consequently reduced to less than half of its already-diminished volumes, just as Kingston was struggling to rebuild from the fire. To make matters worse, a cholera epidemic struck in 1850, claiming some 5,000 of the city's poorest residents over the next two years, so that its populace stood at a mere 27,400 by 1861. The mid-nineteenth century has been described as "the dark age of Jamaican history," the depths of its poverty and uncertainty finally climaxing with the Morant Bay rebellion of October 1865.

Lacking the means to resolve such difficulties, the island assembly finally abdicated in favor of Crown Colony status that same year, and the corporation of the City of Kingston was dissolved as well. Colonial officers were duly dispatched from England to inject a measure of stability into Jamaica's administrative and fiscal affairs, and among their reforms was the expansion of the municipal boundaries northward in 1867 to encompass the race course and new suburbs of Smith Village, Hannah Town, and Fletcher's Town. Public health services were furthermore overhauled two years later, the privately owned waterworks company being purchased in 1871 and upgraded to provide filtered water. The status of capital was officially transferred back to Kingston from Spanish Town the following year, the Jamaican legislature being installed into the former mansion of Thomas Hibbert's family on Duke Street, which was renamed Headquarters House.

Kingston's courthouse on election day, ca. 1850. (Duperly, *Daguerian Excursions in Jamaica*)

More significantly still, however, the new governors' residence, or King's House, was relocated northeast of Half Way Tree in adjacent St. Andrew Parish, amid the Liguanea Plain, so that the city expanded in that direction as old sugar estates were bought up by wealthy businessmen to be converted into country mansions. Tramway or streetcar service was also inaugurated as of 1876, greatly facilitating access to all of Kingston's suburbs, while a modern slaughterhouse was erected as well. As the nineteenth century drew to a close, Britain gradually became displaced by the United States and Canada as the island's prime trading partners, Jamaican exports to English ports declining from 78 percent of its total in 1870 to a mere 19 percent four decades later. A few small tanneries, tobacco factories, and bottling plants also appeared around Kingston.

Thanks to such modest innovations, impoverished country dwellers began migrating into the capital once more in quest of employment opportunities, so that its population rebounded to 38,566 inhabitants by 1881—of whom 13 percent were classified as whites, 36.5 percent as mulattoes, and 50 percent as blacks—with another 34,982 people scattered about the adjoining St. Andrew Parish. The city corporation was reinstated four years later, yet Jamaica's overall poverty levels remained so high that many people began emigrating over the next few decades, seeking better prospects in the United States, Panama, or Cuba. Kingston's old role as a major British naval base also faded once the Royal Navy adopted a "blue water" strategy during the late nineteenth century, whereby powerful fleets would operate directly out of Britain, touching only briefly at a few select, strongly fortified overseas bases. As Kingston's anchorage was too small to accommodate large numbers of massive battleships, the last Port Royal commodore hauled down his flag in 1905, a withdrawal that led to the swift decay or demolition of its dockyard facilities—although the offshore town itself continued to enjoy a certain measure of prosperity as a pleasant tourist retreat. That same year of 1905, almost 1,900 dwellings in Kingston were connected to its new sewage system, representing about one-sixth of all city houses.

The Kingston Parish Church, ca. 1850. (Duperly, *Daguerian Excursions in Jamaica*)

Earthquake and Resurrection (1907–1938)

A series of heavy jolts struck just after 3:30 P.M. on 14 January 1907, claiming some 1,750 lives as the city's southern and eastern sectors suffered extensive damage. The entire commercial district south of the Parade was gutted by the fires that spread amid the wooden debris thrown down by this catastrophe. Port Royal was also shaken and flooded in its western part, although losses were otherwise largely confined to the capital and its immediate environs, the remainder of Jamaica emerging relatively unscathed. Foreign aid flowed in, and a grant of £150,000 and a loan of £800,000 were secured from Parliament in London to finance the replacement of Kingston's official buildings, as well as to supplement private reconstruction efforts.

The city was to undergo a noticeable architectural transformation as a result of this process, reinforced-concrete structures being widely introduced in the hope of minimizing future losses; sturdier new designs were also produced, such as the public offices erected along King Street between Barry and Tower streets. Life slowly returned to normal for the inhabitants, who numbered 59,674 people according to the census of 1911. Jamaica was to remain largely unaffected by World War I, which started three years later, and the capital became electrified at the conclusion of hostilities in 1918 by the West Indies Electric Company. Five years later, that firm was taken over by the Jamaica Public Service Company, a subsidiary of a larger Canadian corporation that increased generation capacity and broadened the distribution network; this not only helped to better illuminate Kingston, but also encouraged an increase in light industry. The population within the old city boundaries grew modestly to 62,700 inhabitants by 1921, yet, when combined with that of St. Andrew Parish, it now totaled 117,000 people and occupied areas as far east as the Mental Hospital, as far north as Up Park Camp, and as far west as Jones Town.

Two years later this metropolitan sprawl was finally addressed when the administration of both entities was amalgamated into a single "Kingston and St. Andrew Corporation." Marshy areas in the southwestern quadrant of Liguanea Plain around Trench Pen, Maxfield, and Tower Hill Pen were gradually filled in and converted to residential use, as was the district north of Cross Roads. Another economic downturn occurred during the Great Depression years of the early 1930s: per capita incomes declined across the island throughout that

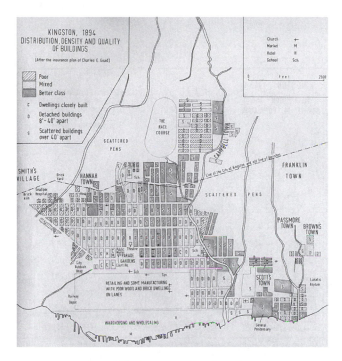

Modern copy of an 1894 insurance plan for Kingston. (Charles E. Goad)

decade, eventually sparking popular unrest spearheaded by the charismatic leader Alexander Bustamante's Industrial Trade Union, which in 1938 organized workers and unemployed alike into a series of assemblies. These often riotous marches demanded "a better life here and now, in a country of which they formed the majority, but from whose society they had been actively excluded." British troops were deployed to quell the disturbances, and a West India Royal Commission was dispatched from London to investigate the conditions that had precipitated the outburst.

Modern Boom (1939–Present)

Reforms were postponed when Britain became entangled in conflict against Nazi Germany in Europe early in September 1939, the Crown soon finding itself so hard pressed that the next year it allowed the U.S. government to establish bases on British possessions throughout the Western Hemisphere in exchange for fifty old destroyers. One such small U.S. Army Air Force base was installed on Jamaica, but the densest concentration of American military deployment in the Caribbean was to be on Puerto Rico and Trinidad.

Two months after the United States was drawn into the fighting by the Japanese attack on Pearl Harbor, the relative tranquillity of the West Indian theater was shattered when Japan's German allies unleashed a submarine offensive codenamed Operation Neuland, on 16 February 1942, immediately sowing panic among the Caribbean shipping lanes. Kingston

Street scene in Kingston, ca. 1905. (Keane, *Central and South America*)

The spire of Kingston's parish church, heavily damaged by the 1907 earthquake. (Lloyd, *Twentieth Century Impressions of the West Indies*)

was not directly threatened, because of its strong defenses and shallow approaches, while the Allies gradually gained air superiority and brought U-boat attacks under control over the next several months.

With Britain distracted by its struggle in Europe, and the United States widely extolling the virtues of egalitarian democracy, Jamaican leaders such as Bustamante and the mulatto lawyer Norman Manley renewed their demands for some measure of local self-government, with the aim of eventually achieving independence. Wartime production had caused the combined population of Kingston and St. Andrew Parish to double to 237,000 people by 1943, but although the city now extended as far east as Long Mountain, as far northeast as Matilda's Corner, as far north as Cross Roads, and westward beyond Hagley Park Road, less than 2.5 percent of the capital's

109,000 core residents were white. Furthermore, most blacks were crammed into dilapidated tenements in the poorest sections of West Kingston, with unemployment running higher than 20 percent. The next year, Britain agreed to allow the first island-wide election held on the basis of universal adult suffrage, in which Bustamante's newly created Jamaica Labour Party (JLP) garnered 41.4 percent of the vote. Manley's People's National Party (PNP)—a more socialist, academic-oriented group appealing to the middle classes—received 23.5 percent.

The end of the global war in the spring of 1945 ushered in a period of British "decolonization," during which a more liberal administration in London—beset by their own ruined economy, plus U.S. disapproval of any lingering presence in the Caribbean—began dismantling the last vestiges of the old imperial apparatus so as to clear the way for regional independence. In 1947, negotiations were initiated toward forming a Federation of the British West Indies, Jamaican autonomy intended to be gradually phased in as part of this undertaking by withdrawing Crown-appointed officials in favor of local replacements throughout the early 1950s. A modest economic boom also occurred, Kingston's public transit becoming more efficient as streetcars were superseded by buses, while the number of private automobiles more than doubled.

Bustamante's rather conservative JLP, though, failed to develop any coherent program to meet these changing circumstances or to handle such unexpected crises as the hurricane that struck in August 1951, killing about 150 people across the island and causing extensive damage to the capital. Manley's PNP, in contrast, took advantage of these shortcomings by divesting itself of its more radical, Marxist elements the next year and was voted into office in 1955 on a platform coupling greater economic development with an all-out push toward federation. Jamaica's bauxite mining, tourism, agriculture, and industrialization were all actively promoted, along with a broadening of public education.

A modest program of slum clearance was also commenced in Kingston, by applying the £2.25 million in hurricane aid provided by the British government to build some 2,700 new dwellings at Long Mountain Pen and Norman Range in the east, as well as Tower Hill, Cockburn Pen, and Majesty Pen to the west. Thanks to a steady influx of migrants attracted from the countryside, the population of the metropolitan area soared from 289,200 inhabitants in 1953 to 379,600 seven years later, representing almost one-quarter of the island's total. Construction could not keep pace with such a press of arrivals, so that urban expansion into the foothills of the Blue Mountains even resulted in the first suburb beyond the Liguanea Plain when Harbour View was created just east of Long Mountain. Many structures were now being built of more durable concrete, although wooden shantytowns with corrugated iron roofs still abounded—especially in impoverished West Kingston—along with tiny squatter shacks.

Aerial view of the new middle-income suburb of Harbour View in the foreground, looking westward past the cement factory and Long Mountain to the city of Kingston on distant Liguanea Plain, 1961. (Jamaican Board of Tourism)

Yet despite progress on social issues such as literacy and the modernization of certain sectors of the island economy, Manley's efforts were undermined by excessive spending and inflation, while benefits seemed to accrue most directly among the lighter-skinned middle class, provoking resentment among the masses of poor urban blacks. Disillusioned by their seemingly unaltered plight within Jamaica's emergent new society, thousands of blacks in West Kingston—especially in the slums of Back O'Wall and Trench Town on the foreshore—were attracted into the "Ras Tafari" cult, a loosely defined religion that had originated in the 1930s as a protest movement by rejecting all trappings of white civilization in favor of a black repatriation to Africa. (The Ethiopian emperor Haile Selassie, or Ras Tafari, was venerated as their god, hence the name.)

Rastafarian preachers began repudiating Manley's new social model, soon gaining so much impetus in West Kingston that Communist agitators also joined, hoping to channel alienated black followers for their own revolutionary purposes. Noting the trepidation with which police regarded Rastafarian strength within the crowded squatter camps—many of which had been fortified against evictions—criminals swelled the movement's ranks as well, adding a reputation for violence. In September 1961, a referendum was held to determine whether Jamaica would join the newly created West Indies Federation the following year, with a capital to be created at Chaguaramas,

outside Port of Spain (Trinidad). Many poor blacks in Kingston spurned such a notion, feeling that it would merely perpetuate the status quo ante trend of replacing British rulers with a mulatto elite; their negative votes provided the small margin for rejecting the proposal.

Having staked his party's reputation upon the outcome, Manley and the PNP were subsequently voted out of office in favor of Bustamante's JLP, which led Jamaica into full-fledged independence as of 6 August 1962. In order to meet its obligations as the capital of the new nation, Kingston's civic authorities launched an ambitious drive to improve berthing facilities by constructing a vast complex called Newport just west of its old "finger" piers, so as to receive and more speedily discharge larger container ships. Once completed in 1966, this project in turn allowed for the rezoning of the city's cramped old commercial core, replacing its dilapidated infrastructure with modern facilities intended to cater to tourist cruise ships and ferry passengers to and from Palisadoes International Airport. Some public housing was also created by clearing the former squatter camps at Trench Town and Back O'Wall, while private businessmen started another commercial center called "New Kingston" north of Half Way Tree Road that concentrated shopping plazas and retail outlets to cater to wealthier suburban customers. A private corporation was moreover formed in 1969 to build a causeway and bridge westward from Kingston, linking the city to Dawkins Pond and the Hellshire Hills, where a new suburb called Portmore emerged.

These improvements helped moderate urban conditions, although no amount of government or private funds could entirely reverse the city's accumulated ills. Despite Jamaica's natural beauty and glittering tourist resorts, its capital was to remain plagued by poverty, slums, high unemployment, crime, and racial tension. Riots directed against Chinese and other small business owners had erupted in 1965, and "black power" sentiments radicalized politics for a considerable period there-after. According to the census taken in 1970, Kingston and its suburbs encompassed a population of 506,200 inhabitants, roughly 27.2 percent of the island total, which percentage changed little when another census was taken a dozen years later. That count gave a total of 524,000 urban residents, of whom slightly more than 104,000 still lived within the city's original seventeenth-century boundaries.

For further reading on the history of Kingston or Jamaica, please consult the Select Bibliography at the end of this volume.

Martinique

Fort-de-France
City specifically created to serve as a capital because of its natural impregnability.

Antecedents (1000–1634)
This mountainous island, 40 miles long by 21 miles at its widest point, was originally populated by Arawak tribesmen migrating north up the Lesser Antillean chain out of the Orinoco River Basin in Venezuela. Around the year 1000, they in turn were supplanted by another wave of a more aggressive South American indigenous group known as Caribs, who—like their predecessors—settled down to a subsistence existence based upon fishing and the cultivation of root crops such as manioc, preferring to live in the cooler highlands rather than along the hotter and more exposed coastline. (The island's tallest point is the 4,430-foot volcano at its northwestern tip, which would later become known as Mont Pelée [Bald Mountain], while the Pitons-du-Carbet, with peaks rising to 3,960 feet, lie in the center. The southeastern lowlands are dominated by 1,160-foot Vauclin Mountain.) The weather is warm year-round, with dry seasons running from mid-January through mid-July, followed by hot tropical storms that last until mid-October, and then a relatively mild rainy season until the next January.

When Christopher Columbus and other explorers passed through the Caribbean in the late 1490s, they chose to establish their headquarters on the much larger Hispaniola (modern Haiti and the Dominican Republic), deeming Matinia—as Martinique was apparently called by its inhabitants—unsuitable for colonization. Its Carib residents were left undisturbed except for sporadic slaving raids, and the Spaniards eventually concentrated all their efforts into the conquest of the Aztec and Incan empires on the American mainland during the 1520s and 1530s. As a result, sailors from other West European nations found "Martinica" still unclaimed when they began visiting during the latter half of the sixteenth century—men such as James Langton, who paused for three days in August 1593 with his trio of Elizabethan privateering vessels to refresh provisions and capture the Portuguese caravel of Domingo Díaz before steering away toward Margarita Island.

Such masters soon found that they could obtain exotic produce through barter with the local islanders, profiting so

Panoramic view over Fort-de-France, with its citadel in the distance, ca. 1920. (Franck, *Roaming Through the West Indies*)

163

handsomely upon their return to Europe that private companies began forming during the early decades of the seventeenth century to secure permanent footholds in unwanted corners of the Americas, to be developed as commercial outposts. For instance, Thomas Warner reached the island of Saint Christopher, or "St. Kitts," with sixteen English settlers late in January 1624, having been financed by a London merchant to establish a tobacco colony. This group erected a crude fort and some huts, then began planting crops, being joined shortly thereafter by a group of French colonists driven out of Guiana by hostile Indians. Because of their small numbers and mutual fear of the Caribs, the two groups agreed to share St. Kitts.

In September 1625, a damaged French brigantine under Capt. Urbain du Roissey, Sieur de Chardonville, and his friend Pierre Belain d'Esnambuc also sought refuge on St. Kitts after a losing battle against a Spanish galleon off Cuba. Welcomed, they built another tiny fort at the island's northern extremity and remained for six months, before sailing to France with a rich cargo of tobacco. Inspired by such easy profits, they persuaded the chief royal minister—Cardinal Armand-Jean du Plessis de Richelieu—to allow them to create the Compagnie de Saint Christophe (St. Christopher Company) in October 1626, for the exploitation of this and adjacent islands, with Richelieu acting as its principal shareholder.

After recruiting more than 500 settlers, d'Esnambuc and du Roissey returned to St. Kitts on 8 May 1627, hoping to convert it into a French colony. However, their transatlantic crossing having been difficult, fully half of their following arrived dead or dying; the Anglo-French inhabitants of St. Kitts had also endured various Carib assaults during their absence, so that both factions signed a partition and defense treaty on 13 May.

Two years later, six French men-of-war arrived at St. Kitts under François de Rotondy, Sieur de Cahuzac, sent by Richelieu to aid the French settlers against their English neighbors, who were now much more numerous and contentious. After a brief confrontation the latter sued for terms, and boundaries on the island were more clearly defined. Cahuzac thereupon proceeded to Sint Eustatius to install another French colony, yet shortly thereafter news arrived from Nevis that a formidable Spanish fleet under Adms. Martín de Vallecilla and Fadrique de Toledo would soon descend upon St. Kitts. The Spaniards duly materialized and stormed the principal English defense on the western coast, Fort Charles, easily overrunning it. Du Roissey and d'Esnambuc meanwhile evacuated 400 people aboard two ships from the northwest of the island, leaving the rest of their scattered populace to surrender. The raiders leveled every structure and departed with 3,100 prisoners, leaving only a few frightened survivors to emerge from hiding.

D'Esnambuc returned with a few followers and began rebuilding, but so did many Englishmen, so that the French soon found themselves heavily outnumbered; what's more, they were so poorly supported by their private backers in France that they began disposing of their tobacco crops to Dutch or English traders. Starved of profits, the Compagnie de St. Christophe in Paris was consequently dissolved by Richelieu and replaced in February 1635 by the Compagnie des Îles d'Amérique (Company of the Islands of America); this new corporation undertook not only to reinforce the old firm's assets on St. Kitts but to also expand onto nearby islands.

Such growth was to be spearheaded by the ambitious Charles Liénard, Sieur de l'Olive, who had been appointed as d'Esnambuc's lieutenant governor on St. Kitts in 1631. During his tenure, l'Olive had sent his able young assistant Guillaume d'Orange to reconnoiter nearby Guadeloupe, Dominica, and Martinique. Judging this first island ripe for settlement, l'Olive and d'Orange had thereupon sailed to France, chancing to meet the former naval captain Jean Duplessis, Sieur d'Ossonville—a veteran of Cahuzac's West Indian campaign—as they arrived at Dieppe late in 1634. Forming a partnership with this officer, who owned a stout ship, l'Olive approached the Company of the Islands of America the next spring in Paris and received authorization to colonize a new Antillean island, of which he was to become governor. (He would still, however, remain subordinate to d'Esnambuc, who was simultaneously commissioned governor-general over all the French West Indies by King Louis XIII on 7 March 1635.)

L'Olive, Duplessis, and d'Orange departed Dieppe on 25 May 1635 with more than 500 colonists aboard a pair of ships, sighting Martinique as they entered the Caribbean one month later. Wondering whether this island might not prove a superior choice, they decided to go ashore, disembarking at the mouth of what would later be called the Carbet River. But although l'Olive and Duplessis performed a ceremony laying claim to Martinique for France, this particular stretch of coastline seemed too rugged for easy clearance and cultivation, so that the group decided to proceed for Guadeloupe, as intended, three days later.

Early French Foothold (1635–1638)

When d'Esnambuc learned of the arrival of these rival colonists, he gathered 150 picked subjects at St. Kitts and crossed over to Martinique himself by 1 September 1635, so as not to risk seeing his prestige as governor-general eventually overshadowed by these larger islands. Anchoring off its northwestern shore, he started work on a rough, 3-gun fortress on the northern bank of a large river mouth; it was to become christened Fort Saint-Pierre in his honor during a ceremony held upon its completion two weeks later. Having thus established his own claim over Martinique, d'Esnambuc installed the veteran Jean du Pont as his governor with 100 men, before departing in mid-November to deposit other small contingents on Dominica and Saba during his return passage toward St. Kitts.

Du Pont's garrison was promptly beset by hostile local Caribs, who summoned more than 1,000 allies from neighboring islands to expel these interlopers from Martinique. The

View of St. Pierre, ca. 1898; until it was leveled by the volcanic eruption of Mont-Pelée in May 1902, this was the island's largest city. (Hill, *Cuba and Porto Rico*)

French remained watchful within their fort, though, until this army was at last lured directly beneath the outpost's artillery; as they burst from the jungle, the Carib warriors received a punishing volley of grape. Such carnage shattered their resolve, after which du Pont succeeded in winning their confidence over the next several months, establishing sufficiently good relations that his band could begin clearing land to plant food crops, as well as some tobacco for export. Although most seaborne contact was maintained northward from Saint-Pierre toward St. Kitts, the French settlers soon began to expand down Martinique's western coastline, while the Caribs remained in the mountains or on the island's eastern side.

The following year, du Pont was captured by the Spaniards while sailing toward St. Kitts. D'Esnambuc, before succumbing to old age in December 1636, appointed his own nephew, Jacques Dyel, Sieur du Parquet—a young former infantry captain recently arrived from France—as Martinique's interim governor. Du Parquet consequently reached St.-Pierre from St. Kitts to assume office as of 20 January 1637, and notwith-

standing his inexperience, he proved so able an administrator that he was confirmed in the post by Paris as of 2 December. Thanks to his enthusiastic leadership, tobacco cultivation increased, and several hundred new settlers were attracted to the island; and despite commencing his own fortified brick mansion on an isle at the mouth of the Carbet River, south of Saint-Pierre, he realized that Martinique needed a more secure anchorage, so that he laid the foundation for a proper seaport that was to eventually evolve into the city of Fort-de-France.

Initial Stockade (1639–1668)
Southeast of the principal town of Saint-Pierre, the island's coastline opens up into a vast bay, enclosed on three sides by hills and a peninsula, which offered ideal shelter against the prevailing trade winds and seasonal storms; this bay's northern bank moreover featured a stony, 100-foot-high promontory jutting out into the harbor, beside which lay a shallow inlet, known as the Carénage, suitable for careening or repairing ships. Du Parquet therefore decided to take advantage of this

natural configuration by erecting a palisaded stockade called Fort-Royal atop this promontory, thus transforming its bay into a protected anchorage called Cul-de-Sac Royal. He encouraged visits by foreign vessels by spreading word that this harbor would be open to all flags during the hurricane months of July to September, and he stationed a permanent pilot on Martinique's southwestern coastline so as to guide new arrivals around the headland and into its channel.

By the time a new governor-general for the West Indies—Commo. Philippe de Lonvilliers de Poincy, knight commander of the Order of Saint John of Malta—called at Fort-Royal in early February 1639 while proceeding toward St. Kitts to replace d'Esnambuc, du Parquet was able to greet him with fired salutes from his completed stockade, plus a modest parade of troops. Yet since most of Martinique's farms, churches, and dwellings were still clustered around the main settlement of Saint-Pierre, and visiting merchantmen preferred its open roadstead for quickly unloading or loading cargoes, the governor had also directed that its fortress be strengthened with masonry and expanded so as to accommodate up to ten gun embrasures. Once those alterations were finished, he began using Fort Saint-Pierre as his official headquarters, so that Saint-Pierre remained the island capital,

while Fort-Royal remained merely a reserve anchorage protected by its coastal keep.

Economic woes now beset the fledgling colony, as a glut of tobacco on European markets provoked a drop in prices. The Compagnie therefore attempted to introduce sugarcane on Martinique as an alternative crop, but that took several decades to implement fully because its cultivation required knowledgeable operators, plus the acquisition of expensive milling equipment and large numbers of African slaves as field hands. The several hundred French settlers on Martinique therefore continued to eke out a subsistence existence, but such large-scale commercial expansion was impossible so long as their overseas trade did not improve. Dissensions grew—especially after Richelieu died in December 1642, followed by Louis XIII five months later.

A ship anchored off Fort-Royal on 16 November 1645, bearing a new governor-general for the French West Indies: the youthful Noël Patrocles, Seigneur de Thoisy. Realizing that this inexperienced appointee stood little chance of compelling the hard-bitten de Poincy to relinquish his office, du Parquet decided to back the new royal claimant by sailing against St. Kitts in de Thoisy's support. But the tough de Poincy was able to defeat du Parquet's landing in late January 1646 and

St. Pierre's waterfront, ca. 1898; note the long, shoaling beach, ideal for manhandling cargoes. (Hill, *Cuba and Porto Rico*)

imprison him. The rebuffed young nobleman retreated to Guadeloupe, while sentiment began taking hold among the islands' residents in favor of his entrenched predecessor; a mutiny furthermore erupted against the new governor-general on Martinique on 26 June, led by a former Parisian glove maker nicknamed General Beaufort. After a chaotic fortnight, the island's Acting-Gov. Jerome du Sarrat, Sieur de la Pierrière, suffocated this rebellion by luring Beaufort and twenty associates to a meeting within Fort Saint-Pierre, where they were murdered.

However, the troubles nonetheless spread to Guadeloupe, where the would-be governor-general's residence was besieged by several hundred armed men, until the youthful de Thoisy finally fled back to Martinique on the night of 31 December 1646 aboard a hired Portuguese caravel. Taking sanctuary with the Jesuits on its southern shoreline by 3 January 1647, he was overtaken ten days later by an 800-man expedition sent from St. Kitts by de Poincy, who offered to restore Governor du Parquet to Martinique in exchange for the young pretender. De Thoisy thereupon surrendered, and this turmoil subsided.

Du Parquet henceforth concentrated on increasing his island's productivity, as well as other material improvements; he even set sail from Saint-Pierre on 14 March 1649 with 145 well-equipped colonists aboard two ships to occupy Grenada, farther to the south. In June 1650, he sent another small contingent to do the same on neighboring St. Lucia, as the Compagnie in Paris had by now become so discouraged by its lack of control and profits that it was willing to sell all Antillean properties to the local governors. Du Parquet therefore traveled to France and purchased Martinique, St. Lucia, Grenada, and the Grenadines for 41,500 francs in September 1650, further receiving the title of governor-general over this grouping from the Crown the following August. The prosperity of his principal island of Martinique was moreover boosted when 300 Dutch refugees from Recife, Brazil, arrived in the summer of 1654 and—notwithstanding their Protestant and Jewish faiths—received land titles within Cul-de-Sac Royal because of their skill in the management of tropical sugar plantations.

That same autumn of 1654 a major Carib onslaught swept over Martinique, both French and Dutch enclaves along its western coast being reduced to a desperate struggle for survival against 2,000 roving warriors, plus black rebel slaves. Du Parquet became besieged within his own fortified mansion at Le Carbet, and this onslaught was checked only thanks to the chance arrival at Saint-Pierre of four large Dutch merchantmen that disembarked 300 men to assist the beleaguered colonists. Three years of uneasy guerrilla warfare ensued, until the French—under the wily direction of the veteran d'Orange—finally triumphed, compelling the islanders to sue for terms in October 1657. Martinique was to be split as a result, with a boundary running through the mountains from Macouba in the north.

Du Parquet died of old age on 3 January 1658, being interred in Saint-Jacques Church at his capital of Saint-Pierre. His widow, Marie, attempted to rule in the name of their young children but was deposed in early August of that same year. Médéric Rolle, Sieur de Gourselas—who had assumed the title of interim governor—then launched a ruthless campaign in September 1658 to drive the Caribs from the island, but despite some relief achieved by that heartless measure, Martinique nonetheless remained underdeveloped because its fractious private owners were incapable of providing the necessary stability and resources for a full flourishing. Over the next few years, some 1,000 settlers consequently abandoned the island.

The new king, Louis XIV, and his chief minister, Jean-Baptiste Colbert, thereupon decided to intervene by summoning members of the defunct Compagnie to present papers pertaining to their sale of Antillean islands before a special commission in Paris in April 1664. A new Compagnie des Indes Occidentales (West India Company) was subsequently chartered the following month, with the aim of uniting all of France's American colonies under the joint administration of the Crown and this new corporation. An officer named Alexandre de Prouville, Marquis de Tracy, had already sailed with the titles of civilian governor-general and military lieutenant-general to reimpose government rule over these scattered private settlements. His small squadron dropped anchor before Fort Saint-Pierre at the beginning of June to announce that the island's current owners were to be bought out. According to a census taken in that same year of 1664, there were 2,694 whites and 2,710 blacks living on Martinique.

A new island governor—Robert Le Frichot des Friches, Seigneur de Clodoré—arrived from France early the next year, taking office by 17 March 1665. Six weeks later a huge Dutch battle-fleet under Adm. Michiel Adriaenszoon de Ruyter materialized off Saint-Pierre, asking to effect repairs after being battered during a bombardment of Barbados. Although well received, this visit also heralded an ominous escalation in the competition between Britain, France, and The Netherlands to dominate the Lesser Antilles.

On 26 January 1666, Louis XIV honored his treaty obligations to the Dutch by declaring war against England back in Europe; when news of this outbreak reached Martinique on 19 March, Governor de Clodoré began feverishly refurbishing its coastal defenses—Fort Saint-Pierre being expanded into a stout rectangular citadel with twin towers facing inland. He subsequently sailed to help fight the English on St. Kitts, and upon his return he proposed organizing an expedition from the vessels anchored within Cul-de-Sac Royal—five Compagnie ships with a total of 140 guns, plus five Dutch ships bearing 80 guns between them—to seize Nevis. This project was deferred, however, at a council-of-war held on 30 May; two months later a large enemy counterexpedition prowled past Saint-Pierre, having been sent from Barbados. The French shipping huddled beneath its batteries, while Clodoré's recent defensive measures discouraged any disembarkation. The

Crude map of Martinique, a dotted line showing how it was to be shared between the French settlers on its western half and Caribs to its east; also note the prominence accorded "Cul-de-Sac Royal," the huge natural harbor on whose shores stood Fort-Royal. (Du Terte, *Histoire generale des Antilles, 1667*)

defenders' good fortune continued to hold, as a hurricane swept through the archipelago on 4–5 August, causing some damage on Martinique. Most ships managed to creep down its coast in time into the safety of Cul-de-Sac Royal, but the storm utterly destroyed the enemy armada off the Saintes.

To bolster the 400 regulars of the Navarre and Normandie infantry regiments already serving in the West Indies, reinforcements began arriving from France as of 11 August 1666, accompanied by the military engineer Nicolas François Blondel, plus a new lieutenant-general for the region, Antoine Lefebvre, Seigneur de La Barre. After gathering local volunteers he set sail on 25 October to successfully attack the English on Antigua, returning more than a month later to concentrate upon strengthening Martinique's defenses; he then assembled another large force that struck southeastward on 4 February 1667 to overrun Montserrat. But the British responded by rushing a fleet out to the West Indies under Rear Adm. Sir John Harman, who re-established the Royal Navy's supremacy and compelled the French fleet to retire into the Carénage beside

Fort-Royal. The chance arrival of a small Dutch squadron under Commo. Abraham Crijnssen (known to the English as "Captain Crimson") at Saint-Pierre on 7 May 1667 inspired de La Barre to attempt a joint expedition against Nevis, which departed one week later. This Franco-Dutch formation, however, was repelled, and Crijnssen parted company, the French being chased back into Martinique.

Harman thereupon bore down against Saint-Pierre on 29 June 1667 with nine ships-of-the-line, a fire ship, and an auxiliary to attack the nineteen Compagnie vessels and fourteen island traders anchored beneath its batteries. Although driven off, he resumed his efforts the next afternoon, then again on 2 July; a fourth assault occurred two days later and another on 6 July. Then there came a final point-blank bombardment the following day. The defenders' resolve had been sorely depleted by these persistent thrusts, the Saint-Robert battery at the southern end of town (near the De la Touche River mouth) already lying demolished, so that de Clodoré and d'Orange could resist only from the adjacent Saint-Sébastien battery.

When Harman withdrew an hour and a half later, virtually every French vessel was left sinking or burning. As the least damaged hulks were being refloated and towed to the Carénage over the next few weeks for repair, word arrived from Europe that a treaty was being finalized that called for all hostilities to cease by the end of the same year.

Martinique and Fort-Royal were to undergo considerable change in the aftermath. Firstly, the Compagnie had been bankrupted by its losses and would be entirely supplanted within the next few years by the Crown. Secondly, a new royal governor-general for the French West Indies—Jean-Charles de Baas-Castelmore—arrived on 4 February 1669 and chose to establish his official headquarters at Saint-Pierre rather than at the traditional residence on St. Kitts, so that Martinique became the de facto administrative center for the entire French archipelago (with Guadeloupe subordinated to it). And thirdly, amid de Baas's numerous instructions for improving colonial rule was a clause directing that at least one impregnable stronghold be erected on each island, which meant an enhanced prominence for Fort-Royal.

City Foundation and Dutch Assault (1669–1674)

Given that Saint-Pierre's open roadstead had been revealed as vulnerable to enemy attack by Harman's persistence, the original stockade at Fort-Royal was strengthened according to designs left by the departed engineer Blondel, while de Baas furthermore elevated the tiny clutch of shacks and ware-houses around the Carénage to the status of a city on 3 October 1669, and even temporarily took up residence there. Still, few additional property owners were attracted, as its surrounding terrain was unappealingly low and marshy; most people not directly involved with its garrison or maritime duties therefore preferred developing farmlands at select points around Cul-de-Sac Royal, traveling into Fort-Royal by boat only as their needs dictated.

But despite its indifferent appeal, Fort-Royal proved its strategic worth when Louis XIV declared war against The Netherlands in the spring of 1672. Upon receipt of news of this outbreak, Martinican forces—in conjunction with their English allies—captured several small Dutch islands, although this initial impetus soon faltered when de Baas failed to carry Curaçao in March 1673. A small Dutch fleet under Commos. Jacob Binckes and Cornelis Evertsen de Jongste, or "the Youngest" (nicknamed "Kees the Devil"), blockaded Cul-de-Sac Royal this same May, after which the British withdrew from the hostilities in March 1674.

Now free to concentrate their considerable naval might against France alone, the Dutch sent an expedition against Martinique. On the afternoon of 19 July 1674, Admiral de Ruyter materialized out of the Atlantic with more than thirty warships, a half dozen storeships, plus fifteen transports bearing 3,400 troops under Col. Jan van Uyttenhove. The defenders hastily mustered at Saint-Pierre, expecting the main enemy blow to fall against their most populous center, but

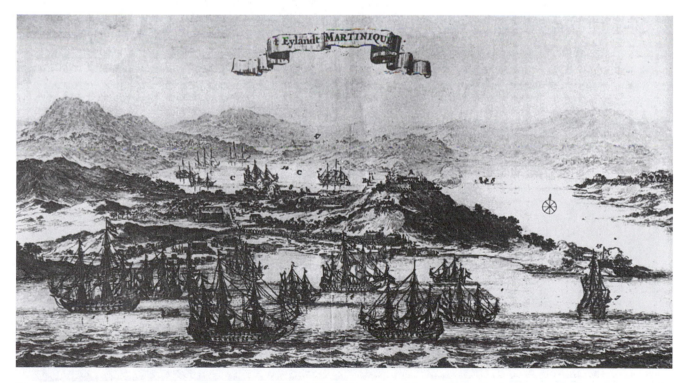

Engraving of the failed Dutch assault against Fort-Royal, 20 July 1674; de Ruyter's warships are depicted in the foreground, disgorging troops who are circling inland, only to become caught in a cross fire between the hilltop citadel and anchored French vessels in the Carénage beyond. At this time, the city only consisted of a few dwellings and warehouses. (Prinz Hendrik Museum, Rotterdam)

inasmuch as de Ruyter was familiar with the island—as well as being accompanied by the Huguenot turncoat Charles de Birac of Gascony—the Dutch admiral instead steered directly for Fort-Royal, remembering it as a lightly guarded outpost that he hoped to secure as an anchorage before disgorging van Uyttenhove's army.

The attackers failed to enter its roadstead that afternoon only because their fleet became becalmed, allowing a scratch force of 160 Frenchmen to work frantically overnight shoring up Fort-Royal's defenses, supplemented by crews from the few ships at anchor within the Carénage: the royal frigate *Jeux* of 44 guns and 150 men under Capt. Thomas Claude Renart de Fuch Samberg, Marquis d'Amblimont, plus the 22-gun merchantmen *Saint-Eustache* and *Sagesse.* Two smaller vessels were scuttled as block-ships, and booms were stretched across the Carénage's entrance, while Martinique's governor, Antoine André de Sainte Marthe de Lalande, hurriedly arrived by boat to assume command, and the veteran d'Orange directed the outer batteries. (The archipelago's governor-general, de Baas, was lying ill at Saint-Pierre.)

When de Ruyter's fleet finally bore down upon the morning of 20 July 1674, it was greeted by heavy gunfire. Van Uyttenhove's troops nonetheless disembarked by 9:00 A.M. to the west of Fort-Royal—in an inlet known ever afterward as the Baie des Flamands (Flemish Bay)—only to then be unexpectedly checked by a circuit of palisades 18 feet tall that guarded the promontory. As the Dutch columns swelled to more than 1,000 men, they became caught in a cross fire between the citadel's batteries and the anchored *Jeux* and *Saint-Eustache* out in the Carénage. Lacking scaling-ladders or any support fire from de Ruyter's more distant warships, the attackers' discipline collapsed altogether when van Uyttenhove was wounded and a rum warehouse was breached, obliging them to retreat to their boats by 11:00 A.M.

Vice Adm. Evertsen and Rear Adm. Engel de Ruyter led a second disembarkation at 2:00 P.M., but this attempt suffered heavy losses as well so that they were recalled two hours later by Michiel de Ruyter's 80-gun flagship *Zeven Provinciën.* Dutch casualties totaled 143 killed and 318 wounded, as opposed to only five French dead (among them d'Orange) and fifteen injured. Unaware that they had won a great victory, the French abandoned Fort-Royal's stockade that night, while the masters of *Saint-Eustache* and *Sagesse* set their ships ablaze and slipped ashore. D'Amblimont maintained a nervous watch from aboard his royal frigate in anticipation of doing the same, yet dawn of 21 July 1674 revealed the Dutch fleet staggering north toward Dominica.

Stronghold (1675–1691)

Martinique was to remain unthreatened over the next several years of this conflict, and a French battle-fleet under Vice Adm. Jean, Comte d'Estrées, even arrived on 19 January 1677 with the intent of attacking the Dutch garrison on Tobago. Five days later, while local volunteers were still being gathered, Governor-General de Baas expired at his Fond Capot estate just south of Le Carbet. D'Estrées subsequently set sail on 12 February with his ten men-of-war plus numerous auxiliaries bearing more than 4,000 men, but he lost most of these in a bloody assault against the anchored Dutch fleet three weeks later. He therefore limped back into Martinique before hastening across to France to receive command of a second fleet from Louis XIV that same autumn.

With this new formation, d'Estrées then won a resounding victory at Tobago in December 1677, before parading triumphantly through the Lesser Antilles. His third-in-command, Rear Adm. Charles de Courbon, Seigneur de Romegeux and Comte de Blénac, had furthermore brought out the title of new governor-general in succession to the deceased de Baas. The signing of the Treaty of Nijmegen in August 1678 brought an end to this struggle and ushered in a peaceful decade during which life on Martinique—already the most prosperous French West Indian colony—was significantly improved thanks to Blénac's vigorous leadership. The office of *Intendant* was also created by the Crown, being a semiautonomous

Depiction of Fort-Royal's headland in 1679 by Jean Barbot, as seen from the Carénage; the ten-year-old city at right would soon be expanded by Governor-General de Blénac's efforts. (British Library)

civilian administrator who—although subordinate to the governor-general in strategic matters—nonetheless had jurisdiction over a broad range of public works, as well as the archipelago's judicial system.

More important for Fort-Royal, however, Blénac took an active and personal interest in the tiny town's development, even taking up residence there rather than at Saint-Pierre, so as to stimulate the stronghold's growth. Wishing to expand its urban area beyond the untidy clump of buildings crowded along the banks of the Carénage, he ordered its encroaching bogs either drained or filled in so that a more ample street grid might be laid out, centered around a main square that was to be remembered as the Savane (Swamp); he also started work on a church and other structures, while the citadel's defenses were reinforced so that numerous migrants were drawn into the district as permanent residents.

By 1686, Martinique's total population had increased to 15,194 people, and the governor-general could report to the king:

> I do not believe that you have in the islands of America a colonist better established than I am in Cul-de-Sac at Fort-Royal. There were not more than three sugar-refineries when I arrived; there are presently 57. There was not a single hen; now it is filled with cattle, pigs, horses, and poultry. I have made you a town and a church constructed of stone. . . . I have made you a fort which provides security for all these islands.

Although founded by du Parquet, Fort-Royal can truly be said to have taken shape under Blénac. His labors were put in hazard, however, when France declared war against Holland again in December 1688, and then against Spain by April 1689; England and the so-called "Grand Alliance," or League of Augsburg, joined in May of that same year. Initially, this renewal of hostilities was enthusiastically endorsed on Martinique, Blénac being able to raise large expeditions at Fort-Royal to surprise both Sint Eustatius in the spring of 1689 and St. Kitts later that same summer. But a regiment of British regulars reinforced Antigua toward year's end, allowing Sir Christopher Codrington—new governor-general for the English Leeward Islands—to counterattack against Saint-Barthélemy, Marie-Galante, and Saint Martin. Stung by criticisms of his inaction during these enemy offensives, Blénac resigned as governor-general on 29 January 1690, returning to France to seek vindication before the king. British forces, meanwhile, had reconquered St. Kitts and Sint Eustatius by July.

Martinique was not relieved until a new French governor-general—François d'Alesso, Marquis d'Eragny—reached Fort-Royal on 5 February 1691 with fourteen men-of-war, spending the next two months trying to alleviate its many wants and strengthen its defenses. That April, Codrington and Commo. Lawrence Wright overran Marie-Galante, then pushed a few thousand men ashore on Guadeloupe, trapping its last

French defenders within Fort Saint-Charles. This desperate plight was reversed when the marquis set sail from Fort-Royal in late May with a small squadron bearing two infantry companies and 600 buccaneers, whose arrival caused the invaders—their morale sapped by disease and torrential rains—to abandon Guadeloupe. Yet despite this success, there was scant celebration when the expedition regained Martinique; yellow fever broke out and claimed many lives—including that of d'Eragny, who succumbed by 18 August.

Elevation to Regional Capital (1692–1758)

When word of the death reached Paris, Blénac was reappointed on 24 November 1691 and set sail early the following year with reinforcements. He had also persuaded Louis XIV that because of the critical situation in the Lesser Antilles, its official capital should be transferred from Saint-Pierre to the much more defensible Fort-Royal. Blénac consequently arrived on 5 February 1692 with orders for the *Intendant,* council, and all other royal administrators to move into the island's southern town. Its fortifications were moreover to be strengthened yet again, as Blénac had been accompanied from France by the military engineer de Caylus. Local residents assisted in these labors with their slaves, while Blénac sortied with his fleet on 2 March to skirmish against an approaching enemy fleet, which proved to be merely a Jamaica-bound merchant convoy escorted by Commo. Ralph Wrenn.

The next spring, however, the British massed all their regional forces for a descent against Martinique, and Blénac's strategic choice of Fort-Royal was justified. On 11 April 1693 a huge fleet under Rear Adm. Sir Francis Wheler circled around the northern tip of the island; Gov. Nicolas de Gabaret braced to receive this host at Saint-Pierre, but the English swept past and also avoided Blénac's concentration at Fort-Royal, instead putting in to Cul-de-Sac Marin in the island's more sparsely populated, southeasterly corner—where there were no defenses and scarcely sixty local militiamen to oppose their disembarkation. The next morning Gen. John Foulke landed 2,300 troops and 1,500 sailors at Anse de Sainte-Anne, intending to secure a base from which to roll up Martinique's other defenses.

The first major clash occurred on the morning of 13 April 1693, when English boats pushed westward from Sainte-Anne and overran the settlement at Rivière-Pilote; two days later, the invaders leapfrogged still farther west and devastated more plantations. They were then joined by ten additional vessels and 1,300 men under Governor-General Codrington on 19 April, but Foulke's main army was by now becoming sickly; the English consequently decided to abandon their slow overland strategy and re-embarked three days later to probe instead the mouth of Cul-de-Sac Royal. After several unsuccessful tries, Wheler steered north and threw his marines ashore a week later at Canouville, just north of Fort Saint-Pierre, only to be contained by militia cavalry hastily deployed by Col. François de Collart and infantry units arriving under Blénac. Checked at every turn, the English stood away from Martinique on the evening of 30 April, having suffered 800 killed, wounded, or captured, plus many others desperately ill.

But the defenders too lay exhausted by their exertions, so that both sides refrained from any more offensives for the duration of these hostilities. Occasionally, small French squadrons touched at Fort-Royal on their way through the Antilles—such as the half dozen warships of Bernard Renau d'Elissagaray (better known as Petit-Renau), who visited in the spring of 1696, or a similar-size force under Commo. Chevalier des Augiers that same October—but major fighting was otherwise confined elsewhere in the Americas. Governor-General de Blénac did not live to see the war's conclusion, falling sick at Fort-Royal on 8 June 1696 and dying two days afterward; he was buried in the church that he had ordered built.

The Treaty of Rijswijk restored peace in September 1697, and notwithstanding the hardships endured, Martinique emerged from this struggle relatively unscathed; for unlike most of its Antillean neighbors, it had suffered no crippling

A Martinican *métisse,* ca. 1890, wearing the traditional island head-kerchief, known as a madras *calendé.* (Hearn, *Two Years in the French West Indies*)

invasion and was now the undisputed administrative and commercial center for the French West Indies. Its populace had increased to roughly 7,000 white inhabitants and 13,300 blacks, double the number on Guadeloupe, its next-largest sister colony. Saint-Pierre furthermore remained the main trading outlet for both islands, enjoying a virtual monopoly over arrivals by transatlantic merchantmen and slavers.

Peace proved fleeting, though, for Spain's last Hapsburg monarch died without issue in November 1700, leaving the Bourbon princeling Philip of Anjou—grandson to Louis XIV—as sole heir to the Spanish empire. Unwilling to accept such a powerful combination, other European governments united to contest this succession, backing a rival claimant to the Spanish Crown. Fears of a renewed war soon spread to the West Indies, as Vice Adm. John Benbow arrived with ten Royal Navy warships to patrol this theater, visiting Martinique in late November 1701 before wintering at Jamaica.

Concerned that this deployment might initiate hostilities by the preemptive seizure of a Spanish-American treasure convoy, a French battle-fleet was also hurried across the Atlantic under Vice Adm. François Louis Rousselet, Comte de Château-Renault, who entered Fort-Royal on 2 January 1702 and provided its first real test as a naval base; for his fleet was composed of thirty-seven warships bearing 12,500 seamen and marines, straining every local resource, although there was ample space within the anchorage itself. Three weeks later, Château-Renault was instructed to attack Barbados, but feeling that such an enterprise lay beyond his capabilities, he decided instead to sail toward Havana to provide an escort for the Mexican plate-fleet. His fleet got under way from Fort-Royal by 22 February, and war with Britain and The Netherlands erupted that same May.

The small island capital was once more thrust into its familiar role of assembling expeditions, which sailed to the relief of Guadeloupe in April 1703, in addition to making descents against St. Kitts in February 1706 and Nevis that same April (this latter raid netting Martinique almost 4,600 black slaves). Fort-Royal was also briefly threatened by a privateer flotilla that rounded Pointe-Arlet in December 1704 but that glided up the coast past Saint-Pierre making minor captures before disappearing. As during previous conflicts, the bulk of major fighting occurred elsewhere, until the veteran privateer Jacques Cassard of Nantes arrived in July 1712—just as peace terms were being negotiated in Europe—with a small squadron supplied by the king and financed by private subscribers, to profit from some last-minute captures. Having also been appointed as a captain in France's Royal Navy, Cassard was able to raise 1,500 Martinican volunteers aboard thirty vessels, and he departed three days later to attack Antigua, Montserrat, Surinam, and Berbice. A second venture against Dutch Sint Eustatius and Curaçao in January–February 1713 proved equally successful, although not quite so remunerative, after which hostilities ceased on 11 April.

Although Saint-Domingue was subsequently separated from the governor-general's jurisdiction by a bureaucratic reorganization in 1714—a new administration for the Iles sous le Vent (Leeward Islands) being created—Fort-Royal nonetheless remained the capital for the Iles du Vent (Windward Islands) in the Lesser Antilles, and furthermore enjoyed several decades of peaceful economic development. Sugar emerged as Martinique's predominant export during this interlude, and the well-irrigated flatlands deeper inside Cul-de-Sac Royal—especially around Lamentin—proved ideally suited for harvesting and processing large-scale commercial crops. Maritime traffic increased noticeably, thousands of African slaves being imported as large plantations and mills gradually supplanted many of Martinique's smaller family farms; this transformation was furthermore accelerated when the first coffee trees were introduced as of 1723 and came to be reflected demographically as well—for although the island population more than trebled to 72,000 by 1742, only 16,000 of them were now white, as the percentage of slave-laborers had increased exponentially.

A renewed round of warfare against Britain was briefly feared in October 1740, when Vice Adm. Antoine François de Pardaillan de Gondrin, Marquis d'Antin, passed through Fort-Royal with a large fleet, having been sent out by Paris to attack English interests in support of Spain, which had become embroiled in the War of Jenkins's Ear against the British; however, after reprovisioning and taking on 1,200 Martinican reinforcements, d'Antin merely sailed westward to Port Saint-Louis (modern Les Cayes, Haiti), then failed to act.

France was not drawn into this Anglo-Spanish conflict until 15 March 1744, after which Fort-Royal's garrison was strengthened by the arrival of a new governor-general—Charles de Tubières, Chevalier de Caylus—in April 1745. However, its port was not menaced by anything more than sporadic blockades. For example, a forty-three-ship convoy escorted by Commo. Hilarion Josselin, Comte Duguay, was intercepted offshore on 11 November of that same year by Vice Adm. Isaac Townsend's squadron, suffering fourteen captures before gaining the protection of Fort-Royal's batteries; Commo. Hubert de Brienne, Comte de Conflans, fared much better, by safely guiding 214 merchantmen into harbor in mid-June 1746, before a squadron under Commo. Fitzroy Henry Lee could take up station outside. Conflans then slipped out again after these blockaders retired on 3 July, leading a significant portion of his charges on to Saint-Domingue (Haiti). Lee exacted some small measure of vengeance by snapping up six prizes from the convoy of Commo. Emmanuel Auguste de Cahideuc, Comte Dubois de La Motte, as it circled north of Martinique in late November 1746, but no more incidents occurred before hostilities finally wound down in the spring of 1748.

Martinique emerged well from this struggle, its population being measured at 79,000 three years later. Saint-Pierre had also maintained its stranglehold over regional trade and was the dominant city in the archipelago with its 15,000 inhabitants; Fort-Royal, in contrast, only had 4,000. Global conflict soon resumed as London declared war against Paris in May 1756, unleashing another round of commercial dislocation from attacks against shipping by naval blockaders and regional privateers, until a large British expedition—some 3,700 or 3,800 regulars under Maj.-Gen. Peregrine Thomas Hopson—reached Barbados in early January 1759, with specific orders to conquer Martinique.

English Conquest and Resurgence (1759–1788)

Reinforced by local auxiliaries, this force set sail from Bridgetown aboard more than 100 vessels a fortnight later, materializing off Martinique's southern coast by the afternoon of 15 January 1759 and probing the defenses within Case-Navires Bay (west of Fort-Royal) the next day. By the morning of 17 January, Hopson had almost 4,400 men ashore, but he felt that they were insufficient to deal with the militia units massing under Gov.-Gen. François de Beaumont, Comte de Beauharnois. The British landing force was also devoid of food and water and faced with toiling through dense underbrush under sniper-fire, so that Hopson asked Moore whether an attack might be attempted closer in to Fort-Royal. That notion was rejected after a hasty conference, at which time Hopson ordered a stealthy re-embarkation for that same night. The English expedition then ventured northwest toward Saint-Pierre, sounding its entrance and engaging its batteries on 19 January before sailing away in frustration to Guadeloupe.

Fort-Royal's defenses had in fact been much weaker than the attackers realized, Beauharnois having slightly fewer than 600 regulars, while morale on his blockaded island was particularly low. He managed to muster only two privateer vessels with 400 volunteers to assist Guadeloupe, scarcely enough to prevent this enormous British force from gradually subduing most of that island. Not even the arrival of eight French ships-of-the-line and three frigates at Fort-Royal on 8 March 1759 under Commo. Maximin de Bompar (himself a former governor-general) could prevent Guadeloupe's fall, its hard-pressed defenders requesting terms by 21 April. Beauharnois sailed six days later with another 600 volunteers aboard eighteen coasters, escorted by two of Bompar's frigates, but this belated reinforcement could not affect the outcome. It withdrew by 29 April, and Guadeloupe capitulated two days later, after which the English occupied Marie-Galante as well.

Martinique spent an uneasy year and a half surrounded by enemies, until a much larger expedition of 13,000 soldiers and 1,000 auxiliaries was marshaled at Bridgetown under Rear Adm. George Brydges Rodney and Maj.-Gen. Robert Monckton, who appeared off Saint-Pierre on 7 January 1762. They detached a diversionary unit the following day to reconnoiter Petite Anse-d'Arlet near the entrance to Cul-de-Sac Royal, plus another group of five frigates against La Trinité on the island's eastern coast. Masked by these distractions, the main British disembarkation then occurred at Saint-Luce on 10 January, although its terrain proved too difficult, so that the invaders instead re-embarked and bore directly down upon Fort-Royal.

On 16 January 1762, Royal Navy warships silenced the batteries in Cas des Navires Bay, allowing the entire British army to be landed there the next day. After fortifying a seaside base camp, the British advanced against the city, intending to capture the hills above Fort-Royal and install siege artillery to shell its defenses. Morne-Tartenson was overrun first on the morning of 24 January; Morne-Garnier was taken by midnight of 27–28 January, at which time Gov.-Gen. Louis Charles Le Vassor de La Touche, rather than see his main force become trapped on the fortified promontory, left 1,000 men to hold its citadel, while retiring north with the bulk of his men toward Saint-Pierre. The invaders gained yet another battery atop Morne-Capuchin shortly thereafter, compelling Fort-Royal's garrison to beat for terms by the evening of 3 February, its 800 survivors surrendering the next day, along with 170 guns and fourteen vessels anchored in the harbor.

With Cul-de-Sac Royal now entirely within their power and Fort-Royal renamed as "Fort Edward," the English dispatched a small squadron with 500 seamen and marines to seize La Trinité, and the remainder of Martinique capitulated by 16 February 1762, the conquest having cost the British 500 casualties. Capt. George Darby of HMS *Devonshire* and Maj. Horatio Gates—later an American Revolutionary War hero—were delegated to convey the dispatches announcing this victory to London, where each was rewarded with £500 from a young and grateful George III.

Fort-Royal and Martinique remained in British hands for more than a year, until all Antillean colonies were restored to France by the Treaty of Paris of 1763, and François-Louis de Salignac arrived to take office as the new governor. Numerous modest reforms in the administration of the West Indies were implemented with this restoration that were aimed at strengthening the islands' economies and making overseas colonies more attractive for migrants. The islands' first official delegate—Jean-Baptiste Dubuc of Martinique—even traveled to Versailles, where the following year he was appointed Premier Commis du Bureau des Colonies (First Commissioner of the Colonial Office) and succeeded in liberalizing trade—especially by limiting the old, onerous monopoly called l'Exclusif, whereby the West Indies could trade only with certain French ports.

Having lost its largest outposts in India, Canada, and Louisiana by the ruinous terms of the peace, the Crown now lavished attention upon the Caribbean, with Saint-Domingue emerging as France's richest overseas colony. But Martinique also benefited from this attention, soon coming to import swelling numbers of African slaves through Fort-Royal and exporting enhanced commercial volumes of coffee, cacao, and cotton. In 1771, transatlantic traffic was further broadened and Guadeloupe was separated from Martinique's jurisdiction so that it began to develop independently. Ship arrivals at Fort-Royal multiplied throughout this decade, and the port city was able to shrug off the damages from a hurricane that struck the island on 25 August 1775.

Fort-Royal also proved its worth as a strategic base when France declared war against Great Britain again in August 1778, in support of the War of Independence launched by the Thirteen Colonies. Shortly after that news had reached the city, Gov.-Gen. Claude François Amour, Marquis de Bouillé du Chariol, decided to launch a surprise attack against Dominica, for which he raised 1,200 troops and 1,000 volunteers aboard three frigates, plus numerous lesser vessels, and captured that English colony by 7 September. More important, though, Fort-Royal was then able to receive and maintain even such large fleets as that of Vice-Adm. Charles-Henri, Comte d'Estaing, which put in on 25 November to counter an expected British offensive out of Barbados. Less than three weeks later, this enemy formation fell upon Saint Lucia, and an American privateer carried word to d'Estaing, who sortied with his fleet and numerous auxiliaries under the governor-general; their arrival at Saint Lucia proved too late, however, so that they re-entered Fort-Royal by 30 December.

D'Estaing sallied once more on 11 January 1779 to confirm that Saint Lucia's English occupiers had been reinforced by an additional fleet before retiring into his base. He was bolstered in turn by the arrival of four French ships-of-the-line on 19 February under Adm. François-Joseph Paul, Comte de Grasse Tilly, plus two more on 26 April under Commo. Louis-Philippe Rigaud, Marquis de Vaudreuil. Fort-Royal's facilities accommodated and sustained even this increased fleet, which now totaled nineteen ships-of-the-line and many auxiliaries, in addition to thousands of seamen.

When the rival English fleet bore away southward to escort a large merchant convoy from Grenada early in June, d'Estaing availed himself of the opportunity to detach a small squadron to capture Saint Vincent. He was then joined by another French convoy under Commo. Toussaint Guillaume Picquet de La Motte (better known as the Comte de Lamotte-Picquet) on 27 June, so consequently exited Fort-Royal four days later with a main strength of twenty-five ships-of-the-line and 2,500 troops aboard transports, hoping to fall upon Barbados. Contrary winds impeded d'Estaing's advance, however, so that his fleet instead veered round to seize Grenada. The English fleet reappeared and was repelled on 6 July, after which the French also occupied the Grenadines; the triumphant d'Estaing proceeded then toward Saint-Domingue (Haiti) and North America.

Fort-Royal remained undisturbed until early December 1779, when Lamotte-Picquet returned with a half dozen warships from North America to effect repairs and spend the winter. On 18 December, an approaching convoy of twenty-six French vessels was intercepted offshore by a Royal Navy squadron, obliging Lamotte-Picquet to sortie with the only ships available to him—the *Annibal*, *Réfléchi*, and *Vengeur*—which proved powerless to prevent the English from capturing ten merchantmen and driving another four aground. The commodore subsequently sailed to reinforce Saint-Domingue on 13 March 1780, as naval strength once more began to grow at Fort-Royal.

Vice Adm. Luc Urbain du Bouexic, Comte de Guichen, arrived ten days later, and then exited on 13 April 1780 with his entire fleet and 3,000 troops under the Marquis de Bouillé to attempt another descent against Barbados. However, this expedition was sighted by Adm. Sir George Brydges Rodney's fleet as it stemmed the Martinique Passage opposite Dominica three days later and was constrained to retire into Guadeloupe after a hard-fought battle. The two fleets then circled each other menacingly for several days, before de Guichen finally returned into Fort-Royal by 22 May. Early that same June, a Spanish frigate entered to advise that Adm. José Solano y Bote was approaching with a dozen ships-of-the-line and a half dozen lesser consorts, escorting sixty-two transports bearing 12,400 soldiers under Lt.-Gen. Victorio de Navía Osorio, plus thirty-eight merchantmen and seven privateers. De Guichen sortied with his fifteen French ships-of-the-line to greet this allied armada on 8 June, persuading its commander to put into Fort-Royal with his main body the following day, while simultaneously refreshing his convoy at Guadeloupe. Yet despite the massive strength of this anchored host, the two admirals could not agree upon a concerted plan of action against the English, and disease began to spread aboard the crowded transports. The two fleets therefore merely sailed together toward their respective destinations of Cuba and Saint-Domingue.

On 28 April 1781, another twenty French ships-of-the-line and a trio of frigates arrived off Martinique from Brest under Admiral de Grasse, escorting a merchant convoy. They learned shortly before sundown that Fort-Royal was blockaded by eighteen English warships under Rear Adm. Samuel Hood and subsequently paused off Salines Point to gather intelligence from an officer set ashore at Sainte-Anne. The French expedition then resumed its progression the next morning and sighted Hood's formation by 8:00 A.M. While the formation bore down to attack, de Grasse screened his charges. The 74-gun *Victoire* and the 64-gun *Caton*, *Solitaire*, and *Réfléchi* also slipped their cables to sortie from Fort-Royal in support. Some broadsides were exchanged, but de Grasse's convoy entered port safely, while Hood drew off that same evening and was briefly pursued toward St. Kitts by de Grasse on 30 April, before the French battle-fleet returned into Fort-Royal on 6 May. A pair of squadrons then departed two days later, one to reconnoiter occupied Saint Lucia with 1,200 men under Gov.-Gen. de Bouillé, plus another to assail Tobago with 1,300 troops under Col. Philibert François de Rouxel de Blanchelande.

The governor-general captured 100 prisoners and regained Fort-Royal by 15 May 1781, where a week later he and de

Grasse learned that English formations were moving to reinforce Tobago. The entire French fleet consequently quit harbor with additional troops under de Bouillé, preventing a British squadron from assisting Tobago's defenders, then helping compel its garrison to surrender by 2 June. Rodney belatedly arrived off this captive island two days later from Barbados with twenty-one ships-of-the-line, being powerless to attack de Grasse's twenty-three anchored warships, and so retired. The victorious French thereupon returned into Fort-Royal, from where de Grasse's fleet eventually set sail on 5 July with a 200-ship convoy, escorting it as far as Cap-François (modern Cap-Haïtien) before continuing for North America, while pursued by Hood.

Governor-General de Bouillé ventured from Fort-Royal with 1,200 men aboard two frigates and several privateer craft on 16 November 1781 to wrench the Dutch islands of Sint Eustatius, Sint Maarten, and Saba back from their English captors. Ten days later, Admiral de Grasse's battle-fleet returned into Fort-Royal from Chesapeake Bay, and both commanders then sallied together on 5 January 1782 with twenty-six ships-of-the-line and a troop convoy to reconquer St. Kitts, returning successfully by 26 February. The Royal Navy responded by massing in strength at Saint Lucia until 8 April, when de Grasse emerged from Fort-Royal again with thirty-three ships-of-the-line, protecting the departure of a 123-ship Martinican convoy before confronting Rodney and Hood off Dominica on 12 April. The French were defeated, suffering more than 3,000 men killed, wounded, or captured aboard five vessels (not including another four ships-of-the-line overtaken a few days later); British losses were 237 killed and 766 wounded, but no ships, reasserting their domination in the Lesser Antilles.

Fort-Royal and Martinique were subsequently blockaded, and one of the last major actions occurred on 6 December 1782, when Rear Adm. Sir Richard Hughes intercepted a small approaching convoy and beat the 64-gun *Solitaire* of Capt. Jean-Charles de Borda into submission. Peace preliminaries were signed at Versailles by 20 January 1783, ending hostilities two months later in the Americas. Fort-Royal had proven to be a most successful naval base throughout this conflict. Its commercial traffic also resurged once peace was reestablished, and the island's main commercial center of Saint-Pierre was declared a "free port" in 1784, licensed to receive foreign merchantmen as well. Martinique entered another interlude of prosperity so that according to the census taken four years afterward, there were 10,603 whites on the island, 2,326 "free colored," and 83,414 black slaves—all of whose lives were about to become transformed by a dramatic series of events in distant Paris.

"Républiqueville" and British Occupations (1789–1814)

France's long-simmering social discontent exploded with the assault upon the Bastille of 14 July 1789, which effectively brought down royal rule three days later and ushered in the chaotic "democracy" of the Estates-General. When news of this upheaval reached the West Indian island that same September, Martinicans initially reacted with joy, holding a festival at Fort-Royal to celebrate the "new alliance between the King and the Nation." However, it soon became apparent that such changes meant different things to different people and that the island moreover contained its own unique social rifts.

Wealthy white estate-owners, or *planteurs,* naturally tended to uphold the traditional ways that ensured their privileged status, while bourgeois whites and Creole freedmen—most concentrated at Saint-Pierre—selectively embraced certain egalitarian ideals in hopes of personal advancement, while ignoring the needs of the tens of thousands of slaves. As Crown authority eroded over the ensuing year and conflicting decrees began to arrive from Paris, local animosities deepened and some violence erupted. On 21 February 1790, an excited mob seized two officers at Saint-Pierre for having allegedly trampled upon a revolutionary cockade; as its garrison had already been withdrawn into Fort-Royal, the uneasy city authorities requested support from Guadeloupe, which arrived—but failed to assuage the growing tensions. A second incident occurred on 3 June, when the troops stationed in Fort-Louis and Fort-Bourbon proclaimed their allegiance to the revolutionary ideals being espoused at Saint-Pierre, thus contributing to monarchist fears; afterward, a Guadeloupan contingent disembarked and marched upon the capital that September, only to be defeated on the 25th near Acajou Plantation outside Lamentin by an army raised by local planters, killing or capturing 900 of their revolutionary opponents and seizing their artillery train.

Stability was temporarily restored with the arrival of a new governor-general—Jean-Pierre Antoine de Béhague—on 12 March 1791, who deported the most mutinous troops; yet the embittered planters subsequently refused to send any trade through Saint-Pierre, instead routing all their traffic through Fort-Royal, which created such dire economic hardships for the northern city that they sent a delegation to protest before the National Assembly in Paris. This latter institution had meanwhile continued to be radicalized by its Jacobin leadership, and in September 1792 it dispatched an expedition under the "Commissioner" Donatien Marie-Joseph de Vimeur, Vicomte de Rochambeau, to fully implement its policies on Martinique.

Local authorities refused to allow Rochambeau and his men to disembark, though, instead writing directly to the hapless king to reassert their loyalty to the Crown. Proponents of change fled Saint-Pierre during this reactionary period for the safety of Dominica, and when a naval expedition appeared offshore on 1 December 1792 under Capt. Jean-Baptiste Raymond, Baron Lacrosse—with explicit orders from the Convention in Paris to impose republican rule—Martinique's monarchists became openly defiant, even declaring war against the new government. This gesture proved vain, however, as the royalists lacked overseas allies or popular support. Lacrosse merely retired to Saint Lucia, from where he issued a stream of proclamations extolling the benefits of liberty to the general populace, until opposition in the Colonial Assembly finally voted to recognize the Republic on 9 January 1793.

Outmaneuvered, Governor-General de Béhague and his monarchist followers sought sanctuary with the Spanish on Trinidad, allowing Rochambeau to enter Fort-Royal on 3 February 1793. Amid the euphoria, the city was renamed Républiqueville, while its main defenses were changed from Fort-Louis and Fort-Bourbon to Fort-de-la-République and Fort-de-la-Convention, respectively; the city and its district became commonly known as Fort-de-la-République. Yet despite such submissiveness, and the fact that Rochambeau installed his headquarters there, the city was nonetheless punished for its former monarchist sentiments when its rival, Saint-Pierre, was designated as the only port on the island authorized to receive merchant traffic.

In Paris, the Directorate had meanwhile executed the captive Louis XVI on 21 January 1793, then declared war against both England and Spain. As a result, a small Royal Navy squadron under Rear Adm. Alan Gardner set sail from Barbados in late April, bearing a contingent of monarchists and British troops in a joint attempt to wrest Martinique from republican control. This surprise attack miscarried, the royalists being unable to raise much local assistance when they landed in Cas-des-Navires Bay on 7 May and subsequently being abandoned to their fate when the British warships withdrew. Despite its failure, this disembarkation nonetheless goaded Rochambeau into more drastic measures on the island, its Colonial Assembly being dissolved and a Revolutionary Tribunal installed, monarchist and clerical properties confiscated, and so forth. On 26 October, Martinique officially became a Département, subdivided into four administrative districts.

A more concerted British effort was organized by Vice Adm. Sir John Jervis (later the Earl of St. Vincent), who materialized offshore on 5 February 1794 with eighteen warships and two auxiliaries, having escorted a troop convoy across from Barbados bearing 6,100 soldiers under Lt.-Gen. Sir Charles Grey. Finding only the 32-gun French frigate *Bienvenue* anchored before Fort-de-la-République and an 18-gun corvette at Saint-Pierre, the British disembarked at three different locations with little opposition, overrunning Saint-Pierre by 16 February and then closing in on Rochambeau's main concentration at the capital. The 600 defenders became besieged within Fort-de-la-République and Fort-de-la-Convention by 16 March, the rest of the island being already in English hands (at a cost of 71 redcoats dead, plus 196 wounded or missing). Fort-de-la-République was stormed on 20 March, and once its garrison fell Rochambeau requested terms two days later, marching out of Fort-de-la-Convention by 23 March to be sent to the United States.

View from the southwest of the British assaults against Fort-de-la-République and Fort-de-la-Convention, March 1794; engraved by Samuel Alken, based upon an original drawing by the Reverend C. Willyams. (National Maritime Museum, Greenwich)

The British declared that they had occupied Martinique on behalf of the monarchy, which they expected would be restored to the throne of France. Wealthy plantation-owners and royalists were therefore assuaged, and Governor-General de Béhague was allowed to return from exile to reassume office as a titular head. The island was to be administered by its English governors in accordance with the laws and practices that had existed prior to the fall of the ancien regime—the ten-month term of Governor Milnes in 1795–1796 proving especially enlightened. Fort-Royal also regained its original name in the process, its harbor serving the Royal Navy as a valuable marshaling area for further West Indian offensives, as well as a privateering base after the installation of a prize court.

Its commerce flourished as well, as the island now enjoyed ample maritime access for both its imports and exports, without being too burdened by defense concerns. British merchants took up residence, and neutral American vessels were made welcome, providing much of occupied Martinique's food and lumber in exchange for rum and molasses. A small counter-expedition of 1,100 Jacobin troops from France under Commissioner Victor Hugues—soon dubbed the "Colonial Robespierre"—had succeeded in reconquering Guadeloupe in December 1794; after being further bolstered by 3,000 more reinforcements in early January 1795, they began making

descents on the Martinican coast and other British islands. The English occupiers responded by mustering royalist militia units, and even Martinican privateers, for the island's defense, which proved so successful that Hugues was constrained to change tactics as of mid-1796, concentrating on attacks against merchant shipping (with so many American vessels being intercepted as to contribute significantly to the outbreak of the so-called Quasi-War with France). Fort-Royal remained a busy harbor, despite occasional disorders among plantation slaves elsewhere on the island.

After eight years of occupation, Martinique was restored to French rule by the Treaty of Amiens, signed on 27 March 1802. Under its terms, a new governor—Vice Adm. Louis Thomas, Comte Villaret de Joyeuse—arrived to take office by 14 September, and a few uneasy royalists emigrated to Trinidad prior to his arrival. The capital was renamed Fort-de-France at this juncture, while its principal citadel was changed from Fort-de-la-République into Fort-Desaix in honor of Gen. Louis Desaix (a favorite of First Consul Napoleon Bonaparte, who had been killed during the Battle of Marengo on 14 June 1800). Because its social composition had been left largely unchanged during the British interlude, the island was spared the turmoil that gripped other French Antillean possessions during this restoration phase; the liberties won by bourgeois whites,

Statue of Empress Joséphine in Fort-de-France's main square, or La Savane, ca. 1890. The statue was positioned so as to gaze across the bay toward her family's old sugar plantation of La Pagerie on the opposite shore. (Hearn, *Two Years in the French West Indies*)

on 6 January 1804, Commo. Samuel Hood's 74-gun flagship HMS *Centaur* anchored off Rocher du Diamant (Diamond Rock)—a small and steep-sided islet three-quarters of a mile off the southern headland—and next morning deposited a party of British seamen, who installed heavy batteries. Martinique's defenders were unable to muster any effective countermeasures against this intrusive presence until 14 May 1805, when Vice Adm. Pierre Charles Silvestre de Villeneuve unexpectedly arrived from across the Atlantic with an enormous Franco-Spanish battle-fleet.

Fifteen days later, two French ships-of-the-line, a frigate, a brig, and a schooner towed eleven gunboats crammed with 240 soldiers out of Fort-de-France to assault Diamond Rock, compelling its 128-man British garrison to capitulate by 3 June. Villeneuve's main fleet then weighed two days later to ravage British colonies throughout the Lesser Antilles as a diversionary tactic before hastening back toward Europe. But upon capturing fifteen English merchantmen off Antigua on 8 June, the French admiral learned that a pursuing battle-fleet under Vice Adm. Horatio Nelson had arrived at Barbados four days earlier, so he decided to abandon his diversionary scheme in favor of a direct return toward Europe.

Having reclaimed supremacy at sea, the Royal Navy then reimposed its blockade around Martinique, inevitably followed by another invasion. On the morning of 30 January 1809, Rear Adm. Sir Alexander Cochrane appeared with twenty-seven warships, escorting a troop convoy bearing the army of Lt.-Gen. George Beckwith. The British took Cul-de-Sac Marin, thousands of redcoats coming ashore there and at Saint-Luce, to circle inland around the inner shoreline of Cul-de-Sac Royal in twin columns. Governor Villaret de Joyeuse decided to evacuate Fort-de-France and make his stand with 2,250 men inside the greatly expanded Fort-Bourbon, which commanded the high ground above the city. Beckwith consequently instituted a formal siege, his first heavy batteries opening fire against this hilltop fort's western side by 19 February. As more artillery sprouted along the surrounding Surirey Heights, the French commander finally requested terms on 23 February, his garrison laying down their arms two days later.

Martinique passed under British control for the third time, Beckwith being elevated to the Order of the Bath for this success, while Cochrane was promoted to vice admiral. The English remained in possession for more than five years, during which Fort-de-France enjoyed a renewed flow of commercial traffic until Napoleon was defeated in Europe and the island was ceremoniously restored to French control. Vice Adm. Pierre René Marie, Comte de Vaugiraud, assumed office as royal governor on 10 December 1814, at which time the main citadel was renamed Fort Saint-Louis, although some uneasiness was experienced the following spring when the emperor escaped from his confinement on Elba and briefly regained the French throne, only to meet his final defeat at Waterloo.

mulattoes, and even some blacks were rolled back on orders from Napoleon, who furthermore crowned himself emperor on 2 December 1804.

Fighting then flared anew less than a year later back in Europe, and Fort-de-France was menaced by a different threat:

Martinique's Celebrated Daughter

Marie-Joséphe Rose Tascher de La Pagerie—the lovely and kindly woman nicknamed "Joséphine," who would become Napoleon's first wife and empress of France—was born at Trois-Ilets opposite Fort-Royal in 1763, into the island's planter aristocracy. At the age of sixteen she wed the governor-general's son Alexandre, Vicomte de Beauharnais (himself born in the Martinican capital three years prior to his bride), and the young couple moved to France that same year of 1779. Two children resulted from this union: Eugène, a son born two years afterward, and a daughter, Hortense, delivered in 1783.

Five years later, Joséphine became separated from her husband and returned with her young daughter to the family estate of La Pagerie, opposite Fort-Royal. When the turbulence unleashed by the Revolution spilled over into Martinique shortly thereafter, she sailed for France again and disembarked at Toulon in November 1790. Her husband had since become a deputy in the Estates-General and was a rising political figure, so Joséphine rejoined him. However, the vicomte—while acting as commander of the Army of the Rhine in 1793—was unable to prevent the fall of Mayence, so he was tried by a revolutionary tribunal and executed.

Joséphine was also imprisoned and might have shared his fate, except for the timely overthrow and death in late July 1794 of the driving force behind the Reign of Terror, Maximilien Robespierre. Upon her release, the young widow found her teenage boy (a future viceroy of Italy) apprenticed to a carpenter, and her girl (a future queen of Holland) working for a seamstress. Joséphine therefore attached herself to the man who had brought down Robespierre—Paul-François, former vicomte Barras—and became his mistress, thus an influential personage in the new circles of power.

Her beauty, charm, and grace attracted another rising star, the young artillery Gen. Napoleon Bounaparte (spelling of his name at the time), who courted his "sweet and matchless Joséphine" passionately despite their six-year difference in age and convinced her to marry him in a civil ceremony performed on 9 March 1796. He departed at the end of that same month to assume command over the Army of Italy, winning a series of spectacular victories that eventually propelled him to power. Joséphine was to enjoy the material riches of his ascent—compensating for her previous penury, for example, by spending more than a million francs a year on her clothing alone—although she was frequently troubled by the bluntness of her partner, her inability to bear him an heir, as well as the jealousy of his family and underlings.

His infatuation with her remained strong, though, and he crowned Joséphine as empress in Notre-Dame Cathedral in Paris before Pope Pius VII on 2 December 1802. Napoleon also agreed to adopt Eugène as his son four years afterward, but for reasons of state he began to desire to found his own dynasty. Having sired several children—including a son—with mistresses, Napoleon finally resolved to divorce his beloved but barren Joséphine so as to marry a royal princess and produce a universally recognized male heir.

The emperor consequently returned to Fontainebleau from a victorious campaign against Austria on 20 October 1809, and when the empress arrived to join him that same evening, she found the connecting door between their bedrooms walled up. Divorce proceedings were concluded by mid-December, and he married the nineteen-year-old Austrian princess Marie-Louise the following April Fool's Day. Joséphine retired to the magnificent Malmaison Palace outside Paris and died there late in 1814, without ever having beheld Martinique again.

Stagnation (1816–1901)

This restoration of peace, unfortunately, was to initiate a difficult interlude for the history of Fort-de-France and the entire Antillean archipelago. The drop in sugar prices on international markets resulting from competition from much larger producers on the mainlands of America, Africa, and Asia utterly crippled Martinique's export-based economy, and it never fully recovered. The island was also racked by slave revolts in 1816 and entered into a prolonged spiral of depression and neglect.

The installation of the liberal Second Republic in Paris in 1848 led to an emancipation from slavery on this overseas colonial outpost, so that most of Martinique's blacks made a joyful exodus from the island plantations, but large numbers had to return almost immediately to seek employment as wage laborers because sugar cultivation still remained the only viable business. As the best lands were controlled by the island's large estates, a majority of workers had to depend upon seasonal work during harvest times, the small parcels of land that some were able to obtain being too small to provide even the most basic subsistence.

The first road running through the tropical forest from the capital to the north end of the island was also opened in 1850 and was named La Trace. The following year, though,

An itinerant pastry seller, ca. 1890. (Hearn, *Two Years in the French West Indies*)

bark *Agrippina* slipped into its harbor on the evening of 11 November 1862, bearing coal and provisions intended to covertly resupply the Confederate commerce-raider *Alabama* of Capt. Raphael Semmes. This elusive warship appeared one week later, depositing fifty-three prisoners ashore; but at 7:00 A.M. on 19 November, the powerful Federal steamer USS *San Jacinto* of Capt. Ronckendorff—having learned of the *Alabama*'s clandestine rendezvous—also materialized outside Fort-de-France and mounted watch. Concerned, the island Gov. Antoine Marie Ferdinand de Maussion de Candé ordered the French batteries manned, and he stationed a small steamer between the two belligerents, so as to preclude any hostilities within French territorial waters. However, Semmes feinted toward the fort's inner anchorage that same sunset, only to slip out the southern side of the bay after darkness fell, leaving *San Jacinto* vainly maintaining watch outside the empty harbor for another thirty-six hours.

The first regular transatlantic steamship line was inaugurated in 1862, and that same year Fort-de-France regained some of its former strategic usefulness by serving as a staging area for the French expeditions bound to Mexico to place the Archduke Maximilian upon its throne. However, that venture ended in failure, and the island subsequently slid back into its former state of official neglect. After the fall of the Second Empire, republican institutions were restored to Martinique during the 1870s, despite vehement opposition from its white Creole elite, and the port city resumed its somnolent existence as a colonial backwater. When a devastating hurricane struck in 1891, Fort-de-France was rebuilt in part because of the personal intervention of the famed Parisian architect Henri Picq (married to a Martinican), who imported the Schoelcher Library piece by piece from his Tuileries exhibit and redesigned its Saint Louis Cathedral by 1895. However, the city was to actually be revived and transformed by a wholly unexpected series of events.

Eruption and Recovery (1902–1938)

The traditional concentration of Martinique's inhabitants and commerce were to be dramatically rearranged after the cataclysmic eruption of Mont-Pelée at the northern end of the island. This long dormant volcano had begun to show signs of activity as early as January 1902, but the population of nearby Saint-Pierre—only 4 miles away—did not exhibit any particular alarm until 23 April when minor explosions began belching ash and sulphurous gases down upon their city, and frightened snakes and insects swarmed through their dwellings. As tremors multiplied over the next couple of weeks, the water in the Etang Sec crater lake overheated and finally burst its rim on 5 May, destroying a rum distillery with twenty-three laborers inside before cascading into the sea. Nevertheless, Governor Louis Mouttet was reassured by an inspection that no volcanic explosion seemed imminent; he ordered the publication of positive and reassuring newspaper

government policies throughout the French West Indies underwent a dramatic reversal after the conservative coup d'état in Paris of 1–2 December 1851 that resulted in the establishment of the Second Empire as President and Prince Louis Napoleon ascended the throne with the title of Emperor Napoleon III. Slavery was not reimposed, yet universal manhood suffrage was abolished on Martinique in 1854 as a result, while the local election of councilors was replaced by imperial nominations from among the island's dominant white upper class. Large numbers of indentured laborers moreover began to be brought in from abroad to bolster certain specialized sectors of the economy, so that some 25,000 East Indians, 10,000 Africans (nicknamed Congos), 1,000 Chinese, and 500 Annamites arrived between 1852 and 1894—complicating the chronic local problem of underemployment.

Sleepy Fort-de-France was to witness a dramatic byplay of the U.S. Civil War, starting when the neutral English merchant articles and had troops stationed along the road leading toward Fort-de-France to prevent a stampede of refugees.

However, at about 7:50 A.M. on 8 May 1902, Mont-Pelée erupted with an enormous roar. A superheated cloud of gas, ash, and rock swept down through Saint-Pierre a minute later and killed virtually all its 28,000 inhabitants, additional thousands in adjoining farmlands, as well as sinking twenty vessels anchored offshore. Such a horrifying eradication of 15 percent of Martinique's total population, coupled with continual signs of danger from the volcano (more eruptions occurring on 20 May, 6 June, and 30 August), created a wholesale retreat and reaccommodation of most island interests into the bay around Fort-de-France.

As calm slowly returned in the wake of this cataclysm, the tiny capital took on new life and importance. The revival was generated by the influx of many new residents and government funds, both of which spurred modern municipal services such as bus routes that were inaugurated in 1903 and the construction of a grand new Palais de Justice in 1906 and an 800-seat public theater by 1912. Port activities also took on added impetus as ship movements began to increase throughout the entire Caribbean after 1903 when American interests helped Panama gain its independence and then committed enormous resources to completing a trans-Isthmian canal by August 1914. The demand for so many laborers and supplies indirectly benefited Martinique, while Fort-de-France was able to upgrade its bunkering facilities to serve as a coaling station for transient vessels.

The cultivation of bananas and pineapples was also introduced into the island economy in an attempt to reduce its total dependence upon the sugar trade, but the latter nevertheless remained Martinique's predominant export through Fort-de-France. Not even restrictions placed upon the importation of Martinican rum into France in 1922, as well as sugar itself a dozen years later (because of complaints from the cognac and sugar beet interests in Paris, respectively), could reverse the island's small but favorable balance of trade. And although Mont-Pelée erupted again in 1929–1930, causing widespread consternation, the island did not suffer nearly as much loss of life or material damages because its demographic and commercial concentrations radiated out from Fort-de-France by that time.

World War II Difficulties (1939–1943)
However, the city and the entire island were to suffer as a result of the unexpectedly swift conquest of France by Adolf Hitler's Nazi armies at the beginning of World War II. Two weeks after the outbreak of hostilities, Vice Adm. Georges Joseph Robert arrived at Fort-de-France, on 15 September 1939, aboard the 6,500-ton training cruiser *Jeanne d'Arc,* bearing the joint titles of haut commissaire (high commissioner) and military commander-in-chief for the French Antilles and Guiana. Although Martinique initially remained

Street scene in Fort-de-France, ca. 1920, its cathedral spire looming in the distance. (Franck, *Roaming Through the West Indies*)

untroubled by the distant European conflict, circumstances worsened once the German Blitzkrieg (lighting offensive) had overrun northern France the next spring, bringing about the wholesale collapse of its government.

According to the capitulation terms signed on 22 June 1940, the defeated French authorities were to retain control over only the central portion of their nation, as well as its Mediterranean coastline, overseas colonies, and navy (although many of its best warships were also to be handed over to the German victors as indemnization, prompting Britain—France's recent ally—to destroy a large French fleet anchored at the North African port of Mers-el-Kebir near Oran on 3 July, with grievous loss of life). When delegates of the defeated administration gathered at the small French city of Vichy to ratify their nation's humiliating surrender to the Nazis, Pierre Laval persuaded them to create a wholly new regime on 11 July, the elderly Marshal Henri Pétain emerging as president and Adm. Jean Darlan as one of his cabinet ministers. This so-called Vichy government was soon to engender widespread odium abroad because of its close collaboration with the Germans.

At Fort-de-France, meanwhile, Robert had been joined on 22 June 1940 by the 22,100-ton aircraft carrier *Béarn*, which had reversed course in the mid-Atlantic while bound from Halifax toward France with 107 aircraft purchased from the United States. Then, two days later, the 5,900-ton light cruiser *Émile Bertin* had also entered port bearing 300 tons of the Bank of France's gold reserves, which were deposited underground in Fort Desaix for safekeeping. Upon learning of the British attack against Mers-el-Kebir on 3 July—during which 1,300 French sailors had lost their lives—Robert immediately ordered the visiting cruiser HMS *Fiji* to depart, then placed his forces upon alert against any similar assault.

Robert was personally loyal to his naval superior Darlan, and as a result his 2,500-man squadron ensured that Martinique and all other French colonies in the New World remained firmly in the Vichy camp and somewhat ill disposed toward the English; indeed, as a direct consequence of the Oran raid, the French squadron even had standing orders to fire upon any approaching Royal Navy formation. Maritime traffic from Fort-de-France toward Casablanca (Morocco) tentatively resumed, despite the naval battles raging in the North Atlantic between British convoys and German submarines. In 1940, Martinique was able to export 75,000 tons of sugar to France via Morocco, as well as other produce; soon, though, the Royal Navy began intercepting and impounding such vessels, so as to tighten their blockade of Continental Europe.

When the United States became drawn into the conflict after the Pearl Harbor attack of 7 December 1941 by the Japanese—Germany's and Italy's Axis partner—U.S. Rear Adm. F. J. Horne negotiated an arrangement with Robert later that same month whereby no French warship would sortie without advance notification to the Allies. But given the Vichy government's pro-German proclivities, Washington nonetheless soon began to suspect that the Martinicans were collaborating with the enemy.

Such distrust was seemingly confirmed when German submarines unleashed a new offensive against Allied shipping in the West Indies as of 16 February 1942, inflicting heavy casualties and creating widespread panic amid these vulnerable sea-lanes. Two days later, the *U-156* of Lt. Werner Hartenstein entered Fort-de-France to deposit a wounded crew member, then reprovisioned with fresh fruit and vegetables. Although there was no proof that the U-boat had furthermore been refueled by Vichy sympathizers, the Allies suspected that it had, so that when a second wave of submarine attacks began inflicting even heavier losses, in May of 1942, Washington dispatched the destroyers USS *Blakeley* and *Ellis,* plus a small patrol cutter, to inspect every vessel entering or departing Fort-de-France for evidence of clandestine contacts.

Ironically, not only had the Martinican authorities refused Hartenstein undue assistance, but in addition the Germans had detached two of their own submarines to attack vessels standing into the same port: Hartenstein's *U-156,* which sank the small Dominican freighter *Presidente Trujillo* 10 miles out-

USS *Blakeley* (DD-150) staggering into Fort-de-France's harbor on 25 May 1942 after being torpedoed by *U-156;* this photo was most likely taken from aboard the anchored French aircraft carrier *Béarn.* (U.S. Naval Historical Center, Washington, D.C.)

side Fort-de-France on 21 May 1942, and *U-68* of Ulrich Graf, which unsuccessfully fired its deck-gun at a freighter running inside the next day. Then, on the morning of 25 May, *U-156* spotted the USS *Blakeley* patrolling inshore and blew off its bow with a torpedo. The heavily damaged American destroyer limped into port, while Hartenstein requested permission by wireless from U-boat headquarters in Lorient to enter Fort-de-France's anchorage and finish it off; permission was denied, though, so that the *Blakeley* was rescued shortly thereafter by U.S. naval reinforcements.

A huge U.S. expedition subsequently landed in Morocco and Algeria on 8 November 1942, encountering no resistance from its French colonial garrisons. The Vichy minister of marine, Jean Darlan, who happened to be in Algiers at that time, even switched allegiances and ordered the main French battle-fleet to escape from Toulon and join the Allied cause, whose flight was prevented when the Germans quickly overran the remainder of France and incorporated the entire nation into their Reich.

Given such changed circumstances—France now being completely occupied by Germany, its Vichy administration openly cooperating with the Nazis—Washington began to grow increasingly impatient with Admiral Robert's continual refusal to align himself with the Free French movement. On 13 November 1942, constrictive diplomatic pressure compelled him to immobilize his warships and remove propellers from his planes at Fort-de-France, after which the U.S. Navy instituted a blockade against Martinique, Guadeloupe, and French Guiana. Cut off from all sea traffic, the latter colony opted to join the Free French cause in March 1943, while the United States menacingly marshaled combat aircraft on the island of St. Lucia and assembled a task force around their new fleet carrier USS *Essex* to prevent any countercoup by Robert's squadron sortieing from Martinique. No such attempt was made, however, the only ship to violate the American blockade being the *Couventeur Mouttete,* which brought a group of dispossessed Vichy Loyalists into Fort-de-France from Guiana.

Eventually, U.S. forces on Puerto Rico and Trinidad began large-scale exercises in June 1943 heralding a projected invasion of Martinique, openly advising the French defenders of their intent: two U.S. regiments were to land on the beaches immediately south of Fort-de-France and assault Fort Desaix, while a parachute regiment would seize Lamentin Airport north of the town and other regiments would be disembarked on the eastern shores of the island at Le Robert. Already disheartened by their isolation, their will to resist collapsed altogether before the prospect of resisting the U.S. attack on behalf of an increasingly unpopular regime; many officers thus deserted to the Free French cause—including the commanders of Martinique's colonial infantry regiment and artillery regiment, as well as Robert's own second-in-command, Rear Adm. Robert Marie-Joseph Battet. Robert himself requested terms by 30 June 1943, sailing for Puerto Rico on 15 July with his remaining staff and Vichy supporters to surrender to the U.S. authorities, after which Martinique passed peacefully into the hands of the Free French forces under General Jessy.

Modern Evolution (1944–Present)

A year after World War II ended in 1945, the restored French government decided to revise old colonial practices by elevating Martinique to the status of a department of France, a policy that went into full effect as of 1948. This implementation was accompanied by considerable infusions of funds, in the form of both government grants and private investments, that artificially stimulated the growth of commerce and light industry—yet it failed to elevate the island into a self-sustaining economy. In fact, Martinique was to become ever more dependent upon France—seemingly prosperous, yet actually operating at a deficit and with a negative balance of trade.

Still, the resultant public and private construction booms began transforming Fort-de-France, whose population reached

Émile Bertin in dry dock; probably photographed at Fort-de-France, ca. 1942–1943, as proof that this French light cruiser had been effectively "demilitarized," so as to pose no threat to Allied interests in the West Indies. (U.S. Naval Historical Center, Washington, D.C.)

60,648 by 1954—out of a total of approximately 275,000 inhabitants on the island, of whom only 1.25 percent were Békés, or descendants of the old dominant white colonial elite; another 30,512 residents were scattered among the city's suburbs, plus satellite towns such as Schoelcher, Saint-Joseph, Case-Pilote, and Lamentin. Thanks to regular supplements in the form of French bureaucratic jobs, make-work projects, and social security checks, a wave of rural workers moreover began forsaking farm life to migrate into the capital, whose combined metropolitan population ballooned to 122,791 by 1961 and 141,369 by 1967, representing more than 35 percent of the island's total. Without having to depend upon sugar exports any longer, island production dropped commensurately from a high of 93,000 tons in 1963 to little more than 14,000 tons eleven years later, while unemployment and underemployment spread.

In 1970, the increasingly crowded capital and its surrounding district were hit by tropical storm Dorothy, which was detected forming out in the Atlantic on 17 August. Unlike previous storms, Dorothy approached the island via an unusually circuitous route, swinging round Martinique's southeastern tip to come ashore directly above Fort-de-France, soaking the city and its barren foothills with a foot of torrential rainfall during the night of 20–21 August. As a result, Madame River became heavily swollen, sending torrents of water and mud spewing down through the low-lying city streets, claiming scores of lives and leaving thousands more homeless.

Fort-de-France nonetheless recovered and by 1982, the population within the capital's old boundaries stood at 97,814 inhabitants—known on the island as Foyalais—and grew to 101,540 seven years later. Bulk exports of sugar through port facilities continued to taper off, most produce instead being converted locally into rum, although banana shipments to France rose steadily. Martinique still remains economically dependent upon French subsidies, though, as well as having to import most foodstuffs, while tourism has emerged as its primary service industry. The modern municipal boundaries radiate out from its ancient stronghold of Fort Saint-Louis only as far as the Madame River canal, the public park called La Savane, and Général de Gaulle Boulevard, with numerous satellite communities and tourist resorts now clustered along the nearby shorelines.

For further reading on the history of Fort-de-France or Martinique, please consult the Select Bibliography at the end of this volume.

Puerto Rico

San Juan

Lonely Spanish outpost, oft coveted by foreign enemies, which has evolved into one of the largest metropolises of the modern Antilles.

Establishment as "Caparra" (1508–1520)

The beautiful island called Borinquen by its Taino-speaking inhabitants—signifying "Land of the Great Lord"—was sighted by Christopher Columbus on 16 November 1493, during his second voyage to the New World. Three days later, he stepped ashore near the Culebrinas River mouth, dubbing the island San Juan Bautista (Saint John the Baptist) in honor of Spain's Crown Prince Juan, before proceeding westward to install a permanent colony on Hispaniola. Borinquen was to be visited only sporadically over the next dozen years by transient Spanish vessels pausing to take on wood and water.

The Catholic king Ferdinand granted a license on 24 April 1505 to Vicente Yáñez Pinzón to settle the island, although the explorer failed to carry out such a colonization project, instead probing the South American mainland. It was not until early August 1508 that Juan Ponce de León actually set sail from the eastern coast of what is today the Dominican Republic with fifty would-be occupiers, disembarking upon San Juan Bautista's semiarid southwestern shore and establishing friendly contacts with the local chieftain Agüeybaná. Venturing inland with his new ally, Ponce de León learned that several gold-bearing rivers emptied onto the island's more verdant northern coast, so he circled round its eastern tip aboard his *caravelón* (large caravel).

After two abortive attempts at finding a suitable settlement site, Ponce de León entered a spacious, almost landlocked bay that he dubbed Puerto Rico (Rich Port), then pushed 2 miles inland to erect a small fortified camp by December 1508. Crops were planted in token of possession, a little gold was garnered,

and two Spaniards remained behind when Ponce de León departed for Santo Domingo on 1 May 1509 to report to Nicolás de Ovando, governor-general for the Spanish West Indies.

De Ovando acknowledged his subordinate's accomplishment by appointing him acting-governor and chief justice for the newly acquired island (subject to confirmation from Spain), and he suggested that its capital be called Caparra after an ancient Roman city in the Spanish province of Extremadura. Ponce de León obliged upon regaining his settlement and constructed a whitewashed, stone *casa fuerte* (strong house) to act as his official residence. His authority, though, was abruptly voided when Diego Columbus—son and heir to the great admiral and de Ovando's successor as governor-general—arrived at Santo Domingo that same summer and designated a member of his own retinue, Juan Cerón, as new Puerto Rican governor in October 1509.

De Ovando had this second title reversed upon regaining Spain, so that Ponce de León and his original deputy governor, Cristóbal de Sotomayor, were reinstated. Transatlantic ships bound for Hispaniola were moreover ordered to call at Puerto Rico during their passage by a royal decree issued in 1510, so that tiny Caparra prospered modestly by receiving a few more settlers—including its first doctor, Gaspar de Villalobos, as well as "Micer Geron," or Gerónimo, an émigré from Brussels who operated its gold smelter as of that October.

Yet a local uprising and Carib raids claimed Sotomayor's life early in 1511, as well as those of eighty other Spanish residents scattered about the island, before finally being put down by Ponce de León with 100 troops. His commission was then invalidated for a second time when Diego Columbus successfully petitioned the Spanish Crown on behalf of his own nominee, Cerón, who arrived at Caparra to reassume office as governor on 28 November 1511. Although nominally left in

Panoramic view from atop El Morro headland, looking southwest across San Juan over its inner harbor, ca. 1898. (Hill, *Cuba and Porto Rico*)

185

command of the island militia, a disappointed Ponce de León sailed northwestward in March 1513 to search for the mythical "Fountain of Youth," in the process discovering Florida.

Relocation (1521–1585)

Caparra's population had grown to perhaps 175 Spanish residents by 1515, yet they were increasingly disenchanted with their settlement's remove from the sea, being inconveniently separated from all shipborne traffic by a muddy and hilly jungle track wending toward the distant anchorage. Citizens therefore secured permission in September 1519 to relocate their community to the coast, despite the strenuous objections of Ponce de León, who had since resumed residence.

After a survey of the harbor shoreline, the western side of its 3-mile-long barrier island was chosen as the locale for a new city, being apparently blessed with abundant wood and water (although both would soon become depleted). Its narrow entrance channel and eastern shallows moreover promised to be easily defensible, so that about eighty town plots were allocated by 1521 to Spanish residents and their dependents—representing roughly 320 people. A clutch of thatched-roofed, wooden houses and *bohíos* (shacks) emerged within the urban compound, which measured 700 yards in length by 450 in width; the relocated city was christened San Juan Bautista de Puerto Rico, soon shortened into San Juan de Puerto Rico.

However, the conquest of the Mexican empire by Hernán Cortés that same autumn stunted the fledgling city's development, as reports of the spectacular wealth available on the American mainland lured away many West Indian residents. San Juan's citizens were also alarmed by a royal dispatch in 1522 that warned that a trio of French privateering vessels was preparing to raid the Antilles, so that a bulwark of logs had to be extemporized at their harbor entrance. A sturdy brick-and-mortar Dominican monastery dedicated to Saint Thomas of Aquinas was also commenced on the city's northern fringe in 1523 (being converted centuries later into a military headquarters called the Cuartel de San Juan, after the Dominican Order had been suppressed by the Spanish authorities in 1837), and a six-bed city hospital named Nuestra Señora de la Concepción was added in 1524, thanks to a donation from Pedro de Herrera.

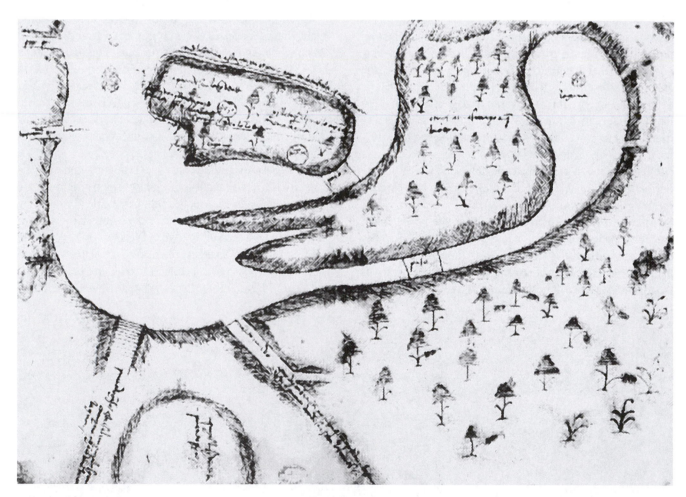

Sketch of the city's proposed new site, as surveyed in September 1519 by Lic. Rodrigo de Figueroa, in anticipation of transferring Caparra's residents to the harbor. (Archive of Indies, Seville)

Yet much of the nascent city, including its log-and-thatch cathedral, was flattened by a storm on 4 October 1526, remembered as the *huracán de San Francisco* (Saint Francis's hurricane) because it had struck upon that particular feast day of the Church calendar. By the following year, 129 homes had been reconstructed—although fewer than a half dozen made of stone—to shelter some 500 residents, who were furthermore startled when 240 Carib warriors stole into their harbor before dawn on 18 October 1529 aboard eight seagoing *piraguas* (dugouts), seizing a boat from the Bayamón River and slaying three black crewmen before being driven off by shore fire. Fear of future penetrations spurred the completion of the Ponce family's stone strong-house in 1530 to act as a communal sanctuary nicknamed the Casa Blanca (White House); it resisted two more heavy storms that leveled virtually every other dwelling that same July and August.

A second major depopulation ensued when discouraged Spanish residents were drawn away by news of Francisco Pizarro's campaign against the rich Incan empire of Peru. Puerto Rican officials strove to staunch this exodus by enacting harsh penalties against would-be emigrants. Funds were also allocated in March 1533 by the *real audiencia* (royal tribunal) at Santo Domingo for Gov. Francisco Manuel de Lando to commence work the next year on an 8-gun stone emplacement enclosed by a wooden stockade to cover San Juan's anchorage at Santa Catalina Inlet. It was officially christened Fort Santa Catalina upon its completion in May 1540, although better known simply as La Fortaleza (The Fortress), later supplanted by Santa Catalina Palace. Two dismantled brigantines were received from Spain to act as regional patrol vessels.

A pair of 3-gun batteries and a stout blockhouse were added atop the 120-foot rocky heights of El Morro headland during the early 1540s, while a new stone cathedral was initiated within the city core by Bishop Rodrigo de Bastidas. Yet the island's gold mines were now exhausted, and only small amounts of sugar could be produced for export; *sanjuaneros* therefore found sea-traffic routinely bypassing their port in favor of more lucrative destinations on the mainland. Their isolation deepened after the plate-fleet system was implemented from Seville, and galleons grew so voluminous that masters were reluctant to brave San Juan's narrow entry for the sake of its meager commerce. Instead, they merely touched at Puerto Rico's western coastline to refresh provisions before proceeding with their voyages.

San Juan was visited only sporadically as of the mid-sixteenth century, and by smaller vessels detached from these convoys. The Crown provided one of the few sources of local revenue by financing construction of the wooden San Antonio Bridge across Condado Lagoon during the late 1550s and early 1560s, featuring a stockade at one end and a removable mid-section for emergencies. The visiting Adm. Pedro Menéndez de Avilés moreover installed a battery between El Morro headland and La Fortaleza to protect the inner harbor, which would eventually evolve into Santa Elena Bastion; yet the Puerto Rican capital otherwise stagnated, its neglected residents even turning to foreign smugglers for relief. According to an ecclesiastical survey taken in 1582, the urban populace remained virtually unchanged at 170 Spanish households, totaling perhaps 800 to 850 people, including fourteen priests.

Beleaguered Stronghold (1586–1648)

A destructive sweep through the Caribbean by an English privateering fleet under Sir Francis Drake in 1585–1586 galvanized Madrid into strengthening San Juan's defenses to provide both a haven for transient galleons, as well as a regional base for retaining the Lesser Antilles. Annual *situados* (subsidies) from the Mexican exchequer were instituted as of 1586, and upon the official declaration of hostilities a couple of years later, the Italian-born royal engineer Batista Antonelli made an inspection tour and suggested replacing the small batteries crowning El Morro headland with a castle—a project assigned a year and a half later to Capt. Pedro de Salazar. By August 1591, a 32-gun fortress had been partially completed, christened San Felipe del Morro in honor of King Philip II.

San Juan's garrison had also been augmented, from 50 to 400 troops; San Antonio Bridge had been fortified, becoming known as the Puente de los Soldados (The Soldiers' Bridge); a new 4-gun battery named Fort Santiago was installed to cover the shallow Boquerón (Mouth) of Condado Lagoon; and the inner harbor's old battery was upgraded to become Santa Elena Bastion. Yet, notwithstanding these measures, the English privateers William King and William Richards slipped into San Juan's roadstead one spring night in 1592 to liberate a 70-ton English merchantman.

Then the 973-ton galleon *Nuestra Señora de Begonia*, flagship of Adm. Sancho Pardo y Osorio's plate-fleet, staggered into port on 9 April 1595, having been damaged by a storm while bound from Havana toward Seville. Millions of pesos in silver bullion were ferried into Gov. Pedro Suares's residence at La Fortaleza for safekeeping, while an *aviso* (dispatch vessel) hastened across the Atlantic to request that a squadron be sent to rescue the treasure. Five Spanish frigates duly arrived under Commo. Pedro Tello de Guzmán on 13 November, but only a short distance ahead of a much larger enemy fleet under Drake and Sir John Hawkins, the secret of the crippled galleon having also reached England. San Juan's 400-man garrison was reinforced by *Begonia*'s 300 seamen, 500 from Tello de Guzmán's frigates, plus 300 Puerto Rican militiamen, stretching a log-boom between El Morro and Cañuelo Key, as well as repositioning the galleon and frigates close up to the entrance to be sunk as block-ships.

The English came within sight of Escambrón Point by dawn of 22 November 1595. They drew fire from the Boquerón's Santiago battery, before gliding west to anchor off Cabrón Inlet that same afternoon, where Hawkins succumbed to the diseases ravaging the British crews. The 5-gun Cabrón battery of Capt. Alonso Vargas also opened fire at 5:00 P.M., smashing a round into Drake's cabin aboard his flagship *Defiant* that killed an officer and wounded three others, so that the admiral shifted his anchorage again to Cabras Island. The raiders spent 23 November reconnoitering San Juan's approaches, then dispatched two dozen boats bearing several hundred men into its harbor after nightfall to attack the anchored Spanish ships.

The defenders fired back blindly, unable to prevent the English from burning the frigates *Santa Isabel, Santa Magdalena,* and *Santa Clara.* But the flames also illuminated the attackers, so that counterfire from the shore batteries drove the English off with fifty dead or missing, plus a similar number wounded, compared with only forty Spanish dead. The next morning, Drake circled out to sea and then steered toward San Juan's harbor mouth that same afternoon, only to halt upon seeing the galleon and remaining two frigates scuttled to prevent access. The English probed as far east as the Boquerón on 25 November 1595, intercepting a Spanish caravel that was driven on to Cangrejos Beach (modern Santurce, 12 to 14 miles east of San Juan); yet Drake and his men had become so disheartened that they sailed away in quest of easier prey, leaving San Juan's garrison exultant.

The English fared better when twenty vessels and 1,700 men suddenly materialized offshore on the morning of 16 June 1598 under George Clifford, Third Earl of Cumberland, disgorging 700 men at Cangrejos Bay who pushed westward until checked at nightfall by ten Spanish regulars and eighty Puerto Rican militiamen holding the San Antonio Bridge gatehouse under Capt. Bernabé de Sierra Alta (who was killed during this clash). Having suffered twenty deaths of their own and a like number wounded, the invaders used boats to outflank that strongpoint the following morning, covering their landing at Escambrón Point with a simultaneous bombardment of the Boquerón's Santiago battery—nicknamed Red Fort by the English because of the distinctive hue of its coral blocks.

Cumberland swept unopposed into San Juan's unpaved and sandy streets on 18 June 1598, finding its citizenry fled, while 250 soldiers were ensconced within El Morro citadel under Gov. Antonio de Mosquera. This castle was besieged with artillery ferried ashore from the English fleet, until Mosquera's garrison surrendered on 1 July and was deported to Cartagena a few weeks later. Yet disease claimed so many English lives that Cumberland decided to forgo his occupation plans, instead sailing for England on 14 August with part of his fleet and was followed on 23 September by the balance under his convalescent second-in-command, Sir John Berkeley. The failed conquest had cost 700 English lives: 60 the result of battle, 40 from accidents, the rest from illness.

San Juan's citizens returned to find their capital ransacked, pillagers having carried away the cathedral bells, eighty cannons, plus a great deal of other booty. Reconstruction did not begin until a relief force arrived from Spain in 1599 under

gov.-designate Alonso de Mercado, who initially concentrated his efforts upon rendering El Morro more secure by the addition of new ramparts, cisterns, magazines, storerooms, quarters, and the like. The gutted city below did not receive any official attention until the tenure of his successor, Sancho Ochoa de Castro, Conde de Salvatierra, who reinvigorated a few civilian projects such as a new *cabildo* (municipal building) that was initiated in 1602 and completed six years later.

Yet royal attention remained fixated upon San Juan's defensive capabilities, King Phillip III even referring to the island capital as the "vanguard of all my West Indies." Gov. Gabriel de Torres expanded El Morro Castle further during his tenure from 1608 to 1614; his successor, Felipe de Beaumont y Navarra, during his six-year term finished a small, square battery called Fort San Juan de la Cruz on Cañuelo Key opposite and a stone watchtower at the eastern end of San Antonio Bridge. Such labors were to be tested when the United Provinces of The Netherlands declared war against Spain in April 1621, and the Westindische Compagnie (West Indian Company) sent seventeen Dutch ships under Adm. Boudewijn Hendricksz that surprised the refortified city on the afternoon of 24 September 1625.

The new governor, Juan de Haro, had not been in office a month when, expecting an immediate enemy disembarkation in Escambrón Inlet, he sent his predecessor, Juan de Vargas, to man the Boquerón with a militia contingent. Yet Hendricksz sailed brazenly into San Juan's harbor the next afternoon, exchanging shots with El Morro Castle before anchoring off Puntilla Point (modern La Marina). Panic-stricken civilians fled, while the governor gathered 220 soldiers and 110 auxiliaries inside El Morro. Hendricksz brought 700 to 800 men ashore on 26 September 1625 to occupy the empty capital, plus tiny Fort San Juan de la Cruz on Cañuelo Key two days later; but the rebuilt Morro was now much more difficult to storm, so that the Dutch dug sap lines and installed six siege guns atop Calvario Heights by 29 September.

Hendricksz called upon de Haro to surrender the following morning but was rebuffed, after which a bombardment commenced while Capt. Jan Jasperz de Laet's *West Kappel* exited on 1 October 1625 to chase away an approaching Spanish resupply vessel. Two columns of forty men each sallied from El Morro under Capts. Sebastián de Avila and Andrés Vázquez Botello de Carrera on the night of 3–4 October, accomplishing little; yet fifty men under Capt. Juan de Amézquita y Quixano succeeded in destroying the advance Dutch siege-works at noon on 5 October, in the process killing ten sappers. Guerrillas from the interior also troubled the besiegers, slaying *Nieuw Nederlandt*'s captain and a twenty-man boat party in the harbor that same night. A similar detachment was eliminated up the Bayamón River on 15 October, and two boatloads of thirty Puerto Rican militiamen reclaimed Fort San Juan de la Cruz the next day with fire pots, killing two Dutch occupiers and capturing fourteen.

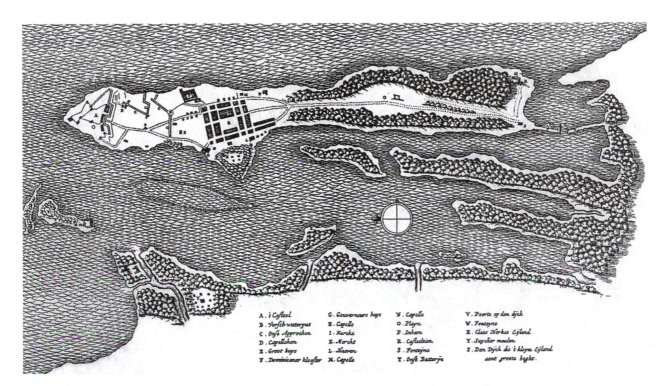

A .	i Casteel	G .	Gouverneurs huys	N .	Capelle	V .	Poorte op den dijck
B .	Versch-watergat	H .	Capelle	O .	Playn	W .	Fonteyne
C .	Onse Approchen	I .	Kercke	P .	Inham	X .	Claes Workes Eyland
D .	Capellcken	K .	Mercht	R .	Casteelcien	Y .	Suycker meulen
E .	Groot huys	L .	Haeven	S .	Fonteyne	Z .	Den Dijck die 't kleyn Eyland
F .	Dominicaner klooster	M .	Capelle	T .	Onse Batterye		aen't groote beght .

Dutch map of the unfortified city and El Morro's defenses during Hendricksz's attack, September 1625; north is toward upper left. (Johannes de Laet, *Historie ofte iaerlijck verhael,* 1644)

Hendricksz therefore vainly called once more for de Haro to capitulate on 21 October 1625 before setting San Juan's empty buildings ablaze the following dawn and re-embarking his land forces. (According to Spanish reports, forty-six stone and fifty-two wooden edifices were consumed by these flames, while the city's bishopric, Dominican convent, and La Fortaleza also suffered extensive damage.) Now trapped inside the harbor, the Dutch did not rush past the gauntlet of Spanish artillery until 2 November, abandoning their 30-gun, 450-ton *Medemblik* when it ran aground. A cannon near Governor de Haro exploded during these final exchanges, spraying him with two dozen fragments and causing his death—one of 17 Spanish fatalities, compared with 200 Dutch dead.

Elated by this successful resistance, Madrid agreed to make El Morro even stronger, so that by 1630 it boasted 100 artillery pieces, 86 of bronze and 14 of iron. The Crown also decided to enclose the city of San Juan itself with stone ramparts, its most vulnerable southern side between Santa Catalina Inlet and La Fortaleza being fortified as of July 1634 by Gov. Enrique Enríquez de Sotomayor, to plans drawn up by Juan Bautista Antonelli (son of the earlier royal engineer). A second section of walls, extending between La Fortaleza to San Pedro Bastion at La Marina or Puntilla, was constructed from 1636 to 1638 under Gov. Iñigo de la Mota Sarmiento, knight of the Order of Santiago, plus a third section running toward a new northern redoubt called San Cristóbal.

All these ramparts were to be massive, averaging 24 feet in height by almost 20 feet in thickness at their bases, so that the city's 250 reconstructed edifices and 100 shacks became slowly enclosed as of the mid-1640s. The burned San Juan de la Cruz fortress was also replaced by 1647, and the removable midsection of San Antonio Bridge was substituted by a drawbridge and its entire wooden length rebuilt of stone by Gov. José de Novoa y Moscoso in 1655–1669.

Imperial Backwater (1649–1765)
Yet despite such large-scale fortification projects, San Juan continued to languish in almost complete commercial neglect, not being visited by a single merchantmen between 1651 and 1662, and by precious few even after that date. The island's meager output of sugar, ginger, tobacco, and cocoa could not multiply into any significant volumes without an infusion of slave labor, which its penniless landowners could not afford. Mexican subsidies too became so irregular, because of the empire's bankruptcy and decay, that hard currency was scarce, most items or services being acquired at San Juan through barter.

Its urban populace remained largely unchanged throughout that bleak interlude, being measured in 1673 at 820 Spanish residents and 971 mulattoes and blacks. Their circumstances worsened as *tabardillo* (spotted fever)—smallpox and measles—swept through the island in 1689–1690, killing 631

Some of the city ramparts as they appeared, ca. 1920. (Franck, *Roaming Through the West Indies*)

whites and slaves. Smuggling and privateering were the only profitable ventures available for ambitious islanders, abetted by frequent outbreaks of Caribbean warfare.

It was not until Spain's new Franco-Bourbon monarchy finally loosened the old monopolistic trade restrictions early in the eighteenth century that the Puerto Rican economy began to struggle back to life. Coffee trees were introduced from Santo Domingo as of 1736, promising to provide a valuable cash crop; yet the city garrison had not changed in size from a century and a half earlier, being constituted at 336 infantrymen and 64 gunners as late as April 1757. Eventually, though, Spain's humiliating defeat at the hands of Great Britain five years later, during the closing phases of the French and Indian War, goaded Madrid into reforming its West Indian administrative policies.

Revival (1766–1796)

Royal Commissioner and Field Marshal Alejandro, Conde de O'Reilly, visited San Juan aboard the frigate *Aguila* in April–June 1765, his inspection recording 4,506 inhabitants living within the capital plus another 40,300 scattered about the island, of whom 5,000 were slaves. To spark an economic rebirth, he recommended that labors be reinvigorated upon

the city defenses as of January 1766, bolstered by a 100,000-peso increment in the 80,000-peso annual subsidy from Mexico; that figure was soon raised to 300,000 pesos. These extra funds, coupled with huge wooden *barracones* (large barracks) erected at San Justo Inlet that same year to receive and re-export thousands of African slaves on behalf of the Caracas Company, helped stimulate Puerto Rico's commerce. Trade licenses from Spain were also eased, bringing more merchantmen into San Juan, whose harbor and shops remained the only entities on the island authorized to receive overseas vessels.

Within a decade, the capital's defenses were substantially enhanced in accordance with plans drawn up by the Galway-born military engineer Col. Tomás O'Daly, while its populace swelled to 6,605 by 1776, with another 63,400 spread about the island. A powerful hurricane struck that same 19 September—remembered as the *huracán de San Genaro* (Saint Genaro's Hurricane)—yet San Juan quickly recuperated. An eight-year project even culminated with the inauguration of a new 500-bed hospital in 1782, and its defensive circuit was finished the following year. Some open spaces for gardens, orchards, and breeding small livestock still existed inside the 62-acre enclosure, although most foodstuffs had to be imported—along with firewood, ferried across from Cangrejos or tiny inlets around Miraflores and Isla Grande. The *abasto forzoso* (compulsory supply) of meat, a military dictate requiring that all island municipalities contribute cattle for San Juan's garrison and maritime needs, was especially resented.

By the closing decades of the eighteenth century, the capital consisted of four main *cuarteles* (sectors) encompassing fifty-eight city blocks that in turn were interspersed by a grid of five narrow streets running east-west, plus a like number north-south. Access was restricted to three fortified entries: San Juan Gate facing the bay, San Justo Gate facing the docks, and Santiago or the "Tierra" Gate facing eastward. Some streets began to be paved over with smooth river-flagstones as of 1784, although lack of funds soon halted that undertaking; public education was encouraged, and economic prospects brightened still further after France's West Indian sugar industry collapsed seven years later because of the violent emergence of a radical new revolutionary government in Paris that dislocated all transatlantic movements, the shortfall causing a price boom on European markets.

As tensions escalated, the Crown dispatched the Cantabria Regiment to reinforce the city regiment in 1791, and the next year ordered Gov. Miguel Antonio Ustariz to commence work on a new redoubt to better protect the Boquerón entrance, dubbed Fort San Jerónimo. Puerto Rico's population had more than doubled to 150,000 inhabitants by the time the Republic of France declared war against Spain, Great Britain, and other monarchies the following January. But when Madrid was

defeated in August 1795, then realigned itself with the French Directorate against England as of 6 October 1796, San Juan's prosperity was abruptly curtailed by the imposition of a Royal Navy blockade.

Loyal Outpost (1797–1897)

Worse followed when sixty English vessels suddenly materialized offshore under Rear Adm. Henry Harvey on 17 April 1797, bearing a small army under Lt.-Gen. Sir Ralph Abercromby, fresh from conquering the Spanish West Indian island of Trinidad. The attackers reconnoitered the shoreline before anchoring off Cangrejos Beach that same evening, disembarking their troops the next morning against only slight opposition. Despite commanding no more than 200 regular troops within San Juan, the governor—Brig. Ramón de Castro—counted upon the barrier island's difficult eastern shallows, plus 6,000 militia volunteers raised from the city and its hinterland.

Fort San Jerónimo, San Antonio Bridge, and other defenses were manned, a half dozen floating batteries being additionally launched into Condado Lagoon under frigate captain Francisco de Paula Castro to check the enemy advance overland, while 100 visiting French privateersmen under Capts. Barron and Paris were also pressed into service. Abercromby could not ford past the Boquerón strongpoints to invest the city proper, so his progress stalled and disease spread among the English ranks. When de Paulo Castro launched a counterattack with 800 militiamen and two troops of cavalry on the

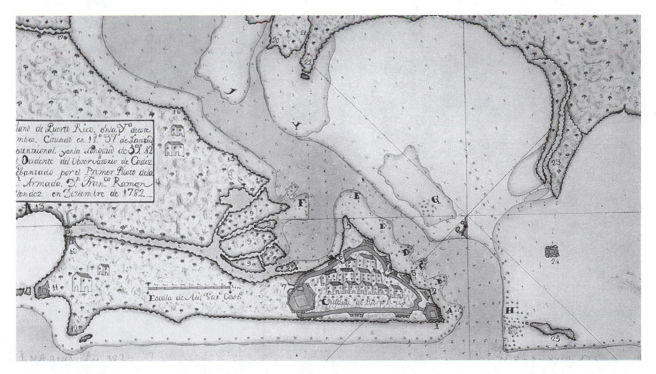

Chart of San Juan's harbor and shoreline, as surveyed by the senior naval pilot Francisco Ramón Méndez of the warship *San Juan Nepomuceno* in December 1782; north is toward bottom. (Archivo General de Simancas, Spain)

night of 29–30 April 1797, the British broke camp the following day and sailed away by 2 May, having suffered 31 dead, 70 wounded, and 124 captured or missing.

Yet despite this successful defense, San Juan still had trouble exporting its island sugar and coffee, eventually resorting to neutral American vessels (to such an extent that Washington even appointed a permanent consular agent at the port as of 1807). Peace was restored briefly in March 1802, but European hostilities flared anew only twenty months later, so that commerce was again curtailed. The capital's populace was measured at 7,835 residents by 1803, out of a total of 174,902 people on Puerto Rico, numbers that continued to climb after Spanish refugees began arriving from Santo Domingo following its occupation by French forces, as well as from Louisiana after its sale to the United States by Napoleon Bonaparte. It is believed that a French émigré even brought the first printing press to San Juan, its first newspaper—*La Gaceta de Puerto Rico*—appearing in 1808.

Napoleon, now emperor of France, sent an army into Spain to depose his hapless ally King Charles IV in May 1808,

prompting a realignment with Great Britain, so that Puerto Rico was freed from Royal Navy blockaders. Two years later, word also reached San Juan of the first antimonarchist stirrings at Caracas, Venezuela, which quickly engulfed the viceroyalty of New Granada (modern Colombia) and launched another wave of refugees—mostly expelled royalist officers and officials—into the Puerto Rican capital. But when the revolutionaries invited San Juan's leaders to join their revolt, the latter demurred, instead remaining loyal to the liberal Cortes (Parliament) in Spain.

Notwithstanding a few separatist sentiments expressed among its Creole elite, San Juan was to remain unswervingly loyal to the Crown throughout the ensuing decade and a half of continental turmoil, its harbor serving as a marshaling area for Spanish counterexpeditions. The Puerto Rican population had swollen to 220,982 by 1814, although most new arrivals had resettled into rural areas to concentrate upon cultivation, so that the capital's numbers remained at a modest 8,900 residents.

The tide of warfare eventually turned against the monarchist cause on the mainland, so that San Juan was beset by

A state funeral cortege wending through one of Old San Juan's narrow colonial-era streets, ca. 1898. (Hill, *Cuba and Porto Rico*)

insurgent privateers—many American mercenaries—and its trade suffered once again. Mexican subsidies ended after the viceroyalty of New Spain collapsed as of 1820, only Cuba and Puerto Rico remaining as Spanish colonies in the Americas. San Juan lived in trepidation of a possible invasion orchestrated by one of these emergent new republics, a feeble effort being made when a Franco-German mercenary named Louis du Coudray-Holstein outfitted a band of adventurers from New York and Philadelphia in 1822; his Puerto Rican collaborators were denounced to the authorities, however, and executed before he could arrive, so that he retreated into Dutch Curaçao.

Fear of such an attack caused San Juan's garrison to overreact when Commo. David D. Porter's sixteen U.S. warships arrived before the port on 5 March 1823, dispatched by Washington to scour the Caribbean for renegade privateers. As his auxiliaries *Greyhound* and *Fox* approached the harbor entrance with an explanatory note for the Spanish governor, El Morro's jittery gunners opened fire, killing one of *Fox*'s officers. Angry recriminations ensued, during which the U.S. Navy astonished *sanjuaneros* with their paddle steamer *Seagull,* the first such vessel seen off the island.

Because of its lost Spanish-American contacts, San Juan's population declined by 1824 to 8,453, who were then further battered by a tempest on the night of 26–27 July 1825, remembered as the *huracán de Santa Ana* (Saint Ann's Hurricane). Sufficient economic recuperation nonetheless occurred for the population to rise to 9,266 three years later, not including a garrison of 3,300 soldiers and sailors. Gov. Miguel de la Torre initiated a series of public works that included the erection of the city's first municipal theater, while the Crown authorized the creation of Puerto Rico's own *real audiencia* (royal tribunal) to adjudicate local cases in July 1832.

Patrols of *serenos* (night watchmen) were instituted as of 16 October 1837, while concerns about potential sedition among the black and mulatto majority caused Madrid to encourage the migration of loyal Canary Islanders and Catalans to Puerto Rico, so as to ensure Spain's firm hold. Control over the crowded capital was also tightened by replacing its poorest slums with new civil structures; dislocated residents were recongregated outside the ramparts—most often into *arrabales* (shantytowns) along the city's southeastern fringe, as plans for subsidized housing in the Puerta de Tierra sector never materialized. Capt.-Gen. Juan Prim y Prats eventually enacted a harshly restrictive *Código Negro* (Black Code) in 1848 that delimited the activities of all mulattoes and blacks.

Spain's first transatlantic steamer, *Tridente,* entered San Juan on 21 October 1848, inaugurating a new era in sea travel that required an upgrade in harbor facilities, so as to include coaling stations and metal shops. A few other municipal enhancements ensued, such as the commencement of a *carretera central* (central highway) toward Caguas in 1852, the opening of a new public market in the city's northeastern Santa Bárbara sector the following year (where the city arsenal and slaughterhouse also stood), initiation of steamboat ferry service to bayside communities, erection of a new barracks in the northwestern city sector of Ballajá in 1854, plus replacement of the thirty-five-year-old olive oil public lighting system with petroleum lamps the next year.

Peace was shattered when the disgruntled artillery company manning Fort San Cristóbal mutinied on the evening of 13 April 1855 because their enlistments had not been reduced by two years, as with fellow servicemen in Spain. The new captain-general, Lt.-Gen. Andrés García Camba, deployed the Valladolid, Cádiz, and Madrid Infantry regiments to intercept a mutineer contingent sent to seize the San Gerónimo arsenal, wounding two and capturing eight. Fearful of being caught in an exchange within the densely packed city confines, panic-stricken civilians fled into the countryside, and three women and a child drowned. García Camba succeeded in persuading the mutineers to lay down their arms without further bloodshed, and seven were eventually executed. A cholera epidemic also struck San Juan early in December of that same year, claiming at least 549 victims within the span of three weeks.

Progress resumed as hydrogen gas lamps were introduced in 1857, and the city's first telegraph went into operation the following year. San Juan's population had reached 18,132 by 1860, and they were now beginning to sprawl beyond the tight confines of the city's old colonial-era ramparts. The percentage of black residents slowly declined after slave importations were banned, and San Juan profited as a neutral harbor during the U.S. Civil War years. Conversely, the Confederate surrender in the spring of 1865 caused an economic downturn, and Puerto Rican delegates joined a Cuban representation to air their joint grievances before a board of inquiry in Madrid the following year, complaining of burdensome taxes, lack of input toward shaping policy, as well as inequality regarding appointments and privileges.

The conference collapsed in 1867, and San Juan was struck by a hurricane on 29 October and then an earthquake on 18 November that inflicted considerable damage. The city painstakingly rebuilt, and an underwater telegraph cable was laid to Saint Thomas in the Virgin Islands by 1870. But political turmoil was renewed when a new administration in Madrid moved to abolish slavery throughout all Spanish territories the next year. A riot consequently erupted in the Puerto Rican capital between contending factions on 26 July 1871, requiring the intervention of militia companies and the imposition of martial law for five days before that reform could finally be promulgated on 5 August 1872. Partly because of that anarchic outburst, as well as a secessionist rebellion in Cuba, Puerto Rico's stern new captain general, José Laureano Sanz, abolished all municipal councils two years later and replaced San Juan's ineffectual watchmen with a more professional police force—also more unwaveringly loyal to Spain.

A census taken in 1874 revealed 21,847 people now crowded within the city, plus another 600,000 scattered about the island. The capital's first steam-powered tramway was inaugurated on 31 July 1880, running as far as Río Piedras, while its populace continued a slow ascent to 25,685 inhabitants by 1883 and 27,020 four years afterward. Early in May 1893, San Juan provided a splendid reception to the *Infantes* (royal princes) Doña María Eulalia and Don Antonio María de Orleans as they were bound to the United States and Chicago's World Fair aboard the warship *Reina María Cristina*. Electric streetlights illuminated the Puerto Rican capital that same year, while its first telephone went into service by 1897.

American Occupation (1898–Present)

Conflict with the United States was to impose profound changes upon both the city and the island. Three weeks after the outbreak of the Spanish-American War, Rear Adm. William T. Sampson approached San Juan out of the northeast before dawn on 12 May 1898 with his battleships *Iowa* and *Indiana*, heavy cruiser *New York*, light cruisers *Detroit* and *Montgomery*, monitors *Amphitrite* and *Terror*, torpedo boat *Porter*, and the armed tug *Wompatuck*. They opened fire at 5:17 A.M., slowly circling offshore for the next three hours while exchanging salvos with two dozen Spanish artillery pieces ashore. Marksmanship proved poor on both sides, only minor damage being inflicted; yet Sampson's real intent was to determine whether Rear Adm. Pascual Cervera y Topete's squadron had arrived from Spain, and realizing that it was not inside, he reversed course westward and left the 11,600-ton armed auxiliary *Saint Louis* of Capt. Caspar F. Goodrich to mount a blockade.

The next day, Goodrich dragged the seabed a few miles east of San Juan to cut its underwater telegraph cable with Saint Thomas, then was relieved by the 11,600-ton armed auxiliary *Saint Paul* of Capt. Charles D. Sigsbee (surviving commander of the battleship *Maine*). At 1:00 P.M. on 22 June 1898, the 1,130-ton Spanish cruiser *Isabel II* and 380-ton destroyer *Terror* sortied from San Juan's harbor to chase the American blockader away. After pausing briefly beneath the shore batteries, the Spanish destroyer dashed at *Saint Paul*, only to be hit by heavy counterfire, so that *Terror* was beached on Puntilla Shoal (eventually to be refloated), and *Isabel* retired into port. Three days later, Sigsbee's watch was replaced by the 6,200-ton armed auxiliary *Yosemite* (formerly *El Sol*), which intercepted the 3,460-ton Spanish steamer *Antonio López* and drove it aground on Salinas Point on 30 June, despite a belated sally by *Isabel II* and the gunboat *General Concha*.

Puerto Rico was subsequently invaded by a 3,400-man U.S. army under Maj.-Gen. Nelson A. Miles, detached from the main force that had captured Santiago de Cuba. Although originally aiming to disembark 25 to 30 miles east of San Juan near Cape Fajardo, Miles's expedition landed instead near Ponce on 25 July 1898, gradually swelling to 17,000 men, while pushing inland toward the capital in the face of increasingly feeble

opposition from 8,000 demoralized Spanish soldiers. A small party from the blockading ship *Amphitrite* also seized the lighthouse outside San Juan on 6 August repulsing a counterattack on the night of 8–9 August, before withdrawing. But the Spanish units holding the passes out of Puerto Rico's interior nonetheless collapsed over the next few days, retreating into the capital, while the U.S. forces occupied Mayagüez by 11 August and then hammered out a peace treaty in Europe the next day.

Unlike a majority of the island's impoverished rural residents, the more cosmopolitan and conservative San Juan had remained intrinsically loyal to Spain throughout this struggle, so that the initial reception in the capital to the American invaders was cool. Spanish forces and officials were repatriated, and a census taken in 1899 revealed the capital's population at 32,048 out of a Puerto Rican total of more than 950,000. On 8 August of that same year, another huge hurricane—*el huracán de San Ciriaco*—crashed across the island, claiming more than 3,000 lives and sowing great destruction. The city was painstakingly rebuilt and modernized, its first aqueduct being inaugurated by the spring of 1900. The Escuela Normal—precursor of the modern University of Puerto Rico—opened its doors three years later, and a vast new hospital complex was created at Santurce between 1906 and 1909.

Thanks to more effective health measures, economic investment, and various municipal improvements, San Juan's urban populace entered a notable period of growth, increasing from 48,716 in 1910 to 71,443 a decade later. Another huge storm—*el huracán de San Felipe*—struck on 13 September 1928, but because of timely intervention by the authorities only 300 lives were lost, despite the leveling of some 250,000 homes across the island. San Juan's populace continued its rapid rise from 114,715 residents in 1930 to 169,247 a decade later, then benefited further by serving as a crucial U.S. base during World War II.

German submarines inaugurated an offensive dubbed OPERATION NEULAND in the West Indies on 16 February 1942, and Puerto Rico was to serve as a crucial U.S. outpost during the ensuing struggle against the U-boats. A vast complex of bases was developed under U.S. Vice Adm. John Hoover, regional commander for the so-called Caribbean Sea Frontier, and frequent air patrols were flown by the 204th Squadron out of Naval Air Station San Juan until these underwater German raiders were driven from the Americas within a year. Some minor incursions persisted, such as when *U-218* of Cmdr. Klaus Becker slipped into San Juan's harbor early in March 1944 to sow a few mines, but they were detected and harmlessly destroyed.

Widespread industrialization in and around the city began after World War II. Puerto Rico remained a U.S. dependency until November 1948, when islanders were at last allowed to elect their own governor. The 1950 census revealed 223,949

View across the rooftops of San Juan, ca. 1905. (Keane, *Central and South America*)

residents living within the city boundaries (now extended to include Santurce), while the following year the capital also absorbed the neighboring municipality of Río Piedras, with its additional 143,897 inhabitants, producing a combined total of almost 368,000 people. By 1967 that number had soared to 845,000; it had reached 1,222,316 inhabitants by 1990—although only 437,745 now actually remained within the old colonial-era limits. They endured considerable damage from Hurricane Hugo in September 1989.

For further reading on the history of San Juan or Puerto Rico, please consult the Select Bibliography at the end of this volume.

Trinidad-Tobago

Port of Spain

Sheltered West Indian anchorage that despite its relatively late start has evolved into an exceptionally cosmopolitan city.

Discovery and Colonization Attempts (1498–1570)

On his third voyage to the New World, Christopher Columbus approached the Caribbean with a trio of vessels via a more southerly heading, in hopes of spotting the chimerical Asian continent that had thus far eluded him. Instead, on the afternoon of 31 July 1498, his lookouts espied rising above the horizon three peaks of an island that the explorer auspiciously named Trinidad in honor of the Holy Trinity. As he drew near, its southeastern cliffs furthermore looked like a galley under full sail, so that he named this particular headland Cabo de la Galera (Galley Cape—modern Galeota Point).

The next day a watering party went ashore at what is today Erin Point, finding signs of human habitation, although contact with the island residents themselves proved to be fleeting. Columbus therefore refreshed provisions and on 4 August 1498 penetrated into the southern entrance of the Gulf of Paria, dubbing it Boca de la Sierpe (Serpent's Mouth) because of the powerful currents churned up by the nearby Orinoco River delta. He emerged into the more placid waters of the inner gulf, but similarly high seas greeted his exit nine days later through the northern gap, prompting him to dub it Bocas del Dragón

View northeastward across the original city core, as it appeared during the late 1960s. Port of Spain's metropolitan area already extended for several miles in both directions. (Noel P. Norton, *Organization of American States*)

197

(Dragon's Mouths) before proceeding with his voyage toward Hispaniola.

Other explorers subsequently coasted through Trinidad's waters—Alonso de Ojeda, Juan de la Cosa, Américo Vespucci, Pedro Alonso Niño, and Cristóbal Guerra during the summer of 1499, Vicente Yáñez Pinzón and Diego de Lepe the following year, and so forth—yet aside from garnering small quantities of pearls and tobacco, there was nothing to attract any permanent Spanish settlers to this poor and torrid isle. Slavers from Santo Domingo made sporadic descents over the next couple of decades (such as Juan Bono's cruel raids of 1515–1516, decried by the reformist priest Bartolomé de las Casas), yet the Spaniards otherwise exhibited no interest in Trinidad. The veteran colonizer Rodrigo de Bastidas was authorized by the governor of Santo Domingo to attempt to subjugate the island in 1520, but Columbus's grandson Diego Colón quickly contested this license; and there is no evidence that it was ever acted upon, as Hernán Cortés was just then diverting attention by his conquest of the fabulously wealthy Aztec empire in Mexico, luring hundreds of Spanish adventurers in his wake.

A decade later, the Council of Indies in Spain granted Antonio Sedeño—former *Contador Real* (royal accountant) at Puerto Rico—a twenty-year lease to settle Trinidad and act as its governor, so that he appeared offshore in November 1530 with two caravels bearing sixty Spaniards and a band of indigenous allies from the Venezuelan mainland. He installed twenty-five men into a small earthen fort on the western side of the Dragon's Mouths, before proceeding to Puerto Rico for reinforcements. During Sedeño's absence, another rival Spanish colonizer, Diego de Ordás, also entered the gulf in February 1531, displacing his Dragon's Mouths garrison with fifty of his own men and rechristening the site as San Miguel de Paria on 14 June, before departing himself to probe the Orinoco River. When Sedeño learned of this usurpation, he complained to the Council of Indies and had his original title upheld in January 1532—although simultaneously enjoined to establish himself on Trinidad proper, rather than merely at San Miguel on the Paria peninsula, as well as to aid Ordás in his mainland endeavors.

Sedeño therefore returned to the island in late spring of 1533 with eighty men aboard a half-dozen vessels, fighting his way ashore near a beach named Cumucurapo (meaning Place of the Silk-Cotton Trees in the local dialect; modern Mucurapo), only to withdraw shortly thereafter because of a lack of provisions. His third attempt began more promisingly, a host of hostile tribesmen being defeated at Mucurapo on 13 September 1533, before Sedeño and his men became beleaguered within a miserable base camp, finally mutinying in March 1534 and compelling him to retire again. Because of Francisco Pizarro's subjugation of the rich Incan empire of Peru around that same time, Spaniards were once more being lured out of this region, so that little zeal remained for occupying primitive Trinidad with its fierce warriors.

A Peruvian named Juan Francisco Sedano was apparently granted a license in 1553 to attempt another disembarkation, yet he did not put it into effect; Juan Trejo Ponce de León, however—a descendant of the Juan Ponce de León who had left Puerto Rico a generation earlier to scour Florida for the Fountain of Youth—actually landed on Trinidad in January 1570 with a small band of colonists, only to have most of them quit nine months later because of starvation and disease. The island was relegated to transient visits by foreign seamen throughout the remainder of the sixteenth century who paused to refresh provisions after their Atlantic traverses and barter with its tribesmen, before penetrating more deeply into the Caribbean for plunder or trade along the Spanish Main. Yet none attempted any permanent occupation.

The true catalyst for Trinidad's colonization was to be provided by the ancient Venezuelan legends of El Dorado (The Golden Man), an allusion to the Chibcha coronation ritual in which a new leader appeared at dawn, standing on a raft in sacred Lake Guatavita, coated with resin and gold dust, to dive into the water and emerge as overlord. Inspired by this tale, the veteran Spanish adventurer Antonio de Berrio y Oruña led the first of three overland expeditions out of Tunja in the Colombian Andes in 1584, hoping to find this wondrous source of gold.

Foundation and Early Vicissitudes (1592–1637)

De Berrio y Oruña finally succeeded in navigating the entire length of the Orinoco and emerging onto Venezuela's Atlantic coast during his third attempt in 1590–1591. He touched at Trinidad on 1 September 1591, before proceeding to Margarita for reinforcements to secure this strategically placed island as an advance base for further mainland explorations. His subordinate Domingo de Vera Ibargüen (or Ibargoyen) returned with the first Margarita contingent, landing at Mucurapo Beach on 15 May 1592 to claim the whole island for de Berrio, who was to become governor over both "Guiana and Trinidad." De Vera Ibargüen then pushed some 7 miles up the Caroní River, away from the hot and humid gulf shoreline and into the more densely wooded and hilly interior, reaching the seat of Chief Goanagoanare four days later, formally reconstituting it into a town christened San José de Oruña (modern St. Joseph).

The traditional Spanish-American urban grid-pattern was laid out and individual plots assigned, although his superior de Berrio did not actually reach the island with more men until some time later, renaming the anchorage near Mucurapo Puerto de España (Port of Spain) before delegating de Vera to continue exploring up the Orinoco for El Dorado. De Berrio personally tended to the development of his fledgling inland capital of San José de Oruña by granting estates in the fertile Maracas and Santa Cruz valleys, and also remained behind to rebuff any attempts by the rival governor, Francisco de Vides of Cumaná, to void his claim over Trinidad.

The Spaniards estimated the island's total indigenous population at 35,000 in 1593, depleting to only 15,000 two years later because of disease and flight. De Berrio's toehold was moreover threatened when the twenty-year-old English nobleman Robert Dudley anchored off Cedros Bay with a trio of vessels on 9 February 1595, bent upon charting Trinidad and the Orinoco River delta for potential conquest. Although he departed on 22 March, Dudley was followed on 1 April by Sir Walter Raleigh with another pair of English vessels. Three days later, Raleigh disembarked 100 soldiers to seize the small stockade at Puerto de España, before pushing inland to capture San José de Oruña and de Berrio. After inspecting the island for a fortnight, Raleigh was joined by two more ships, raising his total complement to 300–350 men, allowing him to steer southward across to the mainland and conduct a detailed reconnaissance of the Orinoco delta as well, before circling westward to invest Cumaná briefly on 22 June, depositing de Berrio there before sailing away.

The few Spaniards still remaining on Trinidad after this sweep by Elizabethan privateers were left in a very compromised position, beset by hostile islanders and diseases, as well as the fearful possibility of an English return. The island consequently did not recuperate, and San José de Oruña was soon sharing the title of joint Trinidadian-Guianese "capital" with a new, more defensible mainland town called Santo Tomé on the Orinoco (originally installed near Jaya Island, between the Caroní confluence and Atamaya Point, 6 miles west of Los Castillos). Even after a peace treaty was signed with England in the spring of 1604, the Spanish presence on Trinidad remained minuscule. Its handful of residents were so far removed from the mainstream galleon traffic bound toward Cartagena or Veracruz that they only had limited outlets for whatever tobacco they harvested nor could they attract migrants to their steamy tropical backwater.

Instead, foreign enclaves began to sprout throughout the region, which Trinidad's Spaniards resisted as best they could. In August 1613, twelve men and a priest departed to rendezvous with another twenty men from Santo Tomé, jointly expunging two Dutch intruder settlements up the Corantin and Essequibo rivers in Guiana. Yet the interlopers continued to multiply, and Raleigh even returned to Galeota Point with fifteen vessels in mid-November 1617. Now sixty-five years of age, he had been released after thirteen years' incarceration in the Tower of London by King James I, on the understanding that he would secure El Dorado for England without antagonizing Spain. Because of sickness ravaging his fleet, Raleigh detached a force under Lawrence Keymis up the Orinoco to storm Santo Tomé, killing its recently installed Trinidadian-Guianese governor, Diego Palomeque de Acuña, as well as several other Spaniards before a counterassault obliged the English to retreat. In anguish over

the death of his twenty-five-year-old son Walter and facing personal ruin, Raleigh's fleet thereupon disintegrated, various captains parting company to prowl the Caribbean, while he returned to London to face execution.

When the new governor, Luis de Monsalve, reached San José de Oruña on 24 May 1624, he found only forty able-bodied Spanish men living on Trinidad, and they were in such want that they were compelled to barter with foreign smugglers. The tiny neglected community even had to be assisted in May 1633 from the larger Spanish settlement on Margarita Island: three militia companies and fifty native auxiliaries under Julián Alvarez de Eulate set sail to capture eleven English Catholic settlers under Sir Henry Colt who were clearing an advance base camp near Galera Point on northeastern Trinidad. A second such Spanish foray in December 1636 proved disastrously counterproductive, however, as Capt. Martín Mendoza de la Hoz Berrio combined 400 militiamen and 3,000 native auxiliaries from Margarita, San José de Oruña, and Santo Tomé to raze a new intruder fort at Galera Point, plus two more on neighboring Tobago. They brought 160 captives of diverse nationalities back early the next year to face harsh punishment.

Such severity, though, resulted in swift and devastating retribution. A Dutch counterexpedition destroyed Santo Tomé on 22 July 1637, then surprised the sleepy anchorage of Puerto de España less than an hour before dawn on 14 October before pressing inland to ransack and burn San José de Oruña to the ground. After these raiders retired, the few score Spanish survivors on Trinidad learned that the islanders had also turned against them, resulting in a bloody massacre at Mount Tamana.

Isolation and Stagnation (1640–1775)

It was not until Mendoza returned with a small military contingent in 1640 that the Spanish presence on the island could be restored, San José de Oruña and its tiny seaport of Puerto de España being shakily reconstituted. Yet since Spain's military and economic power had by now collapsed overseas, they were to be left unsupported by the Crown for more than a century. When the Earl of Warwick installed a small English enclave on the island's southeastern coast that same year of 1640, it went unchallenged, although unilaterally abandoned five years later. The nominal Spanish capital and its unfrequented seaport almost faded into oblivion: when Diego Jiménez de Aldana arrived as new governor in August 1670, he counted only eighty Spanish heads-of-household on Trinidad, with a like number of Christianized tributaries, plus 500 captive Indian slaves. (The twin capital of Santo Tomé on the mainland was even more diminished, having only ten Spanish households in addition to its forty-seven-man garrison.)

By the time Capt. Sebastián de Roteta arrived as governor in 1684, he found merely four Spanish plantation owners ruling over some 300 Christianized islanders inland, plus a dozen unhappy residents clustered around Puerto de España. He initiated an extremely modest revival by reconstituting the latter into an independent town, as well as by persuading the Capuchin Order to send missionaries—undeterred by the fact that the galleon *Ballestera,* which brought one such contingent from Seville, was almost immediately captured by a pair of French privateers off Puerto de España on 24 June 1690 after loading an export cargo of cocoa beans. De Roteta even convinced King Carlos II to elevate San José de Oruña to the status of a city on 1 April 1691, although its inability to seat the requisite four *regidores* (councilors) would cause recurrent problems.

The forlorn Spanish colonists eked out a subsistence existence on the fringes of empire, exporting what little cocoa or tobacco they could—mostly aboard foreign vessels—while enduring frequent setbacks such as the cocoa plant blight of 1725. When Pedro de la Moneda arrived as new island governor in 1757, he found a total population of 400 people, his assigned "official residence" at San José de Oruña being a dilapidated grass shack. Unwilling to live in a such a humble setting, he rented a private home on the eastern edge of the village of Puerto de España, which consisted of but two streets called Príncipe and Infante (later renamed Nelson and Duncan), traveling up into San José only occasionally to transact business. By 1773 the island's population had increased to

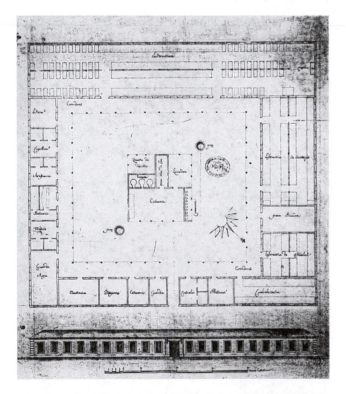

Diagram and profile view of a proposed new 200-bed hospital at Puerto España, as designed by the military engineer José del Pozo y Sucre, November 1786. (Servicio Histórico Militar, Madrid)

scarcely 1,000 people, mostly Christianized islanders tended by a few missionaries.

Emergence as a City (1776–1796)

Spain became committed to developing unexploited Trinidad and Puerto de España because of the lucrative benefits that other European powers were reaping from their West Indian sugar colonies during the last quarter of the eighteenth century. Under its reformist Bourbon monarch Charles III, Madrid was inspired to attempt the same. This new policy was inaugurated when the king signed a royal decree on 3 September 1776 that relaxed many immigration requirements, while at the same time promising free land, religious tolerance, and no taxation for a number of years to any Caribbean resident willing to relocate to Trinidad and take out Spanish citizenship. This edict was translated into English and French for distribution throughout the Antilles. Yet although a few score converts were lured from St. Lucia at the end of 1777—raising the total Trinidadian population to 1,410, of whom 340 were classified as whites, 870 as free mulattoes, and 200 as black slaves, not including a couple of thousand native islanders—all movement was interrupted by the American War of Independence, which embroiled both France and Spain in hostilities against England as of August 1778 and June 1779, respectively. When the military engineer Brig. Agustín Crame inspected the island the following year, he moreover judged it unworthy of a major colonization effort, despite its sheltered anchorages, fine stands of trees, and tar pits at La Brea (modern Pitch Lake)—the latter being especially valuable assets for any shipyard.

Still, Madrid revived its plans at the conclusion of this conflict in March 1783, designating the junior naval captain José María Chacón as new governor three months later, with instructions to promote the colony's development. Its capital was also officially transferred down from San José de Oruña into Puerto de España as part of this administrative overhaul, its first *cabildo* (city council) meeting being celebrated on 12 December 1783. By the time Chacón finally arrived on 30 August 1784 and assumed office two days later, he found that Trinidad's inhabitants had already more than doubled in number thanks to renewed interest in the Crown's resettlement offer, the population increasing from 2,763 people in 1783 to 6,503 by late December 1784; of them, 1,025 now resided in the burgeoning capital, increasingly referred to by its shortened name of "Puerto España." Many of the new arrivals were French colonists displaced from the Lesser Antilles, who had brought 2,100 slaves with them; in addition to cultivating cotton, they began clearing new sugar, coffee, and cacao plantations a few years later in the fertile valleys and alluvial terraces of the island's northwestern section.

Puerto España therefore benefited from a rapid increase in its traffic volumes, blossoming into a functional port as its populace grew to some 3,000 residents and its 78 wooden structures multiplied into almost 600. Two new streets were created, named San José and Santa Ana (later George and Charlotte streets), while Crown and church edifices were commenced and other large-scale projects undertaken. One was a 1.5 mile-long channel begun in 1787 along the base of La Ventilla (the Laventille Hills) northwest of the city so that the Santa Ana (modern Dry) River might flow more easily through: 1,000 laborers toiled upon that dig under the supervision of the recently arrived royal engineer José del Pozo y Sucre.

The city's economy was furthermore bolstered by a Crown decision to develop Chaguaramas and Carenero bays into a major naval base and shipyard, fortifying both anchorages—located 7.5 and 5 miles west of Puerto España, respectively—so as to create a regional stronghold in support of Spain's claims over the adjacent South American coastline. Funds were provided from the Venezuelan and Mexican exchequers to protect both anchorages by erecting batteries on Chaguaramas peninsula and Gaspar Grande Island during the years 1787–1791 under the supervision of the military engineer Esteban Aymerich, who was sent over from Puerto Cabello (Venezuela). Two batteries and a powder magazine were also constructed to defend Puerto España itself, while another significant municipal enhancement was the 750-foot mole-and-wooden quay projecting out from its waterfront (modern South Quay), protected by its own half-moon battery called Fort San Andrés.

As a result of all this activity, Puerto España soon boasted eleven paved streets, while the island population almost doubled from 7,446 inhabitants in 1785 to 9,022 the next year,

11,533 by 1787, and 13,053 by 1789. Because of the high percentage of French émigrés among these resettled peoples—now constituting 190 of Trinidad's 284 major landowners—Chacón experienced some qualms when news arrived that same year of a revolution in Paris that spawned a radical new republic that would soon challenge Europe's monarchies. However, most former French colonists transposed to Trinidad rejected such egalitarian policies, so that their commitment to the Spanish Crown remained unwavering even after the radical Directorate in Paris declared war against Spain and Britain in January 1793. The island's population even grew again as many French Loyalists fled the turmoil unleashed on Saint-Domingue (Haiti), Martinique, and other New World colonies, Trinidad's figure rising from 14,744 residents in 1793 to 17,718 four years later—and of the latter, 4,525 were now clustered at Puerto España, a sizable majority being black or mulatto females. The city garrison was also bolstered when Commo. Gabriel de Aristizábal visited on 29 March 1795 with three ships-of-the-line, four frigates, and a brigantine, disembarking 200 troops.

British Conquest (1797–1807)

Despite a brief economic boom fueled by a spectacular rise in international sugar prices, Puerto España's growth was to be abruptly curtailed by Spanish reversals overseas. After being bested by Republican French armies in Europe, Madrid was pressured into realigning itself with Paris as of 18 August 1796, risking war against Britain. Rear Adm. Sebastián Ruiz de Apodaca consequently entered Chaguaramas Bay on 14 September with the 80-gun warship *San Vicente,* the 74-gun

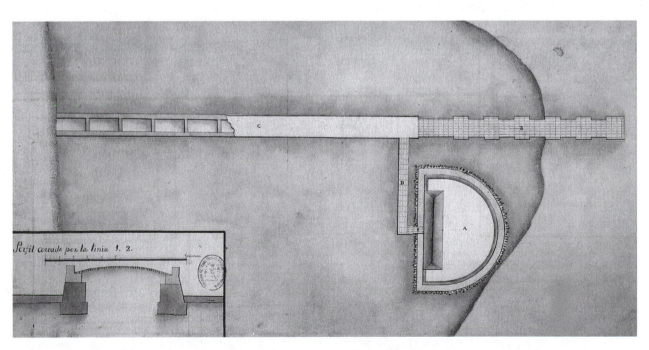

Diagram of the new wooden jetty and half-moon battery, ca. 1787, by the military engineer José del Pozo y Sucre. (Servicio Histórico Militar, Madrid)

San Dámaso and *Gallardo,* the 68-gun *Arrogante,* and the 34-gun frigate *Santa Cecilia,* bearing orders to deposit sixty-seven artillery pieces plus other armaments, and then remain on station at Trinidad with his first two ships while the *Gallardo* and *Arrogante* were to convey 700 troops on to Cartagena and the frigate to reinforce La Guaira. Faced with an imminent threat of war, Governor Chacón persuaded Ruiz de Apodaca to instead keep his entire squadron intact within Chaguaramas Bay to aid the feverish strengthening of island defenses; moreover, within a short span his crews were halved by disease—suffering more than 850 sick, of whom 700 died, along with another 200 ashore—so that any departure became impossible.

London imposed an embargo against all Spanish shipping because of Madrid's realignment with France, and war erupted by 6 October 1796, the news reaching Trinidad by the end of that same month. With the West Indies already largely in British hands, Rear Adm. Henry Harvey was able to muster overwhelming force for a strike against the Spanish island, his dozen warships being sighted approaching the Gulf of Paria's northern entrance shortly before noon on 16 February 1797, escorting forty transports bearing 6,250 soldiers under Lt.-Gen. Ralph Abercromby. Clearing the Boca Grande channel by 3:30 P.M., the invaders then sighted Ruiz de Apodaca's squadron lying inside Chaguaramas Bay. Harvey's 100-gun flagship *Prince of Wales* and main battle-fleet thereupon anchored opposite, while Abercromby's transports and lighter auxiliaries penetrated deeper into the gulf, anchoring about 5 miles short of Puerto España.

The defenders were so demoralized that Ruiz de Apodaca ordered his warships scuttled and batteries spiked that same night, retreating overland to join Chacón. The British were surprised to see the Spanish men-of-war burst into flames at 2:00 A.M. on 17 February 1797, managing to save only *San Dámaso* the next morning. Abercromby thereupon disembarked his troops at Cucurito (modern Cocorite) 3 miles outside Puerto España, advancing in twin columns to occupy the abandoned capital by that same evening. There was no opposition from the 300 Spanish regulars and 300 urban militiamen who had retreated inland through La Ventilla foothills along with Chacón, in the vain hope of organizing a resistance around San José de Oruña and Acarigua. Realizing the hopelessness of his plight, the governor met with Abercromby on the morning of 18 February, surrendering the entire island. His feeble defense—losses having totaled only seven Spanish dead and one Briton wounded—led to both his and Ruiz de Apodaca's being cashiered upon their repatriation to Spain.

Harvey's and Abercromby's main forces quickly re-embarked and withdrew from Trinidad by 1 March 1797, having installed Lt.-Col. Sir Thomas Picton (later slain at the Battle of Waterloo) as military governor at Puerto España with a 500-man garrison, in addition to a Royal Navy frigate and two other vessels stationed offshore under Capt. Thomas Webster.

As occupiers, the British behaved humanely and did not unduly perturb local customs, so that although a number of Spanish and former French landowners chose to emigrate with their households to La Guaira, Venezuela, a majority were content to remain behind under British rule. As the island was now freed of blockaders and could gain access to new overseas markets, its economic life soon revived as well, sugar exports through Puerto España rising to 4,000 tons by 1799. A wave of migrants from older, more congested Caribbean isles were attracted by Trinidad's untapped potential and proximity to the Spanish-American mainland—a lucrative outlet for smugglers—so that the number of departures was more than offset by new arrivals.

When the Treaty of Amiens was signed on 27 March 1802, marking a brief respite in European hostilities, Trinidad was the only major Antillean conquest retained by Britain. Its capital—henceforth to become known by its translated name of "Port of Spain"—had doubled in size during five years of military occupation, its urban populace now approaching 10,000 inhabitants, out of a total of 28,372 people on the island. Such swift and dense concentration, especially having to intermingle its previous Spanish, French, and free mulatto residents with an influx of Britons and black slaves, proved somewhat difficult to manage, so that Port of Spain's council voted on 9 March 1803 to open up the muddy flatlands south of the city for development, carting earth down from the Laventille Hills to help fill in the marshlands. Export trade was slowed yet not halted when war with France resumed that same May, and the island capital's growth stabilized.

Great Fire and Resurrection (1808–1869)

Tragically, a dreadful conflagration erupted at about 10:00 P.M. on 24 March 1808, when a German immigrant apothecary apparently fell asleep inside his wooden outhouse with a lighted candle. The flames quickly fanned through the city's 5,000 sun-bleached structures, claiming roughly 3,000 of them by the next noon. Twelve entire blocks of Port of Spain were consumed, plus another nine partially damaged, and although only two individuals perished, it was recorded that 3,647 inhabitants—615 of them white, 1,004 free mulattoes and blacks, plus 2,028 slaves—were left homeless. Moreover, every public building was lost—the government house, customshouse, town hall, treasury, hospital, Protestant church, jail, and so forth—so that virtually an entire new city had to be rebuilt from the ashes, during which process its last Spanish vestiges were erased. In order to prevent future recurrences of such a calamity, the municipal authorities passed an ordinance on 4 April that prohibited the erection of wooden houses; yet although major structures and businesses were to be rebuilt of stone, necessity compelled many poorer residents to ignore the measure.

The gutted city did not truly revive until the administration of the vigorous Sir Ralph Woodford, who governed from 1813 to 1828. Despite a regionwide depression after the conclusion of the Napoleonic Wars, he managed to institute numerous hygienic improvements, beautification projects, as well as an urban police force and public schools. (Among his most enduring legacies was to be the purchase of an old sugar plantation just north of the city in 1817, which—rather than become subdivided into plots for habitation—was converted into a park dubbed the Savannah.) This burst of activity, at a time when other more densely populated Antillean islands were plunged into poverty and unemployment, helped maintain a steady influx of migrants into Trinidad, whose population increased to 41,673 residents by 1829. That same year, an aqueduct was built to bring piped water down from the St. Ann's River directly into the city center, supplementing its numerous private wells. Exports totaled 25,000 tons of sugar, 1,100 of cocoa beans, and 113 of coffee. The Colonial Bank opened at Port of Spain as of 1837, while its population was measured the following year at 11,707—of whom slightly more than a third were immigrants.

Parliament's gradual abolition of slavery during the 1830s seemingly brought an end to the island's plantation-based economy, and many freed blacks resettled around the outskirts

Two Hindus of Trinidad, ca. 1920. (Franck, *Roaming Through the West Indies*).

of the capital. Yet a few years later, estate owners turned to indentured workers and coolies hired from the Far East as an alternative pool of cheap labor; the first of tens of thousands—usually contracted for three years' service—arrived from India in 1845. Although the vast majority of these employees were destined for inland plantations, where many subsequently chose to settle, Port of Spain's populace nonetheless doubled to approximately 22,000 by 1850, out of an island total of 75,000. In order to accommodate such renewed growth, several more abandoned sugar estates around its periphery were expropriated and converted into suburbs, while a new hospital was added.

Municipal services were overwhelmed when a cholera epidemic swept through the crowded city from August to October 1854, infecting one in every five inhabitants and claiming 2,112 lives. As a result of that frightening outbreak, hydrants from the newly expanded water system—which tapped a dam in Maraval Valley, on the far side of the Mucurapo River—were routinely opened afterward to help wash down city streets, while an underground sewage system was begun in 1861. Port of Spain's first horse-drawn cab appeared the next year.

Tentative Modernization (1870–1939)

Exports through Port of Spain resurged notably as of the 1870s, causing its populace to grow from 23,561 inhabitants in 1871 to 31,858 a decade later. A railway running eastward to Arima was laid down by 1876 and soon sprouted numerous spurs, the resultant upsurge in goods funneling through the capital adding to its prosperity. And some new urban amenities arrived: public lighting with kerosene lamps was inaugurated on Christmas Eve 1878, for example, while the first telephones and mule-drawn streetcars appeared five years later and electric power by 1887. As commercial sugar operations spread ever more deeply into southwestern Trinidad, and cocoa groves higher up into the central highlands and onto the eastern coastline, the rural population of Trinidad grew more rapidly than that of Port of Spain, whose figure remained relatively static at 33,787 residents in 1891.

Yet after Tobago was merged with Trinidad into a single administrative entity in 1898, Port of Spain entered its "golden age" under colonial rule so that its urban population reached 55,000 three years later. The first automobile—a steam-driven two-seater, capable of traveling up to 5 miles an hour—had appeared in its streets by March 1900, while rich estate owners also now had fine mansions lining the Savannah. In addition, new suburbs were being cleared north and west of the city at Belmont, Woodbrook (both officially annexed by the municipality in 1905 and 1907, respectively), and Mucurapo. Petroleum also began to be exploited at the southern tip of the island.

Trinidad served as the advance British base for a joint Anglo-German blockade of Venezuela in December 1902 that

View across the rooftops of Port of Spain, ca. 1905. (Keane, *Central and South America*)

was precipitated when President Cipriano Castro reneged on his country's foreign debts. At the very onset of this campaign, the cruiser HMS *Charybdis* of Capt. R. A. J. Montgomerie captured the Venezuelan gunboat *Bolívar*, while the British sloop *Alert* took the troopship *Zamora* and the gunboat *23 de Mayo* in the Gulf of Paria, conveying both into Port of Spain for internment. Larger battle squadrons under British Vice Adm. Sir Archibald Lucius Douglas and German Commo. Georg Scheder subsequently seized numerous other vessels while patrolling from Trinidad as far as Maracaibo, before the crisis was resolved in February 1903.

The very next month, Port of Spain suffered a serious riot when public dissatisfaction over a proposed water distribution system erupted into violence on 23 March 1903: the Red House was burned to the ground during an outburst in which sixteen people were killed and forty-two wounded. A more agreeable event occurred five years later, when Port of Spain was visited early in 1908 by sixteen U.S. battleships under Rear Adm. Robley Evans—dubbed the "Great White Fleet" because of their peacetime color scheme—which had been dispatched by President Theodore Roosevelt on a global circumnavigation. The city's population stood at 60,000 people by 1911, plus another 5,000 living in nearby Mucurapo—now connected to Port of Spain by a broad, paved avenue. Another riot occurred on 3 December 1919, when a stevedores' strike degenerated into bloodshed.

Two years later, the population for the entire metropolitan area—now including Mucurapo and the western slopes of the Laventille Hills, where mansions had begun springing up—totaled 70,500 people. Unfortunately, the island's cocoa plantations were struck by a series of droughts beginning in 1925,

Rope tobacco sellers, ca. 1914; throughout much of its early history, Port of Spain's urban population was to consist of an unusually high percentage of female residents. (Lloyd, *Twentieth Century Impressions of the West Indies*)

combined with a blight nicknamed "Witches' Broom," which brought this era of prosperity to an end by greatly reducing the volume of exports through Port of Spain. The island's economic plight worsened after the Great Depression started with the New York stock market crash of October 1929, so that some planters even turned to citrus fruits or coconuts as alternate crops.

Col. Charles Lindbergh visited Port of Spain during this difficult interlude to inaugurate the Pan American World Airways service, the first passengers actually landing at Cocorite Field west of the capital on 12 January of the following year (six days before the first talking motion picture was also exhibited at the Empire Theatre; the German dirigible *Graf Zeppelin* visited on 22 October 1933). The urban population had reached 83,000 inhabitants by 1931, with 114 acres of Mucurapo being officially renamed "St. James" and incorporated into the city the next year, followed by 49 acres from St. Clair in 1937. A deep water channel was dredged off the city's waterfront, making it more accessible for oceangoing ships.

World War II and Independence (1940–Present)

The greatest change to Port of Spain resulted from Trinidad's role in World War II. Early on during that conflict, the British government—standing alone against Nazi Germany in Europe, almost a year after the eruption of hostilities—agreed in August 1940 to allow Washington to lease bases on British possessions throughout the Western Hemisphere, in exchange for fifty old U.S. destroyers. One such naval base was to be installed at Chaguaramas Bay, west of the existing Royal Navy base designated as HMS Benbow, while an airbase was also to be manned on the northeastern corner of the island by advance elements of the 11th U.S. Infantry Regiment and 252nd Coast Artillery Regiment (eventually becoming Fort Reid). However, as the United States had not yet become directly involved in any fighting, the first units were received coolly in March–May 1941 by the island's governor, Sir Hubert Young.

Such inhospitality ceased when German submarines inaugurated a surprise offensive in the West Indies code-named OPERATION NEULAND early the following year: Lt. Albrecht Achilles's *U-161* stealthily penetrated the Gulf of Paria on 18 February 1942 to torpedo the 7,400-ton American freighter *Mokihana* and the British tanker *British Consul* off Port of Spain at 11:35 P.M., before escaping into the night in the resultant confusion. The next afternoon, the 7,200-ton British freighter *Scottish Star* was also sunk east of Trinidad by the Marconi-class Italian submarine *Luigi Torelli* of Captain de Giacomo, while at 10:00 P.M. that same night, *U-129* of Nicoli Clausen destroyed the small Norwegian tanker *Nordvangen* 2 miles off Galera Point.

Over the next several months, Trinidad was alarmed by prowling submarines intent upon disrupting the flow of bauxite exports from the Guianas—traffic so vital to the war effort

that Allied strategic planners decided to counter by transforming the island into a major base. Because local U.S. commanders had initially been outranked by their British counterparts, cooperation sputtered until Governor Young was recalled to England on 8 June 1942, to be replaced by the more amenable Sir Bede Clifford. Construction battalions arrived and cleared vast tracts to accommodate a U.S. garrison that would eventually swell to more than 20,000 men, as well as to build a new aerodrome 15 miles due east of the capital at Arima (named Waller Field in honor of U.S. Maj. Alfred J. Waller, killed in a 1937 crash at Langley, Virginia). Roads, railroads, and dockyard facilities radiating out of Port of Spain were all vastly expanded and improved, in a construction boom that expended millions of dollars and employed thousands of local laborers.

The U-boat menace was soon defeated by air patrols crisscrossing the Caribbean, and President Franklin D. Roosevelt visited Waller Field on his way to his historic Casablanca Conference with Britain's prime minister, Winston Churchill, in January 1943. The enclosed waters of the Gulf of Paria furthermore proved an excellent training area for huge naval and amphibious exercises, with thousands of trainees being temporarily bivouacked ashore before proceeding to combat overseas. Most garrison units were finally transferred elsewhere during the closing phases of the war, and when hostilities ceased in the spring of 1945, the bases themselves were reduced to skeleton establishments or closed outright. (Waller Field, for example, was abandoned four years later.)

Port of Spain had nonetheless been transformed by this massive external influx, its populace measuring 92,793 inhabitants by 1946, with another 11,000 in adjacent suburbs; health and birthrates had also improved as the Laventille marshlands were drained and diseases such as malaria were eradicated. But what is more significant, the metropolitan area now extended northwestward and—most especially—eastward through many newly built-up towns along the Eastern Main Road toward Arima and Waller Field, spanning roughly 20 miles and encompassing a total of perhaps 200,000 people.

This dense concentration of laborers around the seaport—coupled with a commensurate growth in Trinidad's petroleum and tourism industries—helped foment the postwar establishment of industrial parks, banks, insurance companies, and the like around Port of Spain during the 1950s, notwithstanding the severe earthquake that struck on 4 December 1954, injuring eighty-nine persons and causing considerable material damage. British colonial officials sought to assist such commercial development and responded to the growing sentiments in favor of national independence by granting the island limited autonomy in 1956. Two years later, Trinidad was even touted as a potential site for the capital of a "British West Indian Federation," with a legislative complex to be created southeast of Port of Spain at "Federation Park."

But that notion proved stillborn: Trinidad and Tobago

Panoramic view over Port of Spain, ca. 1914. (Lloyd, *Twentieth Century Impressions of the West Indies*)

voted for their own independence on 31 August 1962, along with most other British Caribbean colonies. The new administration was to govern a fractious nation consisting of 47 percent black citizens, 35 percent East Indians, 14 percent of mixed heritage, 2.7 percent whites, and 1 percent Chinese. In order to reduce overcrowding and other urban problems within the old city limits of Port of Spain, immigration from other Antillean islands was curtailed and a subsidized program was introduced to encourage city residents to move out into other parts of Trinidad. That reduced the city's core pop-

ulation to perhaps 60,000 people by 1973 (although this figure is considered unreliable, and its extended metropolitan area still contained as many as 400,000 people—44 percent of the island total—when all its satellite towns were included). But by actively pursuing such a policy, the estimated numbers for the capital core at least declined to a little more than 44,000 residents by 1994.

For further reading on the history of Port of Spain or Trinidad-Tobago, please consult the Select Bibliography at the end of this volume.

MEXICO

One does not require witnesses from heaven to demonstrate that they [indigenous Americans] were political peoples, with towns, inhabited places of large size, villas, cities, and communities.

—Bartolomé de las Casas (1474–1566)

Acapulco

Lonely port-of-call for the galleons traversing the Pacific Ocean from Manilathat, in the twentieth century, has blossomed into one of the world's great tourist destinations.

Origins (1521–1550)

Prior to the Spanish conquest of the Aztec capital in Mexico's central highlands, Acapulco and its narrow coastal plain were inhabited by primitive tribesmen subordinate to the Cuitlatecan kingdom of Mexcaltepec, all of whom paid tribute to the distant Mexican emperors. The name *Acapulco* appar-

ently signifies "Place of Thick Cane" in Náhuatl, the language of the Aztecs. Local residents, who spoke Tlapanecan, maintained their principal community some distance inland from the ocean, amid the cooler foothills of the encircling mountains at a spot today called La Sabana, or Ciudad Perdida (Lost City).

After the fall of the Aztec capital in August 1521, the victorious Hernán Cortés dispatched Spanish columns to subjugate the empire's outlying vassal states. It is possible that Acapulco was visited by the expedition of Rodrigo Alvarez Chico that same autumn; however, its region was not fully brought under

The great natural harbor of Acapulco, as surveyed by Félix Dayot in 1808. (Archivo General de la Nación, Mexico)

Spanish control until the campaign of Gonzalo de Sandoval's small army in the spring of 1523. After that sweep, administration over the district was assigned to the conquistador Juan Rodríguez de Villafuerte, who established his headquarters farther west at Zacatula.

Because of the torrid, humid weather that gripped Acapulco every May through November, no Spaniards initially chose to occupy its shoreline, believing such climates to be insalubrious. Their fears were further exacerbated by the epidemics, unwittingly introduced by the Spaniards themselves, that soon began decimating the indigenous population. Nevertheless, the magnificent natural bay, sheltered from ocean currents and storms by its rocky headlands and deep, narrow channel, provided such an ideal anchorage that a few ships were being launched from extemporized yards around Acapulco's wooded shoreline as early as 1528, as well as from adjacent Puerto del Marqués. A major naval expedition set sail to explore northwestward from Acapulco under Diego Hurtado de Mendoza in May 1532; another such venture departed seven years later under Francisco de Ulloa while Domingo del Castillo charted much of the coastline in 1540. Still, Huatulco—located 300 miles farther east-southeast in the modern state of Oaxaca—remained New Spain's principal Pacific port, as it lay astride the most direct route for passengers and goods traveling to and from Central America, Panama, or Peru.

Foundation (1550–1566)

Another terrible epidemic ravaged Acapulco's Indian populace between 1545 and 1548. Yet the overall volume of Pacific sea traffic nonetheless increased so steadily that its district officer soon became designated as *alcalde mayor* of the port of Acapulco in addition to his other duties, although no new municipality was actually created within the harbor, that official continuing to be headquartered inland at the highland village of Acamutla. It was not until early 1550 that Fernando de Santa Ana arrived with a small band of settlers to establish a town within the bay itself and appoint Pedro Pacheco as Acapulco's first mayor.

However, the greatest impetus to the town's evolution was to be provided by Miguel López de Legaspi, who in November 1564 departed with an expedition from Puerto de la Navidad—375 miles farther northwest, near modern Manzanillo—to traverse the Pacific and establish a trading outpost in the Far East. Ever since Christopher Columbus's day, Spain had aspired to tap the riches of the Orient, which was finally achieved when Legaspi's subordinate Fr. Andrés de Urdaneta returned across the ocean aboard the galleon *San Pedro*, touching at Puerto de la Navidad on 1 October 1565 before entering Acapulco Bay one week later. A new trade route to Asia had thus been opened, and Crown officials in Mexico and Spain furthermore decided—on Urdaneta's recommendation—to funnel all future traffic through the port of Acapulco.

Emergence as a Transpacific Terminal (1567–1614)

The first scheduled galleon to arrive was the *San Juan* of master Rodrigo de la Isla, which entered Acapulco Bay in November 1567 from what were still known as the Islas del Poniente (Western Islands), although soon they were renamed the "Philippines" in honor of King Philip II. Because of difficulties in conveying the requisite men, accoutrements, munitions, provisions, medicines, and money down from the viceregal capital over the intervening 200 miles of precipitous Sierra Madre del Sur mountain trails, this vessel did not clear for its return voyage until fourteen months later.

A census taken in 1569 revealed only fifty Spanish families and 1,589 indigenous tributaries scattered around Acapulco Bay, as well as a few score black slaves tending to small cacao plantations and many runaways eking out an existence as fugitives in the surrounding territory. Realizing that such a limited population base could never adequately sustain port activities, receiving and refurbishing the ships that were to carry annual reinforcements and supplies to Legaspi's fledgling colony on the far side of the ocean, the exchequer hired specialized workers such as shipwrights and carpenters and financed construction of a shoreline cluster of edifices, including a customshouse, warehouses, and a church. The Hippolytean Order of Fr. Bernardino Alvarez—a soldier of fortune who had amassed great wealth in Peru before turning to charitable works—also erected the wooden Hospital de Nuestra Señora de la Consolación (Hospital of Our Lady of Consolation) in the port sometime prior to 1575 for members of his hospitaler order to tend to sick transients.

Acapulco's indigenous population was thinned by another epidemic in 1576–1579, and when the great Elizabethan adventurer Francis Drake penetrated into the Pacific during his circumnavigation, he sacked Huatulco in April 1579, yet bypassed Acapulco. His countryman Thomas Cavendish duplicated this tactic in 1587, sacking the former port and circling past Acapulco to take up station off Cabo San Lucas at the southern tip of Baja California to await the Manila galleon. On 14 November 1587, Cavendish's pair of small craft intercepted the 700-ton *Santa Ana* of Capt. Tomás de Alzola, relieving it of 40 tons of expensive goods before striking out across the Pacific.

Soon, however, the Philippine galleons began arriving at Acapulco with increasingly valuable cargoes of Eastern luxuries for sale—Asian spices, Chinese silks and ivories, and so forth—that commanded fantastic prices in silver-rich Mexico. Merchants quickly showed themselves willing to make the difficult descent to the pestilential coast from the capital in order to barter for such exotic merchandise, while vessels also arrived from as far away as Peru to join in this traffic. Therefore, when the second English privateer had materialized offshore, the Spaniards had responded to this latest incursion by digging trenches and earthen gun emplacements to help

Modern shoreline of Acapulco Bay, lined with luxury hotels, 1999. (Jan Butchofsky-Houser/Corbis)

defend Acapulco's anchorage, although no permanent battery was installed until several years later.

The galleons meanwhile resumed their regular annual crossings, and in 1592 the Viceroy Luis de Velasco II ordered improvements made to the highway leading inland. Four years later, the explorer Sebastián Vizcaíno departed Acapulco on the first of his celebrated voyages to chart the coasts of California and the Pacific Northwest. Meanwhile, Acapulco's original wooden, barracklike hospital had burned down that same year of 1596 and was ordered replaced—at Crown expense—by a stone building, completed two years afterward with a capacity for fifty beds.

In addition to their commercial traffic, the galleons departing Acapulco also maintained a vital flow of supplies, money, and reinforcements for the Spanish colonists in the Philippines, ensuring the survival of that outpost. In 1610 a vessel furthermore arrived directly from Japan, bearing a group of shipwrecked Spaniards. Vizcaíno was delegated to visit this Oriental kingdom in turn, setting sail from Acapulco on 22 March 1611 aboard his galleon *San Francisco* and returning aboard the Japanese *Mutsu Maru* on 25 January 1614, accom-

panied by a diplomatic delegation headed by Capt. Tsunenaga Rokuemon Hasekura that proceeded overland toward Mexico City, Havana, and Spain. (Unfortunately, this transoceanic contact proved short-lived, as the Spanish Crown had already decreed that all future exchanges with the Japanese should be conducted through Manila.)

Dutch Incursions and Fortification (1615–1624)

On the evening of 10 October 1615, Acapulco received a less welcome visitor when the five-ship squadron of Dutch Commo. Joris van Spilbergen appeared outside, having rounded the Strait of Magellan and fought its way up South America. Light winds delayed their entry into Acapulco Bay until the next afternoon, yet fire from the lone Spanish battery inside proved so desultory that rather than reply, these intruders merely sent a boat inshore, under flag of truce, requesting permission to buy supplies. Surprised, Acapulco's garrison commander, Gregorio de Porres, agreed to a cessation of hostilities, and van Spilbergen's crews spent the next week refreshing themselves on the beautiful beaches (further delighted to meet several Spanish officers who spoke their

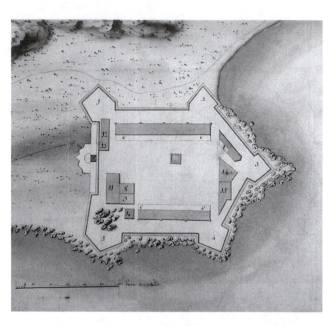

Pen-and-ink diagram with watercolor highlights of old Fort San Diego, 1772. (Servicio Geográfico del Ejército, Madrid)

language, having served in Flanders). The rovers eventually departed on 18 October, continuing up the coast toward California in the hope of intercepting the Manila galleon before steering out into the open Pacific.

Chastened by the ease with which these interlopers had occupied the port, the Viceroy Diego Fernández de Córdoba, Marqués de Guadalcázar, ordered an engineer down to the coast to improve Acapulco's defenses. Ironically, that individual proved to be none other than Adrian Boot, himself a Dutchman, who had been hired two years previously to supervise the drainage of the Valley of Mexico. On 24 November 1615 he wrote to suggest the construction of a large pentagonal fortress atop a rocky outcrop protruding from Acapulco's beach that would be capable of housing numerous artillery pieces, a governor's residence and Crown offices, plus barracks for 300 troops. His proposal was duly approved, and Fort San Diego was completed by 15 April 1617 (despite setbacks caused by an earthquake the previous autumn); it received its regular garrison of five officers, fifteen gunners, and forty infantrymen, who were to be supplemented by the 100 militiamen maintained by the small town.

Lamentably, though, when a second Dutch squadron, under Commo. Gheen Huygen Schapenham, forced its way into Acapulco Bay on 28 October 1624, this new fortress was so ill supported from the interior—because of an insurrection in Mexico City that had deposed the unpopular Viceroy Diego de Pimentel, Marqués de los Gelves, thus paralyzing all government activities—that its garrison commander, Pedro de Legorreta, had to leave the Dutch in uncontested possession for

a week before they, too, headed northwest in search of the annual galleon.

Seasonal Occupation (1625–1775)

Notwithstanding this embarrassing debut, Fort San Diego was soon strengthened with extra battlements that effectively prevented any further irruptions into the bay, although foreign aggressors still attempted to waylay galleons out at sea. By now a system had evolved whereby two pairs of vessels—each consisting of a galleon flagship and smaller *patache,* or auxiliary—took turns circulating between the Philippines and Mexico. Departures from Manila normally occurred in summertime, the vessels touching at the Marianas before continuing along the North Pacific currents to emerge off uninhabited California by Christmastime.

Coasting southeastward, a courier known as the *gentilhombre de los pliegos* (gentleman of the dispatches) would then be set ashore near Cabo Corrientes, to be hastened on toward Mexico City by relays of mounts, with news of the galleons' imminent arrival at Acapulco. Only then would the port's non-resident governor, plus numerous other Crown officials and a host of merchants, begin the arduous trek from the capital down to the coast. The vessels meanwhile would be received at Acapulco by its local lieutenant-governor, their crews being

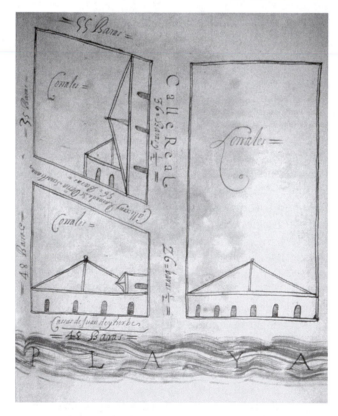

Crude drawing of the new customs building erected at Acapulco, 1627. (Archivo General de la Nación, Mexico)

allowed ashore to recuperate while the cargo holds (sealed upon clearing Manila) would remain locked until the governor's actual arrival. Finally, merchandise would be lightered into the customshouse, duties would be paid, and a great commercial fair would ensue upon the beaches.

The tiny, somnolent town was therefore transformed every winter by a massive influx of people, its few hundred residents servicing thousands of visitors, as well as preparing the galleons and their crews for the homeward leg. It was impossible to lodge so many transients, most people camping under the stars, favored by the clear days and balmy nights of that season. So much Chinese merchandise was offered for sale that these vessels were commonly referred to throughout Mexico as the *naos de China* (China merchantmen), while the catchphrase *venida en nao* (come upon the merchantman) was applied to any item held in especially high esteem. As mule trains started inland with the first purchases that had been made, others began arriving in the opposite direction with provisions (most often ships' biscuits and cheeses from Puebla) for the return passage. Fresh meat was provided by local ranchers, who bid every few years for that *asiento* (exclusive privilege).

Once bartering began to subside, the refurbished galleons would prepare to receive their passengers, as well as groups of soldier-conscripts and *forzados* (convict deportees) who had been marched down from Mexico City. Last to arrive would be the chests containing hundreds of thousands of silver pesos from the viceregal mint, which were to be shipped across to the Philippines as the *situado* (subsidy) for its Crown and church employees. With the addition of the merchants' accrued profits, galleons routinely departed with millions in treasure aboard.

Ideally, they set sail southward in late March or early April to catch the prevailing winds and currents, which would waft them back across the Pacific. No other craft was allowed to depart Acapulco until they had dropped below the horizon, after which the governor and his retinue, plus any other private individuals, were free to return to the capital, leaving the port quiet once more. Only a few coastal traders called throughout the remainder of the year, activities reviving shortly before the next pair of galleons was scheduled to arrive. This routine was largely observed for two and a half centuries, interrupted only by shipwrecks or reports of enemy raiders. For example, Acapulco was alarmed during the mid-1680s by news of Anglo-French buccaneers pushing out of the West Indies across the Isthmus of Panama into the Pacific. Their numbers proved too insignificant to directly threaten the port, though, although five French vessels under Pierre le Picard did briefly occupy Tehuantepec in late August 1687, then looked into Acapulco's bay a few weeks later.

During Queen Anne's War early the next century, a pair of English privateers under Capts. Woodes Rogers and Stephen Courtney—piloted by the former buccaneer William Dampier—captured the 20-gun auxiliary *Nuestra Señora de la Encarnación* (alias *Desengaño,* or "Deception") off Cabo San Lucas on 1 January 1710, yet failed to subdue its wealthier, 60-gun galleon flagship *Nuestra Señora de Begonia* five days later. Another pair of English privateers—George Shelvocke and John Clipperton—hovered outside Acapulco in May 1721, hoping to snap up the galleon *Santo Cristo de Burgos,* which lay inside. However, after arguing over prize shares, Clipperton slipped away one night to head across the Pacific and wait in the Philippines, compelling Shelvocke to abandon his own watch a few days later. A generation later, Commo. George Anson materialized near Acapulco with the British warships HMSS *Centurion* and *Gloucester* in late February 1742, anticipating the arrival of the galleon *Nuestra Señora de Covadonga,* which had already entered Acapulco from Manila on 6 January. Eventually tiring of his blockade, Anson struck out across the Pacific three months later, finally intercepting *Covadonga* in the San Bernardino Strait.

Earthquake and Recovery (1776–1809)

A census taken in 1743 revealed that Acapulco's population had grown to approximately 3,000 to 4,000 residents, spread mostly among 541 indigenous and 578 non-Indian households—the vast majority of the latter being free mulattoes. On 21 April 1776, a massive quake leveled the town, collapsing virtually every dwelling and heavily damaging Fort San Diego. Within a month, the military engineer Miguel Costanzó arrived from the capital, conducting an inspection that concluded that its original structure would have to be replaced by an entirely new edifice. The next year a forty-eight-man construction crew arrived under the military engineer Ramón Panón to demolish the old citadel and erect an improved version upon its foundations. After removing the rubble, work commenced on a brand-new pentagonal building in mid-March 1778 that was completed—despite numerous delays because of illness—by 7 July 1783. The structure was thereupon officially designated Fort San Carlos in honor of Spain's reigning monarch, Charles III, although the old name of Fort San Diego soon reasserted itself. This new citadel boasted sixty cannons and could hold as many as 2,000 people during a siege.

The 1792 census found only 122 Spaniards residing in Acapulco and its jurisdiction, compared with 5,557 mulattoes and blacks, plus a couple of thousand Indians (568 indigenous households being registered in 1804). In addition to the Manila galleons, the port was also visited by the Spanish naval corvettes *Descubierta* and *Atrevida* in 1791, during their Pacific cruise under Capt. Alejandro Malaspina. The celebrated German scientist Alexander, Baron von Humboldt, furthermore arrived from South America on 22 March 1803 aboard the frigate *Orúe,* remaining five days before continuing overland toward Mexico City. During his layover, Humboldt calculated

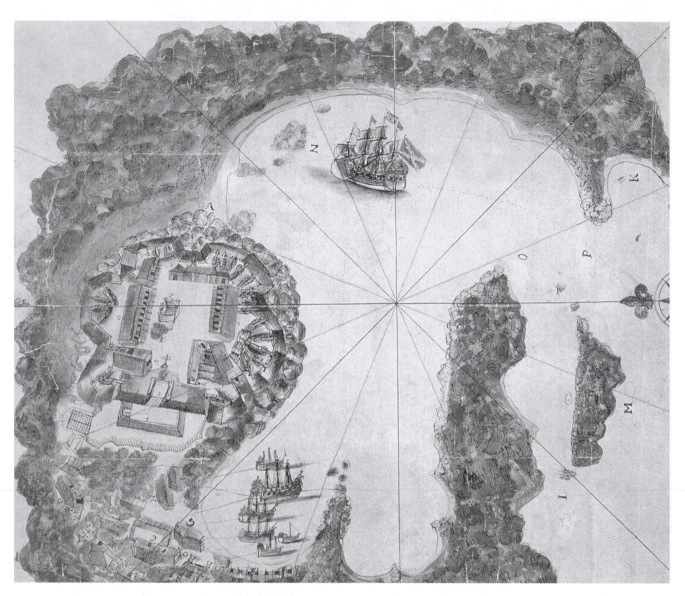

Chart of Acapulco Bay in November 1712, by garrison commander Miguel Gallo; note that while Fort San Diego and its shore installations have been accurately rendered, the harbor itself is shown disproportionately small. (Archive of Indies, Seville)

the port's population at 4,000 permanent inhabitants, with another 5,000 visitors present for its commercial fair. Four years previously, Charles IV had elevated the town into a city, with the name of Ciudad de los Reyes de Acapulco (apparently because its original sixteenth-century parish had been called Santos Reyes de Acapulco).

Revolutionary Disruption (1810–1821)

However, Mexico's struggle to gain its independence from Spain would drastically alter Acapulco's fortunes, first by ending its transpacific trade. Early on during this rebellion—on 9 November 1810—the fiery rebel priest José María Morelos y Pavón invested Acapulco with a swarm of ill-armed insurgents, returning again on 1 December with 3,000 men; how-

ever, he proved incapable of carrying its defenses because of his lack of trained soldiers or a heavy siege train. Nevertheless, his arrival had cut off the travel routes leading toward the capital, and twelve days later his subordinate Julián de Avila ambushed an approaching relief column at La Sabana, while Morelos himself surprised 3,000 royalists encamped at nearby Tres Palos on the night of 4–5 January 1811, inflicting 400 casualties. Thus heartened, the guerrilla chieftain assaulted Fort San Diego for a third time on 8 February, believing he had bribed the gunner José Gago to cripple its artillery; instead, the insurgents were received with grapeshot, suffering fourteen dead before retreating out of range. By mid-March the royalist garrison under Nicolás Cosío began making a few sallies, defeating some of Morelos's

Panoramic view across Acapulco Bay in 1791 by Tomás Suria, an artist attached to the Malaspina expedition, as seen from the Hippolytean hospital. The corvettes *Atrevida* and *Descubierta* are anchored offshore, and to the right can be seen the town, as well as the large *ceiba* tree where the Manila galleons traditionally moored. (Museo Naval, Madrid)

followers at Las Cruces Point on 4 April, only to then be bloodied against the main insurgent positions at La Sabana on 30–31 April.

Shortly thereafter Morelos marched his army northward, but although Acapulco was no longer threatened directly, it nonetheless remained isolated because of the guerrilla bands controlling the mountain roads. No merchants from Mexico City had been able to attend that year's fair, and after a lengthy wait the galleon returned to Manila with no profits or supplies. On 6 April 1813, Morelos reappeared with 1,500 men, occupying Iguanas and the Mira Heights outside Acapulco and bombarding the town for six days with a few field pieces. Finally, its royalists evacuated their Casamata bulwark and the fortified Nuestra Señora de la Consolación Hospital (which was consumed by flames when its powder dump exploded), regrouping inside Fort San Diego under garrison commander Pedro Antonio Vélez. The insurgents thereupon instituted a close siege, seizing Roqueta Island offshore by 9 June, then eventually tightening their stranglehold sufficiently on 17 August to compel the fort's defenders to capitulate three days later.

This rebel triumph lasted for only a few months, as after Morelos's twin defeats at Valladolid and Puruarán the next year, he straggled back into Acapulco in early March 1814 with only 100 survivors. Learning a month later that royalist forces were closing in under Gabriel Armijo, Morelos burned the city of Acapulco, hanged more than 100 Spanish captives, and then disappeared into the Atijo Mountains with a few loyal adher-

ents. The monarchists reoccupied Acapulco's smoldering remnants on 14 April, retaining control over the port until the very end of the war, although it was no longer able to receive galleons.

At last, victorious Mexican forces under Isidro Montes de Oca and Juan N. Alvarez besieged the final royalist holdouts within Fort San Diego in early September 1821, obliging them to surrender by 15 October. The national struggle for independence was now concluded, although the port continued to be the scene of a few minor international incidents, such as on 29 January 1822, when the British mercenary Thomas, Lord Cochrane, appeared offshore with a Chilean squadron, hunting for the Spanish frigates *Venganza* and *Prueba;* but when he learned three days later that they were at Guayaquil, he steered southeast. Also, the 64-gun Spanish ship-of-the-line *Asia*—its crew having mutinied in the Marianas—traversed the Pacific and capitulated to the Mexican authorities at Acapulco early in 1825.

Stagnation (1822–1926)

Although now a free port within an independent republic, Acapulco nonetheless declined dramatically over the next century, being unable to find any substitute for its lost Philippine traffic. Modest amounts of local produce were exported, but larger markets deeper inland remained inaccessible because of the barrier of the Sierra Madre Occidental mountain range. Its very remoteness occasionally made

Mid-nineteenth-century depiction of the sleepy port; note the imposing mountain range barring access to the interior. (Author's Collection)

Acapulco a stronghold during the frequent insurrections that racked the new republic: in December 1829, for example, the war hero Nicolás Bravo occupied the tiny port city in support of Vice President Anastasio Bustamante, who had mutinied against President Vicente Guerrero in the interior. The latter fled his capital and in turn mounted a tenacious guerrilla campaign throughout southern Mexico, only to eventually be lured aboard the anchored Genoese brigantine *Colombo* at Acapulco on 15 January 1831, whose captain, Francesco Picaluga, had been offered a 50,000-peso bounty by Bustamante to kidnap his predecessor. Rather than receiving the anticipated luncheon, Guerrero was instead sailed to Huatulco and shot. Also in November 1834, the veteran Gen. Juan Alvarez revolted against the presidency of Antonio López de Santa Anna, besieging Acapulco and clashing with Bravo.

Almost two decades later, Acapulco was again thrust into the national limelight when on 1 March 1854 the garrison at nearby Ayutla mutinied against Santa Anna, incensed—like many other Mexicans—by his territorial concessions to the United States with the signing of the Gadsen Treaty. Ten days later, the troops at Acapulco joined this insurrection, under their highly respected former customs collector, Ignacio Comonfort. Santa Anna reacted swiftly, marching out of Mexico City on 16 March at the head of 5,000 troops. Despite heavy guerrilla resistance and the daunting mountain terrain, his

army appeared before Acapulco on 20 April, attempting to surprise Comonfort's defenders within Fort San Diego. But after six days' fruitless bombardment and siege, the dictator was compelled to retire because of disease and lack of supplies, burning numerous dwellings as he retreated. This ignominious withdrawal encouraged other rebellions throughout Mexico, while the victorious Comonfort moreover sailed to San Francisco to raise American financing. Eventually, Santa Anna was obliged to resign from office on 4 August 1855 and go into exile.

During the French intervention into Mexico in the early 1860s, Acapulco's poverty and physical remove spared it any direct overland threats, although it was twice attacked from out at sea: Firstly, it was bombarded by a French squadron on 10–11 January 1864 that drove its terrified inhabitants inland and allowed French sailors to occupy the abandoned city for three days. Secondly, it was approached on 3 June of that same year by five French warships that set a battalion of Algerian *tireurs* ashore next day, then pushed 400 troops inland six days later to seize La Sabana Pass as well. However, these forces remained in possession only until the end of 1864, after which the port resumed its former somnolent existence. Little else of consequence occurred until Acapulco was struck by a heavy earthquake and tidal wave in April 1907, causing considerable damage; two years later, its population was estimated at 5,800 residents, virtually unchanged from its colonial days.

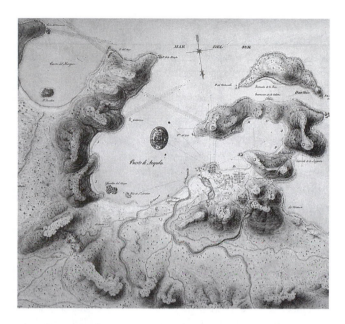

Acapulco Bay and its surrounding district in 1820; north is toward bottom. (Servicio Histórico Militar, Madrid)

Tourist Haven (1927–Present)

Decades of neglect were finally reversed during the late 1920s and early 1930s, when a campaign was implemented to take advantage of Acapulco's great natural beauty and wonderful winter climate by transforming it into a tourist mecca. With tropical diseases now controlled by modern improvements in medicine, the first step was to construct a highway down from the capital. A convoy of a dozen automobiles duly reached the port on the evening of 11 November 1927, an asphalt highway being completed four years later (followed by a four-lane expansion in 1954). The first airport was constructed southeast of the city in 1928, and passenger service from Mexico City was inaugurated the following year; a system of drinking water drawn from the Santa Cruz Springs went into operation by 1930.

Notwithstanding the economic hardships brought on by the worldwide effects of the Great Depression, work on Acapulco's first major hotel—El Mirador, overlooking the spectacular La Quebrada—was begun in 1933, soon followed by a half dozen others. Mexico's federal government supplemented such efforts by installing a telephone system as of April 1936 and an electric plant somewhat later, as well as by straightening and paving most of the old meandering, sandy streets. Soon Acapulco's occupied urban area began to expand, its population being estimated at 30,000 in 1950, and the 1960 census officially tabulated 49,149 residents.

That figure more than tripled to 174,378 within the next ten years, spurred by an explosive growth in both international and domestic air travel. The city hosted 1,446,788 visitors in 1970, 1,753,114 in 1971, and more than 3 million by 1973 (roughly half of them being foreigners). Ironically, such a dramatic upsurge in business strained the pristine city's services to the breaking point and was thus accompanied by the

Two Mexican beauties painted by Diego Rivera, ca. 1950, relaxing with Acapulco Bay featured in the background; this famed muralist often visited the resort town, convalescing here late in life. (Anahuacalli Collection, Mexico City)

appearance of the first slums around Acapulco's periphery, such as La Laja, Santa Cruz, El Jardín, and La Garita. Even beach frontage became scarce, having to be allocated under government scrutiny. Nevertheless, undaunted migrants continued to arrive in great numbers from throughout southern Mexico, the tourism boom offering them better prospects than conditions in the countryside, and the urban population figure eventually topped 515,000 by 1990.

Although today still a beautiful resort, Acapulco has suffered from its own success, now straining under a population of more than 1 million and sprawling for more than 10 miles both inside and outside its bay. Its 250 hotels and many luxurious restaurants and shops are increasingly surrounded by congested streets, noise, pollution, and crime. Floods and mud slides caused by Hurricane Pauline in 1997 inflicted extensive damage throughout poorer neighborhoods, resulting in several score deaths and thousands more being left homeless. Still, repairs were quickly effected, and it is today estimated that during peak periods—such as the Semana Santa or Easter holidays—a flight departs Mexico City for Acapulco every three minutes.

For further reading on the history of Acapulco or Mexico, please consult the Select Bibliography at the end of this volume.

Campeche

Mayan coastal city that served as the main Spanish colonial sea outlet for the Yucatán Peninsula, then emerged as capital of its own separate state.

Contact (1517–1518)

Two Spanish brigantines under Francisco Hernández de Córdoba, dispatched by the governor of Cuba on a reconnaissance mission, spotted the sprawling indigenous city on the low, steamy shoreline of the Gulf of Mexico on 22 March 1517. Pausing nearby to refresh their water supply, the explorers noted that this teeming community lay at the edge of a fertile jungle plain, encircled by a natural amphitheater formed by several small hills. The city's core contained many fine whitewashed temples and at least 3,000 dwellings, housing perhaps 35,000 residents who lived from fishing, agriculture, and trading pursuits.

The Spaniards learned that the city's Mayan name was Ah K'in Pech, or Kampech, signifying the patrilineal fiefdom of the Pech family (although some Spaniards later misconstrued the term to mean "Tick-Serpent," as its principal temple idol was crowned by a coiled serpent with a tick atop its head). Hernández de Córdoba dubbed the metropolis San Lázaro upon his chart, in honor of that particular feast day on the Church cal-

Aerial photograph looking northeastward across Campeche, ca. 1950; note how the city had only recently begun expanding beyond its ancient walls. (Compañía Mexicana Aerofoto, S.A.)

endar, before proceeding southwestward to be bloodily repulsed a few days later at Champotón.

More than a year later, a larger Spanish expedition appeared from Cuba under Juan de Grijalva, sighting Campeche on 25 May 1518 and drawing water nearby the next day, before continuing along the coast and eventually encountering the wealthy inland empire of the Aztecs. Grijalva did not reverse course until several months later, regaining "San Lázaro" by early September to reprovision with water, firewood, and corn for his return to Cuba.

Stillborn Occupation (1531–1535)

Over the next several years, the conquistadors remained engrossed in subduing the powerful Aztecs in central Mexico, so that Campeche was bypassed. But on 8 December 1526, Francisco de Montejo—one of Grijalva's former lieutenants, and now an associate of the victorious Hernán Cortés—received permission from the Crown to seize the Yucatán Peninsula, although his invasion of its eastern shoreline the following year proved unsuccessful.

A second attempt started when Montejo occupied Champotón and used it as an advance base from which to press forward and overrun Kampech, defeating its defenders in a pitched battle in June 1531. He renamed the captive city Salamanca de Campeche in honor of his birthplace in Spain, but penetrations farther northeastward across the arid limestone plains of the central peninsula were repelled by fierce Mayan resistance, so that all Spanish probes ceased by late 1534. News of Francisco Pizarro's simultaneous conquest of the rich Incan empire of Peru moreover lured away many adventurers, so that Gonzalo Nieto—alcalde (municipal magistrate) at Campeche—was compelled to withdraw his depleted garrison into Tabasco early the next year, after which the first Franciscan missionaries were also chased out of Champotón.

Spanish Refoundation (1540–1632)

A third and final attempt was not made until Francisco de Montejo "el Mozo" ("the Younger") disembarked at Champotón a half-decade later with 100 Spanish mercenaries, plus hundreds of Mexican auxiliaries and Chontal Maya allies. As Campeche had meanwhile been depopulated by the previous Spanish incursions and contagious diseases, it submitted tamely to this latest offensive, so that by 4 October 1540—a date still disputed by some scholars—the younger Montejo was able to reconstitute it formally as a Spanish town, with yet another new name: San Francisco de Campeche.

Montejo subsequently fought his way inland and established his headquarters at the Mayan capital of Tihó by early 1542, renaming it Mérida de Yucatán. But the peninsula's oppressively hot climate and lack of mineral riches caused many of his conquistadors to depart in disillusionment, so that Campeche's jittery municipal council even passed an ordinance on 2 December 1542 trying to stem all emigration. In a

further desperate bid to retain his followers, the younger Montejo allowed these mercenaries to enslave hostile Indians, a dispensation that was so widely abused that the province soon became threatened with the loss of all laborers, obliging him to rescind the order.

Stable administration was not imposed at Campeche until the elder Montejo arrived on 25 December 1546 to supersede his son as regional governor, accompanied by a half dozen Franciscan friars and a few civilian colonists. While pausing at the port, he reorganized its urban layout by concentrating its handful of Spanish residents into a seaside core; the shrunken remnants of its original Mayan population were recongregated a mile and a half farther northeast, around the new Franciscan monastery of San Francisco Kinpech—also known as Campechuelo (Little Campeche). Aztec allies were separated into a distinct new southwestern suburb called San Román.

A census taken in 1548 revealed twenty Spanish households at Campeche, serviced by perhaps 2,000 indigenous vassals in outlying satellite communities. Most agricultural operations

Young Mayan women, ca. 1914. (Underwood and Underwood)

were scattered more deeply inland, among the tropical rain forest tracts, and haciendas (estates) in those regions soon began to ship modest amounts of cotton and *palo de tinte* (dyewood) down the *camino real* (royal highway) into Campeche's port for transshipment toward Veracruz or Havana. Overland communication with the main Mexican viceroyalty was virtually nonexistent, except for a few faint jungle tracks.

Although Campeche was the best anchorage along an otherwise lengthy stretch of reef-lined Yucatecan coastland, its shallow roadstead nevertheless lay exposed to the strong northers that blew across the Gulf of Mexico every October through April, while its bar furthermore prevented vessels drawing more than 9 feet from entering via its two narrow channels. As a result of these geographical constraints, plus the meager value of Yucatán's exports, port traffic consisted merely of seasonal visits by a few medium-size vessels, as well as the activities of small coasters or fishing boats manufactured locally from the abundant stands of wood.

And because of its small population base and lack of defenses, Campeche proved vulnerable enough to tempt a trio of Huguenot (French Protestant) privateer vessels during a Caribbean foray, as part of the ongoing Franco-Spanish hostilities back in Europe. About thirty raiders disembarked on the night of 7–8 July 1561 and slipped into the sleeping town, driving its citizenry into the darkness. But upon perceiving the raiders' limited numbers the next morning, the inhabitants—Spanish households having since doubled in number to forty—counterattacked as the French tried to retire aboard a captured bark laden with booty and five female prisoners, killing fifteen rovers and capturing five; the rest swam back out to their waiting ships.

Administration of the Yucatán Peninsula passed from private hands to Crown control shortly thereafter, its first royal-appointed governor arriving to assume office at Mérida as of mid-November 1565. He in turn delegated a deputy to rule over the province's strategic outlet at Campeche, yet who promptly became embroiled in jurisdictional disputes with its fractious *cabildo* (town council). Throughout the colonial era, Campeche's leading citizens would be quick to complain to the viceroys in Mexico City or to the authorities in distant Madrid about any perceived infringement upon their privileges, so that Yucatecan governors resorted to often devious methods to retain control over their provincial port.

Commercially, Campeche expanded modestly over the next several decades, yet it could never hope to compete with the much busier Gulf ports of Veracruz or Havana, which served as terminals for the great annual plate-fleets from Spain. Still, the town's Spanish families again doubled in number to eighty by the time that hostilities with Elizabethan England erupted in 1588, although its indigenous population had dwindled to fewer than 1,500 people. A raid was endured during the second week of June 1589, when the 70-ton English privateer *Black Dog* of Capt. William Michelson—under the temporary command of his pilot, Roger Kingson, and master, William Mace—stole upon a merchantman loading off Campeche, only to be repulsed. When Kingson and Mace attempted to extort a ransom of 5,000 ducats not to mount a blockade, they were lured aboard by the Spaniards and stabbed. Mace managed to swim back to *Black Dog* with two or three survivors.

A much more serious assault occurred on 21 September 1597, when the veteran rover William Parker appeared out in the Gulf with his 120-ton flagship *Prudence,* the 25-ton *Adventure* of Richard Henne, plus a pinnace. Feigning a retirement, the raiders returned after dark and—guided by a Spanish turncoat named Juan Venturate—stole ashore through the San Román suburb to surprise the town. Campeche's garrison commander, Capt. Antonio de Alcalá, and a handful of men mounted a desperate resistance from within its tiny Bonete strong house, while noncombatants fled toward the Franciscan monastery at Campechuelo. The next dawn, rural volunteers rallied at the estate of alcalde Francisco Sánchez, marching upon the town and being joined by a sally from the convent under his fellow official Pedro de Iterián to drive the English back aboard their ships after two hours' heavy fighting around the main square in which Parker and many others were wounded. (One convalescent left behind was the traitor Venturate, who was summarily put to death by red-hot tongs.)

The defenders thereupon commandeered a merchant frigate with which to pursue the fleeing raiders, along with a coast guard frigate dispatched from nearby Caucel by the governor of Yucatán. The two vessels cornered *Adventure,* subduing it after a ferocious exchange during which eleven of its sixteen crewmen were killed. The *campechanos* returned into port triumphantly with their prize, followed by Parker, who remained outside for seventeen days vainly trying to ransom his captive colleagues.

Once the Elizabethan conflict ended in August 1604, local citizens were able to address their more mundane concerns. Four years later, Campeche's *cabildo* requested permission from the Yucatecan governor, Carlos de Luna y Arellano, to replace their aged parish church—a small stone structure with a thatched roof—with a more fitting edifice, capable not only of ministering to the town's 306 Spanish residents but also of providing refuge against future attacks. This petition was forwarded to Spain, while de Luna authorized the construction of a stone blockhouse called Fort San Benito in 1611 to protect Campeche's vulnerable southwestern flank. It was intended to supplement the town's only other defense: a twin-towered enclosure around its main square.

Enemy Raids (1633–1685)

Neither redoubt could stem the next enemy onslaught, which resulted from an eruption of hostilities with The Netherlands in Europe. On 11 August 1633, thirteen vessels came up over

Engraving of van Hoorn's and Jol's attack against Campeche in August 1633, published eleven years later in Johannes de Laet's *Historie ofte iaerlijck verhael*. (Royal Library, The Hague)

the horizon under the Dutch commodore Jan Janszoon van Hoorn. More than 500 men swarmed ashore the next morning to advance under van Hoorn's peg-legged subordinate Capt. Cornelis Jol (known to the Spaniards as *Pie de Palo*) and the renegade Cuban corsair Diego the Mulatto. Their initial charge was repelled by Fort San Benito's three artillery pieces plus fifty harquebusiers under Capt. Domingo Galván Romero in a long trench. But when the attackers recoiled, the defenders rashly chased them into open country, where Galván and a dozen others were shot down.

The freebooters thereupon regrouped and circled around into the town, carrying it after a close-quarters firefight against 300 defenders in its main square that ended with more than three dozen Spanish deaths and many captures, while survivors ran toward Campechuelo. The Dutch retained possession of Campeche for the next two days, stripping it of everything of value and twenty-two anchored vessels, before sailing a dozen miles up the coast to release their prisoners.

This ordeal galvanized the authorities into upgrading Campeche's defenses: Fort San Benito's trench was made a permanent, stone-lined structure; another 15-gun pentagonal fortress was erected atop a nearby hill (officially christened Fort Santa Cruz, better known as Eminencia Fort); and a new bastion called San Bartolomé was constructed at the town's northeastern corner. The Order of San Juan de Dios was furthermore invited to take over the ruined Nuestra Señora de los Remedios Hospital on the eastern edge of town in 1635, and a census undertaken four years later revealed that there were

approximately 300 householders in Campeche, many now being categorized as mestizos (a term describing the offspring of Spaniards and local inhabitants, being a garbling of the Latin term *mixticius,* or "mixed").

Once the Dutch conflict ceased, in 1648, the Spanish empire collapsed from economic decay, so that even Campeche's parish project was halted eight years later for lack of funds. Disturbing reports were also received that same year of 1656 regarding the English conquest of Jamaica, prompting the erection of yet another new redoubt between Forts San Benito and Santa Cruz named Fort Santo Cristo de San Román in honor of that suburb's patron saint. Unfortunately, such efforts once again proved futile, as the Jamaican Council—wishing to retaliate against Spain's American colonies for their unrelenting hostility, despite a separate peace concluded back in Europe—authorized the naval commodore Christopher Myngs to raise a privateer expedition in late December 1662 to strike against Mexico.

Myngs materialized southwest of Campeche on the night of 8–9 February 1663 with his 46-gun flagship HMS *Centurion* and a small flotilla under the veteran buccaneer Edward Mansfield, disembarking almost 1,000 men at Jámula Beach to steal the 4 miles overland into town. At first light Campeche's lookouts perceived the anchored English vessels, yet as the alarm was being sounded, Myngs's army burst out of the nearby jungle. Despite being surprised and outnumbered, the town's 150 militiamen put up a spirited resistance, and the English commodore received serious wounds during the initial charge. Mansfield consequently assumed command, subduing the defenders after two hours of fighting in which 30 invaders and more than 50 *campechanos* were killed and 170 captives taken.

The following morning the only Spanish official still at large—*regidor* Antonio Maldonado de Aldana—agreed to a truce that left the English undisturbed within the gutted and burned town until 17 February 1663, at which time a recuperated Myngs released four captives with a message offering to spare all of Campeche's remaining buildings and free his prisoners, if the raiders could water at the nearby Lerma wells before departing. Maldonado acceded, and the enemy formation got under way six days afterward, carrying away much booty and fourteen prizes.

For a second time, *campechanos* were reduced to repairing their battered town and bolstered its defenses by enclosing its northeastern and southwestern sides with moated stockades. The old Bonete citadel, the main church, and Fort San Benito were also replaced by stouter structures, while coastal residents as far southwest as Champotón were withdrawn into Campeche's environs, so as to deny approach roads and wells to future enemy incursions. Yet foreign logwood poachers soon ensconced themselves amid the dense mangroves of the Laguna de Términos, 100 miles farther down the coast, gaining such intimate knowledge of local conditions as to mount a clever raid a decade and a half later.

Two sloops and eight large piraguas (dugouts) under Capts. George Spurre and Edward Neville anchored opposite Jaina on 6 July 1678, bearing commissions from the French governor of Saint-Domingue (modern Haiti), whose nation was just then at war against Spain. Slipping ashore with 160 freebooters the next day, the captains instructed their vessels to bear down upon Campeche two mornings later, while they themselves stealthily marched the 18 miles southwestward in nocturnal stages with their land force, capturing every person that they chanced to meet.

One such prisoner was tortured to deceive Campeche's watch, so that an hour before daybreak on Sunday, 10 July 1678, the disguised raider column materialized before one of the new northeastern gates, their terrorized captive answering the sentinel's challenge and thus gaining them access. In the gloom the sentry assumed the shadowy figures to be Indians come early to market, so that the infiltrators were able to advance into the central plaza and fire a volley directly into the governor's residence, taking the nine soldiers quartered inside—rather than the usual sixty—utterly by surprise. *Sargento mayor* (garrison commander) Gonzalo Borrallo was seized in his nightshirt, along with virtually every other leading citizen, after which the buccaneer flotilla appeared and two huts were fired as a signal for them to anchor. Captives were subsequently brutalized and buildings ransacked, before Spurre and Neville withdrew on the evening of 12 July with three prizes, much booty, and 250

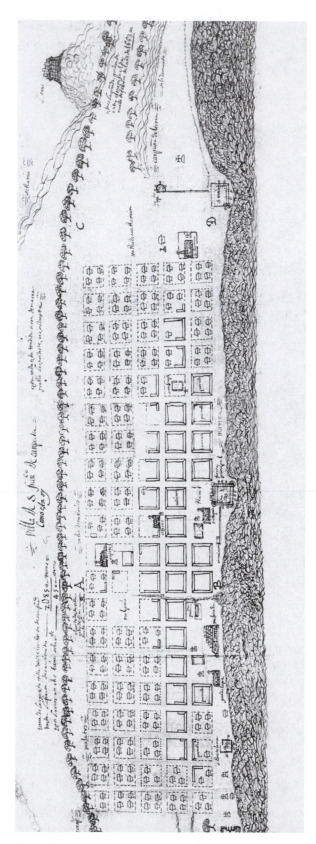

Map of Campeche by its *sargento mayor* or "garrison commander" Pedro Frías Salazar, indicating some possible defensive improvements following the February 1663 raid by Jamaican buccaneers; north is toward lower right. (Archive of Indies, Seville)

black, mulatto, and Indian townspeople to sell as slaves at the Laguna de Términos.

Yucatán's governor, Antonio de Layseca y Alvarado, belatedly arrived with a relief column from the interior, then remained to supervise the repair of Bonete citadel. During his stay he noted that many surviving citizens now balked at resurrecting their Campeche homes, preferring to resettle their families inland; concerned that such a depopulation might cripple the port's effectiveness, the governor requested that the Crown finance the erection of a 2-mile circuit of stone walls and eight bastions around the town, which was approved by Madrid in April 1682. Unfortunately, the engineer assigned to that project—Martín de la Torre—died during its early stages, so that the town remained vulnerable.

In the spring of 1685, reports began arriving of a large pirate fleet gathering off Isla Mujeres under the *boucanier* chieftains François Grammont and Laurens de Graaf. On the afternoon of 6 July, thirty-three craft materialized a half dozen miles offshore, disgorging 700 freebooters who began rowing in toward land. They were checked when 200 Campeche militiamen exited and positioned themselves opposite the intended disembarkation point. But the following morning, the rovers dashed ashore on the very outskirts of the town itself, while its defenders—their morale shaken when Capt. Cristóbal Martínez de Acevedo's coast guard frigate *Nuestra Señora de la Soledad* was deliberately detonated out in the harbor—retreated inside Bonete citadel to continue resisting.

The invaders ferried siege artillery ashore and commenced bombarding that stronghold by dawn of 12 July 1685, only to be interrupted when two relief columns appeared out of the northeast. Unfazed, the raiders veered round and manned Campeche's ramparts, driving the Yucatecan militia off in disarray by late afternoon, once Grammont had circled behind them. The disheartened Bonete garrison consequently deserted after nightfall, so that the besiegers gained control over the entire city; Grammont then organized troops of mounted buccaneers to ravage the countryside as far as 10 miles inland.

The rovers remained in possession of Campeche for the next two months, although frustrated because most of its plunder had been withdrawn prior to their assault. Moreover, Yucatán's governor, Juan Bruno Téllez de Guzmán, his army headquartered at Hecelchakán, prohibited all payments of ransom to redeem Spanish captives. Grammont's *flibustiers* eventually celebrated their monarch Louis XIV's feast day on 25 August 1685, then the next morning began preparations to depart: a message was sent inland demanding 80,000 pesos and 400 head of cattle to leave Campeche's buildings intact. This was rejected by Téllez de Guzmán, so that the town was torched the following day at dawn. Grammont thereupon sent another missive threatening the captives themselves, received the same response, and so paraded the prisoners amid the smoldering ruins of the main square on 28 August, executing a half-dozen before de Graaf interceded and the pirates at last departed.

Fortification (1686–1738)

Shaken by this brazen and ruinous occupation, many citizens refused to resume residency at Campeche, instead choosing to re-establish their homes at a safer remove inland. As late as 29 May 1688, the municipal council was complaining to the Crown that its urban populace remained shrunken to a mere third of the number of inhabitants prior to the buccaneer sack; hopes of resuming work upon its defensive perimeter under the military engineer Capt. Manuel Jorge Cáceres had also proven stillborn, because the port's lack of economic activity was generating no revenue. The German-born royal engineer Jaime Franck nevertheless did arrive from Veracruz the next year and used some private donations to reinvigorate labors, adopting the proposed 2-mile, hexagonal enclosure dotted with eight bastions as designed by *sargento mayor* Pedro Osorio de Cervantes, leaving ample space within the perimeter for private orchards and garden plots.

Ironically, the port's very poverty spared it further attacks during King William's War—nine years of conflict during which Spain, England, and Holland were allied against France—for although seven West Indian corsair vessels did appear offshore briefly on 30 June 1692, they chose to raid Jaina instead. And when hostilities against the English and Dutch erupted early in the eighteenth century (becoming known as Queen Anne's War), Campeche had its garrison augmented to 200 regular soldiers, with barracks, a customshouse, and government offices being added. The small town's enclosure with its 8-foot-thick, 25-feet-high walls was largely completed by 1704 and inspected by the French military engineer Louis Bouchard de Becour one year later; still, four enemy privateer vessels anchored offshore with impunity on 18 January 1708 under a commander nicknamed *Barbillas* or *Bigotes* (Spanish for "Little Whiskers" or "Mustache"), setting a party ashore that sacked and burned Lerma, then intercepted Yucatán's arriving governor-designate, Fernando Meneses Bravo de Saravia, holding him and his family for ransom, so that Campeche's garrison was augmented to 300 troops in 1709.

Once that particular conflict ceased, the town's security was more fully ensured when *sargento mayor* Alonso Felipe de Andrade led a sizable flotilla in December 1716 against the English logwood establishments in the Laguna de Términos, eradicating that foreign enclave and erecting a fortress to bar all future access. Thanks to the bureaucratic and commercial reforms introduced by the new Bourbon monarchy out of Madrid, as well as to the vigorous regional administration provided during 1726 to 1733 by the Yucatecan governor, Antonio de Figueroa y Silva, Campeche's defenses and roads were improved, so that trade volumes gradually rebounded and even diversified to include such additional commodities as salt, hides, and tobacco.

Late Colonial Heyday (1739–1821)

Campeche attained an enhanced legal standing during the War of Jenkins's Ear against England, when its previously delegated office of deputy governor was elevated by royal decree in 1744 to a full *Tenientazgo del Rey* (king's lieutenancy), indicating that this office was to henceforth be appointed directly from Spain and rank second only to that of the provincial governors. As commercial traffic throughout the Gulf of Mexico and Caribbean Sea resurged once peace was restored, the town revived so significantly that a report submitted in 1756 indicated that fishermen and sailors were even beginning to erect houses outside its walls. Two years later the royal powder magazine was relocated about a mile southeast of its walls to prevent accidents.

Although Campeche was spared any direct blockade when war erupted against Great Britain in 1762, Spain's rapid defeat during that conflict prompted a shaken King Charles III to finance the upgrading of all Crown installations throughout the Americas, so that Campeche's defenses were improved. More significantly, trade throughout the Spanish empire was further liberalized, opening up transatlantic and Gulf traffic so that transportation costs came down and prices for imported merchandise declined; exports of Yucatecan produce through the port also gathered greater impetus, and in 1777 the town was elevated by the Crown to the full status of a city. Its defenses continued to be strengthened, especially during the American War of Independence, resulting in considerable expenditures financed by the general prosperity engendered throughout Spain's empire by the Bourbon economic reforms.

An institution to treat leprosy, called the Hospital de San Lázaro, was created south of the city in September 1796 (later being immortalized in the Justo Sierra novel *Un año en el hospital de San Lázaro*). By the end of the eighteenth century, the population of the city and its suburbs had soared to approximately 17,000 people, being classified as 8,200 Spaniards or Spanish-American Creoles, 1,800 blacks and mulattoes, plus 7,000 Indians—the latter figure calculated according to the Church registry of 1803, which enumerated 1,747 indigenous families.

Yet despite its resurgence, Campeche still remained a relatively minor port. Trade slowed during the French Revolutionary Wars, and on 19 February 1805 the British frigate HMS *Surveillante* captured two vessels outside its anchorage, then two days later sent boat parties in to cut out another four. Campeche was also such a political backwater that it was to remain unaffected by Mexico's struggle for independence from Spain, which exploded in the much more densely populated central highlands as of September 1810. A liberal faction called the *sanjuanistas* and a conservative group known as the *rutineros* engaged in a local war of words at Campeche, yet the

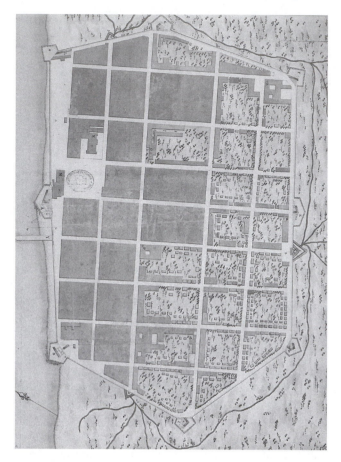

Map of Campeche as surveyed in 1772, then copied seven years later by the military engineer Brig. Agustín Crame; north is toward upper left. (Servicio Histórico Militar and Servicio Geográfico del Ejército, Madrid)

city submitted to an approaching insurgent expedition under Gen. Juan A. Fernández on 13 September 1821, embracing full Mexican independence four days later.

Yucatecan Dominance (1822–1856)

Loyalist holdouts in Mérida refused to acquiesce, however, so that Campeche seceded from Yucatán on 5 November 1821, inaugurating a strained "tug-of-war" period during which the port city upheld the new central government while the province of Yucatán oscillated between loyalty to Spain and outright nationhood. Campeche's commerce was to be directly affected by this schism, because the Yucatecans dealt exclusively with Spanish Cuba through Sisal, while *campechanos* were reduced to trading with Veracruz and New Orleans. Early in 1824 the Mérida authorities further dispatched a 1,500-man army under Col. José Segundo Carvajal—called the Columna Volante de la Unión (Flying Column of the Union)—to reclaim their breakaway port, but this so-called Guerra de la Columna (War of the Column) ended without

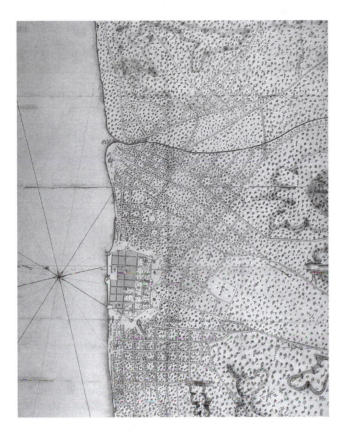

The city and its surrounding environs, ca. 1779; north is toward upper left. (British Museum and Servicio Histórico Militar, Madrid)

4,000 troops under Vicente Miñón pushed northeast through Champotón, Seybaplaya, and Lerma without encountering resistance to invest the 3,500 Yucatecans holding Campeche under Santiago Méndez. Yet despite overrunning La Atalaya, Eminencia Hill, and the San Román suburb by November, this federal host could not fully carry the city itself and so became bogged down in a stalemate. Eventually Miñón was recalled on 29 January 1843 and replaced by the federal general Matías de la Peña y Barragán, who decided to reinvigorate operations that March by outflanking the secessionists and disembarking 2,500 troops at Telchac in north-central Yucatán to threaten Mérida from its rear. Instead, though, he was checked at Tixcocob by López de Llergo on 10 April, then compelled to request terms two weeks later, sailing away in defeat by 26 May. One month later Gen. Pedro Ampudia lifted the federal siege of Campeche, leaving it still in Yucatecan hands. The city was to chafe under their domination, launching several abortive insurrections, while Yucatán remained neutral in the ensuing war between Mexico and the United States from 1846 to 1848.

Struggle for Statehood (1857–1867)

Eventually, a 150-man coup organized by the young liberal politicians Leandro Domínguez and Pedro Baranda seized Campeche's Maestranza (factory district) on the night of 6–7 August 1857, backed by Col. Alejandro García's artillery battery. Three days later, the Yucatecan garrison retired to Sisal, and Campeche withstood yet another siege from late September through November before finally winning its freedom from Yucatán and achieving full statehood within the Mexican Republic by May 1858.

Some conservative factions in Yucatán refused to accept this separation of their province's traditional sea outlet, however, so that during the French military intervention into central Mexico five and a half years later, Campeche became blockaded by the squadron of Capt. Georges Charles Cloué, then invested shortly before Christmas of 1863 by a small conservative Yucatecan army under Gen. Felipe Navarrete. Heavy bombardments and assaults from 4 to 15 January 1864 claimed several hundred lives on both sides, after which liberal Gov. Pablo García requested terms. A series of parleys resulted in the city's capitulation to the French by 26 January, so that it subsequently became reincorporated into Yucatán as part of Mexico's new conservative empire. The tour made by the French-installed Empress Carlota visited Campeche between 11 and 16 November 1865, but when the imperial government's fortunes began to wane a couple of years later, García was able to disembark near Lerma on 23 December 1866 with 500 liberal troops and raise enough local volunteers to besiege Gen. Juan Espejo's conservative garrison inside Campeche four days afterward. A Yucatecan relief column was beaten off, and after a 155-day encirclement, the liberals stormed the ramparts on 1 June 1867 and reclaimed their city.

any assault against Col. Ignacio de la Roca's defiant garrison within Campeche.

On 20 May 1824, Antonio López de Santa Anna reached the port, having been sent from Mexico City to bring the recalcitrant province of Yucatán peacefully into the republic. His diplomacy proved largely successful, although four years after his departure, Yucatán again broke away from Mexico in November 1829—provoking renewed frictions with Campeche, which again stood by the central government. On 4 August 1834 a small Campechan army under Francisco de Paula Toro (Santa Anna's brother-in-law) fought its way into the provincial capital of Mérida, temporarily restoring it to federal rule. But six years afterward, the roles were reversed when Yucatán seceded once more, this time invading Campeche. First a naval blockade was imposed, then on 2 April 1840 a small expedition appeared under Sebastián López de Llergo and Santiago Imán, besieging the city. After a lengthy bombardment, Campeche's garrison requested terms on 6 June, capitulating ten days later. Henceforth, the city was to suffer appreciably from two decades of Yucatecan occupation, not least by being cut off from its usual Mexican market at Veracruz.

Finally, late in August 1842, a counterexpedition organized by the federal government captured El Carmen, and

Porfirian Modernization (1868–1910)

Campeche was at last free of Yucatecan control, yet the decades of warfare had taken their toll: the 1869 census revealed only 80,366 inhabitants living in the entire state of Campeche—a decrease of 6,089 people from nine years before—and a figure that would only increase to 85,799 by 1874. Five years later, the capital's population was measured at 15,190 residents.

As a result of the emergence of Gen. Porfirio Díaz as the nation's new strongman in Mexico City, however, turmoil diminished over the next several decades, allowing the port city to take some modest steps toward modernization. Its first telegraph went into operation as of 16 September 1871; roads were improved; a naval base was established at Lerma in October 1883 to take advantage of its slightly deeper waters; and the old colonial era ramparts began to be torn down as of a decade later, to permit more unimpeded access to the city jetty and fishermen's wharf. However, Campeche's anchorage still remained so shallow—being a mere 10 feet deep—that seagoing ships had to hover almost 10 miles out in the Gulf to discharge their cargoes by lighter; thus, the bulk of regional produce was soon being exported through the rival ports of Sisal or Progreso. Inland, Campeche's state economy continued to be dominated by large agricultural concerns that exploited peasant laborers almost to the point of slavery.

From 1892 to 1902 the coastal capital bore the official name of Campeche de Baranda, in honor of the state's founding father, Pedro Baranda. Yet its unrelenting poverty and underdevelopment were underscored by the census of 1900, which found that the state population had again diminished to 82,286 people—approximately 18,000 of whom resided in the capital—while three years later another study revealed that less than 19 percent of the total could read or write. The Bank of Campeche was founded in June 1903, yet little other progress ensued before Porfirio Díaz was finally driven from Mexico City by the Revolution of 1910, which ushered in another period of national upheaval.

Modern Era (1911–Present)

Campeche was initially unaffected by the revolts and countercoups that gripped Central Mexico and eventually exploded into the Mexican Revolution, until the rebel chieftain Venustiano Carranza four years later appointed Col. Joaquín Mucel Acereto as new state governor. He arrived with a small army on 9 September 1914 and began implementing much-needed social reforms, such as the freeing of indentured plantation workers and improved public education. As a minor backwater of the troubled nation, Campeche was spared any direct involvement in the continuous fighting until 12 December 1923, when the 40th Infantry Battalion under Lt.-Col. José María Vallejo joined the national army's mutiny in support of Adolfo de la Huerta against President Alvaro Obregón. Within a few weeks, however, the rebels were cor-

nered in Tabasco, and Campeche was restored to federal control by 19 April 1924.

By 1950 the city's population had grown to 31,279 inhabitants, out of a total of 122,098 within the entire state, and it was finally linked by rail the next year with both Mexico City and Mérida. Twenty years later, the capital's population was measured at 69,506 residents. Curiously, having been bypassed by so many modern urbanization efforts, Campeche has retained much of its colonial charm—being adorned with ancient fortresses and churches, colorful buildings, plus shady squares—and its population in 1990 stood at a manageable 150,518 inhabitants.

For reading on the history of Campeche or Mexico, please consult the Select Bibliography at the end of this volume.

Guadalajara

Mexico's second-largest city and the core of its cultural heartland, as exemplified by such archetypal symbols as tequila, mariachi music, broad-brimmed *charro* cowboy hats, and the *jarabe tapatío* (Mexican hat dance).

Initial Settlements (1531–1541)

At the time of Hernán Cortés's subjugation of Mexico City in August 1521, this territory lay beyond the scope of the Aztec empire, so that its seminomadic Chichimecan tribesmen had to be subjugated once the victorious Spaniards began to disperse. The particular motivation behind this penetration into the northern highlands ensured that they would become a distinct new Spanish jurisdiction. Late in December 1529, the president of the governing *Audiencia* (high tribunal) in Mexico City, Nuño Beltrán de Guzmán—uneasy at the prospect of Cortés's impending return after a lengthy stay in Spain, during which the local *Audiencia* had often acted against his interests—decided to resign from office and lead an army of 500 Spanish conquistadors and 7,000 to 8,000 Mexican auxiliaries to carve out a semiautonomous fiefdom of his own.

Guzmán began his invasion by a devastating sweep through communities of Coca-speaking Tecuexe farmers, capturing their religious capital of Tonalá by 25 March 1530 and securing its queen, along with numerous lesser subchieftains. He installed a small garrison and pressed deeper into Chichimecan territory, soon writing to Emperor Charles V in Madrid to lay claim to a vast new province, which he hoped would be named New Galicia after his natal province in Spain (comprising most of the modern-day states of Jalisco, Zacatecas, and Nayarit). The Crown responded favorably by the end of that same year by appointing Guzmán as governor.

Guzmán's subordinate Juan de Oñate was thereupon commissioned on 15 October 1531 to found New Galicia's first Spanish settlement near Nochistlán, to be named Guadalajara after Guzmán's birthplace in Spain (originally a corruption of

Modern rendering of Guadalajara's sixteenth-century coat of arms. (Luis Páez Brotchie)

the Arabic term *Wad-al-Hidjara* or "River of Stones"). The new town was officially constituted as of 5 January 1532, yet only grew to sixteen blocks in size before Guzmán ordered it relocated to a more accessible site on 24 May 1533, lower down in the mountains. As a result, Guadalajara's colonists departed that June and began resettling farther southwest at Tonalá by 8 August of that same year.

However, the *Audiencia* in Mexico City then claimed that this latter town lay within its jurisdiction, even dispatching a *corregidor* (municipal magistrate) to assume office over the reconstituted community and its district. Guadalajara was therefore shifted again in February 1535 to north of the Santiago River—the purported borderline between both territories, then called the Espíritu Santo River—and resettled by 12 March into Tlacotán, 3 miles west of modern Tlacotlán. A church and thirty blocks of wooden homes and straw shacks were duly erected there over the next several years, while Guadalajara's *cabildo* (town council) enjoyed considerable autonomy because of the administrative strife prevailing between both rival authorities, which finally culminated when Guzmán was arrested and sent captive to Spain in 1538 by his Crown-appointed successor, Gov. Diego Pérez de la Torre.

On 8 November 1539, councilman Santiago de Aguirre succeeded in obtaining a royal decree that restored the lands south of the Santiago River to New Galicia's control, while

simultaneously elevating Guadalajara to the status of a city, entitled to its own coat of arms. Less than a year and a half later, a major Indian insurrection erupted at Nochistlán, swiftly spreading as far southwest as the Nayarit Range and becoming known as the Mixtón War. Many isolated ranchers retreated toward Guadalajara, while Spanish reinforcements rushed to their aid from other parts of Mexico. The first two such companies, under Lt.-Gov. Cristóbal de Oñate and the veteran conquistador Pedro de Alvarado, were defeated, however, so that the rebel leader Tenamaxtle, or "Diego el Zacateco"—emboldened by these successes—pushed south out of his mountain fastnesses and attacked Guadalajara itself on 28 September 1541. Despite heavy losses and considerable material damage, its garrison managed to repel this assault, although once the warrior throngs withdrew two days later (leaving behind thousands of casualties, mostly because of disease and malnourishment), Guadalajara's frightened Spanish survivors—inspired by an impassioned speech from the female householder Beatríz Hernández—decided to abandon the exposed locale and transfer 15 miles farther southwest, beyond a large ravine in the safer Atemajac Valley.

Foundation (1541–1559)

The Tlacotán site was therefore emptied on 8 October 1541, and the next day plots were distributed among sixty-three new residents representing twenty households at the new clearance near the loyal Tecuexe village of Mezquitán, a tributary of larger Atlemaxaque farther to its west. Thirteen days later the viceroy, Antonio de Mendoza, quit Mexico City with an army of 600 Spanish troops and 50,000 indigenous auxiliaries to crush the insurrection. Brushing aside smaller rebel units, he invested 12,000 of Tenamaxtle's followers at their main mountain stronghold of Nochistlán by 19 November, fighting his way to the top five days later and taking 8,000 captives. On 8 December another major bastion fell at the nearby Mixtón de Juchipila, some 1,500 Chichimecans being slain during the initial onslaught, while many others among the 3,000 prisoners were savagely executed afterward as a deterrent against future uprisings. Both assaults brought large-scale fighting to an end, columns being then detached to pursue lesser groupings, while de Velasco turned to implementing further measures to secure this frontier province against hostile acts before returning to Mexico City. A string of tiny keeps was duly established along the *camino real* (royal highway) to provide sanctuaries for Spanish travelers, while the new city of Guadalajara was also strengthened to furnish a rallying point against future troubles.

Its residents had already settled in along the eastern banks of the San Juan de Dios Creek and were joined by the Franciscan friar Antonio de Segovia with his missionaries and 500 Christianized Indians, transferred from Tetlán into a new suburb called San Juan Bautista Analco (later changed to Asunción de Analco, then finally to San José Analco). On 5 February 1542

Panoramic view over the city from its cathedral rooftop, ca. 1880–1897; note the flat landscape extending toward the distant mountains. (Library of Congress)

Guadalajara's new city councilors held their first official meeting; then in May a large contingent of Mexican auxiliaries were furthermore given lands along the western banks of its creek as a reward for their services during the Mixtón war, this suburb becoming known as Mexicaltzingo. Such a concentration of forces provided the necessary nucleus for Guadalajara to take firm root, its populace constituting perhaps eighty Spanish households—approximately 300 people—plus a like number of blacks and mulattoes and 3,000 Indians in adjoining suburbs.

The new city's geographic setting also proved to be most amenable, as it overlooked a fertile and almost level plain falling off gently northward into the Valley of Atemajac. Because of the elevation at 5,100 feet above sea level, its climate was pleasantly mild, the greatest heat of the summer months being alleviated by cooling rains. The surrounding expanse of grassland was perfect for grazing livestock and growing wheat, while the Santiago and Verde rivers that intersected near the fledgling city were two of the only major waterways in the region, proving invaluable for irrigation and hydraulic pur-

poses. The first threshing mill to produce flour and bread was established in October 1543 by Juan Saldívar, and that same year the residents of Compostela, Guadalajara, Culiacán, and La Purificación jointly petitioned Charles V to have New Galicia separated by the Pope from the bishopric of Michoacán so as to create their own independent diocese.

The emperor approved, and also expanded Guadalajara's municipal boundaries in 1545 to incorporate Tetlán and Atlemaxaque. So attractive was the city's landscape that when the first bishop appointed to New Galicia—the bespectacled Pedro Gómez Maraver, a former dean of the Oaxaca cathedral—reached Guadalajara on 13 December 1546, he chose it as his future see rather than the nominal provincial capital of Compostela in Nayarit, which was envisioned in the papal bull *Super specula militantes Ecclesiae* of 13 July 1548. Guadalajara's adobe, thatched-roof church—dedicated to San Miguel Arcángel in honor of the townspeople's survival against Tenamaxtle's assault on 28 September 1541, and today supplanted by the Santa María de Gracia church—was consequently elevated into a cathedral on 12 December 1548.

However, that same summer a major silver strike occurred in the mountains at Zacatecas, which reduced the number of Guadalajara's Spanish householders to a mere thirty-five, as dozens of men departed to seek their fortunes as prospectors. Still, the diminished city remained sufficiently viable because of its fertile setting and it retained perhaps 250 Spanish residents according to an estimate made in 1554. They even managed to import a cathedral organ from Mexico City two years later and found a hospital dedicated to the Santa Veracruz (Holy Cross) by 1557. When the Franciscan Pedro de Ayala arrived as New Galicia's second bishop two years afterward, he also chose to reside at Guadalajara, despite the fact that the city was still not officially designated as his see.

Provincial Capital (1560–1809)

The locale seemed so ideal that even New Galicia's *Audiencia* transferred into the city from Compostela in December 1560, transforming Guadalajara into the de facto provincial capital—although such a move was not legally sanctioned until King Philip II at last issued a decree from Toledo on 10 May 1562, which approved the shift of all administrative, ecclesiastical, and fiscal offices into the city.

Various setbacks were then endured: In 1565 a splendid new cathedral was commenced under the supervision of Alonso de Rubalcava, which featured stone foundations, adobe walls, plus a wooden ceiling and floor, but it had scarcely been completed when it burned down on 30 May 1574 during the celebration of Pascua del Espíritu Santo (the Feast of the Holy Spirit—that is, Pentecost Sunday), after a salute carelessly fired in an adjacent corral at the height of the service sparked a conflagration. The indigenous population also declined noticeably throughout much of that same period, on account of frequent outbreaks of typhus and other epidemics, so that suburban Analco's tributaries, for example, plunged from 1,000 heads of households in 1570 to 373 by 1582 and a mere 160 by 1644.

Still, Guadalajara's Spanish population had stabilized at approximately 300 by 1586 (roughly a quarter the size of Zacatecas at that time), so that the following year its bishop, Fr. Domingo Arzola, founded the twenty-bed Hospital Real de San Miguel, the Crown financed the expansion of the Santa Veracruz Hospital in 1588, and the recently arrived Jesuits opened a school called the Colegio de Santo Tomás de Aquino two years afterward. Gradually, *haciendas* (rural estates) began to radiate outward from the city into the interconnected series of flat-floored, ancient lake basins that comprised its agricultural domain, an area measuring roughly 60 miles wide by 120 miles long, so that by the end of the sixteenth century, Guadalajara boasted approximately 500 to 600 Spanish residents spread among 160 households, plus a thousand or so free mulattoes and black slaves and 600 Indians. The Order of San Juan de Dios assumed the administration of Santa Veracruz Hospital in 1606, increasing its capacity to forty beds, while a

new cathedral was completed by the architect Martín Casillas and reconsecrated as of 19 February 1618.

Two years later, a visitor estimated that the number of Spanish households had increased to 200, while New Galicia's small capital was now conducting sufficient commerce to sustain the activities of a score of wealthy merchants. However, most Spanish residents still remained occupied in various minor judicial, administrative, fiscal, or military roles, while blacks and Indians toiled as laborers, which meant that the bucolic city did not experience any significant additional growth. As a result, the new Virgen de las Mercedes church proposed by Bishop Francisco de Rivera in 1626 was not actually completed until 95 years later, while a building intended as the Casas Reales (Royal Offices)—commenced in 1643 to a design by Juan Francisco Espino—could not be completed until a century and a half afterward. As Guadalajara was safely removed from any seaborne descents by foreign raiders along the coasts or Indian war-bands roaming the interior mountain ranges, it did not require the expense of fortifications, so that its development throughout the remainder of the seventeenth century was to only be restricted by meager local resources, occasional outbreaks of disease or earthquakes, as well as its relative isolation so far from the main hub of economic life in central Mexico.

The decay of Spain's overseas empire under the last Hapsburg monarchs further hampered Guadalajara's development during the latter half of the seventeenth century, its urban population estimated to have increased to a mere 500 Spanish households, a like number of mulattoes and black slaves, and as many Indian tributaries by 1700. A small college called the Seminario Conciliar de San José was founded the next year (today the Guadalajara museum), while the neglected Hospital Real de San Miguel was ceded by New Galicia's penniless *Audiencia* in 1704 to the Bethlemite Order. The Bethlemites increased its capacity to forty-five beds and vastly improved its services under the name of Hospital Real de San Miguel de Belén.

It was to be the invigorating spirit of Spain's reformist new Bourbon rulers in Madrid that truly injected life into the backwater provincial capital, along with the entire viceroyalty. As Mexico's mining, agricultural, and trade volumes steadily escalated, the city benefited by serving as a clearinghouse for its own rich hinterland, as well as being the sole local source of credit or capital. Such commercialization soon spurred the displacement of small farmers by ever larger estates throughout the valley system, resulting in enhanced bulk traffic through the city. This rise in prosperity in turn helped fund the completion of such projects as the Santa Mónica convent by 1733, while an ecclesiastical census conducted five years later indicated that Guadalajara's population had soared to more than 10,000 inhabitants, who weathered a measles epidemic in 1747, as well as a heavy earthquake three years later that damaged the cathedral and numerous other edifices. Commerce

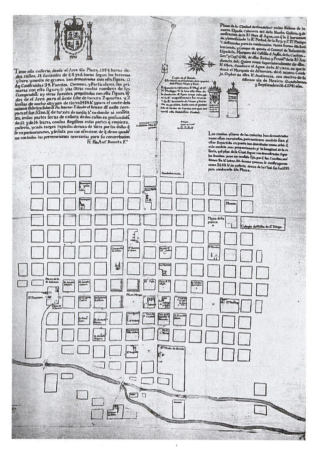

Map of Guadalajara in September 1741 by Fr. Pedro Antonio Buzeta, showing how a new aqueduct was to distribute water from Colli Hill to two dozen fountains placed throughout the city; north is to the right. Note the even grid pattern of city blocks set upon flat terrain and unrestricted by any military defenses. (Archive of Indies, Seville)

increased still further after the first textile factories appeared by 1765, supplementing the output already being generated by the city's existing tanneries and soap works.

By 1770, Guadalajara's population had risen to 23,768 residents, and its urban area expanded modestly northward under the vigorous impulse of its bishop, Fr. Antonio Alcalde, who oversaw the construction of new religious structures—such as Guadalupe church, commenced in 1777—as well as housing for the poor, which resulted in the creation of the new parishes of Nuestra Señora de Guadalupe by 1782 and San Juan Bautista Mexicalcingo seven years afterward. A civilian intendancy was created despite an outbreak of disease in 1786; the Casas Reales were completed four years afterward; and a census in 1792 recorded a total of 24,249 inhabitants spread among Guadalajara and its indigenous suburbs of Analco, Mezquitán, Tetlán, and Mexicalcingo. The inhabitants were classified as 9,572 Spaniards or Spanish-American Creoles, 6,538 mulattoes and blacks, 3,898 "mixed castes," and 4,241 Indians. In addition, Guadalajara's Real Universidad Lit-

eraria (Royal Literary University) was opened in March 1792 to supplant the former Jesuit College of Santo Tomás; the city's first printing press went into operation the next year; and Bishop Alcalde inaugurated a new 1,000-bed Hospital Real de San Miguel de Belén in May 1794, although the *Audiencia* president accused its Bethlemite administrators of malfeasance in 1793, so that the order withdrew their services and the vast institution was idled. Nonetheless, as a sign of the city's growing wealth and influence, local merchants were granted the right to form their own *consulado* (merchant guild) by the Crown in June 1795, enhancing their ability to conduct trade independent of Mexico City. And the gifted Manuel Tolsá—the most famous architect in all of New Spain—was hired to design a Hospicio in his polished neoclassical style to serve as a city orphanage, although an economic downturn then delayed its construction.

The Spanish government had become embroiled with the French revolutionary movement, thereby spurring the Royal Navy to impose a crippling Atlantic blockade. Guadalajara and its Pacific coast jurisdiction were to be less adversely affected over the next several years than other regions of the viceroyalty, especially after a French army furthermore invaded Spain and deposed Ferdinand VII in the summer of 1808, which meant the British instead became allies and some new seaborne contacts were permitted. By 1810 Guadalajara was at the peak of its colonial splendor and influence with a population of approximately 35,000 residents. Its judicial authority now extended as far afield as California, embracing 600,000 subjects scattered throughout western New Spain, and its cultural amenities attracted many visitors from among the provincial elites.

Independence and Early Republican Era (1810–1840)
The loosening of Spain's imperial ties, however, because of the French occupation of the homeland, had sparked a movement toward Mexican independence. The viceroyalty's mixed-heritage Creoles had grown especially resentful of the preferments routinely accorded peninsular-born Spaniards, as well as the heavy burdens of taxation. Consequently, when the village priest Miguel Hidalgo y Costilla ignited a revolt at Guanajuato in September 1810, Guadalajara was taken in the initial wave of patriot euphoria by the insurgents José Antonio Torres and Miguel Gómez Portugal. Additionally, when the rebel chieftain Hidalgo was subsequently defeated in his attempts to march upon Mexico City and Querétaro, he arrived at Guadalajara in mid-November with 7,000 riders to establish a new headquarters (as well as to execute 400 royalist sympathizers). However, this occupation of the city proved short-lived, as a monarchist army under Gen. Félix María Calleja fought its way through the central highlands, threatening to retake Guadalajara by the second week of January 1811. Over the objections of his military adviser, Capt. Ignacio Allende, Hidalgo led his 35,000 ill-disciplined followers 20

miles outside the unfortified city to offer battle at Calderón Bridge. On 17 January, Calleja's 14,000 royalists drove into these rebel positions, being briefly checked before an insurgent grenade accidentally detonated one of their own ammunition wagons, creating widespread panic. A monarchist cavalry charge thereupon carried the day, although Hidalgo and Allende retired in good order, despite suffering 3,000 casualties. Calleja—who had lost only 400 men killed or wounded—was slow to pursue, not entering Guadalajara until four days later and installing Brig. José de la Cruz as its new royalist governor.

The city was to remain under the control of monarchist forces for the remaining decade of this struggle, and the security it afforded in such troubled times prompted many rural residents to seek refuge in Guadalajara, so that its urban population grew to an estimated 39,700 residents by 1813. Conditions in the crowded capital became even more difficult after a major earthquake struck on 31 May 1818, many of its buildings damaged, including the cathedral, whose towers and facade collapsed. Nevertheless, more waves of refugees, generated during the final offensives of the war for independence, caused its population to soar to beyond 60,000 inhabitants by the time its royalist defenders finally surrendered, without a fight, in the summer of 1821.

Although the independent young nation was beset by many economic and political problems in the aftermath of the fall of Spanish rule, Guadalajara's fertile surroundings and unexploited coastlines afforded considerable venues for recuperation. As Veracruz was no longer legally recognized as Mexico's primary port, goods could now flow more freely through diverse Pacific ports, while foreign developers invested funds and introduced technological innovations. As a result, Guadalajara experienced such remarkable growth during this boom period that it eclipsed Puebla as Mexico's second-largest city, with a population figure that remained stable at roughly 40,000 inhabitants throughout the decade of 1820–1830.

Sieges and Ordeals (1841–1875)

Such economic development was to also bring Guadalajara to the very forefront of the political rivalries afflicting the young nation. On 8 August 1841, the city's military commander—Brig. Mariano Paredes y Arrillaga—rose in a prearranged coup against President Anastasio Bustamante, being joined shortly thereafter by several other generals (including Santa Anna at Veracruz). Together the rebels drove upon Mexico City and forced Bustamante from office by the end of September. Three years later Paredes used his position at Guadalajara to spearhead a second revolt, this time against Santa Anna's new regime, by rebelling on 30 October 1844 and quickly gathering adherents throughout neighboring states. When Santa Anna marched northwestward out of the national capital the next month to check Paredes's advancing forces in the state of Querétaro, the Mexico City garrison

mutinied behind him on 6 December, so that Santa Anna surrendered power by early January 1845.

Later that same year Paredes was placed in command of the army being raised at San Luis Potosí to contest the forthcoming annexation of Texas by the United States. He revolted in frustration at the inadequate support from the central government and was acclaimed president in the national capital by January 1846, only to then suffer the indignity of yet another revolt emanating out of Guadalajara when his local governor and garrison commander were arrested on 20 May and replaced by the liberal politician Juan N. Cumplido, with support from Cols. José María Yáñez, J. Guadalupe Montenegro, and Santiago Xicoténcatl. Notwithstanding the fact that the Mexican-American War had erupted a few weeks previously, Paredes was obliged to divert a 6,000-man army to besiege the rebellious city, whose vanguard arrived on 12 June and initiated a protracted encirclement. Wishing to invigorate this siege operation against Guadalajara so as to free up his troops to counteract the American invasion, Paredes was preparing to depart Mexico City at dawn on 5 August when he too was deposed by a mutiny, paving the way for Santa Anna's return.

Consequently, Guadalajara was not to be featured in the U.S. campaign that seized Veracruz and Mexico City and ended with the Treaty of Guadalupe Hidalgo, ceding the largely empty Mexican provinces of California, Nevada, Utah, Colorado, Arizona, and New Mexico by May 1848. Bitter recriminations thereupon ensued between the defeated nation's conservative and liberal factions, the former wishing to eliminate the weakness and anarchy of republican rule by imposing a strong centralized authority, while liberals called for broader sociopolitical reforms so as to include more citizens in their country's affairs. Many skirmishes flared locally, such as when the conservative "Plan del Hospicio" was proclaimed at Guadalajara on 20 October 1852, the city briefly besieged by the liberal forces of General J. Vicente Miñón that same December.

The liberals eventually fought their way into national power when Santa Anna was driven from the presidency for the fifth and final time in August 1855, so that liberal officials such as Gen. Santos Degollado came to be installed into office as governor of Jalisco. He initiated a modest series of urban reforms intended to highlight the change of administrative philosophies, such as selling off the colonial-era *ejidos* (commons) so as to raise funds for a fine new public theater in San Agustín square, designed by Jacobo Gálvez. Yet the much more drastic reforms announced in February 1857 by the national congress in Mexico City sparked a general conservative uprising, so that President Ignacio Comonfort fled into exile and his successor, Justice Minister Benito Juárez, retired into Guanajuato to begin organizing liberal resistance. Meanwhile, Brig. Félix María Zuloaga was acclaimed as a rival conservative president in Mexico City and dispatched an army of 5,400 regulars under Gen. Luis G. Osollo.

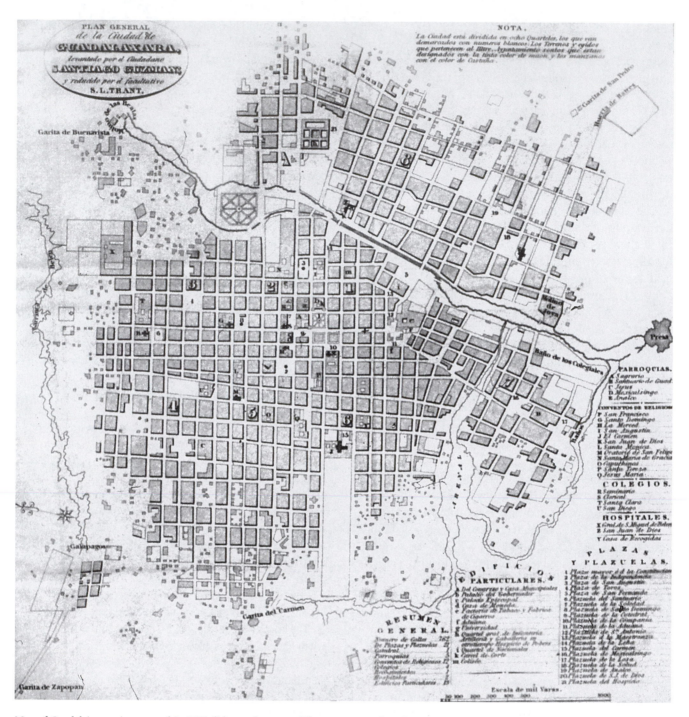

Map of Guadalajara as it appeared in 1800; lithograph executed forty-two years later by S. L. Trant, based upon an original drawing by Santiago Guzmán. North is toward the left. (Archivo General de la Nación, Mexico)

On 15 February 1858, the fugitive Juárez retreated into Guadalajara to reinstall his liberal government, after which Osollo's regulars crushed a liberal militia throng under Gen. Anastasio Parrodi the next month at Salamanca, forcing the vanquished back upon Jalisco's capital. News of this defeat led the city garrison to mutiny on 13 March, parading Juárez and his cabinet before a firing squad, only to be saved at the last moment by the eloquence of Minister Guillermo Prieto, who persuaded the soldiers to lower their weapons. The president was nonetheless compelled to flee toward the Pacific coast one week later with ninety liberal troopers, leaving Parrodi to surrender the city to Osollo's approaching conservative army on 21 March, which entered triumphantly two days later.

Guadalajara was to be contested as a political prize when

Street scene in Guadalajara, ca. 1880–1897, looking north toward the distant cathedral spires; note the trolley tracks recently laid amid the old cobblestones. (Library of Congress)

liberal forces moved to counterattack from outlying regions, their 1st Division arriving a month later under Gens. Degollado and Pedro Ogazón Rubio to threaten an assault, only to be checked by conservative Gens. Francisco García Casanova and José María Blancarte, who obliged the attackers to withdraw by 13 June. Undeterred by this repulse, in additon to their defeat early the following month by Brig. Miguel Miramón at Atenquique ravine (near modern Ciudad Guzmán), other liberal forces managed to reimpose a siege upon Guadalajara on 3 July, fighting their way in as far as the Hospicio before being obliged to retire on 21 July when Miramón reappeared.

The city remained in conservative hands for the next couple of months until Miramón had to forsake Jalisco altogether to bolster the hard-pressed conservative army of Gen. Leonardo Márquez Araujo in central Mexico. During his absence, the liberals initiated a third offensive against Guadalajara when Degollado bested Casanova at Cuevitas near Techaluta on 21 September 1858 and then marshaled numerous for-

mations outside the city six days later to again attempt to carry it by storm. After repeated onslaughts against its extemporized defenses, the conservative garrison commander Blancarte agreed to capitulate on 28 October with the victors entering the next day amid great disorder. Many prominent conservatives were lynched, Blancarte was summarily shot, and looting and pillaged raged.

Guadalajara also suffered from punitive measures enacted by its liberal occupiers, such as expropriating and tearing down ancient church properties to make way for public thoroughfares. Two months later, conservative armies under Miramón and Márquez began to fight their way back into Jalisco, prompting liberals to evacuate the gutted capital rather than become trapped behind its frail defenses. In a series of freewheeling encounters along the banks of the Santiago River, from Puente Grande near Tolotlán as far as Atequiza, the advancing conservatives bested Degollado and Ogazón until a clash at a San Miguel ranch 3 miles from Poncitlán on 14

December finally allowed Miramón and Márquez to reoccupy the battered city that same day.

The reconquest of Mexico's second-largest city resulted in Miramón being offered the conservative presidency early in January 1859, which he initially refused, while long-suffering Guadalajara endured yet another calamity when a powder magazine exploded inside its municipal palace on 10 January, ruining the edifice. Miramón subsequently accepted the presidency on 2 February, his rival Márquez remaining behind as governor and military commander of Guadalajara. When Miramón marched down from the national capital to besiege the fugitive Juárez in Veracruz, a liberal army under Degollado took advantage by attempting to surprise Mexico City in late March 1859. Márquez rushed across with his Guadalajaran forces to effect a timely rescue, crushing Degollado on 10 April in the battle of Tacubaya, then had himself immodestly crowned with golden laurels in the cathedral upon his triumphal return into Jalisco's capital that May.

When a subsequent lull in the war was broken by Miramón's defeat of Degollado outside the city of Querétaro in mid-November 1859, the conservative president followed up his victory by marching into Guadalajara shortly thereafter and jealously arresting Márquez on a charge of theft. Yet no sooner did Miramón depart Jalisco to once again besiege Juárez in Veracruz than liberal Gen. José López Uraga arrived outside Guadalajara with 8,000 men, calling upon its conservative garrison commander—the French-born veteran Adrián Woll—to surrender. The latter refused, and López Uraga was wounded and captured during the ensuing assault. His successor, the bespectacled young Brig. Ignacio Zaragoza, withdrew in early June upon learning of the approach of Miramón's main conservative army.

Notwithstanding their repeated battlefield successes, the conservatives could not stem a rising tide of liberal support. When Miramón sortied from Guadalajara on 8 June 1860 with 6,000 soldiers to pursue Zaragoza, he was surprised to find the liberals dug into impregnable positions atop Zapotlán's crest between Ciudad Guzmán and Sayula. Then, 3,000 conservatives marching through Aguascalientes as reinforcements were scattered by liberal Gen. Jesús González Ortega, forcing the worried, conservative commander-in-chief to leave 5,000 men to hold Guadalajara under Gen. Severo del Castillo, while he hastened northeastward on 27 June to concentrate his remaining troops at Lagos de Moreno to bar the road leading into the national capital.

Disparate liberal formations coalesced into a vast host that pulverized Miramón's overmatched army at Silao on 10 August 1860 and then marched upon Guadalajara. Realizing that a major battle for the city was imminent, General del Castillo spent the next six weeks strengthening its defenses, even stripping its cathedral of precious ornaments to pay for these labors. The vanguard of González Ortega's weary, rain-sodden army finally appeared on 22 September, joined at San Pedro Tlaquepaque four days later by Ogazón's corps, which gradually raised the besiegers' numbers to 20,000 men. Their first siege opened fire on 27 September.

Over the ensuing month, hapless Guadalajara was pounded by 7,500 heavy shells, its water supply cut, hundreds of buildings destroyed or damaged, fires and diseases raged, paving stones were torn up, and bodies were buried in makeshift graveyards. Del Castillo arranged a truce on 29 October 1860 to allow for the evacuation of the pathetic remnants of the civilian population, after which 125 liberal fieldpieces resumed their bombardment and their infantry slowly pushed into the smoldering city. The conservative defenders' last hope of relief was extinguished when Márquez was defeated at nearby Zaplotanejo on 1 November, surrendering his 3,000 men and eighteen cannons to the encircling army. Del Castillo capitulated to González Ortega's subordinate Zaragoza two days later, receiving generous terms.

With the fall of Guadalajara, all liberal armies were now free to close in upon Mexico City, overwhelming Miramón's last stand outside its gates on 22 December 1860 and bringing an end to the so-called War of the Reform. Guadalajarans were left to painfully begin the reconstruction of their devastated city, many of whose colonial-era edifices were totally lost. The victorious liberal administration also expropriated even more church properties for public usage, even seizing the libraries of all religious institutions so as to lay the foundation for the first public library (not actually inaugurated until 1874).

However, Mexico's defeated conservatives had meanwhile secretly allied themselves with France, so that when Juárez's restored government defaulted on its foreign debts shortly thereafter, an expeditionary force disembarked at Veracruz in January 1862 and spearheaded a joint Franco-conservative effort to entirely supplant the republican form of government with an imperial regime. Columns battered their way into central Mexico over the next year and a half, occupying the national capital and eventually gaining Guadalajara without opposition on 8 January 1864. Liberal resistance nonetheless persisted throughout the countryside, until the imperial gains were reversed a couple of years later, and Jalisco's capital was evacuated by the retreating conservatives before their final defeat at Querétaro in May 1867.

Jalisco's capital slowly rebounded from these protracted ordeals, further hampered by the liberal government's insolvency and simmering political discontent. When the increasingly unpopular Juárez announced his re-election plans in 1871, another rash of military outbreaks ensued. Guadalajara was moreover struck by a major earthquake on 11 March 1875, which damaged many of its buildings; and when Juárez's successor as president, Sebastián Lerdo de Tejada, announced that same year that he too would run for a second term—thereby perpetuating his faction's stranglehold—the country was plunged into another period of rebellions, which propelled the war hero General Porfirio Díaz into office by November 1876.

Guadalajara's cathedral, ca. 1891. Its lower portions date from the early seventeenth century, yet the spires at left were added by the architect Manuel Gómez Ibarra to replace the pair that had collapsed during the May 1818 earthquake; its main cupola had also been reconstructed by Domingo Torres, repairing damage sustained by the March 1875 quake. (Library of Congress)

Porfirian Era and Mexican Revolution (1876–1920)

Surprisingly, strongman Díaz inaugurated an efficient regime, stifling all subsequent outbreaks of destabilizing unrest, while at the same time encouraging the industrialization and modernization of the war-weary nation. Guadalajara was to benefit from this enforced period of peaceful growth, although its agricultural-based economy did not expand as spectacularly as that of some other Mexican cities.

Nevertheless, Jalisco's capital experienced sufficient growth for its municipal boundaries to be enlarged when the state legislature allocated funds in 1885 to purchase the nearby Agua Azul springs from Antonio Álvarez del Castillo, which were drawn upon to meet increased city needs. La Joya swamp was also drained, and many new promenades and parks were cre-

ated for public recreation. More significantly, the first railway was inaugurated on 16 April 1888, linking Guadalajara with ever more distant markets. From 1879 to 1909, the urban population rose from 78,600 inhabitants to approximately 125,000.

Unfortunately, the economic strength and influx of foreign investment gained under the Porfirian regime was undermined by the resentment that also accumulated against the inequitable distribution of wealth, lack of broad-based social advancement, or any significant political participation. When Díaz stood for his eighth presidential term in 1910 he ordered the arrest of his rich and high-minded political opponent, Francisco Ignacio Madero. This tactic showed his refusal to campaign actively or justly, thereby causing a widespread national movement that drove him from office by the spring

Crowded market scene in Guadalajara, ca. 1880–1897, looking east toward the cathedral. Note the prevalence of two-story buildings. (Library of Congress)

of 1911. The country thereupon descended into the chaos of the Mexican Revolution, and Guadalajara was to change hands three times during one of the war's major offensives.

Early in July 1914, the revolutionary Gen. Alvaro Obregón's Ejército del Noroeste (Army of the Northwest) bore down upon the city out of the west to invest its Huertista garrison under Gen. José María Mier—who sallied to await his opponent at the rural La Vega railway station rather than offer resistance from within Guadalajara itself. Through bold maneuvering around the Tequila range, Obregón surprised Mier's rear stronghold on 6 July, then pulverized his paralyzed train convoy at Orendáin with long-range artillery fire. The trapped federal army disintegrated by dawn of 7 July, desperate units breaking away in hopes of at least regaining the state capital. Rather than pursue each fleeing unit individually, Obregón entered Zapopan that same evening, thereby barring all access

into the city and preventing the dispersed Huertistas from regrouping. When Mier attempted to flee from Guadalajara southward on 8 July with his 3,000 remaining men, he furthermore found Brig. Lucio Blanco's revolutionary cavalry blocking his escape route at El Castillo, and he was killed attempting to fight his way through. Obregón entered Guadalajara in triumph that same day, having achieved a spectacular victory that had cost the Huertistas 2,000 dead, 1,000 wounded, 5,000 captured, as well as sixteen fieldpieces, eighteen trains, and forty locomotives.

This setback helped convince the usurper Gen. Victoriano Huerta to vacate Mexico's presidential throne a week later, but other revolutionary leaders subsequently refused to acknowledge the succession of Obregón's superior, Venustiano Carranza, so that warfare renewed and Guadalajara once more became targeted. On 12 December 1914, its Carrancista garrison under Gen. Manuel M. Diéguez evacuated the uneasy city for Ciudad Guzmán, allowing a large army loyal to Pancho Villa to occupy the capital, uncontested, five days later. However, Diéguez's retirement proved to have been merely a strategic retreat, as he united with another small Carrancista army under Gen. Francisco Murguía to produce a combined force of 9,000 Carrancistas, which he led back through central Jalisco to invest the city on 17 January 1915.

In a two-day battle raging over Cuatro, Gachupín, and Santa María hills, Diéguez succeeded in defeating Guadalajara's 10,000 Villista defenders under Gens. Julián Medina, Melitón F. Ortega, and Calixto Contreras, thereby reclaiming the capital and holding it for the remainder of this conflict. (In a curious historical sidelight, a young painter serving as an officer on Diéguez's staff—David Alfaro Siqueiros—subsequently struck up friendships with numerous local artists during his four years of garrison duty, contributing to the evolution of a vigorous muralist style in the postrevolutionary era.)

Modern Expansion (1921–present)

The return to peace facilitated a spectacular rise in Guadalajara's fortunes. As the hub of a large and fertile region, the addition of modern rail facilities and an integrated highway system fueled a period of almost unbridled growth, the city's traditional economic producers—such as the tanneries and soap factories clustered around its old urban core— being encouraged to diversify and relocate to more ample grounds by such measures as passage of the Ley de Fomento Industrial (Industrial Development Law) in 1939, which would lead to the erection of numerous new factories producing cement, fertilizers, glass, and many other products in a new industrial park extending between kilometers 7 to 10 along the highway running toward Tequila.

The following year, Guadalajara's population was measured at 229,235 inhabitants, a figure that would soar exponentially over the next few decades as its economy multiplied in strength and rural-to-urban migration patterns accelerated throughout western Mexico. Such explosive growth caused Gov. Agustín Yáñez to begin converting the large wasteland south of the city into yet another new industrial park in 1957 with purpose-built rail connections and feeder highways. The ancient San Juan de Dios market in the urban core also made way for the 1,500-stall Mercado Libertador in December 1958, a relocation that would free the increasing volumes of traffic to flow westward out of the city center along Javier Mina Street. Municipal projects during Gov. Juan Gil Preciado's tenure from 1959 to 1965 also struggled to keep up with the demographic explosion that the city was undergoing, straining many services. From 1970 to 1990, the population more than doubled from 1,196,218 residents to 2,870,417 within the entire metropolitan area, a figure that reached an estimated total of 4 million by the year 2000 (although only 1,737,334 were recorded as living within the actual munici-

pal limits). Guadalajara's size, coupled with its historical association with traditional Mexican values, prompted it to serve as a cultural counterweight to the centralist domination in Mexico City.

For further reading on the history of Guadalajara and Mexico, please consult the Select Bibliography at the end of this volume.

Guanajuato

Mining camp that blossomed during the late colonial era into one of the world's wealthiest cities, then became the cradle of Mexican independence.

Origins (1539–1679)

After the surrender of the Aztec capital in central Mexico in 1521, columns of conquistadors fanned out to subdue the fallen empire's outlying vassal states, encountering particularly stiff resistance from the seminomadic Chichimec hunter-gatherer tribes of the stark northern highlands. Rich mineral deposits and fertile agricultural pockets nonetheless enticed Spanish settlers into this hostile region, and one hardy pioneer—Rodrigo Vázquez—was granted title twenty-five years later to found a cattle ranch in the territory "of the Chichimecans, near the source of a river which was called *Guanajuato*" by its Guamare-speaking natives (Guanajuato apparently being a Tarascan term signifying "Hills of the Frogs"). A few other ranchers may have preceded Vázquez into that narrow and sparsely populated mountain gorge, perhaps as early as 1539, although confirmatory documentation is today missing.

According to popular legend, a party of muleteers en route to the recently discovered mines of Zacatecas in 1548 chanced to encamp on Cubilete Hill beside the Guanajuato River, and their fire revealed silver streaks in the surrounding stone. But modern research has discounted this anecdotal evidence and instead determined that the actual discovery was more likely made four years later, during a chance patrol by military Capt. Juan de Jaso, who consequently decided to install a small garrison atop Cuarto Hill by 1554—one of several such outposts being created as way stations for a new road running northwest out of Mexico City.

It was not until early 1557 that portions of Guanajuato's main San Bernabé mineral vein were at last discovered (eventually being determined to extend 18 miles from southeast to northwest, averaging 200 feet in width), sparking an onrush of prospectors accompanied by their Tarascan, Otomí, and Aztec laborers. Francisco Velázquez de Lara, regional *alcalde mayor* (municipal magistrate) at Pátzcuaro, visited this booming mining camp to legally register its various claims and attempt to impose some civic order that same May, although his authority was soon challenged by rival officials. While this jurisdictional wrangle was being appealed to Mexico City, the great Mellado mine initiated operations on 15 May 1558, followed

Panoramic view across the city from atop San Miguel Hill, ca. 1909; note the *hacienda de beneficio* or "mineral treatment plant" in right foreground, as well as the century-old—yet still formidable—Alhóndiga de Granaditas granary looming at left center, with Cuarto Hill just to the north beyond it. (Carson, *Mexico: The Wonderland of the South*)

the next day by the Rayas mine (named for its owner Juan de Rayas).

Municipal government over this disperse agglomeration of properties, though, could not truly be imposed until the Viceroy Luis de Velasco "the Elder" resolved all jurisdictional disputes by appointing Perafán de Rivera as Guanajuato's *juez y superintendente* (judge and superintendent) in 1559, and that official arrived and took up residence in the tiny fort atop Cuarto Hill. Having also been furnished by the Crown with an ancient wooden icon of the Virgin of the Rosary—allegedly concealed in Santa Fe de Granada throughout its Moorish occupation—this new frontier-community henceforth became known as Santa Fe y Real de Minas de Guanajuato (Holy Faith and the Royal Mining District of Guanajuato).

Because of its far-flung extension, with private mines and mills dotting the undulating landscape, no single town could immediately be formed, although Cuarto Hill remained a strategic rallying point against occasional raids by Chichimec war parties. A small church was also completed as part of Santa Fe's hospital compound during 1560–1565 (whose foundations are still visible today beneath the western grounds of the modern Universidad de Guanajuato); when the viceroy Martín Enríquez de Almanza paid a visit five years later he recorded

the presence of roughly 600 Spanish mine owners, whose holdings now spread as far westward as Santa Ana.

In order to support the highland community's development, the viceroy ordered the creation of a town called Celaya farther to its southeast in 1571, whose residents were to exploit the surrounding fertile plains—soon dubbed the Bajío (Lowlands)—by planting wheat and raising livestock, so as to provide Guanajuato with a regular flow of provisions, as well as teams of horses and mules and the variety of leather goods necessary for its labors. Enríquez moreover elevated the mining camp itself to the status of an *alcaldía mayor* in 1574, so that its first *ayuntamiento* (municipal government) could be formed and impose its authority as far southwest as Silao and Irapuato.

Chichimec depredations declined after the Jesuit missionary Gonzalo de Tapia convinced them to settle peacefully at San Luis de la Paz in 1590; the total number of people living throughout Guanajuato's 2,000-square-mile district a decade later stood at roughly 4,000. New *casas reales* (royal offices) were completed at its administrative hub of Santa Fe by 1610, but silver output subsequently faltered because of the exhaustion of many surface deposits, floods at lower mine levels, a lack of steady capitalization, and the chaotic work methods used by the swarms of *buscones* (literally, "searchers")—free-lance miners hired to dig independently, retaining half of any ore that they found. Although Guanajuato's production never ceased altogether, it nonetheless lagged noticeably behind that of other mining centers. Zacatecas, for example, consumed fully a third of all the *azogue* (quicksilver) mercury used to treat Mexican ores in 1636, compared with only 7 percent at Guanajuato. Three years later, a mere eighty-five Spaniards remained as permanent Guanajuatan property owners, and no recognizable town as yet existed.

Guanajuato's council knew that the gangs of roughneck miners, notorious for starting "terrible riots and tumults over the simplest causes," were a disincentive to honest migrants, and so they welcomed a Franciscan delegation to Santa Fe in January 1663 in the hope of instilling a more sober civic consciousness and work ethic. These clerics began by laying the foundation of their San Diego Convent, and within the next five years an urban core started to take shape between this emerging edifice and the original Nuestra Señora de Belén Hospital (an area encompassing modern Sopeña, San Francisco, Campanero, and San Pedro streets). A massive new *parroquia* (parish church) was also commenced by 1671, plus the Salgado Chapel the following year, so that Santa Fe could be temporarily conferred with the legal status of a town on 16 October 1679, a fact that was confirmed from Spain five years later.

Prosperity (1680–1809)

Guanajuato and its district supported roughly 16,000 inhabitants by the close of the seventeenth century, and the burgeoning town of Santa Fe slowly began expanding from its three small squares along the riverbank—the triangular Plaza Mayor (Main Square, renamed La Paz in 1898), plus San Diego and San Roque—as well as with shacks creeping up the southern slope of the Sierra de la Media Luna (Half-Moon Range). Because this core settlement was low lying and hemmed in by barren hills, an irregular and twisting street pattern evolved, still characterized today by many sloping or curved avenues. The community lies at 6,660 feet above sea level, and thus its climate is cool and moderate, with only a sparse annual rainfall.

Urban development was greatly spurred when Francisco Matías de Busto struck a bonanza with his Cata mine in 1724 and José Joaquín de Sardaneta y Legaspi also acquired the old Rayas mine three years later, driving its shafts to more productive depths through the creative use of blasting powder. The resultant economic boom came to be reflected in the appearance of Guanajuato's first cluster of private mansions, as well as completion of such public institutions as the Cata Church in 1725 and San Roque next year. The Bethelemite friar Francisco de la Asunción could even initiate work on an entirely new Belén hospital and school by the summer of 1727, upon grounds ceded from the Cervera treatment-mill by the wealthy

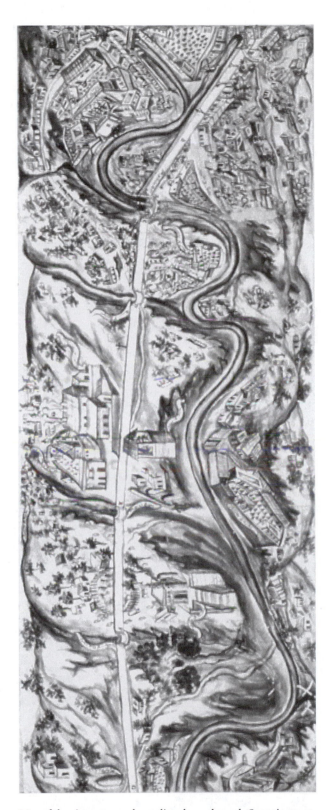

Map of the river-course channeling down through Guanajuato, ca. 1785–1787; because of its vulnerable position, the city was subjected to occasional flash floods. (Archivo General de la Nación, Mexico)

Isabel Hurtado de Mendoza. The Jesuit Order arrived five years later and—thanks to a 60,000-peso endowment from María Josefa Teresa de Busto y Moya, sister of Cata's owner Busto, who had since become ennobled as the Marqués de San Clemente—started their own Santísima Trinidad hospice and school. The latter would soon evolve into a vast monastery (renamed Purísima Concepción during the late eighteenth century), today forming part of the modern Universidad de Guanajuato campus. The royal accountant Agustín de la Rosa furthermore financed the completion of Guadalupe Church by November 1733.

The town of Santa Fe de Guanajuato really began taking shape during this prosperous interlude, lots being surveyed and properly demarked for the first time, while main thoroughfares were paved over with cobblestones, and an aqueduct system was inaugurated by 1738. Councilors petitioned the Crown the following year to be recognized as a city and commenced construction of La Olla Grande Dam in 1741 to prevent flash floods. The total population for the district had mushroomed to 48,750 people by 1742, and Santa Fe now boasted eighty large stores; two years later, its Jesuit-run Santísima Trinidad school was elevated to the status of a college, while the royal title of city was received from Spain on 3 July 1746, sparking a monthlong celebration. (This document had actually been signed by King Phillip V on 8 December 1741,

but delivery was delayed by the Atlantic blockade enforced during the War of Jenkins's Ear against England.)

Mining suffered another major slump during the 1750s, when loans from Mexico City bankers to renovate the Mellado and Sirena mines went unpaid, resulting in an overall loss of credit. To compound difficulties, the city endured its first great flood on 27 July 1760, torrents from a sudden deluge cascading down the hills and along the river course at the narrow gorge bottom, inflicting great loss of life and property. The new Belén Hospital was entirely washed away during the catastrophe, its surviving personnel and patients being temporarily lodged in the Jesuit college until an adobe replacement could be extemporized. The city's mining deputation wrote to the viceroy on 30 October of that calamitous year that the "population was obviously declining and was very poor, that most of the known mines were not being worked, and that their owners were losing money and abandoning business."

The monarchy attempted to rectify Guanajuato's plight by announcing a series of reforms in July 1766 that were aimed at upgrading civic life—but that were also to be financed through new excise taxes on many food staples, plus a royal tobacco and gunpowder monopoly, so that a mob of 6,000 angry miners stormed Guanajuato's royal treasury in protest, being mollified afterward by a few retractions. An even more serious disturbance exploded in July 1767 when the Jesuit

Early twentieth-century photograph of the ancient La Valenciana mine just north of the city of Guanajuato; note the arid, mountainous terrain. (Author's Collection)

Order was abruptly expelled from all Spanish dominions; many miners, who had toiled freely to help complete the magnificent Jesuit monastery only eighteen months before, roamed through Guanajuato's streets over the next three days in an ugly mood, before being put down with 600 arrests by troops. Nine individuals were subsequently hanged, 31 transported abroad, and 148 sentenced to incarcerations ranging between six and ten years.

In order to stifle future outbursts, a new municipal excise duty was imposed upon all maize and flour entering the city to pay for raising and maintaining the aristocratic El Príncipe Militia Regiment and a forty-six-man police force, plus erecting an arsenal and powder magazine (dubbed the Casa-Mata when finished six years later). Martial law had significantly curtailed the aimlessness of independent miners, and a phenomenal economic turnaround thereupon ensued when Antonio de Obregón y Alcocer hit another rich deposit in 1768–1769, after eight years of patiently deepening his old Valenciana mine. Not only was a vast amount of new high-grade ore uncovered, but Obregón's laborers additionally accepted toiling for modest yet regular shares. This was against the customary practice of working fitfully and unsystematically, then squandering any proceeds on useless luxuries or debauchery—a practice that perpetuated a lack of financial continuity within the city.

In contrast, Obregón was able to invest most of Valenciana's profits into large-scale expansion and other ancillary businesses, without resorting to usurious loans from Mexico City bankers. So great were the sums available to him that Valenciana soon had more than 3,300 miners digging in its lengthened tunnel system, with enough capital left over for the rest of Guanajuato to attain some measure of financial autonomy as well. Not even the floods of 16 September 1770 and 2 September 1772 could impede the city's rise; a bridge called San Juan Nepomuceno (modern Rastro) was completed by 1773, along with a new avenue leading out to Guadalupe Church two years later and a wholesale reconstruction of the Belén Hospital complex.

As the effects of this Valenciana bonanza spread, mansions again began to multiply within the city, such as the magnificent Churrigueresque-style residence erected on Pósitos Street by Vicente Manuel de Sardaneta in 1776 (two years after he, too, had obtained the title of first Marqués de San Juan de Rayas). More streets were paved over, an attempt was made to introduce public lighting, a theater called the Coliseo y Corral de Comedias opened by April 1778, and Los Santos Dam was finished at nearby Marfil that same November.

Another major flood occurred on 27 July 1780, burying the old San Diego Convent and many other edifices in a sea of mud, but the Valenciana mine continued to produce so strongly that these damages were soon made good. In fact, Guanajuato's mining tribunal even noted the next year: "Almost alone, this famous mine has maintained the town's growing number of workers, refiners, and merchants." Obregón, now ennobled as the Conde de Valenciana, paid for half the restoration costs of San Pedro de Alcántara Church, plus many other repairs; a new San Diego Convent—in Churrigueresque style—was completed by 1784. A regional drought thereupon gripped the city with famine, so cruelly during its final phase that desperate councilors borrowed funds in 1786 to purchase emergency stocks and encourage the planting of new crops. But notwithstanding their efforts, an estimated 19,000 inhabitants of Guanajuato and vicinity died because of starvation or related maladies.

Recovery was accelerated by a general administrative overhaul throughout the Spanish empire, which converted Guanajuato into the capital of a new provincial intendancy as of December 1786; this new jurisdiction was to be composed of its own former *alcaldía mayor,* plus those of Celaya, León, Salvatierra, San Luis de la Paz, and San Miguel el Grande (roughly equivalent to the boundaries of the modern state of Guanajuato). Urban amenities increased as a result of the city's enhanced prestige, including the unveiling of a new clock on the baroque parish church by October 1790, as well as completion of Los Pozuelos Dam in June of the following year.

The able and cultured former naval officer Juan Antonio de Riaño y Bárcena arrived as intendant in late January 1792, and he promptly set about constructing new royal offices, as well as properly naming all city streets, numbering its houses, and subdividing the capital into eleven wards (each to be presided over by its respective *alcalde de barrio*—ward magistrate). A military census taken that same year revealed 21,766 residents within the city limits, of whom 314 were peninsular-born Spaniards; 7,132 *criollos* (Creoles), Mexicans of Spanish descent; 6,454 mixed-heritage *castas;* 4,385 pure-bred Indians; and 3,481 mulattoes or blacks. An additional 30,000 people were scattered among the numerous satellite communities, engaged in either mining or refining.

Although another flood swept through on 1 August 1794, Guanajuato had by now become the leading producer of silver in the world, its annual output of more than 5 million pesos constituting one-sixth of all the bullion mined in the New World and equal to the entire production from the viceroyalties of Buenos Aires and Peru. The German scientist Alexander, Baron von Humboldt, visited less than a decade later and was impressed by the city's many "grand and beautiful buildings," although rather incongruously set amid its shacks and a stark mountain backdrop.

Guanajuato's district now boasted more than 1,800 mining claims, with 9,000 workers employed directly in either mineral extraction or refinement at any one of its 366 treatment plants or 116 mills. The nearby Bajío lowlands had furthermore become a prosperous breadbasket, with a population density second only to that of the Valley of Mexico, plus significant manufacturing output of its own: woolen textiles from

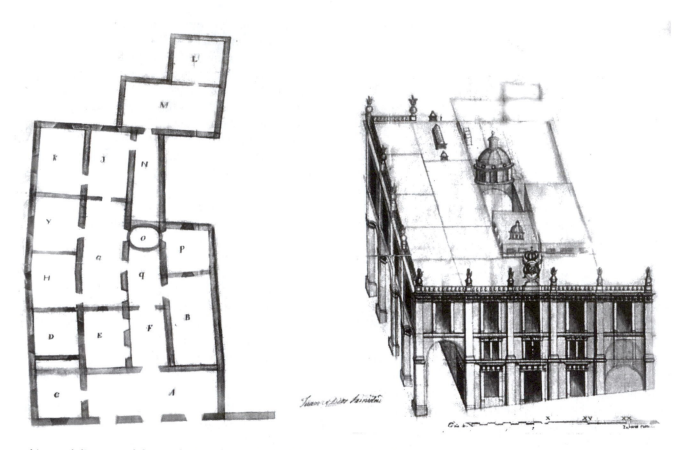

Architectural diagram and drawing by Juan de Dios Trinidad Pérez, of Guanajuato's new *casa real* or "royal government house," 1792. (Archivo General de la Nación, Mexico)

San Miguel el Grande and Querétaro, cottons from Celaya and Salamanca, leather goods from León, and so forth. Much of this agricultural bounty was drawn into the stores and markets of the rich intendancy capital, enhancing the quality of Guanajuato's urban life.

As a crowning glory, Riaño and the city council commissioned a local *alarife* (mason) named José Alejandro Durán y Villaseñor to design a massive new stone granary to replace the existing structure on Alonso Street. His plans and budget were submitted by March 1796, being forwarded to the viceroy in Mexico City that August and—after a few alterations suggested by the architect José del Mazo y Avilés—approved by July 1797, so that work on a massive new two-story edifice could commence as of 5 January 1798. The result, ten years later, was an imposing fortresslike building in neoclassical style that was to become known as the Alhóndiga de Granaditas (Granaditas Granary), because it had been raised atop the remnants of a treatment plant of that same name.

Sack and Stagnation (1810–1821)
That summer of 1808, when the Alhóndiga was inaugurated, the city was furthermore astonished to learn that the French emperor Napoleon I had sent an army into Spain to depose Ferdinand VII in favor of his brother Joseph Bonaparte. Like most other Spanish-American subjects, Guanajuatans repudiated this crude usurpation of power, and moreover became engrossed in their own local problems: another severe drought and food shortages. However, this loosening of overseas imperial ties eventually opened the door for thoughts of Mexican independence, mixed-heritage Creoles having grown especially resentful of the preferments routinely accorded peninsular-born Spaniards by Crown or Church officials in distant Madrid, as well as by heavy taxation.

As a result, word reached Riaño on 13 September 1810 of a Creole conspiracy being hatched 20 miles east-northeast of Guanajuato by the village priest of Dolores—the fifty-seven-year-old Miguel Hidalgo y Costilla—with the intention of fighting for Mexico's liberty. The intendant immediately ordered this firebrand's arrest, but a warning was carried to the cleric by his fellow conspirator Lt. Juan Aldama on the evening of 15 September. Hidalgo therefore roused his followers at dawn on Sunday the 16th by pealing Dolores's church bells, then marching southward against San Miguel el Grande with 400 riders and 400 men on foot under Capt. José Ignacio María de Allende y Unzaga. The rebels encountered no resistance and were joined by hundreds more supporters as they forged into

A corner of the Alhóndiga de Granaditas, ca. 1978; note the steep incline of its street. (Flora L. Phelps, *Organization of American States*)

Celaya by 20 September, from where Hidalgo called upon Riaño to surrender the provincial capital.

Although commanding only a small number of troops and a few hundred peninsular Spaniards, the intendant refused, sending out appeals for help while strengthening his unfortified city as a swelling mass of insurgents swept through Salamanca, Irapuato, and Silao for an assault. After issuing another surrender demand on 27 September 1810, Hidalgo's 20,000 to 25,000 unruly followers swarmed through Marfil, splitting around Cuarto and San Miguel Hills before storming down Nuestra Señora de Guanajuato Avenue directly into the capital the following afternoon. Riaño and several hundred frightened adherents sought shelter inside the Alhóndiga, but they were overwhelmed when a young Mellado miner named Juan José María de los Reyes "El Pípila" Martínez crawled through a hail of bullets with a stone slab tied to his back, setting its wooden doors ablaze with a torch by nightfall. The insurgents slaughtered every monarchist defender by dawn, then sacked and burned the hapless city, noncombatants being murdered or imprisoned before Hidalgo could restore order.

This sensational capture of the viceroyalty's wealthiest city

inspired similar insurrections elsewhere, although the accompanying excesses also clouded the rebellion's reputation, alienating the less radical segments of Mexican society. Hidalgo meanwhile raised two volunteer regiments as a garrison for Guanajuato, created a *casa de moneda* (mint) at San Pedro Hacienda opposite the Regimiento del Príncipe barracks, established an artillery foundry under the direction of mathematics professor Rafael Dávalos, appointed José Francisco Gómez as insurgent "*intendant corregidor*" on 8 October 1810, and then departed two days later to lead his host of followers in a decisive advance against Mexico City. His undisciplined forces, though, were routed within a month by Loyalist armies, then pursued back through the central highlands by the victorious Gen. Félix María Calleja del Rey. Hidalgo retreated toward Guadalajara with his survivors, while Allende evacuated Guanajuato on 24 November, after first executing all its monarchist detainees.

Calleja entered the devastated city the next day and in turn shot numerous rebel sympathizers—including Gómez, who was supplanted as royal intendant by Fernando Pérez Marañón—before allowing his army a six-week respite and then advancing to expel Hidalgo from Guadalajara early the following year. The rebel chieftain was eventually overtaken and executed in Chihuahua City on 30 July 1811, his pickled head (along with those of Allende, Aldama, and other subordinates) being shipped back to Guanajuato to be exposed in iron cages at the corners of the Alhóndiga, as a gruesome warning to other would-be dissidents.

Yet despite this defeat, the insurgency proved to be so deep rooted and resilient that resistance continued smoldering in the countryside, Guanajuato being unable to recuperate its former mining glory because of interrupted communications, damaged installations, lack of Crown or private capital, as well as an unreliable workforce. Deep depression persisted for the next decade, mansions being offered rent-free to anyone willing to merely tend to them, while weeds sprouted in city streets and the urban populace contracted to as few as 6,000 inhabitants. The royalist garrison was briefly threatened on 25 October 1817 by 1,400 insurgent guerrillas under Francisco Javier Mina y Larrea and Pedro Moreno, but these attackers were repulsed and hunted down two days later, so that Guanajuato experienced no more assaults.

The insurgent cause eventually triumphed elsewhere in Mexico, prompting the regional royalist commanders Luis de Cortazar and Anastasio Bustamante to switch allegiances and march jubilantly into the capital on 24 March 1821 to remove the heads of Hidalgo and the other martyrs from the Alhóndiga. The supreme insurgent commander, Gen. Agustín Iturbide, then entered Guanajuato on 26 April to create a provisional government, retaining the services of such former Loyalist luminaries as Pérez Marañón and José Mariano Sardaneta y Llorente, second Marqués de San Juan de Rayas. Mexico's independence was acclaimed locally on 8 July.

Revival and Uncertainty (1822–1867)

Mining had been severely dislocated by this protracted struggle for independence, imports of vital metallurgical ingredients such as mercury having been interrupted, knowledgeable operators having departed, mines having flooded, and mills having been neglected. Peace nonetheless ushered in a brief boom for Guanajuato as operations were resumed with foreign—especially British—assistance, whose overseas investors dispatched their own experts and equipment into its district in the hope of reaping high profits.

The city was also designated as capital of a new "Free State of Guanajuato" by Mexico's national congress in March 1824, its first printing press being imported that same year. A census ordered by Gov. Carlos Montes de Oca in 1825 indicated that the population of Guanajuato and its immediate municipality had resurged to 33,000 residents. Construction of a grand new theater was even undertaken the following year, public lighting was restored by May 1827, the Colegio de la Purísima Concepción was renamed Colegio del Estado (State College) and resumed classes by February 1828, and a public library was inaugurated three years afterward.

But unfortunately, further progress was hampered by nationwide political and fiscal chaos, as factions jealously dislodged each other through coups. Guanajuato's governorship soon began to change hands frequently, while a dreadful cholera epidemic added to its citizenry's woes in 1833. Because of its physical remove deep in the central highlands, Guanajuato was spared any occupation during the U.S. invasion of Mexico in 1846–1848; its mining economy even experienced a brief resurgence shortly thereafter, reflected in such modest municipal improvements as the creation of a new public fountain in June 1852 to draw water from La Olla Dam, plus Cantador ("Singer") Park two years later (allegedly named after the wealthy eighteenth-century miner José Carpio, who was reduced to becoming a minstrel after suffering a bankruptcy). Mansions in the French neoclassical style also began to spring up, blocks were surveyed anew and more accurately delineated, while urban boundaries were expanded beyond the old San Agustín treatment mill for the first time. The Santa Casa de Loreto was also inaugurated, and the total population for the municipality now exceeded 40,000.

Mexico's liberal and conservative factions descended into a bitter civil war a half decade later, the city becoming embroiled in this conflict—known as the War of the Reform,

Panoramic view across the city, ca. 1891. (Library of Congress)

or Three-Year War—when Acting-Pres. Benito Juárez was driven from the national capital and reached Guanajuato on 17 January 1858, being recognized as legitimate ruler by the state's Gov. Manuel Doblado. Two days later Juárez created a liberal government in exile with Guanajuato as his capital, receiving support from eight sister states. But the approach of 5,400 conservative regulars under Gen. Luis G. Osollo compelled him to depart for Guadalajara that same 14 February, so that Guanajuato fell to his opponents by mid-March. Before this struggle finally ceased with a liberal triumph two and a half years later, the city changed hands eight more times.

The nation had scarcely started to recuperate when the defeated conservatives allied themselves with France and encouraged the disembarkation of an expeditionary force at Veracruz in January 1862 to spearhead a thrust aimed at supplanting Mexico's republican form of government with an imperial regime, which was to be headed by the foreign figurehead Archduke Maximilian of Austria. It took more than a year for this invasion force to drive Juárez and his liberal administration from central Mexico again, after which a Franco-conservative army fought its way into the Bajío lowlands. Doblado abandoned Guanajuato on 6 December 1863, and a committee of neutral representatives was organized the next day by the British vice consul, John H. Glass, to ensure a peaceful transition, the city being occupied on 8 December by a conservative cavalry vanguard under Gen. Tomás Mejía.

Once again, Guanajuato experienced a short-lived economic boom thanks to an infusion of foreign funds and modern technologies, such as its first telegraph line, laid from the national capital by June 1864. Nevertheless, widespread resentment against the French-imposed imperial apparatus helped sustain a persistent guerrilla struggle, while Washington exerted pressure upon Napoleon III in Paris to withdraw his supporting regiments. Once the latter began retiring from their Mexican occupation, republican armies closed in upon the imperial garrisons, and conservative Gen. Feliciano Liceaga was compelled to mount a stand outside Guanajuato with 1,500 troops and twenty-two artillery pieces, only to meet defeat at the hands of republican Gen. Florencio Antillón, who was able to reoccupy the long-suffering state capital by 26 January 1867.

Reduced Circumstances (1868–Present)

As a war hero, Antillón was elected governor three times over the ensuing decade, and he drew upon Guanajuato's modest resurgence in profitability to finance a few reforms such as restoration of its police force, improvements to its water distribution system, purchase of English steam engines for its

Modern panorama of the city of Guanajuato, crowded into its narrow valley confines. (Danny Lehman/Corbis)

mint, encouragement of public education, the construction of a highway across the state, and so forth. However, he resisted the revolt that swept Gen. Porfirio Díaz into power as president of Mexico in November 1876 and was deposed the following January in favor of the Porfirian appointee Gen. Francisco Z. Mena. Minor progress continued during the latter's administration, the first railway line into Guanajuato being laid (eventually connecting it with Celaya and León), as well as a few other innovations; a census taken in 1879 revealed that the total population for the city and its municipality stood at 56,112.

On the night of 7 June 1885, Guanajuato once again suffered a major flood, so that construction was initiated on La Esperanza Dam, just west of the city, under the direction of the engineer Ponciano Aguilar and was completed eight years later. Díaz had meanwhile implemented a surprisingly effective national regime, ruthlessly fomenting the industrialization and modernization of Mexico. Guanajuato benefited from the overall prosperity and stability that this policy engendered, its mining industry in particular achieving enhanced returns thanks to mechanization and more up-to-date technologies. But with silver no longer commanding high prices on international markets, its other resources proved so meager that what had once been among the country's most populous and wealthiest cities now became far outstripped by manufacturing hubs such as Guadalajara, Puebla, and Monterrey.

Some growth nevertheless continued: better edifices were created at Guanajuato, and a new public cemetery was cleared atop nearby Trozado Hill. Work on a two-story Palacio de Gobierno (government palace)—designed by the local architect Luis Long—also commenced as of 1897 on a site once occupied by mansions belonging to the Marqués de San Clemente and Conde de Valenciana. This structure was inaugurated, along with the grand Teatro Juárez, during a ceremonial visit by President Díaz in October 1903. Then, another terrible flood swept through the densely packed city on 1 July 1905, drowning 200 people. Recovery efforts included the completion of the first railway spur from Silao to the terminal just west of Guanajuato by 1908, while the iron-framed Hidalgo Market—erected by Ernesto Brunel on the former grounds of the Gavira Bullring—opened in September 1910.

The Porfirian era ended when Díaz, now approaching eighty years of age, stood for his eighth presidential term that same year. Despite the economic progress achieved, resentment had accumulated throughout Mexico against his regime's inequitable distribution of wealth and lack of social advancement, or any significant political voice for most citizens. When his young and high-minded opponent Francisco Ignacio

The "mummies" of Guanajuato, ca. 1909; because land had become so scarce in this crowded mountain city, corpses interred for five years in its public cemetery atop nearby Trozado Hill—having become desiccated in the unusually dry subsoil—were exhumed and stood up in these vaults to make way for fresh burials. (Carson, *Mexico: The Wonderland of the South*)

Madero escaped confinement and called for a general uprising on 20 November 1910, federal power was sapped within an astonishingly short period by rebel outbreaks in northern Mexico under leaders such as Francisco "Pancho" Villa and by Emiliano Zapata's peasant revolt southwest of the national capital. Díaz fled Mexico City by late May 1911, being succeeded by Madero, who was in turn murdered by the former Porfirian general Victoriano Huerta in February 1913. Another wave of revolutionary anarchy engulfed Mexico, during which the rebel general Pablo González led a column unopposed into Guanajuato in July 1914 to supplant its Huertista governor.

Notwithstanding the interruptions to its commerce and frequent changes in administration, the small mining city had otherwise remained largely unaffected by this unrest. It became more directly involved after Gen. Alvaro Obregón dissolved the Huertista administration and installed Venustiano Carranza as president in Mexico City, leading to a break with other rebel factions. Obregón advanced northwestward in March 1915 to confront Villa, prompting Guanajuato's anti-Carrancista governor, Abel B. Serratos, to propose transferring the state capital to León. This decision was rescinded when Obregón crushed Villa's counterthrust at Celaya the following month, then sent a detachment to occupy Guanajuato on 25 April while his main force circled across the Bajío lowlands to crush Villa outside León.

Guanajuato returned to being a political backwater over the next dozen years as the revolution ran its course, although the office of state governor switched hands seventeen times during that unsettled interlude. Eventually, though, sufficient tranquillity was restored for its university to be created in 1945 on the grounds of the old Casa Municipal and former Jesuit buildings in the city core. Gov. José Aguilar y Maya then initiated a concerted program of urban modernization that included the ambitious project of improving vehicular traffic flows through its narrow and winding streets, by taking advantage of an existing 2-mile labyrinth of tunnels to create a unique subterranean thoroughfare called Belaunzarán, which traversed beneath the wards of Matavacas, Manuel Doblado, Cantarranas, Baratillo, and Pósitos.

Population figures for the city and municipality nonetheless remained virtually unchanged from previous centuries, rising from 55,107 residents in 1960 to a mere 65,309 a decade later, despite a phenomenal upsurge in rural-to-urban migration patterns elsewhere in Mexico and Latin America. Yet precisely because of its quaint size, historical reputation, and attractive colonial-era architecture, civic leaders were able to supplement their traditional mining income by catering to a growing international tourist trade through such measures as laying a scenic road from the San Renovato Basin and La Olla Dam up to a lookout point atop San Miguel Hill. Theater productions called *cervantinas*—because they mostly staged works by Miguel Cervantes and other classical authors—have also been celebrated since 1972 in beautiful open-air venues

Palm tree nestled beside the ancient Parroquia de San Miguel Arcangel. (Karen Huntt/Corbis)

such as San Roque Square, while university faculties have furthermore organized their own mendicant musical troupes called *estudiantinas,* thus adding to Guanajuato's allure. Today, the city still retains much of its intimate colonial charm, its population total of 73,100 inhabitants in 1990 having increased to only 76,900 a dozen years later.

For further reading on the history of Guanajuato or Mexico, please consult the Select Bibliography at the end of this volume.

Mexico City

Already a great metropolis at the time of its Spanish conquest and that today ranks as one of the largest cities on earth.

Origins (1325–1519)

The Mexica were Náhuatl-speaking hunter-gatherers who migrated into the temperate, 7,500-foot-high valley of Anáhuac from out of the northwest early during the twelfth century C.E., finding that this fertile and well-irrigated basin—measuring roughly 70 by 45 miles and ringed by mountains densely forested with oak, cedar, and pine—was already populated by other tribes under the dominion of the Culhua kings of Culhuacán. As latecomers, the Mexica or Aztecs were driven from successive encampments near Zempoala, Tula, Chapultepec, and Contitlán before finally settling down to eke out a miserable existence amid the marshes and tiny islands that bordered the western banks of the valley's great saline lake.

A band of Mexica hunters prowling one of these islands reputedly chanced upon an eagle devouring a serpent atop a cactus, which—according to Aztec lore—represented the spot where they were to create a permanent home. The city of México-Tenochtitlán was therefore erected upon the largest of these islands around 1325 C.E., its name signifying the "place of the divine cactus where the Mexitli are to be found." (The Aztecs regarded themselves as mythic sons of the moon and sun, celestial bodies that caused dawn to break by hunting and capturing the stars.)

Because of their capital's unique name, the Aztecs also became known as Tenochcas, and although their city was initially subordinate to the Tepanecan capital of Azcapotzalco, its physical remove, far out over the lake, provided enough security for its inhabitants to forge alliances with larger city-states and grow in strength. The capital expanded accordingly, spreading out on to several adjoining islands through the use of *chinampas*—enormous wooden rafts covered with loamy soil and vegetation that took root once they became anchored in the shallow sediment of the lake bed.

By the mid-fifteenth century, the Aztecs had surpassed their allied city-states of Texcoco and Tlacopan (modern Tacuba) to emerge as the valley's dominant tribe. They then carved out an empire extending beyond the mountains through military conquests during the reigns of their fifth and sixth monarchs—Moctezuma Ilhuicamina from 1440 to 1469, and Axayácatl from 1469 to 1483—as well as by crushing a rebellion in their neighboring city of Tlaltelolco during the early 1470s. All these campaigns were inspired by the Aztecs' practice of sacrificing prisoners to their fierce war god Huitzilopochtli, which had seemingly brought an end to a drought in 1455 and needed to be continually appeased

Panoramic view looking eastward across the valley of Anáhuac toward Mexico City in 1894, by the famed landscape artist José María Velasco; note the snow-capped Ixtaccíhuatl and Popocatépetl volcanoes in the distance. (Private Collection, Mexico City)

through a constant state of *xochiyáoyotl* (ritualized warfare) against outlying nations.

Yet despite being feared for their martial aggressiveness and bloodthirsty religion, the Mexica also developed many qualities of an advanced civilization, reflected in their capital's sophisticated palaces, grand temples, beautiful causeways and canals, a freshwater system running underground from springs atop Chapultepec Hill, as well as a valleywide system of dams and dykes to control lake levels and limit floods (such as the one that inundated the low-lying city in 1501).

By the time Moctezuma Xocoyotzin ascended the throne as ninth *hueytlatoani* (emperor), México-Tenochtitlán had evolved into a densely packed, 4-square-mile city of perhaps 250,000 to 400,000 inhabitants, with another million or so allies and vassals crowded around the shores of Lake Texcoco, plus several million more scattered throughout the empire. The capital's largest edifices, such as its great pyramid crowned by a *teocalli* (temple) or Moctezuma's sumptuous two-story palace, were magnificent stone structures covered in gleaming plaster, while lesser neighborhoods were crisscrossed by canals and serviced by thousands of canoes, in addition to four broad causeways that connected the city to the mainland. Its markets offered an abundance of fish and waterfowl, harvests from terraced fields, plus many other goods imported over immense distances. Urban amenities included a spectacular zoo and aviary, ball courts, and many popular diversions.

Spanish Conquest (1519–1521)

Disturbing rumors began reaching the Aztec leaders of a powerful new presence in the Caribbean, reminiscent of an ancient prophecy that their civilization would be destroyed by white sun-gods out of the east. In the spring of 1519, several hundred Spanish troops under Hernán Cortés disembarked at Veracruz, the easternmost fringe of the Aztec empire. Moctezuma showered these strangers with rich gifts in the hope that they would withdraw, but the Spaniards were instead enticed by such a display of wealth into visiting Tenochtitlán, pushing implacably inland despite every Aztec disincentive. During this progression, Cortés forged alliances with many lesser tribes, while astounding the local populations with his troops' sophisticated steel weaponry, artillery, and cavalry.

Finally, the advancing army crested the 13,000-foot-high gap between the 21,000-foot volcanoes Ixtaccíhuatl and Popocatépetl (a path deliberately chosen because the sun rises between both peaks) and descended into the valley, to be welcomed into the capital by a reluctant Moctezuma on 8 November 1519. The Spaniards were dazzled by the city's wonders, the conquistador Bernal Díaz del Castillo later recording that "among us were soldiers who had been in many parts of the world, in Constantinople, and in Italy and Rome" without beholding anything comparable. After six days' entertainment Cortés received word of a clash between a detachment that he had left behind on the Gulf coast and an Aztec army, so he took the emperor from his palace under armed guard and transferred him into the Spaniards' quarters. This bold arrest created a sensation among Tenochtitlán's citizenry, further heightened when the offending Aztec commanders were brought in a few days later on Cortés's orders and burned alive in its main square.

The Spaniards nonetheless spent the next several months peaceably in the capital, learning everything about its empire, reconnoitering outlying provinces, and receiving vast amounts of tribute. But in April 1520 word was received of a rival Spanish expedition of 1,400 men off Veracruz under Pánfilo de Narváez sent to detain Cortés for having absconded from Cuba. Cortés departed the Aztec capital to confront this challenger in May, leaving behind 120 soldiers as a holding force under his subordinate Pedro de Alvarado. The latter, uneasy when a large crowd gathered to celebrate the Toxcatl festival on 16 May, misconstrued their dances as a prelude to a surprise attack and massacred the celebrants—an act that precipitated

Modern rendering of the Aztec capital of Tenochtitlán, connected to the mainland by causeways. (Museo de la Ciudad de México)

a vengeful descent upon the Spanish garrison, abating only when Alvarado forced Moctezuma onto a rooftop to quell the angry Aztec mobs.

When Cortés regained Tenochtitlán on 24 June 1520 with more than 1,000 Spanish soldiers and a host of Tlaxcaltecan allies, having outwitted Narváez and incorporated his troops into his own ranks, he found Alvarado's garrison isolated. Wanting the city markets reopened so as to feed his army, Cortés released Moctezuma's brother Cuitláhuac, Lord of Ixtapalapa, the following day, but that chieftain only fueled Aztec resolve. When 300 Spaniards sallied into the narrow streets, they were attacked and chased back into their quarters. Cortés again directed Moctezuma to address the throngs from a rooftop, but this time the unhappy emperor was stoned and died shortly thereafter. Thirst and hunger eventually compelled the Spaniards to attempt to cut their way out of Tenochtitlán after midnight on 30 June–1 July, being beset along the Tacuba Causeway by thousands of warriors, who inflicted 600 fatalities among the Spaniards before they could gain the mainland town of Popotla.

Cortés and his survivors retreated toward Tlaxcala, while the Aztecs fortified their capital. Cuitláhuac was officially elected emperor on 7 September 1520, but he died two and a half months later from smallpox, which the Spanish had unwittingly introduced into the valley. Cortés meanwhile rebuilt his army to 550 Spanish troops thanks to a steady trickle of ships arriving from the West Indies, then advanced against Tenochtitlán again on 27 December, backed by 10,000 Tlaxcaltecans. Encountering scant opposition, his army reached Texcoco four days later and destroyed Ixtapalapa on 4 January 1521, despite the Aztecs' best efforts to prevent the assault.

Their past tyrannies now redounded, as many subject cities turned against their former Aztec overlords. Cuitláhuac's cousin Cuauhtémoc led an army down the eastern shores of Lake Texcoco to cow vassals back into submission, but Cortés replied with countersweeps of his own, before a 6-mile-long column of 10,000 Tlaxcaltecan bearers staggered into Texcoco on 15 February 1521 with timbers to be assembled into a fleet of flat-bottomed Spanish brigantines, armed with iron cannon and bronze swivels. These were intended to cut off the Aztec capital's waterborne supplies, before three land columns assaulted the towns guarding the Tacuba, Ixtapalapa, and Coyoacán causeways. (The fourth causeway, which exited at Tepeyac, was deliberately left open to tempt Aztec noncombatants into flight.)

On 29 April 1521, the four-day ceremonial marking Cuauhtémoc's coronation culminated within the beleaguered capital, and a month later the Spaniards launched their final offensive. Tenochtitlán's water system was destroyed, then Cortés defeated a large fleet of war canoes on 1 June, effectively cutting off most staples. Spanish conquistadors and their allied hordes slowly pressed into the city despite heroic Aztec

resistance, gaining Tenochtitlán's main square by 10 June, only to be thrown back at nightfall. During a second penetration five days later, Cortés's indigenous auxiliaries razed many buildings so that his cavalry and artillery might have better play, in the process depriving defenders of high positions from which to pelt down missiles. Cortés continued these destructive incursions over the next couple of weeks, until half of Tenochtitlán lay flattened.

All three land columns then launched a concerted drive against the last Aztec concentration in the northern suburb of Tlaltelolco on 30 June 1521, but 73 Spaniards, 2,000 allies, four horses, and a brigantine were lost. Shaken, the invaders hung back over the next four days, while local auxiliaries quit in fright and some outlying tribes even switched allegiances. The loyal Tlaxcaltecans, though, launched a foray into devastated Tenochtitlán that netted a large catch of Aztec captives, after which the local peoples began returning; Alvarado's contingent fought its way into the very heart of Tlaltelolco by 27 July. Pressed into a small northwestern enclave of their once-magnificent capital, thousands of Aztec noncombatants were massacred in another vicious assault on 12 August, before resistance collapsed the next afternoon. Cuauhtémoc fled aboard a canoe with a score of retainers, only to be overtaken by a Spanish brigantine and brought before Cortés.

Resurrection (1521–1532)

Such protracted fighting had left the city in ruins and most of its inhabitants either dead or dispersed. The victors consequently chose to remain at their mainland camp of Coyoacán, while Juan Rodríguez de Villafuerte temporarily assumed the title of military governor over the devastated and almost deserted island capital.

Soon, Spanish columns were dispatched to subdue other vassal states outside the valley, and it was assumed that Tenochtitlán would be forsaken in favor of a new capital on the mainland. But when Cristóbal de Tapia unexpectedly arrived at Veracruz that same December 1521 with instructions from Spain to supersede Cortés as "Governor of New Spain," the latter countered by quickly constituting an *ayuntamiento* (municipal government) at Tenochtitlán, with himself as its *alcalde mayor,* Cristóbal de Olid as his deputy, Pedro de Alvarado as chief magistrate, and so forth—a legal fiction designed to allow Cortés to appeal directly to the Crown against his deposal as an independent titleholder.

Such recourse proved unnecessary, however, as de Tapia was soon mollified and dismissed; yet when Cortés began preparing for a military incursion into northeastern Mexico late in January 1522, he announced that New Spain's capital was in fact to be erected atop Tenochtitlán's ruins, later explaining to Emperor Charles V that he had "debated with himself as to whether to establish another town within the circuit of the lakes" before finally opting to rebuild upon the original site. Such an island stronghold would not only offer the outnumbered Spaniards a more defensible position in case of an insurrection but also the blatant superimposition of Spanish institutions upon the shattered Aztec remnants would undeniably embody the finality of conquest.

Charles granted broad powers to the city's *ayuntamiento* via a royal decree on 15 October 1522, after which Cortés and Tenochtitlán's "municipal council"—all officers in his army, still headquartered at Coyoacán—assigned Alonso García Bravo and Bernardino Vázquez de Tapia to draw up a *traza* (plan) for razing the damaged Aztec city and replacing it with European-style edifices and streets. The captive Cuauhtémoc's influence was used to raise tens of thousands of conscript laborers from throughout the valley, who toiled under the direction of the *cihuacoatl* (vice emperor) Tlacotzin in clearing away debris. Large chunks of masonry were reused as foundations for new buildings, while smaller pieces helped to level out low spots or fill in canals. The old underground water system from Chapultepec was repaired, but most initial construction was concentrated in erecting a triple-towered water fort on the city's eastern shoreline to serve as a Spanish citadel and berth their brigantines.

Once that structure, known as the Ataranzas (Shipyards) at San Lázaro Point, was completed late in 1523, Cortés informed his monarch:

> I considered that it was safe to proceed with my plan, which was to repopulate the city, and therefore took up my quarters with all of my people within it. The various lots of land were divided out [early in 1524] among the inhabitants and to each one of the conquistadors I gave, in Your Majesty's name, a plot for which he had labored, in addition to that which he was entitled to receive as a settler and citizen . . .

A grid of eighteen north-south and seven east-west streets gradually emerged, encompassing slightly more than a square mile of 100 blocks and crisscrossed by eight major canals. The new Spanish core's boundaries extended as far north as modern Perú and Peña y Peña streets; east to Leona Vicario, Santísima, Alhóndiga, and Roldán streets; south to San Pablo and San Jerónimo; and west to San Juan de Letrán, Juan Ruiz de Alarcón, Aquiles Serdán, and Gabriel Leyva (as well as incorporating a narrow corridor along the Tacuba Causeway as an escape route).

Fears of an indigenous uprising meant that the first mansions erected by Cortés and his officers were two-story fortress-residences with extremely thick walls, massive wooden doors, and tiny windows. Sites were also allocated for a future cathedral, royal and municipal offices, a prison, slaughterhouse, public granary, monasteries, markets, fountains, wooden bridges, sewers, and the like. Water distribution was deemed a municipal service, being piped into two huge tanks for redistribution through four public fountains, as well as directly into certain major residences. Street paving and gut-

ters were to be privately maintained by each individual householder.

Outside this central Spanish core, the remnants of Tenochtitlán's four original sectors were repopulated and rechristened Santa María Tlaquechiucan (or Cuepopan) in the northwest, San Sebastián Atzcualco in the northeast, San Pablo Teopan (as well as Zoquipan or Xochimilco) in the southeast, plus San Juan Moyotla in the southwest. The old Tezontlalli Canal that had divided the Aztec capital from its sister city of Tlaltelolco was also redug to create a fifth *parcialidad* (ward).

Neighborhoods east of the new Spanish main square were the first to revive because of their proximity to the strategic Ataranzas and lakeborne commerce, while the city's western side (modern Ribera de San Cosme) remained largely empty marshland, where Cortés and others planted orchards known as the Huertas de San Antonio. Work continued for many months, on such a Herculean scale that when a band of Franciscan missionaries reached Mexico City on 18 June 1524, Fr. Toribio Paredes de Benavente—who would soon change his surname to Motolinía, the Aztec term for "humility"—recorded that the "songs and voices" of thousands of workers "scarcely ceased at night." One year later, the first Crown-appointed *regidor perpétuo* (councilor for life) also arrived from Spain, marking the commencement of direct royal control over municipal affairs.

By the time Cortés departed to visit Spain in October 1526, he was able to report that his redesigned capital held more than 30,000 inhabitants, of whom approximately 2,000 were Spaniards, as most Iberians arriving on the torrid Gulf coast

Boatmen plying through the *chinampas* or "floating gardens" of Xochimilco, ca. 1902–1904. (Gadow, *Through Southern Mexico*)

preferred ascending into the brisk climes of the central highlands. Animals such as cattle and pigs imported from the Caribbean had also begun to multiply throughout the fertile valley of Anáhuac, along with wheat plantings. As the number of the city's Spanish inhabitants continued to grow, its boundaries were expanded the following year to incorporate more mainland *ejidos* (commons), while estate owners developed farms stretching between Coyoacán and Tenayuca. Even indigenous losses resulting from disease were temporarily checked, so that their traditional produce trade resurged as well, along with overland traffic from more distant regions.

Because of the prestige of its founding members—Cortés and virtually every other prominent conquistador—Mexico City's municipal *ayuntamiento* had initially claimed jurisdiction over all of New Spain, although such a grandiose notion was soon curtailed as other Spanish jurisdictions began to emerge. Still, the city's role was enhanced when Mexico's first bishop—Fr. Juan de Zumárraga—took up residence in the capital in 1528 and a small eastward-facing cathedral was completed by the builder Martín de Sepúlveda four years later. A legislative *real audiencia* (royal tribunal) arrived from Spain in January 1532 to officially inaugurate Crown rule, and although a small *cabildo* (city hall) structure was completed that same 10 May, its councilors were disappointed to learn that their authority had been restricted to a radius of only 5 leagues, or 15 miles.

Vicissitudes (1533–1555)

Water levels in Lake Texcoco had begun dipping soon after the Spanish conquest, yet because all bodies of water throughout the valley were quite shallow, unusually heavy rainfalls could cause sudden rises, a consequence that caused Mexico City to be unexpectedly flooded in 1533. Recent Iberian arrivals were so disillusioned by this problem that many became tempted by reports of Francisco Pizarro's conquest of the Incan empire to instead emigrate to Peru, leaving the city council worriedly reporting the next year that the number of Spanish residents was "less than half what they had been."

The arrival of the able Antonio de Mendoza as New Spain's first Crown-appointed viceroy in November 1535, however, restored some measure of confidence. He enacted many improvements, such as importing the city's first printing press, encouraging education by establishing such schools for the indigenous population as Santa Cruz de Tlaltelolco and San Juan de Letrán, creating a *Casa de Moneda* (mint), as well as extending the capital's municipal jurisdiction to a radius of 45 miles four years later. Native craftsmen had by then become so adept at producing European-style manufactures that the capital boasted weavers, tailors, blacksmiths, tanners, saddlers, shoemakers, carpenters, glaziers, hatters, masons, candle makers, and more. However, a hard frost devastated crops throughout the valley in 1541, causing a famine the following

year; then the local population was ravaged by another dreadful epidemic in 1545, reducing their numbers by more than a third over the next three years.

A *real universidad* (royal university) opened its doors on 25 January 1553, but as Lake Texcoco's shoreline had by then receded farther east and some northern lakes had been entirely drained by a canal dug between Zumpango and Xaltocan, a daylong downpour in October 1555 inundated the city again—so badly, in fact, that people could only circulate through its streets for the next three or four days in canoes. The new viceroy, Luis de Velasco, asked the Indian governors of Tenochtitlán, Tacuba, and Texcoco "for the ancient paintings showing the foundation of the city, and the methods they and their ancestors had used for protecting it from floods." After studying these, along with several proposals from Spanish officials, de Velasco decided to address the problem "as the Indians used to do"; he personally turned the first shovelful of dirt to rebuild a great *albarrada* (dyke) along Mexico City's eastern edge, which was completed the next year.

Transformation (1556–1602)

The capital began to undergo a pronounced economic, social, and demographic change as of the late 1550s thanks to a boom in New Spain's silver output, the development of a new amalgamation process in distant mining zones augmenting the flow of crude bars exponentially into its Real Casa de Moneda (royal mint) for assay, taxation, and export. Revenues derived from this immensely rich traffic helped transform Mexico City from a densely packed indigenous metropolis with a small, superimposed Hispanic presence into a full-blown Spanish-American city.

Numerous municipal projects could additionally be financed. For example, new freshwater sources were tapped and diverted to supplement Chapultepec's supply, San Hipólito Hospital was erected in 1567 and San Lázaro Hospital five years later, the Holy Office of the Inquisition was established, and work on a massive new cathedral was commenced in 1573 under the direction of the architect Claudio de Arciniega. The city's newfound wealth even came to be reflected in an increased use of red-colored *tezontle* stone or decorative tiles for its private homes.

The first Crown-appointed *corregidor* (magistrate) arrived from Spain in 1574, instituting several additional reforms such as bulk purchases of maize to stabilize prices for the urban poor, as well as expanding the tiny *ayuntamiento* building eight years later to incorporate a larger *alhóndiga* (public granary) and a new prison. (In theory, a *corregidor* governed over only a single community, while an *alcalde mayor* ruled over an entire district, although there was otherwise little difference in their functions.) Mansions also increased in number and styles, while the capital's religious institutions expanded or were beautified, and many new ones came to be founded: the Balvanera nunnery in 1573, the Jesuit college of

Cutaway view of the inner courtyard of the Inquisitorial headquarters in 1792, by the architect Antonio Velázquez. (Archivo General de la Nación, Mexico)

San Pedro y San Pablo the next year, the San Gregorio and San Diego monasteries in 1576, Jesús María Convent in 1578, and San Cosme three years later.

Yet in contrast to this prosperity among Spanish residents, indigenous fortunes continued to decline because of disease and poverty. The valley's total population had plummeted to roughly 325,000 to 350,000 people by the early 1570s, of whom an estimated 85,000 to 90,000 lived within the municipal jurisdiction of Mexico City—more than 75,000 being Indians. Another major typhoid epidemic in 1576 claimed a quarter of their number over the next five years, and a major flood engulfed the capital in 1580; as a result, chieftains could no longer raise the requisite levies of laborers to perform public works, and criminals or slaves had to be substituted. The indigenous population's diminution became so pronounced that Spanish citizens began acquiring properties in desolate Indian neighborhoods, a practice that had previously been forbidden.

Native farms also dwindled throughout the valley, while Spanish landholdings expanded, dramatically altering the environment during the 1580s. Having already claimed the richest and deepest soils low down in the basin and diverted watercourses to irrigate their crops or power their mills, estate owners now began pasturing their cattle or sheep among the brushy grasslands of the volcanic and alluvial deposits higher up the valley slopes. The more labor-intensive terrace farming previously practiced at those higher elevations by the original population dwindled as surviving bands shifted down into depopulated sectors among the freshwater streams along the lakeshores to more easily plant crops upon *chinampas.*

Consequently, the total acreage of arable land contracted as topsoils from unmaintained terraces and from grasslands cropped bare by grazing herds were washed down into the basin, leaving behind barren gullies. The chilly, uppermost reaches of the valley had always been lined with only shallow-soiled forests, whose trees were now felled in huge numbers to serve as construction materials—being especially prized as *estacas* (pilings) driven deep into the soft subsoil beneath the city—as well as for fuel. Such wanton deforestation increased the general desiccation and runoff into the valley, which in turn imperceptibly elevated the lake beds, threatening worse floods during future rainy seasons.

Still, Mexico City was seemingly flush with economic and agricultural success by the end of the sixteenth century, receiving silver and other consignments from throughout its viceroyalty, while at the same time distributing merchandise imported from Europe and local manufactures. Its eastern sector was now fully developed as far as modern Anillo de Circunvalación, while more than a thousand canoes plied into its *acequia* (canal) system from Lake Texcoco every day, some measuring up to 50 feet in length and bearing several tons of produce. A public park dubbed the Alameda (Poplar Grove) had been planted a few years previously on land beside the Santa Veracruz Hermitage, and other beautification efforts were made; nevertheless, the municipality's populace was calculated at only 58,500 inhabitants by 1600, because of a continual attrition of indigenous residents.

Floods (1603–1691)

The capital suffered such a bad flood during the winter of 1603–1604 that removing the viceregal administration to the higher-elevated satellite city of Tacubaya was seriously considered; instead, though, work intensified on a dig previously initiated by the Franciscans at Huehuetoca, aimed at creating a water-exit at the valley's lowest point. Another rainy autumn three years later produced so much more flooding that the city fathers offered a bounty for a better solution, the winner being a Hamburg-born printer, mathematician, and cosmographer named Heinrich Martin, or Enrico Martínez, who had arrived eighteen years previously in the train of Viceroy Luis de Velasco II. Martínez and a Jesuit named Juan Sánchez Vaquero were put in charge of a new dig at Nochistongo in November 1607, intended to divert the Cuautitlán River— largest of the watercourses flowing into the valley.

Completed within a year, this new outlet failed to live up to expectations during the winter of 1610–1611, so that Martínez was temporarily arrested; a Dutchman named Adrian Boot was moreover contracted at Paris, arriving in New Spain by October 1614 to supervise all work as "royal engineer." Mexico City had meanwhile been struck by an earthquake in August 1611, bringing down several structures and causing extensive damage. Drought further caused a famine in the summer of 1616 and again seven years later, slowing work on the drainage project.

A jurisdictional dispute occurred early in 1624 between the viceroy, Diego Carrillo de Mendoza y Pimentel, Marqués de los Gelves y Conde de Priego, and archbishop Juan Pérez de la Cerna. When the latter was ordered deported to Spain, he retaliated by halting all religious services, sparking a riot that besieged the viceregal palace with an infuriated throng on 15 January 1624. Gelves tried to summon the capital's 4,000 militiamen to aid his handful of ceremonial guards, but the citizenry ignored his repeated appeals. The mob fought its way inside by evening, and the viceroy fled in disguise to a Franciscan monastery, leaving New Spain to be governed by its *Audiencia* until the new viceroy, Rodrigo Pacheco y Osorio, Marqués de Cerralvo, could arrive from Spain late that same October.

After the city was struck by another flood in 1626, then again the next year, Boot and Martínez were directed to resume work on the suspended drainage project. However, huge thunderclouds gathered on 21 September 1629 (Saint Matthew's

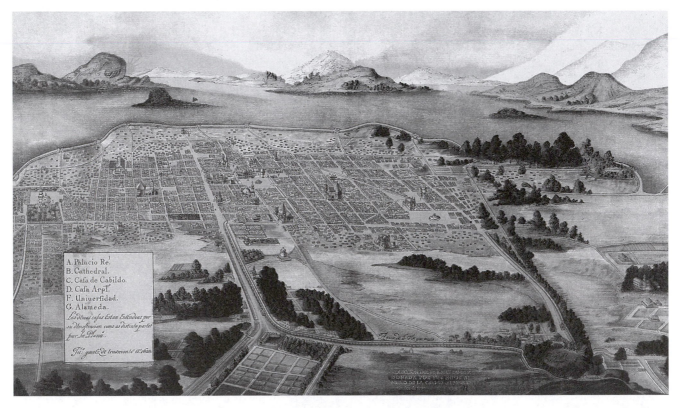

Panorama looking eastward across Mexico City in 1628, reproduced from an original drawing by the architect and engineer Juan Gómez de Trasmontes. In the foreground appears the 900-arch Santa Fe Aqueduct, initiated 22 years previously to bring water down from Chapultepec Hill, while the remains of Lake Texcoco lie behind the *albarrada* or "dyke" in the distance. (Author's Collection)

Day on the Church calendar) and unleashed a thirty-six-hour deluge that plugged the Huehuetoca cut, burst the embankments, and almost entirely inundated the city, drowning hundreds of residents—especially in its lowest-lying areas, where levels rose more than 6 feet. Survivors sought refuge atop their homes, waiting to be rescued by canoes, while the waters did not recede because of that unusually wet autumn. Most officials and civilians transferred over to the mainland, one contemporary estimating that only 400 of the capital's 20,000 families remained behind, and only 27 of its 340 taverns were still open. Elaborate wooden walkways were erected for people to pass above the waters from building to building, with spaces left beneath for boats to glide under, while religious processions were rowed through the streets.

This calamity greatly stultified Mexico City's economic, political, and social life. Water levels rose once more during the rainy season of 1630, and Martínez was arrested to placate angry residents (although soon released); the notion of shifting the capital to a better locale was again seriously entertained. The rains eventually lost their intensity, however, so that the crisis had abated by May 1634. Martínez having died, Boot was superseded as supervisor of the drainage project in August 1637 by the Franciscan friar Luis Flores, after which the Dutch specialist was arrested and succumbed in prison.

Another strong earthquake rattled the unhappy viceregal capital on 27 January 1637, while famine and disease added to its citizenry's woes during the summers of 1639 and 1641–1642. Although Juan Lozano de Balbuena arrived as new royal engineer to provide renewed impetus for the 3,000 Indian laborers, 6,000 mules, 2,800 oxen, and 200 carts employed upon the drainage dig, his efforts could not prevent Mexico City from flooding again in 1647. By the mid-seventeenth century, the entire municipality's population had declined to 70,000 people, scarcely enough to sustain the capital's 52 Franciscan, 30 Dominican, 26 Augustinian, 26 Mercedarian, 18 Carmelite, and 14 convents of other orders. Furthermore, Spain had entered a protracted period of decay overseas that would stunt development in the viceregal capital for several decades to come.

In a cost-cutting effort, the viceroy Luis Enríquez de Guzmán, Conde de Alba de Aliste, shifted the expense of maintaining Mexico City's canals and streets over to its citizenry, which provoked much resentment. Droughts, famines, and diseases reoccurred during the summers of 1653, 1661, 1663, and 1667–1668, as well as some flooding during the winter of 1673–1674. More hunger was experienced in 1678 and 1686, adding to the misery—especially acute among the capital's once-teeming indigenous suburbs of Texcoco, Tacuba, Coyoacán, Cuautitlán, and Ixtapalapa.

Tumult (1692–1700)
During one of the periodic shortages of corn and wheat, Indian petitioners appeared outside the viceregal palace of Gaspar de la Cerda, Conde de Galve, on the afternoon of Sunday, 8 June 1692, bearing a dead woman killed by distributors at the public granary. Receiving no satisfaction, as the viceroy was absent visiting the San Francisco Convent with his family, the complainants withdrew into Tepito in the native sector of Santiago Tlaltelolco for her funeral, but a couple of hundred of men returned at 6:00 P.M. to pelt the palace windows with rocks, then overwhelmed the ten soldiers on guard duty.

As evening fell, full-scale rioting engulfed the heart of Mexico City, mobs torching the criminal courts and jail in the viceregal complex's southwestern quadrant, plus its adjacent city hall, the lower floor of the *Audiencia* building, and 280 wooden *cajones* (merchant kiosks) in the main square. The viceroy issued emergency decrees for food supplies to be brought overnight from private warehouses at Chalco and Celaya to help ease the lower classes' want, then rode through the smoldering capital center on the morning of 9 June 1692 with an escort of 200 mounted noblemen. A few score people had died during this outburst, and a dozen executions over the next few days concluded matters. But the city administration was entirely overhauled as a result, in an effort to preclude future unrest.

Many municipal regulations were reissued, redefining the boundaries of the Spanish core and restricting residential areas for Indians. The capital's outer fringes were also expanded to incorporate more common-lands for cultivation, pushing Mexico City's jurisdiction more deeply into territories previously controlled by Ixtapalapa, Ixtacalco, and other indigenous communities to the south; some of the former lake beds had now dried sufficiently to be used as common pasturelands as well. For added security, a cavalry barracks was erected where the burned merchant kiosks had stood in the main square; most government business had to be conducted from extemporized quarters over the next several years, as Crown offices required extensive repairs. (Even the viceroy was obliged to house his court in the mansion of the Marqués del Valle de Oaxaca, a descendant of Cortés; the viceregal palace was not fit for rehabitation until late 1699.)

A hard frost in September 1695 once again devastated crops throughout the valley, resulting in more shortages and famine the following year. The capital's population was nonetheless calculated at 105,000 people by 1700, the same year in which the last Hapsburg monarch, Charles II, died without issue in Spain, leaving the sixteen-year-old French Bourbon princeling Philip of Anjou to succeed him on the throne, so that the empire's long decline finally began to be reversed.

Bourbon Resurgence (1701–1758)
The change of ruling houses was exemplified for citizens of Mexico City when the viceregal palace's ceremonial guards paraded in new French-style uniforms on 6 January 1703, creating a sensation. More practical reforms, however, had to

wait until after the War of the Spanish Succession could conclude in Europe. On 16 August 1711, the capital was moreover struck by a heavy earthquake, damaging hundreds of its edifices. The new viceroy, Fernando de Alencastre, Duque de Linares, responded by dividing the city into six *cuarteles* (sectors), so as to better concentrate resources for the reconstruction effort. The next year, he moreover sold the damaged cavalry barracks in the main square to the Guild of Philippine Merchants, so as to become converted into a *Parián* (mercantile exchange—so named because of a similar institution in Manila).

A slow but steady economic upsurge throughout the viceroyalty allowed the viceroy Juan de Acuña, Marqués de Casafuerte, to allocate funds for upgrading the city water system and redesigning Alameda Park; for resurrecting the Santa Cruz College in Tlaltelolco by November 1728; for having Luis Díez Navarro design and erect a splendid new *Aduana* (customshouse) in Santo Domingo Square by late June 1730; for an extensive reconstruction of the royal mint by 1734; and so forth. A new Inquisitorial headquarters was also initiated two years later, while the capital's first newspaper—the short-lived *Gaceta de México*—was issued by 1736. Renovations were made to numerous existing religious establishments, such as Santo Domingo and La Merced, while a distinctly Mexican baroque architectural style called *churrigueresco* had furthermore emerged, inspired by Jerónimo de Balbás's beautiful redesign for the cathedral. Private mansions multiplied, and the city even expanded southward, its first clusters of homes appearing beyond the Chimalpopoca Causeway; the stone

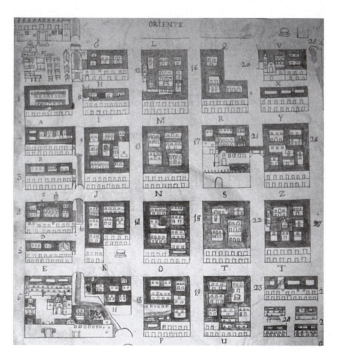

Detailed drawing of a section of the viceregal capital, 1752. (Archivo General de la Nación, Mexico)

Santa Fe Aqueduct coursed down from Chapultepec Hill, while Lake Texcoco continued to recede.

Unfortunately, the capital and its district endured yet another three-year epidemic as of late 1736, starting around Tacubaya and claiming almost 40,000 lives before abating and prompting many survivors to flee. (Six years later, the total number of inhabitants left in the valley was estimated at only 120,000.) A major conflagration gutted a significant portion of the capital's core on 24 February 1742, while the official chronicler José Antonio Villaseñor y Sánchez noted four years later in his *Theatro americano* that Mexico City had not grown in extension in more than a century and a third, "but the structures of its temples have been beautified, and its houses built with greater care." He furthermore added that the capital boasted more than 3,000 vehicles, and "there is no street, not even in the outlying slums, which does not have three or four taverns."

Late Colonial Heyday (1759–1794)

The viceregal capital was to flourish during the latter third of the eighteenth century, after the ascension of the enlightened King Charles III and the acceleration of reforms after the conclusion of hostilities against Great Britain in 1763. As New Spain's silver output also peaked during that period, ample funds were to become available for a host of projects, starting with the 1771–1779 administration of the energetic viceroy Antonio María de Bucareli y Ursúa, who ordered extensive repairs undertaken upon the royal mint, customshouse, and Acordada Jail as of 1772; converted the expropriated Jesuit properties into hospitals and other charitable institutions; established a Crown-run *Monte de Piedad* (pawnshop) to ensure fair treatment for debtors; planted a grand tree-lined Paseo Nuevo (New Boulevard) directly into the city (modern Paseo de Bucareli); had large, flat flagstones replace the older, smaller *tenayucas* (globular stones) from the Tacubaya River as street-paving materials; and completed the long-delayed Belén Aqueduct, which ended at the Salto del Agua fountain on modern Chapultepec Avenue.

Despite distractions caused by a renewed war against Great Britain and a deadly smallpox outbreak, Viceroy Martín de Mayorga was able to found New Spain's first lending institution—the Banco Real de San Carlos (Royal Saint Charles Bank)—and subdivide the capital into eight major and thirty-two minor administrative wards as of 1782. The most populous and impoverished sectors were now clustered to the southeast, nearest to the city's last accessible stretch of waterfront, while its more arid northern sectors—once home to tens of thousands of Indian descendants—had become quite desolate. Exceptionally severe frosts in August–September 1785 once again devastated crops throughout the valley, resulting in shortages and famine next year. But the arrival in late October 1789 of yet another excellent viceroy—Juan Vicente de Güemes Pacheco de Padilla Horcasitas y Aguado, Second

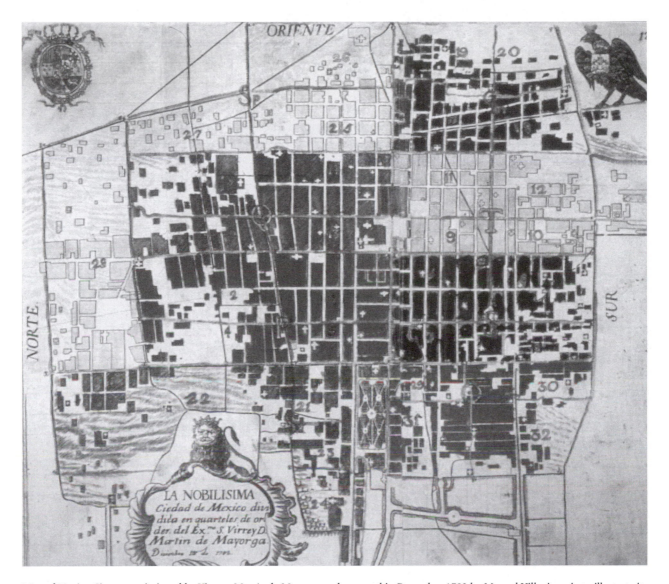

Map of Mexico City, commissioned by Viceroy Martín de Mayorga and executed in December 1782 by Manuel Villavicencio to illustrate its municipal reorganization; north is toward left. (Archivo General de la Nación, Mexico)

Count of Revillagigedo—reinvigorated Mexico City's urban renaissance.

Public lighting, police, and street repair ordinances were revised and enforced, and the architect Ignacio de Castera was commissioned to redesign the façade of the Ayuntamiento (Municipal Hall). Yet Revillagigedo's most lasting act was to order Mexico City's main plaza cleared of its unsightly cluster of kiosks, a beautification measure that the architect José Damián Ortiz de Castro completed four years later, having repaved the square entirely in flagstones, added proper drainage and public fountains at each of its four corners, and refurbished the cathedral's façade. (While excavating the plaza's foundations, important pre-Hispanic artifacts had moreover been recovered, such as the famous stone "Aztec calendar.")

Revillagigedo also ordered a census taken, in 1790, that registered a total population—exclusive of military personnel—of 112,926 in the capital: 2,335 being classified as Spaniards; 50,371 as *criollos* (Creoles), Mexicans of Spanish descent; 25,603 as pure-bred Indians; 19,357 as mixed-heritage *castas;* 8,166 as ecclesiastics; and 7,094 as mulattoes or blacks. That same year, the military engineer Lt.-Col. Miguel Costansó (alternate spelling: Costanzó) took time off from his service as municipal director of Street Paving and Public Works to initiate work on San José Church, while the gifted sculptor Manuel Tolsá arrived from Spain in 1791 to assume a teaching position at the recently created San Carlos Academy of the Three Arts.

A man of exceptional talents, Tolsá was soon hired to completely redesign the cathedral interior in his polished neoclassical style, as well as to create magnificent public fountains and statues—such as a huge equestrian figure of King Charles IV, nicknamed El Caballito (The Little Horse)—and design major new edifices, such as private mansions and a School of Mines (commenced in 1797 and completed by 1813). His genius even extended to the manufacture of fine furniture, carriages, ceramics, and artillery pieces. But more importantly, his refined style inspired many emulators, who left an indelible mark upon the architecture of the city and its viceroyalty. Revillagigedo moreover commissioned de Castera to plan for the capital's future growth, although the viceroy's term expired before any cohesive instruction could be given.

Stagnation (1795–1821)

Funds for large-scale municipal projects evaporated once revolutionary France declared war against Spain and various other European monarchies in January 1793. Madrid was defeated and compelled to realign itself with the radical Directorate in Paris three and a half years later, so that England imposed a crippling transatlantic blockade as of October 1796. Early in the nineteenth century, the visiting German naturalist Alexander, Baron von Humboldt, estimated Mexico City's population at 137,000 inhabitants, with another 138,000 scattered among lesser satellite communities throughout its valley. Private homes continued to extend in a westerly direction along Bucareli Boulevard toward the Ciudadela (Citadel), an armory and magazine converted in 1807 by Costansó from the existing Real Fábrica del Tabaco (Royal Tobacco Factory), as well as north toward San Antonio El Pobre Hermitage.

Uncertainty gripped municipal activities after the French emperor Napoleon I sent an army into Spain in the summer of 1808, deposing Ferdinand VII in favor of his own brother Joseph Bonaparte. Such a crude usurpation of power was widely rejected, yet it contributed to a loosening of imperial ties and the first stirrings toward outright independence among Mexican-born Creoles. Fearful that the viceroy José de Iturrigaray might separate New Spain from their homeland, 300 armed peninsular Spaniards led by the conservative merchant Gabriel de Yermo stormed the viceregal palace on the night of 15–16 September, deposing him in favor of the retired octogenarian Field Marshal Pedro de Garibay.

But a much more serious rebellion erupted exactly two years later in the central part of the viceroyalty, spearheaded by the rural priest Miguel Hidalgo y Costilla. His adherents quickly swelled to 80,000 poorly armed, ill-disciplined insurgents, who marched upon Mexico City and reached Toluca by 28 October. Two days later, they clashed at a mountain pass called Monte de las Cruces with 7,000 Loyalists under Lt.-Col. Torcuato Trujillo, who inflicted 5,000 casualties among the rebels' ranks before being forced back through sheer weight of numbers. Yet although victorious, Hidalgo's army was so bloodied that it instead veered northwestward on 2 November, rather than brave a direct assault against the capital's defenses.

A protracted guerrilla war raged throughout the viceroyalty over the ensuing several years, preventing any significant improvements to Mexico City. Droughts and frosts also blighted harvests throughout its valley, and an epidemic claimed more than 17,000 lives between the viceregal capital

Mexico City's main square as it appeared in 1793, after the beautification efforts of Viceroy Conde de Revillagigedo; the viceregal palace is on the righthand side, with the cathedral to the north, at the far end. (Archivo General de la Nación, Mexico)

and Puebla in 1813. Loyalist fortunes revived two years later, after the restoration of Ferdinand VII to the Spanish throne; yet royal power eventually deteriorated so badly that province after province fell to the Mexican insurgents.

Desperate, the artillery general Francisco Novella and a group of royalist officers deposed the viceroy Juan Ruiz de Apodaca, Conde del Venadito, in Mexico City on 5 July 1821 for his seeming inability to contain the insurrection. Some 5,000 soldiers were thereupon mustered to make a last stand within the capital, but when the new viceroy-designate, Lt.-Gen. Juan O'Donojú, reached Veracruz three weeks later, he recognized that further resistance would be futile and so signed a treaty in August that recognized Mexican independence. An additional meeting was then held on 13 September at Pateza Hacienda outside the capital between the viceroy, Novella, and the supreme insurgent commander Agustín Iturbide, so that Mexico City might be surrendered without bloodshed. A triumphal parade two weeks later, in which 9,000 patriot infantrymen and 7,000 cavalrymen passed below O'Donojú's review balcony in the viceregal palace, marked an official end to three centuries of colonial rule.

Republican Chaos (1822–1846)

Yet although Mexico and its capital were now independent, development continued to languish because of lost Spanish contacts that could not be remedied by a penniless and disorganized new administration. Stable political and economic leadership would prove especially elusive, for after learning that Spain had refused to recognize Mexico's independence, troopers from the 1st Cavalry Regiment abandoned their San Hipólito barracks on the evening of 18 May 1822, in a contrived gesture to urge Iturbide to accept the mantle of emperor. Congress was bullied into ratifying such an arrangement the next morning, so that Agustín I was proclaimed; yet his imperial experiment proved short-lived, for despite dissolving the congress with the help of Gen. Luis de Cortazar's troops that same 31 October, a mutiny at the end of the year by Gen. Antonio López de Santa Anna in Veracruz fanned a widespread uprising against the emperor's undemocratic rule. Virtually all troops in Mexico City rose against Agustín on 9 February 1823, obliging him to shift his headquarters to

Ixtapalucan three days later, while imprisoned congressmen were released.

The emperor finally abdicated on 19 March 1823, leaving the congress to install a temporary triumvirate of Gens. Nicolás Bravo, Guadalupe Victoria, and Pedro Celestino Negrete, while a republic was being crafted. After contentious debates, a new constitution was promulgated on 31 January 1824, Guadalupe Victoria being elected as Mexico's first president on 10 October. Democracy proved frail, though, as the narrow electoral victory won four years later by moderate Gen. Manuel Gómez Pedraza was contested by the second-place finisher, Vice President Guerrero. The "Tres Villas" Battalion of Col. Santiago García rose in support from the Acordada barracks on 30 November 1828, so that full-fledged fighting erupted within the capital's streets two days later; its old *Parián* was ransacked and numerous executions were carried out on 3 December before Gómez Pedraza at last fled.

Hapless Mexico City became a political prize, Guerrero being driven from office a year later by his vice president, Anastasio Bustamante, who in turn was challenged early in 1832 by Santa Anna. The capital welcomed that victorious rebel general on 3 January 1833; he officially took office on 1 April, with the liberal politician Dr. Valentín Gómez Farías as his vice president. A few years later, Bustamante regained the presidency, and the capital was racked by exceptionally violent fighting when Gen. Juan José Urrea, incarcerated in its old Inquisitorial cloisters for having abetted a recent French disembarkation at Veracruz, was broken out of confinement at 2:00 A.M. on 15 July 1840 to lead the 5th Battalion and Comercio Militia Regiment in an assault against Bustamante's palace, capturing the president while he slept. The army chief-of-staff, Gabriel Valencia, plus Gens. Antonio Mozo and Juan Nepomuceno Almonte, launched a counterattack from the Ciudadela barracks, opening fire upon the mutineers with artillery. Bustamante cut his way free with twenty-eight dragoons during the night of 15–16 July, and after a fortnight of street battles that inflicted many civilian casualties, he compelled Urrea to retire.

Bustamante did not fare as well the next year, when garrisons rose against him throughout the country, then were joined by Valencia's 1,200 men from the Ciudadela and Acordada barracks. The beleaguered president nonetheless fought

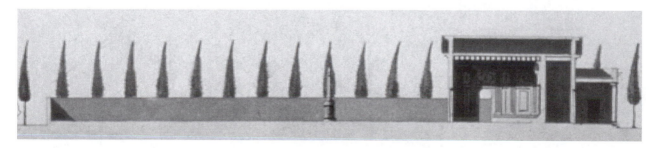

Cutaway view of a proposed "model cemetery" for the city, as drafted by the architect Manuel Tolsá on orders from Viceroy José de Iturrigaray in 1808; no such public burial-ground was actually created until fifteen years later. (Archivo General de la Nación, Mexico)

back with 2,000 loyal troops and a dozen guns, while Mexico City's frightened civilians once more fled out of the line of fire. Although reinforcements eventually raised Bustamante's numbers to 3,500 men, he was driven from the capital on 20 September 1841, resigning nine days later to go into exile. Santa Anna regained power but was also obliged to march northwest from Mexico City in late November 1844 to confront the rebel brigadier Mariano Paredes y Arrillaga, so that the Batallón de Reemplazos (Reserve Battalion) revolted in the Acordada barracks during his absence on 6 December.

The capital nevertheless experienced some growth spurts during these difficult decades, its grand Teatro Nacional (National Theater) being completed by the architect Lorenzo de la Hidalga that same year of 1844, while its total population was estimated at 240,000 inhabitants the following year. They were rattled by a strong earthquake in 1845, after which President José Joaquín de Herrera was successfully toppled by Paredes, who entered on 2 January 1846 to assume office. His administration proved short-lived, though, as the United States declared war that same May to annex Texas, and the city of Guadalajara also rebelled. At dawn on 5 August, as Paredes was preparing to depart Mexico City to invigorate his troops, Gen. José Mariano Salas mutinied at the Ciudadela, deposing him to make way for the return of Santa Anna.

The former dictator timed his reappearance from exile to coincide with Mexico's independence day celebrations on the eve of 15 September 1846, being escorted jubilantly into the capital the next morning by Salas's troops. Santa Anna departed shortly thereafter to gather a large army and attempt to hurl back the U.S. invasion force occupying northeastern Mexico under Gen. Zachary Taylor, and the capital's garrison revolted during his absence against the liberal vice president Gómez Farías on 27 February 1847, who had introduced new taxes upon church properties. Defeated at the Battle of Buena Vista, Santa Anna returned with his two best surviving divisions on 21 March, resolving the dispute before continuing eastward to contest a second U.S. front that had been opened when Gen. Winfield Scott's army disembarked at Veracruz.

Santa Anna failed to stem that second penetration as well, so that the American invaders seized Puebla and gathered strength for a final thrust against Mexico City.

American Occupation (1847–1848)

Scott launched his long-anticipated offensive on 7 August 1847, departing Puebla with 14,000 troops. Santa Anna responded three days later by directing 7,000 men to begin entrenching with thirty cannon atop El Peñón Hill, 10 miles east of the capital. But when the advance U.S. cavalry units probed a Mexican battery at San Antonio (3 miles south of Churubusco) on 18 August, finding it could not be outflanked because of an impassable lava field to its west called El Pedregal, the invaders instead slipped around these prepared defenses along a small road reconnoitered by a youthful Capt. Robert E. Lee.

To contain this flanking maneuver, Santa Anna redeployed 5,500 soldiers and twenty-two guns into San Angel under General Valencia, plus another 3,500 under Gen. Francisco Pérez into Coyoacán, 2 miles farther east. Valencia, however—believing his contingent would see no action—took up station 5 miles southwest of his allotted position, in the crossroads village of Padierna. Early on the afternoon of 19 August 1847, the U.S. vanguard encountered his lines, and Brig. Gideon J. Pillow committed 3,500 men into capturing the adjoining hamlet of San Gerónimo, hoping to thereby cut Valencia off from the main Mexican army. Santa Anna countermoved late in the day, but the U.S. troops entrenched a screen force in San Gerónimo, while continuing behind Valencia's positions under cover of darkness. Next dawn, their surprise attack from Valencia's rear scattered his demoralized troops after only seventeen minutes, inflicting 700 dead and capturing 813 men and all their artillery.

The subsequent American pursuit of this broken formation carried as far northeast as San Angel and Coyoacán, spreading panic among other Mexican units. Brig. William J. Worth took advantage by wheeling a brigade behind the Mexicans' San Antonio stronghold, whose garrison fled north toward

Cutaway view by Manuel Tolsá of Mexico City's bullring in 1793, indicating the changes made to its viceregal box. (Archivo General de la Nación, Mexico)

Churubusco rather than risk being cut off. Morale in Santa Anna's disperse divisions collapsed, every man struggling to recross the river at Coyoacán or Churubusco, while the invaders pressured both bridgeheads. The last Mexican strongpoint—the fortified San Mateo Convent, held by Irish-American deserters who had been reformed into the so-called San Patricio Battalion—fell after more than two hours' heavy fighting, thirty of their sixty-nine survivors later being court-martialed and executed.

Santa Anna regained the panic-stricken capital by midafternoon of 20 August 1847, having suffered 4,000 killed or wounded, plus another 3,000 captured (including two former presidents and six generals). Scott's casualties totaled 139 dead, plus more than 900 wounded or missing; yet although the rapidly emptying city lay at his mercy, the U.S. commander granted Santa Anna a truce on Sunday, 22 August, hoping to conclude a general armistice. After two weeks of fruitless talks, Scott informed the Mexican authorities on 6 September that his army would resume offensive operations the following noon. Expecting to easily brush aside the defenders holding Molino del Rey (King's Mill) and its adjacent stone Casa Mata on the morning of 8 September, the U.S. commander was instead surprised when his 3,500-man thrust endured 116 killed and 671 wounded in a fierce two-hour fight before finally rooting out the Mexican garrisons.

Scott regrouped, then directed his artillery to commence bombarding the hilltop Chapultepec Castle at dawn of 12 September 1847, whose 260 defenders under old Gen. Nicolás Bravo included 50 young cadets from Mexico's Military College, plus 600 troops in its surrounding woods. The next morning U.S. columns charged eastward from Molino del Rey to overwhelm Chapultepec's lower defenses in hand-to-hand fighting, after which Col. Joseph E. Johnston's Voltigeur Regiment scaled the heights and unfurled the Stars and Stripes atop the fortress. (A half dozen cadets fought to the death rather than surrender, one—Fernando Montes de Oca—leaping off the ramparts with the Mexican flag clutched in his arms; all six are today remembered as Mexico's *Niños Héroes* or "Boy Heroes.")

Twin U.S. columns thereupon swept past, toward the capital's western gates. By nightfall Santa Anna had suffered 1,800 casualties, compared with Scott's 450, so that at 1:00 A.M. he gave the order for his surviving troops to evacuate Mexico City northward via Guadalupe. The invaders pushed their way through sporadic resistance into the city's main square by noon of 14 September 1847, after which a couple of days' looting and rioting gutted many buildings. Brig. John A. Quitman was appointed military governor and finally restored order, U.S. forces remaining in possession of the sparsely populated capital over the next eight months, until the Treaty of Guadalupe Hidalgo was ratified and the United States received the largely empty provinces of California, Nevada, Utah, Colorado, Arizona, and New Mexico in exchange for ending their occupation.

Troubled Recuperation (1849–1862)

Mexico City recovered slowly from this difficult episode, its revival further hampered by the bitter recriminations exchanged between Mexico's conservative and liberal factions, who blamed each other for their nation's defeat. A new bullring was nonetheless completed by 1851, before the capital witnessed yet another coup when Gen. Manuel María Lombardini toppled Pres. Juan Bautista Ceballos on 7 February 1853, recalling Santa Anna from Colombian exile to reassume the title on 20 April. The aged dictator was in turn driven from power—for the last time—in early August 1855, and a new political force emerged upon the scene when the victorious liberal Gen. Juan N. Alvarez entered the capital a few days later, becoming provisional president that same October, then convening a constitutional congress to overhaul all national institutions.

The congress's first pronouncement—an abolition issued on 23 November 1855 by Justice Minister Benito P. Juárez against the ancient tribunals catering exclusively to the military and clergy—sparked an angry conservative reaction throughout Mexico that was subsequently contained by liberal troops. More decrees followed, including the expropriation of vast church properties in Mexico City in September 1856,

Engraving of Mexican street vendors, the woman selling foodstuffs, and the man straw mats; reproduced from an 1880 photograph by the French traveler Desiré Charnay. (*América pintoresca*, 1884)

which were cleared so as to widen streets for traffic and furnish more space for urban development.

But all progress halted when the liberal congress unveiled their "reformed" constitution on 5 February 1857, setting off an even angrier wave of conservative denunciations. Moderate individuals such as Gen. Ignacio Comonfort, interim president after Alvarez's resignation, even refused to accept office under its terms. His protégé Brig. Félix María Zuloaga finally led a mutiny by the Mexico City garrison on 17 December that recognized Comonfort's election but called for a new congress to draft a less radical constitution.

Comonfort accepted two days later, while the liberal civilian minister Juárez—legally next in line of succession to the presidency under the old constitution—was jailed. But after three more weeks of chaos, conservative Gen. José de la Parra launched a second mutiny with his Tacubaya garrison on 11 January 1858, driving Comonfort into exile after a brief spate of fighting around Mexico City's Ciudadela. Zuloaga was thereupon acclaimed president on 22 January and abolished all previous liberal reforms, while Juárez was released from prison and traveled clandestinely to the city of Guanajuato to organize resistance as a rival president.

The nation plunged into the three-year Guerra de la Reforma (War of the Reform), during which the capital remained under conservative control. In October 1858, a small liberal army under Gen. Miguel Blanco advanced from Morelia through the valley of Toluca to threaten Mexico City, but Brig. Leandro Valle's thrust into its suburb of San Antonio Abad was bloodily repulsed, so that the attackers retreated. An anti-Zuloaga mutiny by conservative Gens. Miguel María Echegaray and Manuel Robles Pezuela deposed the president that same 23 December, after which the office was refused in early January 1859 by the conservative champion in Jalisco—Gen. Miguel Miramón—before he eventually relented and reached Mexico City on 2 February to assume the mantle.

The next month, a 6,000-man liberal army under Gen. Degollado advanced from Querétaro, occupying the suburbs of Tacubaya and Chapultepec by 22 March 1859. However, conservative Gen. Ramón Corona's 4,000 defenders were well entrenched around the capital's fringes, and they were heartened by news that Gen. Leonardo Márquez Araujo's army was hastening to their relief. Degollado did not try an assault until 2 April, probing the Tlaxpana and San Cosme defenses without success. A few days later, Márquez arrived and crushed Degollado near Tacubaya on 10 April, sending the liberals reeling southwestward in defeat. (Márquez marred his triumph by ordering every liberal captive executed, including medical personnel and civilians, thus earning the sobriquet "Tiger of Tacubaya.")

But despite that successful defense, conservative fortunes gradually faded throughout the country. After a string of liberal victories, their armies coalesced under Gen. Jesús González Ortega, closing in upon Mexico City in December 1860 for a final showdown. President Miramón marshaled his few thousand remaining troops at San Miguel Calpulalpan on the outskirts of the capital, but he was routed on 22 December, fleeing back through the city into exile. González Ortega's victorious liberals made a triumphal entry on Christmas Day, after which Juárez was summoned from Veracruz and officially assumed office as president on 11 January 1861, bringing an end to hostilities.

Few urban changes had been attempted during those three years of strife, and when the liberal administration resumed their efforts to enact some municipal improvements—such as clearing a new satellite *colonia* (ward) at Santa María la Ribera—lack of funds crippled most of their aims. Mexico's defeated conservatives had meanwhile secretly allied themselves with France, so that when Juárez's government defaulted on its foreign debts shortly thereafter, an expeditionary force was encouraged to disembark at Veracruz in January 1862 and spearhead a joint Franco-conservative effort to supplant the republic with an imperial regime.

Improvements to the capital had to be deferred again—even after the first French incursion inland was repulsed at Puebla on 5 May 1862—as more troops arrived from overseas and a second, 25,000-man, Franco-conservative advance under Gen. Elie Frédéric Forey besieged Puebla by early 1863, compelling its garrison to capitulate on 17 May. As Mexico City was deemed virtually indefensible against such a large, well-equipped, modern army, its 12,000-man liberal garrison retired northward with President Juárez on 31 May.

Imperial Capital (1863–1867)

The vanguard of Forey's army, the Chasseurs de Vincennes Battalion, reached the San Lázaro suburb on 4 June 1863, discovering that the republican defenders had already withdrawn. To appeal to popular sentiment, the invaders waited until allied Mexican troops under conservative General Márquez joined them to lead the triumphal parade into Mexico City six days later. A new government was extemporized as of 15 June, authorizing Franco-conservative forces to continue subduing the rest of the nation, while an "imperial" crown was offered to the foreign figurehead Archduke Maximilian of Austria, who was to become a permanent constitutional monarch.

As military columns fanned out into the country, Mexico City experienced a number of municipal innovations, intended to showcase the new regime's modern resources. Few, however, were practicably implemented, and none proved as popular as the simple inauguration of Tivoli gardens around San Rafael, which were to be enjoyed by capital residents for many years to come. The youthful Maximilian and his consort Charlotte (Carlota) reached Mexico City on 12 June 1864, to be crowned amid a generally warm reception. The next year he ordered the creation of a grand new Calzada del Emperador (Emperor's Highway) to run diagonally into the city out of the southwest;

Mexico City, shortly after passing under French rule in June 1863; note the projected railway lines, not actually laid down until several years afterward. (Archivo General de la Nación, Mexico)

it would eventually become transformed into the magnificent Paseo de la Reforma.

Yet no significant upgrading of the capital's infrastructure was possible, as Juárez's fugitive administration sustained a tenacious guerrilla resistance throughout Mexico, discouraging any long-term urban planning. Mexican commoners soon came to resent the foreign presence, and once the U.S. Civil War concluded in 1865, Washington began exerting pressure upon Paris to withdraw Maximilian's supporting French troops. Republican successes multiplied throughout the north the following year, as well as in the southern state of Oaxaca under Gen. Porfirio Díaz, until Maximilian marched forth from Mexico City in February 1867, at the head of 4,000 troops raised by Márquez, to make a stand at Querétaro against his advancing northern foes.

Díaz besieged Puebla the next month, cutting the capital off from its vital sea-communications at Veracruz. Then in late April 1867 his small army appeared outside Mexico City and occupied the towns of Chapultepec, Tacubaya, and Guadalupe, although not strongly enough to overwhelm the entrenched imperial garrison of Gen. Ramón Tabera. Nevertheless, when news arrived of the emperor's capture, the imperial commander met Díaz on the afternoon of 20 June and surrendered Mexico City the next day. Many conservatives were subsequently executed before Juárez made his own triumphal return to reassume office by 15 July.

Porfirian Era (1867–1910)

Bankruptcy and political turmoil continued to dog the capital and the country, however, especially when the increasingly unpopular Juárez announced his re-election plans in 1871. A group of dissident officers tried to raise an insurrection by seizing the arsenals in Belén Jail and La Ciudadela that same 1 October, but they were quickly put down by troops loyal to the government. The retired national hero Porfirio Díaz also proclaimed his own opposition to the president, persisting with a rural guerrilla struggle until Juárez died of natural causes on 18 July 1872, leaving Sebastián Lerdo de Tejada as his successor.

The latter announced that he, too, would run for a second term three years later—thus perpetuating his faction's stranglehold upon power—so that Díaz revolted again in Oaxaca on 10 January 1876, defeating a small army loyal to Lerdo de Tejada's government at Tecoac by 16 November, the president fleeing Mexico City into exile ten days later. The cycle of destructive strife seemed about to repeat itself, but Díaz clamped an unexpectedly efficient regime upon the nation after being elected in May 1877, wielding power uninterruptedly over the next third of a century. Would-be usurpers and other disruptive elements were ruthlessly stamped out, while industrialization and modernization were encouraged, along with foreign investment and trade.

Under Díaz's iron-fisted rule, war-weary Mexico enjoyed a protracted period of peaceful development for the first time since its colonial era, and the capital flourished. Railway and telegraph links multiplied, factories were built, hydroelectric power was introduced, streets became paved, telephones appeared, the valley was properly drained, and so forth. In addition, the city's perimeter expanded, extending by 1891 from Cerrada del Sabino in the northwest to San Simón, Colonia Ex-Hipódromo de Peralvillo, Juventino Rosas, Ixnahualtongo, "Diagonal 20 de Noviembre," Niño Perdido, Dr. Márquez, Cuauhtémoc and Chapultepec avenues, Versalles, General Prim, Sullivan, Melchor Ocampo, Unidad Tlatilco, and the Colonia Santa María la Ribera. Architecturally, its aspect also changed, thanks to the introduction of new construction techniques such as iron framing and poured concrete, which permitted much larger and stronger designs. Spanish-colonial styles also became superseded by more current European models; wealthy citizens erected fine Mansard-style homes in such fashionable new neighborhoods as Colonia Juárez, while a French-style, sixty-four-building medical complex called the General Hospital was commenced in 1896.

The population rose notably from 541,000 inhabitants in 1900 to 721,000 a decade later, finding outlet in a southerly direction with the creation of the Colonias Hidalgo, Roma, and Obrera, as residential expansion to the north and northwest was constrained by an array of rail lines. As 1910 was to mark the centennial of Mexico's independence from Spain, grandiose civic projects were undertaken to showcase the country's progress, such as the new marbled Palacio de Bellas Artes (Palace of Fine Arts) designed by the Italian architect Adamo Boari; a colossal legislative palace envisioned by the Frenchmen Emil Bénard and Maxime Roisin; a palatial headquarters for the secretariat of Communications and Public Works, designed by the Italian Silvio Contri; and a beautiful Renaissance-style post office.

At left, the late eighteenth-century School of Mines in Mexico City, with the Renaissance-style post office beyond, and part of the Palace of Fine Arts at right, as seen from the balcony of the secretariat of Communications and Public Works, ca. 1968. (Ing. Salvador Peña Slane)

Revolutionary Era (1910–1920)

Yet despite the economic prosperity and modernization achieved under the Porfirian regime, resentment had also accumulated against its inequitable distribution of wealth, lack of broad-based social advancement, or significant political participation. When Díaz—now approaching eighty years of age—stood for his eighth term in 1910, the rich and high-minded political neophyte Francisco Ignacio Madero opposed him as head of an "anti-reelectionist" party, but the strongman ordered him arrested on 6 June; by the time the primary election day of 21 June dawned, 5,000 of the challenger's supporters were in prison. When the final election was held on 8 July, an estimated 60,000 were behind bars.

Díaz was officially reinaugurated in Mexico City on 27 September 1910, yet his rule was essentially doomed when Madero escaped from loose confinement on 4 October and gained Texas, calling for a general uprising by 20 November. With astonishing speed, federal power was sapped by a rash of rebellions throughout northern Mexico under leaders such as Pancho Villa, plus a peasant revolt southwest of the capital under Emiliano Zapata. Shaken by such widespread opposition, Díaz offered to resign on 7 May 1911; two and a half weeks later, after rioting had erupted outside the presidential palace itself in Mexico City's main square, he fled into exile. Madero made a triumphal entry on 7 June, only scant hours after a heavy earthquake had killed 207 people. He won a rescheduled election and was legally installed into office by 6 November.

However, not all his revolutionary adherents were mollified, Zapata continuing to expropriate estates to be distributed among his impoverished peasant followers. In such a troubled atmosphere, Gens. Manuel Mondragón and Gregorio Ruiz mutinied against Madero at dawn of Sunday, 9 February 1913, by marching from Tacubaya toward the presidential palace with three cavalry regiments and an artillery regiment totaling 2,400 men, six cannon, and fourteen machine guns. En route, one column released Gen. Bernardo Reyes from imprisonment at Santiago Tlaltelolco, while another freed Brig. Félix Díaz—the former dictator's nephew—from Lecumberri Penitentiary. A group of 600 cadets from the Tlalpan Military College also preceded the mutineers into the capital's main square and briefly occupied the presidential palace before being overwhelmed by 500 loyal troops under the elderly Gen. Lauro Villar.

The latter also arrested Ruiz when the first mutineer column reached the Zócalo, sparking a burst of gunfire that killed Reyes and 300 other people—including many curious civilian onlookers. The mutineers then forced their way into the Ciudadela at 1:00 P.M., executing most of its garrison. Meanwhile, President Madero arrived from Chapultepec Castle and appointed the former Porfirian general Victoriano Huerta to replace the badly wounded Villar. Huerta ordered Ruiz and all the rebel cadets executed, while Madero traveled to Cuernavaca to summon 1,000 more troops under Brig. Felipe Angeles. There ensued a tense standoff on 10 February, shattered at 10:00 A.M. the next morning by an artillery duel with the mutineers ensconced inside the Ciudadela, during which another 500 civilians were killed. (Eventually, exchanges within the close confines of the crowded city would cause 5,000 deaths, an ordeal remembered as the Decena Trágica or "Tragic Fortnight.")

Huerta soon had 6,000 troops arrayed against the 1,800 rebels remaining to Mondragón and Díaz, yet he seemed incapable of reducing the ancient fortress, fanning doubts as to his loyalty. After five more days of long-range shelling, Madero's youngest brother, Gustavo, arrested Huerta at 2:00 A.M. on 18 February 1913, accusing him of treachery. Unconvinced, the president ordered the general released. But at 1:30 P.M. that same afternoon, Huerta in turn detained Gustavo Madero, the president, Vice Pres. José María Pino Suárez, and most members of the cabinet. Huerta and Díaz met that same evening at the residence of U.S. ambassador Henry Lane Wilson—a vocal critic of Madero—to sign a pact whereby the former temporarily assumed the presidency. Despite being promised safe conduct into Cuban exile, Madero was murdered at Lecumberri Penitentiary on the night of 22 February. (For his

Mexican street-vendors, the woman selling charcoal, and the man basins; reproduced from an 1880 photograph by the French traveler Desiré Charnay. (*América pintoresca,* 1884)

role in this treachery, Wilson was shortly thereafter recalled to Washington and forced to retire.)

The death of Madero unleashed another wave of anarchy throughout Mexico, factions rising everywhere in opposition to Huerta, while the capital became little more than a political football disputed by contending generals. After defeats at Zacatecas and Guadalajara, Huerta resigned on 14 July 1914, seeking asylum in Spain. Gen. Alvaro Obregón's 18,000-man Ejército del Noroeste (Army of the Northwest) arrived one month later, and he signed a treaty with a representative from the federal government at Teoloyucan outside Mexico City on 13 August that dissolved the Huertista administration and much of the regular army, before marching triumphantly into the capital five days later. Obregón's political superior, Venustiano Carranza, appeared by 20 August, assuming office as president the following day. But Villa and Zapata refused to recognize his authority, so warfare resumed.

Obregón's depleted 4,000-man garrison was compelled to abandon Mexico City for Veracruz on 24 November 1914, so that Zapata occupied the capital's southern suburbs two days later. Then, on 1 December, Villa also appeared at Tacuba, combining his army with Zapata's to parade as many as 50,000 revolutionaries through the city streets five days later; however, as neither leader had any coherent political agenda, their occupation proved short-lived. Obregón re-entered Mexico City unopposed on 28 January 1915, finding its citizenry on the brink of starvation. He continued north by 10 March, smashing Villa's army in two huge battles in the state of Guanajuato. A detachment of 4,000 cavalrymen under Villa's henchman Rodolfo Fierro launched a diversionary counterthrust toward the capital that same June, so successfully that Obregón's subordinate Pablo González even vacated Mexico City. During his absence, a Zapatista contingent under Gen. Amador Salazar advanced upon the capital, only to be defeated on 30 July, permitting González to return eleven days later.

Obregón's subsequent string of victories throughout the interior of the country ensured that the capital remained firmly under Carranza's administrative control. A series of destructive sweeps were launched into Zapata's home state of Morelos in May 1916, obliging the guerrilla chieftain to attempt to relieve pressure upon his followers by advancing across the mountains to threaten the capital again late that same September. He retired, however, after seizing only the Xochimilco pumping station on 4 October and temporarily cutting off much of the city's water supply.

The revolution began to wind down after Zapata was killed in 1919, while Villa had already been reduced to little more than a bandit nuisance in the north. The troubled epoch finally ended when the increasingly unpopular Carranza fell out with retired general Obregón in April 1920, who quickly rallied numerous colleagues and closed in upon the capital. Carranza departed Mexico City for Veracruz on 7 May aboard a 15-mile-long train convoy bearing 10,000 adherents and the

national treasury, only to be intercepted en route and assassinated two weeks later.

Modern Boom (1921–Present)

As the threat of military descents receded, life in Mexico City quickly revived. Despite the recent shortages and upheavals, its population nonetheless stood at 906,000 inhabitants by 1921, and a resurgence in its commercial and industrial activities even allowed for a wealthy new neighborhood called Lomas de Chapultepec (Chapultepec Heights) to be created by the renowned architect José Luis Cuevas two years later. There followed the Colonia Hipódromo as of 1927—also designed by Cuevas and another distinguished architect, José G. de la Lama—and then Anzures and Polanco. Municipal projects complemented this private construction boom, so that public buildings multiplied, while many streets were widened, extended, or created.

Population figures soared from 1,230,000 residents in 1930 to 1,760,000 a decade later, while the capital's urban boundaries also expanded significantly during and immediately after World War II as industrialization gathered greater impetus because of Mexico's participation on the Allied side during that conflict. A vast campus for the Universidad Nacional Autónoma de México (National Autonomous University of Mexico) was cleared in 1950–1953, by which time the city's population had skyrocketed to 3,480,000 inhabitants, and the new Colonias Federal, Moctezuma, and Jardín Balbuena had taken shape to its east; the ancient towns of Azcapozalco, Ticomán, Zacatenco, and Santa Isabel Tola were being absorbed to its north; while the wealthy Lomas de Chapultepec neighborhood was already sprawling as far westward as the adjoining state of Mexico.

By 1960 the capital's population had swollen to 4,374,000 residents, a figure that would rise to 6,874,165 within a decade. Rural-to-urban migration patterns accelerated exponentially throughout central Mexico as the need for manual laborers dwindled in the countryside because of increased mechanization; workers therefore felt constrained to seek employment at a living wage, in addition to better residential conditions around the fringes of the metropolis. Unbridled growth of the city within its bowl-shaped valley only accentuated such modern ills as pollution, traffic congestion, crime and corruption, as well as shortages of essential services such as water, electricity, and housing. With relatively few high-rise buildings erected because of its frequent earthquakes, Mexico City sprawled into a leviathan, spilling so dramatically beyond its boundaries into the state of Mexico that its population was measured at 8,235,744 residents by 1990—or 15,047,685 if the entire metropolitan area were included. By the dawn of the twenty-first century, estimates as to the total number of inhabitants fluctuated between 21 and 25 million.

For further reading on the history of Mexico City, please consult the Select Bibliography at the end of this volume.

Monterrey

Sun-baked frontier outpost that blossomed into an industrial powerhouse during the late nineteenth century.

Stillborn Settlements (1577–1587)

After the capture of the Aztec capital in central Mexico in 1521, Spanish conquistadors fanned out to subdue the fallen empire's outlying vassal states, encountering particularly stiff resistance from the autonomous and seminomadic Chichimec tribes of the stark northern highlands. Rich mineral deposits and fertile desert oases nonetheless enticed Spanish adventurers into this region over the next several decades, paving the way for hardy bands of permanent settlers.

In 1577, Capt. Alberto del Canto probed northeastward from his recently founded town of Saltillo in quest of a passage through the towering limestone massif known as the Sierra Madre Oriental, so as to open a cart trail down to the Gulf of Mexico. At the point where this range broke up and abruptly veered westward, he discovered a relatively easy descent through a picturesque and fertile valley that he dubbed the Valle de Extremadura (Extremadura Valley). A tiny way station called Santa Lucía was consequently established on its flood plain, 1,765 feet above sea level on the banks of the eastward-flowing Santa Catarina River, near a freshwater source that soon became known as the Ojos de Santa Lucía (Santa Lucía

Springs). But del Canto was recalled the next year by the *real audiencia* (royal tribunal) at Guadalajara, and the settlement failed to flourish.

In May 1579, the converted Portuguese Sephardic Jew, former slaver, and veteran conquistador Luis de Carvajal y de la Cueva secured a commission from King Phillip II in Spain to penetrate this same territory out of the east—from his already existing fiefdom along the Gulf coast—and carve out a new province to be called Nuevo Reino de León (New Kingdom of León). De Carvajal returned to Mexico the next year, eventually pushing inland from Tampico to re-establish a community called San Luis Rey de Francia on the northern banks of the Santa Lucía Springs by early 1582. Gaspar Castaño de Sosa became this community's first *alcalde mayor* (municipal magistrate), governing not only this tiny would-be capital but San Luis's surrounding piedmont district as well, which was nestled between dramatically serrated mountain ridges to its south and west nicknamed the Dientes (Teeth). There was also an isolated prominence to its east—called the Silla (Saddle) Mountain because of its distinctive shape.

Spanish settlers hunted down the primitive tribesmen who roamed throughout the valley to be sold as slaves, and also began planting wheat and raising livestock. They enjoyed considerable success with the latter two endeavors, given the semiarid climate with its cool and wet winters and stifling

Panoramic view eastward across Monterrey, as seen from its late eighteenth-century Obispado or "Bishop's Palace" in the right foreground; the distinctive Silla or "Saddle" Mountain looms in the distant background. (Ober, *Travels in Mexico,* 1884)

summers. Yet Governor de Carvajal was frequently absent, busily persuading friends and compatriots in adjacent districts to shift over into his sparsely populated jurisdiction. The viceroy finally summoned him in 1586 to answer complaints from rival authorities about his infringements, ordering him to restore more than twenty villages to their original jurisdictions, while San Luis's settlers were to desist from enslaving Indians.

The indigenous population furthermore counterattacked the following year, massacring any Spaniard who did not flee from the valley, then torching their crude dwellings and wheat fields, as well as running off the cattle. Lesser Spanish settlements at Cerralvo and La Cueva were also abandoned by 1588, so that the region was left almost entirely depopulated.

Foundation and Early Struggles (1596–1751)

After de Carvajal succumbed in an Inquisitorial jail in 1590, and Castaño and his adherents were arrested or dispersed from Almadén (modern Monclova, Coahuila) the next year, Diego de Montemayor—a veteran of Captain del Canto's original penetration—led thirty-four people constituting twelve families back up to this potentially bountiful site. They reestablished a community at Santa Lucía Springs on 20 September 1596 with the new name of Ciudad de Nuestra Señora de Monterrey (City of Our Lady of Monterrey)—

specifically chosen to ingratiate this unauthorized venture with the reigning Mexican viceroy, Gaspar de Zúñiga y Acevedo, Conde de Monterrey. One month later, de Montemayor left Alfonso de Barreda as *alcalde mayor* and traveled to Mexico City to obtain that dignitary's blessing, which was grudgingly granted in February 1599.

The tiny "city" of Monterrey claimed a municipal district radiating for 30 miles in every direction as the capital of a reconstituted New Kingdom of León (a name eventually shortened into Nuevo León); however, few migrants traveled up to its remote desert locale, the lone priest, Lic. Cebrián de Acevedo Ovalle, not receiving support from a delegation of Franciscan missionaries out of Zacatecas until 1602, when they founded the community's first convent (San Andrés, better remembered as San Francisco). Otherwise, Monterrey remained a precarious frontier outpost, its few inhabitants eking out a subsistence existence by capturing Indians as slaves, in addition to some planting or ranching. Governor de Montemayor died in April 1611, and a downpour that same year inundated the squalid settlement so badly that his acting successor—*justicia mayor* (chief magistrate) Diego Rodríguez—shifted the community across from the northern to the southern banks of the springs in 1612, laying out a new grid pattern of urban plots around a central square (modern Plaza de Zaragoza).

The next year, the viceroy officially conferred the gover-

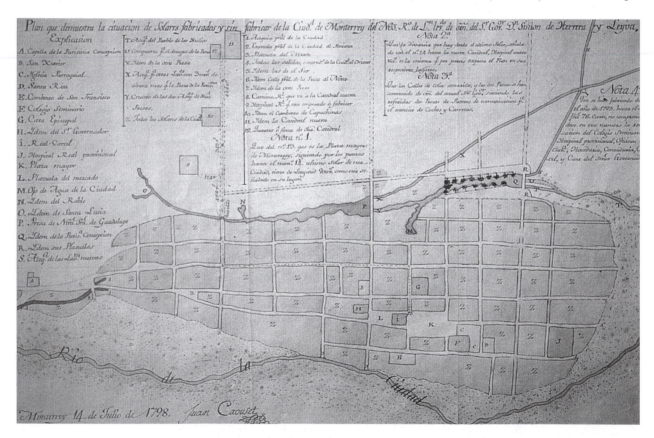

Map drawn by Juan Crouset in 1798, on orders from Gov. Simón de Herrera y Leyva, to identify fully developed city plots and thus be able to contribute toward the construction of a new cathedral. (Archivo General de la Nación, Mexico)

norship of Nuevo León upon the rich Zacatecan miner Agustín de Zavala, who never actually visited Monterrey during his tenure, although he did sporadically send supplies to its twenty or thirty households. However, when Zacatecas's mines suffered an economic decline during the ensuing decade, de Zavala ceded the title of governor of Nuevo León to his illegitimate son Martín. The latter in turn arrived at Monterrey on 8 August 1626 with more than 150 new settlers, as well as cattle and mining equipment and the first clerical beneficiary to minister to its Spanish populace; the Franciscan missionaries were to continue tending to the indigenous population.

Martín de Zavala found fewer than 200 Spanish, mulatto, or mestizo residents scattered throughout his district. Monterrey had no municipal offices or church, only the stout San Andrés Convent with its "strong tower" (which had helped repulse a dawn raid by the Indian chieftain Guajuco only two years previously) and some "very good bells." The few homes were "far from each other . . . without order nor continuity, streets, police, nor commerce," so that the new governor—having committed himself to establishing two new towns in Nuevo León—tried to reconstitute the insubstantial capital as the "town of Cerralvo," although its offended citizenry got that decision rescinded two years later.

Despite its lack of urban development, Monterrey and the valley nonetheless served as an invaluable springboard for prospectors scouring the nearby mountain ranges for mineral deposits, as well as missionaries seeking converts; it also welcomed numerous sheep farmers out of the south, plus large horse- and cattle-herders, so that ranches began to multiply and its vast municipality gradually contracted as new rural hamlets were created. Unfortunately, this brief upsurge in activity was offset by a damaging flood and smallpox epidemic in 1636, plus another outbreak of that same disease in 1646–1648 that decimated the few score peaceful indigenous *rancherías* (encampments) dotted around the valley and reduced the overall population figure to perhaps 400 residents. Governor de Zavala was even obliged to instruct all property owners to maintain their homes in the neglected capital on pain of forfeiture, while its municipal offices began to be slowly rebuilt as of February 1653.

Smallpox recurred in 1660–1662, slowing the reconstruction of the church initiated the next year under Capt. Juan Cavazos, and the mason Juan de Montalvo de Zavala himself died on 8 August 1664. When Nicolás de Azcárraga arrived as new governor three years later, he found Nuevo León's valley core inhabited by perhaps 150 Spanish households. Monterrey itself consisted of a half dozen blocks of crude adobe dwellings clustered around three unpaved streets (modern Morelos, Hidalgo, and P. Mier). De Azcárraga attempted to improve matters by introducing a regulated tax system, using the resultant funds to clear the city's encroaching bogs and scrubland; he also requested the issuance of a city coat of arms in late September 1667, which was granted by the Crown on 9 May 1672.

The reconstruction of the lone church was completed the next year.

A large military expedition was raised by Gen. Alonso de León to strike northward into Texas in 1686, but Monterrey otherwise remained in bucolic isolation for the remainder of the seventeenth century, its inhabitants now numbering roughly 1,300 people. Work on a large new stone church commenced early the next century, while the Jesuits' San Francisco Javier Convent—initiated in 1702 at the northwestern corner of modern Morelos and Escobedo streets—served as a temporary parish. One of the city's periodic floods occurred eight years later and provoked a modest population shift westward, where some planted orchards upon a higher stretch of urban plots.

Disaster and Resurrection (1752–1845)

Monterrey suffered a major flood in 1752, collapsing or weakening virtually every major edifice and driving so many families to emigrate northeastward into the recently opened territory of Nuevo Santander (modern Tamaulipas) that the capital's population plummeted from 3,334 residents to 800 over the next four years. However, Pedro de Barrio Junco y Espriella reassumed the governorship and maintained Monterrey alive through such measures as erecting new *casas reales* (royal offices) on the higher ground to its east (a building that later became known as the Casa del Campesino).

Still, when Nuevo León was elevated to a diocese by the papal bull *Relata semper* on 15 December 1777, Monterrey remained such an unprepossessing seat that its first bishop—the Franciscan Antonio de Jesús Sacedón—chose to be invested two years later at the more centrally located town of Linares, where a new cathedral was to be erected. But as the only city within the region, Monterrey was eventually restored to full prominence by King Charles III's decision to reorganize the administration of New Spain in late 1786, which included elevating Monterrey to the headquarters of a new northern department to be called the Provincias Internas (Internal Provinces). The city was then furthermore placed under direct military control by the viceroy in Mexico City as of November 1792, who provided funding to help erect new public buildings, as well as to bolster its primitive economy.

The ecclesiastical authorities had already made a similar commitment, Sacedón's successor—Bishop Rafael José Verger—authorizing the construction of a sumptuous new Episcopal residence called Nuestra Señora de Guadalupe (although more commonly known as the Obispado or Bishop's Palace, later the Museo Regional) atop Chepe Vera Hill in 1786–1787. He also had waters from the Santa Catarina River diverted down into the city via an aqueduct. The stone *parroquia* (parish church) was also concluded by 1791, although its façade was not completed until nine years later; the energetic Andrés Ambrosio Llanos y Valdés arrived as bishop in 1792, making the city his de facto seat and further boosting development by hiring the master architect Juan Crouset to lay out a new northern suburb around Nuestra Señora del Roble Chapel. Llanos also founded a *Colegio Seminario* (seminary college) and a Capuchin nunnery, as well as initiating work on a huge new hospital dedicated to Nuestra Señora del Rosario in 1793 (in the former home of the former governor, Ignacio Wessel, or "Ussel," at the corner of modern Abasolo and Mina streets). Moreover, the bishop initiated a vast new cathedral project at the intersection of today's Juárez and Tapia streets.

Simón de Herrera y Leyva arrived as governor in 1795 and added two new municipal dams, plus the Alameda park and a market (today's Plaza de Hidalgo); lesser public amenities—such as posted street names—were also implemented for the first time. Yet royal funding dried up as Spain was subsequently dragged into a protracted struggle in Europe, so that Monterrey's growth became stunted. Its hospital was not even functioning when a smallpox epidemic struck in 1798, so that local authorities had to request keys to its empty structure from church officials and personally assist Fr. Antonio de la Vera y Gálvez in administering vaccinations. A yellow-fever epidemic also broke out in 1802–1803, but the city's population was nonetheless measured at 6,412 inhabitants in that latter year, and Bishop Primo Feliciano Marín de Porras was able to inaugurate the city's first school.

Because of its remove far from the viceroyalty's commercial and political mainstream, Monterrey remained undisturbed by the deposal of Ferdinand VII by the French emperor Napoleon I in the summer of 1808; the subsequent revolt that Miguel Hidalgo y Costilla launched in central Mexico to win outright independence from Spain in September 1810 also found only modest support around Monterrey. The rebel chieftain Mariano Jiménez sent columns from Saltillo under "Brigs." Juan Bautista Carrasco and Ignacio Camargo to occupy the city peacefully on 17 January 1811, yet Hidalgo was defeated, betrayed, and executed in Coahuila shortly thereafter, so that monarchist rule was reimposed.

Despite a guerrilla descent made by the Texan leader José Herrera on 2 July 1813, repelled by Monterrey's garrison under Capt. Francisco Bruno Barrera, the city was not seriously menaced again during the ensuing eight years of internecine warfare. Its first printing press was even introduced (captured from insurgents), and Monterrey became a regional royalist stronghold after Col. Joaquín de Arredondo y Muñiz established his headquarters in 1814. Its population flourished modestly, and a few more municipal improvements were implemented, such as converting its abandoned San Francisco Javier Convent into the Palacio de Gobierno (Government Palace) and paving over several streets the next year, as well as encouraging urban expansion along Roble Street as of 1817. Eventually, however, the insurgency triumphed elsewhere in Mexico, so that de Arredondo fled and the city unilaterally embraced independence as of 3 July 1821.

Regrettably, liberty did not result in any appreciable urban growth or modernization, as the fledgling nation was plunged into factional strife, the first round occurring after the victorious insurgent Gen. Agustín Iturbide crowned himself "emperor" in Mexico City in May 1822. He was soon deposed, and Monterrey—now with a population of 12,282—officially became recognized as the capital of the new "State of Nuevo León" on 7 May 1824, its government issuing the first newspaper (the *Gazeta Constitucional de Nuevo León*) by August 1826. Still, a rancorous split developed between conservative elements—often personified by clerics—who wished to maintain colonial-era institutions intact, while liberal forces headed by such local leaders as the city mayor and state governor Manuel María de Llano proposed sweeping social change.

Nuevo León, like the rest of the young republic, became so riven that Monterrey changed hands several times in coups and countercoups, so that reform could proceed only fitfully. Oil lamps for public illumination, for example, were installed in 1832, although a proposed new water fountain was never completed. The city was then most unexpectedly thrust into international prominence after the U.S. Congress voted on 1 March 1845 to accede to American settlers' wishes and annex the Republic of Texas, which Mexico regarded as a breakaway province. Relations with Washington were consequently severed, and tensions along the disputed border between Texas and Mexico heightened when Gen. Zachary Taylor pushed

Profile and cutaway views by Crouset of a proposed new public jail, 1794. (Archivo General de la Nación, Mexico)

south from Corpus Christi with 3,500 troops in March 1846 to establish U.S. sovereignty.

Early the next month, Mexican major-general (and former president) Mariano Arista was appointed to lead the so-called Ejército del Norte (Army of the North) from Monterrey to challenge Taylor's incursion. Arista set out with several thousand troops, his vanguard under Gen. Pedro Ampudia y Grimarest reaching Matamoros by 11 April 1846. This force was defeated by Taylor the following month in the twin battles of Palo Alto and Resaca de la Palma, marking the opening of the Mexican-American War. Matamoros was duly abandoned, Arista replaced, Texas and California secured by the United States, and Monterrey reinforced. But despite having achieved its primary goal, Washington was unable to bring the Mexican government to the bargaining table and so instructed Taylor to increase pressure by forging southwestward and investing Monterrey.

American and French Occupations (1846–1866)

The U.S. Army started its cross-desert trek from Matamoros on 4 August 1846, approaching Monterrey via Camargo and Mier. Hundreds of civilians fled in anticipation of a full-fledged assault, while Ampudia built up the defenders' strength to 4,000 regulars and 2,000 to 3,000 state militiamen, plus forty-six poor-quality cannon. Although almost 5,000 invaders were left behind during their march because of harsh conditions, Taylor was able to launch his final thrust from Cerralvo on 12 September with 3,200 regulars and a like number of militiamen.

The U.S. forces came within sight of Monterrey on the morning of 19 September 1846, being fired upon by its 8-gun Ciudadela (citadel), which was actually the still incomplete cathedral, dubbed the "Black Fort" by the invaders. The next afternoon, Brig. William Jenkins Worth swung west in a flanking maneuver with Col. John C. Hays's Texas Cavalry Regiment, Lt.-Col. Thomas Staniford's 1st Infantry Brigade, and Col. Persifor F. Smith's 2nd Brigade, being confronted early on 21 September by 1,500 Mexican cavalrymen and infantrymen under Lt.-Col. Juan N. Nájera. The latter were scattered, so that Worth cut Monterrey's supply line by straddling the Saltillo road, then continued east up Blanca Hill to overrun its Federación and El Soldado strongpoints by nightfall.

Taylor's main body meanwhile mounted a direct assault against Monterrey's northeastern suburbs, Col. David E.

Crude watercolor, by the American soldier Samuel Chamberlain, of street fighting in the approaches to Monterrey's cathedral, September 1846. (West Point Museum)

Twiggs's 1st Division—temporarily commanded by Lt.-Col. John Garland—and other units becoming enfiladed, suffering 394 casualties. Despite such punishment, U.S. forces captured the 200-man Fortín de las Tenerías (Tanneries Redoubt), then rested throughout the rainy day of 22 September 1846, while Worth stole up Independencia Hill and installed a 12-pound howitzer atop its 800-foot summit to dislodge the 200 Mexican troops of Lt.-Col. Francisco Berra who were holding the Obispado, prompting a discouraged Ampudia to call in his outposts that night.

When the main U.S. body noticed that the Rincón or Diablo strongpoint lay abandoned the next morning, it was quickly seized by the 1st Mississippi Rifle Regiment under Col. Jefferson Davis (the future Confederate president). Supporting units thereupon fought their way house by house into the heart of Monterrey, while a similar offensive moved out of the west under Worth. Most of the city was in American hands by dawn of 24 September 1846, when Ampudia requested terms from his headquarters inside the stout walls of the unfinished cathedral. Taylor agreed to permit the surviving Mexican troops to march out the following morning with their arms and six guns, retreating beyond Rinconada Pass, while both sides observed a temporary cessation of offensive operations throughout the theater.

Monterrey's conquest had cost the invaders 120 dead and 368 wounded, compared with 700 casualties among the defenders. Taylor subsequently used the battered city as a base from which to resume his push southwestward on 13 November 1846, occupying Saltillo three days later without resistance. But rather than proceed more deeply across the desert into the teeth of a Mexican army waiting at San Luis Potosí under President Antonio López de Santa Anna, Washington decided to open a second front by sending Maj.-Gen. Winfield Scott with a seaborne expedition to invade Veracruz. Taylor therefore returned into Monterrey with his main army to press southeastward against Ciudad Victoria, but he learned on 18 December that Santa Anna was moving north to assail Worth's small garrison at Saltillo. U.S. reinforcements were therefore hastened across, prompting Santa Anna to cancel this operation until February 1847, when he finally advanced and was defeated by Taylor at the Battle of Buena Vista.

Monterrey remained in U.S. hands until Mexico's national capital fell to Scott, and its government capitulated by the spring of 1848. Monterrey was thereupon restored, repaired, and revived somewhat under Gov. José María Parás, who rebuilt some municipal buildings and expanded urban boundaries both southeastward and southward (this suburb becoming known as San Luisito or "Little San Luis," because of the number of new migrants arriving from San Luis Potosí); the total urban population was measured at 26,795 residents by 1853. But Mexico's political life once more descended into anarchy as conservatives and liberals fell out, the former calling for a strong traditional oligarchy to avoid the divisive weakness of republican rule, while liberals felt that social strictures should instead be loosened further so that more citizens might participate in civic affairs.

Coups and countercoups resumed at Monterrey, until liberal Gen. Santiago Vidaurri seized the governorship on 22 May 1855, then used the city as his headquarters for campaigns into central Mexico during the so-called Guerra de la Reforma (War of the Reform). He was defeated at the Battle of Ahualulco de los Pinos near San Luis Potosí in late September 1858, and his administration fled Monterrey for Galeana the following year, until the conservatives were in turn driven from national office early in January 1861. The latter thereupon allied themselves with France and encouraged the disembarkation of an expeditionary force at Veracruz in January 1862 that spearheaded a drive to eradicate the republican form of government in favor of an imperial administration.

Mexico's liberal republican president Benito P. Juárez was driven north to San Luis Potosí, then retreated into Saltillo by late December 1863 and—after deposing Vidaurri on 29 March 1864 for hinting at switching sides—transferred his provisional government into Monterrey five days later. A pursuing Franco-conservative offensive under Gen. Armand Alexandre de Castagny eventually caused Juárez to decamp on 5 August, after which Monterrey's new imperial rulers introduced a few civic improvements, such as a new fountain by Mateo Mattei in its main square, numerous beautification efforts, and the hiring of Isidoro Epstein as city engineer. A republican counterthrust by Gen. Miguel Negrete briefly reoccupied the city without opposition on 12 April 1865, but imperial forces reclaimed it after defeating the liberals two months later at the Battle of La Angostura.

A more damaging incursion into Monterrey began on 23 November 1865, when its imperial garrison launched a sally to drive away a concentration of republican guerrillas under Gen. Mariano Escobedo, who were operating from nearby Guadalupe Hill. This sortie was checked by Col. Jerónimo Treviño's republican cavalry, permitting Escobedo to lead twin columns in a counterattack against the city's Carlota and Pueblo strongpoints two days later, fighting their way into Monterrey's main square, only to be interrupted by the unexpected arrival of an imperial relief column from Saltillo under French Foreign Legion major La Hayrie. Learning that Gen. Pierre-Jean Joseph Jeannigros was not far behind with another 800 imperial soldiers, Escobedo and his followers melted into the mountains. Imperial fortunes eventually waned elsewhere in Mexico, however, so that Jeannigros abandoned Monterrey without a fight on 6 July 1866, and republican rule was restored.

Porfirian Industrialization (1867–1909)

Despite the toll exacted by these invasions, the small city's commercial prospects had nonetheless brightened, as its geographic isolation had been ended by growing trade relations with the Confederate states—especially nearby Texas, whose

Panoramic view from the Bishop's Palace, looking across the burgeoning city of Monterrey toward La Silla Mountain in the far distance, ca. 1919. (Library of Congress)

cotton brokers had diverted shipments through Mexican conservative sympathizers so as to circumvent the Union blockade imposed during the U.S. Civil War. Branch offices had been created at Monterrey as a result, and its first textile mill—La Fama, located in its western hamlet of Santa Catarina—had been opened by 1865. Southern entrepreneurs also immigrated into its district after the Confederacy was defeated, evincing particular interest in the nonprecious metal and coal deposits dotting nearby mountain ranges.

Treviño was elected state governor in 1867, and he instructed Monterrey's new city engineer, Francisco Leonides Mier, to pursue Epstein's earlier plan of expanding the capital in a northerly direction; residences also multiplied around the Colegio Civil and El Roble Chapel. But the nation's bankruptcy and political turmoil continued to hamstring its progress, especially after the increasingly unpopular Juárez announced his re-election plans in 1871, provoking widespread military opposition. Treviño joined this insurrection, being defeated by Gen. Diódoro Corella at the Battle of San Bernabé del Topo Chico outside Monterrey on 30 May 1872. But when Juárez's successor, Sebastián Lerdo de Tejada, announced that he too would run for a second term three years later—thus perpet-

uating his faction's stranglehold upon power—another widespread revolt brought Gen. Porfirio Díaz to power by November 1876.

Surprisingly, Díaz inaugurated a ruthlessly effective regime, stifling all unrest while encouraging the industrialization and modernization of the war-weary nation. Monterrey benefited from this interlude of peaceful stability, its population doubling from 15,300 inhabitants in 1879 to 33,356 only four years later, while railway, electric, telephone, and streetcar services were all introduced within that same span. However, it was not to be until Díaz was re-elected president in 1885 and imposed the dynamic Gen. Bernardo Reyes upon Nuevo León as provisional governor that the city's boom truly gathered impetus; for although local resentment forced Reyes's withdrawal by October 1887, he was reinstated two years later and successfully promoted the city's evolution from a trading, agricultural, and light manufacturing hub into a major industrial center.

One hundred new companies were created in the state during Reyes's tenure in the 1890s, two of which grew so large as to ensure Monterrey's preeminence: the Cuauhtémoc *cervecería* (brewery) group, established in 1891 by diverse Mexican and foreign entrepreneurs, which diversified into the mass production of glass, cardboard, and numerous ancillary products; and the Fundidora de Fierro y Acero (Iron and Steel Smelter) conglomerate, established nine years later by a similar multinational group, which expanded capacity at the city's three small metallurgical works by laying rail lines to import minerals and coal from nearby mines and to export finished products throughout Mexico and into the United States. Banks and financial institutions flourished in Monterrey during this upsurge, while its population mushroomed from 40,703 people in 1891 to 72,936 by the end of the decade. So many American businessmen visited or took up temporary residence in the rapidly expanding city that an English-language newspaper called *The Monterrey News* appeared as early as April 1892, published by the transplanted Col. J. A. Robertson.

The resultant bonanza of tax revenues moreover allowed Reyes to upgrade municipal services, installing modern water, sewage, and penal systems; opening two grand new avenues called Unión and Progreso (modern Madero and Pino Suárez); and commencing the construction of monumental structures such as a two-story, red granite Government Palace (completed thirteen years after its foundation stone was laid in August

1895). The city expanded northeastward, and its population rose commensurately to more than 78,000 by 1909, the same year in which another major flood occurred. However, much worse was to ensue after Díaz—now seventy-nine years of age—stood for his eighth presidential term in 1910, ignoring many Mexicans' simmering resentment about their lack of an equitable distribution of wealth or social advancement.

Revolutionary Era (1910–1929)

When Díaz arrested his opponent—the much-revered northern magnate Francisco Ignacio Madero—rather than campaign actively, uprisings erupted throughout the nation, driving the aged dictator into exile by May 1911. Yet Madero was also beset by so much dissension upon assuming office that Mexico descended into chaos after he was assassinated by Gen. Victoriano Huerta in February 1913, and Monterrey's economy was crippled by repeated interruptions to its rail traffic. Rural rebel bands coalesced into a regional army under Gen. Pablo González, who advanced upon the city on 23–25 October 1913, only to hesitate because of the strength of its garrison under Gens. Alfonso Iberri and J. Refugio

Nocturnal view of the new Sears Roebuck store in Monterrey, ca. 1954, reflecting the city's emergence as a modern manufacturing and economic powerhouse. (Library of Congress)

Velasco. A second, more determined assault drove out its defenders on 24 April 1914; then the former bandit Francisco "Pancho" Villa launched a third attack in January 1915, after having fallen out with a rival revolutionary faction led by Venustiano Carranza and Gen. Alvaro Obregón.

The latter eventually emerged triumphant, gaining the presidency and reimposing some measure of national stability, after which Monterrey's industrial productivity painstakingly revived, its population increasing from 88,305 inhabitants in 1921 to 137,387 nine years later. Jesús María Salinas proved an especially active city mayor during his 1927–1928 tenure, initiating many public works projects such as new schools, markets, hospitals, and street paving. In March of 1929, garrison commander Gen. José Gonzalo Escobar joined

a brief nationwide rebellion against President Emilio Portes Gil, but loyal troops quickly advanced north from Mexico City under Gen. Juan Andrew Almazán to suffocate this outburst.

Modern Boom (1930–Present)

Despite another economic downturn caused by the New York stock market crash of October 1929, as well as by a destructive five-year cycle of Santa Catarina River floods beginning in 1933, Monterrey nonetheless continued to expand and modernize. The state-financed Universidad de Nuevo León began offering classes as of that same September, while the outbreak of World War II a few years later increased both national and international demand for the city's industrial output. Monterrey hosted a meeting between Presidents

Soccer stadium on the grounds of the University of Nuevo León, ca. 1970, silhouetted against the distant mountains. (*Enciclopedia de México*)

Monterrey's modern Faro del Comerico or "Beacon of Commerce," framed against the cathedral and Silla Mountain in the distance. (Randy Faris/Corbis)

Manuel Avila Camacho and Franklin D. Roosevelt in April 1943, and the city's spectacular economic rise can really be dated from this era, as an influx of rural migrants—mostly from the neighboring states of Coahuila and San Luis Potosí—began arriving in quest of wartime employment in its plants, swelling the population from 190,074 in 1940 to 333,422 only ten years later (plus another 22,000 in adjoining communities such as Guadalupe, San Nicolás de los Garza, Garza García, and Santa Catarina, which were soon to become absorbed into an agglomeration known as "Metropolitan Monterrey").

This manufacturing boom financed the installation of a massive system of canals during 1949–1952 to curtail future flooding and supply the ever-expanding city with a more reliable source of potable water, as well as to build numerous new thoroughfares and bridges. Industrial enterprises multiplied from 1,310 in 1940 to 5,839 three decades later, while demographic growth kept pace with that expansion in output; the population was measured at 601,086 inhabitants by 1960—or 708,400, if the whole metropolitan area was included—while the respective figures for ten years later ascended to 835,837

and 1,185,349, representing 80 percent of Nuevo León's total residents and 90 percent of the entire state's economic activity. The city had by this time become nicknamed the Sultana del Norte (Sultaness of the North) because of its financial might, its humble origins now forgotten in the rush to modernity. By 1980 the population within the old city limits was measured at 1,084,696, with several hundred thousand more in its sprawling suburbs.

For further reading on the history of Monterrey or Mexico, please consult the Select Bibliography at the end of this volume.

Oaxaca

Ancient city set in a bountiful pocket of flat terrain, amid an otherwise dense mountain range.

Antecedents (ca. 100 B.C.E.–1528)

Because of its semitropical and fecund climate, this sheltered and fertile plain—its floor lying at 5,000 feet above sea level, at the confluence of three river valleys completely ringed by the Sierra Madre del Sur—has been inhabited continuously since at least 8000 B.C.E. Trade with other Mesoamerican regions became increasingly important to its Zapotec inhabitants between 1200 and 900 B.C.E., so that its first major urban concentrations evolved. The most impressive was the mountaintop city of Monte Albán, whose ruins lie just outside modern Oaxaca City, which flourished between 100 B.C.E. and 750 C.E., and at its peak sprawled over 15 square miles.

However, Zapotec power declined, and Monte Albán was abandoned by 1000 C.E., the valley being subsequently invaded out of the west by Mixtec tribesmen, who erected their own capital 7 to 8 miles farther southwest at Cuilapan. The Mixtecs in turn became subordinated to the Aztecs shortly after the commencement of the reign of their expansionistic emperor Ahuítzotl in 1486, who sent 600 families to establish a new garrison town called Huaxyácac near the ancient Zapotec capital of Monte Albán. But aside from gathering regional tributes, this small occupying force seldom intervened in Mixtec-Zapotec affairs, preferring to remain ensconced around their compound.

In August 1521 the distant Aztec capital fell to a Spanish army under Hernán Cortés, who in order to secure its southeastern tributary provinces delegated his subordinate Francisco de Orozco to subdue "Guaxaca" as well (the rather difficult Náhuatl rendering of Huaxyácac was to be so often garbled by the conquistadors that it eventually became reduced to "Oaxaca"). De Orozco consequently departed Tepeaca in November of that same year with 30 cavalrymen, 80 foot soldiers, and 4,000 indigenous allies, defeating the 4,000 to 5,000 Aztecs living within the square-mile compound at Huaxyácac, plus several thousand of their Mixtec vassals. De Orozco thereupon marked this victory by having his chaplain, Juan Díaz, celebrate a Mass atop San Juan Chapultepec Hill opposite, on the southwestern banks of the Atoyac River.

The Spaniards were delighted to find approximately 350,000 indigenes distributed throughout the Valley of Oaxaca, 80 percent of whom were docile Zapotecs, inclined to submit to this latest takeover. Indeed, Cortés wished to retain this populous and lucrative valley as his own personal fiefdom, and so he ordered de Orozco to settle some of his native allies in tribal groupings around Huaxyácac, in the process creating new satellite towns such as San Martín Mexicapan and Santo Tomás Xochimilco. The bulk of de Orozco's Spanish force continued toward the torrid Pacific coast to help another expedition under Pedro de Alvarado conquer the fierce warriors of Tututepec, and by early 1522 established a frontier outpost there called Segura de la Frontera.

Panoramic view across the ancient city of Oaxaca, veiled by a misty sunrise. (Michael S. Yamashita/Corbis)

However, de Alvarado had promised estates in the much more amenable Valley of Oaxaca to many soldiers, so that a small group led by Juan Cedeño and Hernando de Badajoz deserted the hostile environs of Segura de la Frontera to return and take up residence overlooking Huaxyácac. They settled in a new village, which they renamed Tepeaca (modern San Matías Jalatlaco), on the northeastern bank of the narrow Jalatlaco River. Cortés angrily ordered these interlopers removed, then officially reserved the entire valley for his own use in his subsequent distribution of Mexican lands and booty. But he proved unable to take personal possession of this vast landholding because of numerous other demands upon his time, and when he had to leave New Spain in October 1524 to put down an uprising in Honduras, Cortés's political foes Pedro Almíndez Chirinos and Gonzalo de Salazar—ruling from Mexico City in his name—dispatched a force the following year into the valley to combat Mixtec rebels. They then furthermore authorized the re-establishment of a Spanish town at Huaxyácac to act as a regional stronghold.

This latter measure was even sanctioned by a royal decree issued in Spain on 14 September 1526, yet before its confirmatory documentation could reach Mexico, Cortés unexpectedly returned from his Honduran adventure and uprooted the second town's fifty families late that same year. Nevertheless, as his authority was now being so frequently flouted, Cortés sailed for Seville in March 1528 to regain his influence with the Emperor Charles V.

Uncertain Beginnings (1529–1551)

During Cortés's second absence, Mexico's governing *Audiencia* (high tribunal) in Mexico City once again moved to create a Spanish stronghold and way station for Pacific travelers at Oaxaca, by approving a proposal from Nuño de Mercado (or possibly Juan Núñez de Mercado)—and who moreover, in a sycophantic gesture aimed at ingratiating himself with the *Audiencia* president, Nuño Beltrán de Guzmán, suggested naming this new community Antequera, in honor of the latter's birthplace near Málaga in Spain. As a result, Juan Peláez de Berrio (brother of the *Audiencia*'s *oidor*, or justice, Diego Delgadillo) was appointed *alcalde mayor* (municipal magistrate) for this future city and its district by 7 June 1529, and set forth from Mexico City the next month with eighty settlers. A directive was also promulgated throughout the valley of Oaxaca by the *Audiencia,* enjoining its *encomenderos* (landowners) to set up their households in Antequera or else forfeit their estates.

Upon arriving outside Huaxyácac, Peláez de Berrio convened a *cabildo* (town council) meeting and took formal possession of its central core as Antequera de Oaxaca on 24 July 1529. Indigenous residents were displaced into a new northwestern suburb so that the old Aztec street maze could be razed and replaced by a new Spanish-style grid pattern designed by the architect Alonso García Bravo (who had previously laid out

Zapotec "plume dancer," so-called because of his traditional feather headdress, 1901. (Francisco Belmar, *Reseña histórica del Estado de Oaxaca*)

Antigua Veracruz and Mexico City). A new Plaza de Armas (Main Square) was cleared at the halfway point between the Atoyac and Jalatlaco rivers, to be lined on its northern side by a future cathedral, on its southern side by government offices, plus a hospital and other structures; the old indigenous ceremonial center two blocks away meanwhile became transformed into a marketplace called San Juan de Dios Plaza (later Santa Catalina or Catarina). The Dominican missionaries Gonzalo Lucero and Bernardino de Minaya started work on a crude monastery that would eventually evolve into San Pablo Convent, while the distant *Audiencia*—still seeking to assist this fledgling community—attached several score valley villages to its municipal jurisdiction in October 1529, so as to furnish its coffers with additional revenues.

But Antequera's very existence was threatened when Cortés returned from Spain in mid-July 1530 with the title of Marqués del Valle de Oaxaca (marquis of the Valley of Oaxaca), reasserting his rights over its principal Cuatro Villas (Four Towns) of Cuilapan, Etla, Tecuilabacoya (later Tlapacoya), and Oaxaca. As his claim to this latter site conflicted with the *Audiencia* grant, it was only—as a compromise—applied with regard to indigenous communities, so that Oaxaca's suburban satellites of Mexicapan, Xochimilco, and Jalatlaco passed under the marquis's control, along with the new suburb of displaced Aztecs called Villa de Oaxaca (which heretofore became known as the Villa del Marqués, with an independent *alcalde mayor* appointed by Cortés).

However, although the newly created Spanish community of Antequera was thus allowed to remain intact, its residents were now almost completely encircled by the marquis's properties, so that the town councilors sent their own representative before the king the following year, who managed to get their *Audiencia* grant upheld. Antequera even obtained full status as a city by a royal decree issued on 25 April 1532, although the traditional 3-mile urban radius was then successfully contested by Cortés so that access to common pasturelands would continue to be obstructed over the next couple of decades.

A few roads were nevertheless built to improve communications with Mexico City, Cuernavaca, Veracruz, and Huatulco, while Antequera was also chosen as a diocesan see in compliance with the papal bull *Illius fulciti praessidio,* issued on 21 June 1535. Juan López de Zárate arrived two years later to be invested as its first district bishop in San Juan de Dios Church. Still, Antequera's economy sputtered and its Spanish populace failed to prosper, as they suffered from crippling shortages of foodstuffs and funds. A little local gold smelting was authorized in 1538, but the inhabitants were otherwise reduced to planting fig trees and grapevines in their patios to eke out a miserable existence. The number of *vecinos* (householders) dwindled to scarcely thirty by 1544, while six years later discouraged councilors even petitioned the viceroy to transfer their moribund city to a more favorable locale.

Full Emergence (1552–1749)

Rather than abandon this strategic outpost, the Crown instead took measures to foment its growth. In 1552 the patchwork of *corregimientos* and other disparate titles scattered throughout the valley were reconstituted into a single province, to be administered by the city mayor—thus providing a fresh source of tax revenues; the viceroy, Luis de Velasco, moreover suggested that major marquisate towns such as Oaxaca and Cuilapan be placed under the *alcalde mayor*'s direct control as well, although that latter recommendation was rejected. But of equally great benefit, Antequera also received license to dye and weave silk rather than ship its raw produce to the mills of Mexico City or Puebla, resulting in a brief boom that in turn encouraged large-scale harvesting of the spidery *cochinilla* (cochineal) mites from nopal cacti, an excellent source of red colorants and eventually the city's major export.

Relations with Cortés's successor, Martín, the second marquis, began to ease as well, despite occasional litigious outbursts such as the suit lodged against him in 1554 for trying to enlarge his stranglehold through the purchase of more properties around Antequera. His marquisate, however, languished as an underdeveloped economic rival, while the reinvigorated city began to expand as surrounding lands fell vacant with the decimation of indigenous communities throughout the valley by epidemics. A new cathedral was completed at Antequera by 1555, and three years later the Dominicans acquired twenty-four contiguous city lots to initiate a long-term project of creating a monumental monastery. The Franciscan and Jesuit orders also established lesser institutions—including the educational Colegio, or Seminario de San Juan, in 1579—while a defensive wall was raised around the new Episcopal see as early as 1560. Municipal authorities furthermore addressed the periodic flooding of Antequera's marshy southern sector by employing 500 native laborers the next year to divert the Atoyac River 550 yards farther southward.

The valley's total population had been reduced to an estimated 150,000 inhabitants by 1568, of whom only one-fifth were still under the marquisate's control; that in contrast to the roughly 350 Spaniards, 480 mixed-heritage residents, 500 indigenes, and 150 black slaves now living at Antequera in 200 homes. A fifty-bed Hospital Real de San Cosme y San Damián was founded two years later by its council (albeit only in a crude adobe building with a wooden roof), while shortly thereafter the marquis's towns were taken from him by the Crown, as punishment for his involvement in an alleged conspiracy. As the administration of these towns was shifted to the *alcaldes mayores* of Antequera, territorial disputes were consequently settled in the city's favor, so that satellites such as San Matías Jalatlaco and San Felipe del Atarjea became permanently reattached to municipal control as of 1574, marking an end to Antequera's encirclement.

The city began to blossom, construction of new council offices commencing two years later, and the Santa Catalina de Sena nunnery was also established. Another calamitous epidemic further reduced the number of indigenous tributaries outside the city, thereby rendering more land available for the development of larger ranches and farms, so that—despite these deaths, the collapse of the silk industry, and reduced trade volumes flowing through Antequera—its citizenry were at least able to become more self-sufficient agriculturally. By 1595 the municipality's total population—including indigenous suburbs—was estimated at 500 Spanish residents, 3,500 dependents, 500 free mulattoes, and 1,000 slaves, making Antequera the third-largest urban concentration in the viceroyalty of New Spain, after Mexico City and Puebla. It moreover now boasted numerous fine stone edifices, as well as a half dozen churches and a like number of religious institutions.

Because of its safe remove inland, Antequera was not threatened during the fifteen-year sea struggle against Elizabethan England, although it did suffer extensive damage from a series of earthquakes that struck in December 1603, March

1604, and on 8 January 1608 (the latter calamity prompting the Dominicans, who had taken refuge at Cuilapan after the roof of their old San Pablo Convent had collapsed, to move into their partially completed Santo Domingo complex). Recuperation efforts were further hampered by agents of the restored marquisate, who took advantage of this setback to found four new encroaching villages in Antequera's environs shortly before 1611. Two years later, the hard-pressed city council—at the behest of Bishop Juan Cervantes—also ceded the administration of the municipal San Cosme y San Damián Hospital to the Hippolytean Order, while the title of university granted by Pope Paul V to the Santo Domingo Convent in March 1619 could not be implemented.

Nevertheless, reconstruction slowly proceeded, so that the urban populace totaled approximately 2,000 residents by the 1620s, although they endured repeated droughts and famines over the next two decades. Valley ranches and estates meanwhile grew in size, so that the region could at least survive through exporting modest amounts of hides, wool, and other agricultural produce. The administration of the valley by Antequera's often venal *alcalde mayores* proved so unpopular as to provoke a two-year Indian uprising in a score of towns on 22 March 1660. An earthquake that same 7 June also collapsed the city's Franciscan convent and Santo Domingo's

spires, in addition to inflicting other damage. When the Bethelemite Order was offered a building in 1678 in which to found a new hospital, seven years elapsed before that offer could be acted upon because of a lack of qualified personnel. (Fr. Francisco de la Ascensión finally arrived with four colleagues in October 1685 to found their hospital and school in the old burned-out ruins of Nuestra Señora de Guadalupe Hermitage.) Droughts and famines recurred throughout the 1680s, leading unhappy city residents to establish their own *alhóndiga* (granary) soon after 1690 to stockpile supplies against such emergencies, while another earthquake in August 1696 damaged the cathedral, La Merced Church, and other edifices.

By the beginning of the eighteenth century, the total population of Antequera and its indigenous suburbs stood at 6,000 inhabitants. The wealthy rancher and trader Manuel Fernández de Fiallo single-handedly set about funding civic improvements, such as an aqueduct running down from San Felipe del Agua Hill into various public fountains, the reconstruction of the *ayuntamiento* (municipal hall), the expansion of the jail and slaughterhouse, and repairs to various churches. He also supplemented the endowment that had been furnished by Capt. Antonio Díaz Maceda for Fr. Juan de Loranca of the Order of San Juan de Dios to found the Hospital de Santa Catarina

View of the Main Plaza, ca. 1909, showing some of the *portales* or "covered walkways" at right, which were erected all around the square during the seventeenth century to provide shade. (Carson, *Mexico: The Wonderland of the South*)

Mártir in 1702, so that a pharmacy might be added and its total capacity increased to twenty-five beds.

As the eighteenth century progressed, urban life gradually improved, despite another earthquake in 1727. There were increasing numbers of construction projects throughout the city: the magnificent new San José nunnery was initiated in June 1728, for example, the Calvario was completed the next February, and a reconstructed cathedral by Christmas 1730. Municipal authorities also inaugurated a fine new public fountain in the main square by October 1739, then started work on a major new aqueduct that was finished a decade and a half later. But it was to be a spectacular boom in the cochineal trade, starting during the 1740s, that revived the local textile industry and transformed Antequera from a sleepy farming community into a significant commercial center.

Prosperity (1750–1807)

Thanks to an overhaul of the Spanish empire's restrictive commercial policies by its new Bourbon rulers, trade became increasingly vibrant as of the mid-eighteenth century, resulting in substantial benefits for cities with abundant local resources such as Antequera—in particular, its virtual monopoly over cochineal harvests from throughout the Valley of Oaxaca. As demand for this red dye in Spain and Western Europe could now be more easily satisfied through an enhanced flow of transatlantic shipping, export volumes quickly multiplied, reaching a peak by 1774 and coming to represent the viceroyalty's second most valuable product after silver.

This upsurge caused the city to treble in size and its new-found wealth to become reflected in numerous new mansions, many of which were built of the beautiful pale green stone quarried from nearby Santa Lucía del Camino (described by one observer as "very solid, yet soft enough to be carved with a knife"). The Crown had furthermore purchased a large clock from Robert Markham of London as long ago as 1755 and installed it into the cathedral's southern façade. The city's population was measured at 18,558 inhabitants by 1777, the same year in which the Frenchman Nicolas Joseph Thièry de Menonville—drawn by reports of Antequera's agricultural success—visited and noted:

> Nothing can be conceived more magnificent than the site of Guaxaca. . . . It is amply furnished with cereal products, and fruits of all kinds from the plain; the foot of the slope on which it is built (San Felipe del Agua Hill) is bathed by a beautiful river; and well-planned aqueducts supply it with abundance of water of the utmost excellence.

Although bulk exports of raw cochineal declined from 1779 to 1783 because of a Royal Navy blockade imposed during the American War of Independence, as well as natural disasters such as droughts, famine, and a smallpox epidemic,

Antequera's merchants nonetheless compensated by diverting their harvests into the local manufacture of dyed silks, cottons, and linens, which eventually proved to be even more profitable.

This early phase of industrialization was further encouraged when King Charles III ordered that New Spain be subdivided into twelve intendancies in October 1786, Antequera being designated the following year as the capital of a greatly enlarged jurisdiction (roughly equivalent to the modern state of Oaxaca) and headed by the progressive-minded intendant Antonio de Mora y Peysal, who was eager to stimulate commerce. The city prospered throughout the remainder of the eighteenth century, despite suffering an earthquake in 1787, an epidemic two years later, more tremors in 1794 and on 23 March 1795, another outbreak of contagious disease the next year, as well as one more quake on 15 October 1801. A majority of its adult populace came to be employed among the weaving plants or on hundreds of individual looms, as well as ancillary businesses of the clothing industry.

Independence and Turmoil (1808–1876)

Overseas trade declined again when hostilities erupted between Madrid and London in October 1796, and the entire viceroyalty was further gripped by unease a dozen years later when Spain was invaded by a French army and King Ferdinand VII was deposed by Napoleon Bonaparte. The resultant vacuum of power sparked the first stirrings toward Mexican independence, although Antequera failed to respond to the initial insurgency launched at Guanajuato in September 1810. Indeed, when rebel forces penetrated its province a year later, they were routed at the siege of Cuautla. But the insurgent leader José María Morelos y Pavón then regrouped 5,000 rebels at Tehuacán and pretended to march against the royalist bastion of Acapulco.

Instead, though, his army suddenly materialized a dozen miles north-northwest of Antequera on 24 November 1812, sending a message on ahead calling upon its 2,000 monarchist defenders under Lt.-Gen. Antonio González Sarabia to surrender. That demand was rejected, so that the insurgent columns began their assault the next morning. Eugenio Montaño led a cavalry charge into the Xochimilco suburb to cut off any escape northeastward, before storming the city defenses at La Merced. Ramón Sesma meanwhile drove against the fortified La Soledad Church with his San Lorenzo Battalion, under covering fire from Manuel de Mier y Terán's artillery, while the rebel priest Mariano Matamoros assaulted El Carmen and Hermenegildo Galeana carried the huge Santo Domingo Convent.

When Morelos entered the devastated city on the afternoon of 25 November 1812, he ordered summary executions of most royalist officials, then installed an insurgent government for both the city and province that was to be headed by José María Murguía y Galardi and garrison commander Benito Rocha. Columns were dispatched to subdue lesser towns, while

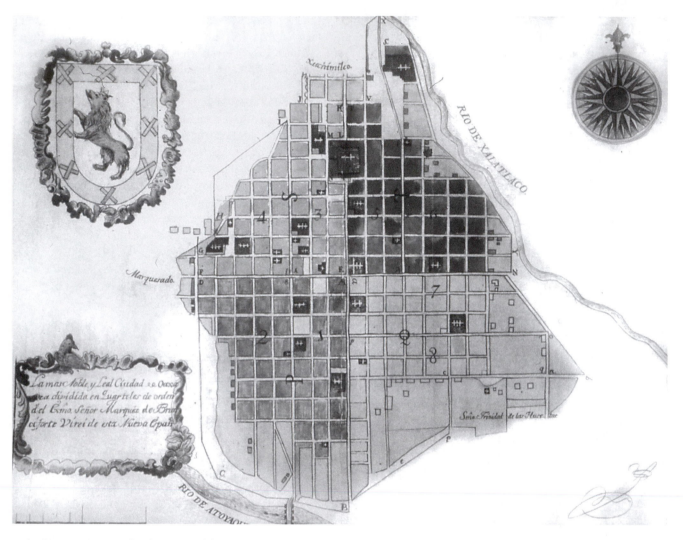

Map of Oaxaca City, 1795. (Archivo General de la Nación, Mexico)

Morelos supervised the recasting of church bells into artillery pieces, the confiscation of all loyalist goods, and even started a short-lived newspaper called *El Correo del Sur* (*The Southern Mail*). By 7 February 1813 he was ready to march westward with the bulk of his army to attack Acapulco, leaving behind Rocha with a 1,000-man garrison.

Antequera remained in rebel hands for a year, Matamoros fending off a feeble royalist counterthrust out of Guatemala in the spring of 1813. But insurgent defeats elsewhere eventually sapped the defenders' resolve, so that when Col. Melchor Alvarez advanced from Tepeaca with 2,000 monarchist troops early in 1814, Antequera's occupiers simply stripped and abandoned it, allowing Alvarez to enter uncontested on 29 March. Ruined by this ordeal, as well as by their lost overseas trade, the city populace found itself reduced to 15,700 people by 1815, whose prospects scarcely improved during the remaining six years of this struggle. Eventually, monarchist fortunes collapsed throughout Mexico, and the royalist Capt. Antonio de

León revolted against Crown authority in June 1821 with his Huajuapan garrison, marching against Antequera and defeating its last Loyalist defenders under Col. Manuel Obeso at Etla on 29 July, so that the city fell two days later.

Notwithstanding Mexico's national freedom, Antequera and its district continued to suffer as its cochineal exports could no longer compete with cheaper produce emanating out of Guatemala, while Mexico was furthermore plunged into prolonged factional strife, handicapping all recuperation and modernization efforts. The first round of fighting occurred after the insurgent Gen. Agustín Iturbide crowned himself "emperor" in May 1822, sparking a widespread revolt that prompted de León and his fellow rebel Gen. Nicolás Bravo to march once more against Antequera and reoccupy it without resistance on 9 June 1823. Determined to break completely with the colonial past, they proclaimed a "Free and Sovereign State of Oaxaca" on 1 July, and the name Antequera was officially replaced by that of Ciudad de Oaxaca (Oaxaca City).

Diagrams and profile views by Miguel Vendrell y Puig, of a proposed new guardhouse for Oaxaca's Casa Mata or "Casemate," 1810. (Archivo General de la Nación, Mexico)

A centralist army compelled this separatist movement to rejoin the Mexican federation in September 1823, so that only a few modest attempts at liberalization could be implemented over the next few years, such as supplementing the old elitist church educational system with new secular schools (most particularly, the Instituto de Ciencias y Artes del Estado or "State Institute of Sciences and Arts," whose first law graduate would be the full-blooded Zapotec Indian Benito Juárez). But the capital's garrison commander, Col. Santiago García,

revolted against central rule on 20 December 1827, obliging de León to reclaim Oaxaca City with his troops on 28 December and reinstall Gov. José Ignacio Morales by 15 January 1828.

Riots erupted that same August 1828 against the imminent election of Gen. Manuel Gómez Pedraza as president, and on 6 November the rebellious army of Antonio López de Santa Anna also entered the city. One week later a rival army under Gen. José Antonio Rincón appeared outside Oaxaca City and besieged Santa Anna inside its Santo Domingo Convent, until Gómez Pedraza finally departed Mexico City into exile in early December. Santa Anna consequently retained control over Oaxaca's capital until relieved by de León in January 1829, then marched in support of Vicente Guerrero's successful bid for the presidency. The latter was subsequently betrayed and imprisoned in Oaxaca City in February 1831, then executed at Cuilapan. Two and a half years later, another rebellious army under the conservative Gen. Valentín Canalizo briefly threatened the state capital before being dispersed by a rival force under liberal Gen. Esteban Moctezuma.

Oaxaca City was also ravaged by a cholera epidemic in 1833, then assaulted on 27 June 1836 by a throng of liberal rebels, who ransacked stores around its central plaza as conservative Gen. Luis Quintanar retreated inside Santo Domingo with his garrison. A relief column under Gen. Canalizo compelled the liberals to end their occupation by 2 July. A serious drought ensued during 1838–1839, and the disgruntled city garrison mutinied briefly in September 1841 and December 1842. Both the capital and state had been utterly bankrupted by such relentless unrest, while the tentative reforms attempted as of May 1844 by Governor de León—such as re-establishing judicial courts and public health services, clearing roads, encouraging silk production, and reopening schools—were undone by earthquakes that struck on 9 March and 7 April 1845.

Chaos once more descended, exacerbated by the U.S. invasion of central Mexico. De León died helping defend the national capital and was succeeded as governor in November 1847 by Juárez, whose term was characterized by honesty and the elimination of public debt, the opening of hundreds of new schools, the initiation of the first bridge across the Atoyac River, the building of more roads, and repairs to the Palacio de Gobierno (Government Palace). Unfortunately, cholera recurred in August 1850, claiming 1,146 lives in and around Oaxaca City (plus another 9,500 throughout the remainder of the state). After Juárez ascended to national politics two years later, misfortune once more befell Oaxaca as another cholera outbreak killed 20,000 people between August and December 1853, and the capital was leveled by another heavy earthquake on 5 May 1854.

Meanwhile, Juárez chaired a liberal congress in the national capital aimed at reforming Mexico's constitution but whose very first pronouncement on 23 November 1855—abolishing the exclusive tribunals catering to the military and clergy—

Typical nineteenth-century Mexican kitchen. (Secretaría de Hacienda y Crédito Público, Mexico)

provoked a violent conservative backlash throughout the country and caused Oaxaca's governor, José María García, to mutiny on 11 December. This revolt was put down after two days of intense street fighting, after which Juárez returned to reassume office as governor on 9 January 1856 with several hundred troops, confiscating many of the 814 church properties within Oaxaca City. The new constitution that he had helped to draft was finally unveiled in February 1857, plunging the country into three years of warfare known as the Guerra de la Reforma (War of the Reform).

During these hostilities Oaxaca City was sacked when a conservative army under Gens. José María Cobos and José María Moreno penetrated on 28 December 1857, besieging its 1,000 defenders under Col. Ignacio Mejía until a sally drove the attackers to back out on 16 January 1858. A second occupation occurred when liberal fortunes declined elsewhere, so that local authorities were obliged to quit their state capital on 4 November 1859 and suffer Cobos's army to re-enter uncontested two days later. His garrison was in turn harried as of 2 February 1860 by liberal guerrillas under Gen. Vicente Rosas Landa before being driven from the surrounding foothills three months later. But when the conservative cause finally suffered serious reverses in central Mexico, a liberal army under Col. Porfirio Díaz and his brother Lt.-Col. Félix Díaz—sons of

an Oaxacan innkeeper—reclaimed the city on 5 August 1860, Cobos and his few retainers demolishing a wall in the Santo Domingo Convent to escape.

Oaxaca had scarcely begun to recuperate when Mexico's defeated conservatives allied themselves with France and encouraged the disembarkation of an expeditionary force at Veracruz in January 1862 to spearhead a thrust aimed at replacing the republican form of government with an imperial regime headed by the foreign figurehead Archduke Maximilian of Austria. It took more than a year for this invasion force to drive President Juárez and his liberal administration from central Mexico, at which time the battered 2,800-man army of Gen. Porfirio Díaz retreated into Oaxaca City on 1 December 1863 to continue their resistance. The next summer, two French and two imperial columns approached out of the northwest, but were obliged to retreat shortly after penetrating into republican territory when Díaz slipped between the French contingents with 2,000 men and struck their rear. After reassembling at Nochistlán (60 miles northwest of Oaxaca City), the Franco-imperial forces furthermore learned that the state capital had been heavily fortified, and so they withdrew altogether.

A more determined three-pronged offensive was launched in December 1864 by Gen. Curtois d'Hurbal, who easily gained Etla before being superseded on 17 January 1865 by Gen. François Achille Bazaine. Fearful of becoming trapped, almost 10,000 of the capital's 24,500 inhabitants fled when Bazaine started his final advance against Oaxaca City with 4,000 infantrymen, 1,000 cavalrymen, 200 sappers, 500 auxiliaries, and 80 gunners. The Franco-imperial vanguard clashed with republican pickets just north of the city a couple of days later, prompting Díaz to order 700 dragoons to exit under his brother, Col. Félix Díaz, while preparing his remaining 3,000 regulars and 4,000 militiamen to resist. Col. José Guillermo Carbó sallied with a couple of republican battalions on 21 January to battle some French units at Aguilera Hacienda, but once the siege artillery—a dozen 12-pounders and six mortars—were installed opposite the city and atop Mogote and Pelado hills on 1 February, no more sorties were made. The garrison's morale collapsed within a week, so that Díaz surrendered by 9 February and was marched into captivity along with more than a hundred of his officers.

The Mexican conservative Juan Pablo Franco was installed as governor, or "imperial prefect," while Gen. Carlos Oronoz became garrison commander. The half-empty city was little changed from colonial days, being described by the historian Charles R. Berry as consisting:

> . . . of one-story adobe and plaster homes, joined one against the other, so that someone walking down a street saw nothing but a solid and long wall, painted in various colors, pierced by grilled windows and heavy wooden doors. Towering above the low dwellings were the many churches and

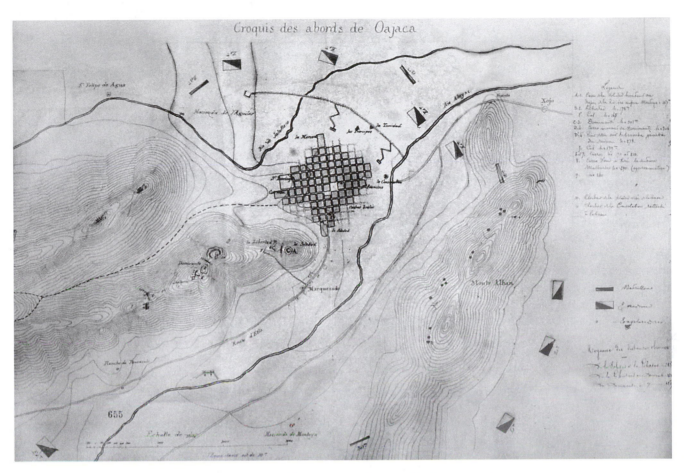

Hand-drawn map of Oaxaca City and its environs during the Franco-conservative siege of early 1865. (Archivo General de la Nación, Mexico)

monasteries with their ornately carved façades and towers covered in tiles of white, yellow, and blue. . . .

Liberal survivors soon started a guerrilla campaign in the hills, being bolstered when Díaz escaped confinement in September 1865 and organized a new army. As Franco-imperial fortunes began to wane throughout the rest of Mexico, Díaz routed Oronoz at Miahuatlán on 3 October 1866, then two days later sent his republican cavalry storming back into Oaxaca City under his brother Félix, followed on 6 October by his main body.

Several hundred imperial defenders were besieged inside Santo Domingo, El Carmen Alto, La Soledad, and several other churches. Díaz sortied on the night of 16 October 1866 to defeat an approaching relief column of 1,500 Austrian and imperial troops at La Carbonera, then resumed his siege of the 350 disheartened imperial holdouts, who agreed to capitulate on 31 October. With Oaxaca City once more in republican hands, Díaz used it as a springboard from which to clear the Isthmus of Tehuantepec that same December, then to reclaim Puebla and the national capital the following year, helping bring an end to Maximilian's regime.

As a war hero, Félix Díaz was elected governor of the state of Oaxaca in November 1867, while Porfirio Díaz went into retirement. But political infighting flared anew when the increasingly unpopular Juárez announced four years later that he would seek yet another presidential term. The Díaz brothers mounted one of several major revolts throughout Mexico, but they were subdued in December 1871 by a federal army under Gen. Ignacio Alatorre, who entered Oaxaca City on 8 January 1872. Félix Díaz was subsequently caught in the hills and executed.

When Juárez died of natural causes in Mexico City that same July 1872, the occupied state capital was officially renamed Oaxaca de Juárez. But when his successor, Sebastián Lerdo de Tejada, announced late in 1875 that he too would run for another term—thus perpetuating his faction's stranglehold upon power—Díaz mounted a second, more successful rebellion on 10 January 1876 that deposed the president by 20 November of that same year.

Porfirian and Revolutionary Eras (1877–1924)
Although the cycle of destructive factional strife seemed destined to repeat itself with this latest insurrection, Díaz most

unexpectedly imposed an efficient regime upon the war-weary nation, ruthlessly stamping out all hints of unrest. Consequently, Oaxaca City was to enjoy a protracted period of peaceful development for the first time since the colonial era, as Díaz—after his first presidential term expired on 30 November 1880—won uncontested election as state governor a year later then started implementing some much-needed civic improvements, such as the capital's first public oil lamps in February 1882 and a new railway running toward Tehuantepec that same August.

He reassumed the presidency in 1884 and ruled Mexico uninterruptedly over the next twenty-six years, remorselessly driving the country toward modernization and industrialization. Oaxaca benefited from improved railway and telegraph services, new public markets, foreign investment, hydroelectric power, paved streets, a new Palacio Federal (on the site of its old Episcopal Palace), a new jail and university, proper sewers, a new theater, and telephone service. But the state did not enjoy the great natural mineral resources of other parts of the country, so that its urban center lagged behind national development economically. Only the rural Oaxacan textile industry prospered through industrialization, while the state capital itself remained relatively small and poor, with a population rising from 26,228 inhabitants in 1879 to a mere 40,000 thirty years later.

Despite the undoubted progress achieved during the Porfirian era, many Mexicans eventually came to resent their lack of a commensurate social advancement or equitable distribution of wealth, while wearying of the dictator's heavy-handed

Map of Oaxaca City, ca. 1909; note how its boundaries had expanded since 1795. (*Terry's Mexico*)

repression and partiality toward foreign interests. When Díaz—now seventy-nine years of age—stood for his eighth term in 1910, then arrested his high-minded opponent Francisco Ignacio Madero rather than campaign actively, uprisings occurred throughout the state of Oaxaca and the nation. As these rebellions gained momentum and fear gripped the state capital, Maj. Félix Díaz (the president's nephew) took over as governor in early May 1911, only to be driven out a month later after his uncle too had been exiled.

Madero tentatively assumed power in Mexico City, but he was beset by so much dissension that Col. Pedro León's "Sierra Juárez" Battalion—on garrison duty in Oaxaca City—mutinied against his authority on 26 April 1912, only to be driven out into the countryside a few days later. Banditry continued to plague the district until Madero was assassinated in Mexico City by Gen. Victoriano Huerta, after which Fidencio Hernández and Guillermo Meixueiro—conservative backers of Félix Díaz—raised three brigades and captured Etla and Tlacolula on 10 July 1914, compelling the Huerta-appointed governor to resign five days later. The presidential challenger, Venustiano Carranza, tried to impose his authority upon the state by ordering Gen. Luis Jiménez Figueroa to seize Oaxaca City on 14 November, but four days later this occupying force became besieged inside El Fortín citadel north of the capital by three brigades of local revolutionaries under Meixueiro, who chased Jimémez Figueroa out after nightfall.

Because of the lack of an acknowledged national leader, Oaxaca declared itself to be a sovereign state on 3 June 1915, refusing to recognize the authority of Carranza or any other federal pretender. To reassert centralist rule, the Carrancista Gen. Jesús Agustín Castro was ordered from Chiapas that same November, pushing inland from Puerto Angel with a small army until his subordinate Gens. Macario M. Hernández and Juan José Baños could defeat a separatist concentration and occupy the deserted capital on 5 March 1916. Félix Díaz returned from exile in mid-May to lead a force of separatist guerrillas, but he was also soundly beaten by Carrancista forces in June–July, after which the federalist garrison holding the capital gradually subdued all rural resistance. The state Gen. Alberto Córdova was captured and executed in Oaxaca City on 8 February 1918; the head of its separatist governor, José Inés Dávila, was put on public display at the end of May 1919, while Meixueiro—the last remaining separatist leader—surrendered by 27 December of that same year.

State forces did not regain Oaxaca City until Carranza was overthrown by his rival, Gen. Alvaro Obregón, in May 1920, who in turn became president. Obregón then was confronted by his own insurrection in early December 1923, when Adolfo de la Huerta challenged him for the office. Oaxaca's governor, Manuel García Vigil, and garrison commander, Gen. Fortunato Maycotte, sided with de la Huerta, along with more than half of Mexico's 110,000-man army, but Obregón's control over the treasury ensured abundant supplies of modern weaponry for

A 1932 photograph showing a portion of Oaxaca City, as seen from atop its cathedral belfry. (Author's Collection)

his Loyalists so that the mutiny was doomed. Although a guerrilla assault on Oaxaca City by Onofre Jiménez was easily repelled on 12 January 1924, the approach of a well-armed federal division under Gen. Juan Andrew Almazán caused the mutineers to abandon it without a struggle on 1 March, after which Gen. Isaac M. Ibarra was installed as its Obregónista governor two days later.

Modern Era (1925–Present)

Although electoral irregularities allowed Jiménez to exercise power briefly, he was deposed on 6 November 1925, and Oaxaca's decade and a half of political turbulence finally ended. Modest attempts at recuperation and modernization were interrupted by a series of earthquakes on 9 February, 20 March, 16 April, 16 July, 4 August, and 8 October 1928; then another major quake leveled three-quarters of Oaxaca's buildings on 13 January 1931.

The city was once again rebuilt, its highway communica-tions upgraded, and a water purification plant erected at El Fortín during the early 1940s. But because of Oaxaca's economic dependence upon such nonindustrial exports as textiles, pottery, and ranch produce, it did not experience the prodigious growth in size and wealth of many other urban centers throughout Mexico after World War II. Oaxaca's population nevertheless more than doubled from 46,741 inhabitants in 1950 to 99,509 twenty years later, reaching 294,961 by 1990. Its small size, tranquil charm and beauty, plus magnificent baroque architecture made it a popular tourist destination, famous for such seventeenth-century treasures as its Santo Domingo and San Agustín convents, La Soledad Church, the San José Convent—converted into the Escuela Oaxaqueña de Bellas Artes (Oaxacan School of Fine Arts)—and many other ancient structures.

For further reading on the history of Oaxaca or of Mexico, please consult the Select Bibliography at the end of this volume.

Puebla

Throughout much of the colonial era, Mexico's second-largest and most splendid city.

Foundation and Relocation (1531–1532)

In the decade after the fall of the Aztec empire in 1521, Mexican fiefdoms and vassals were distributed among the victorious conquistadors and the hundreds of adventurers who arrived in their wake. Soon there were no significant holdings left to be granted, while the Indian population declined precipitously because of disease, the shock of defeat, and unaccustomed new forms of servitude. Madrid and its Crown representatives in Mexico City—the *real audiencia* (royal tribunal), headed by such visionary clerics as Bishop Sebastián Ramírez de Fuenleal and Vasco de Quiroga—consequently decided in 1530 to encourage the establishment of a European-style city not dependent upon tribute from indigenous inhabitants, but which would rather attract landless Spaniards and develop its own economy, thus helping introduce Spanish agricultural and commercial practices. This new city was also to be strategically situated between the Gulf coast and the highland capital, so as to serve as a stronghold in case of insurrection.

After a careful study, an uninhabited site was chosen in a valley nestled approximately 7,000 feet above sea level amid the Sierra Madre Oriental mountain range, some 80 miles east-southeast of Mexico City, between the old Aztec satellite city of Cholula and the semiautonomous city of Tlaxcala. The spot—its horizon dominated by the 14,500-foot Matlalcuéyatl (Malinche) Volcano to its northeast and the 17,000-foot Popocatépetl and Ixtaccíhuatl volcanoes and other snow-capped peaks farther west—had been known by the Aztec name of Cuetlaxcoapan (River of the Hairy Snakes), but the Franciscan delegate and future bishop Fr. Julián Garcés allegedly saw angels hovering about the spot in a dream, so that the settlement was to be named Puebla de los Angeles (Town of the Angels).

A party of fifty Spaniards was recruited and conducted there from Tlaxcala by the regional *corregidor* (municipal magistrate), Hernando de Elgueta, who officially constituted the town of Puebla on 16 April 1531 by distributing urban plots among these settlers, as well as farmlands around its periphery. A small group of Indian laborers, provided by the Franciscan missionaries, helped to erect the first adobe-and-wood shacks on the eastern shore of a stream named San Francisco in the order's honor, the resultant community being laid out on the southern folds of an eminence named San Cristóbal (modern Loreto and Guadalupe Hills).

Unfortunately, these early residents suffered serious setbacks when heavy rains collapsed many of their crude dwellings, and an early frost killed their first crops. The thirty-four householders who remained therefore transferred their town over to the more favorable western bank of the San Fran-cisco River on 29 March 1532, although half of them then became so discouraged by their want and distress, even at this new site, that they departed for Peru, drawn by news of Francisco Pizarro's campaign against the alluringly rich empire of the Incas.

Meanwhile, in Spain, Emperor Charles V had already become so convinced of this fledgling settlement's potential that he had issued a *real cédula* (royal decree) on 20 March 1532 granting Puebla the title of a city and exempting its residents from paying most taxes for thirty years. The *Audiencia* expanded upon this measure by delegating their colleague Juan de Salmerón to visit Puebla that same December; he further assisted the seventeen surviving inhabitants by granting them new farmlands in the better sheltered and warmer Atlixco Valley and by temporarily assigning each householder thirty indigenous vassals to assist in improving their Puebla residences, plus another twenty to tend to their distant crops.

Flourishment (1533–1649)

Wheat proved to be especially amenable to the Atlixco Valley, so that water-powered mills soon sprang up in Puebla to grind harvests, while sheep, pigs, and cattle multiplied throughout the district as well. The city blossomed as a result, the number of its householders swelling to sixty-eight by 1534, while municipal government was reconstituted into a ten-member *cabildo* (council) elected from among married property owners. Sufficient funds were soon garnered to commence construction of administrative offices that same year, in addition to a slaughterhouse. An intricate system of clay troughs diverted a flow of water into the San Francisco del Alto neighborhood as early as the following year, while a rudimentary cathedral was started by the Indians of Calpa in 1536. The number of city officials increased to a dozen the next year, although henceforth they were all to be appointed directly by the Crown. Puebla was granted its official crest on 20 July 1538, depicting a golden city with five towers upon a green field, with two white-clad angels hovering above, plus the initials "KV" for Karolus V—the Latinized form of Charles the Fifth.

Puebla's farmlands and orchards proved so bountiful, and its taxes so low, that migrants continued to be attracted to the city. But perhaps its greatest asset was its location: a new highway leading up from the coast was soon diverted through Puebla, so that recently disembarked sea travelers—after making the weary ascent from the torrid and humid Gulf coast into the beautiful central highlands—were favorably struck by Puebla's cool and benign climate, very reminiscent of Spain. By 1540, Fr. Toribio de Motolinía (one of the city's original Franciscan founders) could note that it now had "many completed homes, and long and straight streets, and beautiful façades on the houses." The next year, its San Juan de Letrán Hospital received a handsome bequest from Rodrigo de Madrid and so was significantly expanded. Many artisans and

Pictographic map by Nicolás de Zamudio of the newly created city, plus its mountainous district extending as far as Izúcar, in 1533. (Archivo General de la Nación, Mexico)

tradesmen opted to settle into such a welcoming urban landscape, and Puebla's first textile mill opened that same year of 1541 to produce woolens from the district's thriving flocks of sheep. The glassmaker Rodrigo de Espinosa took up residence in 1542, and Puebla's first school started giving classes that same year.

Allotments of Indian vassals had been largely phased out by the *Audiencia* by 1543, yet indigenous migrants nonetheless continued to throng into the burgeoning city's outskirts, seeking employment as local commerce expanded. Three years later the city council attempted to regularize these Indian suburbs by assigning individual plots and exempting owners from paying tribute so long as they remained for five years and performed certain minor communal tasks in addition to their paid labors. The number of Spanish households within Puebla's core mushroomed to 300 by 1547, and manufacturing diversified with the introduction of the city's first looms the next year to treat raw silk grown around Tepejí de la Seda and other southern hamlets. A group of potters also arrived shortly thereafter from the town of Talavera de la Reina in Spain, initiating production of glazed Majolica-ware in a distinctive

blue-on-white Moorish pattern; their plates and tiles would soon become famous throughout Mexico and Spanish America under the name of Talavera de Puebla.

The municipal authorities reorganized the teeming indigenous suburbs along tribal lines in 1550, so as to reduce frictions between groups by congregating peoples from Tlaxcala, for example, into Tlaxcaltecapan or San Francisco del Alto de los Tlaxcaltecas; Cholulans into Cholultecapan or Santiago de los Cholultecas; Aztecs into Mexicapan or San Pablo de los Mexicanos; Huejotzingans into Huejotzingocapan or San Sebastián de los Huejotzincas; and so forth. Puebla was now so established as to manifest its prosperity by boasting a clock tower and a theater, as well as by inaugurating a public fountain in its Plaza Mayor (Main Square) by 1555, while its prestige was further enhanced when the Crown declared it to be a *Noble y Leal Ciudad* (Noble and Loyal City) three years later.

Yet it was to be the enormous growth of transatlantic plate-fleet traffic between Seville and Veracruz as of the 1560s, with ever larger fleets of galleons arriving to receive the proceeds of Mexico's dramatically augmented silver production—thanks to a new amalgamation treatment for ores called the

Panoramic view looking westward across the city from its outskirts, ca. 1909, with the snow-capped Popocatépetl Volcano visible in the distance. (Carson, *Mexico: The Wonderland of the South*)

patio process—that crowned Puebla's success. The Gulf coast being wholly unable to feed such massive seasonal influxes by thousands of sailors and passengers, foodstuffs such as flour, pork, beef, and cheese were instead regularly contracted from Puebla; the city also provided a welcome stopover for the stream of teamsters, merchants, and travelers circulating to and from the viceregal capital. Royal highway maintenance furthermore benefited Puebla by reducing the transportation costs of its other bulk exports such as textiles, Talavera pottery, *cochinilla* cactus pellets (used to produce red dyes), and soaps.

The number of its Spanish *vecinos* (citizens) escalated to 800 by 1570, and the city evolved into a major trade hub over the next few decades by exporting produce as far east as Cuba, as far south as Guatemala, and as far west as Acapulco. Nonperishable manufactures such as its woolens, pottery, and silks went farther still, reaching Peru and Spain. The resultant business upsurge allowed for a grand new cathedral to be commenced as of 1575 under the direction of the noted architect from Extremadura, Francisco Becerra, while the four major mendicant orders—Franciscans, Dominicans, Augustinians, and Jesuits—expanded or beautified their original monasteries, thus adding to the city's grandeur. (One surviving example is the Casa del Deán at the corner of modern 16 de Septiembre and 7 Poniente avenues, whose owner—the

cathedral's dean, Tomás de la Plaza—directed native artisans to paint murals depicting scenes from Petrarch.) The next year Puebla was granted the additional title of *Muy Noble y Muy Leal Ciudad* (Very Noble and Very Loyal City), and its populace more than doubled over the ensuing quarter century as smiths, masons, woodworkers, silversmiths, jewelers, and many other skilled tradesmen continued to swell its labor pool. Black slaves were also imported in large numbers to handle specialized tasks, and the Hippolytean Order established the Hospital de San Roque in 1592 to tend to travelers.

Located a safe distance from the coast, Puebla remained largely unaffected by the war against Elizabethan England that lasted from 1588 to 1604, despite occasional interruptions in plate-fleet traffic. By the conclusion of those hostilities, it could boast more than 1,500 Spanish households, for a total of some 20,000 people spread out over 120 city blocks (although not all were entirely occupied, numerous orchards and tilled fields still dotting the urban landscape). Black slaves and mulatto residents now outnumbered white Spaniards, and five large textile factories—employing as many as 400 laborers apiece—were in full operation, as well as more than two dozen lesser works. Silk manufacture had decreased because of competition from superior materials now being imported from the Philippines, but Puebla was nonetheless universally

View looking northward from atop the cathedral, ca. 1880–1897. (Library of Congress)

recognized as the viceroyalty of New Spain's second-largest and most important city, enjoying a wide variety of urban amenities plus a rich cultural life based upon its diverse painters, musicians, and writers.

Its religious institutions also grew in number, wealth, and influence as the seventeenth century began, eventually acquiring many properties and businesses through bequests. Nunneries such as Santa Teresa, Santa Clara, Santísima Trinidad, Santa Inés de Montepoliciano, and Santa Mónica became established, while the Order of San Juan de Dios opened the Hospital de San Bernardo in 1632, naming it in honor of Bishop Gutierre Bernardo de Quirós. The first printing press was installed sometime around 1640, and the vigorous Juan de Palafox y Mendoza gave further impetus to ecclesiastical ascendancy when he arrived as bishop that same year, melding the seminaries of San Juan, San Pedro, and San Pablo into a single institution with a well-stocked library (later known as the Biblioteca Palafoxiana). He also reinvigorated work on the massive cathedral project, stalled since thirty years previously, with help from the Crown, the participation of his own personal artist, Pedro García Ferrer, and an improved configuration prepared by the architect Juan Gómez de Trasmonte, so that it could at least be consecrated by 18 April 1649—shortly before this prelate returned to Spain. In fact, its façade

and twin spires were not actually completed until several decades later.

Decline and Revival (1650–1809)

Physically, the city had now taken full shape, being characterized by large, ornate churches decorated with gold leaf; most other prominent structures consisted of low, two- or three-story stone buildings. A majority of residences were single-story dwellings, while adobe shacks with thatched roofs predominated among the indigenous suburbs. But despite the city's evolution, Spain and its empire were in a state of ruin by the middle of the seventeenth century, with the Crown bankrupt and the imperial economy on the verge of collapse. Plate-fleet traffic had tapered off drastically, so that Puebla suffered a downturn in its export of provisions. Galleons arrived less frequently and in smaller groups, and demand for the city's woolen products had also declined; Mexico's mining industry slumped in the interior, and inter-American trade dried up.

Although agriculturally self-sufficient, Puebla's inhabitants—who numbered 68,800 by 1678—endured a prolonged period of commercial stagnation, only religious institutions benefiting somewhat under such straitened circumstances by accumulating ever more properties as local businesses failed and the populace shrank. Eventually, the Church controlled turn its attention to overhauling the viceroyalty's decayed administrative apparatus, soon incrementing government expenditures and encouraging commerce.

Puebla—like the rest of Spain's empire—benefited from such reforms, its shipments of provisions to Veracruz and Cuba growing significantly as overall trade revived, although other markets within New Spain (such as the Valley of Mexico) had now become less dependent upon its exports. Despite some minor disturbances in the city in 1729 and August 1743, Puebla's prosperity resurged as the eighteenth century progressed. The practice of incorporating Talavera tiles as decorative pieces into church domes and the façades of private mansions took hold as of 1750 and uniquely beautified the city. (One famous example was the Casa de los Muñecos or "Doll House" on modern 2 Norte Street, whose owner ordered special tiles glazed with caricatures depicting his enemies as a permanent form of ridicule.) Puebla's grand Coliseo de Comedias Theater was completed by the master architect José Miguel de Santa María and opened in 1759 on San Roque Square—today the Teatro Principal, on the Plazuela del Boliche—while a new Tribunal de Justicia (courthouse) was completed three years later. Advanced medical research was conducted at the ancient Hospital Real de San Pedro.

The pace of urban improvements increased notably during the enlightened administrations of Mayors Esteban Bravo de Rivero from 1764 to 1771 and José Merino Ceballos from 1771 to 1777, who organized the first system of public lighting, expanded the city jail, erected the San Miguel water fountain in the city's Main Square by 1777, and installed wooden stalls for a better regulated public market. Only their efforts to pave Puebla's streets failed, thwarted by resistance from religious institutions that were "owners of the most and best part of the possessions within the city."

The Paseo (Promenade) bordering the San Francisco River was beautified by planting shade trees in 1780, and a dragoon barracks was completed the following year. The Mexican viceroyalty's fortunes peaked as the eighteenth century drew to a close, Puebla achieving its greatest splendor under the protracted term from 1786 to 1811 of the energetic civilian intendant Manuel Flon, Conde de la Cadena, who finally succeeded in getting its central avenues paved. Although the city's population measured 56,859 by 1793—12,000 fewer than in the previous century—residents nonetheless enjoyed a better quality of life and steady demands for city exports of foodstuffs and manufactures. Trade with Veracruz, the Caribbean, and Spain was curtailed when Madrid reluctantly aligned itself with the French Directorate in Paris as of August 1796, goading England into declaring war by 6 October, so that a blockade was clamped upon all transatlantic movement. Ironically, the intendant began transferring Puebla's merchant houses that same year from the Main Square to the Parián (Exchange) on the banks of the San Francisco River.

Despite this downturn in overseas traffic, the city—

One of the naves in the cathedral, ca. 1900–1950. (Library of Congress)

roughly two-thirds of all urban or suburban lots. Puebla's reputation for piety and ecclesiastical learning was increased during this interlude by some fine choral works, composed and performed at its magnificent Cathedral Chapel. But it was not to be until the last Hapsburg monarch, Charles II, died in Spain on 30 November 1700, and the sixteen-year-old French Bourbon princeling Philip of Anjou succeeded him, that the empire's long decline could finally be halted and the city's fortunes slowly revived as part of a gradual policy of reforms.

Even as the fighting was still raging overseas against this change of ruling houses—known as the War of the Spanish Succession, England and Holland disputing this far-reaching political realignment—Puebla's *alcalde mayor* (municipal magistrate), Juan José de Veytia Linaje, was able to order two brick bridges built across the Atoyac River and a wooden span across the San Francisco River into Analco. As Puebla's structures were damaged by an earthquake in 1711, he also started construction on a new Palacio del Ayuntamiento (Municipal Palace) the year after hostilities ceased in 1713. Spain became embroiled again against the Quadruple Alliance of England, Holland, France, and Austria from 1718 to 1720, then almost went to war against Britain in 1727. But as this overseas opposition abated, the new Bourbon administration was able to

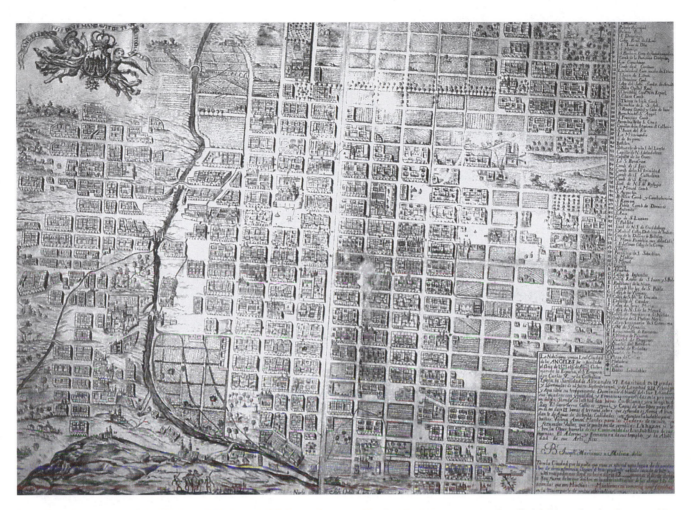

Map of Puebla as surveyed in 1754 by José Mariano de Medina and engraved by José Ortíz Carnero; note the tilled fields and orchards around its periphery. North is toward bottom. (Archivo General de la Nación, Mexico)

according to a survey conducted in 1804—still boasted fourteen watermills, two textile plants, a pair of glass factories, three major warehouses, an *alhóndiga* (granary), a slaughterhouse, and various tanneries. It also had 45 stores that sold imported goods, 39 dealing in local products, 102 groceries, 39 bakeries, 286 wine shops, and 4 haberdasheries.

Independence Era (1810–1846)

Like the rest of Spanish America, Puebla was astonished to learn that the French emperor Napoleon I had sent an army into Spain in the summer of 1808, deposing Ferdinand VII in favor of his own brother Joseph Bonaparte. This crude usurpation of power was widely rejected throughout Spanish America, yet the ensuing period of political uncertainty loosened old imperial ties and stoked the first stirrings toward independence among Mexican-born Creoles. A revolt erupted in the central part of the viceroyalty by mid-September 1810, spearheaded by Miguel Hidalgo y Costilla, that launched a decade of internecine warfare.

The socially conservative city of Puebla remained a Loyalist stronghold throughout this struggle, dispatching several thousand troops under such noteworthy commanders as Ciriaco de Llano to uphold the monarchist cause elsewhere in Mexico. Its commerce suffered, however, while municipal funds were diverted into erecting defenses such as Forts Loreto and Guadalupe atop the heights commanding the city. Eventually, the insurgents won the upper hand throughout the rest of Mexico, so that late in the conflict a small rebel army under Gens. José Joaquín de Herrera and Nicolás Bravo advanced from Córdoba to besiege Puebla in early July 1821. Only a few weeks later the last vestiges of royalist resistance collapsed when the viceroy, Juan O'Donojú, capitulated to Agustín Iturbide, ending Spanish rule forever.

A new state legislature was installed into Puebla's converted *alhóndiga* by 1824, while its old Espíritu Santo College was transformed into a Colegio del Estado (State College) the next year. Some other municipal improvements were also attempted—such as the creation of a museum in 1827 and a

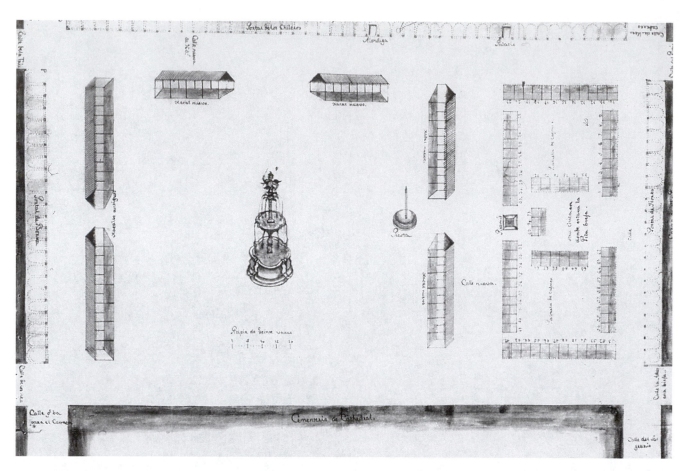

Diagram of the wooden market-stalls installed in Puebla's main square as of 1779 as part of Mayor José Merino Ceballos's urban reforms. Also note the baroque San Miguel water fountain featured at its center, installed two years previously by José Antonio de Santa María, which was to remain in this spot until modern times. (Archivo General de la Nación, Mexico)

medical school four years afterward—although economic dislocation persisted as the city's traditional Crown contracts and export trade had been ruptured; also, the nation's new republican administration was racked by instability and lack of funds. The Church still controlled much real estate in the city, figures in 1832 estimating that 1,484 of its 2,966 urban lots were in ecclesiastical hands. Veracruz was no longer Mexico's primary port, as goods could now be imported directly through numerous lesser ports, resulting in a reduced volume of transient highway traffic through Puebla. Foreign developers who were bringing more modern technologies into Mexico tended to bypass Puebla in favor of such once-rich silver centers as Guanajuato or Zacatecas, while Guadalajara experienced such remarkable growth during this boom period that it soon surpassed Puebla as Mexico's second-largest city.

Political unrest also contributed to city problems, as national factions wrangled repeatedly over the young nation's constitutional configuration and future course. In one such outbreak, Gen. Antonio López de Santa Anna revolted at Veracruz in 1832 against the presidency of Gen. Anastasio Bustamante, a rebellion that spread and obliged Bustamante to

march out of Mexico City at the head of his army by mid-August to confront rebel concentrations in central Mexico. Santa Anna took advantage of this distraction to press inland from Veracruz, overwhelming the garrison in Puebla under Col. Manuel Andrade by early December, then clashing so successfully against Bustamante's main force on 21 December that the latter resigned from office two days later.

Santa Anna proceeded triumphantly into Mexico City and was installed into office by 1 April 1833—only then to share this same fate as revolts erupted against his administration as well. His Puebla garrison was consequently besieged from 3 to 10 July 1833 by a small mutinous army under Gens. Mariano Arista and Gabriel Durán; then a more serious investiture occurred the next year, when a rebel army of 7,000 troops and thirty field-pieces appeared under Gen. Luis Quintanar on 1 June 1834, besieging the 3,000 defenders and fourteen guns under Gov. Cosme Furlong for two months. During this encirclement the city was shelled but not assaulted, and its garrison was finally starved into submission by 31 July, marching out the next day with full honors of war.

A brief interlude of peace allowed the local industrialist

Passengers resting in the Hotel Diligencias, ca. 1880–1897. Puebla's role as a layover point gradually faded as the volume of overland travel between Veracruz and Mexico City declined. (Library of Congress)

Esteban de Antuñano to establish Puebla's first modern textile mill—called La Constancia Mexicana (Mexican Constancy)—at his Santo Domingo watermill on the banks of the Atoyac River by 1835, using English equipment and technicians. He also imported French and Belgian experts to establish glass and paper factories three years later, while the state authorities could initiate some major construction projects of their own, starting a solid new *penitenciaría* (penitentiary) as of 1840, as well as remodeling the Main Square two years later and creating the Paseo Bravo (Bravo Boulevard) in 1844. During yet another round of political fighting, though, Puebla was besieged again from 1 to 11 January 1845—this time by Santa Anna's defeated forces as he was retreating toward the coast following a series of reverses.

American Occupation (1847–1848)
Two months after this incident, the new Mexican government severed diplomatic relations with Washington to protest a vote by the U.S. Congress approving the annexation of the Republic of Texas—which Mexico still regarded as a breakaway province. Border tensions between the two countries escalated, leading to an outbreak of hostilities by spring of 1846. The United States successfully invaded northern

Mexico, then opened a second front by disembarking an army under Gen. Winfield Scott at Veracruz in March 1847. Santa Anna (since restored to office) countered by marshaling 12,000 troops and forty-three field-pieces 4 miles outside Jalapa at Cerro Gordo to contest Scott's advance into the interior. However, the 8,500 U.S. soldiers smashed through this position on 18 April, obliging Santa Anna to retreat hastily into the Valley of Mexico to prepare for a last stand, leaving Puebla undefended.

On 6 May 1847, the American vanguard—Brig. William Jenkins Worth's 1st Division—pushed up the main highway from Jalapa and entered the deserted city on 15 May, being followed into Puebla thirteen days later by Scott's main body. But the invaders paused, as seven volunteer regiments had quit after the Battle of Cerro Gordo because their enlistments had expired, leaving Scott only 5,820 effectives—too few to press on into the teeth of the Mexican defenses. The U.S. forces therefore rested in Puebla until they were reinforced by 4,500 more troops on 8 July, then another 2,400 on 6 August (the latter under the command of future president Franklin Pierce), permitting them to resume their penetration toward Mexico City the next day, while a small garrison held Puebla. The national capital was overrun by mid-September, after which Santa

Anna—so disgraced by his repeated defeats that he had resigned the presidency—circled back through the mountains, making toward his home state of Veracruz on the Gulf coast.

On 21 September 1847, the former president appeared outside Puebla with 3,200 irregular cavalrymen and 2,500 militiamen, calling upon its garrison commander—Col. C. F. Childs—to surrender. The latter refused, at which point the Mexicans—lacking any artillery, except for two small fieldpieces—instituted a half-hearted siege, threatening U.S. communications until they were surprised on 8 October by Samuel Walker's "Texas Rangers," who were acting as scouts for Brig. Joseph Lane's approaching 2,500-man brigade. Santa Anna's pickets were chased back into his main encampment at Huamantla and scattered, so that Lane paraded triumphantly into Puebla the next day. U.S. troops remained in possession of the city for another eight months, until the Treaty of Guadalupe Hidalgo was finally ratified and the United States received the largely empty provinces of California, Nevada, Utah, Colorado, Arizona, and New Mexico in exchange for withdrawing from Mexico.

Cinco de Mayo *and French Invasion (1849–1867)*

The period immediately following this humiliating capitulation was marked by bitter recriminations throughout Mexico, as conservatives and liberals fell out over how best to rectify their country's malaise. The former—who had sought to maintain colonial-era mores intact, especially with regard to social status, land tenure, predominance of the Catholic faith, and so forth—preferred a strong constitutional monarchy so as to avoid the divisive anarchy of republican rule. Liberals, conversely, felt that such old strictures should instead be loosened further, so that more citizens might participate in civic affairs. They set about implementing just such a policy after Gen. Juan N. Alvarez was propelled to the presidency in October 1855 by the Ayutla Revolution and convened a constitutional congress to reform Mexico's institutions.

This body's first pronouncement was issued on 23 November 1855, when Justice Minister Benito P. Juárez abolished the ancient tribunals catering exclusively to members of the military and clergy. Conservative protests erupted throughout the country under the banner of ¡Religión y fueros! (Religion and Privileges), and the revolt in Puebla proved so tenacious that liberal Gen. Antonio de Haro y Tamariz besieged the city in January 1856. Gen. Ignacio Comonfort did the same for another forty-one days until finally Gen. Tomás Moreno concluded matters with a third successful investment from 28 October to 6 December, after which the liberals avenged themselves by enacting numerous anticlerical decrees. (Included among them were such punitive measures as driving a street right through the grounds of the Dominicans' Santo Domingo Convent, which was symbolically named the Callejón de la Reforma or "Reform Alley.")

Yet despite such suppression in Puebla and elsewhere, the new liberal constitution unveiled in February 1857 sparked three more years of open conflict throughout Mexico, known as the Guerra de la Reforma (War of the Reform). Puebla remained occupied and thus was spared any more fighting during this struggle, which concluded with a liberal victory and Juárez's installation as president by January 1861. However, the defeated conservatives then secretly allied themselves with France and encouraged the disembarkation of an expeditionary force at Veracruz by January 1862 that was to spearhead a joint effort to replace republican government with an imperial administration (to be headed by a mutually agreed upon foreign figurehead, Archduke Maximilian of Austria).

Because of its location, Puebla lay in the path of the 6,600-man French army of Gen. Charles Ferdinand Latrille, Comte de Lorencez, which pushed inland that same spring and reached Amozoc without opposition by 4 May 1862, to await Mexican conservative forces rallying under Gen. Leonardo Márquez Araujo. France being regarded as the preeminent military power in the world at that time, it was assumed that the antiquated liberal forces would be unable to resist this modern army's advance. But the bespectacled, thirty-three-year-old Gen. Ignacio Zaragoza had spent the previous several weeks preparing to defend Puebla, evacuating its noncombatants and entrenching his 5,000-man garrison: 1,200 soldiers from the division of Gen. Miguel Negrete, plus 3,100 from the brigades of Gens. Felipe Berriozábal, Porfirio Díaz, and Juan N. Méndez. The city also contained 500 cavalrymen, small artillery and engineering companies, as well as some militia auxiliaries.

When Lorencez's conservative allies failed to rendezvous with the invaders at Amozoc, the French general resumed his progression at dawn the next day—5 May (in Spanish: Cinco de Mayo)—reaching Los Alamos Hacienda by 9:00 A.M. and expecting to overrun Puebla easily. A bombardment of Loreto and Guadalupe Hills commenced two and a half hours later, and then the French artillery shifted closer to Lorencez's headquarters at Oropeza Ranch. But despite expending 1,000 rounds—almost half their total supply—they were unable to breach the Mexican defenses, so that when two Zouave columns charged against Guadalupe Hill in midafternoon, they were checked by heavy counterfire. Lorencez committed two more Zouave companies, but a sudden rainstorm made it impossible for them to ascend the slippery slope, and they were then further struck in the right flank by hidden Mexican cavalry.

Having suffered 117 killed and 305 wounded, Lorencez beat an orderly retreat as far as Acultzingo by 11 May 1862; Mexican losses totaled 83 dead and 232 injured, but they were elated by this unexpected victory, which raised morale throughout the entire nation. However, Zaragoza was mauled when he subsequently overtook the retreating French near Orizaba, then died of typhoid fever in Puebla by September. The French meanwhile were reinforced from overseas by more troops under Gen. Elie Frédéric Forey, and their conservative allies

Lithograph of the French siege of Puebla, spring 1863. (Archivo General de la Nación, Mexico)

finally mustered in full strength, so that a cavalry brigade could push out of Orizaba by 3 February 1863 to again probe the road leading inland toward Puebla. Forey's main army followed twenty days later, merging with two other converging columns under his subordinates Charles Abel Douay and François Achille Bazaine, to create a Franco-conservative concentration of 25,000 men.

This host's vanguard captured Amozoc by 8 March 1863, Forey's main body entering two days later; the liberals braced to resist this second incursion within Puebla, having massed 25,000 troops and 180 guns inside the deserted city under Gen. Jesús González Ortega, plus another 8,000 troops and 40 field-pieces among the nearby Uranga Hills under Gen. Comonfort. Forey's advance units reached Los Alamos Hacienda by 15 March, beginning to encircle Puebla the next afternoon, and completing its isolation when they occupied San Juan Hill unopposed at noon of 18 March. Two liberal cavalry brigades managed to escape three days later, but French siege lines and batteries were completely laid out by 22 March, and an intense bombardment commenced two days afterward.

At dawn of 28 March 1863, three French columns stormed the San Javier Monastery—converted into "Fort Iturbide"—being initially repelled, although carrying that strongpoint the following afternoon at a cost of 600 casualties. Gen. Tomás O'Horan slipped out of the beleaguered city with 2,500 more republican troopers on the night of 13 April to join Comonfort's army at nearby San Jerónimo; then six days later, the besiegers stormed the southeastern portions of Puebla, and Santa Inés Convent changed hands several times in fierce fighting. On the night of 20 April a supply column attempted to sneak into the city, but it was mistakenly fired upon in the darkness. At dawn of 24 April, French sappers detonated mines beneath Santa Inés Convent and tried to overrun the stronghold the next morning, only to be thrown back.

On 5 May 1863—anniversary of Zaragoza's famous victory—Comonfort's republican army presented itself at San Lorenzo, hoping to break the siege lines at La Cruz Hill and thus resupply the hard-pressed defenders. But after clashing inconclusively with Márquez's conservative contingent the next day, Comonfort saw his left flank suddenly driven in at dawn of 8 May by a surprise French counterattack led by Bazaine that scattered the small republican army and left behind 2,000 killed, wounded, or captured. Forey released prisoners into Puebla the following day to report upon this demoralizing defeat, and González Ortega finally requested terms on 16 May, capitulating the next afternoon. Forey was generous, but the defenders nonetheless destroyed their materiel and attempted to disband their units so as not to be considered prisoners of war; still, the French seized 1,000 officers and 16,000 troops, of whom 5,000 soon joined the victorious conservative ranks.

Puebla had been badly battered by this protracted siege, and it staggered back to life slowly as its citizenry returned to their pillaged homes. Franco-conservative armies meanwhile pressed inland to seize Mexico City by 10 June 1863, then set about expanding their stranglehold over the country while offering the title of "emperor" to Maximilian one month later. The archduke and his Belgian-born wife, Charlotte (called Carlota in Mexico), made a triumphal passage through Puebla in early June 1864 while proceeding inland to be crowned. But despite their benevolence and the fall of the last major republican garrison at Oaxaca City by February 1865, most Mexicans resented this foreign-imposed "imperial" administration, and some conservatives furthermore deplored their idealistic young monarch's more liberal views. Guerrilla warfare persisted. Washington also exerted heavy pressure upon Emperor Napoleon III to withdraw his French supporting troops, and the republican Gen. Porfirio Díaz managed to escape from confinement in the Jesuit monastery at Puebla on 21 September 1865 to mount an effective counterinsurgency in southern Mexico the following year.

Once Paris had bowed to U.S. pressure, and the withdrawal of French soldiers accelerated in January 1867, republican armies began defeating remote imperial-conservative garrisons and closing in upon Mexico City, persuading Maximilian to march north to confront this approaching host at Querétaro. Díaz took advantage of the emperor's distraction to move out of the south and materialize atop San Juan Hill west of Puebla by 9 March with 3,000 troops, assisting local contingents in besieging its 3,000-man imperial garrison under Gen. Manuel Noriega. The city's San Javier and Penitenciaría redoubts were seized in costly assaults, but the republicans were unable to overwhelm all its defenders. News then arrived on 31 March that conservative Gen. Márquez had quit Mexico City the previous day with a relief column of 3,000 imperial troops and seventeen field-pieces. Thus, Díaz assembled three assault columns of 300 men apiece to storm Puebla's main stronghold—El Carmen Convent—plus thirteen companies of approximately 100 men each to stealthily approach other strongpoints scattered around the city.

At 2:00 A.M. on 2 April 1867, the three-pronged attack was launched against El Carmen; after an hour and a half of noisy fighting—long enough for Noriega to commit his reserves—

Porfirio Díaz and his troops recapturing Puebla's main square and cathedral at dawn of 2 April 1867. (Museum of History, Chapultepec Castle, Mexico City)

Díaz signaled from San Juan Hill for his 1,300 hidden soldiers to initiate their other individual attacks, which broke through everywhere, despite losses of 253 dead and 233 wounded. The few imperial survivors took refuge in the Loreto and Guadalupe convents but were compelled to capitulate two days later, after which Díaz veered westward to check Márquez's approaching relief column, eventually investing Mexico City by late April. Maximilian was defeated at Querétaro and executed on 19 June, thus bringing an end to Mexico's imperial experiment.

Porfirian Era (1868–1910)

Puebla had suffered extensive war damage from its repeated investitures throughout the conflict, especially in the western half of the city. Many of its splendid colonial-era convents and churches—San Agustín, La Merced, Santa Inés, San Javier, San Ildefonso, San Ignacio, San Sebastián, San Matías, San Juan Centepec, Guadalupe, San Marcos, and San Diego el Pobre—had been reduced to gutted shells, a new boulevard named Cinco de Mayo even being driven through the ruined grounds of the first-named. Also, many ecclesiastical properties were expropriated by the victorious liberal government for secular uses—such as the old San Juan de Dios Hospital, which was converted into a temporary jail because of the *penitenciaría's* destruction, while Santa Rosa became an insane asylum. The city's name was also officially changed, from Puebla de los Angeles into Puebla de Zaragoza, in memory of its fallen defender.

Yet despite the utter collapse of the conservative cause, national politics still remained confused and volatile until the war hero Díaz led a rebellion in November 1876 that toppled the bankrupt government of Juárez's successor, President Sebastián Lerdo de Tejada. Díaz then implemented a surprisingly effective new administration after being elected into office the next May, stamping out disruptive elements with ruthless efficiency while encouraging the modernization of the war-weary nation and restoring strength to its financial institutions. Gradually, foreign trade and commerce flourished under his iron-fisted rule, and a protégé of the president—the one-armed Gen. Manuel González—succeeded Díaz in office in December 1880 for a four-year term; González was subsequently re-elected and held office uninterruptedly over the next twenty-six years.

By 1879, Puebla's population had rebounded to 64,588 residents—virtually the same as in colonial times—and urban improvements multiplied as the national economy resurged. Its first municipal cemetery was inaugurated the following year; streetcar service began in 1881; public education allowances were increased; the *zócalo* (main square) was significantly beautified as of 1883, the same year in which the first suburban development—Colonia de los Remedios—was built east of the city limits; more than a hundred turpentine lamps were suspended throughout Puebla to provide public lighting two years later, in turn giving way to electric lights as of 1888; and more. Agricultural and manufacturing exports benefited from rail lines laid throughout Mexico during that same decade—although much initial construction was done locally by small private firms, rather than as a broad-based national effort. (Puebla's complex of rails was not joined to the main Mexico City–Veracruz trunk line until more than a decade later, when the federal government began consolidating all such operations.)

The old San Juan College was transformed into the Palacio de Gobierno (Government Palace) in 1891, the same year in which a new *penitenciaría* was inaugurated and other urban amenities appeared: a velodrome by 1893, a new bullring, and the Pescaditos and Elíseo Tivoli Gardens. More improvements were carried out under the vigorous administration of Mayor Leopoldo Gavito from 1895 to 1900, under whose direction a grand new railway station was completed by 1897, as well as starting construction of a proper, purpose-built Palacio del Ayuntamiento (Municipal Palace) that same year, in "Spanish Renaissance" style. Some of Puebla's streets were furthermore asphalted for the first time, while sidewalks were laid using

Some of the extensive war damage suffered during the French siege and capture of the city in May 1863; note the oil lamp still suspended above this intersection. (Museo de la No Intervención, Puebla)

stone slabs, and the unsanitary colonial-era canals were filled in. Urban boundaries also expanded southward with the annexation of Rancho de la Magdalena in 1898, and westward by taking over the Matadero or Necoechea suburb the next year, transforming it into the Colonia del Pensador Mexicano.

Public works accelerated during the 1907–1911 term of Mayor Francisco de Velasco, the most significant being the city's new water distribution system, which tapped into the Cieneguilla and Rentería Springs and diverted that flow into tanks atop Loreto and Guadalupe Hills, for distribution into Puebla through metal pipes. Three new hospitals—Corazón de Jesús, General del Estado, and Beneficencia Española—were also constructed, plus numerous banks, office buildings, and mansions. The city's population had increased to 91,899 residents by 1908, and the fine Victoria Market was opened two years later.

Modern Era (1911–Present)

But despite the undoubted economic improvements and modernization achieved during the Porfirian era, many Mexicans resented their lack of a commensurate social advancement or equitable distribution of wealth, while wearying of the regime's heavy-handed political repression and partiality toward foreign interests. When the seventy-nine-year-old Díaz stood for his eighth term in 1910, he arrested his high-minded opponent Francisco Ignacio

Madero rather than campaign actively. And when the latter escaped loose confinement and called for a general uprising for 20 November, Díaz's power was quickly sapped by a rash of rebellions in northern and southern Mexico, driving him into exile by late May 1911.

Puebla had been peacefully occupied by the peasant troops of Emiliano Zapata's southern movement during this insurrection and endured its only significant outburst of fighting when, on 12 July 1911, these occupiers began arresting civilians believed to be implicated in a plot to assassinate Madero during a forthcoming electoral visit. Col. Aureliano Blanquet, commander of the local federal garrison—on orders from the interim president, Francisco León de la Barra, Díaz's former foreign minister—consequently attacked the Zapatista encampment within Puebla's bullring the next day, killing 80 and wounding 200 in a ferocious exchange of gunfire. But the city was spared any further action during the revolution, although its economy suffered as a result of this nationwide upheaval.

Late in 1914, Zapata and the northern rebel Pancho Villa combined their forces against President Venustiano Carranza, driving him from Mexico City. But Carranza's able military commander—Gen. Alvaro Obregón—succeeded in defeating their regional contingents and entering Puebla peaceably on 5 January 1915, before driving on toward the capital with his well-disciplined 12,000 troops, eventually crushing those rivals in a protracted series of battles in central Mexico.

After Obregón's final victory and his election as president in November 1920, revolutionary fervor waned, so that modernization efforts could resume. Puebla's first passenger airline flight was made to Mexico City two years later, while its first modern highway into the capital was completed by 1926. A few more church properties were expropriated by Obregón's anticlerical successor, Plutarco Elías Calles: its Palacio Episcopal, for example, becoming the Palacio Federal; its Colegio del Sagrado Nombre de Jesús a state institute; and Santa Mónica Convent an art museum.

However, the city's textile and pottery industries, as well as its overall export trade, benefited thanks to an improved transportation infrastructure, plus the numerous construction projects funded to celebrate Puebla's 400th anniversary in 1931. Its municipality had achieved a population of 124,063 inhabitants by that time, having expanded by annexing the 30 square miles of the neighboring municipality called Ignacio Zaragoza. As manufacturing and industrialization gained speed during World War II, the total population exploded to 211,285 by 1950 and 297,257 a decade later. Puebla's last orchards and tilled fields disappeared during that growth spurt, and urban sprawl began creeping outward as more adjoining municipalities were annexed in October 1962,

The former Palacio Episcopal as it appeared, ca. 1975; its glazed-tile exterior had been designed and completed in 1768 by the master architect José Miguel de Santa María. (Author's Collection)

trebling the metropolitan area to almost 90 square miles. An ambitious scheme of urban road construction was also commenced around that time, and the San Francisco River was diverted into a subterranean tunnel—a project that unfortunately razed some of the oldest sectors of the city, without fully resolving the problem of occasional flash floods.

The German automotive corporation Volkswagen installed a huge complex of plants in Puebla's new "industrial corridor" during the decade of the 1960s, which in turn spawned numerous other ancillary businesses. The population of its expanded metropolitan area therefore leaped to 532,744 residents by 1970, 772,908 a decade later, and 1,266,258 by 1990 as smaller outlying communities continued to become engulfed by its unbridled growth. Modern problems such as air pollution and traffic congestion appeared, threatening many colonial-era architectural treasures, as well as shortages in drinking water, sewer treatment, and public lighting.

For further reading on the history of Puebla or Mexico, please consult the Select Bibliography at the end of this volume.

Veracruz

Mexico's principal seaport for transatlantic and Caribbean traffic throughout the colonial era.

Foundation at Quiahuiztlan (1519–1524)

This low and marshy coastline had been populated by Totonac tribes since remote times, although they preferred congregating on natural levees or higher spots deep within the interior rain forest, tending to their crops rather than enduring prolonged exposure to the heat, humidity, insects, and storms along the seashore. Seasonal fishing was also practiced, but the flat and treeless landscape around what is today the city of Veracruz was especially inhospitable, its terrain interspersed with only shallow and turbid rivers and stagnant lagoons; thus, no permanent indigenous settlement ever existed in the region.

Eventually, the Totonacs were decimated by epidemic diseases and conquered when the Aztecs pushed down out of the central highlands during the third quarter of the fifteenth century under their expansionistic emperor Axayácatl. Thousands of inland tribesmen were thereupon resettled into this coastal region, and the entire district was placed under the authority of the Texcocan, or Aculúacan, branch of the Aztec empire, which gathered tributes through a *calpixqui* (tribune) commanding a garrison at Cuetlaxtlan (modern Cotaxtla), more than 30 miles from the sea.

But on 17 June 1518, four Spanish vessels bearing more than 200 men appeared offshore under Juan de Grijalva, having coasted westward from Yucatán on a reconnaissance mission organized by Gov. Diego Velázquez of Cuba. De Grijalva touched at a deserted offshore island where there were signs of recent human sacrifices to the Aztec deity Quetzalcóatl, naming the place Sacrificios Island before contacting some Totonacs who chanced to appear along the mainland. Hoping to ingratiate themselves with these powerful new strangers and perhaps throw off Aztec rule, the Totonacs gave the Spaniards such an elaborate welcome that on 24 June—Saint

Aerial photo of Veracruz, ca. 1945, not including its offshore island fortress of San Juan de Ulúa; note the flat, sterile terrain. (Aerofoto)

John's feast day in the Church calendar—de Grijalva formally laid claim to the largest offshore island and named it San Juan de Ulúa (Saint John of Ulúa), having apparently confused the term "Aculúacan" for the region's name.

His subordinate Pedro de Alvarado was detached a few days later to return to Cuba with a report and some booty for Velázquez, while a single Spaniard—Miguel de Zaragoza—remained ashore among the Totonacs. The rest of de Grijalva's scouting force then pressed northwestward as far as Cape Rojo before finally turning back themselves. A much larger expedition of almost 600 Spanish soldiers and several hundred Cuban porters and black slaves followed up this discovery by dropping anchor off San Juan de Ulúa on 20 April 1519, their leader, Hernán Cortés, having abruptly quit Cuba rather than allow himself to be superseded by Velázquez. On Good Friday, two days after anchoring, Cortés's army disembarked on the mainland opposite San Juan de Ulúa and was given a friendly reception at the nearby Totonac hamlet of Chalchicueyecan.

A like welcome was extended a few days later by Teutliltzin, the Aztec tribune at Cotaxtla, who assigned 2,000 vassals to wait upon the Spaniards and offered rich presents to their leader. But these dazzling gifts unwittingly excited the Spaniards' greed, so that the Aztecs would try in vain to dissuade the strangers from visiting their inland capital of Tenochtitlán (modern Mexico City). While Cortés awaited a formal invitation from Emperor Moctezuma II, he also received de Zaragoza and a Totonac delegation from nearby Cempoala, who revealed that many subject tribes resented Aztec rule. Teutliltzin reappeared shortly thereafter and withdrew the indigenous servants, thus cutting off the Spaniards' food supply, but Cortés instructed Alvarado to probe inland with a column while two brigantines circled northwestward to search for a better anchorage.

Convinced of the richness of the Aztec empire, Cortés devised a ruse to free himself of his obligations to Velázquez by convening a meeting of his soldiery on 18 May 1519 and persuading them to found a new Spanish settlement on Mexican soil to be called Villa Rica de la Vera Cruz (Rich Town of the True Cross), with Cortés as its *justicia mayor* (chief magistrate—that is, mayor) and his officers appointed as its *ayuntamiento* (municipal government). No civilian community was ever actually contemplated, this ceremony being merely a legal fiction concocted to permit Cortés to report directly to King Charles I in Spain, bypassing the Cuban governor. Once his two brigantines returned to report on discovering a suitable harbor, called Quiahuiztlan or Quiahuahuiztlan, 40 miles farther northwest in friendly Cempoalan territory, the conquistador abandoned his encampment at Chalchicueyecan by striking overland with his army on 7 June, making a stately three-week progression—during which he forged alliances with local tribes—while his fleet circled round by sea.

Upon reuniting with his ships at Quiahuiztlan on 28 June 1519, Cortés found its harbor dominated by a fortified Cempoalan village atop a hill, but he chose to establish his own "town" of Villa Rica de la Vera Cruz on a plain about a mile from this sea outlet. Although a street grid was laid out and lots assigned for a future church, main square, shipyards, and so forth, urban touches were ignored; his troops simply concentrated on throwing up a compound enclosed by a ditch, palisades, bastions, and gun embrasures. While this stronghold was taking shape, Cortés encouraged the Cempoalans to refuse to pay tribute to the Aztecs, who in turn mustered warriors menacingly at their nearby garrison town of Tizapancingo. Cortés sallied and easily routed them, thus gaining the adherence of the Cempoalans. Then, on 16 July, he ordered three vessels to sail toward Europe with messages and bullion for the king, while simultaneously persuading the masters of his other nine anchored ships to beach and disassemble their craft, so that Cortés's soldiers could see that there would be no retreat.

Leaving Juan de Escalante as Villa Rica's garrison commander, Cortés moved inland on 8 August 1519 with his main force, returning shortly thereafter with 100 men to repel four rival Spanish vessels sent from Jamaica. Resuming his advance into the interior, Cortés was eventually greeted at the Aztec capital in early November, then shortly thereafter his Quiahuiztlan garrison clashed with an Aztec contingent from Nautla, resulting in many Cempoalans and seven Spaniards slain (among them de Escalante). Upon receiving this news in distant Tenochtitlán, Cortés detained Moctezuma and had the offending Aztec commander brought in captive from the coast to be burned alive in its main square.

The main Spanish army spent the next several months in the wary Aztec capital, until a rival expedition—seventeen vessels bearing 1,400 men under Pánfilo de Narváez—materialized off San Juan de Ulúa on 19 April 1520, having been sent from Cuba by a vengeful Governor Velázquez. Narváez disembarked and marched his host as far as Cempoala, before being defeated by a clever nocturnal attack in late May that allowed Cortés to absorb virtually the whole expedition into his own ranks. Upon regaining Tenochtitlán, Cortés learned that the Aztecs had risen against the garrison he had left behind under Alvarado, so that the Spaniards had to cut their way out with heavy losses and spend the next year subduing the Mexican capital.

Quiahuiztlan proved instrumental throughout this campaign, furnishing Cortés with a steady stream of reinforcements from the Spanish ships that materialized offshore. But no actual town developed around its stronghold, most men simply being hastened up into the mountains, while once Aztec resistance collapsed in August 1521, the victors fanned out to claim large towns and estates throughout central Mexico. The coastal region—already depopulated because the Totonacs had been decimated by a smallpox epidemic unleashed from Narváez's army—remained largely ignored, having no deposits of precious metals; most Spaniards preferred the cool highlands to this torrid shoreline.

Cortés scuttling his vessels off Quiahuiztlan in July 1519, so that his troops might commit wholeheartedly to the forthcoming conquest of the Aztec empire; a romanticized 1887 oil painting by Rafael Monleón y Torres. (Museo Naval, Madrid)

The sea and wind currents flowing into the Gulf of Mexico moreover brought vessels within sight of San Juan de Ulúa first, so that it naturally became the preferred anchorage, while the Quiahuiztlan site was often flooded as well at high tide. Cortés therefore decided, during an inspection tour in 1523, to shift Veracruz 25 miles farther south and bolster its few citizens by adding others from an equally ineffectual inland township called Medellín, creating a united community near the former Aztec town of Mitlancuautla only 15 miles from the strategic anchorage of San Juan de Ulúa. (By coincidence, the king had also granted Veracruz-Quiahuiztlan full title as a city on 4 July of that same year, with a crest depicting a golden city upon a green field above, two white columns on a blue field below, a red cross over all, plus thirteen blue stars in a golden border. This title naturally transferred to the new settlement.)

"Antigua" Veracruz (1524–1599)

The Quiahuiztlan site was officially abandoned as of 1524, being remembered afterward as Villa Rica la Vieja (The Old Rich Town), while the new establishment was created early the following year and quickly began to take shape as settlers felled trees along its riverfront to build houses. Only a mile upriver from the coast, goods could now be lightered directly from San Juan de Ulúa by boat and disgorged at the city quays for inspection, storage, and dispatch inland. Passengers rode the intervening distance overland and after a brief respite continued due westward up the 260-mile road leading through La Rinconada and Jalapa toward Mexico City and the central plateau.

Veracruz's relocation—virtually completed by 1525—was hardly an unusual occurrence during the early stages of Mexico's occupation; numerous other Spanish communities shifted into more favorable locales as well. Moreover, Veracruz's transfer was legally justifiable, for its original town charter had encompassed an immense expanse of unallotted territory—from Perote in the west, to the Huasteca in the north, and Coatzacoalcos in the southeast—so that its few score citizens were merely moving within those broadly defined urban boundaries. (Such a move would not be possible even a few years later, after more villages and estates had begun to spring up, thus contracting its jurisdiction.)

In addition to urban lots, citizens also received outlying properties on which to plant crops and raise livestock, while the native population continued fishing out in the Gulf. However, the principal livelihood was derived from ships anchoring 15 miles away at San Juan de Ulúa. Crude government offices were erected to process arrivals, private dwellings multiplied, and a Franciscan monastery was established as early as 1529 to minister to the stream of transients. Procedures became better regularized once the first Crown-appointed viceroy for Mexico—Antonio de Mendoza, Conde de Tendilla—passed through Veracruz en route to his capital in October 1535. He also bore instructions from Madrid to erect a permanent "fortress and shelter for vessels" at San Juan de Ulúa, as well as to search for a more suitable anchorage along the Gulf coast. Fifteen years later de Mendoza reported to his successor that it had been impossible to find a harbor better than San Juan de Ulúa, "as bad as it is."

A seasonal pattern began to develop once the plate-fleet system was introduced during the mid-1540s, with individual sailings gradually becoming supplanted by annual convoys departing from Seville. With the foreknowledge that a fleet would not be expected until late summer, Veracruz's few permanent residents could now tend to their rural properties, returning into the city only when a convoy was due to employ their slaves as supplementary boatmen or stevedores for the Crown workforce maintained at San Juan de Ulúa. Residences were converted into inns to accommodate hundreds of disembarking passengers and sailors, as well as traders and *arrieros* (teamsters) descending from central Mexico to acquire imported goods for resale in the interior. Food, drink, and fodder were all sold to these throngs, and once this commercial fair abated and the glut of visitors receded inland, *veracruzanos* resumed their agricultural and ranching pursuits—until a second upsurge occurred early the next spring when the anchored plate-fleet was prepared to receive another influx of passengers and cargo and depart for Spain.

The city suffered extensive damage when a massive hurricane swept down the coast on 2–4 September 1552, causing its river to overflow, collapsing numerous homes and warehouses, and leaving Veracruz's streets deep with silt. The storm also flattened most structures on the low-lying and more exposed island of San Juan de Ulúa, drowning many people and sinking twelve of fifteen recently arrived (and thus almost fully laden) merchantmen. Because of these losses, the Crown accepted a proposal from García de Escalante Alvarado to construct a high stone wall with imbedded iron rings upon San Juan de Ulúa, so that ships might be moored in its lee. Veracruz was also rebuilt, its resurrection being hastened by a tripling of Mexican silver output toward the end of that same decade, thanks to a remarkable new amalgamation treatment for ores called the *patio* process.

The volume and value of transatlantic traffic mushroomed as a result, the city prospering as fleets of ever-larger galleons wended into San Juan de Ulúa's narrow and reef-bound entrance. When ten vessels were sighted at dusk on 15 September 1568, island lookouts assumed that they were advance

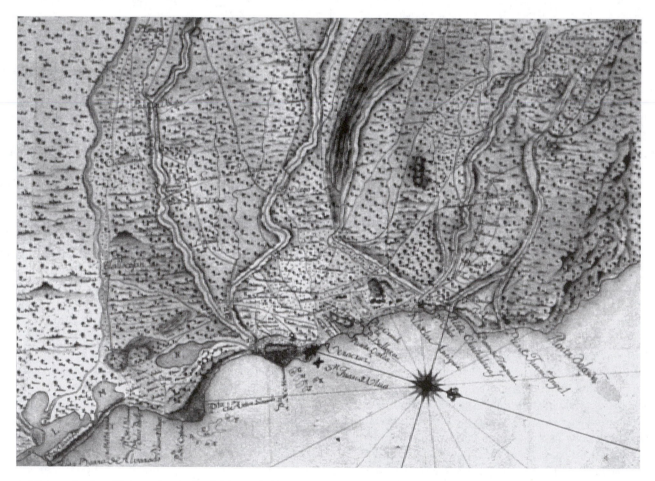

A 1784 map by the military engineer Miguel del Corral, showing the major routes leading inland from Veracruz; note the undeveloped surroundings, two and a half centuries after the city's foundation. North is toward lower right. (Archivo General de la Nación, Mexico)

elements of an anticipated plate-fleet. But the next morning these ships lured its pilot-boat close enough for capture, then glided past its batteries—busily firing salutes—and tied up at its rings before the *alcaide* (keep commander), Antonio Delgadillo, realized that they were actually illegal English traders under the command of John Hawkins, seeking sanctuary after being storm damaged while trying to exit the Caribbean.

Seizing San Juan de Ulúa, Hawkins sent a message to the authorities 15 miles away at Veracruz, promising to depart once his repairs were complete. But at sunrise on 17 September 1568, Adm. Francisco Luján appeared offshore with a dozen galleons; among his passengers was the new viceroy-designate for New Spain, Martín Enríquez de Almanza. Hawkins warned the approaching plate-fleet that they too must allow him to refit or else he would dispute their entrance. Short on food and water and hovering off a dangerous lee shore, Luján and Enríquez had no choice but to comply. Contrary winds prevented their entry until 21 September, but once the two fleets became moored side by side, Spanish troops slipped under cover of darkness aboard a dismasted hulk near the interlopers.

Suspicious, Hawkins opened fire at 10:00 A.M. on 23 September 1568, all his ships being destroyed or captured during a daylong exchange, except for his flagship *Minion* and the tiny auxiliary *Judith,* commanded by his youthful kinsman Francis Drake. This incident created enormous resentment when reported in England, leading to a deterioration in relations. Mexican officials meanwhile sought to strengthen San Juan de Ulúa's defenses against future penetrations, the stonemasons and brothers Juan Sánchez and Ginés Talaya being hired to enlarge its ramparts and bastions, as well as to install the captured English artillery, while the garrison was furthermore augmented to 50 soldiers and 150 black slaves under a full *castellano* (fort commander).

Veracruz was unaffected by this dramatic yet distant encounter, its populace being estimated at 200 Spanish citizens and 600 blacks by 1571, most of whom still resided only seasonally within the city. A few more monasteries had been erected, and there were now three hospitals: at Santiago; a charity institution established two years previously by the Hippolytean Order; and Nuestra Señora (established as early as 1560 by free and enslaved blacks). The small number of residents could scarcely cope with the thousands of transients now routinely passing through every spring and autumn, so that

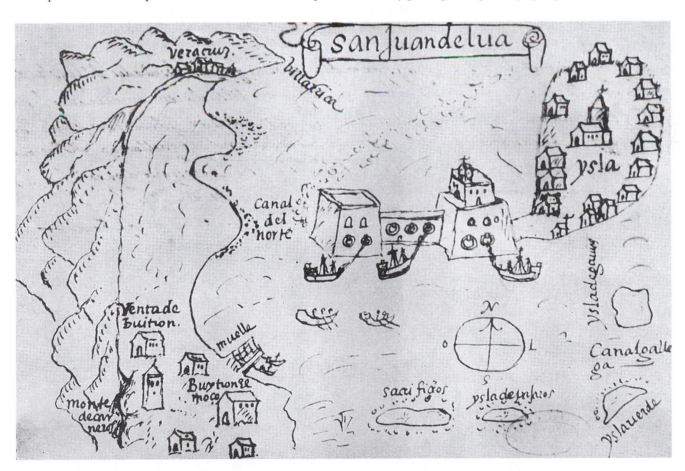

Crude drawing from a Spanish sea-atlas, ca. 1585–1590, which depicts the Ventas de Buitrón—site of the future city of Nueva Veracruz—at lower left, while the island fortress of San Juan de Ulúa is featured at center right, and what is today Antigua Veracruz appears 15 miles in the distance at upper left. (Real Academia de la Historia, Madrid)

camps had to be extemporized in every direction outside Veracruz, while mules and horses grazed for miles around.

In order to immediately cater to travel-weary passengers as they disembarked from San Juan de Ulúa onto the mainland opposite, a few plots were claimed during the latter half of the 1570s, one such being granted in 1585 to the *veracruzano* Juan Buitrón—and another somewhat later to his relation Juan González de Buitrón, better known as Buitrón el Mozo (Buitrón the Younger)—who both erected hostels near a wooden jetty that quickly became so famous that this landing spot was soon referred to as Ventas de Buitrón (Buitrón's Inns), as well as the Banda de Buitrón (Buitrón's Shoreline).

When Drake led a destructive privateering sweep through the Caribbean early in 1586 and war with Elizabethan England flared two years later, the Spanish Crown realized that San Juan de Ulúa remained worrisomely vulnerable, so that the Italian-born royal engineer Batista Antonelli was sent across from Havana to suggest improvements in January 1590. Given that the island was now crowded with customs offices, a church, a twelve-bed hospital, a prison, a cistern, and twenty crude dwellings, Antonelli recommended that a new city be created on the mainland opposite around Ventas de Buitrón, so as to handle all nonmilitary matters and thus clear space on San Juan de Ulúa for its proper enclosure with ramparts. In addition, he judged the ferrying of merchandise to and from undefended Veracruz as needlessly risky and inefficient, so he added that the distant city's *casas reales* (royal offices)—where all cargoes were received, taxed, and released to consignees—should be shifted into the proposed new city as well, so that goods might be released for direct transportation overland via a new road.

Because of the English conflict these recommendations were only fitfully implemented, construction of new edifices proving especially difficult because of a lack of available materials. (Large timbers and stone blocks, for example, had to be imported by sea from Campeche.) San Juan de Ulúa's *castellano* nevertheless began issuing grants to his island personnel and a few private individuals along the Banda de Buitrón, while work was also commenced on a two-story structure to accommodate the new *casas reales,* complete with a central patio ample enough to process voluminous ship cargoes.

The pace of the future city's development accelerated after a road running northwestward from it was finished in the mid-1590s, so that merchants began actively soliciting plots in hopes of eliminating the expense of leasing storage space and accommodations in distant Veracruz; they preferred to erect their own private residence-warehouses at the new site. Religious orders also requested tracts along the Banda de Buitrón, the Carmelites obtaining a large space in June 1597; the Augustinians in December (their monastery serving as the new city's first parish until San Sebastián Church could be completed); the Jesuits receiving their first plot in April 1598; while the Dominicans initiated a monastery that same July (although not actually finished until 1656).

"Nueva" Veracruz (1600–1682)

The old city quickly emptied, as *veracruzanos* realized that they risked losing their livelihoods if they failed to move into this new harborside community. Municipal administration was initially split between both sites, because although Nueva Veracruz (New Veracruz) had a population of roughly 200 Spanish citizens and was fully functional by the summer of 1600, the office of *alcalde mayor* was still legally retained at the old site—San Juan de Ulúa's *castellano* having been empowered by the Crown to serve as an independent *justicia mayor* at the new locale.

Nueva Veracruz did not receive its own separate office of *corregidor* until a few years later, after which commerce boomed again as plate-fleet traffic resumed once peace with England was restored in August 1604. (Theoretically, a *corregidor* governed only a town, while an *alcalde mayor* ruled over a district; yet there was otherwise little difference in their functions.) Two years later, the viceroy, Juan Manuel de Mendoza y Luna, Marqués de Montesclaros, provided funds to purchase a plot to transfer the old city's charity hospital—which was renamed Hospital de San Juan de Montesclaros upon being reconstituted in his honor—with a capacity of sixty beds.

Only eight Spaniards and a few free blacks remained by 1609 at Vieja Veracruz (Old Veracruz—a term that would later devolve into Antigua Veracruz or "Ancient Veracruz"). But despite the new city's ascendancy, it was to remain plagued by a lack of freshwater and a shortage of construction materials. So many wooden structures had to be erected as a result that it became derisively known as the Ciudad de Tablas (City of Boards), while its haphazard layout left plots clustered along the barren sandy beach, uncomfortably exposed to the elements as they were only a few feet above water level.

The climate was light and benign during the spring months of April and May, but heat and humidity soon grew into the crushing intensity of the *caniculares* (dog days) of summer, exacerbated by a lack of breezes. Hot southern winds would eventually spring up in mid-August, presaging the advent of strong *nortes* (northers) that dropped temperatures sharply, increasing in strength and frequency throughout the winter months of November to March. Each successive gale—some lasting for as long as a fortnight—threatened moored vessels and sent hissing whitecaps against Nueva Veracruz's waterfront, spraying the frail dwellings with clouds of spinning drift and sand. (Gales that coincided with a rising tide were known as *nortes chocolateros* or "chocolate northers" because their roiling effects churned up sediment from the harbor floor.)

Residents recognized the orange or reddish-colored skies that were harbingers of storms, while the early departure of

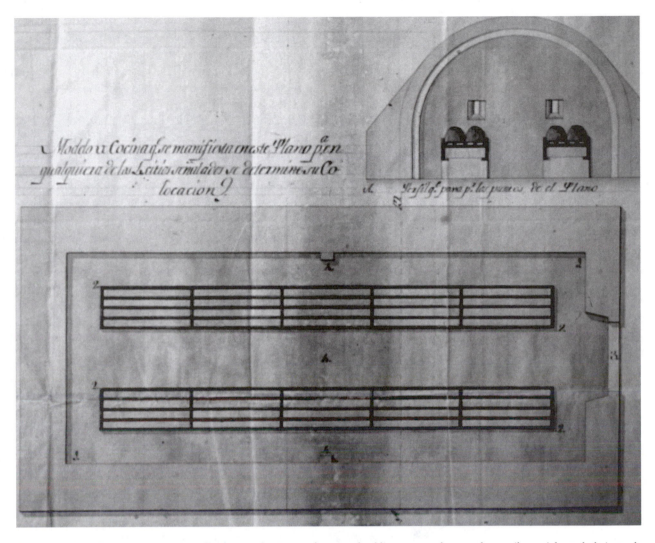

Diagram and profile view by the military engineer Pedro Ponze of proposed public ovens, so that merchant sailors might cook their meals while in port, 1792. (Archivo General de la Nación, Mexico)

land birds far out over the Gulf signaled a fair day. Heavy rainfall usually occurred at night, when the breezes blew offshore, often turning the city's unpaved streets and overland roads into such impassable quagmires that the normal two-week sojourn by mule train to Mexico City could become elongated into five weeks. Such unpleasant conditions, plus calamities such as the conflagration that consumed virtually every building in the city in December 1616, including La Merced and Santo Domingo convents, convinced most citizens to continue their practice of withdrawing to their farms once a convoy had been received or dispatched. The city would be left to a small coterie of mulatto and black retainers, plus the unhappy garrison on San Juan de Ulúa, reduced to a peacetime complement of only twenty-five men.

Yet the needs of plate-fleet traffic meant that Nueva Veracruz remained in existence. Even before a convoy appeared,

Mexico City merchants would begin amassing bulk exports such as sugar, cotton, tobacco, wool, cochineal, and dyewoods in Veracruz's warehouses. News of the actual sighting of an approaching fleet would be sped to the capital and proclaimed throughout New Spain by criers, prompting scores of traders to descend into Veracruz to acquire imported wines, textiles, wrought iron, leather goods, hardware, crystal, weaponry, furniture, books, and many other sundries that would be conveyed inland by caravans of hired teamsters. Once the commercial frenzy subsided, the throngs dispersed, sailors leaving their anchored galleons empty while traveling up into the more benign mountain climes. Labors would renew the next spring in anticipation of a convoy's departure, climaxing with the arrival of gold, silver, and copper consignments from the Real Casa de Moneda (Royal Mint) in Mexico City, plus an order from the viceroy for the fleet to sail.

Veracruz also received annual ships from Spain bearing *azogue* (mercury), a vital ingredient for treating mineral ores, as well as dispatch boats called *avisos*. Slavers frequently called as well, an estimated 220,000 Africans passing through the port between 1595 and 1640, while dignitaries such as viceroys and bishops were often greeted as they traveled through, among thousands of lesser passengers. Notwithstanding the new locale's physical shortcomings, Veracruz still derived great profit from handling this crush of business, its population swelling to roughly 500 Spaniards and 3,000 slaves by 1624. (The English Dominican friar Thomas Gage, in transit through the city the next year, nonetheless noted that almost all of its structures were still "built with boards and timber, the walls of the richest man's house being made but of boards, which . . . hath been cause that many times the town hath been for the most part of it burnt down to the ground.")

Its municipal office of *corregidor* was upgraded in 1629 from a secondary appointment made by the viceroys in Mexico City to a royal commission issued directly from Madrid, while the increase of Dutch naval activity in the Gulf—especially the devastating raid against Campeche by Jan Janszoon van Hoorn and Cornelis Jol in August 1633—galvanized work on a defensive perimeter of wooden stockades and bastions around the city. A new stone customshouse, with a Doric design highlighted by a large central archway, was also completed fifteen years later.

But commercial traffic declined after Spain endured a quarter century of debilitating naval warfare against The Netherlands, emerging as a ruined power once peace was restored in January 1648. Imperial bankruptcy resulted in a drastic curtailment in plate-fleet movements for the remainder of the seventeenth century, while a severe yellow-fever epidemic also struck Veracruz in 1648, adding to the inhabitants' woes. Seven years later England seized Jamaica, spawning such fear of freebooters roving unchecked throughout the Caribbean that the Mexican viceroy hired the Flemish-born engineer Marcos Lucio in May 1656 to suggest improvements for San Juan de Ulúa's fortifications. A hurricane razed much of Veracruz on the night of 14 August 1661, while major buccaneer descents by the Jamaican naval commodore Christo-

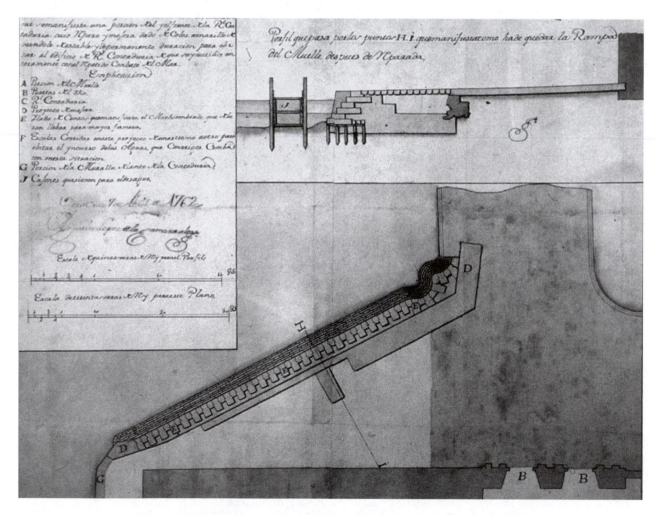

Diagram and cutaway view by the military engineer Agustín López de la Cámara-Alta, suggesting improvements to the city wharf, 1762; because of constant wave action, this jetty had to be frequently repaired or replaced. (Archivo General de la Nación, Mexico)

pher Myngs against Santiago de Cuba in October 1662 and Campeche in February 1663 engendered nervousness among *veracruzanos*.

Madrid bolstered all Caribbean defenses by dispatching a naval squadron called the Armada de Barlovento (Windward Fleet) into the West Indies that used Veracruz as its financial and logistical base. Commo. Agustín de Diústegui's 572-ton flagship *San Felipe* and 412-ton *Magdalena* entered port in the autumn of 1667, while the armada's second-in-command, Alonso de Campos, patrolled off Santo Domingo and southern Cuba with three other warships. But this force was annihilated in a battle against Henry Morgan's buccaneer fleet inside Lake Maracaibo in April 1669, so that as a precaution, Veracruz's garrison was augmented to 300 regular troops the following year. Its 400 civilian militiamen were furthermore reformed, and all free mulattoes and blacks were exempted from paying tribute. There were also an additional 300 soldiers stationed offshore on San Juan de Ulúa.

A second armada could not be reconstituted until seven years later, and although this squadron also drew the bulk of its payments and supplies from the Mexican exchequer, Veracruz's open roadstead and lack of a shipyard meant that these vessels spent much of their time circulating between other Spanish-American ports. Such absences were not deemed critical, as the city had not been directly menaced by an enemy in more than a century and peace prevailed in Europe. Consequently, when lookouts sighted a pair of approaching sails on the afternoon of 17 May 1683, which broke off after closing within 10 miles, it was assumed that they were Spanish merchantmen fearful of chancing the dangerous approaches at sundown.

Buccaneer Raid and Recuperation (1683–1728)

But the vessels were actually captive Spanish prizes bearing the French *boucanier* chieftain François Grammont of Saint-Domingue (modern Haiti), his Dutch-born colleague Laurens de Graaf (a deserter from the armada, highly familiar with local conditions), and the aggrieved Dutch slaver Nikolaas van Hoorn, operating together with a French letter of reprisal against Spanish interests because van Hoorn had been illegally divested of his ship at Santo Domingo. Having determined that the annual plate-fleet had not yet appeared, so that the city was quiet and uncrowded, de Graaf piloted his two ships back inshore that night and landed with 200 freebooters at the Vergara River mouth, a mile and a half due west. While his vanguard stole upon the sleeping city, Grammont and van Hoorn brought another 600 buccaneers ashore 3 miles northwest at Punta Gorda and followed.

Knowing that Veracruz's palisades were low and neglected, de Graaf was able to lead the raiders silently in over a sand dune, deploying undetected within the unlit streets. The pirate attack erupted at dawn of 18 May 1683, overwhelming Veracruz's startled defenders, while houses were randomly pep-

pered to cow its few thousand civilians. Within a half hour half-dressed captives were being herded into La Merced Church, all buildings being ransacked and numerous prisoners tortured over the next four days to reveal their riches as San Juan de Ulúa's garrison watched helplessly from across the harbor and appealed for help out of Mexico's interior. Before relief columns could appear, de Graaf and Grammont marched their captives 2 miles southeast down the coast and transferred offshore to Sacrificios Island, beyond reach of any rescuers, then began loading booty aboard their ships while awaiting payment of a ransom to release their wealthiest prisoners. Shortly after that sum was received, the *flibustiers* gathered hundreds of blacks and mulattoes from among the Sacrificios Island captives, carrying them off to be sold as slaves.

Even though the engorged pirate fleet encountered that year's plate-fleet as they stood out to sea, Adm. Diego Fernández de Zaldívar refused combat, preferring to allow the fearsome predators to escape so as to enter port unchallenged. The city had been reduced to shambles, with 300 of its inhabitants dead, more than a quarter of its population carried off into bondage, and its dwellings and warehouses stripped of millions in merchandise. The viceroy, Tomás Antonio de la Cerda y Aragón, Conde de Paredes, descended from Mexico City to inspect the devastation in August 1683, ordering the city's mile-long perimeter upgraded by installing additional bastions, fortified gates, and higher palisades by mid-April 1685; a few homes lying outside its circuit were also demolished.

Yet despite recuperating from this ordeal, Veracruz's unhappiness deepened when crews from the Armada de Barlovento

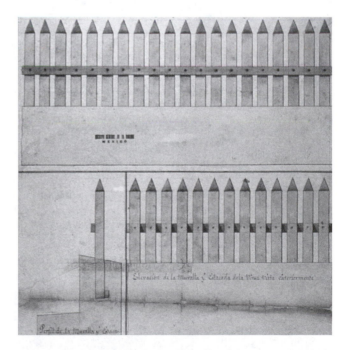

Drawings by the engineer Felipe León Maffey of the improved palisade design to be installed atop a 3-foot stone parapet around the city's perimeter, late March 1727. (Archivo General de la Nación, Mexico)

rioted in May 1687 because of their arrears in pay, enforced idleness, and competition from a squadron of recently arrived Biscayan privateers. Some 200 armada sailors and marines therefore deserted en masse, the rest being put down with three fatalities. When the Italian traveler Giovanni Francesco Gemelli Careri passed through the city in November 1697, he found it still "very small and poor, inhabited by few Spaniards and mostly blacks and mulattoes, so that whites are seen only when a fleet arrives." He additionally recorded that its cost of living was exceptionally high because its arid district could not sustain the city, while its fortifications and shabby wooden dwellings were once again half-buried by blowing sand.

Veracruz did not experience any significant economic resurgence until Spain's long decline began to reverse when the last Hapsburg monarch—the deformed invalid Charles II—died on 30 November 1700, being succeeded by the sixteen-year-old French Bourbon princeling Philip of Anjou. Other European nations, fearful that this union would concentrate too much power in a single dynasty, sought to contest the succession, so that a British fleet was sent to prowl the Caribbean late in 1701. Paris and Madrid, convinced that hostilities would be initiated by a preemptive strike against a Spanish plate-fleet, sent out a huge French counterexpedition under Vice Adm. François Louis Rousselet, Comte de Château Renault, who

reached Veracruz on 5 May 1702 to escort home the bullion convoy of Adm. Luis Manuel de Velasco. The seven French warships and fourteen Spanish vessels set sail on 10–11 June, yet despite being joined by more ships at Havana and traversing the Atlantic, they were cornered in Vigo Bay (Spain) by an Anglo-Dutch fleet under Adm. Sir George Rooke, their resultant capture precipitating the War of the Spanish Succession, or Queen Anne's War.

Veracruz's defenses were strengthened and its garrison upgraded by an additional 200 cavalrymen during this eleven-year struggle, as well as when Madrid was subsequently drawn into a war against the "Quadruple Alliance" of England, France, Holland, and Austria from 1718 to 1721. City administration was simplified the next year by merging its governorship with that of San Juan de Ulúa, when Juan de Acuña y Bejarano, Marqués de Casafuerte, passed through en route to assuming office as viceroy in Mexico City. He furthermore directed that a new seawall be completed along Veracruz's waterfront, plus a new fortified land gate dubbed Puerta Nueva (New Gate), or Puerta de Acuña (Acuña's Gate), upon its inauguration in 1727.

Overseas commerce also benefited as Bourbon-inspired reforms gradually began to take effect, especially for Veracruz, by supplementing the sporadic arrivals of plate-fleets with increasing use of so-called *navíos de registro* (registry ships)

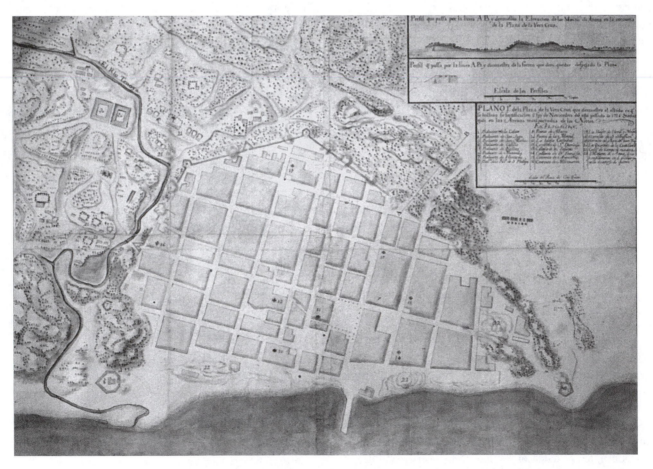

Map by Maffey of the city as it appeared late in 1726; north is toward lower right. (Archivo General de la Nación, Mexico)

authorized to sail and trade semiautonomously, as well as by annual visits by English slavers. Exports of Mexican produce to Campeche, Havana, and New Orleans grew as a result, although one particular reform seemed to threaten the city's existence: when the Crown decided to shift plate-fleet fairs from Veracruz to the inland city of Jalapa in April 1720. Merchants and teamsters had long complained about the arduous descent to the hot and pestilential coast, while Veracruz's inadequate accommodations and provisions often resulted in sickness among the thousands of crowded congregants. Ingrained practice nonetheless got this directive rescinded two years later, although it was then reissued in November 1724—with Orizaba now designated as the fair's locale—before Jalapa was finally appointed again in April 1728, hosting its first commercial fair the next year.

Colonial Heyday (1729–1794)

Despite being reduced to a mere entrepot, Veracruz compensated for its lost plate-fleet business by the growing number of registry ships that began arriving, as well as by more numerous exports to other Gulf ports and the Caribbean. The first of many solid new edifices was created when the city's Parroquia (Parochial Church) was consecrated on 13 June 1734, dedicated to the veneration of Our Lady of the Assumption. And while Jalapa's fairs declined when plate-fleet traffic was interrupted during the War of Jenkins's Ear from 1739 to 1748, Veracruz still received blockade runners. Additional work became available as port defenses were strengthened, while the city and island garrisons mushroomed to 4,250 troops, resulting in the establishment of Veracruz's own Regimiento Fijo de la Corona (Fixed Crown Regiment).

Private construction of whitewashed stone buildings continued once peace was restored in the autumn of 1748, allowing maritime trade to resume. A census taken six years later revealed that Veracruz's populace consisted of 2,751 Spaniards and 3,065 "persons of color," divided among 1,645 households; there were an additional 325 troops and Crown personnel stationed upon San Juan de Ulúa, where a new lighthouse was erected in 1755. An aqueduct was begun the next year to bring water into the city, but this project failed—as had a private attempt organized forty years previously by Fr. Pedro Buzeta—

and Veracruz's population suffered a slight dip when it was swept by typhus and smallpox in 1761.

The port's military role was dramatically enhanced when war erupted again against Great Britain the following year, the viceroy, Joaquín de Monserrat, Marqués de Cruillas, coming down from the capital to suggest improvements in May 1762. Such efforts were greatly spurred when a huge English expedition captured Havana that same August, so that thousands of Mexican troops hastened down to the coast to prevent a similar disembarkation along the Gulf shore. This massive influx into the tight confines of Veracruz—3,200 soldiers being billeted within the grounds of four large commandeered homes, while 470 mounts were crammed into seven city corrals—caused an epidemic that utterly overwhelmed the Bethelemite and Loreto hospitals, so that a new military institution had to be extemporized between the two grounds. This expanded hospital was made permanent two years later under the name Hospital Real y Militar de San Carlos (Royal and Military Hospital of San Carlos), eventually growing into a 500-bed complex capable of tending to 1,000 patients.

When hostilities against England ceased in early 1763, King Charles III—shaken by Spain's easy defeat—authorized the erection of new barracks and other Crown installations at Veracruz. San Juan de Ulúa was significantly upgraded as well, a couple of nearby coastal quarries being tapped for construction materials, while the city's ancient lime kilns were also revived. Yet the greatest improvement to Veracruz's infrastructure came from a Crown decision to liberalize trade throughout the Spanish empire, opening up transatlantic traffic to more carriers as of 1765. As the flow of goods gathered impetus, transportation costs came down, so that prices for merchandise lowered at Veracruz. The ancient system of plate-fleet sailings was suspended in 1772, and the long-held monopoly by Mexico City merchants over bulk imports from Spain was at last broken six years later, when many of the most restrictive customs procedures were finally relaxed.

Middlemen in Veracruz could consequently begin acting as wholesale distributors for the goods and produce now flowing more regularly through their city, profiting accordingly over the remainder of the eighteenth century. Thanks to this boom, Veracruz took on a more robust character, lots along its

A 1758 cutaway view by the military engineer and brigadier, Lorenzo de Solís, of a proposed new barracks capable of housing up to six companies of troops or 400 convicts. Its whitewashed exterior and high ceilings, designed to resist the oppressive heat, were typical features of the large stone structures erected in Veracruz during the last quarter of the eighteenth century. (Archivo General de la Nación, Mexico)

waterfront rising in value and many more stately stone edifices being erected. Trade contracted somewhat when war against Great Britain flared anew in June 1779—Veracruz being simultaneously smitten by a yearlong outbreak of typhus and smallpox—but prosperity nonetheless returned once peace was restored early in 1783.

Despite another yellow-fever epidemic two years later, Veracruz's wealth and prestige had by now become so manifest as to justify numerous urban innovations. For example, another aqueduct project was authorized by the Crown, while its first streets were paved over with stone in 1786—the same year in which houses were assigned address numbers. Governors received the additional title of district intendant, with authority over a much broader inland jurisdiction. Trade accelerated three years later, after the Crown authorized Spanish vessels to also call at foreign ports, broadening the variety of imports while cutting down on freight commissions and insurance rates. The highway leading inland toward the viceregal capital was improved as well, so that regular coach service could be inaugurated. Veracruz's first public cemetery was established outside the city in 1790, and despite the smallpox epidemic that struck three years later, the printer Manuel López Bueno imported its first press by 1794, and local businessmen succeeded in creating their own *consulado* (merchant guild) by January 1795.

Difficulties (1795–1837)

Unfortunately, Madrid was compelled to submit to invading French republican armies that same August of 1795, and Veracruz's trade almost completely evaporated after Spain became realigned with the radical French Directorate a year later, an accommodation that plunged the empire into conflict against England as of 6 October, when powerful Royal Navy squadrons imposed a transatlantic and Caribbean blockade. In order to counter this stranglehold, the Spanish government permitted the shipping of cargoes aboard neutral vessels the following year, resulting in numerous American merchantmen calling at Veracruz.

Yet trade volumes nevertheless declined, and the city was gripped by another smallpox epidemic in 1797–1798. *Maestros de albañería* (master masons) Francisco Antonio Díaz and José María Rodríguez proposed remedying such recurrent outbreaks by expanding the city's perimeter southwestward in 1800, so that breezes might play more easily through the crowded streets—although the project was rejected by the Crown as too expensive. When peace was tentatively restored in March 1802, Veracruz suffered another two-year outbreak of yellow fever. The German naturalist Alexander, Baron von Humboldt, passing through at the end of his celebrated Spanish-American tour in February–March 1804, was disappointed to note that while the city's 16,000 inhabitants enjoyed illuminated streets, as well as several schools and hospitals, many shabby wooden structures still remained—as well as stifling heat, blowing sand, and lack of running water (yet another attempt at installing an aqueduct having failed in 1802).

Hostilities against Great Britain resumed on 12 December 1804, so that Veracruz once more became blockaded, its population receding to perhaps 15,000 people, according to a petition submitted to the Crown by its merchant guild the next year. So many ship interceptions occurred at sea that all commercial traffic was effectively halted as of September 1805, export produce being left to rot in city warehouses. And after Vice Adm. Horatio, Viscount Nelson, won a smashing victory over the combined Hispano-French navies at the Battle of Trafalgar that same October, Mexico's authorities—fearful of a possible English invasion—massed 11,000 troops at Veracruz, adding to the citizens' hardships.

Misery persisted until the summer of 1808, when residents were astonished to learn that the French emperor Napoleon I had sent an army into Spain, deposing King Ferdinand VII in favor of his own brother Joseph Bonaparte. Like all other Spanish American subjects, *veracruzanos* rejected this crude usurpation of power, instead supporting an interim *junta* (council) established at Aranjuez that same September to uphold their captive monarch's cause. Veracruz also benefited from the subsequent lifting of the Royal Navy blockade, as Britain became allied with Spain against the French, so that a couple of hundred ships entered port in 1809 and sparked a brief economic revival.

Yet this loosening of imperial ties with Spain allowed for the first stirrings toward outright Mexican independence, many mixed-heritage Creoles having become resentful of the preferments routinely accorded peninsular-born Spaniards by the Crown or Church. A rebellion therefore erupted at Guanajuato in September 1810 that quickly engulfed many parts of the viceroyalty, although Veracruz remained loyal because of its strong garrison. Col. Joaquín de Arredondo y Muñiz set sail in mid-March 1811 with 500 troops (including a teenaged ensign born in Jalapa and named Antonio López de Santa Anna) to help put down rebel forces in southern Texas and Tamaulipas. But despite the fact that Mexico's insurgency was soon confined to rural areas, it nevertheless diminished the volume of exports, so that the annual number of ship arrivals at Veracruz plummeted to only forty.

Overland routes became seriously disrupted as of April 1812, so that royal officers had to organize cumbersome mule trains to be escorted through rebel territory by military detachments, while some merchants even bribed partisan chieftains to ensure safe passage for their goods, both measures adding significantly to costs. The danger was underscored when a young guerrilla named Nicolás Bravo ambushed one such convoy traveling from Veracruz to Puebla on 20 August, slaughtering most of its 360 guards under Lt.-Col. Juan Labaqui. Bravo's superior—the patriot leader José María Morelos y Pavón—then boldly assaulted Orizaba on 29 October, torching a valuable tobacco consignment before disappearing into the mountains; Bravo did much the same against Alvarado and Jalapa early in November.

News had meanwhile reached Veracruz on 7 September 1812 of a new liberal constitution for the Spanish empire that Gov. Juan María Soto enacted by installing the city's first semi-autonomous *ayuntamiento* on 5 December. But the city's status as district capital was lost the next year when all intendancies were suppressed, after which its isolation deepened further when a severe yellow-fever outbreak struck in 1814. Also, insurgent privateers—mostly American or British West Indian mercenaries who had taken out republican commissions after being left unemployed at the conclusion of the War of 1812—began prowling into the Gulf. Royalist fortunes nonetheless revived, and the Veracruz garrison remained sufficiently resolute for Commo. Francisco Berenguer to set sail against nearby Soto la Marina in mid-May 1817 with his frigate *Sabina,* as well as the schooners *Belona* and *Proserpina,* to sink insurgent vessels that had deposited an antimonarchist expedition under the Spanish adventurer Francisco Javier Mina y Larrea. Colonel de Arredondo followed the following month with more than 1,600 royalist soldiers, mopping up Mina's survivors and incarcerating them within the grim confines of San Juan de Ulúa.

But the withering of trade had made civilians forsake Veracruz, so that its population fell to roughly 11,000 by 1820, by which time the insurgency was gaining inexorably throughout Mexico's interior. When news reached the port in April that same year of an army mutiny in Spain calling for the restoration of the liberal constitution, the remaining merchants compelled garrison commander Gen. José Dávila to acclaim that decree on 26 May. But such belated liberalization could not save the flagging Loyalist cause, so that Santa Anna—a recent convert to the rebellion, now promoted to insurgent lieutenant-colonel—attempted to overwhelm the city garrison on 2 July 1821, his assault being checked in its streets and ejected five days later at a cost of half his troops. Still, a tight siege was imposed, so that when Lt.-Gen. Juan O'Donojú arrived from Spain on 30 July as viceroy-designate, he realized that New Spain was lost; he thus procured a safe-conduct from Santa Anna on 3 August to proceed inland and conclude a treaty with the supreme insurgent commander Agustín Iturbide, recognizing Mexican independence a month and a half later.

The royalist Gen. Dávila, however, refused to comply, retiring with his city garrison across the bay into San Juan de Ulúa on the night of 25–26 October 1821 to hold out against the troops that subsequently entered Veracruz under its new Mexican governor, José Manuel Rincón. As a result of this standoff, port traffic continued to languish, the anchorage being inaccessible to merchantmen, so that they were instead diverted to Antigua, Alvarado, Campeche, Tampico, and elsewhere. Jalapa was furthermore chosen as the new state capital when a republican government was created in January 1822 because Veracruz was unavailable.

Iturbide, who crowned himself Mexican "emperor" in May 1822, remained indifferent to the port's plight, so that it was Santa Anna who tried in vain to wrest the island fortress from its Spanish occupiers by a surprise attack on 26 October. This failure, coupled with conversations he apparently sustained with U.S. ambassador Joel R. Poinsett about creating a more democratic form of government, caused the emperor to recall Santa Anna on 16 November. But the youthful officer refused and instead revolted on 6 December, fortifying Veracruz against an imperial land offensive. Such an army duly appeared by January 1823, but after briefly investing the city its commanders switched over to Santa Anna's republican uprising on 1 February, being joined by other disgruntled units in central Mexico until Iturbide was compelled to abdicate by March and be deported from Antigua aboard the frigate *Rawlins.*

A redoubled effort was thereupon made by the insurgent war hero "Guadalupe Victoria" (born Manuel Félix Fernández) to dislodge the Spaniards still holding San Juan de Ulúa, which unfortunately produced a damaging exchange of shot for Veracruz on 21–25 September 1823. An English visitor estimated that the battered city's populace had dwindled to approximately 7,000 inhabitants, their misery not abating until San Juan de Ulúa's obstinate Spanish holdouts finally capitulated on 23 November 1825.

Despite being free to receive oceangoing ships again, Veracruz struggled to revive economically as its colonial-era monopoly no longer applied, having to henceforth compete with rival ports along both coasts. The young republic's government was also handicapped by uncertain political and financial footing, so that the city governor, Rincón, revolted against State Gov. Miguel Barragán on 30 July 1827. Santa Anna arrested Barragán during a similar insurrection that same Christmas, launching his own ill-fated rebellion against a tightly contested presidential campaign that had seen the moderate Gen. Manuel Gómez Pedraza elected in September 1828.

Sebastián Camacho was chosen as state governor in late January 1829, but Santa Anna overturned that decision in April, serving as governor himself when a Spanish expedition, three months later, deposited 3,500 troops farther north under Brig. Isidro Barradas. That force was intended to reconquer Mexico, but it was defeated by a concentration of *veracruzano* and other Mexican armies. Vice President Anastasio Bustamante then deposed President Vicente Guerrero in December 1829, sending Santa Anna—a Guerrero appointee—into retirement at his Manga de Clavo estate near Veracruz. Camacho reassumed office as state governor in March 1830 and transferred the capital down from Jalapa into Veracruz that same year, only to have Santa Anna lead the city garrison in a revolt against Bustamante on 2 January 1832. Despite its sputtering start, this revolt gradually spread throughout central Mexico and ended with the president's displacement by Santa Anna in March 1833.

Oil painting by Pedro Gualdi of Veracruz's main square, ca. 1840, looking northeast toward the island fortress of San Juan de Ulúa in the middle distance and the Gulf of Mexico beyond. (Museum of History, Chapultepec Castle, Mexico City)

Veracruz benefited modestly from his ascendancy: stagecoach service with Mexico City was renewed as of 1835, as were a few other amenities. But the nation's incessant upheavals and lack of fiscal responsibility had also bankrupted the republic and inflicted discouraging losses upon foreign investors. The latter lodged bitter complaints with their home countries, resulting in the dispatch of Pierre Lemoine, Baron Deffaudis, as a plenipotentiary from France in 1837 to demand full compensation from the Mexican authorities. This claim was rejected with the argument that it lay beyond the scope of any government to spare foreigners the vicissitudes that even its own citizens must endure; Deffaudis consequently quit the talks by 1 January 1838 and fifteen days later took ship from Veracruz.

French Bombardment and Aftermath (1838–1845)
Deffaudis soon returned with a French squadron, anchoring off Sacrificios Island on 21 March 1838 and sending an ultimatum ashore from its flagship *Herminie.* (When this note was delivered in Mexico City, it was erroneously believed to include a claim for pastries taken from the French owners of the Remontel Restaurant in Tacubaya by Santa Anna's troops in 1832; the subsequent hostilities thus became mockingly known among Mexicans as the Guerra de los Pasteles or "War of the Cakes.") When no satisfaction was forthcoming, these warships clamped a limited blockade upon Veracruz as of 16 April, restricting the importation of certain items so as to deprive the Mexican government of revenues.

Rear Adm. Charles Baudin arrived from France to assume overall command, while other countries also dispatched men-of-war to look after their interests. The city spent the next six months under such restrictions, until Baudin deposited another communication on 21 October 1838, which led to a meeting with Mexico's foreign minister, Luis G. Cuevas, at Jalapa on 17 November. Negotiations broke down when the admiral demanded an additional 200,000 pesos to compensate his government for the expeditionary costs, so that Baudin returned to his squadron. Two Mexican officers went aboard his flagship *Néréide* with a counteroffer from Cuevas at 9:00 A.M. on 27 November, only to have the French admiral reject the proposal five and a half hours later.

A mere five minutes afterward, while the Mexican emissaries were still being rowed back toward Veracruz, the frigates *Néréide, Iphigénie, Gloire,* corvette *Créole,* and bomb vessels *Cyclope* and *Vulcain* opened fire against San Juan de Ulúa, using newly developed Paixhans explosive shells. This bombardment lasted until 8:00 P.M., when garrison commander Antonio Gaona requested a truce to tend to his wounded; his forces suffered 224 casualties among his 1,186 defenders—plus 20 of his 153 guns dismounted—compared with only 4 French dead and 39 injured. The attackers informed Gaona that they would resume shelling and completely level his fortress if he did not surrender; he subsequently consulted with Governor Rincón in the city and then evacuated his garrison. The French seized the island next morning, along with a half dozen vessels moored beneath its walls. Rincón and Santa Anna (who had arrived from his nearby Manga de Clavo estate) furthermore agreed to a cessation of hostilities that would allow Baudin's men ashore to refresh their provisions, while French citizens were to be granted compensation, the blockade was to be lifted, and each nation's remaining grievances were to be submitted to diplomatic resolution.

But when news of Rincón's and Gaona's capitulation of San Juan de Ulúa reached Mexico City on 30 November 1838, furious government ministers ordered both officers arrested and the truce voided, while declaring war against France. Santa Anna was informed on 3 December and assumed command over the 700 to 800 soldiers within Veracruz, advising Baudin the next morning, so that both leaders agreed to resume hostilities by 8:00 A.M. on 5 December. Gen. Mariano Arista entered the city the night of 4 December to consult with Santa Anna, having left his 871-man relief column encamped some 8 miles away at Santa Fe. Both Mexican commanders went to bed at 2:00 A.M. on 5 December, only to be awakened a few hours later by gunfire as Baudin swept down upon Veracruz's waterfront in a three-pronged surprise attack.

Boatloads of French marines and sailors stormed the Santiago and Concepción bastions at the city's southeastern and northwestern corners, while others disgorged directly at its wharf and poured into the main square. Santa Anna narrowly escaped from his headquarters at Coliseo and Damas streets, but Arista surrendered to the prince of Joinville. Baudin vainly peppered the stout doors of the fortresslike barracks in La Merced Square before deciding to retire an hour later, hoisting a white flag to call for a truce. Angered by the surprise attack, the Mexicans ignored this request, so that the French had to fight their way back to the wharf with their wounded. Santa Anna charged their re-embarkation with 200 hastily formed men, being checked by a blast from a field-piece that killed nine of his followers and blew off his left leg below the knee, as well as a finger from his right hand.

Baudin, having suffered eight killed and sixty wounded, regained his warships and pounded Veracruz for another two hours, until its defenders retreated out of the devastated city into the dunes. The blockade was thereupon resumed, but passions at last began to cool. When the neutral British ambassador, Richard Pakenham, reached Veracruz from Mexico City on 22 December 1838 to mediate a resolution—backed by eleven Royal Navy warships that anchored offshore under Vice Adm. Sir Charles Paget four days later—he eventually arranged a meeting that produced a treaty by 9 March 1839. Mexico agreed to pay 600,000 pesos in compensation, while France restored San Juan de Ulúa and withdrew its squadron.

First U.S. Occupation (1846–1848)

Veracruz was to be featured once again in an international conflict when the U.S. Congress voted in March 1845 to accede to American settlers' wishes and annex the Republic of Texas, which the Mexican government regarded as a breakaway province. Diplomatic relations were severed, and a U.S. naval squadron under Commo. David Conner prowled off Veracruz for the next six months as Washington and Mexico City sought to resolve their differences. The unhappy city garrison also mutinied in November 1845, after which full hostilities exploded along the Texan border the following spring. The U.S. Navy imposed a blockade when the 10-gun, 1,700-ton paddle steamer *Mississippi* appeared off Veracruz on 20 May 1846.

Fighting was to be concentrated in northern Mexico for almost a year, with only a few noteworthy events occurring off the port: Conner, for example, contrived to permit the Mexican schooner *Criolla* to slip into its harbor as a spy ship on 26 November 1846, running past the blockading brig *Somers* of Lt. Raphael Semmes, but the latter sent eight volunteers to cut it out from under San Juan de Ulúa's guns after nightfall, burning the schooner and escaping through a hail of gunfire with seven prisoners. Semmes (later captain of the famed Confederate commerce raider *Alabama*) fared much worse when pursuing another blockade runner on 8 December: his *Somers* accidentally overturned and sank, drowning thirty-two of its seventy-six crew members; seven others were captured, and the remainder were rescued by neutral warships anchored off Sacrificios Island.

The next spring, though, Veracruz became directly involved when Washington—having failed to bring the Mexican government to the bargaining table by occupying the northern portion of the country—decided to open a new front by disembarking an 8,600-man army under Maj.-Gen. Winfield Scott to invade nearer Mexico City. His forty transports began anchoring between Antón Lizardo and Salmedina Island on 4 March 1847, and he personally reconnoitered the proposed landing site at Collado Beach 3 miles southeast of Veracruz two days later aboard a tiny steam vessel (accompanied by such future luminaries as Capts. Robert E. Lee and Joseph E. Johnston, plus Lts. Pierre G. T. Beauregard and George G. Meade). After transferring the invasion force aboard navy boats, Conner's gunboats bombarded Collado Beach, allowing all the soldiers and a 1,200-man naval contingent to come ashore by nightfall of 9 March.

U.S. siege-batteries shell the beleaguered city of Veracruz, March 1847. (U.S. Naval Historical Center)

Because of their inferior armaments, the city's 3,360 defenders and eighty-six guns under Maj.-Gen. Juan Morales waited behind its ramparts, backed by an additional 1,030 men and 135 artillery pieces on San Juan de Ulúa. At dawn of 10 March 1847, the 3-gun paddle-steamer *Spitfire* of Cmdr. Josiah Tattnall made a diversionary attack against the island fortress, while Scott's troops fanned out to encircle the city. Gen. David E. Twiggs's division reached the sea northwest of Veracruz shortly after midday on 13 March; Gen. Robert Patterson's division had taken up position in the center, with Gen. William Jenkins Worth's division farther southeast. The American units dug formal siege works, their first heavy batteries being ready to open fire by noon on 21 March, so that Scott called upon Morales to capitulate the next afternoon. The offer being rejected, a concerted bombardment erupted at dawn on 23 March, seconded from offshore by naval warships (now under the command of Commo. Matthew Calbraith Perry, destined to "open Japan" seven years later).

The besiegers, at a cost of fourteen dead and fifty-nine wounded, increased their rate of fire until dawn on 26 March 1847, when Gen. José Juan Landero—who had succeeded as garrison commander after Morales fell ill—requested terms. The battered city and San Juan de Ulúa were surrendered on 29 March, its defenders being paroled inland. Scott thereby

gained a secure base of operations that could be resupplied by sea, detaching Gen. John A. Quitman's brigade and a naval squadron the next afternoon to also seize nearby Alvarado and Tlacotalpan. The U.S. forces then marshaled, their vanguard emerging from Veracruz on 8 April to initiate the long march up toward Jalapa, Scott following three days later with the balance of his troops. His Veracruz garrison maintained supply lines intact, until Scott's army pushed into the central highlands and eventually captured Mexico City.

Mexico's faction-riven national government agreed to sign the Treaty of Guadalupe Hidalgo by 2 February 1848, whereby the United States wrested away the largely empty provinces of California, Nevada, Utah, Colorado, Arizona, and New Mexico. Veracruz remained under American occupation even after this agreement was ratified by Congress in Washington on 10 March and by the Mexican legislature on 19 May, serving as the re-embarkation point for most U.S. forces as they retired. Mexican authority was not restored over the city until 11 June, and its last U.S. contingents did not withdraw until the evening of 30–31 July.

Conservative Sieges (1849–1860)
Mexico's humiliating defeat caused bitter recriminations throughout the country, conservatives and liberals falling out over how best to rectify their nation's malaise. The former

called for a strong traditional oligarchy to avoid the divisive weakness of republican rule, while liberals felt that social strictures should instead be loosened even further, to allow for more civic participation. When the liberal Gen. Juan N. Alvarez was propelled to the presidency in October 1855, he convened a congress aimed at rewriting Mexico's constitution. But the resultant pronouncements so incensed conservative opinion that the presidency changed hands several times in coups. Finally, liberal justice minister Benito P. Juárez laid claim to the office in January 1858, igniting a civil war that saw him driven from the capital.

After fleeing through Panama, Havana, and New Orleans, Juárez and his fugitive cabinet reached Veracruz aboard the American steamer *Tennessee* on 4 May 1858, being welcomed by Gov. Manuel Gutiérrez Zamora, so that the port city became the provisional liberal capital. Distracted by fighting in central Mexico, the rival conservative president, Miguel Miramón, could not lead his army out of Mexico City to besiege Veracruz until nine months later. Slowed by numerous guerrilla strikes during his progression down to the coast, his sappers did not begin erecting siege works until 17 March 1859; news then arrived of a large liberal army driving upon Mexico City, so that Miramón withdrew at the end of that same month.

Immediately thereafter, the U.S. representative, Robert H. MacLane, reached Veracruz and five days later recognized Juárez's government, which issued the first so-called *leyes de Reforma* (reform laws) on 12 July 1859, calling for the confiscation of most church properties by the state (in part to raise money to pay for promised American aid). MacLane signed an agreement with Foreign Minister Melchor Ocampo on 14 December whereby the United States committed to provide the liberal government with $4 million in exchange for permission to lay rail lines across Mexico to be guarded by American troops—which treaty eventually failed to win ratification in the U.S. Senate.

Miramón marched out of Mexico City again on 8 February 1860 to besiege Veracruz once more, establishing his headquarters at Antón Lizardo by 6 March. The conservative Rear Adm. Tomás Marín simultaneously appeared offshore with the steam vessels *General Miramón* and *Marqués de la Habana,* hired at Havana (with covert Spanish backing) to mount a blockade. But when these ships glided menacingly past San Juan de Ulúa without displaying any ensign, liberal officials ashore declared them to be piratical craft, subject to seizure by any vessel. Availing himself of that excuse, Comm. Turner of the U.S. frigate *Saratoga*—stationed at Veracruz as part of Washington's support for the liberal regime—sortied and captured both vessels, passing their artillery and ammunition, as well as 4,000 Cuban rifles, over to the defenders.

Miramón initiated a desultory bombardment of the city on

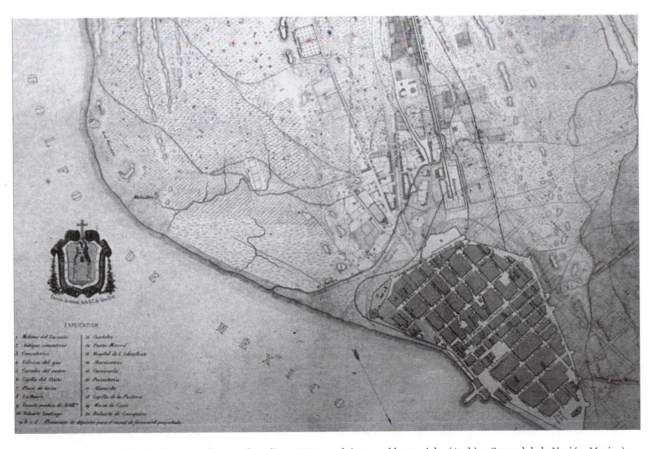

Lithograph by Salazar of the city's proposed new railway lines, 1864; north is toward lower right. (Archivo General de la Nación, Mexico)

15 March 1860, but soon ran out of heavy rounds, and so withdrew six days later. His government fell by Christmas, when liberal armies converged upon Mexico City, so that Juárez could depart Veracruz in triumph on 5 January 1861 and assume the presidency six days later.

French Intervention (1861–1867)

Veracruz enjoyed little respite, however, as the liberal government became embroiled in yet another international conflict when it suspended all payments on Mexico's foreign debt in July 1861. Britain, Spain, and France severed diplomatic relations in protest, then prepared an expedition to occupy Veracruz and garnishee customs dues until those obligations were met. Bracing for such an attack, local authorities shifted the state capital back into Jalapa on 3 December, one week before Spanish Adm. Joaquín Gutiérrez de Rubalcava anchored off Antón Lizardo with thirteen warships and ten transports bearing 5,800 soldiers under Gen. Manuel Gasset y Mercader. De Rubalcava contacted the anchored English frigate HMS *Ariadne* and French *Foudre* to propose a joint seizure of the half-empty port city, but their captains demurred; the Spaniards then delivered a unilateral ultimatum on 14 December, prompting Gov. Ignacio de la Llave to evacuate Veracruz and San Juan de Ulúa, leaving them to be occupied three days later.

On 7 January 1862, six English warships also arrived with the plenipotentiary Sir Charles Lennox Wyke, plus four French warships bearing their representative, Alphonse Dubois de Saligny, and 2,000 troops. The diplomats sent an offer inland to Mexico City one week later, hinting at a resolution; Foreign Minister Manuel Doblado responded in kind, but excessive demands by the French delegation hampered progress. The latter moreover facilitated the return of exiled conservative opponents of Juárez's liberal regime through Veracruz, trying to foment an uprising in the interior.

Disease soon felled hundreds of foreign troops, so that the new Spanish commander-in-chief—Gen. Juan Prim—informed the Mexican authorities on 2 February 1862 that his expedition would have to advance inland to healthier cantonments. Rather than allow this foreign bridgehead to be expanded from Veracruz, Doblado accelerated his negotiating efforts, so that a preliminary accord was signed at Orizaba on 19 February. But without waiting for the agreement to be ratified, the French contingent unexpectedly moved inland six days later, being reinforced by the disembarkation on 6 March of 4,500 more troops under Gen. Charles Ferdinand Latrille, Comte de Lorencez.

It was now evident that France was pursuing its own separate agenda. In fact, the French were secretly intending to back the conservatives in toppling Juárez's liberal administration, so as to entirely replace Mexico's republican form of government with a puppet monarchy headed by the figurehead Archduke Maximilian of Austria, a policy that prompted Britain and

Spain to dissolve their association on 9 April 1862 and set sail from Veracruz with their squadrons nine days later. The French continued to press inland, and although repulsed by a liberal army defending Puebla on 5 May, they were reinforced by thousands more troops under Gen. Elie Frédéric Forey in August–September and eventually fought their way into the capital the following year. Many officials, developers, and adventurers streamed through Veracruz in their wake, until Maximilian and his Belgian-born wife, Charlotte, arrived aboard the frigate *Novara* on 28 May 1864, proceeding inland to be crowned as emperor and empress.

Juárez, however, resolutely maintained republican resistance with his fugitive liberal government, and ordinary Mexicans' resentment against this foreign-imposed regime gradually coalesced into an effective guerrilla movement. Washington moreover pressured Paris to remove its French troops once the distracting U.S. Civil War had ended in the spring of 1865, so that most of the emperor's military mainstay was withdrawn by late 1866. Republican forces recaptured many cities, including Jalapa and Orizaba, until Maximilian and his remaining conservative supporters were finally defeated by a massive liberal concentration outside Querétaro early the next year, so that the empire fell. Veracruz's garrison—the last imperial holdout of this war—surrendered to republican forces on 27 June 1867.

Porfirian Modernization (1868–1913)

Veracruz was restored to its status as state capital within the next few months, and its new governor, Francisco Hernández y Hernández, implemented a public education system in 1868 to replace the old church-run schools. But like the rest of the war-weary nation, the city remained mired in poverty and underdevelopment because of limited resources and uncertain prospects for investors. One of the few private innovations attempted was a railway line running inland, which made a short inaugural run in January 1873 with Juárez's successor—the *Jalapeño*-born president Sebastián Lerdo de Tejada—as honorary passenger. Yet this track did not extend even as far as Jalapa until June 1875 and did not enjoy locomotive power along its entire length, so that port traffic volumes still remained quite small.

The nation's political chaos seemed destined to perpetuate itself when the war hero Porfirio Díaz launched a rebellion that toppled the bankrupt government of Lerdo de Tejada in November 1876, but Díaz quite unexpectedly implemented a ruthlessly efficient new regime that drove Mexico toward modernization and industrialization. In the case of Veracruz, Díaz named his protégé Luis Mier y Terán as state governor on 15 March 1877, who in turn stamped out all hints of opposition or social turmoil. The city populace of roughly 10,000 residents grew swiftly under such iron-fisted rule, the demolition of the vestiges of its encumbering colonial-era walls beginning in mid-July 1880 to allow the urban area to expand. As the flow

Pedestrians in Veracruz, ca. 1909; despite having modernized the port's shipping facilities, note the open sewers still exposed in midstreet, plus the buzzards lining the rooftops. (Carson, *Mexico: The Wonderland of the South*)

of imports and exports gathered greater impetus through the port, a bank was created nine years later—the Banco de Veracruz, later the Banco Mercantíl—while the number of inhabitants had almost doubled to 18,200 by 1890, the same year in which the Ferrocarril Interoceánico (Interoceanic Railway) was completed to link Veracruz with Puebla and Mexico City.

The city re-emerged as Mexico's prime seaport after an English contractor, Sir Weetman Pearson (later Viscount Cowdray), was hired to upgrade its harbor facilities, enclosing its anchorage with four long concrete *rompeolas* (breakwaters) by March 1902, which meant that vessels no longer had to put out to sea at any approaching storm. The 95-foot Benito Juárez Lighthouse—its glow visible from 15 miles out at sea—plus another 76-foot tower atop San Juan de Ulúa added to safety measures, while rail spurs and warehousing capabilities were greatly enhanced. Foreign investors now committed funds eagerly into Mexico, and the city's export trade of textiles, sugar, rum, tobacco, soap, and agricultural produce flourished so remarkably that its population exploded from 29,164 people at the turn of the century to 48,633 by 1910.

Revolution and Second U.S. Occupation (1910–1920)

Yet while Díaz's rule had imposed stability and generated prosperity, many Mexicans resented their lack of a commen-surate social advancement or equitable distribution of wealth. When Díaz—at seventy-nine years of age—stood for his eighth presidential term in 1910 and then arrested his high-minded opponent, Francisco Ignacio Madero, rather than campaign actively, popular discontent crystallized into a broad-based insurrection in November of that same year that drove the dictator into exile from Veracruz aboard the German liner *Ypiranga* by late May 1911.

The port city was not directly affected by the sociopolitical unrest that subsequently convulsed the country, except briefly when the departed president's nephew—Brig. Félix Díaz—led a mutiny by the San Juan de Ulúa garrison on 16 October 1912, which was contained within a week by the appearance of forces loyal to Madero, who arrested Félix Díaz by 23 October. But trade volumes declined because of the country's uncertain business climate, especially after Madero was betrayed and assassinated in the capital by Gen. Victoriano Huerta in February 1913, sparking another round of bitter factional fighting throughout Mexico.

On 9 April 1914, eight unarmed U.S. seamen from the gunboat *Dolphin* were detained when they ventured ashore at Tampico, whose Huertista garrison was under siege by rebel forces. Rather than accept the prompt release and regrets expressed by its garrison commander, Rear Adm. Henry

Thomas Mayo insisted that the infractors be punished and there be a formal apology issued in writing and a U.S. flag saluted ashore with a 21-gun salvo. Upon being refused, the administration of President Woodrow Wilson (who disliked Huerta because of his brutal usurpation of power) began massing warships off Mexico's Gulf coast five days later to punish the dictator.

Veracruz was chosen as a target, because a shipment of 200 machine guns and 15 million rounds of ammunition for Huerta were scheduled to arrive aboard the liner *Ypiranga;* Rear Adm. Frank Friday Fletcher was therefore directed to disembark and intercept the consignment. Gen. Gustavo Maass, commander of the Veracruz garrison—600 soldiers of the 18th and 19th battalions—plus naval Commo. Alejandro Cerisola's 160 gunners and seamen on San Juan de Ulúa were advised not to offer any resistance by the authorities in Mexico City, instead withdrawing 10 miles inland by train to Tejería, while the state government was once more shifted into Jalapa.

When the 800 U.S. seamen and marines headed inshore at 11:00 A.M. on 21 April 1914 under Capt. William R. Rush of the USS *Florida* and marine Lt.-Col. Wendell C. ("Buck") Neville, only a few civilian snipers and ninety naval cadets remained to open fire against the invaders as they stepped ashore at La Terminal shortly before noon. Hearing gunshots, 400 reinforcements were promptly rushed ashore from the USS *Utah,* and all resistance was subdued by 3:00 P.M., with four Americans dead and twenty wounded.

Ypiranga was detained upon its arrival at 2:00 P.M. that same afternoon, although its armaments proved to have orig-inated from the Remington Company in the United States rather than from German sources. Rear Adm. Charles J. Badger's battleships *Arkansas, New Hampshire, South Carolina, Vermont,* and *New Jersey* arrived from Hampton Roads, Virginia, after midnight on 21–22 April 1914, setting an additional 1,500 sailors and marines ashore the following dawn. Sporadic sniper fire resumed, but the deserted city was firmly under U.S. control by 11:00 A.M. on 23 April, when marine Col. John J. Lejeune disembarked from USS *Hancock.* Shortly before midnight on 27 April, Brig. Frederick Funston also arrived from Texas City with four transports bearing his 5th Reinforced Army Brigade—4th, 7th, 19th, and 28th Infantry regiments—to garrison the city, while San Juan de Ulúa was occupied the next day by a marine company from the battleship *North Dakota.* Eventually, 3,300 U.S. sailors and 2,500 marines held the city, 126 Mexicans having perished and another 195 being wounded during the invasion, compared with a total of 17 U.S. dead and 63 wounded.

Yet despite being directed against Huerta, this occupation was resented by all Mexicans. When the dictator was defeated elsewhere by rebel armies and resigned on 14 July 1914, he left behind a vacuum of power: Venustiano Carranza laid claim to the presidency, only to be immediately challenged by the powerful rebel chieftains Pancho Villa and Emiliano Zapata. Bereft of any recognizable government with which to open negotiations, U.S. Secretary of State William Jennings Bryan had no other choice but to announce unilaterally on 13 November that Veracruz would be evacuated ten days later; Carrancista Gen. Cándido Aguilar's division arrived at noon on the appointed day to reassert Mexican control over the city.

American landing craft being towed from the battleship USS *Utah* into Veracruz's harbor under small arms fire, 21 April 1914; the island fortress of San Juan de Ulúa lies deserted in the background. (Clendenen Papers, Hoover Institution)

On 26 November 1914, Carranza—having been driven from Mexico City by his rivals—also arrived at the port to set up his own provisional government. His able general Alvaro Obregón promptly reversed the military situation by recapturing Puebla and Mexico City, so that Carranza regained use of the national capital by early the next year. Eventually Villa was defeated and Zapata killed in 1919, after which Carranza fell out with Obregón, who finished off his former superior in May 1920 and was elected president himself that same November.

Modern Evolution (1921–Present)

This destructive cycle of revolutionary violence had now mostly ended, so that some modest steps could be taken toward Veracruz's modernization, such as starting work in 1921 on an asphalt highway leading toward Jalapa, which still retained the title of state capital. The port city became embroiled in a brief resurgence of insurrectionism in early December 1923, when Adolfo de la Huerta—Obregón's disaffected former finance secretary—traveled down from Mexico City secretly by train to challenge his former fellow cabinet minister Plutarco Elías Calles as designated successor to the president. Veracruz's garrison commander Gen. Guadalupe Sánchez and more than half of Mexico's 110,000-man federal army sided with de la Huerta, but Obregón's control over the treasury ensured abundant supplies of modern weaponry for his Loyalists; thus the mutiny was short-lived and Sánchez was defeated at the Battle of Esperanza in late January 1924, after which de la Huerta fled Veracruz on 5 February.

The city's urban boundaries expanded, and its population grew from 54,225 inhabitants in 1921 to 67,801 by 1930, thanks to a revival of trade and steadily increasing economic activity along the Gulf coast resulting from the discovery and development of rich oil fields. These were expropriated from foreign ownership in March 1938, and global demand peaked once World War II erupted in Europe in September 1939. Veracruz's authorities consequently had abundant revenues to complete a highway link with Mexico City by the next year and erect modern shipyards on San Juan de Ulúa. Two successive *veracruzano* governors also used their state's financial success to gain the presidency: Miguel Alemán Valdés and Adolfo Ruiz Cortines.

A trio of idled German merchantmen was impounded at Veracruz in April 1941, before Mexico actually declared war against the Axis powers on 22 May 1942 because of sinkings of its neutral oil tankers by German submarines. Shortly after the conclusion of that conflict, three and a half years later, a concerted program was initiated to begin replacing and upgrading the port's cargo-handling system and warehouse facilities, so as to expedite national trade. Ships of up to 7,000 tons' burden were soon being received at any of three main docks, while the city population reached 101,469 residents by 1950. A dry-dock was also completed the following year, plus

a highway extending into the oil-rich municipality of Poza Rica. Veracruz's harbor was blasted and dredged in 1953, a new concrete breakwater was built extending from its northwestern shoreline, and its naval school was transferred to Antón Lizardo.

As the Republic of Mexico entered a period of protracted industrialization and modernization, Veracruz benefited by handling large-scale imports of mechanized equipment and raw materials, while exporting a wide variety of agricultural produce and finished products. The city continued to expand as a result, its population rising from 214,072 inhabitants in 1970 to 351,000 by 1980 and 472,657 by 1990.

For further reading on the history of Veracruz or Mexico, please consult the Select Bibliography at the end of this volume.

Zacatecas

Small mining city, which—together with Guanajuato—transformed New Spain into the world's leading silver producer during the colonial era.

Discovery and Foundation (1546–1548)

After the fall of the Aztec capital in the autumn of 1521, bands of Spanish conquistadors fanned out throughout Mexico to subdue its outlying vassal states, encountering especially stiff resistance from the seminomadic Chichimecan tribes who roamed the barren, inhospitable plateaus of the north-central highlands. After a quarter century of probes and partial colonization in the region, a lone Spanish prospector named Juan de Tolosa—nicknamed Barbalonga (Long-Beard)—was attracted to a valley of Zacateco-speaking Indians after being given a chunk of silver ore at Tlaltenango by a local, then guided to this spot as its source.

De Tolosa and his guide arrived on 8 September 1546 (the feast day of Nuestra Señora de los Remedios or "Our Lady of Remedies" on the Church calendar), pausing only long enough to load 3 mules with mineral samples before departing southward that same afternoon toward the relative safety of the main Spanish stronghold at Nochistlán. When assayed before Lt.-Gov. Cristóbal de Oñate, these rocks proved to be of such exceptionally high grade that de Tolosa immediately decided to return to the valley to claim the site, accompanied by his fellow miners Diego and Miguel de Ibarra plus a few other prospectors. He identified the 500-foot promontory at whose foot this sample had been gathered as La Bufa—a Basque nickname signifying "Pig's Bladder"—because of its peculiar shape.

The chill temperatures and winds in this 8,000-foot-high ravine, plus the scarce forage because of its low annual rainfall, meant that the first band endured considerable hardship in their extemporized shelters during the winter of 1546–1547 while they vainly scoured the surrounding hills for the mother lode. During an exploration southeastward from his base camp, de Tolosa chanced upon a village of friendly Indians at

Panoramic view across the city of Zacatecas, from atop La Bufa Hill, ca. 1905. (Keane, *Central and South America*)

Tepezalá that had recently endured attacks from hostile Huachichil war bands; he therefore sent a message back to his companions, suggesting that they erect a strong-house in case the Spanish encampment should also be assaulted. Instead, this warning so disheartened the prospectors that they buried their tools and hastened south toward Nochistlán, until de Tolosa overtook them at Mocotabasco (later called Mecatabasco or Tabasco, and since renamed García de la Cadena) and persuaded the Ibarras, plus a few others, to return with him the next day.

The Spaniards' base was in fact spared, and a small stone fortress (believed to have been laid out somewhere between modern García Square and the former San Agustín Convent) was commenced by late 1547, while de Tolosa had furthermore established a primitive *hacienda de beneficio* (treatment plant) to mill and refine the few ores being garnered. The most widely accepted date for the town's actual foundation came when Lt.-Gov. de Oñate made an inspection tour of this remote new settlement, officially constituting it as a permanent community on 20 January 1548 in a ceremony attended by de Tolosa, Diego de Ibarra, Baltazar Tremiño de Bañuelos, and a handful of other prospectors. Their crude and disperse dwellings, stake claims, and mills were to become collectively known as the Minas de Nuestra Señora de los Remedios en la Provincia de

los Zacatecas (Mines of Our Lady of the Remedies in the Province of the Zacatecans), soon shortened to Nuestra Señora de los Zacatecas, or merely Zacatecas.

"Boom-and-Bust" Evolution (1548–1809)
The first major strike occurred when the San Bernabé Mine was discovered on 11 June 1548, followed shortly thereafter by another rich vein—Albarrada de San Benito—farther north at Vetagrande, and yet more discoveries at Pánuco. Despite the difficulties in reaching Zacatecas's mountainous region, word of this bonanza soon attracted many more migrants, so that by the end of 1549 an *alcalde mayor* (municipal magistrate) had been appointed for the district by the ruling *Audiencia* (high tribunal) of New Galicia, there being perhaps 250 Spanish miners now scattered throughout Zacatecas's hills and ravines. Relatively few had brought their families with them, because of lingering dangers from Chichimecan war bands and the lack of amenities, although most had been accompanied by black or Indian slave laborers. Numerous free or indentured Zacatecans had also gathered to profit from this boom, as well as Indians from more distant provinces, while itinerant traders made visits from as far away as Mexico City.

Santa Veracruz Hospital was inaugurated by 1550, the same year in which the first priest arrived to officiate over regular Masses (although a parish beneficiary was not actually appointed by New Spain's clerical authorities until nine years later). The number of property owners scattered throughout the environs was calculated at 300 by 1554, with another 1,000 transient Spaniards toiling away at lesser occupations, and the community was sufficiently well developed to mount military campaigns into other frontier regions. Mineral treatment also escalated significantly toward the end of this same decade because of the introduction of the *patio* process, a more effective amalgamation method for treating lower-grade ores. Franciscan missionaries founded a hospice at Zacatecas by 1558, developing it into a major monastery over the next nine years; they were also assigned indoctrination of the Indian *barrio* (neighborhood) of Santa María (Concepción) Tlacuitlapan, all non-Zacatecan Indians having been congregated into satellite settlements according to their linguistic groupings. Náhuatl-speaking Mexicans, for example, were settled at Mexicalpan—later merging with the Tlaxcaltecans of Tlacuitlapan—while Tarascans occupied Chepingue, Tecuexes were allocated San Diego Tonalá, Texcocans at El Niño or Dulce Nombre de Jesús, and so forth.

A new cathedral devoted to Our Lady of Remedies was laid out in November 1567 on the original *parroquia* (parish) site, while five years later a report estimated that there were now 300 Spanish property owners resident within the broad boundaries of the mining town, plus another 50 farther north at Pánuco, which had evolved into its own distinct community. There were also 1,500 Indians and 500 black slaves distributed

Zacatecas's crest, issued in July 1588. It depicts Our Lady of Remedies, the city's patron saint, superimposed upon La Bufa Hill, while below tiny mining figures gambol above the motto *Labor vincit omnia* or "Labor overcomes all." (Author's Collection)

between the two places. A *justicia* (justice) was appointed by the Crown in May 1573. Two years later, Pascual Carrasco opened a new cart road leading southward, while the Augustinians furthermore established a monastery at Zacatecas by 1575 and were given doctrinal charge the next year over Chepingue, San Diego Tonalá, and Dulce Nombre de Jesús.

An epidemic during 1576–1577 caused so many Indian deaths that mineral production slowed, yet the ramshackle town remained sufficiently viable as to have its office of *alcalde mayor*—previously appointed from Guadalajara—replaced as of 1580 by a royal *corregidor* named directly by the Council of Indies in Spain. (Although in theory a *corregidor* governed only a town, while an *alcalde mayor* ruled over an entire municipality, there was otherwise little difference in their legal functions.) Zacatecas's first public water fountain was also inaugurated the next year, and a clock tower was installed by 1585.

King Philip II granted the burgeoning town the status of a city on 17 April 1585, which decree was duly received and

promulgated the next year, after which a coat of arms was also issued by the Crown on 20 July 1588. Given its wealth and new-found prominence, a *cabildo* (town hall) was formally inaugurated on 8 September 1593 with great pageantry, fireworks, festivities, and bullfights. Two years later, an Inquisitorial report estimated that the district's total population stood at 1,000 Spaniards and 3,000 mixed-race or black slaves, and expeditions were even striking out toward distant New Mexico. The Dominicans under Bartolomé Bravo de Acuña began erecting a grand monastery at Zacatecas in 1604 (modern "Pedro Coronel" Museum), while the city population was calculated the following year at 300 major mine or mill owners, 100 to 200 merchants or tradesmen, 800 black slaves, and 1,500 Indian laborers. Missionaries from the medical order of San Juan de Dios arrived in 1608 and took over the twenty-four-bed Santa Veracruz Hospital two years later, while the city's first recognized medical doctor—Duarte Lope de Vega—began practice in 1609; the Jesuits appeared seven years later.

Several problems combined to hinder Zacatecan development, most especially the flooding of mine shafts, which had to be driven ever deeper in quest of new deposits. Construction was also hampered because nearby hills had been denuded of their few trees, while the city's overdependence upon imported commodities—painstakingly conveyed up the long and perilous mountain roads—made its cost of living unusually high, even for such a silver-rich community. Zacatecas was moreover shaken by a series of earthquakes from 6 May to 22 August 1622, necessitating extensive repairs to many edifices, including its cathedral (the construction of which was not completed until 8 December 1625). A drought and epidemic moreover coincided to decimate its population in 1628–1629, just as a rich new mineral strike was being reported farther northwest at Parral; that news tempted so many residents to emigrate that Zacatecas's *corregidor* even published an edict threatening dire punishment for any citizen trying to depart without permission.

The city's population stabilized at around 500 Spanish heads of household and 800 slaves by 1640, although they suffered a further calamity when the San Francisco Convent was consumed by an accidental fire on 7 December 1648. Still, the total number of inhabitants rebounded to 15,000–16,000 people by 1667, before once more being thinned by an outbreak of pulmonary disease. Another mining upsurge revived the local economy between 1670 and 1690, before another slump ensued until 1705. The city's buildings had by now begun sprawling irregularly down its original deep and narrow ravine, numerous pink stone churches and flat-roofed houses towering above one another amid its steep and winding streets. Mail service with the distant viceregal capital had also been regularized as of 1696, when Capt. Antonio Bermúdez had been appointed Zacatecas's first *correo mayor* or "postmaster." Prior to that date, only Crown officials and wealthy

Girls' classroom at Zacatecas, ca. 1890. (Author's Collection)

individuals had been able to hire dispatch-riders or Indian runners.

Another economic expansion occurred between 1705 and the early 1730s, during which public structures such as the city jail, several bridges and roads, and numerous churches were either rebuilt or refurbished. Zacatecas's first private school for young women opened in February 1722—the Colegio de los Mil Angeles Marianos (College of the Thousand Marian Angels)—while a grand new cathedral was also commenced in early 1730. More than 6,000 carts now entered the city annually, and its population mushroomed to perhaps 40,000 by the mid-1730s, although they suffered yet another noteworthy decline as a result of the typhus epidemic of 1737–1739, which claimed so many lives that many residents fled and the Bracho Cemetery became completely filled. The populace had been reduced to a mere 24,000 inhabitants by the end of that

same decade, a number that would continue to decline. The census of 1754 enumerated only 21,250 inhabitants—7,000 Spaniards or Spanish-American Creoles; 9,950 Indians; plus 4,300 members of other races—and a mere 16,260 inhabitants by 1770.

The famous entrepreneur José de la Borda reached Zacatecas at this particularly low point in its fortunes, determined to recoup the personal wealth he had earlier enjoyed at Taxco and Tlalpujahua (mining centers in southern Mexico). An experienced and skillful engineer, he reopened seven mines at Vetagrande, eventually striking it rich with La Esperanza, whose profits allowed him to purchase the huge Sauceda refining mill and the Malpaso estate, which furnished provisions for his hundreds of workers, as well as fodder for 1,400 mules. De la Borda then launched another ambitious venture in 1775, successfully draining the Quebradilla Mine, which ushered in the last of Zacatecas's great colonial booms and provided employment for more than 2,500 laborers.

Although ill health soon obliged de la Borda to retire to Cuernavaca, where he died at the age of seventy-nine in 1778, his drainage techniques were copied by other Zacatecan mine owners, permitting many old shafts to be pumped out and reworked to much lower levels. The Crown supported such efforts by dispatching experts from Europe, such as the delegation headed by the Saxon engineer Friedrich Sonneschmidt, which visited the city in November 1788. Zacatecas revived accordingly, its population swelling from 19,480 people in 1772 to 24,966 by 1793—despite a smallpox epidemic that struck in 1780—and to 32,720 residents by 1798. Urban amenities also improved, the former Jesuit College called Santo Domingo, for example, being reconstituted as Zacatecas's first university in 1795 with the name of Real Colegio de San Luis Gonzaga. Four years later the city was also formally subdivided into eight administrative *cuarteles* (quarters), despite some difficulty because of its irregular shape.

Independence and Early Republican Era (1810–1863)

Like all other urban centers in Spanish America, Zacatecas was astonished to learn that the French emperor Napoleon I had sent an army into Spain in the summer of 1808, deposing Ferdinand VII in favor of his brother Joseph Bonaparte. Most vassals in the New World rejected this crude usurpation of power, instead supporting an interim *junta* (council) established at Aranjuez that same September to uphold their captive monarch's cause. Yet the ensuing period of relaxed imperial ties and political uncertainty also stoked the first stirrings toward Mexico's independence, which many mixed-heritage Creoles had come to yearn for as they resented the preferments routinely accorded peninsular-born Spaniards by the Crown or church officials in distant Madrid.

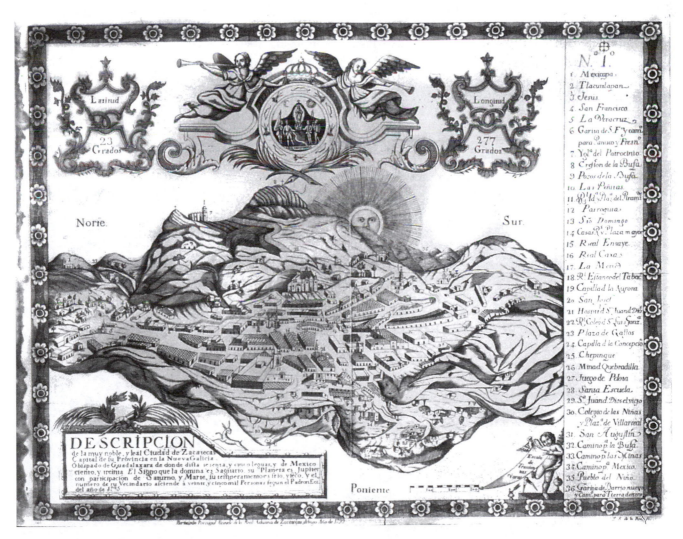

Zacatecas at the peak of its colonial splendor, as drawn by the customs and excise officer Bernardo Portugal in 1799. The city crest, above, is supported by a pair of angels, while the sun rises auspiciously from behind La Bufa Hill. (Archivo General de la Nación, Mexico)

Word furthermore reached the city on 21 September 1810 that a rebellion had erupted at Guanajuato, spearheaded by the rural priest Miguel Hidalgo y Costilla. Zacatecas's population of a few hundred Spaniards, 11,000 Creoles, 9,500 Indians, plus 12,500 mulattoes and blacks responded sympathetically to this uprising, and the intendant could count on the support of so few loyal peninsulars that he tried to impose martial law and a curfew. But without troops to enforce his dictates, he was obliged to quit the city with a handful of retainers by 8 October, leaving its administration to the wealthy Creole Manuel Rivero, Conde de Santiago de la Laguna.

Hidalgo's undisciplined rebel throng was defeated shortly thereafter while attempting to march upon Mexico City, so that the rebel chieftain retreated into Zacatecas by 27 January 1811, pausing a week before resuming his flight northward with a few hundred surviving adherents. A pursuit column of 600 royalist cavalrymen and 300 Indian archers under Lt.-Col. José María Ochoa reoccupied Zacatecas on 17 February, chasing after Hidalgo one month later. During the royalists' absence, 300 insurgents under Ignacio López Rayón swept back into the city in a surprise attack on 15 April, holding it for two weeks before fleeing again when the main monarchist army approached under Gen. Félix María Calleja del Rey, Conde de Calderón. His force entered on 3 May and executed a dozen rebel sympathizers, leaving Zacatecas firmly under Crown control when it resumed its march thirteen days later.

Although Zacatecas's encircling mountains were to harbor insurgent guerrilla bands for the remaining ten years of this conflict—men such as Víctor Rosales, who led twenty-five riders in a wild raid against the city garrison on 25 September 1813—Zacatecas did not actually change hands again until Mexico's independence from Spain was fully consummated elsewhere and fealty to a new national government sworn on 4 July 1821. The city's economy had been severely dislocated during this protracted struggle, its overseas outlets having been lost, imports of vital metallurgical ingredients such as *azogue* (quicksilver) interrupted, and mines flooded; knowledgeable operators and large numbers of citizens had also departed, and its mills were neglected. Foreign (especially British) investors attempted to revive the city's prospects by dispatching their own experts and equipment into the district, but progress proved painfully slow, complicated by the nationwide political and financial chaos as contending factions sought to dislodge each other through coups and countercoups.

Certain improvements were nonetheless achieved, the city's first printing press being imported by Pedro Ipiña in 1824, so that the newspaper *El Correo Político (The Political Post)* could appear by April of the next year, published by a cultural association called the Sociedad Patriótica de Amigos del País (Patriotic Society of Friends of the Nation). The women's paper *El Abanico (The Fan)* appeared by May 1826, followed shortly thereafter by *El Censor,* while the population struggled

back to a total of 15,800 residents. Slavery was abolished by the new state legislature as of 26 June 1826, while the first public library opened in 1832 (with a collection of 3,033 books), at which time the population was measured at 18,938. Zacatecas's old jail was torn down that following year to make way for the 2,000-seat Calderón Theater, although a dreadful cholera epidemic thereupon broke out, claiming 3,500 out of roughly 19,000 lives within the capital proper, plus another 8,500 throughout the remainder of the state.

Military intervention also portended after the federal congress in Mexico City passed a law on 14 February 1835 on behalf of President Antonio López de Santa Anna, restricting each state's militia forces to just one soldier per every 500 inhabitants, in the hope of curtailing the young republic's incessant regional uprisings. Zacatecas, with 4,000 men under arms and another 16,000 in reserve, was one of several states that refused to comply, instead increasing its armaments production at both the capital and Saltillo while appointing Gen. Francisco García Salinas as its militia commander-in-chief. Having anticipated just such a reaction, Santa Anna suddenly materialized amid the Tolosa Hills less than 9 miles east of the city on 10 May with 4,000 federal troops, defeating García Salinas the following day near Guadalupe, killing 81 of his men and capturing 2,700 before penetrating into the defenseless

Young woman typesetter at Zacatecas, early twentieth century. (Author's Collection)

city of Zacatecas. After a celebratory *Te Deum* in its cathedral on 17 May, the president's army stripped many buildings of valuables in a calculated act of punishment, then departed ten days later.

Zacatecas recuperated slowly from this brutal sack, as well as the vindictive separation of the adjoining territory of Aguascalientes from its jurisdiction, the city populace being reduced to a mere 13,803 inhabitants by 1836. Some measure of prosperity finally returned after the English enterprises operating at Bolaños, Vetagrande, and Fresnillo improved the roads leading into the main smelters at Guadalupe in 1842 and then assumed a fourteen-year lease over Guanajuato's neglected Casa de Moneda (mint). Three years later, the city had rebounded sufficiently to open its first music conservatory, while the Argentine "aeronaut" José María Flores thrilled spectators by staging several balloon ascents that same year; population figures resurged to almost 25,000 residents.

Because of its safe remove in north-central Mexico, the city was spared any direct hostilities during the U.S. invasion of 1847–1848. It was also relatively untouched by the subsequent three-year internal conflict known as the War of the Reform, which erupted early in 1858 after changes to the national constitution by liberal politicians such as Benito Juárez had sparked a conservative backlash. When Juárez was ejected from Mexico City and Guadalajara early during that struggle, a conservative column under Brig. Miguel Miramón defeated a liberal concentration near Ahualulco de los Pinos on 17 April 1858, then entered Zacatecas City two days later. But that proved to be the conservatives' northernmost thrust, as liberal Brig. Juan Zuazua recaptured the city ten days later, defeating its defenders atop La Bufa Hill. Over the next two and a half years, conservative armies were gradually pressed back into south-central Mexico, until Juárez finally reclaimed the presidency on 11 January 1861.

French Occupation and Aftermath (1864–1876)

Mexico's conservatives, however, allied themselves with France and were reinforced by an expedition that disembarked at Veracruz in January 1862, to push inland and displace the republican form of government with an imperial administration under a foreign figurehead: Archduke Maximilian of Austria. Despite stubborn patriot resistance, the invaders and their conservative cohorts gained Mexico City by the summer of 1863, after which joint Franco-conservative armies spread out to subdue the entire country. One such column slowly forged northwestward under Gen. Charles Abel Douay, compelling liberal Gen. Jesús González Ortega to abandon the unfortified city of Zacatecas and retreat toward Fresnillo with his 3,000 troops on 5 February 1864. Douay entered unopposed the next afternoon, his 600 French troops and conservative auxiliaries being greeted festively with pealing church bells.

Two months later, Col. Edmond L'Heriller was appointed

Zacatecas's military governor, and French enterprises soon dominated its mining industry and other lesser trades. A few urban improvements were introduced during their two-and-a-half-year occupation, a diocese being created on 26 January 1863 by the papal bull *Ad universam agridominici* and the city's first bishop, Dr. Ignacio Mateo Guerra Alba, being consecrated on 5 June 1864. A grand new bullring was also inaugurated on 15 September 1866, a date deliberately chosen to coincide with the nationwide celebrations marking Mexico's independence from Spain. Still, most citizens had come to resent their occupiers, who because of Franco-conservative defeats elsewhere, were obliged to evacuate Zacatecas on the morning of 20 November 1866. That same afternoon a contingent of republican troops under Gen. Miguel Auza reentered the city, and on 22 January 1867 it furthermore greeted Juárez, who temporarily installed his government in exile.

The presence of the patriot president tempted Miramón into leading 2,000 conservative horsemen in a daring ride from Querétaro; they burst into the city five days later—Sunday, 27 January 1867—only to find that their quarry had been alerted and had decamped toward Fresnillo. Four days later, Juárez reappeared with a much larger republican army under Gen. Mariano Escobedo, who chased Miramón back out of Zacatecas and crushed his column on 1 February at San Diego

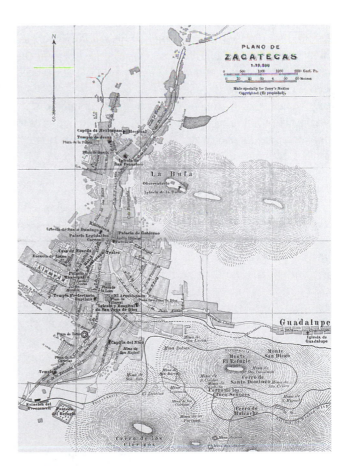

Map of the city, ca. 1909. (*Terry's Mexico*)

Hacienda, on the road between San Jacinto and San Francisco de Adames. The president thereupon resumed residence at Zacatecas until 17 February, when he pressed southeastward in the wake of his advancing army and reassumed office in the national capital by 15 July.

Once more the city had to recuperate from wartime vicissitudes, its first telegraph line being completed to San Luis Potosí on 4 December 1868. But political unrest soon flared anew, the increasingly unpopular Juárez announcing less than two and a half years later that he would seek yet another term, which ignited an abortive coup in Mexico City on 1 October 1871 and similar insurrections throughout the country—most of which were put down. However, one of the few successful rebellions occurred when Gens. Gerónimo Treviño and José Trinidad García de la Cadena fought their way into Zacatecas City on 29 January 1872 with 9,000 ill-equipped troops after an hour and a half exchange with its federal garrison, then imposed a forced loan of 200,000 pesos upon its municipal authorities, before digging in atop La Bufa, El Grillo, and Bolsas hills to await Juárez's inevitable counterattack. That materialized in the form of a federal army under Gen. Sóstenes Rocha, who smashed the rebels on 2 March and regained control over the city.

Juárez died of natural causes in Mexico City on 18 July 1872, leaving Sebastián Lerdo de Tejada as his successor. When the latter announced late in 1875 that he too would run for another term—thus perpetuating his faction's stranglehold over power—Gen. Porfirio Díaz, a retired hero of the struggle against the French, rose in opposition and deposed Lerdo de Tejada by 20 November 1876. Díaz then set about imposing his own iron-fisted dictatorship upon the warweary nation, enforcing political and fiscal discipline so as to encourage its industrialization and modernization through foreign investment.

Porfirian Era (1877–1909)

Díaz inaugurated his ruthless new regime by installing loyal henchmen throughout all branches of government—men such as General García de la Cadena, whom Díaz appointed as governor of Zacatecas on 25 March 1877, two months before he himself was sworn into office as president. (Ironically, García de la Cadena would soon be replaced and summarily executed nine years later for plotting a revolt.) Modern amenities multiplied rapidly throughout the small city, thanks to this stable new business environment. Zacatecas's first telephone system was inaugurated as of 13 October 1878—using the already existing telegraph lines toward nearby Guadalupe—while its first 4-mile stretch of narrow-gauge railway was laid by 5 May 1880. Electric lights illuminated the Plaza de Armas (Main Square) three years later, while full international train service between Mexico City to the south and Texas to the north was inaugurated in March 1884.

The city's "Zaragoza" Public Library opened on 5 May 1886, with 20,000 volumes and a collection of ancient manuscripts, while a fine three-story *mercado principal* (main market) designed by the engineer Carlos Suárez Fiallo was unveiled just south of its cathedral on 16 September 1889. (This market accidentally burned down on 8 December 1901, being replaced by a single-story edifice as of 15 September 1902.) The old Calderón Theater was furthermore consumed by a fire on 3 October 1889, and a six-year reconstruction effort was started on 5 May 1891. Work on a new hospital was initiated by 1 January 1890, while electric service was extended throughout the entire city when the new Vergel Nuevo plant went on line as of 5 February 1891; the financial institution called the Banco de Zacatecas came into existence that same December.

Disease continued to pose a threat to public health, however, the typhoid epidemic of 1892 claiming 3,000 lives within the capital alone before eventually being checked through Draconian measures. The first movie theater opened in 1898, mule-drawn streetcars appeared the next year, and the first automobile was imported from France by Genaro Carrillo to

The Mercado Principal or "Main Market," inaugurated on 16 September 1889 and destroyed by an accidental fire on 8 December 1901. (Author's Collection)

Public water fountain in Zacatecas, July 1892. (Author's Collection)

wend through the narrow, winding streets by 1902. Two years afterward, the cathedral's second spire was completed, and more significantly still, Gov. Eduardo G. Pankhurst inaugurated a modern new water system by March 1906 that provided citizens with a steady supply by pumping directly from nearby mines through 3-inch iron pipes and discharging into various public fountains. Thanks to this innovation the crippling effects of droughts abated, while sanitary conditions improved somewhat because the old and insalubrious stone aqueducts—which had discharged into crude clay cisterns with wooden covers—were no longer employed.

Yet notwithstanding such steps, plus increased mineral output thanks to enhanced treatment methods, mechanization, and bulk rail shipments, the city's population scarcely rose, from 32,000 inhabitants in 1877 to only 34,438 three decades later. An outbreak of typhoid furthermore claimed almost a thousand lives in 1910, the same year that Mexico's discontent under the elderly dictator peaked when he won his eighth presidential election, after having first arrested his high-minded political opponent Francisco Ignacio Madero. A rural revolt consequently exploded that same November, sparking a revolution with tragic consequences for Zacatecas.

Devastation (1910–1920)
After numerous hit-and-run raids against isolated federal outposts and towns, the city became the first significant prize

to fall to rebel forces when the guerrilla chieftain Luis Moya made a surprise descent upon Zacatecas on 9 April 1911—Palm Sunday—encamping unopposed with his 400 followers in the grounds of the Mercedes treatment plant in its northern suburbs before disappearing northward. So many other insurrections occurred throughout the disgruntled nation that Díaz was driven from power one month later, being succeeded by Madero. Zacatecas's Porfirian-appointed governor, Francisco de Paula Zárate, consequently resigned on 25 May and was followed in office by Lic. Jesús María Castañeda, whose attempts at reform were crippled by political uncertainty and lack of funds.

Less than two years later, Madero was betrayed and murdered in Mexico City by Gen. Victoriano Huerta, renewing the revolutionary struggle. Much of the state of Zacatecas was again overrun by rebel bands, so that refugees crowded into its capital to escape their depredations. Its very outskirts were then stormed at dawn on 5 June 1913 by 1,500 riders under the former rural police corporal Pánfilo Natera, being repelled by the 400-man city garrison and four field-pieces under Col. Miguel Rivero. The next dawn, however, Natera's second wave succeeded in penetrating into Zacatecas, its surviving federal troops being massacred while attempting to escape from their stronghold atop La Bufa Hill for Aguascalientes.

This rebel occupation of the city proved short-lived, melting away before the Huertista Gen. José Refugio Delgado could reclaim Zacatecas with 1,300 federal soldiers two weeks later. Late in October, the rebel chieftain Natera—now promoted to "brigadier" by the revolutionary "president" Venustiano Carranza of Sonora—once more threatened the city with 2,500 to 3,000 guerrillas, circling at a distance and firing upon its outer ring of defenses for twenty-four hours before finally being chased away by Delgado's artillery. Rebel and federal armies thereupon began building up throughout the state in anticipation of an earnest showdown, Zacatecas standing directly in the path of a rebel advance upon the national capital.

The military engineer Brig. Alberto Canseco arrived to assume office as Huertista governor on 1 November 1913 and began fortifying the city to resist a direct assault. Natera was finally ordered by Carranza on 10 June 1914 to push southeast from Fresnillo once again and assail Zacatecas with the 15,000 poorly equipped troops of his so-called División del Centro (Central Division). His irregular cavalrymen duly probed the defenses in the city's encircling hills for four days, until Gen. Luis G. Medina Barrón's garrison was reinforced by yet more federal troops from San Luis Potosí under Gen. Benjamín Argumedo (nicknamed El Orejón or "Jug-Ears"), bloodying an ill-coordinated rebel thrust against the Guadalupe suburb on 14 June. Natera gingerly resumed his probes the next day, but with Zacatecas's defenders now totaling more than 12,000 federal soldiers, backed by thirteen artillery pieces and ninety machine guns, greater revolutionary strength would be required.

One of about ninety federal machine-gun nests, placed in the heights above Zacatecas, June 1914. (Museo de la Toma de Zacatecas)

Carranza therefore telegraphed Pancho Villa at Torreón and ordered him to send reinforcements from his much larger, better-equipped División del Norte (Northern Division). Villa did not wish to divert any of his men to another general's command, so he suggested that he personally spearhead this assault. When Carranza spitefully refused, Villa ignored his nominal "commander-in-chief" and began moving his entire División del Norte southward on 16 June 1914. Three days later, his vanguard under Gen. Felipe Angeles appeared outside Zacatecas and began bombarding its outer ring of defenses at dawn on 20 June, thus providing a screen for the main body under Gen. Tomás Urbina to deploy over the next two days. By the time Villa arrived on the afternoon of 22 June, his subordinates had massed 25,000 troops and fifty guns around the city, most infantry and cavalry being to its east at Guadalupe or to its south-southwest, while the main artillery batteries were emplaced at Vetagrande to its northeast. The defenders' guns under Huertista artillery Gen. Guillermo Rubio Navarrete included a mobile 80-mm piece nicknamed *El Niño* (The Boy), mounted upon a railway flatcar.

At 10:00 A.M. on 23 June 1914, Villa launched a massive assault by directing an artillery barrage against the federal strong points atop La Bufa, Loreto, and La Sierpe heights, while his main force advanced against the fortified El Grillo Hill. This

isolated federal outpost west of Zacatecas began to run low on ammunition by 1:00 P.M. and was carried a half hour later. Santa Clara, La Sierpe, Cantarranas, and La Cebada were then rolled up an hour afterward, followed by Bolsas and Clérigos, while the lynchpin redoubt atop La Bufa Hill fell at 4:00 P.M. Such an inexorable string of losses created a panic-stricken stampede of defeated *federales* through the city, which worsened when demolition charges began leveling public buildings at 4:30 P.M. The revolutionaries entered an hour and a half later amid considerable slaughter, total losses being estimated later at 6,000 dead Huertistas, 5,000 captured (2,500 of whom were wounded), plus almost 2,000 civilians slain. Wounded in his left leg, Medina Barrón was lucky to escape southward into Soledad with fourteen men.

Villa's casualties came to 1,500 dead and 2,500 wounded, and he furthermore executed 60 of his own men the next day in an attempt to stem the pillaging of the hapless, smoldering city. Stacks of bodies were burned to prevent outbreaks of disease, before Villa boarded his personal train at Guadalupe Station on 26 June 1914 to resume his advance southeastward, delegating Lt.-Col. Manuel Carlos de la Vega to be Zacatecas's new revolutionary "governor." The battered city remained under martial law for the next two years, painstakingly repairing its worst damage while further handicapped by a typhoid epidemic, drought, and economic paralysis.

Some of the city-wide devastation left by the June 1914 battle for Zacatecas, this particular photo showing the ruined Palacio Federal, leveled by demolition charges during the defenders' flight. (Museo de la Toma de Zacatecas)

Modern Era (1921–Present)

Zacatecas suffered no further attacks during the remainder of the Mexican Revolution, and even experienced a modest revival after "El Bote" Mine resumed large-scale operations in 1921. Contacts with the rest of the nation gradually improved as well, the first commercial airliner landing at its Guadalupe aerodrome in August 1929, while highways also began radiating out from the city in every direction—although none were actually to be paved over in its entirety until December 1939. That following year, a modern new urban water distribution system was inaugurated as well, greatly easing the citizens' needs. But El Bote went bankrupt in April 1940, leaving 1,200 workers unemployed and plunging the local economy into a depression that persisted until well after the conclusion of World War II five years later.

Gov. Leobardo Reynoso instituted various municipal reforms during his 1944–1950 term, such as clearing land for the new Sierra de Alica suburb, extending Hidalgo Avenue and other main arteries, improving highways by encouraging the creation of the first interstate trucking and bus companies, granting suffrage to women voters, overhauling the telephone system, and inaugurating the city's first radio station. Still, Zacatecas's population stood at a mere 24,254 residents by 1950, significantly less than during its great colonial heyday. More municipal projects were undertaken during the 1956–1962 administration of Gov. Francisco E. García, the most important being the channeling of La Plata Creek so as to minimize city floods from sudden downpours.

Modern cyanidation and flotation treatment plants were built in the early 1960s to help upgrade the city's refining capacity, and federal funds were granted to its rail and highway haulage network so that Zacatecas's mining industry staged a modest comeback. The city's central core was moreover restored to its colonial splendor, so as to tap into Mexico's burgeoning tourist trade. Yet despite such efforts, Zacatecas had nonetheless been far outstripped in both size and industrial development by many other cities throughout the nation, while local resources for developing any kind of significant manufacturing infrastructure remained severely limited. Many Zacatecans consequently continued to migrate elsewhere in quest of seasonal or full-time employment, the capital's population slowly growing from 58,323 inhabitants in 1970 to only 100,100 twenty years later and 113,900 by the dawn of the twenty-first century.

For further reading on the history of Zacatecas or Mexico, please consult the Select Bibliography at the end of this volume.

CENTRAL AMERICA

Much have I traveled in the realms of gold,
And many goodly states and kingdoms seen . . .

—John Keats (1795–1821)

Costa Rica

San José

Despite a late start, this farm town evolved into the national capital, as well as Costa Rica's leading commercial and financial center.

Antecedents (1502–1737)

Notwithstanding its lush vegetation and alluring name—*Costa Rica* signifies "Rich Coast," because Columbus had been met by gold-necklaced tribesmen during his initial landfall near Limón in September 1502—this territory actually proved to be one of Spain's poorest imperial possessions, containing no significant mineral deposits nor highly developed civilizations to attract the initial wave of conquistadors subduing the mainland. Instead, after the populace along its Pacific coast had been depleted by European diseases, a few Spanish settlers under Juan de Cavallón pushed up into the broad, fertile *meseta central* (central plateau) in 1561, founding a capital city called Cartago three years later. Local inhabitants retreated eastward into the densely forested Talamanca Mountains, leaving the Spaniards to clear and claim estates in the Guarco and Asserí valleys—which failed to flourish because of a lack of workers and suitable outlets for their produce.

Throughout the first century of its existence, Costa Rica remained an impoverished, sparsely populated, remote backwater of the Spanish empire, its residents subsisting modestly from their agricultural efforts. A minor boom in cacao exports emanating from the steamy Matina plains into the West Indies began around 1650–1660, abetted by the introduction of a few thousand black slave laborers, yet otherwise Costa Rica's residents lived a simple, secluded, and rustic life. A trip on horseback to the regional capital of Guatemala City might take up to three months to complete.

Foundation and Colonial Evolution (1738–1821)

A group of settlers migrated 14 miles west-northwestward from Cartago in 1737 to found a new town called San José de la Boca del Monte (Saint Joseph at the Mouth of the Highlands) the following year, this name being chosen to honor the first parish originally established in the Asserí Valley. Their municipal jurisdiction stretched northwest as far as the Virilla River; 15 miles due east to the folds of La Carpintera Hill and the 11,260-foot eminence of Irazú Volcano; and southward to Escazú, Candelaria, and Puriscal hills. This outpost was for some time thereafter referred to as Villa Nueva (New Town), as well as Villita (Little Town), to distinguish it from another, earlier settlement called Villa Vieja (Old Town; modern Heredia), which had been founded some miles farther north-northwest twenty years previously.

Located at 3,900 feet above sea level, San José had a climate that proved to be wonderfully temperate, while its rolling terrain was fertile, well drained, and abundantly supplied with water: rainfalls occurred regularly from May through November. An ecclesiastic visitor in 1751 described it as consisting of a cluster of "eleven tiled houses and fifteen thatched huts, without any formal plaza or street"; this lack of development was addressed four years later, when orders were issued from Cartago that every Asserí Valley landowner must establish a permanent residence at San José or else face severe punishments such as fines, banishment, or even the burning of their *chácaras* (ranches). Thanks in part to this Draconian decree, the town boasted a primitive square and *casa de cabildo* (municipal hall) by 1760.

More migrants continued to arrive into its district, especially after another minor agricultural boom based upon tobacco exports started about ten years later; also, a general lack of restrictions in this frontier territory allowed individuals to profit from trafficking in smuggled contraband. A new church was completed by 1776, and San José surpassed Heredia in population shortly thereafter, its growth accelerating still further when San José was licensed by the Crown to establish a tobacco "factory" two years later, securing a virtual monopoly over all local processing of harvests as of 1784. The town enjoyed considerable prosperity throughout the remaining few decades of the colonial era, a few score double-story homes made of whitewashed adobe bricks appearing around its main square, while its populace grew much more rapidly than even Cartago, its nominal superior.

Costa Rica nevertheless remained a bucolic backwater in Spain's dominions, and so it was left relatively undisturbed by the struggle for independence that erupted throughout the Americas as of 1808. Parish records indicate that there were 8,316 congregants in San José and its district that same year. A town council was elected in December 1812 as part of the widespread implementation of a liberal new Spanish constitution, enacting a few local urban improvements such as better streets and the creation of the Santo Tomás Casa de Enseñanza (School), which was suppressed two years later upon the restoration of the reactionary King Ferdinand VII.

Regional Capital (1821–1840)

When news arrived on 13 October 1821 that the Guatemalan authorities had declared all of Central America free, Costa Ricans gradually divided into two contending factions to decide their country's fate. A conservative group, centered around Cartago and Heredia, felt that their province should merge with Agustín Iturbide's newfangled Mexican "empire" for protection, while a more liberal group, headquartered at

San José and Alajuela, preferred the formation of a distinct Central American federation. The dispute climaxed on 17 March 1823 when republican delegates achieved a majority in the Costa Rican assembly, prompting the conservatives to seize power at Cartago. The republicans under Gregorio José Ramírez thereupon responded and triumphed in a three and a half hour clash fought at Ochomogo Pass near Cartago on 5 April, in which twenty people were killed. Their victory became irreversible when it was subsequently learned that Iturbide had been deposed in Mexico City.

This occasion marked the true beginning of San José's ascension to national prominence, being designated as provincial capital that same year, after which the liberal lawyer Juan Mora Fernández was installed as interim president in 1824. Among numerous other reforms, he brought the first printing press into the country and founded its first newspaper. A census that year revealed 15,472 inhabitants in San José, sur-

Costa Rican farm-owner, ca. 1925, his saddlebags thrown over his shoulder while shopping in the capital. (Carpenter, *Lands of the Caribbean*)

passing the other three towns. Resentment against its growing predominance quickly coalesced the trio of rivals into a league that chose their own president in late September 1835, dispatching a small army to besiege San José. After three battles San José again emerged triumphant, the census of the following year registering 17,965 residents—including those of the recently absorbed villages of Curridabat and Asserí—which total rose to 19,245 by 1838. In May 1838 the anticlerical leader and former president Braulio Carrillo launched a military coup with Capt. José Manuel Quirós's troops from the San José barracks, thereby withdrawing Costa Rica from the strife-torn "Central American Federation," a doomed entity that collapsed shortly thereafter, leading to the nation's outright independence by 1840.

Republican Capital (1840–1949)

Unfortunately, San José's new role began somewhat inauspiciously when it was struck by a heavy earthquake on 2 September 1841, killing twenty-two residents and bringing down more than 900 houses, while damaging another 1,000. The ruined city was to be briefly contested as a political prize as well, the deposed federation leader Francisco Morazán exacting vengeance for its rejection by invading Costa Rica in April 1842 and toppling Carrillo, only to see his forces routed at San José; he faced execution by 15 September. Still, the country underwent fewer disturbances than many of its Central American neighbors, and the contending numbers remained relatively small. (According to the 1843–1844 census, there were only 61,714 people living in the entire Central Valley, of whom 6,497 were resident at San José, 5,630 in Cartago, 2,478 at Heredia, and 1,834 in Alajuela.)

The national economy began to rebound, thanks to a great new demand for coffee on international markets, which Costa Rica's jungle farmlands were ideally suited to meet—especially after a new road was completed down to the Pacific port of Puntarenas in 1845, permitting large-scale exports aboard English vessels. With their ready access to credit, San José merchants reaped the lion's share of these benefits. A brief rebellion at Alajuela and Heredia three years later was put down, after which a republican form of government was promulgated for the entire country. A new national palace was consequently commenced at San José in 1850, as well as the neoclassical Teatro Mora; its old Universidad de Santo Tomás also received a brand-new building by 1854. Not even the worrisome machinations of the American filibuster William Walker in neighboring Nicaragua could dim the country's economic prospects, so that its capital soon blossomed with its first hotels, restaurants, clubs, and pharmacies. Coffee merchants constituted San José's new elite, their plantations radiating out in every direction from the city, so closely packed that during springtime the landscape appeared to turn white from the plants' blossoms and red during winter as the beans ripened.

The first telegraph was installed in 1869, while exports were

Amenities also kept pace, electric power being introduced as of 1884 (initially displacing the oil lamps used for public lighting, then later spreading into private homes); telephones appeared two years later. The police force and educational system were overhauled, and streetcar service was instituted as of 1889. In that same year, the Laguna Swamp northeast of the city was drained, opening up more land for development, eventually leading to the construction of the Barrio Amón (Amon Ward), a model project named after its French promoter, Amon Duplantier. A national library, museum, and archive were all created around that same time, such works climaxing with the dedication of a magnificent neoclassical Teatro Nacional in 1897, reminiscent of the Paris Opera House. (When contrasted to San José's otherwise unpretentious, single-story shops and dwellings, the grandiosity of this Teatro Nacional moved a visiting Spanish critic to describe the capital as "a city built around a theater.")

San José's grid pattern had furthermore been reorganized so that thoroughfares running east-west became *Avenidas* (avenues), while those running north-south became *Calles*

Coffee beans being dried and sorted, ca. 1925. (Carpenter, *Lands of the Caribbean*)

given further impetus after the American railway magnate Minor Cooper Keith began improving the national system in 1884. Six years later he completed a new line eastward to the Caribbean port of Limón that ended in a grand station called Estación del Atlántico on the northeastern edge of San José (an older station for the line running down to the Pacific port of Limón had been built on its southernmost fringe in 1878, the Estación del Pacífico). The urban population continued to increase throughout the remainder of the nineteenth century, rising from 8,863 inhabitants in 1864—spread among eighty city blocks—to 13,484 people by 1883 and 19,326 by 1892. Such an increase naturally entailed a physical expansion of the city as well, a modern public market having been inaugurated due west of the core as early as 1880. Wealthy residents began recongregating into a new northeastern suburb shortly thereafter, away from the poorer sections huddled beneath the massive San Juan de Dios Hospital in its southwestern quadrant.

The National Theater in San José, ca. 1925. (Carpenter, *Lands of the Caribbean*)

(streets). Avenues north of the Avenida Central were moreover given odd numbers, while those to the south were given even numbers, just as streets east of the Calle Central were given odd numbers and those to its west even ones, so as to make direction finding easier (although individual houses still remained unnumbered). Coffee prices subsequently plunged on the international market, bringing this late nineteenth-century Golden Age to a close. Some farmers switched to growing bananas in order to turn a profit, and exports gradually revived. San José's population stood at 24,228 people by 1904, spread among 4,400 dwellings encompassing 259 city blocks; four years later a visitor calculated the number of residents at 26,700, while its former rival of Heredia held a mere 7,000, plus 6,000 apiece for Cartago and Alajuela. (Cartago's decline was further exacerbated by a violent earthquake on 4 May 1910 that claimed hundreds of lives and brought down many of its buildings, requiring extensive reconstruction.)

On 27 January 1917, Costa Rica suffered a rare coup when its young, reform-minded president, Alfredo González Flores, was deposed by his war minister and former confidant, Federico Tinoco Granados. U.S. president Woodrow Wilson refused to acknowledge this irregular change of government, invoking Washington's 1909 Non-Recognition Policy; however, thanks to support from Costa Rica's upper classes and American companies, plus a vigorously pro-Allied stance throughout the remainder of World War I, Tinoco was able to retain power. He was eventually driven into exile on 12 August 1919 by a wave of popular discontent (tacitly supported by the U.S. government, which had dispatched the 1,200-ton gunboat USS *Castine* to Limón). A major earthquake struck San José on 4 March 1924, causing widespread damage; nevertheless, its population was still measured at 50,580 three years later, representing almost 11 percent of the country's total.

A heated electoral campaign and fifteen-day general strike created another constitutional crisis in February 1948, when Rafael Angel Calderón Guardia—candidate of the ruling Partido Nacional Republicano (National Republican Party), better known as the PNR—was defeated by opposition leader Otilio Ulate Blanco of the Partido Democrático Social (Social Democratic Party). The outgoing PNR president, Teodoro Picado Michalski, refused to honor these results, calling out the 340-man army. Ulate fled to Guatemala, but Col. José Figueres Ferrer rose in his support on 12 March, his so-called Caribbean Legion defeating the Costa Rican regulars within a month in a campaign costing 1,600 lives. A truce was subsequently arranged on 20 April, and Santos León Herrera was proclaimed interim president until Ulate could return from exile, Figueres's troops entering the capital eight days later.

When a new constitution was drafted the following year, Costa Rica's army was abolished and replaced by an all-volunteer Guardia Civil (Civil Guard) that proved sufficient to repel an invasion of its northern provinces in January 1955 by the exiled Calderón Guardia, backed by the dictators Anastasio Somoza of Nicaragua and Rafael Trujillo of the Dominican Republic. Figueres—now president of Costa Rica—quickly mobilized 16,000 volunteers and secured the support of both Washington and the Organization of American States to drive the invaders back.

Modern Boom (1950–Present)

With the increasing pace of urbanization that has taken place throughout Latin America since World War II, San José came to expand prodigiously, its role on the national scene becoming ever more dominant. Its population, which stood at 86,718 in 1950, multiplied to approximately 150,000 by March 1963, when the 11,260-foot Irazú Volcano erupted 15 miles due east of the capital. Despite the millions of tons of gritty ash that were spewed over the entire Central Plateau during the next several months, San José continued to thrive. By 1980 it held approximately 250,000 residents, which number rose to 968,367 by 1997 (or 1,220,412, if its whole administrative district was included). This growth has created such a dramatic urban sprawl that distinctions between the country's original four central cities have become blurred, Heredia-Cartago-Alajuela having blended into one great megalopolis with the capital, embracing almost one-half this nation's total populace.

An aerial view of San José, 1995. (Kevin Schafer/Corbis)

Guatemala

Guatemala City

Beautiful highland capital, which has been relocated various times during its lengthy history.

Foundation (1524–1527)

Two years after the Spanish forces of Hernán Cortés had subdued the Aztec empire in Mexico, a detached army of conquistadors pushed southeast under his subordinate Pedro de Alvarado to overrun Central America. Upon penetrating into Guatemalan territory, Alvarado forged a temporary alliance with the Cakchiquel Mayas against their Quiché neighbors, helping defeat those rivals, then peaceably entering the fortified Cakchiquel city of Iximché by mid-April 1524. Judging it to be highly defensible, being situated atop a hill protected by deep ravines, Alvarado installed a small garrison, then departed with his main army to continue his Central American campaign.

Rumors of a possible Cakchiquel uprising prompted Alvarado to return unexpectedly on 21 July 1524, extorting a punitive ransom from Iximché's frightened inhabitants. Four days later he formally renamed the city Santiago de los Caballeros de Guatemala—25 July being the feast-day of Santiago (Saint James) on the Church calendar. Three days afterward, he wrote to Emperor Charles V in Spain to request the title of ruler over a vast new fiefdom encompassing the modern republics of Costa Rica, Nicaragua, Honduras, El Salvador, Guatemala, and the Mexican state of Chiapas, with its capital to be located at Santiago de los Caballeros.

Yet that Spanish "city" was little more than a legal fiction, Iximché-Santiago being merely a temporary base camp for Alvarado's troops. When its Cakchiquel inhabitants fled into the jungle on 26 August 1524, the Spaniards gave chase and fought a pitched battle on 5 September yet could not prevent their vassals from melting into the wilderness and initiating a six-year guerrilla struggle. Deprived of Indian laborers and servants, the Spaniards consequently forsook the settlement, shifting their army headquarters—along with the nominal title of Santiago de los Caballeros—to Xepau near Olintepeque, then on to Chijxot near San Juan Comalapa.

First Permanent Site (1527–1542)

It was not until Alvarado was formally granted the title of governor over his huge Central American claim in 1527 that his brother and lieutenant governor, Jorge de Alvarado, chose an actual seat for its administration, laying out a new city on 22 November a mile east of the village of Bulbuxyá in an intermontane basin known as the Almolonga Valley. This new community lay on the banks of the Guacalate River—

Panoramic view across Guatemala City, at the capital's third and final locale, ca. 1888. (Curtis, *The Capitals of Spanish America*)

renamed the Magdalena—between the active12,582-foot Fuego (Fire) Volcano and the dormant 12,310-foot Agua (Water) Volcano.

Also known as Santiago en Almolonga, this capital grew to some 150 households before burning down in 1538, although its rustic wooden dwellings and thatched-roof huts were quickly replaced. However, just before dawn on 11 September 1541—after three days of dense rainfall—a torrent of mud gushed down the steep northern flanks of the Agua Volcano, smothering 700 of Santiago de los Caballeros's residents in their sleep and leaving its Spanish core utterly submerged. Less than a month and a half later, its survivors—acting upon the advice of their bishop, Francisco Marroquín, and Francisco de la Cueva—agreed to re-establish their capital 3 miles farther north-northeast, in the fertile but narrow Panchoy or Tuerto Valley. The Almolonga site was thereupon vacated by early 1543, its ruins being remembered as the Ciudad Vieja (Old City).

Second Capital (1543–1773)

The transplanted Santiago de los Caballeros de Guatemala consisted of a grid of streets radiating out from a central square, with spaces left along that plaza's southern face for *casas reales* (royal offices), a cathedral to its east, a *cabildo* (city hall) to its north, and *portales* (commercial arcades) to its west. All urban thoroughfares ran north-south or east-west, while Indian suburbs such as Jocotenango sprang up around the northwestern fringe of the Spanish core, along with San Felipe to its north, Santa Inés to its east, and Santa Isabel and Santa Ana to its southeast. The reconstituted city's first official council meeting was celebrated on 10 March 1543, and in addition, Madrid had united all Central American provinces into a single administrative entity, known as a captaincy-general, to be ruled by the Guatemalan governor as "president" of a *real audiencia* (royal tribunal) installed at Santiago de los Caballeros.

The capital's Mayan population soon plummeted in numbers as a result of epidemics, notwithstanding desperate curative measures attempted by various religious orders; many surviving natives also slipped away into rural areas to avoid paying tribute to the Spaniards or being conscripted to perform manual labor. Eventually, all serfs were emancipated by order of the *Audiencia* president, Alonso López de Cerrato, in 1549–1550; yet few returned and their half-deserted city suburbs were subsequently infiltrated by Spaniards, mulattoes, blacks, and mestizos (the latter term referring to the offspring of whites and Indians, being a corruption of the Latin term *mixticius,* or "mixed"). Santiago de los Caballeros consequently expanded to the north, south, and east during the 1550s and 1560s, although its *Audiencia* headquarters was transferred to the busier and more accessible port of Panama early in 1565.

Having no mineral wealth or significant commercial traffic, Guatemala's farmlands nonetheless produced bountiful harvests, and livestock multiplied. Despite some damage suffered from tremors that same year of 1565 and on 30 November 1577, as well as from a major earthquake that almost completely leveled Santiago de los Caballeros on 23 December 1586, its citizens persevered and thrived in their highland setting. The valley's temperate climate of warm days and cool nights was complemented by regular rainfalls, which nourished crops by growing progressively heavier from May to October. The capital therefore evolved into a regional clearinghouse for exports of hides, cochineal, indigo, cacao, and tobacco, as well as a distribution hub for imported goods from Spain, the Caribbean, or the Pacific—activities that also spurred the development of a sizable multiethnic workforce of urban artisans.

Because of its remove, deep within the jungle highlands, the small and unfortified city was spared any direct threats during Spain's conflict against Elizabethan England from 1588 to 1603, although privateers did sporadically dislocate its overseas trade. A municipal census taken in late July 1604 revealed that Santiago de los Caballeros's population had blossomed into some 2,700 Spanish residents spread among 762 households, in addition to 400 free mulattoes and blacks; 220 mestizos; 1,750 Indian laborers; 1,625 black and mulatto slaves; and several hundred suburban Indians, for a total figure of slightly more than 7,000 people inhabiting ninety city blocks. Most wealthy merchants were clustered in the northeastern quadrant known as Santo Domingo (where Santa Teresa Convent would later stand), while town houses for older *encomenderos* (estate-owners) were in the San Francisco neighborhood in the city's southeastern part. Artisans lived in its northwestern section.

All endured heavy losses when another devastating earthquake struck on 9 October 1607, yet the Central American capital recuperated. Because of the lush valley vegetation and lack of defensive ramparts, it lay nestled from view; two decades later, the English Catholic friar Thomas Gage was surprised to emerge directly from the wilderness beside the city's rebuilt San Sebastián parish church. In July 1650, Capt. Martín de Alvarado y Guzmán led a contingent of Guatemalan troops in a vain attempt to dislodge an English intruder settlement from Roatan Island off the Caribbean coast that had been menacing the captaincy-general's seaborne commerce.

Santiago de los Caballeros endured yet more damage from powerful earthquakes on 18 February and 13 April 1651, while the Spanish empire had also entered a protracted period of decay, stunting almost all its maritime traffic to the Americas. The Guatemalan capital's agricultural self-sufficiency and local workshops nevertheless permitted it to continue flourishing modestly, its first printing press being imported by 1660. San Carlos University was founded a decade later; a new cathedral was initiated in 1680; stouter, whitewashed masonry buildings with red-tiled roofs appeared; and a few streets were paved over with flagstones.

Painting by Antonio Ramírez Montúfar, looking eastward across Santiago de los Caballeros de Guatemala's main square, ca. 1678; the bustling public market can be glimpsed in the foreground, while the quake-damaged cathedral undergoes reconstruction behind. (Private collection, Cuernavaca, Mexico)

Tremors recurred in March 1679, on 22 July 1681, in May 1683, August 1684, and September–October 1687. An epidemic also claimed more than a tenth of all urban inhabitants in 1686–1687 and was followed by another exceptionally heavy earthquake on 12 February 1689 that inflicted widespread damage. Yet Santiago de los Caballeros emerged from the seventeenth century as a city whose population had more than doubled to 15,000 residents, remaining sufficiently dominant that Capt.-Gen. Toribio Cosío was able to march against Chiapas with a small Guatemalan army late in 1712 to put down a revolt by its Tzeltal Indians, crushing the rebels and regaining Santiago de los Caballeros by March 1713.

The city was subjected to devastating earthquakes again from 17 August to 29 September 1717, as well as on 4 March 1751; yet thanks to a gradual overhaul of the Spanish empire's restrictive old policies by its new Bourbon rulers in Madrid, trade revived, resulting in such substantial economic benefits for Guatemala that a new palace for its captains-general was initiated during the late 1750s and completed by 1764. However, the resurgent capital was then wracked by such a frightening quake on the afternoon of 29 July 1773—Saint Martha's Day on the Church calendar—followed by yet another cataclysm on the night of 13–14 December that its authorities finally opted to once more shift their seat of government.

Third Colonial Capital (1774–1823)
A survey of the Llano de la Virgen (The Virgin's Plain) identified a potential new site 25 miles east of the ruined capital, amid an isolated tableland called Las Vacas Valley at 4,900 feet above sea level. Its immediate topography, surrounded on all sides except one by deep *barrancas* (gullies), was deemed by the experts of that day to be insulated from seismic activity, so that the Crown sanctioned a wholesale move.

It took a couple of years to convince the old capital's 23,500 residents to commence transferring to this new spot in the parish of Ermita, their reluctance at being uprooted from their

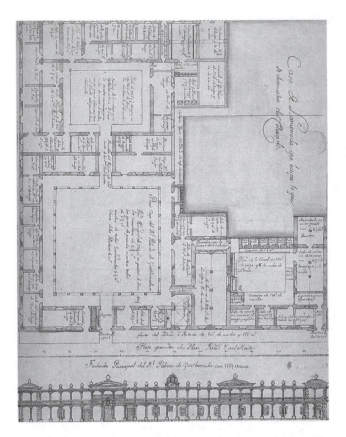

Floor plan and profile view of the proposed new Captain-General's Palace in Santiago de los Caballeros, ca. 1755. (Servicio Geográfico del Ejército, Madrid)

could be erected, incorporating statuary and paintings rescued from the old city's main temple. The Dominicans, Franciscans, Mercedarians, and Capuchins erected fine new monasteries, while the Carmelites created two: a hermitage nicknamed Carmen del Cerro atop a hill northeast of the new capital and a church within its urban boundaries known as Carmen el Bajo (The Lower Carmen). Eventually only a few thousand impoverished people remained amid the ruins of the distant old capital, which became known as Antigua Guatemala (or the parish of San Miguel Escobar).

Spanish America enjoyed a boom during the closing decades of the eighteenth century, Guatemalan merchants profiting particularly after they were granted their own *consulado* (guild) by the Crown in 1793, enhancing their business potential. But the emergence of a radical new French government in Paris disrupted peaceful development around the globe, as Spain was invaded and compelled to realign itself with the Directorate by August 1796, joining the ongoing hostilities against England by 6 October. Royal Navy squadrons quickly imposed Atlantic and Caribbean blockades, so that Guatemalan exports and imports sagged; the country's traditional output of indigo and cacao was furthermore undermined, as rival producers emerged elsewhere in the world.

After a brief interlude of peace in 1802–1803, the colony was astonished to learn that the French emperor Napoleon I had sent an army to depose Ferdinand VII in favor of his brother Joseph Bonaparte in the summer of 1808. Such a crude usurpation of power was repudiated by most Latin American vassals, yet the subsequent loosening of imperial ties paved the way for independence movements to spring up throughout the

traditional habitations exacerbated by the onerous expense involved in such a distant exodus, plus the lack of readily available water at their new settlement. As an inducement to relocate, however, municipal authorities promised not to collect taxes for a decade, and seventeen Indian communities were forcibly resettled at the new clearance to plant crops and provide a labor pool for the Spanish citizenry who were to follow.

Despite stiff clerical and civilian opposition, the capital was formally refounded as Nueva Guatemala de la Asunción (New Guatemala of the Assumption) on 2 January 1776; yet when a census was conducted two years later, only 10,841 inhabitants were registered within the new city limits, and its last royal offices were not actually transferred until 1779. Capt.-Gen. Matías de Gálvez was moreover distracted by an outbreak of hostilities against Great Britain, which required him to lead relief columns to recuperate the Caribbean port of Omoa from an English expedition that same November, plus Fort Inmaculada Concepción or "San Juan Castle" (modern El Castillo, Nicaragua) from a youthful Capt. Horatio Nelson in April 1780.

All the religious orders did not resettle into Nueva Guatemala de la Asunción until 1782, Santa Rosa Church serving as its temporary cathedral until a grand new structure

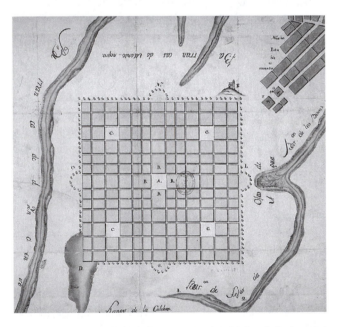

Map of Nueva Guatemala de la Asunción, the third and final capital city, as it appeared in 1787; note its symmetrical layout. (Archive of Indies, Seville)

Americas, as mixed-heritage Creoles reacted against the preferments routinely accorded peninsular-born Spaniards. Guatemala remained loyal to the monarchy throughout the ensuing years of struggle, its *Audiencia* president, José de Bustamante y Guerra, even repressing a Creole insurrection launched at San Salvador in November 1811 by the priest and jurist José Matías Delgado, as well as a conspiracy centered around the Bethelemite religious order in New Guatemala in December 1813. There then occurred a second Salvadoran uprising, spearheaded by the rebel priest Manuel José Arce, in January 1814.

But depression and poverty nonetheless gripped the capital as its traffic with other Spanish-American colonies evaporated, so that the first slums began sprawling north and south from its urban core. When Loyalist fortunes finally collapsed altogether and the Mexican general Agustín de Iturbide switched allegiances, calling in February 1821 for outright independence for the entire viceroyalty—albeit tempered by a continued predominance of the Catholic faith and close ties with Spain—Guatemala's Creoles were stirred to respond in kind. José Cecilio del Valle proclaimed a similar "declaration of independence" at New Guatemala on 15 September, then contacted Iturbide to formally request joining his cause by 29 December.

All of Central America nominally became annexed to Mexico according to a limited local plebiscite conducted on 5 January 1822 and ratified by a declaration issued three days later by the former royal captain-general, Gabino Gaínza; yet not all provinces accepted Guatemala's lead, so that Iturbide sent a small army under the Italian-born brigadier Vicente Filisola in June 1822 to impose his rule directly, while simultaneously assuming the title of "Emperor Agustín I" in Mexico City. Filisola succeeded in maintaining Central America united, yet Iturbide was driven from office by a republican uprising in Mexico in February 1823; his detached general consequently called on 29 March for a constitutional assembly to meet in Guatemala City and peacefully decide the region's fate.

Diminished Standing (1823–1872)

Representatives from throughout the old captaincy-general convened in its capital on 24 June 1823 and—with the exception of Chiapas, which opted to remain a part of Mexico—established an independent federation on 1 July that was to become known as the United Provinces of Central America. The newfangled Mexican Republic formally acknowledged this act of secession on 1 August 1824, so that Filisola's army departed. A provisional Central American council presided over by the former rebel priest and jurist Delgado thereupon promulgated a Central American constitution on 22 November, based upon the U.S. model. No capital was specifically designated, yet Guatemala City remained the de facto seat of power, with a population of 28,000.

Its lost commerce, public debts, and administrative chaos, however, precluded any significant improvements in urban conditions, while liberal dictates enacted by the federation's first president, Salvador's former rebel priest Arce—such as the abolition of slavery and establishment of free trade—merely contributed to a growing sense of discontent. Civil war erupted when Salvador rose against the federation in December 1826, soon joined by Honduras, Nicaragua, and Costa Rica. An army under Gen. Francisco Morazán fought its way into Guatemala City by 13 April 1829, expelling numerous prominent citizens, confiscating Church properties, and imposing a dictatorship once that strongman became president in 1830. Morazán's regime nonetheless made some attempts to foster education, trade, and industry, opened the federation to foreigners, and overhauled its outdated administration. Yet Guatemala City's status was downgraded when the title of Central American capital was officially transferred to San Salvador in 1835.

Local dissatisfaction led to a counterrevolt, forces under an illiterate mestizo leader named Rafael Carrera driving out the federal occupiers by January 1838, then helping to create an autonomous yet austerely conservative republic that same June. Guatemala City revived and expanded south toward its slaughterhouse and bullring, while Fort San José was erected to its southwest in 1842; its urban population rebounded to some 40,000 inhabitants by 1850. Public lighting was introduced shortly thereafter, and Fort San Rafael de Matamoros was completed northwest of the capital in 1858.

Unfortunately, international demand for cochineal plummeted during the late 1850s because of the development of cheap synthetic dyes overseas, drastically curtailing Guatemala's exports. The impoverished and backward nation struggled to replace its lost income by substituting larger harvests of coffee and cacao, and when the president for life, Carrera, eventually died in April 1865, his conservative regime was perpetuated by Gen. Vicente Cerna. But liberal opposition resurged, and a series of revolts finally succeeded in unseating him by May 1871, after which the reactionary archbishop Dr. Bernardo Piñol y Aycinena and the Jesuit Order were also expelled from the capital.

Modernization (1873–1917)

The liberal leader Justo Rufino Barrios succeeded the provisional president, Miguel García Granados, in 1873, and despite another destructive tremor that rattled Guatemala City the following year, he inaugurated a program of forced modernization. Church properties were once again expropriated, and a national bank was created; private foreign banks were also authorized to operate as of 1877. Local coffee exports were fomented by the building of roads toward such refurbished Caribbean outlet-ports as Livingston, Izabal, and Puerto Barrios, while contracts were signed with foreign steamship lines as of 1880 to ensure regular visits.

The capital benefited significantly, public gaslights being

Fort San José southwest of the city, ca. 1888. (Curtis, *The Capitals of Spanish America*)

introduced as of 1879, the same year in which the ancient municipality of Jocotenango was absorbed, raising the total urban populace to 55,728 inhabitants according to a census taken the next year. The suburban villages of Candelaria and La Parroquia were annexed in 1881; horse-drawn streetcars appeared the next year; and a new residential development called Santa Elena was constructed in 1883, along with a boulevard running out of the west into the city, from the national penitentiary and around Fort San José, past the public cemetery. A 75-mile-long, German-built railway called the Ferrocarril del Sur (Southern Railroad) was completed to the Pacific port of San José by September 1884; telephone service was inaugurated; and the municipality of San Pedro Las Huertas was absorbed in 1885 (becoming the *cantón* La Independencia, later La Palmita). Electric power was moreover introduced, and the public cemetery relocated.

President Barrios had invaded El Salvador with the hope of reviving the Central American federation, but he died at the Battle of Chalchuapa on 2 April 1885. His successor, Gen. Manuel Lisandro Barillas, made peace with the nation's enemies, and modernization efforts resumed after Gen. José María Reyna Barrios was elected president in 1892—especially with

regard to the erection of city hospitals. The following year the capital's population was measured at 67,818, its wealthiest citizens now occupying the southernmost sectors, having forsaken the crowded, colonial-era core. After Reyna Barrios's assassination on 8 February 1898, Manuel Estrada Cabrera was elected president that same October, and he initiated a twenty-year reign that saw the government become increasingly aligned with oligarchic coffee interests and foreign investors.

Large-scale banana cultivation was introduced to Guatemala when a contract was signed in 1904 with the American-owned United Fruit Company, a conglomerate that, along with the International Railways of Central America, came to dominate the national economy. Light industry increased in the capital, and an influx of rural job seekers almost doubled its population to 112,000 residents by 1917, although the vast majority still remained mired in poverty and illiteracy.

Devastation and Metropolitan Boom (1918–Present)
The capital was razed by a series of massive earthquakes that struck from Christmas Day 1917 through January 1918, necessitating large-scale reconstruction. Because of the hardships involved—almost half the urban population still being

housed in temporary shelters two years afterward—the dictator, Estrada Cabrera, was compelled to resign by worker unrest in April 1920 in favor of the wealthy landowner Carlos Herrera, who in turn was supplanted two years later by the election of Gen. José María Orellana. The subsequent collapse of coffee prices on international markets and the global crisis engendered by the Great Depression served only to aggravate Guatemala's problems, retarding all major renovations until Gen. Jorge Ubico came to power in February 1931 and imposed an iron grip upon the country.

Under his dictatorial rule, many damaged structures were replaced by modern constructions—such as a new police headquarters, chamber of deputies, and central post office—some even in a copied "colonial" style, such as his Palacio Nacional (National Palace) on the north side of the Parque Central, done in a light green stone. City authorities also availed themselves of this opportunity to relieve the congested core by clustering a new Municipalidad (Municipal Building), the Palacio de Justicia (Hall of Justice), the Banco de Guatemala, and other offices into a new Centro Cívico (Civic Center) in the shadow of the old southwestern Fort San José and Teatro Nacional. Private construction practices had also changed, as single-story edifices were now preferred, and clumsy streetcars had been supplanted by more mobile buses, both of which developments would unwittingly contribute to

urban sprawl eastward and westward; the traditional red-tile roofs were also replaced with lighter corrugated zinc.

The national economy gradually rebounded, and Guatemala allied itself with the United States during World War II against Japan as of 8 December 1941, so that its capital industrialized and flourished. However, a student strike erupted in June 1944, quickly mushrooming into a general work stoppage. Soldiers fired upon a crowd and killed a demonstrator, so that the unpopular Ubico was obliged to resign by 1 July, being succeeded by a military triumvirate headed by Gen. Federico Ponce Vaides; he too was overthrown, on 20 October, by young dissident officers, seconded by unionists and students, and replaced by army captain Francisco Javier Arana and Maj. Jacobo Arbenz Guzmán, plus the civilian Jorge Toriello Garrido.

Elections resulted in the installation of the populist Juan José Arévalo as president by 15 March 1945; he inaugurated numerous social reforms, especially in the areas of public education and workplace regulation. Several failed counterconspiracies occurred, the most serious being in July 1949, during the highly charged atmosphere prior to the next presidential election. Arbenz, in his capacity as defense minister, attempted to arrest the rival political candidate Francisco Arana—senior commander of the army—on charges of plotting a coup, resulting in the latter's death when he resisted. That

Guatemala City's beautiful baroque cathedral—erected 1782–1815—as it appeared, ca. 1908. (Winter, *Guatemala and Her People of To-day*)

action sparked a series of minor uprisings by Arana supporters such as the one led by Col. Carlos Castillo Armas.

Arbenz emerged as the new president, quickening the pace of social change by such measures as an agrarian reform law that proposed expropriating large estates to be subdivided among the peasantry. Convinced that such policies masked a socialist intent, Washington persuaded the Organization of American States in March 1954 to authorize action against "communist aggression" in the Americas, then raised an antigovernment "army" in Honduras under the exiled Castillo Armas and Miguel Ydígoras Fuentes. Arbenz responded by declaring martial law in Guatemala City by early June, arresting numerous conservatives. But when Castillo Armas occupied the border town of Esquipulas on 18 June with 160 to 200 men, then used aircraft provided by the U.S. Central Intelligence Agency to bombard the capital, Arbenz's regime disintegrated. Diplomatically isolated and with many officers defecting to the opposition, he resigned on 27 June, allowing Castillo Armas to enter Guatemala City aboard a U.S. embassy plane and assume the presidency by 8 July.

Some 9,000 Guatemalans were subsequently imprisoned or fled into exile, and 8,000 peasants were killed over the ensuing weeks, as a rightist dictatorship was clamped upon the poor and backward nation. Such brutal repression was resisted by rural guerrillas, which along with numerous rightist coups hampered Guatemala's development over the next several decades. Its capital nonetheless grew throughout this difficult interlude, its population doubling from 284,276 inhabitants in 1950 to 572,671 by 1964.

Guatemala City suffered considerable damage when a heavy earthquake rumbled through the central portion of the country at 2:50 A.M. on 4 February 1976, claiming a total of 20,000 lives throughout the nation and leaving 1.25 million homeless. The capital was nevertheless rebuilt and continued to grow exponentially, boasting 1.1 million residents by 1991—or 1.7 million, if all outlying satellite towns were included. Unfortunately, such unbridled growth had also left the capital overcrowded, smog-bound, and congested by traffic, while ironically the ruined former capital of Antigua Guatemala had been restored and transformed into an attractive archaeological and tourist center, with a population of 43,000.

For further reading on the history of Guatemala City, please consult the Select Bibliography at the end of this volume.

Panama

Panama City

Way-station for passengers and cargoes traversing the narrowest portion of Central America between the Caribbean Sea and the Pacific Ocean.

Discovery (1514–1519)

Vasco Núñez de Balboa's claim of the Pacific in September 1513 sparked feverish excitement throughout the Hispanic communities of the West Indies, so that many would-be conquistadors descended upon his base camp of Santa María la Antigua del Darién to participate in the forthcoming subjugation of this vast new expanse. Further probes were duly dispatched across the jungly Isthmus, and by November 1514 a 110-man column under Capt. Antonio Tello de Guzmán paused to rest at a tiny hamlet on the Pacific side called *Panamá*—apparently signifying "Fishing Place" in the local Cueva dialect, although that interpretation has been the subject of considerable scholarly debate.

The site did not seem remarkably different from other coastal locales, until a detachment under Tello de Guzmán's subordinate Diego de Albítez emerged due north the following year at the Caribbean harbor of Nombre de Dios, thereby pioneering a more accessible overland route. Two Spaniards named Bartolomé Hurtado and Hernán Ponce de León were consequently granted license to settle the village of Panama in 1517, although no city would actually start to emerge until Balboa's successor—Gov. Pedro Arias de Avila, more commonly referred to as Pedrarias Dávila—jealously arrested and executed his young predecessor, then ordered the transfer of the entire Santa María la Antigua colony over to the Pacific shore.

Foundation and Early Evolution (1519–1564)

Pedrarias Dávila reached Taboga Island in the summer of 1519 with one contingent of settlers, contacting the few Spaniards already resident ashore, while awaiting the arrival of another 300-man column that was forging overland under his subordinate Gaspar de Espinosa. Both groups reunited that July, at which time the governor selected a site about a mile from Panama's original fishing village for his new capital. Hoping to transform this virgin settlement into a major

Aerial photograph of the old seventeenth-century core of Panama City as it appeared in 1944; north is toward right. (Organization of American States)

347

Panoramic view eastward across Panama City, from atop Ancón Hill, ca. 1900. (Heald, *Picturesque Panama*)

springboard for future conquests, Pedrarias Dávila ignored its rather swampy terrain, steamy heat, torrential downpours from May through November, and lack of fresh drinking water. He instead focused upon its stands of trees—essential for shipbuilding—as well as its small natural harbor, which was sheltered by a low headland soon dubbed Judas Point and fed by the Gallinero (modern Abajo) River.

The city of Nuestra Señora de la Asunción de Panamá (Our Lady of the Assumption of Panama) was formally established on 15 August 1519—so named as the date coincided with the day of the Assumption on the Church calendar—and consummated by a ceremonial distribution of land plots to approximately 100 Spanish soldiers and their dependents. However, because of the expeditions that Pedrarias Dávila was continuously to dispatch westward and southeastward over the next several years in quest of indigenous kingdoms, his new capital did not evolve much beyond a transient military camp, most of its dwellings merely extemporized huts and its "citizens" constantly departing.

A visitor who arrived in 1529 over the newly completed *camino real* (royal highway) from Nombre de Dios described Panama City as a clutch of seventy-five wooden shacks with thatched roofs. After Francisco Pizarro ventured south a couple of years later to seize the immensely rich Incan empire of Peru, that vast territory was to lure away so many Panamanian residents that the flimsy city became even further depleted. Late in 1533 its new governor, Francisco de Barrio Nuevo, lamented that only thirty-three Spaniards remained as permanent inhabitants, supervising perhaps 500 Indian slaves who toiled as stevedores, porters, teamsters, and laborers in bringing across the isthmus a steady stream of equipment, supplies, and passengers, most of whom immediately pressed on for the new Peruvian viceroyalty.

Few Castillians chose to linger in Panama's sweltering, pestilential heat when enormous tracts of land, rich mines, and thousands of potential vassals could be secured in the more temperate Andean highlands. Barrio Nuevo himself absconded shortly thereafter, leaving the citizenry to endure a fire in late July 1539 that consumed most of their frail structures, including the four-year-old cathedral, which contained an organ and a clock. In addition, an earthquake struck on 21 November 1541; yet despite such setbacks and its overall lack of allure, Panama retained great strategic importance as a transshipment point because of its vital placement. This fact was exemplified when Pizarro's brother Gonzalo overthrew the first Crown-appointed viceroy of Peru, then sent a rebel contingent north under Capt. Hernando de Bachicao to occupy Panama City in December 1544. This rebel fleet of 500 men and twenty-six vessels departed four months afterward, only to return later that same year under Gen. Pedro Alonso de Hinojosa; it was to remain in possession of Panama until 1546.

Four years later, the tiny city underwent an even greater ordeal when the rebellious Nicaraguan brothers Hernando and Pedro de Contreras—Pedrarias Dávila's grandsons—materialized 5 miles southwest of Panama at Ancón Bay on 22 April 1550, disgorging from their pair of frigates 262 men, who surprised the sleeping residents at midnight. The interlopers then brought their frigates into La Tasca anchorage the next morning to seize the two best anchored vessels and cripple the rest. The Contreras brothers had hoped to intercept the royal emissary Lic. Pedro de la Gasca, who was returning toward Spain with vast treasure after crushing Pizarro's Peruvian revolt. Yet that officer had proceeded overland toward Nombre de Dios two days previously, accompanied by Panama's governor, Sancho de Clavijo. Hernando de Contreras therefore took forty horsemen in pursuit, while his second-in-command, Juan Bermejo, followed with 200 foot soldiers; Capt. Rodrigo Salguero led another twenty-five down a secondary road toward the isthmian way-station of Venta de Cruces.

During their absence, the leading citizen Martín Ruiz de Marchena organized an armed band of Panamanians to prevent the rebels' return. They fought a stiff action around the city square when Bermejo's infantry—having been rebuffed by another royalist muster farther north, at Capira—reappeared at midnight of 23–24 April 1550. The weary rebels were driven atop Matanza Hill by dawn and slaughtered, thirty-seven survivors being led back into Panama City to be garroted, after which Hernando de Contreras attempted to escape past the city with his few remaining riders to rejoin his brother Pedro's ships offshore. However, he slipped down an embank-

ment and drowned, while Pedro was beaten by a flotilla under Capt. Zamorano and his crews executed.

Panama City quickly recuperated from these assaults, the value and volume of transisthmian trade increasing rapidly during the early 1550s as enormous amounts of silver began flowing out of Peru. Because of this bullion's crucial importance to the Spanish imperial economy, a convoy system soon evolved whereby a pair of royal warships would escort a merchant fleet across the Atlantic from Seville every spring, touching at Cartagena before entering Nombre de Dios. Peruvian vessels would simultaneously arrive at Panama City from Callao, bearing the king's silver from the Lima mint, plus wealthy traders with South American produce to sell. A great commercial fair would then be celebrated at Nombre de Dios, during which Spanish merchants sold European wares and bought American goods for the return passage, while their Peruvian counterparts did the inverse. All transactions ceased once the royal bullion was lightered aboard the warships, signaling that the Sevillean convoy was about to depart, at which time the Peruvians would bring their purchases back through Panama City for shipment toward South America.

The city profited by serving as an intermediary for this rich traffic, its *recuas* (mule trains) shuttling consignments between coasts, while its warehouses stockpiled merchandise, and its ranches reprovisioned both fleets. Goldfields in the nearby province of Veragua, plus pearl fisheries in the Gulf of Panama, eventually added to this prosperity, so much business being transacted that trading firms soon began maintaining *factores* (agents) year-round in the city, while large numbers of Africans were imported and sold as slaves by an Italian consortium. (For centuries thereafter Panama's slave mart was to remain known as the Casa de los Genoveses or House of the Genoese, because of the nationality of these early traffickers.)

A slave revolt had occurred in the city as early as 1549, under a leader nicknamed Felipillo (Little Phillip); five years later, another uprising erupted under a leader called Bayano, who was not captured by Capt. Pedro de Urzúa and deported to Seville until 1558. More dangerous still, though, was the steady trickle of individual *negros cimarrones* (renegade blacks) who escaped into the surrounding jungles, settling amid the hostile Indians to pose a constant threat to transisthmian travelers.

A Spanish revolt also occurred in Panama on 4 December 1562, when the city notary Rodrigo Méndez Guzmán—availing himself of the temporary absence at Nombre de Dios of Gov. Luis de Guzmán—rose with 350 followers, only to see his movement undermined by the opposition of Bishop Juan de Vaca, eventually costing Méndez and his lieutenants their lives. A nocturnal conflagration that originated in a blacksmith's shop consumed forty of Panama's houses in early March 1563, although thanks to a decade of vigorous economic activity, that number represented only 10 percent of all dwellings within the city and were promptly replaced.

Panama's city crest, issued at Burgos on 15 September 1521 by the Emperor Charles V of Spain. (Archive of Indies, Seville)

Colonial Heyday (1565–1640)

Panama was elevated to the full status of isthmian capital when the regional *real audiencia* (royal tribunal) was transferred from Guatemala and reinstalled at Panama as of 15 May 1565. Its governors, who also served as presidents of this court, would thenceforth be referred to by the honorific title of "president," like their peers at Santo Domingo or Quito. Five years later the total number of edifices in the city was calculated at almost 500, while it was reported in 1575 that they housed 500 Spanish inhabitants—most originating from Seville—plus 3,000 black slaves.

The tonnage of arriving Peruvian vessels had also increased so dramatically that the original anchorage—nicknamed La Tasca (The Pocket) because its shallow bottom left even medium-size vessels beached at low tide—was no longer adequate. The deepwater anchorage off Perico Island farther to the southwest therefore had to be substituted, soon becoming dubbed Naos (Merchantmen) Island. Cargoes had to be lightered across the intervening 7 miles of water into Panama's *casas reales* (royal offices) by boats that for many years would remain known as *embarcaciones de La Tasca* (Tasca craft), despite the fact that the latter anchorage had silted up through disuse by the 1650s. Shipwrights were also kept busy repairing vessels anchored off Perico Island that became riddled by teredo worms in the warm tropical waters, while epidemics among the weakened disembarking passengers and crews kept medical practitioners gainfully employed.

Such wealth and activity also attracted unwelcome attention from abroad. Four-score Englishmen raided Nombre de Dios at dawn on 29 July 1572 under a youthful Francis Drake, who returned on 22 February 1573 to march inland and—aided by black *cimarron* allies—surprise the Venta de Cruces way-station, although failing to secure the silver-ladened mule train that was his target. Drake enjoyed better success on his third attempt, netting considerable booty when he ambushed another mule train just outside Nombre de Dios on 1 April 1573.

Two escaped Spaniards reached Panama City by canoe on 6 March 1577 with even more troubling news, for Drake's colleague John Oxenham had traversed the isthmus farther east by rafting down the Chucunaque and Tuira rivers with fifty Englishmen and ten *cimarrones,* disgorging into the Gulf of San Miguel and gaining the Pearl Islands. The *Audiencia* president, Dr. Gabriel de Loarte, ordered an immediate muster of all militiamen, which dissuaded Oxenham from attacking the city when his intruders materialized offshore the next evening. De Loarte then dispatched 200 men in pursuit under Pedro de Ortega Valencia aboard a half dozen boats on 13 March, while two frigates were also detached from Vice Adm. Miguel de Eraso's anchored plate-fleet at Nombre de Dios plus a Panamanian coast guard frigate and brigantine to cut off Oxenham's retreat on the Caribbean side. These interlopers were eventually captured far up the Chucunaque, thirteen executed

in Panama City in April 1578, while Oxenham and four others met the same fate at Lima.

Panamanian security improved somewhat after the local authorities made peace with a large *cimarron* band led by Luis de Mozambique in 1580, allowing them to settle at Santiago del Príncipe (modern Palenque) on the Caribbean coast. The next year, another 300 black renegades under Antón de Mandinga were granted that same privilege at Pacora, 9 miles outside the capital itself. Nevertheless, Drake's destructive descents early in 1586 against Santo Domingo and Cartagena so worried Panama that a small militia army of 50 riders and 800 foot soldiers, including numerous free mulattoes or blacks, was formally constituted within the city.

Transisthmian traffic continued to grow even after war with Elizabethan England erupted two years later, so that the urban population stood at 600 Spaniards and almost 4,000 total residents by 1595. The following year they experienced a fright when Drake seized Nombre de Dios on 6 January 1596 with his fleet, its few defenders being pursued inland by 600 to 700 English troops under Col.-Gen. Thomas Baskerville. These invaders penetrated the isthmus as far as the Venta de la Quebrada way-station, before being checked on the morning of 9 January by 70 Spanish troops under Capt. Juan Enríquez Conabut dug in atop Capirilla Hill near the San Pablo way-station. The defenders held that narrow pass until reinforced by an additional 50 harquebusiers under Capt. Hernando de Lierno Agüero, obliging the English to retire the following day. Ill and demoralized, Drake torched and quit Nombre de Dios by 25 January, dying shortly thereafter.

As a result of the devastation experienced by that anchorage at the hands of the raiders, the Panamanian authorities decided to shift all future plate-fleet operations into the more defensible harbor of Portobelo, although transisthmian access would not prove as direct or convenient. Commercial fairs were suspended roughly every other year for the remainder of the Elizabethan conflict, yet business revived fully once peace was established in August 1604. Three years afterward, Panama's *Audiencia* reported that the city's population had risen to 1,000 Spaniards, 300 free mulattoes and blacks, plus 3,700 slaves, while its infrastructure now consisted of eight substantial, stuccoed buildings—among them, six convents—plus hundreds of permanent wooden structures. Natural dangers still recurred, though, many people perishing during a heavy earthquake that struck at 5:00 P.M. on 2 May 1621, prompting a short-lived debate about relocating the city farther southwest to the foot of Ancón Hill.

Decline and Sack (1641–1671)

The Panamanian economy thrived, as plate-fleets were received every year between 1616 and 1640, the total number of inhabitants topping 8,000 by that latter year. They remained undeterred even after eighty of their buildings, including the cathedral, were consumed by an arson fire set at

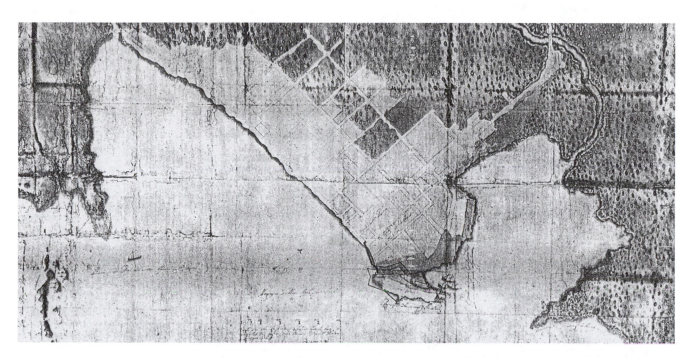

Map of the city as surveyed in 1609 by the Italian-born engineer Batista Antonelli's nephew, Cristóbal de Roda; north is toward upper right. (Archive of Indies, Seville)

9:00 P.M. on 21 February 1644, plus another that claimed three more buildings two nights later. However, Spain had now entered into a protracted period of decay, manifested at Panama by a downturn in its traffic and less frequent commercial fairs, which were held only every other year until 1654, after which their pattern became ever more erratic.

In addition to economic depression, the palpable weakness of Spain's forces in the New World tempted the Jamaican rover Henry Morgan to seize Portobelo with a few hundred buccaneers on 11 July 1668, holding it defiantly for a month, despite the transisthmian march of 800 Panamanian troops under interim Gov. Agustín de Bracamonte—who succeeded in regaining possession of this vital Caribbean outlet only through paying a ransom of 100,000 pesos. Two and a half years later, Morgan launched an even more ambitious scheme by capturing Chagres on 7 January 1671, then pushing up its river twelve days later against Panama City itself.

The *Audiencia* president—fifty-two-year-old Juan Pérez de Guzmán, knight of the Order of Santiago—sortied from his capital with 800 militiamen on 21 January 1671, camping at Guayabal to monitor the enemy's progression through the jungle, while small units of scouts harried Morgan's column. But the veteran West Indian rovers came on relentlessly, compelling the governor to retire into Panama three days later and order every able-bodied man to muster atop Matasnillos rise (modern Antiguo Golf Club development), 2.5 miles southwest of the city, as the unfortified capital could not otherwise be defended. Morgan's 1,200 buccaneers came into view toward evening of 27 January, advancing next morning against Pérez

de Guzmán's 1,200 waiting infantrymen—mostly mulattoes and blacks in a line six deep—plus two companies of 200 riders apiece on each flank.

The 300-man freebooter vanguard under Lt.-Col. Laurens Prins and Maj. John Morris were still ascending a hillock on the Spaniards' right when the undisciplined defenders launched a wild charge. Being much better armed, the invaders smashed this rush with dense fusillades, more than 100 Panamanians succumbing to the first volley. The inexperienced volunteers thereupon broke and fled, leaving 400 to 500 casualties upon the field (as opposed to only 15 buccaneers). Pérez de Guzmán was swept back into the city during that precipitate flight, ordering its magazines blown as he rode through. Panama burst into flames as the triumphant raiders entered through its northwestern Matadero suburb, across a span known ever after as the Puente de Morgan (Morgan's Bridge). But although they remained in undisputed possession for the next four weeks, the frustrated mercenaries could find no great treasures hidden among the ashes, most riches and noncombatants having been removed previously. Despite detaching columns throughout the district that inflicted cruel tortures upon every refugee that they caught, relatively little booty could be garnered before the disappointed occupiers retraced their route to Chagres and departed the north coast in mid-March.

Spanish survivors crept back into Panama City immediately thereafter, finding that only the Augustinian convent and a few shacks along its northern fringe had escaped outright destruction by the flames, most other edifices having been reduced to gutted ruins. Disease quickly appeared as well, a total of more

Remnants of the Puente de Morgan or "Morgan's Bridge," as it appeared on the outskirts of Old Panama, ca. 1913. (Abbot, *Panama and the Canal*)

than 3,000 of its 10,000 inhabitants perishing as a result of this ordeal, in addition to another 600 marched off as captives by the buccaneers. An eight-ship relief convoy of 2,500 Peruvian reinforcements finally appeared in April 1671, affording the frightened citizenry sufficient peace of mind to consider rebuilding their homes.

Relocation (1672–1740)

The Peruvians left behind 750 troops as added security upon their departure, and when Antonio Fernández de Córdoba y Mendoza, knight of the Order of Santiago, subsequently arrived from Cadiz as new Panamanian president in mid-January 1672, it was decided to abandon the city-site altogether. Instead, the old project was revived of shifting the capital 5 miles southwest into the shadow of 560-foot Ancón Hill, whose protruding La Punta headland could be readily converted into a defensive position by erecting ramparts along its narrow breadth; its flanks were furthermore protected by a ring of reefs. Fresh water was available from Chorrillo Spring, just to its west, while the Perico Island anchorage would lay much closer, so that cargoes would have to be lightered only 2 miles to be deposited at El Taller beach.

Peruvian merchants consequently donated 40,000 pesos toward this relocation project, so that work might commence within a year on clearing the new site. By the time official con-firmation was received from Madrid, it only remained for Gov. Fernández to distribute plots to the first 300 residents in a formal ceremony celebrated on 21 January 1673 and for the original city—henceforth called Panamá la Vieja (Old Panama)—to become gradually depopulated. (Although not without some delays, as moving proved expensive for people who had so recently lost everything, while Fernández moreover died in the diseased older city on 8 April, being succeeded by the corrupt *oidor* [justice] Luis de Lozada, who diverted public funds into a palatial private residence for himself, while also expropriating unclaimed plots for his personal use.) In addition to financing the construction of a new defensive perimeter, the Crown also augmented the permanent city garrison from 200 to 500 royal troops, plus 300 seamen.

By 1675, this new city still contained only 1,600 residents, but the transfer proved justified when a flotilla of 330 Caribbean buccaneers appeared offshore in early May 1680, having followed Oxenham's old route across the eastern isthmus. The Spaniards feverishly tried completing Panama's unfinished stone circuit with earthen ramparts, while sending out a scratch naval force to offer battle, which was overwhelmed in a three-hour fight, yet displayed such spirited resistance that the interlopers dispersed to pillage weaker towns. Four years later another Jamaican contingent gained the Pacific via this same route and occupied the offshore Pearl

Proposed street layout for the new city, as it was to be reconstituted on La Punta headland at the foot of Ancón Hill, after Morgan's raid had devastated the original city early in 1671; north is toward right. (Archive of Indies, Seville)

Islands, being joined by reinforcements until by mid-April 1685 six vessels and almost 1,000 freebooters were awaiting the annual treasure-fleet from Peru. They were frustrated when Lt. Gen. Tomás Palavacino slipped past into Panama City on 3 June with 1,400 men aboard four warships and three hired merchantmen, resupplied its starving garrison, and then sortied four days later to scatter the blockaders after a two-day running fight off Pacheca Island.

But although this particular pirate fleet had disbanded, individual commanders continued to prowl the Pacific for several more years, rendering trade unsafe and Panama isolated. On 22 July 1686, Capt. Francis Townley's Anglo-French buccaneers even made a descent upon the outskirts of the new Panamanian capital, seizing a mule train reputedly worth 1.5 million pesos—only to lose it to a Spanish counterambush. Still, his landing force had also brought off 300 captives, which Townley used to brutally extort a truce by sending two heads to the *Audiencia* president with a demand that his rovers be given a daily subsistence of cattle, sheep, and flour.

This uneasy stranglehold persisted for a month, until 240 Panamanians emerged from the Perico Island anchorage aboard three ships and attempted to surprise Townley's anchored flotilla on 22 August 1686. Their assault was repelled, two of their three ships being boarded and only sixty-five

attackers escaping death or injury. The infuriated Townley—wounded during this exchange—sent twenty more heads ashore to protest this violation of the truce, until Panama's archbishop placated him by delivering 10,000 pesos on 4 September, along with a promise that henceforth all English prisoners would be considered Catholics and so enjoy the protection of the Church. Townley died of his wounds four days later, being buried near Otoque Island, after which his freebooters vanished southward.

Constant alarms had galvanized the Panamanians into completing their new city's enclosure with granite walls, plus a dry moat and several batteries, yet they could not as easily compensate for the decrease in plate-fleet arrivals on the Caribbean side. This decline in transatlantic movement so reduced local incomes and tax gathering that the annual *situados* (subsidies) remitted from the Peruvian exchequer had to be almost quadrupled—from 105,000 pesos in 1670 to 406,000 two decades later—merely to sustain Panama's garrison and royal establishment intact, without any additional consideration for the cost of fortification works. Many foodstuffs had furthermore been regularly imported into the city from South America, and they became increasingly unaffordable as the number of ship arrivals decreased.

This predicament worsened, as commercial fairs were held only in 1691, 1698, and 1708, Panama's president even being driven to the drastic expedient of expropriating a silver consignment bound for the king's coffers in Spain later that summer so as to avert a mutiny by his penniless troops. Only three more fairs could be celebrated—in 1721, 1726, and 1730—while the one scheduled for 1737 was canceled after a huge fire consumed two-thirds of Panama's buildings on the evening of 2 February. Two years later the War of Jenkins's Ear erupted against England, and a British naval expedition under Vice Adm. Edward Vernon pulverized the defenses at both Portobelo and Chagres during the initial operations of 1739–1740. These attacks rendered both ports useless as havens for anchored merchantmen and diverted the flow of South American commercial traffic away from Panama altogether, toward the safer venues offered by Cartagena and other ports.

Stagnation (1741–1847)

Despite painstakingly refurbishing the defenses of its commercial outlets at Portobelo and Chagres once peace was restored in October 1748, Panama failed to recoup even its depleted prewar trade volumes over the ensuing decades because the Crown policy of annual treasure fleets had become a thing of the past. Individual vessels continued to call at the isthmus with more modest cargoes, yet the great commercial gatherings were now irretrievably lost. Some Panamanian merchants managed to survive the ensuing lean interlude by smuggling in foreign goods through the ancillary Caribbean port of Bastimentos—located 10 miles northwest of Portobelo—but without any natural resources

Panama's main square as it appeared in February 1748, lined with grandstands to view bullfights by day and other festivities at night, in honor of Ferdinand VI's ascension to the Spanish throne. At lower right can be seen the cathedral framework, still under reconstruction following the city's great fire of eleven years previously; this edifice was not reconsecrated until April 1796. (Archive of Indies, Seville)

or manufactures of their own, prospects for Panama's citizenry remained dim.

Accidental fires that damaged the capital in 1756 and 1781 increased the feeling of despondency, plunging to its lowest level once Buenos Aires was licensed to handle South American exports as of the late 1770s; after that, trade restrictions were also gradually eased throughout Spanish America, resulting in still more alternative outlets. The population of Panama City had remained static throughout most of the eighteenth century, being measured at only 7,000 inhabitants by 1790, of whom a contemporary observer noted that "having no commerce, nor industry, nor agriculture, its natives emigrate to Peru."

Ironically, South America's struggle for liberty from Spain produced a short-lived revival at Panama, as the declarations of independence by Argentina and Colombia in May 1810 meant that Buenos Aires and Cartagena were denied to royal vessels, so that the isthmian route had to be revived by the Crown in order to hasten reinforcements and materiel to sustain its Loyalist garrisons in Peru, Ecuador, and Chile. Two years later, the viceroy-designate for New Granada—Benito Pérez—even declared Panama City to be his official capital, because he was unable to take up residence in rebel-controlled Bogotá.

Yet as royalist fortunes waned throughout the Spanish-American empire, so did this military flow across the isthmus, and the city finally joined the insurgent cause on 28 November 1821 and became part of Simón Bolívar's newly created "Republic of Gran Colombia." Because of its midcontinental position and easy accessibility by sea, Panama hosted an inter-American congress at which Bolívar received delegates from Mexico, Peru, and Central America from 22 June to 15 July 1826, resulting in pledges of mutual defense against European intervention and the elimination of the slave trade. Yet a paucity of merchant traffic meant that the city remained a virtual backwater for the next two decades.

Isthmian Crossroads (1848–1902)

Panama blossomed again thanks to the California Gold Rush, which abruptly elevated it into a transit point for thousands of prospectors eager to hurry from the eastern United States to San Francisco after 1848, bypassing the tedious overland treks or voyages around Cape Horn. A plan had been drafted earlier by an American company to lay down a railway line between the city and its new Caribbean terminus of Colón on the northwestern coast, which became galvanized by this sudden crush of travelers. Construction was well under way by 1850 and concluded in January 1855, spanning 47 miles of swamps, rivers, and rugged tropical terrain. Soon, so many foreigners were being brought across the isthmus to take ship from the port city that its first English-language newspaper—the *Star and Herald*—had appeared in 1849 (still published today as *La Estrella de Panamá*).

Servicing of the first oceangoing steamships on the Pacific side also meant that Perico was abandoned as Panama's anchorage in favor of Taboga, while the sudden business upsurge furthermore encouraged the capital's population to rebound from 8,000 to 10,000–12,000 inhabitants within the next couple of years. But although prospering, its citizens—most of whom were impoverished blacks—endured considerable difficulties as a result of the continual demands from hundreds of thousands of transients, plus unpleasant treatment at the hands of racist white travelers.

On the evening of 15 April 1856, a drunken outward-bound Forty-Niner named Jack Oliver snatched a watermelon slice from a vendor in the city's new railway station, refusing to pay, then wounding a bystander with his pistol when a crowd angrily gathered. The incident quickly escalated into a citywide rampage, during which fifteen American citizens were killed and sixteen wounded, compared with two Panamanians dead and thirteen injured. Derisively dubbed the "Watermelon War" by U.S. newspapers, it eventually goaded Washington into ordering the warships USS *Independence* and *St. Mary's* to anchor offshore on 19 September, disembarking a detachment under Cmdr. William Mervine to occupy the railway station for three days. New Granada's government was also pressured into paying more than $412,000 in damages three years later.

The city's economic boom evaporated once the U.S. transcontinental railroad was completed at Promontory Point, Utah, in 1869, obviating the roundabout route through Panama. Another depression therefore ensued, until the French company of Ferdinand de Lesseps was formed in 1881 to implement the long-held dream of digging a ship canal between the capital and the Caribbean. Panama's population quickly doubled to 24,000 as this project gained headway, and various urban innovations came to be made—such as the creation of the city's first fire department in 1887 and the introduction of limited electric power the next year. This resurgence collapsed, however, once disease began seriously decimating workers' ranks, so that the corporation had to declare bankruptcy and suspend labors as of May 1889.

Panamanians were now thoroughly disillusioned by these boom-and-bust cycles, as well as by their misgovernment from distant Bogotá, which ignored their needs and appointed avaricious place-seekers as governors. The isthmian state had already halfheartedly tried to secede from New Granada in November 1840 and in 1853, but it was not until a debilitating civil war erupted in Colombia between liberal and conservative factions in October 1899 that Panama at last had a realistic chance of achieving full-fledged independence. During the initial stages of the conflict, the port city became a contested

Offices of the French Canal Company in the city's Cathedral Plaza, ca. 1889, the same year in which this corporation declared bankruptcy and the initial dig became suspended. (Abbot, *Panama and the Canal*)

strategic prize, its conservative Colombian garrison under Gen. Albán mounting an unsuccessful defense at Calidonia Bridge on 24 July 1900 before capitulating to liberal besiegers two days later. Yet victories elsewhere eventually reimposed conservative rule, and Colombia's so-called War of the Thousand Days culminated with the execution of liberal general Victoriano Lorenzo in the city's Chiriquí (modern Francia) Square on 15 May 1903.

Yet an expansionistic U.S. administration under President Theodore Roosevelt had signed a treaty with Colombia's conservative rulers on 22 January 1903, aimed at reanimating the canal project. Panamanian hopes of reaping an economic bonanza from the deal were dashed, however, when the senate in Bogotá rejected the agreement, then adjourned that same October. The resultant disappointment in Panama led to yet another proclamation of independence, on 3 November, provoking the dispatch of a counterexpedition of Colombian troops to Colón. But that force was denied transit across the isthmus by the American-owned railway company, backed by the intimidating presence of the USS *Nashville* and 400 marines under Maj. John A. Lejeune. A Panamanian delegate was meanwhile swiftly received at Washington, and the country's liberty was recognized as of 13 November.

Independence (1903–Present)

Five days later, a long-term treaty was concluded between the United States and this fledgling "Republic of Panama," whereby all canal properties were to be leased for ninety-nine years in exchange for a $10 million down payment, plus annual rents of $250,000. Almost immediately, this American investment proved materially beneficial for Panama City; its streets became paved, garbage collection was regularized, water and sewage systems were installed by U.S. Army engineers, and fumigation efforts were organized to eradicate mosquitoes and reduce recurrent outbreaks of yellow fever and malaria. Residents also profited from the protracted construction of a 40-mile series of canals, locks, and dams stretching across the isthmus from the brand-new port of Balboa—formerly La Boca, located just west of their city—to Limón Bay on the northwestern coast, concluded by 3 August 1914. During this vast undertaking the capital's populace had more than doubled, from 22,000 residents in 1905 to 46,500 by 1911.

George Davis, the U.S. governor for the autonomous "Canal Zone," had also swiftly intervened when Panama's army commander, Gen. Esteban Huertas—backed by the Liberal Party, then in opposition—called for the resignation of two ministers in the cabinet of conservative president Manuel Amador on 28 October 1904. Worried that this threat might have portended a troublesome coup in the host republic, Davis brought a detachment of marines from Empire to Ancón just outside the capital, then requested additional support from Washington. On 14 November, Adm. Caspar F. Goodrich anchored off Panama City with the battleship USS *New York,* cruiser *Boston,*

and gunboat *Bennington,* pressuring Huertas into accepting early retirement four days later, after which the republic's 250-man army was disbanded on 19 November and replaced by a police force.

As the city's birthrate and health standards improved, and ship traffic through the canal escalated during the 1920s and 1930s, Panama attracted many Antillean, Spanish, Italian, Colombian, and Greek immigrants seeking work or modest business opportunities; its population therefore mushroomed again, from 49,500 inhabitants in 1920 to 74,400 a decade later and 111,800 by 1940 (plus another 15,000 at Ancón, which lay inside the U.S.-controlled Canal Zone). Thus despite its newfound prosperity and attractiveness, the burgeoning city found itself increasingly hemmed in by the Zone and unable to find outlets for expansion, a constraint that engendered such friction that protest strikes had occurred in 1925 and 1932 against high rents, overcrowding, and dilapidation.

Resentment against the U.S. presence grew, especially as other treaty provisions began to prove irksome with the passage of time: the U.S. government, for example, reaped an enormous bounty in passage tolls, yet refused to adjust the original low rental agreement with the host republic to compensate for inflation or devaluations; merchants in the Zone—benefiting from a duty-free status—routinely undersold their Panamanian competitors; locals were excluded from any significant managerial positions in canal operations and were oftentimes treated condescendingly (or worse) by low-grade American employees; and Washington still retained the ominous right to intervene militarily or to expropriate lands "in defense of the canal."

As a result, Panamanians—30 percent of whom were black—had come to feel that their country was little more than a U.S. protectorate and resented being treated as second-class citizens, as well as being denied a voice in the canal's stranglehold over their urban economy. Washington ignored the republic, focusing merely upon the canal's strategic importance. When the nationalistic, profascist president Arnulfo "El Hombre" Arias opposed U.S. plans to lease new air bases in 1940, he was deposed on 9 October of the following year by the pliant local assembly, with tacit approval from the U.S. government. Panama subsequently fought as an ally during World War II, furnishing bases for air patrols and training sites for many thousands of U.S. servicemen, while the canal served as a valuable military conduit.

Yet once that conflict ceased, in August 1945, a trade slump ensued, and anti-U.S. sentiment grew ever more strident. Riots erupted in the capital on 11 December 1947 against Washington's plan to extend the leases on many wartime bases with such fervor that President Enrique A. Jiménez was obliged to reject the deal eleven days later. Although peacetime traffic through the canal gradually rebounded and a measure of prosperity returned to the adjacent city, living conditions became more problematical as its populace ballooned as a

"Fumigation Brigade," ca. 1913, organized by the American health authorities to help reduce Panama's perennial blight of disease-bearing mosquitoes. (Abbot, *Panama and the Canal*)

result of a new wave of migrants from rural areas. Another disturbance injured 120 people during independence day celebrations on 3 November 1959, having to be quelled by Panamanian national guardsmen and U.S. troops. The bloodiest clash occurred after canal authorities refused to honor a symbolic arrangement to fly the Panamanian flag beside the Stars and Stripes over the Zone on 9 January 1964. Diplomatic relations were severed with Washington the following day, and 4 U.S. soldiers and 24 Panamanians were killed during four days of anarchy; 85 American citizens and 200 Panamanians were also wounded.

Negotiations to address the republic's grievances dragged on fruitlessly until the administration of President Jimmy Carter, who signed a revised treaty with strongman Col. Omar Torrijos Herrera in 1977 that replaced the Panama Canal Company (a wholly owned U.S.-government corporation) with a commission of five U.S. and four Panamanian directors. Approximately 60 percent of Zone territory was simultaneously restored to local control, with a pledge to hand over the entire canal by 31 December 1999. As tensions eased following that accommodation, the capital enjoyed another economic

boom, having in the interim also become a significant world financial center, with subsidiaries of major international banks having been established since the 1960s to take advantage of its very liberal tax laws.

Unfortunately, a few of those institutions subsequently became compromised by money-laundering operations for Colombian drug cartels, with the complicity of Torrijos's corrupt successor, Brig. Manuel Antonio Noriega. Relations between President George Bush and this strongman grew increasingly strained until 16 December 1989, when four unarmed marine officers were attacked at a checkpoint near the general's *comandancia* (headquarters) in the teeming capital, one being slain. The next day, President Bush authorized the dispatch of 11,000 soldiers from the United States to join the 13,000 servicemen already guarding the canal. Together they launched Operation Just Cause at 1:00 A.M. on 20 December, seconded by paratroop drops and air cover flown in from the United States, that swiftly secured strongpoints throughout Panama City and its adjacent airports.

Battle damage in this confined urban setting proved extensive ($1–2 billion in total), especially in the densely populated

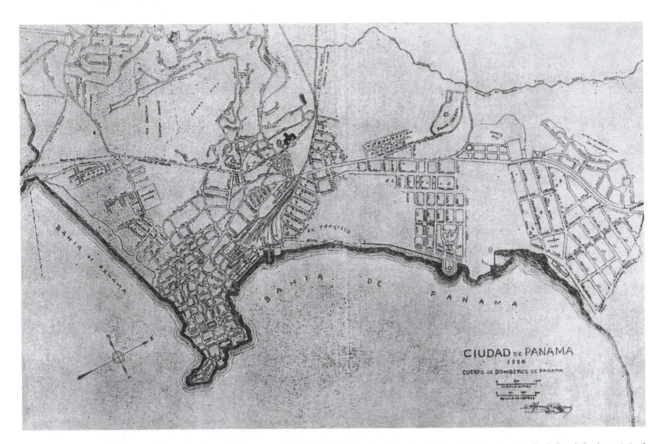

Map of the city and its expanding suburbs, as they appeared in 1928; the mouth of the canal lies at Balboa just to the left, while the original "Old Panama" ruins lay half covered by tropical growth at right. (Alfonso Lavergne)

El Chorrillo slums to the west of Panama's downtown core, where flames spread after a particularly vigorous exchange. Sporadic sniper fire did not cease until the morning of 21 December 1989, while looting and rioting were not curtailed until two days later, with the arrival of an additional 2,000 U.S. troops. Noriega finally emerged from his sanctuary in the papal embassy on 3 January 1990, being flown off to stand trial in Miami for drug trafficking. Casualties from this campaign were later estimated at 23 U.S. dead and 330 wounded; 297 Panamanian soldiers killed, 123 wounded, and several hundred captured; plus 500 civilians killed, hundreds more injured, and 18,000 left homeless out of a metropolitan population of perhaps 450,000 residents. Once again in its history, Panama City had to rebuild from a military assault.

For further reading materials on the history of Panama, please consult the Select Bibliography at the end of this volume; additional sources can be found under "Regional Works on Mexico and Central America," as well as under "General Works on Latin America."

Portobelo

Isthmian seaport that blossomed into a world-famous plate-fleet terminal during the early seventeenth century before fading into virtual oblivion.

Antecedents (1510–1596)

After the first Spanish explorers had probed Panama's northern coastline, dubbing it Castilla del Oro (Golden Castle), Diego de Nicuesa approached these shores with five vessels and 700 men in 1509 to establish a permanent settlement. However, his squadron was scattered and his flagship lost during a storm, so that the depleted survivors regrouped at the Belén River mouth on the Mosquito Coast to try again. This second attempt succeeded in disembarking at Portobelo, yet was so fiercely beset by local inhabitants that Nicuesa shifted 15 miles farther east to Nombre de Dios in October 1510, establishing another shaky foothold amid its unremittingly hostile tribesmen. Three months later, Nicuesa forsook this beleaguered second outpost as well to sail still farther east in the hope of displacing the unlicensed Vasco Núñez de Balboa as leader of a much more successful Spanish enclave at Santa María la Antigua del Darién, only to be greeted by strenuous protests and rejected.

The charismatic Núñez de Balboa spent the next couple of years pacifying northeastern Panama, before approaching uninhabited Portobelo in September 1513 with his small army, disembarking at the nearby port of Acla to fight his way across the isthmus and lay claim to the Pacific Ocean by the end of that same month. The discovery of that spectacular

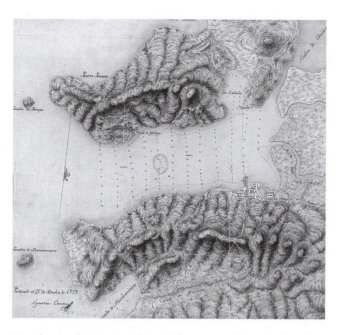

Map showing the tiny city of Portobelo ensconced deep inside its harbor, as surveyed by the military engineer and brigadier, Agustín Crame, in January 1779. The Farallón del Draque or "Drake's Beacon" is featured on the island to the left of the headland. (Servicio Histórico Militar, Madrid)

expanse of virgin coastline sparked feverish excitement throughout the Spanish West Indies; an onrush of would-be conquistadors arrived to participate in its forthcoming subjugation. Although Núñez de Balboa was officially superseded as acting governor of the nominal capital of Santa María del Darién late in June 1514 by the seventy-two-year-old Crown-appointed Pedro Arias de Avila (whose name was commonly contracted, both during his lifetime and afterward, as Pedrarias Dávila), the youthful discoverer nonetheless retained the more coveted title of *adelantado* or military commander for the imminent campaigns into the Pacific.

In mid-July 1514, one of Pedrarias Dávila's subordinates—Capt. Juan de Ayora—ventured westward from Santa María del Darién with a ship and three or four caravels, pillaging the friendly tribes along the Caribbean coast that summer. Simultaneously, a 110-man exploratory column under Capt. Antonio Tello de Guzmán penetrated across to the Pacific and occupied the tiny fishing hamlet called Panamá that same November, and a detachment under Diego de Albítez re-emerged due north at Nombre de Dios early in 1515, opening up a new transisthmian passage. In order to lay claim over this vital exit point, Pedrarias Dávila dispatched Capts. Gonzalo de Badajoz and Alonso Pérez de la Rúa westward from Santa María del Darién early in April 1515; they disembarked at Portobelo and began fighting their way inland—only to be defeated, Pérez de la Rúa being killed along with almost half of this Spanish force. When news of the disaster reached

Pedrarias Dávila, he sent Capt. Gaspar de Espinosa with 200 men to cruelly ravage Portobelo's interior.

But as the Pacific Ocean remained the true allure, Pedrarias Dávila eventually arrested and executed his youthful precursor Núñez de Balboa, then abandoned his capital of Santa María del Darién altogether in favor of shifting his entire administration over into Panama City by the summer of 1519. Albítez was simultaneously granted formal title to the tiny settlement that he had founded with a wooden stockade at Nombre de Dios, which, because of Santa María del Darién's eradication, was to thereafter serve as the main transisthmian transit point. Despite some doubts regarding the easy accessibility of the harbor at Nombre de Dios, a "highway" was nonetheless completed through the mountainous jungle ten years later, over which a steady stream of adventurers and goods traveled.

The volume of this traffic multiplied exponentially once the wealth of the recently conquered Incan empire of Peru began to be fully tapped during the late 1540s and early 1550s, silver bullion flowing out of the Pacific in prodigious amounts and attracting thousands of migrants through Nombre de Dios. Ship movements escalated so remarkably that a convoy system soon evolved, whereby a pair of royal warships would escort a merchant fleet across the Atlantic every spring from Seville, refreshing at Cartagena before entering Nombre de Dios, to be met by a throng of Peruvian and Panamanian traders so as to celebrate a great commercial fair, noteworthy for its wealth. All transactions concluded when the king's bullion from the Lima mint was conveyed across the isthmus from Panama City, so that the plate-fleet might weigh for Europe.

Over the next few decades, business swelled so remarkably that transatlantic galleons increased in size until they could no longer traverse the shallow, reef-lined bar at Nombre de Dios without first off-loading part of their cargoes. Its exposed anchorage moreover offered scant protection against Caribbean storms, while the tiny town of only thirty wooden structures surrounded by swamps flooded during any tropical cloudburst; also, its overland trails were unsuitable for bulk haulage—especially when compared with the shipments ferried by boat along the coastline to the lesser port of Chagres, 50 miles away.

As a result, when the king's Italian-born engineer Batista Antonelli made an inspection tour of the West Indies in 1585–1587, it was assumed that transisthmian service at Nombre de Dios would be relocated, and some officials even proposed a site as far away as Puerto Caballos (modern Puerto Cortés, Honduras). Antonelli, though, recommended that operations be shifted instead only around Point Manzanillo into Portobelo, describing the new port's attributes as its deep, safe anchorage with "clean ground or sand" at bottom, free of dangerous rocks or reefs; its high, protective headland; solid terrain upon which to found a city; abundant freshwater from a dozen small streams; large stands of trees for ship repairs; and greater proximity to Chagres.

Survey of the installations being erected around Portobelo's shorelines, ca. 1597, possibly rendered by the military engineer Batista Antonelli. Note how the highway to Panama City was to run eastward from the city-site at bottom center. (Archive of Indies, Seville)

Because of the slowness of administrative decisions referred across the Atlantic to Spain, in addition to the increased drain placed upon the royal exchequer by the outbreak of hostilities against Elizabethan England in 1588, authorization for this project and the allocation of the requisite funds—initially estimated at 100,000 ducats, to be raised out of new taxes—was not approved by Madrid until late December 1593. A "commission of constructions and fortifications" was thereupon appointed, consisting of Portobelo's designated new *alcalde mayor* (municipal magistrate) Miguel Ruiz del Duayen plus some other Panamanian officials, who were to supervise the planning and execution of all labors. These were to consist of the erection of defenses at both Portobelo and Chagres; the opening of a new highway; and construction of the new city itself, which the Crown indicated was to be christened San Felipe de Portobelo (Saint Philip of Fair Port).

Clearing the future urban site commenced in 1594 by 100 black slaves toiling under a few Spanish overseers who had been privately contracted by the rich merchant captains Juan de Magán and Melchor Suárez, because no official funds had as yet been raised for such a purpose. Antonelli himself did not reach Panama from his other fortification projects at Havana until Christmas 1594, then fell ill two days later, further delaying

progress. Nevertheless, some significant work was already under way by the next year, in particular the shore batteries at Portobelo and Chagres, despite the lack of slaves and equipment and outbreaks of disease. Moreover, many Panamanian merchants were proving reluctant to support these efforts actively, being unhappy at the prospect of relinquishing the properties that they had so painstakingly nurtured at Nombre de Dios.

Ironically, it was the English sea rover Sir Francis Drake who spurred matters, by boldly sailing into the latter port with a large fleet on 6 January 1596. Its outnumbered defenders retreated into the jungle, pursued past the way-station of Venta de la Quebrada by 600 to 700 Englishmen under Col.-Gen. Thomas Baskerville, until these invaders were checked by 70 Spanish troops dug in atop Capirilla Hill under Capt. Juan Enríquez Conabut on the morning of 9 January. Illness subsequently thinned English ranks at Nombre de Dios, so that they laid waste the town and departed westward on 25 January, pausing off Veragua to reprovision before reversing course on 2 February to assail the emergent installations at Portobelo.

Although Drake died of dysentery as his flagship *Defiance* was closing upon its entrance—his body being committed to the waves off an island that has been remembered ever since as the Isla de Draque—Portobelo's incomplete defenses were incapable of keeping out his fleet, which easily pushed past and occupied the fledgling town for eleven days. They noted that it consisted of only eight to ten dwellings, "besides a great new house" that was being erected as a government palace, the whole protected by a very strong battery "with flankers of great trees and stones filled with earth." The raiders threw down or burned everything before departing on 18 February.

Plate-Fleet Terminal (1597–1667)

Galvanized by these twin disasters, as well as by the need to reconstitute at least one defensible port quickly, so as to receive the annual convoy expected from Seville, the Spaniards had decided on 26 January 1596 to forsake Nombre de Dios in favor of concentrating all their reconstruction efforts at Portobelo. The royal crier duly read out a decree at Panama City that ordered all Nombre de Dios property owners to erect a new dwelling at Portobelo "with a tiled roof and not of straw" within fifteen days of being assigned a plot or else lose their land titles. Moreover, anyone who rebuilt at Nombre de Dios would have that structure torched at his own expense, plus be fined 500 pesos. A private counterpetition raised in hopes of deferring this directive was rejected, and even the subsequent arrival of that year's plate-fleet under Adm. Juan Escalante de Mendoza at the traditional Nombre de Dios anchorage on 23 April failed to rescind the relocation order.

Antonelli—who had been supervising entrenchment work at Chagres when Drake died—set about resurrecting Portobelo's 8-gun earthen battery as of 15 July 1596, then also better aligned its town plots, as well as directing the cutting of a new transisthmian road. A few private buildings soon began to emerge, plus a Mercedarian convent designed by Juan de Avendaño, while the *cabildo* (town council) was formally transferred from Nombre de Dios and reconstituted at Portobelo by Francisco Valverde y Mercado as of 20 March 1597 (leaving the remnants of Nombre de Dios to become overgrown by jungle, not being reinhabited until the twentieth century).

The royal engineer then turned his attention to further strengthening Portobelo's harbor defenses by initiating construction on 11 September 1597 of a 4-gun fortress atop its northern headland that was to be named San Felipe de Sotomayor in honor of both Philip II of Spain and the youthful governor of Panama, Alonso de Sotomayor y Andia, knight of the Order of Santiago. Large chunks of brain coral were extracted from the waters for this purpose, proving easy to cut while fresh; yet once set with lime and baked by the sun, they dried into such solid blocks that the resultant edifice soon became nicknamed Todo Fierro (All Iron) Castle. Its arches, and domes such as watchtower roofs, were made of small clay bricks lacquered with red wash, while the exterior walls were coated with lime and whitewashed, giving a dazzling appearance.

View northwestward from the ruined ramparts of Santiago de la Gloria Castle, ca. 1913, looking across Portobelo's anchorage toward Fort San Felipe de Sotomayor, as it was being demolished and removed from its headland. (Abbot, *Panama and the Canal*)

Labors paused in mid-September 1598 to receive the battle-fleet of Adm. Luis Faxardo, which arrived to convey a vital shipment of Peruvian bullion across to the hard-pressed Spanish exchequer, after which construction resumed. The same building materials were used to supplant the earthen battery beside the town with a stout new redoubt christened Santiago de la Gloria (Saint James of Glory). The first scheduled plate-fleet entered Portobelo on 10 March 1599, followed on 16 April by yet another battle squadron under Adm. Francisco Coloma. By this time, Antonelli had grown so old and infirm as to be allowed to return to Europe, being succeeded as engineer by Hernando de Sotomayor, who expanded Fort San Felipe by adding gun platforms for twenty artillery pieces close to its waterline, plus several more tiers and towers above.

Such work was still proceeding when the English privateer William Parker stole into Portobelo's harbor in February 1601 with his 120-ton flagship *Prudence,* accompanied by the 60-ton *Pearl* of Capt. Robert Rawlins and a 20-ton pinnace, to slip 200 men into the unwary town and chase its 100 defenders under *castellano* (garrison commander) Capt. Pedro Meléndez inland, before setting fire to the Triana suburb and escaping with 10,000 ducats' worth of booty. Alarmed by the ease of this penetration only four months prior to the arrival of Portobelo's second commercial plate-fleet, Crown authorities even considered relocating the town to a site called San Cristóbal at the eastern end of the bay. There, a protective circuit of walls might be added, but they were deemed impractical at the San Felipe site because of the narrow expanse left between its beachfront and the encroaching hills.

Nevertheless, abandoning so many brand-new buildings proved a deterrent, while the shallowness of the stinking mud flats at the Cascajal River mouth would have further complicated the task of servicing galleons, which would have to continue anchoring in the middle of the bay. Therefore, the engineer Hernando de Montoya suggested replacing Santiago de la Gloria Battery atop Chorrillo Hill with a fort to better defend the existing town. By January 1603 his successor—Capt. Eriburcio Españolés—was able to report this project well advanced, the San Antonio and San Francisco bastions having already been completed, four cannon installed into its tower, and living quarters for transient dignitaries about to be added.

When hostilities against England finally ceased in late August 1604, Portobelo's nominal population had stabilized at fifty to sixty Spanish households comprising several hundred people, plus more than 300 slaves who toiled as stevedores; its garrison was supposed to be maintained at 300 soldiers to defend both its San Felipe and Santiago de la Gloria strongholds. However, military complements were to remain chronically understrength because of repeated bouts of disease or desertion, while leading citizens also preferred avoiding the stifling, pestilential coastal town during its *tiempo muerto* (dead time) prior to the anticipated plate-fleet arrival every spring, residing instead more comfortably at Panama City. (During his inspection tour in 1622, Gov. Rodrigo de Vivero y Velasco

Remnants of the once busy *camino real* or "royal highway" outside Portobelo, ca. 1913. (Abbot, *Panama and the Canal*)

reported that only thirteen Spaniards actually lived at Portobelo year-round; other major Spanish-American ports such as Cartagena, or Veracruz and Acapulco in Mexico, experienced similar seasonal absences.)

Large merchant companies also preferred warehousing their goods in the greater safety of the capital, sending commodities across the isthmus once word was received that the galleons had reached at Cartagena. Two routes were available: overland by mule train or with lighters via the Chagres River. As this latter method was only half or one-third the cost, despite being monopolized by a handful of boat owners, traders usually preshipped bulk items early in the year so as to have an inventory on hand at Portobelo. Pack animals carried such loads the 18 steep and tortuous miles from Panama City up the Río Grande Valley and down Obispo Valley on the far side of the Continental Divide, into a way-station called Venta de Cruces. There, they were transferred by coolies aboard some of the 30- to 35-ton *chatas*—or smaller *bongos* of 15 tons apiece—that sailed down the snaking river to exit 44 miles away at Chagres, then hug the open coast as far as Portobelo. Such consignments normally took two weeks to arrive, if spring droughts had not dried up the river course, which would require additional portages.

Once the Peruvian silver convoy reached Panama City and the galleons from Spain actually dropped anchor at Portobelo, the port sprang into life and transisthmian traffic accelerated. The 1,000 to 2,000 mules engaged in *trajín* (literally "haulage," a term applied to the conveyance of all goods back and forth) became fully committed to shuttling bullion and other high-value items directly overland, taking roughly four days to complete each traverse. Once the commercial fair concluded, these same teams—consisting of approximately thirty mules and nine teamsters apiece—would resume servicing the bulk river traffic via the Cruces way-station, as traders began bringing their purchased cargoes back upriver (oftentimes retarded by the strong countercurrents that developed during the rainy season of June through December, especially along the final 4.5-mile stretch between Gorgona and Cruces).

Portobelo's fairs were celebrated every year between 1616 and 1640, constituting the town's glorious heyday. Once an *aviso* (dispatch-boat) arrived with news that a plate-fleet had reached Cartagena, and the Peruvian convoy appeared off Panama City, hundreds of traders, Crown officials, soldiers, teamsters, and slaves began streaming up the jungle trails to initiate the fair. Only a fortunate few could find shelter in Portobelo's handful of dwellings, most transients having to extemporize grass shacks in a designated area between the town and Santiago de la Gloria Castle. Thousands more sailors, passengers, and merchants were disgorged as each galleon anchored, their cargoes being lightered ashore to be landed on the beach below Santiago de la Gloria or in front of the town's main *aduana* (customshouse), as Portobelo had no jetty. They were then inspected and hauled by carts into separate corrals in the main square, shaded from the scorching sunlight by galleon sails and illuminated at night by ships' lanterns.

Both groups of travelers, weakened by their respective transatlantic or transisthmian traverses, in addition to Portobelo's own hot and humid climate, were prone to illnesses amid the unsanitary living conditions of these crowded cantonments, frequently resulting in hundreds of deaths. Even Panamanian governors, with standing orders to be present so as to prevent tax fraud and adjudicate disputes, were not immune. Iñigo de la Mota Sarmiento succumbed in Portobelo in 1642, which same fate befell Juan Bitrián Navarra y Biamonte on 6 December 1651. Yet the spectacular riches transacted by South American and Spanish commercial houses ensured attendance and made the tropical seaport's name a universal byword for wealth, Portobelo being referred to by the modern Latin American historian Juan Manuel Zapatero as the *teatro del mayor mercado del orbe* (theater for the greatest market on the globe).

Panamanian governors commonly served as spokesmen for the Peruvian merchants, while fleet admirals did the same on behalf of the Spanish representatives, who were prohibited from venturing beyond Portobelo. Crates, bales, and boxes commonly piled up in the town's narrow streets until they could be shipped toward Chagres or ferried aboard the anchored galleons. After a month and a half, sales typically wound down and the royal bullion arrived across the isthmus to be loaded aboard the warship escorts for departure. Revenues derived from housing, feeding, and tending to such a plentiful concurrence helped finance the erection of numerous new private and municipal edifices in Portobelo, work even commencing in 1653 on an additional water fort to the east of town—a full-blown castle that was to become designated as San Gerónimo or San Jerónimo. It was envisioned as eventually supplanting Santiago de la Gloria, as the new fort's position out in shallow water would render it immune to land assaults or close-range naval bombardment.

However, Spain's fortunes began to plummet dramatically during the second half of the seventeenth century, so that plate-fleets would call at Portobelo only every other year or so between 1651 and 1663, and incomes became irregular. Eventually, the water fort's *castellano* (garrison commander), Pedro de Arredondo, deemed all outstanding labors as too costly for the exchequer, so that its design was scaled back and downgraded into a smaller *fortaleza*. In April of that same year of 1663, the town also suffered a great calamity when fire consumed forty-six of its buildings, and Panama's governor, Fernando Ibáñez de la Riva Agüero, died while attending the annual fair. Worse still, this was to be the last plate-fleet to visit Portobelo for another thirteen years, as Spain's imperial economy had utterly collapsed, curtailing most transatlantic traffic. As the enfeebled Crown strove to expel rival foreign outposts springing up throughout the Caribbean, a hostile backlash came to be directed against the once great Spanish seaport.

Overgrown ruins of Portobelo's seventeenth-century Casa Real or "Royal Office," as it appeared, ca. 1913. (Abbot, *Panama and the Canal*)

Morgan's Raid and Commercial Decline (1668–1738)

Late in 1667, Gov. Thomas Modyford of the burgeoning English colony of Jamaica commissioned Henry Morgan—recently promoted colonel of the Port Royal militia—"to draw together the English privateers (throughout the West Indies) and take prisoners of the Spanish nation, whereby he might inform of the intention of that enemy to invade." Such an open-ended license was also meant to bestow the unofficial mantle of buccaneer "admiral" upon Morgan, as mercenaries flocked to his banner from throughout the region.

The next year, his four frigates and eight sloops anchored at Bocas del Toro on the Central American coast, transferring several hundred men aboard twenty-three piraguas and smaller boats to stealthily row 150 miles eastward against the contrary winds and currents, arriving undetected just west of Portobelo on the afternoon of 10 July 1668. That night his flotilla disgorged its landing parties, and Morgan led them in

a swift overland march, taking the stunned Spanish citizenry completely by surprise at daybreak and overrunning the town without suffering a single casualty. The eighty-man garrison holding Santiago de la Gloria citadel resisted for a couple of hours longer, until Morgan rounded up a group of captives—including the town's *alcalde mayor,* two friars, and several women and nuns—who acted as human shields for a party of buccaneers that charged the castle's wooden gate bearing torches and axes. The defenders reluctantly opened fire, wounding two clerics and killing an Englishman, yet were unable to prevent the sappers from reaching the portal.

Simultaneously, another band of buccaneers used scaling ladders to enter unobserved on the far side of the fortress, carrying it by storm; at least 45 Spanish soldiers perished during a vicious bloodbath, the rest being wounded. The following morning, Morgan led 200 buccaneers across the bay to subdue the 50 soldiers watching from the San Felipe harbor-castle, thereby allowing his ships to enter from the Bocas del Toro anchorage. At a cost of 18 buccaneers dead, Portobelo had been seized, after which its wealthiest citizens were tortured to reveal their hidden treasures and many other excesses committed. Morgan thereupon sent a letter on 14 July to the acting president of Panama's *Audiencia*, Agustín de Bracamonte, saying: "Tomorrow we plan to burn this city to the ground and then set sail with all the guns and munitions from the castles." However, the freebooter offered to spare Portobelo for a ransom of 350,000 pesos, which the president—already marching to its relief at the head of 800 militiamen—refused.

Morgan consequently dug in and wrote back that he now intended to resist, adding that he was releasing all his Spanish captives, "since I do not believe that you have sufficient men to fight with me tomorrow." Much to Bracamonte's chagrin, his army proved too weak to assault the buccaneers inside Portobelo when he arrived outside the next day so that his troops were forced to encamp for a miserable week in the jungle. Finally, the president ordered a retreat on 24 July 1668, leaving a subordinate to negotiate the ransom, which was eventually set at 100,000 pesos and paid during the first days of August. After that, Morgan sailed away to a hero's welcome at Port Royal.

Already weakened by commercial decline, Portobelo struggled to recuperate from this rapacious raid, and when news of it reached Madrid, Queen Regent Mariana furthermore authorized all Spanish-American officials on 20 April 1669 to issue privateering commissions against English vessels, deepening regional tensions. Less than two years later, Morgan made another descent that seized Portobelo's subsidiary port of Chagres, from where he led an army across the isthmus to sack and burn Panama City in late January 1671. Transisthmian trade did not begin to revive significantly until a treaty could be concluded between Madrid and London, allowing Spanish plate-fleets to once again celebrate fairs in Portobelo in 1676 and 1679.

But in January 1680, the Jamaican privateer John Coxon gathered eight English and French *flibustier* captains at Golden Island off northeastern Panama for another piratical assault, bringing 330 men in boats into the Gulf of San Blas from where they stole afoot down the Cascajal River Valley to avoid Spanish coast watchers. After three days, they were spotted by a tribesman in a village 3 miles short of Portobelo, who set off at a run to warn its Spanish inhabitants. The footsore buccaneers trotted in pursuit, yet the Indian arrived a half hour before them and raised the alarm. The pirate vanguard was still able to sweep Portobelo unopposed, as the Spaniards withdrew inside Santiago de la Gloria, leaving their dwellings and warehouses to be ransacked over the next two days. Coxon's raiders then retired 10 miles northeast to a coastal hamlet known as Bastimentos, entrenching themselves with a few prisoners on a cay a half mile offshore to await their ships. Three days later, several hundred Spanish militiamen hastened

across the isthmus from Panama City and began firing upon the pirates from the beach, yet they were unable to exact any vengeance before Coxon's vessels appeared. The pirates subsequently imposed a brief blockade upon Portobelo, intercepting a pair of coastal craft before distributing their booty and dispersing.

Despite lingering fears, plate-fleet fairs were held successfully at Portobelo in 1682 and 1686; nor did France's declaration of war in April 1689 unduly discomfit the town, as Spain was aligned in a strong naval alliance with England and Holland that allowed another commercial fair to be celebrated in 1691. However, during the closing phases of that conflict six years later, the strategic port of Cartagena was devastated by a French expedition under Adm. Bernard Jean-Louis de Saint Jean, Baron de Pointis, complicating the traffic patterns bound in and out of Portobelo. Another plate-fleet was nonetheless received in 1698, the year after peace had been restored in Europe, although trade volumes were now considerably depleted because of Spain's continual insolvency.

A small group of Scottish colonizers established an intruder settlement at nearby Darién that same year, requiring Adm. Andrés de Pez to hasten into Portobelo from Cartagena on 16

San Blas Indians, ca. 1925. (Carpenter, *Lands of the Caribbean*)

January 1699 with four warships of the Spanish West Indian squadron (the Armada de Barlovento). He left his vessels at anchor in the harbor while leading 500 seamen in an overland trek that stalled 6 miles short of its objective because of heavy rain and impassable terrain. Pez then retreated back into Portobelo because of reports of an approaching English squadron under Rear Adm. John Benbow, and although that proved to be only a peaceful diplomatic overture, the Spanish commander had nonetheless lost ninety men through desertion, plus another eighty because of illness.

Despite being ordered to remain anchored at Portobelo by the *Audiencia* president, Pedro Luis Enríquez, Conde de Canillas de Torneros, Pez sailed for Cartagena that same summer, obliging the president to personally lead a company of soldiers across the isthmus in April 1701 to defend the port against any contemplated British descents. Canillas died in Portobelo on 14 October, and it was subsequently learned that the Scots had abandoned Darién because of disease, dissent, and lack of profits. Yet a threat recurred when Benbow returned into the Caribbean the following month with a large fleet, as the major European powers were now openly maneuvering to dispute the succession of the French princeling Philip of Anjou to the Spanish throne, and war was imminent.

Portobelo's trade was once again interrupted and no plate-fleet could dash across the hostile Atlantic until the winter of 1707–1708, when a convoy at last arrived under Adm. José Fernández de Santillán, Conde de Casa Alegre. His dozen vessels and five accompanying French privateers were waylaid on their return leg into Cartagena on 8 June by Commo. Charles Wager's four Royal Navy warships, Casa Alegre's 64-gun flagship *San José* being sunk and a rich 44-gun merchantman captured. The British subsequently started a brisk smuggling trade at Bastimentos, while maintaining such a close blockade of Portobelo that when its Spanish traffic cautiously attempted to resume three years later, Commo. James Littleton made yet another successful interception outside Cartagena on 6 August 1711.

Once the War of the Spanish Succession, or Queen Anne's War, finally ceased two years afterward, Portobelans hoped to benefit from an overhaul of the ramshackle imperial system being initiated by the new Bourbon rulers in Madrid. In 1717, for example, the provinces that today constitute Panama, Colombia, Venezuela, and Ecuador were separated from Peruvian control and merged into a new "Viceroyalty of New Granada," and a plate-fleet was received at Portobelo in 1721. Yet this new viceroyalty's creation was rescinded two years afterward, and when another plate-fleet entered port in 1726, Portobelo was to become beleaguered as a pawn in a festering diplomatic rift in Europe.

The British government, concerned that Madrid's recent alliance with Austria might lend added weight to its claims for the restoration of Gibraltar and Minorca, forged a coalition of its own with France, Hanover, and Prussia (later joined by Hol-

land, Sweden, and Denmark). Worried that another war loomed, Spain's ministers countered at the end of March 1726 by ordering their American officials to confiscate English goods. Vice Adm. Francis Hosier consequently appeared off Bastimentos on 16 June with eleven ships-of-the-line, a frigate, plus three smaller consorts, presenting such a threat to the treasure-fleet waiting to be loaded at Portobelo that the *Audiencia* president inquired the reason for Hosier's presence. The English admiral replied that he had come to escort home the South Sea Company slaver *Royal George* from an authorized visit into port; yet even after that vessel had cleared, the Royal Navy fleet hovered menacingly in the distance, so that the Spaniards canceled their convoy's departure. Hosier thereupon instituted a close blockade of luckless Portobelo, preventing all ships from entering or departing until mid-December, when he finally retreated to Jamaica with his crews ravaged by disease.

Open warfare was narrowly averted, thanks to a diplomatic resolution in Europe, so that the delayed convoy was finally able to sail early the next year; another plate-fleet visit was made by Adm. Manuel López Pintado in 1730–1731. Nevertheless, Portobelo's best days were now clearly behind it, repeated interruptions in transatlantic traffic having stunted any hopes of urban development; its population remained only a few score residents, a few hundred slaves, and a couple of hundred disgruntled soldiers clustered inside its steamy harbor, eking out a meager subsistence by servicing small coastal craft or fishing boats without any of the great windfall profits previously obtained from the thousands of transients accompanying the plate-fleets.

Yet to British traders, increasingly frustrated by Madrid's impediments to opening its Spanish-American markets, Portobelo's vaunted reputation was to make it a target for retribution. When the plate-fleet of Vice Adm. Blas de Lezo—a pair of warships and seven merchantmen bearing almost 1,900 tons in goods—unexpectedly reached Cartagena in March 1737, the promised fair had to be postponed, as a huge fire had destroyed two-thirds of Panama City, and Peru's traders in its aftermath proved slow to replace their lost consignments. War with Britain threatened the next spring, and the Peruvian convoy did not clear Callao for Panama until 28 June 1739; before Lezo's plate-fleet could complete its crossing into Portobelo to initiate trading, the sloop of José de Barandica hastened into the Panamanian harbor from Cuba on 8 November with news that Britain had declared war.

Devastation (1739–1748)

Notwithstanding this alert, Vice Adm. Edward Vernon was able to emerge undetected 7–8 miles northeast of Portobelo on 1 December 1739, his half dozen warships and two tenders weathering the Salmedina Group next dawn, before rushing directly into Portobelo's harbor that afternoon. The startled garrison of Fort San Felipe—referred to as "Iron Castle" by

Sleepy street scene in Portobelo, ca. 1913. (Abbot, *Panama and the Canal*)

the English—were caught so unprepared that fifty-three Spanish marines under naval Lt. Juan Francisco Garganta had to be rowed across from the anchored coast guard vessels to raise its strength to ninety men; yet only nine of San Felipe's thirty-two guns were also serviceable, quickly reduced to four by the British bombardment. By 4:30 P.M., as English boat parties closed in upon the battered citadel, scarcely five Spanish officers and thirty-five men remained to surrender, the rest having fled.

The invaders thereupon shifted their fire against Santiago de Gloria Castle, sinking a Spanish sloop and doing other damage before eventually halting action at nightfall. At 5:30 on the morning of 2 December 1739, Vernon's squadron began working more deeply into the bay, only to be greeted by a launch sent by Lt.-Gov. Francisco Javier Martínez de la Vega y Retes to request terms. Vernon allowed until 3:00 P.M. for his conditions to be accepted, while continuing to warp his ships into the roadstead. Many Portobelans having already fled inland, drunken looters were ransacking empty dwellings by the time the town capitulated that same afternoon. The English met no resistance, their casualties having totaled three dead and six wounded.

Vernon brought a halt to all plundering, then reassured the few remaining inhabitants that Britain's fight was against the Spanish Crown, not the Portobelans themselves. On 3 December 1739 he furthermore addressed letters to the authorities at Panama and Cartagena, announcing that Portobelo was to be left unoccupied and unblockaded as a neutral seaport, so long as Spanish officials and *guardacostas* permitted free trade. He also requested the release of Francis Humphreys and other detained members of the South Sea Company from the isthmian capital.

The *Audiencia* president, Dionisio Martínez de la Vega, agreed to only this latter demand twelve days later, hoping thereby to spare Portobelo from being destroyed, along with the large amounts of cacao and vicuna wool already accumulated in its warehouses. The port's royal accountant, Francisco García Vicente, was consequently dispatched across the isthmus with the captives, which Vernon was pleased to acknowledge on 20 December 1739. However, in keeping with London's global objectives, he nonetheless ordered all major defenses thrown down and every artillery piece ferried aboard his ships so as to leave Portobelo "an open and defenseless bay" before withdrawing four days afterward. The Spanish soon reasserted control but were powerless to prevent Vernon from re-entering the unprotected harbor on 25 March 1740 to water his squadron before proceeding to Chagres to level its fortifications as well.

Portobelo suffered another descent two years later, when the veteran West Indian rover George Lowther—brevetted as a Royal Navy lieutenant, and in command of the sloop *Triton*—proposed to Vernon that a regiment of 500 to 600 men be landed at Nombre de Dios to hasten inland and cut off the Portobelo-to-Panama highway, thus intercepting any reports of a subsequent disembarkation by another 2,500 redcoats at Portobelo to traverse the isthmus and seize Panama City itself. However, Vernon was obliged to sail directly into Portobelo Bay at 4:30 P.M. on 8 April 1742, allowing its garrison commander Juan José Colomo ample time to retire into the interior with his 80 Spanish regulars and 300 militiamen, as well as to dispatch a warning overland to the capital. When the English came ashore and discovered that the defenders had already melted into the jungle, as well as having almost 1,000 redcoats fall sick, the English army commanders lost heart and departed for Jamaica aboard their transports on 20 April, fol-

lowed five days later by Vernon's eight ships-of-the-line and three lesser craft.

The unhappy and gutted town once again returned to Spanish domination, but when Dionisio Alsedo y Herrera succeeded Martínez de la Vega as governor of Panama and inspected Portobelo's ruined defenses in late June 1743, he deemed any major reconstruction efforts as impracticable because of the ongoing hostilities, so that only a few entrenchments and redoubts were dug along its shoreline. These proved so unprepossessing that when the English merchant captain William Kinghill appeared on 2 August 1744, demanding the return of one of his ships, he was able to batter the town with a prolonged and unopposed bombardment as punishment.

Loss of Monopoly (1749–1809)

It was not until peace with Britain was finally restored in October 1748 that Spanish Crown officials could begin making a concerted effort to reconstitute Portobelo. Remembering the vital strategic link once provided by the north isthmian port, Peru's viceroy, José Antonio Manso y Velasco, Conde de

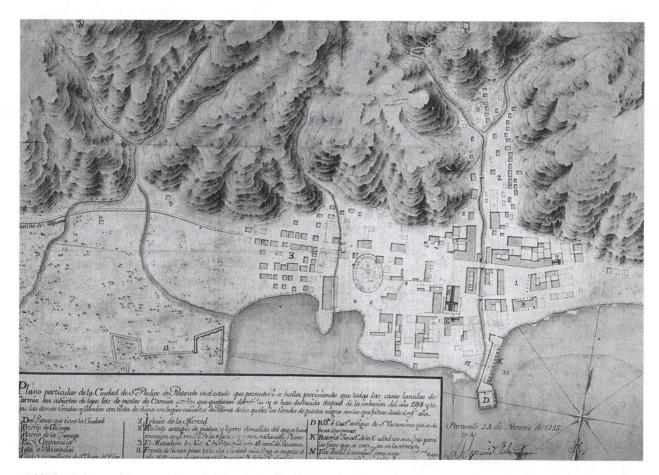

Highly detailed map of the town of Portobelo as surveyed in January 1753 by the military engineer, Brigadier Ignacio de Sala, as its harbor defenses were about to be resurrected from damages inflicted by the English assaults of more than a decade earlier, during the War of Jenkins's Ear. North is toward bottom. (Servicio Histórico Militar, Madrid)

Superunda, subsidized a large-scale resurrection of the harbor defenses from the Lima treasury as of the mid-1750s; Portobelo's permanent garrison was also augmented to a full infantry regiment and artillery company, while new heavy guns were brought round Cape Horn from Spain to be installed.

Yet Vernon's raids had also revealed that the plate-fleet system had become outdated and should not be reinstituted. Spanish ministers had already noted how the 1,900 tons of goods that de Lezo's fleet had conveyed into Cartagena had been easily diverted up the Magdalena River for sale into the interior of the viceroyalty of New Granada—some even traveling as far as Honda, to be sold to Peruvian merchants who had withdrawn their funds from Panama City and circled round via the Pacific port of Guayaquil, expressly to meet these consignments. Madrid therefore realized that it would be more advantageous to dispense with the cumbersome, centuries-old practice of annual convoys, and instead gradually inaugurate a policy of independent sailings to more diverse destinations such as Cartagena and Buenos Aires. Such widespread traffic would moreover preclude any enemy descent against a single economic choke point during times of war.

Yet for Portobelo, such a policy shift effectively ended its role as a commercial entrepot and doomed its future evolution as a city. The individual vessels called *registros sueltos* that replaced the treasure fleets bore relatively modest cargoes, and most steered for more accessible and profitable destinations such as La Guaira, Cartagena, Buenos Aires, and even around Cape Horn. The few persistent Portobelans soon understood that even their depleted prewar trade volumes could never be reattained and so abandoned their once flourishing businesses. As early as the 1760s, Manuel Amat y Junient—Superunda's successor as Peruvian viceroy—was lamenting that Panama's Pacific traffic had been reduced to a mere single slaver a year, while its merchants struggled to survive by smuggling foreign goods in through Bastimentos. Despair reached its lowest level once Buenos Aires was licensed to handle vast amounts of South American exports as of the late

Overgrown graveyard for American canal workers, beside old Fort San Fernando, ca. 1913. (Abbot, *Panama and the Canal*)

1770s, and trade restrictions generally began to be eased throughout the continent. Portobelo was one city that would fail to profit significantly from the late-colonial economic upsurge that these measures generated.

False Revival (1810–1821)

Ironically, it was to be the eruption of many South American insurgencies seeking independence from Spain as of 1808 that produced an unexpected revitalization in Panamanian traffic—most especially after the declarations of independence by Argentina and Colombia in May 1810, which denied the major ports of Buenos Aires and Cartagena to Spanish vessels. The transisthmian route had to be renewed by the Crown as an alternative means of dispatching the troops and materiel needed to sustain Loyalist holdouts in Peru, Ecuador, and Chile. In 1812 the viceroy-designate for New Granada, Benito Pérez, even took up temporary residence in Panama City because his official capital of Bogotá lay in rebel-controlled territory.

Yet once royalist fortunes began to wane in the early 1820s, so did the flow of military personnel, money, and supplies across the isthmus, and Portobelo was to relapse into even deeper torpor after Panama joined the insurgent cause on 28 November 1821 and became incorporated as a province into Simón Bolívar's ramshackle "Republic of Gran Colombia."

Desolation (1822–Present)

With the collapse of the Spanish empire, interest in Portobelo evaporated for the next two decades, leaving the once proud city utterly destitute, except for its tiny local fisheries. Transisthmian traffic finally revived when gold was discovered in California in 1848, bringing thousands of seaborne prospectors to Panama's shores for transshipment, but the foreign firms that sought to profit from this onrush by carving a faster passageway across to the Pacific bypassed Portobelo, through sheer ill luck.

Initially, the New York financier William H. Aspinwall formed the Pacific Mail Steamship Company, then dispatched a survey team to Navy Bay to find a suitable spot for a Caribbean railway terminal; his rival George Law of the United States Mail Steam Line meanwhile sent "Colonel" Albert Zwingle as his confidential agent to Portobelo, who bought options all along that community's coastline within a matter of days. However, when Law subsequently attempted to use this property to extort a huge block of stock from Aspinwall, as well as to wrest a seat upon the board of his newly constituted Panama Railroad Company, the latter refused to submit and instead insisted upon establishing his railhead on territory that he controlled—pestilential Manzanillo Island, opposite the ominously named Black Swamp—rather than share ownership with Law. Portobelo's prospects were therefore dashed, and the withered city plunged back into neglect, being ignored as enormous throngs of passengers traversed the isthmus via Aspinwall's chosen route.

Even during the construction of the Panama Canal in the first decade of the twentieth century, Portobelo continued to be overlooked, except for a decision to level its San Felipe harbor-castle and a goodly portion of its northern headland with dynamite, so that the resultant stony rubble might be used to prevent erosion by lining the banks of the canal's Gatún Passage. A temporary work camp dubbed "New Portobelo" was established at the foot of San Felipe Hill for this purpose, a plot beside its old San Fernando Fort being converted into a graveyard for the scores of American workers who succumbed during the ensuing months of heavy labor.

In modern times, an initiative has been launched to tap into the forgotten city's romantic past by upgrading Portobelo's infrastructure and elevating it into a major tourist destination, with luxury hotels sprouting around its sheltered bay, beside the ruins of such ancient historical structures as Forts Santiago and San Jerónimo.

For further reading on the history of Portobelo or of Panama, please consult the Select Bibliography at the end of this volume.

Select Bibliography

General Studies and Specialized Journals

Abrams, Charles. *Housing in the Modern World: Man's Struggle for Shelter in an Urbanizing World.* Cambridge and London: Massachusetts Institute of Technology Press and Faber and Faber, 1964.

Alden, John, editor. *European Americana: A Chronological Guide to Works Printed in Europe Relating to the Americas, 1493–1776.* New York: Readex Books, 1980–1988, six volumes.

Bairoch, Paul. *Cities and Economic Development: From the Dawn of History to the Present.* Chicago: University of Chicago Press, 1988.

Bennett, Ralph, editor. *Settlements in the Americas: Cross-Cultural Perspectives.* Newark: University of Delaware Press, 1991.

Blumenfeld, Hans. *The Modern Metropolis: Its Origins, Growth, Characteristics, and Planning.* Cambridge: Massachusetts Institute of Technology Press, 1967.

Blumenfeld, Hans, editor. *Internal Structure of the City: Readings on Urban Form, Growth and Policy.* New York: Oxford University Press, 1982 re-edition of 1971 original.

Bourne, Larry S. *The Geography of Housing.* London: Arnold, 1981.

Breese, Gerald. *Urbanization in Newly Developing Countries.* Englewood Cliffs, NJ: Prentice-Hall, 1966.

Briggs, Asa. *Victorian Cities.* Harmondsworth: Penguin, 1968.

Buisseret, David J., editor. *Envisioning the City: Six Studies in Urban Cartography.* Chicago: University of Chicago Press, 1998.

Burnett, John. *A Social History of Housing, 1815–1985.* New York: Methuen, 1986.

Burns, E. Bradford. "Visual History." *Américas [Organization of American States]* 26, Number 8 (August 1974): 5–12.

Calendar of State Papers: Colonial Series, America and West Indies. London: Her Majesty's Stationery Office, 1860–1969, forty-four volumes.

Carter, H. *An Introduction to Urban Historical Geography.* London, 1983.

Castells, Manuel. *City, Class, and Power.* New York: St. Martin's Press, 1978.

———. *The City and the Grassroots: A Cross-Cultural Theory of Urban Social Movements.* Berkeley: University of California Press, 1983.

Chapin, F. S., Jr., and S. F. Weiss. *Urban Growth Dynamics in a Regional Cluster of Cities.* New York: Wiley, 1962.

Conway, D. "Changing Perspectives on Squatter Settlements, Intraurban Mobility, and Constraints on Housing Choice of the Third World Urban Poor." *Urban Geography* 6 (1985): 170–192.

Davis, Kingsley. "The Urbanization of the Human Population." *Scientific American* 213 (September 1965): 40–53.

———. *World Urbanization, 1950–1970, Volume I: Basic Data for Cities, Countries, and Regions.* Berkeley: Institute of International Studies, University of California, 1969.

De la Croix, Horst. *Military Considerations in City Planning: Fortifications.* New York: G. Braziller, 1972.

Duncan, Otis Dudley, et al. *Statistical Geography.* New York: Free Press, 1961.

Eames, Edwin, and Judith Granich Goode. *Anthropology of the City: An Introduction to Urban Anthropology.* Englewood Cliffs, NJ: Prentice-Hall, 1977.

Elliot, James. *The City in Maps: Urban Mapping to 1900.* London: British Library, 1987.

Fox, Richard. *Urban Anthropology: Cities in Their Cultural Settings.* Englewood Cliffs, NJ: Prentice-Hall, 1977.

Gutkind, E. A. *International History of City Development.* New York and London: Collier-MacMillan, 1970–1972, six volumes.

Hall, Peter. *The World Cities.* New York: McGraw-Hill, 1966.

Harvey, David. *Consciousness and the Urban Experience: Studies in the History and Theory of Capitalist Urbanization.* Baltimore: Johns Hopkins University Press, 1985.

Hatt, Paul K., and Albert J. Reiss, Jr., editors. *Cities and Society: The Revised Reader in Urban Sociology.* New York: Glencoe, 1957.

Hauser, Philip M., and Leo F. Schnore, editors. *The Study of Urbanization.* New York: Wiley, 1965.

Home, Robert. *Of Planting and Planning: The Making of British Colonial Cities.* London, 1997.

Hughes, Thomas P. *Networks of Power: Electrification in Western Society, 1880–1930.* Baltimore: Johns Hopkins University Press, 1983.

Johnston, R. J. *Urban Residential Patterns: An Introductory Review.* London: Bell, 1971.

Jones, Ronald, editor. *Essays on World Urbanization.* London: George Philip, 1975.

Kidder Smith, G. E. *Source Book of American Architecture: 500 Notable Buildings from the 10th Century to the Present.* Princeton: Princeton University Press, 1996.

Klemp, Egon. *America in Maps Dating from 1500–1856.* New York: Holmes and Meier, 1976.

Knight, Franklin W., and Peggy K. Liss, editors. *Atlantic Port Cities: Economy, Culture, and Society in the Atlantic World, 1650–1850.* Knoxville: University of Tennessee, 1991.

Lavedan, Pierre. *Histoire de l'urbanisme.* Paris: H. Laurens, 1959, two volumes.

Lees, Andrew. *Cities Perceived: Urban Society in European and American Thought, 1820–1940.* Manchester, UK: Manchester University Press, 1985.

Ley, David. *The New Middle Class and the Remaking of the Central City.* New York: Oxford University Press, 1995.

McGee, T. G. *The Urbanization Process in the Third World.* London: Bell, 1971.

McGrath, Dorn C., Jr., and Manuel Ungaro Zevallos. "A Silence Broken." *Américas [Organization of American States]* 31, Number 2 (February 1979): 16–25.

McShane, Clay. "The Origins and Globalization of Traffic Control Signals." *Journal of Urban History* 25, Number 3 (March 1999): 379–404.

Mora, Gilles. "Walker Evans et la ville." *Revue française d'études américaines [France]* 14, Number 39 (1989): 57–62.

Moses, Robert. *Public Works: A Dangerous Trade.* New York: McGraw-Hill, 1970.

Pinto, John. "Origins and Development of the Ichnographic City Plan." *Journal of the Society of Architectural Historians* 35 (1976): 35–50.

Ports of the World, 1972. London: Benn Brothers, 1971.

Potter, Robert B. *Urbanisation and Planning in the Third World: Spatial Perceptions and Public Participation.* New York: St. Martin's Press, 1985.

Rasmussen, Eiler. *Towns and Buildings.* Liverpool: University of Liverpool Press, 1951.

Rondinelli, Dennis, et al. "The Changing Forces of Urban Economic Development: Globalization and City Competitiveness in the 21st Century." *Cityscape* 3, Number 3 (1998): 71–105.

Santos, Milton. *Les villes du Tiers Monde.* Paris: Génine, 1971.

Schaedel, Richard P., et al., editors. *Urbanization in the Americas from Its Beginnings to the Present.* The Hague: Mouton, 1978.

Sjoberg, Gideon. *The Preindustrial City, Past and Present.* New York: Free Press, 1960.

Taylor, John H., et al., editors. *Capital Cities, Les Capitales: Perspectives Internationales, International Perspectives.* Ottawa: Carleton University Press, 1993.

Thomson, Guy P. C. "America and the Americas: Mexico and Philadelphia." *History Today [UK]* 34 (May 1984): 29–35.

Tooley, Ronald Vere, compiler. *Dictionary of Mapmakers.* New York: Alan R. Liss, 1979.

Turner, John F. C. *Housing by People: Toward Autonomy in Building Environments.* London: Marion Boyars, 1976.

Van Hartesveldt, Fred R., editor. *The 1918–1919 Pandemic of Influenza: The Urban Impact in the Western World.* Lewiston, NY: Edwin Mellen Press, 1992.

Van Vliet, Willem, editor. *The Encyclopedia of Housing.* Beverly Hills, CA: Sage, 1998.

Vance, James E., Jr. *The Continuing City: Urban Morphology in Western Civilization.* Baltimore: Johns Hopkins University Press, 1990.

Weber, Adna Ferrin. *The Growth of Cities in the Nineteenth Century: A Study in Statistics.* Ithaca, NY: Cornell University Press, 1963.

General Works on the Dutch in the Americas

Araúz Monfante, Celestino Andrés. *El contrabando holandés en el Caribe durante la primera mitad del siglo XVIII.* Caracas: Volumes 168–169 of the Series "Fuentes para la Historia Colonial de Venezuela" published by the Academia Nacional de la Historia, 1984.

———. "La acción ilegal de los holandeses en el Caribe y su impacto en las Antillas y Puerto Rico durante la primera mitad del siglo XVIII." *Revista/Review Interamericana [Puerto Rico]* 14, Numbers 1–4 (1984): 67–79.

Böhm, Günther. "The First Sephardic Synagogues in South America and in the Caribbean Area." *Studia Rosenthalia [The Netherlands]* 22, Number 1 (1988): 1–14.

Coolhaas, W. Ph. *A Critical Survey of Studies on Dutch Colonial History.* The Hague: Martinus Nijhoff for the Koninklijk Instituut voor Taal-, Land- en Volkenkunde, 1980 re-edition of 1960 original, revised by G. J. Schutte.

Diepraam, Willem. *The Dutch Caribbean: Foto's uit Suriname en de Nederlandse Antillen.* Amsterdam: Arbeiderspers, 1978.

Gastmann, A. L. *The Politics of Surinam and the Netherlands Antilles.* Rio Piedras: Institute of Caribbean Studies [Monograph Number 3], University of Puerto Rico, 1968.

Goslinga, Cornelis Ch. *The Dutch in the Caribbean and on the Wild Coast, 1580–1680.* Gainesville: University of Florida Press, 1971.

———. *A Short History of the Netherlands Antilles and Surinam.* The Hague: Martinus Nijhoff, 1979.

———. *The Dutch in the Caribbean and in the Guianas, 1680–1791.* Dover, NH: Van Gorcum, 1985.

Handboekje voor Suriname en Curaçao. Amsterdam, 1938.

Hiss, Philip Hanson. *Netherlands America: The Dutch Territories in the West.* New York: Duell, Sloan and Pearce, 1943.

Jacobs, H. J., and Fr. Oudschans Dentz. *Onze West in beeld en woord.* Amsterdam: De Bussy, 1929.

Maronier, J. H. *Pictures of the Tropics: A Catalogue of Drawings, Watercolours, Paintings, and Sculptures in the Collection of the Royal Institute of Linguistics and Anthropology in Leiden.* 's-Gravenhage: Nijhoff, n.d.

Postma, Johannes. "The Dimension of the Dutch Slave Trade from Western Africa." *Journal of African History* 13, Number 2 (1972): 237–248.

Schrieke, B. J. O., and Van M. J. Heemstra, editors. *Ons Koninkrijk in Amerika: West Indiën.* 's-Gravenhage: Van Hoeve, 1947.

Walle, J. van de. *De Nederlandse Antillen; land, volk, cultuur.* Baarn: Wereldvenster, 1954.

General Works on the French in the Americas

Aboucaya, Claude. *Les intendants de la marine sous l'ancien régime.* Gap: Louis-Jean, 1958.

Aboucaya, Claude, and Jacques Merlande, editors. *Documents d'histoire antillaise et guyanaise, 1814–1914.* [N.p., n.p.], 1979.

———. *Histoire des communes Antilles-Guyane.* Fort-de-France: Pressplay, 1986, six volumes.

Aldrich, Robert, and John Connell. *France's Overseas Frontier: Départements et territoires d'Outre-Mer.* Cambridge, UK, and New York: Cambridge University Press, 1992.

Atlas des Départements d'Outre-Mer. Paris: Centre National de la Recherche Scientifique, 1979.

Balesi, Charles J. *The Time of the French in the Heart of North America, 1673–1818.* Chicago: Alliance Française, 1992.

Bataillon, Claude. *Villes et campagnes.* Paris: Anthropos, 1971.

Berthet, Thierry. *Seigneurs et colons de Nouvelle France: l'émergence d'une société distincte au XVIIIe siècle.* Cachan: L'E.N.S., 1993.

Berthiaume, Pierre. "Le tremblement de terre de 1663: les convulsions du verbe ou la mystification du logos chez Charlevoix." *Revue d'histoire de l'Amérique française [Canada]* 36, Number 3 (1982): 375–387.

Bonnel, Ulane. *La France, les États-Unis et la guerre de course, 1797–1815.* Paris: Éditions Latines, 1961.

Bougaineville, Louis-Antoine de. *Adventures in the Wilderness: The American Journals of Louis-Antoine de Bougaineville, 1756–1760.* Norman: University of Oklahoma Press, 1964, translation by Edward P. Hamilton.

Boyer, Pierre, et al. *Les Archives nationales, état général des fonds [Tome III: marine et outre-mer].* Paris: Archives Nationales, 1980.

Devèze, Michel. *Antilles, Guyanes, la Mer des Caraïbes de 1492 à 1789.* Paris: SEDES, 1977.

"Documents: Journal of a French Traveller in the Colonies, 1765, I." *American Historical Review* 26, Number 4 (July 1921): 726–747.

Dormoy, M. *Architecture française.* Paris: Vincent Fréal, 1951.

Duflot de Mofras, Eugène. *Duflot de Mofras' Travels on the Pacific Coast.* Santa Ana, CA: The Fine Arts Press, 1937 translation and re-edition by Marguerite Eyer Wilbur, two volumes.

Eccles, William J. *France in America.* East Lansing: Michigan State University Press, 1990 re-edition of 1972 original published in New York by Harper and Row.

Germain, Annick, and Jean-Claude Marsan. *Aménager l'urbain, de Montréal à San Francisco: politiques et désign urbain.* Montreal: Méridien, 1987.

Goodman, Morris F. *A Comparative Study of Creole French Dialects.* The Hague: Mouton, 1964.

Griffiths, Naomi. *The Acadians: The Creation of a People.* Toronto: McGraw-Hill Ryerson, 1973.

Huetz de Lemps, Christian. *Géographie du commerce de Bordeaux à la fin du règne de Louis XIV.* Paris: Mouton, 1975.

Huret, Jules. *En Amérique.* Paris: "Bibliothèque Charpentier," Eugène Fasquelle, 1904–1905, two volumes.

Julien, Charles-André. *Les français en Amérique au XVIIe siècle.* Paris: SEDES/CDU, 1976.

———. *Les français en Amérique de 1713 à 1784.* Paris: SEDES/CDU, 1977.

Le Moël, Michel, and Claude-France Rochat. *Catalogue général des cartes, plans et dessins d'architecture: Série N,* Volume IV. Paris: Archives Nationales, 1974.

Lussagnet, Suzanne, editor. *Les français en Amérique pendant la deuxième moitié du XVIe siècle.* Paris: Presses Universitaires de France, 1953.

Margry, Pierre, compiler and editor. *Mémoires et documents pour servir à l'histoire des origines françaises des pays d'outre mer: découvertes et établissements des françaises dans l'ouest et dans le sud de l'Amérique Septentrionale.* Paris, 1879–1887, six volumes.

Mollat, Michel. *Les explorations du XIIIe au XVIe siècles: premiers regards sur des mondes nouveaux.* Paris: CTMS, 1992.

Pastoreau, Mireille. *Voies océanes: cartes maritimes et grandes découvertes.* Paris: Bibliothèque Nationale, 1992.

Pluchon, Pierre, and Denise Bouche. *Histoire de la colonisation française.* Paris: Fayard, 1991, two volumes.

Queuille, Pierre. "Les diplomaties anglaise et américaine vis-à-vis de la France vaincue (1940–1942): un schéma d'ensemble." *Revue d'histoire diplomatique [France]* 94, Numbers 1–3 (1980): 230–250.

Rochat, Claude-France, and Michel Le Moël. *Catalogue général des cartes, plans et dessins d'architecture: Série NN.* Paris: Archives Nationales, 1978.

Saussure, Henri de. *Voyage aux Antilles et au Mexique, 1854–1856.* Geneva: Olizane, 1993 re-edition by Louis de Roguin and Claude Weber.

Stein, Robert Louis. *The French Slave Trade in the Eighteenth Century: An Old Regime Business.* Madison: University of Wisconsin Press, 1979.

———. *The French Sugar Business in the Eighteenth Century.* Baton Rouge: Louisiana State University Press, 1988.

Taillemite, Étienne. *Inventaire analytique de la correspondance générale avec les colonies, 1654–1715.* Paris: Ministère de la France d'Outre-Mer, 1959.

Thevet, André. *André Thevet's North America, A Sixteenth-Century View.* Kingston and Montreal: McGill-Queens University Press, 1986 re-edition and translation by Roger Schlesinger and Arthur P. Stabler.

Thwaites, Reuben Gold, editor. *The Jesuit Relations and Allied Documents: Travels and Explorations of the Jesuit Missionaries in New France, 1610–1791.* New York: Pageant, 1959 reprint of 1896–1901 originals published by Arthur H. Clarke in Cleveland, seventy-three volumes.

Villes portuaires, acteurs de l'environnement. Le Havre, France: Association Internationale Villes et Ports, 1994.

Wright, Gwendolyn. *The Politics of Design in French Colonial Urbanism.* Chicago: University of Chicago, 1991.

General Works on Latin America

Acosta, Antonio, and Juan Marchena Fernández, editors. *La influencia de España en el Caribe, la Florida y la Luisiana, 1500–1800.* Madrid: Instituto de Cooperación Iberoamericana, 1983.

Aguilera Rojas, Javier, and Luis J. Moreno Rexach, compilers. *Urbanismo español en América.* Madrid: Editora Nacional, 1973.

Alba, Victor. *Politics and the Labor Movement in Latin America.* Palo Alto, CA: Stanford University Press, 1968.

Albi, Fernando. *El corregidor en el municipio español bajo la monarquía absoluta: ensayo histórico-crítico.* Madrid, 1943.

Alcedo, Antonio de. *Diccionario geográfico-histórico de las Indias Occidentales o América.* Madrid: Atlas, 1967 reprint of 1786–1789 original published by Benito Cano, four volumes.

Alomar, Gabriel, editor. *De Teotihuacán a Brasilia: estudios de historia urbana iberoamericana y filipina.* Madrid: Instituto de Estudios de Administración Local, 1987.

Altamira y Crevea, Rafael, compiler and editor. *Colección de documentos inéditos para la historia de Ibero-América* [or *Hispano-América*]. Madrid: Ibero-América, 1927–1932, fourteen volumes.

Altamira y Crevea, Rafael, et al. *Contribuciones a la historia municipal de América.* Mexico City: Instituo Panamericano de Geografía e Historia, 1951.

Altman, Ida. "Immigrants and Society: An Approach to the Background of Colonial Spanish America." *Comparative Studies in Society and History [UK]* 30, Number 1 (1988): 170–190.

———. *Emigrants and Society: Extremadura and Spanish America in the Sixteenth Century.* Berkeley: University of California Press, 1989.

Alvarez Terán, María Concepción. *Mapas, planos y dibujos (1503–1805) del Archivo General de Simancas.* Valladolid: Ministerio de Cultura, 1980.

América colonial: población y economía. Santa Fe, Argentina: Instituto de Investigaciones Históricas de la Universidad Nacional del Litoral, 1967.

América pintoresca: descripción de viajes al nuevo continente, 1884. Madrid: Colección Erisa Ilustrativa, 1980 facsimile reprint of graphic materials.

Andrews, George Reid. "Latin American Urban History." *History Teacher* 19, Number 4 (August 1986): 499–515.

Angulo Iñiguez, Diego. *Planos de monumentos arquitectónicos de América y Filipinas existentes en el Archivo General de Indias.* Seville: Laboratorio del Arte, Universidad de Sevilla, 1933–1940, six volumes.

———. *Bautista Antonelli: las fortificaciones americanas en el siglo XVI.* Madrid: Hauser y Menet, 1942.

———. *Historia del arte hispanoamericano.* Barcelona: Salvat, 1945–1956, three volumes.

Armus, Diego, and John Lear. "The Trajectory of Latin American Urban History." *Journal of Urban History* 24, Number 3 (March 1998): 291–301.

Avellá Vives, Joaquín. *Los cabildos coloniales.* Madrid, 1934.

Ayala, Manuel José de, compiler. *Diccionario de gobierno y legislación de Indias.* Madrid: Cultura Hispánica and the Instituto de Cooperación Iberoamericana, 1988, twenty-two volumes.

Bagú, Sergio. *Economía de la sociedad colonial: ensayo de historia comparada de América Latina.* Buenos Aires: El Ateneo, 1949.

———. *Estructura social de la colonia: ensayo de historia comparada de América Latina.* Caracas and Buenos Aires: El Ateneo, 1952.

Barbier, Jacques A., and Allan J. Kuethe, editors. *The North American Role in the Spanish Imperial Economy, 1760–1819.* Manchester, UK: Manchester University Press, 1984.

Bastide, Roger. *Las Américas negras: las civilizaciones africanas en el Nuevo Mundo.* Madrid: Alianza Editorial, 1969.

Baudot, Georges. *La vie quotidienne dans l'Amérique espagnole de Philippe II, XVIe siècle.* Paris: Hachette, 1981.

Bayitch, S. A. *Latin America and the Caribbean: A Bibliographical Guide to Works in English.* Coral Gables, FL: University of Miami Press, 1967.

Bayle, Constantino. *Los cabildos seculares en la América Española.* Madrid: Sapientia, 1952.

Bayón, Damián. *Sociedad y arquitectura colonial en América Latina.* Madrid: Gustavo Gili, 1975.

Belliter, Erika. *Fotografía latinoamericana: desde 1860 hasta nuestros días.* Madrid: El Viso, 1982.

Beneyto Pérez, Juan. *Historia de la administración española e hispanoamericana.* Madrid: Aguilar, 1958.

Bernaldo de Quirós, Constancio. *La picota en América (contribución al estudio del derecho penal indiano).* Reprint: Havana, 1947.

Bernales Ballesteros, Jorge. *El urbanismo sevillano de los siglos XVI-XVII y su proyección en Indias.* Seville: Real Academia de Bellas Artes de Santa Isabel de Hungría, 1972.

Beyer, Glenn H., editor. *The Urban Explosion in Latin America: A Continent in Process of Modernization.* Ithaca, NY: Cornell University Press, 1967.

Bonet Correa, Antonio. *Monasterios iberoamericanos.* Madrid: El Viso, 2001.

Borah, Woodrow. "Trends in Recent Studies of Colonial Latin American Cities." *Hispanic American Historical Review* 64, Number 3 (1984): 535–554.

Bourdé, Guy. *Urbanisation et immigration en Amérique Latine.* Paris: Aubier-Montaigne, 1974.

Boyd-Bowman, Peter. *Indice geobiográfico de cuarenta mil pobladores españoles de América en el siglo XVI.* Bogotá and Mexico City: Instituto Caro y Cuervo and Academia Mexicana de Genealogía y Heráldica, 1964–1968, respectively, two volumes.

———. "La procedencia de los españoles de América." *Historia Mexicana* 17, Number 1 (1967): 37–71.

———. *Patterns of Spanish Emigration to the New World, 1493–1580.* Buffalo: Council on International Studies, State University of New York [SUNY], 1973.

———. "Patterns in Spanish Emigration to the Indies, 1579–1600." *The Americas: A Quarterly Review of Inter-American Cultural History [Academy of American Franciscan History]* 33, Number 1 (1976): 78–95.

———. *Indice geobiográfico de 56 mil pobladores españoles de la América Hispánica.* Mexico City: Instituto de Investigaciones Históricas of the Universidad Nacional Autónoma de México [UNAM], and the Fondo de Cultura Económica, 1985.

Boyer, Richard E., and Keith A. Davies. *Urbanization in Nineteenth-Century Latin America: Statistics and Sources.* Berkeley: University of California Press, 1973.

Brading, David A., and Harry E. Cross. "Colonial Silver Mining: Mexico and Peru." *Hispanic American Historical Review* 52, Number 4 (November 1972): 545–579.

Braun, Georg, and Franz Hogenberg [with an introduction by Raleigh A. Skelton]. *Civitates Orbis Terrarum: The Towns of the World, 1572–1618.* Amsterdam: Van Hoeve, 1980 facsimile reprint of 1623 edition, three volumes.

Bronner, Fred. "Urban Society in Colonial Spanish America: Research Trends." *Latin American Research Review* 21, Number 1 (1986): 3–72.

Brown, Jonathan. *The Word Made Image: Religion, Art, and Architecture in Spain and Spanish America, 1500–1600.* Hanover: University Press of New England, 1998.

Burkholder, Mark A., and D. S. Chandler. *From Impotence to Authority: Spain and the American Audiencias.* Columbia: University of Missouri Press, 1977.

———. *Biographical Dictionary of Audiencia Ministers in the Americas, 1687–1821.* Westport, CT: Greenwood, 1982.

Burns, E. Bradford, and Thomas E. Skidmore. *Elites, Masses, and Modernization in Latin America, 1850–1930.* Austin: University of Texas Press, 1979.

Burzio, Humberto F. *Diccionario de la moneda hispanoamericana.* Santiago de Chile: Fondo Histórico y Bibliografico José Toribio Medina, 1958, three volumes.

Buschiazzo, Mario J. *Estudios de arquitectura colonial hispanoamericana.* Buenos Aires: Guillermo Kraft, 1943.

———. *Historia de la arquitectura colonial en Hispano América.* Reprint, Buenos Aires: Emecé, 1961.

Bushnell, David, and Neil Macaulay. *The Emergence of Latin America in the Nineteenth Century.* New York: Oxford University Press, 1988.

Butterworth, Douglas, and John Chance K. *Latin American Urbanization.* Cambridge, UK: Cambridge University Press, 1981.

Carrière, Jean, et al., editors. *The State, Industrial Relations and the Labour Movement in Latin America.* New York: St. Martin's Press, 1989, two volumes.

Cartografía de ultramar. Madrid: Servicios Geográfico e Histórico del Ejército, 1949–1957, ten volumes.

Casariego Fernández, Jesús Evaristo. *El municipio y las cortes en el imperio español de Indias.* Madrid, 1946.

Casasco, Juan A. "Slums of Hope and Despair." *Américas [Organization of American States]* 21, Number 6 (June 1969): 13–20.

Castañeda, Carlos E. "The Corregidor in Spanish Colonial Administration." *Hispanic American Historical Review* 9 (1929): 446–470.

Castells, Manuel, editor. *Imperialismo y urbanización en América Latina.* Barcelona: Gustavo Gili, 1973.

Chance, John K. "Recent Trends in Latin American Urban Studies." *Latin American Research Review* 15 (1980): 183–188.

Chiaramonte, José Carlos. *Formas de sociedad y economía en Hispanoamérica.* Mexico City: Grijalbo, 1984.

Chiaramonte, José Carlos, editor. *Pensamiento de la ilustración: economía y sociedad iberoamericanas en el siglo XVIII.* Caracas: Biblioteca Ayacucho, 1979.

Chueca Goitia, Fernando. *Invariantes castizos de la arquitectura española.* Madrid: DOSSAT, 1947.

———. *Breve historia del urbanismo.* Madrid: Alianza, 1981 reprint.

Chueca Goitia, Fernando, with Leopoldo Torres Balbás and Julio González y González, compilers. *Planos de ciudades iberoamericanas y filipinas existentes en el Archivo de Indias.* Madrid: Instituto de Estudios de Administración Local, Seminario de Urbanismo, 1951, two volumes.

Clement, Jean-Pierre. "El nacimiento de la higiene urbana en la América española del siglo XVIII." *Revista de Indias [Spain]* 171 (1983): 77–96.

Cline, Howard F. "The *Relaciones geográficas* of the Spanish Indies, 1577–1648." *Handbook of Middle American Indians* 12 (1972): 183–242.

Colección de documentos inéditos relativos al descubrimiento, conquista y organización de las antiguas posesiones españolas de ultramar. Madrid: Real Academia de la Historia, 1885–1932, twenty-five volumes.

Collier, George A., et al., editors. *The Incan and Aztec States, 1400–1800: Anthropology and History.* Boston: Academic Press, 1982.

Collier, Ruth Berins, and David Collier. *Shaping the Political Arena: Critical Junctures, the Labor Movement, and Regime Dynamics in Latin America.* Princeton: Princeton University Press, 1991.

Conniff, Michael L., editor. *Latin American Populism in Comparative Perspective.* Albuquerque: University of New Mexico Press, 1982.

Connolly, Mark. "Adrift in the City: A Comparative Study of Street Children in Bogotá, Colombia, and Guatemala City." *Child and Youth Services* 14, Number 1 (1990): 129–149.

Contribuciones para el estudio de la historia de América: homenaje al doctor Emilio Ravignani. Buenos Aires: Jacobo Peuser, 1941.

Cook, Noble David, and W. G. Lovell, editors. *"Secret Judgements of God": Old World Disease in Colonial Spanish America.* Norman: University of Oklahoma Press, 1992.

Cornelius, Wayne A., and Robert V. Kemper, editors. *Metropolitan Latin America: The Challenge and the Response.* Beverly Hills, CA: Sage, 1978.

Cotler, Julio, editor. *Clases populares, crisis y democracia en América Latina.* Lima: Instituto de Estudios Peruanos, 1989.

Crouch, Dora P., et al. *Spanish City Planning in North America.* Cambridge, UK: Cambridge University Press, 1982.

Cuesta Domingo, Mariano. *Alonso de Santa Cruz y su obra cosmográfica.* Madrid: Instituto "Gonzalo Fernández de Oviedo," Consejo Superior de Investigaciones Científicas, 1983.

Cueto, Marcos, editor. *Salud, cultura y sociedad en América Latina: nuevas perspectivas históricas.* Lima: Instituto de Estudios Peruanos and the Organización Panamericana de la Salud, 1996.

Curtis, William Eleroy. *The Capitals of Spanish America.* New York: Harper and Brothers, 1888.

Das, Man Singh, and Clinton J. Jesser, editors. *The Family in Latin America.* New Delhi: Vikas, 1980.

Dawson, Frank Griffith. *The First Latin American Debt Crisis: The City of London and the 1822–25 Loan Bubble.* New Haven: Yale University Press, 1990.

De la Torre, Carlos. "Génesis y desarrollo de la teoría de la localización." *Revista Interamericana de Planificación* 8, Numbers 28–29 (1973–1974): 63–79.

Díaz Plaja, Fernando. *La sociedad española desde 1500 hasta nuestros días.* San Juan: University of Puerto Rico Press, 1968.

Domínguez, Jorge. *Insurrection or Loyalty: The Breakdown of the Spanish American Empire.* Cambridge: Harvard University Press, 1980.

Domínguez Ortiz, Antonio. *La sociedad española en el siglo XVIII.* Madrid: Consejo Superior de Investigaciones Científicas, 1955.

———. "Concesión de 'naturalezas' para comerciar con Indias." *Revista de Indias [Spain]* 19, Number 76 (1959): 227–239.

———. *Sociedad y estado en el siglo XVIII.* Madrid: Ariel, 1976.

Domínguez y Compañy, Francisco. *El urbanismo en las Leyes de Indias: estudio histórico jurídico social.* Havana, 1945.

———. *Los pueblos de indios.* Havana, 1958.

———. *La vida en las pequeñas ciudades hispanoamericanas de la Conquista, 1494–1549.* Madrid: Cultura Hispánica del Centro Iberoamericano de Cooperación, 1978.

———. "Contenido urbanístico de las actas de fundación, 1520–1573." *Revista de Historia de América [Mexico]* 91 (1981): 9–27.

———. *Política de poblamiento de España en América: la fundación de ciudades.* Madrid: Instituto de Estudios de Administración Local, 1984.

Durston, Alan. "Un régimen urbanistico en la América hispana colonial: el trazado en damero durante los siglos XVI y XVII." *Historia [Chile]* 28 (1994): 59–115.

Elkin, Judith Laikin. *The Jews of Latin America.* New York: Holmes and Meier, 1998.

Encinas, Diego de, compiler. *Cedulario indiano.* Madrid: Cultura Hispánica, 1945–1946 facsimile reprint of 1596 original, published by the Imprenta Real of Madrid in four volumes.

Fernández de Navarrete, Martín, et al., compilers and editors. *Colección de documentos inéditos para la historia de España.* Madrid: Viuda de Calero for the Real Academia de la Historia, 1842–1895, 113 volumes.

Fisher, John R. *Commercial Relations between Spain and Spanish America in the Era of Free Trade, 1778–1796.* Liverpool: Centre for Latin American Studies at the University of Liverpool, 1985.

Florescano Mayet, Enrique, editor. *Ensayos sobre el desarrollo económico de México y América Latina.* Mexico City: Fondo de Cultura Económica, 1979.

Fox, David John, and David James Robinson. *Cities in a Changing Latin America: Two Studies of Urban Growth in the Development of Mexico and Venezuela.* London: Latin American Publications Fund, 1969.

French, John D., and Daniel James, editors. *The Gendered Worlds of Latin American Women Workers: From Household and Factory to the Union Hall and Ballot Box.* Durham, NC: Duke University Press, 1997.

García, Juan Agustín. *La ciudad indiana.* Santa Fe, Argentina: Editorial Claridad, 1954 re-edition of 1900 original.

García-Baquero, Antonio. *Cádiz y el Atlántico (1717–1778).* Seville: Escuela de Estudios Hispano-americanos, 1976, two volumes.

Gibson, Charles. *Spain in America.* New York: Harper and Row, 1966.

Gil Munilla, Ladislao. "La ciudad hispanoamericana." *Anuario de Estudios Americanos [Spain]* 10, Number 48 (1955): 295–310.

Gilbert, Alan. *In Search of a Home: Rental and Shared Housing in Latin America.* London: UCL Press, 1993.

———. *The Latin American City.* New York: Monthly Review Press, 1998 revised edition.

Gilbert, Alan, and Peter M. Ward. *Housing, the State, and the Poor: Policy and Practice in Three Latin American Cities.* Cambridge, UK: Cambridge University Press, 1985.

Gómez Pérez, Carmen. *El sistema defensivo americano: siglo XVIII.* Madrid: MAPFRE, 1992.

Góngora, Mario. *Studies in the Colonial History of Spanish America.* New York: Cambridge University Press, 1975 translation by Richard Southern.

González González, Enrique. "Royal Patronage and Private Support in the Emergence of Spanish American Universities." *Paedagogica Historica [Belgium]* 34, Number 2 (1998): 507–525.

Greenfield, Gerald Michael. "New Perspectives on Latin American Cities." *Journal of Urban History* 15, Number 2 (February 1989): 205–214.

Greenfield, Gerald Michael, editor. *Latin American Urbanization: Historical Profiles of Major Cities.* Westport, CT: Greenwood, 1994.

Greenfield, Gerald Michael, and Sheldon L. Maran, editors. *Latin American Labor Organizations.* Westport, CT: Greenwood, 1987.

Griffin, Charles C., and J. Benedict Warren, editors. *Latin America: A Guide to the Historical Literature.* Austin: University of Texas Press, 1971.

Guarda, Gabriel. *Santo Tomás de Aquino y las fuentes del urbanismo indiano.* Santiago: Academia Chilena de la Historia, 1965.

———. "Tres reflexiones en torno a la fundación de la ciudad indiana." *Revista de Indias [Spain]* 32, Nos. 127–130 (January–December 1972): 89–106.

Guillén y Tato, Julio Fernando. *El fichero fotográfico del Museo Naval.* Madrid: Museo Naval, 1933.

———. *Monumenta chartografica indiana.* Madrid: Ministerio de Asuntos Exteriores, 1942.

Gutiérrez, Ramón. *Notas para una bibliografía hispanoamericana de arquitectura (1526–1875).* Madrid: Resistencia, 1972.

———. *Arquitectura del siglo XIX en Iberoamérica (1800–1850).* Madrid: Resistencia, 1979.

———. *Arquitectura colonial: teoría y praxis.* Madrid: Resistencia, 1980.

———. *Arquitectura y urbanismo en Iberoamérica.* Madrid: Cátedra, 1983.

Gwynne, R. N. *Industrialization and Urbanization in Latin America.* London: Croom Helm, 1985.

Halperín Donghi, Tulio. *Hispanoamérica después de la independencia: consecuencias sociales y económicas de la emancipación.* Buenos Aires: Paidós, 1972.

———. *Reforma y disolución de los imperios ibéricos, 1750–1850.* Madrid: Alianza, 1985.

Hamel, P., et al. "Urban Heritage in Puebla and Montreal: Assessment of Strategies and Interpretative Elements." *Canadian Journal of Urban Research* 5, Number 1 (1996): 18–50.

Handbook of Latin American Studies. Austin: University of Texas Press, 1936–.

Hanke, Lewis, and Celso Rodríguez, editors. *Los virreyes españoles en América durante el gobierno de la Casa de Austria.* Madrid: Volumes 273–277 and 280–286 of the "Biblioteca de Autores Españoles," 1976–1980.

Hardoy, Jorge Enrique. *Pre-Columbian Cities.* New York: Walker, 1973 translation of 1964 original *Ciudades precolombinas.*

———. *Urban Planning in Pre-Columbian America.* New York: George Braziller, 1968.

———. "El modelo clásico de la ciudad colonial hispanoamericana." *Actas del XXXVIII Congreso Internacional de Americanistas [Stuttgart 1968],* Volume IV (1972): 143–182.

Hardoy, Jorge Enrique, editor. *Las ciudades en América Latina: Seis ensayos sobre la urbanización contemporánea.* Buenos Aires: Paidós, 1972.

———. *Urbanization in Latin America: Approaches and Issues.* Garden City, NY: Anchor Books and Doubleday, 1975.

Hardoy, Jorge Enrique, and Carmen Aranovich. "Urbanización de América hispánica entre 1580 y 1630." *Boletín del Centro de Investigaciones Históricas y Estéticas de la Universidad Central de Venezuela* 11 (May 1969): 9–89.

Hardoy, Jorge Enrique, and Richard P. Schaedel, compilers. *Las ciudades de América Latina y sus áreas de influencia a través de la historia.* Buenos Aires: SIAP, 1975.

———. *Asentamientos urbanos y organización socioproductiva en la historia de América Latina.* Buenos Aires: SIAP, 1977.

Hardoy, Jorge Enrique, and Carlos Tobar. *La urbanización en América Latina.* Buenos Aires: Instituto Di Tella, 1969.

Hargreaves-Mawdsley, William N. *Spain under the Bourbons, 1700–1833.* Columbia: University of South Carolina Press, 1973.

———. *Eighteenth-Century Spain, 1700–1788: A Political, Diplomatic and Institutional History.* London and Totowa, NJ: Macmillan, and Rowman and Littlefield, 1979.

Haring, Clarence H. *The Spanish Empire in America.* New York: Oxford University Press, 1947.

Harris, Walter D., Jr., and Humberto L. Rodríguez-Camilloni. *The Growth of Latin American Cities.* Athens: Ohio University Press, 1971.

Hauser, Philip M., editor. *Urbanization in Latin America.* New York: International Documents Service, 1961.

Hernández, José, compiler and editor. *Catálogo de los fondos americanos del Archivo de Protocolos de Sevilla.* Madrid: Companía Ibero-americana de Publicaciones for the Instituto Hispano-Cubano de Historia de América, 1930–1932, three volumes.

Higueras Rodríguez, M. D., compiler and editor. *Catálogo crítico de los documentos de la Expedición Malaspina (1789–1794) del Museo Naval.* Madrid: Museo Naval, 1985.

Hoberman, Louisa S., and Susan Migden Socolow, editors. *Cities and Society in Colonial Latin America.* Albuquerque: University of New Mexico Press, 1986.

Howse, Derek, and Norman J. W. Thrower, editors. *A Buccaneer's Atlas: Basil Ringrose's South Sea Waggoner. A Sea Atlas and Sailing Directions of the Pacific Coast of the Americas 1682.* Berkeley: University of California Press, 1992.

Humboldt, Baron Alexander von, and Aimé Bonpland. *Personal Narrative of Travels to the Equinoctial Regions of the New Continent during the Years 1799–1804.* New York: AMS Press, 1966 reprint of translation by Helen M. Williams originally published in London by Longman in 1826, seven volumes.

Humphreys, Robert A. *British Consular Reports on the Trade and Politics of Latin America.* London: Royal Historical Society, 1940.

Jacobsen, Nil, and Hans-Jürgen Puhle, editors. *The Economies of Mexico and Peru during the Late Colonial Period, 1760–1810.* Berlin: Biblioteca Ibero-Americana, 1986.

Jaksic, Ivan. "The Politics of Higher Education in Latin America." *Latin American Research Review [UK]* 20, Number 1 (1985): 209–221.

Johnson, John J. *Political Change in Latin America: The Emergence of the Middle Sectors.* Palo Alto, CA: Stanford University Press, 1958.

Johnson, Lyman L., and Enrique Tandeter, editors. *Essays on the Price History of Eighteenth-Century Latin America.* Albuquerque: University of New Mexico Press, 1990.

Junquera y Mato, Juan José. "Reflexiones sobre el urbanismo canario y sus relaciones con Hispanoamérica." *Revista de Historia Canaria [Spain]* 37 (1980): 249–251.

Kaplan, Marcos. *Estado y urbanización en América Latina.* Valparaíso: CIDU, 1967.

Karrow, Robert W., Jr. *Mapmakers of the Sixteenth Century and Their Maps: Bio-Bibliographies of the Cartographers of Abraham Ortelius, 1570.* Chicago: Speculum Orbis Press for The Newberry Library, 1993.

Keane, A. H. *Central and South America.* London: Edward Stanford, 1909, two volumes.

Keeler, Mary Frear. "The Boazio Maps of 1585–1586." *Terrae Incognitae [The Netherlands]* 10 (1978): 71–80.

Kelemen, Pál. *Baroque and Rococo in Latin America.* New York: Dover, 1967 reprint of 1951 original published by Macmillan, two volumes.

Kicza, John E. "Patterns in Early Spanish Overseas Expansion." *William and Mary Quarterly,* Third Series, Volume 49, Number 2 (April 1992): 229–253.

———. "The Social and Political Position of Spanish Immigrants in Bourbon America and the Origins of the Independence Movements." *Colonial Latin American Review* 4, Number 1 (1995): 105–128.

Kinsbrunner, Jay. *Petty Capitalism and Spanish America: The Pulperos of Puebla, Mexico, Caracas, and Buenos Aires.* Boulder: Westview, 1987.

Kirkpatrick, F. A. "Municipal Administration in the Spanish Dominions in America." *Transactions of the Royal Historical Society [UK],* Third Series, Volume 9: 95–110.

Klein, Herbert S. *African Slavery in Latin America and the Caribbean.* New York: Oxford University Press, 1986.

Konetzke, Richard, editor. "Legislación sobre inmigración de extranjeros en América." *Revista Internacional de Sociología [Spain]* 3, Number 9 (1945): 269–299.

———. "Documentos para la historia y crítica de los registros parroquiales en las Indias." *Revista de Indias [Spain]* 25 (1946): 581–586.

———. "Las fuentes para la historia demográfica de Hispano-América durante la época colonial." *Anuario de Estudios Americanos [Spain]* 5 (1948): 267–323.

———. *Colección de documentos para la historia de la formación social de Hispanoamérica, 1493–1810.* Madrid: Consejo Superior de Investigaciones Científicas, 1953–1962, four volumes.

Kubler, George A., and Martín S. Soria. *Art and Architecture in Spain and Portugal and Their American Dominions, 1500 to 1800.* Harmondsworth: Penguin, 1959.

Langue, Frédérique. "Hombres e ideas de la Ilustración en dos ciudades consulares: Caracas y Veracruz." *Historia Mexicana* 45, Number 3 (1996): 467–500.

Latorre, Germán, editor. *Relaciones geográficas de Indias.* Seville: Centro Oficial de Estudios Americanistas, 1920.

Lavrín, Asunción. "Women, the Family, and Social Change in Latin America." *World Affairs* 150 (1987): 109–128.

Lavrín, Asunción, editor. *Latin American Women: Historical Perspectives.* Westport, CT: Greenwood, 1978.

León Tello, Pilar. *Mapas, planos y dibujos de la Sección de Estado del Archivo Histórico Nacional.* Madrid: Dirección General de Archivos y Bibliotecas, 1969.

Leonard, Irving A., editor. *Colonial Travellers in Latin America.* New York: Knopf, 1972.

Les villes dans le monde ibérique. Paris: Institut des Hautes Études de l'Amérique Latine or IHEAL, Centre National de la Recherche Scientifique, 1982.

Liagre, Leone, compiler. *Guide des sources de l'histoire de l'Amérique Latine conservées en Belgique.* Brussels: UNESCO, 1967.

Lockhart, James M., and Stuart B. Schwartz. *Early Latin America: A History of Colonial Spanish America and Brazil.* Cambridge, UK: Cambridge University Press, 1983.

Lockhart, James M., and Enrique Otte, editors and translators. *Letters and People of the Spanish Indies: Sixteenth Century.* Cambridge, NY: Cambridge University Press, 1976.

Lohmann Villena, Guillermo. *Los americanos en las ordenes nobiliarias (1529–1900).* Madrid: Instituto "Gonzalo Fernández de Oviedo," 1947, two volumes.

López de Velasco, Juan. *Geografía y descripción universal de las Indias.* Madrid: Ediciones Atlas as Volume 247 of the "Biblioteca de Autores Españoles," 1971 reprint of 1574 original.

Luján Muñóz, Jorge. *Los escribanos en las Indias occidentales.* Guatemala City: Instituto Guatemalteco de Derecho Notarial, 1977 re-edition.

Lynch, John. *The Spanish-American Revolutions, 1808–1826.* London: Weidenfeld and Nicolson, 1973.

Lyn-Hilton, Sylvia. *Bibliografía hispanoamericana y filipina: manual de repertorios bibliográficos para la investigación de la historia y la literatura hispanoamericana y filipina.* Madrid: Fundación Universitaria Española, 1983.

Mangin, William. "Latin American Squatter Settlements: A Problem and a Solution." *Latin American Research Review* 2, Number 3 (1967): 65–98.

Mapas españoles de América, siglos XV-XVII. Madrid: Hauser y Menet for the Real Academia de la Historia, 1951.

Marchena Fernández, Juan, and Carmen Gómez Pérez. *La vida de guarnición en las ciudades americanas de la Ilustración.* Madrid: Ministerio de Defensa, 1992.

Marco Dorta, Enrique. *Fuentes para la historia del arte hispano-americano.* Seville: Escuela de Estudios Hispano-americanos, 1951.

Marichal, Carlos. *A Century of Debt Crises in Latin America: From Independence to the Great Depression, 1820–1930.* Princeton: Princeton University Press, 1989.

Mellafe, Rolando. *The Latifundio and the City in Latin American History.* Toronto: University of Toronto Press, 1971.

Menéndez Pidal, Ramón, and Juan Manzano, editors. *Recopilación de leyes de Indias.* Madrid: Cultura Hispánica, 1973 facsimile reprint of 1681 original published by Julián Paredes.

Millares Carlo, Agustín. *Los archivos municipales de Lationamérica: libros de actas y colecciones documentales, apuntes bibliográficos.* Maracaibo: Universidad de Zulia, 1961.

Miller, John, and Ralph A. Gakenheimer, editors. *Latin American Urban Policies and the Social Sciences.* Beverly Hills, CA: Sage, 1971.

Molina, Raúl A. *La ciudad hispanoamericana.* Santo Domingo: II Congreso Hispanoamericano de Historia, 1957.

Monteiro, Palmyra V. M. *A Catalogue of Latin American Flat Maps, 1926–1964.* Austin: Institute of Latin American Studies, University of Texas Press, 1967.

Morales Padrón, Francisco. *Fisonomía de la conquista indiana.* Seville: Escuela de Estudios Hispano-americanos, 1953.

———. "Descubrimiento y toma de posesión." *Anuario de Estudios Americanos [Spain]* 12 (1955): 321–380.

Morales Padrón, Francisco, compiler. *Historia y bibliografía americanista, 1967.* Seville: Escuela de Estudios Hispano-americanos, 1969.

Moreno Fraginals, Manuel, editor. *L'Afrique en Amérique Latine.* Paris: UNESCO, 1984.

Mörner, Magnus. *Estratificación social hispanoamericana durante el período colonial.* Stockholm: Instituto de Estudios Ibero-Americanos, 1980.

Mörner, Magnus, editor. *Race Mixture in the History of Latin America.* Boston: Little, Brown, 1967.

———. *La corona española y los foráneos en los pueblos de indios de América.* Stockholm: Almquist and Wiksell for the Instituto de Estudios Ibero-Americanos, 1970.

———. *Race and Class in Latin America.* New York: Columbia University Press, 1970.

———. "Economic Factors and Stratification in Colonial Spanish America with Special Regard to Elites." *Hispanic American Historical Review* 63, Number 2 (1983): 335–369.

Mörner, Magnus, and Harold Sims. *Adventurers and Proletarians: The Story of Migrants in Latin America.* Pittsburgh: University of Pittsburgh Press, 1985.

Morse, Richard McGee. "Some Characteristics of Latin American Urban History." *Hispanic American Historical Review* 67, Number 2 (1962): 321–322.

———. "Recent Research on Latin American Urbanization: A Selective Survey with Commentary." *Latin American Research Review* 1, Number 1 (fall 1965): 35–74.

———. "Trends and Issues in Latin American Urban Research, 1965–1970." *Latin American Research Review* 6, Number 1 (spring 1971): 3–52 and Number 2 (summer 1971): 19–76.

———. "A Prolegomenon to Latin American Urban History." *Hispanic American Historical Review* 52, Number 3 (1972): 359–394.

———. "Trends and Patterns in Latin American Urbanization, 1750–1920." *Comparative Studies in Society and History [UK]* 16, Number 4 (September 1974): 416–447.

———. "Latin American Intellectuals and the City, 1860–1940." *Journal of Latin American Studies [UK]* 10 (1978): 221–227.

———. "The Urban Development of Colonial Spanish America." Volume 2 of *The Cambridge History of Latin America,* edited by Leslie Bethell. Cambridge, UK: Cambridge University Press, 1984, 67–104.

Morse, Richard McGee, editor. *Las ciudades latinoamericanas.* Mexico City: Volumes 96–97 of the Series "Sep-Setentas" published by the Secretaría de Educación Pública or SEP, 1973.

Morse, Richard McGee, et al., editors. *The Urban Development of Latin America, 1750–1920.* Palo Alto, CA: Stanford University Press, 1971.

Morse, Richard McGee, and Jorge Enrique Hardoy, editors. *Repensando la ciudad de América Latina/Rethinking the Latin American City.* Baltimore: Johns Hopkins University Press for the Woodrow Wilson Center in Washington, DC, 1992.

Muro Orejón, Antonio, compiler. *Cedulario americano del siglo XVIII: colección de disposiciones legales indianas desde 1680 hasta 1800, contenidas en los cedularios del Archivo General de Indias.* Seville: Escuela de Estudios Hispano-americanos, 1956.

Musset, Alain, and Pablo Emilio Pérez-Mallaína Bueno, editors. *De Séville à Lima.* Paris: Laboratoire de Géographie Urbaine, Université de Paris X-Nanterre, 1997.

Navarro García, Luis. *Intendencias en Indias.* Seville: Escuela de Estudios Hispano-americanos, 1959.

Nutall, Zelia. "Royal Ordinances Concerning the Laying Out of New Towns." *Hispanic American Historical Review* 4 (1921): 743–753 and Volume 5 (1922): 249–254.

Ocaña, Fr. Diego de. *Un viaje fascinante por la América Hispana del siglo XVI.* Madrid: Studium, 1969 re-edition by Fr. Arturo Alvarez, O.F.M.

Ots Capdequí, José María. *Las instituciones sociales de la América española en el período colonial.* La Plata: Biblioteca Ilumindades, 1935.

———. *El régimen municipal hispanoamericano del período colonial: concejos y ciudades.* Madrid and Valencia: Salvat, 1936–1937.

———. *El estado español en las Indias.* Reprint, Mexico City: Fondo de Cultura Económica, 1957.

Pacheco, Joaquín F., Francisco de Cárdenas, and Luis Torres de Mendoza, compilers. *Colección de documentos inéditos relativos al descubrimiento, conquista y colonización de las posesiones españolas en América y Oceanía, sacados en su mayor parte del Real Archivo de Indias.* Madrid: Imprenta de Manuel B. de Quirós, 1864–1884, forty-two volumes.

Pastor, José M. F. "Streets and Spaces." *Américas [Organization of American States]* 19, Number 10 (October 1967): 5–11.

Paz, Julián. *Catálogo de manuscritos de América existentes en la Biblioteca Nacional.* Madrid: Tipografía de Archivos for the Patronato de la Biblioteca Nacional, 1934.

Piel, Jean, et al. *Regiones y ciudades en América Latina.* Mexico City: Volume 111 of the Series "Sep-Setentas" published by the Secretaría de Educación Pública or SEP, 1973.

Pierson, W. W. "Some Reflections on the Cabildo as an Institution." *Hispanic American Historical Review* 5 (1922): 573–596.

Pike, Frederick B. "Algunos aspectos de la ejecución de las leyes municipales en la América española durante la época de los Austrias." *Revista de Indias [Spain]* 72 (1958): 201 et seq.

———. "The Municipality and the System of Checks and Balances in Spanish American Colonial Administration." *The Americas: A Quarterly Review of Inter-American Cultural History [Academy of American Franciscan History]* 15 (1958): 139 et seq.

———. "Aspects of Cabildo Economic Regulations in Spanish America under the Hapsburgs." *Inter-American Economic Affairs* 13 (1960): 67–86.

Pineo, Ronn F., and James A. Bayer, editors. *Cities of Hope: People, Protests, and Progress in Urbanizing Latin America, 1870–1930.* Boulder: Westview, 1998.

Ponce Leiva, Pilar. "Publicaciones españolas sobre cabildos americanos, 1939–1989." *Revista de Indias [Spain]* 50, Number 188 (1990): 77–81.

Portes, Alejandro, and John Walton. *Urban Latin America: The Political Condition from Above and Below.* Austin: University of Texas Press, 1976.

Quesada, Santiago. *La idea de ciudad en la cultura hispana de la edad moderna.* Barcelona: Universitat de Barcelona Publicacions, 1992.

Rabinovitz, F. F., and F. M. Trueblood, editors. *Latin American Urban Research.* Beverly Hills, CA: Sage, 1970–1978, six volumes.

Recopilación de leyes de los reinos de las Indias. Madrid: Consejo de la Hispanidad, 1943, three volumes.

Relaciones históricas de ultramar. Madrid: Servicios Geográfico e Histórico del Ejército, 1955, two volumes.

Ricard, Robert. "La plaza mayor en España y en América española: notas para un estudio." *Estudios geográficos* 11 (1950): 301–327.

Richert, Gertrud. *Johann Moritz Rugendas.* Berlin: Rembrandt, 1959.

Robinson, David James, editor. *Social Fabric and Spatial Structure in Colonial Latin America.* Ann Arbor: University of Michigan Press, 1979.

———. *Studies in Spanish American Population History.* Boulder: Westview, 1981.

———. *Migration in Colonial Spanish America.* Cambridge, UK: Cambridge University Press, 1990.

Roessingh, M. P. H. *Guide to the Sources in The Netherlands for the History of Latin America.* The Hague: Government Publishing Office, under the auspices of UNESCO and the International Council on Archives, 1968.

Romano, Ruggiero, editor. *Governare Il Mondo: L'Impero di Spagna dal XV al XIX secolo.* Palermo, Italy, 1992.

Romero, José Luis. *Latinoamérica: las ciudades y las ideas.* Buenos Aires: Siglo XXI, 1976.

Rothenberg, Irene Fraser. "National Intervention and Urban Development in Colombia and Mexico." *Publius* 12, Number 2 (1982): 111–134.

Rout, Leslie B., Jr. *The African Experience in Spanish America: 1502 to the Present.* New York: Cambridge University Press, 1976.

Rubio Moreno, Luis, compiler. *Colección de documentos inéditos para la historia de Hispanoamérica.* Madrid: Inventario General de Registros de Cedularios, 1928.

Saint-Lu, André, and Marie-Cécile Bénassy-Berling, editors. *La ville en Amérique espagnole coloniale.* Paris: Université de la Sorbonne for the Séminaire Interuniversitaire sur l'Amérique Espagnole Coloniale, 1984.

Sáiz, Blanca, compiler. *Bibliografía sobre Alejandro Malaspina y acerca de la expedición Malaspina y de los marinos y científicos que en ella participaron.* Madrid: El Museo Universal, 1992.

Sáiz, Blanca, editor. *Alejandro Malaspina: la América imposible.* Madrid: Compañía Literaria, 1994.

Sala Catalá, José. "El agua en la problemática científica de las primeras metrópolis coloniales hispanoamericanas." *Revista de Indias [Spain]* 49, Number 186 (1989): 257–281.

Salvatore, Ricardo Donato, and Carlos Aguirre, editors. *The Birth of the Penitentiary in Latin America: Essays on Criminology, Prison Reform, and Social Control, 1830–1940.* Austin: University of Texas Press, 1996.

Sánchez-Albornoz, Nicolás. *The Population of Latin America: A History.* Berkeley: University of California Press, 1974 translation by W. A. R. Richardson of 1973 original *La población de América Latina desde los tiempos precolombinos al año 2000.*

Sánchez Bella, Luis. *Guía del Archivo Histórico Nacional.* Madrid: Dirección General de Archivos y Bibliotecas, 1958.

Sanz Fernández, Jesús, editor. *Historia de los ferrocarriles de Iberoamérica, 1837–1995.* Madrid: Centro de Estudios y Exermientación de Obras Públicas or CEDEX, 1998.

Schaedel, Richard P. "The Anthropological Study of Latin American Cities in Intra and Interdisciplinary Perspective." *Urban Anthropology* 3 (1974): 139–170.

Schteingart, Martha, editor. *Urbanización y dependencia en América Latina.* Buenos Aires: SIAP, 1973.

Segre, Roberto. *América Latina en su arquitectura.* Mexico City: Siglo XXI, 1975.

———. *Las estructuras ambientales de América Latina.* Mexico City: Siglo XXI, 1977.

Serrano y Sanz, Manuel, editor. *Colección de libros y documentos referentes a la historia de América.* Madrid: V. Suárez, 1904–1929, twenty-one volumes.

———. *Relaciones históricas de América, primera mitad del siglo XVI.* Madrid: Sociedad de Bibliófilos Españoles, 1916.

Simposio de geografía urbana. Rio de Janeiro: Instituto de Geografía e Historia, 1968.

Smith, Robert C. "Colonial Towns of Spanish and Portuguese America." *Journal of the Society of Architectural Historians* 14, Number 4 (1953): 1 et seq.

Smith, T. Lynn. "The Changing Functions of Latin Cities." *The Americas: A Quarterly Review of Inter-American Cultural History [Academy of American Franciscan History]* 25 (July 1968): 70–83.

Smith, T. Lynn, editor. *Studies of Latin American Societies.* New York: Anchor, 1970.

Socolow, Susan Migden, and Lyman L. Johnson. "Urbanization in Colonial Latin America." *Journal of Urban History* 8, Number 1 (1981): 27–59.

Sofer, Eugene F., and Mark D. Szuchman. "City and Society: Their Connection in Latin American Historical Research." *Latin American Research Review* 14, Number 2 (1979): 113–129.

Solano Pérez-Lila, Francisco de. "Urbanización y municipalización de la población indígena." *Revista de Indias [Spain]* 32, Numbers 127–130 (January–December 1972): 241–268.

———. "Introducción al estudio del abastecimiento de la ciudad colonial." *Atti del XL Congreso Internazionale degli Americanisti [Italy]* 4 (September 1973).

Solano Pérez-Lila, Francisco de, editor. *Estudios sobre la ciudad iberoamericana.* Madrid: Instituto "Gonzalo Fernández de Oviedo," Consejo Superior de Investigaciones Científicas, 1975.

———. *Estudios sobre la ciudad americana.* Madrid: Instituto "Gonzalo Fernández de Oviedo," Consejo Superior de Investigaciones Científicas, 1983.

Solaún, Mauricio, and Michael Quinn. *Sinners and Heretics: Patterns of Military Intervention in Latin America.* Urbana: University of Illinois Press, 1973.

Solórzano y Pereyra, Juan de. *Política indiana.* Madrid: Ediciones Atlas, 1972, five volumes.

Spalding, Hobart A., Jr. "The Parameters of Labor in Hispanic America." *Science and Society* 36 (summer 1972): 202–216.

———. *Organized Labor in Latin America.* New York: New York University Press, 1977.

Spalding, Karen, editor. *Essays in the Political, Economic, and Social History of Colonial Latin America.* Newark: University of Delaware Press, 1982.

Stanislawski, Dan. "Early Spanish Town Planning in the New World." *Geographical Review* 37 (1947): 94–105.

Stern, Malcolm H. "Portuguese Sephardim in the Americas." *American Jewish Archives* 44, Number 1 (1992): 141–178.

Subero, Efraín. *La ciudad y las ciudades.* Reprint, Caracas: Lafarge, 1997.

Torres Lanzas, Pedro. *Relación descriptiva de los mapas, planos, etc., de Panamá, Santa Fé y Quito existentes en el Archivo General de Indias.* Madrid : Revista de Archivos, Bibliotecas y Museos, 1904.

Tricart, Jean. "Quelques caractéristiques générales des villes latinoamericaines." *Annales: économies, sociétés, civilisations [France]* 15, Number 1 (1965): 15–30.

Tudela de la Orden, José. *Los manuscritos de América en las bibliotecas de España.* Madrid: Cultura Hispánica, 1954.

"The Urban Population Explosion." *Américas [Organization of American States]* 27, Numbers 11–12 (November–December 1975): 11–16.

Urbanización y proceso social en América. Lima: Instituto de Estudios Peruanos, 1972.

Vázquez de Espinosa, Antonio. *Compendium and Description of the West Indies.* Washington, DC: Smithsonian Institution, 1948 translation by Charles Upson Clark.

Vila Vilar, Enriqueta. *Hispanoamérica y el comercio de esclavos: los asientos portugueses.* Seville: Escuela de Estudios Hispano-americanos, 1977.

Villamarín, Juan A., and Judith E. Villamarín. *Indian Labor in Mainland Colonial Spanish America.* Newark : University of Delaware Press, 1975.

Villes et nations en Amérique Latine. Paris: Institut des Hautes Études de l'Amérique Latine or IHEAL, Centre National de la Recherche Scientifique, 1983.

Villes et régions en Amérique Latine. Paris: Institut des Hautes Études de l'Amérique Latine or IHEAL, Centre National de la Recherche Scientifique, 1970.

Vindel, Francisco. *Mapas de América en los libros españoles de los siglos XVI al XVIII (1503–1798).* Reprint, Madrid: Ministerio de Asuntos Exteriores, 1991.

Walter, Richard J. "Recent Works on Latin American Urban History." *Journal of Urban History* 16, Number 2 (February 1990): 205–214.

Ward, James S. *Yellow Fever in Latin America: A Geographical Study.* Liverpool: Centre for Latin American Studies at the University of Liverpool, 1972.

Watriss, Wendy, and Lois Parkinson Zamora. *Image and Memory: Photography from Latin America, 1866–1994.* Austin: University of Texas Press, 1998.

Welch, Thomas L., et al., compilers. *Travel Accounts and Descriptions of Latin America and the Caribbean, 1800–1920: A Selected Bibliography.* Washington, DC: Columbus Memorial Library of the Organization of American States, 1982.

Wilhelmy, Herbert. "Appearance and Functions of the Large Latin-American Cities in the Past and Present." *Geoforum* 3 (1970): 31–38.

Yujnosky, Oscar. *La estructura interna de la ciudad: el caso latinoamericano.* Buenos Aires: SIAP, 1971.

Zavala, Silvio. *El mundo americano en la época colonial.* Mexico City: Editorial Porrúa, 1967, two volumes.

Zéndegui, Guillermo de. "City Planning in the Spanish Colonies." *Américas [Organization of American States]* 29, Number 2 (February 1977): supplementary pp. 1–12.

CARIBBEAN
Regional Studies and Journals

Aarons, John, introduction. *The Catalogue of the West India Reference Library.* Millwood, NY: Kraus International Publications, 1980, six volumes.

Ashdown, Peter. *Caribbean History in Maps.* London: Longman Caribbean, 1979.

Augier, F. Roy, and Shirley C. Gordon. *Sources of West Indian History.* London: Longman Caribbean, 1962.

Baa, Enid M., compiler. *Theses on Caribbean Topics, 1778–1968.* San Juan: Institute of Caribbean Studies and the University of Puerto Rico Press, 1970.

Boswell, Thomas D., et al. "A Comparison of Net Migration Patterns in Puerto Rico and the Bahamas." *Revista/Review Interamericana [Puerto Rico]* 11, Number 3 (1981): 351–365.

Boucher, Philip P. *Cannibal Encounters: Europeans and Island Caribs, 1492–1763.* Baltimore: Johns Hopkins University Press, 1992.

Butel, Paul. *Les négociants bordelais, l'Europe et les îles au XVIIIe siècle.* Paris: Aubier-Montaigne, 1974.

———. *Les Caraïbes au temps des flibustiers, XVIe-XVIIe siècles.* Paris: Aubier-Montaigne, 1982.

———. "Succès et déclin du commerce colonial français, de la Révolution à la restauration." *Revue économique [France]* 40, Number 6 (1989): 1079–1096.

Caribbean Geography. Annual published by the Education and Geography Departments at the Mona, Jamaica, Campus of the University of the West Indies, 1983–.

Caribbean Quarterly. Published by the Department of Extra-Mural Studies at the Mona, Jamaica, Campus of the University of the West Indies, 1951–.

Caribbean Studies. Quarterly published by the Institute of Caribbean Studies and University of Puerto Rico Press [Rio Piedras], 1961–.

Clarke, Colin G. "Urbanization in the Caribbean." *Geography* 59, Number 3 (1974): 223–232.

Clarke, Colin G., editor. *Caribbean Social Relations.* Liverpool: Centre for Latin American Studies at the University of Liverpool, 1978.

Cohen Stuart, B. A. *Women in the Caribbean: An Annotated Bibliography.* Leiden: Department of Caribbean Studies of the Royal Institute of Linguistics and Anthropology, 1979.

Comitas, Lambros, compiler. *The Complete Caribbeana, 1900–1975: A Bibliographic Guide to the Scholarly Literature.* New York: KTO Press, 1977, four volumes.

Corzani, J., editor. *Dictionnaire encyclopédique des Antilles et de la Guyane.* Fort-de-France: Désormeaux, 1992, seven volumes.

Craton, Michael. "The Bahamian Self and the Haitian Other: The Migration of Haitians to and through the Bahamas, 1950–2000." *Immigrants and Minorities [UK]* 14, Number 3 (1995): 265–288.

Cross, Malcolm. *Urbanization and Urban Growth in the Caribbean: An Essay on Social Change in Dependent Societies.* London: Cambridge University Press, 1979.

Crouse, Nellis Maynarde. *The French Struggle for the West Indies, 1665–1713.* New York: Octagon, 1966 reprint of 1943 original.

———. *French Pioneers in the West Indies, 1624–1664.* New York: Octagon, 1977 reprint of 1940 original.

Debien, Gabriel. *La société coloniale aux XVIIe et XVIIIe siècles: les engagés pour les Antilles, 1634–1715.* Paris: Armand Collin, 1952.

———. "Réfugés de Saint-Domingue à Cuba, 1793–1815." *Revista de Indias [Spain]* 13 (1953): 559–605 and 14 (1954): 11–36.

———. *Études antillaises: XVIIIe siècle.* Paris: Armand Collin, 1956.

———. *Les esclaves aux Antilles françaises.* Fort-de-France: Société d'Histoire de la Martinique, 1974.

Delson, Roberta Marx, editor. *Readings in Caribbean History and Economics: An Introduction to the Region.* New York: Gordon and Breach, 1981.

Doran, Edwin, Junior. "The West Indian Hip-Roofed Cottage." *California Geographer* 3 (1962): 97–104.

Doucet, Louis. *Quand les français cherchaient fortune aux Caraïbes.* Paris: Fayard, 1981.

Felhoen Kraal, Johanna L. G. "Libraries and Archives for Research in West Indian History, with an Appendix on a Collection of Curaçao Plantation Archives." *De West-Indische Gids [The Netherlands]* 37 (1956–1957): 71–92.

Fermor, Patrick Leigh. *The Traveller's Tree: A Journey through the Caribbean Islands.* New York: Harper, 1950.

Gaspar, David Barry, and David Patrick Geggus, editors. *A Turbulent Time: The French Revolution and the Greater Caribbean.* Bloomington: Indiana University Press, 1997.

Gauthier, Arlette. *Les soeurs de Solitude: la condition féminine dans l'esclavage aux Antilles du XVIIe au XIXe siècle.* Paris: Editions Caribéennes, 1985.

Gisler, Antoine. *L'esclavage aux Antilles françaises, XVIII–XIXe siècle.* Paris: Karthala, 1981.

Guerra, Francisco. "The Influence of Disease on Race, Logistics, and Colonization in the Antilles." *Journal of Tropical Medicine and Hygiene* 69 (1966): 23–52.

Hannau, Hans. *The Caribbean Islands.* Miami: Argos, ca. 1966.

Hoetink, Hermannus R. or "Harry." *The Two Variants in Caribbean Race Relations: A Contribution to the Sociology of Segmented Societies.* London: Oxford University Press for the Institute of Race Relations, 1967.

———. *Caribbean Race Relations: A Study of Two Variants.* London: Oxford University Press for the Institute of Race Relations, 1971.

Hope, Kempe Ronald. "Urban Population Growth in the Caribbean." *Cities* 1, Number 2 (1983): 167–174.

Journal of Caribbean History. Biannual publication issued jointly by the History Departments of the University of the West Indies at Mona [Jamaica], Port of Spain [Trinidad and Tobago], and Cave Hill [St. Michael, Barbados], 1970–.

Journal of Caribbean Studies. Official publication of the Association of Caribbean at the University of Miami [Coral Gables], 1980–.

Kelshall, Gaylord T. M. *The U-Boat War in the Caribbean.* Annapolis: Naval Institute Press, 1994.

Kiple, Kenneth F. *The Caribbean Slave: A Biological History.* Cambridge, NY: Cambridge University Press, 1984.

———. "Cholera and Race in the Caribbean." *Journal of Latin American Studies [UK]* 17 (1985): 157–177.

Kiple, Kenneth F., and Virginia H. Kiple. "Deficiency Diseases in the Caribbean." *Journal of Interdisciplinary History* 11 (autumn 1980): 197–215.

Labat, Jean-Baptiste [abridged and translated by John Eaden]. *The Memoirs of Père Labat, 1693–1705.* London: Frank Cass, 1970 reprint of 1931 version published by Constable; 1722 French original *Nouveau voyage aux îles de l'Amérique* consisted of eight volumes.

Langley, Lester D. *Struggle for the American Mediterranean.* Athens: University of Georgia Press, 1976.

————. *The United States and the Caribbean, 1900–1970.* Athens: University of Georgia Press, 1980.

————. *The Banana Wars: United States Intervention in the Caribbean, 1898–1934.* Chicago: Dorsey Press, 1988 revised edition.

Lewis, Gordon K. *The Growth of the Modern West Indies.* London: MacGibbon and Kee, 1968.

————. *Main Currents in Caribbean Thought: The Historical Evolution of Caribbean Society in Its Ideological Aspects, 1492–1900.* Baltimore: Johns Hopkins University Press, 1983.

Lloyd, Reginald, et al., editors. *Twentieth Century Impressions of the West Indies: Their History, People, Commerce, Industries, and Resources.* London: Lloyds Great Britain Publishing, 1914.

Macpherson, John. *Caribbean Lands.* London: Longman Caribbean, 1980 re-edition of 1963 original.

Martínez-Fernández, Luis. *Torn between Empires: Economy, Society, and Patterns of Political Thought in the Hispanic Caribbean, 1840–1878.* Athens: University of Georgia Press, 1994.

Mason, Keith. "Demography, Disease and Medical Care in Caribbean Slave Societies." *Bulletin of Latin American Research* 5 (1986): 109–119.

May, Robert E. *The Southern Dream of a Caribbean Empire, 1854–1861.* Athens: University of Georgia Press, 1989 reedition of 1973 original published in Baton Rouge by the Louisiana State University Press.

Moreno Fraginals, Manuel, et al., editors. *Between Slavery and Free Labor: The Spanish-Speaking Caribbean in the Nineteenth Century.* Baltimore: Johns Hopkins University Press, 1985.

Munro, Dana Gardner. *Intervention and Dollar Diplomacy in the Caribbean, 1900–1921.* Princeton: Princeton University Press, 1964.

————. *The United States and the Caribbean Republics, 1921–1933.* Princeton: Princeton University Press, 1974.

Ortiz, Altagracia. *Eighteenth-Century Reforms in the Caribbean.* Rutherford, NJ: Fairleigh Dickinson University Press, 1981.

Ramalho Massena, Rosa Maria. *Étude urbaine de deux villes antillaises: Kingston et Santo Domingo.* Bordeaux, 1971.

Revista/Review Interamericana. Quarterly published by the Inter-American University at San Juan, Puerto Rico, 1971–.

Slater, Mary. *The Caribbean Islands.* New York: Viking, 1968.

Social and Economic Studies. Quarterly published by the Institute of Social and Economic Research at the Mona [Jamaica] Campus of the University of the West Indies, 1953–.

Szulc, Tad, editor. *The United States and the Caribbean.* Englewood Cliffs, NJ: Prentice-Hall, 1971.

Tarr, Jashina Alexandra. "The Architecture of the Caribbean: Great Houses, Sugar Mills, and Fortresses." *Américas [Organization of American States]* 30, Numbers 6–7 (June–July 1978): 37–43.

Tarrade, Jean. *Le commerce colonial de la France à la fin de l'Ancien Régime: l'évolution du régime de 'l'exclusif' de 1763 à 1789.* Paris: Presses Universitaires de France, 1972.

Tavares K., Juan Tomás. *Los indios de Quisqueya.* Santo Domingo, República Dominicana: Taller, 1988.

Vilaire, Patrick, et al. *Images d'Espanola et de St. Domingue.* Port-au-Prince: Henri Deschamps, 1981.

Welch, Thomas L., et al., compilers. *Travel Accounts and Descriptions of Latin America and the Caribbean, 1800–1920: A Selected Bibliography.* Washington, DC: Columbus Memorial Library of the Organization of American States, 1982.

Williams, Eric, editor. *Documents of West Indian History, 1492–1655.* Port-of-Spain: PNM, 1963.

Bahamas
Nassau
Early History (1666–1897)

Beerman, Eric. "The Last Battle of the American Revolution: Yorktown, No, the Bahamas!" *The Americas: A Quarterly Review of Inter-American Cultural History [Academy of American Franciscan History]* 45, Number 1 (1988): 79–95.

Bruce, Peter Henry. *Bahamian Interlude.* London: R. H. Johns, 1949 re-edition.

Johnson, Howard. "Social Control and the Colonial State: The Reorganisation of the Police Force in the Bahamas, 1888–1893." *Slavery and Abolition [UK]* 7, Number 1 (1986): 46–58.

————. "Slave Life and Leisure in Nassau, Bahamas, 1783–1838." *Slavery and Abolition [UK]* 16, Number 1 (1995): 45–64.

Lewis, James A. *The Final Campaign of the American Revolution: Rise and Fall of the Spanish Bahamas.* Columbia: University of South Carolina Press, 1991.

Little, Bryan. *Crusoe's Captain: Being the Life of Woodes Rogers, Seaman, Trader, Colonial Governor.* London: Odhams, 1960.

Oldmixon, John. *The Isle of Providence.* London: R. H. Johns, 1949 reprint.

Pelzer, John, and Linda Pelzer. "'Cotton, Cotton, Everywhere!': Running the Blockade to Nassau." *Civil War Times Illustrated* 19, Number 9 (1981): 10–17.

Settlements in New Providence. Nassau: Department of Archives exhibition handbook, 1982.

Townsend, Dr. P. S. *Nassau, Bahamas, 1823–24.* Nassau: Bahamas Historical Society, 1980 reedition.

Modern History (1898–Present)

Albury, Paul. *The Paradise Island Story.* London: Macmillan Caribbean, 1984.

Bloch, Michael. *The Duke of Windsor's War: The Windsors in the Bahamas, 1940–1945.* New York: Coward, McCann and Geoghegan, 1982.

Boswell, Thomas D. "The Characteristics of Internal Migration to and from New Providence Island (Greater Nassau), Bahamas, 1960–1970." *Social and Economic Studies [Jamaica]* 35, Number 1 (March 1986): 111–150.

DeMarigny, Alfred, and Mickey Herskowitz. *A Conspiracy of Crowns: The True Story of the Duke of Windsor and the Murder of Sir Harry Oakes.* New York: Crown, 1990.

Francis, Carlene. "The Offshore Banking Sector in the Bahamas." *Social and Economic Studies [Jamaica]* 34, Number 4 (1985): 91–110.

Johnson, Howard. "Bahamian Labor Migration to Florida in the Late Nineteenth and Early Twentieth Centuries." *International Migration Review* 22, Number 1 (1988): 84–103.

Leasor, James. *Who Killed Sir Harry Oakes?* Boston: Houghton Mifflin, 1983.

Palmer, C. A. "Tourism and Colonialism: The Experience of the Bahamas." *Annals of Tourism Research* 21, Number 4 (1994): 792–811.

Pye, Michael. *The King over the Water.* New York: Holt, Rinehart and Winston, 1981.

Saunders, D. Gail. "The 1942 Riot in Nassau: A Demand for Change?" *Journal of Caribbean History [Barbados]* 20, Number 2 (1985–1986): 117–146.

———. "The Role of the Coloured Middle Class in Nassau, Bahamas, 1890–1942." *Ethnic and Racial Studies* 10, Number 4 (October 1987): 448–465.

———. "The 1958 General Strike in Nassau: A Landmark in Bahamian History." *Journal of Caribbean History [Barbados]* 27, Number 1 (1993): 81–107.

———. "The Changing Face of Nassau: The Impact of Tourism on Bahamian Society in the 1920s and 1930s." *New West Indian Guide [The Netherlands]* 71, Numbers 1–2 (1997): 21–42.

Barbados
Bridgetown
Colonial Era (1628–1903)

Campbell, P. F. "St. Ann's Fort and the Garrison." *Journal of the Barbados Museum and Historical Society* 35, Number 1 (1975): 3–16.

Ludlum, David M. "The Great Hurricane." *Journal of the Barbados Museum and Historical Society* 31, Number 3 (1965): 127–131.

McAllister, George C. "The Hurricane of August 1831." *Journal of the Barbados Museum and Historical Society* 31, Number 4 (1966): 180–189.

Powell, John Rowland. "Sir George Ayscue's Capture of Barbados in 1651." *The Mariner's Mirror [UK]* 59 (August 1973): 281–290.

Richardson, Bonham C. *Economy and Environment in the Caribbean: Barbados and the Windwards in the Late 1800s.* Gainesville: University Press of Florida, 1997.

Shilstone, E. M. "Some Notes on Early Printing Presses and Newspapers in Barbados." *Journal of the Barbados Museum and Historical Society* 26, Number 1 (November 1958): 19–33.

———. "The Jewish Synagogue, Bridgetown, Barbados." *Journal of the Barbados Museum and Historical Society* 32, Number 1 (1966): 3–15.

Shilstone, E. M., and Wilfred Samuel, editors. *Jewish Monumental Inscriptions in Barbados.* London: Jewish Historical Society and University College, 1956.

Welch, Pedro. "The Slave Family in the Urban Context: Views from Bridgetown, Barbados, 1780–1816." *Journal of Caribbean History [Barbados]* 29, Number 1 (1995): 11–24.

Early Maps and Depictions
of Bridgetown, 1675–1847

The Quaker surveyor Richard Ford drew a map of Barbados in 1675 that was published in London a few years later by Phillip Lea and John Sellers, including a small inset plan of "The Bridg Toun"—originals held by the British Museum and the Council Chambers in Barbados, among other sources

View of the city waterfront as engraved in 1695 by Jan Kip, based upon a drawing by Samuel Copen—original held by the Library of Congress with call number: PGA - Kip—A prospect of Bridgetown (E size) [P&P], plus other sources

Map of the island as surveyed in 1717–1721 by Maj. William Mayo and published in London in 1722, including insets of "A Plan of the Bridge Town, With Explanation" and "A Prospect of Codrington College"—originals held by the British Museum, the Public Records Office [archival provenance: Calendar of State Papers, Colonial Series, 28/17. 57 i (a)], plus other sources

Map of Barbados with an inset "Plan of Bridgetown and Carlisle Bay," engraved by J. Lodge for the 15 January 1782 issue of the *Political Magazine* in London—held by the British Museum, plus other sources

Plans drawn by the military officer Capt. F. de Barralier in 1818, showing how Carlisle Bay, Bridgetown, and its suburbs might be upgraded into a major naval base—originals held by the Barbados Museum, plus other sources

Plan of Bridgetown as surveyed in February 1847 by the architect Blayney William Walsh, showing the "Extent of the Fire of 3 Feby. 1846, with proposed improvements according to the approved plan for rebuilding that portion of the City"—originals held by the Colonial Office in London, plus the Barbados Museum

Modern History and General Works (1904–Present)

Alleyne, Warren. *Historic Bridgetown.* Bridgetown: Barbados National Trust, 1978.

Barrow, Christine. "Reputation and Ranking in a Barbadian Locality." *Social and Economic Studies [Jamaica]* 25, Number 2 (June 1976): 106–121.

Connell, Neville. "Hotel Keepers and Hotels in Barbados." *Journal of the Barbados Museum and Historical Society* 33, Number 4 (November 1970): 162–185.

Fletcher, W. E. L. "The Barbados Railway." *Journal of the Barbados Museum and Historical Society* 28, Number 3 (1961): 86–98.

Jones, A. "The Housing Experience of Barbados." *Cities* 4 (1987): 52–57.

Jones, Huw R. "Metropolitan Dominance and Family Planning in Barbados." *Social and Economic Studies [Jamaica]* 26, Number 3 (September 1977): 327–338.

Potter, Robert B. "Industrial Development and Urban Planning in Barbados." *Geography* 66 (1981): 225–228.

———. "Congruence between Space Preferences and Socio-Demographic Structure in Barbados, West Indies: The Use of Cognitive Studies in Third World Urban Planning and Development." *Geoforum* 14, Number 3 (1983): 249–265.

———. "Urban Development, Planning and Demographic Change, 1970–1980, in Barbados." *Caribbean Geography [Jamaica]* 1, Number 1 (1983): 3–12.

———. "Housing Upgrading in Barbados: The Tenantries Programme." *Geography* 71 (1986): 255–257.

———. "Urban Housing in Barbados, West Indies." *Geographical Journal [UK]* 155, Number 1 (1989): 81–93.

Potter, Robert B., and Muriel L. Hunte. "Recent Developments in Planning the Settlement Hierarchy of Barbados: Implications Concerning the Debate on Urban Primacy." *Geoforum* 10 (1979): 355–362.

"The 350th Anniversary of Bridgetown." *Bajan and South Caribbean* 296 (July 1978): 4–59.

Cuba
General Studies

Acosta, Maruja, and Jorge E. Hardoy. *Urban Reform in Revolutionary Cuba.* New Haven: Yale University Press for the Antilles Research Program, 1973 translation by Mal Bochner.

Aguirre, Yolanda. *Influencias económicas en la arquitectura colonial de Cuba.* Havana: Editorial Pueblo y Educación, 1974.

Ameringer, Charles D. *The Cuban Democratic Experience: The Autentico Years, 1944–1952.* Gainesville: University Press of Florida, 2000.

Ames, David W. "Negro Family Types in a Cuban Solar." *Phylon* 11, Number 2 (1950): 159–163.

Angulo Pérez, Andrés. *Curso de historia de las instituciones locales de Cuba.* Havana: Cultural, 1943.

———. *El municipio en Cuba y América: facetas de su vida.* Havana, 1948.

Atlas nacional de Cuba. Havana, 1970.

Bergad, Laird W., et al. *The Cuban Slave Market, 1790–1880.* New York: Cambridge University Press, 1995.

Bourdé, Guy. "Sources et méthodes de l'histoire démographique à Cuba (XVIIIe et XIXe siècles)." *Annales de démographie historique [France]* (1972): 385–424.

Casanovas, Joan. *Bread, or Bullets! Urban Labor and Spanish Colonialism in Cuba, 1850–1898.* Pittsburgh: University of Pittsburgh Press, 1998.

Castillo Meléndez, Francisco. "La hacienda municipal indiana: el caso de La Habana y Santiago de Cuba hasta 1700." *Anuario de Estudios Americanos [Spain]* 42 (1985): 501–547.

Catálogo de los fondos existentes en el Archivo Nacional. Havana: Archivo Nacional, 1957.

Chomsky, Ariva. "'Barbados or Canada?' Race, Immigration, and Nation in Early Twentieth-Century Cuba." *Hispanic American Historical Review* 80, Number 3 (August 2000): 415–462.

Corbitt, Duvon C. "*Mercedes* and *Realengos:* A Survey of the Public Land System in Cuba." *Hispanic American Historical Review* 19, Number 3 (August 1939): 263–269.

Corwin, Arthur F. *Spain and the Abolition of Slavery in Cuba, 1817–1886.* Austin: University of Texas Press, 1967.

Díaz Martínez, Yolanda. "Dos ejércitos en lucha: tácticas y estructuras militares en la guerra de Cuba, 1895–1898." *Revista Complutense de Historia de América [Spain]* 20 (1994): 257–274.

Domínguez, Jorge I. "Seeking Permission to Build a Nation: Cuban Nationalism and U.S. Response under the First Machado Presidency." *Cuban Studies* 16 (1986): 33–48.

Dubesset, Eric. "Le tourisme à Cuba: une industrie en pleine expansion." *Les cahiers d'Outre-Mer [France]* 48, Number 189 (January–March 1995): 35–54.

Eblen, Jack Ericson. "On the Natural Increase of Slave Populations: The Example of the Cuban Black Population, 1775–1900." In *Race and Slavery in the Western Hemisphere: Quantitative Studies,* edited by Stanley Engerman and Eugene Genovese (Princeton: Princeton University Press, 1975).

Estrade, Paul. "Las huelgas de 1890 en Cuba." *Revista de la Biblioteca Nacional José Martí [Cuba]* 21, Number 1 (1979): 27–51.

Fitchen, Edward D. "1300 Cuban Teachers in Boston." *Américas [Organization of American States]* 26, Number 2 (February 1974): 13–19.

Fountain, Anne. "Questions of Race and Gender: Evangelina Cisneros and the Spanish-Cuban-American War." *Secolas Annals* 30 (1999): 36–43.

Franco, José Luciano. *Proceso y triunfo de la intermunicipalidad.* Havana: Instituto Interamericano de Historia Municipal e Institucional, 1956.

———. *Instituciones locales; urbanismo.* Havana: Instituto Interamericano de Historia Municipal e Institucional, 1959.

———. *Apuntes para una historia de la legislación y administración colonial en Cuba, 1511–1800.* Havana: Editorial de Ciencias Sociales, 1985.

Fuente García, Alejandro de la. "Población y crecimiento en Cuba (siglos XVI y XVII): un estudio regional." *European Review of Latin American and Caribbean Studies [The Netherlands]* 55 (1993): 59–93.

García del Pino, César, and Alejandro de la Fuente García. "Introducción a la cultura en Cuba en los siglos XVI y XVII: elementos para un nuevo enfoque." *Revista de la Biblioteca Nacional José Martí [Cuba]* 31, Number 2 (1989): 5–33.

García Santana, Alicia, et al. "Fuentes y antecedentes de la arquitectura tradicional cubana." *Revista de la Biblioteca Nacional José Martí [Cuba]* 25, Number 2 (1983): 145–181.

Gavira, Carmen. "La configuración del espacio colonial en Cuba." *Revista de la Biblioteca Nacional José Martí [Cuba]* 24, Numbers 1–2 (1982): 63–95.

González, Alfonso. "The Population of Cuba." *Caribbean Studies [Puerto Rico]* 11, Number 2 (1971): 74–84.

Guerra y Sánchez, Ramiro, et al., editors. *Historia de la nación cubana.* Havana, 1952, ten volumes.

Gugler, Josef. "A Minimum Urbanism and a Maximum Ruralism: The Cuban Experience." *Studies in Comparative Development* 15, Number 2 (1980): 27–44.

Healy, David F. *The United States in Cuba, 1898–1902.* Madison: University of Wisconsin Press, 1963.

Hitchman, James H. *Leonard Wood and Cuban Independence, 1898–1902.* The Hague: Martinus Nijhoff, 1971.

Humboldt, Baron Alexander von. *Ensayo político sobre la isla de Cuba.* Havana: Archivo Nacional, 1960 reprint of Spanish translation.

Kiple, Kenneth F. *Blacks in Colonial Cuba, 1774–1899.* Gainesville: University of Florida Press, 1976.

Kuethe, Allan J. *Cuba, 1753–1815: Crown, Military, and Society.* Knoxville: University of Tennessee Press, 1986.

———. "La fidelidad cubana durante la edad de las revoluciones." *Anuario de Estudios Americanos [Spain]* 55, Number 1 (1998): 209–220.

Lapique Becali, Zoila. *Música colonial cubana en las publicaciones periódicas, 1812–1902.* Havana: Letras Cubanas, 1979.

Lebroc, Reyneiro G. *Cuba: iglesia y sociedad (1830–1860).* Madrid, 1976.

Le Riverend Brusone, Julio. *Historia económica de Cuba.* Havana: Editorial de las Ciencias Sociales, 1985 reprint of 1965 original published by the Editora Universitaria.

León y Canales, Benito, and Manuel Pérez Beato, compilers and editors. *Archivo de Indias: ingenieros cubanos, siglos XVI, XVII y XVIII.* Havana: Imprenta Compañía Editora de Libros y Folletos for the Archivo Histórico, 1941.

Lloyd, Reginald, et al., editors. *Twentieth Century Impressions of Cuba: Its History, People, Commerce, Industries, and Resources.* London: Lloyds Great Britain Publishing, 1913.

Lockmiller, David A. *Magoon in Cuba: A History of the Second Intervention, 1906–1909.* New York: Greenwood, 1969 reprint of 1938 original published by the University of North Carolina Press.

Los censos de población y viviendas en Cuba. Havana: Instituto de Investigaciones Estadísticas, 1988.

Macías Domínguez, Isabelo. *Cuba en la primera mitad del siglo XVII.* Seville: Escuela de Estudios Hispano-americanos, 1978.

Marieu, Jean. "Quelques données récentes sur la population cubaine." *Les cahiers d'Outre-Mer [France]* 27, Number 106 (April–June 1974): 128–167.

Marrero y Artiles, Leví. *Cuba: economía y sociedad.* Madrid and San Juan de Puerto Rico: Playor, 1972–1988, fourteen volumes.

Martínez Alier, Verena. *Marriage, Class, and Colour in Nineteenth-Century Cuba: A Study of Racial Attitudes and Sexual Values in a Slave Society.* New York: Cambridge University Press, 1974.

Millett, Allan R. *The Politics of Intervention: The Military Occupation of Cuba, 1906–1909.* Columbus: Ohio State University Press, 1968.

Mohl, Raymond A. "A Scotsman in Cuba, 1811–1812." *The Americas: A Quarterly Review of Inter-American Cultural History [Academy of American Franciscan History]* 29, Number 2 (1972): 232–245.

Murray, David R. *Odious Commerce: Britain, Spain, and the Abolition of the Cuban Slave Trade.* New York: Cambridge University Press, 1980.

———. "The Slave Trade, Slavery, and Cuban Independence." *Slavery and Abolition [UK]* 20, Number 3 (1999): 106–126.

Naranjo Orovio, V. Consuelo. "Análisis histórico de la emigración española a Cuba, 1900–1959." *Revista de Indias [Spain]* 44, Number 174 (1984): 505–527.

Nieto y Cortadellas, Rafael. *Dignidades nobiliarias en Cuba.* Madrid: Cultura Hispánica, 1954.

Olivera, Otto. *Viajeros en Cuba (1800–1850).* Miami: Ediciones Universal, 1997.

Oostindie, Gert J. "Cuban Railroads, 1803–1868: Origins and Effects of Progressive Entrepreneurialism." *Caribbean Studies [Puerto Rico]* 20, Numbers 3–4 (1988): 24–45.

Paquette, Robert. *Sugar Is Made with Blood: The Conspiracy of La Escalera and the Conflict between Empires over Slavery in Cuba.* Middletown, CT: Wesleyan University Press, 1988.

Pérez, Louis A., Jr. *Intervention, Revolution, and Politics in Cuba, 1913–1921.* Pittsburgh: University of Pittsburgh Press, 1978.

———. *Cuba between Empires, 1878–1902.* Pittsburgh: University of Pittsburgh Press, 1983.

———. "Insurrection, Intervention, and the Transformation of Land Tenure Systems in Cuba, 1895–1902." *Hispanic American Historical Review* 65, Number 2 (1985): 229–254.

———. *Cuba: Between Reform and Revolution.* New York: Oxford University Press, 1988.

———. *Cuba and the United States: Ties of Singular Intimacy.* Athens: University of Georgia Press, 1990.

———. *The War of 1898: The United States and Cuba in History and Historiography.* Chapel Hill: University of North Carolina Press, 1998.

Pérez de la Riva, Juan. "La population de Cuba et ses problèmes." *Population* 22, Number 1 (January–February 1967): 99–110.

———. "Presentación de un censo ignorado: el padrón general de 1778." *Revista de la Biblioteca Nacional José Martí [Cuba],* Tercera Epoca, Volume 19, Number 3 (1977): 5–16.

Pérez Stable, Marifeli. "Estrada Palma's Civic March: From Oriente to Havana, April 20–May 11, 1902." *Cuban Studies* 30 (1999): 113–121.

Pichardo Viñals, Hortensia, editor. *Documentos para la historia de Cuba.* Havana: Consejo Nacional de Universidades and Editorial Ciencias Sociales, 1965–1973, three volumes.

Prat Puig, Francisco. *El prebarroco en Cuba: una escuela criolla de arquitectura.* Havana: Burgay, 1947.

Rallo, Joaquín, and Roberto Segre. *Introducción a las estructuras territoriales y urbanas de Cuba, 1519–1959.* Havana: Facultad de Arquitectura, 1981.

Rigol, Jorge. *Apuntes sobre la pintura y el grabado en Cuba.* Havana: Editorial Letras Cubanas, 1982.

Sánchez Baena, Juan José. "Noticias sobre el mundo del libro en Cuba antes del desarrollo de la imprenta, 1525–1763." *Contrastes [Spain]* 9–10 (1994–1997): 181–205.

Sánchez de Fuente y Peláez, Eugenio. *Cuba monumental, estatuaria y epigráfica.* Havana: Solana y Compañía, 1916–1917, two volumes.

Sánchez Ramírez, Antonio. "Notas sobre la Real Hacienda de Cuba, 1700–1760." *Anuario de Estudios Americanos [Spain]* 34 (1977): 465–486.

Santa Cruz y Mallen, Francisco Xavier de. *Historia de familias cubanas.* Miami: Hércules, 1986–1989 re-edition of 1940–1950 originals, nine volumes.

Schroeder, Susan. *Cuba: A Handbook of Historical Statistics.* Boston: G. K. Hall, 1982.

Schwartz, Rosalie. *Pleasure Island: Tourism and Temptation in Cuba.* Lincoln: University of Nebraska Press, 1997.

Scott, Rebecca J. *Slave Emancipation in Cuba: The Transition to Free Labor, 1860–1899.* Princeton: Princeton University Press, 1985.

Segre, Roberto. "Significación de Cuba en la evolución tipológica de las fortificaciones coloniales de América." *Revista de la Biblioteca Nacional José Martí [Cuba],* Año 59, Tercera Epoca, Volume 10, Number 2 (May–August 1968): 5–46.

———. "Continuidad y renovación en la arquitectura cubana del siglo XX." *Santiago [Cuba]* 41 (March–May 1981): 9–35.

Smith, Robert S. "Twentieth-Century Cuban Historiography." *Hispanic American Historical Review* 44 (1964): 44–73.

Suárez y Romero, Anselmo. *Artículos de costumbres cubanos del siglo XIX.* Havana: Arte y Literatura, 1974 compilation of nineteenth-century originals.

Tornero Tinajero, Pablo. *Crecimiento económico y transformaciones sociales: esclavos, hacendados y comerciantes en la Cuba colonial (1760–1840).* Madrid: Ministerio de Trabajo y Seguridad Social, 1996.

Ward, Fred. "Inside Cuba Today." *National Geographic* 151, Number 1 (January 1977): 32–69.

Weiss y Sánchez, Joaquín E. *Arquitectura colonial cubana: colección de fotografías de los principales y más característicos edificios erigidos en Cuba durante la dominación española.* Havana: Editorial Arte y Literatura, 1972 reprint of 1936 original published by Editorial Cultural, two volumes.

White, Peter T. "Cuba at a Crossroads." *National Geographic* 180, Number 2 (August 1991): 90–121.

Yebra, Rita. "Proceso de urbanización en Cuba en dos décadas de revolución." *Revista de la Biblioteca Nacional José Martí [Cuba]* 21, Number 2 (1979): 77–88.

Zanetti, Oscar, and Alejandro García. *Sugar and Railroads: A Cuban History, 1837–1959.* Chapel Hill: University of

North Carolina Press, 1998 translation by Franklin W. Knight and Mary Todd of 1987 original.

Havana
Early Colonial Era (1508–1761)

Arrate y Acosta, José Martín Félix de. *Llave del Nuevo Mundo, antemural de las Indias Occidentales: La Habana descripta: noticias de su fundación, aumentos y estados.* Mexico City: Fondo de Cultura Económica, 1949 reprint of mid-eighteenth-century original, first published in Havana by the Imprenta Andrés Pego in 1876.

Arriaga Mesa, Marcos D. "Un acercamiento al comportamiento del precio de los esclavos en La Habana en la segunda mitad del siglo XVI." *Anuario de Estudios Americanos [Spain]* 56, Number 1 (1999): 15–40.

Artiles, Jenaro. *La Habana de Velázquez.* Havana: Cuadernos de Historia Habanera, 1946.

Berthe, Jean-Pierre, and Juan Pérez de la Riva, editors. "La Habana de fines del siglo XVII visto por un italiano: Gemelli Careri." *Revista de la Biblioteca Nacional José Martí [Cuba],* Tercera Epoca, Volume 13 (May–August 1971): 63–86.

Blanes Martín, Tamara. "La Habana vieja: mapas y planos en los archivos de España." *Revista de la Biblioteca Nacional José Martí [Cuba]* 27, Number 2 (1985): 184–185.

Carbonell, Néstor, and Joaquín Llaverías, compilers and editors. *Papeles existentes en el Archivo de Indias relativos a Cuba y muy particularmente a La Habana.* Havana: Imprenta El Siglo XX for the Academia de la Historia, 1931, two volumes.

Cruz Hermosilla, Emilio de la. "Lorenzo Montalvo, figura señera de la Armada." *Revista General de la Marina [Spain]* 202 (January 1982): 17–23.

Domínguez, Lourdes. "Arqueología del sitio colonial Casa de la Obrapía o de Calvo de la Puerta, Habana Vieja." *Santiago [Cuba]* 41 (March–May 1981): 63–82.

Dunn, Oliver. "Trouble at Sea: The Return Voyage of the Fleet of New Spain and Honduras in 1622." *Terrae Incognitae* 11 (1979): 29–41.

Fuente García, Alejandro de la. "Los matrimonios de esclavos en La Habana, 1585–1645." *Ibero-Amerikanisches Archiv [Germany]* 16, Number 4 (1990): 507–528.

———. "El mercado esclavista habanero, 1580–1699: las armazones de esclavos." *Revista de Indias [Spain]* 50, Number 189 (1990): 371–395.

———. "Indices de morbilidad e incidencia de enfermedades entre los esclavos en La Habana, 1580–1699." *Asclepio [Spain]* 43, Number 2 (1991): 7–22.

———. "Los ingenios de azúcar en La Habana del siglo XVII (1640–1700): estructura y mano de obra." *Revista*

de Historia Económica [Spain] 9, Number 1 (1991): 35–67.

Fuente García, Alejandro de la, César García del Pino, and Bernardo Iglesias Delgado. "Havana and the Fleet System: Trade and Growth in the Periphery of the Spanish Empire, 1550–1610." *Colonial Latin American Review* 5, Number 1 (1996): 95–115.

"Fundación del convento de Santo Domingo, en La Habana." *Boletín del Archivo Nacional [Cuba]* 8 (1909): 15–24 and 57–64.

García del Pino, César. "El combate entre Knowles y Reggio en 1748." *Santiago [Cuba]* 36 (1979): 197–220.

———. "¿Dónde se fundó la villa de San Cristóbal?" *Revista de la Biblioteca Nacional José Martí [Cuba]* 21, Number 1 (1979): 5–26.

———. "Toma de La Habana por Jacques de Sores." *Universidad de La Habana* 218 (1982): 5–16.

———. "Los combates navales de Cabañas en 1638." *Santiago [Cuba]* 67 (1987): 63–71.

———. "Notas sobre la propiedad de la tierra en la jurisdicción de La Habana en 1680." *Universidad de La Habana* 229 (1987): 7–13.

Herrera López, Pedro A. "El maestro mayor Francisco de Calona, primer arquitecto municipal de La Habana, 1528–1607." *Universidad de La Habana* 233 (1988): 67–86.

La Habana vieja: mapas y planos en los archivos de España. Madrid: Ministerio de Cultura, 1985.

Lague, Guillermo. *El primer hospital de La Habana.* Havana: Neptuno, 1952.

LaRosa Corzo, Gabino. "El hospital para cimarrones en La Habana: notas para un estudio." *Universidad de La Habana* 228 (1986): 193–204.

———. "Apuntes sobre el hospital para los cimarrones de La Habana." *Estudios de Historia Social [Spain]* 1–4 (1988): 561–568.

Marley, David F. "A Fearful Gift: The Spanish Naval Build-Up in the West Indies, 1759–1762." *The Mariner's Mirror [UK]* 80, Number 4 (November 1994): 403–417.

McNeill, John Robert. *Atlantic Empires of France and Spain: Louisbourg and Havana, 1700–1763.* Chapel Hill: University of North Carolina Press, 1985.

Oglesby, J. C. M. "Spain's Havana Squadron and the Preservation of the Balance of Power in the Caribbean, 1740–1748." *Hispanic American Historical Review* 49, Number 3 (1969): 473–488.

Otero Lana, Enrique. "Un avance en la construcción naval: las fragatas construídas en La Habana hacia 1600." *Revista de Historia Naval [Spain]* 9, Number 34 (1991): 87–94.

Roig de Leuchsenring, Emilio, compiler. *Actas capitulares del ayuntamiento de La Habana, 1550–1578.* Havana: Municipio de La Habana, 1937–1946, three volumes.

Rojas, María Teresa de. *Indice y extractos del Archivo de Protocolos de La Habana.* Havana, 1947–1957, three volumes.

Smith, Octavio. "El capitán Santiago Pita de Figueroa, las viejas milicias habaneras." *Revista de la Biblioteca Nacional José Martí [Cuba]* 18, Number 1 (1976): 79–84.

Stibi, Ferdinand. "El 'libro de barajas' de la catedral de La Habana." *Hidalguía [Spain]* 21, Number 118 (1973): 241–272 and Number 119: 603–644.

Torriente, Juan. *El castillo del Morro.* Havana: Editora del Ministerio de Educación, 1964.

Venegas Fornias, Carlos. "La Habana proclama un rey." *Revista de la Biblioteca Nacional José Martí [Cuba]* 23, Number 1 (1981): 105–117.

Wright, Irene Aloha. *Historia documentada de San Cristóbal de La Habana en el siglo XVI* and *Historia documentada de San Cristóbal de La Habana en la primera mitad del siglo XVII.* Havana: Siglo XX, 1927–1930, two volumes.

Early Maps and Depictions of Havana, 1584–1798

Pen-and-ink drawing of proposed improvements to the town's defenses, ca. 1584–1586—original held by the Archive of Indies at Seville, call number: Mapas y Planos de Santo Domingo, 4 [archival provenance: Audiencia de Santo Domingo, Legajo 101]

Pen-and-ink drawing with watercolor highlights, of a property whose confiscation was contested by the royal engineer Cristóbal de Roda in the 1590s—original held by the Archive of Indies at Seville, call number: Mapas y Planos de Santo Domingo [archival provenance: Indiferente General, Legajo 1381]

Pen-and-ink drawing with watercolor highlights by De Roda, of proposed stone ramparts for the city perimeter, 1603—original held by the Archive of Indies at Seville, call number: Mapas y Planos de Santo Domingo, 20 [archival provenance: Audiencia de Santo Domingo, Legajo 100]

Pen-and-ink drawing with watercolor highlights of the city core in 1691—original held in the "Colección Cubana" of the Biblioteca Nacional José Martí in Havana

Pen-and-ink drawing by the military engineer Bruno Cavallero and signed by Gov. Dionisio Martínez de la Vega in February 1730, indicating a proposed new site for Havana's cathedral—original held by the Archive of Indies at Seville, call number: Mapas y Planos de Santo Domingo, 160 [archival provenance: Audiencia de Santo Domingo, Legajo 385]

Survey of Havana and its surroundings, May 1733—original held by the Archive of Indies at Seville, call number: Mapas y Planos de Santo Domingo, 176 [archival provenance: Audiencia de Santo Domingo, Legajo 1588]

Pen-and-ink drawing with watercolor highlights by Antonio de Arredondo, illustrating a plan to drain rain-waters from the city, December 1739—original held by the Archive of Indies at Seville, call number: Mapas y Planos de Santo Domingo, 204 [archival provenance: Audiencia de Santo Domingo, Legajo 531]

Pen-and-ink diagram with watercolor highlights of Havana's harbor by naval Capt. José Montero de Espinosa, June 1749—original held by the Archivo General de Simancas in Spain, call number: Mapas, Planos y Dibujos, VII-132 [archival provenance: Marina, Legajo 401]

Anonymous, undated map of Havana and its harbor in the mid-eighteenth century—original held by the Servicio Geográfico del Ejército in Madrid, call number: 88

"A new and correct chart of the harbour of Havana" by Capt. James Phelps, ca. 1758—original held by the Library of Congress in Washington, call number: American Maps, Volume 2, Number 52

Map of the city and harbor, ca. 1760—original held in the "Colección Cubana" of the Biblioteca Nacional José Martí in Havana

More than a dozen oil paintings by Dominique Serres the Elder, progressively depicting the English siege and capture of Havana, June–August 1762—eleven originals held by the National Maritime Museum in Greenwich, London [call numbers: BHC 0408 through 0418], plus numerous lithographic reproductions

Anonymous Spanish map, drawn in ink with watercolor highlights, of the English conquest of the city in 1762—original held by the National Maritime Museum in Greenwich, London [call number: PAI 6040]

Pen-and-ink map with watercolor highlights detailing the improvements needed to strengthen Havana's walls and harbor defenses, April 1764—original held by the Archivo General de Simancas in Spain, call number: Mapas, Planos y Dibujos, V-180 [archival provenance: Secretaría y Superintendencia de Hacienda, Legajo 2342]

Diagram, plus profile and cutaway views by the military engineer Silvestre Abarca, of the new San Carlos Castle atop La Cabaña heights, 1764—original held by the Servicio Geográfico del Ejército in Madrid, call number: 112

Map of the city and its defenses, published in the 1764 *Petit atlas maritime* by the French naval engineer and cartographer Jacques-Nicolas Bellin—numerous sources

Two pen-and-ink diagrams with watercolor highlights by Ramón Ignacio de Yoldi of Havana's old Royal Tobacco Factory, and a proposed replacement, June 1772—original held by the Archivo General de Simancas in Spain, call numbers: Mapas, Planos y Dibujos, XI-32 and XI-48

[archival provenance: Secretaría y Superintendencia de Hacienda, Legajo 1844]

Pen-and-ink diagram with watercolor highlights of Havana's new arsenal, July 1773—original held by the Archivo General de Simancas in Spain, call number: Mapas, Planos y Dibujos, V-199 [archival provenance: Marina, Legajo 350]

Pen-and-ink chart with watercolor highlights, of how the harbor was to be dredged, November 1773—original held by the Archivo General de Simancas in Spain, call number: Mapas, Planos y Dibujos, VIII-152 [archival provenance: Marina, Legajo 385]

Diagram and profile view of a proposed new paving system, using hard wooden blocks, 1773—original held by the Archive of Indies at Seville, call number: Mapas y Planos de Santo Domingo, 383

Diagram of a small new fort called Atarés, to be erected atop Soto Hill south-southwest of Havana, ca. 1776—original held by the Archive of Indies at Seville, call number: Mapas y Planos de Santo Domingo, 401

Pen-and-ink drawing with watercolor highlights by Luis Huet, of Abarca's fortification efforts outside the city, 8 May 1776—original held by the Archive of Indies at Seville, call number: Mapas y Planos de Santo Domingo, 412 [archival provenance: Audiencia de Santo Domingo, Legajo 1226]

Pen-and-ink map with watercolor highlights by Huet, of suggested wartime measures for the city's defense, 11 May 1776—originals held by the Archive of Indies at Seville, call numbers: Mapas y Planos de Santo Domingo, 418 and 418bis [archival provenance: Audiencia de Santo Domingo, Legajos 1226 and 1227]

Street diagrams by Mariano de la Rocque, March 1777—originals held by the Archive of Indies at Seville, call number: Mapas y Planos de Santo Domingo [archival provenance: Audiencia de Cuba, Legajo 1229]

Pen-and-ink diagram and profile view with watercolor highlights by Huet, of Fort Príncipe, June 1779—original held by the Archivo General de Simancas in Spain, call number: Mapas, Planos y Dibujos, I-47 [archival provenance: Guerra Moderna, Legajo 3222]

Pen-and-ink map with watercolor highlights of Havana in 1783 by naval Lt. José de San Martín, then copied seven years later by the pilot José Soto Villa—original held by the Library of Congress in Washington, call number: G 4922.H3 1783.B6 Vault

Four pen-and-ink diagrams with watercolor highlights of a proposed new two-story militia barracks, May 1787—originals held by the Archivo General de Simancas in Spain, call numbers: Mapas, Planos y Dibujos, V-4, VII-86, VIII-6, and VIII-8 [archival provenance: Guerra Moderna, 6840]

Pen-and-ink drawing with watercolor highlights of the naval arsenal, 1788—original held by the Museo Naval in Madrid

Pen-and-ink diagram with watercolor highlights of the arsenal, ca. 1790—original held by the Library of Congress in Washington, call number: G 4924.H3P55 17—.P5 Vault

Pen-and-ink diagram with watercolor highlights by Cayetano Paveto, of the Nogales Redoubt, June 1791—original held by the Archivo General de Simancas in Spain, call number: Mapas, Planos y Dibujos, XIX-69 [archival provenance: Guerra Moderna, 7247]

Map of the city and its harbor by José del Río, 1794—original held by the Museo Naval in Madrid, call number: Sección de Cartografía, XVI-C-11

Sketch map of Havana's anchorage, including depth soundings, 1798—original held by the Archive of Indies at Seville, call number: Mapas y Planos de Santo Domingo, 607

English Occupation (1762–1763)

Bachiller y Morales, Antonio. *Cuba: monografía histórica que comprende desde la pérdida de La Habana hasta la restauración española.* Havana: Oficina del Historiador de la Ciudad, 1962 reprint of 1883 original published by Miguel de Villa.

Castillo Manrubia, Pilar. "Pérdida de La Habana." *Revista de Historia Naval [Spain]* 8, Number 28 (1990): 61–77.

Grabados de Dominique Serres sobre la toma de La Habana en 1762. Havana: Biblioteca Nacional José Martí, 1962.

Guiteras, Pedro J. *Historia de la conquista de La Habana por los ingleses.* Havana: Oficina del Historiador de la Ciudad, 1962 reprint of 1932 original published by Editorial Cultural.

Hale, Edward E., editor. *The Capture of Havana in 1762 by the Forces of George III.* Boston: Lend-A-Hand, 1898.

Jiménez Pastrana, Juan. "Balance de la dominación inglesa en La Habana, 1762–1763." *Revista de la Biblioteca Nacional José Martí [Cuba]* 29, Number 3 (1987): 78–97.

Llaverías, Joaquín, compiler. *Papeles sobre la toma de La Habana por los ingleses en 1762.* Havana: Archivo Nacional de Cuba, 1948.

Marley, David F. "Havana Surprised: Prelude to the British Invasion, 1762." *The Mariner's Mirror [UK]* 78, Number 3 (August 1992): 293–305.

Martínez Dalmau, Eduardo. *La política colonial y extranjera de los reyes españoles de la casa de Austria y de Borbón y la toma de La Habana por los ingleses.* Havana: Siglo XX, 1943.

Nuevos papeles sobre la toma de La Habana por los ingleses en 1762. Havana: Archivo Nacional de Cuba, 1951.

Parcero Torre, Celia María. *La pérdida de La Habana y las reformas borbónicas en Cuba, 1760–1773*. Valladolid, Spain: Junta de Castilla y León, 1998.

Pérez de la Riva, Juan, et al., editors. *Documentos inéditos sobre la toma de La Habana por los ingleses en 1762.* Havana: Biblioteca Nacional José Martí, 1963.

Plasencia Moro, Aleida, editor. *La dominación inglesa vista por el pueblo de La Habana.* Havana: Biblioteca Nacional José Martí, 1965.

Pocock, Tom. "The Capture of Havana, 1762," *History Today [UK]* 12 (1962): 580–586.

Rodríguez, Amalia A., compiler and editor. *Cinco diarios del sitio de La Habana.* Havana: Biblioteca Nacional José Martí, 1963.

Roig de Leuchsenring, Emilio, compiler. *La dominación inglesa en La Habana: libros de cabildo, 1762–1763.* Havana: Molina for the Municipio de La Habana, 1929.

Syrett, David, compiler and editor. "American Provincials and the Havana Campaign of 1762." *New York History* 49, Number 4 (1968): 375–390.

———. *The Siege and Capture of Havana, 1762.* London: Navy Records Society, 1970.

The Two Putnams, Israel and Rufus, in the Havana Expedition 1762 and in the Mississippi River Exploration 1772–1773. Hartford: Connecticut Historical Society, 1931.

Zurbarán, Juana. "Biblioteca de la toma de La Habana por los ingleses." *Revista de la Biblioteca Nacional José Martí [Cuba],* Tercera Epoca, Volume 2 (1960): 44–53.

Bourbon Revival (1764–1797)

Abarca, Silvestre. *Proyecto de defensa de la plaza de La Habana y sus castillos.* Havana: Oficina del Historiador de la Ciudad, 1961 edition of eighteenth-century document.

Aranda y Antón, Gaspar de. "Las maderas de América en la arquitectura naval del siglo XVIII." *Revista de Historia Naval [Spain]* 10, Number 38 (1992): 7–31.

Beerman, Eric. "El marino que trasladó los restos de Colón de Santo Domingo a La Habana: Gabriel de Aristizábal, 1743–1805." *Revista de Historia Naval [Spain]* 9, Number 34 (1991): 13–48.

Campbell, John F. "The Havana Incident." *American Neptune* 22, Number 4 (1962): 264–276.

Cruz Hermosilla, Emilio de la. "Los restos de Colón." *Revista General de Marina [Spain]* 201 (November 1981): 435–441.

Delgado, Jaime. "El conde de Ricla, capitán general de Cuba." *Revista de Historia de América [Mexico]* 55–56 (1963): 1–75.

"Documentos sobre el correo en Cuba." *Boletín del Instituto de Historia y del Archivo Nacional [Cuba]* 64 (1964): 3–35.

DuBouchet, Jorge. "Antiguallas habaneras: la dote de una marquesa." *Revista de la Biblioteca Nacional José Martí [Cuba]* 30, Number 3 (1988): 215–224.

García Marruz, Fina. "Obras de teatro representadas en La Habana en la última década del siglo XVIII según el 'Papel Periódico'." *Revista de la Biblioteca Nacional José Martí [Cuba]* 14, Number 2 (1972): 95–125.

García Ricardo, José. "Los impresores Boloña." *Revista de la Biblioteca Nacional José Martí [Cuba]* 28, Number 2 (1986): 141–154.

González-Aller Hierro, José Ignacio. "El navío *San Hermenegildo,* alias *Meregildo.*" *Revista de Historia Naval [Spain]* 2, Number 4 (1984): 75–81.

———. "El navío de tres puentes en la armada española." *Revista de Historia Naval [Spain]* 3, Number 9 (1985): 45–76.

Harbron, John D. "The Spanish Ship of the Line." *Scientific American* 251, Number 6: 116–124.

Johnson, Sherry. "'La guerra contra los habitantes de los arrabales': Changing Patterns of Land Use and Land Tenancy in and around Havana, 1763–1800." *Hispanic American Historical Review* 77, Number 2 (May 1997): 181–209.

Lewis, James A. "Nueva España y los esfuerzos para abastecer La Habana, 1779–1783." *Anuario de Estudios Americanos [Spain]* 33 (1976): 501–526.

López Sánchez, José. "Manuscritos sobre fiebre amarilla en la Biblioteca Nacional José Martí." *Revista de la Biblioteca Nacional José Martí [Cuba]* 28, Number 1 (1986): 123–137.

Navarro, Diego José. "Bando de buen gobierno." *Boletín del Archivo Nacional [Cuba]* 28 (1949): 83–84.

Nunes Días, Manuel. "Le mouvement des 'navires de registre' entre La Havane et les ports d'Espagne à l'époque du 'commerce libre', 1787–1789." *Revue d'histoire économique et sociale [France]* 45, Number 1 (1967): 87–104.

Ortega Pereyra, Ovidio. *La construcción naval en La Habana bajo la dominación colonial española.* Havana: Academia de Ciencias de Cuba, 1986.

Peraza, Fermín. "El 'Papel Periódico de La Havana' y los orígenes del periodismo en Cuba." *Revista Interamericana de Bibliografía* 8, Number 4 (1958): 368–378.

Pérez Cabrera, José Manuel. "Un gran editor del siglo XVIII, el capitán don Diego de la Barrera y Navarro." *Revista de Historia de América [Mexico]* 60 (1965): 125–159.

Perotin, Anne. "Los planes económicos de los grandes hacendados habaneros." *Revista de la Biblioteca Nacional José Martí [Cuba]* 19, Number 2 (1977): 5–50.

Pichardo Viñals, Hortensia. *Biografía del colegio de San Cristóbal de La Habana.* Havana: Academia de Ciencias de Cuba, 1979.

Rodríguez Vicente, María Encarnación. "El comercio cubano y la guerra de emancipación norteamericana." *Anuario de Estudios Americanos [Spain]* 11 (1954): 61–106.

Sánchez Agustí, María. *Edificios públicos de La Habana en el siglo XVIII.* Valladolid, Spain: Universidad de Valladolid Press, 1984.

Sánchez de Neyra Mille, Antonio. "En torno a los restos de Colón." *Revista General de Marina [Spain]* 186, Number 3 (1974): 297–300.

Simpson, Renate. "Francisco de Arango y Parreño: sus esfuerzos en pró de la educación científica y técnica en Cuba." *Revista de la Biblioteca Nacional José Martí [Cuba]* 18, Number 3 (1976): 13–51.

Topping, Aileen Moore. "Alexander Gillon in Havana: 'This Very Friendly Port.'" *South Carolina Historical Magazine* 83, Number 1 (1982): 34–49.

Torres Ramírez, Bibiano. "Alejandro O'Reilly en Cuba." *Anuario de Estudios Americanos [Spain]* 24 (1967): 1357–1388.

Valero González, Mercedes. "La Real Expedición Botánica a Nueva España y los intentos de creación del Jardín Botánico de La Habana." *Asclepio [Spain]* 47, Number 2 (1995): 67–78.

Venegas Fornias, Carlos. *Dos etapas de colonización y expansión urbana.* Havana: Editora Política, 1979.

———. *La urbanización de las murallas: dependencia y modernidad.* Havana: Letras Cubanas, 1990.

———. "La Habana y su región: un proyecto de organización espacial de la plantación esclavista." *Revista de Indias [Spain]* 56, Number 207 (1996): 333–366.

Late Colonial Era (1798–1898)

Abbot, Abiel. *Cartas.* Havana: Consejo Nacional de Cultura, 1965 Spanish translation of 1828 original.

Acevedo, Luciano de, compiler. *La Habana en el siglo XIX, descrita por viajeros extranjeros.* Havana: Sociedad Editorial Cuba Contemporánea, 1919.

Altschuler, José, and Miguel González. "El alumbrado eléctrico en La Habana del siglo XIX." *Quipú [Mexico]* 2, Number 2 (1985): 213–249.

Argüelles Espinosa, Luis Angel. "La abolición de la esclavitud a través de algunos diarios habaneros de la época: 1880 y 1886." *Universidad de La Habana* 230 (1987): 5–19 and *Anuario de Estudios Americanos [Spain]* 43 (1986): 241–257.

Arriaga Mesa, Marcos D., and Andrés Delgado Valdés. "Contribución al estudio de la vivienda pobre en La Habana del siglo XIX: ciudadelas y accesorias." *Revista de Indias [Spain]* 55, Number 204 (1995): 453–483.

"Bando de buen gobierno." *Boletín del Instituto de Historia y del Archivo Nacional [Cuba]* 64 (1964): 43–47.

Barras y Prado, Antonio de las. *La Habana a mediados del siglo XIX.* Madrid: Ciudad Lineal, 1925.

Cabrera Leiva, Guillermo. "First Railroad in Latin America." *Américas [Organization of American States]* 26, Number 4 (April 1974): 8–14.

Charon, Euridice. "El asentamiento de emigrantes árabes en Monte (La Habana, Cuba), 1890–1930." *Awraq [Spain]* 13 (1992): 35–68.

Dalleo, Peter T. "Thomas McKean Rodney, U.S. Consul in Cuba: The Havana Years, 1825–1829." *Delaware History* 22, Number 3 (1987): 204–218.

Debien, Gabriel. "Refugiés de Saint-Domingue expulsés de La Havane en 1809." *Anuario de Estudios Americanos [Spain]* 35 (1978): 555–610.

Del Regato, J. A. "Carlos Finlay and the Carrier of Death." *Américas [Organization of American States]* 20, Number 5 (May 1968): 30–38.

Deschamps Chapeaux, Pedro. *El negro en la economía habanera del siglo XIX.* Havana: Unión de Escritores y Artistas de Cuba, 1971.

———. "Testamentaría de pardos y morenos libres en La Habana del siglo XIX." *Revista de la Biblioteca Nacional José Martí [Cuba]* 14, Number 2 (1972): 45–54.

Diego García, Emilio de. "El ferrocarril La Habana-Güines." *Cuadernos de Historia Moderna [Spain]* 4 (1983): 59–77.

Drake, F. C. "The Cuban Background of the *Trent* Affair." *Civil War History* 19, Number 1 (1973): 29–49.

Egea López, Antonio. "Angel Laborde, comandante del apostadero de La Habana." *Revista de Historia Naval [Spain]* 8, Number 28 (1990): 7–30.

Fraile, Pedro. "La necesidad de remodelar un espacio: La Habana bajo el general Tacón." *Estudios de Historia Social [Spain]* 1–4 (1988): 577–594.

García del Pino, César. "La Habana en los días de Yera." *Revista de la Biblioteca Nacional José Martí [Cuba]* 20, Number 2 (1978): 149–172.

García González, Armando C. "La obra botánica de Antonio Parra." *Asclepio [Spain]* 47, Number 2 (1995): 143–157.

García González, Armando C., and Consuelo Naranjo Orovio. "Antropología, racismo e inmigración en la Sociedad Económica de Amigos del País de La Habana." *Asclepio [Spain]* 43, Number 2 (1991): 139–163.

García González, Armando C., and García González with Armando Rangel Rivero. "El Museo Anatómico de La Habana: la enseñanza de la anatomía, cirugía y obstetricía, 1823–1842." *Asclepio [Spain]* 43, Number 2 (1991): 23–57.

García Pons, César. *El obispo Espada y su influencia en la cultura cubana.* Havana: Ministerio de Educación, 1951.

Garfield, Evelyn Picon. "Periodical Literature for Women in Mid-Nineteenth Century Cuba: The Case of Gertrúdis Gómez de Avellaneda's *Album Cubano de lo Bueno y lo*

Bello." *Studies in Latin American Popular Culture* 11 (1992): 13–28.

González del Valle, Francisco. *La Habana en 1841.* Havana: Oficina del Historiador de la Ciudad, 1952.

González González, Francisco José. "La rectificación de las coordenadas geográficas de La Habana mediante señales telegráficas en 1868: una interesante colaboración entre el United States Naval Observatory y la Comisión Hidrográfica de las Antillas." *Llull [Spain]* 16, Number 31 (1993): 493–504.

González Jiménez, José Miguel. "La casa de vivienda de Osma." *Revista de la Biblioteca Nacional José Martí [Cuba]* 15, Number 3 (1973): 125–136.

Humboldt, Alexander von. *Ensayo político sobre la isla de Cuba.* Havana: Oficina del Historiador de la Ciudad, 1959 Spanish translation.

"Instrucción para el servicio de las tres expediciones diarias del correo interior de la ciudad y sus barrios extramuros." *Boletín del Instituto de Historia y del Archivo Nacional [Cuba]* 64 (1964): 37–41.

Iznaga, Diana, and Yolanda Vidal. "Apuntes para la historia de la Sociedad Económica de Amigos del País de La Habana durante la época colonial." *Revista de la Biblioteca Nacional José Martí [Cuba]* 23, Number 1 (1981): 153–173.

Karras, Bill J. "Yankee Carpenter in Cuba, 1848." *Américas [Organization of American States]* 30, Numbers 6–7 (June–July 1978): 17–23.

Jameson, Francis Robert. "Cartas habaneras 1820." *Revista de la Biblioteca Nacional José Martí [Cuba],* Year 57, Volume 8, Number 2 (July–September 1966): 43–75.

Labarre, Roland. "La conspiración de 1844: un 'complot por lo menos dudoso' y una 'atroz maquinación.'" *Anuario de Estudios Americanos [Spain]* 43 (1986): 127–141.

Lapique Becali, Zoila, et al. "La primera imprenta litográfica en Cuba." *Revista de la Biblioteca Nacional José Martí [Cuba]* 12, Number 3 (1970): 35–47.

Le Roy y Gálvez, Luis F. "Aspecto jurídico del 27 de noviembre de 1871." *Revista de la Biblioteca Nacional José Martí [Cuba]* 18, Number 3 (1976): 93–108.

———. "Documentos desconocidos sobre el proceso de los estudiantes del 27 de noviembre de 1871." *Revista de la Biblioteca Nacional José Martí [Cuba]* 20, Number 3 (1978): 33–73.

Long, John Sherman. "Glory-Hunting Off Havana: Wilkes and the *Trent* Affair." *Civil War History* 9, Number 2 (1963): 133–144.

Martínez Fernández, Luis. "The Havana Anglo-Spanish Mixed Commission for the Suppression of the Slave Trade and Cuba's *Emancipados.*" *Slavery and Abolition [UK]* 16, Number 2 (1995): 205–225.

———. "Life in a 'Male City': Native and Foreign Elite Women in Nineteenth-Century Havana." *Cuban Studies* 25 (1995): 27–49.

———. *Fighting Slavery in the Caribbean: The Life and Times of a British Family in Nineteenth-Century Havana.* Armonk, NY: M. E. Sharpe, 1998.

Merino, Luz. "Apuntes para un estudio de la Academia San Alejandro." *Revista de la Biblioteca Nacional José Martí [Cuba]* 18, Number 1 (1976): 117–142.

Merlin, María de las Mercedes Santa Cruz y Montalvo, Comtesse de. *Viaje a La Habana.* Havana, 1922 translation of 1844 French original published by Dayhot in Paris as *La Havane.*

Miranda Cancela, Elina, and Amaury Carbón Sierra. "La educación clásica de un joven habanero de la segunda mitad del siglo XIX." *Revista de la Biblioteca Nacional José Martí [Cuba]* 27, Number 3 (1985): 79–94.

Misas Jiménez, Rolando E. "La Real Sociedad Patriótica de La Habana en el rescate de la variedad 'naturalizada' del trigo de Villa Clara." *Asclepio [Spain]* 43, Number 2 (1991): 117–128.

Pruna, Pedro M. "La vacunación homeopática contra la fiebre amarilla en La Habana, 1855." *Asclepio [Spain]* 43, Number 2 (1991): 59–68.

———. "National Science in a Colonial Context: The Royal Academy of Sciences of Havana, 1861–1898." *Isis* 85, Number 3 (1994): 412–426.

Pruna, Pedro M., and Ovidio Ortega. "La composicián de la Real Academia de Ciencias de La Habana." *Quipú [Mexico]* 2, Number 2 (1985): 251–262.

Rey, Francisco. "Gran teatro de La Habana: 150 aniversario." *Revista de la Biblioteca Nacional José Martí [Cuba]* 29, Number 2 (1988): 192–196.

Rodríguez Exposito, César. "El ingeniero Francisco de Albear, artífice del Canal de Vento." *Finlay [Cuba]* 7 (1966): 5–38.

Socarras Matos, Martín. "Los transportes habaneros, 1519–1868: algunas consideraciones." *Revista de la Biblioteca Nacional José Martí [Cuba]* 25, Number 2 (1983): 193–204.

Tylden, John Maxwell. "La Habana en 1814–1815, según Sir John Maxwell Tylden." *Revista de la Biblioteca Nacional José Martí [Cuba]* 14, Number 2 (1972): 81–94.

Valdés Domínguez, Fermín. *Tragedy in Havana: November 17, 1871.* Gainesville: University Press of Florida, 2000 translation by Consuelo E. Stebbins.

Valero González, Mercedes. "Estudios de plantas medicinales publicados por la Academia de Ciencias Médicas, Físicas y Naturales de La Habana de 1899 a 1958." *Asclepio [Spain]* 43, Number 2 (1991): 89–100.

Vizcaíno, Juan F. "Carlos J. Finlay, gloria americana." *Journal of Inter-American Studies* 7, Number 4 (1965): 493–502.

Wogan, Daniel, editor. "La Habana vista por un mexicano en 1817–1829." *Revista de la Biblioteca Nacional [Cuba]* 6, Number 1 (1955): 27–41.

American Occupations (1898–1909)

Abel, Christopher A. "Controlling the Big Stick: Theodore Roosevelt and the Cuban Crisis of 1906." *Naval War College Review* 40, Number 3 (1987): 88–98.

Allen, Thomas D. "Remember the *Maine*?" *National Geographic* 193, Number 2 (February 1998): 92–111.

———. "What Really Sank the *Maine*?" *Naval History* 12, Number 2 (1998): 30–39.

Arvy, Lucie. "Clara Louise Maass (1876–1901) et la fièvre jaune." *Clio Medica [The Netherlands]* 13, Numbers 3–4 (1979): 277–282.

Barcia Zequeira, María del Carmen. "El 98 en La Habana: sociedad y vida cotidiana." *Revista de Indias [Spain]* 58, Number 212 (1998): 85–99.

Basoco, Richard M. "What Really Happened to the *Maine*?" *American History Illustrated* 1, Number 3 (1966): 12–22.

Bybee, John D. "Blind Tiger: The U.S.S. *Maine* in Havana Harbor." *Periodical: Journal of America's Military Past* 24, Number 4 (1998): 70–76.

Calleja Leal, Guillermo G. "La voladura del *Maine*." *Revista de Historia Militar [Spain]* 34, Number 69 (1990): 163–196.

Duncan, John E. "Remember the *Maine*, One More Time." *Naval History* 4, Number 2 (1990): 58–62.

Eggert, Gerald G. "Our Man in Havana: Fitzhugh Lee." *Hispanic American Historical Review* 47, Number 4 (1967): 463–485.

González Echevarría, Roberto. *The Pride of Havana: A History of Cuban Baseball.* New York: Oxford University Press, 1999.

Hammersmith, Jack L. "Raising the Battleship *Maine*." *Industrial Archaeology [UK]* 15, Number 4 (1980): 318.

Haydock, Michael D. "'This Means War!'" *American History* 32, Number 6 (1998): 42–50 and 62–63.

Miller, Tom. "Remember the *Maine*." *Smithsonian* 28, Number 11 (1998): 46–57.

Samuels, Peggy, and Harold Samuels. *Remembering the "Maine."* Washington, DC: Smithsonian Institution Press, 1995.

Stepan, Nancy. "The Interplay between Socio-Economic Factors and Medical Science: Yellow Fever Research, Cuba and the United States." *Social Studies of Science [UK]* 8, Number 4 (1978): 397–423.

Taylor, John M. "Remembering the *Maine*." *American History Illustrated* 13, Number 1 (1978): 34–41.

Wegner, Dana, and Laurence A. Arnot, compilers. "Raising *Maine* and the Last Farewell." *Nautical Research Journal* 42, Number 4 (1997): 220–236.

Modern Era (1910–Present)

Baquero, Gastón. "Recuerdos sobre exiliados españoles en La Habana." *Cuadernos Hispanoamericanos [Spain]* 473–474 (1989): 211–220.

Butterworth, Douglas. *The People of Buena Ventura: Relocation of Slum Dwellers in Post-Revolutionary Cuba.* Urbana: University of Illinois Press, 1980.

Chailloux Cardona, Juan M. *Síntesis histórica de la vivienda popular: los horrores del solar habanero.* Havana: Editorial Obispo for the Biblioteca de Historia, Filosofía y Sociología, 1954.

Chaline, Claude. "La Havane: urbanisme de rupture ou de rattrapage?" *Annales de géographie [France]* 96, Number 534 (1987): 171–185.

Garnier, Jean-Pierre. *Une ville, une révolution: La Havane, de l'urbain au politique.* Paris: Anthropos, 1973.

Gellman, Irwin F. "The *St. Louis* Tragedy." *American Jewish Historical Quarterly* 51, Number 2 (1971): 144–156.

Gimbel, Wendy. *Havana Dreams: A Story of Cuba.* New York: Knopf, 1998.

Halperin, Maurice. *Return to Havana: The Decline of Cuban Society under Castro.* Nashville: Vanderbilt University Press, 1994.

Konovitch, Barry J. "The Fiftieth Anniversary of the *St. Louis:* What Really Happened." *American Jewish History* 79, Number 2 (1989–1990): 203–209.

LeShane, Albert A., Jr. "Aeromarine Airways, Inc." *American Aviation Historical Society Journal* 25, Number 3 (1980): 162–180.

Moore, Robin. *Nationalizing Blackness: "Afrocubanismo" and Artistic Revolution in Cuba, 1920–1940.* Pittsburgh: University of Pittsburgh Press, 1998.

Nickel, Annegret. "El casco histórico de La Habana: la situación de vivienda y los conceptos de renovación." *Revista Geográfica [Mexico]* 112 (1990): 75–90.

Nieves Rivera, Dolores. "Apuntes para una historia de la lucha insurreccional en la ciudad de La Habana: años 1957–1958." *Universidad de La Habana* 234 (1989): 25–49.

Otero, Lisandro, translated by Nancy Westrate. "Utopia Revisited." *South Atlantic Quarterly* 96, Number 1 (1997): 17–30.

Rodríguez, Eduardo Luis. *The Havana Guide: Modern Architecture, 1925–1965.* New York: Princeton Architectural, 2000 translation by Lorna S. Fox.

Salwen, Michael B. "Gaspar Pumarejo: Pre-Castro Cuba's 'Number Two' Television Tycoon." *Studies in Latin American Popular Culture* 14 (1995): 209–223.

Sánchez Porro, Reinaldo. "Tradición y modernidad: los judíos en La Habana." *Cuadernos de Historia Contemporánea [Spain]* 18 (1996): 175–189.

Smith, Rebecca. "The Visual Record: Travel Aboard the *Queen of the Caribbean*." *South Florida History Magazine* 23, Number 1 (1995): 14–19.

General Works

Arquitectura [Cuba] 340, Number 3 (1971), entire issue devoted to Havana's history.

Blanes Martín, Tamara. *Castillo de los Tres Reyes del Morro de La Habana: historia y arquitectura.* Havana: Letras Cubanas, 1998.

Bradley, Hugh. *Havana: Cinderella's City.* Garden City, NJ: Doubleday, 1941.

Corbitt, Duvon C. "Historical Publications of the Oficina del Historiador de la Ciudad de La Habana." *Hispanic American Historical Review* 35, Number 4 (1955): 492–501.

Fernández Santalices, Manuel. *Las calles de La Habana intramuros: arte, historia y tradiciones en las calles y plazas de La Habana Vieja.* Miami: Saeta, 1985.

Fernández Simón, Abel. *La Zanja Real.* Havana, 1957.

Judge, Joseph. "The Many Lives of Old Havana." *National Geographic* 176, Number 2 (August 1989): 278–300.

Le Riverend Brusone, Julio. *La Habana: biografía de una provincia.* Havana: Academia de la Historia de Cuba, 1960.

Le Roy y Cassá, Jorge, and Luis F. Le Roy y Gálvez. *Historia del hospital San Francisco de Paula.* Havana, 1958.

Le Roy y Gálvez, Luis F. *La Universidad de La Habana: síntesis histórica.* Havana, 1960.

———. *La Real y Pontificia Universidad de San Jerónimo.* Havana, 1965.

———. *La Real y Literaria Universidad de La Habana.* Havana, 1966.

———. *La Universidad de La Habana en su etapa republicana.* Havana, 1966.

Leal Spengler, Eusebio. *La Habana intramuros.* Havana: Oficina del Historiador de la Ciudad, 1975.

———. *La Habana, ciudad antigua.* Havana: Letras Cubanas, 1988.

Lobo Montalvo, María Luisa. *Havana: History and Architecture of a Romantic City.* New York: Monacelli, 2000 translation by Lorna S. Fox.

Morales y Pedroso, Luis. *El abasto de agua en la ciudad de San Cristóbal de La Habana.* Havana, 1938.

Núñez Jiménez, Antonio, and Carlos Venegas Fornias. *La Habana.* Madrid: Agencia Española de Cooperación Internacional e Instituto de Cooperación Iberoamericana, 1989 re-edition.

Paloscia, Raffaele. "L'Avana: note sulla costruzione di una identità urbana." *Storia Urbana [Italy]* 22, Numbers 82–83 (1998): 133–149.

Parajón, Mario. "Birth of a Plaza." *Américas [Organization of American States]* 28, Number 3 (March 1976): 2–4.

Peraza, Lilian, and Carlos Venegas Fornias. "Plaza Vieja: historia e identidad." *Islas [Cuba]* 70 (1981): 79–146.

Pérez Beato, Manuel. *La Habana antigua: apuntes históricos.* Havana: Seoane y Fernández, 1936, two volumes.

Pérez de la Riva, Francisco. "La construcción de buques en el arsenal de La Habana." *Revista Cubana* 31, Number 2 (1957): 91–101.

Pérez Guzmán, Francisco. *La Habana: clave de un imperio.* Havana: Editorial de Ciencias Sociales, 1997.

Roberts, Walter Adolphe. *Havana: Portrait of a City.* New York: Coward-McCann, 1953.

Roig de Leuchsenring, Emilio. *Historia de La Habana.* Havana: Municipio de La Habana, 1938.

———. *Los monumentos nacionales de la República de Cuba.* Havana: Junta Nacional de Arqueología y Etnología, 1957–1959, two volumes.

———. *La Casa de Gobierno o Palacio Municipal de La Habana.* Havana: Municipio de La Habana, 1961.

———. *La Habana: apuntes históricos.* Havana: Consejo Nacional de Cultura, 1963 reprint of 1938 original published by the Municipio de La Habana, three volumes.

Romero Estebánez, Leandro S. "Estudio histórico del sitio arqueológico de la maestranza de artillería de La Habana." *Universidad de La Habana* 228 (1986): 145–176.

Segre, Roberto, et al. *Havana: Two Faces of the Antillean Metropolis.* New York: Wiley, 1997.

Torre, José María de la. *Lo que fuimos y lo que somos, o La Habana antigua y moderna.* Santo Domingo: Ediciones Históricos Cubanos, 1986 facsimile re-edition of 1857 original published in Havana.

Universidad de La Habana 222 (January–September 1984): 7–417, entire issue devoted to Havana, in honor of the city's 465th anniversary.

Valdés, Antonio José. *Historia de la isla de Cuba y en especial de La Habana.* Havana: Comisión Nacional Cubana de la UNESCO, 1963 reprint of 1813 original published by the Oficina de la Cena.

Santiago De Cuba

Colonial Era (1515–1898)

Benítez Rojo, Antonio. "Para una valoración del libro de viajes y tres visitas a Santiago." *Santiago [Cuba]* 26–27 (June–September 1977): 275–300.

Callejas, José María. *Historia de Santiago de Cuba, compuesta y redactada en vista de los manuscritos originales e inéditos de 1823.* Havana: La Universal, 1911.

Cejudo, Célida. "Acerca de la fecha en que se introdujo la imprenta en Santiago de Cuba." *Santiago [Cuba]* 26–27 (June–September 1977): 203–209.

Duharte Jiménez, Rafael. "Santiago visto por un pintor inglés del siglo XIX." *Santiago [Cuba]* 54 (June–August 1984): 97–105.

———. "La esclavitud en la ciudad de Santiago de Cuba durante el siglo XIX." *Santiago [Cuba]* 64 (1987): 127–137.

———. "Apuntes para la manumisión de esclavos en Santiago de Cuba." *Secuencia [Mexico]* 13 (1989): 106–116.

"Esteban de Salas y Castro en el Archivo Nacional." *Boletín del Archivo Nacional [Cuba]* 57 (1958): 119–126.

Feliú Herrera, Virtudes. "Juan París, sucesor de Esteban Salas en la capilla de música de la catedral de Santiago de Cuba, 1805–1855." *Revista de la Biblioteca Nacional José Martí [Cuba]* 27, Number 3 (1985): 5–26.

Franco, José Luciano. *Las minas de Santiago del Prado y la rebelión de los cobreros, 1530–1800.* Havana: Editorial de Ciencias Sociales, 1975.

García del Pino, César. "Corsarios, piratas y Santiago de Cuba." *Santiago [Cuba]* 26–27 (June–September 1977): 101–178.

———. "Baltasar Díaz de Priego: un matemático santiaguero del siglo XVIII." *Santiago [Cuba]* 47 (September–November 1982): 115–149.

García Santana, Alicia, et al. "Fuentes y antecedentes de la arquitectura tradicional cubana." *Revista de la Biblioteca Nacional José Martí [Cuba]* 25, Number 2 (1983): 145–181.

González Loscertales, Vicente, and Inés Roldán de Montaud. "La minería del cobre en Cuba: su organización, problemas administrativos y repercusiones sociales." *Revista de Indias [Spain]* 159–162 (January–December 1980): 255–299.

González-Ripoll Navarro, María Dolores. "Una aproximación a la expedición 'secreta' de Ventura Barcaiztégui (1790–1793) y los reconocimientos de la parte oriental de Cuba." *Asclepio [Spain]* 43, Number 2 (1991): 165–179.

Goodman, Walter. *Un artista en Cuba.* Havana: Consejo Nacional de Cultura, 1965 translation of 1873 original published in London.

"La agricultura comercial en el proyecto expedicionario de Mopóx a Cuba." *Revista Complutense de Historia de América [Spain]* 20 (1994): 277–285.

Le Roy y Gálvez, Luis F. "Burriel, el *Virginius* y Sir Lambton Loraine." *Santiago [Cuba]* 26–27 (June–September 1977): 339–387.

Maluquer de Motes, Jordi. "La formación del mercado interior en condiciones coloniales: imigración y comercio catalán en las Antillas españolas durante el siglo XIX." *Siglo XIX [Mexico]* 2, Number 4 (1987): 161–181.

Marrero y Artiles, Leví. *Los esclavos y la Virgen del Cobre: dos siglos de lucha por la libertad de Cuba.* Miami: Cuba y sus Jueces, 1982.

Martínez Arango, Felipe. *Próceres de Santiago de Cuba.* Havana: Imprenta de la Universidad de La Habana, 1946.

———. Misas Jiménez, Rolando E. "Trascendencia del trigo recolectado por la expedición de Mopóx en Cuba, 1797–1799." *Asclepio [Spain]* 47, Number 2 (1995): 211–220.

Morales, María Caridad, et al. "Vestigios de la temprana arquitectura colonial de Santiago de Cuba." *Santiago [Cuba]* 65, Number 1 (1987): 63–77.

Muguercia, Alberto. "Músicos santiagueros del siglo XIX." *Santiago [Cuba]* 66 (1987): 67–78.

Myngs, Vice Admiral Sir Christopher. "Account of the Taking of St. Iago upon Cuba, October 1662." London: Historical Manuscripts, Commission Reports, Heathcote Mss, HMC, 1899.

Pérez Guzmán, Francisco. "Documentos sobre las fortalezas militares de Santiago de Cuba." *Santiago [Cuba]* 26–27 (June–September 1977): 181–200.

Pichardo Viñals, Hortensia. "Noticias de Cuba." *Santiago [Cuba]* 20 (December 1975): 7–44.

Portuondo Zúñiga, Olga. "Trayectoria histórica de Santiago de Cuba, 1515–1707." *Santiago [Cuba]* 26–27 (June–September 1977): 9–32.

Prat Puig, Francisco, et al. "La arquitectura santiaguera de estirpe tradicional con aportes neoclásicos." *Santiago [Cuba]* 54 (June–August 1984): 35–67.

Roldán de Montaud, Inés. "Organización municipal y conflicto en la villa de El Cobre, 1827–1845." *Santiago [Cuba]* 60 (December 1985): 121–145.

Sánchez Martínez, Guillermo. "Dias cubanos de Santiago Sawkins." *Santiago [Cuba]* 48 (December 1982): 137–146.

Wright, Irene Aloha. "Los orígenes de la minería en Cuba: las minas de Santiago del Prado hasta 1600." *Reforma Social [Cuba]* 7, Number 4 (July 1916).

———. *Santiago de Cuba and Its District, 1607–1640.* Madrid: Felipe Peña Cruz, 1918.

Yacou, Alain. "Los franceses de Saint-Domingue en el cinturón cafetalero de Santiago de Cuba, 1790–1815." *Revista de Ciencias Sociales [Puerto Rico]* 30, Numbers 1–2 (1993): 91–107.

Early Maps and Depictions of Santiago, 1668–1813

Diagram of a proposed new hexagonal citadel for the city center, by the ayudante de ingeniero or "assistant engineer" Capt. Juan de Siscara, 1668—original held by the Archive of Indies at Seville, call number: Mapas y Planos de Santo Domingo, 63

Map showing the new forts at Santiago Bay's entrance, plus the city itself, 1669—original held by the Archive of Indies at Seville, call number: Mapas y Planos de Santo Domingo, 66

Five hand-drawn diagrams with watercolor highlights by the military engineers Francisco Pérez and Louis Bouchard de Becour, outlining suggested reconstruction of the harbor entrance's defenses, 1704–1707—originals held as Illustrations 359–363 in the Archivo General de la Nación in Mexico City, photographic negative numbers: 977/0346 through 977/0349, plus 977/3014 [archival provenance: Serie Historia, Volume 346, Expediente 4, Folios 107–108, 117–118, and 138]

Detailed map of Santiago and its bay, drawn in July 1712 by the military engineer Lt. José del Monte y Messa, on orders from Gov. Pedro Ferrer—original held by the Archive of Indies at Seville, call number: Mapas y Planos de Santo Domingo, 121 [archival provenance: Audiencia de Santo Domingo, Legajo 408]

Bird's-eye-view depiction of the ruins of San Francisco Citadel and its surrounding buildings, 1729—original held by the Archive of Indies at Seville, call number: Mapas y Planos de Santo Domingo, 155 [archival provenance: Indiferente General, Legajo 1884]

Santiago and environs, as surveyed in 1751 by Baltasar Díaz de Priego—original held by the Archive of Indies at Seville, call number: Mapas y Planos de Santo Domingo, 284

French map of the harbor entrance and its defenses, ca. 1764—published in Paris on page 55 of the first volume of Jacques-Nicolas Bellin's Petit atlas maritime: recueil et plans des quatre parties du monde, several sources

"A Sketch of the harbour of St. Iago de Cuba," ca. 1765—original held by the Library of Congress in Washington, call number: G 4922.S3P5 1765.S5 Howe 37

Map of the harbor and its shoreline, as surveyed in 1776 by Ventura Buzella—original held by the Archive of Indies at Seville, call number: Mapas y Planos de Santo Domingo, 404

Map of the city in 1813—original held by the Archive of Indies at Seville, call number: Mapas y Planos de Santo Domingo, 643 [archival provenance: Ultramar, Legajo 34]

American Invasion (1898–1902)

Feuer, A. B. *The Santiago Campaign of 1898: A Soldier's View of the Spanish American War.* Westport, CT: Praeger, 1993.

García del Pino, César. "La acción naval de Santiago de Cuba en 1898." *Santiago [Cuba]* 30 (June–August 1978): 99–171.

Heinl, Robert D., Jr. "How We Got Guantanamo." *American Heritage* 13, Number 2 (February 1962): 18–21 and 94–97.

Kindsvatter, Peter S. "Santiago Campaign of 1898: Joint and Combined Operations." *Military Review* 73, Number 1 (1993): 3–14.

Pérez, Louis A., Jr. "The Siege of Santiago de Cuba, 1898: A View from Within." *Inter-American Review of Bibliography* 43, Number 4 (1993): 633–640.

Ullman, Bruce L. "The War Balloon Santiago." *Aerospace Historian* 32, Number 2 (1985): 117–129.

Modern Era and General Works (1903–Present)

Bacardí y Moreau, Emilio. *Crónicas de Santiago de Cuba.* Havana, 1972–1973 reprint of 1906–1908 original published by Carbonell y Esteva in Barcelona, ten volumes.

Barrero, Amparo, and Bertha Del Castillo. "Apuntes sobre los espectáculos culturales en Santiago de Cuba, 1910–1930." *Santiago [Cuba]* 54 (June–August 1984): 109–128.

Buch López, Ernesto. *Santiago de Cuba: ciudad de heroísmo y de leyenda.* Havana: Lex, 1947.

Forment, Carlos E. *Crónicas de Santiago de Cuba.* Santiago: Arroyo, 1953.

Henríquez Hureña, Max. *El libro de Santiago de Cuba.* Santiago: Ediciones Archipiélago, 1931.

Jerez Villarreal, Juan. *Oriente: biografía de una provincia.* Havana: Siglo XX, 1960.

Tamayo Rodríguez, Carlos. "Notas para el estudio de las publicaciones periódicas en Santiago de Cuba, 1900–1930." *Santiago [Cuba]* 49 (March–May 1983): 125–159.

Vázquez, Antonio. "Cuartel Moncada: represión vs revolución." *Santiago [Cuba]* 11 (June–August 1973): 9–33.

Curaçao
Willemstad
Early History (1521–1816)

Aizpurua, Ramón. *Curazao y la costa de Caracas: introducción al estudio del contrabando en la provincia de Venezuela en tiempos de la Compañía Guipuzcoana, 1730–1780.* Caracas: Volume 222 of the Series "Fuentes para la Historia Colonial de Venezuela," Academia Nacional de la Historia, 1993.

Araúz Monfante, Celestino Andrés. *Kerkgeschiedenis van Curaçao, 1742–1776.* Curaçao, 1967.

———. *El contrabando holandés en el Caribe durante la primera mitad del siglo XVIII.* Caracas: Volumes 168–169 of the Series "Fuentes para la Historia Colonial de Venezuela," Academia Nacional de la Historia, 1984.

———. "La acción ilegal de los holandeses en el Caribe y su impacto en las Antillas y Puerto Rico durante la primera mitad del siglo XVIII." *Revista/Review Interamericana [Puerto Rico]* 14, Numbers 1–4 (1984): 67–79.

Brada, W. M. *Kerkgeschiedenis van Curaçao, 1680–1707.* Curaçao, 1961.

Felice Cardot, Carlos. *Curazao hispánico: antagonismo flamenco-español.* Caracas: Volume 115 of the Series "Fuentes para la Historia Colonial de Venezuela," Academia Nacional de la Historia, 1973.

Gaay Fortman, B. de. "Een belangrijk dagboek." *De West-Indische gids [The Netherlands]* 6 (1924–1925): 241–270.

———. "Brieven van den Commissaris-Generaal voor de Nederlandsche West-Indische bezittingen J. van den Bosch aan den Minister voor de marine en koloniën, 1827–1829." *Bijdragen en mededeelingen van het Historisch Genootschap [Utrecht 1930]:* 189–335.

———. "Curaçao in 1782." *De West-Indische gids [The Netherlands]* 17 (1935–1936): 349–364.

———. "Nieuwe gegevens over de inbezitneming van Curaçao op den Nieuwjaarsdag." *De West-Indische gids [The Netherlands]* 25 (1943): 193–247.

———. "De kolonie Curaçao onder Engelsch bestuur van 1807 tot 1816." *De West-Indische gids [The Netherlands]* 26 (1945): 229–246.

Gehring, Charles T., and Jacob A. Schiltkamp, translators and editors. *Curaçao Papers, 1640–1665.* Interlaken, NY: Heart of the Lakes Publishing, 1987.

Goslinga, Cornelis Ch. *The Dutch in the Caribbean and on the Wild Coast, 1580–1680.* Gainesville: University of Florida Press, 1971.

———. "Curaçao as a Slave-Trading Center during the War of the Spanish Succession, 1702–1714." *Nieuwe West-Indische gids [The Netherlands]* 52, Numbers 1–2 (1977): 1–50.

———. *The Dutch in the Caribbean and in the Guianas, 1680–1791.* Dover, NH: Van Gorcum, 1985.

Hamelberg, J. H. J. *De Nederlanders op de West-Indische eilanden: Documenten.* Amsterdam: 1901 and 1909, two volumes.

Hering, J. H. *Beschrijving van het eiland Curaçao.* Amsterdam, 1969 reprint of 1779 original published by J. van Selm.

Kaplan, Yosef. "The Curaçao and Amsterdam Jewish Communities in the 17th and 18th Centuries." *American Jewish History* 72, Number 2 (1982): 193–211.

Klooster, Wim. "Contraband Trade by Curaçao's Jews with Countries of Idolatry, 1660–1800." *Studia Rosenthaliana [The Netherlands]* 31, Numbers 1–2 (1997): 58–73.

———. "Subordinate but Proud: Curaçao's Free Blacks and Mulattoes in the Eighteenth Century." *New West Indian Guide [The Netherlands]* 68, Numbers 3–4 (1994): 283–300.

Kooyman, Jan. "De wallen van Willemstad, Curaçao, omstreeks 1750." *De West-Indische gids [The Netherlands]* 38 (1958): 168–173.

Meeteren, Nicolaas van. *Noodlotsdagen: grepen uit de geschiedenis van Curaçao, 1799–1800.* Willemstad: De Stad, 1944.

———. *De oude vestingwerken, forten en batterijen van Curaçao en de capitulatievoorwaarden, zoals gepubliceerd in de Columbian Centinel van 19 november 1800.* Willemstad, 1951.

Oudschans Dentz, Frederik. "De aanval op Curaçao in 1673." *De West-Indische gids [The Netherlands]* 7 (1925–1927): 279–285.

Paula, A. F. *1795, De slavenopstand op Curaçao: Een bronnenuitgave.* Willemstad: Centraal Historisch Archief, 1974.

Postma, Johannes. "The Dimension of the Dutch Slave Trade from Western Africa." *Journal of African History* 13, Number 2 (1972): 237–248.

Smidt, J. Th. de, et al., compilers and editors. *West Indisch plakaatboek: Publikaties en andere wetten alsmede de oudste resoluties betrekking hebbende op Curaçao, Aruba, Bonaire, 1638–1782 en 1782–1816.* Amsterdam: S. Emmering, 1978, two volumes.

Early Maps and Depictions of Willemstad, 1634–1860

Draft of a pentagonal fort to guard the entrance into Santa Anna Bay, 1634—original held by the Algemeen Rijksarchief at The Hague, call number: Inventaris Leupe 595 [accompanying text found in *Bijlagen* or "Appendix," page 259]

Detailed map of Willemstad in 1707, by the artillery officer Jacob Daniel Gebhardt—original held by the Algemeen Rijksarchief at The Hague, call number: Inventaris Leupe 1440

General map of Curaçao published in Amsterdam by Gerard van Keulen, ca. 1715, including small inserts of Willemstad and Fort Amsterdam—original held by the Algemeen Rijksarchief at The Hague, call number: Buitenlanden kaarten 590, plus other sources

Anonymous mid-eighteenth-century panorama of Willemstad's wharf district, as seen from Otrabanda—original held by the Scheepvaartmuseum at Amsterdam

Map of Willemstad and its surroundings, as surveyed in November 1751 on orders from Lt.-Gen. G. A. van Burmania—original held by the Algemeen Rijksarchief at The Hague, call number: Inventaris Leupe 1452

Profile and cross-sectional views of a proposed new town gate, designed by Godfried Carel Esdré in June 1754—originals held by the Algemeen Rijksarchief at The Hague, call number: Inventaris Leupe 1480–1481

Engraving by B. Mourik of Willemstad's new Lutheran church, published in the October 1766 issue of the Dutch *Mercurius*—several sources

Crude drawing of the port of Willemstad, as seen from out at sea, 1786—original held by the National Maritime Museum at Greenwich, England

Drawing of the port of Willemstad as seen from out at sea, 1791—original held by the Scheepvaartmuseum at Amsterdam

Map of Willemstad and its harbor, published in London by A. Arrowsmith in 1807—original held by the Servicio Histórico Militar at Madrid, among numerous other sources

British-occupied Willemstad as seen from the hills to its northeast; an 1812 aquatint made by Thomas Hall of Boydell & Company in London, from an eye-witness drawing by James Belt—original held by the Koninklijk Instituut voor de Tropen in The Netherlands, among other sources

Panoramic view of part of Santa Anna Bay and the Schottegat, during the British occupation; 1812 aquatint by Hall, from a drawing by Belt—original held by the Koninklijk Instituut voor de Tropen in The Netherlands, among other sources

Lithograph based upon a drawing by Maj. Reinier Frederik van Raders, looking northeastward up Santa Anna Bay toward the Schottegat, ca. 1822—various sources

Diagrams and cross-sectional views of the capstan used to extend and retract the boom across the Santa Anna Bay entrance, November 1835—originals held by the Ministerie van Rijksdelen Overzee in The Netherlands, call number: Bibliotheek, map Ninaber

General map of Curaçao published in Amsterdam by the Widow of Gerard Hulst van Keulen in 1836, including an insert of Willemstad and the Schottegat—original held by the University of Leiden Library, call number: Bodel Nyenhuis, portef. 63, numbers 32 and 33, plus other sources

Watercolor of a militia parade on the flatland to the east of Willemstad, ca. 1850—original held by the Foto Fischer Archive of Curaçao

Lithograph by J. E. van Heemskerck van Beest of the harbor-forts guarding the Santa Anna Bay entrance as seen from Otrabanda, ca. 1860, based upon an original drawing by naval Lt. G. W. C. Voorduin—various sources

Lithograph by van Heemskerck van Beest of the Waaigat beside Willemstad, ca. 1860, based upon a drawing by Voorduin—various sources

Modern Era (1816–Present)

Aanzet tot een beleidskader voor de Nederlandse Antillen in de jaren tachtig. 's-Gravenhage: Staatsuitgeverij, 1979.

Album van het eiland Curaçao, inhoudende 50 foto's. Willemstad: Sluyter, ca. 1920.

Anderson, William Averette, and Rusell R. Dynes. *Social Movements, Violence and Change: The May Movement in Curaçao.* Columbus: Ohio State University, 1975.

Bouman, L. F. *K.L.M.'s Caribbean Decade, 1934–1944: The Story of the Operations of Royal Dutch Airlines in the West Indies since December 1934.* New York, 1944.

Cerruti, James. "The Netherlands Antilles: Holland in the Caribbean." *National Geographic* 137, Number 1 (January 1970): 115–146.

De Meidagen van Curaçao. Willemstad: Scherpenheuvel for the Algemeen Cultureel Maandblad *Ruku,* 1970.

Dupuis, Jacques. "Les paradoxes de Curaçao: à travers les provinces de l'Empire Shell." *Les cahiers d'Outre-mer [France]* 22, Number 85 (January–March 1969): 63–74.

Fenzi, J. *Port of Call: Sights and Sounds of Curaçao's Busy Harbor.* Willemstad, 1972.

Gaay Fortman, B. de. *Het Curaçaosch faillissementsbesluit 1931.* 's-Gravenhage: Algemeene Landsdrukkerij, 1931.

———. *Het Curaçaosch wetboek van burgerlijke vordering.* 's-Gravenhage: Algemeene Landsdrukkerij, 1931.

———. *Algemeene bepalingen der wetgeving van de kolonie Curaçao.* 's-Gravenhage: Algemeene Landsdrukkerij, 1932.

———. *Het Curaçaosch wetboek van burgerlijke van koophandel.* 's-Gravenhage: Algemeene Landsdrukkerij, 1935.

———. *Wetboek en strafrecht voor de kolonie Curaçao.* 's-Gravenhage: Algemeene Landsdrukkerij, 1936.

Goslinga, Cornelis Ch. *Curaçao and Guzmán Blanco: A Case Study of Small Power Politics in the Caribbean.* 's-Gravenhage: Nijhoff, 1975.

Hartog, Johannes. *Het verhaal der Maduro's en foto-album van Curaçao, 1837–1962.* Aruba: De Wit, 1962.

———. *Curaçao: From Colonial Dependence to Autonomy.* Aruba: De Wit, 1968 translation of 1961 Dutch original *Curacao: Van kolonie tot autonomie.*

———. *U.S. Consul in 19th Century Curaçao: The Life and Works of Leonard Burlington Smith.* Oranjestad, Sint Eustatius: Van Dorp, 1971.

———. *Curaçao in oude ansichten.* Zaltbommel: Europese Bibliotheek, 1974.

Marks, A. F. *Male and Female in the Afro-Curaçaon Household.* The Hague: Martinus Nijhoff, 1976.

Meilink-Roelofsz, M. A. P. "A Survey of Archives in the Netherlands Pertaining to the History of the Netherlands Antilles." *De West-Indische gids [The Netherlands]* 35 (1954): 1–38.

Soest, J. J. van. *Trustees of the Netherlands Antilles: A History of Money, Banking and Economy, with Special Reference to the Centrale Bank van de Nederlandse Antillen, 1828–February 1978.* Curaçao, 1978.

General Works

Coolhaas, W. Ph. *A Critical Survey of Studies on Dutch Colonial History.* The Hague: Martinus Nijhoff for the Koninklijk Instituut voor Taal-, Land- en Volkenkunde, 1980 re-edition of 1960 original, revised by G. J. Schutte.

Emmanuel, Isaac S. *Precious Stones of the Jews of Curaçao: Curaçaoan Jewry, 1656–1957.* New York: Bloch, 1957.

Emmanuel, Isaac S., and S. A. Emmanuel. *History of the Jews of the Netherlands Antilles.* Cincinnati: American Jewish Archives, 1970–1971, two volumes.

Gedenkboek Nederland-Curaçao, 1634–1934. Amsterdam: De Bussy, 1934.

Goslinga, Cornelis Ch. *A Short History of the Netherlands Antilles and Surinam.* The Hague: Martinus Nijhoff, 1979.

Hartog, Johannes. *Geschiedenis van de Nederlandse Antillen.* Oranjestad, Sint Eustatius, 1956–1964, five volumes.

Hoetink, Hermann R. *Het patroon van de Curaçaose samenleving.* Assen: Van Gorcum, 1958.

Hoetink, Hermann R., editor. *Encyclopaedie van de Nederlandse Antillen.* Amsterdam-Brussels: Elsevier, 1969.

Karner, Francis P. *The Sephardics of Curaçao: A Study of Socio-Cultural Patterns in Flux.* Assen: Van Gorcum, 1969.

Keur, John Y., and Dorothy L. Keur. *Windward Children: A Study in Human Ecology of the Three Dutch Windward Islands in the Caribbean.* Assen: Van Gorcum, 1960.

Krafft, A. J. C. *Historie en oude families van de Nederlandse Antillen: Het Antilliaans patriciaat.* 's-Gravenhage: Martinus Nijhoff, 1951.

Nagelkerke, Gerard A. *Netherlands Antilles: A Bibliography, 17th Century–1980.* The Hague: Smits Drukkers for the Department of Caribbean Studies of the Royal Institute of Linguistics and Anthropology at Leiden, 1982.

Ozinga, Murk Daniel. *De monumenten van Curaçao in woord en beeld.* 's-Gravenhage: Stichting Monumentenzorg Curaçao, 1959.

Römer, René A. *Curaçao.* Unica, 1981.

Swetschinski, Daniel M. "Conflict and Opportunity in 'Europe's Other Sea': The Adventure of Caribbean Jewish Settlement." *American Jewish History* 72, Number 2 (1982): 212–240.

Van der Mark, E. Abraham. "Marriage and the Family in a White Caribbean Elite: The Impact of Descent for the Ethnic Persistence of the Sephardic Jews in Curaçao." *Anthropologica [Canada]* 22, Number 1 (1980): 119–134.

Van Soest, J. J. "Archival Sources to the History of the Netherlands Antilles: A Challenge for Archivists and Historians." *Nieuwe West-Indische gids [The Netherlands]* 54, Number 2 (1980): 73–93.

Dominican Republic
General Studies

Alemar, Luis E. *Fortificaciones antiguas de Santo Domingo.* Santo Domingo, [n. d.].

Amiama, Manuel A. "La población de Santo Domingo." *Clio [Dominican Republic]* 27, Number 115 (1959): 116–134.

Atkins, G. Pope. *Arms and Politics in the Dominican Republic.* Boulder: Westview, 1981.

Atkins, G. Pope, and Larman C. Wilson. *The United States and the Trujillo Regime.* New Brunswick, NJ: Rutgers University Press, 1972.

Becker, Jerónimo. "La cuestión de Santo Domingo." *Eme [Dominican Republic]* 3, Number 14 (1974): 72–103.

Bell, Ian. *The Dominican Republic.* Boulder: Westview, 1981.

Benot, Yves. "Comment Santo Domingo n'a pas été occupé para la République Française en 1795–1796 (An III–IV)." *Annales historiques de la Révolution Française [France]* 311 (1998): 79–87.

Beras, Francisco Elpidio, compiler and editor. "Antecedentes de la anexión." *Clio [Dominican Republic]* 36, Number 123 (1968): 26–35.

Black, Jan Knippers. *The Dominican Republic: Politics and Development in an Unsovereign State.* Boston: Allen and Unwin, 1986.

Bosch, Juan. *The Unfinished Experiment: Democracy in the Dominican Republic.* New York: Praeger, 1965.

Campillo Pérez, Julio G. "La primera independencia americana." *Clio [Dominican Republic]* 128 (1972): 127–142.

Cassá, Roberto. *Historia social y económica de la República Dominicana.* Santo Domingo: Alfa y Omega, 1991 re-edition, two volumes.

Cassá, Roberto, and Genaro Rodríguez Morel. "Consideraciones alternativas acerca de las rebeliones de esclavos en Santo Domingo." *Anuario de Estudios Americanos [Spain]* 50, Number 1 (1993): 101–131.

Cerruti, James. "The Dominican Republic: Caribbean Comeback." *National Geographic* 152, Number 4 (October 1977): 538–565.

Cordero Michel, Emilio. "Gregorio Luperón y Haití." *Anuario de Estudios Americanos [Spain]* 49 (1992): 497–528.

"Descripción de la colonia española en 1716 en un informe de un oficial francés que viajó por la isla en ese año." *Eme [Dominican Republic]* 3, Number 15 (1974): 130–146.

D'Esposito, Francesco. "Portuguese Settlers in Santo Domingo in the Sixteenth Century (1492–1580)." *Journal of European Economic History [Italy]* 28, Number 2 (1998): 315–329.

Domínguez, Jaime de Jesús. *Economía y política: República Dominicana, 1844–1861.* Santo Domingo: U.A.S.D., 1977.

———. *La anexión de la República Dominicana a España.* Santo Domingo: U.A.S.D., 1979.

———. *Notas económicas y políticas dominicanas sobre el período julio 1865-julio 1886.* Santo Domingo: U.A.S.D., 1983–1984, two volumes.

Dyer, Donald R. "Distribution of Population on Hispaniola." *Economic Geography* 30, Number 4 (October 1954): 335–346.

Franco, Franklin J. "Gérmenes de una burguesía colonial en Santo Domingo, siglos XVI al XVIII." *Revista de Ciencias Sociales [Puerto Rico]* 12, Number 4 (1968): 527–539.

García, José Gabriel. *Compendio de la historia de Santo Domingo.* Santo Domingo: ¡Ahora!, 1968, two volumes.

Garrido, Víctor. *Política de Francia en Santo Domingo, 1844–1846.* Santo Domingo: Editora del Caribe for the Academia Dominicana de la Historia, 1962.

Geraldini, Alessandro. *Itinerario por las regiones subequinocciales.* Santo Domingo: Editora del Caribe for the Fundación Rodríguez Demorizi, 1977 Spanish translation of 1631 Latin original *Itinerarium ad regiones sub æquinoctiali,* published in Rome.

Gil-Bermejo García, Juana. *La Española: anotaciones históricas, 1600–1650.* Seville: Escuela de Estudios Hispanoamericanos, 1983.

Goiscorí Henriquez, Máximo. *Historia de Santo Domingo.* Ciudad Trujillo: Montalvo, 1938.

González y González, Julio. *Catálogo de planos y mapas de Santo Domingo.* Madrid: Dirección General de Archivos y Bibliotecas, 1972.

Hartlyn, Jonathan. *The Struggle for Democratic Politics in the Dominican Republic.* Chapel Hill: University of North Carolina Press, 1998.

Hazard, Samuel. *Santo Domingo Past and Present, with a Glance at Hayti.* Santo Domingo: Sociedad Dominicana de Bibliófilos, 1974 reprint of 1873 original published in London by Sampson Low, Marston, Low, and Searle.

Hidalgo, Dennis. "Charles Sumner and the Annexation of the Dominican Republic." *Itinerario [The Netherlands]* 21, Number 2 (1997): 51–65.

Hoetink, Hermannus R. or "Harry." *The Dominican People, 1850–1900.* Baltimore: Johns Hopkins University Press, 1982 translation by Stephen K. Ault.

Incháustegui Cabral, Joaquín Marino, compiler. *Documentos para estudio: marco de la época y problemas del Tratado de Basilea de 1795, en la parte española de Santo Domingo.* Buenos Aires: Academia Dominicana de la Historia, 1957, two volumes.

———. *Reales cédulas y correspondencia de gobernadores de Santo Domingo.* Madrid: Colección Histórico-Documental Trujilloniana, 1958, five volumes.

Larrazábal Blanco, Carlos. *Los negros y la esclavitud en Santo Domingo.* Ciudad Trujillo: Postigo e Hijos, 1967.

Latortue, Paul R. "La migración haitiana a Santo Domingo." *Estudios Sociales [Dominican Republic]* 18, Number 59 (1985): 43–59.

Lebrán Savinón, Mariano. *Historia de la cultura dominicana.* Santo Domingo: Universidad Nacional "Pedro Henríquez Ureña," 1982.

Lemonnier-Delafosse, J. B. *Segunda campaña de Santo Domingo: guerra dominico-francesa de 1808.* Santo Domingo: Editora de Santo Domingo for the Sociedad Dominicana de Bibliófilos, 1975 translation by Armando Rodríguez of *Seconde campagne de Saint-Domingue,* originally published in Havre by Brindeau in 1846.

Lockward, Alfonso, editor. *Documentos para la historia de las relaciones dominico americanas (1837–1860).* Santo Domingo: Corripio, 1987.

Logan, Rayford W. *Haiti and the Dominican Republic.* London: Oxford University Press for the Royal Institute of International Affairs, 1968.

Madruga, José Manuel. "Azúcar y fuerza de trabajo en la República Dominicana." *Estudios Sociales [Dominican Republic]* 18, Number 59 (1985): 31–42.

Malagón Barceló, Javier. *El distrito de la Audiencia de Santo Domingo en los siglos XVI y XVII.* Ciudad Trujillo, 1942.

Marte, Roberto. *Estadísticas y documentos históricos sobre Santo Domingo (1805–1890).* Santo Domingo: Museo Nacional de Historia y Geografía, 1984.

Martínez, Rufino. *Diccionario biográfico-histórico dominicano, 1821–1930.* Santo Domingo: Universidad Autónoma, 1971.

Martínez-Fernández, Luis. "Caudillos, Annexationism, and the Rivalry between Empires in the Dominican Republic, 1844–1874." *Diplomatic History* 17, Number 4 (1993): 571–597.

Mejía, Gustavo Adolfo. *Historia de Santo Domingo.* Ciudad Trujillo: Pool y Hermanos, 1952.

Millett, Richard, and G. Dale Gaddy. "Administering the Protectorates: The Occupation of Haiti and the Dominican Republic." *Revista/Review Interamericana* 6, Number 3 (fall 1976): 383–402.

Moreau de Saint-Méry, Médéric-Louis-Élie. *Descripción de la parte española de Santo Domingo.* Ciudad Trujillo: Montalvo, 1944 Spanish translation of French original *Description topographique et politique de la partie espagnole de l'isle de Saint-Domingue,* published by the author in two volumes in Philadelphia in 1796.

Moya Pons, Frank. *Historia colonial de Santo Domingo.* Santiago: Universidad Católica Madre y Maestra, 1974.

Nelson, William J. *Almost a Territory: America's Attempt to Annex the Dominican Republic.* Newark: University of Delaware Press, 1990.

Palm, Erwin Walter. *Los monumentos arquitectónicos de La Española.* Ciudad Trujillo: Universidad de Santo Domingo, 1955, two volumes.

Prince Mars, Jean. *La República de Haití y la República Dominicana.* Madrid, 1953.

Puente García, Esteban de la. "1861–1865: anexión y abandono de Santo Domingo." *Revista de Indias [Spain]* 22, Numbers 89–90 (1962): 411–472.

Rodríguez Demorizi, Emilio. *Relaciones históricas de Santo Domingo.* Ciudad Trujillo: Montalvo, 1957 re-edition of 1943–1945 originals, three volumes.

————. *Documentos para la historia de la República Dominicana*. Ciudad Trujillo: Montalbo, 1944.

————. *Invasiones haitianas de 1801, 1805 y 1822*. Ciudad Trujillo: Academia Dominicana de la Historia, 1955.

————. *La era de Francia en Santo Domingo: contribución a su estudio*. Ciudad Trujillo: Editora del Caribe, 1955.

————. *Cesión de Santo Domingo a Francia*. Ciudad Trujillo, 1958.

————. *Mapas y planos de Santo Domingo*. Santo Domingo: Editora Taller, 1979.

Roorda, Eric Paul. "Genocide Next Door: The Good Neighbor Policy, the Trujillo Regime, and the Haitian Massacre of 1937." *Diplomatic History* 20, Number 3 (1996): 301–319.

Ruiz Tejada, Manuel Ramón. *Estudio sobre la propriedad inmobiliaria en la República Dominicana*. Ciudad Trujillo: Editora del Caribe, 1952.

Sánchez Ramírez, Juan. *Diario de la Reconquista*. Ciudad Trujillo: Academia Militar "Batalla de las Carreras," 1957 re-edition by Cipriano de Utrera.

Santiago, Pedro J. *Estudios sobre comercio marítimo, naufragios y rescates submarinos en la República Dominicana*. Santo Domingo: Museo de las Casas Reales, 1978.

Silie, Rubén. *Economía, esclavitud y población: ensayo de interpretación histórica de Santo Domingo español en el siglo XVIII*. Santo Domingo, 1976.

————. "La trata de negros en Santo Domingo, siglo XVIII." *Islas [Cuba]* 78 (1984): 67–79.

Tansill, Charles C. *The United States and Santo Domingo, 1798–1873: A Chapter in Caribbean Diplomacy*. Baltimore: Johns Hopkins University Press, 1938.

Utrera, Cipriano de. *Noticias históricas de Santo Domingo*. Santo Domingo: Editora Taller, 1978–1979, four volumes.

Walton, William, Jr. *Estado actual de las colonias españolas*. Santo Domingo: Editora de Santo Domingo for the Sociedad Dominicana de Bibliófilos, 1976 translation by Nora Read Espaillat and Tony Rodríguez Cabral of the *Present State of the Spanish Colonies, Including a Particular Report of Hispañola or the Spanish Part of Santo Domingo*, originally published in London by Longman, Hurst, Rees, Orme, and Brown in 1810, two volumes.

Wilson, Samuel M. *Hispaniola: Caribbean Chiefdoms in the Age of Columbus*. Gainesville: University Press of Florida, 1992.

Wucker, Michele. *Why the Cocks Fight: Dominicans, Haitians, and the Struggle for Hispaniola*. New York: Hill and Wang, 1999.

Zéndegui, Guillermo de, compiler. "The Dominican Miracle." *Américas [Organization of American States]* 23, Number 9 (September 1971), supplementary pp. 1–24.

Santo Domingo

Early Colonial Era (1496–1654)

Cassá, Roberto. "Cuantificaciones sociodemográficas de la ciudad de Santo Domingo en el siglo XVI." *Revista de Indias [Spain]* 56, Number 208 (1996): 637–657.

Hampe Martínez, Teodoro. "Lecturas de un jurista del siglo XVI." *Anuario de Estudios Americanos [Spain]* 41 (1984): 143–193.

Hernández Tapia, Concepción. "Despoblaciones de la isla de Santo Domingo en el siglo XVII." *Anuario de Estudios Americanos [Spain]* 27 (1970): 281–320.

Huerga, Alvaro. "El concilio provincial de Santo Domingo, 1622–1623." *Horizontes [Puerto Rico]* 32, Numbers 63–64 (1988–1989): 54–69.

Incháustegui Cabral, Joaquín Marino. "Apuntes para una biografía del adelantado don Bartolomé Colón, fundador de la ciudad de Santo Domingo." *Clio [Dominican Republic]* 29–30, Numbers 118–119 (1961): 19–27.

Keeler, Mary Frear, editor. *Sir Francis Drake's West Indian Voyage, 1585–86*. London: Hakluyt, 1981.

Liriano, Alejandra V. "Presencia de mujeres negras en el comercio de esclavos hasta Santo Domingo." *Estudios Sociales [Dominican Republic]* 23, Numbers 79–80 (1990): 61–76.

Lugo, Américo. "Baltasar López de Castro y la despoblación del norte de La Española." *Revista de Historia de América [Mexico]* 23 (1947).

————. *Historia de Santo Domingo desde el 1556 hasta el 1608*. Ciudad Trujillo: Librería Dominicana, 1952.

Moya Pons, Frank. *La Española en el siglo XVI, 1493–1522: trabajo, sociedad y política en la economía del oro*. Santiago, Dominican Republic: Universidad Católica Madre y Maestra, 1971.

————. *Historia colonial de Santo Domingo*. Santiago, Dominican Republic: Universidad Católica Madre y Maestra, 1977.

Paredes Vera, María Isabel. "San Nicolás de Bari, en La Española, primer hospital de América." *Anuario de Estudios Americanos [Spain]* 33 (1976): 933–948.

Rodríguez Demorizi, Emilio. *El pleito Ovando-Tapia: comienzos de la vida urbana en América*. Santo Domingo: Editora del Caribe, 1978.

Rodríguez Morel, Genaro, compiler and editor. "Cartas privadas de Hernando Gorjón." *Anuario de Estudios Americanos [Spain]* 52, Number 2 (1995): 203–233.

Varela, Consuelo. "La Isabela, vida y ocaso de una ciudad efímera." *Revista de Indias [Spain]* 47, Number 181 (1987): 733–744.

Vigneras, Louis-André. "Diego Méndez, Secretary of Christopher Columbus and Alguacil Mayor of Santo Domingo: A Biographical Sketch." *Hispanic American Historical Review* 58, Number 4 (1978): 676–696.

Early Maps and Depictions of Santo Domingo, 1531–1809

Diagram of an intersection near the San Francisco Convent, 1531—original held by the Archive of Indies at Seville [archival provenance: Indiferente General, Legajo 1382-A]

Engraving of Sir Francis Drake's assault in 1585, published three years later in Leyden by Batista Boazio, as part of *Le Voyage de Messire François Drake, Chevalier, aux Indes Occidentales;* it also appeared in Walter Bigges's *A Summarie and True Discourse of Sir Francis Drake's West Indian Voyage,* published in London in 1589—several sources

Hand-colored, pen-and-ink sketch of the city in 1592 by the military engineer Batista Antonelli, identifying its principal structures and incorporating proposals for improving its defenses—original held by the Biblioteca Nacional at Madrid, call number: MIV.–235

Map showing proposed changes and additions to the city's outer defenses, January 1608—original held by the Archive of Indies at Seville, call number: Mapas y Planos de Santo Domingo, 22 [archival provenance: Audiencia de Santo Domingo, Legajo 52]

Map of the city and its environs in 1619, drawn by Bernardo de Silva to be included in a report by Gov. Diego Gómez de Sandoval—original held by the Archive of Indies at Seville, call number: Mapas y Planos de Santo Domingo, 29 [archival provenance: Audiencia de Santo Domingo, Legajo 54]

Pen-and-ink drawing of a proposed new fort to replace the stone tower at Puntilla Point, 1625—original held by the Archive of Indies at Seville, call number: Mapas y Planos de Santo Domingo, 33 [archival provenance: Audiencia de Santo Domingo, Legajo 55]

Crude pen-and-ink sketch with watercolor highlights of the city and its adjacent coastline in 1632, by Nicolás de Cardona—original held by the Biblioteca Nacional at Madrid, call number: Sección de Manuscritos, 2468

Before-and-after maps of the city and its coastline, drawn by Capt. Francisco Vicente Durán in February 1656 to demonstrate the state of its defenses—original held by the Archive of Indies at Seville, call number: Mapas y Planos de Santo Domingo, 52 [archival provenance: Audiencia de Santo Domingo, Legajo 58]

Pen-and-ink map by the military engineer Juan Bautista Ruggero, detailing a proposed expansion of the city walls in 1674—original held by the Archive of Indies at Seville, call number: Mapas y Planos de Santo Domingo, 67 [archival provenance: Audiencia de Santo Domingo, Legajo 92]

Two hand-colored, pen-and-ink sketches by Ruggero of his revised proposal for expanding the defenses, 1679—originals held by the Archive of Indies at Seville, call numbers Mapas y Planos de Santo Domingo, 75 and 76 [archival provenance: Audiencia de Santo Domingo, Legajos 92 and 294]

Pen-and-ink map describing the terrain and defenses between the city and the Haina River mouth, 1679—original held by the Archive of Indies at Seville, call number: Mapas y Planos de Santo Domingo, 77 [archival provenance: Audiencia de Santo Domingo, Legajo 92]

Crude pen-and-ink diagram sketched in Spain, to demonstrate to the Council of Indies the proposed improvements to the city walls, 1679—original held by the Archive of Indies at Seville, call number: Mapas y Planos de Santo Domingo, 78 [archival provenance: Audiencia de Santo Domingo, Legajo 72]

Pen-and-ink diagram sketched in Spain, to demonstrate to the Council of Indies the improvements made to Fort San Gerónimo, 1679—original held by the Archive of Indies at Seville, call number: Mapas y Planos de Santo Domingo, 79 [archival provenance: Audiencia de Santo Domingo, Legajo 72]

Pen-and-ink diagram showing the improvements made to Fort San Gerónimo by Governor Segura y Sandoval, 1679—original held by the Archive of Indies at Seville, call number: Mapas y Planos de Santo Domingo, 80 [archival provenance: Audiencia de Santo Domingo, Legajo 92]

Pen-and-ink map of Santo Domingo and its environs, drawn in 1717 by the Frenchman Buttet—original held by the Bibliothèque Nationale in Paris

Two hand-drawn French maps of the city and its river in the early eighteenth-century, containing numerous inaccuracies—originals held by the Bibliothèque Nationale at Paris, stamped with the anchor-crest seal of the "Dêpot des Colonies Françaises"

Map of the city, ca. 1728, by the French engraver d'Anville—original found on page 223 of the first volume of Pierre-François-Xavier de Charlevoix's *Histoire de l'Isle Espagnole ou S. Domingue,* published in Paris by Hippolyte-Louis Guérin in 1730–1731

Numerous diagrams, plus profile and cutaway drawings by the military engineer Félix Prosperi, of proposed repairs and improvements to Santo Domingo's defenses in 1732—originals held by the Servicio Geográfico del Ejército at Madrid

Hand-colored diagram of Santo Domingo's main plaza in 1737, by Fernando Gerónimo Pineda—original held by the Archive of Indies at Seville

Hand-drawn French map of the city and its harbor in the mid-eighteenth century—original held by the Bibliothèque Nationale at Paris

Map of the city, ca. 1755, engraved in Leipzig by C. F. Fritzsch after an original drawing by Quintin-Pierre Chedel—original held by the Library of Congress in Washington, call number: G 4954.S8A3 1755.F7 Vault

Engraved Italian map of Santo Domingo, found in Giuseppe Pazzi's *Il gazzetiere americana del Nuovo Mondo,* published in Livorno by Marco Cortellini in 1763—original held by the Biblioteca Nacional at Madrid, call number M26V, plus other sources

Street map of the city's northern section, drawn by Luis José Peguero in 1764—original held by the Archive of Indies at Seville

Two highly detailed, almost identical French maps of the city in 1764, drawn by Daniel Lescallier as part of his *Itineraire géographique, historique et politique* of the island—originals held by the Bibliothèque Nationale at Paris

Diagram by Alonso González de Villamar and José de Esineas, depicting the seating arrangement for Audiencia members in Santo Domingo's main church, 30 December 1766—original held by the Archive of Indies at Seville, call number: Mapas y Planos de Santo Domingo, 341 [archival provenance: Audiencia de Santo Domingo, Legajo 978]

Floor plan, plus profile and cutaway views, for converting the abandoned ruins of Christopher Columbus's ancient Casa del Almirante into a royal jail, 1770—original held by the Archive of Indies at Seville, call number: Mapas y Planos de Santo Domingo, 370 [archival provenance: Audiencia de Santo Domingo, Legajo 981]

Diagram by Antonio Alvarez Barba, detailing some proposed improvements to the city riverfront, 10 October 1772—original held by the Archive of Indies at Seville, call number: Mapas y Planos de Santo Domingo, 378 [archival provenance: Audiencia de Santo Domingo, Legajo 983]

Diagram and profile views by Barba of the city's new riverfront barracks, March 1773—original held by the Servicio Geográfico del Ejército at Madrid

Map of Santo Domingo's anchorage in 1773, by Capt. José Antonio Puig—original held by the Museo Naval at Madrid

Hand-colored, pen-and-ink map of the city and its harbor, ca. 1776—original held by the Servicio Histórico Militar at Madrid, call number: K b 2 14–5713

Another hand-colored, pen-and-ink map of the city and its harbor, ca. 1776—original held by the Servicio Histórico Militar at Madrid

Map of the city's coastline and environs, drawn in November 1778 by Antonio Ladrón de Guevara—original held by the Servicio Histórico Militar at Madrid

Three detailed drawings and a floor plan of the San Nicolás de Bari Hospital, 1783—originals held by the Archive of Indies at Seville, call number: Mapas y Planos de Santo Domingo, 487 [archival provenance: Audiencia de Santo Domingo, Legajo 989]

Floor plans and cutaway views by Ladrón de Guevara of a proposed new powder magazine that was to be built outside the city, 21 September 1783—originals held by the Archive of Indies at Seville, call number: Mapas y Planos de Santo Domingo, 488 [archival provenance: Audiencia de Santo Domingo, Legajo 1096]

Map of the city, published in Madrid by the royal geographer Tomás López in 1785—original held by the Museo Naval at Madrid [call number: XX-D-8], plus other sources

Diagram by Ladrón de Guevara of the San Nicolás de Bari Hospital, 1786—original held by the Archive of Indies at Seville, call number: Mapas y Planos de Santo Domingo, 523 [archival provenance: Audiencia de Santo Domingo, Legajo 989]

Diagram of the city's *real fuerza* or "royal citadel," drawn in 1792 by Alvarez Barba—original held by the Servicio Histórico Militar at Madrid

Diagram of the improved waterfront, ca. 1792—original held by the Servicio Histórico Militar at Madrid

Map by Pedro Roig de Lluis of the pastureland outside the capital, 23 June 1792—original held by the Archive of Indies at Seville, call number: Mapas y Planos de Santo Domingo, 566 [archival provenance: Audiencia de Santo Domingo, Legajo 997]

Two highly detailed diagrams and profile views by the Frenchman Moulut, of Fort San Gerónimo in 1795—originals held by the Bibliothèque Nationale at Paris

French map of Dessalines's siege of the city, March 1805—original held by the Library of Congress in Washington, call number: G 4954.S8:2P2 1805.P48 Vault

French map of Santo Domingo and its defenses, ca. 1805—original held by the Library of Congress in Washington, call number: G 4954.S8 1805.P5 Vault

Floor plan and profile view of the changes and repairs made to the Government Palace on orders from Gen. Jean-Louis Ferrand, September 1807—original held by the Library of Congress in Washington, call number: G 4954.S8:2P2 1807.P5 Vault

Engraved map of the city and its river, 1808—original held by the Colección Pérez Montas, plus other sources

Map of the route followed by Maj.-Gen. Hugh Lyle Carmichael's invading British army, June 1809—published in William Walton, Jr.'s *Present State of the Spanish Colonies,* 1810

Engraved map by the retired officer George de Bois St. Lys of the siege of the French garrison, 27 November 1808–7 July 1809—published in Gilbert Guillermin's *Diario histórico,* 1811

Engraved map of the 1805 and 1809 sieges of the French garrison inside Santo Domingo—published in J. B. Lemonnier Delafosse's *Segunda campaña de Santo Domingo,* 1846

English Assault and Revival (1655–1800)

Gascón, Margarita. "The Military of Santo Domingo, 1720–1764." *Hispanic American Historical Review* 73, Number 3 (1993): 431–452.

Gutiérrez Escudero, Antonio. *Población y economía en Santo Domingo, 1700–1746.* Seville: Artes Gráficas Padura, 1985.

Incháustegui Cabral, Joaquín Marino. *La gran expedición inglesa contra las Antillas Mayores.* Mexico City: Gráfica Panamericana, 1953.

Rodríguez Demorizi, Emilio. *Invasión inglesa de 1655: notas adicionales de Fray Cipriano de Utrera.* Ciudad Trujillo: Montalvo, 1957.

———. "Invasión inglesa en 1655." *Boletín del Archivo General de la Nación [Dominican Republic]* 20, Number 92 (January–March 1957): 6–70.

Sevilla Soler, María Rosario. *Santo Domingo: tierra de frontera, 1750–1800.* Seville: Escuela de Estudios Hispanoamericanos, 1980.

Taylor, S. A. G. *The Western Design: An Account of Cromwell's Expedition to the Caribbean.* London: Solstice Productions, 1969.

Vandecasteele, Maurits. "Involvement of the Spanish Netherlands in the Population Problems of Santo Domingo at the End of the Seventeenth Century." *Bulletin de l'Institut historique belge de Rome [Belgium]* 62 (1992): 165–173.

Wright, Irene Aloha, editor and translator. "Spanish Narratives of the English Attack on Santo Domingo, 1655." *Camden Miscellany* 14 (1926).

Franco-Haitian Occupations and First Republic (1801–1860)

Alfau Durán, Vetilio. "Apuntaciones en torno al 27 de febrero de 1844." *Clio [Dominican Republic]* 28, Number 116 (1960): 55–107.

Beerman, Eric. "El marino que trasladó los restos de Colón de Santo Domingo a La Habana: Gabriel de Aristizábal, 1743–1805." *Revista de Historia Naval [Spain]* 9, Number 34 (1991): 13–48.

Bell, Ian. "Santo Domingo's Struggle for Independence from Haiti." *History Today [UK]* 31 (April 1981): 42–48.

Bonnel, Ulane. "Histoire de la station navale de Santo-Domingo de 1803 à 1809." *Revue historique, économique et sociale [France]* 40, Number 1 (1962): 48–89.

Bryan, Patrick. "The *Independencia Efímera* of 1821 and the Haitian Invasion of Santo Domingo in 1822: A Case of Pre-Emptive Independence." *Caribbean Quarterly [Jamaica]* 41, Numbers 3–4 (1995): 15–29.

Cruz Hermosilla, Emilio de la. "Los restos de Colón." *Revista General de Marina [Spain]* 201 (November 1981): 435–441.

Evanson, Philip. "The Third Dominican-Haitian War and the Return of General Pedro Santana: Part of a Long Story." *Caribbean Studies [Puerto Rico]* 4, Number 1 (1964): 13–23.

Guillermin, Gilbert. *Diario histórico.* Santo Domingo: Editora de Santo Domingo for the Sociedad Dominicana de Bibliófilos, 1976 translation by Armando Rodríguez of *Précis historique des derniers événemens de la partie de l'est de Saint-Domingue depuis le 10 août 1808, jusqu'a la capitulation de Santo-Domingo,* originally published in Paris by Arthus-Bertrand in 1811.

Moya Pons, Frank. "Notas sobre la primera abolición de la esclavitud en Santo Domingo." *Eme [Dominican Republic]* 3, Number 13 (1974): 3–26.

———. "The Haitian Revolution in Santo Domingo, 1789–1809." *Jahrbuch für Geschichte von Staat, Wirtschaft und Gesellschaft Lateinamerikas [Germany]* 28 (1991): 125–162.

Sánchez de Neyra Mille, Antonio. "En torno a los restos de Colón." *Revista General de Marina [Spain]* 186, Number 3 (1974): 297–300.

Spanish Reoccupation (1861–1865)

Borrell Merlín, María Dolores. "Santo Domingo y España: historia de una reincorporación fallida." *Revista de Historia Naval [Spain]* 11, Number 42 (1993): 45–60.

De la Puente, Esteban. "1861–1865: anexación y abandono de Santo Domingo: problemas críticos." *Revista de Indias [Spain]* 22, Numbers 89–80 (1962): 411–472.

Egan, Clifford L. "The Monroe Doctrine and Santo Domingo in Spanish-American Diplomacy, 1861–1865." *Lincoln Herald* 71, Number 2 (1969): 55–66.

Goico Castro, Manuel de Jesús. "El 2 de mayo de 1861: primer episodio de la restauración." *Clio [Dominican Republic]* 33, Number 122 (1965): 10–25.

Guerrero Cano, María Magdalena. "La biblioteca de la Secretaría del Gobierno Superior Civil de Santo Domingo, 1862–1864." *Anuario de Estudios Americanos [Spain]* 45 (1988): 317–341.

Robles Muñóz, Cristóbal. "Reforma moral y conflicto cultural en Santo Domingo, 1862–1865." *Hispania Sacra [Spain]* 40 (July–December 1988): 867–889.

Rodríguez Demorizi, Emilio, compiler and editor. "Antecedentes de la anexión." *Clio [Dominican Republic]* 36, Number 123 (1968): 36–43.

Sánchez Diana, José María. "Anexación de la isla de Santo Domingo a España bajo el reinado de Isabel II." *Anuario de Estudios Americanos [Spain]* 11 (1954): 381–412.

*Independence and First American
Occupation (1865–1924)*

Baughman, C. C. "United States Occupation of the Dominican Republic." *United States Naval Institute Proceedings* 51, Number 274 (December 1925): 2306–2327.

Calder, Bruce J. *The Impact of Intervention: The Dominican Republic during the U.S. Occupation of 1916–1924.* Austin: University of Texas Press, 1984.

Castro García, Teófilo. *Intervención yanqui, 1916–1924.* Santo Domingo: Editora Taller, 1978.

Fuller, Stephen M., and Graham A. Cosmas. *Marines in the Dominican Republic, 1916–1924.* Washington, DC: U.S. Marine Corps, 1974.

Grieb, Kenneth J. "Warren G. Harding and the Dominican Republic: U.S. Withdrawal, 1921–1923." *Journal of Inter-American Studies* 11, Number 3 (July 1969): 425–440.

Hoepelman, Antonio, and Juan A. Senior, compilers and editors. *Documentos históricos que se refieren a la intervención armada de los Estados Unidos de Norte-América y a la implantación de un gobierno militar en la República Dominicana.* Santo Domingo: Librería Dominicana, 1973 reprint of 1922 original.

Hoetink, Hermann R. *El pueblo dominicano, 1850–1900: apuntes para su sociología histórica.* Santiago de los Caballeros: Universidad Católica Madre y Maestra, 1971.

Juarez, Joseph Robert. "United States Withdrawal from Santo Domingo." *Hispanic American Historical Review* 42, Number 2 (May 1962): 152–190.

Lane, Rufus H. "Civil Government in Santo Domingo in the Early Days of the Military Occupation." *Marine Corps Gazette* 7, Number 2 (June 1922): 127–146.

Lozano, Wilfredo. *La dominación imperialista en la República Dominicana, 1900–1930.* Santo Domingo: Universidad Autónoma, 1976.

Pitre, Merline. "Frederick Douglass and the Annexation of Santo Domingo." *Journal of Negro History* 62, Number 4 (1977): 390–400.

Sutton, Walter A. "The Wilson Administration and Scandal in Santo Domingo." *Presidential Studies Quarterly* 12, Number 4 (1982): 552–560.

*American Reoccupation and
Modern Era (1925–Present)*

Alemán, José Luis. "La prostitución: sus determinantes económicos." *Estudios Sociales [Dominican Republic]* 7, Number 4 (1974): 201–210.

Corten, André. "Como vive la otra mitad de Santo Domingo: estudio de dualismo estructural." *Caribbean Studies [Puerto Rico]* 4, Number 4 (1965): 3–19.

Draper, Theodore. "The Dominican Intervention Reconsidered." *Political Science Quarterly* 86, Number 1 (1971): 1–36.

Duarte, Isis. "Fuerza laboral urbana en Santo Domingo, 1980–1983." *Estudios Sociales [Dominican Republic]* 16, Number 53 (1983): 31–53.

Greenberg, Lawrence M. "The U.S. Dominican Intervention: Success Story." *Parameters* 17, Number 4 (1987): 18–29.

Pacini Hernández, Deborah. *Bachata: A Social History of Dominican Popular Music.* Philadelphia: Temple University Press, 1995.

Slater, Jerome. *Intervention and Negotiation: The United States and the Dominican Revolution.* New York: Harper and Row, 1970.

Tolentino Rojas, Vicente. *Reseña geográfica, histórica y estadística de la República Dominicana.* Ciudad Trujillo: Impresora Dominicana, 1954.

Vega, Bernardo. *Trujillo y las fuerzas armadas norteamericanas.* Santo Domingo: Fundación Cultural Dominicana, 1992.

Wiarda, Howard J. *Dictatorship and Development: The Methods of Control in Trujillo's Dominican Republic.* Gainesville: University of Florida Press, 1968.

General Works

Alemar, Luis E. *Santo Domingo-Ciudad Trujillo: historia de sus calles.* Santiago de los Caballeros, 1943.

Amiama, Manuel A. "La población de Santo Domingo." *Clio [Dominican Republic]* 27, Number 115 (1959): 116–134.

Balaguer, Joaquín. *Guía emocional de la ciudad romántica.* Santo Domingo: ALPA, 1969 and República Dominicana, 1974.

Bearse, Grace M. "History Is Alive and Well and Living in Santo Domingo." *Américas [Organization of American States]* 31, Number 9 (September 1979): 33–39.

"First Scenario of the New World: Museum of the Casas Reales." *Américas [Organization of American States]* 28, Number 10 (October 1976), supplementary pp. 1–12.

González, Julio. *Mapas y planos de Santo Domingo.* Madrid: Dirección General de Archivos y Bibliotecas, 1973.

Moya, Casimiro N. de. *Atlas de la isla y de la ciudad de Santo Domingo.* Santo Domingo: Editora Taller, 1978.

Santiago, Pedro J. *La isla de Santo Domingo: mapas y planos.* Santo Domingo: Museo de las Casas Reales, 1976.

Suro, Darío. "Baroque in Santo Domingo." *Américas [Organization of American States]* 16, Number 6 (June 1964): 15–21.

Zéndegui, Guillermo de. "Columbus' Castle." *Américas [Organization of American States]* 20, Number 7 (July 1968): 1–10.

———. "Hostal Nicolás de Ovando." *Américas [Organization of American States]* 29, Number 8 (August 1977): 21–28.

Haiti

General Studies

Adams, Thomas K. "Intervention in Haiti: Lessons Relearned." *Military Review* 76, Number 5 (1996): 45–56.

Allman, James, and John May. "Fertility, Mortality, Migration and Family Planning in Haiti." *Population Studies* 33, Number 3 (November 1979): 505–521.

Anglade, Georges. *L'espace haïtien.* Montreal: Presses de l'Université de Montréal, 1974.

———. *Atlas critique d'Haïti.* Montreal: Erce and CRC, 1982.

Ardouin, Beaubrun. *Etudes sur l'histoire d'Haïti.* Port-au-Prince: 1958 re-edition by Dr. François Dalencour, eleven volumes in one.

Atlas d'Haïti: une image de la réalité nationale. Talence: Centre d'Etudes de Géographie Tropicale, 1985.

Barros, J. *Haïti, de 1804 à nos jours.* Paris: L'Harmattan, 1984.

Baur, John Edward. "Mulatto Machiavelli: Jean-Pierre Boyer and the Haiti of His Day." *Journal of Negro History* 32, Number 3 (July 1947): 307–353.

———. "Faustin Soulouque, Emperor of Haiti: His Character and His Reign." *The Americas: A Quarterly Review of Inter-American Cultural History [Academy of American Franciscan History]* 6 (1949): 131–166.

Bausman, Frédéric, et al. *The Seizure of Haiti by the United States.* New York: Foreign Policy Association, 1922.

Begouën-Demeaux, Maurice, editor. *Mémorial d'une famille du Havre: Stanislas Foache, négociant de Saint-Domingue, 1737–1806.* Paris: Société des Colonies Françaises and Librairie Larose, 1951.

———. *Jacques-François Begouën, 1734–1831.* Le Havre: Ancienne Imprimerie M. Etaix, 1957.

Bellegarde-Smith, Patrick. *Haiti: The Breached Citadel.* Boulder: Westview, 1989.

Bennett Patterson, Carolyn. "Haiti: Beyond Mountains, More Mountains." *National Geographic* 149, Number 1 (January 1976): 70–97.

Bird, Mark Baker. *The Black Man; or, Haitian Independence.* Freeport, NY: Books for Libraries, 1971 reprint of 1869 original.

Bissainthe, Max, compiler. *Dictionnaire de bibliographie haïtienne.* Washington, DC: Scarecrow Press, 1951.

———. *Dictionnaire de bibliographie haïtienne: premier supplément.* Metuchen, NJ: Scarecrow Press, 1973.

Bonhomme, Colbert. *Révolution et contre-révolution en Haïti de 1946 á 1957.* Port-au-Prince: Imprimerie de l'État, 1957.

Brasseaux, Carl A., and Glenn R. Conrad, editors. *The Road to Louisiana: The Saint-Domingue Refugees, 1792–1809.* Lafayette: University of Southwestern Louisiana, 1992.

Brown, Jonathan. *The History and Present Condition of St. Domingo.* London: Frank Cass, 1972 reprint of 1837 original published by Marshall in Philadelphia.

Brutus, Edner. *Instruction publique en Haïti, 1492–1945.* Port-au-Prince: Imprimerie de l'Etat, 1948.

Candler, John. *Brief Notices of Hayti: With Its Conditions, Resources, and Prospects.* London: Frank Cass, 1972 reprint of 1842 original published by Thomas Ward and Company.

Césaire, Aimé. *Toussaint-Louverture: la révolution et le problème colonial.* Paris: Club Français du Livre, 1960.

Chambers, Frances, compiler. *Haiti.* Oxford, England, and Santa Barbara, CA: "World Bibliographical Series," ABC-CLIO, 1983.

Chernush, Kay. "Haitian Portfolio." *Américas [Organization of American States]* 30, Number 2 (February 1978): 33–40.

Cobb, Charles E., Jr. "Haiti: Against All Odds." *National Geographic* 172, Number 5 (November 1987): 644–671.

Cole, Hubert. *Christophe: King of Haiti.* New York: Viking, 1967.

Cooper, Anna Julia. *Slavery and the French Revolutionists, 1788–1805.* Edwin Mellen Press, 1988 translation by Frances Richardson Keller.

Cornevin, Robert. *Le théâtre haïtien des origines à nos jours.* Montreal: Leméac, 1973.

Croizat, Victor J. "Mission to Haiti—1958." *Marine Corps Gazette* 71, Number 6 (1987): 23–25.

Dash, J. Michael, editor. *Haiti and the United States: National Stereotypes and the Literary Imagination.* New York: St. Martin's Press, 1997.

David, Placide. *L'héritage colonial en Haïti.* Paris: Presses Nationales, 1959.

De Ville, Winston. *Saint Domingue: Census Records and Military Lists, 1688–1720.* Ville Platte, Louisiana: Self-published, 1988.

Debien, Gabriel. "Les sources manuscrites de l'histoire et de la géographie de Saint-Domingue." *Revue de la Société d'histoire et de géographie d'Haïti* 6 (1937): 13–62.

———. "Notes bibliographiques sur l'histoire de Saint-Domingue." *Revue de la Société d'histoire et de géographie d'Haïti* 14 (1943): 25–42.

———. "Les cimetières à Saint-Domingue." *Conjonction* 105 (1967): 27–40.

———. "Une nantaise à Saint-Domingue, 1782–1786." *Revue de Bas-Poitu et des provinces de l'Ouest [France]* 83 (1972): 413–436.

———. "Un officier du regiment de Forez à Saint-Domingue en 1764." *Conjonction* 124 (1974): 115–139.

———. "Pour ameliorer les cases, les hospitaux et la nourriture des esclaves à Saint-Domingue à la fin du XVIIIe siècle." *Revue de la Société haïtienne d'histoire et de géographie* 39, Number 131 (1981): 1–17.

Descourtilz, M. E. *Voyage d'un naturaliste en Haïti, 1799–1803.* Paris: Librairie Plon, 1935 re-edition by Jacques Boulenger.

Diederich, Bernard, and Al Burt. *Papa Doc: The Truth about Haiti Today.* New York: McGraw-Hill, 1969.

Dodge, R. A. "Massacre in Haiti." *Proceedings of the U.S. Naval Institute* 120, Number 11 (1994): 60–64.

Dumerve, Constantin. *Histoire de la musique en Haïti.* Port-au-Prince: Imprimerie des Antilles, 1968.

Dunham, Katherine. *Island Possessed.* Garden City, NJ: Doubleday, 1969.

Duvivier, Ulrich. *Bibliographie générale et méthodique d'Haïti.* Port-au-Prince: Imprimerie de l'État, 1941, two volumes.

Fauriol, Georges. "The Duvaliers and Haiti." *Orbis* 32, Number 4 (1988): 587–607.

Ferguson, James. *Papa Doc, Baby Doc: Haiti and the Duvaliers.* Oxford: Basil Blackwell, 1987.

Fiehrer, Thomas. "Saint-Domingue/Haiti: Louisiana's Caribbean Connection." *Louisiana History* 30, Number 4 (1989): 419–437.

Fouchard, Jean. "Les joies de la lecture à Saint-Domingue." *Revue d'histoire des colonies [France]* 41 (1954): 103–111.

———. *Artistes et répertoire des scènes de Saint-Domingue.* Port-au-Prince: Imprimerie de l'État, 1955.

———. *Le théâtre à Saint-Domingue.* Port-au-Prince: Imprimerie de l'État, 1955.

———. "Les joies de la table à Saint-Domingue." *Revue de la Société haïtienne d'histoire at de géographie* 27 (1955): 59–63.

———. *Plaisirs de Saint-Domingue: notes sur sa vie sociale, littéraire et artistique.* Port-au-Prince: Imprimerie de l'État, 1955.

———. *The Haitian Maroons: Liberty or Death.* New York: Blyden, 1981.

Franco, José Luciano. *Historia de la Revolución de Haití.* Santo Domingo: Editora Nacional, 1971 re-edition.

Franco, José Luciano, compiler. *Documentos para la historia de Haití en el Archivo Nacional de Cuba.* Havana: Archivo Nacional de Cuba, 1954.

Franklin, James. *The Present State of Hayti (Saint Domingo) with Remarks on Its Agriculture, Commerce, Laws, Religion, Finances, and Populations, Etc.* London: Frank Cass, 1971 reprint of 1828 original published by Murray.

Frostin, Charles. "L'intervention britannique à Saint-Domingue en 1793." *Revue française d'histoire d'Outre-Mer [France]* 49 (1962): 293–365.

———. "Les 'Enfants Perdus de l'État' ou la condition militaire à Saint-Domingue aux XVIIIe siècle." *Annales de Bretagne [France]* 80 (1973): 317–343.

———. *Les révoltes blanches à Saint-Domingue aux XVIIe et XVIIIe siècles: Haïti avant 1789.* Paris: L'École, 1975.

Gaillard, Roger. *Les cent-jours de Rosalvo Bobo; ou, une mise à mort politique.* Port-au-Prince: Presses Nationales, 1973.

Garrigus, John D. "Catalyst or Catastrophe? Saint-Domingue's Free Men of Color and the Battle of Savannah, 1779–1782." *Revista/Review Interamericana [Puerto Rico]* 22, Numbers 1–2 (1992): 109–125.

Geggus, David Patrick. "Yellow Fever in the 1790s: The British Army in Occupied Saint Domingue." *Medical History* 23, Number 1 (January 1979): 38–58.

———. *Slavery, War and Revolution: The British Occupation of Saint-Domingue, 1793–1798.* Oxford: Clarendon Press, 1982.

———. *Unexploited Sources for the History of the Haitian Revolution,* 1983.

———. "Racial Equality, Slavery, and Colonial Secession during the Constituent Assembly." *American Historical Review* 94 (1989): 1290–1308.

Girod, François. *Une fortune coloniale sous l'Ancien Régime: la famille Hecquet à Saint-Domingue, 1724–1796.* Paris: Les Belles Lettres, 1970.

———. "Les villes dans la partie française de Saint-Domingue au XVIIIe siècle." *Procès-verbaux et mémoires de l'Académie des sciences, belles-Lettres et arts de Besançon [France]* 179 (1971): 225–250.

———. *La vie quotidienne de la société créole: Saint-Domingue au XVIIIe siècle.* Paris: Hachette, 1972.

Goubert, Pierre. "Une belle enquête: Saint-Domingue au XVIIIe siècle." *Annales: économies, sociétés, civilisations [France]* 7 (1952): 329–331.

Griggs, Earl Leslie, and Clifford H. Prator, editors. *Henry Christophe and Thomas Clarkson: A Correspondence.* New York: Greenwood, 1968 reprint of 1952 original published by the University of California Press at Berkeley.

Haiti: Urban Sector Survey. Washington, DC: World Bank, 1979.

Healy, David F. *Gunboat Diplomacy in the Wilson Era: The U.S. Navy in Haiti, 1915–1916.* Madison: University of Wisconsin Press, 1976.

Heinl, Nancy Gordon. "Return to Haiti—June 1986." *Marine Corps Gazette* 71, Number 6 (1987): 26–27.

Heinl, Robert Debs, Jr., and Nancy Gordon Heinl. *Written in Blood: The Story of the Haitian People, 1492–1971.* Boston: Houghton Mifflin, 1978.

Hickey, Donald R. "America's Response to the Slave Revolt in Haiti, 1791–1806." *Journal of the Early Republic* 2, Number 4 (1982): 361–379.

Hoffman, Léon-François. "An American Trader in Revolutionary Haiti: Simeon Johnson's Journal of 1807." *Princeton University Library Chronicle* 49, Number 2 (1988): 182–199.

Houdaille, Jacques. "Quelques données sur la population de Saint-Domingue au XVIIIe siècle." *Population [France]* 28, Numbers 4–5 (July–October 1973): 859–872.

Hunt, Alfred N. *Haiti's Influence on Antebellum America: Slumbering Volcano in the Caribbean.* Baton Rouge: Louisiana State University Press, 1988.

James, C. L. R. *The Black Jacobins: Toussaint L'Ouverture and the San Domingo Revolution.* London: Alison and Busby, 1980 revised edition.

Johnston, Harry. "Haiti: The Home of Twin Republics." *National Geographic* 38, Number 6 (December 1920): 483–496.

Labelle, Micheline. *Idéologie de couleur et classes sociales en Haïti.* Montreal: Presses de l'Université de Montréal, 1978.

Lacerte, Robert K. "The First Land Reform in Latin America: The Reforms of Alexandre Pétion, 1809–1914." *Inter-American Economic Affairs* 28, Number 4 (spring 1975): 77–85.

Lachance, Paul F. "The 1809 Immigration of Saint-Domingue Refugees to New Orleans: Reception, Integration and Impact." *Louisiana History* 29, Number 2 (1988): 109–141.

Lacombe, Robert. *Histoire monétaire de Saint-Domingue et de la République d'Haïti jusqu'en 1874.* Paris: Larose, 1958.

Laguerre, Michel S. *The Complete Haitiana: A Bibliographic Guide to the Scholarly Literature, 1900–1980.* Millwood, NY: Kraus International, 1982, two volumes.

———. *Urban Life in the Caribbean: A Study of a Haitian Urban Community.* Cambridge, MA: Schenkman, 1982.

———. *Voodoo and Politics in Haiti.* New York: St. Martin's Press, 1989.

———. *The Military and Society in Haiti.* Knoxville: University of Tennessee Press, 1993.

Laurent, Gérard M. *Trois mois aux archives d'Espagne.* Port-au-Prince: Imprimerie "Les Presses Libres," 1956.

———. *Documentation historique pour nos étudiants.* Port-au-Prince: La Phalange, 1959.

———. *Le Commissaire Sonthonax à Saint-Domingue.* Port-au-Prince: Imprimerie La Phalange, 1965, two volumes.

Léon, Rulx. *Propos d'histoire d'Haïti.* Port-au-Prince: Imprimerie de l'Etat, 1945.

Lerebours, Michel-Philippe. "The Indigenist Revolt: Haitian Art, 1927–1944." *Callaloo* 15, Number 3 (summer 1992): 711–725.

Leyburn, James G. *The Haitian People.* New Haven: Yale University Press, 1955 reprint of 1941 original.

Lobb, J. "Caste and Class in Haiti." *American Journal of Sociology* 46 (1940): 23–34.

Logan, Rayford W. *The Diplomatic Relations of the United States with Haiti, 1776–1891.* Chapel Hill: University of North Carolina Press, 1941.

———. *Haiti and the Dominican Republic.* 1968.

Lugo, Américo. *Recopilación diplomática relativa a las colonias española y francesa de la isla de Santo Domingo, 1640–1701.* Ciudad Trujillo: Editorial La Nación, 1944.

MacKenzie, Charles. *Notes on Hayti, Made during a Residence in That Republic.* London: Frank Cass, 1972 reprint of 1830 Colburn and Bentley original, two volumes.

Maclean, Frances. "'They Didn't Speak our Language; We Didn't Speak Theirs.'" *Smithsonian* 23, Number 10 (1993): 44–55.

MacLeod, Murdo J. "The Soulouque Regime in Haiti, 1847–1859: A Re-Evaluation." *Caribbean Studies [Puerto Rico]* 10, Number 3 (October 1970): 35–48.

Manigat, Leslie. *L'Avènement à la Présidence d'Haïti du Général Salomon.* Port-au-Prince: Imprimerie de l'Etat, 1957.

Mathurin, Augustin. *Assistance sociale en Haïti, 1804–1972.* Port-au-Prince: Imprimerie des Antilles, 1972.

Matthewson, Tim. "Jefferson and Haiti." *Journal of Southern History* 61, Number 2 (1995): 209–248.

———. "Jefferson and the Nonrecognition of Haiti." *Proceedings of the American Philosophical Society* 140, Number 1 (1996): 22–48.

McCronklin, James H. *Garde d'Haïti: Twenty Years of Organization and Training by the United States Marine Corps.* Annapolis: U.S. Naval Institute Press, 1956.

McIntosh, Malcolm E., and Bernerd Clarke Weber, editors. *Correspondance familiale au temps des troubles de Saint-Domingue: lettres du marquis et de la marquise de Rouvray à leur fille (Saint-Domingue-États-Unis, 1791–1796).* Paris: Société de l'Histoire des Colonies Françaises and Librairie Larose, 1959.

Ménier, Marie-Antoinette. "Les sources de l'histoire de la partie française de l'île de Saint-Domingue aux Archives Nationales de France." *Conjonction* 140 (1978): 119–135.

Ménier, Marie-Antoinette, and Gabriel Debien. "Journaux de Saint-Domingue." *Revue d'histoire des colonies [France]* 36 (1949): 424–475.

Montague, Ludwell Lee. *Haiti and the United States, 1714–1938.* New York: Russell and Russell, 1966 reprint of 1940 original published by Duke University Press.

Montas, Michele. *Haïti.* Papeete: Éditions du Pacifique, 1975.

Moral, Paul. "La maison rurale en Haïti." *Les cahiers d'Outre-Mer [France]* 10, Number 38 (April–June 1957): 117–130.

Moreau de Saint-Méry, Médéric-Louis-Élie, edited by Blanche Maurel and Étienne Taillemite. *Description physique, civile, politique et historique de la partie française de l'isle de Saint-Domingue, avec des observations générales sur sa population, sur le caractère et les mæurs de ses divers habitans; sur son climat, sa culture, ses productions, son administration, etc., etc.* Paris: Société d'Histoire des Colonies Françaises and Librairie Larose, 1958 republication of the 1797–1798 original issued in Philadelphia in three volumes; also republished in 1984 by the Société Française d'Histoire d'Outre-Mer.

———. *A Civilization That Perished: The Last Years of White Colonial Rule in Haiti.* Lanham, MD: University Press of America, 1985 translated re-edition by Ivor D. Spencer.

Morley, Morris, and Chris McGillion. "'Disobedient' Generals and the Politics of Redemocratization: The Clinton Administration and Haiti." *Political Science Quarterly* 112, Number 3 (1997): 363–384.

Morris, Justin. "Force and Democracy: UN/US Intervention in Haiti." *International Peacekeeping [UK]* 2, Number 3 (1995): 391–412.

Munro, Dana Gardner. "The American Withdrawal from Haiti, 1929–1934." *Hispanic American Historical Review* 49, Number 1 (February 1969): 1–26.

Nicholls, David. *From Dessalines to Duvalier: Race, Colour and National Independence in Haiti.* Cambridge, NY: Cambridge University Press, 1979.

Niles, Blair. *Black Haiti: A Biography of Africa's Eldest Daughter.* New York: Putnam's, 1926.

Ott, Thomas O. *The Haitian Revolution, 1789–1804.* Knoxville: University of Tennessee Press, 1973.

Pamphile, Leon D. "America's Policy-Making in Haitian Education, 1915–1934." *Journal of Negro Education* 54, Number 1 (1985): 99–108.

———. "The NAACP and the American Occupation of Haiti." *Phylon* 47, Number 1 (1986): 91–100.

Parham, Althea de Puech, editor and translator. *My Odyssey: Experiences of a Young Refugee from Two Revolutions.* Baton Rouge: Louisiana State University Press, 1959.

Perusse, Roland I. *Historical Dictionary of Haiti.* Metuchen, NJ: Scarecrow Press, 1977.

Pluchon, Pierre. *Vaudou: sorciers empoisonneurs de Saint-Domingue à Haïti.* Paris: Karthala, 1987.

Plummer, Brenda Gayle. *Haiti and the Great Powers, 1902–1915.* Baton Rouge: Louisiana State University Press, 1988.

———. *Haiti and the United States: The Psychological Moment.* Athens: University of Georgia Press, 1992.

Rainsford, Marcus. *An Historical Account of the Black Empire of Hayti; Comprehending a View of the Principal Transactions in the Revolution of Saint Domingo, with Its Ancient and Modern State.* London: Frank Cass, 1972 reprint of 1805 original published by Cundee.

Recensement général de la population et du logement, août 1971. Port-au-Prince: Département des Finances et des Affaires Économiques of the Institut Haïtien de Statistique, 1975.

Reid, Stuart. "Brigands and the Black Vomit: The Royal Scots on San Domingo, 1794–1797." *Journal of the Society for Army Historical Research [UK]* 74, Number 299 (1996): 155–165.

Revue de la Société haïtienne d'histoire et de géographie [quarterly]. Port-au-Prince, 1925–.

Richard, Robert. "À propos de Saint-Domingue: la monnaie dans l'économie coloniale, 1674–1803." *Revue d'histoire des colonies [France]* 42 (1954): 22–46.

Rodman, Selden. "Letter from Haiti." *Architecture Plus* 2, Number 4 (July–August 1974): 10 ff.

———. *Haiti: The Black Republic.* Old Greenwich, CT: Devin-Adair, revised 1980 edition of 1954 original.

Rotberg, Robert. *Haiti: The Politics of Squalor.* Boston: Houghton Mifflin, 1971.

Roussier, Paul, editor. *Lettres du Général Leclerc.* Paris: Société des Colonies Françaises and Librairie Ernest Leroux, 1937.

Rubin, Vera, and Richard P. Schaedel, editors. *The Haitian Potential: Research and Resources of Haiti.* New York: Teachers College Press, 1975.

Saint-Vil, Jean. "Villes et bourgs de Saint-Domingue au XVIIIe siècle: essai de géographie historique." *Conjonction* 138 (1978): 5–32 and *Les cahiers d'Outre-Mer [France]* 31, Number 123 (July–September 1978): 251–270.

Schéma d'aménagement du territoire: diagnostic et image à long terme. Port-au-Prince: Secrétariat d'État au Plan, Direction de l'Aménagement du Territoire et Protection de l'Environnement, 1981.

Schmidt, Hans. *The United States Occupation of Haiti, 1915–1934.* New Brunswick, NJ: Rutgers University Press, 1971.

Scofield, John. "Haiti: West Africa in the West Indies." *National Geographic* 119, Number 2 (February 1961): 227–259.

Shannon, Magdaline W. "Bibliography of Saint-Domingue, Especially for the Period of 1700–1804." *Revue de la Société haïtienne d'histoire et de géographie* 37, Number 125 (1979): 5–55.

Spector, Robert M. *W. Cameron Forbes and the Hoover Commissions to Haiti (1930).* Lanham, MD: University Press of America, 1985.

Suggs, Henry Lewis. "The Response of the African American Press to the United States Occupation of Haiti, 1915–1934." *Journal of Negro History* 73, Numbers 1–4 (1988): 33–45.

Thésée, Françoise, and Gabriel Debien. "Un colon niortais à Saint-Domingue: Jean Barré de Saint-Venant,

1737–1810." *Bulletin de la Société historique et scientifique des Deux Sèvres [France]* 7 (1974): 355–523.

Trammond, Joannès. *Saint-Domingue en 1756 et 1757 d'après la correspondance de l'ordonnateur Lambert.* Paris: Société de l'Histoire des Colonies Française, 1928; version also published in the *Revue d'histoire coloniale française* 4 (1927): 509–542.

Trouillot, Hénock. *La condition des nègres domestiques à Saint-Domingue.* Port-au-Prince: Collection Haitiana, 1955.

Trouillot, Michel-Rolph. *Haiti: State against Nation.* New York: Monthly Review Press, 1990.

Weddle, Ken. *Haiti in Pictures.* New York: Sterling, 1974.

Wilson, Samuel M. *Hispaniola: Caribbean Chiefdoms in the Age of Columbus.* Gainesville: University Press of Florida, 1992.

Wingfield, Roland, and Vernon J. Parenton. "Class Structure and Class Conflict in Haitian Society." *Social Forces* 43, Number 3 (March 1965): 338–347.

Zéndegui, Guillermo de. "Magical Haiti." *Américas [Organization of American States]* 24, Number 3 (March 1972), supplementary pp. 1–24.

Cap-Haïtien
Colonial Era (1492–1803)

Deagan, Kathleen A., editor. *Puerto Real: The Archaeology of a Sixteenth-Century Spanish Town in Hispaniola.* Gainesville: University Press of Florida, 1995.

Debien, Gabriel. "Une maison d'éducation à Saint-Domingue: 'Les Religieuses' du Cap." *Revue d'histoire de l'Amérique française [Canada]* 2 (1949): 557–575.

Ewen, Charles R. *From Spaniard to Creole: The Archaeology of Cultural Formation at Puerto Real, Haiti.* Tuscaloosa: University of Alabama Press, 1991.

Hassal, Mary. *Secret History; or the Horrors of St. Domingo, in a Series of Letters Written by a Lady at Cape François to Colonel Burr, Late Vice-President of the United States, Principally during the Command of General Rochambeau.* Freeport, NY: Books for Libraries Press, 1971 reprint of 1801 original published by Bradford and Inskeep of Philadelphia.

Hernández Tapia, Concepción. "Despoblaciones de la isla de Santo Domingo en el siglo XVII." *Anuario de Estudios Americanos [Spain]* 27 (1970): 281–320.

Landers, Jane. "Jorge Biassou, Black Chieftain." *Escribano* 25 (1988): 85–100.

Loker, Zvi. "Un cimetière juif au Cap-Haïtien, Haïti." *Revue des études juives [France]* 136, Numbers 3–4 (1977): 425–427.

Lugo, Américo. "Baltasar López de Castro y la despoblación del norte de La Española." *Revista de Historia de América [Mexico]* 23 (1947).

McClellan, James E., III. *Colonialism and Science: Saint Domingue in the Old Regime.* Baltimore: Johns Hopkins University Press, 1992.

Mercier, L. "La vie au Cap Français en 1789." *Revue d'histoire des colonies [France]* 21 (1933): 101–130.

Pluchon, Pierre. "Le cercle des philadelphes du Cap-Français à Saint-Domingue: seule académie coloniale de l'Ancien Régime." *Mondes et cultures [France]* 45 (1985): 157–191.

Varela, Consuelo. "La Isabela, vida y ocaso de una ciudad efímera." *Revista de Indias [Spain]* 47, Number 181 (1987): 733–744.

Early Maps and Depictions of Cap-François, 1728–1791

Panoramic view and map of the city and its harbor, ca. 1728, by the French engraver d'Anville—found on page 238 of the second volume of Pierre-François-Xavier de Charlevoix's *Histoire de l'Isle Espagnole ou S. Domingue* (Paris: Hippolyte-Louis Guérin, 1730–1731), various sources

Spanish map and profile views of "Guarico," copied in 1756 by Juan Linares, a student at Cadiz's *Real Escuela de Navegación* or "Royal School of Navigation"—original held by the Library of Congress, call number: G4944.C3A1 1756.L5 Vault

Oil painting by John Cleveley "the Elder" of Commo. Arthur Forrest's naval action off Cap-François, 21 October 1757—original held by the National Maritime Museum at Greenwich, England, negative number: BHC 0382

Map of the city, engraved by P. Croisey as illustration 65 in the first volume of Jacques-Nicolas Bellin's *Petit atlas maritime: recueil et plans des quatre parties du monde,* published in 1764—available from the Library of Congress [call number: G4944.C3 1764.B4 Vault], plus numerous other sources

Pen-and-ink map with watercolor highlights, entitled "A sketch of the harbour of Port Francoise on the island of Hispaniola," drawn during the 1760s—original held in the Howe Map Collection of the Library of Congress, call number: G4944.C3P55 176-.S5 Howe 46

Hand-tinted manuscript drawing of Cap-François's La Charité Hospital, after its expansion in 1777–1782—original held by the Centre des Archives d'Outre-Mer of the Archives Nationales at Aix-en-Provence, France

Map of *El Guarico, alias el Cabo Francés,* drawn in 1783 by master's mate José María Sánchez of the Royal Spanish Navy—original held by the Library of Congress, call number: G4944.C3A1 1783.S2 Vault [three anonymous, undated versions can also be found under call numbers G4944.C3A1 17—.G8 Vault; G4944.C3A1 17—.P8 Vault; and G4944.C3A1 17—.P9 Vault]

Hand-colored map of Cap-François, possibly engraved by Dupuis, ca. 1785–1787—original held by the American

Philosophical Society in Philadelphia, plus various other sources

Cadastral map of Cap-François's district, as surveyed by René Phelipeau in 1786—original held by the Library of Congress, call number: G4944.C3G46 1786.P5 Vault

Numerous views of the city, engraved by Nicolas Ponce from original drawings by Ferdinand de la Brunière and published in Paris in 1791, as illustrations for Médéric-Louis-Élie Moreau de Saint-Méry's *Recueil de vues des lieux principaux de la colonie françoise de Saint-Domingue*—originals held by the Bibliothèque Nationale in Paris, the National Maritime Museum at Greenwich, the New York Public Library, etc.

Independence and General Works (1804–Present)

Bernardin, Antoine. *Silhouettes d'hier: portraits et anecdotes.* Port-au-Prince: Henri Deschamps, 1985.

Cap-Haïtien: ville des merveilles. Port-au-Prince, 1953.

"Considerations sur la ville du Cap Français." *Revue de la Société haïtienne d'histoire et géographie* 37 (1972): 44–56.

"The Cathedral at Cape Haytien, St. Domingo, as Restored by Messrs. Cummings and Sears, Architects, Boston." *American Architect and Building News* 4, Number 154 (December 1878): 189.

Enquête sur la population de La Fossette (Cap-Haïtien). Port-au-Prince: Volume 3 of the Series "Études démographiques, économiques et sociologiques" published by the Service de la Population, 1961.

Péan, Marc. *Vingt-cinq ans de vie capoise, 1890–1915.* Port-au-Prince: Henri Deschamps, ca. 1977–1993, three volumes respectively subtitled *L'illusion héroïque, L'échec du firminisme,* and *La ville éclatée.*

Peltier, Norman A. "The Haitian Expedition of 1929." *Marine Corps Gazette* 71, Number 6 (1987): 25–26.

Rebelle, Hugues. *Les nuits chaudes du Cap Français.* Paris: Jérôme Martineau, 1966 reprint of 1927 original published by Henri Jonquier.

Wilson, Victor-Emmanuel Roberto. "The Forgotten Eighth Wonder of the World." *Callaloo* 15, Number 3, Part 2 (summer 1992): 849–856.

Wood, Harold A. *Northern Haiti: Land, Land Use, and Settlement: A Geographical Investigation of the Département du Nord.* Toronto: University of Toronto Press, 1963.

Zéndegui, Guillermo de. "The Great Haitian Epic." *Américas [Organization of American States]* 22, Number 6 (June 1970): 2–11.

Port-au-Prince

Cauna, Jacques. "La révolution à Port-au-Prince (1791–1792) vue par un bordelaise." *Annales du Midi [France]* 101, Numbers 185–186 (1989): 169–200.

Comhaire-Sylvain, Jean, and Suzanne Comhaire-Sylvain. "Urban Stratification in Haiti." *Social and Economic Studies [Jamaica]* 8, Number 2 (June 1959): 179–189.

Corvington, Georges, Jr. *Port-au-Prince au cours des ans, 1749–1934.* Port-au-Prince: Henri Deschamps, 1970–1987, five volumes.

Devauges, Roland. "Une capitale antillaise: Port-au-Prince, Haïti." *Les cahiers d'Outre-mer [France]* 7, Number 26 (1954): 105–136.

Étude d'améliorations physiques des Cités Simone, Jean-Claude, Linthau, Brooklyn, Boston et Wharf. Port-au-Prince: Fondation Cooperative de l'Habitat, 1981.

Godard, Henry R. "Port-au-Prince, Haïti: Les 'quartiers' et les mutations récentes du tissu urbain." *Les cahiers d'Outre-mer [France]* 38, Number 149 (January–March 1985): 5–24.

Grimoüard, Nicolas-Henri-René, vicomte de. *L'Amiral de Grimoüard au Port-au-Prince.* Paris: Société de l'Histoire des Colonies Françaises et Librairie Larose, 1937.

Jan, Jean-Marie. *Port-au-Prince: Documents pour l'histoire religieuse.* Port-au-Prince: Henri Deschamps, 1956.

May, L. F. "Port-au-Prince, 1749–1950." *Revue d'histoire des colonies [France]* 36, Number 3 (1949): 225–237.

Plan de développement de Port-au-Prince et de sa région métropolitaine. Port-au-Prince: Conseil National de Développement et de Planification, 1974–1975, six volumes.

Rigaud, Candelon. *Promenades dans les rues de Port-au-Prince.* Port-au-Prince: Chéraquit, 1927.

Saint-Gérard, Y. *Haïti: L'enfer au paradis.* Toulouse: Eché, 1984.

Jamaica
Kingston

Barham, A., et al. *Survey of Trench Town and Victoria Town: A Preliminary Report.* Kingston: Department of Sociology of the University of the West Indies, 1965.

Black, Clinton V. *Port Royal.* Kingston, 1970.

Buisseret, David J. "Port Royal, 1655–1725." *Jamaican Historical Review* 6 (1966): 21–28.

———. *The Fortifications of Kingston, 1655–1914.* Kingston: Bolivar Press, 1971.

Cadbury, Henry J. "Conditions in Jamaica in 1687." *Jamaican Historical Review* 3, Number 2 (1959): 52–57.

———. "Quakers and the Earthquake at Port Royal, 1692." *Jamaican Historical Review* 8 (1971): 19–31.

Clarke, Colin G. *Kingston, Jamaica: Urban Development and Social Change, 1692–1962.* Berkeley: University of California Press, 1975.

Cumper, Gloria. "New Pattern for Kingston." *Geographical Magazine* 40, Number 7 (1967): 588–598.

Davison, Betty. "No Place Back Home: A Study of Jamaicans Returning to Kingston, Jamaica." *Race* 9 (1967–1968): 499–509.

Jacobs, H. P. "French Interlopers in 1555." *Jamaican Historical Review* 1, Number 2 (December 1948): 234–246.

———. "Port Royal in Decline." *Jamaican Historical Review* 8 (1971): 34–59.

Link, Marion Clayton. "Exploring the Drowned City of Port Royal." *National Geographic* 117, Number 2 (February 1960): 151–183.

Matley, Charles. *The Geology and Physiography of the Kingston District, Jamaica.* Kingston: Government Printing Office, 1951.

Maunder, W. F. "Kingston Public Passenger Transport." *Social and Economic Studies [Jamaica]* 2, Number 4 (1954): 5–36.

———. *Employment in an Underdeveloped Area: A Sample Survey of Kingston, Jamaica.* New Haven: Yale University Press, 1960.

Official Souvenir Album of the City of Kingston. Kingston: Kingston and St. Andrew Corporation, 1964.

Pawson, Michael, and David J. Buisseret. *Port Royal, Jamaica.* Oxford: Clarendon Press, 1975.

Port Royal, Jamaica: Excavations, 1969–70. Kingston: National Trust Commission, 1972.

Report on the Harbour of Kingston. Toronto: Ewbank and Partners, Limited, 1961.

Roberts, George W. "Provisional Assessment of Growth of the Kingston–St. Andrew Area, 1960–1970." *Social and Economic Studies [Jamaica]* 12 (1963): 432–441.

———. "Urbanization and the Growth of Small Towns in Jamaica." *Jamaica Architect* 1, Number 3 (1967–1968): 69–71.

Roberts, W. Adolphe, editor. *The Capitals of Jamaica.* Kingston: Pioneer Press, 1955.

Sesqui-Centennial Anniversary of the Granting of the Charter to Kingston, 1802–1952. Kingston, 1952.

Simpson, George Eaton. "Begging in Kingston and Montego Bay." *Social and Economic Studies [Jamaica]* 3, Number 2 (1954): 197–211.

———. "Political Cultism in West Kingston, Jamaica." *Social and Economic Studies [Jamaica]* 4 (1955): 133–149.

Smith, M. G., et al. *The Ras Tafari Movement in Kingston, Jamaica.* Kingston: Institute of Social and Economic Research at the University of the West Indies, 1960.

Steers, J. A. "The Cays and Palisadoes of Port Royal, Jamaica." *Geographical Review* 106 (1940): 279–295.

Stone, Carl. *Race, Class and Political Behavior in Urban Jamaica.* Kingston: Institute of Social and Economic Research at the University of the West Indies, 1973.

The Town and Country Planning Development Order, 1966. Kingston: Government Printing Office, 1966.

Williams, Wilma. "Old Kingston." *Jamaica Journal* 5, Numbers 2–3 (1971): 3–9.

Wright, Irene Aloha. "The Spanish Version of Sir Anthony Sherley's Raid on Jamaica, 1597: Extracts from Four Heretofore Unpublished Documents Existing in the Archivo de Indias." *Hispanic American Historical Review* 5 (1922): 227–248.

Young, J. G. "Who Planned Kingston?" *Jamaica Historical Review* 1 (1946): 144–153.

Zahedieh, Nuala. "The Merchants of Port Royal, Jamaica, and the Spanish Contraband Trade, 1655–1692." *William and Mary Quarterly* 43, Number 4 (October 1986): 570–593.

———. "A Frugal, Prudential and Hopeful Trade: Privateering in Jamaica, 1655–1689." *Journal of Imperial and Commonwealth History* 18, Number 2 (1990): 145–168.

Martinique

General Studies

Achéen, René. "Conflits des institutions républicaines à la Martinique: les blancs créoles et la question du pouvoir, 1870–1885." *Cahiers du Centre d'études régionales Antilles-Guyane* or *CERAG* 30 (1975): 15–63.

Affergan, Francis. *Anthropologie à la Martinique.* Paris: Fondation Nationale des Sciences Politiques, 1983.

Annuaire de la vie martiniquaise. Fort-de-France: Imprimerie Officielle, 1947, two volumes.

Blérald, Alain-Philippe. *Histoire économique de la Guadeloupe et de la Martinique du XVIIe siècle à nos jours.* Paris: Karthala, 1986.

Bonniol, Jean-Luc, editor. *L'Historial Antillais: Guadeloupe et Martinique, des îles aux hommes.* Fort-de-France: Dajani, 1980.

Burton, Richard D. E. *Assimilation or Independence?: Prospects for Martinique.* Montreal: McGill University Press for the Centre for Developing-Area Studies, 1978.

Celma, Cécile. "Deux formes de sociabilité de la population de couleur en Martinique et en Guadeloupe à la fin du XIXe siècle: la mutualité et le syndicat." *Revue française d'histoire d'Outre-mer* 74, Number 2 (1987): 207–233.

Césaire, Aimé. "La révolte des esclaves du Carlet à la Martinique, octobre–novembre 1822." *Revue française d'histoire d'Outre-mer* 80, Number 301 (October 1993): 551–584.

Constant, Fred P. "White Minority Power in Martinique and Guadeloupe." *Caribbean Affairs [Trinidad]* 7, Number 6 (1997): 115–128.

Cottias, Myriam. "La Martinique: Babylone fertile ou terre stérile? Des discours sur la fécondité aux indicateurs démographiques et sociaux, XVIIe–XIXe siècle." *Annales de démographie historique [France]* (1992): 199–215.

————. "'Forgetting the Past' for 'Citizenship': Barter and Resentment in Martinique, 1848–1946." *New Contree [South Africa]* 42 (1997): 155–168.

Cottrel, René, and Théodore Baude, compilers. *Tricentenaire des Antilles, Guadeloupe-Martinique, 1635–1935: documents.* Fort-de-France, 1935.

Darsières, Camille. *Les origines de la nation martiniquaise.* Pointe-à-Pitre, Guadeloupe: Désormeaux, 1974.

Dessalles, Pierre. *Sugar and Slavery, Family and Race: The Letters and Diary of Pierre Dessalles, Planter in Martinique, 1808–1856.* Baltimore: Johns Hopkins University Press, 1996 translation by Elborg Foster and Robert Forster.

Dubreuil, Guy. *La famille martiniquaise: analyse et dynamique.* Montreal: Université de Montréal Presses for the Centre des Recherches Caraïbes, 1970.

Ferre, Jean-François. "L'économie sucrière et rhumière martiniquaise en péril, 1950–1980." *Les cahiers d'Outre-mer [France]* 34, Number 136 (October–December 1981): 321–360.

Hermann, B., and C. Maillard. *Martinique.* Paris: Éditions du Pacifique, 1975.

Labrousse, Paul. *Deux vieilles terres françaises.* Colombes, 1935.

Leiris, Michel. *Contacts des civilizations en Martinique et en Guadeloupe.* Paris: UNESCO, 1955.

Leridon, H. *Fécondité et famille en Martinique.* Paris: Presses Universitaires de France, 1970.

Murch, Arvin W. "Migration in Martinique." *Revista/Review Interamericana [Puerto Rico]* 11, Number 3 (1981): 335–350.

Piriou, Jean-Pierre. "Robert Challe: une chronique martiniquaise." *Proceedings of the Annual Meeting of the French Colonial Historical Society* 15 (1992): 36–45.

Renard, Rosamunde. "Labour Relations in Martinique and Guadeloupe, 1848–1870." *Journal of Caribbean History [Barbados]* 26, Number 1 (1992): 37–61.

Revert, Eugène. *La Martinique, étude géographique.* Paris: Nouvelles Editions Latines, 1949.

Salandre, H., and R. Cheyssac. *Histoire et civilisation des Antilles françaises: Guadeloupe et Martinique.* Paris: Fernand Nathan, 1962.

Schmidt, Nelly. "1848 dans les colonies françaises des Caraïbes: ambitions républicaines et ordre colonial." *Revue française d'histoire d'Outre-mer* 85, Number 3 (1998): 33–69.

Slater, Miriam. *The Caribbean Family: Legitimacy in Martinique.* New York: St. Martin's Press, 1977.

Thompson, D. G. "General Ricci and the Suppression of the Jesuit Order in France, 1760–1764." *Journal of Ecclesiastical History [UK]* 37, Number 3 (1986): 426–441.

————. "The Lavalette Affair and the Jesuit Superiors." *French History [UK]* 10, Number 2 (1996): 206–239.

Tomich, Dale W. "'Liberté ou Mort': Republicanism and the Slave Revolt in Martinique, February 1831." *History Workshop Journal [UK]* 29 (1990): 85–91.

————. *Slavery in the Circuit of Sugar: Martinique and the World Economy, 1830–1848.* Baltimore: Johns Hopkins University Press, 1990.

Fort-de-France

Banbuck, C. A. *Histoire politique, économique et sociale de la Martinique sous l'Ancien Régime.* Fort-de-France: Société de Distribution et de Culture, 1972 re-edition of 1935 original published in Paris by Rivière.

Boswall, Capt. John Donaldson. "Narrative of the Capture of the Diamond Rock, Effected by Sir Samuel Hood in the *Centaur.*" *United Service Journal [UK]* 55 (June 1933): 210–215.

Cazes, Georges. "Problèmes de population et perspectives économiques en Martinique et en Guadeloupe." *Les cahiers d'Outre-mer [France]* 23, Number 92 (October–December 1970): 379–424.

Chauleau, L. *La Société de la Martinique au XVIIe siècle, 1635–1713.* Paris: Librairie Orientale et Américaine, 1966.

Cormack, William S. "The French Navy and the Revolt of Martinique and Guadeloupe in 1792–1793." *Consortium on Revolutionary Europe 1750–1850: Selected Papers* (1994): 237–243.

Desse, Michel. "Hierarchies et polarisations urbaines récentes en Guadeloupe, Martinique et Réunion." *Les cahiers d'Outre-mer [France]* 51, Number 201 (January–March 1998): 65–88.

Fewster, Joseph M. "The Jay Treaty and British Ship Seizures: The Martinique Cases." *William and Mary Quarterly* 45, Number 3 (1988): 426–452.

François, Y. *La croissance des villes et l'organisation de l'espace urbain en milieu tropical: la cité Dillon, zone d'extension récente de Fort-de-France.* Bordeaux, 1970.

Geggus, David Patrick. "Esclaves et gens de couleur libres de la Martinique pendant l'époque Révolutionnaire et Napoléonienne: trois instants de résistance." *Revue historique [France]* 295, Number 1 (1996): 105–132.

Horowitz, Michael M. *Morne-Paysan: Peasant Village in Martinique.* New York: Holt, Rinehart and Winston, 1967.

Jenkins, H. J. K. "Martinique: The British Occupation, 1794–1802." *History Today [UK]* 31 (November 1981): 35–39.

————. "Guadeloupe, Martinique and Commerce Raiding: Two Colonies in Conflict, 1797–1798." *Revue française d'histoire d'Outre-mer* 78, Number 4 (1991): 465–475.

Levy, Joseph-Josy. *Un village du bout du monde: modernisation et structures villageoises aux Antilles françaises.* Montreal: Université de Montréal Presses, 1976.

MacLeish, Kenneth. "Martinique: Liberté, Egalité, and Uncertainty in the Caribbean." *National Geographic* 147, Number 1 (January 1975): 124–148.

Merli, Frank J. "Caribbean Confrontation: Letters on the *Alabama,* November 1862." *Journal of Confederate History* 6 (1990): 161–174.

Miles, William F. S. "The Jews of Martinique." *Midstream* 32, Number 2 (1986): 31–33.

Ranely Verge-Depre, Colette. "Quinze années de conteneurisation des trafics maritimes aux Antilles françaises: éléments d'un bilan." *Les cahiers d'Outre-mer [France]* 50, Number 198 (April–June 1997): 151–170.

Robert, Georges. *La France aux Antilles de 1939 à 1943.* Paris: l'Annuaire, 1978 reprint of 1950 original published in Paris by Plon.

Rowbotham, W. B. "The British Occupation of the Diamond Rock, 1804–1805." *Naval Review [UK]* 37 (1949): 385–395 and Volume 39 (1950): 53–64.

Sirivine, Jean-Michel. "La tempête tropicale 'Dorothy' à la Martinique, 20–21 août 1970." *Les cahiers d'Outre-mer [France]* 25, Number 99 (July–September 1972): 338–346.

Smelser, Marshall. *The Campaign for the Sugar Islands, 1759: A Study of Amphibious Warfare.* Chapel Hill: University of North Carolina Press, 1955.

Thomas, Gordon, and Max Morgan Witts. *Day the World Ended.* New York: Stein and Day, 1969.

Puerto Rico
General Studies

Abbad y Lasierra, Iñigo. *Historia geográfica, civil y natural de la isla de San Juan Bautista de Puerto Rico.* Río Piedras: Editorial Universitaria, 1979 re-edition.

Bearse, Grace M. "The Pride of Puerto Rico." *Américas [Organization of American States]* 30, Number 1 (January 1978): 17–24.

Cabán, Pedro A. *Constructing a Colonial People: Puerto Rico and the United States, 1898–1932.* Boulder: Westview, 1999.

Campos Lacasa, Cristina. *Historia de la Iglesia en Puerto Rico.* San Juan, 1977.

Chardon, Jean-Pierre. "Le rôle de Puerto Rico dans les relations maritimes de la Caraïbe." *Les cahiers d'Outre-Mer [France]* 28, Number 110 (April–June 1975): 137–161.

Chinea, Jorge L. "Race, Colonial Exploitation and West Indian Immigration in Nineteenth Century Puerto Rico, 1800–1850." *The Americas: A Quarterly Review of Inter-American Cultural History [Academy of American Franciscan History]* 52, Number 4 (1996): 510–513.

Cifré de Loubriel, Estela. *La inmigración a Puerto Rico durante el siglo XIX.* San Juan: Instituto de Cultura Puertorriqueña, 1964.

————. *La formación del pueblo puertorriqueño: la contribución de los catalanes, baleáricos y valencianos.* San Juan: Instituto de Cultura Puertorriqueña, 1975.

Clark, Truman R. *Puerto Rico and the United States, 1917–1933.* Pittsburgh: University of Pittsburgh Press, 1975.

Córdova, Pedro Tomás de. *Memorias geográficas, históricas, económicas y estadísticas de la isla de Puerto Rico.* San Juan: Coquí, 1968 facsimile re-edition of 1825 original.

Cruz Monclova, Lidio. *Historia de Puerto Rico (siglo XIX).* Río Piedras: Editorial Universitaria, 1952–1964, three volumes.

Díaz Soler, Luis Manuel. *Historia de la esclavitud negra en Puerto Rico, 1493–1890.* Río Piedras: Editorial Universitaria, 1967 re-edition of 1953 original published in Madrid.

Dietz, James L. *Economic History of Puerto Rico: Institutional Change and Capitalist Development.* Princeton: Princeton University Press, 1986.

El proceso abolicionista en Puerto Rico: documentos para su estudio. San Juan: Centro de Investigaciones Históricas del Instituto de Cultura de la Universidad de Puerto Rico, 1974–1978, two volumes.

Fernández Méndez, Eugenio, editor. *Crónicas de Puerto Rico desde la conquista hasta nuestros días (1493–1955).* Río Piedras: Editorial Universitaria, 1981.

Guerra, Lillian. *Popular Expression and National Identity in Puerto Rico: The Struggle for Self, Community and the Nation.* Gainesville: University Press of Florida, 1998.

Hatt, Paul K. *Backgrounds of Human Fertility in Puerto Rico.* Princeton: Princeton University Press, 1952.

Huetz de Lemps, Christian. "La place des plantations dans l'économie portoricaine." *Les cahiers d'Outre-Mer [France]* 24, Number 96 (October–December 1971): 329–393; 25, Number 97 (January–March 1972): 57–97; and 25, Number 98 (April–June 1972): 142–163.

Lewis, Gordon K. *Puerto Rico: Freedom and Power in the Caribbean.* New York: Harper and Row, 1968.

López Cantos, Angel. *Historia de Puerto Rico, 1650–1700.* Seville: Escuela de Estudios Hispano-americanos, 1975.

Morales Carrión, Arturo, et al. *Auge y decadencia de la trata negrera en Puerto Rico (1820–1860).* San Juan: Centro de Estudios Avanzados de Puerto y el Caribe e Instituto de Cultura Puertorriqueña, 1978.

————. *Puerto Rico: A Political and Cultural History.* New York: Norton, 1983.

Negroni, Héctor A. *Historia militar de Puerto Rico.* Madrid: Sociedad Estatal Quinto Centenario, 1992.

Picó, Fernando. *Historia general de Puerto Rico.* Río Piedras: Huracán, 1986 re-edition.

Quintero Rivera, Angel G. *Patricios y plebeyos: burgueses, hacendados, artesanos y obreros (las relaciones de clase en el Puerto Rico de cambio de siglo).* Río Piedras: Huracán, 1988.

Richards, Bill. "The Uncertain State of Puerto Rico." *National Geographic* 163, Number 4 (April 1983): 516–543.

Rosario Rivera, Raquel. *Los emigrantes llegados a Puerto Rico procedentes de Venezuela entre 1810–1848.* San Juan: Comisión Celebración del Quinto Centenario de América y Puerto Rico, 1992.

Santiago Marazzi, Rosa. "El impacto de la inmigración a Puerto Rico, 1800 a 1830: análisis estadístico." *Revista de Ciencias Sociales [Puerto Rico]* 18, Numbers 1–2 (1974): 1–44.

———. "La inmigración de mujeres españolas a Puerto Rico en el período colonial español." *Homines* 10, Number 2 (August 1986–February 1987): 154–165.

Scarano, Francisco. "Población esclava y fuerza de trabajo: problemas del análisis demográfico de la esclavitud en Puerto Rico, 1820–1873." *Anuario de Estudios Americanos [Spain]* 43 (1986): 3–25.

———. *Puerto Rico, cinco siglos de historia.* Bogotá: McGraw-Hill, 1993.

Scarano, Francisco, editor. *Inmigración y clases sociales en Puerto Rico del siglo XIX.* Río Piedras: Huracán, 1981.

Seda Bonilla, Eduardo. "Who Is Puerto Rican: Problems of Socio-Cultural Identity in Puerto Rico." *Caribbean Studies [Puerto Rico]* 17, Numbers 1–2 (1977): 105–121.

Steward, Julian H., editor. *The People of Puerto Rico.* Urbana: University of Illinois Press, 1956.

Taylor, Milton C. "Tax Exemption and New Industry in Puerto Rico." *Social and Economic Studies [Jamaica]* 4 (1955): 121–132.

Vivó, Paquita, editor. *The Puerto Ricans: An Annotated Bibliography.* New York: Bowker, 1973.

Wagenheim, Kal. *Puerto Rico: A Profile.* New York: Praeger, 1970.

San Juan
Early Colonial Era (1508–1807)

Abril, Mariano. "El primer diario de San Juan." *Revista del Instituto de Cultura Puertorriqueña* 4, Number 13 (1961): 54–55.

Cabrillana, Nicolás. "Las fortificaciones militares en Puerto Rico." *Revista de Indias [Spain]* 27, Numbers 107–108 (January–June 1967): 157–188.

Castillo Manrubia, Pilar. "La defensa de Puerto Rico, 1797." *Revista de Historia Naval [Spain]* 9, Number 35 (1991): 29–43.

Dávila, Arturo V. "El escultor habanero en San Juan: el maestro José Valentín Sánchez, 1771–1829." *Revista del Instituto de Cultura Puertorriqueña* 4, Number 13 (1961): 22–25.

Díaz Melián, Mafalda Victoria. "La condición jurídica y social del negro en Puerto Rico a través de las actas del cabildo de San Juan Bautista de Puerto Rico,

1775–1810." *Revista Chilena de Historia del Derecho* 12 (1986): 277–303.

———. "Contribución al conocimiento de las costumbres carcelarias en Puerto Rico entre los años 1785–1810: exámen de las actas del cabildo de la ciudad de San Juan Bautista de Puerto Rico." *Revista Chilena de Historia del Derecho* 14 (1991): 189–206.

Geibel Sabat, Fernando J. *Balduino Enrico: asedio de la ciudad de San Juan de Puerto Rico por la flota holandesa.* Barcelona, 1934.

Hewitt, G. R. "Drake at San Juan de Puerto Rico." *The Mariner's Mirror [UK]* 50 (August 1964): 199–204.

Joseph, J. W., and Stephen C. Bryne. "Socio-Economics and Trade in Viejo San Juan, Puerto Rico: Observations from the Ballajá Archaeological Project." *Historical Archaeology* 26, Number 1 (1992): 45–58.

"La catedral de San Juan de Puerto Rico." *Boletín de la Academia Puertorriqueña de la Historia* 2, Number 7 (1971): 59–62.

Lédru, André-Pierre. *Viaje a la isla de Puerto Rico en el año 1797.* Río Piedras: Editorial Universitaria, 1957 re-edition of Julio L. Vizcarrondo's translation from the French.

Moscoso, Francisco. *Lucha agraria en Puerto Rico, 1541–1545: un ensayo de historia.* San Juan: Ediciones Puerto, 1997.

"Notas sobre el convento dominico Santo Tomás de Aquino." *Boletín de la Academia Puertorriqueña de la Historia* 2, Number 7 (1971): 41–58.

Rigau Pérez, José G. "Surgery at the Service of Theology: Postmortem Caesarean Sections in Puerto Rico and the Royal Cédula of 1804." *Hispanic American Historical Review* 75, Number 3 (1995): 377–404.

Szászdi, Adam. "Credit—Without Banking—In Early Nineteenth-Century Puerto Rico." *The Americas: A Quarterly Review of Inter-American Cultural History [Academy of American Franciscan History]* 19, Number 2 (1962–1963): 149–171.

———. "Apuntes sobre la esclavitud en San Juan de Puerto Rico, 1800–1811." *Anuario de Estudios Americanos [Spain]* 24 (1967): 1433–1477.

Tió, Aurelio. "Doña Leonor Ponce de León: la primera puertorriqueña." *Boletín de la Academia Puertorriqueña de la Historia* 2, Number 7 (1971): 21–26.

———. "Puerto Rico: Site of the Primordial University of the Americas." *Revista/Review Interamericana [Puerto Rico]* 4, Number 4 (1974–1975): 484–492.

Williamson, George Charles. *George, Third Earl of Cumberland, 1558–1605: His Life and Voyages.* Cambridge, NY: Cambridge University Press, 1920.

Zeno, Francisco M., compiler. *Actas del cabildo de San Juan Bautista de Puerto Rico, 1730–1821.* San Juan:

Administración General de Suministros, Oficina de Servicios, División de Imprenta, 1949–, eight volumes.

*Early Maps and Depictions
of San Juan, 1519–1793*

Crude sketch of the city's proposed new site as surveyed in September 1519 by Licenciate Rodrigo de Figueroa, in anticipation of transferring Caparra's residents to the port—original held by the Archive of Indies at Seville [archival provenance: Estante 2, Cajón 1, Legajo 2]

Diagram by Capt. Pedro de Salazar of the completed and future fortification works on El Morro headland, August 1591—original held by the Archive of Indies at Seville [archival provenance: Patronato Real, Legajo 176]

Dutch map of San Juan and its defenses during Hendricksz's attack, September 1625—published nineteen years later in Leiden in Johannes de Laet's *Historie ofte iaerlijck verhael van de verrichtingen der Geoctroyeerde West-Indische Compagnie,* several sources

Map of the city published at Havana in De Rueda's *Atlas americano,* 1766—several sources

Chart of the bay and city by the military engineer Col. Tomás O'Daly, 1776—original held by the Museo Naval in Madrid, call number: Plano B.ª XXII, C.ª A, Número 9

Pen-and-ink chart with watercolor highlights of San Juan's harbor and shoreline by Francisco Ramón Méndez, senior pilot of Capt. José de Pereda's royal warship *San Juan Nepomuceno,* December 1782—originals held by the Archivo General de Simancas in Spain, call number: Mapas, Planos y Dibujos, XVIII-133 [archival provenance: Marina, Legajo 387], as well as by the Servicio Histórico Militar at Madrid, call number: Plano 1.ª–4.ª–2.ªb–164 [archival provenance: Proyecto de Defensa, Documento 4-1-7-2]

Pen-and-ink chart with watercolor highlights of a harbor survey conducted by naval Capt. José Montero de Espinosa, November 1785—original held by the Library of Congress in Washington, call number: G 4974.S5P55 1785.M6 Vault

Map of the city and its bay by the Spanish naval Capt. Cosme Damián de Churruca, 1793—engraved and published the next year as *Plano Geométrico del Puerto Capital de la Isla de Puerto Rico,* several sources

Late Colonial Era (1808–1898)

Aponte, Gilberto. *San Mateo de Cangrejos, comunidad cimarrona en Puerto Rico: notas para su historia.* San Juan: Comité de Historia de los Pueblos, 1985.

Asenjo, Federico. *Las fiestas de San Juan.* San Juan: Coquí, 1972 re-edition of 1868 original.

Carrillo Alvarez, Ana María. "El consulado de Puerto Rico: aportaciones a la historia de su creación." *Anuario de Estudios Americanos [Spain]* 41 (1984): 617–718.

Castro de Dávila, María de los Angeles. *Arquitectura en San Juan de Puerto Rico, siglo XIX.* Río Piedras: Editorial Universitaria, 1980.

Córdova Landrón, Arturo. "San Juan en 1880." *Revista del Instituto de Cultura Puertorriqueña* 2, Number 5 (1959): 42–45.

Iturregui, Juan R. "Antecedentes de la medicina en Puerto Rico hasta la llegada de Betances." *Revista/Review Interamericana [Puerto Rico]* 18, Numbers 3–4 (1988): 79–84.

Kinsbrunner, Jay. "Caste and Capitalism in the Caribbean: Residential Patterns and House Ownership among the Free People of Color of San Juan, Puerto Rico, 1823–1846." *Hispanic American Historical Review* 70, Number 3 (August 1990): 433–461.

———. *Not of Pure Blood: The Free People of Color and Racial Prejudice in Nineteenth-Century Puerto Rico.* Durham, NC: Duke University Press, 1996.

Lalinde Abadía, Jesús. *La administración española en el siglo XIX puertorriqueño.* Seville: Escuela de Estudios Hispano-americanos, 1980.

Martínez Vergne, Teresita. "The Allocation of Liberated African Labour through the Casa de Beneficencia: San Juan, Puerto Rico, 1859–1864." *Slavery and Abolition [UK]* 12, Number 3 (1991): 200–216.

———. *Shaping the Discourse on Space: Charity and Its Wards in Nineteenth-Century San Juan, Puerto Rico.* Austin: University of Texas Press, 1999.

Matos Rodríguez, Félix V. "Spatial and Demographic Change in Nineteenth-Century San Juan, Puerto Rico, 1800–1868." *Journal of Urban History* 25, Number 4 (May 1999): 477–513.

———. *Women and Urban Change in San Juan, Puerto Rico, 1820–1868.* Gainesville: University Press of Florida, 1999.

Mayo Santana, Raúl, et al. "La familia esclava urbana en San Juan en el siglo XIX." *Revista de Ciencias Sociales [Puerto Rico]* 30, Numbers 1–2 (1993): 163–197.

———. "Esclavos libertos: el trabajo en San Juan pre y post-abolición." *Revista de Ciencias Sociales [Puerto Rico]* 30, Numbers 3–4 (1995): 1–48.

Modern Era (1899–Present)

Cafferty, Pastora San Juan. "Puerto Rican Return Migration: Its Implications for Bilingual Education." *Ethnicity* 2, Number 1 (1975): 52–65.

Davis, Martha Ellen. "The Social Organization of a Musical Event: The Fiesta de Cruz in San Juan, Puerto Rico." *Ethnomusicology* 16, Number 1 (1972): 38–62.

Dooley, Edwin L., Jr. "Wartime San Juan, Puerto Rico: The Forgotten American Home Front, 1941–1945." *Journal of Military History* 63, Number 4 (1999): 921–938.

Fischman, Jerome. "The Church in Politics: The 1960 Election in Puerto Rico." *Western Political Quarterly* 18, Number 4 (1965): 821–839.

Grosfoguel, Ramón. "World Cities in the Caribbean: The Rise of Miami and San Juan." *Review (Fernand Braudel Center)* 17, Number 3 (1994): 351–381.

Lewis, Lawrence. "The 1960–70 Spatial Patterns of Population within Puerto Rico." *Revista/Review Interamericana [Puerto Rico]* 11, Number 3 (1981): 366–375.

Lewis, Oscar. *La Vida: A Puerto Rican Family in the Culture of Poverty—San Juan and New York.* New York: Random House, 1965.

Morse, Richard. "The Sociology of San Juan: An Exegesis of Urban Mythology." *Caribbean Studies [Puerto Rico]* 5, Number 2 (1965): 45–55.

Okraku, Ishmael O. "The Family Life-Cycle and Residential Mobility in Puerto Rico." *Sociology and Social Research* 55, Number 3 (1971): 324–340.

Quintero Rivera, Angel G. *Patricios y plebeyos: burgueses, hacendados, artesanos y obreros: las relaciones de clase en el Puerto Rico de cambio de siglo.* Río Piedras: Huracán, 1988.

Safa, Helen Icken. "The Female-Based Household in Public Housing: A Case Study in Puerto Rico." *Human Organization* 24, Number 2 (1965): 135–139.

———. *The Urban Poor of Puerto Rico: A Study in Development and Inequality.* New York: Holt, Rinehart and Winston, 1974.

———. "Class Consciousness among Working Class Women in Latin America: A Case Study in Puerto Rico." *Politics and Society* 5, Number 3 (1975): 377–394.

Santiago, Victor A. "Patrones de delitos tipo 1 en San Juan, Puerto Rico, 1983–1985." *Revista/Review Interamericana [Puerto Rico]* 20, Numbers 1–2 (1990): 10–30.

Stevens, Robert William, et al. "Los arrabales de San Juan: una perspectiva histórica." *Revista de Ciencias Sociales [Puerto Rico]* 24, Numbers 1–2 (1985): 155–197.

General Works

Arrivi, Francisco. "El antiguo San Juan y el teatro Tapia." *Revista del Instituto de Cultura Puertorriqueña* 12, Number 45 (1969): 40–44.

Castro de Dávila, María de los Angeles. "The Place of San Juan de Puerto Rico among Hispanic American Cities." *Revista/Review Interamericana [Puerto Rico]* 6, Number 2 (1976): 156–173.

Galis Menéndez, Julio. "Una joya urbanistica colonial: el edificio del Archivo y Biblioteca General de Puerto Rico." *Revista/Review Interamericana [Puerto Rico]* 12, Number 4 (1982–1983): 534–541.

Gómez Canedo, Lino. "El convento de San Francisco en el viejo San Juan." *Revista del Instituto de Cultura Puertorriqueña* 56 (1972): 36–43.

Gómez-Sicre, José. "San Juan Muralists." *Américas [Organization of American States]* 23, Number 8 (August 1971): 2–9.

Hostos, Adolfo de. *Historia de San Juan, ciudad murada: ensayo acerca del proceso de la civilización en la ciudad española de San Juan Bautista de Puerto Rico, 1521–1898.* Havana: Lex, 1948, and San Juan: Instituto de Cultura Puertorriqueña, 1966 and 1983 re-editions.

Manucy, Albert, and Ricardo Torres Reyes. *Puerto Rico and the Forts of Old San Juan.* Riverside, CT: Chatham, 1973.

Marrero Núñez, Julio. "Breve asedio a los fuertes de San Juan de Puerto Rico." *Castillos de España [Spain]* 17, Number 68 (1970): 54–60.

Nadel, Barbara A. "El Morro: Caribbean Citadel." *Periodical: Journal of America's Military Past* 23, Number 1 (1996): 33–37.

Negrón Portillo, Mariano, and Raúl Mayo Santana. *La esclavitud urbana en San Juan de Puerto Rico.* Río Piedras: Huracán and the Centro de Investigaciones Sociales of the Universidad de Puerto Rico, 1992.

Sepúlveda Rivera, Aníbal. *San Juan: historia ilustrada de su desarollo urbano, 1508–1898.* San Juan: Centro de Investigaciones Carimar, 1989.

Stevenson, Robert. "Music in the San Juan, Puerto Rico Cathedral to 1900." *Revista/Review Interamericana [Puerto Rico]* 8, Number 4 (1978–1979): 546–569.

"The World of Art, Pan America: Visit to La Fortaleza." *Art in America* 51, Number 1 (1963): 116–117.

Zéndegui, Guillermo de. "A New Museum from an Old House." *Américas [Organization of American States]* 20, Number 1 (January 1968): 20–25.

Zeno, Francisco M. *Historia de la capital de Puerto Rico.* San Juan: Oficina de Actividades Culturales del Gobierno de la Capital, 1959, two volumes.

Trinidad-Tobago
Port of Spain
Spanish Era (1592–1797)

Morales Padrón, Francisco. "Descubrimiento y papel de Trinidad en la penetración continental." *Anuario de Estudios Americanos [Spain]* 14 (1957): 93–159.

———. "Trinidad en el siglo XVII." *Anuario de Estudios Americanos [Spain]* 17 (1960): 133–180.

Newson, Linda A. *Aboriginal and Spanish Colonial Trinidad: A Study in Culture Contact.* New York: Academic Press, 1976.

———. "Foreign Immigrants in Spanish America: Trinidad's Colonisation Experiment." *Caribbean Studies [Puerto Rico]* 19, Numbers 1–2 (April–July 1979): 133–151.

Noel, Jesse A. *Trinidad, provincia de Venezuela: historia de la administración española de Trinidad.* Caracas: Volume 109 of the Series "Fuentes para la Historia Colonial de Venezuela," Academia Nacional de la Historia, 1972.

Pérez Aparicio, Josefina. *Pérdida de la isla de Trinidad.* Seville: Escuela de Estudios Hispano-americanos, 1966.

*Early Maps and Depictions of Port of
Spain during Its Spanish Era, 1733–1787*

Cutaway view by the military engineer, Sub Lt. Pablo Díaz Faxardo, of a proposed new redoubt, 1733—original held by the Servicio Geográfico del Ejército at Madrid

Diagram and cutaway view by Juan Antonio Perelló of a proposed new extemporized redoubt above the city, ca. 1760–1780—original held by the Servicio Geográfico del Ejército at Madrid

Diagram and cutaway view by Perelló of a proposed new circular battery at the Caroni River mouth, ca. 1760–1780—original held by the Servicio Geográfico del Ejército at Madrid

Diagram and cutaway view by Perelló of a proposed new seaside battery, ca. 1760–1780—original held by the Servicio Geográfico del Ejército at Madrid

Map of the island of Trinidad by the military engineer Brig. Agustín Crame, April 1780—original held by the Archive of Indies at Seville [archival provenance: Caracas, 152 and Estado, 66]

Map of Chaguaramas Bay and its adjacent coastline, February 1785—original held by the Archivo General de Simancas in Spain, call number: Mapas, Planos y Dibujos, VIII-47 [archival provenance: Guerra Moderna 7236]

Exterior view of Port of Spain's church by the military engineer José del Pozo y Sucre, April 1786—original held by the Servicio Histórico Militar in Madrid

Diagram and profile view by del Pozo of a proposed new barracks and storehouse, November 1786—original held by the Servicio Histórico Militar in Madrid

Diagram and profile view by del Pozo of a proposed new 200-bed hospital, November 1786—original held by the Servicio Histórico Militar in Madrid

Diagram by del Pozo of a new wooden jetty and half-moon battery, ca. 1787—original held by the Servicio Histórico Militar in Madrid

Diagrams and profile views by the military engineer Esteban Aymerich of various new military installations, ca. 1787–1790—originals held by the Servicio Histórico Militar at Madrid

British Era and Independence (1797–Present)

Becker, Truman. "Migration in Reverse: Trinidadians Opt for Life on the Farm." *Américas [Organization of American States]* 31, Numbers 6–7 (June–July 1979): 53–57.

Brereton, Bridget. *Race Relations in Colonial Trinidad, 1870–1900.* Cambridge, NY: Cambridge University Press, 1979.

———. *A History of Modern Trinidad, 1783–1962.* London: Heinemann, 1981.

Campbell, Carl. "Jonas Mohammed Bath and the Free Mandingos in Trinidad: The Question of Their Repatriation to Africa, 1831–1838." *Pan-African Journal* 7, Number 2 (summer 1974): 129–152.

Elkins, W. F. "Black Power in the British West Indies: The Trinidad Longshoremen's Strike of 1919." *Science and Society* 33, Number 1 (winter 1969): 71–75.

Laird, Colin. "Trinidad Town House, or the Rise and Decline of a Domestic Architecture." *Caribbean Quarterly [Jamaica]* 3, Number 4 (August 1954): 188–198.

Laurence, K. O., editor. "The Trinidad Water Riots of 1903: Reflections of an Eye-Witness." *Caribbean Quarterly [Jamaica]* 15, Number 4 (December 1969): 5–22.

Lieber, Michael. *Street Life: Afro-American Culture in Urban Trinidad.* Cambridge, MA: Schenkman, 1981.

Maqid, Alvin. *Urban Nationalism: A Study of Political Development in Trinidad.* Gainesville: University Press of Florida, 1988.

Martin, Tony. "Revolutionary Upheaval in Trinidad, 1919: Views from British and American Sources." *Journal of Negro History* 58, Number 3 (July 1973): 313–326.

Taper, Bernard. "Letter from Port of Spain." *New Yorker Magazine* (23 October 1965): 203–226.

General Works

Giacottino, Jean-Claude. "Le développement des villes principales aux Antilles: l'exemple de Port of Spain." *Etudes de géographie tropicale offertes à Pierre Gourou.* Paris: Mouton, 1972, 507–538.

Ottley, Carlton Robert. *The Story of Port of Spain, Capital of Trinidad, West Indies, from the Earliest Times to the Present Day.* Port of Spain: Self-published, 1962.

———. *A Historical Account of the Trinidad and Tobago Police Force from the Earliest Times.* Port of Spain: Self-published, 1964.

MEXICO
General Studies

Acuña, René, editor. *Relaciones geográficas del siglo XVI.* Mexico City: Instituto de Investigaciones Antropológicas of the Universidad Nacional Autónoma de México or UNAM, 1981–1988, ten volumes.

Aguilar, Adrián Guillermo, et al. *Las ciudades intermedias y el desarrollo regional en México.* Mexico City: Consejo Nacional para la Cultura y las Artes, El Colegio de México, and the Instituto de Geografía of the Universidad Nacional Autónoma de México or UNAM, 1996.

Aguirre Beltrán, Gonzalo. *La población negra de México, 1519–1810: estudio etnohistórico.* Mexico City: Fondo de Cultura Económica, 1972 republication of 1946 original.

Ajofrín, Fr. Francisco de. *Diario del viaje que hicimos a México Fr. Francisco de Ajofrín y Fr. Fermín de Olite, capuchinos.* Mexico City: Instituto Cultural Hispano-Mexicano, 1964 republication of 1763–1764 manuscript.

Altman, Ida, and James M. Lockhart, editors. *Provinces of Early Mexico: Variants of Spanish American Regional Evolution.* Los Angeles: Issue Number 36 by the Latin American Studies Center of the University of California, 1976.

Anderson, Arthur J. O., et al. *Beyond the Codices: The Nahua View of Colonial Mexico.* Berkeley: University of California Press, 1976.

Anna, Timothy E. "Inventing Mexico: Provincehood and Nationhood after Independence." *Bulletin of Latin American Research [UK]* 15, Number 1 (1996): 7–17.

Arbingast, Stanley A., et al. *Atlas of Mexico.* Austin: University of Texas Press, 1975.

Arcila Farías, Eduardo. *Reformas económicas del siglo XVIII en Nueva España.* Mexico City: Volumes 117–118 of the Series "Sep-Setentas" published by the Secretaría de Educación Pública or SEP, 1974.

Arregui, Domingo Lázaro de. *Descripción de la Nueva Galicia.* Seville: Escuela de Estudios Hispano-americanos, 1946 re-edition by François Chevalier.

Arreola, Daniel D. "Nineteenth-Century Townscapes of Eastern Mexico." *Geographical Review* 72, Number 1 (1982): 1–19.

Baird, Joseph Armstrong, Jr. *The Churches of Mexico, 1530–1810.* Berkeley: University of California Press, 1962.

Bassols Batalla, Angel. *La división económica regional de México.* Mexico City: Universidad Nacional Autónoma de México or UNAM, 1967.

———. *Recursos naturales (climas, aguas, suelos).* Mexico City: Nuestro Tiempo, 1969.

Baudot, Georges. "La population des villes du Mexique en 1595, selon une enquête de l'Inquisition." *Caravelle: cahiers du monde hispanique et luso-brésilien [France]* 37 (1981): 5–18.

———. *Utopía e historia en México: los primeros cronistas de la civilización mexicana, 1520–1569.* Madrid: Espasa-Calpe, 1983.

Bazant, Jan. *Los bienes de la Iglesia en México, 1856–1875: aspectos económicos y sociales de la revolución liberal.* Mexico City: El Colegio de México, 1971.

Benjamin, Thomas, and Mark Wasserman, editors. *Provinces of the Revolution: Essays on Regional Mexican History, 1910–1929.* Albuquerque: University of New Mexico Press, 1990.

Berlandier, Jean-Louis. *Journey to Mexico during the Years 1826–1834.* Austin: Texas State Historical Society, 1980 translation of French original by Sheila M. Ohlendorf.

Bertrand, Michel. "De la richesse en Amérique: la genèse des patrimonies familiaux des officiers de finances de Nouvelle-Espagne, XVIIe-XVIIIe siècles." *Revue d'histoire moderne et contemporaine [France]* 41, Number 2 (1994): 221–236.

Bobb, Bernard E. *The Vice-Regency of Antonio María Bucareli in New Spain, 1771–1779.* Austin: University of Texas Press, 1962.

Bonet Correa, Antonio. *Arquitectura de la época porfiriana en México.* Murcia, Spain, 1966.

Borah, Woodrow W. *New Spain's Century of Depression.* Berkeley: University of California Press, 1951.

———. *The Aboriginal Population of Central Mexico on the Eve of the Spanish Conquest.* Berkeley: University of California Press, 1963.

Borah, Woodrow W., and Sherburne F. Cook. *The Population of Central Mexico in 1548: An Analysis of the "Suma de visitas de pueblos."* Berkeley: University of California Press, 1960.

Bosch García, Carlos. *Historia de las relaciones entre México y los Estados Unidos, 1819–1848.* Mexico City: Volume 3 of the Third Series of the "Archivo Histórico Diplomático Mexicano" published by the Secretaría de Relaciones Exteriores, 1974.

Boyd-Bowman, Peter. "Negro Slaves in Early Colonial Mexico." *The Americas: A Quarterly Review of Inter-American Cultural History [Academy of American Franciscan History]* 26, Number 2 (1969): 134–151.

———. "Spanish and European Textiles in Sixteenth-Century Mexico." *The Americas: A Quarterly Review of Inter-American Cultural History [Academy of American Franciscan History]* 29, Number 3 (1973): 334–358.

Brachet, Vivian. *La población de los estados mexicanos, 1824–1895.* Mexico City: "Colección Científica" of the Instituto Nacional de Antropología e Historia or INAH, 1976.

Brading, David A. "Government and Elite in Late Colonial Mexico." *Hispanic American Historical Review* 53, Number 3 (August 1973): 389–414.

———. "The Historical Demography of Eighteenth-Century Mexico: A Review." *Bulletin of the Society for Latin American Studies* 25 (1976): 3–17.

———. "Facts and Figments in Bourbon Mexico." *Bulletin of Latin American Research* 4, Number 1 (1985): 61–64.

Brading, David A., editor. *Caudillo and Peasant in the Mexican Revolution.* Cambridge, NY: Cambridge University Press, 1980.

Bradley, Benedict. "El estado en México en la época de los hapsburgos." *Historia Mexicana* 23, Number 4 (1974): 551–610.

Brady, Robert L. "The Domestic Slave Trade in Sixteenth-Century Mexico." *The Americas: A Quarterly Review of Inter-American Cultural History [Academy of American Franciscan History]* 24, Number 3 (1968): 281–289.

Brown Villalba, Celis Lourdes, and Miguel Messmacher. *El territorio mexicano.* Mexico City: Instituto Mexicano del Seguro Social or IMSS, 1982.

Bullock, William. *Six Months' Residence and Travels in Mexico.* Port Washington, NY: Kennikat, 1971 reprint of 1824 London original.

Burrus, Ernest J. *La obra cartográfica de la provincia mexicana de la Compañía de Jesús, 1567–1967.* Madrid: "Colección Chimalistac" published by José Porrúa Turanzas, 1967, two volumes.

Calderón de la Barca, Frances, or "Fanny" Erskine Inglis. *Life in Mexico.* New York: Doubleday, 1966 reedition by Howard T. Fisher and Marion Hall Fisher.

Calderón Quijano, José Ignacio. *Historia de las fortificaciones en Nueva España.* Seville: Escuela de Estudios Hispano-americanos, 1953.

———. *Los virreyes de Nueva España en el reinado de Carlos III.* Seville: Escuela de Estudios Hispano-americanos, 1967, two volumes.

———. *Nueva cartografía de los puertos de Acapulco, Campeche y Veracruz.* Seville: Escuela de Estudios Hispano-americanos, 1969.

Cameron, Sarah. *Mexico and Central America Handbook.* Chicago: Passport, 1998.

Características principales de la migración en las grandes ciudades del país. Mexico City: Consejo Nacional de Población or CONAPO, 1987.

Carmagnani, Marcello. "Demografía y sociedad: la estructura social de los centros mineros del norte de México, 1600–1720." *Historia Mexicana* 21 (1972): 419–459.

Carr, Barry. *El movimiento obrero y la política en México, 1910–1929.* Mexico City: ERA, 1981.

———. *Marxism and Communism in Twentieth-Century Mexico.* Lincoln: University of Nebraska Press, 1992.

Carrasco, David, and Eduardo Matos Montezuma, editors. *Moctezuma's Mexico: Visions of the Aztec World.* Niwot: University Press of Colorado, 1992.

Carrera Stampa, Manuel. *Los gremios mexicanos: la organización gremial en Nueva España, 1521–1816.* Mexico City: Volume I of the "Colección de Estudios Histórico-Económicos" published by the Cámara Nacional de la Industria de Transformación, 1954.

———. "El obraje novohispano." *Memorias de la Academia Mexicana de la Historia* 20, Number 2 (April–June 1961): 148–171.

Carson, W. E. *Mexico: The Wonderland of the South.* New York: Macmillan, 1910.

Castro Aranda, Hugo. *Primer censo de población de la Nueva España, 1790: censo de Revillagigedo, "un censo condenado."* Mexico City: Dirección General de Estadística, 1977.

Cervantes de Salazar, Francisco. *Tres diálogos latinos: México en 1554.* Mexico City: Universidad Nacional Autónoma de México or UNAM, 1984 reprint of 1939 translation from the original Latin by Joaquín García Icazbalceta.

Chandler, D. S. *Social Assistance and Bureaucratic Politics: The Montepíos of Colonial Mexico, 1767–1821.* Albuquerque: University of New Mexico Press, 1991.

Chapman, A. M. *Desarrollo urbano en México: caminos.* Mexico City: Secretaría de Asentamientos Humanos y Obras Públicas or SAHOP, 1982.

Chaunu, Pierre, and Huguette Chaunu, editors. *Colección de documentos para la historia del comercio exterior de México.* Mexico City: Banco Nacional de México or BANAMEX, 1966, two volumes.

Chávez Orozco, Luis, editor. *Documentos para la historia económica de México.* Mexico City: Secretaría de la Economía Nacional, 1933–1938, twelve volumes.

Chevalier, François. "Les municipalités indiennes en Nouvelle Espagne, 1520–1620." *Anuario de Historia del Derecho Español [Spain]* 15 (1944): 352–376.

———. *Land and Society in Colonial Mexico: The Great Hacienda.* Berkeley: University of California Press, 1966.

Ciudad Real, Antonio de. *Tratado curioso y docto de las grandezas de la Nueva España.* Mexico City: Instituto de Investigaciones Históricas of the Universidad Nacional Autónoma de México or UNAM, 1976, two volumes.

Cline, Howard F. "Civil Congregations of the Indians in New Spain, 1598–1640." *Hispanic American Historical Review* 29 (1949): 349–369.

———. "The Ortelius Maps of New Spain, 1579, and Related Contemporary Materials, 1560–1610." *Imago Mundi* 16 (1962): 98–115.

———. *Mexico: Revolution to Evolution, 1940–1960.* Oxford University Press, 1963.

———. "A Census of the *Relaciones geográficas* of New Spain, 1579–1612." *Handbook of Middle American Indians* 12 (1972): 324–369.

———. "The *Relaciones geográficas* of Spain, New Spain, and the Spanish Indies: An Annotated Bibliography." *Handbook of Middle American Indians* 12 (1972): 370–395.

Coatsworth, John H. "Obstacles to Economic Growth in Nineteenth-Century Mexico." *American Historical Review* 83, Number 1 (February 1978): 80–100.

———. *Los orígenes del atraso: nueve ensayos de historia económica de México en los siglos XVIII y XIX.* Mexico City, 1990.

"Conventos del siglo dieciséis," *Artes de México,* Numbers 86–87. Mexico City: Frente Nacional de Artes Plásticas and the Universidad Nacional Autónoma de México or UNAM, 1966.

Cook, Sherburne F. *The Indian Population of Central Mexico, 1531–1610.* Berkeley: University of California Press, 1960.

———. *The Population of the Mixteca Alta, 1520–1960.* Berkeley: University of California Press, 1968.

Cook, Sherburne F., and Woodrow W. Borah. *Essays in Population History: Mexico and the Caribbean.* Berkeley: University of California Press, 1971–1979, three volumes.

Cornelius, Wayne A. "Urbanization as an Agent in Latin American Political Instability: The Case of Mexico." *American Political Science Review* 63, Number 4 (1969): 833–857.

Corona Núñez, José, editor. *Antigüedades de México.* Mexico City: Secretaría de Hacienda y Crédito Público, 1964, seven volumes.

Costeloe, Michael P. *Church Wealth in Mexico: A Study of the "Juzgado de Capellanías" in the Archbishopric of Mexico, 1800–1856.* Cambridge University Press, 1967.

———. *The Central Republic in Mexico, 1835–1846: Hombres de Bien in the Age of Santa Anna.* Cambridge, NY: Cambridge University Press, 1993.

Cuevas, Mariano, compiler. *Documentos inéditos del siglo XVI para la historia de México.* Mexico City, 1975 reprint of 1914 original issued by the Museo Nacional.

Davidson, David M. "Negro Slave Control and Resistance in Colonial Mexico, 1519–1650." *Hispanic American Historical Review* 46, Number 3 (1966): 235–253.

Davies, Keith A. "Tendencias demográficas urbanas durante el siglo XIX en México." *Historia Mexicana* 21, Number 3 (January–March 1972): 481–524.

Dávila Padilla, Agustín. *Historia de la fundación y discurso de la provincia de Santiago de México.* Mexico City: Editorial Ac. Literaria, 1955 reprint of 1625 Belgian re-edition of 1596 original published by Pedro Madrigal.

Denham, James M., and Keith L. Huneycutt. "With Scott in Mexico: Letters of Captain James W. Anderson in the Mexican War, 1846–1847." *Military History of the West* 28, Number 1 (1998): 19–48.

Dinámica de la población de México. Mexico City: Centro de Estudios Económicos y Demográficos, 1981.

Documentos para la historia del México colonial. Mexico City, 1955–1961, seven volumes.

Edwards, Mike. "Mexico: A Very Beautiful Challenge." *National Geographic* 153, Number 5 (May 1978): 612–647.

Enjalbert, Henri. "Le peuplement du Mexique." *Les cahiers d'Outre-Mer [France]* 24, Number 93 (January–March 1971): 5–15.

Erwin, Sarah. "The Printed Book in Mexico." *Gilcrease Journal* 1, Number 2 (1993): 58–64.

Evolución de las ciudades en México, 1900–1994. Mexico City: Consejo Nacional de Población or CONAPO, 1994.

Farris, N. M. *Crown and Clergy in Colonial Mexico, 1759–1821.* London: University of London Press, 1968.

Flandrau, Charles Macomb. *Viva Mexico!* New York: Appleton, 1936 reprint of 1908 original.

Flannery, Kent N. *The Early Mesoamerican Village.* New York: Academic Press, 1976.

Florescano, Enrique, and Isabel Gil, editors. *Descripciones económicas generales de Nueva España, 1784–1817.* Mexico City: Secretaría de Educación Pública or SEP and the Instituto Nacional de Antropología e Historia or INAH, 1973.

———. *Descripciones económicas regionales de Nueva España: provincias del centro, sudeste y sur, 1766–1830.* Mexico City: Secretaría de Educación Pública or SEP and the Instituto Nacional de Antropología e Historia or INAH, 1976, three volumes.

Fowler, Will. *Mexico in the Age of Proposals, 1821–1851.* Westport, CT: Greenwood, 1998.

Frankl, Víctor. "Hernán Cortés y la tradición de las Siete Partidas." *Revista de Historia de América [Mexico]* 53–54 (1962): 9–74.

"Fundación de pueblos en el siglo XVI." *Boletín del Archivo General de la Nación [Mexico],* Primera Serie, Volume 6, Number 3 (May–June 1935): 321–360.

Gadow, Hans. *Through Southern Mexico, Being an Account of the Travels of a Naturalist.* New York: Charles Scribner's, 1908.

García, Virginia, and Gerardo Suárez. *Los sismos en la historia de México.* Mexico City: Centro de Investigaciones y Estudios Superiores en Antropología Social, 1996.

García Zambrano, Angel J. "El poblamiento de México en la época de contacto, 1520–1540." *Mesoamérica [Costa Rica]* 14, Number 24 (December 1992): 239–296.

Gardiner, C. Harvey. "Foreign Travellers' Accounts of Mexico, 1810–1910." *The Americas: A Quarterly Review of Inter-American Cultural History [Academy of American Franciscan History]* 8, Number 3 (January 1952): 321–351.

Gardiner, C. Harvey, editor. *Mexico, 1825–1828: The Journal and Correspondence of Edward Thornton Tayloe.* Chapel Hill: University of North Carolina Press, 1959.

Garner, Richard L. "Silver Production and Entrepreneurial Structure in Eighteenth-Century Mexico." *Jahrbuch für Geschichte von Staat, Wirtschaft und Gesellschaft Lateinamerikas [Germany]* 17 (1980): 157–185.

———. "Price Trends in Eighteenth-Century Mexico." *Hispanic American Historical Review* 65, Number 2 (1985): 279–325.

Gemelli Careri, Giovanni Francesco. *Viaje a la Nueva España.* Mexico City: Universidad Nacional Autónoma de México or UNAM, 1976.

Gerhard, Peter. *A Guide to the Historical Geography of New Spain.* Norman: University of Oklahoma Press, 1993.

———. *The North Frontier of New Spain.* Norman: University of Oklahoma Press, 1993.

———. *The Southeast Frontier of New Spain.* Norman: University of Oklahoma Press, 1993.

Gierloff-Emden, H.-G. *Mexico, eine Landeskunde.* Berlin: Walter de Gruyter, 1970.

Gilbert, Alan. *Housing and Land in Urban Mexico.* San Diego: University of California Press, 1989.

Gilbert, Alan, and Ann Varley. "The Mexican Landlord: Rental Housing in Guadalajara and Puebla." *Urban Studies* 27, Number 1 (1990): 23–44.

———. *Landlord and Tenant: Housing and the Poor in Urban Mexico.* London: Routledge, 1991.

Gilly, Adolfo. *La revolución interrumpida: México, 1910–1920.* Mexico City: El Caballito, 1974.

Godoy Dárdano, Félix E. "La electrificación del alumbrado en las principales ciudades de México, 1880–1910: transferencia de nuevas tecnologías." *Siglo XIX: Cuadernos de Historia [Mexico]* 5, Number 15 (1996): 39–58.

Goetzmann, William F. "Our First Foreign War." *American Heritage* 17, Number 4 (June 1966): 18–27 and 85–99.

Gómez Canedo, Lino. *La educación de los marginados durante la época colonial.* Mexico City: Porrúa, 1982.

Gómez Mayorga, Mauricio. "La arquitectura contemporánea en México." *Artes de México,* Number 36. Mexico City: Frente Nacional de Artes Plásticas and the Universidad Nacional Autónoma de México or UNAM, 1961.

González Claverán, Virginia. "La expedición Malaspina y la cartografía novohispana." *Revista de Historia Naval [Spain]* 5, Number 19 (1987): 91–112.

González Dávila, Gil. *Teatro eclesiástico de la primitiva iglesia de la Nueva España en las Indias Occidentales.* Madrid: José Porrúa, 1958–1959 reprint of 1649–1655 original, two volumes.

González de Cossío, Francisco, editor. *El libro de las tasaciones de pueblos de la Nueva España, siglo XVI.* Mexico City: Archivo General de la Nación, 1952.

González Navarro, Moisés. *Población y sociedad en México, 1900–1970.* Mexico City: Universidad Nacional Autónoma de México or UNAM, 1974, two volumes.

Gouy, P. *Pérégrinations des "Barcelonnettes" au Mexique.* Grenoble: Presses Universitaires de Grenoble, 1980.

Grajales, Gloria. *México y la Gran Bretaña durante la Intervención, 1861–1862.* Mexico City: Volume 15 of the Second Series of the "Archivo Histórico Diplomático Mexicano" published by the Secretaría de Relaciones Exteriores, 1962.

Grajales, Gloria, compiler. *Guía de documentos para la historia de México en archivos ingleses, siglo XIX.* Mexico City: Instituto de Investigaciones Bibliográficas of the Universidad Nacional Autónoma de México or UNAM, 1969.

Greenleaf, Richard E. "The Obraje in the Late Mexican Colony." *The Americas: A Quarterly Review of Inter-American Cultural History [Academy of American Franciscan History]* 22, Number 1 (1967): 227–250.

Haber, Stephan. *Industry and Underdevelopment: The Industrialization of Mexico, 1890–1940.* Stanford, CA: Stanford University Press, 1989.

Hall, Barbara J. *Mexico in Pictures.* New York: Sterling, 1964.

Hall, Linda. *Oil, Banks, and Politics: The United States and Postrevolutionary Mexico, 1917–1924.* Austin: University of Texas Press, 1995.

Hamill, Hugh, Jr. *The Hidalgo Revolt: Prelude to Mexican Independence.* Gainesville: University of Florida Press, 1966.

Hamnett, Brian R. "The Appropriation of Mexican Church Wealth by the Spanish Bourbon Government: The 'Consolidación de Vales Reales', 1805–1809." *Journal of Latin American Studies [UK]* 1, Number 2 (1969): 85–113.

———. "The Economic and Social Dimensions of the Revolution of Independence in Mexico, 1800–1824." *Ibero-Amerikanisches Archiv [Germany]* 8, Number 1 (1980): 1–27.

Hardy, Robert William Hale. *Travels in the Interior of Mexico in 1825, 1826, 1827, and 1828.* Glorieta, NM: Rio Grande Press, 1977 reprint of 1829 original published in London.

Hart, John Mason. *Anarchism and the Mexican Working Class, 1860–1931.* Austin: University of Texas Press, 1978.

———. *Revolutionary Mexico: The Coming and Process of the Mexican Revolution.* Berkeley: University of California Press, 1987.

Hernández Sáenz, Luz María. *Learning to Heal: The Medical Profession in Colonial Mexico, 1767–1831.* New York: Peter Lang, 1997.

Hernández y Dávalos, Juan E., editor. *Colección de documentos para la historia de la Guerra de Independencia de México de 1808 a 1821.* Nendeln, Liechtenstein: Kraus Reprint, 1968 re-edition of 1877–1882 Mexican original, six volumes.

Hoberman, Louisa S. "Merchants in Seventeenth-Century Mexico: A Preliminary Portrait." *Hispanic American Historical Review* 57, Number 3 (August 1977): 479–503.

Humboldt, Baron Alexander von. *Political Essay on the Kingdom of New Spain.* New York: AMS Press, 1966 reprint of 1811 original published in London by Longman, four volumes.

Indice de documentos de Nueva España existentes en el Archivo de Indias de Sevilla. Mexico City: Secretaría de Relaciones Exteriores, 1929–1931, four volumes.

Israel, Jonathan Irvine. *Race, Class and Politics in Colonial Mexico, 1610–1670.* New York: Oxford University Press, 1975.

Joseph, Gilbert M., and Daniel Nugent, editors. *Everyday Forms of State Formation: Revolution and the Negotiation of Rule in Modern Mexico.* Durham, NC: Duke University Press, 1994.

Katzman, Israel. *Arquitectura del siglo XIX en México.* Mexico City, 1973.

Kemper, Robert V., and Anya P. Royce. "Mexican Urbanization since 1821: A Macro-Historical Approach." *Urban Anthropology* 3 (winter 1979): 267–290.

Knight, Alan. "The Working Class and the Mexican Revolution, ca. 1900–1920." *Journal of Latin American Studies [UK]* 16, Part 1 (May 1984): 51–79.

———. *The Mexican Revolution.* Cambridge, NY: Cambridge University Press, 1986.

Kubler, George A. "Mexican Urbanism in the Sixteenth Century." *The Art Bulletin* 24 (June 1942): 160–171.

———. *Mexican Architecture of the Sixteenth Century.* Westport, CT: Greenwood, 1972 reprint of 1948 original issued by Yale University Press, two volumes.

Ladd, Doris. *The Mexican Nobility at Independence, 1780–1826.* Palo Alto, CA: Stanford University Press, 1972.

Lavrín, Asunción, and Edith Couturier. "Dowries and Wills: A View of Women's Socioeconomic Role in Colonial Guadalajara and Puebla, 1640–1790." *Hispanic American Historical Review* 59, Number 2 (1979): 280–304.

Leal, Fernando. "La litografía mexicana en el siglo XIX." *Artes de México* 3, Number 14. Mexico City: Frente Nacional de Artes Plásticas, 1956.

Lemus, M., editor. *Ciudades mexicanas.* Mexico City: Fundación Cambio XXI, 1994.

Leonard, Irving A. *Baroque Times in Old Mexico: Seventeenth-Century Persons, Places, and Practices.* Ann Arbor: University of Michigan Press, 1959.

Liss, Peggy K. *Mexico under Spain, 1521–1556: Society and the Origins of Nationality.* Chicago: University of Chicago Press, 1984.

Lomnitz, Larissa. *Networks and Marginality: Life in a Mexican Shantytown.* New York: Academic Press, 1977.

Lomnitz, Larissa, and Marisol Pérez Lizaur. "The History of a Mexican Urban Family." *Journal of Family History* 3, Number 4 (winter 1978): 392–409.

López Jiménez, Eucario, editor. *Cedulario de la Nueva Galicia.* Guadalajara, 1971.

López Rosado, Diego G. *Historia del peso mexicano.* Mexico City: Fondo de Cultura Económica, 1987.

Löschner, Renate, et al. *El México luminoso de Rugendas.* Mexico City: Cartón y Papel, S.A., 1985.

Luque Alcaide, Elisa. *La educación en Nueva España en el siglo XVIII.* Seville: Escuela de Estudios Hispanoamericanos, 1970.

Lyon, George Francis. *Journal of a Residence and Tour in the Republic of Mexico in the Year 1826.* Port Washington, NY: Kennikat, reprint of 1828 London original, two volumes.

MacLachlan, Colin M. *Criminal Justice in Eighteenth-Century Mexico: A Study of the Tribunal of the Acordada.* Berkeley: University of California Press, 1974.

Marichal, Carlos. "La historiografía económica reciente sobre el México borbónico: los estudios del comercio y las finanzas virreinales, 1760–1820." *Boletín del Instituto de Historia Argentina y Americana "Dr. Emilio Ravignani"* 2 (1990): 161–180.

McAlister, Lyle N. *The "Fuero Militar" in New Spain, 1764–1800.* Westport, CT: Greenwood, 1957.

McAndrew, John. *The Open-Air Churches of Sixteenth-Century Mexico: Atrios, Posas, Open Chapels, and Other Studies.* Cambridge: Harvard University Press, 1965.

Melville, Elinor G. K. *A Plague of Sheep: Environmental Consequences of the Conquest of Mexico.* Cambridge, NY: Cambridge University Press, 1994.

Mentz, Brigida von. *México en el siglo XIX visto por los alemanes.* Mexico City: Instituto de Investigaciones Históricas of the Universidad Nacional Autónoma de México or UNAM, 1982.

Meyer, Lorenzo. *Mexico and the United States in the Oil Controversy, 1917–1942.* Austin: University of Texas Press, 1977.

Middlebrook, Kevin. *The Paradox of Revolution: Labor, the State, and Authoritarianism in Mexico.* Baltimore: Johns Hopkins University Press, 1995.

Millon, René. *Urbanization at Teotihuacán.* Austin: University of Texas Press, 1973.

Miranda, José. *Humboldt y México.* Mexico City: Universidad Nacional Autónoma de México, 1962.

Moreno Toscano, Alejandra. "Cambios en los patrones de urbanización en México, 1810–1910." *Historia Mexicana* 22, Number 2 (1972): 160–187.

Moreno Toscano, Alejandra, and Richard E. Boyer. "Las ciudades mexicanas." *Historia Mexicana* 22 (1973): 142–159.

Mota y Escobar, Alonso de la [introduction by Joaquín Ramírez Cabañas]. *Descripción geográfica de los reinos de Nueva Galicia, Nueva Vizcaya y Nuevo León.* Mexico City, 1940.

Mullen, Robert James. *Architecture and Its Sculpture in Viceregal Mexico.* Austin: University of Texas Press, 1997.

Mundy, Barbara E. *The Mapping of New Spain: Indigenous Cartography and the Maps of the "Relaciones Geográficas."* Chicago: University of Chicago Press, 1996.

Nava Otero, Guadalupe. *Cabildos y ayuntamientos de la Nueva España en 1808.* Mexico City: Volume 78 of the Series "Sep-Setentas" published by the Secretaría de Educación Pública or SEP, 1973.

Navarrete, E., and Vera M. Navarrete, coordinators. *Población y sociedad.* Toluca: El Colegio Mexiquense, 1994.

Navarro y Noriega, Fernando. *Memoria sobre la población del Reino de Nueva España escrita en el año 1814.* Llanes, Spain: José Porrúa Turanzas, 1954.

O'Crouley, Pedro Alonso. *A Description of the Kingdom of New Spain, 1774.* San Francisco: John Howell Books, 1972 translation and re-edition by Séan Galvin.

Olivera, Ruth R., and Liliane Crété. *Life in Mexico under Santa Anna, 1822–1855.* Norman: University of Oklahoma Press, 1991.

Ollivier, Emile. *Expedición de México.* Mexico City: Cámara de Diputados, 1972 translation of the nineteenth-century French original by Manuel Puega y Acal.

Orendáin, Leopoldo I., and Salvador Reynoso, editors. *Cartografía de la Nueva Galicia.* Guadalajara: Banco Industrial de Jalisco, 1961.

Ortiz Escamilla, Juan. "Las elites de las capitales novohispanas ante la guerra civil de 1810." *Historia Mexicana* 46, Number 2 (1996): 325–357.

Ouweneel, Arij. "Growth, Stagnation, and Migration: An Explorative Analysis of the Tributario Series of Anáhuac, 1720–1800." *Hispanic American Historical Review* 71, Number 3 (1991): 531–577.

Palmer, Colin A. *Slaves of the White God: Blacks in Mexico, 1570–1650.* Cambridge, NY: Cambridge University Press, 1976.

Paso y Troncoso, Francisco del, compiler and editor. *Papeles de Nueva España.* Mexico City, 1905–1948, nine volumes.

———. *Epistolario de Nueva España, 1505–1818.* Mexico City: Series 2 of the "Biblioteca Histórica Mexicana de Obras Inéditas," 1939–1942, sixteen volumes.

Pérez Herrero, Pedro. "El crecimiento económico novohispano durante el siglo XVIII: una revisión." *Revista de Historia Económica* 7, Number 1 (1989): 69–110.

"Pintura popular y costumbrista del siglo XIX." *Artes de México,* Number 61. Mexico City: Frente Nacional de Artes Plásticas and the Universidad Nacional Autónoma de México or UNAM, 1965.

Potash, Robert A. *Mexican Government and Industrial Development in the Early Republic: The Banco de Avío.* Amherst: University of Massachusetts Press, 1983.

Reber, James Q. "Mexican Portfolio: Landscape, Art, People." *Américas [Organization of American States]* 27, Number 5 (May 1975): 19–30.

Rees, Peter W. "Origins of Colonial Transportation in Mexico." *Geographical Review* 65, Number 2 (1975): 323–334.

Rees Jones, Ricardo. *El despotismo ilustrado y los intendentes de la Nueva España.* Mexico City, 1979.

Rodríguez, Victoria E., and Peter M. Ward. "Opposition Politics, Power and Public Administration in Urban Mexico." *Bulletin of Latin American Research [UK]* 10, Number 1 (1991): 23–36.

Rodríguez O., Jaime E., and Colin M. MacLachlan. *The Forging of the Cosmic Race: A Reinterpretation of Colonial Mexico.* Berkeley: University of California Press, 1980.

Romero de Terreros, Manuel. *Paisajes mexicanos de un pintor inglés.* Guadalajara: Banco Industrial de Jalisco, 1949.

Rosell, Lauro E. *Iglesias y conventos coloniales de México.* Mexico City, 1961.

Rubio Mañé, José Ignacio. *El virreinato.* Mexico City: Universidad Nacional Autónoma de México or UNAM and Fondo de Cultura Económica, 1983, four volumes.

Ruiz, Ramón Eduardo. *Labor and the Ambivalent Revolutionaries.* Baltimore: Johns Hopkins University Press, 1976.

———. *The Great Rebellion: Mexico, 1905–1924.* New York: Norton, 1980.

Salvucci, Richard J. *Textiles and Capitalism in Mexico: An Economic History of the Obrajes, 1539–1840.* Princeton: Princeton University Press, 1987.

Saravia Viejo, María Justina. *El juego de gallos en Nueva España.* Seville, 1972.

Sartorius, Carl Christian. *Mexiko: Landschaftsbilder.* Stuttgart: Brockhaus, 1961 reprint [also available as the English translation *Mexico about 1850*].

Scholes, France V., and Eleanor B. Adams, compilers and editors. *Documentos para la historia del México colonial.* Mexico City, 1961.

Schroeder, Susan, editor. *Native Resistance and the Pax Colonial in New Spain.* Lincoln: University of Nebraska Press, 1998.

Schwaller, John Frederick. *The Church and Clergy in Sixteenth-Century Mexico.* Albuquerque: University of New Mexico Press, 1987.

Seed, Patricia A. *To Love, Honor, and Obey in Colonial Mexico: Conflicts over Marriage Choice.* Stanford, CA: Stanford University Press, 1988.

Sims, Harold D. *La expulsión de los españoles de México, 1821–1828.* Mexico City: Fondo de Cultura Económica, 1976.

———. *Descolonización en México: el conflicto entre mexicanos y españoles, 1821–1831.* Mexico City: Fondo de Cultura Económica, 1982.

Smith, Bradley. *Mexico: A History in Art.* Garden City, NJ: Doubleday, 1968.

Tamayo, Jorge L. *Geografía general de México.* Mexico City, 1962, four volumes and an atlas.

Tannenbaum, Frank. *Peace by Revolution: Mexico after 1910.* New York: Columbia University Press, 1966.

Tardiff, Guillermo, editor. *Historia general del comercio exterior: antecedentes, documentos, glosas y comentarios, 1503–1847.* Mexico City, 1968–1970, two volumes.

Tenenbaum, Barbara A. "Merchants, Money and Mischief: The British in Mexico, 1821–1862." *The Americas: A Quarterly Review of Inter-American Cultural History [Academy of American Franciscan History]* 35, Number 3 (1979): 317–340.

Torres Lanzas, Pedro. *Relación descriptiva de los mapas, planos, &, de México y Floridas existentes en el Archivo General de Indias.* Seville: El Mercantil, 1900, two volumes.

Toussaint, Manuel. *Arte colonial en México.* Mexico City, 1948.

———. *Pintura colonial en México.* Mexico City: Imprenta Universitaria, 1965.

Toussaint, Manuel, editor. *La litografía en México en el siglo XIX.* Mexico City: Biblioteca Nacional, 1934.

Tovar y de Teresa, Guillermo. *México barroco.* Mexico City: Secretaría de Asentamientos Humanos y Obras Públicas or SAHOP, 1981.

Tutino, John. "Power, Class, and Family: Men and Women in the Mexican Elite, 1750–1810." *The Americas: A Quarterly Review of Inter-American Cultural History [Academy of American Franciscan History]* 39, Number 3 (1983): 359–381.

Ugalde, Antonio. *The Urbanization Process of a Poor Mexican Neighborhood.* Austin: University of Texas Press, 1974.

Ulloa, Berta. *La revolución intervenida: relaciones diplomáticas entre México y los Estados Unidos, 1910–1914.* Mexico City: El Colegio de México, 1971.

Unikel, Luis. *El desarrollo urbano de México: diagnóstico e implicaciones futuras.* Mexico City: El Colegio de México, 1976 re-edition.

Van Oss, A. C. "Architectural Activity, Demography and Economic Diversification: Regional Economies of Colonial Mexico." *Jahrbuch für Geschichte von Staat, Wirtschaft und Gesellschaft Lateinamerikas [Germany]* 16 (1979): 97–145.

Vaughan, Mary Kay. *The State, Education, and Social Class in Mexico, 1880–1928.* DeKalb: Northern Illinois University Press, 1982.

———. "Primary Education and Literacy in Nineteenth-Century Mexico: Research Trends, 1968–1988." *Latin American Research Review* 25, Number 1 (1990): 31–66.

Vázquez de Warman, Irene. "El pósito y la alhóndiga en la Nueva España." *Historia Mexicana* 17, Number 3 (1968): 395–426.

Velasco Avila, Cuauhtémoc, et al. *Estado y minería en México (1767–1910).* Mexico City, 1988.

Vélez Ibáñez, Carlos G. *Rituals of Marginality: Politics, Process, and Cultural Change in Urban Central Mexico, 1969–1974.* Berkeley: University of California Press, 1983.

Vetancourt, Agustín de. *Teatro mexicano: descripción breve de los sucesos, ejemplos históricos y religiosos del nuevo mundo de las Indias, crónica de la provincia del Santo Evangelio de México.* Mexico City: Porrúa, 1971 facsimile reprint of 1698 original published by Doña María de Benavides, viuda de Juan de Ribera.

Vigneaux, Ernesto de. *Viaje a México.* Guadalajara: Banco Industrial de Jalisco, 1950.

Vila Vilar, Enriqueta, and María Justina Sarabia Viejo, compilers and editors. *Cartas de cabildos hispanoamericanos: audiencia de México.* Seville: Escuela de Estudios Hispano-americanos, 1985, two volumes.

Villaseñor y Sánchez, José Antonio. *Theatro americano: descripción general de los reinos y provincias de la Nueva España y sus jurisdicciones.* Mexico City: Editora Nacional, 1952 facsimile reprint of 1746–1748 original, two volumes.

Weckmann, Luis. *Las relaciones franco-mexicanas, 1823–1867.* Mexico City: Volumes 1–2 and 5 of the Second Series of the "Archivo Histórico Diplomático Mexicano" published by the Secretaría de Relaciones Exteriores, 1961–1972, three volumes.

Weismann, Elizabeth Wilder. *Art and Time in Mexico.* New York: Harper and Row, 1985.

West, Robert C. "The *Relaciones geográficas* of Mexico and Central America, 1740–1792." *Handbook of Middle American Indians* 12 (1972): 396–439.

Whitmore, Thomas M. *Disease and Death in Early Colonial Mexico: Simulating Amerindian Depopulation.* Boulder: Westview, 1991.

Wolcott, Roger, editor. *The Correspondence of William Hickling Prescott, 1833–1847.* Cambridge: Massachusetts Historical Society, 1925.

Zárate Toscano, Verónica. "Los conflictos de 1624 y 1808 en la Nueva España." *Anuario de Estudios Americanos [Spain]* 53, Number 2 (1996): 35–50.

Zavala, Silvio, and M. Castelo, compilers and editors. *Fuentes para la historia del trabajo en Nueva España.* Mexico City: Fondo de Cultura Económica, 1939–1946, eight volumes.

Acapulco

Colonial Era (1550–1815)

Bauzon, L. *Deficit Government: Mexico and the Philippine Situado, 1606–1804.* Tokyo: Press Company, 1981.

Bjork, Katharine. "The Link That Kept the Philippines Spanish: Mexican Merchant Interests and the Manila Trade, 1571–1815." *Journal of World History* 9, Number 1 (1998): 25–50.

Carrera Stampa, Manuel. "La Nao de la China." *Historia Mexicana* 9, Number 1 (1959): 97–118.

Chaunu, Pierre. *Les Philippines et le Pacifique des Ibériques.* Paris: École Pratique des Hautes Études, 1960–1966, two volumes.

El fuerte de San Diego en Acapulco, Gro. Mexico City: Instituto Nacional de Antropología e Historia or INAH, 1960.

Mathes, W. Michael. *Vizcaíno and Spanish Expansion in the Pacific Ocean, 1580–1630.* San Francisco: Historical Society of California, 1968.

McCarthy, William J. "Between Policy and Prerogative: Malfeasance in the Inspection of the Manila Galleons at Acapulco, 1637." *Colonial Latin American Historical Review* 2, Number 2 (1993): 163–183.

Rubio Mañé, José Ignacio. "La expedición de Miguel López de Legaspi a Filipinas." *Boletín del Archivo General de la Nación [Mexico],* Segunda Serie, Volume 5, Numbers 3–4 (July–December 1964): 427–798.

Sales Colín, Ostwald. "El movimiento portuario de Acapulco: un intento de aproximación, 1626–1654." *Revista Complutense de Historia de América [Spain]* 22 (1996): 97–119.

Schurz, William Lytle. *The Manila Galleon.* New York: Dutton, 1939, reprinted in 1959, as well as in 1985 by the Historical Conservation Society of Manila.

Sluiter, Engel. "The Fortification of Acapulco, 1615–1616." *Hispanic American Historical Review* 39, Number 1 (February 1940), Part I: 69–80.

Velázquez, María del Carmen. "La navegación transpacífica." *Historia Mexicana* 70 (1968): 159–178.

Williams, Martha N., and John Hoyt. "The Route to Riches." *Américas [Organization of American States]* 36, Number 6 (1984): 24–29.

Yuste López, C. *El comercio de la Nueva España con Filipinas, 1590–1785.* Mexico City: Instituto Nacional de Antropología e Historia or INAH, 1984.

Early Maps and Depictions of Acapulco, 1614–1820

Crude drawing of Acapulco Bay as seen from atop El Grifo headland, drawn by garrison commander Capt. Nicolás de Cardona, ca. 1614—original held by the Biblioteca Nacional at Madrid, call number: Manuscritos de América 2468, Folios 116–117

Imaginary Dutch view of the attack by Joris van Spilbergen's squadron, October 1615—published in *The East and West Indian Mirror, Being an Account of Joris van Spilbergen's Voyage Round the World,* 1906 Hakluyt Society re-edition by J. A. J. de Villiers, also available as a 1967 Kraus reprint

Panoramic view of the bay and its adjacent shoreline by the Dutch-born engineer Adrian Boot, ca. 1617—original held by the Imperial Library at Vienna, while the British Museum holds a different version under call number L.R. 265, c.7, Folios 161–162, from François Valentyn's *Oud en Nieuw Oost-Indien* (published in Amsterdam by Joannes van Braam in 1724); a reproduction of the Viennese original was also commissioned in the late nineteenth century by the Mexican historian Francisco del Paso y Troncoso and executed by the Florentine engraver Alejandro Ruffoni

Drawing of Acapulco's new customshouse, 1627—original held as Illustration 615 of the Archivo General de la Nación in Mexico City, photographic negative number 977/0816 [archival provenance: *Tierras,* Volume 87, Expediente 1, Folio 178]

Imaginary Dutch engraving of Acapulco—original found in Dr. Oliver Dapper's *Amerika,* published in Amsterdam by Jacob von Meurs in 1673 and reissued numerous times afterward, for example, see version held by the Bibliothèque Nationale in Paris under call number Cartes et Planes 171, 1, 6/1; another done by Pieter Schenk; etc.

Crude late seventeenth-century drawing of Acapulco harbor, plus adjoining Puerto Marqués—original held by the Biblioteca Nacional at Madrid, call number: Manuscritos de América 2957

Simplistic map of Acapulco and its coastline, copied in 1687 by William Hack from a Spanish pilot's chart book, captured a half dozen years previously in the South Pacific by English buccaneers—original held by the British Museum, call number: Sloane Manuscripts 45, Folios 3 vto.–4

Hand-drawn and a simple printed English map of Acapulco Bay and its coastline, eighteenth century—originals held by the Bibliothèque Nationale at Paris, call numbers: Cartes et Plans (Collection d'Anville), Ge. DD 2987, 8894 and 8895

Eighteenth-century hand-drawn Spanish maps of the bay and its coastline—originals held by the Bibliothèque Nationale at Paris, call numbers: Cartes et Plans 171, 6, 2 and 3

Eighteenth-century French map of the bay and its coastline by Lemoine—original held by the Bibliothèque Nationale at Paris, call number: Cartes et Plans 171, 6, 4

Drawing of the bay by Acapulco's garrison commander Miguel Gallo, November 1712—original held by the Archive of Indies at Seville, old Torres Lanzas call number: Mapas y Planos de México, 106 [archival provenance: México, 563]

Diagram by Juan de San Pedro Saldaña of office space in the *real caja* or "royal treasury," 1717—original held as Illustration 425 of the Archivo General de la Nación in Mexico City, photographic negative 977/0414 [archival provenance: *Historia,* Volume 390, Folio 313]

Drawing by the military engineer Francisco Alvarez Barreiro of Fort San Diego and other official buildings, late 1729 or early 1730—original held by the Archive of Indies at Seville, old Torres Lanzas call number: Mapas y Planos de México, 125 [archival provenance: Guadalajara, 144]

Simple English map of Acapulco Bay, 1730—original held by the British Museum, call number: Additional Manuscripts 5415, G. 12

Inaccurate French drawing of Acapulco, 1730—original held by the Bibliothèque Nationale at Paris, call number: Cartes et Plans 171, 1, 6

Diagrams and profile view of Fort San Diego by the military engineer Ens. José González, June 1766—originals held by the Archive of Indies at Seville, old Torres Lanzas call numbers: Mapas y Planos de México, 230 and 231 [archival provenance: México 2453]

Pen-and-ink diagram with watercolor highlights of Fort San Diego, 1772—original held by the Servicio Geográfico del Ejército at Madrid, call number: LM-8.ª–1.ª-a–86

Two pen-and-ink diagrams with watercolor highlights by the military engineer Miguel Costanzó, of proposed reconstruction plans for Fort San Diego, August–September 1776—originals held by the Servicio Histórico Militar at Madrid, call number K-b–5–8, and Servicio Geográfico del Ejército at Madrid, call numbers: LM-8.ª–1.ª-a–84 and LM-8.ª–1.ª-a–85

Chart of the bay as sounded by naval Lt. Juan Francisco de la Bodega y Quadra and Ens. José de Cañizares, March 1777—original held by the Servicio Geográfico del Ejército at Madrid, call number: J-9.ª–2.ª-a–26

Diagram by the military engineer Ramón Panón, of proposed reconstruction of Fort San Diego, December 1777—originals held by the Servicio Geográfico del Ejército at Madrid under call number LM-8.ª–1.ª-a–87, and as Illustration 133 of the Archivo General de la Nación in Mexico City, photographic negative 977/0121 [archival provenance: *Correspondencia de Virreyes, Primera Serie*, Volume 105, Expediente 6, Folio 80]

Diagram and profile views by Panón of progress on Fort San Diego's reconstruction, 30 June 1779—originals held by the Archive of Indies at Seville under the old Torres Lanzas call number Mapas y Planos de México, 351, and as Illustration 145 of the Archivo General de la Nación in Mexico City, photographic negative 977/0133 [archival provenance: *Correspondencia de Virreyes, Primera Serie*, Volume 122, Expediente 28, Folio 104]

Rough diagram of Acapulco's defenses, late eighteenth century—original held by the Biblioteca del Palacio Real at Madrid, call number: Manuscritos de América, 979; an Italian version also exists under call number Mapas M-XIII-B.^{a} 9, plus a Franco-Dutch version in the Bibliothèque Nationale at Paris with call number: Cartes et Plans (Collection d'Anville), Ge. DD 2987, 8896

Pen-and-ink diagram with watercolor highlights of the reconstruction of Acapulco's eroded wharf, under supervision by acting garrison commander Rafael Vasco, December 1782—original held by the Archivo General de Simancas in Spain, call number: Mapas, Planos y Dibujos, XVI-158 [archival provenance: Guerra Moderna 6986]

Diagram by José González of proposed improvements to Fort San Diego, 1783—original held by the Archive of Indies at Seville, old Torres Lanzas call number: Mapas y Planos de México, 391

Six diverse paintings and sketches of Acapulco by the Malaspina expedition artists Fernando Brambila, Tomás Suría, and José Cardero, 1791—originals held by the Museo Naval at Madrid, call number: Manuscritos 794

Harbor chart, as sounded during the visit of Malaspina's corvettes *Atrevida* and *Descubierta,* 1791—originals held by the Servicio Histórico Militar in Madrid, call number: K-b–1–48, and Bibliothèque Nationale in Paris, call number: Cartes et Plans 171, 6, 6

Franco-Dutch engraving of Acapulco's entrance as seen from out at sea, presumably derived from a drawing made during Malaspina's visit, 1791—original held by the Bibliothèque Nationale at Paris, call number: Cartes et Plans (Collection d'Anville), Ge. DD 2987, 8898

Diagram by Pío Quinto Balzares of the new *alhóndiga* or "granary," 1793—original held as Illustration 4156 of the Archivo General de la Nación in Mexico City, photographic negative number 978/2259 [archival provenance: *Civil,* Volume 1624, Folio 138]

Diagrams and profile views by Juan Camargo Caballero of a proposed new naval headquarters, 1796—original held by the Servicio Histórico Militar in Madrid, call number: P-b–11–39

Chart of Acapulco Bay by Félix Dayot, 1808—original held as Illustration 424.1 of the Archivo General de la Nación in Mexico City, photographic negative 979/2725 [archival provenance: *Historia,* Volume 382, Folio 218]

Chart and drawing of the coastline by pilots of Capt. Juan Vernacci's Manila galleon *Magallanes,* 1808—original held by the Archive of Indies at Seville, old Torres Lanzas call numbers: Mapas y Planos de México, 497 or Carpeta de Mapas, 13

Cross-sectional views by the *agrimensor* or "surveyor" Manuel Agustín Mascaró, of Fort San Diego's cistern and drawbridge, 1808—originals held as Illustrations 424.2 and 424.3 of the Archivo General de la Nación in Mexico City, photographic negatives 979/2726 and 979/2727 [archival provenance: *Historia,* Volume 382, Folios 305–306]

Detailed map of the harbor and its surrounding district, 1820—original held by the Servicio Histórico Militar in Madrid, call number: K-b–1–58 or 4980, hoja 1/D. 9–40

Modern History and General Works (1816–Present)
Alessio Robles, Vito. *Acapulco en la historia y en la leyenda.* Mexico City: Mundial, 1932.

Benítez, José R. *Guía histórica y descriptiva de la carretera México-Acapulco.* Mexico City, 1928.

Cerruti, James. "The Two Acapulcos." *National Geographic* 126, Number 6 (December 1964): 848–878.

Enríquez, H. *En el Mar del Sur, Acapulco: narraciones, historia, guía.* Mexico City: Bolívar, 1945.

Oteiza Iriarte, Tomás. *Acapulco: la ciudad de las naos de Oriente y de las sirenas modernas.* Mexico City: Diana, 1973.

Rojas, Pedro. *Acapulco.* Mexico City: Hermes, 1961.

Campeche

Colonial Era (1519–1821)

Barrera Vásquez, Alfredo, et al. *Diccionario Maya Cordemex.* Mérida, Yucatán: Cordemex, 1980.

Calderón Quijano, José Antonio. *Las murallas de Campeche.* Campeche, 1968.

Chamberlain, Robert S. *The Conquest and Colonization of Yucatan, 1517–1550.* Washington, DC: Carnegie Institution, 1948.

Contreras Sánchez, Alicia del C. "El palo de tinte, motivo de un conflicto entre dos naciones, 1670–1802." *Historia Mexicana* 37, Number 1 (1987): 49–74.

Eugenio Martínez, María Angeles. *La defensa de Tabasco, 1600–1717.* Seville: Escuela de Estudios Hispano-Americanos, 1971.

Juárez Moreno, Juan. *Piratas y corsarios en Veracruz y Campeche.* Seville: Escuela de Estudios Hispano-americanos, 1972.

Pérez Martínez, Héctor. *Piraterías en Campeche: siglos XVI, XVII y XVIII.* Mexico City: Porrúa, 1937.

Piña Chan, Román. *Campeche en el período colonial.* Mexico City: Secretaría de Educación Pública or SEP and the Instituto Nacional de Antropología e Historia or INAH, 1977.

Rubio Mañé, José Ignacio. "Movimiento marítimo entre Veracruz y Campeche, 1801–1810." *Boletín del Archivo General de la Nación [Mexico],* Primera Serie, Volume 24, Number 4 (October–December 1953): 595–676.

———. "Las jurisdicciones de Yucatán: la creación de la plaza de teniente de Rey en Campeche, año de 1744." *Boletín del Archivo General de la Nación [Mexico],* Segunda Serie, Volume 7, Number 3 (July–September 1966): 549–631.

Early Maps and Depictions of Campeche, 1609–1804

Map of the city's central core, indicating the proposed site and design of its new parish church, January 1609—original held by the Archive of Indies at Seville, call number: Mapas y Planos de México, 686 [archival provenance: Escribanía de Cámara de Justicia, Legajo 305-A]

Crude drawing of Campeche, ca. 1614, by Capt. Nicolás de Cardona—original held by the Biblioteca Nacional at Madrid, call number: Manuscritos de América 2468, Folio 56

Dutch engraving of Van Hoorn and Jol's seaborne attack, 1633—published eleven years later in Leiden as part of Johannes de Laet's *Historie ofte iaerlijck verhael van de verrichtingen der Geoctroyeerde West-Indische Compagnie;* copies held by the Royal Library at The Hague, plus various other sources

Panoramic view of Campeche as seen from offshore in the seventeenth century—original held by the Bibliothèque Nationale in Paris, call number: Cartes et Plans 141, 8, 1

Maps depicting improvements made to the city fortifications, July 1658—originals held by the Archive of Indies at Seville, old Torres Lanzas call numbers: Mapas y Planos de México, 57 and 57 bis [archival provenance: Audiencia de México, Legajo 1006]

Map of the city, and diagram of proposed improvements to its core fortifications, by *sargento mayor* or "garrison commander" Pedro Frías Salazar, after the devastating Jamaican raid of February 1663—originals held by the Archive of Indies at Seville, old Torres Lanzas call numbers: Mapas y Planos de México, 60 and 61 [archival provenance: Audiencia de México, Legajo 1006]

Proposal for fortifying Campeche's central core by the military engineer Ens. Martín de la Torre, May 1680—original held by the Archive of Indies at Seville, old Torres Lanzas call number: Mapas y Planos de México, 72 [archival provenance: Audiencia de México, Legajo 1009]

Proposed design by the German-born royal engineer Capt. Jaime Franck, for completing the central core's fortification, June 1690—original held by the Archive of Indies at Seville, old Torres Lanzas call number: Mapas y Planos de México, 87 [archival provenance: Audiencia de México, Legajo 1009]

Map of Campeche and its outer defenses, plus a diagram of proposed improvements to its city ramparts, by the French-born engineer Louis Bouchard de Becour, October 1705—originals held by the Archive of Indies at Seville, old Torres Lanzas call number: Mapas y Planos de México, 98 and 99 [archival provenance: Audiencia de México, Legajo 1009]

Pen-and-ink map with watercolor highlights of Campeche, March 1734—original held by the Servicio Geográfico del Ejército at Madrid, call number: LM-8.ª-1.ª–114

Diagram by Juan de Villa Juana of the fortified city, September 1751—original held by the Archive of Indies at Seville, old Torres Lanzas call number: Mapas y Planos de México, 195 [archival provenance: Audiencia de México, Legajo 3009]

Detailed map with watercolor highlights of Campeche and its defenses, copied in May 1779 by the chief military engineer Brig. Agustín Crame, from a version seven years previously—originals held by the Servicio Geográfico del Ejército at Madrid [call number: LM-8.ª-1.ª-a–53], as well as the Servicio Histórico Militar at Madrid, call number: M, b, II, 9 or 5127, hoja 4/D. 12–3

Companion map by Crame, of the city and its surrounding territory, ca. 1779—originals held by the British Library [call number: Additional Manuscripts 17654; B] and the

Servicio Histórico Militar at Madrid, call number: K-b-4-49 or 5146, hoja 1/D. 13-2

Map, diagram, and cutaway view by the volunteer military engineer, Sub-Lt. Juan José de León, of Campeche's environs as far southwest as the extemporized San Roberto Battery, June 1781—original held by the Servicio Histórico Militar at Madrid, call number: M, b, II, 3

Diagrams by De León of proposed new locations for Campeche's customshouse and other official buildings, October 1786—originals held as Illustration 4612 of the Archivo General de la Nación in Mexico City, photographic negative 979/1087 [archival provenance: *Alcabalas,* Volume 182, Folio 22bis], as well as the Archive of Indies at Seville, old Torres Lanzas call numbers: Mapas y Planos de México, 402 and 403

Diagram and drawings by the military engineer Rafael Llobet, of a proposed new city barracks and armory, 1788—original held by the Servicio Histórico Militar at Madrid, call number: K, b, 6, 47

Proposed new city slaughterhouse, designed by De León after his promotion to *ingeniero mayor de brigada* or "senior brigade engineer," 1789—original held as Illustration 3519.1 of the Archivo General de la Nación in Mexico City, photographic negative 980/2908 [archival provenance: *Mercados,* Volume 6, Folio 27]

Diagram and profile view by De León of proposed new second story to be added to Campeche's barracks, June 1802—original held by the Servicio Histórico Militar at Madrid, call number: K, b, 6, 47, 1.[a]

Diagram and profile views by de León of new guard-station at the city's sea gate, July 1802—original held by the Servicio Histórico Militar at Madrid, call number: K, b, 6, 47

Proposed new layout by De León for the city slaughterhouse, 1804—original held as Illustration 3520 of the Archivo General de la Nación in Mexico City, photographic negative 978/2247 [archival provenance: *Mercados,* Volume 6, Folio 64]

Independence and General Works (1822–Present)

Abud Flores, José Alberto. *Campeche: revolución y movimiento social, 1911–1923.* Mexico City: Instituto Nacional de Estudios Históricos de la Revolución Mexicana, 1992.

Arjona Uribe, Rosendo. *Breve monografía del Estado de Campeche.* Mexico City: Sociedad Mexicana de Geografía y Estadística, 1967.

"Campeche." *Artes de México,* Number 246 (1999), entire volume.

Cornelio Sosa, Roger Elías. *Historia del movimiento obrero de Campeche, 1540–1990.* Campeche: Federación de Trabajadores, 1990.

Konrad, Herman W. "Capitalismo y trabajo en los bosques de las tierras bajas tropicales mexicanas: el caso de la industria del chicle." *Historia Mexicana* 36, Number 3 (1987): 465–505.

Müller, F. *Campeche.* Mexico City: Instituto Nacional de Antropología e Historia or INAH, 1960.

Guadalajara

Colonial Era (1541–1809)

Actas de cabildos de la ciudad de Guadalajara, Volumen Primero: 1607–1635. Guadalajara: N.p., 1870.

Benítez, José R. *Conquistadores de Nueva Galicia, fundadores de Guadalajara.* Guadalajara: Imprenta Universitaria, 1942.

Calvo, Thomas. "Document: un regard clinique jeté sur la ville de Guadalajara au début du XIXème siècle." *L'ordinaire du mexicaniste [Institut des Études Mexicaines, Perpignan, France]* 57 (May 1981): 50–56.

Castañeda, Carmen. "Los archivos de Guadalajara." *Historia mexicana* (1975): 143–162.

———. "El impacto de la Ilustración y de la Revolución Francesa en la vida de México: finales del siglo XVIII, 1793 en Guadalajara." *Caravelle: cahiers du monde hispanique et luso-brésilien [France]* 54 (1990): 61–87.

Cook, Sherburne F. "The Hunger Hospital in Guadalajara: An Experiment in Medical Relief." *Bulletin of the History of Medicine* 8 (1940): 533–545.

Gálvez Ruiz, María Angeles, and Pedro Sánchez Rodrigo. "La creación de la Universidad de Guadalajara, México: ilustración y conciencia regional." *Chronica Nova [Spain]* 21 (1993–1994): 161–190.

Greenleaf, Richard. "The Little War of Guadalajara." *New Mexico Historical Review* (1968): 119–135.

Greenow, Linda L. *Credit and Socioeconomic Change in Colonial Mexico: Loans and Mortgages in Guadalajara, 1720–1820.* Boulder: Westview, 1983.

Iguíniz, Juan Bautista. "Los gobernantes de Nueva Galicia: datos y documentos para sus biografías." *Memorias de la Academia Mexicana de la Historia* 7 (1948): 296–312.

Iguíniz, Juan Bautista, compiler. *Guadalajara a través de los tiempos.* Guadalajara, 1950, two volumes.

López Jiménez, José Eucario, compiler. *Cedulario de la Nueva Galicia.* Guadalajara: Lex, 1971.

Páez Brotchie, Luis. *Guadalajara, Jalisco, México: su crecimiento, división y nomenclatura durante la época colonial, 1542–1821.* Guadalajara, 1951.

———. *Guadalajara de Indias y otras monografías históricas regionales.* Guadalajara: Banco Industrial de Jalisco, 1957.

Parry, John H. *The Audiencia of New Galicia in the Sixteenth Century.* Cambridge, NY: Cambridge University Press, 1948.

Ramírez Flores, José. *El Real Consulado de Guadalajara: notas históricas.* Guadalajara: Banco Refaccionario de Jalisco, 1952.

Razo Zaragoza, José Luis, compiler. *Crónicas de la conquista de Nueva Galicia y memoria de Guzmán.* Guadalajara: Instituto Jaliscience de Antropología e Historia, 1963.

Serrera Contreras, Ramón María. *Guadalajara ganadera: estudio regional novohispano, 1760–1805.* Seville: Escuela de Estudios Hispano-americanos, 1977.

Van Young, Eric. *Hacienda and Market in Eighteenth-Century Mexico: The Rural Economy of the Guadalajara Region, 1675–1820.* Berkeley: University of California Press, 1981.

Early Maps and Depictions of Guadalajara, 1689–1808

Drawings of the façade, side-door, and interior of its cathedral, June 1689—originals held by the Archive of Indies at Seville, old Torres Lanzas call numbers: Mapas y Planos de México, 82 to 84

Map of the city and environs, 1732—original held by the Archive of Indies at Seville, old Torres Lanzas call number: Mapas y Planos de México, 127 [archival provenance: Guadalajara, 420]

Diagrams by José de Tapia Palacios, of proposed repairs and reconstruction of the *casas reales* or "royal offices," March 1734—originals held by the Archive of Indies at Seville, old Torres Lanzas call numbers: Mapas y Planos de México, 128 to 130

Map by Fr. Pedro Antonio Buzeta, of the new aqueduct and water-distribution system, September 1741—original held by the Archive of Indies at Seville, old Torres Lanzas call number: Mapas y Planos de México, 138 [archival provenance: Guadalajara, 420]

Map of the water-distribution system in 1745, by Juan Francisco de Espino—original held by the Archive of Indies at Seville, old Torres Lanzas call number: Mapas y Planos de México, 153 [archival provenance: Guadalajara, 106]

Diagram by Francisco Oxea de Bóbeda, of improvements to the city seminary, November 1746—original held by the Archive of Indies at Seville, old Torres Lanzas call number: Mapas y Planos de México, 160

One large and six small maps of Guadalajara, drawn in August 1753—originals held by the Archive of Indies at Seville, old Torres Lanzas call number: Mapas y Planos de México, 201 [archival provenance: Guadalajara, 229]

Diagrams of the new government palace and jail, under construction in 1756—originals held by the Archive of Indies at Seville, old Torres Lanzas call numbers: Mapas y Planos de México, 203–204

Diagram by Salvador González of a proposed new tobacco factory, 1778—original held as Illustration 4927 of the Archivo General de la Nación at Mexico City, photographic negative 979/2014 [archival provenance: *Tabaco,* Volume 506, Expediente 201, Folio 21]

Diagram by Manuel Conique of a proposed new tobacco factory, 1779—original held as Illustration 4928 of the Archivo General de la Nación at Mexico City, photographic negative 979/2015 [archival provenance: *Tabaco,* Volume 506, Expediente 201, Folio 26]

Diagram of the new *aduana* or "customs and excise" building, 1781—original held as Illustration 4632 of the Archivo General de la Nación at Mexico City, photographic negative 979/1106 [archival provenance: *Alcabalas,* Volume 532, Expediente 22, Folio 13]

Diagrams by Conique and Juan José de la Hoz, of proposed improvements to Guadalajara's *aduana,* 1790—originals held as Illustrations 4623–4624 of the Archivo General de la Nación at Mexico City, photographic negatives 979/1098 and 979/1099 [archival provenance: *Alcabalas,* Volume 486, Expediente 1, Folios 3 and 6]

Two diagrams outlining proposed improvements to the *aduana* building, 1791—originals held as Illustrations 4625–4626 of the Archivo General de la Nación at Mexico City, photographic negatives 979/1100 and 979/1101 [archival provenance: *Alcabalas,* Volume 486, Expediente 1, Folios 37 and 38]

Diagram by Francisco Gutiérrez of proposed improvements to the *aduana,* 1792—original held as Illustration 4627 of the Archivo General de la Nación at Mexico City, photographic negative 979/1102 [archival provenance: *Alcabalas,* Volume 486, Expediente 1]

Diagram by the *maestro de arquitectura* or "master architect" Pedro José Siprés of a city granary, 1793—original held as Illustration 3374 of the Archivo General de la Nación at Mexico City, photographic negative 978/1843 [archival provenance: *Indiferente de Guerra,* Volume 460-A, Folio 10]

Diagram by *maestro mayor de obras* Luis González, of proposed improvements to the *aduana,* 1795—original held as Illustration 4628 of the Archivo General de la Nación at Mexico City, photographic negative 979/1105 [archival provenance: *Alcabalas,* Volume 486, Expediente 1]

Six diagrams, plus exterior and cutaway views, of the reconstructed *aduana,* 1795—originals held as Illustrations 4635–4640 of the Archivo General de la Nación at Mexico City, photographic negatives 979/1110 through 979/1115 [archival provenance: *Alcabalas,* Volume 607, Expediente L 2, Folios 29–34]

Diagram by González of the Astillero *garita* or "sentry station," 1795—original held as Illustration 4634 of the Archivo General de la Nación at Mexico City, photographic negative 979/1109 [archival provenance:

Alcabalas, Volume 607, Expediente L 2, Number 22, Folio 21]

Diagrams by Siprés of a large building that was to serve as granary, military barracks, and meat storage, 1797—originals held as Illustrations 4178–4179 of the Archivo General de la Nación at Mexico City, photographic negatives 979/0701 and 979/0702 [archival provenance: *Civil,* Volume 2040, Expediente 7, Folios 33bis and 34bis]

Map of Guadalajara as surveyed by Santiago Guzmán in 1800, although not issued until 42 years later as a lithograph by Loreto, Ancira y Hermano—originals held by the Museo del Estado de Jalisco in Guadalajara and as Illustrations 4671–4672 of the Archivo General de la Nación at Mexico City, photographic negatives 979/0647 and 979/0648 [archival provenance: *Bienes Nacionales,* Legajo 178, Folios 16 and 23]

Diagram by Siprés of the clerical seminary, 1802—original held as Illustration 4171 of the Archivo General de la Nación at Mexico City, photographic negative 979/0693 [archival provenance: *Civil,* Volume 2009, Expediente 2, Folios 67bis]

Diagram by Siprés of the Mesquitán *garita* or "sentry station," 1806—original held as Illustration 4621 of the Archivo General de la Nación at Mexico City, photographic negative 979/1096 [archival provenance: *Alcabalas,* Volume 478, Expediente 49, Folio 19 vuelta]

Diagram, plus profile and cutaway views by the architect José Gutiérrez, of the *Puente Verde* or "Green Bridge" near Guadalajara, 1808—original held as Illustration 2685 of the Archivo General de la Nación at Mexico City, photographic negative 978/1339 [archival provenance: *Obras Públicas,* Volume 12, Expediente 17, Folio 291]

Independence Era (1810–Present)

Anderson, Rodney D. "Race and Social Stratification: A Comparison of Working-Class Spaniards, Indians, and Castas in Guadalajara, Mexico, in 1821." *Hispanic American Historical Review* 68, Number 2 (May 1988): 209–243.

Arroyo, Jesús, editor. *Impacto regional de la apertura comercial: perspectivas del Tratado de Libre Comercio en Jalisco.* Universidad de Guadalajara Press, 1993.

Ibáñez, E., and D. Vázquez. *Guadalajara: un análisis urbano.* Guadalajara: CCUVG, 1970.

Logan, Kathleen. *Haciendo Pueblo: The Development of a Guadalajaran Suburb.* University: University of Alabama Press, 1984.

Mayo, John. "Consuls and Silver Contraband on Mexico's West Coast in the Era of Santa Anna." *Journal of Latin American Studies [UK]* 19, Number 2 (1987): 389–411.

McDowell, Bart. "The Most Mexican City: Guadalajara." *National Geographic* 131, Number 3 (March 1967): 412–441.

Ornelas Mendoza y Valdivia, Nicolás de. *Crónicas de la provincia de Santiago de Xalisco.* Guadalajara: Instituto Jaliscience de Antropología e Historia, 1962.

Ramírez Flores, José. *El gobierno insurgente en Guadalajara, 1810–1811.* Guadalajara: Publicaciones del Ayuntamiento, 1969.

Rivière d'Arc, Hélène. *Guadalajara y su región: influencias y dificultades de una metrópoli mexicana.* Mexico City: Volume 106 of the Series "Sep-Setentas" published by the Secretaría de Educación Pública or SEP, 1973 translation of the French original by Carlos Montemayor and Josefina Anaya.

Siembieda, William J. "Looking for a Place to Live: Transforming the Urban Ejido." *Bulletin of Latin American Research [UK]* 15, Number 3 (1996): 371–385.

Tello, Fray Antonio. *Crónica miscelánea de la Sancta Provincia de Xalisco.* Guadalajara: Gobierno del Estado de Jalisco and Universidad Autónoma de Guadalajara, 1968–1973 re-edition, two volumes.

General Works

Chávez Hayhoe, Arturo. *Guadalajara de antaño.* Guadalajara: Banco Industrial de Jalisco, 1960.

Cornejo Franco, José. *Reseña de la catedral de Guadalajara.* Guadalajara: Vera, 1960.

Cuarto centenario de la fundación del obispado de Guadalajara, 1548–1946. Guadalajara: Artes Gráficas, 1948.

Dávila Garibi, José Ignacio. *Apuntes para la historia de la Iglesia en Guadalajara.* Mexico City: Editorial Cultura, 1957–1967, six volumes.

Franco Fernández, R. *Monumentos históricos y artísticos de Jalisco.* Guadalajara, 1971.

"Guadalajara." *Artes de México,* Numbers 94–95 (1967), entire volume.

Orozco y Jiménez, Francisco, editor. *Colección de documentos históricos inéditos o muy raros referentes al arzobispado de Guadalajara.* Guadalajara, 1922–1928, six volumes.

Guanajuato

Colonial Era (1539–1821)

Arenas Sánchez, José. *Historia de la Alhóndiga de Granaditas.* Guanajuato City: Archivo Histórico de la Universidad de Guanajuato, 1969.

Bernstein, Henry. "A Provincial Library in Colonial Mexico." *Hispanic American Historical Review* 26 (1946): 162–183.

Brading, David A. *Miners and Merchants in Bourbon Mexico, 1763–1810.* Cambridge, NY: Cambridge University Press, 1971.

———. "Grupos étnicos, clases y estructura ocupacional en Guanajuato, 1792." *Historia Mexicana* 21, Number 3 (January–March 1972): 460–480.

Casas históricas de la ciudad de Guanajuato. Guanajuato City: Ayuntamiento Constitucional, 1939.

Chávez Orozco, Luis. *Más datos para la historia de la Alhóndiga de Granaditas.* Mexico City, 1954.

Díaz Berrio, Salvador. *El templo de la Compañía de Jesús en Guanajuato: proyecto de restauración.* Guanajuato City, 1969.

Hamnett, Brian R. "Royalist Counterinsurgency and the Continuity of Rebellion: Guanajuato and Michoacán, 1813–1820." *Hispanic American Historical Review* 62, Number 1 (1982): 19–48.

Macías, Carlos. "El retorno a Valencia: las familias Pérez Gálvez y Rul. *Historia Mexicana* 36, Number 4 (1987): 643–659.

Early Maps and Depictions of Guanajuato, 1706–1802

Diagram by the *maestros de alarifes y de cantera* or "master masons and quarriers" Baltazar de los Reyes and José Hernández, of the city's new *real caja* or "royal treasury," 1706—original held as Illustration 2679 of the Archivo General de la Nación in Mexico City, photographic negative 978/1333 [archival provenance: *Obras Públicas,* Volume 6, Expediente 2, Folio 64]

Modern drawing by José Recuerte Ledesma of how the city must have appeared, ca. 1750—original held by the Archivo de Culhuacán in Mexico City [call number: CCX-48], plus numerous other sources

Hand-drawn map of the district's mining camps, 1754–1755—original held by the Archivo General de la Nación in Mexico City, archival provenance: *Inquisición,* Volume 937, Folios 270–271 and 375–378

Diagram by the *maestro de arquitectura* or "master architect" Felipe Bruno de Ureña and *maestro mayor de albañería* or "master mason" Manuel Ventura de la Cerda, of a *hacienda de beneficio* or "mineral-treatment plant," 1775—original held as Illustration 2760 of the Archivo General de la Nación in Mexico City, photographic negative 978/1396 [archival provenance: *Minería,* Volume 36, Expediente 1, Folio 57]

Diagrams by De Ureña of the new church, convent, and infirmary to be operated by the Hospital de Belén, 1778—originals held as Illustrations 4249–4250 of the Archivo General de la Nación in Mexico City, photographic negatives 979/1153 and 979/1154 [archival provenance: *Hospitales,* Volume 20, Folio 287]

Diagram by the surveyor Manuel Ignacio Zerrato of the "Señor San Juan Nepomuceno" *hacienda de beneficio,* 1779—original held as Illustration 2762 of the Archivo

General de la Nación in Mexico City, photographic negative 978/1398 [archival provenance: *Minería,* Volume 37, Expediente 1, Folio 62]

Diagram of the city *matadero* or "slaughterhouse," 1781—original held as Illustration 4345 of the Archivo General de la Nación in Mexico City, photographic negative 979/0034 [archival provenance: *Ayuntamientos,* Volume 142, Expediente 3, Folio 49]

Three maps of the river-course running through Guanajuato City, ca. 1785–1787—originals held as Illustrations 331–333 of the Archivo General de la Nación in Mexico City, photographic negatives 977/0318 to 977/0320 [archival provenance: *Historia,* Volume 279, Expediente 1, Folios 1–3]

Crude drawing of the city, ca. 1788–1808, as seen from atop San Miguel Hill to its west—original held by the Archive of Indies at Seville, old Torres Lanzas call number: Mapas y Planos de México, 601 [archival provenance: Indiferente General, Legajo 1783]

Diagram and drawing by Juan de Dios Trinidad Pérez, of the grand new *casa real* or "royal office," 1792—original held as Illustration 2709 of the Archivo General de la Nación in Mexico City, photographic negative 979/0033 [archival provenance: *Obras Públicas,* Volume 31, Folio 249]

Diagram by José Guadalupe Ribera of a proposed new military barracks, 1798—original held as Illustration 3393 of the Archivo General de la Nación in Mexico City, photographic negative 978/1862 [archival provenance: *Indiferente de Guerra,* Volume 473-A, Folio 17]

Diagram by Ribera of the almost completed barracks for the Provincial "del Príncipe" Cavalry Regiment, 1799—original held as Illustration 3398 of the Archivo General de la Nación in Mexico City, photographic negative 978/1867 [archival provenance: *Indiferente de Guerra,* Volume 473-A, Folio 100]

Diagram by José Alejandro Durán y Villaseñor of the city's El Hormiguero *garita* or "sentry station," 1802—original held as Illustration 4616 of the Archivo General de la Nación in Mexico City, photographic negative 979/1091 [archival provenance: *Alcabalas,* Volume 293, Folio 9]

Modern Era (1822–Present)

Blanco, Mónica. *Revolución y contienda política en Guanajuato, 1908–1913.* Mexico City: El Colegio de México, 1995.

Herr, Robert Woodmansee. *An American Family in the Mexican Revolution.* Wilmington, DE: Scholarly Resources, 1999.

Rankine, Margaret E. "The Mexican Mining Industry in the Nineteenth Century, with Special Reference to Guanajuato." *Bulletin of Latin American Research [UK]* 11, Number 1 (1992): 29–48.

Rodríguez Fraustro, Jesús. *Orígenes de la imprenta y el periodismo en Guanajuato.* Guanajuato City, 1961.

Serrano O., José Antonio. "El ascenso de un caudillo en Guanajuato: Luis de Cortázar, 1827–1832." *Historia Mexicana* 43, Number 1 (1993): 49–80.

Thompson, Angela Tucker. "Children and Schooling in Guanajuato, Mexico, 1790–1840." *Secolas Annals* 23 (1992): 36–52.

———. "To Save the Children: Smallpox Innoculation, Vaccination, and Public Health in Guanajuato, Mexico, 1797–1840." *The Americas: A Quarterly Review of Inter-American Cultural History [Academy of American Franciscan History]* 49, Number 4 (1993): 431–455.

———. "Mexico's Other Wars: Epidemics, Disease, and Public Health in Guanajuato, Mexico, 1810–1867." *Annales de démographie historique [France]* (1996): 169–194.

General Works

Aguilar, Rosalía, et al. "Guanajuato, una bibliografía comentada, 1750–1917." *Secuencia [Mexico]* 8 (1987): 111–144.

Cervantes, Enrique A. *Bosquejo del desarrollo de la ciudad de Guanajuato.* Mexico City, 1942.

Cobb, Charles E., Jr. "Mexico's Bajío: The Heartland." *National Geographic* 178, Number 6 (December 1990): 122–143.

Leal, Manuel. *Breviario gráfico e histórico de Guanajuato.* Guanajuato City, 1951.

Ortiz Macedo, Luis, and Gonzalo Obregón, editors. "Guanajuato." *Artes de México,* Numbers 73–74, 1965, entire volume.

Ponce de León, Salvador. *Guanajuato en el arte, en la historia y en la leyenda.* Mexico City, 1967.

Rodríguez Fraustro, Jesús. *Guía de gobernantes de Guanajuato.* Guanajuato City: Archivo Histórico de la Universidad de Guanajuato, 1965.

Vargas, Fulgencio. *Proceso histórico de la metrópoli guanajuatense.* Mexico City, 1948.

Mexico City

Aztec Era (1325–1521)

Carrasco, David. "City as Symbol in Aztec Thought: The Clues from the Codex Mendoza." *History of Religions* 20, Number 3 (1981): 199–223.

Caso, Alfonso. "Los barrios antiguos de Tenochtitlán y Tlatelolco." *Memorias de la Academia Mexicana de la Historia* 15, Number 1 (1956): 7–62.

Davies, Nigel B. *The Aztecs.* London: Macmillan, 1973.

Gillespie, Susan D. *The Aztec Kings: The Construction of Rulership in Mexica History.* Tucson: University of Arizona Press, 1989.

Gómez Aparicio, Luis. *Plano reconstructivo de la región de Tenochtitlán.* Mexico City: Instituto Nacional de Antropología e Historia or INAH, 1973.

González Aparicio, Luis. *Plano reconstructivo de la región de Tenochtitlán.* Mexico City: Instituto Nacional de Antropología e Historia, 1973.

Lenz, Hans. *México-Tenochtitlán, ciudad lacustre.* Mexico City: Libros de México, 1969.

Lombardo de Ruiz, Sonia. *Desarrollo urbano de México-Tenochtitlán, según las fuentes.* Mexico City: Secretaría de Educación Pública and the Instituto Nacional de Antropología e Historia or SEP-INAH, 1973.

Matos Moctezuma, Eduardo. "New Finds in the Great Temple." *National Geographic* 158, Number 6 (December 1980): 766–775.

McDowell, Bart. "The Aztecs." *National Geographic* 158, Number 6 (December 1980): 704–751.

Molina Montes, Augusto F. "The Building of Tenochtitlán." *National Geographic* 158, Number 6 (December 1980): 752–765.

Palerm, Angel. *Obras hidráulicas prehispánicas en el valle de México.* Mexico City: Secretaría de Educación Pública and the Instituto Nacional de Antropología e Historia or SEP-INAH, 1973.

Rojas, José Luis de. "Cuantificaciones referentes a la ciudad de Tenochtitlán en 1519." *Historia Mexicana* 36, Number 2 (1986): 213–250.

Soustelle, Jacques. *Daily Life of the Aztecs.* Stanford, CA: Stanford University Press, 1970 translation of French original by Patrick O'Brian.

Valero de García Lascurain, Ana Rita de. "Los indios en Tenochtitlán, la ciudad imperial mexica." *Anuario de Estudios Americanos [Spain]* 47 (1990): 29–63.

Van Zantwijk, Rudolf. *The Aztec Arrangement: The Social History of Pre-Spanish Mexico.* Norman: University of Oklahoma Press, 1985.

*Early Maps and Depictions
of Mexico City, 1524–1795*

Many inaccurate woodcuts were rushed into print when news of the Aztec capital's conquest reached Europe, being featured in such works as *La preclara narratione di Ferdinando Cortese della Nuova Hispagnia,* published in Venice by Bernardino de Viano for Baptista de Pederzani in 1524, or Benedetto Bordonne's *Libro . . . de tutte l'isole del mondo,* printed in Venice by Niccolo d'Aristotile four years later—originals available from the British Library; Rare Books and Manuscripts Division of the New York Public Library; etc.

Native map representing Tenochtitlán's foundation, painted by Aztec artists for the Codex Mendoza, ca. 1542—

original held by the Bodleian Library at Oxford University, call number: MS. Arch. Selden. A. 1, fol. 2r

Map of *Tenuxtlitan-Mexico* by a native artisan, ca. 1545—original held by the University of Uppsala in Sweden

Pen-and-ink drawing by Juan Garcés, of buildings around the capital's *plaça mayor* or "main square," ca. 1580—original held by the Archive of Indies at Seville, old Torres Lanzas call number: Mapas y Planos de México, 3 [archival provenance: Indiferente General, Legajo 1579]

Diagram of the main plaza drawn in 1596 by the *regidor* or "alderman" Francisco Guerrero, protesting against proposed erections of commercial kiosks—original held by the Archive of Indies at Seville, old Torres Lanzas call number: Mapas y Planos de México, 47 [archival provenance: Indiferente General, Legajo 1414]

Map of several empty lots just off Mexico City's main square that Pedro Cortés, Marqués del Valle de Oaxaca, wished to sell in order to house a new silk exchange, November 1603—original held by the Archive of Indies at Seville, old Torres Lanzas call number: Mapas y Planos de México, 52 [archival provenance: Patronato Real 17, Ramo 17]

Pen-and-ink map with watercolor highlights by Fray Baltasar de Medina, of the capital and its environs, 1618—original held by the Real Academia de la Historia in Madrid, call number: Colección Boturini, Volume 14

Depiction of the city from atop Chapultepec Hill by the architect and engineer Juan Gómez de Trasmonte, 1628—numerous modern reproductions

Drawing of the Santa Fe Aqueduct by Cristóbal de Medina Vargas, January 1688—original held by the Archive of Indies at Seville, old Torres Lanzas call number: Mapas y Planos de México, 81

Three diagrams of the city's viceregal palace, 1709—originals held by the Archive of Indies at Seville, old Torres Lanzas call number: Mapas y Planos de México, 105

Map drawn in 1750 by José de Villaseñor y Sánchez on orders from the viceroy, Francisco de Güemes y Horcasitas, First Conde de Revillagigedo, of a proposed city division into four *subalcaldías* or "submayoralties" so as to introduce a *ronda* or "night watch," plus other municipal services—original held by the Archive of Indies at Seville, old Torres Lanzas call number: Mapas y Planos de México, 178 [archival provenance: Audiencia de México, Legajo 543]

Detailed drawing of a sector of the capital, 1752—original held as Illustration 4150 of the Archivo General de la Nación in Mexico City, photographic negative 978/2132 [archival provenance: *Civil,* Volume 1496, Folio 242]

Map of the city and its surroundings, ca. 1760—original held by the Servicio Geográfico del Ejército in Madrid, call number: LM-8.ª–1.ª-a–116

Crude map of the city and its lakes, drawn in December 1763 by Ildefonso de Yniesta Bejarano—original held by the Servicio Geográfico del Ejército in Madrid, call number: LM-8.ª–1.ª-a–109

Detailed map of San José parish and its lake, 1768—original held by the Archive of Indies at Seville, old Torres Lanzas call number: Mapas y Planos de México, 247

Map of Mexico City and its valley, copied in 1776 by José Antonio de Alzate y Ramírez from a seventeenth-century original by Carlos de Sigüenza y Góngora; Alzate's reproduction was in turn republished by the royal Spanish cartographer Tomás López in 1785—original held by the Servicio Geográfico del Ejército in Madrid with call number LM-8.ª–1.ª-a–113, plus a print with call number LM-8.ª–1.ª-a–90, plus numerous other sources

Map of the city in 1776 by *maestro mayor de architectura* or "master architect" Ignacio de Castera, republished nine years later in Spain by López—print held by the Servicio Geográfico del Ejército in Madrid, call number: LM-8.ª–1.ª-a–91

Map of *acequias* or "canals" in the Santiago district of the capital by José Eligio Delgadillo, June 1777—original held by the Archive of Indies at Seville, old Torres Lanzas call number: Mapas y Planos de México, 327

Map of the city in December 1782 by Manuel Villavicencio, commissioned by the viceroy, Martín de Mayorga, to illustrate his municipal reforms, then engraved and hand-tinted by the printer Felipe de Zúñiga y Ontiveros—prints held by the Archive of Indies at Seville, old Torres Lanzas call numbers Mapas y Planos de México, 387 and 689 [archival provenance: Audiencia de México, Legajo 1433]; others held as Illustrations 3179 and 4346 of the Archivo General de la Nación in Mexico City, photographic negatives 978/2104 and 979/0783 [archival provenance: *Bandos,* Volume 12, Folio 124 and *Ayuntamientos,* Volume 211, Expediente 3]

Drawing of a proposed new street lamp, 1785—original held by the Archive of Indies at Seville, old Torres Lanzas call number: Mapas y Planos de México, 401

Watercolor of Mexico City's main plaza in 1791 by Fernando Brambila, one of the artists who accompanied Capt. Alejandro Malaspina's scientific expedition into the Pacific—original held by the Museo Naval in Madrid, call number: *Colección de láminas de la expedición Malaspina,* Volume II, Number 50

Three sketches of Mexico City scenes by Juan Ravenet, one of the Italian-born artists who accompanied Malaspina's expedition into the Pacific, 1791—originals held by the Museo Naval in Madrid

Diagram depicting the proposed new botanical garden in Chapultepec Park, 1792—original held by the Archive of Indies at Seville, old Torres Lanzas call number: Mapas y Planos de México, 437

Cross-sectional view of a typical Mexico City street, drawn in 1792 by the *maestro mayor* José Damián Ortíz de Castro to depict suggested improvements in paving techniques—original held by the Archive of Indies at Seville, old Torres Lanzas call number: Mapas y Planos de México, 438

Highly detailed map of Mexico City, drawn in 1793 by dragoon Lt.-Col. Diego García Conde and engraved in 1807—original held by the Servicio Geográfico del Ejército in Madrid, call number: Rollo-Armario N, Núm. 1

Map drawn in 1793 by De Castera to re-establish the boundaries of the ancient Indian communities around the capital, plus street-cleaning and waste-disposal procedures—original held by the Archive of Indies at Seville, old Torres Lanzas call number: Mapas y Planos de México, 444 [archival provenance: Audiencia de México, Legajo 2773]

Drawing of the main square as it appeared in 1793, after the beautification effort ordered by the viceroy, Juan Vicente de Güemes Pacheco de Padilla, Second Conde de Revillagigedo—originals held by the Archive of Indies at Seville: call number Mapas y Planos de México, 446 [archival provenance: Audiencia de México, Legajo 1451], as well as Illustration 229 of the Archivo General de la Nación in Mexico City, photographic negative 977/0215 [archival provenance: *Historia,* Volume 60, Expediente 16, Folio 270]

Map of the valley's drainage system, drawn in 1795 by De Castera—original held as Illustration 3668 of the Archivo General de la Nación in Mexico City, photographic negative 979/0239 [archival provenance: *Desagüe,* Volume 1 Bis, Folio 213]

Early Colonial Era (1521–1692)

Altman, Ida. "Spanish Society in Mexico City after the Conquest." *Hispanic American Historical Review* 71, Number 3 (1991): 413–445.

Apenes, Ola. *Mapas antiguos del valle de México.* Mexico City: Instituto de Historia de la Universidad Autónoma de México or UNAM, 1947.

Bénassy-Berling, Marie-Cécile. "Les couvents de femmes à Mexico au XVIIe siècle." *Cahiers des Amériques latines [France]* 20 (1979): 37–45.

———. "Sor Juana Inés de la Cruz: une expression des élites mexicaines du XVIIe siècle." *Caravelle: cahiers du monde hispanique et luso-brésilien [France]* 67 (1996): 23–36.

Boyer, Richard. "La Ciudad de México en 1628: la visión de Juan Gómez de Trasmonte." *Historia Mexicana* 29, Number 3 (1980): 447–471.

———. "Absolutism Versus Corporatism in New Spain: The Administration of the Marquis of Gelves, 1621–1624." *International History Review [Canada]* 4, Number 4 (1982): 475–503.

Cañeque, Alejandro. "Theater of Power: Writing and Representing the Auto de Fe in Colonial Mexico." *Americas: A Quarterly Review of Inter-American Cultural History* 52, Number 3 (1996): 321–343.

Cervantes de Salazar, Francisco. *Life in the Imperial and Loyal City of Mexico.* Austin: University of Texas Press, 1953 re-edition by Carlos Eduardo Castañeda of sixteenth-century original.

Cline, S. L. *Colonial Culhuacan, 1580–1600: A Social History of an Aztec Town.* Albuquerque: University of New Mexico Press, 1986.

Coe, Michael D., and Gordon Whittaker. *Aztec Sorcerers in Seventeenth Century Mexico.* Albany: Institute for Mesoamerican Studies, State University of New York, 1982.

Cope, R. Douglas. *The Limits of Racial Domination: Plebeian Society in Colonial Mexico City, 1660–1720.* Madison: University of Wisconsin Press, 1994.

Curcio-Nagy, Linda A. "Native Icon to City Protectress to Royal Patroness: Ritual, Political Symbolism and the Virgin of Remedies." *The Americas: A Quarterly Review of Inter-American Cultural History [Academy of American Franciscan History]* 52, Number 3 (1996): 367–391.

Dusenberry, William H. "The Regulation of Meat Supply in Sixteenth-Century Mexico City." *Hispanic American Historical Review* 28 (1948): 38–52.

Flinchpaugh, Steven G. "Economic Aspects of the Viceregal Entrance in Mexico City." *The Americas: A Quarterly Review of Inter-American Cultural History [Academy of American Franciscan History]* 52, Number 3 (1996): 345–365.

Fuentes, Patricia de, editor. *The Conquistadors: First-Person Accounts of the Conquest of Mexico.* New York, 1963.

Gibson, Charles. *The Aztecs under Spanish Rule: A History of the Indians of the Valley of Mexico, 1519–1810.* Stanford, CA: Stanford University Press, 1964.

Guijo, Gregorio M. de. *Diario, 1648–1664.* Mexico City: Porrúa, 1952.

Gurría Lacroix, Jorge. *El desagüe del valle de México durante la época novohispana.* Mexico City: Universidad Nacional Autónoma de México, 1978.

Guthrie, Chester L. "A Seventeenth-Century Ever-Present Granary: The Alhóndiga of Colonial Mexico City." *Agricultural History* 15 (1941): 37–43.

Hassig, Ross. "Conquest or Commerce: The Caballo Ordinance of 1526." *New Mexico Historical Review* 55, Number 4 (1980): 331–333.

Hoberman, Louisa Schell. "Merchants in Seventeenth-Century Mexico City: A Preliminary Portrait." *Hispanic American Historical Review* 57 (1977): 477–503.

———. "Technological Change in a Traditional Society: The Case of the Desagüe in Mexico City." *Technology and Culture* 21, Number 3 (1980): 386–407.

Holler, Jacqueline. "I, Elena de la Cruz: Heresy and Gender in Mexico City, 1568." *Journal of the Canadian Historical Association* 4 (1993): 143–160.

Horn, Rebecca. *Postconquest Coyoacán: Nahua-Spanish Relations in Central Mexico, 1519–1650.* Stanford, CA: Stanford University Press, 1997.

Howard, David A. *The Royal Indian Hospital of Mexico City.* Tempe, AZ: Center for Latin American Studies, 1980.

Kellogg, Susan. "Households in Late Prehispanic and Early Colonial Mexico City." *The Americas: A Quarterly Review of Inter-American Cultural History [Academy of American Franciscan History]* 44, Number 4 (1988): 483–494.

Langue, Frédérique. "De la munifence à l'ostentation: la noblesse de Mexico et la culture de l'apparence, XVIIe–XVIIIe siècles." *Caravelle: cahiers du monde hispanique et luso-brésilien [France]* 64 (1995): 49–75.

Lavrin, Asunción. "La congregación de San Pedro: una cofradía urbana del México colonial, 1604–1730." *Historia Mexicana* 29, Number 4 (1980): 562–601.

Leiby, John S. "San Hipólito's Treatment of the Mentally Ill in Mexico City, 1589–1650." *Historian* 54, Number 3 (1992): 491–498.

———. "The Royal Indian Hospital of Mexico City, 1553–1680." *Historian* 57, Number 3 (1995): 573–580.

León-Portilla, Miguel, and Carmen Aguilera. *Mapa de México-Tenochtitlán y sus contornos hacia 1550.* Mexico City: Celanese, 1986.

Linné, Sigvald. *El valle y la ciudad de México en 1550: relación histórica fundada sobre un mapa geográfico que se conserva en la biblioteca de la Universidad de Uppsala.* Stockholm: Statens Etnografiska Museum, 1948.

Lockhart, James M. *The Nahuas after the Conquest.* Stanford, CA: Stanford University Press, 1992.

Lopes Don, Patricia. "Carnivals, Triumphs, and Rain Gods in the New World: A Civic Festival in the City of México-Tenochtitlán in 1539." *Colonial Latin American Review* 6, Number 1 (1997): 17–40.

López de Gomara, Francisco [translated by Lesley Byrd Simpson]. "The City of the Living God." *American Heritage* 15, Number 3 (April 1964): 67–79.

Martínez, Enrico. *Reportorio de los tiempos.* Mexico City: Secretaría de Educación Pública or SEP, 1948.

Martínez López-Cano, María del Pilar. *El crédito a largo plazo en el siglo XVI.* Mexico City: Universidad Nacional Autónoma de México or UNAM, 1995.

Millares Carlo, Agustín, and J. I. Mantecón. *Indice y extractos de los protocolos del Archivo de Notarías de México, D. F.* Mexico City, 1945–1946, two volumes.

Musset, Alain. "De Tlaloc à Hippocrate: l'eau et l'organisation de l'espace dans le bassin de Mexico, XVIe–XVIIIe siècle." *Annales: économies, sociétés, civilisations [France]* 46, Number 2 (1991): 261–298.

Pescador, Juan Javier. *De bautizados a fieles difuntos: familia y mentalidades en una parroquia urbana: Santa Catarina de México, 1568–1820.* Mexico City: El Colegio de México, 1992.

Porras Muñoz, Guillermo. *El gobierno de la Ciudad de México en el siglo XVI.* Mexico City: Universidad Nacional Autónoma de México or UNAM, 1982.

———. *Personas y lugares de la Ciudad de México, siglo XVI.* Mexico City: Universidad Nacional Autónoma de México or UNAM, 1988.

Reyes García, Luis, et al., compilers and editors. *Documentos nauas de la ciudad de México del siglo XVI.* Mexico City: Centro de Investigaciones y Estudios Superiores en Antropología Social, 1996.

Río Moreno, Justo L., and Lorenzo E. López y Sebastián. "El trigo en la Ciudad de México: industria y comercio de un cultivo importado, 1521–1564." *Revista Complutense de Historia de América [Spain]* 22 (1996): 33–51.

Robles, Antonio de. *Diario de sucesos notables, 1665–1703.* Mexico City: Porrúa, 1972.

Rubio Mañé, José Ignacio. "Gente de España en la ciudad de México, año de 1689." *Boletín del Archivo General de la Nación [Mexico],* Segunda Serie, Volume 7, Numbers 1–2 (January–March 1966): 5–406.

Saucedo Zarco, María del Carmen. "Triunfo parténico de la religiosidad criolla." *Revista Complutense de Historia de América [Spain]* 19 (1993): 93–107.

Schwaller, John Frederick, and Constance Mathers. "A Trans-Atlantic Hispanic Family: The Mota Clan of Burgos and Mexico City." *Sixteenth Century Journal* 21, Number 3 (1990): 411–435.

Serrano, Luis G. *La traza original con que fue construida la Catedral de México.* Mexico City: Universidad Nacional Autónoma de México or UNAM, 1964.

Toussaint, Manuel, et al., compilers and editors. *Planos de la ciudad de México, siglos XVI y XVII: estudio histórico, urbanistico y bibliográfico.* Mexico City: Instituto de Investigaciones Estéticas of the Universidad Nacional Autónoma de México or UNAM, 1938.

Zavala, Silvio. "Una etapa en la construcción de la catedral de México, alrededor de 1585." *Jahrbuch für Geschichte von Staat, Wirtschaft und Gesellschaft Lateinamerikas [Germany]* 20 (1983): 321–330.

Late Colonial Era (1693–1807)

Arnold, Linda. *Bureaucracy and Bureaucrats in Mexico City, 1742–1835.* Tucson: University of Arizona Press, 1988.

————. "Sobre la deducción de evidencia: estratificación en un barrio de la Ciudad de México, 1777–1793." *Estudios de Historia Novohispana [Mexico]* 15 (1995): 87–111.

Arrom, Silvia M. *The Women of Mexico City, 1790–1857.* Stanford, CA: Stanford University Press, 1985.

Báez Macías, Eduardo. "Planos y censos de la ciudad de México, 1753." *Boletín del Archivo General de la Nación [Mexico],* Segunda Serie, Volume 7, Numbers 1–2 (January–March 1966): 407–484 and Volume 8, Numbers 3–4 (October–December 1967): 485–1156.

————. "Ordenanzas para el establecimiento de alcaldes de barrio en la Nueva España: ciudades de México y San Luis Potosí." *Boletín del Archivo General de la Nación [Mexico],* Segunda Serie, Volume 10, Numbers 1–2 (January–June 1969): 51–125 and Volume 12, Numbers 1–2 (January–June 1971): 59–128.

Cooper, Donald B. *Epidemic Disease in Mexico City, 1761–1813: An Administrative, Social, and Medical Study.* Austin: University of Texas Press, 1965.

De Estrada, D. T. "The *Escuelas Pías* of Mexico City, 1786–1820." *The Americas: A Quarterly Review of Inter-American Cultural History [Academy of American Franciscan History]* 31 (1974): 51–71.

Deans-Smith, Susan. "Compromise and Conflict: The Tobacco Workers of Mexico City and the Colonial State, 1770–1810." *Anuario de Estudios Americanos [Spain]* 49 (1992): 271–309.

Flores Marini, Carlos. "City of Palaces." *Américas [Organization of American States]* 23, Number 9 (September 1971): 2–9.

Haslip Viera, Gabriel. *Crime and Punishment in Late Colonial Mexico City, 1692–1810.* Albuquerque: University of New Mexico Press, 1999.

Kicza, John A. "The Pulque Trade of Late Colonial Mexico City." *The Americas: A Quarterly Review of Inter-American Cultural History [Academy of American Franciscan History]* 37, Number 2 (1980): 193–221.

————. "The Great Families of Mexico: Elite Maintenance and Business Practices in Late Colonial Mexico City." *Hispanic American Historical Review* 62, Number 3 (1982): 429–457.

————. *Colonial Entrepeneurs: Families and Business in Bourbon Mexico City.* Albuquerque: University of New Mexico Press, 1983.

————. "Life Patterns and Social Differentiation Among Common People in Late Colonial Mexico City." *Estudios de Historia Novohispana [Mexico]* 11 (1991): 183–200.

Marley, David F., compiler. *Documentos varios para la historia de la Ciudad de México a fines de la época colonial, 1769–1815.* Windsor, ON: Rolston-Bain, 1983.

Miño Grijalva, Manuel. "El censo de la ciudad de México en 1790." *Historia Mexicana* 41, Number 4 (April–June 1992).

Molina del Villar, América. *Por voluntad divina: escasez, epidemias y otras calamidades en la Ciudad de México, 1700–1762.* Mexico City: Centro de Investigaciones y Estudios Superiores en Antropología Social, 1996.

Pérez Toledo, Sonia. *Los hijos del trabajo: los artesanos de la Ciudad de México, 1780–1853.* Mexico City: El Colegio de México, 1996.

Pescador, Juan Javier. "Devoción y crisis demográfica: la cofradía de San Ygnacio de Loyola, 1761–1821." *Historia Mexicana* 39, Number 3 (1990): 767–801.

————. "Vanishing Woman: Female Migration and Ethnic Identity in Late-Colonial Mexico City." *Ethnohistory* 42, Number 4 (1995): 617–626.

Romero de Terreros, Manuel. *La ciudad de México en 1749.* Mexico City: Arte, 1949.

Scardaville, Michael C. "Alcohol Abuse and Tavern Reform in Late Colonial Mexico City." *Hispanic American Historical Review* 60, Number 4 (1980): 643–671.

————. "(Hapsburg) Law and (Bourbon) Order: State Authority, Popular Unrest, and the Criminal Justice System in Bourbon Mexico City." *The Americas: A Quarterly Review of Inter-American Cultural History [Academy of American Franciscan History]* 50, Number 4 (1994): 501–525.

Schroeder, Susan. "Jesuits, Nahuas, and the Good Death Society in Mexico City, 1710–1767." *Hispanic American Historical Review* 80, Number 1 (February 2000): 1–42.

Seed, Patricia. "Social Dimensions of Race: Mexico City, 1753." *Hispanic American Historical Review* 62, Number 4 (1982): 569–606.

Super, John C. "Bread and the Provisioning of Mexico City in the Late Eighteenth Century." *Jahrbuch für Geschichte von Staat, Wirtschaft und Gesellschaft Lateinamerikas [Germany]* 19 (1982): 159–182.

Villaseñor y Sánchez, José Antonio de. *Suplemento al teatro americano: la Ciudad de México en 1755.* Seville: Escuela de Estudios Hispano-americanos, 1980.

Viqueira, Juan Pedro. "Diversiones públicas y cultura popular en la Ciudad de México durante el siglo de las Luces." *Anuario de Estudios Americanos [Spain]* 44 (1987): 195–228.

Voekel, Pamela. "Peeing on the Palace: Bodily Resistance to Bourbon Reforms in Mexico City." *Journal of Historical Sociology [UK]* 5, Number 2 (1992): 183–208.

Independence Era (1808–1876)

Anna, Timothy E. *The Fall of the Royal Government in Mexico City.* Lincoln: University of Nebraska Press, 1978.

Annino, Antonio. "Prácticas criollas y liberalismo en la crisis del espacio urbano colonial: el 29 de noviembre de 1812 en la Ciudad de México." *Boletín del Instituto de Historia Argentina y Americana "Dr. Emilio Ravignani"* 6 (1992): 67–97.

Arrom, Silvia M. "Popular Politics in Mexico City: The Parián Riot, 1828." *Hispanic American Historical Review* 68, Number 2 (1988): 245–268.

Bisbal Siller, María Teresa. *Los novelistas y la Ciudad de México.* Mexico City, 1963.

Costeloe, Michael P. "A Pronunciamiento in Nineteenth Century Mexico: '15 de julio de 1840.'" *Mexican Studies/Estudios Mexicanos* 4, Number 2 (1988): 245–264.

Guedea, Virginia. "México en 1812: control político y bebidas prohibidas." *Estudios de Historia Moderna y Contemporánea de México* 8 (1980): 23–65.

———. "Las primeras elecciones populares en la Ciudad de México, 1812–1813." *Mexican Studies/Estudios Mexicanos* 7, Number 1 (1991): 1–28.

———. "El pueblo de México y la política capitalina, 1808 y 1812." *Mexican Studies/Estudios Mexicanos* 10, Number 1 (1994): 27–61.

Holt, Thaddeus. "Checkmate at Mexico City." *MHQ: The Quarterly Journal of Military History* 2, Number 3 (1990): 82–93.

Houdaille, Jacques, and Hector Gutiérrez. "Exploitation sommaire du recensement de México en 1811." *Population [France]* 36, Numbers 4–5 (1981): 933–938.

Illades, Carlos. "El proceso de organización de los artesanos de la Ciudad de México, 1853–1876." *European Review of Latin American and Caribbean Studies [The Netherlands]* 59 (1995): 59–75.

———. *Hacia la república del trabajo: la organización artesanal en la Ciudad de México, 1853–1876.* Mexico City: El Colegio de México, 1996.

Klein, Herbert S. "The Demographic Structure of Mexico City in 1811." *Journal of Urban History* 23, Number 1 (November 1996): 66–93.

Lozano Armendares, Teresa. *La criminalidad en la Ciudad de México, 1800–1821.* Mexico City: Instituto de Investigaciones Históricas, 1987.

Malo, José Ramón. *Diario de sucesos notables, 1832–1864.* Mexico City, 1948, two volumes.

Moreno Toscano, Alejandra, and Carlos Aguirre Anata. "Migrations to Mexico City in the Nineteenth Century: Research Approaches." *Journal of Inter-American Studies and World Affairs* 17, Number 1 (1971): 42–72.

Pérez Toledo, Sonia. "Los vagos de la Ciudad de México y el Tribunal de Vagos en la primera mitad del siglo XIX." *Secuencia [Mexico]* 27 (1993): 27–42.

Reyes de la Maza, Luis. *El teatro en México en la época de Santa Anna, 1840–1850.* Mexico City: Volume 30 of the Series "Estudios y Fuentes del Arte en México" published by the Instituto de Investigaciones Estéticas of the Universidad Nacional Autónoma de México or UNAM, 1972.

Rodríguez O., Jaime E. "The Struggle for the Nation: The First Centralist-Federalist Conflict in Mexico." *The Americas: A Quarterly Review of Inter-American Cultural History [Academy of American Franciscan History]* 49, Number 1 (1992): 1–22.

Porfirian Era (1877–1910)

Beezley, William. *Judas at the Jockey Club and Other Episodes of Porfirian Mexico.* Lincoln: University of Nebraska Press, 1987.

Blum, Ann S. "Public Welfare and Child Circulation, Mexico City, 1877 to 1925." *Journal of Family History* 23, Number 3 (1998): 240–271.

Johns, Michael. *The City of Mexico in the Age of Díaz.* Austin: University of Texas Press, 1997.

Lear, John. "Mexico City: Space and Class in the Porfirian Capital, 1884–1910." *Journal of Urban History* 22, Number 4 (May 1996): 454–492.

Ludlow, Leonor. "El Banco Nacional Mexicano y el Banco Mercantíl Mexicano: radiografía de sus primeros accionistas, 1881–1882." *Historia Mexicana* 39, Number 4 (1990): 979–1027.

Piccato, Pablo. "*El paso de venus por el disco del sol:* Criminality and Alcoholism in the Late Porfiriato." *Mexican Studies/Estudios Mexicanos* 11, Number 2 (1995): 203–241.

Reyna, María del Carmen. "Las condiciones del trabajo en las panaderías de la Ciudad de México durante la segunda mitad del siglo XIX." *Historia Mexicana* 31, Number 3 (1982): 431–448.

Smith, Phyllis L. "Contentious Voices Amid the Order: The Opposition Press in Mexico City, 1876–1911." *Journalism History* 22, Number 4 (1997): 138–145.

Tenorio Trillo, Mauricio. "1910 Mexico City: Space and Nation in the City of the Centenario." *Journal of Latin American Studies [UK]* 28, Number 1 (1996): 75–104.

Walker, David. "Porfirian Labor Politics: Working Class Organizations in Mexico City and Porfirio Díaz, 1876–1902." *The Americas: A Quarterly Review of Inter-American Cultural History [Academy of American Franciscan History]* 37, Number 3 (1981): 257–289.

Modern Era (1911–Present)

Aguilar, Adrián Guillermo, et al. *El desarrollo urbano de México a fines del siglo XX.* Mexico City: Instituto de Estudios Urbanos de Nuevo León and the Sociedad Mexicana de Demografía, 1995.

Alba, Francisco, and Gustavo Cabrera, editors. *La población en el desarrollo contemporáneo de México.* Mexico City: El Colegio de México, 1994.

Azuela de la Cueva, Antonio. "Low Income Settlements and the Law in Mexico City." *International Journal of Urban and Regional Research [UK]* 11, Number 4 (1987): 522–542.

Bataillon, Claude, and Louis Panabière. *Mexico aujourd'hui, la plus grande ville du monde.* Paris: Publisud, 1988.

Bliss, Katherine. "The Science of Redemption: Syphilis, Sexual Promiscuity, and Reformism in Revolutionary Mexico City." *Hispanic American Historical Review* 79, Number 1 (February 1999): 1–40.

Boraiko, Allen A. "Earthquake in Mexico." *National Geographic* 169, Number 5 (May 1986): 654–675.

Bueno, Gerardo, coordinator. *México: el desafío de largo plazo.* Mexico City: Limusa, 1988.

Calnek, Edward E., et al. *Ensayos sobre el desarrollo urbano de México.* Mexico City: Volume 143 of the Series "Sep-Setentas" published by the Secretaría de Educación Pública or SEP, 1974.

Coll-Hurtado, Atlantida. "L'espace rural face à l'espace urbain: une bataille perdue au centre du Mexique." *Annales de géographie [France]* 98, Number 548 (1989): 421–433.

Corona Rentería, Alfonso. "La economía de la zona metropolitana de la Ciudad de México." *Investigación Económica [Mexico]* 49, Number 193 (1990): 97–124.

Cross, John C. *Informal Politics: Street Vendors and the State in Mexico City.* Stanford, CA: Stanford University Press, 1998.

Czerny, Miroslawa, and Jerzy Makowski. "El desarrollo espacial de las ciudades en América Latina: caso de la Ciudad de México." *Revista Geográfica [Mexico]* 109 (1989): 45–55.

Davis, Charles L., and Kenneth M. Coleman. "Electoral Change in the One-Party Dominant Mexican Polity, 1958–1973: Evidence from Mexico City." *Journal of Developing Areas* 16, Number 4 (1982): 523–541.

Davis, Diane E. "Urban Transport, Dependent Development and Change: Lessons from a Case Study of Mexico City's Subway." *Canadian Journal of Development Studies* 12, Number 2 (1991): 329–355.

———. *Urban Leviathan: Mexico City in the Twentieth Century.* Philadelphia: Temple University Press, 1994.

———. "The Social Construction of Mexico City: Political Conflict and Urban Development, 1950–1966." *Journal of Urban History* 24, Number 3 (March 1998): 364–415.

Díaz Barriga, Miguel, and Karen Kleiber. "The Press and Urban Conflict in Mexico City: A Case Study of Newspaper Reporting on Ecology and Urban Expansion in the Ajusco Region, 1982–1990." *Mexican Studies/Estudios Mexicanos* 12, Number 2 (1996): 273–300.

Durand, Jorge. *La ciudad invade al ejido: proletarización, urbanización y lucha política en el cerro del Judío, D. F.* Mexico City: La Casa Chata, 1983.

Eckstein, Susan. "Formal Versus Substantive Democracy: Poor People's Politics in Mexico City." *Mexican Studies/Estudios Mexicanos* 6, Number 2 (1990): 213–239.

———. "Poor People Versus the State and Capital: Anatomy of a Successful Community Mobilization for Housing in Mexico City." *International Journal of Urban and Regional Research [UK]* 14, Number 2 (1990): 274–296.

"El estado y la organización del suelo urbano." *Boletín del Archivo General de la Nación [Mexico],* 3rd Series, Volume 6, Number 2 (1982): 5–16.

Garza, Gustavo. *Desconcentración, tecnología y localización industrial en México,* Mexico City: El Colegio de México, 1992.

———. "Global Economy, Metropolitan Dynamics and Urban Policies in Mexico." *Cities [UK]* 16, Number 3 (June 1999): 149–170.

———. "Uncontrolled Air Pollution in Mexico City." *Cities [UK]* 13, Number 5 (October 1996): 315–328.

Garza, Gustavo, compiler. *Una década de planeación urbano-regional en México, 1978–1988.* Mexico City: El Colegio de México, 1992.

González, Ronald. "Space for Living: A Modern Proposal." *Américas [Organization of American States]* 25, Number 5 (May 1973): 28–32.

Gussinyer Alfonso, Jordi. "Metro Monuments." *Américas [Organization of American States]* 23, Number 4 (April 1971): 13–19.

Harrison, Margaret E. "Mexico City: The Supply of a Primary Health Care Service." *Bulletin of Latin American Research [UK]* 10, Number 2 (1991): 239–258.

"Las cooperativas de vivienda popular." *Boletín del Archivo General de la Nación [Mexico],* 3rd Series, Volume 6, Number 2 (1982): 25–33.

Loaeza, Soledad. "Perspectivas para una historia política del Distrito Federal en el siglo XX." *Historia Mexicana* 45, Number 1 (1995): 99–158.

Lowe, Arbon Jack. "Mexico's Metro." *Américas [Organization of American States]* 22, Number 7 (July 1970): 30–35.

Maldonado, Victor Alfonso. "Fenómenos de maldesarrollo urbano en México." *Rivista di Studi Politici Internazionali [Italy]* 50, Number 4 (1983): 583–588.

McDowell, Bart. "Mexico's New Museum: Window on the Past." *National Geographic* 134, Number 4 (October 1968): 492–519.

———. "Mexico City: An Alarming Giant." *National Geographic* 166, Number 2 (August 1984): 138–178.

McGehee, Richard V. "The Dandy and the Mauler in Mexico: Johnson, Dempsey, et al., and the Mexico City Press,

1919–1927." *Journal of Sport History* 23, Number 1 (1996): 20–33.

Oldman, Oliver, et al. *Financing Urban Development in Mexico City.* Cambridge: Harvard University Press, 1968.

Parfit, Michael. "Mexico City: Pushing the Limits." *National Geographic* 190, Number 2 (August 1996): 24–43.

Perlo Cohen, Manuel. "Política y vivienda en México, 1910–1952." *Revista Mexicana de Sociología* 41, Number 3 (July–September 1979): 769–835.

Rodríguez, Miguel. "Los tranviarios en los años veinte: sus luchas e incorporación al aparato estatal." *Estudios de Historia Moderna y Contemporánea de México* 8 (1980): 127–178.

Schteingart, Martha. "La promoción inmobiliaria en el área metropolitana de la Ciudad de México, 1960–1980." *Demografía y Economía [Mexico]* 17, Number 1 (1983): 83–105.

Unikel, L., et al. *El desarrollo urbano de México: diagnóstico e implicaciones futuras.* Mexico City: El Colegio de México, 1976.

Varley, Ann. "The Relationship between Tenure Legalization and Housing Improvements: Evidence from Mexico City." *Development and Change [The Netherlands]* 18, Number 3 (1987): 463–481.

Ward, Peter M. "The Squatter Settlement as Slum or Housing Solution: Evidence from Mexico City." *Land Economics* 2, Number 3 (1976): 330–346.

———. "Political Pressure for Urban Services: The Response of Two Mexico City Administrations." *Development and Change [The Netherlands]* 12, Number 3 (1981): 379–407.

Williams, A. R. "Popocatépetl: Mexico's Smoking Mountain." *National Geographic* 195, Number 1 (January 1999): 116–137.

Wirth, Clifford J. "Transportation Policy in Mexico City: The Politics and Impacts of Privatization." *Urban Affairs Review* 33, Number 2 (1997): 155–181.

Zambrano Lupi, Jorge H. "Fecundidad y escolaridad en la Ciudad de México." *Demografía y Economía [Mexico]* 13, Number 4 (1979): 405–448.

General Works

Aguirre, Carlos, et al. *Fuentes para la historia de la Ciudad de México.* Mexico City: Departamento de Investigaciones Históricas of the Instituto Nacional de Antropología e Historia or INAH, 1972.

Apenas, Ola. *Mapas antiguos del valle de México.* Mexico City: Instituto de Historia, Universidad Nacional Autónoma de México or UNAM, 1947.

Bejarano, Ignacio, editor. *Actas del cabildo de la Ciudad de México, 1524–1899.* Mexico City: Various printers for the Municipio Libre, 1889–1913, sixty-three volumes.

Benítez, Fernando. *La Ciudad de México.* Mexico City: Salvat, 1981, two volumes.

Caistor, Nick. *Mexico City: A Cultural and Literary Companion.* New York: Interlink, 2000.

Carrera Stampa, Manuel. *Guía del archivo del antiguo ayuntamiento de la ciudad de México.* Havana: Archivo Nacional de Cuba, 1949.

———. "Planos de la ciudad de México." *Boletín de la Sociedad Mexicana de Geografía y Estadística* 67 (1949): 263–427.

"Centro histórico de la ciudad de México." *Artes de México* (1993), entire volume.

Civeira Taboada, Miguel. *La Ciudad de México en 500 libros.* Mexico City: Departamento del Distrito Federal or DDF, 1973.

Cossío, José L. *Guía retrospectiva de la Ciudad de México.* Mexico City: Privately printed, 1941.

De la Haba, Louis. "Mexico: The City That Founded a Nation." *National Geographic* 143, Number 5 (May 1973): 638–669.

Frost, Elsa Cecilia, et al., editors. *El trabajo y los trabajadores en la historia de México.* Mexico City: El Colegio de México, 1979.

Fuentes para la historia de la Ciudad de México. Mexico City: Instituto Nacional de Antropología e Historia or INAH for the "Seminario de Historia Urbana," 1972.

Garza, Gustavo. *El proceso de industrialización de la ciudad de México, 1821–1970.* Mexico City: El Colegio de México, 1985.

González Obregón, Luis. *The Streets of Mexico.* San Francisco, 1937 translation by Blanche Collet Wagner.

Gruzinski, Serge. *Histoire de Mexico.* Paris: Fayard, 1996.

Illades, Carlos, and Ariel Kuri Rodríguez, editors. *Ciudad de México: instituciones, actores sociales y conflicto político, 1774–1931.* Mexico City and Zamora: Universidad Autónoma Metropolitana and El Colegio de Michoacán, 1995.

Kandell, Jonathan. *La Capital: The Biography of Mexico City.* New York: Random House, 1988.

Marroquí, José María. *La ciudad de México.* Mexico City: Medina, 1969.

Mendoza López, Miguel. *Catálogo general del Archivo del Ayuntamiento de la Ciudad de México.* Mexico City: Instituto Nacional de Antropología e Historia or INAH for the "Seminario de Historia Urbana," 1972.

Morales Díaz, Carlos. *Quién es quién en la nomenclatura de la Ciudad de México.* Mexico City: Costa-Amic, 1962.

Moreno Toscano, Alejandra, and Enrique Florescano. *El sector externo y la organización espacial y regional de México, 1522–1910.* Mexico City: Instituto Nacional de Antropología e Historia or INAH, 1974.

Orozco y Berra, Manuel. *Historia de la Ciudad de México desde su fundación hasta 1854.* Mexico City: Volume 112 of the Series "Sep-Setentas" published by the Secretaría de Educación Pública or SEP, 1973 reprint.

Pérez San Vicente, Guadalupe. *Cedulario de la metrópoli mexicana.* Mexico City: Departamento del Distrito Federal or DDF, 1950.

Romero de Terreros, Manuel. *Bibliografía de cronistas de la Ciudad de México.* Mexico City: Secretaría de Relaciones Exteriores, 1926.

Salas Anzures, Miguel, et al. "La Ciudad de México." *Artes de México,* Numbers 49–50 (1964), 53–54 (1964), 58–59 (1964), 97–98 (1967), 105 (1968), 109–110 (1968), 117 (1969), 136 (1970), 172 (1973), nine volumes.

Sanders, William T., et al. *The Basin of Mexico: Ecological Processes in the Evolution of a Civilization.* New York: Academic Press, 1979.

Toussaint, Manuel, et al. *Planos de la ciudad de México.* Mexico City: Instituto de Investigaciones Estéticas, Universidad Nacional Autónoma de México or UNAM, 1938.

Valle-Arizpe, Artemio de. *El palacio nacional de México.* Mexico City, 1936.

———. *Historia de la Ciudad de México según los relatos de sus cronistas.* Mexico City, 1939.

———. *Calle vieja y calle nueva.* Mexico City, 1949.

Zaldívar Guerra, Sergio. "'El Caballito'." *Jahrbuch für Geschichte von Staat, Wirtschaft und Gesellschaft Lateinamerikas [Germany]* 20 (1983): 501–510.

Monterrey

Early History (1577–1846)

Cavazos Garza, Israel. *Cedulario autobiográfico de pobladores y conquistadores de Nuevo León.* Monterrey: Centro de Estudios Históricos of the Universidad de Nuevo León, 1964.

———. *Catálogo y síntesis de los protocolos del archivo municipal de Monterrey, 1596–1700 y 1700–1725.* Monterrey: Instituto Tecnológico y de Estudios Superiores and Centro de Estudios Históricos of the Universidad de Nuevo León, 1966–1973, two volumes.

Fernández de Jáuregui Uruttia, José Antonio. *Descripción del Nuevo Reino de León, 1735–1740.* Monterrey: Instituto Tecnológico y de Estudios Superiores, 1963 reprint edited by Malcolm D. McLean and Eugenio del Hoyo Cabrera.

Hoyo Cabrera, Eugenio del. *Indice del ramo de causas criminales del Archivo Municipal de Monterrey, 1621–1834.* Monterrey: Instituto Tecnológico y de Estudios Superiores, 1963.

———. *Historia del Nuevo Reino de León, 1577–1723.* Monterrey, 1972, two volumes.

Losada, Juan. *Cuaderno de visita de los conventos y misiones del Nuevo Reino de León, mayo 1739.* Monterrey, 1970 reprint edited by Eugenio del Hoyo Cabrera.

Mendirichaga Cueva, Xavier. *Tres monumentos virreinales de Monterrey: San Francisco, la Catedral, el Obispado.* Monterrey, 1965.

Pérez Maldonado, Carlos. *Documentos históricos de Nuevo León, anotados y comentados, 1596–1811 y 1812–1821.* Monterrey, 1947–1948, two volumes.

———. *El Obispado: monumento histórico de Monterrey.* Monterrey, 1947.

Somonte, Mariano G. *Don Diego de Montemayor.* Mexico City, 1971.

Vizcaya Canales, Isidro. *En los albores de la independencia: las provincias internas de oriente durante la insurrección de don Miguel Hidalgo y Costilla, 1810–1811.* Monterrey, 1976.

Late Eighteenth-Century Maps
and Depictions of Monterrey, 1790–1798

Floor plan and two exterior views sketched by the *maestros de arquitectura* or "master architects" José Antonio Jiménez and José Montalvo in 1790, of the proposed completion of its *parroquia* or "parish church"—originals held as Illustrations 3129–3130 of the Archivo General de la Nación in Mexico City, photographic negatives 978/1791 and 978/1792 [archival provenance: *Templos y Conventos,* Volume 2, Folios 270–271]

Hand-drawn map of Monterrey in 1791 by Cristóbal Bellido Faxardo, *guardián y comisario de misiones*—original held as Illustration 4262 of the Archivo General de la Nación in Mexico City, photographic negative 979/0720 [archival provenance: *Arzobispos y Obispos,* Volume 10, Expediente 3, Folio 384]

Diagram and profile views by the *maestro de arquitectura* Juan Crouset, of a proposed new city jail, 1794—originals held as Illustrations 3537 and 3539 of the Archivo General de la Nación in Mexico City, photographic negatives 978/2099 and 978/2100 [archival provenance: *Presidios y Cárceles,* Volume 31, Folios 253–254]

Two diagrams by Crouset of the layout for the Colegio de Propaganda Fidei, 1796—originals held as Illustrations 3294–3295 of the Archivo General de la Nación in Mexico City, photographic negatives 978/2232 and 978/2233 [archival provenance: *Colegios y Universidades,* Volume 14, Folios 100–101]

Map by Crouset of the central portion of Monterrey, 1796—original held as Illustration 3540 of the Archivo General de la Nación in Mexico City, photographic negative 978/2101 [archival provenance: *Presidios y Cárceles,* Volume 31, Folio 258]

Map of the city in 1798, drawn by Crouset on orders from Gov. Simón de Herrera y Leyva to identify the urban plots capable of contributing toward the new cathedral's construction—original held as Illustration 177 of the Archivo General de la Nación in Mexico City, photographic negative 977/0164 [archival provenance: *Provincias Internas*, Volume 196, Folio 148]

American Occupation (1846–1848)

Dana, Napoleon Jackson Tecumseh. *Monterrey Is Ours! The Mexican War Letters of Lieutenant Dana, 1845–1847.* Lexington: University Press of Kentucky, 1990 re-edition by Robert H. Ferrell.

Dilworth, Rankin. *The March to Monterrey: The Diary of Lt. Rankin Dilworth.* El Paso: Texas Western, 1996 re-edition by Lawrence R. Clayton and Joseph E. Chance.

Michael, Steven. "A Year's Campaign: Dewitt C. Loudon's Mexican War." *Timeline* 9, Number 2 (1992): 18–33.

Spurlin, Charles. "Texas Volunteers in the Monterrey Campaign." *Military History of Texas and the Southwest* 16, Number 1 (1980): 5–22 and Number 2: 137–142.

Modern Era (1848–Present)

Balán, Jorge, et al. *Movilidad social, migración y fecundidad en Monterrey metropolitana.* Monterrey: Centro de Investigaciones Económicas of the Universidad de Nuevo León, 1967.

Beato, Guillermo, and Domenico Sindico. "The Beginning of Industrialization in Northeast Mexico." *The Americas: A Quarterly Review of Inter-American Cultural History [Academy of American Franciscan History]* 39, Number 4 (1983): 499–518.

Bennett, Vivienne. *The Politics of Water: Urban Protest, Gender, and Power in Monterrey, Mexico.* Pittsburgh: University of Pittsburgh Press, 1995.

Buentello Chapa, Humberto. *La inundación de 1909: sus aspectos trágico y político.* Monterrey, 1970.

Cerutti, Mario. "Industrialización y salarios obreros en Monterrey, 1890–1910." *Humánitas [Mexico]* 21 (1980): 443–474.

———. "Poder estatal, actividad económica y burguesía regional en el noreste de México, 1855–1910." *Siglo XIX [Mexico]* 1, Number 1 (1986): 67–134.

———. "El gran norte oriental y la formación del mercado nacional en México a finales del siglo XIX." *Siglo XIX [Mexico]* 2, Number 4 (1987): 53–80.

———. "Monterrey y su ámbito regional, 1850–1910: referencia histórica y sugerencias metodológicas." *Secuencia [Mexico]* 15 (1989): 97–113.

———. "Producción capitalista y articulación del empresariado en Monterrey, 1890–1910." *Siglo XIX [Mexico]* 5, Number 9 (1990): 149–192.

Flores Torres, Oscar. "Revolución mexicana y diplomacia española: la burguesía de Monterrey y los gachupínes en el Nuevo León radical de 1914." *Siglo XIX [Mexico]* 5, Number 9 (1990): 193–222.

———. "Ayuntamiento y poder público en Monterrey: la comuna empresarial, 1915–1917." *Secuencia [Mexico]* 27 (1993): 101–118.

———. "Empresarios, revolución y conflictos laborales en Monterrey: la industria metalúrgica, 1920–1923." *Siglo XIX: Cuadernos de Historia [Mexico]* 3, Number 9 (1994): 83–103.

Gamble, Stephen H. *The Despensa System of Food Distribution: A Case Study of Monterrey, Mexico.* New York: Praeger, 1972.

Hibino, Barbara. "Cervecería Cuauhtémoc: A Case Study of Technological and Industrial Development in Mexico." *Mexican Studies/Estudios Mexicanos* 8, Number 1 (1992): 23–43.

Mauro, Frédéric. "Le développement économiqie de Monterrey, 1890–1960." *Caravelle: cahiers du monde hispanique et luso-brésilien [France]* 2 (1964): 35–133.

Parfit, Michael. "Monterrey: Confronting the Future." *National Geographic* 190, Number 2 (August 1996): 52–61.

Pedraza, Jorge. *Juárez en Monterrey.* Monterrey, 1970.

Puente Leyva, Jesús. *El problema de la vivienda en Monterrey.* Monterrey: Centro de Investigaciones Económicas of the Universidad de Nuevo León, 1967.

———. *Distribución del ingreso en un área urbana: el caso de Monterrey.* Mexico City: Siglo XXI, 1969.

Reséndiz Balderas, José. "Liberalismo y problemas estructurales: el noreste de México a mediados del XIX." *Siglo XIX [Mexico]* 2, Number 3 (1987): 87–111.

Revel-Mouroz, Jean. "Monterrey et le Nord-Est mexicain, croissance urbaine et organisation régionale." *Les cahiers d'Outre-Mer [France]* 22, Number 86 (April–June 1969): 161–190.

Rojas Sandoval, Javier. "Conflictos obreros y legislación laboral en Nuevo León, 1885–1918." *Siglo XIX [Mexico]* 3, Number 6 (1988): 187–213.

Saldaña, José P. *Apuntes históricos sobre la industrialización de Monterrey.* Monterrey: Centro Patronal, 1965.

Saragoza, Alex M. *The Monterrey Elite and the Mexican State, 1880–1940.* Austin: University of Texas Press, 1988.

Vellinga, Menno. *Economic Development and the Dynamics of Class: Industrialization, Power and Control in Monterrey, Mexico.* Assen, The Netherlands: Van Gorcum, 1979.

———. "The Small Margins of Autonomous Development: Cooptation and Control of Urban Social Movements in Monterrey, Mexico." *Boletín de Estudios Latinoamericanos y del Caribe [The Netherlands]* 41 (1986): 53–70.

———. "Actual and Expected Deprivation: Northern Mexico in the 1980s, a Research Note." *Studies in Comparative International Development* 28, Number 3 (1993): 51–66.

General Works

Alessio Robles, Vito. *Monterrey en la historia y en la leyenda.* Mexico City, 1936.

Alisky, Marvin. *Government of the Mexican State of Nuevo León.* Tempe: Arizona State University Press for the Center of Latin American Studies, 1971.

Basave, Agustín. *Constructores de Monterrey.* Monterrey, 1945.

————. *Quién es quién en Monterrey.* Monterrey, 1948.

Cossío, David Alberto. *Historia de Nuevo León.* Monterrey, 1924–1933, six volumes.

Covarrubias, Ricardo. *Las calles de Monterrey.* Monterrey, 1947–1970, three volumes.

León, Alonso de, et al. *Historia de Nuevo León, con noticias sobre Coahuila, Tamaulipas, Téxas y Nuevo México.* Monterrey: Biblioteca de Nuevo León, 1961 re-edition by Israel Cavazos Garza.

León, Gerardo de. "Urbanismo histórico del noreste de México." *Humánitas [Mexico]* 21 (1980): 415–441.

León Garza, Máximo de. *Monterrey: un vistazo a sus entrañas.* Monterrey, 1968.

————. *Grandeza de Monterrey.* Monterrey: Editorial Alfonso Reyes, 1970.

Montemayor, Andrés. *Historia de Monterrey.* Monterrey, 1971.

Roel, Santiago. *Apuntes históricos de Nuevo León.* Monterrey, 1954.

Saldaña, José P. *Estampas antiguas de Monterrey.* Monterrey, 1942.

————. *Grandeza de Monterrey.* Monterrey, 1968.

Oaxaca

Colonial Era (1529–1821)

Alanís Boyso, José Luis. "Introducción al estudio de los corregidores y alcaldes mayores del Marquesado del Valle: títulos de 1590 a 1810." *Boletín del Archivo General de la Nación [Mexico],* 2nd Series, Volume 13 (1972–1976): 5–185.

Baskes, Jeremy. "Coerced or Voluntary?: The Repartimiento and Market Participation of Peasants in Late Colonial Oaxaca." *Journal of Latin American Studies [UK]* 28, Number 1 (1996): 1–28.

Blanton, Richard E., et al. *Ancient Oaxaca: The Monte Albán State.* Cambridge, NY: Cambridge University Press, 1999.

Carmagnani, Marcello. *El regreso de los dioses: el proceso de reconstitución de la identidad étnica en Oaxaca, siglos XVII y XVIII.* Mexico City: Fondo de Cultura Económica, 1988.

Chance, John K. *Race and Class in Colonial Oaxaca.* Stanford, CA: Stanford University Press, 1978.

————. *Conquest of the Sierra: Spaniards and Indians in Colonial Oaxaca.* Norman: University of Oklahoma Press, 1990.

Chance, John K., and William B. Taylor. "Estate and Class in a Colonial City: Oaxaca in 1792." *Comparative Studies in Society and History [UK]* 19, Number 4 (October 1977): 454–487.

Esparza, Manuel, editor. *Relaciones geográficas de Oaxaca, 1777–1778.* Mexico City: Centro de Estudios Mexicanos y Centroamericanos, 1994.

García Martínez, Bernardo. *El Marquesado del Valle: tres siglos de régimen señorial en Nueva España.* Mexico City: El Colegio de México, 1969.

Hamnett, Brian R. "Dye Production, Food Supply, and the Laboring Population of Oaxaca, 1750–1820." *Hispanic American Historical Review* 51, Number 1 (1971): 51–78.

————. *Politics and Trade in Southern Mexico, 1750–1821.* Cambridge, NY: Cambridge University Press, 1971.

Hensel, Silke. *Die Entstehung des Föderalismus in Mexiko: Die Politische Elite Oaxacas zwischen Stadt, Region und Staat, 1786–1835.* Stuttgart: Franz Steiner, 1997.

Paddock, John, editor. *Ancient Oaxaca.* Stanford, CA: Stanford University Press, 1966.

Romero Frizzi, María de los Angeles. *El sol y la cruz: los pueblos indios de Oaxaca colonial.* Mexico City: Centro de Investigaciones y Estudios Superiores en Antropología Social, 1996.

Spores, Ronald. *The Mixtecs in Ancient and Colonial Times.* Norman: University of Oklahoma Press, 1985.

Taylor, William B. *Landlord and Peasant in Colonial Mexico.* Stanford, CA: Stanford University Press, 1972.

Terraciano, Kevin. "Mixtec and Náhuatl in Colonial Oaxaca." *UCLA Historical Journal* 10 (1990): 122–146.

————. "Crime and Culture in Colonial Mexico: The Case of the Mixtec Murder Note." *Ethnohistory* 45, Number 4 (1998): 709–745.

————. "The Colonial Mixtec Community." *Hispanic American Historical Review* 80, Number 1 (February 2000): 1–42.

Travulse, E., editor. *Fluctuaciones económicas en Oaxaca durante el siglo XVIII.* Mexico City, 1978.

Early Maps and Depictions of Oaxaca, 1590–1819

Two diagrams and a single profile view, all in pen-and-ink with yellow watercolor highlights, detailing suggested improvements to the city's *Iglesia colegial* or "Collegial Church," May 1590—originals held by the Archivo General de Simancas in Spain, call numbers: Mapas, Planos y Dibujos, XIII-30, -31, and -32 [archival provenance: Patronato Eclesiástico, Legajo 31]

Diagram by Miguel de Zanabria and Nicolás Merlín of an edifice to serve as city *alhóndiga* or "granary," as well as *aduana* or "customshouse," 1717—original held as Illustration 565 of the Archivo General de la Nación in Mexico City, photographic negative 977/0767 [archival provenance: *Tierras,* Volume 41, Expediente 1bis, Folio 28]

Map of the city in March 1743, by its *alcalde mayor* Martín de Echartena—original held by the Archive of Indies at Seville, old Torres Lanzas call number: Mapas y Planos de México, 141

Diagram and profile view of a proposed new Capuchin nunnery, 1748—original held as Illustration 261 of the Archivo General de la Nación in Mexico City, photographic negative 977/0247 [archival provenance: *Historia,* Volume 98, Expediente 2, Folio 261]

Diagram of the *alhóndiga* or "granary," 1753—original held as Illustration 4939 of the Archivo General de la Nación in Mexico City, photographic negative 980/3581 [archival provenance: *Alhóndigas,* Volume 1, Folio 44bis]

Two maps by the *agrimensor* or "surveyor" José Carrión and by Juan Francisco de Beytia, of properties just outside the city, 1760—originals held as Illustrations 3027–3028 of the Archivo General de la Nación at Mexico City, photographic negatives 978/1672 and 978/1673 [archival provenance: *Hospital de Jesús,* Legajo 119, Expediente 1, Folios 23 and 24 vuelta]

Drawings by de Beytia of the San Jacinto Amilpas, San Juan Chapultepec, Santa Anna, and Santa Anita suburbs, 1760—originals held as Illustrations 3030–3033 of the Archivo General de la Nación in Mexico City, photographic negatives 978/1675 through 978/1678 [archival provenance: *Hospital de Jesús,* Legajo 119, Expediente 2, Folio 18 and Expediente 3, Folios 13–14]

Crude street plan, 1766—found on p. 88 of the second volume of the *Diario del viaje que hizo a la América Septentrional en el siglo xviii el P. Fray Francisco Ajofrín capuchino,* republished in Madrid in 1959

Diagram of a house by the *valuador* or "appraiser" Felipe de Ureña, 1772—original held as Illustration 3172 of the Archivo General de la Nación in Mexico City, photographic negative 978/1784 [archival provenance: *Temporalidades,* Volume 138, Expediente 1, Folio 14]

Hand-colored map of the city, 1777—original held by the Archive of Indies at Seville, old Torres Lanzas call number: Mapas y Planos de México, 556bis [archival provenance: Audiencia de México, Legajos 2589 and 2591]

Drawing of the façade of the *casas reales* or "royal offices" in 1781, demonstrating how these were to be reconstructed by the *corregidor,* infantry Lt.-Col. Nicolás de Lafora—original held by the Archive of Indies at Seville, old Torres Lanzas call number: Mapas y Planos de México, 366 [archival provenance: Audiencia de México, Legajo 1867]

Map of the city, 1795—original held as Illustration 3181.1 of the Archivo General de la Nación in Mexico City, photographic negative 979/2032 [archival provenance: *Bandos,* Volume 18, Folio 182]

Diagram of the *casas reales* by the *maestros alarifes* or "master masons" Manuel Antonio de Vale and Juan Esteban Fernández, 1805—original held as Illustration 3070 of the Archivo General de la Nación in Mexico City, photographic negative 978/1715 [archival provenance: *Hospital de Jesús,* Legajo 348, Expediente 1, Folio 6]

Diagrams and profile views by Miguel Vendrell y Puig of a proposed new guardhouse for the *Casa Mata,* 1810—original held as Illustration 4371 of the Archivo General de la Nación in Mexico City, photographic negative 979/0839 [archival provenance: *Pólvora,* Volume 46, Expediente 245, Folio 3]

Diagram of the *Casa Mata,* 1819—original held as Illustration 3320 of the Archivo General de la Nación in Mexico City, photographic negative 978/1919 [archival provenance: *Indiferente de Guerra,* Volume 61-B, penultimate folio]

Independence and General Works (1822–Present)

Beals, Ralph Leon. *The Peasant Marketing System of Oaxaca, Mexico.* Berkeley: University of California Press, 1975.

Berlin, Heinrich, et al. *Idolatría y superstición entre los indios de Oaxaca.* Mexico City: Toledo, 1988.

Berry, Charles Redmon. *The Reform in Oaxaca, 1856–76: A Microhistory of the Liberal Revolution.* Lincoln: University of Nebraska Press, 1980.

Clarke, Colin G. *Livelihood Systems, Settlements and Levels of Living in "Los Valles Centrales de Oaxaca," Mexico.* Oxford University Press, 1986.

Cook, Scott. *Peasant Capitalist Industry: Piecework and Enterprise in Southern Mexican Brickyards.* Lanham, MD: University Press of America, 1984.

Cook, Scott, and Martin Daskin, editors. *Markets in Oaxaca.* Austin: University of Texas Press, 1976.

Díaz Polanco, Héctor. *El fuego de la inobediencia: autonomía y rebelión india en el obispado de Oaxaca.* Mexico City: Centro de Investigaciones y Estudios Superiores en Antropología Social, 1996.

Dilley, M. "Synoptic Controls on Precipitation in the Valley of Oaxaca, Mexico." *International Journal of Climatology* 16, Number 9 (1996): 1019–1031.

Garner, Paul. "Federalism and Caudillismo in the Mexican Revolution: The Genesis of the Oaxaca Sovereignty Movement, 1915–1920." *Journal of Latin American Studies [UK]* 17, Number 1 (1985): 111–133.

Hamnett, Brian R. "Benito Juárez, Early Liberalism, and the Regional Politics of Oaxaca, 1828–1853." *Bulletin of Latin American Research [UK]* 10, Number 1 (1991): 3–21.

Hendricks, Janet, and Arthur D. Murphy. "From Poverty to Poverty: The Adaptation of Young Migrant Households in Oaxaca, Mexico." *Urban Anthropology* 10, Number 1 (spring 1981): 53–70.

Higgins, Michael James, and Tanya L. Coen. *Streets, Bedrooms, and Patios: The Ordinariness of Diversity in Urban Oaxaca.* Austin: University of Texas Press, 2000.

Kowalewski, Stephen A., and Jacqueline J. Saindon. "The Spread of Literacy in a Latin American Peasant Society: Oaxaca, Mexico, 1890 to 1980." *Comparative Studies in Society and History [UK]* 34, Number 1 (1992): 110–140.

Lemperière, Annick. "La formation des élites libérales au Méxique au XIXe siècle: l'Institut des Sciences et des Arts de l'état de Oaxaca, 1826–1910." *Revue d'histoire moderne et contemporaine [France]* 42, Number 3 (1995): 405–434.

Mahar, C. "An Exercise in Practice: Studying Migrants to Latin American Squatter Settlements." *Urban Anthropology* 21, Number 3 (1992): 275–309.

Martínez, Héctor G., and Francie R. Chassen. "Elecciones y crisis política en Oaxaca: 1902." *Historia Mexicana* 39, Number 2 (1989): 523–554.

Morris, Earl W. "Household, Kin and Non-Kin Sources of Assistance in Home Building: The Case of the City of Oaxaca." *Urban Anthropology* 20, Number 1 (spring 1991): 49–66.

Murphy, Arthur D. "City in Crisis." *Urban Anthropology* 20, Number 1 (1991): 1–13.

Murphy, Arthur D., and Alex Stepnick. *Social Inequality in Oaxaca: A History of Resistance and Change.* Philadelphia: Temple University Press, 1991.

Murphy, Arthur D., and Henry A. Selby. "Poverty and Domestic Cycle in Oaxaca." *Urban Anthropology* 14, Number 4 (winter 1985): 347–365.

Norget, Kristin. "The Politics of Liberation: The Popular Church, Indigenous Theology, and Grassroots Mobilization in Oaxaca, Mexico." *Latin American Perspectives* 24, Number 5 (1997): 96–127.

"Oaxaca." *Artes de México,* Number 70–71 (1965), entire volume.

Pacheco Vásquez, Pedro D., et al. "Neighborhood Type, Housing and Household Characteristics in Oaxaca, Mexico." *Urban Anthropology* 20, Number 1 (spring 1991): 31–47.

Prince, Zack, and Arthur D. Murphy. "Generative and Regulative Organization in Site-and-Services Housing Projects: A Case from Oaxaca, Mexico." *City and Society* 4, Number 2 (December 1990): 180–191.

Rees, Martha W., et al. "Migrants to and in Oaxaca City." *Urban Anthropology* 20, Number 1 (spring 1991): 15–29.

Selby, Henry A. "The Oaxacan Urban Household and the Crisis." *Urban Anthropology* 20, Number 1 (1991): 87–98.

Stepick, Alex, and Arthur D. Murphy. "Comparing Squatter Settlements and Government Self-Help Projects as Housing Solutions in Oaxaca, Mexico." *Human Organization* 39, Number 4 (winter 1980): 339–343.

Whiteford, M. B. "The Patient as Diagnostician: Intracultural Differences in Illness Etiology in a Mexican Neighborhood." *Journal of Developing Societies* 7, Number 2 (1991): 256–268.

Williams, Aubrey, editor. *Social, Political, and Economic Life in Contemporary Oaxaca.* Nashville: Vanderbilt University Press, 1979.

Willis, Katie. "Women's Work and Social Network Use in Oaxaca City, Mexico." *Bulletin of Latin American Research [UK]* 12, Number 1 (January 1993): 65–82.

Winter, Mary, et al. "Planning and Implementation in the Informal Sector: Evidence from Oaxaca, Mexico." *City and Society* 4, Number 2 (December 1990): 131–143.

———. "The Health Status of Women in Oaxaca: Determinants and Consequences." *Social Science and Medicine* 37, Number 11 (1993): 1351–1358.

Puebla

Colonial Era (1532–1820)

Albi Romero, Guadalupe. *La sociedad de Puebla de los Angeles en el siglo XVI.* Cologne, Germany, 1970.

Aranda Romero, José Luis, and Miguel Angel Cuenya. "El mundo del trabajo en una parroquia de Puebla a través de los libros matrimoniales, 1640–1910." *Siglo XIX [Mexico]* 4, Number 7 (1989): 177–217.

Bazant, Jan. "The Evolution of the Textile Industry in Puebla, 1544–1845." *Comparative Studies in Society and History [UK]* 7, Number 1 (1964): 56–69 and Spanish translation in *Historia Mexicana* 13, Number 52 (April–June 1964): 473–516.

Bonet Correa, Antonio. *Retablos del siglo XVII en Puebla.* Madrid, 1963.

Borah, Woodrow. "Archivo de la Secretaria Municipal de Puebla: guía para la consulta de sus materiales." *Boletín del AGNM,* Primera Serie, Vol. 13, Number 2 (April–June 1942): 207–239; Number 3 (July–September 1942): 423–464.

Castro Morales, Efraín. *Francisco Becerra en el Valle de Puebla, México.* Buenos Aires, 1960.

———. *Origen de algunos artistas y artesanos europeos en la región de Puebla-Tlaxcala.* Puebla, 1973.

Chevalier, François. *La significación social de la fundación de Puebla de los Angeles.* Puebla, 1957.

Fee, Nancy H. "*La entrada angelopolitana:* Ritual and Myth in the Viceregal Entry in Puebla de los Angeles." *Americas: A Quarterly Review of Inter-American Cultural History* 52, Number 3 (1996): 283–320.

Hirschberg, Julia. "Social Experiment in New Spain: A Prosopographical Study of the Early Settlement at Puebla de los Angeles, 1531–1534." *Hispanic American Historical Review* 51, Number 1 (1979): 1–33.

Liehr, Reinhard. *Ayuntamiento y oligarquía en Puebla, 1787–1810.* Mexico City, 1976.

Lipsett-Rivera, Sonia. "Water and Bureaucracy in Colonial Puebla de los Angeles." *Journal of Latin American Studies [UK]* 25, Number 1 (1993): 25–44.

———. *To Defend Our Water with the Blood of Our Veins: The Struggle for Resources in Colonial Puebla.* Albuquerque: University of New Mexico Press, 1999.

López de Villaseñor, Pedro. *Cartilla vieja de la nobilísima ciudad de Puebla.* Mexico City, 1961.

Martín Tamayo, Fausto. *La división racial en Puebla de los Angeles bajo el régimen colonial.* Puebla, 1960.

Thomson, Guy P. C. *Puebla de los Angeles: Industry and Society in a Mexican City, 1700–1850.* Boulder: Westview, 1989.

Toussaint, Manuel. *La catedral y las iglesias de Puebla.* Mexico City: Porrúa, 1954.

Zerón Zapata, Miguel. *La Puebla de los Angeles en el siglo XVII.* Mexico City, 1945.

Early Maps and Depictions of Puebla, 1533–1863

Pictographic map of the city and its district by Nicolás de Zamudio, 1533—original held as Illustration 4129 of the Archivo General de la Nación in Mexico City, photographic negative 979/0636 [archival provenance: *Civil,* Volume 1276, Folio 103]

Map by the presbyter Cristóbal de Guadalajara of Puebla and its surroundings, June 1698—original held by the Archive of Indies at Seville, old Torres Lanzas call number: Mapas y Planos de México, 688

Crude colored map on parchment, identifying some properties in Puebla, 1701—original held as Illustration 654 of the Archivo General de la Nación in Mexico City, photographic negative 977/0853 [archival provenance: *Tierras,* Volume 188, Expediente 9, Folio 45]

Crude colored map of the suburb of San Juan Guautinchán, 1704—original held as Illustration 655 of the Archivo General de la Nación in Mexico City, photographic negative 977/0854 [archival provenance: *Tierras,* Volume 190, Expediente 1, Folio 188]

Four diagrams of different houses in Puebla's San Sebastián section, 1727—originals held as Illustrations 1026–1029 of the Archivo General de la Nación in Mexico City, photographic negatives 977/1175.1, 977/1175.3, 977/1175.4, and 977/1175.5 [archival provenance: *Tierras,* Volume 1427, Expediente 18, Folios 8 and 10–12]

Crude sketch of a property in Puebla, signed by the notary public José Montes Gallo, 1728—original held as Illustration 2880 of the Archivo General de la Nación in Mexico City, photographic negative 978/2008 [archival provenance: *Vínculos,* Volume 115, Folio 448]

Diagram by José Eduardo de Herrera of a private residence in the city, 1735—original held as Illustration 4786 of the Archivo General de la Nación in Mexico City, photographic negative 979/2726 [archival provenance: *Bienes Nacionales,* Legajo 1687, Expediente 7, Folio 149]

Diagram of a city brickyard, 1749—original held as Illustration 598 of the Archivo General de la Nación in Mexico City, photographic negative 977/0796 [archival provenance: *Tierras,* Volume 68, Expediente 4, Folio 187]

Highly detailed map of Puebla, drawn in 1754 by José Mariano de Medina, and engraved by José Ortíz Carnero—original held as Illustration 1538 of the Archivo General de la Nación in Mexico City, photographic negative 978/0174 [archival provenance: *Tierras,* Volume 2673, Expediente 1, Folio 19], plus other sources

Diagram and profile view of the Purísima Concepción Church, by the *maestro mayor de arquitectura* José Miguel de Santa María, 1754—original held as Illustration 3126 of the Archivo General de la Nación in Mexico City, photographic negative 978/1788 [archival provenance: *Templos y Conventos,* Volume 2, Folio 173]

Diagrams by Santa María of the city poorhouse and orphanage, 1754—originals held as Illustrations 3127–3128 of the Archivo General de la Nación in Mexico City, photographic negatives 978/1789 and 978/1790 [archival provenance: *Templos y Conventos,* Volume 2, Folios 174 and 224]

Diagram by Vicente de Bargas of the Colegio del Espíritu Santo, 1767—original held as Illustration 3128.1 of the Archivo General de la Nación in Mexico City, photographic negative 979/2050 [archival provenance: Mapoteca]

Drawing of the new public market, 1779—original held as Illustration 4344 of the Archivo General de la Nación in Mexico City, call number: 978/2018 [archival provenance: *Ayuntamientos,* Volume 118, Folio 122]

Diagrams of a two-story residence, surveyed by the architect Francisco Antonio Guerrero Torres in 1780—originals held as Illustrations 2946–2947 of the Archivo General de la Nación in Mexico City, photographic negatives 978/1587 and 978/1588 [archival provenance: *Vínculos,* Volume 266, Expediente 4, Folios 46–47]

Three diagrams by the scribe José Ignacio del Castillo, detailing changes to a private residence, 1788—originals held as Illustrations 4102–4104 of the Archivo General de la Nación in Mexico City, photographic negatives 979/0615, 979/0616, and 979/0617 [archival provenance: *Civil,* Volume 349, Folios 129–131]

Diagram of "Nuestra Señora del Buen Suceso" Orchard in Puebla, 1791—original held as Illustration 4605 of the

Archivo General de la Nación in Mexico City, photographic negative 979/1084 [archival provenance: *Alcabalas,* Volume 21, Expediente 72, Folio 26]

Map of the city, drawn in 1794 by Francisco de la Rosa on orders from the Viceroy Marqués de Branciforte and engraved two years later by José de Nava—originals held as Illustration 3183 of the Archivo General de la Nación in Mexico City (photographic negative 978/2021) and the Archive of Indies at Seville, old Torres Lanzas call number: Mapas y Planos de México, 457

Diagrams by Gerónimo Morales, of a proposed expansion to the *Real Fábrica de la Contaduría de Tabaco,* 1797—original held as Illustration 3794.1 of the Archivo General de la Nación in Mexico City, photographic negative 980/3570 [archival provenance: *Intendencias,* Volume 45, Expediente 3, Folio 4]

Diagram by Ignacio Domenech, of a new street-paving method, 1798—original held as Illustration 4216.1 of the Archivo General de la Nación in Mexico City, photographic negative 979/1830 [archival provenance: *Policía,* Volume 6, Folio 299]

Diagram and frontal view of the Loreto *garita* or "sentry station" by Antonio Santa María Inchaurregui, 1803—original held as Illustration 4643 of the Archivo General de la Nación in Mexico City, photographic negative 979/1118 [archival provenance: *Alcabalas,* Volume 620, Expediente 52, Folio 10]

Diagram by José Ignacio Ramírez, of a *solar* or "lot" in Quintanilla Street, 1845—original held as Illustration 3468 of the Archivo General de la Nación in Mexico City, photographic negative 978/2159 [archival provenance: *Justicia Eclesiástico,* Volume 150, Folio 58]

Map of the roads radiating southwest from the city, 1855—original held as Illustration 3609 of the Archivo General de la Nación in Mexico City, photographic negative 979/0150 [archival provenance: *Fomento Caminos,* Volume 32, Folio 91]

Lithograph of the French siege, spring 1863—original held as Illustration 4935 of the Archivo General de la Nación in Mexico City, photographic negative 980/1573 [archival provenance: *Fondo Reservado Segundo Imperio,* Segundo Estante, Caja 4, Expediente 3]

Independence Era (1821–1910)

Bazant, Jan. "La iglesia, el estado y la sublevación conservadora de Puebla en 1856." *Historia Mexicana* 35, Number 1 (1985): 93–109.

Colín Sánchez, Guillermo. *Ignacio Zaragoza: evocación de un héroe.* Mexico City: Porrúa, 1963.

Fredriksen, John C. "Colonel Childs and His Quadrant: Reflections on the Career of a Distinguished American Soldier." *Military Collector and Historian* 39, Number 3 (1987): 122–125.

Lanusse, Jean-Efrem. *Los vencidos del 5 de mayo.* Mexico City: Fondo de Cultura Económica, 1973 translation by Marte R. Gómez from the French original *Les vaincus du 5 mai.*

Palou, Pedro Angel. *5 de mayo 1862.* Puebla: Heroico Ayuntamiento, 1994.

Ramos y Ortega, Patricio. "Descripción de la batalla ganada al ejército francés en el Cerro de Guadalupe de Puebla el día lunes 5 de mayo de 1862." *Memorias de la Academia Mexicana de la Historia* 3, Number 4 (October–December 1944): 468–489.

Sánchez Lamego, Miguel A. "Fortificación de Puebla." *Historia Mexicana* 11, Number 4 (April–June 1962): 519–526.

———. *La batalla del 5 de mayo.* Mexico City: Sección de Historia de la Sociedad Mexicana de Geografía y Estadística, 1963.

Sommers, Laurie Kay. "Symbol and Style in Cinco de Mayo." *Journal of American Folklore* 98, Number 390 (1985): 476–482.

Téllez Guerrero, Francisco, and Elvia Brito Martínez. "La hacienda municipal de Puebla en el siglo XIX." *Historia Mexicana* 39, Number 4 (1990): 951–978.

Torres Bautista, Mariano E. "De la fiesta monárquica a la fiesta civica: el tránsito del poder en Puebla, 1821–1822." *Historia Mexicana* 45, Number 2 (1995): 221–239.

Vaughn, Mary Kay. "Primary Schooling in the City of Puebla, 1821–1860." *Hispanic American Historical Review* 67, Number 1 (1987): 39–62.

Winders, Richard B. "Puebla's Forgotten Heroes." *Military History of the West* 24, Number 1 (1994): 1–23.

Modern Era and General Works (1911–Present)

Carrasco Puente, Rafael. *Puebla: azulejo mexicano.* Puebla: Ayuntamiento Constitucional, 1971.

Castro Morales, Efraín. *Breve historia de la Universidad de Puebla.* Puebla, 1958.

———. *Desarrollo urbano de la Ciudad de Puebla.* Puebla, 1966.

Fuchs, M. "Puebla: Auswirkungen der Wirtschaftskrise 1994/95 in einer mexikanischen Stadt." *Geographische Rundschau* 51, Numbers 7–8 (1999): 388–392.

Gamboa Ojeda, Leticia. "La epidemia de influenza de 1918: sanidad y política en la Ciudad de Puebla." *Quipú [Mexico]* 8, Number 1 (1991): 91–109.

Germain, Annick, and Mario Polèse. "La structure sociorésidentielle de Puebla, Mexique: essai d'écologie urbaine." *Cahiers de géographie du Québec [Canada]* 39, Number 107 (September 1995): 309–333.

Jones, Gareth A. "The Commercialisation of the Land Market: Land Ownership Patterns in the Mexican City of Puebla." *Third World Planning Review* 13, Number 2 (1991): 129–153.

Jones, Gareth A., and Ann Varley. "The Contest for the City Centre: Street Traders Versus Buildings." *Bulletin of Latin American Research [UK]* 13, Number 1 (1994): 27–44.

———. "The Reconquest of the Historic Centre: Urban Conservation and Gentrification in Puebla, Mexico." *Environment and Planning* 31, Number 9 (1999): 1547–1566.

LaFrance, David G. "Germany, Revolutionary Nationalism, and the Downfall of President Francisco I. Madero: The Covadonga Killings." *Mexican Studies/Estudios Mexicanos* 2, Number 1 (1986): 53–82.

Melé, P. "Cartographier l'illégalité: filières de production de l'espace urbain de la ville de Puebla." *Espace géographique* 17, Number 4 (1988): 257–263.

———. *Puebla: urbanización y políticas urbanas.* Mexico City: Benemérita Universidad Autónoma de Puebla and Universidad Autónoma Metropolitana, 1994.

Palacios, Enrique Juan. *Puebla: su territorio y sus habitantes.* Mexico City, 1917.

Percaz, María. "Fragmentos de vida cotidiana en México: historia de una vecindad." *Historia y Vida [Spain]* 24, Number 277 (1991): 86–90.

Polèse, Mario, et al. "Développement et forme urbaine: le déplacement de l'activité commerciale et industrielle dans la ville de Puebla." *Canadian Journal of Development Studies* 16, Number 1 (1995): 105–130.

"Puebla." *Artes de México* 13, Numbers 81–82 (1966), entire volume.

Toussaint, Manuel. *La Catedral y las iglesias de Puebla.* Mexico City, 1965.

Vanderbush, W. "Assessing Democracy in Puebla: The Opposition Takes Charge of Municipal Government." *Journal of Interamerican Studies and World Affairs* 41, Number 2 (1999): 1–27.

Veracruz

Colonial Era (1519–1821)

Archer, Christon I. "The Key to the Kingdom: The Defense of Veracruz, 1780–1810." *The Americas: A Quarterly Review of Inter-American Cultural History [Academy of American Franciscan History]* 27, Number 4 (1971): 426–449.

Booker, Jackie R. "The Veracruz Merchant Community in Late Bourbon Mexico: A Preliminary Portrait, 1770–1810." *The Americas: A Quarterly Review of Inter-American Cultural History [Academy of American Franciscan History]* 45, Number 2 (1988): 187–199.

———. "Needed but Unwanted: Black Militiamen in Veracruz, Mexico, 1760–1810." *Historian* 55, Number 2 (1992): 259–276.

———. *Veracruz Merchants, 1770–1829: A Mercantile Elite in Late Bourbon and Early Independent Mexico.* Boulder: Westview, 1993.

Carrera Stampa, Manuel. "Las ferias novohispanas." *Historia Mexicana* 2 (1953): 319–342.

Carroll, Patrick J. *Blacks in Colonial Veracruz: Race, Ethnicity, and Regional Development.* Austin: University of Texas Press, 1991.

Chaunu, Pierre. "Veracruz en la segunda mitad del siglo XVI y primera del XVII." *Historia Mexicana* 9, Number 4 (April–June 1960): 521–557.

Corral, Miguel del. *Las fortificaciones de Veracruz en 1786.* Mexico City: Citlaltepetl, 1965 reprint of eighteenth-century original.

Cuenca Esteban, Javier. "Statistics of Spain's Colonial Trade, 1792–1820: Consular Duties, Cargo Inventories, and Balances of Trade." *Hispanic American Historical Review* 61, Number 3 (1981): 381–428.

González, Juan José. *Documentos coloniales de la Nueva Veracruz.* Veracruz, 1943.

Juárez Moreno, Juan. *Piratas y corsarios en Veracruz y Campeche.* Seville: Escuela de Estudios Hispano-americanos, 1972.

Knaut, Andrew L. "Yellow Fever and the Late Colonial Public Health Response in the Port of Veracruz." *Hispanic American Historical Review* 77, Number 4 (1997): 619–644.

Lerdo de Tejada, Miguel. *La fortaleza de San Juan de Ulúa.* Mexico City: Citlaltepetl, 1961 reprint.

Lewis, Michael. "Fresh Light on San Juan de Ullua." *The Mariner's Mirror* 23 (July 1937): 295–315.

Marley, David F. *Sack of Veracruz: The Great Pirate Raid of 1683.* Windsor, ON: Netherlandic Press, 1993.

McCormack, Richard Blaine. "Juárez y la armada norteamericana." *Historia Mexicana* 6, Number 4 (1956–1957): 493–509.

"Oficios del Consulado de Veracruz: capitulación de la ciudad el 26 de octubre de 1821." *Revista de Historia Militar [Spain]* 34, Number 68 (1990): 225–228.

Ortíz de la Tabla Ducasse, L. Javier. *Comercio exterior de Veracruz, 1778–1821: crisis de dependencia.* Seville: Escuela de Estudios Hispano-americanos, 1978.

Ortíz de la Tabla Ducasse, L. Javier, compiler. *Memorias políticas y económicas del Consulado de Veracruz, 1796–1822.* Seville: Escuela de Estudios Hispano-americanos, 1985.

Paso y Troncoso, Francisco del. "Descripción de la Ciudad de Tablas." *Anales del Museo Nacional de Arqueología,*

Historia y Etnografía [Mexico] 1, Fourth Series (1922): 369–388.

Probert, Alan. "Mules, Men and Mining Machinery: Transport on the Veracruz Road." *Journal of the West* 14, Number 2 (1975): 104–113.

Smith, Robert S. "Shipping in the Port of Veracruz, 1790–1821." *Hispanic American Historical Review* 23, Number 1 (1943): 5–20.

Staples, Anne. "Veracruz alrededor de 1821." *Secuencia [Mexico]* 8 (1987): 5–15.

Tatum, Jim C., editor. "Veracruz en 1816–1817: fragmento del diario de Antonio López Matoso." *Historia Mexicana* 73 (1969): 105–124.

Unwin, Rayner. *The Defeat of John Hawkins: A Biography of His Third Slaving Voyage.* London: Allen and Unwin, 1960.

Early Maps and Depictions of Veracruz, 1582–1806

Two crude diagrams of Antigua Veracruz's main church, 1582—originals held as Illustrations 4865.1 and 4865.2 of the Archivo General de la Nación in Mexico City, photographic negatives 980/2479 and 980/2480 [archival provenance: *Inquisición,* Volume 385, Folios 166–167]

Crude depiction of Antigua Veracruz, the island-fortress of San Juan de Ulúa, and the Ventas de Buitrón, as reproduced in a 1585–1590 Spanish sea-atlas—original held by the Library of the Real Academia de la Historia in Madrid, call number: Colección Muñoz, Number 94, Folio 54

Chart of San Juan de Ulúa by the Italian-born royal engineer Batista Antonelli, plus a proposed new mainland city-site at Ventas de Buitrón opposite, January 1590—original held by the Archive of Indies at Seville, old Torres Lanzas call number: Mapas y Planos de México y Floridas, 35 [archival provenance: Audiencia de México, Legajo 257]

Diagram by Capt. Pedro Ochoa de Leguízamo of a proposed new city opposite San Juan de Ulúa and a road leading inland toward Mexico City, February 1590—original held by the Archive of Indies at Seville, old Torres Lanzas call number: Mapas y Planos de México y Floridas, 38 [archival provenance: Audiencia de México, Legajo 257]

Crude depiction of Veracruz's harbor by Nicolás de Cardona, 1614—original held by the Biblioteca Nacional in Madrid, call number: Manuscritos de América 2468

Panoramic view of the city and harbor, ca. 1621–1622, based upon a drawing by the Dutch-born engineer Adrian Boot—print commissioned late in the nineteenth century by the Mexican historian Francisco del

Paso y Troncoso and executed by the Florentine engraver Alejandro Ruffoni

Seventeenth-century drawing of the city, as seen from San Juan de Ulúa—original held by the Bibliothèque Nationale in Paris, call number: Cartes et Plans 141, 6, 1

Two maps by the Flemish-born engineer Marcos Lucio, of proposed improvements to the city's defensive perimeter, November 1663—originals held by the Archive of Indies at Seville, old Torres Lanzas call numbers: Mapas y Planos de México y Floridas, 58 and 59 [archival provenance: Audiencia de México, Legajo 39]

Two maps from a survey conducted by the military engineer Francisco Pozuelo y Espinosa on 13–20 August 1683, of defensive improvements after the devastating pirate raid—originals held by the Archive of Indies at Seville, old Torres Lanzas call numbers: Mapas y Planos de México y Floridas, 74 and 75 [archival provenance: Patronato Real, Legajo 243, Ramo 1]

Diagram by the German-born military engineer Capt. Jaime Franck, of a proposed new mainland fortress, July 1689—original held by the Archive of Indies at Seville, old Torres Lanzas call number: Mapas y Planos de México y Floridas, 85 [archival provenance: Audiencia de México, Legajo 60]

Chart of the harbor approaches, sounded during the May–June 1702 visit by French Vice Adm. François-Louis Rousselet, Comte de Château-Renault—original held by the Bibliothèque Nationale in Paris, call number: Cartes et Plans 141, 6, 6

Sketch of the city and San Juan de Ulúa, drawn during a September 1705 visit by the French slaver Des Marchais—original held by the Bibliothèque Nationale in Paris, call number: Cartes et Plans 141, 6, 7

Eight maps, diagrams, and cutaway views by Felipe León Maffey of proposed improvements to the city defenses, 1726–1727—originals held as Illustrations 376–383 of the Archivo General de la Nación in Mexico City, photographic negatives 977/0364 through 0372 [archival provenance: *Historia,* Volume 362, Expediente 1, Folios 1–2, 107, 119, 171–172, 184, and 228]

Map by the military engineer Lt. Col. Félix Prosperi, of proposed improvements to Veracruz's anchorage, April 1737—original held by the Servicio Geográfico del Ejército in Madrid, call number: LM-8.[a]–1.[a]-a–55

Map by Prosperi of proposed improvements to the city defenses, 1741—original held by the Servicio Geográfico del Ejército in Madrid, call number: LM-8.[a]–1.[a]-a–45

Profile view and diagram by Prosperi of proposed repairs and improvements to the city jetty, December 1748—original held by the Servicio Geográfico del Ejército in Madrid, call number: LM-8.[a]–1.[a]-a–54

Anonymous map, showing the city during the mid-eighteenth century—original held by the Biblioteca Nacional in Madrid

Chart of Veracruz's harbor, as sounded by the naval Capt. Francisco de Villafranca, May 1751—original held by the Archive of Indies at Seville, old Torres Lanzas call number: Mapas y Planos de México y Floridas, 181 [archival provenance: Audiencia de México, Legajo 2447]

Harbor chart as sounded in December 1756 by the pilot Tomás González—original held as Illustration 391 of the Archivo General de la Nación in Mexico City, photographic negative 977/0380 [archival provenance: Historia, Volume 363, Folio 156]

Profile views and diagram by the military engineer Carlos Luxán of a proposed new city jetty, March 1757—original held by the Servicio Geográfico del Ejército in Madrid, call number: LM-8.ª-1.ª-a-56

Cutaway view and two diagrams by the military engineer Brig. Lorenzo de Solís, of a proposed new city barracks, 1758—originals held as Illustrations 302–304 of the Archivo General de la Nación in Mexico City, photographic negatives 977/0288 to 0290 [archival provenance: Historia, Volume 165, Expediente 12, Folios 314–316]

Cutaway views by De Solís of a proposed sea-wall, 1758–1759—originals held as Illustrations 386 and 392 of the Archivo General de la Nación in Mexico City, photographic negatives 977/0375 and 977/0381 [archival provenance: Historia, Volume 363, Folios 148 and 263]

Diagram by De Solís of suggested improvements to the Contaduría waterfront, 1759—original held as Illustration 393 of the Archivo General de la Nación in Mexico City, photographic negative 977/0382 [archival provenance: Historia, Volume 363, Folio 264]

Diagrams by De Solís of the new Concepción Bastion at La Caleta, on the city's northwestern tip, 1759—originals held as Illustrations 404–405 of the Archivo General de la Nación in Mexico City, photographic negatives 977/0393 and 0394 [archival provenance: Historia, Volume 366, Folios 178–179]

Detailed map of the city and harbor by the military engineer Agustín López de la Cámara-Alta, April 1763—original held by the Archive of Indies at Seville, old Torres Lanzas call number: Mapas y Planos de México y Floridas, 220 [archival provenance: Audiencia de México, Legajo 2451]

Diagram by the engineer and architect Manuel de Santiestevan of a proposed new infantry barracks for the northwestern corner of the city, 1763—original held as Illustration 301 of the Archivo General de la Nación in Mexico City, photographic negative 977/0287 [archival provenance: Historia, Volume 165, Expediente 11, Folio 296]

Diagrams by the military engineers Felipe Feringán Cortés and Ricardo Aylmer, of the best site for a proposed new infantry barracks in the northwestern corner of the city, April–May 1764—originals held as Illustrations 305–306 of the Archivo General de la Nación in Mexico City, photographic negatives 977/0292 and 0293 [archival provenance: Historia, Volume 165, Expediente 12, Folios 336–337]

Pen-and-ink map with watercolor highlights by the military engineer Pedro Ponze, of Gov. Félix Ferráz's proposed strengthening of city defenses, September 1764—original held by the Archive of Indies at Seville, old Torres Lanzas call number: Mapas y Planos de México y Floridas, 224 [archival provenance: Audiencia de México, Legajo 2459]

Map with watercolor highlights of Veracruz's coastline in November 1764, by the plate-fleet Commo. Marqués de Casinas of the warship Dragón—original held by the Archivo General de Simancas in Spain, call number: Mapas, Planos y Dibujos, VII-153 [archival provenance: Marina, Legajo 391]

Diagram plus cutaway views by De Santiestevan, of a proposed new royal warehouse for storing timbers, 1764—original held as Illustration 394 of the Archivo General de la Nación in Mexico City, photographic negative 977/0383 [archival provenance: Historia, Volume 365, Expediente 1, Folio 29]

Diagrams and cutaway view of sheds to house boats and timbers in Veracruz's naval arsenal, 1764—originals held as Illustrations 3412–3413 of the Archivo General de la Nación in Mexico City, photographic negatives 978/1882 and 1883 [archival provenance: Indiferente de Guerra, Volume 506A, Folios 79 and 81]

Pen-and-ink maps with watercolor highlights by De Santiestevan, of suggested improvements to city defenses, August 1765—originals held by the Archive of Indies at Seville, old Torres Lanzas call numbers: Mapas y Planos de México y Floridas, 228 and 229 [archival provenance: Audiencia de México, Legajo 2459]

Two diagrams by De Santiestevan of a proposed new military hospital, 1766—originals held as Illustrations 4251 and 4252 of the Archivo General de la Nación in Mexico City, photographic negatives 979/0745 and 0746 [archival provenance: Hospitales, Volume 23, Folios 124–125]

Diagram by De Santiestevan of a proposed expansion of the Loreto Hospital, 1766—original held as Illustration 4253 of the Archivo General de la Nación in Mexico City, photographic negative 979/0747 [archival provenance: Hospitales, Volume 23, Folio 163]

Diagram by De Santiestevan of a proposed "San Joaquín, María y José Hospital," which was never built, 1767—original held as Illustration 4254 of the Archivo General de la Nación in Mexico City, photographic negative 979/0748 [archival provenance: *Hospitales,* Volume 57, Expediente 1, Folio 4]

Diagram by De Santiestevan of the storm-damaged southeastern section of the city sea-wall, November 1779—original held as Illustration 3424 of the Archivo General de la Nación in Mexico City, photographic negative 979/0038 [archival provenance: *Correspondencia de Diversas Autoridades,* Volume 33, Folio 188]

Map by the military engineer Miguel del Corral of Veracruz's district, plus major travel routes leading inland, 1784—original held as Illustration 3543 of the Archivo General de la Nación in Mexico City, photographic negative 979/0084 [archival provenance: *Fomento Caminos,* Volume 1, Folio 91]

Pen-and-ink map with watercolor highlights by Del Corral, of Veracruz and its anchorage, May 1786—original held by the Servicio Histórico Militar in Madrid, call number: P-b–11–33 or 5012, hoja 1/D.10–6

Map by Del Corral of Veracruz's district as far inland as Córdoba and Jalapa, 1787—original held as Illustration 3420 of the Archivo General de la Nación in Mexico City, photographic negative 978/1901 [archival provenance: *Indiferente de Guerra,* Volume 452-A, Last Folio]

Diagram and cutaway view by Del Corral of the artillery repair shop, 1790—original held as Illustration 3369 of the Archivo General de la Nación in Mexico City, photographic negative 978/1838 [archival provenance: *Indiferente de Guerra,* Volume 443-A, Folio 141]

Map of the port and its approaches in 1795–1796, attributed to Bernardo Orta—original held by the Archive of Indies at Seville, old Torres Lanzas call number: Mapas y Planos de México y Floridas, 458 [archival provenance: Audiencia de México, Legajo 2995]

Diagram of San Agustín el Viejo Convent by the *maestro alarife* or "master mason" Francisco de los Reyes, 1796—original held as Illustration 3163 in the Archivo General de la Nación of Mexico City, photographic negative 978/1823 [archival provenance: *Templos y Conventos,* Volume 29, Folio 6]

Diagram by Luis del Toral of a proposed boat-house to shelter eighteen armed coast guard launches, 1797—original held as Illustration 375 of the Archivo General de la Nación in Mexico City, photographic negative 977/0363 [archival provenance: *Historia,* Volume 360, Expediente 1, Folio 3]

French map of the city and its surroundings in 1798, by the military engineer George de Bois St. Lys—original held by the Library of Congress in Washington, call number: G 4414.V46 1798.B6 Vault

Diagrams by De los Reyes of the upper and lower floors of a *nevería* or "ice shop," 1798—originals held as Illustrations 335–336 of the Archivo General de la Nación in Mexico City, photographic negatives 977/0322 and 0323 [archival provenance: *Historia,* Volume 292, Expediente 1, Folios 356–357]

Diagram, plus exterior and cutaway views by Manuel Agustín Mascaró, of a militia barracks, 1798—original held as Illustration 3399 of the Archivo General de la Nación in Mexico City, photographic negative 978/1868 [archival provenance: *Indiferente de Guerra,* Volume 475-A, Folio 96]

Diagram and cutaway view by the military engineer Juan José de León, of the old Regimiento de Castilla barracks, 1799—original held as Illustration 3406 of the Archivo General de la Nación in Mexico City, photographic negative 978/1875 [archival provenance: *Indiferente de Guerra,* Volume 477-A, Folio 277]

Highly detailed map of the city, drawn by Mascaró in March 1800 to demonstrate its proposed expansion—original held by the Archive of Indies at Seville, old Torres Lanzas call number: Mapas y Planos de México y Floridas, 479 [archival provenance: Audiencia de México, Legajo 1815]

Survey maps by Miguel María Márquez and Manuel López Bueno, of the district outside the city, 1802—originals held as Illustrations 2196 and 2197 of the Archivo General de la Nación in Mexico City, photographic negatives 987/0834 and 0835 [archival provenance: *Tierras,* Volume 2788, Expediente 1, Folios 13–14]

Diagram by Miguel Costansó of a guardhouse at Veracruz's sea-gate, 1802—original held as Illustration 521 of the Archivo General de la Nación in Mexico City, photographic negative 977/0677 [archival provenance: *Marina,* Volume 143, Folio 409]

Cutaway view by Costansó of the sea-wall, 1804—original held as Illustration 408 of the Archivo General de la Nación in Mexico City, photographic negative 977/0397 [archival provenance: *Historia,* Volume 369, Folio 123]

Diagram and cutaway view by Mascaró of the sea-wall opposite La Contaduría, 1806—original held as Illustration 3415 of the Archivo General de la Nación in Mexico City, photographic negative 978/1885 [archival provenance: *Indiferente de Guerra,* Volume 510, Folio 70]

American Invasion (1847–1848)

Bauer, Karl Jack. *Surfboats and Horse Marines: U.S. Naval Operations in the Mexican War, 1846–48.* Annapolis: U.S. Naval Institute Press, 1969.

McCaffrey, James M., and George Sanders, editors. "America's First D-Day: The Veracruz Landing of 1847." *Military History of the West* 25, Number 1 (1995): 51–68.

Mulligan, Robert E., Jr. "Letters from a Mexican War Deserter." *Military Collector and Historian* 34, Number 4 (1982): 167.

Smith, Robert P., Jr. "Impossible Campaign Attempted." *Military History* 10, Number 1 (1993): 92–96.

Revolutionary Era and American Reoccupation (1910–1914)

Alexander, J. H. "Roots of Deployment: Vera Cruz, 1914." *Marine Corps Gazette* 66, Number 11 (1982): 71–79.

Blásquez Domínguez, Carmen. "Siglo XIX y revolución en Veracruz: una bibliografía básica." *Secuencia [Mexico]* 6 (1986): 61–98.

Foreman, Michael A. "A Storm in Veracruz." *American History Illustrated* 29, Number 1 (1994): 28–37 and 72.

Haverstock, Mike. "Waiting in Veracruz, 1914." *Américas [Organization of American States]* 35, Number 6 (1983): 34–39.

Owsley, Frank L., Jr., and Wesley Phillip Newton. "Eyes in the Skies." *U.S. Naval Institute Proceedings* (1986 Supplement): 17–25.

Pasquel, Leonardo. *La generación liberal veracruzana.* Mexico City: Citlaltepetl, 1972.

———. *La Revolución en el Estado de Veracruz.* Mexico City: Instituto Nacional de Estudios Históricos de la Revolución Mexicana, 1972.

Quirk, Robert. *An Affair of Honor: Woodrow Wilson and the Occupation of Veracruz.* New York: Norton, 1962.

Sweetman, Jack. *Landing at Veracruz, 1914: The First Complete Chronicle of a Strange Encounter in April 1914, When the United States Navy Captured and Occupied the City of Veracruz, Mexico.* Annapolis: U.S. Naval Institute Press, 1968.

Vanderwood, Paul J. "The Picture Postcard as Historical Evidence: Veracruz, 1914." *The Americas: A Quarterly Review of Inter-American Cultural History [Academy of American Franciscan History]* 45, Number 2 (1988): 201–225.

Modern Era and General Works (1914–Present)

Blásquez Domínguez, Carmen, editor. *Estado de Veracruz: informes de sus gobernadores, 1826–1986.* Jalapa: Estado de Veracruz, 1986, twelve volumes.

Cortés Rodríguez, Martha. "Bailes y carnaval en Veracruz, 1925." *Horizonte: Revista del Instituto Veracruzano de Cultura [Mexico]* 1, Number 1 (March–April 1991): 19–25.

Domínguez, Rafael. *Veracruz en el ensueño y en el recuerdo.* Mexico City, 1946.

Domínguez Pérez, Olivia. *Política y movimientos sociales en el tejedismo.* Jalapa: Universidad Veracruzana, 1986.

Falcón, Romana, and Soledad García Morales. *La semilla en el surco: Adalberto Tejeda y el radicalismo en Veracruz, 1883–1960.* Mexico City: El Colegio de México, 1986.

Franklin, Stuart. "Veracruz: Gateway to the World." *National Geographic* 190, Number 2 (August 1996): 62–69.

García Díaz, Bernardo. *Puerto de Veracruz, Veracruz: imágenes de su historia.* Jalapa: Archivo General del Estado de Veracruz, 1992.

García Mundo, Octavio. *El movimiento inquilinario de Veracruz, 1922.* Mexico City: Series "Sep-Setentas" published by the Secretaría de Educación Pública or SEP, 1976.

Loza, Steven J. "Origins, Form, and Development of the *Son Jarocho:* Veracruz, Mexico." *Aztlán* 13, Numbers 1–2 (1982): 257–274.

Lozano y Nathal, Gema. *Catálogo del archivo sindical del puerto de Veracruz "Miguel Angel Montoya Cortés."* Mexico City: "Fuentes" Collection of the Instituto Nacional de Antropología e Historia or INAH, 1990.

Mancisidor Ortiz, Anselmo. *Jarochilandia.* Veracruz: Self-published, 1971.

Martínez Muñoz, Eugenio. *Los mártires de San Juan de Ulúa.* Mexico City: Instituto de Estudios Históricos de la Revolución Mexicana, 1969.

Melgarejo Vivanco, José Luis. *Breve historia de Veracruz.* Jalapa: Universidad Veracruzana, 1960.

Olivio Lara, Margarita. *Biografías de veracruzanos distinguidos.* Mexico City: Museo Nacional, 1931.

Pasquel, Leonardo. *La ciudad de Veracruz.* Mexico City: 1958, two volumes.

———. *Cincuenta distinguidos veracruzanos.* Mexico City: Citlaltepetl, 1975.

Rees, Peter W. *Transportes y comercio entre México y Veracruz, 1519–1910.* Mexico City: Series "Sep-Setentas" published by the Secretaría de Educación Pública or SEP, 1976.

Siemens, Alfred H. *Between the Summit and the Sea: Central Veracruz in the Nineteenth Century.* Vancouver: University of British Columbia Press, 1990.

Toussaint, Manuel. "Ensayo sobre los planos de la Ciudad de Veracruz." *Anales del Instituto de Investigaciones Estéticas [Mexico]* 15 (1947).

Trens, Manuel B. *Historia de la Heroica Ciudad de Veracruz y de su ayuntamiento.* Mexico City: Enríquez, 1947–1955, six volumes.

Ulloa, Berta. *Veracruz, capital de la nación, 1914–1915.* Mexico City: El Colegio de México, 1986.

"Veracruz: 450 aniversario." *Artes de México* 15, Number 116 (1969), entire volume.

Veracruz: primer puerto del continente. Mexico City: Secretaría de Patrimonio Nacional, 1975.

Wilkerson, Jeffrey K. "Man's Eighty Centuries in Veracruz." *National Geographic* 158, Number 2 (1980): 203–231.

Williams García, Roberto. *Yo nací con la luna de plata: antropología e historia de un puerto.* Mexico City: Costa-Amic, 1980.

Zacatecas

Colonial Era (1546–1821)

Ahumada Sámano, Pedro de. *Relación de los zacatecos y guachichiles, 1562.* Mexico City, 1952.

Alberro, Solange B. de. "Zacatecas, 'zone frontière,' d'après les documents d'Inquisition, XVIe et XVIIe siècles." *Cahiers des Amériques latines [France]* 24 (1981): 185–219.

Bakewell, Peter J. *Silver Mining and Society in Colonial Mexico: Zacatecas, 1546–1700.* Cambridge, NY: Cambridge University Press, 1971.

Brading, David A. "Mexican Silver-Mining in the Eighteenth Century: The Revival of Zacatecas." *Hispanic American Historical Review* 50 (1970): 665–681.

Dávila Garibi, José Ignacio Paulino. *La sociedad de Zacatecas en los albores del régimen colonial: actuación de los principales fundadores y primeros funcionarios públicos de la ciudad.* Mexico City: Antigua Librería Robredo, 1939.

García-Abasolo González, Antonio Francisco. "Resultados de una visita a Nueva Galicia en 1567." *Anuario de Estudios Americanos [Spain]* 36 (1979): 3–39.

Garner, Richard. "Problèmes d'une ville minière mexicaine à la fin de l'époque coloniale: prix et salaires à Zacatecas, 1760–1821." *Cahiers des Amériques latines [France]* 6 (1972): 75–111.

Hoyo Cabrera, Eugenio del, editor. *El primer libro de cabildo de la ciudad de Zacatecas, 1556–1586.* Monterrey, 1972.

Langue, Frédérique. "Del minero rico a la nobleza: el papel de la frontera zacatecana en la formación de una elite económica y social." *Anuario de Estudios Americanos [Spain]* 44 (1987): 173–193.

———. "Mineros y poder en Nueva España: el caso de Zacatecas en vísperas de la Independencia." *Revista de Indias [Spain]* 51, Number 192 (1991): 327–341.

———. "Trabajadores y formas de trabajo en las minas zacatecanas del siglo XVIII." *Historia Mexicana* 40, Number 3 (1991): 463–506.

———. *Mines, terres et société à Zacatecas, Mexique, de la fin du XVIIe siècle à l'indépendance.* Paris: La Sorbonne, 1992.

Lemoine Villacaña, Ernesto. "Miscelánea zacatecana: documentos histórico-geográficos de los siglos XVII al XIX." *Boletín del Archivo General de la Nación [Mexico],* Segunda Serie, Volume 5, Number 2 (1964): 247–329.

Powell, Phillip Wayne. *Soldiers, Indians, and Silver: North America's First Frontier War.* Berkeley: University of California Press, 1969.

Ribera Bernárdez, José de. *Compendio de las cosas más notables contenidas en los libros del cabildo de esta ciudad de Nuestra Señora de los Zacatecas, desde el año de su descubrimiento 1546 hasta 1730.* Mexico City: Academia Mexicana de la Historia, 1940 reprint of 1732 Zacatecan original.

Román G., José Francisco. "Sobre la conquista y colonización de la Nueva Galicia." *Cuadernos de Investigación Histórica [Spain]* 13 (1990): 237–269.

Sánchez Flores, Ramón. "Tecnología minera en México: referencias a Zacatecas." *Quipú [Mexico]* 5, Number 1 (1988): 85–113.

Sescosse, Federico. "Zacatecas en 1550." *Artes de México* 22, Numbers 194–195 (1978), entire volume.

Late Colonial-Era Maps and Depictions of Zacatecas, 1780–1807

Diagram by the architects Guillermo Zavala and Rafael Bravo of its *Casa del Real Ensaye* or "Royal Assay Office," 1780—original held as Illustration 4208 of the Archivo General de la Nación in Mexico City, photographic negative 979/0801 [archival provenance: *Civil,* Volume 209, Folio 13]

Mine survey by Fermín de Reygadas, 1789—original held as Illustration 2766 of the Archivo General de la Nación in Mexico City, photographic negative 978/1404 [archival provenance: *Minería,* Volume 58, Expediente 6, Folio 452]

Two diagrams for transforming the ex–Jesuit college into the Colegio de San Luis Gonzaga, 1792—originals held as Illustrations 3170–3171 of the Archivo General de la Nación in Mexico City, photographic negatives 978/1782 and 978/1783 [archival provenance: *Temporalidades,* Volume 125, Expediente 3, Folios 5 vuelta–6 and 7 vuelta–8]

Drawing of the city, executed in 1799 by customs and excise officer Bernardo Portugal—original held as Illustration 3795 of the Archivo General de la Nación in Mexico City, photographic negative 978/2017 [archival provenance: *Intendentes,* Volume 65, Folio 13]

Map of the city by J. S. de la Rea, 1799—several sources

Diagram by Vicente Larrañaga of the Real Colegio de San Luis Gonzaga's grounds in 1806—original held as Illustration 3168 of the Archivo General de la Nación in Mexico City, photographic negative 978/1780 [archival provenance: *Temporalidades,* Volume 94, Folio 228]

Crude depiction of the city, 1807—original held as Illustration 451.1 of the Archivo General de la Nación in Mexico

City, photographic negative 977/0722 [archival provenance: *Historia*, Volume 552]

Independence and Modern Era (1822–Present)

Candelas Villalba, Sergio. *La batalla de Zacatecas.* Zacatecas, 1989.

Carrasco Puente, Rafael. *Hemerografía de Zacatecas, 1825–1950, con datos biográficos de algunos periodistas zacatecanos.* Mexico City: Secretaría de Relaciones Exteriores, 1951.

De la Peña, Moisés T., editor. *Zacatecas económico.* Mexico City, 1948.

Esparza Sánchez, Cuauhtémoc. *La batalla de Zacatecas.* Zacatecas, 1972.

García González, Francisco. *Conciencia e inteligencia en Zacatecas: sociedad, educación, historia, 1850–1890.* Universidad Autónoma de Zacatecas, 1988.

Hoyo Cabrera, Eugenio del. *La ciudad en estampas: Zacatecas, 1920–1940.* Monterrey: Sierra Madre for the Secretaría de de Servicios Sociales y Culturales del Gobierno del Estado de Nuevo León, 1979.

López Salinas, Samuel. *La batalla de Zacatecas.* Mexico City: Botas, 1964.

Martínez García, Manuel. *Reminiscencias históricas zacatecanas: la batalla de Zacatecas.* Zacatecas: Tipografía Literaria, 1922.

Pérez Toledo, Sonia, and Herbert S. Klein. "La población de la ciudad de Zacatecas en 1857." *Historia Mexicana* 42, Number 1 (1992): 77–102.

Ramos Dávila, Roberto. *Agenda cívica zacatecana.* Zacatecas: Ayuntamiento, 1984.

———. *Plazas, plazuelas y jardines de Zacatecas.* Zacatecas: Ayuntamiento, 1985.

Salinas de la Torre, Gabriel, compiler. *Testimonios de Zacatecas.* Mexico City, 1946.

General Works

Chávez Orozco, Luis. *Bibliografía de Zacatecas.* Mexico City: Secretaría de Relaciones Exteriores, 1932.

Flores Olague, Jesús. *Breve historia de Zacatecas.* Mexico City: El Colegio de México, 1996.

Kuri Breña, Daniel. *Zacatecas, civilizadora del norte: pequeña biografía de una rara ciudad.* Mexico City, 1944.

Vidal, Salvador. *Estudio histórico de la ciudad de Zacatecas.* Zacatecas, 1955.

CENTRAL AMERICA
Regional Studies

Boddam-Whetman, John Whetham. *Across Central America.* London: Hurst and Blackett, 1877.

Cameron, Sarah. *Mexico and Central America Handbook.* Chicago: Passport, 1998.

Cardoso, F. S., and Héctor Pérez Brignoli. *Centroamérica en la economía occidental.* San José: Editorial Universitaria de Costa Rica, 1977.

Fernández Vásques, Rodrigo. "Hacia una interpretación del desarrollo histórico de las ciudades capitales de Centro América, 1870–1930." *Anuario de Estudios Centroamericanos [Costa Rica]* 7 (1981): 5–41.

Fernández Vásques, Rodrigo, and Mario Lungo Uclés, compilers. *La estructuración de las capitales centroamericanas.* San José: EDUCA, 1988.

Flannery, Kent N. *The Early Mesoamerican Village.* New York: Academic Press, 1976.

Gage, Thomas. *The English-American: A New Survey of the West Indies, 1648.* London: George Routledge and Sons, 1928 reprint of 1648 original.

Karnes, Thomas L. *The Failure of Union: Central America, 1824–1960.* Chapel Hill: University of North Carolina Press, 1961.

Landau, Saul. *The Guerrilla Wars of Central America: Nicaragua, El Salvador, and Guatemala.* New York: St. Martin's Press, 1993.

Lassere, Guy. *Les Amériques du Centre.* Paris: Presses Universitaires de France, 1974.

MacLeod, Murdo J. *Spanish Central America: A Socio-Economic History, 1520–1720.* Berkeley: University of California Press, 1973.

Markman, Sidney. *Colonial Central America: A Bibliography.* Tempe: Arizona State University Press, 1977.

Newton, Norman. *Thomas Gage in Spanish America.* London: Faber and Faber, 1969.

Parker, Franklin D., editor. *Travels in Central America, 1821–1840.* Gainesville: University of Florida Press, 1970.

Peraldo Huertas, Giovanni, and Mauricio Mora Fernández. "Las erupciones volcánicas como condicionantes sociales: casos específicos de América Central." *Anuario de Estudios Centroamericanos [Costa Rica]* 21, Numbers 1–2 (1995): 83–110.

Schoonover, Thomas David. *Germany in Central America: Competitive Imperialism, 1821–1929.* Tuscaloosa: University of Alabama Press, 1998.

Serrano y Sanz, Manuel, editor. *Relaciones históricas y geográficas de América Central.* Madrid: V. Suárez, 1908.

Thompson, J. Eric S., editor. *Thomas Gage's Travels in the New World.* Norman: University of Oklahoma Press, 1958.

Torres Rivas, Edelberto. *Interpretación del desarrollo social centroamericano.* San José: EDUCA, 1973.

West, Robert C. "The *Relaciones geográficas* of Mexico and Central America, 1740–1792." *Handbook of Middle American Indians* 12 (1972): 396–439.

Woodward, Ralph Lee, Jr. *Central America: A Nation Divided.* New York: Oxford University Press, 1985.

Guatemala
General Studies

Aparicio y Aparicio, Edgar Juan. *Conquistadores de Guatemala y fundadores de familias guatemaltecas.* Mexico City: Tipografía Guadalajara, 1961 re-edition.

Burgues, Paul. *Biografía de Justo Rufino Barrios.* San José: EDUCA, 1971.

Cambranes, Julio. *Desarrollo económico y social de Guatemala, 1868–1885.* Guatemala City: TIES-USAC, 1969.

————. *El imperialismo alemán en Guatemala.* Guatemala City: TIES-USAC, 1977.

Chinchilla Aguilar, Ernesto. *Historia del arte en Guatemala.* Guatemala City: Ministerio de Educación Pública, 1965 re-edition.

De la Haba, Louis. "Guatemala: Maya and Modern." *National Geographic* 146, Number 5 (November 1974): 660–689.

Estrada Monroy, Agustín. *Datos para la historia de la Iglesia en Guatemala.* Guatemala City: Tipografía Nacional, 1972.

García Peláez, Francisco de Paula. *Memorias para la historia del antiguo Reino de Guatemala.* Guatemala City: Biblioteca "Goathemala," 1968 re-edition of 1851 original, three volumes.

Gil-Bermejo García, Juana, et al., compilers and editors. *Cartas de cabildos hispanoamericanos: audiencia de Guatemala.* Seville: Escuela de Estudios Hispanoamericanos, 1984, two volumes.

Gleijesis, Piero. *Shattered Hope: The Guatemalan Revolution and the United States, 1944–1954.* Princeton: Princeton University Press, 1991.

Grandin, Greg. *The Blood of Guatemala: A History of Race and Nation.* Durham, NC: Duke University Press, 2000.

Guerra Borgues, Alfredo. *Geografía económica de Guatemala.* Guatemala City: Editorial Universitaria, 1969.

Guzmán Beckler, Carlos, and Jean Loup Herbert. *Guatemala: una interpretación histórico social.* Mexico City: Siglo XIX, 1970.

Herrick, Thomas. *Desarrollo económico y político de Guatemala, 1871–1875.* Guatemala City: Editorial Universitaria de la USAC, 1974.

Horst, Oscar H. "1902, año de caos: el impacto político y socioeconómico de las catástrofes naturales en Guatemala." *Mesoamérica [Costa Rica]* 16, Number 30 (1995): 309–326.

Houdaille, Jacques. "Le tremblement de terre de février 1976 à Guatemala: ses effets sur la natalité et la nuptialité." *Population [France]* 37, Number 2 (1982): 429–434.

Immerman, Richard H. *The CIA in Guatemala: The Foreign Policy of Intervention.* Austin: University of Texas Press, 1982.

Kit, Wade. "The Fall of Guatemalan Dictator, Manuel Estrada Cabrera: U.S. Pressure or National Opposition?" *Canadian Journal of Latin American and Caribbean Studies* 15, Number 29 (1990): 105–128.

Kramer, Wendy. *Encomienda Politics in Early Colonial Guatemala, 1524–1544: Dividing the Spoils.* Boulder: Westview, 1994.

Lemmon, Alfred E. "Las obras musicales de dos compositores guatemaltecos del siglo XVIII: Rafael Antonio Castellanos y Manuel José de Quiróz." *Mesoamérica [Costa Rica]* 5, Number 8 (1984): 389–401.

Manson, Anne. *Guatemala.* Lausanne: Editions Rencontre, 1965.

Martínez Durán, Carlos. *Las ciencias médicas en Guatemala.* Guatemala City: Editorial Universitaria, 1964 re-edition.

McDowell, Bart. "Earthquake in Guatemala." *National Geographic* 149, Number 6 (June 1976): 810–829.

Molina, Antonio de. *Cronología guatemalteca del siglo XVII.* Guatemala City: Unión Tipográfica, 1943 re-edition by Jorge del Valle Matheu.

Palomo, Oscar R. "Reseñas biográficas de doña Francisca y doña Beatríz de la Cueva, esposas de Pedro de Alvarado." *Anales de la Academia de Geografía e Historia de Guatemala* 62 (1988): 25–44.

Pardo, J. Joaquín. *Efemérides para escribir la historia de Guatemala.* Guatemala City: Tipografía Nacional, 1944.

Remesal, Antonio de. *Historia general de las Indias occidentales y particular de la gobernación de Chiapa y Guatemala.* Madrid: Ediciones Atlas for the "Biblioteca de Autores Españoles," 1964–1966, two volumes.

Rodríguez Becerra, Salvador. *Encomienda y conquista: los inicios de la colonización en Guatemala.* Guatemala City, 1977.

Rosengarten, Frederic, Jr. "The Death of Flores." *Princeton University Library Chronicle* 44, Number 1 (1982): 42–54.

Sáenz de Santamaría, Carmelo. *El licenciado don Francisco Marroquín, primer obispo de Guatemala (1499–1563).* Madrid, 1964.

————. "La 'reducción a poblados' en el siglo XVI en Guatemala." *Anuario de Estudios Americanos [Spain]* 29 (1972): 187–228.

————. "El año 1776 en Guatemala." *Anales de la Academia de Geografía e Historia de Guatemala* 55 (1981): 139–144.

Sanchíz Ochoa, Pilar. *Los hidalgos de Guatemala: realidad y apariencia en un sistema de valores.* Seville: Seminario de Antropología Americana, 1976.

Schlesinger, Stephen, and Stephen Kinzer. *Bitter Fruit: The Untold Story of the American Coup in Guatemala.* Garden City, NJ: Doubleday, 1982.

Simon, Jean-Marie. *Guatemala: Eternal Spring, Eternal Tyranny.* New York: Norton, 1987.

Smith, Griffin, Jr. "Guatemala: A Fragile Democracy."
  National Geographic 173, Number 6 (June 1988):
  768–803.

Smith, Robert S. "Indigo Production and Trade in Colonial
  Guatemala." *Hispanic American Historical Review* 39
  (1959): 181–211.

Solano, Francisco de. *Tierra y sociedad en el reino de
  Guatemala.* Guatemala City: Universidad de San Carlos,
  1977.

Sullivan González, Douglass. *Piety, Power, and Politics: Religion and Nation Formation in Guatemala, 1821–1871.*
  Pittsburgh: University of Pittsburgh Press, 1998.

Whetten, Nathan L. *Guatemala: The Land and the People.*
  New Haven: Yale University Press, 1961.

Woodward, Ralph Lee, Jr. *Rafael Carrera and the Emergence
  of the Republic of Guatemala, 1821–1871.* Athens: University of Georgia Press, 1993.

Zéndegui, Guillermo de. "The Privileged Land of the Quet-
  zal." *Américas [Organization of American States]* 24,
  Numbers 11–12 (November–December 1972), supplementary pp. 1–24.

Guatemala City

Early Colonial Era (1524–1773)

Annis, Verle Lincoln. *The Architecture of Antigua
  Guatemala, 1543–1773.* Guatemala City: University of
  San Carlos, 1968.

Chinchilla Aguilar, Ernesto. "Evocación del año 1532."
  *Anales de la Academia de Geografía e Historia de
  Guatemala* 55 (1981): 333–339.

Ciudad Suárez, María Milagros. "Poder y religión: la familia
  Alvarez de Vega y el convento de la Limpia Concepción
  de Guatemala, siglo XVII." *Caravelle: cahiers du monde
  hispanique et luso-brésilien [France]* 64 (1995): 31–48.

———. "El colegio de doncellas: una institución femenina
  para criollas, siglo XVI." *Mesoamérica [Costa Rica]* 17,
  Number 32 (1996): 299–314.

De la Peña, José F., and María Teresa López Díaz. "Comercio
  y poder: los mercaderes y el cabildo de Guatemala,
  1592–1623." *Historia Mexicana* 30, Number 4 (1981):
  469–505.

Floyd, Troy S. "The Guatemalan Merchants, the Government, and the *Provincianos,* 1750–1800." *Hispanic American Historical Review* 41 (1961): 90–110.

García Granados, Jorge. *El deán turbulento.* Guatemala City:
  Universidad de San Carlos, 1962.

García Granados, Jorge, editor. *Libro viejo de la fundación de
  Guatemala y papeles relativos a don Pedro de Alvarado.*
  Guatemala City, 1934.

Hussey, Roland D. "Analysis of a Document Concerning a
  Voluntary Donation in Guatemala in 1644." *Hispanic
  American Historical Review* 24 (1944): 699–708.

Jickling, David. "Los vecinos de Santiago de Guatemala en
  1604." *Mesoamérica [Costa Rica]* 3, Number 3 (1982):
  145–231.

Luján Muñoz, Luis. "Una desconocida descripción poética
  de la Ciudad de Guatemala en el siglo XVIII, hecha por
  el jesuita José Ignacio Vallejo." *Anales de la Sociedad de
  Geografía e Historia de Guatemala* 53 (1980): 137–158.

———. "Los primeros asentamientos urbanos en el reino
  de Guatemala." *Anales de la Sociedad de Geografía e Historia de Guatemala* 59 (1985): 69–78.

Lutz, Christopher H. *Santiago de Guatemala, 1541–1773:
  City, Caste, and the Colonial Experience.* Norman: University of Oklahoma Press, 1994.

Markman, Sidney David. *Colonial Architecture of Antigua
  Guatemala.* Philadelphia: American Philosophical Society, 1966.

Pardo, José Joaquín, et al. *Efemérides para escribir la historia
  de la muy noble y muy leal ciudad de Santiago de los
  Caballeros del reino de Guatemala, 1541–1779.*
  Guatemala City: Sociedad de Geografía e Historia, 1944.

———. *Guía de Antigua Guatemala.* Guatemala City: Centro Editorial José de Pineda Ibarra, 1968 re-edition of
  original issued by the Sociedad de Geografía e Historia.

Pérez Valenzuela, Pedro. *Ciudad Vieja.* Guatemala City: Universidad de San Carlos, 1960.

Rubio Sánchez, Manuel. "Primer edificio de la catedral de la
  Ciudad de Samayoa Güevara, Héctor. *Los gremios de
  artesanos en la Ciudad de Guatemala.* Guatemala City:
  Editorial Universitaria, 1962.

———. *Monografía de la ciudad de Antigua Guatemala.*
  Guatemala City: Tipografía Nacional, 1989.

Santiago asentada en Almolonga. "Historial del edificio del
  ayuntamiento de la Ciudad de Antigua Guatemala."
  *Anales de la Sociedad de Geografía e Historia de
  Guatemala* 56 (1982): 15–45.

———. *Anales de la Academia de Geografía e Historia de
  Guatemala* 58 (1984): 37–87.

Webre, Stephen A. "El cabildo de Santiago de Guatemala en
  el siglo XVII: ¿Una oligarquía criolla cerrada y heredi-
  taria?" *Mesoamérica [Costa Rica]* 2 (1981): 1–19.

———. "Water and Society in a Spanish American City:
  Santiago de Guatemala, 1555–1773." *Hispanic American
  Historical Review* 70, Number 1 (1990): 57–84.

Zéndegui, Guillermo de, et al. "Antigua: A Colonial City
  Miraculously Preserved." *Américas [Organization of
  American States]* 17, Number 8 (August 1965): 10–19.

———. "Monumental Cities: Antigua." *Américas [Organi-
  zation of American States]* 26, Number 5 (May 1974),
  supplementary pp. 1–16.

Late Colonial Era (1774–1821)

Acosta, Elías Zamora. "El edificio de la administración de
  correos de la Nueva Guatemala." *Anales de la Academia*

de Geografía e Historia de Guatemala 55 (1981): 145–148.

Aycinena E., Roberto. "Algunas consideraciones sobre el Valle de la Ermita y la fundación de la Ciudad de Guatemala de la Asunción y su desarrollo." *Anales de la Academia de Geografía e Historia de Guatemala* 61 (1987): 245–280.

Brown, Richmond F. *Juan Fermín de Aycinena: Central American Colonial Entrepreneur, 1729–1796.* Norman: University of Oklahoma Press, 1997.

Fernández, Manuel. "Impacto social del traslado de la capital del reino de Guatemala: 1769–1803." *Secolas Annals* 18 (1987): 23–28.

Fernández Molina, José Antonio. "Producción indígena y mercado urbano a finales del período colonial: la provisión de alimentos a la Ciudad de Guatemala, 1787–1822." *Revista de Historia [Costa Rica]* 26 (1992): 9–30.

Galicia Díaz, Julio. *Destrucción y traslado de la Ciudad de Guatemala.* Guatemala City: Imprenta Universitaria, 1968.

Guzmán Chinchilla, Guillermo. "Los acueductos coloniales de Pinula y Mixco de la Nueva Guatemala de la Asunción." *Anales de la Academia de Geografía e Historia de Guatemala* 62 (1988): 231–277.

"La calle real de la Ciudad de Guatemala." *Anales de la Sociedad de Geografía e Historia de Guatemala* 57 (1983): 198–224.

Langenberg, Inge. *Urbanisation und Bevölkerungsstruktur der Stadt Guatemala in der Ausgehenden Kolonialzeit: Eine sozialhistorische Analyse der Stadtverlegung und ihrer Auswirkungen auf die demographische, berufliche und soziale Gliederung der Bevölkerung, 1773–1824.* Cologne-Vienna: Bohlau, 1981.

Luján Muñóz, Luis. "La escultura ecuestre de Carlos III en la plaza mayor de la Nueva Guatemala." *Anales de la Sociedad de Geografía e Historia de Guatemala* 52 (1979): 267–278.

Palma Murga, Gustavo. "Núcleos de poder local y relaciones familiares en la Ciudad de Guatemala a finales del siglo XVIII." *Mesoamérica [Costa Rica]* 7, Number 12 (1986): 241–308.

Pérez Valenzuela, Pedro. *La nueva Guatemala de la Asunción: terremoto de Santa Marta, fundación en el Llano de la Virgen.* Guatemala City: Centro Editorial José de Pineda Ibarra for the Ministerio de Educación Pública, 1964.

Zilbermann de Luján, María Cristina. *Aspectos socioeconómicos del traslado de la Ciudad de Guatemala, 1773–1783.* Guatemala City: Academia de Historia y Geografía de Guatemala, 1987.

Modern Era (1822–Present)

Bogin, Barry, and Robert B. MacVean. "The Relationship of Socioeconomic Status and Sex to Body Size, Skeletal Maturation, and Cognitive Status of Guatemala City Schoolchildren." *Child Development* 54, Number 1 (February 1983): 115–128.

EDOM 1972–2000: plan de desarrollo metropolitano. Guatemala City: Imprenta Municipal for the Dirección de Planificación, 1972.

Espinosa, L., and O. A. López Rivera. "UNICEF's Urban Basic Services Programme in Illegal Settlements in Guatemala City." *Environment and Urbanization* 6, Number 2 (1994): 9–29.

Levenson-Estrada, Deborah. *Trade Unionists against Terror: Guatemala City, 1954–1985.* Chapel Hill: University of North Carolina Press, 1994.

McCreery, David. "'This Life of Misery and Shame': Female Prostitution in Guatemala City, 1880–1920." *Journal of Latin American Studies [UK]* 18, Number 2 (November 1986): 333–353.

Micklin, Michael. "Traditionalism, Social Class, and Differential Fertility in Guatemala City." *América Latina [Brazil]* 12, Number 4 (October–December 1969): 59–78.

Peláez Almengor, Oscar Guillermo. "La economía urbana de la Nueva Guatemala de la Asunción vista a través de los negocios de Francisco Cordón Batres: el abastecimiento de carne, 1871–1898." *Mesoamérica [Costa Rica]* 15, Number 27 (1994): 93–126.

Pérez Sáinz, Juan Pablo, et al. "Trayectorias laborales y constitución de identidades: los trabajadores indígenas en la ciudad de Guatemala." *Estudios Sociológicos [Mexico]* 11, Number 32 (May–August 1993): 515–545.

Roberts, Bryan R. "Politics in a Neighborhood of Guatemala City." *Sociology* 2, Number 2 (May 1968): 185–203.

———. "Protestant Groups and Coping with Urban Life in Guatemala City." *American Journal of Sociology* 73, Number 6 (May 1968): 753–767.

Terrell, Katherine. "An Analysis of the Wage Structure in Guatemala City." *Journal of Developing Areas* 23, Number 3 (April 1989): 405–424.

Van der Tak, Jean, and Murray Gendell. "The Size and Structure of Residential Families, Guatemala City, 1964." *Population Studies* 27, Number 2 (July 1973): 305–322.

Villagran, M., et al. "Seismic Hazard Assessment for Guatemala City." *Natural Hazards* 14, Numbers 2–3 (1997): 189–205.

General Works

Gellert, Gisela. "Ciudad de Guatemala: factores determinantes en su desarrollo urbano, 1775 hasta la actualidad." *Mesoamérica [Costa Rica]* 15, Number 27 (1994): 1–60.

Gellert, Gisela, and Julio C. Pinto Soria. *Ciudad de Guatemala: dos estudios sobre su evolución urbana, 1524–1950.* Guatemala City: Universidad de San Carlos, 1992.

Pinto Soria, Julio C. "Guatemala de la Asunción: una semblanza histórica, 1776–1944." *Mesoamérica [Costa Rica]* 15, Number 27 (1994): 69–92.

Segreda Sagot, Gilda, and Jorge Arriaga. "El proceso histórico en la formación urbana guatemalteca, 1773–1944." *Anuario de Estudios Centroamericanos [Costa Rica]* 7 (1981): 43–69.

Panama
General Studies

Abbot, Willis J. *Panama and the Canal in Picture and Prose.* London, New York, Toronto: Syndicate Publishing, 1913.

Alvarez Rubiano, Pablo. *Pedrarias Dávila.* Madrid: Consejo Superior de Investigaciones Científicas, 1946.

Billard, Jules B. "Panama: Link between Oceans and Continents." *National Geographic* 137, Number 3 (March 1970): 402–440.

Castillero Calvo, Alfredo. *Políticas de poblamiento en Castilla del Oro y Veragua en los orígenes de la colonización.* Panama City, 1972.

———. *Economía terciaria y sociedad: Panamá, siglos XVI y XVII.* Panama City, 1980.

Céspedes del Castillo, Guillermo. "La defensa militar del Istmo de Panamá a fines del siglo XVII y comienzos del XVIII." *Anuario de Estudios Americanos [Spain]* 9 (1952): 235–275.

Conniff, Michael L. *Black Labor on a White Canal: Panama, 1904–1981.* Pittsburgh: University of Pittsburgh Press, 1985.

De la Guardia, R. *Los negros en el istmo de Panamá.* Panama City: Instituto Nacional de Cultura, 1977.

Díez Castillo, Luis A. *Los cimarrones y la esclavitud en Panamá.* Panama City: Instituto Nacional de Cultura, 1975.

Dodd, Thomas J. *La crisis de Panamá: cartas de Tomás Herrán, 1900–1904.* Bogotá: Banco de la República, 1985.

Figueroa Navarro, Alfredo. *Dominio y sociedad en el Panamá colombiano, 1821–1903.* Bogotá: Tercer Mundo, 1978.

Fortune, Armando. "Composición étnica y mestizaje en el Istmo de Panamá durante la colonia." *Lotería [Panama]* 261 (1977): 30–66.

———. "Mestizaje en el Istmo de Panamá a comienzos del siglo XVII." *Lotería [Panama]* 253 (1977): 1–17.

Franco Muñoz, Hernando. *Movimiento obrero panameño, 1914–1921.* Panama City, 1979.

Gandásegui, Marco A., et al. *Las luchas obreras en Panamá, 1850–1978.* Panama City: CELA, 1980.

Gutiérrez, Samuel A. *Arquitectura panameña.* Panama City: Editorial Litográfica, 1967.

Heald, Jean Sadler. *Picturesque Panama: The Panama Railroad, the Panama Canal.* Chicago: Teich, 1928.

Hussey, Roland. "Spanish Colonial Trails in Panama." *Revista de Historia de América [Mexico]* 6 (1936): 47–75.

Jaén Suárez, Omar. *La población del istmo de Panamá del siglo XVI al siglo XX.* Panama City: Instituto Nacional de Cultura, 1979.

———. *Hombres y ecología en Panamá.* Panama City, 1981.

Lemaitre, Eduardo. *Panamá y su separación de Colombia.* Bogotá, 1971.

Lowe, Arbon Jack. "Discovering Panama." *Américas [Organization of American States]* 31, Numbers 11–12 (November–December 1979): 17–24.

McCullough, David. *The Path between the Seas: The Creation of the Panama Canal, 1870–1914.* New York: Simon and Schuster, 1977.

McDowell, Bart. "The Panama Canal Today." *National Geographic* 153, Number 2 (February 1978): 278–294.

Mena García, María del Carmen. *La sociedad de Panamá en el siglo XVI.* Seville, 1983.

Navas, Luis. *El movimiento obrero en Panamá, 1880–1914.* Panama City: Editorial Universitaria, 1974.

Newton, Velma. *The Silver Men: West Indian Labour Migration to Panama, 1850–1914.* Mona, Jamaica: Institute of Social and Economic Research, 1984.

Pearcy, Thomas L. *We Answer Only to God: Politics and the Military in Panama, 1903–1947.* Albuquerque: University of New Mexico Press, 1998.

Serrano y Sanz, Manuel. *El Archivo de Indias y las exploraciones del istmo de Panamá (años 1527 a 1534).* Madrid, 1911.

The Subject Catalog of the Special Panama Collection of the Canal Zone Library-Museum. Boston: Hall, 1964.

Torres Ramírez, Bibiano, et al., compilers and editors. *Cartas de cabildos hispanoamericanos: audiencia de Panamá.* Seville: Escuela de Estudios Hispano-americanos, 1978.

Turner, Jorge. *Raíz, historia y destino de los obreros panameños.* Mexico City: Universidad Nacional Autónoma de México or UNAM, 1970.

Ward, Christopher. "Historical Writing on Colonial Panama." *Hispanic American Historical Review* 69 (1989): 691–713.

Weisberger, Bernard A. "The Strange Affair of the Taking of the Panama Canal Zone." *American Heritage* 27, Number 6 (October 1976): 6–11 and 68–77.

Zéndegui, Guillermo de, compiler. "Center and Juncture of the Americas." *Américas [Organization of American States]* 23, Numbers 11–12 (November–December 1971), supplementary pp. 1–24.

Panama City

Colonial Era (1519–1821)

Blasco de Orozco, Josef. "Diario de lo acontecido en la plaza de Panamá desde el 20 hasta el 25 de septiembre de 1766." *Revista Lotería [Panama]* 350–351 (1985): 163–168.

Castillero, Ernesto J. "Auténtica relación del gobernador de Panamá de la toma de esta ciudad por el pirata Morgan en enero de 1671." *Revista Lotería [Panama]* 217 (1974): 31–39.

———. "El asalto a la Ciudad de Panamá," *Revista Lotería [Panama]* 222–223 (1974): 39–49.

Castillero Calvo, Alfredo. "'La ciudad imaginada': contexto ideológico-emblemático y funcionalidad: ensayo de interpretación de la ciudad colonial." *Revista de Indias [Spain]* 59, Number 215 (1999): 143–169.

Dewey, Stephen. "The Panama Raid." *British History Illustrated [UK]* 5, Number 3 (1978): 20–29.

Earle, Peter. *The Sack of Panamá: Sir Henry Morgan's Adventures on the Spanish Main.* New York: Viking, 1981.

García de Paredes, Luís E. *Mudanza, traslado y reconstrucción de la Ciudad de Panamá en 1673.* Panama City: Concejo Municipal, 1954.

Hampden, Janet, and John Hampden, editors. *Sir Francis Drake's Raid on the Treasure Trains: Being the Memorable Relation of His Voyage to the West Indies in 1572.* London: Folio Society, 1954.

Lussan, Ravenau de. *Journal of a Voyage into the South Seas.* Cleveland: Arthur H. Clark, 1930.

Mena García, María del Carmen. "Censos eclesiásticos y propiedad urbana: una relación conflictiva." *Caravelle: cahiers du monde hispanique et luso-brésilien [France]* 66 (1996): 5–26.

———. "Panamá en el siglo XVIII: trazado urbano, materiales y técnica constructiva." *Revista de Indias [Spain]* 57, Number 210 (1997): 369–398.

Mercado, Pedro. "Historia de la provincia del Nuevo Reino y Quito de la Compañía de Jesús." *Revista Lotería [Panama]* 369 (1987): 179–204.

Moncreith, Alec. "Besieged by Thieves." *Military History* 8, Number 3 (1991): 44–49.

Petrovich, Sandra. "Henry Morgan's Raid on Panama and the French Experience: 1670–1671." *Proceedings of the Annual Meeting of the French Colonial Historical Society* 20 (1994): 36–49.

Zapatero, Juan Manuel. "Las fortificaciones de la Ciudad de Panamá." *Castillos de España [Spain]* 7, Number 74 (1972): 40–51.

———. "La plaza fortificada de Panamá." *Ibero-Amerikanisches Archiv [Germany]*, Neue Folge 2, Number 2 (1976): 227–257.

Colombian Era (1821–1903)

Campbell, Colin D. "Crossing the Isthmus of Panama, 1849: The Letters of Dr. Augustus Campbell." *California History* 78, Number 4 (1999–2000): 226–237.

Conte Porras, Jorge. "Fiesta y miseria en el arrabal." *Revista Lotería [Panama]* 352–353 (1985): 127–137.

Daley, Mercedes Chen. "The Watermelon Riot: Cultural Encounters in Panama City, April 15, 1856." *Hispanic American Historical Review* 70, Number 1 (1990): 85–108.

Figueroa Navarro, Alfredo. "L'oligarchie de la ville de Panama el le commerce avec l'étranger, 1821–1849." *Civilisations [Belgium]* 25, Numbers 1–2 (1975): 99–116.

———. *Los grupos populares de la Ciudad de Panamá a fines del siglo diecinueve.* Panama City: Universidad Santa María la Antigua, 1987.

Jorden, William. *Panama Odyssey.* Austin: University of Texas Press, 1984.

Kemble, John Haskell. *The Panama Route, 1848–1869.* Columbia: University of South Carolina Press, 1990 reedition of 1943 original.

"'La Reina de los Cielos' en la catedral de Panamá." *Revista Lotería [Panama]* 360 (1986): 176–183.

Levy, JoAnn. "The Panama Trail: Short Cut to California." *Overland Journal* 10, Number 3 (1992): 27–34.

Riley, Glenda. "Women on the Panama Trail to California, 1849–1869." *Pacific Historical Review* 55, Number 4 (1986): 531–548.

Schott, Joseph L. *Rails across Panama: The Story of the Building of the Panama Railroad, 1849–1855.* Indianapolis: Bobbs-Merrill, 1967.

Independence (1903–1988)

Acuerdos vigentes expedidos por el Concejo Municipal del Distrito, desde el año de 1908 al de 1911. Panama City: Tipografía Moderna, 1921.

Holguín, Arturo. "La separación de Panamá y la intervención norteamericana en 1903." *Boletín de Historia y Antigüedades [Colombia]* 78, Number 775 (1991): 909–935.

Koster, R. M., and Guillermo Sánchez. *In the Time of the Tyrants: Panama, 1968–1990.* New York: Norton, 1990.

Leonard, Thomas M. "United States Perception of Panamanian Politics, 1944–1949." *Journal of Third World Studies* 5, Number 2 (1988): 112–138.

Major, John. *Prize Possession: The United States and the Panama Canal, 1903–1979.* Cambridge, NY: Cambridge University Press, 1993.

Pippin, Larry LaRae. *The Remón Era: An Analysis of a Decade of Events in Panama, 1947–1957.* Stanford, CA: Stanford University Press, 1964.

Porras, Belisario. "Las elecciones de 1918: intervención o arbitraje por parte de los EE.UU." *Revista Lotería [Panama]* 368 (1987): 157–188.

Quintero, Iván. *El movimiento inquilinario de 1925.* Panama City: Centro de Estudios Latinoamericanos "Justo Arosemena," 1980.

Scranton, Margaret E. *The Noriega Years: U.S.-Panamanian Relations, 1981–1990.* Boulder: Rienner, 1991.

Szok, Peter. "'La Patria es el Recuerdo': Hispanophile Nationalism in Early Twentieth-Century Panama, 1903–1941." *Journal of Caribbean History [Barbados]* 31, Numbers 1–2 (1997): 149–184.

American Invasion and General Works (1989–Present)

Albert, Steve. *The Case against the General: Manuel Noriega and the Politics of American Justice.* New York: Scribner's, 1994.

Briggs, Clarence E., III. *Operation Just Cause: Panama, December 1989, A Soldier's Eyewitness Account.* Harrisburg, PA: Stackpole, 1990.

Collins, Steven N. "Just Cause Up Close: A Light Infantryman's View of LIC [Low Intensity Conflict]." *Parameters* 22, Number 2 (1992): 55–65.

Donnelly, Thomas, et al. *Operation Just Cause: The Storming of Panama.* New York: Lexington Books, 1991.

Kempe, Frederick. *Divorcing the Dictator: America's Bungled Affair with Noriega.* New York: Putnam's, 1990.

Rottman, Gordon L. *Panama, 1989–1990.* London: Osprey, 1991.

Rubio, Angel. *La Ciudad de Panamá: biografía urbana, funciones, diagnosis de la ciudad, paisaje, callejero.* Panama City: Banco de Urbanización y Rehabilitación, 1950.

———. *Panamá: monumentos históricos y arqueológicos.* Mexico City: Instituto Panamericano de Geografía e Historia, 1950.

Sandoya, Rebeca. "La ciudad de Panamá y su área metropolitana." *Revista Geográfica [Mexico]* 110 (1989): 29–56.

Sosa, Juan Bautista. *Panamá la Vieja.* Panama City: Imprenta Nacional, 1955.

Sosa, Tomás. "Breve reseña de la evolución demográfica de la Ciudad de Panamá." *Anuario de Estudios Centroamericanos [Costa Rica]* 7 (1981): 111–128.

Watson, Bruce W., and Peter G. Tsouras, editors. *Operation JUST CAUSE: The U.S. Intervention in Panama.* Boulder: Westview, 1991.

Portobelo

Andrews, Kenneth Raymond. *The Last Voyage of Drake and Hawkins.* Cambridge, NY: Cambridge University Press and the Hakluyt Society, Second Series, Volume 158, 1972.

Castillero Calvo, Alfredo. "Portobelo: apuntes para un libro en preparación." *Revista Patrimonio Histórico [Panama]* 2, Number 1 (1978): 133–200.

King, James Ferguson. "Documents: Admiral Vernon at Portobello, 1739." *Hispanic American Historical Review* 23 (May 1943): 258–282.

Loosley, Allyn C. "The Puerto Bello Fairs." *Hispanic American Historical Review* 13 (1933): 314–335.

Mena García, María del Carmen. "El traslado de la ciudad de Nombre de Dios a Portobelo a fines del siglo XVI." *Anuario de Estudios Americanos [Spain]* (1983): 71–102.

Monasterio, Félix M. *Portobelo: recuerdos de su glorioso pasado, el mejor centro de turismo nacional.* Panama City, 1934.

Moreyra y Paz Soldán, Manuel. *La toma de Portobelo por el almirante Vernon y sus consecuencias económicas.* Lima: *Mercurio Peruano,* entire August 1948 issue.

Vila Vilar, Enriqueta, "Las ferias de Portobelo: apariencia y realidad del comercio con Indias." *Anuario de Estudios Americanos [Spain]* 39 (1982): 275–340.

Ward, Christopher. "The Defense of Portobelo: A Chronology of Construction, 1585–1700." *Ibero-Amerikanisches Archiv [Germany]* 16, Number 2 (1990): 341–386.

Zapatero, Juan Manuel. *Las fortificaciones de Portobelo: estudio asesor para su restauración.* Washington: Organization of American States, 1971.

Zéndegui, Guillermo de. "Portobelo." *Américas [Organization of American States]* 22, Number 8 (August 1970): 20–30.

Zudaire Huarte, Eulogio. "Iniciativas reformistas desde el Nuevo Reino de Granada, año 1773." *Boletín de Historia y Antigüedades [Colombia]* 71, Number 747 (1984): 1007–1032.